I0818473

AMERICA'S
TEST KITCHEN

Also by America's Test Kitchen

Umma

When Southern Women Cook

Cocktails Illustrated

Food Gifts

America's Test Kitchen 25th Anniversary Cookbook

A Very Chinese Cookbook

Boards

Gatherings

The Sheet Pan

The Skillet

Cook It in Your Dutch Oven

Cook It in Cast Iron

Ultimate Air Fryer Perfection

Kitchen Gear

Baking for Two

Everyday Bread

The Cook's Illustrated Baking Book

The Perfect Cookie

The Perfect Pie

The Perfect Cake

The Science of Good Cooking

Cook's Science

The New Cooking School Cookbook: Fundamentals

The New Cooking School Cookbook: Advanced Fundamentals

Mostly Meatless

Vegan for Everybody

Vegan Cooking for Two

Vegetables Illustrated

How Can It Be Gluten Free Cookbook Collection

The Complete Anti-Inflammatory Cookbook

The Complete Plant-Based Cookbook

The Complete Beans and Grains Cookbook

The Complete Mediterranean Cookbook

The Complete Cooking for Two Cookbook, 10th Anniversary Edition

The Complete Diabetes Cookbook

The Complete Vegetarian Cookbook

The Complete One Pot

The Complete Autumn and Winter Cookbook

The Complete Summer Cookbook

The Complete Modern Pantry

The Complete Salad Cookbook

The Complete America's Test Kitchen TV Show Cookbook

The Complete Cook's Country TV Show Cookbook

For a full listing of all our books:

CooksIllustrated.com

AmericasTestKitchen.com

Praise for America's Test Kitchen Titles

"The book is a treasure for its endless kitchen wisdom, heart-filled recipes, and deep-rooted respect for all generations that came before. It showcases home cooking at its best, ranging from sauces, banchan (side dishes), and a slew of kimchi, to gurgling stews, tantalizing meats, and not-too-sweet fare."

Epicurious on *Umma: A Korean Mom's Kitchen Wisdom & 100 Family Recipes*

A Best Cookbook of 2024

Los Angeles Times* on *When Southern Women Cook

"This 'very' Chinese cookbook from a father-son duo is a keeper. The book—ATK's first devoted to Chinese cooking—proves that you can teach and entertain in the same volume . . . All in all, it's one of the most charming works I've seen in years, and I already want to get a second copy."

Washington Post* on *A Very Chinese Cookbook

"An exhaustive but approachable primer for those looking for a 'flexible' diet. Chock-full of tips, you can dive into the science of plant-based cooking or just sit back and enjoy the 500 recipes."

Minneapolis Star Tribune* on *The Complete Plant-Based Cookbook

"This comprehensive guide is packed with delicious recipes and fun menu ideas but its unique draw is the personal narrative and knowledge-sharing of each ATK chef, which will make this a hit."

Booklist* on *Gatherings

"True to its name, this smart and endlessly enlightening cookbook is about as definitive as it's possible to get in the modern vegetarian realm."

Men's Journal* on *The Complete Vegetarian Cookbook

"A mood board for one's food board is served up in this excellent guide . . . This has instant classic written all over it."

Publishers Weekly* (starred review) on *Boards: Stylish Spreads for Casual Gatherings

"Reassuringly hefty and comprehensive, ***The Complete Autumn and Winter Cookbook*** by America's Test Kitchen has you covered with a seemingly endless array of seasonal fare . . . This overstuffed compendium is guaranteed to warm you from the inside out."

NPR on *The Complete Autumn and Winter Cookbook*

"If you're one of the 30 million Americans with diabetes, ***The Complete Diabetes Cookbook*** by America's Test Kitchen belongs on your kitchen shelf."

Parade.com on *The Complete Diabetes Cookbook*

"Another flawless entry in the America's Test Kitchen canon, *Bowls* guides readers of all culinary skill levels in composing one-bowl meals from a variety of cuisines."

BuzzFeed Books on *Bowls*

"***The Perfect Cookie*** . . . is, in a word, perfect. This is an important and substantial cookbook . . . If you love cookies, but have been a tad shy to bake on your own, all your fears will be dissipated. This is one book you can use for years with magnificently happy results."

HuffPost on *The Perfect Cookie*

"The book offers an impressive education for curious cake makers, new and experienced alike. A summation of 25 years of cake making at ATK, there are cakes for every taste."

Wall Street Journal* on *The Perfect Cake

"The go-to gift book for newlyweds, small families, or empty nesters."

Orlando Sentinel* on *The Complete Cooking for Two Cookbook

The New Vegetarian

500+ Recipes for a Lifetime of Great Meals

America's Test Kitchen

Library of Congress CIP data has been applied for.

ISBN 978-1-966027-02-7

America's Test Kitchen
21 Drydock Avenue, Boston, MA 02210

Printed in China
10 9 8 7 6 5 4 3 2 1

Distributed by Penguin Random House Publisher Services
Tel: 800-733-3000

Cover and Featured Illustration:
Sarah Wisbey

Editorial Director, Books: Adam Kowit
Executive Food Editor: Dan Zuccarello
Deputy Food Editor: Stephanie Pixley
Executive Managing Editor: Debra Hudak
Senior Editors: Valerie Cimino, Sacha Madadian, and Sara Mayer
Associate Editor: Claudia Catalano
Senior Photo Test Cook: José Maldonado
Test Cooks: Hannah Smokelin and Stephanie Winter
Kitchen Intern: Canela Almonte
Assistant Editor: Julia Arwine
Additional Editorial Support: Elizabeth Carduff, Elizabeth Wray Emery, Amelia Freidline, Amanda Ngo, and Deri Reed
Creative Director, Editorial: Lindsey Timko Chandler
Associate Art Director and Designer: Molly Gillespie
VP of Imagery: Casey Stenger
Senior Photography Producer: Meredith Mulcahy
Senior Staff Photographers: Steve Klise and Daniel J. van Ackere
Staff Photographers: Kritsada Panichgul and Kevin White
Additional Photography: Beth Fuller, Joseph Keller, and Carl Tremblay
Senior Food Stylist: Christine Tobin
Food Styling: Julia Heffelfinger, Joy Howard, Sheila Jarnes, Catrine Kelty, Chantal Lambeth, Gina McCreadie, Kendra McKnight, Ashley Moore, Christie Morrison, Marie Piraino, Elle Simone Scott, Kendra Smith, Sally Staub, and Janette Zepeda
Project Manager, Books: Kelly Gauthier
Senior Print Production Specialist: Lauren Robbins
Production and Imaging Coordinator: Amanda Yong
Production and Imaging Specialist: Tricia Neumyer
Production and Imaging Assistant: Chloe Petraske
Copy Editor: Karen Wise
Proofreader: Ann-Marie Imbornoni
Indexer: Shapiro Indexing Services

Chief Executive Officer: Dan Suratt
Chief Content Officer: Dan Souza
Senior Content Adviser: Jack Bishop
Executive Editorial Directors: Julia Collin Davison and Bridget Lancaster
Senior Director, Book Sales: Emily Logan

Contents

ix Welcome to America's Test Kitchen

1 Introduction
35 Vegetables Front and Center
90 Salads Big and Small
141 Soups and Stews
181 Burgers, Tacos, and More
221 Pizza, Flatbreads, and Savory Tarts
264 Pasta, Noodles, and Dumplings
327 Rice and Grains
371 Beans and Legumes
405 Tofu and Tempeh
449 Eggs All Day
483 Small Plates and Snacks
522 Simple Vegetables A to Z

582 Nutritional Information for Our Recipes
600 Conversions and Equivalents
603 Index

AMERICA'S
TEST KITCHEN

Welcome to America's Test Kitchen

This book has been tested, written, and edited by the folks at America's Test Kitchen, where curious home cooks become confident cooks. Located in Boston's Seaport District in the historic Innovation and Design Building, it features 15,000 square feet of kitchen space including multiple photography and video studios. It is the home of *Cook's Illustrated* magazine and is the workday destination for more than 60 test cooks, editors, and cookware specialists. Our mission is to empower and inspire confidence, community, and creativity in the kitchen.

We start the process of testing a recipe with a complete lack of preconceptions, which means that we accept no claim, no technique, and no recipe at face value. We simply assemble as many variations as possible, test a half dozen of the most promising, and taste the results blind. We then construct our own recipe and continue to test it, varying ingredients, techniques, and cooking times until we reach a consensus. As we like to say in the test kitchen, "We make the mistakes so you don't have to." The result is our best version of every recipe. We use the same rigorous approach when we test equipment and taste ingredients.

All of this would not be possible without a belief that good cooking, much like good music, is based on a foundation of objective technique. Some people like spicy foods and others don't, but there is a right way to sauté, there is a best way to cook a pot roast, and there are measurable scientific principles involved in producing perfectly beaten, stable egg whites. Our ultimate goal is to investigate the fundamental principles of cooking to give you the techniques, tools, and ingredients you need to become a better cook. It is as simple as that.

Founded in 1992, ATK is the leading multimedia cooking resource serving millions of cooks like you with our trusted expertise. Come inside our kitchens on public television's most-watched cooking shows, *America's Test Kitchen* and *Cook's Country*. Watch every season and our original streaming series on your favorite streaming platforms.

We invite you to explore our app and website for access to thousands of rigorously tested recipes, unbiased product reviews, classes, videos, and more in one easy-to-use, ad-free digital experience.

Download the five-star-rated ATK app today.
cooks.io/subscribe

Keep the inspiration going with our vegetarian newsletter—your weekly dose of plant-based recipes, expert tips, and fresh takes, delivered straight to your inbox. **cooks.io/vegetarian**

Follow us on social

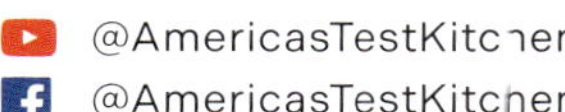

@TestKitchen

@TestKitchen

@AmericasTestKitchen

@AmericasTestKitchen

Introduction

1 The New Vegetarian

2 Making Meals, the New Vegetarian Way

Top 10 Tips for Meal Making

Be Good to Your Produce

» *Make Herbs Last*

» *Scrappy Cooking*

Freeze Building-Block Ingredients

» *25 Freezer-Friendly Meals*

8 Vegetarian Flavors

Read Those Ingredient Labels

13 Go-To Meals to Get Started

When the Cupboard Seems Bare and Time Is Tight

16 Turn Any Vegetable Into a Main Dish

18 Improvise a Sheet Pan Meal

Turn It into Bowl

22 Gatherings for Family and Friends

26 Basic Vegetable Prep

The New Vegetarian

It has been a decade since America's Test Kitchen published our first best-selling comprehensive vegetarian cookbook. Since then, vegetarianism has continued to grow in popularity, so much so that 5 percent of Americans now identify as vegetarian. Their motivations include ethical, health-based, environmental, and economic reasons. Our motivation continues. It is to develop the best recipes that keep vegetables and plant-based proteins at the center of the plate as main course fare. To that end, we've taken vegetarian cooking to the next level by focusing on making vegetables more versatile, more flavorful, and more satisfying. We have explored a wider range of ingredients, found new ways with familiar ingredients, and embraced more global flavors.

Vegetarian meals have become a delightful main event for many of us, regardless of dietary preference, and with no need for those meals to reference or imitate meat. Everyone knows that they should eat more vegetables (and by extension more fiber). This book encourages and supports that effort, serving up a wide variety of vegetables and hearty non-meat proteins that include beans and whole grains, dairy, and eggs, in dishes that are both satisfying and healthful.

Vegetables, beans, tofu and tempeh, eggs, cheese, and grains all shine in myriad ways thanks to inventive techniques that show how to get the most out of every ingredient. We devised a cheese soufflé that can be frozen. We pot roast a whole cauliflower, brine carrots into smoky carrot dogs, sear whole okra for curry, and microwave zucchini into an ultracreamy pasta sauce.

While this collection covers recipes for every time of day and occasion, from quick dishes to celebration-worthy fare, we know that cooking often points to dinner, and often on a weeknight, when time and energy are at a premium. That's why we've focused the majority of the book on recipes that could be dinner (maybe over rice or noodles) on any given night; meals that are creative without being fussy, like Herb Vegetable and Lentil Bake (page 68) and Creamy Broccoli Pasta with Crispy Panko (page 278). These recipes underline how vegetarian food is some of the most exciting food you'll find on any table: Turkish Bulgur and Lentil Soup (page 167), Samosa Gnocchi Chaat (page 303), Chickpea Bouillabaisse (page 378), and East African Tofu and Coconut Curry (page 426).

There are more than just 500 recipes to explore in this new collection. Of those, 269 recipes are vegan (and therefore dairy-free); 380 are naturally gluten-free (find these noted on the nutritional chart starting on page 582). And 303 recipes can be made in 45 minutes or less, helping you get dinner on the table fast. Good cooking is a pursuit to enjoy over a lifetime—and this resource offers approachable meals to cook and share with confidence for years to come. Eating the new vegetarian way makes sense for everyone: It's good for the palate, the wallet, and the planet.

Making Meals, the New Vegetarian Way

One of our goals with this book was to fill it with recipes that lead to dinner. There's a lot to choose from here, from vegetable-centric main courses to pasta- and grain-based meals to soups and stews and beyond.

There are many varied paths to making meals the new vegetarian way, but at the trailhead of these paths, you'll find a garden of core vegetarian ingredients—which formed our starting point for developing these next-level, nextgeneration recipes. Our recipes explore texture and flavor in unexpected yet wholly welcome ways. After trying them, we think you'll look at these core ingredients in a whole new light.

The new vegetarian makes the most of their vegetables. Consider eggplant and mushrooms: Both are long-standing mainstays in the vegetarian kitchen thanks to their satisfying "meatiness." Our Hasselback Eggplant with Muhammara (page 41) uses a technique associated with potatoes to create a sumptuous whole roasted eggplant, its fanned-out slices silky on the inside and crispy at the edges, bursting with spicy-sweet muhammara and drizzled with yogurt sauce to offset eggplant's light bitterness. For our Triple Mushroom Pasta (page 283), we use not one, not two, but three mushrooms, both fresh and dried, to create an intensely flavored but so-easy dish that works for company just as well as it does for a Thursday night.

Carrots, brined and smoked, transform into smoky "hot dogs" worthy of any barbecue (see page 190). Kale meets breakfast when it gets tucked into a breakfast burrito with black beans and eggs (see page 479). Sweet potatoes go fresh and modern when they're stuffed with chipotle-spiked lentils, pickled red onion, and queso fresco (see page 78). Spinach takes a star turn in a pesto-like sauce in Tallarines Verdes (Peruvian Green Noodles) (page 279).

The new vegetarian is always on the lookout for where their protein is coming from. Beans, eggs, cheese, yogurt, tofu, and tempeh are go-to choices for good reason. Legumes of all stripes work everywhere, from Radicchio Chopped Salad with White Beans, Oranges, and Olives (page 118) to Koshari (page 395) to Red Lentil Tacos (page 193). Eggs aren't just for breakfast: Try them in a super-simple Chinese stir-fry with tomatoes and scallions (see page 453) or the beloved Neapolitan dish Pasta Cacio e Uova (Pasta with Cheese and Eggs) (page 278). Instead of egg rancheros, try Tofu Rancheros (page 414). Crumble tofu and add it to Garlicky Tofu Tabbouleh (page 419) to turn this bulgur salad into a main course. You can even make Tofu Croutons (page 178) for your salads and soups. And cheese can play a starring role, as it does in Grilled Halloumi Wraps (page 214), or a supporting role, as in Celery Root Galette with Blue Cheese and Walnuts (page 256).

The new vegetarian explores all the grains now readily available in grocery stores. Farro can be baked into Broccoli Rabe and Farro Gratin (page 70) or be the base of a 45-minute dinner in Hearty Vegetable and Farro Bowls with Goat Cheese (page 85). Teff forms a stuffing for Teff-Stuffed Acorn Squash with Lime Crema and Roasted Pepitas (page 71). Millet makes Curried Millet Burgers with Peach-Ginger Chutney (page 188). And you'll find quinoa in bowls, salads, burgers, wraps, and more.

With hundreds of recipes now at your fingertips, it's time to get going on your own meal-making adventures. Start by taking a look at the test kitchen's top tips for meal making. Then check out our advice for prolonging the life of your produce and avoiding food waste, plus how to create a "freezer pantry" so you'll always have recipe building blocks ready to go to create the meal you want to eat today.

Top 10 Tips for Meal Making

Keep building-block ingredients on hand at all times Having longer-storage components available is smart meal planning. Keep proteins (eggs, firm and soft tofu, feta, halloumi) in the refrigerator. Stock up on your favorite canned and dried beans (they are often interchangeable in recipes). Always have a few good grains at the ready: Bulgur and quinoa work for quick meals, while sturdy grains like farro and wheat berries are great make-ahead choices for salads and bowls. Noodles are always a good option, so stock up on long and short dried pasta, dried rice noodles, shelf-stable gnocchi, fresh or frozen ravioli, and fresh lo mein or other Chinese noodles. And don't forget about pizza and phyllo doughs and puff pastry.

Store long-storage fresh and frozen vegetables Onions and shallots keep a long time (see page 4) and are the starting point for many recipes. Frozen vegetables can be as good as fresh (see page 6) and keep for months.

Build a flavor pantry Beyond building-block ingredients, assembling a pantry of flavorful spices, sauces, syrups, and more makes it easy to elevate even the simplest bowl of rice and beans. See our recommendations on pages 8–11.

Build a freezer pantry Turn to page 6 for our advice on how to stock your freezer with staples that make mealtime easier.

Practice whole-vegetable cooking See page 5 to learn how to use vegetable tops, fronds, and other odds and ends (along with other ingredients), rather than banishing them to the compost heap.

Store produce smartly for maximum freshness See page 4 for advice on what to wash before storing versus what to wash when you're ready to cook, plus when to leave produce in its packaging and when you should remove it.

Don't forget about herbs Herbs aren't afterthoughts; they are often an integral (and nutritious) part of recipes and need slightly different treatment from vegetables to keep them looking and tasting their best. See page 5 to learn more.

Understand your crisper Crisper drawers control humidity levels. Different vegetables and fruits need different humidity levels. How can they all exist in harmony? See page 4 to find out.

Keep your knives good and sharp Learn all about vegetable prep starting on page 26.

Embrace improvisation Sometimes you just want to freestyle dinner. Starting on page 16, we show you how to turn any vegetable into a meal with a few creative additions, as well as how to create a custom sheet pan or bowl meal.

Be Good to Your Produce

. . . and it will be good to you. Following are some best practices on keeping produce in peak condition until you're ready to use it, as well as pointers on not wasting any of it.

Packaging

When you get your gorgeous produce home from the market, don't automatically remove it from its packaging before storing it. For example, though they appear solid, the bags in which many greens are now sold are made of a polymer that allows ethylene to pass through freely, staving off spoilage. Other types of packaging may feature small perforations or other openings. Always remove twist ties from around produce, since those can promote rot if left on. If your produce doesn't come in any kind of packaging, it's a good idea to place it in an open produce storage bag.

In the Crisper Drawer

Crispers provide a more humid environment that helps keep produce with a high water content from shriveling and rotting. The humidity level in the crisper drawer is generated by what you store inside the drawer and how you set the drawer vent. Closing the vent keeps humidity high by trapping air inside, whereas opening the vent allows humid air to escape. Everyone's fridge is different, so experiment with the vents to find the humidity-level sweet spot.

Most vegetables do best in a crisper drawer, including artichokes, beets, broccoli, cabbages, carrots, cauliflower, celery, chiles, cucumbers, green beans, leafy greens, leeks, lettuce, mushrooms, peppers, radishes, scallions, sugar snap peas, summer squash, zucchini, and lemons and limes. We also store corn in the drawer. The sugar in corn begins to convert to starch from the moment the ears are picked; storing corn in the refrigerator will slow the process even more.

Ethylene gas–producing fruits should not be stored in the crisper drawer. Doing so will cause ethylene-sensitive vegetables to spoil faster. Place fruit that is sensitive to chilling injury on shelves at the front of the fridge, where it's a couple of degrees warmer than the back, including melons, oranges, and ripened avocados.

On the Counter

Vegetables that continue to ripen once harvested are called climacteric; these include avocados, eggplant, and tomatoes. In the cold environment of the refrigerator, they can fail to ripen properly and may discolor, so store them on the counter. However, once fully ripe, avocados and tomatoes should be refrigerated in the front of the fridge to halt further ripening and to preserve quality.

In the Pantry

Store long-keeping produce, including garlic, onions, and shallots, potatoes and sweet potatoes, and winter squash, at cool room temperature away from light.

Wait to Wash

Generally, it's best to wash produce just before you use it. Moisture promotes the growth of mold and bacteria, which causes spoilage. If you do wash produce ahead of time, make sure to dry it thoroughly before storing.

Two exceptions to this rule are herbs (see Make Herbs Last, page 5) and fresh berries. While damp berries turn mushy faster than dry berries, we've learned that cleaning these fruits as soon as you bring them home destroys mold spores, ensuring their quality for a longer period of time. We suggest washing them in a bowl with 3 cups of water and 1 cup of distilled white vinegar. Drain them in a colander and rinse under running water. Place the berries in a salad spinner lined with three layers of paper towels, and spin for 15 seconds or until the berries are completely dry. Then you can store the berries in a loosely covered paper towel–lined container at the front of the fridge.

Make Herbs Last

Delicate herbs—cilantro, parsley, dill, tarragon, mint, and basil—are most potent and fragrant with little to no cooking. Use them as a garnish or add them in the last moments on the heat. Hardy herbs—rosemary, thyme, oregano, or sage—can be added at the beginning of cooking.

As soon as you bring them home, gently rinse and dry herbs (a salad spinner works well), wrap in a damp paper towel, and place in a partially open zipper-lock bag in the crisper drawer. The exception here is basil. Don't rinse basil until you need to use it; the added moisture will decrease its shelf life. Instead, wrap it in clean, dry paper towels, place in a partially open zipper-lock bag, and refrigerate.

To freeze fresh herbs, place 2 tablespoons chopped fresh herbs (such as mint, oregano, rosemary, parsley, or thyme) in each well of an ice cube tray and add water to cover (about 1 tablespoon), then freeze. Once frozen, transfer the cubes to a zipper-lock freezer bag. Add the cubes directly to soups, stews, or sauces.

5 Recipes to Use Up Past-Their-Prime Vegetables

- Super Greens Soup with Lemon-Tarragon Cream (page 150)
- Ribollita (page 162)
- Ultimate Veggie Burgers (page 182)
- Sweet Potato Red Flannel Hash with Tempeh (page 441)
- Walkaway Ratatouille (page 58)

Scrappy Cooking

Instead of tossing food scraps and bits of random leftovers, use them up in creative and flavorful ways.

Greens, fronds, and tops Beet greens are tender enough to be sliced and used raw in salads; or add them to green smoothies in place of spinach. They are also delicious sautéed quickly with olive oil and garlic—as are radish greens and turnip greens. Think of fronds as you would any tender herb. For any dish that includes fresh fennel, chop the fronds and sprinkle them on as a garnish. Carrot tops can be used in a similar way as fennel fronds, finely chopped and sprinkled on to finish a dish. Or make a pesto by blending carrot greens with an equal amount of basil leaves (see page 268 for our basil pesto recipe). Save celery tops, leek greens, and potato peels to use in Vegetable Scrap Broth (page 177).

Chop It up Practically any leftover cooked vegetables can be chopped and added to fried rice, simply cooked grains or noodles, loaded baked potatoes, taco fillings, pizza toppings, omelets, and more.

Cheese, please Parmesan (and even Gruyère) rinds, when dropped into soups and tomato sauces, bring their glutamates (and umami flavor) to the finished dish. Likewise, if you have bits and scraps of other cheeses on hand, make fromage fort, a savory spread: Cut 8 ounces assorted cheeses (avoid pungent cheeses such as blue cheese) into 1-inch pieces and combine with 3 tablespoons dry white wine, 1 chopped garlic clove, 1 teaspoon fresh thyme leaves, and ½ teaspoon pepper in a food processor. Process until a creamy spread forms, 1 to 2 minutes. Season with salt and pepper to taste.

Bread alone If you do find yourself with a day-old, half-eaten baguette that's gone hard, remove the crust, tear the bread into rough 1-inch pieces, and blitz in the food processor. Toast the crumbs in a skillet, then sprinkle over finished dishes for textural crunch. (You can freeze these crumbs, too.)

Freeze Building-Block Ingredients

Keeping a stocked freezer means that you always have the building blocks of a great meal at the ready. For some items, like the ones listed here, it's a better storage choice than the refrigerator.

Soaked beans Dried beans benefit from an overnight soak. To save time, soak beans and then drain and freeze. Soaked beans freeze beautifully and are ready to cook without thawing.

Cooked rice and grains Cooked rice and grains can be frozen: Spread in an even layer on a rimmed baking sheet and let cool completely, then transfer to a zipper-lock freezer bag, seal, and lay flat in the freezer.

Vegetables We always keep frozen corn kernels, green peas, spinach, and edamame in the freezer; they're smart, high-quality shortcuts to getting dinner ready. Higher-moisture vegetables (including asparagus, bell peppers, mushrooms, snap peas, and snow peas) don't freeze well, so we suggest avoiding those.

Vegetable scraps Collect fresh vegetable scraps in a zipper-lock freezer bag in the freezer until you have enough to make Vegetable Scrap Broth (page 177). Don't forget about herb stems, and be sure to wash vegetable peels before freezing them.

Cheese Wrap hard and semifirm cheeses such as Parmesan and cheddar tightly in plastic wrap, seal in a zipper-lock freezer bag, and freeze. Thaw in the refrigerator before using. You can freeze Parmesan rinds as well; add them to simmering soups and sauces to enrich and deepen flavor.

Nuts and seeds Due to their high fat content, nuts and seeds go rancid quickly unless frozen. Freeze nuts or seeds in a zipper-lock freezer bag; they'll stay fresh for months. No need to defrost before using.

Homemade broth Pour small amounts of broth into ice cube trays. After broth cubes have frozen, transfer to a zipper-lock freezer bag. Or freeze in nonstick muffin tins for slightly larger portions. Once frozen, store the "cups" in a zipper--lock freezer bag. For even larger amounts, line a 4-cup measuring cup with a zipper-lock freezer bag and pour in the cooled broth. Seal the bag (double up if you wish) and lay it flat to freeze. No matter the size, you can store broth for up to 3 months.

Bread and dough The freezer is a far better place for bread than the refrigerator, where it undergoes a chemical process called retrogradation, essentially becoming stale. We keep crusty bread, sandwich bread, burger buns, pita, and tortillas on hand at all times, and the freezer keeps them fresh. For maximum freshness and ease of use, wrap portions tightly in plastic wrap and then tightly seal (with as little air as possible) in a zipper-lock freezer bag. We also freeze pizza dough (both homemade and store-bought), wrapping dough balls individually in plastic wrap and storing in zipper-lock freezer bags. To thaw dough, place in a lightly oiled bowl, cover with plastic, and let it sit in the refrigerator for 12 to 34 hours.

Butter Refrigerated butter quickly picks up odors and flavors and can turn rancid as its fatty acids oxidize; it keeps for about 2½ weeks in the coldest part of the fridge. In the freezer, well-wrapped butter will keep for up to 4 months.

Pestos and sauces Herb pestos (pages 268–269) and sauces such as No-Cook Pizza Sauce (page 223) will keep in the freezer for up to 1 month.

Chipotle chiles in adobo; tomato paste Spoon out each chipotle chile, along with a couple teaspoons of adobo sauce, onto different areas of a baking sheet lined with parchment paper and freeze. Or do the same with tablespoons of tomato paste. Transfer the frozen mounds to a zipper-lock freezer bag for storage.

Garlic Peel the cloves, mince or press them through a garlic press, and place in a bowl. Add enough neutral-flavored oil to coat the garlic (about ½ teaspoon per clove) and then spoon heaping teaspoons of the mixture onto a baking sheet and freeze. Transfer the frozen portions to a zipper-lock freezer bag. Thaw in the refrigerator (not at room temperature) or use directly from the freezer.

Ginger Simply cut fresh ginger into 1-inch pieces and freeze in a zipper-lock freezer bag. Chop or grate the pieces directly from the freezer (no need to peel or thaw).

25 Freezer-Friendly Meals

- ❊ Vegetable Lasagna (page 58)
- ❊ Eggplant Parmesan (page 60)
- ❊ Pesto Lasagna (page 294)
- ❊ Caramelized Carrot Soup with Coriander-Lemon Browned Butter (soup without browned butter) (page 143)
- ❊ Creamy White Bean Soup with Herb Oil and Crispy Capers (soup without herb oil and capers) (page 159)
- ❊ Red Lentil Soup with Warm Spices (soup without spiced butter and fresh cilantro) (page 159)
- ❊ Turkish Bulgur and Lentil Soup (without yogurt and fresh mint) (page 167)
- ❊ Harira (Moroccan Lentil and Chickpea Soup) (page 168)
- ❊ Best Vegetarian Chili (page 172)
- ❊ Black Bean Chili (page 173)
- ❊ Ultimate Veggie Burgers (formed patties) (page 182)
- ❊ Black Bean Burgers (formed patties) (page 183)
- ❊ Pinto Bean–Beet Burgers (formed patties) (page 187)
- ❊ Fresh Pasta Without a Machine (page 270)
- ❊ Meatless "Meat" Sauce with Chickpeas and Mushrooms (page 292)
- ❊ Three-Cheese Ravioli with Browned Butter–Pine Nut Sauce (formed ravioli) (page 299)
- ❊ Su Shui Jiao (Northern Chinese–Style Cabbage and Mushroom Dumplings) (formed dumplings) (page 323)
- ❊ Bean Bourguignon (page 373)
- ❊ Gigantes Plaki (page 374)
- ❊ Stewed Cranberry Beans with Tomatoes and Sage (page 377)
- ❊ Chana Masala (page 380)
- ❊ Misir Wot (page 400)
- ❊ Make-Ahead Cheese Soufflés (page 458)
- ❊ Scallion Pancakes (page 512)
- ❊ Spring Rolls (Cantonese Egg Rolls) (formed rolls) (page 514)

top | *Scallion Pancakes*
bottom | *Ultimate Veggie Burgers*

Vegetarian Flavors

One of the keys to any great vegetarian meal is incorporating ingredients that add big pops of flavor and varying textures to keep every bite interesting. Here are some of the most-used flavor-packed ingredients in this book, along with some recipe suggestions for using them once you've got them in your pantry.

Umami

Umami—that quality of deep, meaty savoriness—can be subtle, as when you add a bit of tomato paste to Red Lentil Soup with Warm Spices (page 159), or potent, as when you use dried porcini in Triple Mushroom Pasta (page 283).

Hard aged cheeses Umami-producing glutamates in cheese concentrate over time as cheese ages. Many traditionally made aged cheeses use animal rennet in their production, but vegetarian versions are increasing in availability. We call for vegetarian Parmesan throughout this book.

Tomato paste This ultraconcentrated form of tomatoes builds umami in dishes like Mushroom Bourguignon (page 53) and Creamy Chickpea and Sweet Potato Stew (page 170). You can develop its flavor even more by briefly sautéing tomato paste until it darkens and smells fragrant.

Bean pastes Fermented bean pastes are umami bombs. Miso is made from soybeans (along with rice, barley, or rye) and available in multiple types. Generally, the darker the color, the longer it has been fermenting and the stronger the flavor will be. We use it in dressings, and stir it into Miso Mushroom Risotto (page 338). Gochujang is a sweet, savory, and spicy paste made from gochugaru (Korean chile flakes), fermented soybeans, and glutinous rice or barley. We use it to make a bold sauce in Mezzi Rigatoni with Spicy Gochujang Tomato Sauce (page 271) and to flavor Korean rice cakes in Stir-Fried Rice Cakes with Bok Choy and Snow Peas (page 337). Doubanjiang is a Chinese fermented broad bean paste made spicy with chiles; try it in Homestyle Tofu (page 406).

Soy sauce and tamari The base for a multitude of dressings, sauces, marinades, and glazes, soy sauce also deepens the flavor of everything from grain-based dishes like Vegetable Bibimbap with Tempeh (page 334) to our Best Vegetarian Chili (page 172). You can substitute gluten-free tamari.

Dried mushrooms All mushrooms are high in umami, but dried versions deliver intense amounts in small packages. We use dried porcini and shiitakes to build flavor in dishes including Miso-Mushroom Risotto (page 338), Bean Bourguignon (page 373), and Wild Rice and Mushroom Soup (page 156).

Olives and capers The fermentation process for both of these ingredients makes them rich in glutamates, lending umami to Whole Pot-Roasted Cauliflower with Tomatoes and Olives (page 41) and Creamy White Bean Soup with Herb Oil and Crispy Capers (page 159).

Seaweed Kombu is the first food in which umami was clearly recognized. Try steeping a 4-inch piece in your next batch of lentil soup or tomato sauce. Toasted nori makes a delicate topping for Chilled Soba Noodles with Cucumbers, Snow Peas, and Radishes (page 318), as well as egg or rice dishes. Pretoasted seaweed snacks add flavor to dishes including Avocado and Cucumber Salad with Sriracha Mayo (page 112).

Nutritional yeast This deactivated form of yeast adds a funky, nutty, almost salty flavor (though there's no salt in it) that matches cheese in complexity. Try it in Chickpea Noodle Soup (page 169) or Cashew e Pepe e Funghi (page 280).

Spicy and Smoky

Chiles liven things up by contributing warmth, complexity, and aroma to all manner of dishes.

Ground chiles Red pepper flakes and cayenne turn up the heat in dressings, sauces, soups, chilis, and more. Crushed Calabrian chiles (in Calabrian Chile White Beans with Almond Romesco [page 374]) are fiery; Sichuan chili flakes (in Eggplant with Black Bean Sauce [page 45]) offer milder heat. Aleppo pepper conveys gentle heat and raisiny sweetness in Hasselback Eggplant with Muhammara (page 41).

Smoky chiles Canned chipotles in adobo are a go-to for adding smoky chile heat. Chipotle powder is especially delicious sprinkled on roasted sweet potatoes. Smoked paprika comes in sweet and hot versions and can infuse a dish such as Shakshuka (page 461) with smoky complexity.

Chili sauces There's a world of hot sauces, many with specific chile profiles such as habanero or poblano. Chili-garlic sauce and sambal oelek are Southeast Asian staples; the former is made with garlic and chiles and adds zing to Spiced Smashed Chickpea Wraps (page 211), while the latter contains only chiles and creates a powerful glaze in Roasted Tofu and Sweet Potato Bowls with Snap Pea Salad (page 85).

Chili crisp and pastes Chili crisp is highly tactile, with pieces of chiles, garlic, and nuts deep fried and jarred in a spiced oil. It has a tingly crispiness that's superb over noodles, rice, greens, or eggs. Harissa is a popular smoky North African chili paste that will wake up Red Lentil Kibbeh (page 399), as well as vegetables, soups, and more.

Thai curry pastes Combining chile heat with potent aromatics such as lemongrass, galangal, and makrut limes, these are great components in Charred Cabbage Salad with Torn Tofu and Plantain Chips (page 418) and Overstuffed Sweet Potatoes with Tofu and Red Curry Vinaigrette (page 433).

Sweet and Sweet-Tart

Adding a bit of sweetness can balance a dish that has salty, sour, bitter, or spicy elements.

Honey and maple syrup These are best used when you want their flavors featured, whether it's for mixing into a sala dressing or using as a glaze. Both play well with spicy flavors: Check out Spicy Chile-Honey Glazed Eggplant with Burrata and Greens (page 40). Opt for 100 percent maple syrup.

Pomegranate molasses A pantry staple throughout the eastern Mediterranean, pomegranate molasses is made by reducing pomegranate juice to a sticky syrup that layers astringent, floral, and faintly bitter notes over a sweet-tart, fruity flavor profile It can be whisked into vinaigrettes (as in Shaved Celery Salad with Pomegranate-Honey Vinaigrette on page 109), drizzled over vegetables, or pureed into dips (as in Slow-Roasted Eggplant Dip with Pomegranate Molasses and Aleppo Pepper [page 499]).

Mirin This Japanese rice wine has a subtle salty-sweet flavor and light tartness that's prized in marinades, glazes, and sauces. We use it to brighten the flavor of Crispy Teriyaki Tofu (page 421).

Tangy and Acidic

Acidic ingredients can wake up other flavors in any dish.

Citrus A squeeze of lemon or lime cuts through rich or salty food and brightens mild or mellow flavors. While each citrus fruit has a unique flavor, don't omit that splash of acid if you don't have the right one. Swapping one for another can be a nice way to adjust the character of a dish (or use vinegar if you don't have the specified citrus).

Vinegar Red and white wine vinegars are sharp, crisp, and subtly fruity. Sherry vinegar offers warmer, toastier flavors and complements earthy grains such as quinoa and wheat berries. Rice wine vinegar is less acidic than other vinegars and is great in milder salad dressings and stir-fries. Cider vinegar is mellow and slightly sweet; use it in glazes and slaws such as Apple–Celery Root Salad (page 110). Balsamic vinegar brings sweetness and punch. Chinese black vinegar is earthy and complex and makes a great drizzle for dumplings, noodles, and Congee (page 343).

Kimchi This Korean fermented staple conveys tang, umami, heat, and crunch. In addition to serving it as a condiment or side, add it to noodles, soups, or hash. It's a star ingredient in Egg, Kimchi, and Avocado Sandwiches (page 477).

Sauerkraut This tangy fermented food brings bracing freshness to Tempeh Reubens (page 445) and Potato-Sauerkraut Pierogi (page 322).

Creamy and Rich

A cool dollop, spread, schmear, or drizzle can bolster richness, tame spice, and add tangy flavor and velvety texture.

Yogurt If we had to pick one staple in the category of "creamy things to dollop on food," yogurt (Greek or regular) would win. Equally at home with sweet and savory flavors, yogurt is excellent on everything from simple vegetables (Broiled Smashed Zucchini with Garlicky Yogurt [page 580]) to grains (Barley and Lentils with Mushrooms and Tahini-Yogurt Sauce [page 348]) to eggs (Çılbır [Turkish Poached Eggs with Yogurt and Spiced Butter] [page 457]).

Sour cream From soups to enchiladas to baked potatoes, sour cream offers greater richness and more subtle tang than yogurt. Try it in Sweet Potato Soup with Maple Sour Cream (page 146).

Crème fraîche This dairy delight functions in a similar way as sour cream, but it has a higher fat content; a lush, fluid consistency; and complex nutty, tangy flavors. It also can be exposed to higher temperatures without curdling. Try it in Pasta with Creamy Lemon–Sichuan Peppercorn Sauce (page 277), Corn Risotto (page 341), and Lentilles du Puy with Spinach and Crème Fraîche (page 397).

Creamy cheeses (feta, goat, blue, cotija) Keep at least one of these on hand to add creaminess and protein to dishes from eggs and breakfast tacos to salads and flatbreads to pastas and grains. The flavors of each cheese can range from milder to quite bold, so choose what you like best.

Crispy and Crunchy

Textural contrasts take simple vegetables, salads, beans, eggs, and more to the next level.

Flake sea salt Sprinkling a finished dish with flake sea salt, such as Maldon or another coarse salt, adds a delicate crunch and discrete pops of brininess. Sprinkle it on Cherry Tomato Salad with Pita Crisps and Spicy Citrus Dressing (page 123), Chickpea Fries (page 511), or Roasted Fennel (page 551).

Nuts and seeds The pages of this book are sprinkled with nuts and seeds; in addition to crunch, they add protein and richness. They can top Creamy Polenta with Radicchio Agrodolce (page 363), Beet Poke Bowls (page 81), or Lao Hu Cai (Tiger Salad) (page 109); be stirred into Oat Berry Pilaf with Walnuts and Gorgonzola (page 356); or turned into a pasta sauce (see page 280).

Bread crumbs and panko Toasted bread crumbs amp up the crunch factor. Use panko as a breading for Panko-Crusted Tofu with Cabbage Salad (page 424). Combine crumbs with lemon zest to top Lentils with Roasted Broccoli and Lemony Bread Crumbs (page 396) or with Parmesan to top Broccoli Rabe and Farro Gratin (page 70).

Pita and tortilla chips Pita chips add a textured crunch to salads, including Pita Salad with Za'atar Tofu and Chickpeas (page 418), and tortilla chips add a crispy, corny element to chilis.

Fried garlic and shallots Garlic or shallots, quickly "fried" in the microwave, lend delicate crispness and deep allium flavor to dishes including Green Shakshuka (page 462) and Hung Kao Mun Gati (Thai Coconut Rice) (page 342). To learn how to make them, see pages 462 and 89.

Read Those Ingredient Labels

Animal products can hide in surprising places. If you're a strict vegetarian, seek out vegetarian versions of these items.

Some hard cheeses Many traditionally made hard cheeses, including Parmigiano-Reggiano, pecorinos, cheddar, and Comté, are made using animal rennet. Commercial versions made using plant-based or microbial rennet are increasingly available (although not yet for pecorino cheeses, which is why we always suggest Parmesan in the recipes in this book).

Kimchi, Thai curry paste, sambal oelek Commercial versions may include fish sauce or shrimp paste among their ingredients, so read the packaging carefully to be sure the product you're buying is vegetarian.

Condiments Traditional Worcestershire sauce contains anchovies; oyster sauce is in fact made from oyster extract; and fish sauce is made from anchovies and other small fish. Luckily, vegetarian versions of these products are readily available commercially.

Sugar Most conventional sugars (granulated, brown, confectioners', and molasses) are filtered through animal bone char as part of the production process. Some companies use granular carbon instead, but it's impossible to be sure. Consider buying sugar labeled as certified organic, since it is processed without using bone char. Likewise, be on the lookout for convenience foods where conventional sugar lives, such as sandwich bread, condiments, jams and jellies, chocolate, and so on.

Wine Wine fining agents (added to clarify wine) may include gelatin (derived from cows and pigs) and isinglass (derived from fish bladder), and traces of these items can end up in the wine. But many producers now use bentonite clay or activated charcoal instead, both of which are vegetarian-friendly. Check labels for a vegan demarcation or ask a store clerk.

Spicy Chile-Honey Glazed Eggplant with Burrata and Greens

Go-To Meals to Get Started

This book is filled with exciting recipes that are a complete meal in and of themselves. Many recipes may also benefit from adding a second simpler recipe as a side, or even just a good green salad and some crusty bread. Here are some of our favorite go-to meals and pairing ideas to get you started.

One-Pot Meals

- Aloo Gobi (page 48)
- Green Curry with Kale and Butternut Squash (page 50)
- Black Bean Chili (page 173)
- Spinach-Artichoke Macaroni and Cheese (page 277)
- Chickpea Bouillabaisse (page 378)
- Red Lentil Kibbeh (page 399)
- Crispy Teriyaki Tofu (page 421)
- Green Shakshuka (page 462)

Sheet-Pan Meals

- Spicy Chile-Honey Glazed Eggplant with Burrata and Greens (page 40)
- Overstuffed Sweet Potatoes with Tofu and Red Curry Vinaigrette (page 433)
- Baharat Cauliflower and Eggplant with Chickpeas (page 57)
- Charred Cabbage Salad with Torn Tofu and Plantain Chips (page 418)
- Roasted Tofu and Sweet Potato Bowls with Snap Pea Salad (page 85)
- Sheet Pan Cheese Quesadillas (page 194)
- Roasted Vegetable Sandwiches (page 209)
- Sheet Pan White Bean and Sun-Dried Tomato Patties with Lemony Spinach Salad (page 184)
- Baja-Style Cauliflower Tacos (page 191)

Almost Entirely Hands-Off

- Whole Pot-Roasted Cauliflower with Tomatoes and Olives (page 41)
- Walkaway Ratatouille (page 58)
- Hearty Cabbage Soup (page 151)
- Lentil and Escarole Soup (page 160)
- Classic Minestrone (page 161)
- Congee (page 343)
- Oat Berry Pilaf with Walnuts and Gorgonzola (page 356)

Add a Simple Side

- Curry Roasted Cabbage Wedges with Tomatoes and Chickpeas (page 36) + Easy Baked White Rice (page 366)
- Butternut Squash Steaks with Honey-Nut Topping (page 37) + Roasted Fennel (page 551)
- Cauliflower Steaks with Salsa Verde (page 38) + Avocado and Cucumber Salad with Sriracha Mayo (page 112)
- Upside-Down Tomato Tart (page 258) + Kale Caesar Salad (page 92)
- Black Bean and Cheese Arepas (page 199) + Esquites (Mexican Corn Salad) (page 110)
- Miso Mushroom Risotto (page 338) + Quick Collard Greens (page 543)
- Black Bean Burgers (page 183) + Boiled Carrots with Cumin, Lime, and Cilantro (page 537)
- San Francisco–Style Garlic Noodles (page 313) + Broiled Broccoli Rabe (page 532)

Left | *Eggplant with Black Bean Sauce*

Right | *Chile-Spiced Crumbled Tofu with Pineapple Salsa*

Toss with Pasta or Noodles

- ✼ Stir-Fried Tofu and Bok Choy (page 422)
- ✼ Crispy Tempeh with Sambal Sauce (page 436)
- ✼ Eggplant with Black Bean Sauce (page 45)
- ✼ Roasted Fennel with Crunchy Oil-Cured Olives (page 551)
- ✼ Broiled Smashed Zucchini with Garlicky Yogurt (page 580)
- ✼ Mushroom Bourguignon (page 53)
- ✼ Sautéed Corn with Cherry Tomatoes, Ricotta Salata, and Basil (page 545)
- ✼ Espinacas con Garbanzos (Andalusian Spinach and Chickpeas, page 382)

Serve over Rice or Other Grains

- ✼ Stir-Fried Portobellos with Ginger-Oyster Sauce (page 46)
- ✼ Saag Tofu (page 414)
- ✼ Chile-Spiced Crumbled Tofu with Pineapple Salsa (page 420)
- ✼ Jackfruit and Chickpea Makhani (page 378)
- ✼ Xīhóngshì Chao Jīdàn (Chinese Stir-Fried Tomatoes and Eggs) (page 453)
- ✼ Gai Lan with Oyster Sauce (page 552)
- ✼ Braised Eggplant with Soy, Garlic, and Ginger (page 551)
- ✼ Roasted Kale with Garlic, Red Pepper Flakes, and Lemon (page 555)

Make Beans the Center of the Plate

- ✼ Lentils with Roasted Broccoli and Lemony Bread Crumbs (page 396)
- ✼ Lentilles du Puy with Spinach and Crème Fraîche (page 397)
- ✼ Chickpea Curry (page 382)
- ✼ Creamy White Bean Soup with Herb Oil and Crispy Capers (page 159)
- ✼ Calabrian Chile White Beans with Almond Romesco (page 374)
- ✼ Stewed Cranberry Beans with Tomatoes and Sage (page 377)
- ✼ Misir Wot (page 400)
- ✼ Chickpea Salad Sandwiches with Quick Pickles (page 210)

Twofers in Under an Hour

- ✼ Spiced Smashed Chickpea Wraps (page 211) + Chopped Carrot Salad with Mint, Pistachios, and Pomegranate Seeds (page 107)
- ✼ Cutty's-Inspired Eggplant Spuckie (page 205) + Apple–Celery Root Salad (page 110)
- ✼ Beet, Orange, and Chèvre Tartines (page 206) + Wheat Berry Salad with Radicchio, Dried Cherries, and Pecans (page 125)
- ✼ Chickpea and Poblano Quesadillas (page 197) + Broccoli Salad with Avocado Dressing (page 103)
- ✼ Easy Cheddar Omelet (page 466) + Edamame Salad with Mint and Parmesan (page 386)
- ✼ Spicy Cold Tofu (page 407) + Skillet-Charred Green Beans (page 552)
- ✼ Ricotta Toast with Pesto di Prezzemolo and Grapes (page 239) + Cantaloupe Salad with Olives and Red Onion (page 132)

When the Cupboard Seems Bare and Time Is Tight

Creating a satisfying pantry meal from ingredients on hand makes weeknight cooking a little less daunting. All the more reason to keep stocked up on items such as beans and legumes, canned tomatoes, and long-storage vegetables. And when you want to make something really good and really fast, check out the list of the 10 fastest meals in the book below.

Chopped Vegetable and Stone Fruit Salad

Top 15 Pantry-Driven Meals

* Aloo Gobi (page 48)
* Potato Vindaloo (page 55)
* Cheesy Tomato and Bean Bake (page 65)
* Hearty Cabbage Soup (page 151)
* Red Lentil Soup with Warm Spices (page 159)
* Creamy Chickpea and Sweet Potato Stew (page 170)
* Black Bean Burgers (page 183)
* Sheet Pan Cheese Quesadillas (page 194)
* Cast Iron Pan Pizza (page 225)
* Vidalia Onion Pie (page 251)
* Garlicky Spaghetti with Lemon and Pine Nuts (page 272)
* Simple Stovetop Macaroni and Cheese (page 275)
* Green Peas and Dumplings (page 321)
* Calabrian Chile White Beans with Almond Romesco (page 374)
* Crispy Teriyaki Tofu (page 421)

Top 10 Really Fast Meals

* Australian Folded Eggs (10 minutes) (page 454)
* Easy Cheddar Omelet (15 minutes) (page 466)
* Avocado Toast (15 minutes) (page 238)
* Stir-Fried Asparagus with Shiitake Mushrooms (20 minutes) (page 43)
* Chickpea Salad Sandwiches with Quick Pickles (20 minutes) (page 210)
* Breakfast Tacos with Pinto Beans and Cotija Cheese (20 minutes) (page 478)
* Spicy Cold Tofu (20 minutes) (page 407)
* Raw Vegetable Wraps (25 minutes) (page 206)
* Chopped Vegetable and Stone Fruit Salad (30 minutes) (page 126)
* Tempeh Tacos (30 minutes) (page 443)

Turn Any Vegetable into a Main Dish

Vegetables are a vegetarian's best friends. Simply prepared vegetables not only make great sides, they also are creative components that you can use to build a complete dish—beyond merely pairing two or three vegetables on a plate and calling it dinner. Start with a base, add a vegetable, and then drizzle and sprinkle your way to a memorable meal. You can turn any of the simple vegetables from the chart on page 20 or from Chapter 12 into a meal; some of them already have a built-in base or topping. You can also replace many of these components with good store-bought versions.

Mix and Match

This book puts a whole world of recipes for simple vegetables, sauces, and toppings at your fingertips to consider and combine into new and interesting main dishes. Here are five suggestions to get you thinking.

Base	Vegetable	Sprinkle	Drizzle
Whipped Feta	Roasted Cabbage	Savory Seed Brittle	EVOO
Hummus	Simple Sautéed Kale	Frico	Zhoug
Labneh	Skillet-Charred Green Beans	Shichimi Togarashi	Miso-Ginger Sauce
Whipped Boursin	Fried Red Tomatoes	fresh basil	Make-Ahead Balsamic-Fennel Vinaigrette
Romesco	Roasted Celery Root	Crunchy Oil-Cured Olives	All-Purpose Herb Sauce

Improvise a Sheet Pan Meal

A sheet pan is an easy way to make a one-pan meal. While there are a lot of great sheet pan recipes throughout the book, this section will help you improvise creations of your own. We follow these five key steps to sheet pan success: Pick and prepare your ingredients; season; and arrange carefully on the pan. Then all you need to do is slide the sheet pan into the oven to bake in a 450-degree oven with the oven rack set to the lower-middle position.

Pick and Prep

First, choose your sheet pan protein and your vegetable(s) from the charts on page 20 and prep them accordingly. We also list some useful cook times there.

Season

Seasoning is up to you: It can be as simple as salt and pepper, or you can experiment with more complex flavorings. Take inspiration from a cuisine or flavor profile you like to inform your choices. Consider using a spice rub, or add hearty herbs such as fresh rosemary, sage, and thyme.

Arrange

Place vegetables cut side down on the sheet pan for better browning. Heartier ingredients, or any you want to crisp up, should go at the edges of the pan, while easy-to-overcook items should be placed in the center. Don't overcrowd the pan; leave some space between ingredients for heat to circulate.

Cook

Cooking times can vary widely so don't assume you can add everything at once. Use the charts on page 20 as a guide. Flip and toss ingredients when necessary for browning or even cooking. Use the broiler especially for last-minute crisping or browning; your sheet pan should be 6 inches away from the heating element.

Add Fresh Flavor

Once the vegetables and protein are cooked, it's time to get creative with fresh flavors. Simply drizzling with an acid like lemon, lime, or orange juice can add both flavor and brightness; or shower with chopped herbs for color and a burst of flavor. Check out the lists on page 21 for sauces to tie the dish together and toppings that offer texture, eye appeal, and a final flavor flourish.

5 Great Sheet Pan Meals to Try

Sheet Pan 1 tofu, fennel, sweet potatoes, hibiscus vinaigrette, pickled mustard seeds

Sheet Pan 2 feta cubes, green beans, delicata squash, chili crisp, drizzle of honey, fresh cilantro, scallions

Sheet Pan 3 halloumi, zucchini, cilantro-mint chutney, spiced seeds

Sheet Pan 4 tempeh, brussels sprouts, mushrooms, harissa, squeeze of lemon

Sheet Pan 5 chickpeas, butternut squash, chermoula, marinated manchego, crispy onions

Choose Your Protein

Protein	Preparation	Cook Time
Tofu	cut into 1-inch-thick planks, patted dry	12–17 minutes
Tempeh	cut into ½-inch cubes	15–20 minutes
Chickpeas	rinsed and drained	30–35 minutes (at 475 degrees)
Halloumi	cut into ½-inch cubes	10 minutes to warm through; optional 2 minutes broiling
Feta	½ inch cubes	10 minutes to warm through; optional 2 minutes broiling

Choose Your Vegetable(s)

Vegetable	Preparation	Cook Time	Special Notes
Asparagus	trimmed	10–15 minutes	
Beets	peeled and cut into 1-inch pieces or wedges	20–25 minutes	
Bell peppers	stemmed, seeded, and sliced 1 inch thick	8–10 minutes	stir halfway through
Broccoli	cut into 1-inch florets	8–10 minutes	
Brussels sprouts	trimmed and halved	8–10 minutes	arrange cut side down on sheet
Butternut or other winter squash	peeled, seeded, and cut into 1-inch pieces	35–40 minutes	stir halfway through
Cabbage	trimmed and cut into 2-inch pieces	8–10 minutes	stir halfway through
Carrots	peeled and halved lengthwise	20–25 minutes	arrange cut side down on sheet
Cauliflower	trimmed and cut into 1-inch florets	10–15 minutes	
Celery root	peeled and cut into 1-inch pieces	40–45 minutes	stir halfway through
Cherry tomatoes	left whole	20–25 minutes	
Delicata squash	trimmed, halved lengthwise, seeded, and sliced crosswise ½ inch thick	30–35 minutes	stir halfway through
Eggplant	cut into 1-inch pieces	25–30 minutes	stir halfway through
Fennel	stalks discarded, bulbs halved, cored, and sliced into 1-inch-thick wedges	30–35 minutes	
Green beans	trimmed	20–25 minutes	stir halfway through
Mushrooms	trimmed and left whole if small, halved if medium, or quartered if large	40–45 minutes	stir halfway through
Potatoes	cut into 1-inch-thick pieces or wedges	35–40 minutes	arrange cut side down on sheet
Sweet potatoes	cut into 1-inch-thick pieces or wedges	35–40 minutes	arrange cut side down on sheet
Zucchini or summer squash	halved lengthwise and sliced 1 inch thick	20–30 minutes	stir halfway through

Choose a Sauce, Dressing, or Drizzle

- Garlic Yogurt Sauce (page 37)
- Orange-Ginger Vinaigrette (page 86)
- Sesame-Scallion Vinaigrette (page 139)
- Creamless Creamy Roasted Red Pepper and Tahini Dressing (page 139)
- Creamy Avocado Dressing (page 139)
- Hibiscus Vinaigrette (page 353)
- Lemon-Herb Sauce (page 179)
- Cilantro-Mint Chutney (page 213)
- Tomato-Chile Sauce (page 216)
- Quick Chili Oil (page 179)
- Harissa (page 400)
- All-Purpose Herb Sauce (page 524)
- Zhoug (Spicy Middle Eastern Herb Sauce) (page 524)
- Chermoula (page 525)
- Miso-Ginger Sauce (page 526)
- Peanut-Sesame Sauce (page 525)
- Infinite Sauce (page 526)
- Romesco (page 527)
- Spicy Red Pepper Mayonnaise (page 559)
- Cilantro Crema (page 191)
- Spicy Honey (page 573)

Don't Forget a Topping or Garnish

- Dukkah (page 89)
- Shichimi Togarashi (page 88)
- Savory Seed Brittle (page 88)
- Tarragon-Lemon Gremolata (page 88)
- Spiced Seeds (page 179)
- Pickled Mustard Seeds (page 459)
- Pickled Celery (page 179)
- Quick Sweet-and-Spicy Pickled Red Onion (page 213)
- Crispy Onions (page 394)
- Microwave-Fried Shallots (page 89)
- Microwave-Fried Garlic (page 462)
- Crunchy Oil-Cured Olives (page 552)
- Frico (page 489)

Turn It into a Bowl

A well-crafted bowl is another easy route to dinner (and a creative way to use up leftovers). Although there are recipes for specific bowls in the book, you can also prepare a bowl of your choosing by referring to the charts and lists at the left. The test kitchen finds that the most flavorful, texturally interesting bowls have elements from each of these categories: base, protein, vegetable, sauce, crunch. Add a base of cooked rice, grain, or beans, then your protein, pick a sauce or drizzle, add some crunch and/or a topping—and dinner is ready. We've listed some ideas for combinations to get you started.

5 Great Bowl Combinations to Try

1 black rice, gai lan with oyster sauce, shichimi togarashi, orange-ginger vinaigrette, tofu croutons

2 labneh, roasted okra, skillet-roasted cauliflower, zhoug, crispy roasted chickpeas

3 kamut, simple sautéed kale, boiled carrots with lemon and chives, creamy roasted red pepper and tahini dressing, fried garlic, dukkah

4 tempeh, cauliflower, cherry tomatoes, chermoula, chopped toasted walnuts

5 bulgur, broiled smashed zucchini with garlicky yogurt, sweet-and-spicy pickled red onion

Gathering for Family and Friends

We've created these special-occasion menus and meals that are sure to impress all your guests—whether they're vegetarian or not. These are just a start; the possible menu combinations that you can create are endless.

New Year's Eve Cocktail Party

- Warm Marinated Olives (page 485)
- Marinated Manchego (page 485)
- Zucchini Chips with Tzatziki (page 510)
- Seared Tempeh with Tomato Jam (page 437)
- Beet, Orange, and Chèvre Tartines (page 206)
- Lemon-Pickled Radish Toast with Basil and Parmesan (page 238)

New Year's Day Brunch

- Radicchio Chopped Salad with White Beans, Oranges, and Olives (page 118)
- Ricotta Toast with Pesto di Prezzemolo and Grapes (page 239)
- Kol Böreği (Spiraled Spinach and Cheese Pastry) (page 262)
- Tofu Rancheros (page 414)
- Spanish Tortilla with Roasted Red Peppers and Peas (page 467)

Memorial Day Cookout

- Three-Bean Salad (page 114)
- Smoky Carrot Dogs (page 190)
- Grilled Halloumi Wraps (page 214)
- Grilled Tofu with Vegetable Skewers (page 435)
- Cantaloupe Salad with Olives and Red Onion (page 132)

July 4th Barbecue

- Buffalo Cucumber Salad (page 111)
- Tortellini Salad with Broccoli, Cannellini Beans, and Olive-Banana Pepper Dressing (page 302)
- Ultimate Grilled Vegetable Sandwiches (page 209)
- Grilled Peach and Tomato Salad with Burrata and Basil (page 135)

Simple Dinner Party for 6

- Cast Iron-Seared Romaine with Oyster Sauce, Ginger, and Sesame (page 121)
- Pasta with Creamy Lemon-Sichuan Peppercorn Sauce (page 277)
- Sautéed Mushrooms with Soy, Scallion, and Ginger (page 558)

Game Day Gathering

- Garam Masala Peanuts (page 484)
- Fried Brussels Sprouts with Sriracha Dipping Sauce (page 534)
- Baked Pimento Cheese Dip (page 491)
- Black Bean Chili (page 173)

Thanksgiving Menus

Turkey, schmurkey. Here are some fresh holiday menus that are full of fall flavors and color.

Menu 1

- ✻ Bitter Greens, Carrot, and Chickpea Salad with Warm Lemon Dressing (page 98)
- ✻ Creamy White Bean Soup with Herb Oil and Crispy Capers (page 159)
- ✻ Cheese Ravioli with Pumpkin Cream Sauce (page 298)
- ✻ Skillet-Roasted Brussels Sprouts with Maple Syrup and Smoked Almonds (page 533)
- ✻ Swiss Chard and Kale Gratin (page 576)

Menu 2

- ✻ Kale Caesar Salad (page 92)
- ✻ Caramelized Carrot Soup with Coriander-Lemon Browned Butter (page 143)
- ✻ Mushroom and Leek Galette with Gorgonzola (page 254)
- ✻ Cacio e Pepe Beans with Squash, Sage, and Walnuts (page 372)
- ✻ Pan-Seared Beets with Horseradish Cream (page 530)

Menu 3

- ✻ Shaved Celery Salad with Pomegranate-Honey Vinaigrette (page 109)
- ✻ Sweet Potato Soup with Maple Sour Cream (page 146)
- ✻ Vidalia Onion Pie (page 251)
- ✻ Butter-Roasted Carrots with Hazelnut Crumble and Goat Cheese (page 537)
- ✻ Skillet-Charred Green Beans with Crispy Bread-Crumb Topping (page 552)

Menu 1

Menu 2

Menu 3

Basic Vegetable Prep

Some basic vegetable prep is required, whether you are simply steaming a vegetable or making a more involved recipe. After years of peeling, seeding, coring, and chopping in the test kitchen, we've found that the following methods are the easiest and most efficient ways to prepare vegetables for myriad uses.

Asparagus

1. Remove one stalk of asparagus from the bunch and bend it at the thicker end until it snaps.

2. With the broken asparagus as a guide, trim the tough ends from the remaining asparagus bunch using a chef's knife.

Avocados

1. After slicing the avocado in half around the pit with a chef's knife, lodge the edge of the knife blade into the pit and twist to remove.

2. Use a dish towel to hold the avocado steady. Make ½-inch crosshatch incisions in the flesh of each avocado half with a knife, cutting down to, but not through, the skin.

3. Insert a soupspoon between the skin and the flesh and gently scoop out the avocado cubes.

Bell peppers

1. Slice off the top and bottom of the pepper and remove the seeds and stem.

2. Slice down through the side of the pepper.

3. Lay the pepper flat, trim away the remaining ribs and seeds, then cut the pepper into pieces or strips as desired.

Bok choy

1. Trim the bottom 1 inch from the head of bok choy. Wash and pat the leaves and stalks dry. Cut the leafy green portion away from either side of the white stalk.

2. Cut each white stalk in half lengthwise, then crosswise into thin strips.

3. Stack the leafy greens and slice crosswise into thin strips. Keep the sliced stalks and leaves separate.

Broccoli

1. Place the head of broccoli upside down on the cutting board and use a chef's knife to trim off the florets very close to the head. Cut the florets into 1-inch pieces.

2. After cutting away the tough outer peel of the stalk, square off the stalk, then slice it into ¼-inch-thick pieces.

Brussels sprouts

Peel off any loose or discolored leaves and use paring knife to slice off bottom of stem end, leaving leaves attached.

Butternut squash

1. After peeling the squash, use a chef's knife to trim off the top and bottom and then cut the squash in half where the narrow neck and wide curved bottom meet.

2. Cut a strip from the neck to create a stable base. Set the neck on the base and cut it into planks, then into pieces. (Or halve the neck lengthwise and slice each into half moons.)

3. Cut the bottom of the squash in half lengthwise, and scoop out and discard the seeds and fibers. Slice each half into even lengths and then into pieces according to the recipe.

Cabbage

1. Cut the cabbage into quarters, then trim and discard the hard core.

2. Separate the cabbage into small stacks of leaves that flatten when pressed.

3. Use a chef's knife to cut each stack of leaves into thin shreds (you can also use the slicing disk of a food processor to do this).

Carrots

1. Slice the carrot on the bias into 2-inch-long oval pieces.

2. For matchsticks, lay the ovals flat on a cutting board, then slice into 2-inch-long matchsticks, about ¼ inch thick.

Cauliflower

1. Pull off any leaves, then cut out the core of the cauliflower using a chef's knife.

2. Separate the florets from the inner stem using the tip of the knife.

3. Cut larger florets into smaller pieces by slicing through the stem.

Celery root

1. Using chef's knife, cut ½ inch from both root end and opposite end.

2. To peel, cut from top to bottom, rotating celery root while removing wide strips of skin.

Chiles

1. Using a sharp knife, trim and discard the stem end. Slice the chile in half lengthwise.

2. Use a spoon to scrape out the seeds and ribs (reserve if desired). Prepare the seeded chile as directed.

Corn

After removing the husk and silk, stand the ear upright in a large bowl and use a chef's knife to slice the kernels off of the cob.

Cucumbers and Zucchini

Halve the cucumber or zucchini lengthwise. Run a spoon inside each half to scoop out the seeds.

Fennel

1. Cut off the stems and fronds. Trim a thin slice from the base. Remove any tough or blemished outer layers from the bulb.

2. Cut the bulb in half through the base, then use a paring knife to remove the core.

3. Slice each half into thin strips, cutting from the base to the stem end.

Garlic

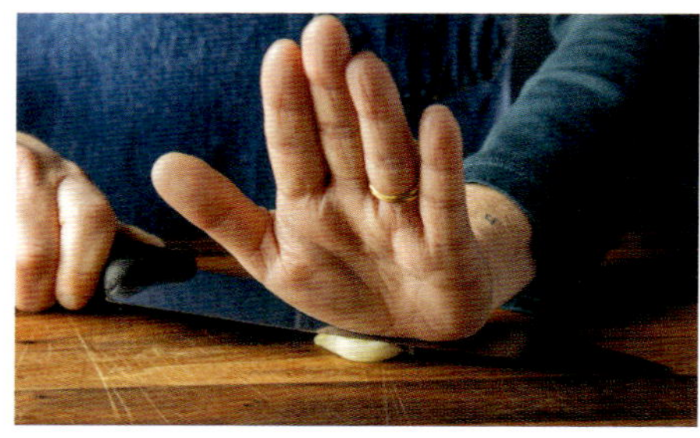

1. Trim off the root end, then crush the clove between the side of the knife and the cutting board to loosen and remove the skin.

2. Resting your fingers on top of the knife blade, use a rocking motion to mince the garlic, pivoting the knife as you work.

Mincing garlic to a paste

Sprinkle the minced garlic with salt, then scrape the blade of the knife back and forth over the garlic until it forms a sticky paste.

Ginger

1. To peel ginger, hold it firmly against the cutting board and use the edge of a dinner spoon to scrape away the skin.

2A. To grate ginger, peel a small section and then grate the peeled portion with a rasp-style grater.

2B. To mince ginger, slice the peeled ginger into thin rounds, cut the rounds into thin strips, and mince the strips.

Hearty greens (Swiss chard, kale, and collard greens)

1. Cut away the leafy portion from the stalk or stem using a chef's knife.

2. Stack several leaves and either slice them crosswise or chop them into pieces according to the recipe.

3. If using chard stems, cut them into pieces as directed. (Discard collard and kale stems.)

Leeks

1. Trim and discard the root and dark green leaves.

2. Cut the trimmed leek in half lengthwise, then slice it crosswise.

3. Rinse the cut leeks thoroughly using a bowl of water or a salad spinner.

Mushrooms

1. Rinse mushrooms just before cooking. Or, if the mushrooms will be eaten raw, simply brush the dirt away with a soft pastry brush or cloth.

2. Tender white button and cremini stems can simply be trimmed. Tough, woody shiitake and portobello stems should be removed.

Onions

1. Halve the onion through the root end, and then peel and trim the top. Make several horizontal cuts from one end of the onion to the other but don't cut through the root end.

2. Make several vertical cuts. Be sure to cut up to but not through the root end.

3. Rotate the onion so the root end is in the back; slice the onion thinly across the previous cuts. As you slice, the onion will fall apart into chopped pieces.

Potatoes

1. Cut a thin sliver from one side of the potato to create a stable base. Set the potato on the cut side and slice it crosswise into even planks.

2. Stack several planks and cut them crosswise, then rotate 90 degrees and cut them crosswise again to create even pieces, or directed in the recipe.

Shallots

1. Make closely spaced horizontal cuts through the peeled shallot, leaving the root end intact.

2. Next, make several vertical cuts through the shallot.

3. Finally, thinly slice the shallot crosswise, creating a fine mince.

Snap peas and Snow peas

Use a paring knife and your thumb to snip off the tip of the pod and pull along the flat side to remove the string at the same time.

Tomatoes

1. Remove the core of the tomato using a paring knife.

2. Slice the tomato crosswise with a sharp chef's knife or serrated knife.

3. Stack several slices of tomato and then cut them into pieces as desired.

Vegetables Front & Center

Steaks and Roasts

36 Curry Roasted Cabbage Wedges with Tomatoes and Chickpeas ■ ●

37 Butternut Squash Steaks with Honey-Nut Topping

37 Garlic Yogurt Sauce ■ ●

38 Cauliflower Steaks with Salsa Verde ■ ●

38 King Trumpet Mushrooms with Smoked Paprika Vinaigrette ●

40 Spicy Chile-Honey Glazed Eggplant with Burrata and Greens ■

41 Hasselback Eggplant with Muhammara ●

41 Whole Pot-Roasted Cauliflower with Tomatoes and Olives

42 Whole Romanesco with Berbere and Yogurt-Tahini Sauce ■ ●

Stir-Fries, Sautés, and Braises

43 Stir-Fried Asparagus with Shiitake Mushrooms ■ ●

45 Eggplant with Black Bean Sauce ■ ●

45 Di San Xian (Stir-Fried Three Treasures)

46 Stir-Fried Portobellos with Ginger-Oyster Sauce
Stir-Fried Portobellos with Sweet Chili-Garlic Sauce

48 Aloo Gobi ●

49 Sautéed Eggplant with Polenta ■ ●

50 Green Curry with Kale and Butternut Squash ●

53 Madras Okra Curry

53 Mushroom Bourguignon ●

55 Potato Vindaloo ●

Bakes

55 Silky Roasted Eggplant with Tomato and Feta

57 Baharat Cauliflower and Eggplant with Chickpeas

57 Baharat ■ ●

58 Walkaway Ratatouille ●

58 Vegetable Lasagna

60 Eggplant Parmesan

62 Baked Pumpkin Kibbeh

63 Skillet Tomato Cobbler

65 Savory Dutch Baby with Portobellos, Roasted Red Peppers, Walnuts, and Feta

65 Cheesy Tomato and Bean Bake

66 Mushroom and White Bean Gratin ●

67 Swiss Chard, Pinto Bean, and Monterey Jack Enchiladas

68 Herb Vegetable and Lentil Bake

69 Charred Cauliflower and Crispy Chickpeas with Romesco ■ ●

70 Broccoli Rabe and Farro Gratin

Stuffed

71 Teff-Stuffed Acorn Squash with Lime Crema and Roasted Pepitas ●

72 Stuffed Delicata Squash ■

72 Eggplant Involtini

75 Stuffed Peppers with Chickpeas, Goat Cheese, and Herbs

75 Chiles Rellenos

77 Stuffed Portobello Mushrooms with Spinach and Gorgonzola

78 Chipotle Lentil–Stuffed Sweet Potatoes

78 Stuffed Tomatoes with Couscous and Zucchini

Bowls

81 Beet Poke Bowls ●

81 Cauliflower Rice Bowls with Sweet Potatoes, Avocados, and Chickpeas ■ ●

82 Spiced Roasted Chickpeas ●

83 Roasted Vegetable Bowls with Bulgur, White Beans, and Arugula ●

85 Hearty Vegetable and Farro Bowls with Goat Cheese ■

85 Roasted Tofu and Sweet Potato Bowls with Snap Pea Salad

86 Rainbow Bowls with Crispy Tempeh ■

86 Orange-Ginger Vinaigrette ■

Toppings for Vegetable Dishes

88 Tarragon-Lemon Gremolata ■ ●

88 Shichimi Togarashi ■ ●

88 Savory Seed Brittle

89 Dukkah ●

89 Microwave-Fried Shallots ■ ●

89 Store-Bought Toppings

■ Fast (45 minutes or less) ● Vegan

top | *Curry Roasted Cabbage Wedges with Tomatoes and Chickpeas*

bottom | *Butternut Squash Steaks with Honey-Nut Topping*

Curry Roasted Cabbage Wedges with Tomatoes and Chickpeas

FAST **VEGAN** Serves 4 Total Time 45 minutes

Why This Recipe Works When you cut cabbage into wedges and roast it, you get charred, crispy edges with tender, sweet layers underneath. We first brush the wedges with a curry-infused oil, including a little sugar to help with browning. Then we cover the cabbage with aluminum foil before putting the baking sheet on the lower rack of a hot oven to steam the wedges and jump-start browning on the undersides. Instead of flipping them, simply uncovering them for the last part of cooking—and adding another drizzle of oil—turns them crispy, browning the upper sides while maximizing browning underneath. To complete our meal, we simmer an aromatic chickpea-tomato curry in a skillet while the cabbage roasts. When slicing the cabbage into wedges, be sure to slice through the core, leaving it intact so the wedges don't fall apart. Smaller 2-pound cabbages work best here; if you have a larger cabbage, you can remove the outer leaves until it weighs about 2 pounds, though it may not brown as well. Serve with Herbed Yogurt Sauce (page 218), if you like.

- 7 tablespoons vegetable oil, divided
- 1 tablespoon curry powder, divided
- 1½ teaspoons sugar
- 1 teaspoon table salt
- ¼ teaspoon pepper
- 1 head green cabbage (2 pounds)
- 2 garlic cloves, minced
- 2 teaspoons grated fresh ginger
- 2 (15-ounce) cans chickpeas, undrained
- 10 ounces grape tomatoes, halved
- ¼ cup chopped fresh cilantro

1. Adjust oven rack to lowest position and heat oven to 500 degrees. Combine ¼ cup oil, 2 teaspoons curry powder, sugar, salt, and pepper in small bowl. Halve cabbage through core and cut each half into 4 approximately 2-inch-wide wedges, leaving core intact (you will have 8 wedges).

2. Arrange cabbage wedges in even layer on rimmed baking sheet, then brush cabbage all over with oil mixture. Cover tightly with aluminum foil and roast for 10 minutes. Remove foil and drizzle 2 tablespoons oil evenly over wedges. Return cabbage to oven and roast, uncovered, until cabbage is tender and sides touching sheet are well browned, 12 to 15 minutes.

3. Meanwhile, heat remaining 1 tablespoon oil in 12-inch skillet over medium-high heat until shimmering. Add garlic, ginger, and remaining 1 teaspoon curry powder and cook, mashing mixture into skillet, until fragrant, about 30 seconds. Add chickpeas and their liquid and tomatoes and bring to simmer. Cook, stirring frequently, until tomatoes begin to break down and mixture has thickened slightly, 7 to 9 minutes.

4. Divide cabbage among individual plates and spoon chickpea mixture over top. Sprinkle with cilantro and serve.

Butternut Squash Steaks with Honey-Nut Topping

Serves 4 Total Time 1 hour

Why This Recipe Works The dense texture of butternut squash makes it a great vegetable to cut into steaks, and here we give it a liberal coating of bold seasonings (think cinnamon, coriander, and Aleppo pepper). For the best texture and browning we use a reverse-searing method, first cooking slabs from the necks of butternut squash through in the oven and then browning and crisping them in a skillet. To serve, we sprinkle toasted pistachios and sesame seeds on the steaks for nuttiness and crunch, then dollop them with tangy garlic yogurt. A drizzle of honey brings all the flavors together, ensuring that every forkful has a balance of sweet, spicy, and savory. We like to pair the squash with a simple side of couscous.

- ¼ cup extra-virgin olive oil, divided
- 2 teaspoons sugar
- 2 teaspoons ground cumin
- 1 teaspoon garlic powder
- 1 teaspoon table salt
- ½ teaspoon ground dried Aleppo pepper
- ½ teaspoon ground coriander
- ½ teaspoon ground cinnamon
- ½ teaspoon pepper
- 2 (3-pound) butternut squashes
- 2 tablespoons chopped toasted pistachios
- 1 tablespoon sesame seeds, toasted
- 2 tablespoons honey
- 1 tablespoon torn fresh mint
- 1 recipe Garlic Yogurt Sauce (recipe follows)
- Lime wedges

1. Adjust oven rack to middle position and heat oven to 450 degrees. Combine 3 tablespoons oil, sugar, cumin, garlic powder, salt, Aleppo pepper, coriander, cinnamon, and pepper; set aside.

2. Working with 1 squash at a time, cut crosswise into 2 pieces at base of neck; reserve bulb for another use. Peel away skin and fibrous threads just below skin (squash should be completely orange, with no white flesh), then carefully cut each piece in half lengthwise. Cut one ¾-inch-thick slab lengthwise from each half. Repeat with remaining squash. (You should have 4 steaks; reserve remaining squash for another use.)

3. Place steaks on wire rack set in rimmed baking sheet and brush evenly with spice mixture. Flip steaks and brush second side with spice mixture. Roast until nearly tender and knife inserted into steaks meets with some resistance, 15 to 20 minutes; remove from oven.

4. Heat remaining 1 tablespoon oil in 12-inch nonstick skillet over medium-high heat until just smoking. Carefully place steaks in skillet and cook, without moving, until well browned and crisp on first side, about 3 minutes. Flip steaks and continue to cook until well browned and crisp on second side, about 3 minutes. Transfer steaks to serving platter

5. Sprinkle steaks with pistachios and sesame seeds. Microwave honey until fluid, about 10 seconds, then drizzle evenly over steaks. Sprinkle with mint and serve with yogurt sauce and lime wedges.

Garlic Yogurt Sauce

FAST VEGAN Makes ½ cup Total Time 5 minutes

To make a drizzleable version of this sauce, use regular plain yogurt. To make this recipe vegan, substitute plant-based yogurt for the dairy yogurt.

- ½ cup plain Greek yogurt
- 1 tablespoon lemon juice
- 1 tablespoon chopped fresh mint
- 1 garlic clove, minced

Combine all ingredients in bowl and season with salt and pepper to taste. Serve. (Sauce can be refrigerated for up to 4 days.)

Cauliflower Steaks with Salsa Verde

FAST VEGAN Serves 4 Total Time 45 minutes

Why This Recipe Works When you cook thick planks of cauliflower they become nutty, sweet, and caramelized. To produce four perfectly cooked cauliflower steaks simultaneously, we opt for a rimmed baking sheet and a scorching oven. We steam the cauliflower briefly by covering the baking sheet with foil, then roast it uncovered on the lowest oven rack, resulting in caramelized seared steaks with tender interiors. To elevate the cauliflower to centerpiece status, we pair it with a vibrant Italian-style salsa verde. Look for fresh, firm, bright white heads of cauliflower that feel heavy for their size and are free of blemishes or soft spots; florets are more likely to separate from older heads of cauliflower. Serve with grated Parmesan cheese.

- 1½ cups fresh parsley leaves
- ½ cup fresh mint leaves
- ½ cup extra-virgin olive oil, divided
- 2 tablespoons water
- 1½ tablespoons white wine vinegar
- 1 tablespoon capers, rinsed
- 1 garlic clove, minced
- ⅛ teaspoon plus ½ teaspoon table salt, divided
- 2 heads cauliflower (2 pounds each)
- ¼ teaspoon pepper, divided
- Lemon wedges

1. Pulse parsley, mint, ¼ cup oil, water, vinegar, capers, garlic, and ⅛ teaspoon salt in food processor until mixture is finely chopped but not smooth, about 10 pulses, scraping down sides of bowl as needed. Transfer salsa verde to small bowl and set aside. (Salsa verde can be refrigerated for up to 2 days.)

2. Adjust oven rack to lowest position and heat oven to 500 degrees. Working with 1 head cauliflower at a time, discard outer leaves of cauliflower and trim stem flush with bottom florets. Halve cauliflower lengthwise through core. Cut one 1½-inch-thick slab lengthwise from each half, trimming any florets not connected to core. Repeat with remaining cauliflower. (You should have 4 steaks; reserve remaining cauliflower for another use.)

3. Place steaks on rimmed baking sheet and drizzle with 2 tablespoons oil. Sprinkle with ¼ teaspoon salt and ⅛ teaspoon pepper and rub to distribute. Flip steaks and repeat with remaining 2 tablespoons oil, remaining ¼ teaspoon salt, and remaining ⅛ teaspoon pepper.

4. Cover baking sheet tightly with aluminum foil and roast for 5 minutes. Remove foil and roast until bottoms of steaks are well browned, 8 to 10 minutes. Gently flip and continue to roast until tender and second sides are well browned, 6 to 8 more minutes.

5. Transfer steaks to platter and brush evenly with ¼ cup salsa verde. Serve with lemon wedges and remaining salsa verde.

Preparing Cauliflower Steaks

1. Trim leaves from cauliflower head and cut stem flush with bottom florets. Halve head lengthwise through core.

2. Cut one 1½-inch-thick slab from each half. Reserve remaining cauliflower for another use.

King Trumpet Mushrooms with Smoked Paprika Vinaigrette

VEGAN Serves 4 Total Time 1 hour

Why This Recipe Works King trumpet mushrooms are large, dense mushrooms with a mild flavor. When cooked, their nutty, earthy flavors shine, and their texture becomes soft and silky. First we halve the mushrooms lengthwise and then crosshatch them, salting their cut surfaces to promote better crisping and seasoning. We then slow-cook them in a generous glug of olive oil before cranking up the heat to crisp them. A simple sauce of pan-roasted garlic, parsley, sherry vinegar, smoked paprika, and the warm, aromatic cooking oil makes these special mushrooms an amazing side dish. You can also serve them as an appetizer with bread and cheese, or chopped and added to an omelet, risotto, or pasta sauce. Look for king trumpet mushrooms, also known as king oyster mushrooms, that are unblemished and firm and weigh about 3 ounces each. You can substitute red or white wine vinegar for the sherry vinegar. You will need a 12-inch nonstick skillet with a tight-fitting lid for this recipe.

- 1¼ pounds king trumpet mushrooms
- 1¼ teaspoons table salt, divided
- ½ cup extra-virgin olive oil
- 8 garlic cloves, lightly crushed and peeled
- 1 sprig fresh rosemary
- ¼ cup minced fresh parsley
- 2 tablespoons sherry vinegar
- ½ teaspoon smoked paprika
- Flake sea salt (optional)

1. Trim bottom ½ inch from mushroom stems, then halve mushrooms lengthwise. Cut ¼-inch crosshatch pattern, about ¹⁄₁₆ inch deep, on cut sides of mushrooms. Sprinkle 1 teaspoon table salt on cut sides of mushrooms and let sit, cut sides up, for 15 minutes.

2. Heat oil, garlic, and rosemary in 12-inch nonstick skillet over medium-low heat until fragrant, about 2 minutes. Arrange mushroom halves, cut sides down, in even layer in pan (pan will appear crowded at first; mushrooms will shrink as they cook). Heat until bubbles begin to form around edges of mushrooms, about 2 minutes.

3. Reduce heat to low, cover, and cook for 10 minutes. Using tongs, flip mushrooms and continue to cook, covered, until paring knife inserted into mushrooms meets little resistance, 8 to 10 minutes longer.

4. Flip mushrooms, cut sides down, in pan. Transfer garlic to cutting board. Increase heat to medium-high and cook, uncovered, until mushrooms are golden brown on cut sides, 4 to 6 minutes. Transfer mushrooms, cut sides up, to serving platter.

5. Mash garlic into paste with side of large knife. Transfer garlic to medium bowl. Carefully pour warm oil from pan into bowl with garlic paste; discard rosemary sprig. Whisk in parsley, vinegar, paprika, and remaining ¼ teaspoon table salt. Drizzle ¼ cup dressing over mushrooms. Sprinkle with flake sea salt, if desired. Serve, passing remaining dressing separately.

King Trumpet Mushrooms with Smoked Paprika Vinaigrette

Spicy Chile-Honey Glazed Eggplant with Burrata and Greens

FAST Serves 4 Total Time 35 minutes

Why This Recipe Works This beautiful dish features vibrant greens, a lush topping of caramelized and glazed rounds of eggplant, and creamy burrata. The sweet heat of Calabrian chiles along with honey glazes the tender eggplant, giving it a delicious char under the broiler. The burrata brings a bit of a cooling counterpoint to the sweet-spicy eggplant. During the first pass under the broiler we simply toss the eggplant with oil and salt, then brush it with the chile-honey mixture, which assures that it will not burn. We reserve a bit of glaze to drizzle over the top of the dressed greens and then top it all with lemon zest, chopped almonds, and flake sea salt for a restaurant-worthy dish you can make in just 35 minutes. Calabrian chiles are spicy chiles from Italy. Harissa paste or chili-garlic sauce can be substituted.

- 1½ pounds eggplant, sliced into ½-inch-thick rounds
- 3 tablespoons extra-virgin olive oil, divided
- 1 teaspoon table salt
- ¼ cup jarred crushed Calabrian chiles
- ¼ cup honey
- 6 cups (6 ounces) mesclun
- 2 teaspoons grated lemon zest plus 1 tablespoon juice
- 8 ounces burrata cheese, room temperature, cut into 1-inch pieces
- ¼ cup chopped toasted almonds
- Flake sea salt

1. Adjust oven rack 6 inches from broiler element and heat broiler. Line rimmed baking sheet with aluminum foil and spray with vegetable oil spray. Toss eggplant with 1 tablespoon oil and table salt in large bowl and arrange in single layer on prepared sheet. Broil eggplant until softened and beginning to brown, 8 to 10 minutes.

2. Combine Calabrian chiles and honey in small bowl. Reserve 4 teaspoons chile mixture for serving. Flip eggplant pieces, brush with remaining chile mixture, and continue to broil until eggplant tops are well browned, 7 to 10 minutes.

3. Toss mesclun, lemon juice, and remaining 2 tablespoons oil in large bowl until evenly coated. Divide mesclun, eggplant, and burrata among 4 plates. Drizzle with reserved chile mixture and sprinkle with lemon zest, almonds, and flake sea salt. Serve.

top | *Spicy Chile-Honey Glazed Eggplant with Burrata and Greens*

bottom | *Hasselback Eggplant with Muhammara*

Hasselback Eggplant with Muhammara

VEGAN Serves 4 Total Time 1¾ hours

Why This Recipe Works Roasty, smoky eggplant typically has a creamy texture from edge to edge. It's delicious, but we also wanted to experience eggplant with textural variety for a substantive main dish. To achieve a creamy interior and crispy edges, we borrow the technique used for Hasselback potatoes. By making slices every ¼ inch crosswise down the length of the eggplant, stopping just short of slicing through, we create a setup that allows steam to escape during cooking so the eggplant gets tender without bursting and turning to mush. Just as important, we're able to pack the spaces between the slices with flavorful, robust muhammara. The sweet-spicy flavor awakens the earthy meatiness and slight bitterness of the eggplant. A creamy yogurt sauce rounds out the richness and is an attractive finishing touch. The eggplants are substantial on their own, but you can also serve them with rice or grains, or a simple side of green beans.

- 2 large eggplants (1½ pounds each)
- 1 teaspoon table salt, divided
- 1 cup jarred roasted red bell peppers, patted dry and chopped
- ¾ cup walnuts, toasted
- 10 tablespoons panko bread crumbs, divided
- 6 scallions, cut into 1-inch pieces
- 3 tablespoons pomegranate molasses
- 2 tablespoons ground dried Aleppo pepper
- 1 tablespoon lemon juice
- 1 teaspoon ground cumin
- 3 tablespoons extra-virgin olive oil
- 2 tablespoons chopped fresh mint
- 1 recipe Garlic Yogurt Sauce (page 37)

1. Adjust oven rack to upper-middle position and heat oven to 400 degrees. Line rimmed baking sheet with aluminum foil and place wire rack in sheet.

2. Trim stem and bottom ¼ inch of eggplants, then halve lengthwise. Working with 1 half at a time, place eggplant cut side down on cutting board and slice crosswise at ¼-inch intervals, leaving bottom ¼ inch intact. Sprinkle eggplant fans evenly with ½ teaspoon salt, making sure to get salt in between slices. Transfer eggplant fanned side up to prepared rack and let sit for 15 minutes.

3. Process red peppers, walnuts, 6 tablespoons panko, scallions, pomegranate molasses, Aleppo pepper, lemon juice, cumin, and remaining ½ teaspoon salt in food processor to coarse paste, about 30 seconds, scraping down sides of bowl as needed. With processor running, slowly add oil until incorporated.

4. Pat eggplant dry with paper towels. Spread 1½ cups muhammara over eggplant, making sure to spread paste in between slices. Roast until eggplant is tender and easily pierced with tip of paring knife and edges are crispy and golden brown, 1 hour to 1 hour 20 minutes.

5. Remove eggplant from oven and heat broiler. Combine remaining ¼ cup panko and remaining muhammara in bowl. Spread panko mixture evenly over top of eggplant and broil until topping is crisp and golden brown, 1 to 3 minutes. Sprinkle with mint. Serve with yogurt sauce.

Whole Pot-Roasted Cauliflower with Tomatoes and Olives

Serves 4 Total Time 1¼ hours

Why This Recipe Works Cauliflower is lovely when pot-roasted and served whole—especially when coated in a vibrant sauce of chunky tomatoes, raisins, and salty capers and olives. To ensure that all of the rich flavors penetrate the dense vegetable, we start by cooking it upside down and spooning some of the sauce into its crevices. Then we flip it right side up, spoon sauce over it again, and leave the pot uncovered to finish cooking. A combination of white miso and nori powder takes the place of anchovies to give the sauce piquancy.

- 2 (28-ounce) cans whole peeled tomatoes
- 2 tablespoons extra-virgin olive oil, plus extra for drizzling
- 6 garlic cloves, minced
- ¾ teaspoon white miso
- ⅛ teaspoon nori powder
- ¼ teaspoon red pepper flakes
- ¼ cup golden raisins
- ¼ cup pitted kalamata olives, chopped coarse
- 2 tablespoons capers, rinsed
- 1 head cauliflower (2 pounds), outer leaves removed, stem trimmed flush with bottom florets
- 1 ounce Parmesan cheese, grated (½ cup)
- ¼ cup minced fresh parsley

1. Adjust oven rack to middle position and heat oven to 450 degrees. Pulse tomatoes and their juice in food processor until coarsely chopped, 6 to 8 pulses.

2. Cook oil, garlic, miso, nori powder, and pepper flakes in Dutch oven over medium heat, stirring constantly, until fragrant, about 2 minutes. Stir in processed tomatoes, bring to simmer, and cook until slightly thickened, about 10 minutes. Stir in raisins, olives, and capers, then nestle cauliflower head, stem side up, into sauce. Spoon some of sauce over top, cover, transfer pot to oven, and roast until cauliflower is just tender (paring knife slips in and out of core with some resistance), 30 to 35 minutes.

3. Uncover pot and, using tongs, flip cauliflower stem side down. Spoon some of sauce over cauliflower, then scrape down sides of pot. Continue to roast, uncovered, until cauliflower is tender, 10 to 15 minutes.

4. Remove pot from oven. Sprinkle cauliflower with Parmesan and parsley and drizzle with extra oil. Cut cauliflower into wedges and serve, spooning sauce over individual portions.

Whole Romanesco with Berbere and Yogurt-Tahini Sauce

FAST **VEGAN** Serves 4 Total Time 45 minutes

Why This Recipe Works Named for its initial appearance in Italy, this dramatically beautiful, fractal-looking vegetable, which is a pale green relative of cauliflower, is a showstopper when cooked and presented whole. Like other brassicas, romanesco has plenty of earthy flavor, so strong seasoning and deep browning are valuable additional touches of drama. We use the broiler to provide the head of romanesco with a nicely charred exterior, but because this large, dense vegetable can burn under the intense heat before it's cooked through all the way, we first parcook it in the microwave. We then brush olive oil over it and transfer it to the broiler to brown. We baste the broiled romanesco with a mixture of more oil and berbere, a warmly aromatic and highly flavorful Ethiopian spice blend. A bright, cooling yogurt sauce with some nutty depth from tahini pleasantly offsets the warm spice coating, and pine nuts provide crunch against the perfectly tender romanesco. Serve with a grain for a hearty meal. To make this recipe vegan, substitute plant-based yogurt for the dairy yogurt.

Yogurt-Tahini Sauce

- ½ cup plain whole-milk yogurt
- 2 tablespoons tahini
- 1 garlic clove, minced
- ½ teaspoon grated lemon zest plus 1 tablespoon juice

Romanesco

- 1 head romanesco or cauliflower (2 pounds), outer leaves removed, stem trimmed flush with bottom florets
- 1 teaspoon plus 3 tablespoons extra-virgin olive oil, divided
- ¼ teaspoon table salt
- ½ teaspoon paprika
- ¼ teaspoon cayenne pepper
- ¼ teaspoon ground coriander
- ⅛ teaspoon ground allspice
- ⅛ teaspoon ground cardamom
- ⅛ teaspoon ground cumin
- ⅛ teaspoon ground black pepper
- 2 tablespoons pine nuts, toasted and chopped
- 1 tablespoon minced fresh cilantro

1. **For the yogurt-tahini sauce** Whisk all ingredients together in bowl and season with salt and pepper to taste. Set aside.

2. **For the romanesco** Adjust oven rack 6 inches from broiler element and heat broiler. Microwave romanesco in covered bowl until paring knife slips easily in and out of core, 8 to 12 minutes.

3. Transfer romanesco stem side down to 12-inch ovensafe skillet. Drizzle romanesco evenly with 1 teaspoon oil and sprinkle with salt. Transfer skillet to oven and broil until top of romanesco is spotty brown, 8 to 10 minutes. Meanwhile, microwave paprika, cayenne, coriander, allspice, cardamom, cumin, pepper, and remaining 3 tablespoons oil in now-empty bowl, stirring occasionally, until fragrant and bubbling, 1 to 2 minutes.

4. Remove skillet from oven, transfer to wire rack, and pour oil mixture over romanesco. Being careful of hot skillet handle, gently tilt skillet so oil pools to 1 side. Using spoon, baste romanesco until oil is absorbed, about 30 seconds.

5. Cut romanesco into wedges and transfer to serving platter. Sprinkle pine nuts and cilantro over top. Serve with yogurt-tahini sauce.

Stir-Fried Asparagus with Shiitake Mushrooms

FAST **VEGAN** Serves 4 Total Time 20 minutes

Why This Recipe Works Asparagus is a natural candidate for stir-frying because it cooks in a flash and the intense heat caramelizes it beautifully, while the short cooking time ensures that it emerges crisp-tender. Here, thinly sliced shiitake mushrooms complement it and add heft, while a potent sauce inspired by Chinese flavors takes this dish to new heights. To ensure that the asparagus and mushrooms cook evenly, we add a bit of water, which creates a small amount of steam that cooks the vegetables through before evaporating, leaving behind a flavorful, clingy glaze. Look for asparagus spears no thicker than ½ inch.

- 2 tablespoons water
- 1 tablespoon soy sauce
- 1 tablespoon Shaoxing wine
- 2 teaspoons packed brown sugar
- 2 teaspoons grated fresh ginger
- 1 teaspoon toasted sesame oil
- 1 tablespoon vegetable oil
- 1 pound thin asparagus, trimmed and cut on bias into 2-inch lengths
- 4 ounces shiitake mushrooms, stemmed and sliced thin
- 2 scallions, green parts only, sliced thin on bias

1. Combine water, soy sauce, Shaoxing wine, sugar, ginger, and sesame oil in bowl.

2. Heat vegetable oil in 14-inch flat-bottomed wok or 12-inch nonstick skillet over high heat until smoking. Add asparagus and mushrooms and cook, stirring occasionally, until asparagus is spotty brown, 3 to 4 minutes. Add soy sauce mixture and cook, stirring twice, until asparagus is crisp-tender, 1 to 2 minutes. Transfer to platter, sprinkle with scallion greens, and serve.

top | *Whole Romanesco with Berbere and Yogurt-Tahini Sauce*
bottom | *Stir-Fried Asparagus with Shiitake Mushrooms*

Eggplant with Black Bean Sauce

A Most Alluring Vegetable

With their dark, luminous skin and many beautiful shapes, eggplants seem a bit mysterious. Technically a fruit and a member of the nightshade family, eggplants were first cultivated in China but have culinary roots in the Mediterranean, the Middle East, and India. Eggplant with Black Bean Sauce is a Chinese recipe with a very un-Chinese method for removing the moisture that plagues so many dishes.

Salt and Steam

Raw eggplants are spongy, with a lot of water tucked away in their flesh. Getting them to that deliciously browned and silky state requires removing this water before cooking. A microwave accomplishes this easily in a third of the time of most other methods. It steams the eggplant and that releases liquid. Salting the eggplant before placing it in the microwave helps accelerate this process. All in all, it takes only 10 minutes to get the eggplant pieces recipe ready.

Sauce Matters

Eggplants are great at soaking up sauces, and here we build a bold Sichuan chili sauce. Heating a wok until smoking, then tossing the eggplant pieces (and sliced green bell pepper) constantly is the secret behind beautifully charred and tender eggplant ready to pair with a sauce. We add a garlic–black bean sauce to the eggplant off the heat to keep its bite and pungency fresh.

Eggplant with Black Bean Sauce

FAST VEGAN Serves 4 Total Time 45 minutes

Why This Recipe Works Eggplants are notorious for exuding water when cooked, and without intervention this usually gets in the way of browning, rendering them mushy. Typically, solving this problem involves salting to draw out the moisture, then blotting the excess liquid. But we found that a microwave accomplishes this in one-third the time. How? The microwave draws out moisture in the form of steam, while salting the eggplant beforehand expedites the process. The result: ready-to-cook eggplant pieces primed to soak up any delicious sauces tossed their way—in this case, a bold Sichuan chili oil with pungent fermented black beans and herbaceous cilantro. Chinese or Japanese eggplant, which both have thinner skin and fewer seeds than globe eggplant, are good options for this dish. If unavailable, globe or Italian eggplant can be substituted.

- 1½ pounds Chinese or Japanese eggplant, cut into 1½-inch pieces
- 1 teaspoon kosher salt
- ⅓ cup plus 3 tablespoons vegetable oil, divided
- 2 garlic cloves, sliced thin
- 1½ tablespoons Sichuan chili flakes
- 1 (½-inch) piece ginger, peeled and sliced thin
- 1 star anise pod
- ¼ cup hoisin sauce
- ¼ cup douchi (fermented black beans), rinsed
- ¼ cup plus 2 tablespoons Shaoxing wine, divided
- 1 tablespoon sugar
- 1 green bell pepper, stemmed, seeded, and cut into 1-inch pieces
- ¼ cup water
- 6 scallions, white parts sliced thin, green parts cut into 1-inch pieces
- 12 sprigs fresh cilantro, cut into 2-inch pieces

1. Toss eggplant with salt in medium bowl. Line large plate with double layer of coffee filters and lightly spray with vegetable oil spray. Spread eggplant in even layer over prepared plate. Microwave until eggplant feels dry and pieces shrink to about 1 inch, about 10 minutes, flipping eggplant halfway through microwaving. Transfer immediately to paper towel–lined plate.

2. Meanwhile, cook ⅓ cup oil, garlic, chile flakes, ginger, and star anise in 14-inch flat-bottomed wok or 12-inch nonstick skillet over medium-high heat until sizzling. Reduce heat to low and gently simmer until garlic and ginger are softened but not browned, about 5 minutes. Transfer oil mixture to medium bowl and let cool for 5 minutes. Stir in hoisin, douchi, 2 tablespoons Shaoxing wine, and sugar. Wipe wok clean with paper towels.

3. Heat now-empty wok over high heat until just beginning to smoke. Drizzle 2 tablespoons oil around perimeter of wok and heat until just smoking. Add eggplant and cook, tossing eggplant slowly but constantly, until pieces are charred on most sides, 5 to 7 minutes. Add remaining 1 tablespoon oil and bell pepper and cook, tossing slowly but constantly, until bell pepper is lightly charred, about 3 minutes.

4. Reduce heat to medium and add remaining ¼ cup Shaoxing wine and water, scraping up any browned bits. Cook, tossing constantly, until liquid is reduced by half, about 15 seconds. Stir in scallion greens and cook, tossing constantly, until slightly wilted, about 15 seconds. Off heat, stir in garlic–black bean sauce until combined. Top with scallion whites and cilantro and serve.

Di San Xian (Stir-Fried Three Treasures)

Serves 4 Total Time 55 minutes

Why This Recipe Works This vibrant, hearty main dish relies on humble ingredients. Di san xian, or stir-fried three treasures (eggplant, potatoes, and bell pepper), is a beloved flavorful dish from Northern China. We start by flash-frying each vegetable, which preserves their color and achieves appealing—and different—textures. The potato crisps and becomes creamy, while the eggplant turns silky and the pepper becomes perfectly tender. Frying in small batches prevents crowding, allowing the wok (or Dutch oven) to maintain high heat for that coveted restaurant-style sear. A simple yet potent sauce of soy sauce, garlic, and aromatics ties the vegetables together, creating layers of savory depth. You can substitute Japanese eggplant for the Chinese eggplant in this recipe, but we don't recommend substituting globe or Italian eggplant. You can use a Dutch oven to fry the vegetables, but you'll need to increase the frying oil to 4 cups. Using a roll cut to cut the eggplant and potatoes creates pieces that cook evenly.

- 1 pound Chinese eggplant
- 2 teaspoons table salt for brining
- 2 Yukon Gold potatoes (8 ounces each), peeled
- ¼ cup soy sauce
- 3 tablespoons vegetarian oyster sauce
- 1 tablespoon sugar
- 4 teaspoons cornstarch, divided
- 3–4 cups peanut or vegetable oil, for frying
- 1 green bell pepper, stemmed, seeded, and cut into 1-inch pieces
- 1 tablespoon vegetable oil
- 2 scallions, white and green parts separated and sliced thin
- 2 garlic cloves, minced

1. Trim stem end of eggplant. Hold knife at about 45 degree angle relative to eggplant and cut 1½ inches from end. Roll eggplant towards you until cut side is facing up, then cut again 1½ inches from end at same angle. Repeat rolling and cutting. (Eggplant pieces should be roughly triangular in shape.) In large bowl, whisk salt into 4 cups cold water to dissolve, then add eggplant. Place plate over eggplant to submerge and let sit for 15 minutes.

2. Meanwhile, quarter potatoes lengthwise. Working with one potato piece at a time, hold knife at about 45 degree angle relative to potato and cut 1 inch from end. Roll potato toward you until cut side is facing up, then cut again 1 inch from end at same angle. Repeat rolling and cutting with remaining potato pieces. (Potato pieces should be roughly triangular in shape.)

3. Whisk ¼ cup water, soy sauce, oyster sauce, sugar, and 2 teaspoons cornstarch together in small bowl; set aside. Drain eggplant and pat dry with paper towels. Dry large bowl and return eggplant to it. Toss with remaining 2 teaspoons cornstarch to coat lightly.

4. Line rimmed baking sheet with triple layer of paper towels. Add peanut oil to 14-inch flat-bottomed wok or Dutch oven until it measures 1-inch deep and heat over medium-high heat to 375 degrees. Add half of eggplant and cook until tender and edges are golden, about 3 minutes. Adjust burner, if necessary, to maintain oil temperature between 350 and 375 degrees. Using spider skimmer or slotted spoon, transfer eggplant to prepared sheet and repeat with remaining eggplant.

5. Add potatoes to oil in pan and cook until tender, about 5 minutes, adjusting burner, if necessary, to maintain oil temperature between 350 and 375 degrees. Using spider skimmer or slotted spoon transfer to sheet with eggplant. Add bell pepper to oil and cook for 30 seconds, then transfer to sheet with vegetables.

6. Heat 1 tablespoon vegetable oil in 12-inch nonstick skillet over medium-high heat until shimmering. Add scallion whites and garlic and cook until fragrant, about 30 seconds. Whisk reserved sauce to recombine, then add to skillet, along with fried vegetables and scallion greens. Stir to coat well and cook until sauce is thickened slightly, about 1 minute. Transfer to platter and serve.

Roll-Cutting Vegetables

1. Hold knife at about 45-degree angle (relative to eggplant or potato) and make diagonal cut 1½ inches from end.

2. Roll vegetable 90 degrees (quarter turn) until cut side is facing up, then cut again 1½ inches from end at same angle to create 2 angled sides.

Stir-Fried Portobellos with Ginger-Oyster Sauce

Serves 3 to 4   Total Time 55 minutes

Why This Recipe Works Portobellos, with their earthy flavor and firm texture, steal the limelight in this vegetable stir-fry. After removing the gills (to keep the mushrooms from tasting leathery and raw), we cut the caps into substantial 2-inch wedges. We cook the mushrooms over medium-high heat until brown and tender, then add a mixture of broth, soy sauce, and sugar and reduce it to a glaze—this provides an intense flavor boost. Accompanying the portobellos here are carrots, snow peas, and napa cabbage. Finally, the sauce—consisting of broth, oyster sauce, soy sauce, cornstarch, and sesame oil—and a heavy dose of ginger tie the dish together, giving the vegetables fantastic flavor. Serve with white rice.

Glaze

- ¼ cup vegetable broth
- 2 tablespoons soy sauce
- 2 tablespoons sugar

Sauce

- 1 cup vegetable broth
- 3 tablespoons vegetarian oyster sauce
- 1 tablespoon soy sauce
- 1 tablespoon cornstarch
- 2 teaspoons toasted sesame oil

Vegetables

- ¼ cup peanut or vegetable oil, divided
- 4 teaspoons minced or grated fresh ginger
- 2 garlic cloves, minced
- 6–8 portobello mushrooms (each 4 to 6 inches), stemmed, gills removed, and cut into 2-inch wedges
- 4 carrots, peeled and sliced ¼ inch thick on bias
- ½ cup vegetable broth
- 3 ounces snow peas, strings removed
- 1 pound napa cabbage (1 small head), cored and cut into ¾-inch strips
- 1 tablespoon sesame seeds, toasted (optional)

1. For the glaze Combine broth, soy sauce, and sugar in small bowl and set aside.

2. For the sauce Combine all ingredients in small bowl and set aside.

3. For the vegetables In small bowl, mix 1 teaspoon oil, ginger, and garlic together; set aside.

4. Heat 3 tablespoons oil in 14-inch flat-bottomed wok or 12-inch nonstick skillet over medium-high heat until shimmering. Add mushrooms and cook without stirring until browned on 1 side, 2 to 3 minutes. Using tongs, flip mushrooms, reduce heat to medium, and cook until second sides are browned and mushrooms are tender, about 5 minutes. Increase heat to medium-high, add glaze, and cook, stirring frequently, until glaze is thick and mushrooms are coated, 1 to 2 minutes. Transfer mushrooms to plate. Rinse pan clean and wipe dry with paper towels.

top | *Di San Xian (Stir-Fried Three Treasures)*

bottom | *Stir-Fried Portobellos with Ginger-Oyster Sauce*

| *Aloo Gobi*

5. Add 1 teaspoon oil to pan and return to high heat until just smoking. Add carrots and cook, stirring frequently, until beginning to brown, 1 to 2 minutes. Add broth, cover, and lower heat to medium. Cook carrots until just tender, 2 to 3 minutes. Uncover and cook until liquid evaporates, about 30 seconds. Transfer carrots to plate with mushrooms.

6. Add remaining 1 teaspoon oil to pan and return to high heat until just smoking. Add snow peas and cook until spotty brown, about 2 minutes. Add cabbage and cook, stirring frequently, until wilted, about 2 minutes.

7. Clear center of pan, add ginger mixture, and cook, mashing mixture into pan, until fragrant, 15 to 20 seconds. Stir ginger mixture into vegetables.

8. Stir in mushrooms and carrots. Whisk sauce to recombine, then add to pan and cook, tossing constantly, until sauce is thickened, 2 to 3 minutes. Transfer to serving platter; sprinkle with sesame seeds, if using; and serve.

Variation

Stir-Fried Portobellos with Sweet Chili-Garlic Sauce

Replace sugar in glaze with 2 tablespoons honey. For sauce, omit vegetarian oyster sauce and toasted sesame oil, reduce broth to ¾ cup, increase soy sauce to 3 tablespoons, and add 2 tablespoons honey, 1 tablespoon rice vinegar, and 1 teaspoon sriracha. For vegetables, increase garlic to 4 cloves.

Aloo Gobi

VEGAN Serves 4 Total Time 50 minutes

Why This Recipe Works Aloo gobi, or "potato cauliflower," is an Indian mainstay that combines these two dense, hearty vegetables to spectacular effect. To tenderize both while retaining some bite, we first shallow-fry them to crisp their exteriors before removing them from the pot. Then, we bloom spices (including asafetida for its savory oniony character, and amchoor for its citrusy fragrance) and aromatics in oil. The veggies go back in, along with water to steam them through. As the water reduces, the potatoes and cauliflower are coated in a flavorful paste. If you are sensitive to spice, seed the serrano chile before using. Look for asafetida, Kashmiri chile powder, and amchoor (also known as aamchur or amchur) at South Asian grocery stores; you might also find them at some well-stocked supermarkets. If you can't find asafetida, you can omit it. If you can't find Kashmiri chile powder, substitute ½ teaspoon paprika plus a pinch of cayenne. If you can't find amchoor, stir 1½ teaspoons lemon juice into the dish at the end of cooking. Serve with roti, basmati rice, or our Chapati (page 213).

- 6 tablespoons vegetable oil
- 1 pound Yukon Gold potatoes, peeled and cut into 1-inch pieces
- 1 pound cauliflower florets, cut into 1-inch pieces
- 1¼ teaspoons cumin seeds
- ¼ teaspoon ground asafetida
- 1 cup finely chopped onion
- 1¼ teaspoons table salt
- 1 serrano chile, halved lengthwise but left intact at stem end
- 1 tablespoon minced garlic
- 1 tablespoon minced fresh ginger
- 1 teaspoon ground coriander
- 1 teaspoon amchoor
- ½ teaspoon ground turmeric
- ½ teaspoon Kashmiri chile powder
- ¾ cup water
- 1 tablespoon chopped fresh cilantro

1. Heat oil in Dutch oven over medium heat until shimmering. Add potatoes and cook, stirring frequently (potatoes may stick to pot), until golden brown in spots, 4 to 5 minutes. Transfer to bowl.

2. Add cauliflower to now-empty pot and cook, gently stirring occasionally, until golden brown in spots, 4 to 5 minutes. Transfer cauliflower to bowl with potatoes.

3. Add cumin seeds and asafetida to now-empty pot and cook, stirring constantly, until fragrant and sizzling, 30 to 60 seconds. Add onion and salt and cook, stirring frequently, until onion is golden brown, 3 to 4 minutes. Add serrano, garlic, ginger, coriander, amchoor, turmeric, and chile powder and cook, stirring frequently, until fragrant, about 1 minute.

4. Return potatoes and cauliflower to pot, along with any excess oil from bowl. Stir in water, scraping up any browned bits. Bring to simmer. Adjust heat to medium-low; cover; and simmer, gently stirring occasionally, until vegetables have absorbed water, 15 to 18 minutes. Transfer to shallow bowl, sprinkle with cilantro, and serve.

Sautéed Eggplant with Polenta

FAST **VEGAN** Serves 4 Total Time 45 minutes

Why This Recipe Works Here, the lushness of a garlicky, silky, tomato sauce and the pungency of a Sicilian caponata mingle with tender bites of stewed eggplant, all served atop a pillow of golden polenta. We cook the wedges of eggplant with sliced onion, olive oil, and garlic, adding a bit of water; the eggplant and onion steam-cook, and when the water evaporates, they become perfectly tender. We cook them a bit more in the now-dry skillet so they can take on some flavorful browning. Meanwhile, we prepare instant polenta, which takes mere minutes once the water boils. Now for the sauce: It's as simple as adding crushed tomatoes to the eggplant mixture, along with raisins, olives, and capers plus red pepper flakes. We cook it all over high heat until the flavors marry and the consistency is lush and thick, perfect for draping over the polenta. Large eggplants disintegrate when braised; using smaller eggplants ensures that the wedges stay intact.

- 2 (8- to 10-ounce) eggplants, trimmed, halved crosswise, and cut into 1-inch-thick wedges
- 2 onions, halved and sliced thin
- 5½ cups water, divided
- ½ cup extra-virgin olive oil, divided
- 4 garlic cloves, sliced thin
- 2½ teaspoons table salt, divided
- 1 cup instant polenta
- 2 cups canned crushed tomatoes
- ¼ cup golden raisins
- ¼ cup pitted kalamata olives, sliced
- 1 tablespoon capers, rinsed
- ¼ teaspoon red pepper flakes

1. Combine eggplants, onions, ½ cup water, ¼ cup oil, garlic, and 1 teaspoon salt in 12-inch nonstick skillet. Cover and cook over medium-high heat, stirring occasionally, until water has evaporated and vegetables are softened, about 10 minutes. Uncover and continue to cook, stirring often, until eggplant and onions are lightly browned, about 8 minutes longer.

2. Meanwhile, bring remaining 5 cups water to boil in large saucepan over medium-high heat. Whisk in polenta, reduce heat to medium-low, and cook until thickened, about 3 minutes. Off heat, stir in 2 tablespoons oil and remaining 1½ teaspoons salt.

3. Stir tomatoes, raisins, olives, capers, and pepper flakes into eggplant mixture and bring to boil over medium-high heat. Reduce heat to medium-low and simmer until slightly thickened, about 8 minutes. Stir in remaining 2 tablespoons oil. Transfer polenta to serving platter. Top with eggplant mixture. Serve.

Green Curry with Kale and Butternut Squash

VEGAN Serves 4 Total Time 1¼ hours

Why This Recipe Works The generous amount of fresh green chiles and aromatics in Thai green curry sauce makes it one of the spiciest and most intense Thai curries. Here we pair it with vegetables to accent the verdant flavors of the sauce. Hearty kale takes well to simmering; the sauce tames the kale's bitter notes and wilts and softens the leaves. To offset the pungent sauce and bitter kale, we introduce butternut squash, which we cut into bite-size cubes so it cooks quickly and evenly in the sauce. We finish the dish with a squeeze of lime juice to brighten the flavor, and a sprinkle of crunchy roasted pepitas to add texture and toasty notes. Light coconut milk can be substituted for regular coconut milk. For a spicier sauce, reserve and add the Thai chile seeds. You will have twice as much green curry sauce as needed for this recipe. You can toss the 2 cups of leftover sauce with cooked vegetables and noodles another night, or use it as a base for braised lentils and beans.

Green Curry Sauce

- ⅓ cup water
- 6 green Thai chiles, stemmed, seeded, and chopped
- 12 garlic cloves, peeled and smashed
- 2 lemongrass stalks, trimmed to bottom 6 inches and sliced thin
- ¼ cup chopped fresh cilantro
- 1 (4-inch) piece ginger, peeled and chopped
- 2 tablespoons vegetable oil
- 2 tablespoons grated lime zest
- 2 teaspoons ground coriander
- 1 teaspoon ground cumin
- ½ teaspoon table salt
- 2 (14-ounce) cans coconut milk
- 2 tablespoons vegetarian fish sauce
- 1 tablespoon packed brown sugar

Vegetables

- 3 tablespoons extra-virgin olive oil
- 2 pounds butternut squash, peeled, seeded, and cut into ½-inch pieces (6 cups)
- ½ teaspoon table salt
- 2 pounds kale, stemmed and chopped
- 1 tablespoon lime juice
- ⅓ cup unsalted roasted pepitas

1. **For the curry sauce** Process water, Thai chiles, garlic, lemongrass, cilantro, ginger, oil, lime zest, coriander, cumin, and salt in blender until finely ground, about 3 minutes, scraping down sides of blender jar as needed.

2. Transfer paste to medium saucepan and cook over medium-high heat, stirring often, until paste is fragrant and begins to sizzle, about 2 minutes. Whisk in coconut milk, fish sauce, and sugar, scraping up any browned bits. Bring to simmer and cook, stirring occasionally, until flavors meld, about 10 minutes. Season with salt to taste. (Sauce can be refrigerated for up to 1 week or frozen for up to 1 month.)

3. **For the vegetables** Heat oil in Dutch oven over medium heat until shimmering. Add squash and salt and cook, stirring occasionally, until squash is just beginning to brown, about 8 minutes; transfer to bowl.

4. Add kale, 1 handful at a time, to now-empty pot and cook over medium heat until just beginning to wilt, about 3 minutes. Stir in 2 cups curry sauce and bring to simmer (reserve remaining sauce for another use). Reduce heat to medium- low, cover, and cook, stirring occasionally, until kale is fully wilted, about 10 minutes.

5. Return squash and any accumulated juices to pot, cover, and simmer until kale and squash are tender and sauce has almost completely evaporated, 10 to 20 minutes. Off heat, stir in lime juice and season with salt to taste. Sprinkle with pepitas and serve.

Trimming Lemongrass

Trim dry top and tough bottom of each stalk. Peel and discard dry outer layer until moist, tender inner stalk is exposed.

Green Curry with Kale and Butternut Squash

The Great Divider

People have strong feelings about okra. Its reputation for being slimy keeps some from ever trying it. And yes, it can become gelatinous, especially when exposed to heat and water. But sometimes that is an advantage, since this can help it act as a thickener—for example, in Cajun gumbo and many other hallmark dishes of the American South (where it is also fried, pickled, stewed, and baked). You can minimize okra's tendency to veer into unpalatable territory by salting it or by cooking it over dry, hot heat. Which is exactly what we do in our recipe for Madras Okra Curry.

A Rich Legacy

Okra came to America from Africa in the days of slavery. It thrives in the heat, so there are many other countries, such as India, where okra is used a lot. This simple curry lets its flavor shine.

Treating It Right

This curry uses 1½ pounds of okra, stemmed but left whole. We cook it in batches until crisp-tender and browned, then set it aside. We then build the sauce in stages, adding creamy coconut milk, honey, and a bit of cornstarch for thickening; we don't use the okra as a thickener because we want it to remain slightly crisp and keep its integrity. This is also why we add the okra to the curry base just to warm it through. The okra makes a big statement in this delicious and beautiful curry.

Madras Okra Curry

Madras Okra Curry

Serves 4 to 6 Total Time 50 minutes

Why This Recipe Works The vivid heat and earthy depth of Madras curry powder make the spice mix a great ingredient to keep on hand for quick, flavorful dinners. The warmth of the seasoning blend (which typically includes spices like coriander, turmeric, and mustard seeds) can add vibrancy and complexity to all sorts of vegetables—including okra, which has a long history in Indian cuisine. Our Madras-style curry pairs a hefty amount of rich sauce with sturdy okra, which can retain some of its pleasurably snappy bite. We start by browning the okra until crisp-tender; searing the pods whole, rather than letting them stew in the sauce, allows them to maintain their slight crunch. We then make a flavor-packed sauce using onion, ginger, garlic, curry powder, and vegetable broth. To thicken the mixture to a velvety consistency, we stir in a mixture of coconut milk, honey, and cornstarch. Fresh cilantro sprigs and bright lime wedges balance out our rich curry. We prefer the spicier flavor of Madras curry powder for this recipe, but you can substitute regular curry powder. Okra pods less than 3 inches long will be the most tender; do not substitute frozen okra here as it does not brown like fresh okra. Serve with white rice.

- 6 tablespoons vegetable oil, divided
- 1½ pounds okra, stemmed, divided
- 1 small onion, chopped fine
- 3 garlic cloves, minced
- 1 tablespoon grated fresh ginger
- 1 tablespoon Madras curry powder
- 2½ cups vegetable broth
- 1 cup canned coconut milk
- 2 teaspoons honey
- 1 teaspoon cornstarch
- ¼ teaspoon table salt
- 10 sprigs fresh cilantro, chopped coarse
- Lime wedges

1. Heat 2 tablespoons oil in 12-inch skillet over medium-high heat until just smoking. Add half of okra to skillet and cook, stirring occasionally, until crisp-tender and well browned on most sides, 5 to 7 minutes; transfer to bowl. Repeat with 2 tablespoons oil and remaining okra; transfer to bowl. Let skillet cool slightly.

2. Heat remaining 2 tablespoons oil in now-empty skillet over medium heat until shimmering. Add onion and cook until softened, about 5 minutes. Stir in garlic, ginger, and curry powder and cook until fragrant, about 1 minute. Stir in broth, scraping up any browned bits, and bring to simmer Cook, stirring occasionally, until reduced to 1¼ cups, 15 to 20 minutes.

3. Whisk coconut milk, honey, and cornstarch in bowl to dissolve cornstarch, then whisk mixture into skillet. Bring to simmer and cook until slightly thickened, about 30 seconds. Stir in okra and any accumulated juices and salt and return to brief simmer to warm through. Season with salt and pepper to taste. Sprinkle with cilantro and serve with lime wedges.

Mushroom Bourguignon

VEGAN Serves 6 to 8 Total Time 1¾ hours

Why This Recipe Works Mushrooms are inherently savory; have the ability to build fond, the rich-tasting browned bits that form on a pot's interior surface; and offer a balance of tenderness and resilience that allows them to turn pleasantly supple when simmered without losing structural integrity. For all these reasons, they're great for featuring in a luxurious, wintry braise such as bourguignon. We start with chunks of meaty, satisfying portobellos, while dried porcini offer a heavy-hitting boost of umami. We add plenty of savory supports such as miso, tomato paste, and soy sauce and classic aromatics and herbs such as carrots, shallot, garlic, and thyme. To achieve the French classic's requisite body and gloss while keeping the stew vegan, we make a modified roux with olive oil and flour. A splash of wine at the end of cooking brings brightness to the dish. Use a good-quality light- to medium-bodied red wine, such as a Pinot Noir or Grenache. You can substitute dried shiitake mushrooms for the porcini and yellow or red miso for white. Leave the mushroom gills intact; they enhance the stew's color and flavor. Serve the bourguignon over polenta, noodles, or mashed potatoes.

top | *Mushroom Bourguignon*
bottom | *Potato Vindaloo*

- 4¾ cups water, divided
- ¼ cup extra-virgin olive oil, divided
- 2½ pounds portobello mushroom caps, cut into 1-inch pieces
- ½ teaspoon table salt
- ¼ teaspoon pepper
- 2 carrots, peeled and sliced ¼ inch thick
- 1 large shallot, chopped
- 4 garlic cloves, smashed and peeled
- 3 tablespoons all-purpose flour
- 1 cup plus 2 tablespoons dry red wine, divided
- 2 tablespoons white miso
- 2 tablespoons soy sauce
- 1 tablespoon tomato paste
- 6 sprigs fresh thyme
- 2 bay leaves
- 1 ounce dried porcini mushrooms, rinsed
- 1 cup frozen pearl onions, thawed
- ¼ cup minced fresh parsley

1. Bring ¼ cup water and 2 tablespoons oil to simmer in Dutch oven over medium-high heat. Add portobello mushrooms, salt, and pepper. Cover and cook, stirring occasionally, until mushrooms have released their moisture, about 10 minutes.

2. Uncover and continue to cook, stirring occasionally, until pot is dry and dark fond forms, 10 to 12 minutes longer. Transfer mushrooms to bowl. Add carrots, shallot, and remaining 2 tablespoons oil to pot and cook, stirring frequently, until vegetables start to brown, 3 to 4 minutes. Add garlic and cook for 1 minute. Stir in flour and cook for 30 seconds. Whisk in 1 cup wine.

3. Add miso, soy sauce, tomato paste, and remaining 4½ cups water and whisk to combine. Add thyme sprigs, bay leaves, and porcini mushrooms and bring to boil over high heat. Reduce heat to maintain vigorous simmer and cook, stirring occasionally and scraping bottom of pot to loosen any browned bits, until sauce is reduced and has consistency of heavy cream, about 25 minutes.

4. Strain sauce through fine-mesh strainer set over large bowl, pressing on solids to extract as much liquid as possible; discard solids. You should have 2 cups sauce. (If you have more, return sauce to pot and continue to cook over medium heat until reduced. If you have less, add enough water to yield 2 cups.) Return sauce to pot. Stir in onions, portobello mushrooms, and remaining 2 tablespoons wine. Cover and cook over low heat, stirring occasionally, until onions are tender, about 20 minutes. Stir in parsley, season with salt and pepper to taste, and serve.

Potato Vindaloo

VEGAN Serves 6 Total Time 1¼ hours

Why This Recipe Works Vindaloo is a complex, spicy dish that blends Portuguese and Indian cuisines into a potent braise featuring warm spices, chiles, red wine vinegar, tomatoes, onions, garlic, and mustard seeds. We set out to translate its comfort food appeal into a hearty vegetarian version. We center our dish around potatoes as they require low and slow cooking to develop complex flavors; to elevate the stew's flavor even more, we use a combination of red and sweet potatoes. Once they are tender we add the tomatoes and vinegar, which otherwise would keep them from softening. To give our vindaloo exceptionally deep flavor, we use a mix of Indian spices plus bay leaves and mustard seeds, and simmer them with the potatoes, which soak up the flavors as they cook. Serve over rice.

- 2 tablespoons vegetable oil
- 2 onions, chopped fine
- 1 pound red potatoes, unpeeled and cut into ½-inch pieces
- 1 pound sweet potatoes, peeled and cut into ½-inch pieces
- 1½ teaspoons table salt, divided
- 10 garlic cloves, minced
- 4 teaspoons paprika
- 1 teaspoon ground cumin
- ¾ teaspoon ground cardamom
- ½ teaspoon cayenne pepper
- ¼ teaspoon ground cloves
- 2½ cups water
- 2 bay leaves
- 1 tablespoon mustard seeds
- 1 (28-ounce) can diced tomatoes
- 2½ tablespoons red wine vinegar
- ¼ cup minced fresh cilantro

1. Heat oil in Dutch oven over medium heat until shimmering. Add onions, red potatoes, sweet potatoes, and ½ teaspoon salt and cook, stirring occasionally, until onions are softened and potatoes begin to soften at edges, 10 to 12 minutes.

2. Stir in garlic, paprika, cumin, cardamom, cayenne, and cloves and cook until fragrant and vegetables are well coated, about 2 minutes. Gradually stir in water, scraping up any browned bits. Stir in bay leaves, mustard seeds, and remaining 1 teaspoon salt and bring to simmer. Cover, reduce heat to medium-low, and cook until potatoes are tender, 15 to 20 minutes.

3. Stir in tomatoes and their juice and vinegar and continue to simmer, uncovered, until flavors are blended and sauce has thickened slightly, about 15 minutes. Discard bay leaves, stir in cilantro, and season with salt and pepper to taste. Serve.

Silky Roasted Eggplant with Tomato and Feta

Serves 4 to 6 Total Time 1¾ hours

Why This Recipe Works This riff on shrimp saganaki—a Greek dish of shrimp stewed in a tomato sauce infused with red pepper flakes and oregano and dotted with chunks of feta—swaps the seafood for vegetarian-friendly eggplant, a substantial vegetable that gives this dish the feeling of a hearty main course. Roasting the eggplant slices allows us to skip the salting and draining step because their excess moisture evaporates in the oven. Baking the browned slices in tomato sauce makes them melt-in-your-mouth tender. Slicing the eggplant at an angle across their fibers ensures that there are no stringy bits. We developed this recipe with Diamond Crystal kosher salt. If using Morton kosher salt, which is denser, use only 1½ teaspoons in step 1. Before flambéing, make sure to roll up long shirt sleeves, tie back long hair, turn off the exhaust fan (otherwise the fan may pull the flames up), and turn off any lit burners (this is critical if you have a gas stove). If flambéing, use a traditional ovensafe skillet rather than a nonstick skillet; the heat produced by igniting the contents of the skillet can damage nonstick coatings.

- ½ cup extra-virgin olive oil, divided
- 2½ pounds eggplant, peeled and sliced ½ inch thick on bias
- 2 teaspoons kosher salt
- ¾ teaspoon pepper
- 1 onion, chopped fine
- 1 tablespoon tomato paste
- 2 garlic cloves, minced
- 1 teaspoon dried oregano
- ½ teaspoon red pepper flakes
- ½ cup dry white wine
- 1 (28-ounce) can crushed tomatoes
- ½ teaspoon sugar
- 8 ounces feta cheese, crumbled (2 cups)
- 2 tablespoons ouzo, grappa, brandy, or vodka (optional)
- ¼ cup minced fresh parsley (optional)
- Crusty bread

Silky Roasted Eggplant with Tomato and Feta

1. Adjust oven racks to upper-middle and lower-middle positions. Heat oven to 450 degrees. Drizzle 2 tablespoons oil over 2 rimmed baking sheets (1 tablespoon per sheet), then use pastry brush to evenly coat sheets. Arrange eggplant slices in even layer over sheets, then brush eggplant evenly with ¼ cup oil. Sprinkle eggplant with salt and pepper.

2. Bake until eggplant slices are golden brown on bottom and tender throughout, about 30 minutes, switching and rotating sheets halfway through baking. Remove sheets from oven and reduce oven temperature to 375 degrees. Let eggplant cool for 5 minutes. Using thin metal spatula, flip each slice and let cool completely on sheets.

3. While eggplant cooks, heat remaining 2 tablespoons oil in 12-inch skillet over medium heat until shimmering. Add onion and cook until softened and beginning to caramelize at edges, 16 to 18 minutes, stirring occasionally. Stir in tomato paste, garlic, oregano, and pepper flakes and cook, stirring occasionally, until fragrant, about 2 minutes. Stir in wine, scraping up any browned bits, and cook until mostly evaporated, about 1 minute. Stir in tomatoes and sugar, increase heat to high, and bring to simmer. Reduce heat to medium-low and simmer until slightly thickened, about 5 minutes. Off heat, season with salt and pepper to taste. Set aside about two-thirds of sauce and spread remaining sauce in even layer in skillet. (Eggplant and tomato sauce can be refrigerated for up to 3 days.)

4. Arrange one-third of cooled eggplant slices in skillet in single layer, spooning some sauce in skillet over eggplant and spreading to cover. Using remaining eggplant slices and reserved sauce, repeat layering 2 more times to make 3 layers. Sprinkle feta evenly over top layer.

5. Transfer skillet to upper rack of oven and bake until sauce is bubbling in center, feta is well browned on top, and tomato sauce is caramelizing at edges of skillet, 35 to 40 minutes. Being careful of hot skillet handle, transfer skillet to wire rack and, if using, drizzle ouzo over top. Wave lit match over skillet until ouzo ignites. When flames subside (15 to 30 seconds), sprinkle with chopped parsley, if using, and serve immediately with crusty bread. (If omitting ouzo, skip flambéing.)

Baharat Cauliflower and Eggplant with Chickpeas

Serves 4 Total Time 1¼ hours

Why This Recipe Works Warm spice and cauliflower are a smart pairing, and here baharat brings out the nuttiness and subtle sweetness of this cruciferous vegetable. We roast the cauliflower with eggplant that's also spiced up for a sheet-pan recipe with contrasting textures and flavors all from vegetables. Stirring chickpeas into the mix turns the roasted vegetables into dinner, and the beans highlight the nuttiness of the dish further. Serving the mix with pickled red onions and a lemony tahini sauce that's a little sweet and a little spicy enlivens this warm-spiced dish. Served with yogurt, this warm meal is made for scooping up with soft, warm pita bread. We prefer our homemade baharat, but you can use store-bought.

- 1½ pounds eggplant, cut into 1½-inch pieces
- 1 teaspoon table salt, divided
- ⅓ cup tahini
- 3 tablespoons water
- 5 tablespoons lemon juice, divided, plus lemon wedges for serving
- 1 small garlic clove, grated
- ½ teaspoon honey
- ⅛ teaspoon cayenne pepper (optional)
- 1 small head cauliflower (1½ pounds), cored and cut into 1½-inch florets
- 1 (15-ounce) can chickpeas, rinsed and patted dry
- ¼ cup extra-virgin olive oil
- 1 tablespoon Baharat (recipe follows)
- ¾ cup chopped fresh cilantro, divided
- Quick Sweet-and-Spicy Pickled Red Onion (page 213)
- Plain yogurt
- Pita bread, warmed

1. Adjust oven rack to lower-middle position and heat oven to 450 degrees. Line rimmed baking sheet with aluminum foil and spray with vegetable oil spray. Toss eggplant with ½ teaspoon salt in colander and let drain for 30 minutes, tossing occasionally. Whisk together tahini, water, 3 tablespoons lemon juice, garlic, honey, and cayenne, if using, until smooth; season with salt and pepper to taste and set aside until ready to serve. (If needed, add more water 1 teaspoon at a time until sauce is thick but pourable.)

2. Pat eggplant dry with paper towels. Toss eggplant, cauliflower, chickpeas, oil, baharat, and remaining ½ teaspoon salt together in large bowl, then spread in even layer on prepared sheet. Roast until vegetables are very tender and beginning to brown in spots, 30 to 40 minutes, stirring occasionally.

3. Gently toss vegetables with ½ cup cilantro and remaining 2 tablespoons lemon juice and season with salt and pepper to taste. Sprinkle with remaining ¼ cup cilantro and serve with reserved tahini sauce, pickled red onion, yogurt, lemon wedges, and pita.

Baharat

FAST VEGAN Makes ½ cup Total Time 10 minutes

Baharat, the Arabic word for "spice," is the name of a spice blend found in dishes across North Africa and the Middle East. It's often also called seven-spice blend, and the seven spices featured in our blend are those most commonly found, though there are regional variations. No matter the combination, the warm blend has an intense profile that befits legumes and hearty vegetables.

- 3 (3-inch) cinnamon sticks, broken into pieces
- 4¾ teaspoons cumin seeds
- 1½ tablespoons coriander seeds
- 1 tablespoon black peppercorns
- 2 teaspoons whole cloves
- 1 tablespoon ground cardamom
- 2 teaspoons ground nutmeg

Process cinnamon sticks in spice grinder until finely ground, about 30 seconds. Add cumin seeds, coriander seeds, peppercorns, and cloves and process until finely ground, about 30 seconds. Transfer to bowl and stir in cardamom and nutmeg. (Baharat can be stored in airtight container for up to 1 month.)

Walkaway Ratatouille

VEGAN Serves 6 to 8 Total Time 2 hours

Why This Recipe Works Classic ratatouille recipes call for cutting vegetables into small pieces, labor- and time-intensive pretreatments such as salting and/or pressing the vegetables to remove excess moisture, and cooking them in batches on the stovetop. Our secret to great yet easy ratatouille? "Overcook" some of the vegetables, barely cook the others—and let the oven do the work. Our streamlined recipe starts with sautéing onions and aromatics and then adding chunks of eggplant and tomatoes before moving the pot to the oven, where the dry, ambient heat thoroughly evaporates moisture, concentrates flavors, and caramelizes some of the veggies. After 45 minutes, the tomatoes and eggplant are meltingly soft, and we mash them into a thick, silky sauce. Zucchini and bell peppers go into the pot last so that they retain some texture. Finishing the dish with fresh herbs, a splash of sherry vinegar, and a drizzle of extra-virgin olive oil ties everything together. This dish is best prepared using ripe, in-season tomatoes. If good tomatoes are not available, substitute one 28-ounce can of whole peeled tomatoes that have been drained, rinsed, and chopped coarse. Serve on its own with crusty bread, topped with an egg, or over pasta or rice. This dish can be served warm, at room temperature, or chilled.

- ⅓ cup plus 1 tablespoon extra-virgin olive oil, divided
- 2 large onions, cut into 1-inch pieces
- 8 large garlic cloves, peeled and smashed
- 1¾ teaspoons table salt, divided
- ¾ teaspoon pepper, divided
- 1½ teaspoons Herbes de Provence (page 122)
- ¼ teaspoon red pepper flakes
- 1 bay leaf
- 1½ pounds eggplant, peeled and cut into 1-inch pieces
- 2 pounds plum tomatoes, peeled and chopped coarse
- 2 small zucchini, halved lengthwise and cut into 1-inch pieces
- 1 red bell pepper, stemmed, seeded, and cut into 1-inch pieces
- 1 yellow bell pepper, stemmed, seeded, and cut into 1-inch pieces
- 2 tablespoons chopped fresh basil, divided
- 1 tablespoon minced fresh parsley
- 1 tablespoon sherry vinegar

1. Adjust oven rack to middle position and heat oven to 400 degrees. Heat ⅓ cup oil in Dutch oven over medium-high heat until shimmering. Add onions, garlic, 1 teaspoon salt, and ¼ teaspoon pepper and cook, stirring occasionally, until onions are starting to soften and have become translucent, about 10 minutes. Add herbes de Provence, pepper flakes, and bay leaf and cook, stirring frequently, for 1 minute. Stir in eggplant and tomatoes. Sprinkle with ½ teaspoon salt and ¼ teaspoon pepper and stir to combine. Transfer pot to oven and cook, uncovered, until vegetables are very tender and spotty brown, 40 to 45 minutes.

2. Remove pot from oven and, using potato masher or heavy wooden spoon, smash and stir eggplant mixture until broken down into sauce-like consistency. Stir in zucchini, bell peppers, remaining ¼ teaspoon salt, and remaining ¼ teaspoon pepper and return to oven. Cook, uncovered, until zucchini and peppers are just tender, 20 to 25 minutes.

3. Remove pot from oven, cover, and let stand until zucchini is translucent and easily pierced with tip of paring knife, 10 to 15 minutes. Using wooden spoon, scrape any browned bits from sides of pot and stir back into ratatouille. Stir in 1 tablespoon basil, parsley, and vinegar. Season with salt and pepper to taste. Transfer to large platter, drizzle with remaining 1 tablespoon oil, sprinkle with remaining 1 tablespoon basil, and serve.

Vegetable Lasagna

Serves 8 Total Time 2 hours, plus 20 minutes cooling

Why This Recipe Works Eggplant and mushrooms are excellent choices for a vegetarian lasagna: Not only do they have a pleasingly chewy texture, but they're also wonderful at taking on seasonings. Microwaving the eggplant and sautéing the mushrooms eliminates excess moisture—ensuring a sturdy and not watery lasagna—and deepens their flavors. Swapping white lasagna noodles for whole-wheat is an easy choice; it gives the lasagna a dose of added fiber, making for a heartier dish. To keep our sauce simple, we puree canned tomatoes with basil, olive oil, and garlic. For the cheesy layers, we blitz part-skim ricotta with spinach and basil in a food processor, which gives us a bright green filling that is rich and milky, yet so ethereally airy it is reminiscent of a soufflé. A mix of mozzarella and Parmesan makes the perfect topping, crisping up in the oven to a delectable golden brown. You will need a 12-inch nonstick skillet with a tight-fitting lid and a 13 by 9-inch baking dish for this recipe.

Walkaway Ratatouille

Tomato Sauce

- 1 (28-ounce) can crushed tomatoes
- 1 (14.5-ounce) can diced tomatoes, drained
- ¼ cup fresh basil leaves
- 1 tablespoon extra-virgin olive oil
- 2 garlic cloves, minced
- ½ teaspoon table salt

Lasagna

- 12 ounces whole-wheat lasagna noodles
- 1¼ teaspoons table salt, divided, plus salt for cooking noodles
- 8 ounces (8 cups) baby spinach
- ⅓ cup fresh basil leaves, plus 2 tablespoons chopped
- 2 tablespoons extra-virgin olive oil, divided
- 8 ounces (1 cup) part-skim ricotta cheese
- 1 large egg
- 1 ounce Parmesan cheese, grated (½ cup), divided
- ¼ teaspoon pepper
- 2 pounds eggplant, peeled and cut into ½-inch pieces
- 1½ pounds cremini mushrooms, trimmed and sliced thin
- 4 garlic cloves, minced
- 4 ounces whole-milk mozzarella cheese, shredded (1 cup)

1. For the tomato sauce Process all ingredients in food processor until smooth, about 30 seconds. Transfer to bowl and set aside.

2. For the lasagna Bring 4 quarts water to boil in large pot. Add lasagna noodles and 1 tablespoon salt and cook, stirring often, until just tender. Drain noodles and set aside. Pulse spinach, whole basil leaves, and 1 tablespoon oil in clean, dry food processor bowl until finely chopped, scraping down sides of bowl as needed, about 6 pulses. Add ricotta, egg, ¼ cup Parmesan, ½ teaspoon salt, and pepper and pulse until just combined, about 6 pulses; transfer to separate bowl and set aside.

3. Adjust oven rack to middle position and heat oven to 375 degrees. Line large plate with double layer of coffee filters and spray with vegetable oil spray. Toss eggplant with ½ teaspoon salt and spread evenly over coffee filters. Microwave eggplant, uncovered, until dry to touch and slightly shriveled, 10 to 12 minutes, stirring once halfway through microwaving.

4. Heat remaining 1 tablespoon oil in 12-inch nonstick skillet over medium-high heat until shimmering. Add mushrooms and remaining ¼ teaspoon salt, cover, and cook until mushrooms release their liquid, 6 to 8 minutes. Uncover, increase heat to high, stir in eggplant, and cook until vegetables are lightly browned, 8 to 10 minutes. Stir in garlic and cook until fragrant, about 30 seconds; remove skillet from heat.

5. Spread 1½ cups tomato sauce evenly over bottom of 13 by 9-inch baking dish. Arrange 4 noodles on top of sauce (noodles will overlap). Spread half of ricotta mixture over noodles in even layer. Spread half of eggplant mixture over ricotta. Repeat layering with 1 cup sauce, 4 noodles, remaining half of ricotta and remaining half of eggplant mixture. For final layer, arrange remaining 4 noodles on top and cover completely with remaining 1½ cups tomato sauce. Sprinkle with mozzarella and remaining ¼ cup Parmesan.

6. Cover dish tightly with greased aluminum foil and bake until edges are just bubbling, about 35 minutes, rotating dish halfway through baking. Remove foil from lasagna, return to oven, and continue to bake until top is lightly browned, 10 to 15 minutes longer. Let lasagna cool for 20 minutes, then sprinkle with chopped basil. Serve.

Eggplant Parmesan

Serves 6 to 8   Total Time 2 hours, plus 30 minutes draining

Why This Recipe Works There is no question about it, eggplant Parmesan takes time, but the result—crisp but creamy rounds of eggplant piled in layers with homemade tomato sauce and mozzarella—is the epitome of a great Italian casserole. The first challenge is making sure that the eggplant keeps its integrity and flavor. To remove moisture from the eggplant, we salt and drain the slices first. A traditional bound breading using homemade bread crumbs (with a bit of Parmesan) is the best way to give the eggplant a crisp coating. Baking the eggplant on preheated and oiled baking sheets results in crisp, golden-brown slices. While the eggplant is in the oven, you can make a quick tomato sauce using canned diced tomatoes. We layer the sauce, eggplant, and mozzarella in a baking dish and leave the top layer mostly unsauced so that it will crisp up in the oven. Use kosher salt when salting the eggplant. We developed this recipe with Diamond Crystal kosher salt. If using Morton kosher salt, which is denser, use only 2¼ teaspoons in step 1.

Eggplant

- 2 pounds globe eggplant (2 medium eggplants), cut crosswise into ¼-inch-thick rounds
- 1 tablespoon kosher salt, for salting eggplant
- 8 slices high-quality white sandwich bread, torn into quarters
- 2 ounces Parmesan cheese, grated (1 cup)
- 1½ teaspoons pepper, divided
- ¼ teaspoon table salt
- 1 cup unbleached all-purpose flour
- 4 large eggs
- 6 tablespoons vegetable oil

Tomato Sauce

- 3 (14.5-ounce) cans diced tomatoes, divided
- 2 tablespoons extra-virgin olive oil
- 4 garlic cloves, minced
- ¼ teaspoon red pepper flakes
- ½ cup coarsely chopped fresh basil
- 8 ounces whole-milk or part-skim mozzarella cheese, shredded (2 cups)
- 1 ounce Parmesan cheese, grated (½ cup)
- 10 fresh basil leaves, torn, for garnish

1. For the eggplant Toss half of eggplant slices and 1½ teaspoons kosher salt in large bowl; transfer salted eggplant to large colander. Repeat with remaining eggplant and remaining 1½ teaspoons kosher salt, placing second batch on top of first; set colander over bowl. Let stand until eggplant releases about 2 tablespoons liquid, 30 to 45 minutes. Spread eggplant slices on triple thickness of paper towels; cover with another triple thickness of paper towels. Press firmly on each slice to remove as much liquid as possible, then wipe off excess salt.

2. While eggplant is draining, adjust oven racks to upper-middle and lower-middle positions, place rimmed baking sheet on each rack, and heat oven to 425 degrees. Process bread in food processor to fine, even crumbs, 20 to 30 seconds. Transfer crumbs to shallow dish and stir in Parmesan, ½ teaspoon pepper, and table salt; set aside. Wipe out workbowl (do not wash) and set aside.

3. Combine flour and remaining 1 teaspoon pepper in large zipper-lock bag; shake to combine. Beat eggs in shallow dish. Place 8 to 10 eggplant slices in bag with flour; seal bag and shake to coat slices. Remove slices, shaking off excess flour; dip into eggs, letting excess egg run off; and coat evenly with bread crumb mixture; set breaded slices on wire rack set over baking sheet. Repeat with remaining eggplant.

Eggplant Parmesan

4. Remove preheated baking sheets from oven; add 3 tablespoons vegetable oil to each sheet, tilting to coat evenly with oil. Place half of breaded eggplant slices on each sheet in single layer; bake until eggplant is well browned and crisp, about 30 minutes, switching and rotating sheets after 10 minutes and flipping eggplant slices with wide spatula after 20 minutes. Do not turn off oven.

5. For the tomato sauce While eggplant bakes, process 2 cans diced tomatoes in food processor until almost smooth, about 5 seconds. Heat oil, garlic, and pepper flakes in large heavy-bottomed saucepan over medium-high heat, stirring occasionally, until fragrant and garlic is light golden, about 3 minutes; stir in processed tomatoes and remaining can of diced tomatoes and their juice. Bring to boil, then reduce heat to medium-low and simmer, stirring occasionally, until sauce is slightly thickened and reduced, about 15 minutes (you should have about 4 cups). Stir in chopped basil and season with table salt and pepper to taste.

6. Spread 1 cup tomato sauce in bottom of 13 by 9-inch baking dish. Layer in half eggplant slices, overlapping slices to fit; distribute 1 cup sauce over eggplant; and sprinkle with half of mozzarella. Layer in remaining eggplant and dot with 1 cup sauce, leaving majority of eggplant exposed so it will remain crisp; sprinkle with Parmesan and remaining mozzarella. Bake until bubbling and cheese is browned, 13 to 15 minutes. Let cool for 10 minutes, scatter basil leaves over top, and serve, passing remaining tomato sauce separately.

Baked Pumpkin Kibbeh

Serves 4 Total Time 1¾ hours

Why This Recipe Works Middle Eastern kibbeh is a finely ground combination of beef or lamb, bulgur, and onions that can be formed into balls and deep-fried, grilled, or pressed into a pan and baked. This vegetarian version of the baked variety matches pumpkin with the hearty bulgur and warm spices. We use a 9-inch springform pan to make slicing and serving easier—plus the thick slices this pan creates bake up extra moist and tender. Because bulgur soaks up liquid as it cooks, when we tried stirring raw bulgur into the squash, the kibbeh turned out dry and crumbly. Soaking the bulgur for 10 minutes solved this problem. A garnish of feta and toasted pine nuts adds some creaminess, tang, and crunch. Serve this hearty meal with a simple salad. You can use medium-grind bulgur here, but the texture of the kibbeh will be coarser and moister. When shopping, don't confuse bulgur with cracked wheat, which has a much longer cooking time and will not work in this recipe.

- 3 tablespoons extra-virgin olive oil, divided
- 1 onion, chopped fine
- 2 garlic cloves, minced
- 1 teaspoon ground coriander
- ¼ teaspoon five-spice powder
- 1 (15-ounce) can unsweetened pumpkin puree
- 1½ cups fine-grind bulgur, rinsed
- ½ cup all-purpose flour
- ¼ cup minced fresh cilantro
- 2 tablespoons minced fresh mint
- 1 teaspoon table salt
- ½ teaspoon pepper
- 4 ounces feta cheese, crumbled (1 cup)
- 2 tablespoons pine nuts, toasted and chopped

1. Adjust oven rack to middle position and heat oven to 400 degrees. Spray 9-inch springform pan with vegetable oil spray. Heat 1 tablespoon oil in 12-inch nonstick skillet over medium heat until shimmering. Add onion and cook until softened, about 5 minutes. Stir in garlic, coriander, and five-spice powder and cook until fragrant, about 30 seconds. Stir in pumpkin puree and cook until slightly thickened, 2 to 4 minutes. Transfer mixture to large bowl and let cool.

2. Meanwhile, place bulgur in second bowl and add water to cover by 1 inch. Let sit until tender, about 10 minutes. Drain bulgur through fine-mesh strainer, then wrap in clean dish towel and wring tightly to squeeze out as much liquid as possible.

3. Stir bulgur, flour, cilantro, mint, salt, and pepper into pumpkin mixture until well combined. Transfer to prepared pan and press into even layer with wet hands. Using paring knife, score surface into 8 even wedges, cutting halfway down through mixture. Brush top with remaining 2 tablespoons oil and bake until golden brown and set, about 45 minutes.

4. Sprinkle with feta and pine nuts and continue to bake until cheese is softened and warmed through, about 10 minutes. Let kibbeh cool in pan for 10 minutes. Run thin knife around inside of springform pan ring to loosen, then remove ring. Slice kibbeh into wedges along scored lines and serve.

Skillet Tomato Cobbler

Serves 6 Total Time 1½ hours, plus 2 hours 20 minutes chilling and cooling

Why This Recipe Works Cobblers are generally of the sweet variety, but this savory version is sure to delight. It is packed full of chunky fresh tomatoes that we season with garlic and thyme and top with a buttery crust. Using a skillet instead of a pie plate is key: You can build a rich tomato filling on the stovetop, let it thicken, and then top it with wedges of buttery homemade crust. Use in-season tomatoes that are ripe but firm; do not use plum tomatoes. We like to dollop servings with sour cream, ricotta, or mascarpone. You will need a 10-inch ovensafe skillet for this recipe.

Crust

- 5 tablespoons unsalted butter, chilled, divided
- ⅔ cup (3⅓ ounces) all-purpose flour, divided
- 1½ teaspoons sugar
- ¼ teaspoon table salt
- 2 tablespoons ice water, divided

Filling

- 1 tablespoon water
- 2½ teaspoons cornstarch
- 2 tablespoons extra-virgin olive oil
- 3 garlic cloves, minced
- 1 tablespoon tomato paste
- 1½ teaspoons minced fresh thyme
- 1½ teaspoons sugar
- ¾ teaspoon table salt
- ½ teaspoon pepper
- 2 pounds tomatoes, cored and cut into ¾-inch pieces
- 1 large egg beaten with 1 tablespoon water and pinch table salt

1. For the crust Grate 1 tablespoon butter on large holes of box grater and place in freezer. Cut remaining 4 tablespoons butter into ½-inch cubes. Pulse ⅓ cup flour, sugar, and salt in food processor until combined, 2 pulses. Add cubed butter and process until homogeneous paste forms, 20 to 30 seconds. Using your hands, carefully break paste into 1-inch chunks and redistribute around processor blade. Add remaining ⅓ cup flour and pulse until mixture is broken into pieces no larger than ½ inch (most pieces will be much smaller), about 3 pulses. Transfer mixture to bowl. Add grated butter and toss until butter pieces are separated and coated with flour.

2. Sprinkle 1 tablespoon ice water over mixture. Toss with silicone spatula until evenly moistened. Sprinkle remaining 1 tablespoon ice water over mixture and toss to combine. Press with spatula until dough sticks together. Wrap dough in plastic wrap and press to form compact, fissure-free 4-inch disk. Refrigerate for at least 2 hours or up to 2 days. Let dough soften on counter for 10 minutes before rolling.

3. For the filling Adjust oven rack to middle position and heat oven to 400 degrees. Whisk water and cornstarch together in small bowl. Heat oil in 10-inch ovensafe skillet over medium heat until shimmering. Add garlic and cook until fragrant, about 30 seconds. Add tomato paste and cook, stirring constantly, until oil is tinted red, about 30 seconds. Add thyme, sugar, salt, and pepper and stir to combine. Add tomatoes and stir until coated. Whisk cornstarch mixture to recombine. Stir into tomato mixture and cook, stirring occasionally, until juice is slightly thickened, 1 to 2 minutes. Remove from heat.

4. Roll dough into 8-inch round on lightly floured counter. Cut into 6 equal wedges. Brush wedges with egg wash. Using bench scraper or spatula, place wedges on filling, spacing rounded edges ½ inch from edge of skillet and leaving gaps between wedges. Bake until crust is deep golden brown, 40 to 45 minutes. Let cool for 20 minutes and serve.

Skillet Tomato Cobbler

Savory Dutch Baby with Portobellos, Roasted Red Peppers, Walnuts, and Feta

Savory Dutch Baby with Portobellos, Roasted Red Peppers, Walnuts, and Feta

Serves 4 Total Time 1 hour

Why This Recipe Works We started with our failsafe Dutch baby, which begins in a cold (turned-off) oven to create dramatically puffed, brown, crisp edges and a plush, custardy middle thick enough to hold lots of toppings. Savory mushrooms, punchy peppers, milky feta, and fresh parsley balance the eggy, buttery Dutch baby. To contrast the pancake's custardy texture and provide some crunch, we finish with toasted walnuts. You will need a 12-inch ovensafe nonstick skillet for this recipe. A traditional 12-inch skillet may be used in place of the nonstick skillet; coat it lightly with vegetable oil spray before using. Note that you will need 2 skillets for this recipe. Prepare the topping while the Dutch baby bakes. We prefer the look and texture of the mushrooms with the gills removed.

Dutch Baby

- 1¾ cups (8¾ ounces) all-purpose flour
- 1 tablespoon sugar
- ½ teaspoon table salt
- 1½ cups milk
- 6 large eggs
- 3 tablespoons unsalted butter

Mushroom Topping

- 3 tablespoons extra-virgin olive oil, divided
- 1¼ pounds portobello mushroom caps, gills removed, sliced thin
- ¾ teaspoon table salt, divided
- ½ teaspoon grated lemon zest plus 2 teaspoons juice
- ¼ teaspoon sugar
- ½ cup chopped jarred roasted red peppers
- 2 ounces feta cheese, cut into ¼-inch cubes (½ cup)
- ½ cup fresh parsley leaves
- ¼ cup walnuts, toasted and chopped

1. **For the Dutch baby** Whisk flour, sugar, and salt together in large bowl. Whisk milk and eggs together in second bowl. Whisk two-thirds of milk mixture into flour mixture until no lumps remain, then slowly whisk in remaining milk mixture until smooth.

2. Adjust oven rack to lower-middle position. Melt butter in 12-inch ovensafe nonstick skillet over medium-low heat. Add batter to skillet, immediately transfer to oven, and set oven to 375 degrees. Bake until edges are deep golden brown and center is beginning to brown, 30 to 35 minutes. Gently transfer Dutch baby to cutting board. Let cool for at least 5 minutes. (Dutch baby will deflate.)

3. **For the topping** While Dutch baby bakes, heat 1 tablespoon oil in 12-inch skillet over medium-high heat until shimmering. Add mushrooms and ½ teaspoon salt and cook, stirring frequently, until mushrooms are tender, 4 to 6 minutes.

4. Whisk lemon zest and juice, sugar, and remaining ¼ teaspoon salt together in bowl. Whisking constantly, slowly drizzle in remaining 2 tablespoons oil. Add red peppers, feta, and parsley and stir to combine.

5. Spread mushrooms over Dutch baby, followed by red pepper mixture and walnuts. Cut into wedges and serve.

Cheesy Tomato and Bean Bake

Serves 4 to 6 Total Time 50 minutes

Why This Recipe Works This cheesy, comforting casserole of hearty cannellini beans, sweet-tangy tomatoes, and gooey mozzarella is one kids and adults alike will ask for and crave. It's also a snap to whip up, relying on pantry-friendly staples and coming together in a single skillet that starts on the stovetop and finishes in the oven. For a savory foundation to our dish, we soften onion in the skillet and season it with garlic, oregano, and red pepper flakes. We then introduce the savory tang of canned tomatoes, which we season with a pinch of sugar to enhance the tomatoes' natural sweetness. After stirring in the creamy canned cannellini beans, mozzarella, and Parmesan, we sprinkle more mozzarella over the top to maximize the ooziness (who can resist a cheese pull?). We finish the dish with a mixture of panko bread crumbs and oil for a topping that browns nicely in the oven into a crisp crust. You will need a 12-inch ovensafe skillet for this recipe.

| Cheesy Tomato and Bean Bake

- 3 tablespoons extra-virgin olive oil, divided
- 1 small onion, chopped fine
- ¾ teaspoon table salt
- 3 garlic cloves, minced
- 1 teaspoon dried oregano
- Pinch red pepper flakes (optional)
- 1 (28-ounce) can crushed tomatoes
- ⅓ cup water
- Pinch sugar
- 2 (15-ounce) cans cannellini beans, rinsed
- 4 ounces mozzarella cheese, shredded (1 cup), divided
- ½ ounce Parmesan cheese, grated (¼ cup)
- ½ cup panko bread crumbs

1. Adjust oven rack to middle position and heat oven to 475 degrees. Heat 1 tablespoon oil in 12-inch ovensafe skillet over medium heat until shimmering. Add onion and salt and cook until softened, about 5 minutes. Stir in garlic; oregano; and pepper flakes, if using, and cook until fragrant, about 30 seconds.

2. Stir in tomatoes, water, and sugar and bring to boil. Reduce heat to medium-low and simmer, stirring occasionally, until slightly thickened, about 10 minutes.

3. Stir in beans and cook until warmed through, about 5 minutes. Remove skillet from heat. Stir in half of mozzarella and Parmesan, then spread beans into even layer. Sprinkle remaining mozzarella evenly over top. Combine panko and remaining 2 tablespoons oil in bowl, then sprinkle evenly over top of cheese in skillet.

4. Bake until cheese is melted and panko is well browned, 5 to 8 minutes. Remove skillet from oven and let cool for 5 minutes. Serve.

Mushroom and White Bean Gratin

VEGAN Serves 4 to 6 Total Time 1½ hours, plus 20 minutes resting

Why This Recipe Works Gratins don't need cheese or dairy to qualify as elevated comfort food. This vegan rendition features creamy white beans, cremini mushrooms, tender carrots, and a crisp, toasty bread layer. We get great flavor from the fond we develop by sautéing mushrooms and aromatics and deglazing the skillet with nutty dry sherry. A combination of flour and starchy bean liquid thickens the sauce. We bake the gratin in a low oven after topping it with seasoned bread cubes. As it bakes, the lower portion of the bread merges with the beans, creating a lovely texture, while the upper portion dries out. Then, by flipping on the broiler for a few minutes, we brown and crisp the top. We prefer a round rustic loaf (also known as a boule) with a chewy, open crumb and a sturdy crust for this recipe. Cannellini or navy beans can be used in place of great northern beans, if desired. You will need a 12-inch ovensafe skillet for this recipe.

- ½ cup extra-virgin olive oil, divided
- 10 ounces cremini mushrooms, trimmed and sliced ½ inch thick
- ¾ teaspoon table salt
- ½ teaspoon pepper, divided
- 4–5 slices country-style bread, cut into ½-inch cubes (5 cups)
- ¼ cup minced fresh parsley, divided
- 1 cup water
- 1 tablespoon all-purpose flour
- 1 small onion, chopped fine
- 5 garlic cloves, minced
- 1 tablespoon tomato paste
- 1½ teaspoons minced fresh thyme
- ⅓ cup dry sherry
- 2 (15-ounce) cans great northern beans, undrained
- 3 carrots, peeled, halved lengthwise, and cut into ¾-inch pieces

1. Adjust oven rack to middle position and heat oven to 300 degrees. Heat ¼ cup oil in 12-inch ovensafe skillet over medium-high heat until shimmering. Add mushrooms, salt, and ¼ teaspoon pepper and cook, stirring occasionally, until mushrooms are well browned, 8 to 12 minutes.

2. While mushrooms cook, toss bread, 3 tablespoons parsley, remaining ¼ cup oil, and remaining ¼ teaspoon pepper together in bowl. Set aside. Stir water and flour in second bowl until no lumps of flour remain. Set aside.

3. Reduce heat to medium, add onion to skillet, and continue to cook, stirring frequently, until onion is translucent, 4 to 6 minutes. Reduce heat to medium-low; add garlic, tomato paste, and thyme; and cook, stirring constantly, until bottom of skillet is dark brown, 2 to 3 minutes. Add sherry and cook, scraping up any browned bits.

4. Add beans and their liquid, carrots, and flour mixture. Bring to boil over high heat. Off heat, arrange bread mixture over surface in even layer. Transfer skillet to oven and bake for 40 minutes. (Liquid should have consistency of thin gravy.)

5. Leave skillet in oven and turn on broiler. Broil until crumbs are golden brown, 4 to 7 minutes. Remove gratin from oven and let sit for 20 minutes. Sprinkle with remaining 1 tablespoon parsley and serve.

Swiss Chard, Pinto Bean, and Monterey Jack Enchiladas

Serves 4 to 6   Total Time 1 hour 40 minutes

Why This Recipe Works Shake up your enchilada game with this recipe that relies on sturdy, flavorful Swiss chard, pinto beans, and bell peppers, We keep things green by wilting the flavorsome Swiss chard and crisp, slightly bitter green peppers with garlic and onions. To add creamy cohesiveness and protein, we mash half a can of pinto beans and mix in our greens; we then stir in the rest of the beans whole for contrasting texture. A quick simmer of convenient canned tomato sauce with aromatics and spices provides a robust sauce to round out the flavors of the filling. Traditional recipes call for frying the tortillas one at a time, but we found that brushing them with oil and microwaving works just as well—and without the mess of frying. A topping of a cilantro sauce or crema and chopped avocado is ideal—tangy, creamy, fresh-tasting, and rich.

Cilantro Sauce

- ¼ cup mayonnaise
- ¼ cup sour cream
- 3 tablespoons water
- 3 tablespoons minced fresh cilantro
- ¼ teaspoon table salt

Enchiladas

- ¼ cup vegetable oil, divided
- 2 onions, chopped fine, divided
- ¾ teaspoon table salt, divided
- 3 tablespoons chili powder
- 2 teaspoons ground cumin
- 2 teaspoons sugar
- 6 garlic cloves, minced, divided
- 2 (8-ounce) cans tomato sauce
- ½ cup water
- 1 pound Swiss chard, stemmed and sliced into ½-inch-wide strips
- 2 green bell peppers, stemmed, seeded, and cut into ½-inch pieces
- 1 (15-ounce) can pinto beans, rinsed, divided
- 12 (6-inch) corn tortillas
- 4 ounces Monterey Jack cheese, shredded (1 cup)
- 1 avocado, halved, pitted, and cut into ½-inch pieces
- ¼ cup fresh cilantro leaves
- Lime wedges

1. **For the cilantro sauce** Whisk all ingredients together in bowl. Cover and refrigerate until ready to serve.

2. **For the enchiladas** Adjust oven rack to middle position and heat oven to 450 degrees. Heat 1 tablespoon oil in large saucepan over medium heat until shimmering. Add half of onions and ½ teaspoon salt and cook until softened, about 5 minutes. Stir in chili powder, cumin, sugar, and half of garlic and cook until fragrant, about 30 seconds. Stir in tomato sauce and water, bring to simmer, and cook until slightly thickened, about 7 minutes. Season with salt and pepper to taste; set aside.

3. Heat 1 tablespoon oil in Dutch oven over medium heat until shimmering. Add remaining onions and remaining ¼ teaspoon salt and cook until softened and lightly browned, 5 to 7 minutes. Add remaining garlic and cook until fragrant, about 30 seconds. Add chard and bell peppers, cover, and cook until chard is tender, 6 to 8 minutes. Using potato masher, mash half of beans coarse in large bowl. Stir in chard-pepper mixture, ¼ cup reserved tomato sauce, and remaining whole beans.

4. Grease 13 by 9-inch baking dish. Spread ½ cup tomato sauce over bottom of prepared dish. Brush both sides of tortillas with remaining 2 tablespoons oil. Stack tortillas, wrap in damp dish towel, and place on plate; microwave until warm and pliable, about 1 minute. Working with 1 warm tortilla at a time, spread ¼ cup chard filling across center. Roll tortilla tightly around filling and place seam side down in dish, arranging enchiladas in 2 columns across width of dish. Cover completely with remaining tomato sauce and sprinkle Monterey jack over top.

5. Cover dish tightly with greased aluminum foil and bake until enchiladas are heated through, 15 to 20 minutes. Let enchiladas cool for 10 minutes. Drizzle with cilantro sauce and sprinkle with avocado and cilantro. Serve with lime wedges.

Herb Vegetable and Lentil Bake

Serves 4 Total Time 1 hour

Why This Recipe Works A garden's worth of vegetables star in this summery meal splashed with timeless flavors. When in season, the fennel, potatoes, zucchini, and tomatoes in this vegetable bake all have a fresh sweetness that benefits from the savor of a cumin rub. Leaving the core in the fennel ensures the pretty wedges stay intact and are easy to flip. Lentils round out the roasted vegetables, and using canned lentils makes things easy. Near the end of roasting, we sprinkle the vegetables with feta for a salty, briny flavor; it softens and browns appealingly over the dish. The finishing touch is a drizzle of an herbaceous oil. Use small potatoes measuring 1 to 2 inches in diameter.

Herb Oil

- ½ cup fresh parsley leaves
- ¼ cup fresh dill
- ¼ cup fresh mint leaves
- ¼ cup extra-virgin olive oil
- 2 tablespoons lemon juice
- 1 garlic clove, minced

Roasted Vegetables

- 8 ounces small Yukon Gold or red potatoes, quartered
- 1 large fennel bulb, stalk discarded, bulb halved, core left intact, and cut through core into ½-inch-thick wedges
- 2 tablespoons extra-virgin olive oil, divided
- ¾ teaspoon ground cumin
- ¾ teaspoon table salt, divided
- ½ teaspoon pepper, divided
- 2 zucchini, cut ½ inch thick on bias
- 8 ounces cherry tomatoes
- 2 shallots, sliced thin
- 1 (15-ounce) can lentils, rinsed and drained well
- 4 ounces feta cheese, crumbled (1 cup)

1. **For the herb oil** Pulse all ingredients in food processor until coarsely chopped, about 10 pulses, scraping down sides of bowl as needed. Transfer to bowl and season with salt to taste; set aside until ready to serve.

2. **For the roasted vegetables** Adjust oven rack to upper-middle position and heat oven to 475 degrees. Toss potatoes, fennel, 1 tablespoon oil, cumin, ½ teaspoon salt, and ¼ teaspoon pepper together in bowl. Arrange vegetables cut side down on rimmed baking sheet and cover tightly with aluminum foil. Roast until vegetables are beginning to brown and are nearly tender, 15 to 20 minutes.

3. Remove foil and flip fennel wedges. Toss zucchini, tomatoes, shallots, lentils, remaining 1 tablespoon oil, remaining ¼ teaspoon salt, and remaining ¼ teaspoon pepper together in bowl. Scatter evenly over top of vegetables on sheet, then sprinkle with feta. Roast until tomatoes blister, feta starts to soften and brown slightly, and vegetables are tender, about 15 minutes. Drizzle with reserved herb oil and serve.

Charred Cauliflower and Crispy Chickpeas with Romesco

FAST **VEGAN** Serves 4 Total Time 40 minutes

Why This Recipe Works This inventive meal is a study in contrasts, with soft cauliflower paired with crispy chickpeas; a bright romesco sauce; and pickled red onion. It's also easy to put together since we roast the cauliflower and chickpeas on a sheet pan. While they're roasting we make the romesco in a food processor. With everything arranged on elegant endive leaves, this dish is a feast for the eyes. You can make the sumac onion in advance. We love the flavor they bring to the dish but you can skip them and just serve lemon wedges.

- 1 head cauliflower (2 pounds), cored and cut into 2-inch florets
- 1 (15-ounce) can chickpeas, rinsed
- 7 tablespoons extra-virgin olive oil, divided
- 1¼ teaspoons table salt, divided
- ⅔ cup jarred roasted red peppers, patted dry
- ¼ cup slivered almonds, toasted
- 6 tablespoons fresh parsley leaves, divided
- 1 tablespoons sherry vinegar
- 1 garlic clove, minced
- 2 heads Belgian endive (4 ounces each), leaves separated
- ½ cup Sumac Onions (page 431)

Herb Vegetable and Lentil Bake

| *Broccoli Rabe and Farro Gratin*

1. Adjust oven rack to middle position and heat oven to 475 degrees. Toss cauliflower, chickpeas, ¼ cup oil, and 1 teaspoon salt together on rimmed baking sheet, then spread into even layer over sheet. Roast until cauliflower is golden in spots, about 20 minutes.

2. Meanwhile, process red peppers, almonds, ¼ cup parsley, vinegar, garlic, remaining 3 tablespoons oil, and remaining ¼ teaspoon salt in food processor until smooth, about 1 minute, scraping down sides of bowl as needed. Season with salt and pepper to taste, and set aside until ready to serve. (Romesco sauce can be refrigerated in airtight container for up to 3 days; bring to room temperature and thin with hot water if needed before serving.)

3. Remove sheet from oven, stir cauliflower and chickpeas, and redistribute evenly over sheet. Return to oven and roast until lightly charred throughout, 8 to 10 minutes. Arrange endive leaves in even layer over platter, then top with roasted cauliflower and chickpeas. Dollop with reserved romesco and sprinkle with sumac onions and remaining 2 tablespoons parsley. Serve.

Broccoli Rabe and Farro Gratin

Serves 4 to 6   Total Time 1¼ hours

Why This Recipe Work This modern gratin features pleasantly bitter broccoli rabe, nutty farro, and creamy white beans. Small white beans blend in nicely with the farro adding creaminess and protein. Blanching the broccoli rabe in salted water tames its bitterness; we then toss it with garlic and pepper flake–infused olive oil for extra flavor. Sun-dried tomatoes add a pop of umami with their sweetness. To bind the filling, we find that miso paste creates a supercreamy sauce and also adds a subtle backbone of flavor. A combo of bread crumbs and Parmesan transforms into a burnished, crunchy topping. Do not substitute pearl, quick-cooking, or presteamed farro (read the ingredient list on the package to determine this) for the whole farro in this recipe.

- 3 tablespoons extra-virgin olive oil, divided
- 1 onion, chopped fine
- ¼ teaspoon table salt, plus salt for cooking vegetables
- 1½ cups whole farro
- 2 cups vegetable broth
- 2 tablespoons white miso
- ½ cup panko bread crumbs
- ¼ cup grated Parmesan cheese

- 1 pound broccoli rabe, trimmed and cut into 2-inch pieces
- 6 garlic cloves, minced
- ⅛ teaspoon red pepper flakes
- 1 (15-ounce) can small white beans or navy beans, rinsed
- ¾ cup oil-packed sun-dried tomatoes, chopped

1. Heat 1 tablespoon oil in large saucepan over medium heat until shimmering. Add onion and salt and cook until softened and lightly browned, 5 to 7 minutes. Stir in farro and cook until lightly toasted, about 2 minutes. Stir in 2½ cups water, broth, and miso; bring to simmer; and cook, stirring often, until farro is just tender and remaining liquid is thickened and creamy, 25 to 35 minutes.

2. Meanwhile, toss panko with 1 tablespoon oil in bowl and microwave, stirring occasionally, until golden brown, 1 to 2 minutes. Stir in Parmesan and set aside.

3. Bring 4 quarts water to boil in Dutch oven. Add broccoli rabe and 1 tablespoon salt and cook until just tender, about 2 minutes. Drain broccoli rabe and set aside. Combine remaining 1 tablespoon oil, garlic, and pepper flakes in now-empty pot and cook over medium heat until fragrant and sizzling, 1 to 2 minutes. Stir in broccoli rabe and cook until well coated, about 2 minutes. Off heat, stir in beans, sun-dried tomatoes, and farro. Season with salt and pepper to taste.

4. Adjust oven rack 10 inches from broiler element and heat broiler. Transfer bean-farro mixture to broiler-safe 3-quart gratin dish (or broiler-safe 13 by 9-inch baking dish) and sprinkle with panko mixture. Broil until lightly browned and hot, 1 to 2 minutes. Serve.

Teff-Stuffed Acorn Squash with Lime Crema and Roasted Pepitas

VEGAN Serves 4 Total Time 1 hour

Why This Recipe Works Stuffed squash is a dish that vegetarians have to mostly suffer through when invited out to dinner, but this recipe is one you will go out of your way to make. Here we use teff, a gluten-free whole grain indigenous to Eritrea and Ethiopia, where it is often ground into flour to make the flatbread known as injera. It has a mildly nutty, earthy flavor, is packed with nutrients, and ranges in color from dark brown to red to white. For this dish we use brown teff, which is the kind most readily available in supermarkets. We cook it pilaf-style and make it the base for a savory stuffing, which we combine with the flesh of the roasted squash. To impart flavor to the squash itself, we brush the cut sides with oil infused with warm spices, oregano, and chipotle chile powder. In keeping with this flavor profile, we add chopped green chiles and cilantro. After spooning the stuffing into the squash, we top it off with lime crema and toasted pepitas to bring freshness and crunch. To make this recipe vegan, substitute plant-based sour cream for the dairy sour cream.

Lime Crema

- ½ cup sour cream
- 2 teaspoons grated lime zest plus 3 tablespoons juice (2 limes)
- ½ teaspoon table salt

Teff-Stuffed Acorn Squash

- 1 tablespoon vegetable oil
- 1 tablespoon chipotle chile powder
- 1 teaspoon table salt, divided
- ½ teaspoon ground cumin
- ½ teaspoon ground coriander
- ½ teaspoon pepper
- ¼ teaspoon dried oregano
- 2 acorn squashes (1½ pounds each), quartered pole to pole and seeded
- 2 cups vegetable broth
- 1 cup teff
- 2 (4-ounce) cans chopped green chiles, drained
- ½ cup minced fresh cilantro
- ¼ cup roasted pepitas

1. **For the lime crema** Whisk all ingredients together in bowl; set aside until ready to serve.

2. **For the teff-stuffed acorn squash** Adjust oven rack to middle position and heat oven to 400 degrees. Line rimmed baking sheet with aluminum foil. Combine oil, chipotle chile powder, ¾ teaspoon salt, cumin, coriander, pepper, and oregano in bowl. Brush flesh side of squash evenly with spice mixture. Place wedges cut side down on prepared sheet and roast until browned on first side, about 20 minutes.

3. Flip wedges so second cut side is in contact with sheet and roast until second side is browned and tip of paring knife slips easily into flesh, about 15 minutes.

4. Meanwhile, bring broth to boil in medium saucepan. Stir in teff and remaining ¼ teaspoon salt, turn heat down to medium-low, cover, and simmer until broth is absorbed, 15 to 20 minutes. Remove from heat and let sit, covered, for 10 minutes. Fluff grains with fork and set aside.

5. Using spoon, scoop flesh from each squash wedge, leaving about ¼-inch thickness of flesh in each shell. Chop squash flesh into rough ½-inch pieces and transfer to large bowl. Gently fold reserved teff, green chiles, and cilantro into squash in bowl, then gently mound teff-squash mixture evenly in squash shells. Drizzle reserved lime crema over top and sprinkle with pepitas. Serve.

Stuffed Delicata Squash

FAST Serves 4 Total Time 45 minutes

Why This Recipe Works Delicata squash offers earthy, autumnal sweetness similar to the flavor of acorn or butternut squash. Its narrow shape and smaller size ensure you won't have to hack through and peel away layers of tough outer skin; its tender skin is thin and perfectly edible. Here, we halve the squash to create boats—ideal for holding a hearty stuffing. To start, we simply season the squash halves and microwave them until the flesh is tender and the skin turns soft—no shell removal required. We then stuff the squash halves with a savory, nutty filling: We cook mushrooms, onion, and spinach in butter to imbue the vegetables with milky richness, then stir in bulgur, toasted pecans, and shredded cheddar for a mixture with plenty of bite and savory flavor. Before broiling the squash, we brush the surfaces of the filling with melted butter to add a bit more richness and to encourage flavorful browning.

- 2 delicata squashes (about 1 pound each), halved lengthwise and seeded
- 1¾ teaspoons table salt, divided, plus salt for cooking bulgur
- ½ teaspoon pepper
- 1 cup medium-grind bulgur
- 4 tablespoons unsalted butter, plus 2 tablespoons melted
- 10 ounces cremini mushrooms, trimmed and chopped
- 1 onion, chopped
- 5 ounces (5 cups) baby spinach, chopped coarse
- 1 teaspoon minced fresh thyme
- ½ cup chopped toasted pecans
- 2 ounces sharp cheddar cheese, shredded (½ cup)

1. Sprinkle cut sides of squash with 1 teaspoon salt and pepper. Microwave in large covered bowl until tender, 12 to 15 minutes. Bring 2 quarts water to boil in large saucepan. Add bulgur and 1 teaspoon salt. Reduce heat to medium-low and simmer until tender, 5 to 8 minutes. Drain.

2. Meanwhile, melt 4 tablespoons butter in 12-inch nonstick skillet over medium-high heat. Add mushrooms, onion, and remaining ¾ teaspoon salt and cook, stirring occasionally, until vegetables are browned, about 10 minutes. Stir in spinach and thyme and cook until wilted, about 3 minutes. Off heat, stir in bulgur, pecans, and cheddar.

3. Adjust oven rack 8 inches from broiler element and heat broiler. Transfer squash, cut side up, to rimmed baking sheet. Tightly pack bulgur mixture into squash halves, mounding bulgur mixture up over squash rims. Brush filling with remaining 2 tablespoons melted butter. Broil until lightly browned, 4 to 5 minutes. Serve.

Eggplant Involtini

Serves 4 to 6 Total Time 1¾ hours

Why this Recipe Works Eggplant involtini is like a lighter and more summery version of eggplant Parmesan, with the flavorful eggplant planks rolled around a creamy ricotta filling. Traditional recipes require a two-step process of salting the eggplant and then frying it, but we skip the breading and instead incorporate the bread crumbs right into the filling. This method allows the eggplant's flavor and meaty texture to take center stage in the dish and also lets us sidestep the salting and draining step; without a coating to turn soggy, we can simply bake the eggplant until its excess moisture evaporates. A bit of Parmesan added to the ricotta contributes flavor without any bulk. Making a simple but bright tomato sauce in a skillet is convenient since we can arrange the eggplant bundles right in it and run the skillet under the broiler—no casserole dish to wash. Select shorter, wider eggplants for this recipe. We like whole-milk ricotta in this recipe, but part-skim may be used. Do not use fat-free ricotta.

Stuffed Delicata Squash

top | *Eggplant Involtini*
bottom | *Stuffed Peppers with Chickpeas, Goat Cheese, and Herbs*

- 2 large eggplants (1½ pounds each), peeled and sliced lengthwise into ½-inch-thick planks (about 12 planks), end pieces trimmed to lie flat
- 6 tablespoons vegetable oil, divided
- 2 teaspoons kosher salt, divided
- ½ teaspoon pepper divided
- 2 garlic cloves, minced
- ¼ teaspoon dried oregano
- Pinch red pepper flakes
- 1 (28-ounce) can whole peeled tomatoes, drained, juice reserved, and tomatoes chopped coarse
- 1 slice hearty white sandwich bread, torn into 1-inch pieces
- 8 ounces (1 cup) whole-milk ricotta cheese
- 1½ ounces Parmesan cheese, grated (¾ cup), divided
- ¼ cup plus 1 tablespoon chopped fresh basil, divided
- 1 tablespoon lemon juice

1. Adjust 1 oven rack to lower-middle position and second rack 8 inches from broiler element. Heat oven to 375 degrees. Line 2 rimmed baking sheets with parchment paper and spray generously with vegetable oil spray. Brush 1 side of eggplant slices with 2½ tablespoons oil, then season with ½ teaspoon salt and ¼ teaspoon pepper. Flip slices over and repeat on second side with another 2½ tablespoons oil, ½ teaspoon salt, and remaining ¼ teaspoon pepper. Arrange eggplant slices in single layer on prepared baking sheets. Bake until tender and lightly browned, 30 to 35 minutes, switching and rotating sheets halfway through baking. Let eggplant cool for 5 minutes, then flip each slice over using thin spatula.

2. Meanwhile, heat remaining 1 tablespoon oil in 12-inch broiler-safe skillet over medium-low heat until just shimmering. Add garlic, ½ teaspoon salt, oregano, and pepper flakes and cook, stirring occasionally, until fragrant, about 30 seconds. Stir in tomatoes and their juice, increase heat to high, and bring to simmer. Reduce heat to medium-low and simmer until thickened, about 15 minutes. Cover to keep warm.

3. Pulse bread in food processor until finely ground, 10 to 15 pulses. Combine bread crumbs, ricotta, ½ cup Parmesan, ¼ cup basil, lemon juice, and remaining ½ teaspoon salt in bowl.

4. With widest short side of eggplant facing you, spoon about 3 tablespoons ricotta mixture over bottom third of each eggplant slice (use slightly more filling for larger slices and slightly less for smaller slices). Gently roll up each eggplant slice and place seam side down in tomato sauce in skillet.

5. Heat broiler. Bring sauce to simmer over medium heat and cook for 5 minutes. Transfer skillet to oven and broil until eggplant is well browned and cheese is heated through, 5 to 10 minutes. Remove from broiler. Sprinkle with remaining ¼ cup Parmesan and let stand for 5 minutes. Sprinkle with remaining 1 tablespoon basil and serve.

Stuffed Peppers with Chickpeas, Goat Cheese, and Herbs

Serves 6 Total Time 1¼ hours

Why This Recipe Works We let our imagination guide us when thinking of creative stuffing mixtures for peppers. Crusty, garlic-infused baguette pieces meet mashed chickpeas for the base of this delicious filling, while a few handfuls of fresh herbs, sliced scallions, and briny capers dial up the bright flavor. We even chop up the bell pepper tops and add them to the chickpeas to add flavor and color. Creamy goat cheese provides richness and its hallmark tanginess while helping bind the other stuffing ingredients together, and lemon zest and juice contribute a fresh brightness. Roasting the bell peppers until they are slightly blistered before stuffing them intensifies their flavors, making them far more than just a vehicle for the stuffing. You can use any color bell peppers in this recipe.

- ½ cup extra-virgin olive oil, divided, plus extra for drizzling
- 6 (7- to 8-ounce) bell peppers
- 1 (15-ounce) can chickpeas, rinsed
- 7 ounces baguette, cut into ½-inch pieces (4 cups)
- 8 garlic cloves, minced
- ¼ teaspoon red pepper flakes
- 1½ teaspoons table salt, divided
- 1 teaspoon pepper
- 8 scallions, sliced
- ¼ cup minced fresh parsley
- ¼ cup minced fresh basil
- 3 tablespoons capers, chopped
- 1 tablespoon grated lemon zest plus 1 tablespoon juice
- 6 ounces goat cheese, crumbled (1½ cups)

1. Adjust oven rack to upper-middle position and heat oven to 475 degrees. Grease 13 by 9-inch baking pan with 1 tablespoon oil. Cut off top ½ inch of bell peppers and reserve; discard stems and seeds. Arrange bell peppers and their tops cut side down in prepared pan. Brush bell peppers and tops with 1 tablespoon oil, then season with salt and pepper.

2. Roast until bell peppers are softened and beginning to blister, about 20 minutes. Flip bell peppers cut side up and let sit until cool enough to handle, about 5 minutes. Season insides with salt and pepper. Reduce oven temperature to 350 degrees.

3. Meanwhile, using potato masher, coarsely mash chickpeas in large bowl. Chop bell pepper tops into ¼-inch pieces and add to bowl with chickpeas.

4. Heat ¼ cup oil in 12-inch nonstick skillet over medium heat until shimmering. Add bread and cook, stirring occasionally, until light golden brown and crispy, 5 to 7 minutes. Push bread to 1 side of skillet and add remaining 2 tablespoons oil to empty spot. Add garlic and pepper flakes to oil and cook until fragrant, about 30 seconds. Stir garlic mixture and ½ teaspoon salt into bread to combine. Transfer to bowl with chickpea mixture and let cool completely, about 10 minutes.

5. Stir scallions, parsley, basil, capers, lemon zest and juice, remaining 1 teaspoon salt, and 1 teaspoon pepper into chickpea mixture. Gently fold in goat cheese until combined.

6. Divide filling evenly among bell peppers, mounding slightly. Bake until filling registers between 100 and 120 degrees and begins to brown on top, 15 to 20 minutes. Drizzle with extra oil before serving.

Chiles Rellenos

Serves 4 to 6 Total Time 1¾ hours

Why This Recipe Works Traditional chiles rellenos are filled with just the right amount of melted cheese and enrobed in a delicate, crispy coating. We use soft, melty Muenster cheese for the filling. Cutting the cheese into cubes rather than long strips makes it easier to stuff into the chiles. Most recipes call for roasting and peeling the peppers before stuffing them, but we skip this step to save time. We simply broil the peppers to soften them and leave their skins on. Instead of a traditional egg white batter, we opt for a batter of flour, cornstarch, baking powder, and beer. For our quick sauce, we rely on pantry staples: chili powder, onion powder, garlic powder, vegetable broth, and tomato sauce. Use a Dutch oven that holds 6 quarts or more. You do not need to remove all of the chile seeds in step 3. Nonalcoholic lagers will also work here. You will need six 4-inch wooden skewers for this recipe.

Sauce

- 1 tablespoon vegetable oil
- 1 teaspoon chili powder
- ½ teaspoon onion powder
- ¼ teaspoon garlic powder
- 1½ cups vegetable broth
- 1 (15-ounce) can tomato sauce
- 1 teaspoon adobo sauce from canned chipotle chiles in adobo sauce
- 1 bay leaf
- 1 tablespoon lime juice

Chiles

- 6 (4- to 5-ounce) poblano chiles
- 8 ounces Muenster cheese, cut into 12 (1-inch) cubes
- 1½ cups all-purpose flour, divided
- 1¼ cups cornstarch
- 2 teaspoons baking powder
- 1 teaspoon table salt
- 1½ cups mild lager, such as Budweiser
- 3 quarts peanut or vegetable oil

1. For the sauce Heat oil in medium saucepan over medium-high heat until shimmering. Add chili powder, onion powder, and garlic powder and cook until fragrant, about 30 seconds. Add broth, tomato sauce, adobo sauce, and bay leaf and bring to boil. Reduce heat to medium and cook at vigorous simmer until reduced to 2 cups, 12 to 15 minutes. Stir in lime juice and season with salt and pepper to taste. Remove from heat, cover, and keep warm. (Discard bay leaf before serving.) (Sauce can be refrigerated for up to 2 days. Microwave for 2 minutes until hot before serving.)

2. For the chiles Meanwhile, adjust 1 oven rack to middle position and second rack 6 inches from broiler element. Heat broiler. Line rimmed baking sheet with aluminum foil. Evenly space poblanos on prepared sheet and broil until skins just begin to blister on first side, 3 to 5 minutes. Flip poblanos and continue to broil until skins are just beginning to blister on second side, about 3 minutes longer. Let poblanos rest on sheet until cool enough to handle, about 10 minutes. Adjust oven temperature to 200 degrees.

3. Peel off any loose skin from poblanos, if desired. Working with 1 poblano at a time, leaving stem intact and starting at top, make 3-inch-long vertical incision down 1 side of chile. Use scissors to cut away interior seed bulb, then use spoon to scoop out and discard bulb and seeds. (Some tearing may occur and is OK.)

4. Place 2 Muenster cubes inside each poblano. Overlap poblano opening and thread with skewer to seal. (Use 1 additional skewer per poblano if necessary.) Allow top of skewer to remain exposed by at least ½ inch for easy removal. (Stuffed poblanos can be refrigerated for up to 24 hours.)

5. Place ½ cup flour in shallow dish. Combine remaining 1 cup flour, cornstarch, baking powder, and salt in medium bowl. Whisk lager into flour mixture until smooth.

6. Set wire rack in rimmed baking sheet and line rack with triple layer of paper towels. Add oil to large Dutch oven until it measures 2 inches deep and heat over medium-high heat to 375 degrees.

7. Working with 3 poblanos at a time, dredge poblanos in flour, shaking gently to remove excess. Holding each poblano by its stem, dunk in batter to evenly coat, then transfer to hot oil. Fry until golden and crispy, 4 to 5 minutes, turning frequently for even cooking. Adjust burner, if necessary, to maintain oil temperature between 350 and 375 degrees.

8. Transfer fried poblanos to prepared wire rack and let drain for 30 seconds. Season poblanos with salt, remove skewers, and transfer sheet to oven to keep poblanos warm. Return oil to 375 degrees and repeat with remaining poblanos and batter. Serve with sauce.

Prepping Chiles

1. After broiling poblanos and peeling away loose skin, cut 3-inch-long vertical slit in each, then cut out seed bulbs with scissors. (Use spoon to scoop away remaining seeds.)

2. Place cheese inside each poblano. Overlap opening and thread with skewer to seal. Then dredge in flour and dunk in batter to coat.

Stuffed Portobello Mushrooms with Spinach and Gorgonzola

Serves 4   Total Time 1¼ hours

Why This Recipe Works Portobello mushroom caps have a wide surface and naturally concave shape that make them ideal for achieving browning and holding robust ingredients. Roasting them gill side down allows any moisture released during cooking to drain away and protects the delicate underside of the mushrooms from burning. While the mushrooms roast, we make an easy stuffing with baby spinach, flavorful Gorgonzola cheese, and toasted walnuts, which we top with panko bread crumbs. Baking the stuffed mushrooms quickly in a superhot oven heats everything through and crisps up the crown of bread crumbs. You can substitute cream sherry with a squeeze of lemon juice for the dry sherry.

- 3 tablespoons extra-virgin olive oil, divided
- 10 large portobello mushroom caps (8 whole, 2 chopped fine)
- ½ teaspoon table salt, divided
- ¼ teaspoon pepper
- 12 ounces (12 cups) baby spinach
- 2 tablespoons water
- 1 onion, chopped fine
- 4 garlic cloves, minced
- ½ cup dry sherry
- 3 ounces Gorgonzola cheese, crumbled (1 cup)
- ½ cup walnuts, toasted and chopped
- ¾ cup panko bread crumbs

1. Adjust oven rack to upper-middle position and heat oven to 500 degrees. Brush rimmed baking sheet with 1 tablespoon oil. Lay whole mushroom caps, gill side down, on prepared baking sheet and brush tops with 1 tablespoon oil. Roast until tender, 10 to 12 minutes. Remove sheet from oven, flip mushrooms gill side up, and sprinkle with ¼ teaspoon salt and pepper.

2. Meanwhile, microwave spinach, water, and remaining ¼ teaspoon salt in covered bowl until spinach is wilted, about 2 minutes. Drain spinach in colander, let cool slightly, then place in clean dish towel and squeeze out excess liquid. Transfer spinach to cutting board and chop coarse.

3. Cook onion and remaining 1 tablespoon oil in 12-inch skillet over medium-high heat until softened, about 3 minutes. Stir in chopped mushrooms and cook until they begin to release their liquid, about 4 minutes. Stir in garlic and cook until fragrant, about 30 seconds. Stir in sherry and cook until evaporated, about 2 minutes. Stir in chopped spinach, Gorgonzola, and walnuts and cook until heated through, about 1 minute. Season with salt and pepper to taste.

4. Spoon filling into roasted mushroom caps, press filling flat with back of spoon, then sprinkle with panko. Bake until panko is golden and filling is warmed through, 5 to 10 minutes. Serve.

Chipotle Lentil–Stuffed Sweet Potatoes

Serves 4 Total Time 50 minutes

Why This Recipe Works One look at these gorgeous stuffed sweet potatoes topped with pickled red onion and jalapeño, crema, and queso fresco will convince you to make them. And these are easier to make than most stuffed potatoes because we microwave them, scoop out their flesh to make the stuffing, and then bake them until beautifully spotty brown. Canned lentils add to this easy and filling stuffing base, which we jazz up with chipotle chiles and cumin. Mexican crema can be found in the dairy section of many supermarkets. If you can't find it, you can substitute sour cream, which has a thicker consistency.

- ½ small red onion, sliced thin
- ¼ cup distilled white vinegar
- 1 small jalapeño chile, stemmed and sliced thin
- 4 small sweet potatoes (8 ounces each), unpeeled, pricked all over with fork
- 1 (15-ounce) can lentils, rinsed
- 1½ tablespoons minced canned chipotle chile in adobo sauce
- 1 teaspoon ground cumin
- 1½ teaspoons table salt, divided
- ¼ cup Mexican crema
- 2 ounces queso fresco, crumbled (½ cup)
- 2 tablespoons chopped fresh cilantro

1. Adjust oven rack to middle position and heat oven to 425 degrees. Combine onion, vinegar, and jalapeño in small bowl. Cover and microwave until hot, about 2 minutes; set aside.

2. Microwave potatoes on large plate until potatoes are very tender and can be easily squeezed with tongs, 12 to 15 minutes, flipping potatoes every 3 minutes. Let cool for 5 minutes.

3. Split each potato lengthwise. Using spoon, scoop about half of flesh from each potato into large bowl. Stir in lentils, chipotle, cumin, 1 teaspoon salt, and 1 teaspoon pickling liquid until combined. Season insides of potatoes with remaining ½ teaspoon salt, then spoon lentil mixture into potatoes. Arrange potatoes on greased rimmed baking sheet, gently pressing halves back together until only partially open. Roast until spotty brown and hot throughout, about 10 minutes. Top with pickled onion mixture, crema, queso fresco, and cilantro. Serve.

Stuffed Tomatoes with Couscous and Zucchini

Serves 4 Total Time 1¼ hours

Why This Recipe Works Round tomatoes look like they're made for stuffing. The problem is that the fruit's watery nature can result in drab stuffed tomatoes with soggy fillings. We core and seed the tomatoes, salt their interiors, and let them drain, drawing out their excess liquid. After 30 minutes, the tomatoes give up most of their liquid so we can pack them with filling without it becoming soggy. The world of stuffed tomato options is large, but here we opt for nutty-tasting couscous and pair it with sautéed zucchini and fennel. Goat cheese and Parmesan add richness and keep the filling cohesive. We sprinkle the stuffed tomatoes with more Parmesan, then bake them until the cheese is browned and the tomatoes are tender. Two tomatoes make a nice meal. Look for round tomatoes of equal size with flat, sturdy bottoms that can sit upright on their own.

Chipotle Lentil-Stuffed Sweet Potatoes

- 8 large tomatoes (8 ounces each)
- ⅛ teaspoon table salt
- 3 tablespoons extra-virgin olive oil, divided
- 1 fennel bulb, stalks discarded, bulb halved, cored, and chopped fine
- 2 shallots, minced
- 1 zucchini (8 ounces), cut into ¼-inch pieces
- 4 garlic cloves, minced
- ⅔ cup couscous
- ¾ cup vegetable broth
- 2 ounces Parmesan cheese, grated (1 cup), divided
- 2 ounces goat cheese, crumbled (½ cup)
- ¼ cup chopped fresh basil

1. Adjust oven rack to upper-middle position and heat oven to 375 degrees. Slice top ⅛ inch off each tomato and carefully remove core and seeds. Sprinkle inside of each tomato with salt. Place upside down on large paper towel–lined plate and let drain for 30 minutes.

2. Meanwhile, heat 2 tablespoons oil in large saucepan over medium heat until shimmering. Add fennel and shallots and cook until softened and lightly browned, 10 to 12 minutes.

3. Stir in zucchini and cook until tender, about 5 minutes. Stir in garlic and cook until fragrant, about 30 seconds. Stir in couscous and cook until lightly toasted, 1 to 2 minutes. Stir in broth and bring to brief simmer. Cover pan and let sit off heat for 5 minutes. Using fork, gently fluff couscous, then stir in ½ cup Parmesan, goat cheese, and basil. Season with salt and pepper to taste.

4. Pat inside of each tomato dry with paper towels. Arrange tomatoes, cut side up, in 13 by 9-inch baking dish lined with aluminum foil. Brush cut edges of tomatoes with remaining 1 tablespoon oil. Mound couscous filling into tomatoes and pack lightly with back of spoon. Sprinkle with remaining ½ cup Parmesan. Bake until cheese is lightly browned and tomatoes are tender, about 15 minutes. Serve.

| *Beet Poke Bowls*

Beet Poke Bowls

VEGAN Serves 4 Total Time 20 minutes, plus 30 minutes chilling

Why This Recipe Works For a vegetarian take on the typical poke bowl we use beets, since their sturdy density, absorbent nature, and bright pink color make them an apt stand-in for the typical seafood. To start, we toss cooked beets in a potent savory-sweet marinade flavored with classic poke seasonings such as rice vinegar, toasted sesame oil, and fresh ginger. The beets must sit in this liquid for at least 30 minutes for the flavors to thoroughly infuse (you can marinate them up to 24 hours ahead). The result is remarkably flavorful and well-seasoned beets. Rather than the more typical rice, we serve the vegetable over chewy, resilient soba noodles, which we toss in a bit of sesame oil to boost their flavor and slurpability. For a texturally dynamic bowl, we embellish with carrots, cucumber, avocado, macadamia nuts, scallions, and a sprinkle of the Japanese seasoning blend furikake. There are many different kinds of furikake; we recommend using one that has dried seaweed (nori and/or kombu), bonito flakes, and sesame seeds. Look for it at Japanese or Asian grocery stores; you might also find it at some well-stocked supermarkets.

- 3 scallions, white and green parts separated and sliced thin on bias
- 2 tablespoons soy sauce
- 2 tablespoons vegetable oil
- 1 tablespoon unseasoned rice vinegar
- 4 teaspoons toasted sesame oil, divided
- 2 teaspoons grated fresh ginger
- 1 garlic clove, minced
- ¾ teaspoon red pepper flakes
- 1 recipe Quick-Cooking Beets (page 103)
- 12 ounces dried soba noodles
- 2 carrots, peeled and cut into 2-inch-long matchsticks
- ½ seedless English cucumber, halved lengthwise and sliced thin crosswise
- 1 ripe but firm avocado, halved, pitted, and sliced ¼ inch thick
- ⅓ cup finely chopped salted dry-roasted macadamia nuts or peanuts
- Furikake (optional)

1. Combine scallion whites, soy sauce, vegetable oil, rice vinegar, 2 teaspoons sesame oil, ginger, garlic, and pepper flakes in large bowl Add cooked beets to bowl and toss well. Refrigerate for at least 30 minutes or up to 24 hours.

2. Meanwhile, bring 4 quarts water to boil in large pot. Stir in noodles and cook according to package directions, stirring occasionally, until noodles are cooked through but still retain some chew. Drain noodles and rinse under cold water until chilled. Drain well

3. Toss noodles with remaining 2 teaspoons sesame oil and divide among individual serving bowls. Top with marinated beets, carrots, cucumber, avocado, macadamia nuts, scallion greens, and furikake, if using. Serve.

Cauliflower Rice Bowls with Sweet Potatoes, Avocados, and Chickpeas

FAST VEGAN Serves 4 Total Time 45 minutes

Why This Recipe Works We forged our own path toward this hearty dinner bowl including a lot of our favorite ingredients in it. Instead of a grain base, we use cauliflower rice, cooking it with red pepper flakes and turmeric to impart both spice and bright color. Roasted sweet potatoes, spinach, and avocado add the perfect balance of flavor and texture. Our Creamless Creamy Roasted Red Pepper and Tahini Dressing is made with soaked cashews, tricking our taste buds with its creamy texture and roasted, smoky flavor. Finally, a generous handful of crispy spiced chickpeas adds bursts of texture. To kick this up a notch, try adding some homemade (page 446) or store-bought sauerkraut. We prefer to make our own cauliflower rice, but you can use store-bought refrigerated or frozen cauliflower rice; reduce the covered cooking time in step 2 to 10 minutes.

- 1 pound sweet potatoes, unpeeled, halved lengthwise and sliced crosswise ¼ inch thick
- 5 teaspoons extra-virgin olive oil, divided
- ½ teaspoon table salt, divided
- 1 head cauliflower (2 pounds), cored and cut into 1-inch florets (6 cups)
- 2 garlic cloves, minced
- ¼–½ teaspoon red pepper flakes
- ½ teaspoon ground turmeric
- 1 cup water
- 2 cups baby spinach
- 2 ripe avocados, sliced thin
- ½ cup Creamless Creamy Roasted Red Pepper and Tahini Dressing (page 139)
- 1 cup Spiced Roasted Chickpeas (recipe follows)

1. Adjust oven rack to middle position and heat oven to 400 degrees. Toss potatoes, 1 tablespoon oil, and ¼ teaspoon salt together in bowl, then spread in even layer on rimmed baking sheet. Roast until potatoes are beginning to brown, 15 to 20 minutes, flipping slices halfway through roasting. Season with salt and pepper to taste and set aside.

2. Meanwhile, working in 2 batches, pulse cauliflower in food processor until finely ground into ⅛- to ¼-inch pieces, 6 to 8 pulses, scraping down sides of bowl as needed. Heat remaining 2 teaspoons oil in large saucepan over medium-low heat until shimmering. Add garlic, pepper flakes, and turmeric and cook until fragrant, about 30 seconds. Stir in cauliflower, water, and remaining ¼ teaspoon salt; cover and cook, stirring occasionally, until cauliflower is tender, 12 to 15 minutes.

3. Uncover and continue to cook, stirring occasionally, until cauliflower rice is nearly dry, about 3 minutes. Stir in spinach and cook until spinach just begins to wilt, about 30 seconds. Season with salt and pepper to taste.

4. Divide cauliflower rice among individual serving bowls, then top with reserved sweet potatoes and avocados. Drizzle with tahini dressing and sprinkle with chickpeas. Serve.

Spiced Roasted Chickpeas

VEGAN Serves 6 Total Time 1 hour 20 minutes, plus 30 minutes cooling

Tossed with an appealing spice mix, roasted chickpeas have a crisp, airy texture that makes them a satisfying snack, a stellar salad topper, or a fitting hummus garnish. Microwaving the chickpeas for about 10 minutes bursts them open at the seams so they release interior moisture. We then bake them in a 350-degree oven. You will need a 13 by 9-inch metal baking pan for this recipe; a glass or ceramic baking dish will result in uneven cooking.

- 2 (15-ounce) cans chickpeas
- 3 tablespoons extra-virgin olive oil
- 2 teaspoons paprika
- 1 teaspoon ground coriander
- ½ teaspoon ground turmeric
- ½ teaspoon ground allspice
- ½ teaspoon ground cumin
- ½ teaspoon sugar
- ⅛ teaspoon table salt
- ⅛ teaspoon cayenne pepper

1. Adjust oven rack to middle position and heat oven to 350 degrees. Place chickpeas in colander and drain for 10 minutes. Line large plate with double layer of paper towels. Spread chickpeas over plate in even layer. Microwave until exteriors of chickpeas are dry and many have ruptured, 8 to 12 minutes.

2. Transfer chickpeas to 13 by 9-inch metal baking pan. Add oil and stir until evenly coated. Using spatula, spread chickpeas into single layer. Transfer to oven and roast for 30 minutes. Stir chickpeas and crowd them toward center of pan. Continue to roast until chickpeas appear dry, slightly shriveled, and deep golden brown, 20 to 40 minutes. (To test for doneness, remove a few paler chickpeas and let cool briefly before tasting; if interiors are soft, return to oven and test again in 5 minutes.)

3. Combine paprika, coriander, turmeric, allspice, cumin, sugar, salt, and cayenne in large bowl. Transfer chickpeas to bowl and toss with spice mixture to coat. Season with salt to taste. Let cool fully before serving, about 30 minutes. (Chickpeas can be stored in airtight container for up to 1 week.)

Roasted Vegetable Bowls with Bulgur, White Beans, and Arugula

VEGAN   Serves 4   Total Time 1 hour

Why This Recipe Works Cannellini beans and roasted vegetables make these bulgur bowls hearty enough for dinner. The cherry tomatoes soften in the high heat of the oven, releasing some of their juices, while chunks of bell pepper and red onion take on some flavorful browning. Then we stir in the beans until they are just heated through. The bulgur cooks quickly but gives us time to make a creamy dressing with yogurt and sambal oelek. Serve bowls topped with chopped pitted kalamata olives, if desired. To make this recipe vegan, substitute plant-based yogurt for the dairy yogurt.

- 10 ounces cherry tomatoes
- 1 red bell pepper, stemmed, seeded, and cut into ¾-inch pieces
- 1 small red onion, cut into ¾-inch pieces
- ½ cup extra-virgin olive oil, divided
- 1¾ teaspoons table salt, divided, plus salt for cooking bulgur
- 1 (15-ounce) can cannellini beans, rinsed
- 1¼ cups medium-grind bulgur
- 1 tablespoon lemon juice
- 5 ounces (5 cups) baby arugula
- ¾ cup plain whole-milk Greek yogurt
- 2 tablespoons sambal oelek

1. Adjust oven rack to middle position and heat oven to 450 degrees. Toss tomatoes, bell pepper, onion, ¼ cup oil, and 1 teaspoon salt together on rimmed baking sheet. Roast until vegetables are softened and spotty brown, about 20 minutes. Stir in beans and roast until heated through, about 5 minutes.

2. Meanwhile, bring 2 quarts water to boil in large saucepan. Add bulgur and 1 teaspoon salt. Reduce heat to medium-low and simmer until tender, 6 to 10 minutes. Drain bulgur in fine-mesh strainer and return to saucepan. Stir in 2 tablespoons oil and ¼ teaspoon salt.

3. Whisk lemon juice, ¼ teaspoon salt, and remaining 2 tablespoons oil together in large bowl. Add arugula and toss to coat. Combine yogurt, sambal oelek, 3 tablespoons water, and remaining ¼ teaspoon salt in second bowl. Divide bulgur, roasted vegetable mixture, and arugula among individual bowls. Drizzle with yogurt mixture and serve.

top | *Cauliflower Rice Bowls with Sweet Potatoes, Avocados, and Chickpeas*

bottom | *Roasted Vegetable Bowls with Bulgur, White Beans, and Arugula*

Roasted Tofu and Sweet Potato Bowls with Snap Pea Salad

Hearty Vegetable and Farro Bowls with Goat Cheese

FAST Serves 4 Total Time 45 minutes

Why This Recipe Works The base of this satisfying dish is nutty farro, which we toss with a lemony vinaigrette while it's still hot so it more easily absorbs the flavors. At the same time we add beautiful carrot ribbons and baby spinach, tossing everything together. While the flavors are melding, we sauté cremini mushrooms until lightly browned and use them for the topping, along with goat cheese.

- 2 cups farro
- ¾ teaspoon table salt, divided, plus salt for cooking farro
- 6 tablespoons extra-virgin olive oil, divided
- 1 teaspoon grated lemon zest plus 3 tablespoons juice
- 1 garlic clove, minced
- ½ teaspoon pepper, divided
- 4 carrots, peeled and shaved with vegetable peeler lengthwise into ribbons
- 4 ounces (4 cups) baby spinach
- 1 pound cremini mushrooms, trimmed and sliced thin
- 2 ounces goat cheese, crumbled (½ cup)

1. Bring 2 quarts water to boil in large saucepan. Add farro and 1 tablespoon salt. Return to boil, turn heat down to medium-low, and simmer until farro is tender with slight chew, 15 to 20 minutes. Drain.

2. Whisk ¼ cup oil, lemon zest and juice, garlic, ½ teaspoon salt, and ¼ teaspoon pepper together in bowl. Add carrots, spinach, and farro and toss to combine.

3. Heat remaining 2 tablespoons oil in 12-inch nonstick skillet over medium-high heat until shimmering. Add mushrooms, remaining ¼ teaspoon salt, and remaining ¼ teaspoon pepper, cover, and cook until mushrooms release their liquid, about 5 minutes. Uncover and continue to cook until liquid has evaporated and mushrooms begin to brown, about 3 minutes longer. Divide farro mixture evenly among 4 serving bowls. Top with goat cheese and mushrooms. Serve.

Roasted Tofu and Sweet Potato Bowls with Snap Pea Salad

Serves 4 Total Time 1¼ hours, plus 20 minutes draining

Why This Recipe Works Bursting with the flavors and textures of many vegetables and starring roasted glazed tofu, this bowl is nourishing, filling, and a feast for the eyes. It is also easy to make thanks to a rimmed baking sheet. Roasting the tofu makes all the difference, as it gives us the opportunity to flavor the tofu at several points along the way. First, before roasting, we toss it with a heady mix of soy sauce, honey, sesame oil, and sambal, which acts as a powerful glaze; the sugars encourage quick browning on the outside, allowing the tofu to stay tender inside. As for the sweet potatoes, we give them a head start on the tofu in a very hot oven because honestly, what is better than sweet potato rounds that are deeply caramelized? Partway through roasting we add more glaze to both the tofu and sweet potatoes, and we use the remaining glaze to make an aromatic drizzling sauce, ensuring that this dish delivers harmonious flavors through and through.

- 28 ounces firm tofu, cut into 1-inch-wide by 1½-inch-long pieces
- 2 pounds sweet potatoes, peeled and cut into 1-inch rounds
- 1 tablespoon vegetable oil
- 2 teaspoons table salt, divided
- 3 tablespoons soy sauce
- 2 tablespoons honey
- 2 tablespoons toasted sesame oil
- 1 tablespoon sambal oelek, plus extra for serving
- 1 tablespoon lime juice, plus lime wedges for serving
- 1 tablespoon vegetarian fish sauce
- 1 teaspoon grated fresh ginger
- 12 ounces sugar snap peas, strings removed, halved on bias
- 1 large red bell pepper, stemmed, seeded, and cut into ¼-inch-wide strips
- 1 cup cilantro leaves and tender stems, chopped coarse, divided
- ⅓ cup dry-roasted peanuts, chopped coarse
- 1 serrano chile, sliced into thin rounds (optional)

1. Adjust oven rack to middle position and heat oven to 475 degrees. Spread tofu over paper towel–lined baking sheet and let drain for 20 minutes. Gently pat dry with paper towels. Toss potatoes with vegetable oil and ¾ teaspoon salt on rimmed baking sheet, then arrange cut side down in single layer over sheet. Roast until deeply browned on bottom, 12 to 16 minutes.

2. Whisk soy sauce, honey, sesame oil, and sambal together in small bowl. Gently pat tofu dry with paper towels, then transfer to large bowl. Toss tofu with 3 tablespoons soy-honey mixture and 1 teaspoon salt. Remove sheet from oven and immediately reduce oven temperature to 375 degrees. Flip potato rounds, shifting to 1 half of sheet, then spread tofu in single layer on empty side. Roast for 15 minutes.

3. Remove sheet from oven and gently stir tofu pieces. Brush potatoes and tofu with 3 tablespoons soy-honey mixture, then return to oven and roast until tofu is golden brown around edges, 14 to 18 minutes.

4. Whisk lime juice, fish sauce, ginger, remaining ¼ teaspoon salt, and remaining soy-honey mixture together in large bowl. Set aside half of dressing for serving, then add snap peas, bell pepper, and half of cilantro to remaining dressing in bowl, tossing to coat. Divide potatoes, tofu, and snap pea salad among individual serving bowls and drizzle with reserved dressing. Top with peanuts; serrano, if using; and remaining cilantro and serve with lime wedges and extra sambal.

Rainbow Bowls with Crispy Tempeh

FAST Serves 2 Total Time 20 minutes

Why This Recipe Works Arranging a rainbow of fruits and vegetables on a bed of greens makes a stunning presentation. Here, cherry tomatoes and a segmented orange offer bright acidity, which we balance with buttery avocado and crisp watermelon radishes for their peppery snap and cheerful pink hue (but you can use any kind of radish). To contrast with all the raw vegetables, we use red beets, cooked to bring out their natural sweetness. A refreshing dressing of orange juice, honey, and ginger highlights our salad. Boiling the tempeh in water and soy sauce seasons it wonderfully, and a quick shallow-fry in oil transforms it into a crunchy umami bomb.

- 1 orange
- 5 ounces (5 cups) baby arugula
- ¼ cup Orange-Ginger Vinaigrette, divided, (recipe follows)
- 4 ounces cherry tomatoes, halved
- ½ ripe avocado, cut into ½-inch pieces
- 4 radishes, trimmed, halved, and sliced thin
- 1½ cups chopped Quick-Cooking Beets (page 103)
- 1 recipe Crispy Tempeh (page 436)

Cut away peel and pith from orange. Holding fruit over bowl, use paring knife to slice between membranes to release segments. Toss arugula with half of vinaigrette to coat, then season with salt and pepper to taste. Divide among individual serving bowls, then top with orange segments, tomatoes, avocado, radishes, and beets. Drizzle with remaining vinaigrette and sprinkle with tempeh. Serve.

Orange-Ginger Vinaigrette

FAST Makes 1 cup Total Time 45 minutes

- 2 cups orange juice (4 oranges)
- 1 tablespoon honey
- 3 tablespoons lime juice (2 limes)
- 1 tablespoon minced shallot
- 1 teaspoon grated fresh ginger
- ½ teaspoon table salt
- ½ teaspoon pepper
- 2 tablespoons extra-virgin olive oil

Bring orange juice and honey to boil in small stainless-steel saucepan over medium-high heat. Reduce heat to maintain simmer and cook until mixture is thickened and measures about ⅔ cup, 15 to 20 minutes. Transfer syrup to medium bowl and refrigerate until cool, about 15 minutes. Whisk in lime juice, shallot, ginger, salt, and pepper until combined. Whisking constantly, slowly drizzle in oil until emulsified. Season with salt and pepper to taste. (Vinaigrette can be refrigerated for up to 1 week; whisk to recombine before using.)

Rainbow Bowls with Crispy Tempeh

Toppings for Vegetable Dishes

A simple topping can really finish a dish. Here are some easy recipes (and store-bought options) that can make a dish even more exciting by adding pops of savory flavor, texture, and color. Let your imagination and culinary instincts be your guide. Deploy this palette of flavors however you wish.

Tarragon-Lemon Gremolata

FAST VEGAN Makes ¼ cup Total Time 5 minutes

Herbs, lemon zest, and garlic are the hallmarks of gremolata, an Italian garnish that is quite versatile. Use it on soups, pasta, roasted vegetables, vegetable casseroles, and more. To avoid harsh garlic flavor, don't mince the garlic until you're ready to mix the gremolata.

- 2 tablespoons minced fresh tarragon
- 2 tablespoons minced fresh parsley
- 2 teaspoons grated lemon zest
- 1 garlic clove, minced

Combine all ingredients in bowl.

Shichimi Togarashi

FAST VEGAN Makes ½ cup Total Time 10 minutes

This Japanese seven-spice mixture adds complexity, texture, and a touch of heat to any dish. Try it as a topping on vegetables, rice, noodles, eggs, tofu, soups, and more.

- 1½ teaspoons grated orange zest
- 4 teaspoons sesame seeds, toasted
- 1 tablespoon paprika
- 2 teaspoons pepper
- ½ teaspoon garlic powder
- ½ teaspoon ground ginger
- ¼ teaspoon cayenne pepper

Microwave orange zest in small bowl, stirring occasionally, until dry and no longer clumping together, about 2 minutes. Stir in sesame seeds, paprika, pepper, garlic powder, ginger, and cayenne. (Spice blend can be stored in airtight container for up to 1 week.)

Savory Seed Brittle

Makes 2 cups Total Time 1¼ hours, plus 1 hour cooling

This seed brittle is packed with both outstanding texture and delicious savory flavor. To achieve the ideal crunchy, brittle texture that breaks into bite-size pieces, we add an egg white and some maple syrup, which also adds just a bit of sweetness to offset all the savory flavors. Do not substitute quick or instant oats in this recipe.

- 2 tablespoons maple syrup
- 1 large egg white
- 1 tablespoon extra-virgin olive oil or vegetable oil
- 1 tablespoon soy sauce
- 1 tablespoon caraway seeds, crushed
- ½ teaspoon table salt
- ¼ teaspoon pepper
- ½ cup old-fashioned rolled oats
- ⅓ cup sunflower seeds
- ⅓ cup pepitas
- 2 tablespoons sesame seeds
- 2 tablespoons nigella seeds

1. Adjust oven rack to upper-middle position and heat oven to 300 degrees. Line 8-inch square baking pan with parchment paper and spray parchment with vegetable oil spray. Whisk maple syrup, egg white, oil, soy sauce, caraway seeds, salt, and pepper together in large bowl. Stir in oats, sunflower seeds, pepitas, sesame seeds, and nigella seeds until well combined.

2. Transfer oat mixture to prepared pan and spread into even layer. Using stiff metal spatula, press oat mixture until very compact. Bake until golden brown and fragrant, 45 to 55 minutes, rotating pan halfway through baking.

3. Transfer pan to wire rack and let brittle cool completely, about 1 hour. Break cooled brittle into pieces of desired size, discarding parchment. (Brittle can be stored in airtight container for up to 1 month.)

Dukkah

VEGAN Makes 2 cups Total Time 1½ hours

Dukkah, an Egyptian condiment used throughout the Middle East, contains roasted chickpeas, nuts, and a variety of seeds that are coarsely ground. It is traditionally added to bread dipped in olive oil, but its uses are boundless: Try sprinkling it on roasted vegetables, hummus, and salads, or stir it into yogurt to make a savory dip in minutes.

- 1 (15-ounce) can chickpeas, rinsed
- 1 teaspoon extra-virgin olive oil
- ½ cup shelled pistachios or unsalted sunflower seeds
- ⅓ cup sesame seeds
- 2½ tablespoons coriander seeds
- 1 tablespoon cumin seeds
- 2 teaspoons fennel seeds
- 1½ teaspoons pepper
- 1¼ teaspoons table salt

1. Adjust oven rack to middle position and heat oven to 400 degrees. Pat chickpeas dry with paper towels and transfer to rimmed baking sheet. Drizzle oil over chickpeas, toss to coat, and spread in even layer. Roast until browned and crisp, 40 to 45 minutes, stirring every 5 to 10 minutes. Transfer to wire rack and let cool completely.

2. Meanwhile, toast pistachios in 8-inch skillet over medium heat, stirring frequently, until lightly browned and fragrant, 3 to 5 minutes; transfer to small bowl and let cool completely. Add sesame seeds to now-empty skillet and toast, stirring frequently, until fragrant, about 1 minute; transfer to separate small bowl and let cool. Add coriander seeds, cumin seeds, fennel seeds, and pepper to now-empty skillet and toast, stirring frequently, until fragrant, about 30 seconds; transfer to food processor.

3. Process spices in food processor until finely ground, 2 to 3 minutes; transfer to medium bowl. Process chickpeas in now-empty processor until coarsely ground, about 10 seconds; add to bowl with spices. Pulse pistachios in now-empty processor until coarsely ground, about 15 pulses; add to bowl with spices. Pulse sesame seeds and salt in food processor until coarsely ground, about 5 pulses; add to bowl with spices.

4. Toss dukkah until well combined. (Dukkah can be stored in airtight container for up to 3 months.)

Microwave-Fried Shallots

FAST **VEGAN** Makes ½ cup Total Time 25 minutes

- 3 shallots, sliced thin
- ½ cup vegetable oil, for frying

Combine shallots and oil in medium bowl. Microwave for 5 minutes. Stir and continue to microwave 2 minutes longer. Repeat stirring and microwaving in 2-minute increments until beginning to brown (4 to 6 minutes). Repeat stirring and microwaving in 30-second increments until deep golden brown (30 seconds to 2 minutes). Using slotted spoon, transfer shallots to paper towel–lined plate; season with salt to taste. Let drain and crisp, about 5 minutes. (Shallots can be stored in an airtight container for up to 1 month.)

Store-Bought Toppings

Simple ingredients can add interest and a bit of flourish to a finished recipe. Here are some ideas for using everyday ones you likely have on hand.

Fresh Herbs: Scattering a handful of chopped or minced fresh herbs is perhaps the easiest way to add eye appeal and flavor all at once.

Citrus Zest: A bit of grated lemon or lime zest adds freshness and intensity to many vegetarian recipes. Scatter some atop roasted vegetables, a grain dish, or vegetable-forward pasta dishes.

Toasted Nuts: Some nuts are available pretoasted, but you can also easily toast them in a skillet with a little olive oil and salt and pepper.

Extra-Virgin Olive Oil: A good olive oil adds instant richness and a fruity, peppery flavor. Drizzle over sautéed vegetables, soups, and more.

Flavored Vinegar: Drizzle a flavored balsamic (like pomegranate or basil) over vegetable dishes, soups, and even fruit salads.

Flake Sea Salt: This finishing salt adds visual interest and a distinct crunch of saltiness. The simpler the recipe, the better, because then these lovely flakes will be visible.

Salads Big & Small

92 Easiest Salad, Ever ■ ●

92 Kale Caesar Salad ●

93 Crispy and Creamy Kale Salad ●

94 Horiatiki Salata (Hearty Greek Salad)

97 Cobb Salad ■

97 Hearty Green Salad with Chickpeas, Pickled Cauliflower, and Seared Halloumi ■

98 Bitter Greens, Carrot, and Chickpea Salad with Warm Lemon Dressing ■

99 Marinated Bean and Asparagus Salad with Preserved Lemon Dressing

100 White Bean and Arugula Salad with Frico Crumble

100 Beet Salad with Spiced Yogurt and Watercress

Beet Salad with Blue Cheese and Endive

103 Quick-Cooking Beets ■ ●

103 Broccoli Salad with Avocado Dressing ■ ●

104 Roasted Butternut Squash Salad with Creamy Tahini Dressing ●

104 Roasted Cauliflower Salad with Arugula and Pear

106 Charred Shaved Brussels Sprout Salad with Sweet Chili–Lime Dressing ■ ●

Charred Shaved Brussels Sprout Salad with Apricot Dressing ■ ●

Charred Shaved Brussels Sprout Salad with Sherry-Honey Dressing ■

107 Chopped Carrot Salad with Mint, Pistachios, and Pomegranate Seeds ■

109 Lao Hu Cai (Tiger Salad) ■ ●

109 Shaved Celery Salad with Pomegranate-Honey Vinaigrette ■

110 Apple–Celery Root Salad ■

110 Esquites (Mexican Corn Salad) ■

111 Buffalo Cucumber Salad ■

112 Avocado and Cucumber Salad with Sriracha Mayo ■

113 Shaved Vegetable Salad with Creamy Miso Dressing

114 Green Bean Salad with Creamy Lemon Sauce and Crispy Capers ■ ●

114 Three-Bean Salad ■

115 Napa Cabbage Slaw with Carrots and Sesame ■ ●

Napa Cabbage Slaw with Apple and Walnuts ■ ●

Napa Cabbage Slaw with Jícama and Pepitas ■

116 Coleslaw Potato Salad

117 Spicy Green Pea Salad ■

118 Radicchio Chopped Salad with White Beans, Oranges, and Olives

118 Romaine and Radicchio Salad with Roasted Squash and Pickled Pears ●

121 Cast Iron–Seared Romaine with Oyster Sauce, Ginger, and Sesame ■

121 Torn Potato Salad with Toasted Garlic and Herb Dressing ●

122 Fingerling Potato Salad with Sun-Dried Tomato Dressing ●

122 Herbes de Provence ■ ●

123 Cherry Tomato Salad with Pita Crisps and Spicy Citrus Dressing ■ ●

125 Tomatillo and Bibb Lettuce Salad with Tomatillo Ranch ■ ●

125 Wheat Berry Salad with Radicchio, Dried Cherries, and Pecans

126 Chopped Vegetable and Stone Fruit Salad ■ ●

126 Bulgur Salad with Curry Roasted Sweet Potatoes and Chickpeas

128 Farro Salad with Asparagus, Radishes, and Parmesan ■

128 Basic Farro ■ ●

129 Kale and Farro Salad with Fennel, Olives, and Parmesan ■

130 Sweet Potato, Lentil, and Kale Salad with Fried Shallots

131 Butternut Squash and Apple Fattoush ●

132 Red Cabbage and Grapefruit Salad

132 Cantaloupe Salad with Olives and Red Onion ■ ●

133 Honeydew Salad with Peanuts and Lime ■

134 Caramelized Plums with Spicy Herb Salad ■ ●

135 Grilled Peach and Tomato Salad with Burrata and Basil ■

136 Grilled Stone Fruit

136 Grilled Watermelon, Halloumi, and Olive Salad

Dressing Up Salads

138 Make-Ahead Vinaigrette ■ ●

Make-Ahead Sherry-Shallot Vinaigrette ■ ●

Make-Ahead Balsamic-Fennel Vinaigrette ■ ●

138 Raspberry Vinaigrette ■ ●

139 Sesame-Scallion Vinaigrette ■ ●

139 Creamless Creamy Herb Dressing ●

Creamless Creamy Roasted Red Pepper and Tahini Dressing ●

139 Creamy Avocado Dressing ■ ●

■ Fast (45 minutes or less)

● Vegan

top | *Easiest Salad, Ever*
bottom | *Kale Caesar Salad*

Easiest Salad, Ever

FAST **VEGAN** Serves 4 to 6 Total Time 5 minutes

Why This Recipe Works Here is a salad-making method that everyone should know as it's a route to making an excellent salad in minutes. The key is to have really good ingredients, starting with the freshest greens, ideally a mix of greens. Adding the two ingredients for the dressing right in the salad bowl and piling the greens on top allows the bowl to be brought to the table when ready and simply tossed there. Tossing the salad too early will just result in wilted greens rather than a fresh-looking salad that glistens.

- Extra-virgin olive oil
- Balsamic vinegar
- 8 ounces (8 cups) lettuce or other greens, torn into bite-size pieces if necessary
- Large pinch flake sea salt

In bottom of large salad bowl, add generous splash of oil and smaller splash of vinegar and mix together with back of large spoon (mixture does not need to emulsify). Add lettuce (toughest greens first so they touch the dressing; delicate greens on top), salt, and pepper. Just before serving, toss greens thoroughly to coat with dressing.

Kale Caesar Salad

VEGAN Serves 4 to 6 Total Time 45 minutes, plus 20 minutes chilling

Why This Recipe Works Kale has closed in on romaine as the Caesar salad green of choice; the hearty leaves, with their pungent earthiness, pair surprisingly well with the tangy dressing—perhaps even better than romaine. But the success of a Caesar salad made with any green rests on its dressing. And given that Caesar dressing traditionally contains anchovies, we knew we'd need a workaround for a vegetarian version—and, while we were at it, a vegan version too. This new dressing uses creamy vegan mayo as its base. To mimic the flavors that anchovies and Parmesan provide, we incorporate briny capers and umami-boosting nutritional yeast. The result? A luxurious dressing that tastes like an exact replica of classic versions. Soaking the kale in a warm water bath for just 10 minutes causes the cell walls of the leaves to break down, tenderizing the hardy greens. Our next step: chilling the dressed salad to cool it down and allow the flavors to meld. We strongly prefer our favorite vegan mayonnaise, Just Mayo, but you can also make your own Vegan Mayonnaise (page 506).

Salad

- 5 ounces baguette, cut into ¾-inch cubes (4 cups)
- 2 tablespoons extra-virgin olive oil
- ¼ teaspoon pepper
- ⅛ teaspoon table salt
- 1 pound curly kale, stemmed and cut into 1-inch pieces

Dressing

- 6 tablespoons vegan mayonnaise
- 1½ tablespoons nutritional yeast
- 1½ tablespoons lemon juice
- 1½ tablespoons capers, rinsed
- 2 teaspoons white wine vinegar
- 2 teaspoons vegan Worcestershire sauce
- 1 garlic clove, minced
- ¾ teaspoon Dijon mustard
- ½ teaspoon table salt
- ½ teaspoon pepper
- 3 tablespoons extra-virgin olive oil

1. For the salad Adjust oven rack to middle position and heat oven to 350 degrees. Toss baguette with oil, pepper, and salt in bowl. Spread on rimmed baking sheet and bake until golden and crisp, about 15 minutes; set aside and let cool completely, about 15 minutes. (Croutons can be stored at room temperature for up to 24 hours.)

2. Place kale in large bowl, cover with warm tap water, and swish to remove grit. Let kale sit for 10 minutes, then remove from water and dry thoroughly.

3. For the dressing Process mayonnaise, nutritional yeast, lemon juice, capers, vinegar, Worcestershire, garlic, mustard, salt, and pepper in blender until smooth, about 30 seconds. With blender running, slowly add oil until emulsified. Toss kale with dressing in large bowl and refrigerate for at least 20 minutes or up to 6 hours. Toss salad with croutons and serve.

Crispy and Creamy Kale Salad

VEGAN   Serves 2 to 4   Total Time 1¼ hours

Why This Recipe Works We love kale for its versatility. It's just as good as a hearty base for a salad as it is when crisped up into crunchy, salty kale chips. So here we combine these two different treatments for a leafy salad with crispy elements: We put kale on kale. Since raw kale can be a bit chewy, we let it soak and soften in its warm rinsing water. Then we bake a portion into crispy kale chips and use the other portion as our leafy salad base. For a crunchy topping, we take inspiration from furikake, a crunchy Japanese seasoning of chopped dried seaweed, sesame seeds, bonito flakes, salt, and sugar. We also use almonds in two ways: We blend some into a bright herb-and-lemon dressing to provide creamy richness, and we use more sliced almonds for crunch in the salad. The result is a simple, hearty, texturally diverse salad. We prefer lacinato kale (aka dinosaur or Tuscan kale) to curly leaf kale in this recipe, but either will work Using half white sesame seeds and half black sesame seeds adds beautiful contrast to the salad, but you can use whichever you have on hand.

Crispy Kale Topping

- 3½ ounces kale, stemmed and cut into 2-inch pieces
- 2 tablespoons vegetable oil
- 4 teaspoons sesame seeds, toasted
- ½ teaspoon kosher salt
- ¼ teaspoon sugar
- ¼ teaspoon cayenne pepper

Salad

- 5 ounces kale, stemmed and cut into 2-inch pieces
- ¾ cup sliced almonds, toasted, divided
- 1½ cups fresh parsley leaves
- 6 tablespoons water
- ¼ cup vegetable oil
- ¼ cup grated Parmesan cheese (optional)
- 3 tablespoons lemon juice
- 2 teaspoons fresh thyme leaves
- ½ teaspoon kosher salt
- ¼ teaspoon sugar

1. For the topping Adjust oven rack to middle position and heat oven to 275 degrees. Line rimmed baking sheet with parchment paper. Place kale in large bowl, cover with warm tap water, and swish to remove grit. Let kale sit for 10 minutes, then remove from water and dry thoroughly. Toss kale and oil in medium bowl until kale is well coated, about 30 seconds. Spread kale evenly on prepared sheet. Wipe bowl clean with paper towels. Bake kale until dry, crispy, and translucent, 30 to 40 minutes, turning leaves halfway through baking. Carefully remove kale and return it to bowl, leaving excess oil on sheet.

2. Combine sesame seeds, salt, sugar, and cayenne in small bowl. Gently toss crispy kale and sesame seed mixture until evenly coated and kale is broken into ½- to 1-inch pieces.

3. For the salad Place kale in large bowl, cover with warm tap water, and swish to remove grit. Let kale sit for 10 minutes, then remove from water and dry thoroughly. Combine kale and ½ cup almonds in large bowl.

4. Process parsley, water, oil, Parmesan, if using, lemon juice, thyme, salt, sugar, and remaining ¼ cup almonds in blender on high speed until smooth and creamy, about 2 minutes, scraping down sides of blender jar halfway through processing. Transfer ¾ cup dressing to bowl with kale mixture; toss until kale is well coated. Season with salt and pepper to taste. Divide salad among shallow bowls or plates, sprinkle with crispy kale topping, and drizzle with remaining dressing. Serve.

Horiatiki Salata (Hearty Greek Salad)

Serves 4 as a main dish or 6 to 8 as a side dish Total Time 25 minutes, plus 30 minutes salting

Why This Recipe Works Imagine bites of sweet tomatoes, briny olives, savory onion, crunchy cucumber, and tangy feta, without any lettuce filler—that's horiatiki salata, the real Greek salad. As with any ingredient-driven dish, sourcing high-quality components and bringing out their best is a must. Ripe, sweet tomatoes are loaded with juice that can flood the salad, so we toss halved wedges (which allow for chunky but manageable bites) with salt and set them in a colander to drain for 30 minutes. Soaking the onion slices in ice water lessens their hot bite by washing away thiosulfinates while maintaining their fresh, crisp texture. Dried oregano, not fresh, is the best choice for this salad as its more delicate flavor complements—but doesn't upstage—the vegetables. A creamy Greek feta, which must be made with at least 70 percent fatty sheep's milk, brings richness to the lean vegetables; we prefer to use feta by Real Greek Feta or Dodoni in this recipe. Use only large, round tomatoes here, not Roma or cherry varieties, and use the ripest in-season tomatoes you can find.

- 1¾ pounds tomatoes, cored, cut into ½-inch-thick wedges, and halved crosswise
- 1¼ teaspoons table salt, divided
- ½ red onion, sliced thin
- 2 tablespoons red wine vinegar
- 1 teaspoon dried oregano, plus extra for seasoning
- ½ teaspoon pepper
- 1 English cucumber, quartered lengthwise and cut into ¾-inch chunks
- 1 green bell pepper, stemmed, seeded, and cut into 2 by ½-inch strips
- 1 cup pitted kalamata olives
- 2 tablespoons capers, rinsed
- 5 tablespoons extra-virgin olive oil, divided
- 1 (8-ounce) block feta cheese, sliced into ½-inch-thick triangles

1. Toss tomatoes and ½ teaspoon salt together in colander set in large bowl. Let drain for 30 minutes. Place onion in small bowl, cover with ice water, and let sit for 15 minutes. Whisk vinegar, oregano, pepper, and remaining ¾ teaspoon salt together in second small bowl.

2. Discard tomato juice and transfer tomatoes to now-empty bowl. Drain onion and add to bowl with tomatoes. Add vinegar mixture, cucumber, bell pepper, olives, and capers and toss to combine. Drizzle with ¼ cup oil and toss gently to coat. Season with salt and pepper to taste. Transfer to serving platter and top with feta. Season each slice of feta with extra oregano to taste. Drizzle feta with remaining 1 tablespoon oil. Serve.

Kale on Kale

In our Crispy and Creamy Kale Salad, we use kale in two ways: raw for the leafy salad base and roasted in the form of kale chips as a crisp topping. We love the contrast in textures this creates because it makes the salad more interesting.

All Hail Kale

Kale has been a vegetarian darling for quite a while and has become so mainstream that it's a common salad base option at the ubiquitous make-your-own salad chains. We have fully embraced this versatile, nutritious hearty green, using it in endless ways.

The King of Salads

We love lacinato kale (also known as dinosaur or Tuscan kale) in salads, as it is a bit less bitter than curly varieties, but both work well, are earthy and sturdy, and can stand up to a variety of hearty ingredients. If you want the kale to really shine, keep your salad simple; don't pile it full of multiple other vegetables.

A Warm Soak

A 10-minute rinsing soak in warm tap water does the trick to tenderize kale. The kale needs to be chopped first to expose the cell walls. When kale is soaked, it becomes softer as some of its bitter-tasting compounds are rinsed away. This results in more appealing kale flavor.

Crispy and Creamy Kale Salad

Cobb Salad

Cobb Salad

FAST Serves 4 Total Time 30 minutes

Why This Recipe Works Most people see Cobb salad as a restaurant treat, given all the work it takes to make it. But this meatless take on the classic will delight you as much as the original. Plus, it's a healthier salad while being just as rich as the original. It is also faster to make, so you can whip it up on a busy weeknight. Soft-poached eggs give the salad a luxurious feel as the creamy yolks mingle with the greens. And the dressing? When this creamy yogurt-dill dressing is draped over the greens and chickpeas, you won't miss the bacon or blue cheese. To finish, simply top each serving with the homemade croutons, eggs, and avocado.

- ¼ cup extra-virgin olive oil, divided
- 3 slices hearty white sandwich bread, cut into ½-inch cubes
- ½ teaspoon table salt, divided
- ½ teaspoon pepper, divided
- ⅔ cup plain whole-milk yogurt
- ¼ cup chopped fresh dill
- 3 tablespoons whole-grain mustard
- 7 ounces (7 cups) mixed greens
- 1 (15-ounce) can chickpeas, rinsed
- 1 avocado, pitted and sliced
- 8 Soft-Cooked Eggs (page 450), peeled

1. Heat 2 tablespoons oil in 12-inch nonstick skillet over medium heat until shimmering. Add bread, ¼ teaspoon salt, and ¼ teaspoon pepper and cook, stirring frequently, until golden brown and crisp, about 10 minutes.

2. Whisk yogurt, dill, mustard, remaining ¼ teaspoon salt, remaining ¼ teaspoon pepper, and remaining 2 tablespoons oil together in large bowl. Add greens and chickpeas and toss to combine. Divide salad among plates. Divide avocado, croutons, and eggs among salads. Serve.

Hearty Green Salad with Chickpeas, Pickled Cauliflower, and Seared Halloumi

FAST Serves 2 Total Time 35 minutes

Why This Recipe Works This salad is vibrant, low-effort, and packed with vegetables; it makes salad a main course and is perfect in the summer when it is just too hot to cook. With a few tricks, this salad becomes dynamic and deeply flavorful. First, we make quick-pickled cauliflower florets and save the vinegar-honey brine to add flavor to a creamy dressing. For the greens we use a mix of green leaf lettuce and radicchio. For heartiness we pan-sear slabs of halloumi until deliciously browned. A creamy dressing made with yogurt, tahini, and the reserved brine takes this salad to new heights. In addition to the pickled cauliflower, we top the greens with the slabs of halloumi, canned chickpeas (tossed first in a bit of the dressing), and juicy grapes for a sweet and unexpected touch. Whole-milk, 2 percent, and 0 percent Greek yogurt will all work here. If Aleppo pepper is unavailable, substitute ⅜ teaspoon of paprika and ⅛ teaspoon of cayenne pepper. This recipe can easily be doubled.

- ¼ cup cider vinegar
- 2 teaspoons honey
- 1 teaspoon table salt, divided
- 2 cups (1-inch) cauliflower florets
- ½ teaspoon plus 2 tablespoons extra-virgin olive oil, divided
- 4 ounces halloumi cheese, cut into 4 slices
- ½ small head green leaf lettuce (4 ounces), torn into bite-size pieces
- ½ small head radicchio (3 ounces), cored and sliced thin
- ⅔ cup canned chickpeas, rinsed
- 3 tablespoons plain Greek yogurt
- 2 tablespoons tahini
- 1 small garlic clove, minced
- ½ teaspoon ground dried Aleppo pepper
- 6 ounces seedless red grapes, halved (1 cup)

1. Whisk vinegar, honey, and ¾ teaspoon salt together in medium bowl. Add cauliflower and stir to coat. Microwave until simmering, 1½ to 2 minutes. Stir, then cover and let sit, stirring occasionally, until cauliflower is crisp-tender, about 5 minutes. Using slotted spoon, transfer cauliflower to small plate, leaving liquid in bowl.

2. Heat ½ teaspoon oil in 8-inch nonstick skillet over medium-high heat until shimmering. Add halloumi and cook until brown on both sides, 60 to 90 seconds per side. Remove from heat and cover to keep warm.

3. Transfer 2 tablespoons pickling liquid to large bowl. Add remaining 2 tablespoons oil and whisk to combine. Add lettuce and radicchio, season with salt and pepper to taste, and toss to combine. Distribute greens evenly between 2 shallow serving bowls. Place chickpeas in now-empty bowl.

4. Add yogurt, tahini, garlic, Aleppo pepper, and remaining ¼ teaspoon salt to remaining pickling liquid and whisk until combined. Add ¼ cup yogurt mixture to chickpeas and toss to combine. Arrange cauliflower, halloumi, and grapes in piles atop greens. Drizzle remaining yogurt mixture over cauliflower, grapes, and halloumi in each bowl. Divide chickpea mixture evenly between bowls and serve.

Bitter Greens, Carrot, and Chickpea Salad with Warm Lemon Dressing

FAST Serves 4 Total Time 40 minutes

Why This Recipe Works Gently wilted greens certainly have their place in the salad repertoire, so we urge you to give them a try. They are more tender and even more flavorful due to contact with heat. But this can be tricky; if you are not careful you'll end up with completely cooked greens. First, get out your Dutch oven, add some oil, and heat until it is just shimmering. Then sauté shredded carrots, raisins, and almonds until the carrots just start to wilt, and pull the pot off the heat so everything cools a bit. Because a Dutch oven holds on to heat even off the stove, we harness that residual heat to wilt bitter, hearty greens perfectly. Warming the dressing and the greens happens in two stages: First, a portion of the vinaigrette goes into the pot, followed by half the greens, and then we repeat with the remaining vinaigrette and greens (along with some fresh mint). At this point the greens are wilted and enveloped with the now warm lemon-infused dressing. Finally, we arrange the greens on a platter and top them with chickpeas (tossed earlier with some dressing) and briny feta. In the midst of the greens are pops of the warm shredded carrots along with the raisins and almonds, which add sweetness and crunch to this beautiful salad. The volume measurement of the greens may vary depending on the variety or combination used.

Vinaigrette

- 2 tablespoons extra-virgin olive oil
- 1 tablespoon grated lemon zest plus 6 tablespoons juice (2 lemons)
- 1 tablespoon Dijon mustard
- 1 tablespoon minced shallot
- ½ teaspoon ground cumin
- ½ teaspoon ground coriander
- ¼ teaspoon smoked paprika
- ¼ teaspoon cayenne pepper
- ¼ teaspoon table salt
- ¼ teaspoon pepper

Salad

- 1 (15-ounce) can chickpeas, rinsed
- Pinch table salt
- 1 tablespoon extra-virgin olive oil
- 3 carrots, peeled and shredded
- ¾ cup raisins, chopped
- ½ cup slivered almonds
- 12 ounces (10–12 cups) bitter greens, such as escarole, chicory, and/or frisée, torn into bite-size pieces
- ⅓ cup mint leaves, chopped
- 1½ ounces feta cheese, crumbled (⅓ cup)

1. **For the vinaigrette** Whisk all ingredients in bowl until emulsified.

2. **For the salad** Toss chickpeas with 1 tablespoon vinaigrette and salt in bowl; set aside. Heat oil in Dutch oven over medium heat until shimmering. Add carrots, raisins, and almonds and cook, stirring frequently, until carrots are wilted, 4 to 5 minutes. Set aside off heat to cool for 5 minutes.

3. Add half of remaining vinaigrette to pot, then add half of greens and toss for 1 minute to warm and wilt. Add remaining greens and mint, followed by remaining vinaigrette, and continue to toss until greens are evenly coated and warmed through, about 2 minutes longer. Season with salt and pepper to taste. Transfer greens to serving platter, top with chickpeas and feta, and serve.

Marinated Bean and Asparagus Salad with Preserved Lemon Dressing

Serves 4 to 6 Total Time 20 minutes, plus 30 minutes marinating

Why This Recipe Works The key to a knockout salad that's quick to prepare is using a short list of ingredients that have big flavors and varied textures. For this recipe, we chose a combination of creamy butter beans and chickpeas, crunchy asparagus and cucumber, fragrant olives, and bright herbs, all tossed in a vinaigrette anchored by bright, floral preserved lemon. It comes together in minutes and is equally at home at a picnic or barbecue or on the dinner table. Letting the salad sit for 30 minutes gives the flavors time to meld. We love the combination of large, creamy butter beans and small firm chickpeas, but you can use whichever beans you prefer. We like a combination of cilantro, parsley, and dill, but you can use any combination of herbs. You can use store-bought preserved lemons or you can make them yourself. If using salt-preserved lemons, be sure to rinse them before using them in this recipe. If using preserved lemons in brine, there's no need to rinse them; just drain them before chopping.

Dressing

- ½ cup extra-virgin olive oil
- ½ cup finely chopped preserved lemon, seeds removed
- 2 tablespoons lemon juice
- 1 tablespoon honey, plus extra for seasoning
- 1 garlic clove, minced
- ½ teaspoon Dijon mustard
- ¼ teaspoon table salt

Salad

- 1 (15-ounce) can butter beans, rinsed
- 1 (15-ounce) can chickpeas, rinsed
- 1 cup pitted Castelvetrano olives, chopped coarse
- 4 ounces thin asparagus, trimmed and sliced crosswise ¼ inch thick
- ½ English cucumber, cut into ¼-inch pieces
- ½ cup coarsely chopped fresh parsley, cilantro, and/or dill
- 1 small shallot, minced

top | *Bitter Greens, Carrot, and Chickpea Salad with Warm Lemon Dressing*

bottom | *Marinated Bean and Asparagus Salad with Preserved Lemon Dressing*

1. For the dressing Whisk oil, preserved lemon, lemon juice, honey, garlic, mustard, and salt together in large bowl. Season with salt and honey to taste. (Dressing can be refrigerated for up to 3 days.)

2. For the salad Add butter beans, chickpeas, olives, asparagus, cucumber, herbs, and shallot to dressing in bowl and toss to combine. Let sit at room temperature for at least 30 minutes or refrigerate for up to 24 hours. (If refrigerating, bring salad to room temperature and season with extra salt and lemon juice to taste before serving.) Serve.

White Bean and Arugula Salad with Frico Crumble

Serves 6 to 8 Total Time 30 minutes, plus 40 minutes steeping and sitting

Why This Recipe Works Adding canned beans to a salad is a terrific way to add protein, texture, and flavor. But without some embellishments they can taste, well, canned. This salad, which is great for a crowd, is all about the beans (and the frico topping). To add flavor to the beans we steep them in a broth with peeled and smashed garlic cloves and a sprig of fresh sage. While the beans are steeping we pickle some shallots, then combine the drained beans and shallots, adding the spicy arugula, minced sage, and a little olive oil. Now this salad is coming into focus, full of texture and sharp flavors. The frico, which we make first and set aside for the topping, takes this salad from good to great. These crispy shards of fried cheese add a ton of flavor and look so appealing scattered across the top of the salad.

Frico Crumble

2 ounces Manchego cheese, grated fine (1 cup)
2 ounces Parmesan cheese, grated fine (1 cup)

Salad

5 tablespoons extra-virgin olive oil, divided
4 garlic cloves, peeled and smashed
1 sprig fresh sage, plus 2 tablespoons minced, divided
1 tablespoon salt for steeping beans
3 (15-ounce) cans cannellini beans, rinsed and drained
¼ cup red wine vinegar
2 shallots, sliced thin (¾ cup)
3 ounces (3 cups) baby arugula

1. For the frico Combine Manchego and Parmesan in bowl. Sprinkle half of cheese mixture evenly over bottom of cold 10-inch nonstick skillet. Cook over medium heat until edges are lacy and light golden, 2 to 3 minutes. Using 2 spatulas, carefully flip frico. Return to medium heat and cook until second side is deep golden brown, about 1 minute. Carefully slide frico onto plate. Wipe skillet clean with paper towels and repeat with remaining cheese. Let frico cool completely, then crumble into bite-size pieces. (Frico can be stored at room temperature for up to 5 days.)

2. For the salad Heat 1 tablespoon oil, garlic, and sage sprig in medium saucepan and cook over medium-high heat until garlic is just beginning to brown, 2 to 3 minutes. Add 2 cups water and 1 tablespoon salt and bring to simmer. Off heat, add beans, cover, and let sit for 20 minutes. Combine vinegar and shallots in large bowl and let sit for 20 minutes.

3. Drain beans and discard garlic and sage sprig. Add beans to shallot mixture and toss until thoroughly combined. Season with salt and pepper to taste. Let sit for at least 20 minutes or up to 6 hours.

4. Add arugula, minced sage, and remaining ¼ cup oil to beans and toss to combine. Transfer to serving platter and top with frico. Serve.

Beet Salad with Spiced Yogurt and Watercress

Serves 6 Total Time 55 minutes

Why This Recipe Works If you aren't making beet salad, you should be. Beets are tailor-made to be the star of any salad given their velvety texture, earthy sweetness, and vibrant color. For a salad plated with panache, we use a yogurt-lime dressing as an ultracreamy landing pad for beets and watercress. Beets are very dense, so roasting whole ones can take up to 2 hours. Here we cut down the wait by peeling and cutting the beets into small chunks and microwaving them. Beets work well with greens and nuts, but instead of tossing the components together, we use yogurt as an anchor for the other ingredients by thinning it with lime juice and water, spreading it on a platter, and topping it with the lightly dressed beets and greens as well as toasted pistachios. The moisture content of Greek yogurt varies, so add the water slowly in step 1. We like to make this salad with watercress, but baby arugula can be substituted. For the best presentation, use red beets here, not golden or Chioggia beets.

- 1¼ cups plain Greek yogurt
- ¼ cup minced fresh cilantro, divided
- 3 tablespoons extra-virgin olive oil, divided
- 2 teaspoons grated fresh ginger
- 1 teaspoon grated lime zest plus 2 tablespoons juice, divided, plus extra juice for seasoning (2 limes)
- 1 garlic clove, minced
- ½ teaspoon ground cumin
- ½ teaspoon ground coriander
- ¼ teaspoon pepper
- ½ teaspoon plus 2 pinches table salt, divided
- 5 ounces (5 cups) watercress, torn into bite-size pieces
- ¼ cup shelled pistachios, toasted and chopped, divided
- 1 recipe Quick-Cooking Beets (page 103), cooled

1. In medium bowl, whisk together yogurt, 3 tablespoons cilantro, 2 tablespoons oil, ginger, lime zest and 1 tablespoon juice, garlic, cumin, coriander, pepper, and ½ teaspoon salt. Slowly stir in up to 3 tablespoons water until mixture has consistency of regular yogurt. Season with salt, pepper, and extra lime juice to taste. Spread yogurt mixture over serving platter.

2. In large bowl, combine watercress, 2 tablespoons pistachios, 2 teaspoons oil, 1 teaspoon lime juice, and pinch salt and toss to coat. Arrange watercress mixture on top of yogurt mixture, leaving 1-inch border of yogurt mixture. Add beets to now-empty bowl and toss with remaining 1 teaspoon oil, remaining 2 teaspoons lime juice, and remaining pinch salt. Place beet mixture on top of watercress mixture. Sprinkle salad with remaining 2 tablespoons pistachios and remaining 1 tablespoon cilantro and serve.

White Bean and Arugula Salad with Frico Crumble

Beet Salad with Spiced Yogurt and Watercress

Variation

Beet Salad with Blue Cheese and Endive

The moisture content of blue cheese varies, so add the water slowly in step 1. Some blue cheese can be quite salty, so taste the cheese mixture carefully before seasoning. You can substitute 5 ounces of baby arugula for the endive, if desired. For the best presentation, use red beets here, not golden or Chioggia beets.

- 4 ounces blue cheese, crumbled (1 cup)
- ¾ cup sour cream
- 3 tablespoons minced fresh chives, divided
- 5 teaspoons lemon juice, divided, plus extra for seasoning
- ¼ teaspoon pepper
- 2 heads Belgian endive (8 ounces), bases trimmed, sliced crosswise into ½-inch-wide pieces
- ¼ cup hazelnuts, toasted, skinned, and chopped, divided
- 1 tablespoon extra-virgin olive oil, divided
- 2 pinches table salt, divided
- 1 recipe Quick-Cooking Beets, cooled (recipe follows)

1. In medium bowl, use silicone spatula to mash together blue cheese, sour cream, 2 tablespoons chives, 2 teaspoons lemon juice, and pepper. Slowly stir in up to 5 tablespoons water until mixture has consistency of regular yogurt. Season with salt, pepper, and extra lemon juice to taste. Spread blue cheese mixture over serving platter.

2. In large bowl, combine endive, 2 tablespoons hazelnuts, 2 teaspoons oil, 1 teaspoon lemon juice, and pinch salt and toss to coat. Arrange endive mixture on top of blue cheese mixture, leaving 1-inch border of blue cheese mixture. Add beets to now-empty bowl and toss with remaining 2 teaspoons lemon juice, remaining 1 teaspoon oil, and remaining pinch salt. Place beet mixture on top of endive mixture. Sprinkle salad with remaining 2 tablespoons hazelnuts and remaining 1 tablespoon chives and serve.

Quick-Cooking Beets

FAST **VEGAN** Serves 6 Total Time 40 minutes

Peeling the beets before cooking cuts the wait for them to cool. Be sure to wear gloves when peeling and cutting the beets to prevent your hands from becoming stained.

- 2 pounds beets, trimmed, peeled, and cut into ¾-inch pieces
- ½ teaspoon table salt

In largest bowl your microwave will accommodate, stir together beets, ⅓ cup water, and salt. Cover with plate and microwave until beets can be easily pierced with paring knife, 25 to 30 minutes, stirring halfway through microwaving. Drain beets. Serve warm, or let cool to use in salads. (Beets can be refrigerated for up to 3 days.)

Broccoli Salad with Avocado Dressing

FAST **VEGAN** Serves 4 to 6 Total Time 25 minutes

Why This Recipe Works Colorful, creamy, and charmingly retro, broccoli salad is great for summertime gatherings, though you can make it year round. The vegetable's grassy flavor and crunch pair seamlessly with chewy, sweet-tangy dried fruit and toasty nuts, adding up to a dynamic dish. We make a lush but light dressing by replacing the usual mayonnaise with avocado and olive oil, buzzing them in a food processor with garlic and lemon so that the flavor is clean, bright, and savory. We also add shallot and tarragon to the salad to balance out the sweet tang and rich toasty flavors of the dried fruit and nuts, respectively. Blanching and shocking the broccoli softens its raw edge, seasons it, and brightens up its color. To ensure that the florets and stems cook evenly, we layer them strategically in the saucepan: denser stems on the bottom, where they are submerged in water, and florets on top, where they steam gently. Be sure to use a fully ripe avocado here.

- 1¼ teaspoons table salt, divided
- 1½ pounds broccoli, florets cut into 1-inch pieces, stalks peeled, halved lengthwise, and sliced ¼ inch thick
- 1 ripe avocado, halved, pitted, and cut into ½-inch pieces
- 2 tablespoons extra-virgin olive oil
- 1 teaspoon grated lemon zest plus 3 tablespoons juice
- 1 garlic clove, minced
- ¼ teaspoon pepper
- ½ cup dried cranberries
- ½ cup sliced almonds, toasted
- 1 shallot, sliced thin
- 1 tablespoon minced fresh tarragon

1. Bring 1 cup water and ½ teaspoon salt to boil in large saucepan over high heat. Add broccoli stalks, then place florets on top of stalks so they sit just above water. Cover and cook until broccoli is bright green and crisp-tender, about 3 minutes. Meanwhile, fill large bowl halfway with ice and water. Drain broccoli well, transfer to ice bath, and let sit until just cool, about 2 minutes. Transfer broccoli to triple layer of paper towels and dry well. Empty and dry bowl and set aside.

2. Process avocado, oil, lemon zest and juice, garlic, pepper, and remaining ¾ teaspoon salt in food processor until smooth, about 30 seconds, scraping down sides of bowl as needed. Season with salt and pepper to taste.

3. Toss broccoli, dressing, cranberries, almonds, shallot, and tarragon in now-empty large bowl until evenly coated. Season with salt and pepper to taste. Serve.

Roasted Butternut Squash Salad with Creamy Tahini Dressing

VEGAN Serves 6 Total Time 1½ hours

Why This Recipe Works This hearty dinner salad is inspired by Israeli-born, London-based chef Yotam Ottolenghi's recipe for roasted butternut squash and red onion with lemon-tahini sauce. To make this recipe our own, we adapted his side dish into a substantial meal, serving the roasted butternut squash and onion (seasoned simply with olive oil, cumin, salt, and pepper) on a bed of baby arugula, which adds color contrast, freshness, and a peppery foil to the sweet roasted vegetables. Whisking mayonnaise into a combination of tahini, lemon juice, and water creates a flavorful dressing with over-the-top creaminess. We top the vegetables with rich, crunchy toasted pecans to add heft and textural intrigue. Briny kalamata olives bring welcome pops of saltiness, further balancing the sweetness of the squash and onion. Finally, we layer on a fistful of vibrant fresh mint. The result is a unique, gorgeous salad that makes a satisfying vegetarian dinner or a beautiful addition to a grand holiday spread. We developed this recipe using Ziyad Tahini Sesame Paste. Using other tahini products may result in a thicker or thinner salad dressing. The dressing should be the consistency of buttermilk (or slightly thicker than heavy cream). If the dressing seems thick, thin it out with water, 1 teaspoon at a time, until it's smooth and pourable. If the dressing seems thin, add extra tahini, 1 teaspoon at a time, to thicken it. You can substitute parsley, dill, or cilantro for the mint, if desired. To make this recipe vegan, substitute plant-based mayo for the mayonnaise.

Roasted Squash

- 1 (2- to 2¼-pound) butternut squash, peeled, seeded, and cut into 1-inch pieces (7 cups)
- 1 red onion, halved and sliced through root end ½ inch thick
- 2 tablespoons extra-virgin olive oil
- 2 teaspoons ground cumin
- 1¼ teaspoons table salt
- ½ teaspoon pepper

Dressing and Salad

- ¼ cup tahini
- ¼ cup water
- 2 tablespoons mayonnaise
- 2 tablespoons lemon juice
- 1 garlic clove, minced
- ½ teaspoon table salt
- ¼ teaspoon pepper
- 5 ounces (5 cups) baby arugula
- ¾ cup pecans, toasted and chopped
- ⅓ cup pitted kalamata olives, chopped
- ¼ cup chopped fresh mint

1. **For the roasted squash** Adjust oven rack to middle position and heat oven to 425 degrees. Toss all ingredients together in bowl. Spread vegetables in single layer on rimmed baking sheet. Roast until squash and onion are browned and tender, 35 to 45 minutes, stirring halfway through roasting. Remove sheet from oven and let cool for 15 minutes. (Cooled roasted vegetables can be refrigerated for up to 24 hours. Let sit at room temperature for 1 hour before assembling salad and serving.)

2. For the dressing and salad Meanwhile, whisk tahini, water, mayonnaise, lemon juice, garlic, salt, and pepper in now-empty bowl until creamy and thoroughly combined, about 30 seconds. (Dressing can be refrigerated for up to 3 days but may thicken over time. If dressing becomes too thick, adjust consistency with water as needed.)

3. Reserve ¼ cup dressing. Add arugula to remaining dressing in bowl and toss to combine. Season with salt and pepper to taste. Spread arugula on large serving platter. Top with squash and onion, pecans, olives, and mint. Drizzle salad with reserved dressing. Serve.

Roasted Cauliflower Salad with Arugula and Pear

Serves 6 Total Time 1 hour

Why This Recipe Works From floret to core, cauliflower is the ideal base for a festive salad. First we roast this hearty brassica in a 425-degree oven. We cover the florets for the first 10 minutes to steam-cook the interiors, then uncover them for another 20 minutes (flipping partway through) to render the exteriors deliciously browned. The core is put to use too; we shave it and pickle the shavings along with a thinly sliced shallot to create a tangy topping. For a simple but remarkably piquant dressing, we blend together Greek yogurt, more arugula, olive oil, and the pickling solution. When it is time to serve, we toss the cauliflower with the dressing in a large bowl, then spread it across a serving platter before combining the arugula and pickled vegetables with chunks of juicy Bartlett pear. If you don't have an immersion blender, use a blender to make the vinaigrette in step 5.

- 1 head cauliflower (2½ pounds)
- ¼ cup extra-virgin olive oil, divided
- 2¼ teaspoons kosher salt, divided
- ½ cup cider vinegar
- 3 tablespoons water, divided
- 1 tablespoon sugar
- ¼ teaspoon coriander seeds
- 2 whole cloves
- 1 shallot, sliced thin
- 1¼ ounces (1¼ cups) arugula, divided
- 2 tablespoons plain Greek yogurt
- 1 ripe Bartlett pear, peeled, halved, cored, and cut into ¼-inch pieces

top | Broccoli Salad with Avocado Dressing
bottom | Roasted Cauliflower Salad with Arugula and Pear

1. Adjust oven rack to middle position and heat oven to 425 degrees. Spray rimmed baking sheet with vegetable oil spray. Trim outer leaves of cauliflower and cut stem flush with bottom of head (discard stem). Turn head cut side down and cut cauliflower into 1-inch-thick slices. Cut around core to remove florets. Cut large florets into 2-inch pieces; reserve core. (You should have about 6 cups florets.)

2. Arrange florets in single layer on prepared baking sheet. Drizzle with 1 tablespoon oil and sprinkle with 1 teaspoon salt. Cover sheet tightly with aluminum foil and roast for 10 minutes. Remove foil and continue to roast cauliflower until sides touching sheet are well browned, about 10 minutes.

3. Using thin metal spatula, flip cauliflower. Return to oven and roast until sides touching sheet are well browned, about 10 minutes longer. (Cauliflower can be refrigerated for up to 2 days; let come to room temperature before using.)

4. Meanwhile, use vegetable peeler to shave cauliflower core lengthwise to create ¼ cup shavings. Discard remaining core. In 2-cup liquid measuring cup, combine vinegar, 2 tablespoons water, sugar, coriander seeds, cloves, and 1 teaspoon salt. Microwave until boiling, about 2 minutes. Add shallot and cauliflower shavings, making sure they're submerged, and let stand for 10 minutes. Transfer pickles to medium bowl. (Pickles can be refrigerated for up to 24 hours.) Reserve 1 tablespoon pickling liquid in measuring cup; discard remaining liquid and spices.

5. Add ¾ cup arugula, yogurt, remaining 3 tablespoons oil, remaining ¼ teaspoon salt, and remaining 1 tablespoon water to measuring cup. Using immersion blender, blend until well combined, 30 to 60 seconds. (Vinaigrette can be refrigerated for up to 24 hours.)

6. Combine roasted cauliflower and vinaigrette in large bowl and toss until cauliflower is evenly coated. Arrange on serving platter in even layer. Add remaining ½ cup arugula to pickles. Scatter pear over arugula and season pear with salt and pepper to taste. Toss to combine. Mound on top of cauliflower and serve.

Charred Shaved Brussels Sprout Salad with Sweet Chili-Lime Dressing

FAST **VEGAN** Serves 4 to 6 Total Time 30 minutes

Why This Recipe Works This intriguing brussels sprout salad features deeply browned sprouts and a pungent dressing. We cook the sprouts in two batches so each can be properly caramelized, making sure to let them cook without turning. This ensures they are browned on the bottom but remain bright green and crisp-tender on the top. Keeping the pan uncovered keeps the sprouts from steaming. The whisk-together sauce made with sweet chili sauce and savory vegetarian fish sauce is a welcome finish to balance the bitter, nutty, subtly sweet brussels sprouts. We prefer to use the slicing disk of a food processor, but you can also slice the brussels sprouts by hand: Cut the sprouts in half lengthwise, arrange the halves cut sides down on a cutting board, then slice crosswise as thin as possible. You can substitute 1½ pounds of preshredded brussels sprouts for the 2 pounds of whole sprouts called for here.

Dressing

- ¼ cup sweet chili sauce
- 1 tablespoon lime juice
- 1 tablespoon vegetarian fish sauce
- 3 garlic cloves, minced

Brussels Sprouts

- 2 pounds brussels sprouts, trimmed and sliced thin
- ¾ teaspoon table salt
- ½ teaspoon pepper
- 6 tablespoons vegetable oil, divided
- ⅓ cup dry-roasted peanuts, chopped
- ¼ cup chopped fresh cilantro

1. **For the dressing** Whisk all ingredients together in small bowl; set aside.

2. **For the brussels sprouts** In large bowl, toss brussels sprouts with salt and pepper.

3. Heat 3 tablespoons oil in 12-inch nonstick skillet over medium-high heat until shimmering. Add half of sprouts in even layer and cook without moving until sprouts are well browned on bottom and bright green on top, 6 to 8 minutes. Transfer sprouts to serving platter, spread into even layer, and drizzle with half of dressing. Repeat with remaining 3 tablespoons oil and remaining sprouts, layering second batch of cooked sprouts on top of first batch, then drizzle with remaining dressing. Sprinkle with peanuts and cilantro. Serve.

Variations

FAST VEGAN Charred Shaved Brussels Sprout Salad with Apricot Dressing

Substitute 3 tablespoons warmed apricot preserves, 1 tablespoon extra-virgin olive oil, 2 teaspoons white wine vinegar, 1 teaspoon lemon juice, and ¾ teaspoon table salt for dressing ingredients in step 1. Increase salt to 1 teaspoon in step 2. Substitute ⅓ cup chopped toasted hazelnuts for peanuts and 2 tablespoons chopped fresh tarragon for cilantro in step 3.

FAST Charred Shaved Brussels Sprout Salad with Sherry-Honey Dressing

Substitute ¼ cup honey, 3 tablespoons sherry vinegar, 1 tablespoon extra-virgin olive oil, 2 teaspoons chopped fresh thyme, 1 minced garlic clove, ¾ teaspoon table salt, and ½ teaspoon smoked paprika for dressing ingredients in step 1. Increase salt to 1 teaspoon in step 2. Omit cilantro and substitute ⅓ cup toasted slivered almonds for peanuts in step 3.

Chopped Carrot Salad with Mint, Pistachios, and Pomegranate Seeds

FAST VEGAN Serves 4 to 6 Total Time 20 minutes

Why This Recipe Works Forget about your grater and your peeler and try this carrot recipe. The result—something like a vivid orange tabbouleh, with carrots in place of cracked wheat—is a surprising and refreshing take on a familiar vegetable. We finely chop the carrots in the food processor instead of grating them by hand. We leave the carrots unpeeled (but scrubbed) because the skins contribute a subtle but pleasant bitterness. For contrasting flavor we incorporate fresh mint, pomegranate seeds, toasted pistachios, and bold spices. If you can, buy carrots with their green tops attached as they boast deeper carrot flavor and are fresher than bagged carrots.

- ¾ cup shelled pistachios, toasted
- ¼ cup extra-virgin olive oil
- 3 tablespoons lemon juice
- 1 tablespoon honey
- 1 teaspoon table salt
- ½ teaspoon pepper
- ½ teaspoon smoked paprika
- ⅛ teaspoon cayenne pepper
- 1 pound carrots, trimmed and cut into 1-inch pieces
- 1 cup pomegranate seeds
- ½ cup minced fresh mint

Pulse pistachios in food processor until coarsely chopped, 10 to 12 pulses; transfer to small bowl. Whisk oil, lemon juice, honey, salt, pepper, paprika, and cayenne in large bowl until combined. Process carrots in now-empty processor until finely chopped, 10 to 20 seconds, scraping down sides of bowl as needed. Transfer carrots to bowl with dressing; add ½ cup pomegranate seeds, mint, and half of pistachios and toss to combine. Season with salt to taste. Transfer to serving platter, sprinkle with remaining pomegranate seeds and pistachios, and serve.

Chopped Carrot Salad with Mint, Pistachios, and Pomegranate Seeds

Lao Hu Cai (Tiger Salad)

Lao Hu Cai (Tiger Salad)

FAST VEGAN Serves 4 as an appetizer or a side dish
Total Time 20 minutes

Why This Recipe Works Celery is in the spotlight in this recipe, underscoring this vegetable's exciting versatility. This vibrant, Northern Chinese salad earns its name, Tiger Salad, for its bold flavors and textures, and is said to stimulate the appetite at the beginning of a meal or to reset the palate between courses. We balance the bracing vinaigrette, piquant scallions, and hot chiles with the herbal freshness of cilantro and the juicy crunch of celery. The earthy sweetness of the nuts and seeds and the rich sesame oil further temper the dish. For a spicier salad, include the chile seeds. For less spice, substitute half of a small green bell pepper (cut into 2-inch-long matchsticks) for the serrano.

- 1 tablespoon unseasoned rice vinegar
- 1 teaspoon sugar
- ½ teaspoon table salt
- ½ teaspoon soy sauce
- ¾ teaspoon toasted sesame oil
- 1 Thai chile, stemmed, halved, seeded, and sliced thin
- 3½ cups fresh cilantro leaves and tender stems, chopped into 2-inch lengths
- 4 celery ribs, sliced on bias ¼ inch thick
- 3 scallions, white and green parts sliced thin on bias
- 1 serrano chile, stemmed, quartered, seeded, and sliced thin
- 2 teaspoons sesame seeds, toasted
- 2 tablespoons chopped salted dry-roasted peanuts

1. In small bowl, stir vinegar, sugar, salt, and soy sauce until sugar and salt are completely dissolved. Add oil and Thai chile and stir to combine.

2. In large bowl, combine cilantro, celery, scallions, and serrano. Sprinkle with sesame seeds and dressing and toss to combine.

3. Transfer salad to serving platter, sprinkle with peanuts, and serve immediately.

Shaved Celery Salad with Pomegranate-Honey Vinaigrette

FAST Serves 4 to 6 Total Time 20 minutes

Why This Recipe Works This delightful shaved celery salad melds thinly sliced celery stalks with the aromatic and anise-tinged flavor of raw celery root. We love how the combination of sweet-tart pomegranate seeds and rich Parmesan cheese boosts the flavors and textures of the celery. Shaving the celery root thin with a vegetable peeler eliminates any need to cook the root. Chopped frisée gives the salad more substance, and toasted walnuts add crunch. For the dressing, we echo the flavor of the pomegranate seeds by whisking pomegranate molasses with red wine vinegar, honey, shallot, and olive oil. Use the large holes of a box grater to shred the Parmesan. A mandoline can also be used to shave the celery root in step 2.

- 2 tablespoons pomegranate molasses
- 1 tablespoon red wine vinegar
- 1 small shallot, minced
- 2 teaspoons honey
- ¼ teaspoon table salt
- Pinch pepper
- 2 tablespoons extra-virgin olive oil
- 14 ounces celery root, trimmed, peeled, and quartered
- 4 celery ribs, sliced thin on bias, plus ½ cup celery leaves
- 1 head frisée (6 ounces), trimmed and cut into 1-inch pieces
- 1½ ounces Parmesan cheese, shredded (½ cup)
- ¼ cup pomegranate seeds, divided
- ½ cup walnuts, toasted and chopped coarse

1. Whisk pomegranate molasses, vinegar, shallot, honey, salt, and pepper together in large bowl. While whisking constantly, slowly drizzle in oil until combined.

2. Using sharp vegetable peeler, shave celery root into thin ribbons. Add celery root, celery ribs and leaves, frisée, Parmesan, and 2 tablespoons pomegranate seeds to bowl with dressing and toss gently to coat. Season with salt and pepper to taste. Sprinkle with walnuts and remaining 2 tablespoons pomegranate seeds. Serve.

Apple–Celery Root Salad

FAST **VEGAN** Serves 8 Total Time 10 minutes

Why This Recipe Works Celery and apples have long been paired together, and no wonder, since sweet apples make a great counterpoint to the herbaceous flavor of celery. And while we will admit to loving the old-fashioned Waldorf salad, this recipe pairs them in a new way, tilting toward the savory side. And we love that this creamy, crunchy, fragrant salad comes together in just 10 minutes. Cutting the celery root and apples into matchsticks makes the pieces easy to spear with a fork. Spiking the mayonnaise with cider vinegar, whole-grain mustard, and capers produces a rich yet bright and tangy slaw-like salad. To make this recipe vegan, substitute plant-based mayo for the mayonnaise.

- ¼ cup cider vinegar
- ¼ cup mayonnaise
- 1 tablespoon whole-grain mustard
- 2 Granny Smith apples, cored and cut into 2-inch-long matchsticks
- 1 small celery root, peeled and cut into 2-inch-long matchsticks
- 2 ounces (2 cups) baby arugula, roughly chopped
- 2 tablespoons capers, chopped

Whisk vinegar, mayonnaise, and mustard together in large bowl. Add apples, celery root, arugula, and capers and toss to combine. Season with salt and pepper to taste. Serve.

Esquites (Mexican Corn Salad)

FAST Serves 6 to 8 Total Time 40 minutes

Why This Recipe Works Inspired by Mexican street corn, this salad incarnation hits all the creamy, cheesy, salty, smoky, and charred notes of the grilled specialty without using a grill, plus it's easier to eat. Our salad features charred kernels; the nutty, slightly bitter flavor from the char complements the natural sweetness of the corn. To achieve that charring on the stovetop, we cook the kernels in a small amount of oil in a covered skillet. The kernels in contact with the skillet's surface brown and char, and the lid prevents the kernels from popping out of the hot skillet and also traps steam, which helps cook the corn. We cook the corn in two batches to allow more kernels to make contact with the skillet and brown. After cooking the corn, we use the hot skillet to bloom chili powder and lightly cook minced garlic to temper its bite. We dress the salad with a creamy, tangy mixture of sour cream, mayonnaise, and lime juice. Letting the corn cool before adding chopped cilantro and spicy serrano chiles preserves their bright colors and fresh flavors. If desired, substitute plain Greek yogurt for the sour cream. We like serrano chiles here, but you can substitute a jalapeño chile that has been halved lengthwise and sliced into ⅛-inch-thick half-moons. Adjust the amount of chiles to suit your taste, and remove the seeds for a less spicy salad. If cotija cheese is unavailable, substitute feta cheese.

- 3 tablespoons lime juice, plus extra for seasoning (2 limes)
- 3 tablespoons sour cream
- 1 tablespoon mayonnaise
- 1–2 serrano chiles, stemmed and cut into ⅛-inch-thick rings
- ¾ teaspoon table salt, divided
- 2 tablespoons plus 1 teaspoon vegetable oil
- 6 ears corn, kernels cut from cobs (6 cups)
- 2 garlic cloves, minced
- ½ teaspoon chili powder
- 4 ounces cotija cheese, crumbled (1 cup)
- ¾ cup coarsely chopped fresh cilantro
- 3 scallions, sliced thin

1. Combine lime juice, sour cream, mayonnaise, serrano(s), and ¼ teaspoon salt in large bowl. Set aside.

2. Heat 1 tablespoon oil in 12-inch nonstick skillet over high heat until shimmering. Add half of corn and spread into even layer. Sprinkle with ¼ teaspoon salt. Cover and cook, without stirring, until corn touching skillet is charred, about 3 minutes. Let stand off heat, covered, for 15 seconds, until any popping subsides. Transfer corn to bowl with sour cream mixture. Repeat with 1 tablespoon oil, remaining ¼ teaspoon salt, and remaining corn.

3. Return now-empty skillet to medium heat and add remaining 1 teaspoon oil, garlic, and chili powder. Cook, stirring constantly, until fragrant, about 30 seconds. Transfer garlic mixture to bowl with corn mixture and toss to combine. Let cool for at least 15 minutes.

4. Add cotija, cilantro, and scallions and toss to combine. Season salad with salt and up to 1 tablespoon extra lime juice to taste. Serve.

Buffalo Cucumber Salad

FAST Serves 4 Total Time 35 minutes

Why This Recipe Works This salad is our interpretation of the fan-favorite dish from Parm restaurant in New York City's Little Italy (and beyond). We use one of our favorite methods of preparing cucumbers: smashing them with a rolling pin before tearing them into bite-size chunks. The craggy edges are perfect for holding on to lots of the buffalo vinaigrette. Salting the cucumbers in a colander pulls out excess moisture so the salad doesn't get watered down. Instead of the usual butter-based buffalo sauce, we use extra-virgin olive oil to keep the vinaigrette from congealing when hitting the cold cucumbers. And extra blue cheese, scattered across the top, adds a creamy, funky contrast to the spicy-cool salad. English cucumbers are the best choice for this recipe. Frank's RedHot Original Cayenne Pepper Hot Sauce is a key element of classic buffalo sauce; the dish might be tasty if made with another sauce, but it won't be "buffalo."

- 2 English cucumbers
- 1 teaspoon table salt
- ¼ cup Frank's RedHot Original Cayenne Pepper Hot Sauce
- 2 tablespoons extra-virgin olive oil
- 1 tablespoon honey
- 1 small shallot, minced
- 2 garlic cloves, minced
- 2 celery ribs, sliced on bias ¼ inch thick
- 3 ounces blue cheese, crumbled (¾ cup), divided

1. Trim and discard ends from cucumbers. Cut each cucumber crosswise into 3-inch lengths. Place pieces in large zipper-lock bag and seal bag. Using small skillet or rolling pin, gently crush cucumbers until flattened and split lengthwise into 3 or 4 spears each.

2. Tear spears into rough 1- to 1½-inch pieces and transfer to colander set in sink. Toss cucumbers with salt and let sit for 15 to 30 minutes.

3. Whisk hot sauce, oil, honey, shallot, and garlic together in large bowl. Add cucumbers, celery, and ½ cup blue cheese and toss to combine. Transfer to serving platter and sprinkle with remaining ¼ cup blue cheese. Serve.

Buffalo Cucumber Salad

top | *Avocado and Cucumber Salad with Sriracha Mayo*
bottom | *Shaved Vegetable Salad with Creamy Miso Dressing*

Avocado and Cucumber Salad with Sriracha Mayo

FAST Serves 4 to 6 Total Time 40 minutes

Why This Recipe Works When culinary inspiration strikes, it often leads to the creation of one-of-a-kind dishes. Take this recipe, for instance. If you love avocado-cucumber sushi rolls, then this salad is for you. Just one bite will hit your taste buds with even more umami than the classic roll. And in salad form, it serves more people, it's scoopable, and it's easier to eat. The ingredients tell the story: chopped cucumber, avocado chunks, soy sauce, pickled ginger, and even crunchy seaweed snacks, a nod to the nori wrapped around sushi rolls. Salting the cucumbers first both helps season them and removes excess moisture. A savory sesame-soy vinaigrette with pickled ginger is tossed with the salad ingredients. A finishing drizzle of spicy sriracha mayo and a sprinkle of crumbled seaweed snacks ties everything together. You can substitute another brand of mayonnaise for the Kewpie. Roasted seaweed snacks are sold in packages that typically range in weight from 0.14 ounces to 0.35 ounces; you will need about 0.28 ounces of plain roasted seaweed snacks for the ½ cup crumbled here. We like to serve this salad with extra seaweed snacks for rolling around scoopfuls of salad.

- 1 English cucumber, cut into ½-inch pieces (3 cups)
- ½ teaspoon table salt for salting cucumber
- 2 tablespoons Kewpie mayonnaise
- 2 teaspoons sriracha
- ½ teaspoon plus 2 tablespoons unseasoned rice vinegar, divided
- 3 scallions, sliced thin on bias
- 1 tablespoon pickled ginger, minced
- 1 tablespoon vegetable oil
- 1 tablespoon soy sauce
- 2 teaspoons sesame seeds, toasted
- ½ teaspoon toasted sesame oil
- 2 ripe avocados, quartered, pitted, and cut into ½-inch pieces
- ½ cup crumbled roasted seaweed snacks, plus extra sheets for serving

1. Toss cucumber and salt together in colander set in large bowl and let sit for 15 to 30 minutes. Whisk mayonnaise, sriracha, and ½ teaspoon vinegar together in small bowl; set aside.

2. Discard cucumber liquid and transfer cucumber to now-empty bowl. Add scallions, pickled ginger, vegetable oil, soy sauce, sesame seeds, sesame oil, and remaining 2 tablespoons vinegar and toss to combine. Gently fold in avocados.

3. Transfer salad to serving platter. Drizzle with sriracha mayo and sprinkle with crumbled seaweed snacks. Serve with extra seaweed snacks.

Safely Removing an Avocado Pit

1. Using sharp knife, cut into avocado from top to bottom (pole to pole), all around pit. As you cut, gently turn avocado, rather than knife, to avoid injury.

2. Slice avocado again from side to side, all around equator. There are now four pieces of avocado. Gently lift pit out of flesh. Use your hand or spoon to separate flesh from peel.

Shaved Vegetable Salad with Creamy Miso Dressing

Serves 6 Total Time 35 minutes, plus 2 hours chilling

Why This Recipe Works Step aside, lettuce. This salad, with its robust, refreshing crunch, is a great counterpoint to the usual green salad. First assemble and slice a kaleidoscope of roots, stalks, and bulbs razor-thin. Beets and carrots provide dense, meaty crunch, while fennel, radishes, and celery add juicy crispness. And here is the key strategy: After slicing the vegetables, we transfer them to a salad spinner, cover them with ice and cold water, and chill them. During that stint in the refrigerator (2 to 16 hours, depending on your schedule), the vegetables absorb some of the cold water, which makes them especially crunchy and refreshing, plus the cold water causes their pectin to firm up. After drying them thoroughly in the salad spinner, we dress the vegetables with a thick, intense dressing. Miso contributes umami and viscosity, the latter of which is bumped up further by tahini and honey; cider vinegar contributes complementary brightness; and pureed garlic, scallion whites, black pepper, and cayenne provide a lasting bold finish. You'll need a salad spinner for this recipe. If small beets are unavailable, use one 6-ounce beet, cut into quarters. The vegetables should be sliced to the thickness of a dime, which is easy using a mandoline; alternatively, you can slice the vegetables with a knife. After trimming and slicing, you should have about 1½ pounds of vegetables. If preferred, you can use an immersion blender to make the dressing, but it won't be quite as smooth.

- 1 (12-ounce) fennel bulb, stalks discarded, bulb halved, cored, and sliced thin
- 3 (2-ounce) red beets, trimmed, peeled, and sliced thin
- 2 celery ribs, sliced thin
- 2 carrots, peeled and sliced thin
- 3 (1½- to 2-inch) radishes, trimmed and sliced thin
- 2 cups ice
- 3 scallions, white parts chopped coarse, green parts cut into 2-inch lengths
- ⅓ cup white miso
- ⅓ cup cider vinegar
- ¼ cup vegetable oil
- 2 tablespoons tahini
- 1 tablespoon honey
- 1 garlic clove, crushed
- ½ teaspoon table salt
- ½ teaspoon pepper
- Pinch cayenne pepper

1. Place fennel, beets, celery, carrots, and radishes in salad spinner basket and place basket in salad spinner bowl. Spread ice over surface of vegetables. Add cold water until vegetables are submerged. Slice scallion greens lengthwise into very thin matchsticks. Sprinkle scallion greens over ice and press lightly to submerge. Cover and refrigerate for at least 2 hours or up to 16 hours.

2. Meanwhile, process miso, vinegar, oil, scallion whites, tahini, honey, garlic, salt, pepper, and cayenne in blender until completely smooth, 1 to 2 minutes (mixture will be thick). Transfer to small bowl, cover, and refrigerate until needed.

3. Using tongs, pluck scallion greens from top of ice water (they will have curled up), and transfer to paper towel–lined plate to drain. If any ice remains on surface of water, skim off and discard. Drain vegetables and spin thoroughly. Lift basket from salad spinner and shake to rearrange vegetables; discard collected water. Repeat spinning and draining until less than 1 teaspoon water collects in bottom of salad spinner, 2 to 3 more times.

4. Transfer three-quarters of vegetables to serving platter. Drizzle three-quarters of dressing over vegetables. Arrange remaining vegetables over dressing, sprinkle scallion greens over salad and serve, passing remaining dressing separately.

Green Bean Salad with Creamy Lemon Sauce and Crispy Capers

FAST VEGAN Serves 4 to 6 Total Time 45 minutes

Why This Recipe Works Green beans are so versatile: You can boil, blanch, stir-fry, and roast them. For tender and deeply seasoned green beans, we blanch them in salted water, then shock them in ice water to stop the cooking process and preserve their vibrant color and texture. For a hit of bold flavor, we toss them in the oil left behind after microwaving capers. To keep the focus on the green beans, we simply drizzle them with an easy-to-make bright and creamy lemon sauce. Topped with the crispy capers and fresh dill, these beans are an impressive make-ahead salad. To make this recipe vegan, substitute plant-based mayo for the mayonnaise.

Fried Capers

- ⅓ cup extra-virgin olive oil
- ¼ cup capers, rinsed and patted dry

Sauce

- ½ cup mayonnaise
- 2 tablespoons lemon juice
- ¾ teaspoon minced fresh thyme
- ⅛ teaspoon pepper

Green Beans

- 1½ pounds green beans, trimmed
- ¼ teaspoon table salt, plus salt for blanching green beans
- ¼ teaspoon pepper
- ¼ cup chopped fresh dill

1. **For the fried capers** Combine oil and capers in 2-cup liquid measuring cup (capers should be mostly submerged). Microwave until capers are darkened in color and have shrunk, about 5 minutes, stirring halfway through microwaving. Using slotted spoon, transfer capers to paper towel–lined plate (they will continue to crisp as they cool); set aside. Transfer 2 tablespoons caper oil to large bowl; set aside. (Reserve remaining caper oil for another use. Fried capers can be stored at room temperature for up to 2 days.)

2. **For the sauce** Combine all ingredients in small bowl. (Sauce can be refrigerated for up to 2 days.)

3. **For the green beans** Bring 3 quarts water to boil in Dutch oven over high heat. Meanwhile, fill large bowl halfway with ice and water. Add green beans and ¼ cup salt to boiling water. Once water returns to boil, cook green beans until crisp-tender, about 3 minutes.

4. Drain green beans, then immediately transfer to ice bath. Let sit until chilled, about 2 minutes. Drain in colander and dry thoroughly with clean dish towels. (Blanched green beans can be refrigerated for up to 2 days.)

5. Just before serving, transfer green beans to large bowl with caper oil. Add salt and pepper and toss until well combined. Arrange green beans in even layer on large platter. Drizzle with sauce and sprinkle with dill and fried capers. Serve.

Three-Bean Salad

FAST Serves 4 to 6 Total Time 30 minutes

Why This Recipe Works Store-bought three-bean salad may be convenient, but it can also be mushy and sugary. Here's our simple take on this summertime classic. We start with fresh Romano beans (also called Italian flat beans or Italian pole beans), which are flatter and broader than regular green beans and have a crisp texture and sweet flavor. We blanch the Romano beans and yellow wax beans to crisp-tender perfection. Canned kidney beans round out our trio, avoiding the need to soak and simmer dried beans for hours. Letting the garlic and onion sit in the vinaigrette while preparing the beans tames the garlic and quick-pickles the onion. A touch of honey in the bright dressing adds the appropriate hint of sweetness reminiscent of classic formulas, and we fold in a generous amount of parsley just before serving for a lively finish. Be sure to set up the ice bath before cooking the wax and Romano beans, as plunging them in the cold water immediately after blanching them retains their bright colors and ensures that they don't overcook.

- ¼ cup cider vinegar
- 3 tablespoons extra-virgin olive oil
- 1 tablespoon honey
- 1 garlic clove, minced
- ½ teaspoon table salt, plus salt for cooking beans
- ⅛ teaspoon pepper
- ½ small red onion, sliced thin
- 8 ounces yellow wax beans, trimmed and halved on bias
- 8 ounces Romano beans, trimmed and halved on bias
- 1 (15-ounce) can red kidney beans, rinsed
- ¼ cup minced fresh parsley

1. Whisk vinegar, oil, honey, garlic, salt, and pepper together in large bowl. Stir in onion and set aside.

2. Bring 4 quarts water to boil in large pot over high heat. Meanwhile, fill large bowl halfway with ice and water. Add wax beans, Romano beans, and 1 tablespoon salt to boiling water and cook until crisp-tender, 3 to 5 minutes. Drain beans, then transfer immediately to ice bath. Let beans cool completely, about 5 minutes, then drain again and pat dry with paper towels.

3. Add wax and Romano beans, kidney beans, and parsley to vinaigrette and toss to coat. Season with salt and pepper to taste. Serve.

Napa Cabbage Slaw with Carrots and Sesame

FAST **VEGAN** Serves 4 to 6 Total Time 45 minutes

Why This Recipe Works While traditional green cabbage has long been the favorite for making coleslaw, napa cabbage is a great alternative. Its crinkly, thin leaves have a more tender texture and a sweeter flavor, but its more delicate structure means that it will leach twice as much liquid as regular cabbage. To avoid a bland, watered-down salad, we make a potent dressing with a high ratio of vinegar to oil. We also cook down some of the vinegar to offset the diluting power of the cabbage's water. Then we toss the cabbage with the dressing and let it sit for about 5 minutes so the slaw reaches the perfect level of bright acidity. Adding

top | *Green Bean Salad with Creamy Lemon Sauce and Crispy Capers*

bottom | *Three-Bean Salad*

carrots for even more crunch, some colorful herbs, and a handful of seeds gives the slaw an additional layer of flavor and texture. This slaw is best served within an hour of dressing it. Use the large holes of a box grater to prepare the carrots.

- ⅓ cup white wine vinegar
- 2 teaspoons toasted sesame oil
- 2 teaspoons vegetable oil
- 1 tablespoon rice vinegar
- 1 tablespoon soy sauce
- 1 tablespoon sugar
- 1 teaspoon grated fresh ginger
- ¼ teaspoon table salt
- 1 small head napa cabbage, sliced thin (9 cups)
- 2 carrots, peeled and grated
- 4 scallions, sliced thin on bias
- ¼ cup sesame seeds, toasted

1. Bring white wine vinegar to simmer in small saucepan over medium heat; cook until reduced to 2 tablespoons, 4 to 6 minutes. Transfer to large bowl and let cool completely, about 10 minutes. Whisk in sesame oil, vegetable oil, rice vinegar, soy sauce, sugar, ginger, and salt.

2. When ready to serve, add cabbage and carrots to dressing and toss to coat. Let stand for 5 minutes. Add scallions and sesame seeds and toss to combine. Serve.

Variations

FAST VEGAN Napa Cabbage Slaw with Apple and Walnuts

Omit sesame oil and increase vegetable oil to 4 teaspoons. Omit soy sauce and ginger. Substitute cider vinegar for rice vinegar. Decrease sugar to 2 teaspoons and increase salt to ¾ teaspoon. Substitute 2 celery ribs, sliced thin on bias, and 1 grated Fuji apple for carrots. Substitute 3 tablespoons minced fresh chives for scallions and ½ cup walnuts, toasted and chopped fine, for sesame seeds.

FAST Napa Cabbage Slaw with Jícama and Pepitas

Omit sesame oil and increase vegetable oil to 4 teaspoons. Omit soy sauce. Substitute lime juice for rice vinegar, honey for sugar, and ½ teaspoon ground coriander for ginger. Increase salt to ¾ teaspoon. Substitute 1 seeded and minced jalapeño for ginger. Substitute 6 ounces jícama, peeled and grated, for carrots. Substitute ¼ cup coarsely chopped fresh cilantro for scallions and ½ cup roasted and salted pepitas, chopped fine, for sesame seeds.

Slicing Napa Cabbage

Napa cabbage leaves come away from core with just a slight tug. Trim base. Stack several leaves and cut thin crosswise. Repeat stacking and cutting for entire head.

Coleslaw Potato Salad

Serves 8 Total Time 1¼ hours, plus 1 hour chilling

Why This Recipe Works For a summer side dish mash-up, we combine two favorites: tangy coleslaw and fluffy, buttery Yukon Gold potatoes. Rather than dicing and then boiling the potatoes, we boil them whole in generously salted water to avoid a soggy, oversaturated slaw. Cooking the potatoes whole allows them to steam inside their skins and keeps the starches from absorbing too much cooking liquid. We mix the cooked potatoes with a buttermilk dressing and stir in shredded cabbage—which we first salt and drain to remove moisture—and carrots to complete the recipe. To save time, shred the cabbage in a food processor fitted with a slicing disk. If you don't have a food processor, slice cabbage wedges crosswise ⅛ inch thick. We recommend using Yukon Gold potatoes that are similar in size, about 6 ounces each, to ensure even cooking.

- 4 cups shredded green cabbage
- 1¾ teaspoons table salt, divided, plus salt for cooking potatoes
- 2 pounds Yukon Gold potatoes, unpeeled
- ¾ cup mayonnaise
- ¼ cup buttermilk
- 3 tablespoons red wine vinegar
- 1 tablespoon sugar
- 1 tablespoon hot sauce
- ½ teaspoon pepper
- ¼ teaspoon celery seeds
- 1 carrot, peeled and shredded (½ cup)
- 3 scallions, sliced thin on bias, divided

1. Toss cabbage and ¾ teaspoon salt together in colander set in large bowl. Let stand, stirring and pressing on cabbage occasionally with silicone spatula, until cabbage has wilted and released at least 2 tablespoons water, about 45 minutes. Discard liquid and transfer cabbage to now-empty bowl.

2. Meanwhile, place potatoes and 3 tablespoons salt in large saucepan, add water to cover by 1 inch, and bring to boil over high heat. Reduce heat to medium and simmer until paring knife inserted into potatoes meets no resistance, 35 to 45 minutes. Drain potatoes in colander and let sit until cool enough to handle but still warm, about 10 minutes.

3. While potatoes cool, whisk mayonnaise, buttermilk, vinegar, sugar, hot sauce, pepper, celery seeds, and remaining 1 teaspoon salt together in second large bowl.

4. Cut potatoes into ¾-inch pieces. Add potatoes, cabbage, carrot, and half of scallions to mayonnaise mixture and toss to coat. Cover and refrigerate until well chilled, at least 1 hour or up to 24 hours.

5. Toss salad to recombine. Season with salt and pepper to taste. Sprinkle with remaining scallions. Serve chilled or at room temperature.

Spicy Green Pea Salad

FAST Serves 6 to 8 Total Time 30 minutes

Why This Recipe Works For a fresh take on a cold summer side salad, we lean into in-season produce by pairing sugar snap peas, snow peas, and cucumbers with a quick tangy dressing. Blanching the peas ensures they are perfectly tender and vividly green. Cumin adds warm flavor to the dressing, which is a combination of cilantro, serrano chile, yogurt, lemon juice, and garlic. The crisp vegetables and punchy dressing make a salad that's equal parts spicy, brightly flavored, and aromatic—a refreshing addition to any cookout. If you're spice averse, remove some or all of the ribs and seeds from the serrano. We prefer whole-milk yogurt here; low-fat or nonfat produces a dressing that is too loose. You can use Greek yogurt if you prefer, but you may need to thin the dressing with a small amount of water after blending.

Napa Cabbage Slaw with Carrots and Sesame

8 ounces sugar snap peas, strings removed
8 ounces snow peas, strings removed
1 teaspoon table salt, plus salt for blanching vegetables
1 cup roughly chopped fresh cilantro leaves and tender stems, plus ¼ cup leaves
½ cup plain yogurt
2 garlic cloves, smashed and peeled
1 serrano chile, stemmed, halved lengthwise, and seeded
2 teaspoons lemon juice
½ teaspoon pepper
½ teaspoon ground cumin
¼ teaspoon ground cardamom (optional)
3 Persian cucumbers, halved lengthwise and sliced crosswise ½ inch thick

1. Bring 2 quarts water to boil in large saucepan. Fill large bowl halfway with ice and water. Add snap peas, snow peas, and 1 tablespoon salt and cook until peas are bright green and crisp-tender, 1 to 2 minutes. Using slotted spoon, transfer peas to ice bath and let sit until cooled. Drain well, then transfer peas to dish towel and pat dry. Cut peas crosswise into 1-inch pieces.

2. Combine 1 cup cilantro, yogurt, garlic, serrano, lemon juice, salt, pepper, cumin, and cardamom, if using, to blender jar and blend until smooth, about 1 minute, scraping down sides of jar as needed. Toss snap peas, snow peas, cucumbers, and dressing together in bowl. Season with salt ad pepper and transfer to serving bowl or platter. Sprinkle with remaining ¼ cup cilantro and serve.

Radicchio Chopped Salad with White Beans, Oranges, and Olives

Serves 4 to 6   Total Time 25 minutes, plus 30 minutes resting

Why This Recipe Works We love a good chopped salad with a mix of hearty ingredients carefully chosen to add flavor, color, and texture. Here, the combination of bitter radicchio and mild crunchy romaine is a winner. Marinated white beans become much more flavorful and lush with our quick marinade, which plays a double role as the dressing as well. It's bold—equal parts oil and acid, with shallot and Dijon to bring it all together. You can substitute 1 cup of drained canned mandarin oranges for the fresh oranges if you prefer. We like the creaminess of cannellini beans, but you can use butter beans for a meatier texture.

¼ cup lemon juice (2 lemons)
1 shallot, minced
1 teaspoon Dijon mustard
1 teaspoon table salt
½ teaspoon pepper
¼ cup extra-virgin olive oil
1 (15-ounce) can cannellini beans, rinsed
2 oranges
12 ounces romaine lettuce hearts, cut into ½-inch pieces (4 cups)
6 ounces radicchio, cut into ½-inch pieces (2 cups)
1 cup walnuts, toasted and chopped
4 ounces feta cheese, cut into ½-inch cubes (1 cup)
¼ cup pitted oil-cured black olives, chopped

1. Whisk lemon juice, shallot, mustard, salt, and pepper in large bowl until smooth. Whisking constantly, drizzle in oil until evenly combined. Stir in beans and let sit at room temperature until flavors meld, about 30 minutes.

2. Meanwhile, cut away peel and pith from oranges. Chop oranges into ½-inch pieces, trimming any remaining pith (you should have about 1 cup orange pieces).

3. Add romaine, radicchio, walnuts, feta, olives, and oranges to bowl with beans and toss to combine. Season with salt and pepper to taste. Serve.

Romaine and Radicchio Salad with Roasted Squash and Pickled Pears

VEGAN   Serves 6 to 8   Total Time 1¼ hours, plus 1½ hours pickling and chilling

Why This Recipe Works When you are looking for an unusual but stunning fall salad to serve when entertaining, this one with pickled Bosc pears, a creamy yet punchy dressing, and chunks of earthy roasted butternut squash will enchant your guests. And you can make all the components ahead and simply assemble the salad when ready—a win-win when you have a whole meal to get on the table. Your guests will be eager to dig in to this salad with its delightful range of textures and flavors. Green leaf lettuce offers a sturdy base to support the hearty add-ins, with a colorful partner in radicchio, whose slight bitterness is a foil for the sweet-tart pears. A final sprinkle of toasted pepitas adds crunchy richness and fall flair. To make this recipe vegan, substitute plant-based mayo for the mayonnaise.

Pickled Pears

- 2 Bosc pears, peeled, halved, cored, and sliced thin crosswise
- ¾ cup cider vinegar
- ¾ cup water
- 2 tablespoons sugar
- 1½ teaspoons table salt
- 1 star anise pod

Dressing

- 1½ tablespoons white wine vinegar
- 1 tablespoon very finely minced shallot
- ¾ teaspoon mayonnaise
- ¾ teaspoon Dijon mustard
- ¼ teaspoon table salt
- 5½ tablespoons extra-virgin olive oil

Salad

- 1½ pounds butternut squash, peeled, seeded, and cut into ½-inch pieces (5 cups)
- 2 tablespoons extra-virgin olive oil
- ½ teaspoon table salt
- ¼ teaspoon pepper
- 1 head green leaf lettuce (12 ounces), torn into bite-size pieces (2 cups)
- 5 ounces radicchio, torn into bite-size pieces (2 cups)
- ⅓ cup roasted unsalted pepitas, toasted, divided

1. For the pears Place pears in medium bowl. Bring vinegar, water, sugar, salt, and star anise to boil in medium saucepan. Pour vinegar mixture over pears and let sit until room temperature, about 30 minutes. Cover and refrigerate until chilled, at least 1 hour or up to 2 days.

2. For the dressing Combine vinegar, shallot, mayonnaise, mustard, and salt in medium bowl and season with pepper to taste. Whisk until mixture is milky in appearance and no lumps of mayonnaise remain. Whisking constantly, very slowly drizzle in oil until glossy and lightly thickened, with no pools of oil visible. (Dressing can be refrigerated for up to 2 days; whisk to recombine before serving.)

3. For the salad Adjust oven rack to lowest position and heat oven to 450 degrees. Toss squash with oil, salt, and pepper. Spread squash on rimmed baking sheet and roast until well browned and tender, 20 to 25 minutes, stirring halfway through roasting. Let cool slightly, about 5 minutes. (Squash can be refrigerated for up to 1 day; bring to room temperature before serving.)

4. Drain pickled pears (discard star anise). Gently toss lettuce, radicchio, squash, pears and half of pepitas together in large bowl. Drizzle with dressing and toss until greens are evenly coated. Season with salt to taste. Transfer to serving platter and sprinkle with remaining pepitas. Serve immediately.

Romaine and Radicchio Salad with Roasted Squash and Pickled Pears

Cast Iron–Seared Romaine with Oyster Sauce, Ginger, and Sesame

Cast Iron–Seared Romaine with Oyster Sauce, Ginger, and Sesame

FAST Serves 4 to 6 Total Time 45 minutes

Why This Recipe Works Romaine lettuce is a good choice for this seared and boldly flavored salad because it holds up just enough to high-heat cooking to keep the lettuce from wilting too far down like cooked spinach. We dry the lettuce thoroughly after washing, then sear it in a preheated cast-iron skillet. This allows it to get slight color and caramelization on the cut side without allowing it to wilt too much while it chars. Since the charred lettuce can stand up to a bold dressing, we create an umami-rich mixture of vegetarian oyster sauce, lemon juice, ginger, garlic, and toasted sesame oil. After searing the romaine, we drizzle it with half the dressing and sprinkle it with sliced scallion greens, sliced Thai chiles, and toasted sesame seeds. Look for tight, dense romaine hearts that are heavy for their size; larger heads can be peeled down to the correct weight. You can substitute other fresh chiles, such as jalapeños, for the Thai chiles, or simply omit them if you prefer a milder dish.

- 3 scallions, white parts minced, green parts sliced thin
- ¼ cup vegetarian oyster sauce
- 1 tablespoon grated fresh ginger
- 1 tablespoon lemon juice
- 1 tablespoon water
- 2 teaspoons toasted sesame oil
- 1 garlic clove, minced
- 3 (8-ounce) romaine lettuce hearts
- 3 tablespoons vegetable oil
- ½ teaspoon table salt
- ½ teaspoon pepper
- 1 tablespoon sesame seeds, toasted
- 1–2 Thai chiles, stemmed and sliced thin

1. Whisk scallion whites, oyster sauce, ginger, lemon juice, water, sesame oil, and garlic together in small bowl; set aside.

2. Line rimmed baking sheet with dish towel. Trim root ends from romaine hearts, leaving bases intact so that layers stay together. Cut romaine hearts in half lengthwise. Rinse thoroughly between layers to remove any dirt. Transfer romaine to prepared sheet, cut sides down, and pat dry with second dish towel.

3. Heat 12-inch cast-iron skillet over medium-high heat for about 10 minutes. Brush romaine evenly with vegetable oil and sprinkle with salt and pepper. Place half of romaine, cut sides down and alternating directions, in pan and cook until well browned, about 4 minutes. Flip romaine and cook until second sides are spotty brown and leaves are softened, about 1 minute. Transfer to serving platter, cut sides up. Repeat with remaining romaine.

4. Drizzle half of dressing over romaine. Sprinkle with sesame seeds, chile(s), and scallion greens. Serve, passing remaining dressing separately.

Torn Potato Salad with Toasted Garlic and Herb Dressing

VEGAN Serves 4 to 6 Total Time 50 minutes

Why This Recipe Works For a new twist on potato salad, rather than slicing and boiling—or boiling and slicing—our potatoes, we boil them whole in generously salted water (which gives them supercreamy interiors and skins that "pop") and then tear them into craggy, irregular pieces. Tearing the potatoes gives them lots of surface area to absorb a creamy toasted garlic dressing, and a handful of fresh herbs provides the salad with a burst of fresh flavor. Look for potatoes that are similar in size, about 2 inches in diameter. You can substitute Red Bliss potatoes for the baby Yukon Gold potatoes and red or white wine vinegar for the sherry vinegar. To make this recipe vegan, substitute plant-based mayo for the mayonnaise.

- 2 pounds baby Yukon Gold potatoes, unpeeled
- 1 teaspoon table salt, plus salt for cooking potatoes
- ¼ cup extra-virgin olive oil
- 6 garlic cloves, sliced thin
- 2 tablespoons mayonnaise
- 1 tablespoon sherry vinegar, plus extra for seasoning
- ½ teaspoon pepper
- ½ cup chopped fresh chives, parsley, cilantro, and/or dill

1. Bring 3 quarts water to boil in large saucepan over high heat. Add potatoes and 3 tablespoons salt; return to boil and cook until potatoes are very tender and easily crushed but not breaking down, 20 to 25 minutes. Drain potatoes in colander and let sit until cool enough to handle but still warm, about 10 minutes.

2. Wipe saucepan clean with damp paper towels. Heat oil and garlic in now-empty saucepan over medium heat, swirling oil constantly once garlic begins to sizzle. Cook until garlic is light golden brown, 3 to 5 minutes. Immediately pour oil and garlic into large bowl. Add mayonnaise, vinegar, salt, and pepper and whisk until smooth.

3. Using your fingertips, gently tear each potato into rough 1-inch pieces and add to bowl with dressing. Add herbs and toss until evenly combined. (Potato salad can be refrigerated for up to 3 days.) Season with salt, pepper, and extra vinegar to taste. Serve warm, at room temperature, or chilled.

Fingerling Potato Salad with Sun-Dried Tomato Dressing

VEGAN Serves 4 to 6 Total Time 50 minutes, plus 30 minutes sitting

Why This Recipe Works Fingerling potatoes (so named for their finger-like shape) are positioned in the middle of the road between waxy and starchy potatoes. Fingerlings don't have to be peeled, don't require a lot of prep work, and have a pleasantly earthy and mildly nutty flavor. The flavors of the South of France are at work in this salad since the potatoes are tossed with herbes de Provence before roasting, and we also use the herb blend in the dressing, which is bright and lively with lots of lemon juice and zest, plus olives and piquant sun-dried tomatoes. Dressing the potatoes while they are hot allows the flavors to soak in more efficiently. Try to find fingerling potatoes that are consistently 2 to 3 inches long and 1 inch in diameter.

- 2 pounds fingerling potatoes, unpeeled, halved lengthwise
- ¼ cup extra-virgin olive oil, divided
- 1½ teaspoons table salt
- 1 teaspoon pepper
- 1 teaspoon herbes de Provence
- ⅓ cup oil-packed sun-dried tomatoes, minced
- ¼ cup pitted kalamata olives, chopped fine
- ¼ cup chopped fresh parsley
- 3 tablespoons finely chopped shallot
- 2 teaspoons grated lemon zest plus 1 tablespoon juice
- 1 garlic clove, minced
- ½ teaspoon red pepper flakes

1. Adjust oven rack to middle position and heat oven to 450 degrees. Toss potatoes, 2 tablespoons oil, salt, pepper, and herbes de Provence in large bowl until potatoes are well coated. Arrange potatoes cut side down in single layer on rimmed baking sheet. Roast until potatoes are tender and cut sides are golden brown, about 20 minutes.

2. Meanwhile, wipe bowl clean with paper towels. Add tomatoes, olives, parsley, shallot, lemon zest and juice, garlic, pepper flakes, and remaining 2 tablespoons oil to now-empty bowl.

3. Transfer hot potatoes to tomato mixture and toss to combine. Let sit for 30 minutes, tossing occasionally. Transfer to platter and serve. (Salad can sit at room temperature for 2 hours before serving.)

Herbes de Provence

FAST **VEGAN** Makes 2½ tablespoons
Total Time 5 minutes

Why This Recipe Works This French-inspired mix of dried herbs—which commonly includes rosemary, marjoram, thyme, lavender, and fennel—lends a balanced, herby flavor to roasted potatoes and other roasted vegetables, soups and stews, and breads. Most supermarkets sell this herb blend, but if you prefer to make your own or can't find it premixed, here's our formula. If you can't find dried lavender, feel free to omit it altogether.

- 2 teaspoons dried marjoram
- 2 teaspoons dried thyme
- 1 teaspoon dried basil
- 1 teaspoon dried rosemary, crumbled
- 1 teaspoon dried sage
- ¼ teaspoon dried lavender (optional)
- ⅛ teaspoon ground fennel

Combine all ingredients in bowl. (Herbes de Provence can be stored at room temperature for up to 1 month.)

Cherry Tomato Salad with Pita Crisps and Spicy Citrus Dressing

FAST **VEGAN** Serves 4 Total Time 40 minutes

Why This Recipe Works We will go so far as to say that this cherry tomato salad is a Mexican riff on Italy's panzanella salad. Honestly,what could be tastier than pieces of bread that soak up the juices of fresh tomatoes dressed with a vibrant and herby vinaigrette? But this recipe takes a new path using toasted pita chips and lots of citrus zest and juice, plus a jolt of Tabasco and thin slices of jalapeño; it's at once spicy and sweet. A shower of dill provides welcome freshness. It is important to lightly crisp the pita pieces in the oven as this keeps them from turning soggy in the salad. This recipe makes more pita crisps than needed; you can toss leftovers into other salads or simply enjoy them as a snack. We prefer the strong heat of Tabasco here, but feel free to use your favorite hot sauce instead.

- 1 (7-inch) pita, cut into ½-inch pieces
- 3 tablespoons extra-virgin olive oil, divided
- ⅛ teaspoon plus ½ teaspoon table salt, divided
- ⅛ teaspoon plus ¼ teaspoon pepper, divided
- ½ teaspoon grated orange zest plus 1 tablespoon juice
- ½ teaspoon grated lime zest plus 1 tablespoon juice
- ½ teaspoon Tabasco sauce
- 1¼ pounds cherry tomatoes, halved
- ½ jalapeño chile, seeded and sliced thin crosswise, divided
- 1 tablespoon chopped fresh dill, divided

1. Adjust oven rack to middle position and heat oven to 400 degrees. Line rimmed baking sheet with parchment paper. Toss pita, 1 tablespoon oil, ⅛ teaspoon salt, and ⅛ teaspoon pepper together on prepared sheet. Spread pita into even layer and bake until golden brown and crisp, 4 to 6 minutes. Let cool on sheet, about 5 minutes.

2. While pita crisps cool, whisk orange zest and juice, lime zest and juice, Tabasco, remaining ½ teaspoon salt, and remaining ¼ teaspoon pepper together in large bowl. Whisking constantly, drizzle in remaining 2 tablespoons oil until combined.

3. To dressing, add tomatoes, half of jalapeño slices, 1½ teaspoons dill, and ½ cup pita crisps, tossing well to combine (reserve remaining pita crisps for another use). Transfer to serving platter and top with remaining jalapeño slices and remaining 1½ teaspoons dill. Season with pepper to taste and serve.

top *Fingerling Potato Salad with Sun-Dried Tomato Dressing*

bottom *Cherry Tomato Salad with Pita Crisps and Spicy Citrus Dressing*

Tomatillos Do Double Duty

Small, spherical, and a lovely shade of pale green, tomatillos, when removed from their husks, resemble miniature green tomatoes, although their versatility and unique tangy flavor puts them in another league. Called tomates verdes in Mexico, where they originated, they are central to many Mexican classics. They are usually served cooked, but in our Tomatillo and Bibb Lettuce Salad they are used raw as part of both the salad and the dressing.

Pale Green Gems

Like tomatoes, tomatillos offer a world of culinary possibilities. They can be roasted, grilled, sautéed, and even pickled. They may look intimidating or mysterious in their papery husks, but once you start using them, they will become a staple in your kitchen. Peel back their husks and the jewel-like round gem within will inspire you to make salsas, enchiladas, tamales, tacos, and more.

A Next-Level Salad

Our Tomatillo and Bibb Lettuce Salad puts raw tomatillos in the spotlight, where they do double duty. We scatter them in thinly sliced rounds on the greens, which we then drape with a spicy, jazzed-up take on creamy ranch dressing made in a blender using quartered tomatillos.

Tomatillo and Bibb Lettuce Salad with Tomatillo Ranch

Tomatillo and Bibb Lettuce Salad with Tomatillo Ranch

FAST **VEGAN** Serves 4 Total Time 30 minutes

Why This Recipe Works Tomatillos, a husked nightshade fruit, have a distinctly firm texture and tart, floral flavor. While tomatillos are usually cooked before serving, our tomatillo salad showcases the unique flavors of the raw fruit. To prepare the tomatillos, we remove the husks and rinse the skins to wash off any sticky residue. Slicing the fruits thin breaks up their skins, exposes more pulp, and reveals a visually stunning cross section. We macerate the slices in salt and sugar to soften the skins, draw out their juices, and season them. Then we toss the tomatillos with Bibb lettuce, which adds crunch without excessive moisture. To create a creamy ranch-style dressing, we blend the tomatillos with mayonnaise, jalapeño, cilantro, chives, dill, and spices (the tomatillos add natural acidity in lieu of buttermilk or vinegar). The final step is drizzling the zippy, spicy dressing atop the salad and garnishing it with pepitas for extra crunch. Use fresh tomatillos (purchased with their husks intact) here. To make this recipe vegan, substitute plant-based mayo for the mayonnaise.

Dressing

- 3 ounces tomatillos, husks and stems removed, rinsed well, dried, and quartered
- ⅔ cup coarsely chopped fresh cilantro leaves and stems
- ⅓ cup mayonnaise
- 1 jalapeño chile, stemmed and chopped
- 2 tablespoons minced fresh chives
- 1 tablespoon chopped fresh dill
- 1 teaspoon granulated garlic
- ½ teaspoon table salt
- ¼ teaspoon pepper

Salad

- 1 pound tomatillos, husks and stems removed, rinsed well, dried, and sliced thin
- 1 teaspoon sugar
- ½ teaspoon table salt
- 1 small (6- to 7-ounce) head Bibb or Boston lettuce, leaves separated
- 2 tablespoons roasted, salted pepitas

1. **For the dressing** Process all ingredients in blender until smooth, about 1½ minutes. (Dressing can be refrigerated for up to 4 days. If separated, stir to recombine before serving.)

2. **For the salad** Toss tomatillos, sugar, and salt together in large bowl and let sit until tomatillos are shiny and slightly juicy, about 10 minutes. Drain tomatillos in colander and return to now-empty bowl (do not rinse).

3. Add lettuce to tomatillos and toss until lettuce is lightly coated with tomatillo juices. Arrange salad in even layer on large serving platter. Drizzle with ½ cup dressing and sprinkle with pepitas. Serve, passing remaining dressing separately.

Wheat Berry Salad with Radicchio, Dried Cherries, and Pecans

Serves 4 to 6 Total Time 1¾ hours

Why This Recipe Works The earthy, nutty flavor and firm chew of whole grains make them an ideal choice for a hearty side dish. We find it easiest (and quickest) to cook the wheat berries like pasta, simply simmering them in a pot of water until they are tender but still chewy. Soaking overnight, while optional, helps shorten the cooking time and prevents the grains from blowing out. Combining the grains with radicchio and parsley and then tossing them with a bright vinaigrette yields a salad that is equally delicious as a side or light main. If using refrigerated grains, let them come to room temperature before making the salad. Any whole grain can be substituted for the wheat berries. Any variety of radicchio can be used.

- 3 tablespoons extra-virgin olive oil
- 2 tablespoons red wine vinegar
- 1 small shallot, minced
- ½ teaspoon table salt
- ½ teaspoon pepper
- 2¾ cups cooked wheat berries
- 1 cup chopped radicchio
- 1 cup loosely packed fresh parsley leaves
- ½ cup pecans, toasted and chopped coarse, divided
- ¼ cup dried cherries
- 1 ounce blue cheese, crumbled (¼ cup)

Whisk oil, vinegar, shallot, salt, and pepper together in large bowl. Add wheat berries, radicchio, parsley, half of pecans, and cherries to dressing and toss to combine. Season with salt and pepper to taste. Sprinkle with blue cheese and remaining pecans. Serve.

Chopped Vegetable and Stone Fruit Salad

FAST **VEGAN** Serves 4 to 6 Total Time 35 minutes

Why This Recipe Works Nearly every cuisine of the eastern Mediterranean serves a refreshing, crunchy, raw chopped vegetable salad with most meals. Whether called shepherd's salad (çoban salatası), as in Turkey; country salad (salata baladi), as in Egypt; Arab salad (salat aravi), as in Israel; or one of many other names, this essential salad consists of finely chopped cucumbers, tomatoes, and parsley, dressed with lemon juice and olive oil. Some renditions add peppers, radishes, red onions, and/or scallions, along with herbs or finishing spices. This version shifts the sweet-tart axis of the salad, substituting stone fruit for the tomatoes. The sweet, juicy, somewhat meaty fruit interplays with the mildly spicy radishes and pepper and cooling cucumber to enliven any dish they accompany. Generous amounts of parsley, mint, and puckery sumac vivify the contrasts. Salting and lightly sugaring the fruit first helps intensify its flavor while also extracting some of the juice that would otherwise create a watery salad.

- 1 pound ripe but firm plums, nectarines, peaches, apricots, or a mix, halved, pitted, and chopped
- ½ teaspoon plus ⅛ teaspoon table salt, divided
- ½ teaspoon sugar
- 2 tablespoons extra-virgin olive oil
- 2 tablespoons lemon juice
- ¼ teaspoon pepper
- 4 Persian cucumbers, quartered lengthwise and chopped
- 1 red bell pepper, stemmed, seeded, and chopped
- 4 radishes, trimmed and chopped
- ¼ cup minced fresh mint
- ¼ cup minced fresh parsley
- 1 shallot, minced
- 2 teaspoons ground sumac

1. Toss plums with ½ teaspoon salt and sugar in bowl. Transfer to fine-mesh strainer and let drain for 15 minutes, tossing occasionally. Drain.

2. Whisk oil, lemon juice, pepper, and remaining ⅛ teaspoon salt together in large bowl. Add plums, cucumbers, bell pepper, radishes, mint, parsley, shallot, and sumac and gently toss to combine. Season with salt and pepper to taste and serve immediately.

Bulgur Salad with Curry Roasted Sweet Potatoes and Chickpeas

Serves 4 Total Time 50 minutes

Why This Recipe Works Curry-spiced sweet potatoes and chickpeas steal the limelight in this hearty bulgur salad. Bulgur is made from wheat berries that have been parcooked, so depending on the grind or the recipe, they must be soaked or cooked. Here we simmer them for about 5 minutes. Then we combine the bulgur with kale and make it more substantial by topping it with nutty chickpeas and spiced sweet potatoes. Tossing the chopped kale with the warm bulgur softens the sturdy leaves. Look for small sweet potatoes that weigh about 8 ounces each. Don't confuse bulgur with cracked wheat, which has a much longer cooking time and will not work in this recipe.

- 1 pound small sweet potatoes, unpeeled, cut lengthwise into 1-inch wedges
- 1 (15-ounce) can chickpeas, rinsed
- ½ cup extra-virgin olive oil, divided, plus extra for drizzling
- 1 tablespoon curry powder
- 1½ teaspoons table salt, divided, plus salt for cooking bulgur
- 1¼ cups medium-grind bulgur
- 5 tablespoons cider vinegar
- 6 ounces kale, stemmed and chopped
- 4 ounces goat cheese, crumbled (1 cup)
- ½ cup walnuts, toasted and chopped
- ⅓ cup dried cranberries

1. Adjust oven rack to middle position and heat oven to 450 degrees. Line rimmed baking sheet with parchment paper. Toss potatoes, chickpeas, 1 tablespoon oil, curry powder, and ½ teaspoon salt together in large bowl. Arrange in single layer on prepared sheet. Roast until potatoes are lightly browned and tender, about 20 minutes.

2. Meanwhile, bring 2 quarts water to boil in large saucepan. Add bulgur and 1 teaspoon salt. Reduce heat to medium-low and simmer until tender, 5 to 8 minutes. Drain.

3. Whisk vinegar, remaining 7 tablespoons oil, and remaining 1 teaspoon salt together in now-empty bowl. Add bulgur and kale and toss to combine. Divide bulgur salad, potatoes, and chickpeas evenly among 4 serving bowls. Top with goat cheese, walnuts, and cranberries. Drizzle with extra oil and serve.

Chopped Vegetable and Stone Fruit Salad

Farro Salad with Asparagus, Radishes, and Parmesan

FAST Serves 6 to 8 Total Time 30 minutes

Why This Recipe Works This fresh and hearty salad looks as good as it tastes, with crisp asparagus, spicy radishes, bright herbs, peppery arugula, and nutty Parmesan cheese. Marinating thinly sliced asparagus in the dressing helps soften the asparagus just enough without cooking and ensures it retains its bright green color. Toasting the farro in oil first brings out its flavor and takes only a few minutes, then we use the pasta method to cook it. Once the farro is cooked, drained, and cooled, it's easy to assemble the salad: Whisk together a bright lemony-shallot dressing, add the vegetables, farro, and herbs, and gently fold in the arugula and half the Parmesan.

- ⅓ cup extra-virgin olive oil
- 3 tablespoons lemon juice
- 3 tablespoons minced shallot
- 1 teaspoon Dijon mustard
- ¾ teaspoon table salt, divided
- ½ teaspoon pepper
- 12 ounces asparagus, sliced thin on bias
- ¼ cup chopped fresh mint
- 3 tablespoons chopped fresh dill
- 1 recipe Basic Farro, cooled completely (recipe follows)
- 5 radishes, trimmed, halved, and sliced thin
- 3 ounces (3 cups) baby arugula
- 2 ounces Parmesan cheese, shaved with vegetable peeler, divided

Whisk oil, lemon juice, shallot, mustard, ½ teaspoon salt, and pepper together in large bowl. Add asparagus, mint, and dill. Let sit for 10 minutes. Add farro, radishes, and remaining ¼ teaspoon salt and toss until thoroughly combined. Fold in arugula and half of Parmesan. Season with salt and pepper to taste. Sprinkle with remaining Parmesan. Serve.

Basic Farro

FAST **VEGAN** Makes 4 cups
Total Time 40 minutes

We developed this recipe using Bob's Red Mill Organic Farro. You can also use whole-grain or semipearl farro here if you can find it, but note that the cooking time will be on the longer side of the range given. To use whole-grain farro, soak it for at least 8 hours or up to 12 hours and drain it thoroughly before starting with step 1. Do not use quick-cooking farro here. To use the farro in one of our salads, omit the parsley and let the finished farro cool completely in the saucepan, about 30 minutes. Or, to speed up the cooling time, spread the farro over a rimmed baking sheet to cool, about 15 minutes. (Farro can be refrigerated for up to 1 day ahead; bring to room temperature before using.)

- 1½ cups pearl farro
- 2 tablespoons extra-virgin olive oil, divided
- ¼ teaspoon table salt, plus salt for cooking farro
- 2 sprigs fresh thyme
- 1 bay leaf
- 2 tablespoons chopped fresh parsley (optional)
- 1 garlic clove, minced

1. Combine farro and 1 tablespoon oil in large saucepan. Cook over medium-high heat, stirring frequently, until farro is fragrant and just starting to darken in color, about 6 minutes.

2. Add 2 quarts water, 1 tablespoon salt, thyme sprigs, and bay leaf. Bring to boil over high heat. Reduce heat to medium and simmer until grains are tender with slight chew, 10 to 20 minutes. Drain well. Discard thyme sprigs and bay leaf.

3. Return farro to saucepan. Stir in parsley, if using; garlic; salt; and remaining 1 tablespoon oil. Season with salt and pepper to taste. Transfer to serving dish and serve.

Kale and Farro Salad with Fennel, Olives, and Parmesan

FAST Serves 4 to 6 Total Time 45 minutes

Why This Recipe Works This occasion-worthy salad marries farro with slightly bitter kale, while fennel accents the dish with its faint licorice aroma. A sharp lemon-shallot vinaigrette and briny olives pull it all together. Tearing the olives gives them craggy edges that up the textural interest. It's best to use whole-grain farro here. You can use pearl farro, but cooking times vary, so start checking for doneness after 10 minutes. Do not substitute quick-cooking farro. Lacinato (aka dinosaur or Tuscan) kale is more tender than curly-leaf kale, but you can substitute curly-leaf kale; if you do, increase the massaging time to 5 minutes. Do not use baby kale.

- 1½ cups whole farro, rinsed
- ½ teaspoon table salt, plus salt for cooking farro
- 5 ounces lacinato kale, stemmed and sliced crosswise ¼ inch thick
- 3 tablespoons extra-virgin olive oil
- 2 tablespoons lemon juice
- 1 small shallot, minced
- ¼ teaspoon pepper
- 1 fennel bulb, fronds minced, stalks discarded, bulb halved, cored, and sliced thin
- ⅓ cup pitted Castelvetrano olives, torn in half
- ¼ cup slivered almonds, toasted, divided
- 1 ounce Parmesan cheese, shaved thin

1. Bring 2 quarts water to boil in large saucepan. Stir in farro and 1 tablespoon salt and simmer until tender, 15 to 20 minutes. Drain well. Spread farro on rimmed baking sheet and let cool for 15 minutes.

2. Vigorously squeeze and massage kale with hands until leaves are uniformly darkened and slightly wilted, about 1 minute. Whisk oil, lemon juice, shallot, salt, and pepper together in large bowl. Add cooled farro, kale, sliced fennel, olives, and 2 tablespoons almonds and toss to combine. (Salad can be refrigerated for up to 24 hours; bring to room temperature before serving.) Season with salt and pepper to taste. Sprinkle with Parmesan, fennel fronds, and remaining 2 tablespoons almonds. Serve.

top | *Farro Salad with Asparagus, Radishes, and Parmesan*
bottom | *Kale and Farro Salad with Fennel, Olives, and Parmesan*

Butternut Squash and Apple Fattoush

Sweet Potato, Lentil, and Kale Salad with Fried Shallots

Serves 6 to 8   Total Time 1¾ hours, plus 1 hour soaking

Why This Recipe Works Black lentils are the caviar of lentils: They're small but possess a unique earthy flavor, plus they hold their shape and almost never turn mushy. In this beautiful salad we pair them with roasted chunks of sweet potato and lacinato kale. A bracing vinaigrette with a touch of mayo unites everything. Topped with crispy shallots and pungent goat cheese, this salad is a riot of colors and flavors.

- ¾ teaspoon table salt, divided, plus salt for soaking lentils
- 1½ cups black lentils, picked over and rinsed
- 1½ pounds sweet potatoes, peeled and cut into ½-inch pieces (5 cups)
- ½ cup plus 2 tablespoons vegetable oil, divided
- ¼ teaspoon pepper
- 3 shallots, sliced thin
- 2 tablespoons sherry vinegar
- 1 teaspoon mayonnaise
- 1 teaspoon Dijon mustard
- 8 ounces lacinato kale, stemmed and sliced into ¼-inch strips (4½ cups)
- 4 ounces goat cheese, crumbled

1. Dissolve 1½ teaspoons salt in 4 cups warm water in bowl. Add lentils; soak at room temperature for 1 hour.

2. Meanwhile, adjust oven rack to lower-middle position and heat oven to 400 degrees. Toss sweet potatoes with 2 tablespoons oil, ½ teaspoon salt, and pepper. Spread sweet potatoes on rimmed baking sheet and roast until well browned and tender, 20 to 25 minutes, stirring halfway through roasting. Let cool slightly, about 5 minutes. (Roasted sweet potatoes can be refrigerated for up to 1 day. Bring to room temperature before using.)

3. Combine shallots and remaining ½ cup oil in medium bowl. Microwave for 5 minutes. Stir and continue to microwave for 2 minutes longer. Repeat stirring and microwaving in 2-minute increments until beginning to brown (4 to 6 minutes). Repeat stirring and microwaving in 30-second increments until deep golden brown (30 seconds to 2 minutes). Using slotted spoon, transfer shallots to paper towel–lined plate; season with salt to taste. Let drain and crisp, about 5 minutes. Set oil aside to cool completely for dressing. (Fried shallots and shallot oil can be stored separately at room temperature for up to 3 days.)

4. Drain lentils well. Bring lentils and 6 cups water to boil in medium saucepan over high heat. Reduce heat and simmer gently until lentils are just tender, 20 to 25 minutes. Drain.

5. Combine vinegar, mayonnaise, mustard, and remaining ¼ teaspoon salt in large bowl and season with pepper to taste. Whisk until mixture is milky in appearance and no lumps of mayonnaise remain. Whisking constantly, very slowly drizzle reserved shallot oil into vinegar mixture until glossy and lightly thickened, with no pools of oil visible. (Dressing can be refrigerated for up to 3 days; whisk to recombine before serving.)

6. Add kale, sweet potatoes, and lentils to dressing and toss to combine. Season with salt and pepper to taste. Transfer to serving platter and sprinkle with goat cheese and fried shallots. Serve.

Butternut Squash and Apple Fattoush

VEGAN Serves 4 to 6 Total Time 1¼ hours

Why This Recipe Works Flatbreads are a mainstay across the Mediterranean, but the thin breads stale quickly, so creative dishes using them up abound. Such recipes are called fatteh, derived from the Arabic word "fatta," meaning "to crumble." Pita bread salad, or fattoush, is a common example—and its appeal goes far beyond leftovers. The vibrant mix is simple but a textural marvel, combining crumbled toasted, fried, or day-old bread with summertime produce (tomatoes and cucumbers), fresh herbs, and greens, all simply dressed with lemon juice and olive oil and lavished with sumac. This recipe is a combination with distinctly fall flavors that also boasts fantastic contrasts in texture. Crisp sweet apples and slightly bitter radicchio provide fresh crunch, while roasted butternut squash gives the salad complexity and serves as a caramelized, soft, creamy foil to the crisp pieces of pita. We prefer a sweeter crisp apple like Pink Lady or Fuji to complement the bright lemony dressing.

- 2 (8-inch) pita breads, halved crosswise
- ½ cup extra-virgin olive oil, divided
- ⅛ teaspoon plus ¾ teaspoon table salt, divided
- ⅛ teaspoon pepper
- 2 pounds butternut squash, peeled, seeded, and cut into ½-inch pieces
- 3 tablespoons lemon juice
- 4 teaspoons ground sumac, plus extra for serving
- 1 garlic clove, minced
- 1 apple, cored and cut into ½-inch pieces
- ¼ head radicchio, cored and chopped (1 cup)
- ½ cup chopped fresh parsley
- 4 scallions, sliced thin

1. Adjust oven racks to middle and lowest positions and heat oven to 375 degrees. Using kitchen shears, cut around perimeter of each pita and separate into 2 thin rounds. Cut each round in half. Place pitas smooth side down on wire rack set in rimmed baking sheet. Brush rough side of pitas evenly with 3 tablespoons oil, then sprinkle with ⅛ teaspoon salt and pepper. (Pitas do not need to be uniformly coated with oil.) Bake on upper rack until pitas are crisp and pale golden brown, 8 to 12 minutes. Let cool completely.

2. Increase oven temperature to 450 degrees. Toss squash with 1 tablespoon oil and ½ teaspoon salt. Spread in even layer on rimmed baking sheet and roast on lower rack until browned and tender, 20 to 25 minutes, stirring halfway through. Set aside to cool slightly, about 10 minutes.

3. Whisk lemon juice, sumac, garlic, and remaining ¼ teaspoon salt together in small bowl and let sit for 10 minutes. Whisking constantly, slowly drizzle in remaining ¼ cup oil.

4. Break cooled pitas into ½-inch pieces and place in large bowl. Add roasted squash, apple, radicchio, parsley, and scallions. Drizzle dressing over salad and toss gently to coat. Season with salt and pepper to taste. Serve, sprinkling individual portions with extra sumac.

Red Cabbage and Grapefruit Salad

Serves 4 to 6 Total Time 25 minutes, plus 30 minutes sitting

Why This Recipe Works This unlikely pairing of ingredients makes for a stellar winter salad. It puts a spotlight on the ever-present red cabbage but livens up the salad with a sweet-tart dressing, red onion, and refreshing grapefruit sections. To make the fruit easier to eat, we cut it into supremes (wedges freed from their bitter membranes). We then squeeze the juice from the remaining pulp and use it as the base for a vinaigrette with grapefruit zest, white wine vinegar, olive oil, and honey. Red onion and cilantro add pungency and sweet herbal freshness that make this salad distinct. We let the dressed salad sit for 30 minutes before serving to soften the cabbage and allow the flavors to meld. For a finishing touch and welcome crunch, we sprinkle the salad with roasted pepitas. You will need about half of a 2-pound cabbage to yield 6 cups. Green cabbage works here, too, but we prefer the slightly sweeter flavor and bright color of red cabbage.

- 1 red grapefruit
- ¼ cup extra-virgin olive oil
- 1½ tablespoons white wine vinegar
- 1 tablespoon honey
- 1½ teaspoons table salt
- ½ teaspoon pepper
- 6 cups thinly sliced red cabbage
- 1 cup thinly sliced red onion, rinsed
- ½ cup fresh cilantro leaves
- ⅓ cup roasted pepitas

1. Using rasp-style grater, grate 1½ teaspoons zest from grapefruit; transfer zest to large bowl. Cut away peel and pith from grapefruit. Holding grapefruit over separate bowl, use paring knife to slice between membranes to release segments; set aside grapefruit segments. Squeeze 2 tablespoons juice from remaining grapefruit pulp and add to bowl with zest.

2. Add oil, vinegar, honey, salt, and pepper to bowl with zest mixture and whisk to combine. Add cabbage, onion, cilantro, and grapefruit segments and toss to combine. Let sit for 30 minutes to allow flavors to meld.

3. Add pepitas and toss to combine. Season with salt and pepper to taste. Serve.

Cutting Citrus Segments

1. Cut thin slice from top and bottom of fruit using a paring knife. Slice off rind, including white pith, by cutting from top to bottom of fruit. Follow fruit's contours closely.

2. Holding fruit over bowl, use paring knife to cut between membranes.

Cantaloupe Salad with Olives and Red Onion

FAST VEGAN Serves 4 to 6 Total Time 20 minutes

Why This Recipe Works This showstopping, next-level melon salad pairs luscious cantaloupe with ingredients you may never have had in such a salad: cured black olives, red onion, and Aleppo pepper. To counter the abundant water that melons release, which inevitably slides to the bottom of the salad bowl, we make a flavorful dressing but skip the oil, which would just slip off the melon's wet surface. Taste the melon before adding any honey to the dressing; if the fruit is sweet enough, you may not need to add any. We leave the melon in large chunks, since fewer cut surfaces means less liquid to water down the dressing. We like the gentle heat and raisiny sweetness of Aleppo pepper here, but if it's unavailable, substitute ¾ teaspoon of paprika and ¼ teaspoon of cayenne pepper. This salad makes a light, refreshing accompaniment to couscous or steamed white rice.

- ½ red onion, sliced thin
- ⅓ cup lemon juice (2 lemons)
- 1–3 teaspoons honey (optional)
- 1 teaspoon ground dried Aleppo pepper
- ½ teaspoon table salt

- 1 cantaloupe, peeled, halved, seeded, and cut into 1½-inch chunks (6 cups)
- 5 tablespoons chopped fresh parsley, divided
- 5 tablespoons chopped fresh mint, divided
- ¼ cup finely chopped pitted oil-cured olives, divided

Combine onion and lemon juice in large bowl and let sit for 5 minutes. Stir in honey, if using; Aleppo pepper; and salt. Add cantaloupe, ¼ cup parsley, ¼ cup mint, and 3 tablespoons olives and stir to combine. Transfer to shallow serving bowl. Sprinkle with remaining 1 tablespoon parsley, remaining 1 tablespoon mint, and remaining 1 tablespoon olives and serve.

Honeydew Salad with Peanuts and Lime

FAST Serves 4 to 6 Total Time 20 minutes

Why This Recipe Works While you would not mistake this dish for a stir-fry, most of the ingredients are similar: Thai chiles, lime, garlic, fish sauce, and cilantro. And surprisingly, they pair well with sweet chunks of honeydew melon, to which we add a bit of sugar and fresh mint for balance. Before doing anything else, we recommend tasting the melon as you cut it up because melons vary in sweetness; this will help you to decide how much sugar to add to the dressing or whether it should be omitted altogether. To counter the abundant water that melons release, we make an intense dressing with assertive ingredients but omit any oil, which would cause the dressing to slide off the melon. Using large chunks of melon also helps cut down on the liquid that could water down the dressing. This salad is especially nice served with steamed white rice.

- ⅓ cup lime juice (3 limes)
- 1 shallot, sliced thin
- 2 Thai chiles, stemmed, seeded, and minced
- 1 garlic clove, minced
- ½ teaspoon table salt
- 1–2 tablespoons sugar (optional)
- 1 tablespoon vegetarian fish sauce
- 1 honeydew melon, peeled, halved, seeded, and cut into 1½-inch chunks (6 cups)
- 5 tablespoons chopped fresh cilantro, divided
- 5 tablespoons chopped fresh mint, divided
- 5 tablespoons salted dry-roasted peanuts, chopped fine, divided

top *Red Cabbage and Grapefruit Salad*
bottom *Honeydew Salad with Peanuts and Lime*

1. Combine lime juice and shallot in large bowl. Using mortar and pestle (or on cutting board using flat side of chef's knife), mash Thai chiles, garlic, and salt to fine paste. Add chile paste; sugar, if using; and fish sauce to lime juice mixture and stir to combine.

2. Add honeydew, ¼ cup cilantro, ¼ cup mint, and ¼ cup peanuts and toss to combine. Transfer to shallow serving bowl. Sprinkle with remaining 1 tablespoon cilantro, remaining 1 tablespoon mint, and remaining 1 tablespoon peanuts and serve.

Cutting Up Melon

1. Trim ¼-inch slice from top and bottom of melon so that it sits flat on cutting board. Using chef's knife, work from top to bottom to carefully cut away rind in long strips.

2. Cut melon in half and scoop out seeds with large spoon.

3. Cut melon into thick slices and then into chunks.

Caramelized Plums with Spicy Herb Salad

FAST **VEGAN** Serves 4 to 6 Total Time 30 minutes

Why This Recipe Works A visit to the skillet helps even less than perfect plums in the flavor and texture department. We found that searing plums teases out their naturally sweet, juicy qualities and mimics a "ripened" feel on the fruit's flesh and skin. To encourage even browning, we toss thick wedges of plums in oil, along with ample sugar and salt to draw out their moisture and heighten their sweetness during cooking. We sear the plums with a cold start in a nonstick skillet, which reduces splatter and slowly softens the plums' flesh while browning. The sugar and salt draw out the plums' juices during cooking, which thickens and creates a glossy, syrupy finish on the deeply browned sides. To showcase the plums, we pair the seared wedges with a bright, complementary mint and cilantro salad, which serves as both a glorified herb garnish and a substantial bed of greens. We toss everything with a lip-puckering, irresistible dressing of lime juice, sugar, sesame oil, and Thai chiles to perk up the naturally zippy, floral notes of the plums and herbs. A sprinkling of sesame seeds and chopped peanuts ties the salad together with a crisp, toasty finish. Both red and black plums work well in this recipe. For a spicier salad, use both Thai chiles.

- ¼ cup vegetable oil, divided
- 3½ teaspoons sugar, divided
- 1 tablespoon lime juice
- 1–2 Thai chiles, stemmed and sliced thin
- 1½ teaspoons grated fresh ginger
- ½ teaspoon toasted sesame oil
- ½ teaspoon table salt, divided
- 1 pound ripe but firm plums, halved and pitted, each half cut into 4 wedges
- 3 cups fresh cilantro leaves and tender stems, cut into 1½-inch lengths
- 2 cups fresh mint leaves, large leaves torn into 1-inch pieces
- 2 tablespoons dry-roasted peanuts, chopped coarse
- 2 teaspoons sesame seeds, toasted

1. Whisk 3 tablespoons vegetable oil, 1½ teaspoons sugar, lime juice, Thai chile(s), ginger, sesame oil, and ¼ teaspoon salt in large bowl until smooth and creamy. Reserve 2 tablespoons dressing in small bowl; set bowls aside.

2. Toss plum wedges with remaining 1 tablespoon vegetable oil, remaining 2 teaspoons sugar, and remaining ¼ teaspoon salt in cold 12-inch nonstick skillet until evenly coated, then arrange wedges cut side down in even layer. Cook over medium-high heat, without moving, until wedges are well browned on first cut side, 4 to 5 minutes.

3. Using tongs, carefully flip wedges and continue to cook until second cut side is well browned, 2 to 3 minutes longer. Remove skillet from heat.

4. Add cilantro and mint to large bowl with dressing and toss until herbs are evenly coated. Arrange herb mixture on serving platter and top with plum wedges. Drizzle plums with reserved dressing. Sprinkle with peanuts and sesame seeds. Serve.

Grilled Peach and Tomato Salad with Burrata and Basil

FAST Serves 4 to 6 Total Time 15 minutes, plus 30 minutes draining

Why This Recipe Works Grilled peaches are a favorite of ours in the summer. That said, grilled peaches alone, while good, are even better when dressed up just a bit. To prevent the peaches from sticking to the grill and to add welcome Maillard browning, we halve them and brush their cut sides with melted butter. For a custardy-soft texture and subtle grill flavor, we grill them over high heat until grill marks form, then move them to a covered baking pan over indirect heat until they are fully softened. Once the peaches are cool, you can remove their skins and cut them into wedges. Tossing the peaches with tomato chunks in a simple vinaigrette of white wine vinegar and extra-virgin olive oil adds flavor and richness. Creamy burrata cheese introduces a luxe element to this summer knockout. This recipe can also be made with nectarines or plums. If burrata is unavailable, sliced fresh mozzarella is a good substitute.

Caramelized Plums with Spicy Herb Salad

- 12 ounces ripe tomatoes, cored and cut into ½-inch pieces
- ¾ teaspoon table salt, divided
- 1 recipe Grilled Stone Fruit (page 136), using peaches, skins discarded
- 1 tablespoon white wine vinegar
- 5 tablespoons extra-virgin olive oil, divided
- 8 ounces burrata cheese, room temperature
- ⅓ cup chopped fresh basil

1. Toss tomatoes with ¼ teaspoon salt and let drain in colander for 30 minutes. Cut each peach half into 4 wedges and cut each wedge in half crosswise.

2. Whisk vinegar and remaining ½ teaspoon salt together in large bowl. Whisking constantly, slowly drizzle in ¼ cup oil. Add tomatoes and peaches and toss gently to combine; transfer to shallow serving bowl. Place burrata on top of salad and drizzle with remaining 1 tablespoon oil. Season with pepper to taste and sprinkle with basil. Serve, breaking up burrata with spoon and allowing creamy liquid to meld with dressing.

Grilled Watermelon, Halloumi, and Olive Salad

Serves 4 to 6   Total Time 1 hour

Why This Recipe Works Grilling the main elements—watermelon, halloumi, and olives—of this midsummer salad transforms them into complex, multi-layered ingredients. Seasoning watermelon with sugar boosts its natural sweetness and pulls out some of the excess moisture, allowing for well-developed char. To retain its bright flavor, we grill the watermelon on only one side. For a salty, savory counterpoint, we add grilled halloumi cheese and grilled olives, while fresh herbs and lemon juice keep the salad lively. Letting the watermelon rest briefly after grilling is important so that it doesn't release all its juices when cut. We call for a mini seedless watermelon (its small size makes slicing a breeze), but you can substitute a larger seedless watermelon; aim for a total weight of 3 pounds of prepped watermelon (sliced, with rind removed, as indicated in step 1). You will need two 12-inch metal skewers for this recipe; flat skewers are helpful because they will prevent the olives from spinning.

Grilled Stone Fruit

Serves 4 to 6   Total Time 1 hour

For the best results, use high-quality, ripe, in-season fruit with a fragrant aroma and flesh that yields slightly when gently pressed. Using a metal baking pan on the cooler side of the grill won't harm the pan, but you can use a disposable aluminum pan if preferred; do not use a glass dish. This makes a great simple side dish.

- 1½ pounds ripe but slightly firm stone fruit, halved and pitted
- 2 tablespoons unsalted butter, melted

1. Brush cut side of fruit with melted butter.

2A. **For a charcoal grill** Open bottom vent completely. Light large chimney starter three-quarters filled with charcoal briquettes (4½ quarts). When top coals are partially covered with ash, pour evenly over half of grill. Set cooking grate in place, cover, and open lid vent completely. Heat grill until hot, about 5 minutes.

2B. **For a gas grill** Turn all burners to high; cover; and heat grill until hot, about 15 minutes. Leave primary burner on high and turn off other burner(s).

3. Clean and oil cooking grate. Arrange fruit cut side down on hotter side of grill and cook (covered if using gas) until grill marks have formed, 5 to 7 minutes, moving fruit as needed to ensure even cooking.

4. Transfer fruit cut side up to 13 by 9-inch baking pan and cover loosely with aluminum foil. Place pan on cooler side of grill. If using gas, turn primary burner to medium. Cover and cook until fruit is very tender and paring knife slips in and out with little resistance, 10 to 15 minutes. When cool enough to handle, remove and discard skins, if desired. Let cool completely. Serve.

¼ cup extra-virgin olive oil, divided
2 tablespoons lemon juice
½ teaspoon table salt
½ teaspoon pepper
1 (6- to 8-pound) mini seedless watermelon
3 tablespoons sugar
½ cup pitted kalamata olives
8 ounces halloumi cheese, sliced into ¾-inch-thick slabs
2 tablespoons chopped fresh basil
2 tablespoons chopped fresh mint

1. Set wire rack in rimmed baking sheet. Whisk 2 tablespoons oil, lemon juice, salt, and pepper together in small bowl; set aside. Using large serrated knife, halve watermelon through equator. Place 1 half cut side down on cutting board and cut into 1-inch-thick slices; discard end pieces of rind. Lay each slice flat on cutting board and cut away rind. (You should have about 3 pounds of trimmed watermelon slabs. Cut slices from second half of watermelon as needed to yield 3 pounds; reserve remaining watermelon for another use.) Place slabs on prepared rack and sprinkle all over with sugar. Let sit while grill heats, at least 15 minutes.

2A. For a charcoal grill Meanwhile, open bottom vent completely. Light large chimney starter filled with charcoal briquettes (6 quarts). When top coals are partially covered with ash, pour evenly over grill. Set cooking grate in place, cover, and open lid vent completely. Heat grill until hot, about 5 minutes.

2B. For a gas grill Meanwhile, turn all burners to high; cover; and heat grill until hot, about 15 minutes.

3. Thread olives (through long sides) onto two 12-inch metal skewers; set aside. Pat tops of watermelon slabs dry and brush evenly with 1 tablespoon oil. Clean and oil cooking grate. Place watermelon on grill, oiled side down, and cook (covered if using gas) until watermelon is well charred on 1 side, 4 to 5 minutes (do not flip). Using spatula, carefully transfer watermelon to now-empty wire rack and let rest while grilling halloumi and olives.

4. Pat halloumi and olives dry, brush all over with remaining 1 tablespoon oil, then place on grill. Cook (covered if using gas) until halloumi and olives are lightly charred on both sides, 6 to 7 minutes, flipping halfway through cooking. Transfer to cutting board. Cut halloumi into ½-inch pieces and remove olives from skewers; transfer halloumi and olives to bowl.

5. Transfer watermelon to now-empty cutting board and cut into 1-inch pieces. Arrange watermelon in even layer on serving platter. Top with halloumi and olives. Whisk dressing to recombine, then drizzle over salad. Sprinkle with basil and mint. Serve.

Grilled Watermelon, Halloumi, and Olive Salad

Dressing Up Salads

This creative yet easy collection of vinaigrettes and creamy dressings will service most of your salad making needs. For a delicious Vegan Ranch Dressing, see page 506. You will also find other dressings within the recipes in the chapter.

To dress a salad, use 1 tablespoon of dressing per 2 cups of washed and dried greens.

Make-Ahead Vinaigrette

FAST **VEGAN** Makes 1 cup Total Time 15 minutes

This versatile vinaigrette is the one to keep on hand for salads or any dish that needs a boost. Mustard and mayonnaise prevent the oil and vinegar from separating, and a surprising ingredient—molasses—is a third stabilizer. Just a tablespoon works wonders without imparting a strong flavor. Do not use blackstrap molasses. This vinaigrette pairs well with nearly any green. To make this recipe vegan, substitute plant-based mayo for the mayonnaise.

- 1 tablespoon regular or light mayonnaise
- 1 tablespoon molasses
- 1 tablespoon Dijon mustard
- ½ teaspoon table salt
- ¼ cup white wine vinegar
- ½ cup extra-virgin olive oil, divided
- ¼ cup vegetable oil

1. Combine mayonnaise, molasses, mustard, and salt in 2-cup jar with tight-fitting lid. Stir with fork until mixture is milky in appearance and no lumps of mayonnaise or molasses remain. Add vinegar, seal jar, and shake until smooth, about 10 seconds.

2. Add ¼ cup olive oil, seal jar, and shake vigorously until combined, about 10 seconds. Repeat with remaining ¼ cup olive oil and vegetable oil in separate additions, shaking vigorously until combined after each addition. Vinaigrette should be glossy and lightly thickened after all oil has been added, with no pools of oil on surface. Season with salt and pepper to taste. (Vinaigrette can be refrigerated for up to 1 week; shake to recombine before using.)

Variations

FAST **VEGAN** Make-Ahead Sherry-Shallot Vinaigrette

Add 2 teaspoons minced shallot and 2 teaspoons minced fresh thyme to jar with mayonnaise. Substitute sherry vinegar for white wine vinegar.

FAST **VEGAN** Make-Ahead Balsamic-Fennel Vinaigrette

Add 2 teaspoons toasted and cracked fennel seeds to jar with mayonnaise. Substitute balsamic vinegar for white wine vinegar.

Raspberry Vinaigrette

FAST **VEGAN** Makes ⅓ cup Total Time 10 minutes

This recipe works nicely for a slightly sweet vinaigrette. It pairs especially well with salads topped with berries or other fruit. Avoid chunky preserves and supersweet jams.

- 2 tablespoons seedless raspberry jam
- 2½ teaspoons red wine vinegar
- 1 teaspoon Dijon mustard
- ⅛ teaspoon table salt
- ⅛ teaspoon pepper
- 3 tablespoons extra-virgin olive oil

Whisk jam in medium bowl until smooth. Add vinegar, mustard, salt, and pepper, whisking until combined. Whisking constantly, slowly drizzle in oil until emulsified. (Vinaigrette can be refrigerated for up to 3 days; whisk to recombine before using.)

Sesame-Scallion Vinaigrette

FAST **VEGAN** Makes ¾ cup Total Time 10 minutes

This simple vinaigrette is light, with a subtle flavor. For an even milder dressing, omit the chili oil.

- ¼ cup soy sauce
- 2 tablespoons rice vinegar
- 2 tablespoons mirin
- 2 tablespoons water
- 1 teaspoon chili oil (optional)
- ½ teaspoon toasted sesame oil
- 1 scallion, minced

Whisk all ingredients together in bowl. (Vinaigrette can be refrigerated for up to 3 days; whisk to recombine before using.)

Creamless Creamy Herb Dressing

VEGAN Makes 2 cups Total Time 15 minutes, plus 1 hour soaking and chilling

For a creamless creamy herb dressing, we use soaked and pureed raw cashews instead of dairy or mayonnaise. Grinding the nuts before soaking allows us to decrease the typical overnight soaking time to just 15 minutes. The dressing is initially warm from the friction of blending, so we chill it before adding minced herbs to prevent them from wilting. You'll need a conventional blender for this recipe; an immersion blender or food processor will produce dressing that is grainy and thin. Use unsalted raw cashews, not roasted, to ensure the proper flavor balance. This dressing works well drizzled over a hearty salad, but it can also be used as a dip for vegetables.

- 1 cup unsalted raw cashews
- ¾ cup water, plus extra as needed
- 3 tablespoons cider vinegar
- 1¼ teaspoons table salt
- 1 teaspoon onion powder
- ½ teaspoon sugar
- ¼ teaspoon garlic powder
- 2 tablespoons minced fresh chives or cilantro
- 1 tablespoon minced fresh parsley
- ½ teaspoon pepper

1. Process cashews in blender on low speed to consistency of fine gravel mixed with sand, 10 to 15 seconds. Add water, vinegar, salt, onion powder, sugar, and garlic powder and process on low speed until combined, about 5 seconds. Let mixture sit for 15 minutes.

2. Process on low speed until all ingredients are well blended, about 1 minute. Scrape down sides of blender jar. Process on high speed until dressing is smooth and creamy, 3 to 4 minutes. Transfer dressing to bowl. Cover and refrigerate until cold, about 45 minutes. Stir in chives, parsley, and pepper. Thin with extra water, adding 1 tablespoon at a time, if needed. (Dressing can be refrigerated for up to 1 week; whisk to recombine before using.)

Variation

VEGAN Creamless Creamy Roasted Red Pepper and Tahini Dressing

Omit chives and parsley. Decrease cashews to ½ cup. Substitute one 12-ounce jar roasted red peppers, drained and chopped coarse, for water; sherry vinegar for cider vinegar; 3 tablespoons tahini for onion powder; 2 teaspoons toasted sesame oil for sugar; and smoked paprika for pepper. Increase salt to 1½ teaspoons and garlic powder to ½ teaspoon and add pinch cayenne pepper.

Creamy Avocado Dressing

FAST **VEGAN** Makes 1 cup Total Time 10 minutes

Rich avocado makes for a deliciously creamy dressing with no dairy needed.

- 1 ripe avocado, halved, pitted, and cut into ½-inch pieces
- 2 tablespoons extra-virgin olive oil
- 1 teaspoon grated lemon zest plus 3 tablespoons juice
- 1 garlic clove, minced
- ¾ teaspoon table salt
- ¼ teaspoon pepper

Process all ingredients in food processor until smooth, about 30 seconds, scraping down sides of bowl as needed. Season with salt and pepper to taste. (Dressing can be refrigerated for up to 5 days; whisk to recombine before using.)

Soups & Stews

142 Pappa al Pomodoro ■ ●

143 Caramelized Carrot Soup with Coriander-Lemon Browned Butter

144 Cauliflower Soup
Hawaij Cauliflower Soup with Zhoug

146 Sweet Potato Soup with Maple Sour Cream

147 Roasted Garlic Soup with Parmesan Croutons

149 Carabaccia (Tuscan Onion Soup)

149 Zucchini Soup with Dill and Sour Cream

150 Super Greens Soup with Lemon-Tarragon Cream

151 Hearty Cabbage Soup

153 Spiced Eggplant and Kale Soup ●

153 Kimchi and Tofu Soup ■ ●

154 Shiitake, Tofu, and Mustard Greens Soup ●

154 Lemongrass-Coconut Soup with Oyster Mushrooms ■ ●

155 Quick Food Processor Gazpacho ●

156 Chilled Peach and Cucumber Soup ■

156 Wild Rice and Mushroom Soup

159 Creamy White Bean Soup with Herb Oil and Crispy Capers ■

159 Red Lentil Soup with Warm Spices ●

160 Lentil and Escarole Soup ●

161 Classic Minestrone

162 Ribollita ●

163 Butternut Squash and White Bean Soup with Sage Pesto

164 Acquacotta (Tuscan White Bean and Escarole Soup)

166 Tanabour (Armenian Yogurt and Barley Soup)

167 Turkish Bulgur and Lentil Soup ■ ●

167 Tomato, Bulgur, and Red Pepper Soup ●

168 Harira (Moroccan Lentil and Chickpea Soup) ●

169 Chickpea Noodle Soup ■ ●

170 Creamy Chickpea and Sweet Potato Stew ■ ●

171 Thai-Spiced Red Lentil Stew with Spinach and Corn ●

171 Green Gumbo ●

172 Best Vegetarian Chili ●

173 Black Bean Chili ●

175 Roasted Poblano and White Bean Chili ●

Building-Block Vegetable Broths

176 Classic Vegetable Broth ●

176 Vegetable Broth Base ■ ●

177 Vegetable Scrap Broth ●

177 Umami Broth ●

Great Garnishes for Soup (and More)

178 Classic Croutons ■
Herbed Croutons ■
Umami Croutons ■ ●

178 Tofu Croutons ■ ●

179 Spiced Seeds ■ ●

179 Pickled Celery ■ ●

179 Quick Chili Oil ●

179 Lemon-Herb Sauce ■

■ Fast (45 minutes or less) ● Vegan

| *Pappa al Pomodoro*

Pappa al Pomodoro

FAST **VEGAN** Serves 6 Total Time 40 minutes

Why This Recipe Works When tomatoes are abundant, it's time for this rustic Tuscan soup with its stunning interplay of simple ingredients: garlic, ripened-to-bursting tomatoes, bread, and a fruity, spicy slick of olive oil on top. We start by grating the tomatoes, which quickly reduces their flesh to pulp without any need to peel or chop them. After gently sautéing sliced garlic in olive oil, we add the pulp, salt, black pepper, red pepper flakes, basil sprigs, water, and thinly sliced rustic bread. Adding water ensures that the dish doesn't end up too dry, and thinly slicing rather than cubing the bread helps it break down and soften quickly and evenly. Finishing with more oil, along with fresh basil and Parmesan cheese, contributes richness and brightness to this luscious and velvety mixture. Do not use plum tomatoes or the dish will be too dry. For the bread, we prefer a round rustic loaf with a chewy, open crumb; fresh or stale bread will work here. Slice the bread as thin as possible; the slices needn't be perfect or fully intact since they will break down during cooking. Serve hot, warm, or at room temperature.

- 3 pounds ripe tomatoes, halved through equator
- 6 tablespoons extra-virgin olive oil, plus extra for drizzling
- 3 garlic cloves, sliced thin
- 1 teaspoon table salt
- ½ teaspoon pepper
- Pinch red pepper flakes
- 2 cups water
- 2 sprigs fresh basil, plus 2 tablespoons chopped
- 6 ounces country-style bread, sliced thin
- Grated Parmesan cheese for serving

1. Place box grater in medium bowl. Rub cut surface of tomatoes against large holes of grater until tomato flesh is reduced to pulp (skins should remain intact). Discard skins. (You should have about 4 cups pulp.)

2. Combine oil and garlic in large Dutch oven and cook over medium heat until garlic is golden at edges, 3 to 4 minutes. Add tomato pulp, salt, pepper, pepper flakes, water, basil sprigs, and bread (tear slices to fit in pot as necessary) and stir to combine so all bread is moistened.

3. Bring to boil over high heat. Adjust heat to medium, cover, and simmer vigorously, stirring and mashing bread occasionally, until bread is fully softened and broken down, 15 to 18 minutes (mixture will not be completely smooth). Off heat, discard basil sprigs. Divide among serving bowls, drizzle with extra oil, and sprinkle with chopped basil. Serve, passing Parmesan separately.

Grating Tomatoes

Halve tomatoes through equator. Place grater in medium bowl and rub cut sides of each tomato on grater's large holes to make tomato puree.

Caramelized Carrot Soup with Coriander-Lemon Browned Butter

Serves 4 to 6 Total Time 55 minutes

Why This Recipe Works Supersimple and surprisingly sophisticated, this soup raises the bar for every carrot soup we've tasted. Rather than add flavors and depth through the usual aromatics, we put our focus on enhancing the carrots through caramelization. First, we cook carrots with butter, a few thyme sprigs, sugar, and salt. As the butter's moisture evaporates, the milk solids start to brown. This occurs around the same time that the carrots begin to caramelize and become well browned. To ensure that this soup can be pureed in a single go, we blend the cooked carrots with just half the liquid and then return the mixture to the Dutch oven and thin it out to our desired consistency with additional broth. As a finishing touch, we created a seasoned browned butter with more fresh thyme, crushed coriander, cayenne, and lemon zest and juice for a n elegant drizzle over each serving. To crush the coriander seeds, place them in a zipper-lock bag and crush with a rolling pin or the heel of a skillet. Look for carrots that are 1 to 1½ inches in diameter at the larger end. You can use an immersion blender to process the soup directly in the pot instead of using a blender.

Soup

- 4 tablespoons unsalted butter
- 2 pounds carrots, peeled and sliced ½ inch thick
- 3 sprigs fresh thyme
- 2 tablespoons sugar
- 2 teaspoons table salt
- 4 cups vegetable broth, divided
- 2 cups water

Browned Butter

- 1 teaspoon coriander seeds, crushed
- 1 teaspoon chopped fresh thyme
- ⅛ teaspoon table salt
- Pinch cayenne pepper
- 4 tablespoons unsalted butter
- 1 teaspoon grated lemon zest plus 1 teaspoon juice

1. **For the soup** Melt butter in Dutch oven over medium heat. Add carrots, thyme sprigs, sugar, and salt and cook, stirring often, until carrots are tender and well browned, 25 to 30 minutes.

2. Stir in 3 cups broth, scraping up any browned bits, and bring to boil over high heat. Cook for 1 minute. Off heat, discard thyme sprigs. Process carrot mixture in blender until smooth, about 1 minute, then return soup base to pot. Whisk in water and remaining 1 cup broth; set aside until ready to serve. (Soup can refrigerated for up to 3 days.)

3. **For the browned butter** Combine coriander, thyme, salt, and cayenne in medium bowl. Melt butter in 8-inch skillet over medium-high heat. Continue to cook, stirring constantly with silicone spatula, until butter is dark golden brown and has nutty aroma, 2 to 4 minutes longer. Immediately transfer browned butter to bowl with coriander mixture and let sit until fragrant, about 30 seconds. Stir in lemon zest and juice; set aside.

4. To serve, bring soup to simmer over medium heat, whisking to recombine as needed, and season with salt and pepper to taste. Serve, drizzling individual bowls with browned butter.

Cauliflower Soup

Serves 4 to 6   Total Time 1 hour

Why This Recipe Works All too often creamy vegetable soups lose sight of the vegetable itself. So for a creamy cauliflower soup that tastes first and foremost of cauliflower, we did away with the distractions—no cream, flour, or overpowering seasonings. Cauliflower, simmered until tender, produces a creamy, velvety smooth puree, without the aid of added cream, thanks to its low insoluble fiber content. For the purest flavor, we cook it in salted water (instead of broth), skip the spice rack entirely, and bolster it with sautéed onion and leek. We add the cauliflower to the simmering water in two stages so our soup offers both the grassy flavor of just-cooked cauliflower and the sweeter, nuttier flavor of long-cooked cauliflower. Finally, we fry a portion of the florets in butter until both the cauliflower and butter are golden brown and use each as a separate, richly flavored garnish. White wine vinegar may be substituted for the sherry vinegar. For the best flavor and texture, trim the core of the cauliflower thoroughly of green leaves and leaf stems, which can be fibrous and contribute to a grainy texture in the soup. You can use an immersion blender to process the soup directly in the pan instead of using a blender.

- 1 head cauliflower (2 pounds)
- 8 tablespoons unsalted butter, cut into 1-tablespoon pieces, divided
- 1 leek, white and light green parts only, halved lengthwise, sliced thin, and washed thoroughly
- 1 small onion, halved and sliced thin
- 1½ teaspoons table salt
- 4½ cups water, plus extra as needed
- ½ teaspoon sherry vinegar
- 3 tablespoons minced fresh chives

1. Pull off outer leaves of cauliflower and trim stem. Using paring knife, cut around core to remove; thinly slice core and reserve. Cut heaping 1 cup of ½-inch florets from head of cauliflower; set aside. Cut remaining cauliflower crosswise into ½-inch-thick slices.

2. Melt 3 tablespoons butter in large saucepan over medium-low heat. Add leek, onion, and salt; cook, stirring frequently, until onion is softened but not browned, about 7 minutes.

3. Increase heat to medium-high, add water, sliced core, and half of sliced cauliflower, and bring to simmer. Reduce heat to medium-low and simmer gently for 15 minutes. Add remaining sliced cauliflower, return to simmer, and continue to cook until cauliflower is tender and crumbles easily, 15 to 20 minutes longer.

4. While soup simmers, melt remaining 5 tablespoons butter in 8-inch skillet over medium heat. Add reserved florets and cook, stirring frequently, until florets are golden brown and butter is browned, 6 to 8 minutes. Remove skillet from heat and use slotted spoon to transfer florets to small bowl. Toss florets with vinegar and season with salt to taste. Pour browned butter in skillet into small bowl and reserve for garnishing.

5. Process soup in blender until smooth, about 45 seconds. Rinse out saucepan. Return pureed soup to saucepan and return to simmer over medium heat, adjusting consistency with up to ½ cup water as needed (soup should have thick, velvety texture but should be thin enough to settle with a flat surface after being stirred) and seasoning with salt to taste. Serve, garnishing individual bowls with browned florets, drizzles of browned butter, and chives and seasoning with pepper to taste. (Soup and browned florets can be refrigerated separately for up to 3 days.)

Variation

Hawaij Cauliflower Soup with Zhoug

Hawaij is a Yemeni spice blend also common to Israeli cuisine. Zhoug (Spicy Middle Eastern Herb Sauce) is a grassy cilantro-chile sauce (page 524).

To make hawaij, process 2½ tablespoons black peppercorns, 2 tablespoons cumin seeds, 1½ tablespoons coriander seeds, 10 cardamom pods, and 6 whole cloves in spice grinder until finely ground, about 30 seconds. Transfer to bowl and stir in 1½ tablespoons ground turmeric. (Hawaij can be stored at room temperature for up to 1 month.) In step 2, stir 1 tablespoon hawaij into softened leek and onion. Cook until fragrant, about 30 seconds, and continue with recipe. In step 4, add ¼ cup zhoug to bowl with reserved florets and toss until well coated. Continue with recipe. To serve, omit drizzles of browned butter and chives and spoon browned florets and additional ¾ cup zhoug over individual serving bowls.

The Cauliflower Advantage

Our Cauliflower Soup is supercreamy—without any cream. This has to do with the amount and the proportion of fiber in cauliflower.

Creamy by Nature

All vegetables have both soluble and insoluble fiber. The former breaks down during cooking; the latter does not. Most pureed vegetable soups need cream to mitigate the effects of insoluble fiber. But cauliflower is very low in insoluble fiber, giving it a creamy quality when cooked.

Timing Is Key

Cooking times have a dramatic effect on cauliflower's flavor. Shorter times bring out its cabbage-y flavor and sulfurous odor. After 30 minutes, it turns nuttier and sweeter. After an hour, cauliflower loses much of its flavor.

Cauliflower Top to Bottom

This soup is basically just cooked cauliflower, water, and flavorings. Browning some of the florets in butter creates a beautiful topping that enhances the soup's texture, richness, and flavor.

Cauliflower Soup

top | *Sweet Potato Soup with Maple Sour Cream*
bottom | *Roasted Garlic Soup with Parmesan Croutons*

Sweet Potato Soup with Maple Sour Cream

Serves 4 to 6 Total Time 1 hour

Why This Recipe Works The secret to creamy sweet potato soup with deep, earthy-sweet flavor is to use the peels. Before simmering and pureeing the peeled potatoes, we coax out more natural sweetness by soaking them in hot water, which converts their large starch molecules into pure sugar. Pureeing some of the skins along with the softened potatoes adds depth to the otherwise sweet soup, a contrast we reinforce with some brown sugar and a touch of cider vinegar. The simple maple–sour cream topping brings a sweet-tangy coolness when serving the soup, and a sprinkling of minced chives adds a pop of color and delicate oniony flavor. You can use an immersion blender to process the soup directly in the pot instead of using a blender.

Maple Sour Cream

- ⅓ cup sour cream
- 1 tablespoon maple syrup

Soup

- 4 tablespoons unsalted butter
- 1 shallot, sliced thin
- 4 sprigs fresh thyme
- 4¼ cups water
- 2 pounds sweet potatoes, peeled, halved lengthwise, and sliced ¼ inch thick, one-quarter of peels reserved
- 1 tablespoon packed brown sugar
- ½ teaspoon cider vinegar
- 1½ teaspoons table salt
- ¼ teaspoon pepper
- 2 tablespoons minced fresh chives

1. For the maple sour cream Combine all ingredients in small bowl and refrigerate until ready to serve.

2. For the soup Melt butter in large saucepan over medium-low heat. Add shallot and thyme sprigs and cook until shallot is softened but not browned, about 5 minutes. Stir in water and bring to simmer over high heat. Off heat, add sweet potatoes and reserved peels and let stand for 20 minutes.

3. Stir in sugar, vinegar, salt, and pepper. Bring to simmer over high heat. Reduce heat to medium-low, cover, and cook until potatoes are very soft, about 10 minutes.

4. Discard thyme sprigs. Working in batches, process soup in blender until smooth, about 1 minute. Return soup to now-empty saucepan. Return to simmer, adjusting consistency with more water if desired. Season with salt and pepper to taste. Serve, topping each portion with sprinkle of chives and drizzle of maple sour cream.

Roasted Garlic Soup with Parmesan Croutons

Serves 4 to 6   Total Time 1¾ hours

Why This Recipe Works It's hard to decide which element of this soup is more crave-worthy: its sweet, garlicky flavor or the exceptional croutons toasted in the reserved garlic oil. First, we roast a whopping 60 cloves of garlic in a half cup of olive oil in a covered saucepan, after which the garlic emerges golden brown, supertender, and mellow. For soup with a luxurious texture, we puree the roasted garlic into a mixture of sautéed onion, vegetable broth, and thyme along with cubed sourdough bread. The bread makes the brothy soup silky and velvety without adding any heaviness or competing flavors that could distract from the focus on the roasted garlic. Finally, we toss more bread cubes with some of the reserved garlic oil and grated Parmesan cheese and bake them to top off the soup. Five to six heads of garlic will yield 60 cloves. You can substitute any crusty bread (such as baguette or ciabatta) for the sourdough. You can use an immersion blender to process the soup directly in the pot instead of using a blender.

- 60 garlic cloves, peeled (1½ cups)
- ½ cup extra-virgin olive oil, divided
- 9 sprigs fresh thyme, divided
- 3 cups thinly sliced onion
- 1 teaspoon table salt, divided
- 6 cups vegetable broth
- 1 (1½-ounce) Parmesan cheese rind, plus 2 ounces Parmesan cheese, grated (1 cup)
- 1 teaspoon pepper, divided
- 6 ounces crusty sourdough bread, cut into ½-inch cubes (5¼ cups), divided
- 1 tablespoon chopped fresh dill

1. Adjust oven rack to middle position and heat oven to 400 degrees. Combine garlic, 6 tablespoons oil, and 3 thyme sprigs in small ovensafe saucepan or 8-inch square baking dish. Cover, transfer to oven, and roast until garlic is tender and golden brown, about 45 minutes, stirring once halfway through roasting. Transfer saucepan to wire rack; discard thyme sprigs. (Leave oven on for croutons.)

2. Meanwhile, heat remaining 2 tablespoons oil in large saucepan over medium heat until shimmering. Add onion and ¾ teaspoon salt and cook, stirring occasionally, until onion is softened and lightly browned, 10 to 14 minutes. Stir in broth, Parmesan rind, ¾ teaspoon pepper, and remaining 6 thyme sprigs and bring to simmer. Cover, reduce heat to low, and simmer for 20 minutes. Off heat, discard thyme sprigs and Parmesan rind.

3. Using slotted spoon, transfer roasted garlic to broth mixture; reserve garlic oil in small saucepan. Stir ¾ cup bread cubes into broth mixture until thoroughly submerged. Working in batches (and filling blender about halfway for each batch), process soup in blender until very smooth, 1½ to 2 minutes per batch; transfer to large bowl. Return soup to now-empty saucepan and cover to keep warm. (Soup can be refrigerated for up to 2 days.)

4. Line rimmed baking sheet with parchment paper and spray parchment lightly with vegetable oil spray. Toss remaining 4½ cups bread cubes with 3 tablespoons reserved garlic oil, remaining ¼ teaspoon salt, and remaining ¼ teaspoon pepper in large bowl. Add grated Parmesan and toss gently to combine.

5. Arrange bread mixture in single, compact layer on prepared sheet. Bake until croutons are browned and crisp on bottoms and Parmesan has melted and turned golden, 12 to 16 minutes. Let cool for 5 minutes. (Croutons and remaining garlic oil can be stored in separate airtight containers at room temperature for up to 2 days.)

6. Rewarm soup over low heat as needed. Serve, topping individual portions with croutons, reserved garlic oil, and dill.

Peeling Garlic in Bulk

Put garlic cloves in zipper-lock bag and seal tight. Beat bag gently with rolling pin to release peels. Separate garlic from peels to use as needed.

The Power of Softened Onions

Onions have incredible range. The pungent bite of a raw one enlivens everything from a veggie burger to chana masala. Caramelizing (technically, Maillard browning) transforms the bulb's sugars and proteins, while charring takes it to a new level of tarry, bitter complexity.

Cook Until Buttery Soft

There's a lesser-known zone of onion flavor that lives between raw and browned. Cooked until they're buttery soft but pale, onions (red, yellow, and white cultivars) turn gently savory—a subtlety that gets drowned out when onions brown but that gives a simple dish such as Carabaccia unmistakable depth.

Developing Flavor

The cause of this softened flavor development is twofold. First, flavor precursors in the onions concentrate when the bulb's juices evaporate, encouraging more flavor-forming reactions among them. Meanwhile, the onions' sulfur compounds, which start to develop when their cells are damaged during cutting, kick into high gear when they cook, forming loads more flavor. Continuing to simmer the onions in the soup allows these flavors to permeate the dish.

Carabaccia (Tuscan Onion Soup)

Carabaccia (Tuscan Onion Soup)

Serves 4 Total Time 1¼ hours

Why This Recipe Works Carabaccia is a simple, centuries-old Tuscan onion soup made by softening (but not browning) and then simmering loads of red onions in water until the liquid is gently savory-sweet; the soup is served with toasted bread, grated Parmesan, and perhaps a poached egg. For our take, we soften 2 pounds of thin-sliced red onions by first simmering them covered, with a little water, salt, and olive oil, so that the moist heat will encourage them to quickly collapse. Then we briefly cook them uncovered to evaporate the liquid and concentrate their flavor; finally, we simmer them with water, sage, and bay leaf to infuse the broth with the onions' sweet savor. Stirring grated Parmesan into the soup enhances its flavor. While the soup simmers, we broil slices of thick-crusted bread. To serve, place a slice of toast in each bowl, top it with a poached egg, and ladle the soup around the bowl. Carabaccia is traditionally made with water, but feel free to use vegetable broth in step 2. Poach the eggs while the soup simmers.

- 2 pounds red onions, halved and sliced through root end ¼ inch thick
- 5 cups water, divided
- 3 tablespoons extra-virgin olive oil, divided
- ¾ teaspoon table salt, divided
- 2 sprigs fresh sage
- 1 bay leaf
- ½ cup (1 ounce) finely grated Parmesan cheese, plus extra for serving
- 4 (½-inch-thick) slices thick-crusted country bread
- 4 Perfect Poached Eggs (page 451)

1. Bring onions, 1 cup water, 2 tablespoons oil, and ½ teaspoon salt to boil in Dutch oven over high heat. Reduce heat to medium, cover, and cook at rapid simmer, stirring occasionally, until onions have fully softened and collapsed, 18 to 20 minutes. Uncover and continue to cook, stirring occasionally, until liquid evaporates (onions should not brown), 6 to 8 minutes. (Onions can be refrigerated for up to 3 days or frozen for up to 1 month.)

2. Add sage sprigs, bay leaf, remaining 4 cups water, and remaining ¼ teaspoon salt. Bring to boil, adjust heat to gentle simmer, cover, and cook for 30 minutes. Remove sage sprigs and bay leaf. Stir in Parmesan. Season with salt and pepper to taste.

3. Meanwhile, adjust oven rack about 6 inches from broiler element and heat broiler. Place bread on aluminum foil–lined rimmed baking sheet, drizzle with remaining 1 tablespoon oil, and season with salt and pepper. Broil until browned, crisp, and starting to char at edges, 2 to 4 minutes. Flip bread and continue to broil until other sides are starting to char, 2 to 4 minutes longer.

4. Place 1 slice bread in bottom of each individual bowl. Top bread with poached egg. Ladle soup into bowl. Serve, passing extra Parmesan separately.

Zucchini Soup with Dill and Sour Cream

Serves 4 Total Time 50 minutes

Why This Recipe Works This silky, verdant soup makes the most of the bounty of summer zucchini (and the gigantic bunches of dill) at farmers' markets. After slicing most of the zucchini thinly, we sauté it with leeks, which form a savory backbone for the soup, along with garlic and red pepper flakes. Once the vegetables are tender, we add a few handfuls of baby spinach and chopped dill, then puree it until smooth. Sour cream adds richness and tang, and swirling a little extra on top of each serving plus small pieces of marinated zucchini makes it irresistible. This soup is also good served cold: After adding the sour cream, refrigerate the soup until chilled, then adjust the consistency with cold water as needed and season with salt and pepper to taste. You can use an immersion blender to process the soup directly in the pot instead of using a blender.

- 3 tablespoons extra-virgin olive oil, divided, plus extra for serving
- 2½ pounds zucchini (2¼ pounds sliced ¼ inch thick, 4 ounces cut into ¼-inch pieces)
- 1 pound leeks, white and light-green parts only, halved lengthwise, sliced ½ inch thick, and washed thoroughly
- 3 garlic cloves, sliced thin
- 1 teaspoon plus pinch table salt, divided
- ½ teaspoon plus pinch pepper, divided
- ¼ teaspoon red pepper flakes
- 4 cups vegetable broth
- 2 ounces (2 cups) baby spinach
- 3 tablespoons chopped fresh dill, plus extra for serving
- ½ cup sour cream, plus extra for serving

1. Heat 2 tablespoons oil in Dutch oven over medium-high heat until shimmering. Add sliced zucchini, leeks, garlic, 1 teaspoon salt, ½ teaspoon pepper, and pepper flakes and cook, stirring occasionally, until vegetables are softened, about 8 minutes. Stir in broth and bring to simmer. Cover and cook until vegetables are tender, about 15 minutes.

2. Meanwhile, combine ¼-inch zucchini pieces, remaining 1 tablespoon oil, remaining pinch salt, and remaining pinch pepper in bowl.

3. Stir spinach and dill into soup until wilted. Process soup in blender until smooth, about 45 seconds. Return soup to now-empty saucepan. Whisk in sour cream. Season with salt and pepper to taste. Serve, garnishing individual portions with marinated zucchini and extra oil, dill, and sour cream.

Super Greens Soup with Lemon-Tarragon Cream

Serves 4 to 6 Total Time 1½ hours

Why This Recipe Works There's a big dose of healthy, hearty greens in this deceptively delicious, ultrasmooth soup. First, we build a flavorful foundation of sweet caramelized onion and earthy sautéed mushrooms. We then add broth, water, and lots of leafy greens (we like a mix of Swiss chard, kale, arugula, and parsley) and simmer the greens until they're tender before blending them into a smooth soup. To thicken the soup without compromising its bright vegetal flavors, we add arborio rice, which gives the soup a velvety consistency. A quick stir-together lemon-tarragon cream drizzled over each bowl adds a vibrant, elegant finish. You can use an immersion blender to process the soup directly in the pot instead of using a blender.

Lemon-Tarragon Cream

- ¼ cup heavy cream
- 3 tablespoons sour cream
- ½ teaspoon minced fresh tarragon
- ¼ teaspoon grated lemon zest plus ½ teaspoon juice
- ¼ teaspoon table salt

Soup

- 2 tablespoons extra-virgin olive oil
- 1 onion, halved and sliced thin
- 1 teaspoon table salt
- ¾ teaspoon light brown sugar
- 3 ounces white mushrooms, trimmed and sliced thin
- 2 garlic cloves, minced
- Pinch cayenne pepper
- 3 cups water
- 3 cups vegetable broth
- ⅓ cup arborio rice
- 12 ounces Swiss chard, stemmed and chopped
- 9 ounces kale, stemmed and chopped
- ¼ cup fresh parsley leaves
- 2 ounces (2 cups) baby arugula

1. **For the lemon-tarragon cream** Whisk all ingredients together in bowl. Cover and refrigerate until ready to serve.

2. **For the soup** Heat oil in Dutch oven over medium-high heat until shimmering. Add onion, salt, and sugar and cook, stirring occasionally, until onion releases some moisture, about 5 minutes. Reduce heat to low and continue to cook, stirring often and scraping up any browned bits, until onion is deeply browned and slightly sticky, about 30 minutes. (If onion sizzles or scorches, reduce heat. If onion does not brown after 15 to 20 minutes, increase heat.)

3. Stir in mushrooms and cook until they have released their moisture, about 5 minutes. Stir in garlic and cayenne and cook until fragrant, about 30 seconds. Stir in water, broth, and rice, scraping up any browned bits, and bring to simmer. Reduce heat to low, cover, and cook for 15 minutes.

4. Stir in chard, kale, and parsley, 1 handful at a time, until wilted. Return to simmer, cover, and cook until greens are tender, about 10 minutes.

5. Off heat, stir in arugula until wilted. Working in batches, process soup in blender until smooth, about 1 minute. Return soup to now-empty pot and bring to brief simmer over medium-low heat. Season with salt and pepper to taste. (Soup can be refrigerated for up to 3 days.) Drizzle individual portions with lemon-tarragon cream before serving.

Hearty Cabbage Soup

Serves 4 to 6 Total Time 1¼ hours

Why This Recipe Works The combination of assertive aromatics and fresh herbs gives cabbage and potatoes an unexpected star quality in this satisfying vegetable soup. Many cabbage soups rely on smoky bacon or sausage for flavor; this vegetarian version uses smoked hot paprika, which gives the soup more backbone and a hint of smokiness. Caraway seeds bring out the sweetness of the cabbage and evoke a hint of sausage flavor. The Yukon Golds add creaminess and a welcome earthy texture, while carrots provide a touch of balancing sweetness and color. You can substitute smoked paprika and a pinch of cayenne for the smoked hot paprika.

- 2 tablespoons unsalted butter
- 1 onion, chopped fine
- ½ teaspoon table salt
- 2 garlic cloves, minced
- 1 teaspoon caraway seeds
- ½ teaspoon minced fresh thyme or ¼ teaspoon dried
- ½ teaspoon smoked hot paprika
- ¼ cup dry white wine or dry vermouth
- 4 cups vegetable broth
- ½ small head green cabbage, halved, cored, and cut into ¾-inch pieces (2 cups)
- 8 ounces red or Yukon Gold potatoes, unpeeled, cut into ¾-inch pieces
- 2 carrots, peeled and cut into ½-inch pieces
- 1 bay leaf

1. Melt butter in Dutch oven over medium heat. Add onion and salt and cook, stirring occasionally, until softened, 5 to 7 minutes. Stir in garlic, caraway seeds, thyme, and paprika and cook until fragrant, about 30 seconds.

2. Stir in wine, scraping up any browned bits, and simmer until nearly evaporated, about 1 minute. Stir in broth, cabbage, potatoes, carrots, and bay leaf and bring to simmer. Reduce heat to medium-low, cover, and simmer gently until vegetables are tender, about 30 minutes. Discard bay leaf and season with salt and pepper to taste. Serve.

top | *Zucchini Soup with Dill and Sour Cream*

bottom | *Hearty Cabbage Soup*

Spiced Eggplant and Kale Soup

Spiced Eggplant and Kale Soup

VEGAN Serves 4 Total Time 50 minutes

Why This Recipe Works When sautéed until softened and browned, chunks of eggplant are so delicious that you may find it hard to resist tasting a few pieces along the way. It is also a vegetable that absorbs spices easily, and this recipe is not shy on them—witness cumin, coriander, ginger, garlic, and Aleppo pepper. We bloom these spices first in shimmering oil to bring out maximum flavor and aroma, then add hearty kale, a great partner for eggplant. The toppings are not just for eye appeal here: They play a starring role in finishing the dish and bringing it to new heights. Sliced almonds add a pleasant crunch, cilantro lends freshness, and a dollop of Greek yogurt provides an unmistakably rich tang. Finally, an additional sprinkle of Aleppo pepper finishes the soup with a striking pop of rich red color against the milky-white yogurt. To make this recipe vegan, substitute plant-based yogurt for the dairy yogurt.

- 6 tablespoons extra-virgin olive oil, divided
- 1¼ pounds eggplant, cut into ½-inch pieces
- 2 garlic cloves, minced
- 1½ teaspoons ground coriander
- 1½ teaspoons ground cumin
- 1 teaspoon grated fresh ginger
- ¾ teaspoon ground dried Aleppo pepper, divided
- ¼ teaspoon ground cinnamon
- ¼ teaspoon table salt
- ¼ teaspoon pepper
- 3 cups vegetable broth
- 1½ cups water
- 2 ounces (2 cups) baby kale, chopped coarse
- ½ cup plain Greek yogurt
- 2 tablespoons sliced almonds, toasted
- 2 tablespoons minced fresh cilantro

1. Heat ¼ cup oil in Dutch oven over medium-high heat until just smoking. Add eggplant and cook, stirring occasionally, until tender and deeply browned, 6 to 8 minutes; transfer to bowl.

2. Heat remaining 2 tablespoons oil in now-empty pot over medium heat until shimmering. Stir in garlic, coriander, cumin, ginger, ½ teaspoon Aleppo pepper, cinnamon, salt, and pepper and cook until fragrant, about 30 seconds. Stir in broth and water, scraping up any browned bits, and bring to simmer. Reduce heat to medium-low, cover partially, and cook until flavors meld, about 15 minutes.

3. Off heat, stir in kale and eggplant, along with any accumulated juices. Let sit until kale is wilted and warmed through, about 2 minutes. Season with salt and pepper to taste. Dollop individual portions with yogurt and sprinkle with almonds, cilantro, and remaining ¼ teaspoon Aleppo pepper before serving.

Kimchi and Tofu Soup

FAST VEGAN Serves 4 to 6 Total Time 40 minutes

Why This Recipe Works This spicy Korean soup is typically served sizzling-hot tableside in an earthenware bowl. To make it at home, without the traditional earthenware serving vessel, we build the soup in a large saucepan. It gets its protein from tofu and its tang and heat from cabbage kimchi and gochujang, a Korean chile-soybean paste. For supple, tender bites, we use silken tofu and keep the pieces large to start. As the soup cooks, we stir it so the tofu breaks into bite-size pieces. If enoki mushrooms are unavailable, substitute thinly sliced white mushrooms. For a spicier dish, use the larger amount of gochujang. Serve with steamed rice.

- 1 tablespoon vegetable oil
- 6 scallions, white parts sliced thin and green parts cut into 1-inch pieces
- 4 garlic cloves, minced
- 2 teaspoons grated fresh ginger
- 1–3 tablespoons gochujang
- 6 cups vegetable broth
- 28 ounces silken tofu, cut into rough 2-inch pieces
- 1 cup cabbage kimchi, drained and chopped coarse
- 8 ounces daikon radish, trimmed and cut into ½-inch pieces
- 2 tablespoons soy sauce
- 2 ounces enoki mushrooms, trimmed

Heat oil in large saucepan over medium-high heat until shimmering. Add scallion whites, garlic, ginger, and gochujang and cook until fragrant, about 2 minutes. Stir in broth, tofu, kimchi, radish, and soy sauce. Bring to simmer and cook, stirring occasionally, until flavors meld, about 15 minutes. Stir in scallion greens and season with salt and pepper to taste. Top individual portions with mushrooms before serving.

Shiitake, Tofu, and Mustard Greens Soup

VEGAN Serves 4 to 6 Total Time 1¾ hours

Why This Recipe Works Peppery mustard greens and a double dose of shiitake mushrooms (fresh and dried) unite for a light, clean-tasting broth in this nourishing soup. To build an aromatic foundation, the first step is to infuse vegetable broth with generous amounts of ginger and garlic. Then we add dried shiitake mushrooms, fresh shiitake stems, and just enough soy sauce to contribute savory character. Simmering and straining the liquid delivers an aromatic broth, but to add more vibrancy, a splash of rice vinegar does the trick, giving the soup subtle sweetness and tang. Sliced shiitake mushroom caps reinforce the umami-rich flavor of the broth, while a hefty amount of mustard greens brings wonderful wasabi-like backnotes that perk up the soup. In lieu of noodles, we add tofu cubes for protein and some meaty bite. A sprinkle of sliced scallions provides the perfect fresh finish. Drizzle with chili oil to ramp up the spicy flavor, if desired.

- 1 tablespoon vegetable oil
- 1 onion, chopped
- ½ teaspoon table salt
- 1 (4-inch) piece ginger, peeled and sliced thin
- 5 garlic cloves, smashed
- 4 cups vegetable broth
- 4 cups water
- 8 ounces shiitake mushrooms, stemmed and sliced thin, stems reserved
- ½ ounce dried shiitake mushrooms, rinsed
- 2 tablespoons soy sauce
- 14 ounces firm tofu, cut into ½-inch pieces
- 8 ounces mustard greens, stemmed and cut into 2-inch pieces
- 2 tablespoons unseasoned rice vinegar
- 3 scallions, sliced thin
- Chili oil (optional)

1. Heat oil in large saucepan over medium-high heat until shimmering. Add onion and salt and cook, stirring occasionally, until softened and lightly browned, 5 to 7 minutes. Stir in ginger and garlic and cook until lightly browned, about 2 minutes.

2. Stir in broth, water, shiitake stems, dried shiitakes, and soy sauce and bring to boil. Reduce heat to low, cover, and simmer until flavors meld, about 1 hour.

3. Strain broth through fine-mesh strainer set over large bowl, pressing on solids to extract as much liquid as possible; discard solids. Wipe saucepan clean with paper towels and return strained broth to saucepan. (Broth can be refrigerated for up to 3 days. Bring broth to simmer over medium-low heat and adjust consistency with hot water, then continue with recipe.)

4. Stir in sliced shiitakes, tofu, mustard greens, and vinegar and cook until mushrooms and tofu are warmed through and greens are wilted, about 3 minutes. Sprinkle individual portions with scallions and drizzle with chili oil, if using. Serve.

Lemongrass-Coconut Soup with Oyster Mushrooms

FAST VEGAN Serves 4 Total Time 45 minutes

Why This Recipe Works Inspired by the Thai dish tom kha, this soup sounds fancy but is very easy to make. It's really a matter of just tossing the tofu with some fish sauce and then simmering everything in a saucepan in two stages. More fish sauce, tangy lime juice, rich coconut milk, and sugar combine in perfect balance; the soup is also fragrant with lemongrass, ginger, and makrut lime leaves. For a flavor more similar to the Thai version, substitute galangal for the ginger. If you can't find makrut lime leaves, simply omit them. For a heartier meal, serve with steamed jasmine rice.

- 14 ounces extra-firm tofu, cut into ½-inch pieces and patted dry
- ¼ cup vegetarian fish sauce, divided, plus extra for seasoning
- 4 cups vegetable broth
- 2 (14-ounce) cans coconut milk
- 2 lemongrass stalks, trimmed to bottom 6 inches and bruised with back of knife
- 1 (2-inch) piece fresh ginger, sliced ¼ inch thick
- 6 makrut lime leaves, torn in half
- 2 tablespoons sugar, plus extra for seasoning
- 8 ounces oyster mushrooms, trimmed and torn into 1-inch pieces
- 1 Thai chile, sliced thin, plus extra slices for serving
- 3 tablespoons lime juice, plus extra for seasoning and wedges for serving
- ¼ cup fresh cilantro leaves

1. Toss tofu with 1 tablespoon fish sauce; set aside. Bring broth, coconut milk, lemongrass, ginger, makrut lime leaves, sugar, and remaining 3 tablespoons fish sauce to simmer in large saucepan over high heat. Reduce heat to medium-low and simmer for 15 minutes. Using slotted spoon, remove solids from pot and discard.

2. Add tofu, mushrooms, and Thai chile to saucepan and simmer until tofu is warmed through and mushrooms are just tender, about 5 minutes. Stir in lime juice. Season with extra sugar, fish sauce, and lime juice to taste. Serve, topping individual portions with cilantro and passing extra sliced Thai chiles and lime wedges separately.

top | *Shiitake, Tofu, and Mustard Greens Soup*

bottom | *Lemongrass-Coconut Soup with Oyster Mushrooms*

Quick Food Processor Gazpacho

VEGAN Serves 4 to 6 Total Time 30 minutes, plus 4 hours chilling

Why This Recipe Works This cold tomatoey soup is a revelation. Traditional recipes for gazpacho call for chopping the vegetables by hand into tiny pieces—with so much knifework, a tedious job at best. With this recipe, we simply cut the vegetables into chunks and let a food processor do the work of turning them all into just the right size. Then we transfer the vegetables to a bowl and stir in tomato juice, sherry vinegar, and a touch of hot sauce. To give the soup some body, we puree 2 cups of the mixture with one slice of white bread and a quarter cup of oil. Garnish the soup with finely chopped bell pepper and cucumber, if desired, or with a mix of chopped radishes, cucumbers, and avocado. Other garnish possibilities include Classic Croutons (page 178), chopped pitted black olives, and chopped Easy-Peel Hard-Cooked Eggs (page 450).

- 12 ounces vine-ripened tomatoes, quartered
- 1 red bell pepper, stemmed, seeded, and cut into 1-inch pieces
- 1 cucumber, halved lengthwise, seeded, and cut into 1-inch pieces
- 2½ cups tomato juice
- 2½ tablespoons sherry vinegar
- 1 teaspoon hot sauce
- 1 teaspoon table salt
- ½ teaspoon pepper
- 1 slice hearty white sandwich bread, torn into pieces
- ¼ cup extra-virgin olive oil, plus extra for serving
- 1 shallot, minced
- 1 garlic clove, minced

1. Pulse tomatoes in food processor until broken into ¼- to ½-inch pieces, about 12 pulses; transfer to large bowl. Pulse bell pepper and cucumber in now-empty processor until broken down into ¼- to ½-inch pieces, about 8 pulses; add to bowl with tomatoes. Stir tomato juice, vinegar, hot sauce, salt, and pepper into tomato mixture.

2. Process bread and 2 cups tomato mixture in now-empty processor until smooth, about 1 minute. With processor running, slowly drizzle in oil until incorporated. Return pureed tomato mixture to bowl with remaining tomato mixture and stir in shallot and garlic. Cover and refrigerate gazpacho for at least 4 hours or up to 2 days before serving.

Chilled Peach and Cucumber Soup

FAST Serves 4 Total Time 40 minutes

Why This Recipe Works Chilled soups can truly make vegetables shine. This outstanding soup pairs cucumbers and peaches, a twist on classic cucumber soup, in starring roles that complement one another. We first combine a pound of peach and cucumber pieces in a blender along with a scallion and a jalapeño plus ice water, which jump-starts the chilling process and puts this soup within reach on a busy weeknight. Whole-milk yogurt adds welcome creaminess and richness, and a dose of seasoned rice vinegar balances out the sweetness of the peaches and adds bright flavor. While the soup is chilling, we whisk together some reserved jalapeño, peach, and cucumber pieces with more rice vinegar for a punchy and unusual topping. Chopped fresh mint and a drizzle of olive oil are the finishing touches for this elegant summery fruit and vegetable soup. You can use an immersion blender to process the soup in a deep bowl instead of using a blender. Serve with goat cheese–topped toasted baguette slices, if desired.

- 1½ pounds yellow peaches, halved and pitted (1 pound cut into 2-inch pieces, remainder cut into ¾-inch pieces)
- 1½ pounds cucumbers, peeled and seeded (1 pound cut into 2-inch pieces, remainder cut into ¾-inch pieces)
- 2 cups ice water, divided
- 1 scallion, chopped
- 2 jalapeño chiles, stemmed, halved, and seeded (1 chopped coarse, 1 chopped fine)
- 1½ teaspoons table salt
- 1 teaspoon sugar
- 1 cup plain whole-milk yogurt
- 3 tablespoons seasoned rice vinegar, divided
- ¼ teaspoon pepper
- 1 tablespoon minced fresh mint, plus shredded mint for serving
- Extra-virgin olive oil

1. Process 2-inch pieces of peach and cucumber, 1 cup ice water, scallion, coarsely chopped jalapeño, salt, and sugar in blender until completely smooth, about 2 minutes. Strain soup through fine-mesh strainer into large bowl, using back of ladle or silicone spatula to press soup through. Whisk in yogurt, 2 tablespoons vinegar, pepper, and remaining 1 cup ice water. Cover and refrigerate to meld flavors, at least 20 minutes or up to 12 hours.

2. Meanwhile, combine ¾-inch pieces of peach and cucumber, finely chopped jalapeño, and remaining 1 tablespoon vinegar in bowl.

3. Stir mint into soup and season with salt and pepper to taste. Serve cold, topping individual portions with peach-cucumber salad and shredded mint and drizzling with oil.

Wild Rice and Mushroom Soup

Serves 6 to 8 Total Time 2¼ hours

Why This Recipe Works Mushrooms and wild rice really complement each other, and here they make a fantastic combo in a creamy soup bursting with umami. This recipe is a testament to building a savory base without relying on meat. Tomato paste, soy sauce, dry sherry, and garlic all amplify the mushrooms' distinctive taste and help deliver a rich, earthy flavor to the soup overall. Cooking the cremini and onion with tomato paste over high heat develops a delicious fond (that we deglaze with sherry), and dried shiitakes deliver more flavor. We cook the wild rice separately in the oven, adding a pinch of baking soda to help it tenderize faster, and reserve the earthy rice cooking liquid to add extra flavor to the soup. We like to use cremini mushrooms here, but you can substitute white mushrooms, if desired.

- 4¼ cups water, divided, plus extra as needed
- 1 sprig fresh thyme
- 1 bay leaf
- 5 garlic cloves, peeled (1 whole, 4 minced)
- 1½ teaspoons table salt, divided
- ¼ teaspoon baking soda
- 1 cup wild rice, rinsed
- 4 tablespoons unsalted butter
- 1 pound cremini mushrooms, trimmed and sliced ¼ inch thick
- 1 onion, chopped fine
- 1 teaspoon tomato paste
- 1 teaspoon pepper
- ⅔ cup dry sherry
- 4 cups vegetable broth
- 1 tablespoon soy sauce
- ¼ ounce dried shiitake mushrooms, finely ground using spice grinder
- ¼ cup cornstarch
- ½ cup heavy cream
- ¼ cup minced fresh chives
- ¼ teaspoon grated lemon zest

1. Adjust oven rack to middle position and heat oven to 375 degrees. Bring 4 cups water, thyme sprig, bay leaf, whole garlic clove, ¾ teaspoon salt, and baking soda to boil in medium saucepan over high heat. Add rice and return to boil. Cover saucepan, transfer to oven, and bake until rice is tender, 35 to 50 minutes. Drain rice in fine-mesh strainer set in 4-cup liquid measuring cup, discarding thyme sprig, bay leaf, and garlic. Add enough water to reserved cooking liquid to measure 3 cups.

2. Melt butter in Dutch oven over high heat. Add cremini, onion, tomato paste, pepper, minced garlic, and remaining ¾ teaspoon salt and cook, stirring occasionally, until vegetables are browned and dark fond develops on bottom of pot, about 15 minutes.

3. Stir in sherry, scraping up any browned bits, and cook until nearly evaporated, about 2 minutes. Stir in broth, soy sauce, shiitakes, and reserved rice cooking liquid and bring to boil. Reduce heat to low, cover, and simmer until onion and mushrooms are tender, about 20 minutes.

4. Whisk cornstarch and remaining ¼ cup water together in bowl. Stir cornstarch slurry into soup and simmer until thickened, about 2 minutes. Off heat, stir in rice, cream, chives, and lemon zest. Cover and let sit for 20 minutes. Season with salt and pepper to taste. Serve.

Chilled Peach and Cucumber Soup

Creamy White Bean Soup with Herb Oil and Crispy Capers

Creamy White Bean Soup with Herb Oil and Crispy Capers

FAST Serves 4 to 6 Total Time 40 minutes

Why This Recipe Works There is no question that bean soups are filling, but they can also be surprisingly sophisticated. For a creamy, smooth, and quick soup, we start by briefly simmering canned great northern beans and their seasoned canning liquid with softened aromatic vegetables and herbs. Heating the beans causes their starches to hydrate, which makes the soup especially creamy (without adding any cream). Blending the beans with a small amount of liquid helps their skins break down so that the puree is completely smooth. To give the soup extra richness, we enhance it with Parmesan and butter. And for an impressive topping also bursting with flavor, herb oil and crispy capers complement the neutral soup base with vibrant color, flavor, and texture. (For an alternative garnish duo, drizzle each portion of soup with 1 teaspoon extra-virgin olive oil and sprinkle with Pickled Celery [page 179].) Use a conventional blender here; an immersion blender will not produce as smooth a soup.

Herb Oil and Crispy Capers

- ⅓ cup extra-virgin olive oil
- ¼ cup capers, rinsed and patted dry
- 2 tablespoons minced fresh parsley
- 1 tablespoon chopped fresh basil

Soup

- 2 tablespoons extra-virgin olive oil
- ½ cup chopped onion
- 1 small celery rib, chopped fine
- 3 sprigs fresh thyme
- 2 garlic cloves, sliced
- Pinch cayenne pepper
- 2 (15-ounce) cans great northern beans, undrained
- 2 tablespoons grated Parmesan cheese
- 2 cups vegetable broth, divided
- 2 tablespoons unsalted butter
- ½ teaspoon lemon juice, plus extra for seasoning

1. **For the herb oil and crispy capers** Combine oil and capers in medium bowl (capers should be mostly submerged). Microwave until capers are darkened in color and have shrunk, about 5 minutes, stirring halfway through microwaving. Using slotted spoon, transfer capers to paper towel–lined plate (they will continue to crisp as they cool); set aside. Reserve caper oil.

2. **For the soup** Heat oil in large saucepan over medium heat until shimmering Add onion and celery and cook, stirring frequently, until softened but not browned, 6 to 8 minutes. Add thyme sprigs, garlic, and cayenne and cook, stirring constantly, until fragrant, about 1 minute. Add beans and their liquid and stir to combine. Reduce heat to medium-low, cover, and cook, stirring occasionally, until beans are heated through and just starting to break down, 6 to 8 minutes. Off heat, discard thyme sprigs.

3. Process bean mixture and Parmesan in blender on low speed until thick, smooth puree forms, about 2 minutes. With blender running, add 1 cup broth and butter. Increase speed to high and continue to process until butter is incorporated and mixture is pourable, about 1 minute.

4. Return soup to now-empty saucepan and whisk in remaining 1 cup broth. Cover and bring to simmer over medium heat, adjusting consistency with up to 1 cup hot water as needed. Off heat, stir in lemon juice. Season with salt and extra lemon juice to taste.

5. Stir parsley and basil into reserved caper oil. Drizzle each portion of soup with herb oil, sprinkle with capers, and serve.

Red Lentil Soup with Warm Spices

VEGAN Serves 4 to 6 Total Time 50 minutes

Why This Recipe Works Green or brown lentils are the more conventional choice when making lentil soup, but this recipe uses colorful, quick-cooking red lentils, which we whisk into a creamy, thick puree after cooking. To begin, we bloom a spice mix of coriander, cumin, ginger, cinnamon, black pepper, and cayenne in the pan after sautéing an onion; this brings a warm complexity to the soup. Tomato paste and garlic complete the base before we add the lentils and a mix of vegetable broth and water to give the soup a full, rounded character. After only 15 minutes of cooking, the lentils are soft enough to puree using just a whisk. A generous dose of lemon juice brings all the flavors into focus, and a drizzle of spice-infused oil and a sprinkle of fresh cilantro complete the transformation of commonplace ingredients into a richly flavored and wholly comforting soup. Dried mint is widely used in Middle Eastern cooking; do not substitute fresh mint, as the flavor will be quite different.

¼ cup extra-virgin olive oil, divided
1 large onion, chopped fine
½ teaspoon table salt
¾ teaspoon ground coriander
½ teaspoon ground cumin
¼ teaspoon ground ginger
¼ teaspoon pepper
⅛ teaspoon ground cinnamon
Pinch cayenne pepper
1 tablespoon tomato paste
1 garlic clove, minced
4 cups vegetable broth, plus extra as needed
2 cups water
10½ ounces (1½ cups) red lentils, picked over and rinsed
2 tablespoons lemon juice
1½ teaspoons dried mint, crumbled
1 teaspoon paprika
¼ cup chopped fresh cilantro

1. Heat 2 tablespoons oil in large saucepan over medium heat until shimmering. Add onion and salt and cook, stirring occasionally, until softened, about 5 minutes. Stir in coriander, cumin, ginger, pepper, cinnamon, and cayenne and cook until fragrant, about 2 minutes. Stir in tomato paste and garlic and cook for 1 minute.

2. Stir in broth, water, and lentils and bring to vigorous simmer. Cook, stirring occasionally, until lentils are soft and about half are broken down, about 15 minutes.

3. Whisk soup vigorously until broken down to coarse puree, about 30 seconds. Adjust consistency with extra hot broth as needed. Stir in lemon juice and season with salt to taste. Cover and keep warm.

4. Heat remaining 2 tablespoons oil in 8-inch skillet over medium heat until shimmering. Off heat, stir in mint and paprika. (Soup can be refrigerated for up to 3 days. Thin soup with water, if desired, when reheating.) Serve soup, drizzling individual portions with 1 teaspoon spiced oil and sprinkling with cilantro.

Lentil and Escarole Soup

VEGAN Serves 4 to 6 Total Time 1¾ hours

Why This Recipe Works This main-course-worthy dish is inspired by the aromatic soups of Umbria, in which lentils often play a starring role. We start by browning our aromatics before stirring in broth, which gives us a deeply savory liquid in which to cook the lentils. We opted for Umbrian lentils or lentilles du Puy, as these varieties hold their shape well during cooking. Supporting ingredients in lentil soup vary throughout Umbria, but we particularly like escarole; adding it toward the end of cooking helps the vegetable hold on to its bite and nutty taste. A rind of Parmesan adds a complex note to the soup as it simmers.

¼ cup extra-virgin olive oil, plus extra for drizzling
1 onion, chopped fine
1 carrot, peeled and chopped fine
1 celery rib, chopped fine
½ teaspoon table salt
6 garlic cloves, sliced thin
2 tablespoons minced fresh parsley
4 cups vegetable broth, plus extra as needed
3 cups water
8 ounces (1¼ cups) Umbrian lentils or lentilles du Puy, picked over and rinsed
1 (14.5-ounce) can diced tomatoes
1 Parmesan cheese rind (optional), plus grated Parmesan for serving
2 bay leaves
½ head escarole (8 ounces), trimmed and cut into ½-inch pieces

1. Heat oil in Dutch oven over medium heat until shimmering. Add onion, carrot, celery, and salt and cook, stirring occasionally, until softened and lightly browned, 8 to 10 minutes. Stir in garlic and parsley and cook until fragrant, about 30 seconds. Stir in broth; water; lentils; tomatoes and their juice; Parmesan rind, if using; and bay leaves and bring to simmer. Reduce heat to medium-low, partially cover, and simmer until lentils are tender, 1 to 1¼ hours.

2. Discard Parmesan rind, if using, and bay leaves. Stir in escarole, 1 handful at a time, and cook until wilted, about 5 minutes. Adjust consistency with extra hot broth as needed. Season with salt and pepper to taste. Drizzle individual portions with extra oil and serve, passing grated Parmesan separately.

Classic Minestrone

Serves 6 to 8   Total Time 1¾ hours

Why This Recipe Works The word "minestrone" translates as "big soup." A great minestrone draws out the flavors of a wide variety of vegetables and captures them all in a bowl. To develop a vegetarian minestrone recipe with a harmonious balance of flavors, we found it best to eliminate both bold and bland vegetables. We keep the standard aromatic vegetables used in most Italian soups—leeks, onions, carrots, and celery—and add zucchini, potatoes, spinach, and tomatoes. The rind from a wedge of Parmesan adds complexity and depth to a soup like this, made with water instead of broth. Creamy canned cannellini beans contribute to the soup's heartiness, while a dollop of pesto adds another delicious layer of flavor. We prefer to use homemade pesto, but you can use store-bought.

- 1 large leek, white and light green parts only, sliced thin crosswise and washed thoroughly
- 2 carrots, peeled and chopped fine
- 2 small onions, chopped fine
- 2 celery ribs, chopped fine
- 1 medium russet potato, peeled and chopped (about 1¼ cups)
- 1 zucchini, trimmed and chopped
- 3 cups spinach leaves, stemmed and cut into thin strips
- 1 (28-ounce) can whole peeled tomatoes, drained and chopped
- 8 cups water
- 1 Parmesan cheese rind (optional)
- 1 teaspoon table salt
- 1 can (15 ounces) cannellini beans, drained and rinsed
- ¼ cup Pesto alla Genovese (Basil Pesto) (page 268)

1. Bring leek; carrots; onions; celery; potato; zucchini; spinach; tomatoes; water; Parmesan rind, if using; and salt to boil in Dutch oven. Reduce heat to medium-low; simmer, stirring occasionally, until vegetables are tender but still hold their shape, about 1 hour. (Soup can be refrigerated for up to 3 days or frozen for up to 1 month.)

2. Add beans and cook just until heated through, about 5 minutes. Off heat, discard Parmesan rind, if using. Stir in pesto. Season with salt and pepper to taste. Serve.

top | *Red Lentil Soup with Warm Spices*

bottom | *Lentil and Escarole Soup*

| *Ribollita*

Ribollita

VEGAN Serves 8 to 10 Total Time 1¾ hours, plus 8 hours soaking

Why This Recipe Works Despite its humble origins, ribollita is arguably the best-known Tuscan soup: Meaning "reboiled" in Italian, this hearty soup was traditionally made by peasants using leftover vegetable soup reheated with leftover bread (sometimes multiple times), creating a mixture that many recipes say should be thick enough to eat with a fork. Here we use Marcella beans, named after Italian chef Marcella Hazan, which are grown in California from Italian seed. These thin-skinned heirloom cannellini have an incredibly creamy texture. While the beans cook on the stovetop, we toast fresh (or stale, if you have it) bread so it will not completely break down when we add it to the hot soup. Lacinato kale and the classic trio of onion, celery, and carrots, browned in fruity extra-virgin olive oil, give deep flavor. A restrained amount of canned tomatoes adds acidity and color, and fresh herbs and a finishing splash of lemon juice bring a bright herbaceous note to balance the earthy flavors. Lacinato kale (also known as Tuscan kale or cavolo nero) is traditional in this recipe, but you can substitute curly kale. You can use dried cannellini beans in place of the Marcella beans.

- 1½ tablespoons table salt for soaking
- 1 pound (2½ cups) dried Marcella beans, picked over and rinsed
- 3 tablespoons extra-virgin olive oil, plus extra for drizzling
- 1 large onion, chopped fine
- 2 carrots, peeled and chopped
- 2 celery ribs, chopped
- 4 garlic cloves, minced
- 4 cups vegetable broth
- 2 bay leaves
- 8 ounces rustic Italian bread, cut into 1-inch pieces
- 1 pound lacinato kale, stemmed and cut into 1-inch pieces
- 1 (14.5-ounce) can whole peeled tomatoes, drained with juice reserved, chopped
- 1½ teaspoons table salt
- 1 teaspoon minced fresh rosemary or ¼ teaspoon dried
- 1 teaspoon minced fresh thyme or ¼ teaspoon dried
- 1 teaspoon pepper
- 4 teaspoons lemon juice

1. Dissolve 1½ tablespoons table salt in 2 quarts cold water in large container. Add beans and soak at room temperature for at least 8 hours or up to 24 hours. Drain and rinse well. (If pressed for time, quick-soak beans: Combine beans with 1½ tablespoons salt in 2 quarts cold water in large Dutch oven and bring to boil. Remove from heat, cover, and let sit for 1 hour. Drain and rinse well.)

2. Adjust oven rack to middle position and heat oven to 250 degrees. Heat oil in large Dutch oven over medium heat until shimmering. Add onion, carrots, and celery and cook, stirring frequently, until onion is browned, 10 to 12 minutes. Stir in garlic and cook until fragrant, about 30 seconds.

3. Stir in soaked beans, broth, 4 cups water, and bay leaves and bring to simmer. Reduce heat to low, cover, and simmer until beans are tender, 25 to 35 minutes.

4. While beans cook, arrange bread in single layer on rimmed baking sheet and bake until bread is dry and crisp, about 30 minutes. Set aside.

5. Stir kale, tomatoes and reserved juice, salt, rosemary, thyme, and pepper into soup. Increase heat to high and return soup to simmer, then reduce heat to low, cover, and cook until kale is tender, about 15 minutes.

6. Off heat, discard bay leaves and stir in bread and lemon juice. Cover and let sit for 15 minutes. Whisk soup vigorously until bread is broken down, about 2 minutes. Serve, drizzling individual servings with extra oil and seasoning with pepper to taste.

Butternut Squash and White Bean Soup with Sage Pesto

Serves 6 to 8 Total Time 1¼ hours

Why This Recipe Works While we love creamy, pureed butternut squash soups, we also like the idea of enlisting the vegetable to make a heartier textured soup. This soup features chunks of squash paired with creamy cannellini beans in an aromatic broth. Adding butter to the broth at the start of its simmering time allows it to fully emulsify, giving the soup base richness and a more velvety texture. We treat the squash like two different vegetables: The bulb portion is difficult to cut into cubes that will cook evenly, and naturally cooks faster than the dense neck portion, so we cut the bulb into wedges and cook them in the broth until soft, then mash them to make a "squash stock" that gives the soup base body and flavor. We then cook chunks of the neck portion in this stock. A swirl of sage pesto, made quickly in the food processor, lends a bright, fresh finish. Be sure to remove the fibrous white flesh below the squash's skin.

Pesto

- ½ cup walnuts, toasted
- 2 garlic cloves, minced
- 1 cup fresh parsley leaves
- ½ cup fresh sage leaves
- ¾ cup extra-virgin olive oil
- 1 ounce Parmesan cheese, grated (½ cup), plus extra for serving

Soup

- 1 (2- to 2½-pound) butternut squash, peeled
- 4 cups vegetable broth
- 3 cups water
- 4 tablespoons unsalted butter
- 1 tablespoon soy sauce
- 1 tablespoon vegetable oil
- 1 pound leeks, white and light green parts only, halved lengthwise, sliced thin, and washed thoroughly
- 1 tablespoon tomato paste
- 2 garlic cloves, minced
- ¾ teaspoon table salt
- ¼ teaspoon pepper
- 3 (15-ounce) cans cannellini beans, undrained
- 1 teaspoon white wine vinegar

1. **For the pesto** Pulse walnuts and garlic in food processor until coarsely chopped, about 5 pulses. Add parsley and sage. With processor running, slowly add oil until incorporated. Transfer to bowl, stir in Parmesan, and season with salt and pepper to taste; set aside.

2. **For the soup** Cut round bulb section off squash and cut in half lengthwise. Discard seeds, then cut each half into 4 wedges.

3. Bring squash wedges, broth, water, butter, and soy sauce to boil in medium saucepan over high heat. Reduce heat to medium, partially cover, and simmer vigorously until squash is very tender and starting to fall apart, about 20 minutes. Off heat, use potato masher to mash squash, still in broth, until completely broken down. Cover to keep warm; set aside.

4. While broth cooks, cut neck of squash into ½-inch pieces. Heat oil in Dutch oven over medium heat until shimmering. Add leeks and tomato paste and cook, stirring occasionally, until leeks are softened and tomato paste is darkened, about 5 minutes. Add garlic and cook until fragrant, about 30 seconds. Add squash pieces, salt, and pepper and cook, stirring occasionally, for 5 minutes. Add squash broth and bring to simmer. Partially cover and cook for 10 minutes.

5. Add beans and their liquid, partially cover, and cook, stirring occasionally, until squash is just tender, 15 to 20 minutes. Stir in vinegar and season with salt and pepper to taste. Serve, passing pesto and extra Parmesan separately.

Acquacotta (Tuscan White Bean and Escarole Soup)

Serves 8 to 10   Total Time 1½ hours

Why This Recipe Works Our version of acquacotta, one of Italy's traditional vegetable soups, features creamy cannellini beans, tender fennel, and faintly bitter escarole. Though acquacotta translates to "cooked water," we use vegetable broth and amp up the flavor with a soffritto, a mixture of sautéed onion, celery, and garlic. A food processor makes quick work of finely chopping these ingredients as well as the canned tomatoes that flavor the broth. Aromatic parsley, oregano, and fennel fronds give our soup its distinctive taste. Finally, we thicken the broth with a mixture of the canned bean liquid and egg yolks and ladle the finished soup over toasted bread, turning a humble vegetable soup into a hearty, one-bowl meal. If escarole is unavailable, you can substitute 8 ounces of kale. If your Parmesan cheese has a rind, slice it off the wedge and add it to the pot with the broth in step 3 (remove it before serving). The traditional way to serve this is spooning a poached or soft-cooked egg on top of the toast before the broth is ladled into the bowl.

Soup

- 1 large onion, chopped coarse
- 2 celery ribs, chopped coarse
- 4 garlic cloves, peeled
- 1 (28-ounce) can whole peeled tomatoes
- ½ cup extra-virgin olive oil
- ¾ teaspoon table salt
- ⅛ teaspoon red pepper flakes
- 8 cups vegetable broth
- 1 fennel bulb, 2 tablespoons fronds minced, stalks discarded, bulb halved, cored, and cut into ½-inch pieces
- 2 (15-ounce) cans cannellini beans, drained with liquid reserved, rinsed
- 1 small head escarole (10 ounces), trimmed and cut into ½-inch pieces (8 cups)
- 2 large egg yolks
- ½ cup chopped fresh parsley
- 1 tablespoon minced fresh oregano
- Grated Parmesan cheese
- Lemon wedges

Toast

- 10 (½-inch-thick) slices thick-crusted country bread
- ¼ cup extra-virgin olive oil

1. For the soup Pulse onion, celery, and garlic in food processor until very finely chopped, 15 to 20 pulses, scraping down sides of bowl as needed. Transfer onion mixture to Dutch oven. Add tomatoes and their juice to now-empty processor and pulse until tomatoes are finely chopped, 10 to 12 pulses; set aside.

2. Stir oil, salt, and pepper flakes into onion mixture. Cook over medium-high heat, stirring occasionally, until light brown fond begins to form on bottom of pot, 12 to 15 minutes. Stir in tomatoes, increase heat to high, and cook, stirring frequently, until mixture is very thick and silicone spatula leaves distinct trail when dragged across bottom of pot, 9 to 12 minutes.

3. Add broth and fennel bulb and bring to simmer. Reduce heat to medium-low and simmer until fennel begins to soften, 5 to 7 minutes. Stir in beans and escarole and cook until fennel is fully tender, about 10 minutes.

4. Whisk egg yolks and reserved bean liquid together in bowl, then stir into soup. Stir in parsley, oregano, and fennel fronds. Season with salt and pepper to taste.

5. For the toast Meanwhile, adjust oven rack about 5 inches from broiler element and heat broiler. Place bread on aluminum foil–lined rimmed baking sheet, drizzle with oil, and season with salt and pepper. Broil until bread is deep golden brown.

6. Place 1 slice bread in bottom of each individual bowl. Ladle soup over toasted bread. Serve, passing Parmesan and lemon wedges separately.

Acquacotta (Tuscan White Bean and Escarole Soup)

top | *Tanabour (Armenian Yogurt and Barley Soup)*
bottom | *Turkish Bulgur and Lentil Soup*

Tanabour (Armenian Yogurt and Barley Soup)

Serves 6 Total Time: 1¾ hours

Why This Recipe Works Tanabour is a nourishing, filling, and thoroughly satisfying Armenian grain-and-yogurt soup. Though tanabour can be made using a wide variety of grains, ours uses pearl (hull-less) barley, which cooks to a tender, plump consistency without breaking down entirely. Greek yogurt gives the soup its requisite thickness and dairy richness without leaving it overly tart. An egg yolk adds further richness and a silky consistency. Finally, we garnish the soup with cilantro and Aleppo pepper–infused melted butter. Dried mint is widely used in Middle Eastern cooking; do not substitute fresh mint, as its flavor is quite different. We prefer the richness of whole-milk Greek yogurt here, but low-fat can be used; avoid nonfat. If Aleppo pepper is unavailable, substitute 1 teaspoon of paprika and a pinch of cayenne pepper. Fresh parsley can be substituted for the cilantro.

- 4 tablespoons unsalted butter, divided
- 1 onion, chopped fine
- 1 teaspoon dried mint
- 1 teaspoon table salt
- ½ teaspoon pepper
- Pinch baking soda
- ¾ cup pearl barley
- 4 cups vegetable broth
- 2 cups water
- 1½ cups plain Greek yogurt
- 1 large egg yolk
- ¼ cup chopped fresh cilantro, divided
- 1 teaspoon ground dried Aleppo pepper

1. Melt 2 tablespoons butter in large saucepan over medium heat. Add onion, mint, salt, pepper, and baking soda. Cook, stirring occasionally, until onion has broken down into soft paste and is just starting to stick to pan, 6 to 8 minutes.

2. Stir in barley. Cook, stirring frequently, until grains are translucent around edges, about 3 minutes. Add broth and water. Increase heat to high and bring to boil. Adjust heat to maintain gentle simmer, partially cover, and cook until barley is very tender, 50 minutes to 1 hour, stirring occasionally. Meanwhile, whisk yogurt and egg yolk together in large bowl.

3. Off heat, gradually add 2 cups barley mixture to yogurt mixture, whisking vigorously. Stirring constantly, return yogurt-barley mixture to saucepan. Cover and let sit for 10 minutes to thicken.

4. Heat soup over medium heat, stirring occasionally, until temperature registers between 180 and 185 degrees (do not allow soup to boil or yogurt will curdle). Remove from heat. Soup should have consistency of buttermilk; if thicker, adjust by adding hot water, 2 tablespoons at a time. Stir in 2 tablespoons cilantro and season with salt to taste.

5. Melt remaining 2 tablespoons butter in 8-inch skillet over medium-high heat. Off heat, stir in Aleppo pepper. Ladle soup into bowls, drizzle each portion with 1 teaspoon spiced butter, sprinkle with remaining 2 tablespoons cilantro, and serve. (Soup can be refrigerated for up to 3 days; reheat gently, being careful not to allow temperature to exceed 180 degrees. If necessary, thin by adding water, 2 tablespoons at a time.)

Turkish Bulgur and Lentil Soup

FAST **VEGAN** Serves 4 Total Time 45 minutes

Why This Recipe Works This very simple bulgur and lentil soup tastes truly impressive without requiring a lengthy ingredient list. The combination of bulgur and quick-cooking red lentils needs only a few ingredients to make it reminiscent of more complex Turkish soups, mainly paprika, Aleppo pepper, and mint. The result is a soup that is heady with warm spices and brimming with fiber-rich bulgur and lentils, making it satisfying enough for a weeknight dinner. First, we cook onion along with tomato paste and enhance this combo with paprika and Aleppo pepper. Tomato paste, when sautéed with aromatics, often gives meatless dishes a full and rounded flavor that they would otherwise miss; here it helps form a strong backbone for the soup. Then we add the lentils and bulgur and toast them in the pan (which brings out their nutty aroma), then the broth and water so all the elements have time to mingle. A shower of fresh mint and a dollop of yogurt offer a cooling contrast to the soup, while lemon wedges bring a burst of brightness. When shopping, don't confuse bulgur with cracked wheat, which has a much longer cooking time and will not work in this recipe. To make this recipe vegan, substitute plant-based Greek yogurt for the dairy Greek yogurt.

- 2 tablespoons extra-virgin olive oil, plus extra for drizzling
- 1 small onion, chopped fine
- 4 teaspoons paprika
- 1 tablespoon tomato paste
- 1 teaspoon ground dried Aleppo pepper
- 1 cup dried red lentils, picked over and rinsed
- ½ cup medium-grind bulgur, rinsed
- 5 cups vegetable broth
- 2½ cups water
- ¼ cup torn fresh mint
- Greek yogurt
- Lemon wedges

1. Heat oil in large saucepan over medium-high heat until shimmering. Add onion and cook, stirring occasionally, until softened and beginning to brown, 5 to 7 minutes. Stir in paprika, tomato paste, and Aleppo pepper and cook until fragrant, about 30 seconds.

2. Stir in lentils and bulgur and toast, stirring constantly, for 1 minute. Add broth and water and bring to boil. Reduce heat to medium-low, partially cover, and cook until lentils are broken down and bulgur is tender, 20 to 25 minutes.

3. Sprinkle individual portions with mint and drizzle with extra oil. Serve with yogurt and lemon wedges.

Tomato, Bulgur, and Red Pepper Soup

VEGAN Serves 6 to 8 Total Time 1 hour

Why This Recipe Works Inspired by Turkish red pepper soups, this one relies mostly on pantry ingredients, but the result is a great soup with layers of flavor. Many soups hailing from the region are enriched with good-for-you grains and legumes that fill you up—and here, bulgur fits the bill. To start, we soften red bell peppers and onion before creating a solid flavor backbone with garlic, tomato paste, white wine, dried mint, smoked paprika, and red pepper flakes. Canned fire-roasted tomatoes add additional smokiness and umami. The bulgur absorbs the surrounding flavors and gives off some of its starch, creating a silky texture. A sprinkle of fresh mint gives the soup a final punch of flavor. (Do not substitute fresh mint for the dried mint in the soup.) When shopping, don't confuse bulgur with cracked wheat, which has a much longer cooking time and will not work in this recipe.

- 2 tablespoons extra-virgin olive oil
- 2 red bell peppers, stemmed, seeded, and chopped
- 1 onion, chopped
- ¾ teaspoon table salt
- ¼ teaspoon pepper
- 3 garlic cloves, minced
- 1 teaspoon dried mint, crumbled
- ½ teaspoon smoked paprika
- ⅛ teaspoon red pepper flakes
- 1 tablespoon tomato paste
- ½ cup dry white wine
- 1 (28-ounce) can diced fire-roasted tomatoes
- 4 cups vegetable broth
- 2 cups water
- ¾ cup medium-grind bulgur, rinsed
- ⅓ cup chopped fresh mint

1. Heat oil in Dutch oven over medium heat until shimmering. Add bell peppers, onion, salt, and pepper and cook, stirring occasionally, until vegetables are softened and lightly browned, 6 to 8 minutes. Stir in garlic, dried mint, paprika, and pepper flakes and cook until fragrant, about 30 seconds. Stir in tomato paste and cook for 1 minute.

2. Stir in wine, scraping up any browned bits, and simmer until reduced by half, about 1 minute. Add tomatoes and their juice and cook, stirring occasionally, until tomatoes soften and begin to break apart, about 10 minutes.

3. Stir in broth, water, and bulgur and bring to simmer. Reduce heat to low, cover, and simmer gently until bulgur is tender, about 20 minutes. Season with salt and pepper to taste. Serve, sprinkling individual bowls with fresh mint.

Harira (Moroccan Lentil and Chickpea Soup)

VEGAN Serves 6 to 8 Total Time 1¼ hours

Why This Recipe Works A popular Moroccan lentil soup, harira features a hearty mix of legumes and tomatoes flavored with warm spices and fresh herbs. We use the traditional spices: coriander, paprika, cumin, cinnamon, and red pepper flakes. Like countless other regional dishes, harira's exact ingredients vary from region to region and often include lamb or chicken. For our vegetarian version, canned chickpeas work well and keep things easy. Fresh greens are a mainstay of harira, and we stir in a generous amount of earthy-sweet Swiss chard at the end of cooking. Finishing the dish with fresh lemon juice helps focus all the flavors. This wonderfully complex, spice-filled soup brings humble lentils to a whole other level. We like to garnish this soup with a small amount of harissa, a fiery North African chili paste, which you can make yourself (page 400) or use store-bought.

- ⅓ cup extra-virgin olive oil
- 1 large onion, chopped fine
- 2 celery ribs, chopped fine
- 5 garlic cloves, minced
- 1 tablespoon grated fresh ginger
- 2 teaspoons ground coriander
- 2 teaspoons smoked paprika
- 1 teaspoon ground cumin
- ½ teaspoon ground cinnamon
- ⅛ teaspoon red pepper flakes
- ¾ cup minced fresh cilantro, divided
- ½ cup minced fresh parsley, divided
- 8 cups vegetable broth
- 1 (15-ounce) can chickpeas, rinsed
- 1 cup brown lentils, picked over and rinsed
- 1 (28-ounce) can crushed tomatoes
- ½ cup orzo
- 4 ounces Swiss chard, stemmed and cut into ½-inch pieces
- 2 tablespoons lemon juice, plus wedges for serving

1. Heat oil in large Dutch oven over medium-high heat until shimmering. Add onion and celery and cook, stirring frequently, until translucent and starting to brown, 7 to 8 minutes. Reduce heat to medium, add garlic and ginger, and cook until fragrant, 1 minute. Stir in coriander, paprika, cumin, cinnamon, and pepper flakes and cook for 1 minute. Stir in ½ cup cilantro and ¼ cup parsley and cook for 1 minute.

2. Stir in broth, chickpeas, and lentils; increase heat to high and bring to simmer. Reduce heat to medium-low, partially cover, and gently simmer until lentils are just tender, about 20 minutes.

3. Stir in tomatoes and pasta, partially cover, and simmer for 7 minutes, stirring occasionally. Stir in chard and continue to cook, partially covered, until pasta is tender, about 5 minutes longer. Off heat, stir in lemon juice, emaining ¼ cup cilantro, and remaining ¼ cup parsley. Season with salt and pepper to taste. Serve, passing lemon wedges separately.

Chickpea Noodle Soup

FAST **VEGAN** Serves 4 to 6 Total Time 45 minutes

Why This Recipe Works This meatless take on chicken noodle soup is easy to make with pantry ingredients. To replace the chicken, hearty, creamy chickpeas work perfectly (and the fun phonetic similarity wasn't lost on us). To capture the underlying "meatiness" in traditional soups, umami-packed nutritional yeast provides instant savoriness far better than other options like miso paste. This seasoning is like savory magic dust; it turns our soup from ordinary to extraordinary. Simmering the chickpeas, sautéed aromatics, and broth together before adding the noodles fully develops the soup's flavor while also softening the chickpeas. In place of traditional egg noodles, small ditalini pasta is a spoon-friendly choice. Lastly, fresh parsley adds an herbaceous accent.

- 2 tablespoons vegetable oil
- 1 onion, chopped fine
- 3 carrots, peeled and sliced ¼ inch thick
- 2 celery ribs, sliced ¼ inch thick
- ¼ teaspoon pepper
- 3 tablespoons nutritional yeast
- 2 teaspoons minced fresh thyme or ¾ teaspoon dried
- 2 bay leaves
- 6 cups vegetable broth
- 2 (15-ounce) cans chickpeas, rinsed
- ½ cup ditalini
- 2 tablespoons minced fresh parsley

1. Heat oil in Dutch oven over medium heat until shimmering. Add onion, carrots, celery, and pepper and cook, stirring occasionally, until softened, 5 to 7 minutes. Stir in nutritional yeast, thyme, and bay leaves and cook until fragrant, about 30 seconds.

2. Stir in broth and chickpeas and bring to boil. Reduce heat to medium-low, partially cover, and simmer until flavors meld, about 10 minutes.

3. Stir in pasta, increase heat to medium-high, and boil until just tender, about 10 minutes. Off heat, discard bay leaves and stir in parsley. Season with salt and pepper to taste and serve.

Chickpea Noodle Soup

top | *Creamy Chickpea and Sweet Potato Stew*
bottom | *Green Gumbo*

Creamy Chickpea and Sweet Potato Stew

FAST **VEGAN** Serves 6 Total Time 45 minutes

Why This Recipe Works Loosely inspired by maafe (Senegalese peanut stew), our chickpea and sweet potato stew is quick and simple but boasts full-on flavor. The recipe starts with sautéing a large chopped sweet potato with onion and red pepper flakes; citrusy coriander and big dollops of fruity tomato paste go into the pot next. A couple cans of chickpeas and their flavorful, viscous cooking liquid (called aquafaba), along with coconut milk and peanut butter, follow. As the chickpeas simmer, they swell to a luscious, buttery smoothness that's central to the appeal of the stew. Fresh cilantro, chopped dry-roasted peanuts, and grated lime zest light up each bowl with freshness and crunch.

- 1 tablespoon vegetable oil
- 1 onion, chopped fine
- 1 large sweet potato, peeled and cut into ½-inch pieces
- ¾ teaspoon table salt
- ¼ teaspoon red pepper flakes
- 3 tablespoons tomato paste
- 1 teaspoon ground coriander
- 2 (15-ounce) cans chickpeas, undrained
- 1 (14-ounce) can coconut milk
- ¾ cup water
- ⅓ cup creamy peanut butter
- 2 teaspoons grated lime zest plus 2 tablespoons juice
- ½ cup dry-roasted peanuts, chopped
- ½ cup minced fresh cilantro

1. Heat oil in large saucepan over medium heat until shimmering. Add onion, sweet potato, salt, and pepper flakes and cook, stirring frequently, until onion begins to brown, 6 to 8 minutes.

2. Add tomato paste and coriander and cook, stirring constantly, until tomato paste slightly darkens, 2 minutes. Stir in chickpeas and their liquid, coconut milk, water, and peanut butter. Increase heat to medium-high and bring to simmer. Cover, adjust heat to maintain simmer, and cook, stirring occasionally, until sweet potato is tender, about 15 minutes.

3. Off heat, stir in lime zest and juice. Season with salt to taste. Serve, passing peanuts and cilantro separately.

Thai-Spiced Red Lentil Stew with Spinach and Corn

VEGAN Serves 4 to 6 Total Time 50 minutes

Why This Recipe Works This easy lentil stew is inspired by the flavors of Thai cuisine, where many dishes are both a little sweet and a little sour. Tomato sauce and coconut milk form the base of this hearty stew, and a mix of freshly ground coriander, mustard, and cumin seeds infuse it with remarkable flavor. It gets another aromatic boost from garlic and a sliced green Thai chile. Tamarind juice concentrate and brown sugar deliver unmistakable sweet-savory notes, while baby spinach and corn are the starring vegetables. Use a Thai tamarind concentrate (look for the words nuoc me chua on the label) and not one from India, which is darker and has a more cooked flavor. If you can only find tamarind pulp, microwave 1 tablespoon in ½ cup water for 1 to 2 minutes, until softened. Pass through a fine-mesh strainer set over a bowl, pressing on the solids to extract as much tamarind as possible, discarding the solids. Add to the pot with the lentils in step 2 and omit the ½ cup water in the ingredient list. To make this recipe vegan, substitute plant-based yogurt for the dairy yogurt.

- 2 teaspoons coriander seeds
- 2 teaspoons brown mustard seeds
- 2 teaspoons cumin seeds
- 2 tablespoons vegetable oil
- 1 onion, chopped fine
- 3 garlic cloves, minced
- 1 green Thai chile, stemmed and sliced thin
- 2 cups vegetable broth
- 1 (15-ounce) can tomato sauce
- 1 (14-ounce) can coconut milk
- ¾ cup red lentils, rinsed
- ½ cup water
- 1 tablespoon tamarind juice concentrate
- 2 teaspoons packed brown sugar, plus extra for seasoning
- 1½ teaspoons table salt
- 2 ounces (2 cups) baby spinach, roughly chopped
- 1½ cups fresh or frozen corn
- Plain yogurt
- Fresh cilantro, chopped
- Roasted and lightly salted peanuts, chopped
- Lime wedges

1. Toast coriander seeds, mustard seeds, and cumin seeds in 8-inch skillet over medium-high heat until fragrant, about 1 minute. Transfer to mortar and pestle or spice grinder and let cool slightly. Grind to coarse powder; measure out 1 teaspoon and set aside separately from remaining ground spices.

2. Heat oil in Dutch oven over medium heat until shimmering. Add onion, garlic, Thai chile, and remaining ground spices and cook, stirring occasionally, until onion is softened, about 5 minutes. Stir in broth, tomato sauce, coconut milk, lentils, water, tamarind juice concentrate, sugar, and salt. Increase heat to high and bring to vigorous simmer. Cover pot, reduce heat to medium, and cook until lentils are tender, about 10 minutes, stirring occasionally.

3. Off heat, stir in spinach, corn, and reserved 1 teaspoon ground spices and let sit until spinach is wilted, 2 to 3 minutes. Season with salt and extra sugar to taste. Garnish individual servings with yogurt, cilantro, peanuts, and lime wedges.

Green Gumbo

VEGAN Serves 6 to 8 Total Time 1 hour

Why This Recipe Works This stew is vegetable heaven in a bowl. Green gumbo, or gumbo z'herbes, was originally a Louisiana Lenten dish signifying abstinence (from meat). It's now served year round, with and without meat. Like most gumbos, it starts with a dark oil-flour roux, which provides thickening power and nutty richness. What sets this gumbo apart from its cousins is all the green vegetables. Some recipes have more than a dozen kinds; to streamline things, we chose a chewier variety (collards, mustard greens, or kale) and a softer one (spinach or Swiss chard) for a balance of fibrousness and silkiness. (Do experiment with whatever greens you have on hand.) Cayenne and smoked paprika echo the smokiness of meaty gumbos. Though not traditional, the addition of okra, green beans, and black-eyed peas make for a heartier and more delicious stew. Don't use fresh okra here, though you can substitute frozen spinach for fresh, if you prefer. Serve over rice.

- ½ cup vegetable oil
- ½ cup all-purpose flour
- 1 large onion, chopped fine
- 2 celery ribs, chopped fine
- 1 green bell pepper, stemmed, seeded, and chopped fine
- 3 garlic cloves, minced
- 1 tablespoon minced fresh thyme or 1 teaspoon dried
- 2¼ teaspoons table salt, divided
- 2 teaspoons smoked paprika
- 1 teaspoon cayenne pepper
- 5 cups water
- 12 ounces collard greens, mustard greens, or kale, stemmed and cut into 1-inch pieces
- 1 cup frozen cut okra
- 1 (15-ounce) can black-eyed peas, rinsed
- 12 ounces curly-leaf spinach or Swiss chard, stemmed and cut into 1-inch pieces
- 6 ounces green beans, trimmed and cut into 1-inch lengths
- 1 tablespoon cider vinegar, plus extra for seasoning
- 2 scallions, sliced thin (optional)

1. Heat oil in Dutch oven over medium-high heat until just smoking. Using silicone spatula, stir in flour and cook, stirring constantly, until mixture is color of peanut butter, 2 to 5 minutes. Reduce heat to medium-low and continue to cook, stirring constantly, until roux has darkened to color of milk chocolate, 5 to 10 minutes longer.

2. Stir in onion, celery, bell pepper, garlic, thyme, 1 teaspoon salt, paprika, and cayenne. Cover and cook, stirring frequently, until vegetables have softened, 8 to 10 minutes.

3. Stir in water, scraping up any browned bits, and bring to boil over high heat. Stir in collard greens, 1 handful at a time; okra; and remaining 1¼ teaspoons salt. Cover, reduce heat to low, and simmer until greens are just tender, 5 to 7 minutes. Stir in black-eyed peas; spinach, 1 handful at a time; and green beans and simmer until green beans and spinach are tender, about 5 minutes. Stir in vinegar and season with salt, pepper, and extra vinegar to taste. Sprinkle with scallions, if using. Serve.

Best Vegetarian Chili

VEGAN Serves 6 to 8 Total Time 4½ hours, plus 1 hour 20 minutes soaking

Why This Recipe Works Vegetarian chilis can be little more than a mishmash of beans and vegetables. To create a robust chili, we found replacements for the different ways in which meat would add depth and savory flavor. Walnuts, soy sauce, dried shiitake mushrooms, and tomatoes add hearty savoriness to this chili. Bulgur gives it a substantial texture. The added oil and nuts lend a richness, for full, lingering flavor. We prefer to use whole dried chiles, but the chili can be prepared with jarred chili powder. If using chili powder, grind the shiitakes and oregano and add them to the pot with ¼ cup of chili powder in step 4. For a spicier chili, use both jalapeños. Pinto, black, red kidney, small red, cannellini, or navy beans can be used here. Serve with lime wedges and your favorite chili garnishes.

- 1¼ teaspoons table salt, plus salt for soaking beans
- 1 pound (2½ cups) dried beans, rinsed and picked over
- 2 dried ancho chiles
- 2 dried New Mexico chiles
- ½ ounce dried shiitake mushrooms, chopped coarse
- 4 teaspoons dried oregano
- ½ cup walnuts, toasted
- 1 (28-ounce) can diced tomatoes, drained with juice reserved
- 3 tablespoons tomato paste
- 1–2 jalapeño chiles, stemmed and chopped coarse
- 6 garlic cloves, minced
- 3 tablespoons soy sauce
- ¼ cup vegetable oil
- 2 pounds onions, chopped fine
- 1 tablespoon ground cumin
- ⅔ cup medium-grain bulgur
- ¼ cup chopped fresh cilantro
- Lime wedges

1. Bring 4 quarts water, 3 tablespoons salt, and beans to boil in Dutch oven over high heat. Remove pot from heat, cover, and let stand for 1 hour. Drain beans and rinse well.

2. Adjust oven rack to middle position and heat oven to 300 degrees. Arrange ancho and New Mexico chiles on rimmed baking sheet and toast until fragrant and puffed, about 8 minutes. Transfer to plate and let cool, about 5 minutes. Stem and seed toasted chiles. Working in batches, grind toasted chiles, shiitakes, and oregano in spice grinder or with mortar and pestle until finely ground.

3. Process walnuts in food processor until finely ground, about 30 seconds. Transfer to bowl. Process drained tomatoes, tomato paste, jalapeño(s), garlic, and soy sauce in food processor until tomatoes are finely chopped, about 45 seconds, scraping down bowl as needed.

4. Heat oil in Dutch oven over medium-high heat until shimmering. Add onions and salt; cook, stirring occasionally until onions begin to brown, 8 to 10 minutes. Lower heat to medium, add ground chile mixture and cumin, and cook, stirring constantly, until fragrant, about 1 minute. Add rinsed beans and 7 cups water and bring to boil. Cover pot, transfer to oven, and cook for 45 minutes.

5. Remove pot from oven. Stir in bulgur, ground walnuts, tomato mixture, and reserved tomato juice. Cover, return to oven, and cook until beans are fully tender, about 2 hours.

6. Remove pot from oven, stir chili well, and let stand, uncovered, for 20 minutes. (Chili can be refrigerated for up to 3 days or frozen for up to 1 month.) Stir in cilantro and serve with lime wedges.

Black Bean Chili

VEGAN Serves 6 to 8 Total Time 2½ hours

Why This Recipe Works This interesting version of black bean chili incorporates chunky bits of white mushrooms for meatiness and a surprising ingredient, mustard seeds, which supply a remarkable amount of instant complexity. Since black beans are the focal point of this chili, we use dried beans. Often we soak dried beans in salted water before cooking to avoid having some of the beans burst open during cooking. For this chili, however, we think that some exploded beans add a nice textural dimension, so we skip the soaking. After blooming spices and sautéing the chopped white mushrooms and aromatics in oil (which gives the chili meaty texture and flavor), we add the beans, along with broth and water, and cook them in the oven until tender and well seasoned. Whole cumin seeds and chipotle add depth and smokiness. A sprinkle of minced cilantro brightens the chili. We strongly prefer the texture and flavor of mustard seeds and cumin seeds in this chili, but you can substitute ½ teaspoon dry mustard and/or ½ teaspoon ground cumin, added to the pot with the chili powder in step 3. Serve with your favorite chili garnishes.

| *Best Vegetarian Chili*

top | *Black Bean Chili*

bottom | *Roasted Poblano and White Bean Chili*

- 1 pound white mushrooms, trimmed and broken into rough pieces
- 1 tablespoon mustard seeds
- 2 teaspoons cumin seeds
- 3 tablespoons vegetable oil
- 1 onion, chopped fine
- 9 garlic cloves, minced
- 1 tablespoon minced canned chipotle chile in adobo sauce
- 3 tablespoons chili powder
- 2½ cups vegetable broth
- 2½ cups water, plus extra as needed
- 1 pound (2½ cups) dried black beans, picked over and rinsed
- 1 tablespoon packed light brown sugar
- ⅛ teaspoon baking soda
- 2 bay leaves
- 1 (28-ounce) can crushed tomatoes
- 2 red bell peppers, stemmed, seeded, and cut into ½-inch pieces
- ½ cup minced fresh cilantro
- Lime wedges, for serving

1. Adjust oven rack to lower-middle position and heat oven to 325 degrees. Pulse mushrooms in food processor until coarsely chopped and uniform in size, about 10 pulses.

2. Toast mustard seeds and cumin seeds in Dutch oven over medium heat, stirring constantly, until fragrant, about 1 minute. Stir in oil, onion, and mushrooms, cover, and cook until mushrooms have released their liquid, about 5 minutes. Uncover and continue to cook until vegetables are browned, 5 to 10 minutes.

3. Stir in garlic and chipotle and cook until fragrant, about 30 seconds. Stir in chili powder and cook, stirring constantly, until fragrant, about 1 minute. Stir in broth, water, beans, sugar, baking soda, and bay leaves and bring to simmer, skimming as needed. Cover, transfer to oven, and cook for 1 hour.

4. Stir in crushed tomatoes and bell peppers, cover again, and continue to cook in oven until beans are fully tender, about 1 hour. (If chili begins to stick to bottom of pot or is too thick, add water as needed.) (Chili can be refrigerated for up to 3 days or frozen for up to 1 month.)

5. Remove pot from oven and discard bay leaves. Stir in cilantro, season with salt and pepper to taste, and serve with lime wedges.

Roasted Poblano and White Bean Chili

VEGAN Serves 4 to 6 Total Time 1¾ hours

Why This Recipe Works White bean chili is a fresher, lighter cousin of the thick red chili most Americans know and love. Because there are no tomatoes to mask the other flavors, the fresh chiles take center stage. A trio of poblanos, Anaheims, and jalapeños provide complexity and modest heat. We broil the poblanos and Anaheims to develop depth and smokiness. To keep the flavor of the jalapeños bright, we chop them, put them in the food processor with onions, and then sauté the mixture. For a flavorful counterpoint to the vegetal flavor of the chiles, we broil fresh sweet corn to add a toasty, caramelized element to them and then simmer the cobs in the chili to extract even more flavor, adding the broiled kernels to the chili just before serving. In addition, simmering the cobs with the beans and chiles creates sweet undertones that permeate the chili. To thicken the chili, we process some of the roasted peppers with a portion of the beans and broth. To make the chili spicier, add the seeds from the chiles. If you can't find Anaheim chiles, add two additional poblanos and one additional jalapeño. Serve with sour cream and tortilla chips, if desired.

- 5 poblano chiles, stemmed, halved, and seeded
- 3 Anaheim chiles, stemmed, halved, and seeded
- 3 tablespoons vegetable oil, divided
- 3 ears corn, kernels cut from cobs and cobs reserved
- 2 onions, cut into large pieces
- 2 jalapeño chiles, stemmed, seeded, and chopped
- 2 (15-ounce) cans cannellini beans, rinsed, divided
- 4 cups vegetable broth, divided
- 6 garlic cloves, minced
- 1 tablespoon tomato paste
- 1 tablespoon ground cumin
- 1½ teaspoons ground coriander
- ½ teaspoon table salt
- 1 (15-ounce) can pinto beans, rinsed
- 4 scallions, green parts only, sliced thin
- ¼ cup minced fresh cilantro
- 1 tablespoon lime juice, plus lime wedges for serving

1. Adjust oven rack 6 inches from broiler element and heat broiler. Toss poblanos and Anaheims with 1 tablespoon oil in large bowl and arrange, skin side up, on aluminum foil–lined rimmed baking sheet. Broil until chiles begin to blacken and soften, about 10 minutes, rotating sheet halfway through broiling. Transfer chiles to bowl, cover with plastic wrap, and let steam until skins peel off easily, 10 to 15 minutes. Peel poblanos and Anaheims, then cut into ½-inch pieces, reserving any accumulated juices.

2. Meanwhile, toss corn kernels with 1 tablespoon oil in medium bowl, spread evenly over now-empty sheet, and broil, stirring occasionally, until beginning to brown, 5 to 10 minutes; let cool on sheet.

3. Pulse onions and jalapeños in food processor to consistency of chunky salsa, 6 to 8 pulses; transfer to separate bowl. Process 1 cup cannellini beans, 1 cup broth, and ½ cup poblano-Anaheim mixture and any accumulated juices in now-empty processor until smooth, about 45 seconds.

4. Heat remaining 1 tablespoon oil in Dutch oven over medium heat until shimmering. Add onion-jalapeño mixture and cook until softened, 5 to 7 minutes. Stir in garlic, tomato paste, cumin, coriander, and salt and cook until tomato paste begins to darken, about 2 minutes. Stir in remaining 3 cups broth, scraping up any browned bits. Stir in bean-chile mixture, remaining roasted chiles, remaining cannellini beans, pinto beans, and corn cobs. Bring to gentle simmer and cook until thickened and flavors meld, about 40 minutes. (Chili can be refrigerated for up to 3 days or frozen for up to 1 month.)

5. Discard corn cobs. Stir in corn kernels and let sit until heated through, about 1 minute. Off heat, stir in scallions, cilantro, and lime juice, and season with salt and pepper to taste. Serve with lime wedges.

Building-Block Vegetable Broths

All of our recipes work with either homemade or store-bought broth, but making your own vegetable broth makes a big difference in flavor and is worth the effort. These homemade broths let vegetal flavors shine. They are interchangeable, so use what works for you: classic broth, a superconvenient frozen broth base, broth that transforms food waste, or a "meaty" supersavory broth.

Classic Vegetable Broth

VEGAN Makes 2 quarts Total time 2½ hours, plus 1 hour cooling

This all-purpose broth is packed with 6 vegetables plus aromatics that give it a robust and balanced flavor. When you make it, you can rest assured that you are starting any soup or stew recipe with a stellar broth.

- 3 onions, chopped
- 2 celery ribs, chopped
- 2 carrots, peeled and chopped
- 8 scallions, chopped
- 15 garlic cloves, peeled and smashed
- 1 teaspoon vegetable oil
- 1 teaspoon table salt
- 12 cups water
- 1 head cauliflower (2 pounds), cored and cut into 1-inch florets
- 1 plum tomato, cored and chopped
- 8 sprigs fresh thyme
- 3 bay leaves
- 1 teaspoon black peppercorns

1. Combine onions, celery, carrots, scallions, garlic, oil, and salt in Dutch oven or large pot. Cover and cook over medium-low heat, stirring often, until golden brown fond has formed on bottom of pot, 20 to 30 minutes.

2. Stir in water, cauliflower, tomato, thyme sprigs, bay leaves, and peppercorns, scraping up any browned bits, and bring to simmer. Partially cover pot, reduce heat to gentle simmer, and cook until broth tastes rich and flavorful, about 1½ hours.

3. Strain broth gently through fine-mesh strainer (do not press on solids). Let broth cool completely. (Broth can be refrigerated for up to 4 days or frozen for up to 1 month.)

Vegetable Broth Base

FAST VEGAN Makes 1¾ cups base, enough for 7 quarts broth Total Time 20 minutes

This broth base is superconvenient, and once it's made you can store it in the freezer for many months to use as you need it. It doesn't freeze solid, making it easy to scoop out whatever quantity you need. And it takes up little space in your freezer, which is a bonus in addition to its fresh vegetal flavor. For the best balance of flavors, measure the prepped vegetables by weight. To make 1 cup of broth, stir 1 tablespoon of fresh or frozen broth base into 1 cup of boiling water. If particle-free broth is desired, let the broth steep for 5 minutes, then strain it through a fine-mesh strainer.

- 2 leeks, white and light green parts only, chopped and washed thoroughly (2½ cups or 5 ounces)
- 2 carrots, peeled and cut into ½-inch pieces (⅔ cup or 3 ounces)
- ½ small celery root, peeled and cut into ½-inch pieces (¾ cup or 3 ounces)
- ½ cup (½ ounce) parsley leaves and thin stems
- 3 tablespoons dried minced onions
- 2 tablespoons kosher salt
- 1½ tablespoons tomato paste
- 3 tablespoons soy sauce

Process leeks, carrots, celery root, parsley, minced onions, and salt in food processor, scraping down sides of bowl frequently, until paste is as fine as possible, 3 to 4 minutes. Add tomato paste and process for 1 minute, scraping down sides of bowl every 20 seconds. Add soy sauce and continue to process 1 minute longer. Transfer mixture to airtight container and tap firmly on counter to remove air bubbles. Press small piece of parchment paper flush against surface of mixture and cover. (Broth base can be frozen for up to 6 months.)

Vegetable Scrap Broth

VEGAN Makes 2 quarts Total Time 1 hour 20 minutes, plus 1 hour cooling

This recipe transforms what might otherwise end up as food waste into a milder-flavored broth that can be used in anything from soups, risottos, pilafs, and sauces to hearty stews and braises. Use it as a template to incorporate scraps you have on hand (like carrot peels and tops, celery leaves and trimmings, corn cobs, onion skins, herb stems and sprigs, and much more). Freeze scraps in zipper-lock bags; avoid saving any that are deeply discolored, overly softened, or beginning to mold. We don't recommend saving potato scraps or scraps from vegetables that have sulfuric or bitter notes, such as broccoli, cauliflower, and cabbage. Consider adding additional flavor with aromatics, such as bay leaves, peppercorns, and citrus zest, or savory elements such as a Parmesan rind, kombu, soy sauce, miso, and tomato paste.

- 1½ pounds trimmings from nearly any vegetable
- 3 quarts water
- 1 tablespoon table salt

Combine all ingredients in large Dutch oven or large pot and bring to boil. Partially cover, reduce heat to medium-low, and simmer gently for 1 hour. Strain broth through fine-mesh strainer into large bowl or container; discard spent scraps. Let broth cool completely. (Broth can be refrigerated for up to 4 days or frozen for up to 2 months.)

Umami Broth

VEGAN Makes 2 quarts Total Time 45 minutes, plus 1 hour cooling

This broth gets its savory depth of flavor from nutritional yeast, miso, and fermented black beans. Look for fermented black beans at Asian grocery stores; if you can't find them, omit them. Do not substitute black bean paste or canned black beans. Straining the broth through a double layer of cheesecloth yields a clearer broth, though some sediment will remain. To add more savoriness to a dish, swap this broth into any recipe that calls for vegetable broth, such as Hearty Cabbage Soup (page 151) or Shiitake, Tofu, and Mustard Greens Soup (page 154).

- 8 cups water
- ¼ cup nutritional yeast
- 2 tablespoons fermented black beans
- 1½ tablespoons soy sauce
- 1 tablespoon white miso
- 1½ teaspoons onion powder
- 1½ teaspoons garlic powder
- ½ ounce dried shiitake mushrooms, rinsed and chopped coarse

1. Combine all ingredients in large Dutch oven or large pot. Bring to boil, then cover, reduce heat to low, and simmer for 30 minutes.

2. Strain broth through fine-mesh strainer lined with double layer of cheesecloth. Let broth cool completely. (Broth can be refrigerated for up to 4 days or frozen for up to 1 month.)

Great Garnishes for Soup (and More)

Sometimes it's a final flourish that can take your soup from good to great. A swirl of something creamy, a drizzle of spicy oil, a shower of flaky sea salt, a sprinkling of flavorful homemade croutons, and even a pickled or crispy vegetable can add drama and flavor. Here is an array of toppings to use on a wide variety of soups. And don't forget that many are good on salads too!

Classic Croutons

FAST Makes 3 cups Total Time 45 minutes

There is just no comparison between store-bought croutons and homemade. They are easy to make and will elevate your soups and salads with their crunch and flavor.

- 6 slices bread, crusts removed, cut into ½-inch cubes (3 cups)
- 3 tablespoons unsalted butter, melted, or extra-virgin olive oil

Adjust oven rack to middle position and heat oven to 350 degrees. Toss bread with melted butter, season with salt and pepper to taste, and spread onto rimmed baking sheet. Bake until golden brown and crisp, 20 to 25 minutes, stirring halfway through baking. Let cool before serving. (Croutons can be stored at room temperature for up to 3 days.)

Variations

FAST Herbed Croutons

Whisk 1 teaspoon minced fresh parsley and ½ teaspoon minced fresh thyme into melted butter before tossing with bread.

FAST VEGAN Umami Croutons

Substitute extra-virgin olive oil for butter and increase amount to ¼ cup. Whisk oil with 3 tablespoons nutritional yeast, 1 teaspoon white or brown miso, 1 teaspoon Dijon mustard, ¼ teaspoon distilled white vinegar, and ⅛ teaspoon table salt before tossing with bread. Reduce baking time to 13 to 15 minutes.

Tofu Croutons

FAST **VEGAN** Makes 2 cups
Total Time 35 minutes

These tofu croutons are crispy on the outside but deliciously creamy inside and are especially good on creamy soups. As a bonus, they also add protein.

- 14 ounces extra-firm tofu, cut lengthwise into 3 equal slabs, divided
- ¼ teaspoon table salt, divided
- ⅛ teaspoon pepper
- 2 tablespoons extra-virgin olive oil

Place tofu on paper towel–lined plate and let drain for 20 minutes, then gently press dry with paper towels. Sprinkle with salt and pepper. Heat oil in large saucepan over medium-high heat until shimmering. Add tofu slabs and cook, flipping as needed, until lightly browned on both sides, 6 to 8 minutes. Transfer tofu to cutting board and cut into ½-inch pieces.

Grab-and-Go Toppings

Widen your topping options with ingredients like these: a drizzle of good olive oil, balsamic vinegar, or sweet-savory pomegranate molasses; toasted nuts and seeds; crumbled cheese such as blue cheese or feta or shaved cheese like Parmesan; a dollop of pesto, sour cream, or yogurt; kale chips; tortilla strips; chopped scallions; citrus zest or juice; and, of course, fresh herbs.

Spiced Seeds

FAST **VEGAN** Makes ½ cup Total Time 10 minutes

Salty, crunchy, spicy, seeds are an easy topping to elevate soups or salads in a snap.

- 2 teaspoons extra-virgin olive oil or vegetable oil
- ½ cup pepitas or sunflower seeds
- ½ teaspoon paprika
- ½ teaspoon ground coriander
- ¼ teaspoon table salt

Heat oil in 12-inch skillet over medium heat until shimmering. Add pepitas, paprika, coriander, and salt. Cook, stirring constantly, until pepitas are toasted, about 2 minutes; transfer to bowl and let cool. (Seeds can be stored at room temperature for up to 5 days.)

Pickled Celery

FAST **VEGAN** Makes ½ cup Total Time 25 minutes

Bits of sweet-savory pickled celery will brighten up pureed soups especially.

- ½ cup rice vinegar
- 1 tablespoon sugar
- ½ teaspoon table salt
- 1 celery rib, chopped fine

Combine vinegar, sugar, and salt in medium bowl and microwave until simmering, 1 to 2 minutes. Stir in celery and let sit for 15 minutes. Drain celery, discarding liquid.

Quick Chili Oil

VEGAN Makes ½ cup Total Time 15 minutes, plus 1 hour cooling

You need only a drizzle of this potent oil to add heat and umami to soups.

- 1 tablespoon soy sauce
- 2 teaspoons sugar
- ½ teaspoon table salt
- ½ cup peanut oil
- ¼ cup red pepper flakes
- 2 garlic cloves, peeled

Combine soy sauce, sugar, and salt in small bowl; set aside. Heat oil in small saucepan over medium heat until just shimmering and registers 300 degrees. Remove pan from heat and stir in pepper flakes, garlic, and soy mixture. Let cool to room temperature, stirring occasionally, about 1 hour. Discard garlic before serving. (Chili oil can be stored in the refrigerator for up to 2 days.)

Lemon-Herb Sauce

FAST Makes ½ cup Total Time 5 minutes

Made with ingredients you likely have, this all-purpose sauce can be drizzled over almost any soup to add richness and bright lemony flavor.

- 6 tablespoons mayonnaise, divided
- 2 scallions, minced, divided
- 3 tablespoons chopped fresh parsley, divided
- 1 tablespoon lemon juice

Whisk all ingredients together in bowl. Season with salt and pepper to taste. (Sauce can be refrigerated for up to 3 days.)

Burgers, Tacos & More

182 Ultimate Veggie Burgers ●

183 Black Bean Burgers

184 Classic Burger Sauce ■ ●

184 Sheet Pan White Bean and Sun-Dried Tomato Patties with Lemony Spinach Salad ■

187 Pinto Bean–Beet Burgers ●

187 Quinoa Burgers with Spinach, Sun-Dried Tomatoes, and Marinated Feta

188 Curried Millet Burgers with Peach-Ginger Chutney

190 Smoky Carrot Dogs ●

191 Baja-Style Cauliflower Tacos ●

191 Cilantro Crema ■ ●

193 Black Bean and Sweet Potato Tacos ●
Black Bean, Sweet Potato, and Poblano Tacos ●

193 Avocado Crema ■ ●

193 Red Lentil Tacos ●

194 Sheet Pan Cheese Quesadillas ■
Sheet Pan Black Bean and Jalapeño Quesadillas ■

195 Spinach and Goat Cheese Quesadillas ■

197 Chickpea and Poblano Quesadillas ■

197 Cheese Pupusas

198 Quick Tomato Salsa ■ ●

199 Black Bean and Cheese Arepas ■
Avocado, Tomato, and Bell Pepper Arepas ■ ●

200 Cheddar-Crusted Grilled Cheese ■
Cheddar-Crusted Grilled Cheese with Tomato ■

203 Marinated Tomato Sandwiches ■ ●

203 Mushroom, Lettuce, and Tomato Sandwiches ●

205 Creamy Mushroom and Pink Pickled Cabbage Sandwiches

205 Cutty's-Inspired Eggplant Spuckie ■

206 Beet, Orange, and Chèvre Tartines ■

206 Raw Vegetable Wraps ■

209 Roasted Vegetable Sandwiches ●

209 Ultimate Grilled Vegetable Sandwiches

210 Chickpea Salad Sandwiches with Quick Pickles ■

211 Spiced Smashed Chickpea Wraps ■ ●

211 Tahini-Yogurt Sauce ■ ●

212 Mumbai Frankie Wraps ●

213 Chapati (Whole-Wheat Wraps) ●

213 Quick Sweet-and-Spicy Pickled Red Onion ●

213 Cilantro-Mint Chutney ■ ●

214 Grilled Halloumi Wraps

215 Falafel ●

216 Tomato-Chile Sauce ■ ●

216 Vospov Kofte (Red Lentil Kofte)

Sandwich Spreads

218 Easy Homemade Mayonnaise ■
Basil-Caper Mayonnaise ■
Lemon-Dill Mayonnaise ■
Spicy Sriracha-Lime Mayonnaise ■

218 Herbed Yogurt Sauce ■ ●

218 Creamy Chipotle Sauce ■ ●

219 Homemade Nut Butter

■ Fast (45 minutes or less) ● Vegan

top | *Ultimate Veggie Burgers*
bottom | *Black Bean Burgers*

Ultimate Veggie Burgers

VEGAN Makes 12 patties Total Time 2½ hours, plus 20 minutes cooling

Why This Recipe Works Making veggie burgers is a labor of love, so they better taste great. For veggie burgers with complex, savory flavor and a satisfyingly robust texture good enough to be worth the effort, we use a base of quick-cooking lentils and bulgur. That combo, paired with aromatic onions, celery, leek, and garlic, give these burgers deep flavor. Cremini mushrooms lend meaty flavor, and a surprising addition of ground cashews amplifies the meatiness even more. Pulsing everything in the food processor makes for a cohesive and even-textured mix, and mayonnaise provides necessary fat to bind the burgers. After forming the mixture into patties, we sear them in a skillet to develop a crunchy, browned exterior. As a bonus, these burgers can be made ahead and frozen for a quick weeknight meal. Do not confuse bulgur with cracked wheat, which has a much longer cooking time and will not work here. To make this recipe vegan, substitute plant-based mayo for the mayonnaise. Serve the burgers with your favorite toppings.

- ¾ cup brown lentils, picked over and rinsed
- 1 teaspoon table salt, plus salt for cooking lentils and bulgur
- ¾ cup medium-grind bulgur, rinsed
- ¼ cup vegetable oil, divided, plus extra as needed
- 2 onions, chopped fine
- 1 celery rib, chopped fine
- 1 small leek, white and light green parts only, halved lengthwise, chopped fine, and washed thoroughly
- 2 garlic cloves, minced
- 1 pound cremini or white mushrooms, trimmed and sliced ¼ inch thick
- 1 cup raw cashews
- ⅓ cup mayonnaise
- 2 cups panko bread crumbs
- 12 hamburger buns, toasted if desired

1. Bring 3 cups water, lentils, and 1 teaspoon salt to boil in medium saucepan over high heat. Reduce heat to medium-low and simmer gently, stirring occasionally, until lentils are just beginning to fall apart, about 25 minutes. Drain lentils, spread out over paper towel–lined rimmed baking sheet, and pat dry; let cool to room temperature.

2. Bring 2 cups water and ½ teaspoon salt to boil in small saucepan. Off heat, stir in bulgur, cover, and let sit until tender, 15 to 20 minutes. Drain bulgur, pressing with silicone spatula to remove excess moisture, and transfer to large bowl; let cool slightly.

3. Heat 1 tablespoon oil in 12-inch nonstick skillet over medium-high heat until shimmering. Add onions, celery, leek, and garlic and cook, stirring occasionally, until vegetables begin to brown, about 10 minutes. Spread vegetable mixture onto second rimmed baking sheet.

4. Heat 1 tablespoon oil in now-empty skillet over high heat until shimmering. Add mushrooms and cook, stirring occasionally, until golden brown, about 12 minutes; add to baking sheet with other vegetables and let cool to room temperature, about 20 minutes.

5. Pulse cashews in food processor until finely chopped, about 15 pulses. Stir cashews into bulgur, then stir in cooled lentils, vegetable-mushroom mixture, and mayonnaise. Working in 2 batches, pulse mixture in now-empty food processor until coarsely chopped, 15 to 20 pulses (mixture should be cohesive but roughly textured); transfer to clean bowl.

6. Stir in panko and salt. Divide mixture into 12 equal portions (about ½ cup each), then tightly pack each portion into ½-inch-thick patty. (Patties can be refrigerated for up to 3 days or frozen for up to 1 month. To freeze, transfer patties to 2 parchment paper–lined rimmed baking sheets and freeze until firm, about 1 hour. Stack patties, separated by parchment paper; wrap in plastic.)

7. To cook burgers: Heat remaining 2 tablespoons oil in 12-inch nonstick skillet over medium-high heat until shimmering. Place 4 patties in skillet and cook until well browned on first side, about 4 minutes. Using 2 spatulas, gently flip patties and continue to cook until well browned on second side, about 4 minutes, adding extra oil as needed if skillet looks dry. Transfer burgers to platter, wipe skillet clean with paper towels, and repeat with extra oil and remaining patties. (If patties were frozen, transfer to wire rack set in rimmed baking sheet and bake in 350-degree oven until heated through, about 10 minutes.) Serve burgers on buns.

Black Bean Burgers

Makes 6 patties   Total Time 1 hour, plus 1 hour chilling

Why This Recipe Works Black bean burgers are often crumbly and tasteless, getting their structure from fillers that rob them of their bean flavor. For a really great nonmeat burger, we turned to convenient canned black beans and harnessed the sticking power of their natural starches. Eggs and flour help hold the burger mix together, and scallions, fresh cilantro, garlic, ground cumin, and coriander contribute some personality. For a dry binder, we grind tortilla chips; their corn flavor adds a pleasing Southwestern flair. We pulse the beans with the chips near the end of processing the chips so the beans maintain some texture. Drying the beans well reduces the moisture content of the burgers so they hold together. Letting the burger mixture sit in the refrigerator gives the starches time to absorb some of the eggs' moisture so the patties are easier to shape. When forming the patties, it is important to pack them together firmly. Serve the burgers with your favorite toppings.

- 2 (15-ounce) cans black beans, rinsed
- 2 large eggs
- 2 tablespoons all-purpose flour
- 4 scallions, minced (¼ cup)
- 3 tablespoons minced fresh cilantro
- 2 garlic cloves, minced
- 1 teaspoon ground cumin
- ½ teaspoon ground coriander
- ¼ teaspoon table salt
- ¼ teaspoon pepper
- 1 teaspoon hot sauce (optional)
- 1 ounce tortilla chips, crushed (½ cup)
- 8 teaspoons vegetable oil, divided
- 6 burger buns, toasted if desired

1. Line rimmed baking sheet with triple layer of paper towels. Spread beans over towels and let stand for 15 minutes.

2. Whisk eggs and flour in large bowl until uniform paste forms. Stir in scallions; cilantro; garlic; cumin; coriander; salt; pepper; and hot sauce, if using, until well combined.

3. Process tortilla chips in food processor until finely ground, about 30 seconds. Add black beans and pulse until beans are roughly broken down, about 5 pulses. Transfer bean mixture to bowl with egg mixture and mix until well combined. Cover and refrigerate for at least 1 hour or up to 24 hours.

4. Divide bean mixture into 6 equal portions. Firmly pack each portion into tight ball, then flatten to 3½-inch patty. (Patties can be wrapped individually in plastic wrap, placed in zipper-lock bag, and frozen for up to 2 weeks. Thaw patties before cooking.)

5. Heat 2 teaspoons oil in 10-inch nonstick skillet over medium heat until shimmering. Carefully lay 3 patties in skillet and cook until bottoms are well browned and crisp, about 5 minutes. Flip patties, add 2 teaspoons oil, and cook second sides until well browned and crisp, 3 to 5 minutes. Transfer patties to buns and repeat with remaining 3 patties and remaining 4 teaspoons oil. Serve burgers on buns.

Classic Burger Sauce

FAST VEGAN Makes 1 cup Total Time 5 minutes

To make this recipe vegan, substitute plant-based mayo for the mayonnaise.

- ½ cup mayonnaise
- ¼ cup ketchup
- 2 teaspoons sweet pickle relish
- 2 teaspoons distilled white vinegar
- 1 teaspoon pepper

Whisk all ingredients together in bowl. Season with salt and pepper to taste. (Sauce can be refrigerated for up to 4 days.)

Sheet Pan White Bean and Sun-Dried Tomato Patties with Lemony Spinach Salad

FAST Makes 4 patties Total Time 45 minutes

Why This Recipe Works Bean burgers and other vegetarian burgers are notorious for easily falling apart. Our sheet-pan method, however, is hands-off, so the patties make it from pan to plate intact. Cannellini beans make up the bulk of these burgers, while sun-dried tomatoes and their flavorful oil add savory depth. We start these bean burgers on a sheet pan preheated on the lower rack of a hot oven, which gives the bottom of the patties a nice crust. Then, instead of flipping the patties, we simply move the pan to a higher rack and broil them for a few minutes to brown the tops. With the extra space on the sheet, we roast some feta and onion to dress up a quick spinach side salad. Drain the beans thoroughly after rinsing. If you don't have sun-dried tomato packing oil, you can substitute vegetable oil.

- ½ cup plain Greek yogurt
- 3 tablespoons plus ¼ cup chopped fresh basil, divided
- ⅓ cup oil-packed sun-dried tomatoes, chopped fine, plus 2 tablespoons oil, divided
- ⅛ teaspoon plus ½ teaspoon table salt, divided
- 2 (15-ounce) cans cannellini beans, rinsed, divided
- 1 large egg
- ⅓ cup panko bread crumbs
- 3 tablespoons extra-virgin olive oil, divided
- 3 ounces feta cheese, cut into ½-inch pieces
- 1 small red onion, halved and sliced ¼ inch thick
- 5 ounces (5 cups) baby spinach
- 1½ tablespoons lemon juice

1. Adjust 1 oven rack to lowest position and second rack 6 inches from broiler element. Place rimmed baking sheet on lower rack and heat oven to 450 degrees. Combine yogurt, 3 tablespoons basil, 1 tablespoon tomato oil, and ⅛ teaspoon salt in bowl; season with salt and pepper to taste and set yogurt sauce aside.

2. Place half of beans in large bowl and mash with potato masher. Add remaining beans and mash until partially broken down. Whisk egg, remaining 1 tablespoon tomato oil, and remaining ½ teaspoon salt together in separate bowl. Stir egg mixture, panko, sun-dried tomatoes, and remaining ¼ cup basil into mashed beans until well combined. Divide mixture into 4 equal portions and lightly pack into ¾-inch-thick patties. Transfer patties to large plate and refrigerate for 10 minutes.

3. Add 2 tablespoons olive oil to hot baking sheet, tilting to coat. Arrange patties on half of sheet and add feta and onion to other half of sheet. Roast on lower rack until patties are browned on bottoms, about 8 minutes. Remove sheet from oven and heat broiler. Brush tops of burgers with remaining 1 tablespoon olive oil. Place sheet on upper rack and broil until patties are lightly browned on top, about 2 minutes.

4. Toss feta, onion, and spinach with lemon juice in large bowl. Serve salad with patties and yogurt sauce.

Sheet Pan White Bean and Sun-Dried Tomato Patties with Lemony Spinach Salad

A Beet Burger Can't Be Beat

You don't often see beets in a vegetarian burger. When shredded and combined with beans and grains in our Pinto Bean—Beet Burgers, the beet becomes tender during cooking and melds seamlessly into the burger, adding an unbeatable earthy flavor and appealing slight sweetness.

More Than a Pretty Color

Beets get their rich red color from water-soluble pigments called betalains, which have antioxidant and anti-inflammatory properties. Beets are low in fat and high in fiber. Beet juice is sometimes used in plant-based beef for its color.

Raw Is Right

Beets are most often consumed cooked, but adding raw shredded beets to our veggie burger brings both a lighter texture and a ton of earthy flavor.

A Reliable Root

Beets are easy to grow and don't have to be harvested right away; they stay in perfectly good condition underground for weeks. Once harvested, beets will keep in the refrigerator for 2 to 3 weeks.

| *Pinto Bean–Beet Burgers*

Pinto Bean–Beet Burgers

VEGAN Makes 8 patties Total Time 1¼ hours

Why This Recipe Works In this modern bean-based vegetarian burger, we use vibrant shredded beet to bring a lighter texture and sweet-earthy flavor. We add substance and heft with bulgur and use ground nuts to provide meaty richness. Plenty of garlic and mustard deepen and unite all the savory flavors. While the bulgur cooks, we pulse the other ingredients in the food processor. To bind the burgers, we hit upon a surprising ingredient: carrot baby food. The pureed carrots add the necessary tackiness to make the patties cohesive, and their subtle sweetness heightens that of the shredded beet. Panko bread crumbs further bind the mixture and help the patties sear up with a nicely crisp crust. Do not confuse bulgur with cracked wheat, which has a much longer cooking time and will not work here. Use the large holes of a box grater or a food processor fitted with a shredding disk to shred the beets. Serve with the burgers with your favorite toppings and Tahini-Yogurt Sauce (page 211), if desired.

- 1½ teaspoons table salt, plus salt for cooking bulgur
- ⅔ cup medium-grind bulgur, rinsed
- 1 large beet (9 ounces), peeled and shredded
- ¾ cup walnuts
- ½ cup fresh basil leaves
- 2 garlic cloves, minced
- 1 (15-ounce) can pinto beans, rinsed
- 1 (4-ounce) jar carrot baby food
- 1 tablespoon whole-grain mustard
- ½ teaspoon pepper
- 1½ cups panko bread crumbs
- 6 tablespoons vegetable oil, divided, plus extra as needed
- 8 hamburger buns, toasted if desired

1. Bring 1½ cups water and ½ teaspoon salt to boil in small saucepan. Off heat, stir in bulgur, cover, and let sit until tender, 15 to 20 minutes. Drain bulgur, spread onto rimmed baking sheet, and let cool slightly.

2. Pulse beet, walnuts, basil, and garlic in food processor until finely chopped, about 12 pulses, scraping down sides of bowl as needed. Add beans, carrot baby food, 2 tablespoons water, mustard, pepper, and salt and pulse until well combined, about 8 pulses. Transfer mixture to large bowl and stir in panko and bulgur.

3. Divide beet-bulgur mixture into 8 equal portions. Using your lightly moistened hands, firmly pack each portion into ¾-inch-thick patty. (Patties can be refrigerated for up to 3 days or frozen for up to 1 month. To freeze, transfer patties to 2 parchment paper–lined rimmed baking sheets and freeze until firm, about 1 hour. Stack patties, separated by parchment paper, wrap in plastic wrap, and place in zipper-lock freezer bag. Do not thaw patties before cooking.)

4. Adjust oven rack to middle position and heat oven to 200 degrees. Set wire rack in rimmed baking sheet. Heat 3 tablespoons oil in 12-inch nonstick skillet over medium-high heat until shimmering. Place 4 patties in skillet and cook until well browned and crisp on first side, about 4 minutes. Using 2 spatulas, gently flip patties and continue to cook until well browned and crisp on second side, about 4 minutes adding extra oil as needed if skillet looks dry. Transfer burgers to prepared rack and keep warm in oven. Wipe skillet clean with paper towels and repeat with remaining 3 tablespoons oil and remaining 4 patties. Serve burgers on buns.

Quinoa Burgers with Spinach, Sun-Dried Tomatoes, and Marinated Feta

Makes 4 patties Total Time 1½ hours, plus 30 minutes chilling

Why This Recipe Works Quinoa's unique texture makes for a super-satisfying burger, and its nutty yet neutral flavor benefits from bright and exciting flavors. For fantastic quinoa burgers, we use white quinoa, which softens enough to be shaped. We mix in chopped sun-dried tomatoes, scallions, delicate baby spinach, and a little lemon zest and juice. We found that the usual toasting step caused the grains to separate, so we skipped it. For patties that stay together in the pan, we use a combination of bread and egg as a binder and also add some Parmesan cheese, which not only helps with binding but also contributes rich flavor. Chilling the patties before cooking further ensures they hold their shape. Cooking the patties on the stovetop over medium-low heat creates a crisp, flavorful crust on the outside but keeps the interior moist. Feta cheese is the perfect topping for these Mediterranean-inspired patties, and a quick marinade allows the cheese to soak up the flavor of fragrant oregano, the citrusy bouquet of fresh lemon zest, and the spicy heat of red pepper flakes. Chopped parsley stirred into the marinated cheese just before serving adds a final burst of freshness to these hearty burgers.

- ⅓ cup plus 2 tablespoons extra-virgin olive oil, divided
- 5 garlic cloves (4 minced, 1 sliced thin)
- ½ teaspoon minced fresh oregano
- 1 teaspoon grated lemon zest, divided, plus 2 teaspoons juice
- ⅛ teaspoon red pepper flakes
- 4 ounces feta cheese, crumbled (1 cup)
- ¼ cup oil-packed sun-dried tomatoes, chopped coarse, plus 1 tablespoon oil
- 4 scallions, chopped fine
- 2 cups water
- 1 cup prewashed white quinoa, rinsed
- 1 teaspoon table salt
- 2 slices hearty white sandwich bread, torn into pieces
- 1 large egg plus 1 large yolk, lightly beaten
- 2 ounces (2 cups) baby spinach, chopped
- 2 ounces Parmesan cheese, grated (1 cup)
- 1 tablespoon chopped fresh parsley
- 8 large iceberg lettuce leaves
- ½ cup Quick Sweet-and-Spicy Pickled Red Onion (page 213)

1. Combine ⅓ cup olive oil, sliced garlic, oregano, ½ teaspoon lemon zest, and pepper flakes in small bowl and microwave until garlic is softened and fragrant, about 1 minute. Gently stir in feta and refrigerate until ready to serve. (Feta mixture can be refrigerated for up to 24 hours.)

2. Line rimmed baking sheet with parchment paper. Heat tomato oil in large saucepan over medium heat until shimmering. Add scallions and cook until softened, 3 to 5 minutes. Stir in minced garlic and cook until fragrant, about 30 seconds. Stir in water, quinoa, and salt and bring to simmer. Cover, reduce heat to medium-low, and simmer until quinoa is tender, 16 to 18 minutes. Off heat, let quinoa sit, covered, until liquid is fully absorbed, about 10 minutes.

3. Pulse bread in food processor until coarsely ground, about 10 pulses. Add egg and yolk and remaining ½ teaspoon lemon zest and pulse until mixture comes together, about 5 pulses. Stir bread mixture, tomatoes, spinach, Parmesan, and lemon juice into cooled quinoa until thoroughly combined. Divide quinoa mixture into 4 equal portions. Using lightly moistened hands, tightly pack each portion into ¾-inch-thick patty and place on prepared sheet. Reshape patties as needed. Cover and refrigerate until chilled and firm, at least 30 minutes or up to 24 hours.

4. Heat remaining 2 tablespoons olive oil in 12-inch nonstick skillet over medium-low heat until shimmering. Place patties in skillet and cook until golden brown and crisp on first side, 5 to 7 minutes. Using 2 spatulas, gently flip patties and cook until browned and crisp on second side, 5 to 7 minutes.

5. Stir parsley into feta mixture. Stack 2 lettuce leaves together to create 4 lettuce wraps. Serve burgers on lettuce wraps, topped with feta mixture and pickled onions.

Curried Millet Burgers with Peach-Ginger Chutney

Makes 4 patties   Total Time 1½ hours, plus 45 minutes cooling and chilling

Why This Recipe Works Millet may not be the first grain you think of to use as the base for veggie burgers, but its nutty, corn-like flavor is the perfect foil for a variety of seasonings. Millet releases a sticky starch as it cooks, so the grain is ideal for making cohesive patties. We combine it with spinach and carrot for vegetal flavor, as well as minced shallot for subtle sweetness and depth. Yogurt and an egg, as binding agents, add moisture and richness. Curry powder gives us a warmly spiced flavor profile that pairs well with a sweet-savory peach chutney; frozen sliced peaches make the condiment easy to whip up. Pan frying the patties is key for a crackly crust and soft interior. These burgers are dense, so we ditch buns in favor of crunchy lettuce leaves.

Peach-Ginger Chutney

- 1 shallot, minced
- 1 tablespoon vegetable oil
- 1 teaspoon grated fresh ginger
- ⅛ teaspoon table salt
- Pinch red pepper flakes
- 1½ cups frozen sliced peaches, thawed and cut into ½-inch pieces
- 2 tablespoons packed light brown sugar
- 2 tablespoons cider vinegar

Burgers

- 1 cup millet, rinsed
- 2 cups water
- 1 teaspoon table salt, divided
- 3 tablespoons vegetable oil, divided
- 1 shallot, minced
- 6 ounces (6 cups) baby spinach, chopped

2 carrots, peeled and shredded
2 teaspoons curry powder
¼ teaspoon pepper
½ cup plain yogurt, divided
1 large egg, lightly beaten
2 tablespoons minced fresh cilantro
8 large iceberg lettuce leaves

1. **For the chutney** Microwave shallot, oil, ginger, salt, and pepper flakes in small bowl, stirring occasionally, until shallot has softened, about 1 minute. Stir in peaches, sugar, and vinegar and microwave until peaches have softened and mixture has thickened, 6 to 8 minutes, stirring once halfway through microwaving. Set aside to cool to room temperature. (Chutney can be refrigerated for up to 3 days; let come to room temperature before serving.)

2. **For the burgers** Line rimmed baking sheet with parchment paper. Combine millet, water, and ½ teaspoon salt in medium saucepan and bring to simmer over medium-high heat. Cover, reduce heat to low, and simmer gently until millet is tender, 15 to 20 minutes. Off heat, let millet sit, covered, until liquid is fully absorbed, about 10 minutes. Transfer millet to large bowl and let cool for 15 minutes.

3. Heat 1 tablespoon oil in 12-inch nonstick skillet over medium heat until shimmering. Add shallot and cook until softened, about 3 minutes. Stir in spinach and carrots and cook until spinach is wilted, about 2 minutes. Stir in curry powder, pepper, and remaining ½ teaspoon salt and cook until fragrant, about 30 seconds; transfer to bowl with millet. Wipe skillet clean with paper towels.

4. Stir ¼ cup yogurt, egg, and cilantro into millet mixture until well combined. Divide mixture into 4 equal portions. Using your lightly moistened hands, firmly pack each portion into ¾-inch-thick patty and place on prepared sheet. Reshape patties as needed. Cover and refrigerate until chilled and firm, at least 30 minutes or up to 24 hours.

5. Heat remaining 2 tablespoons oil in now-empty skillet over medium-low heat until shimmering. Place patties in skillet and cook until golden brown and crisp on first side, 5 to 7 minutes. Using 2 spatulas, gently flip patties and cook until browned and crisp on second side, 5 to 7 minutes.

6. Stack 2 lettuce leaves together to create 4 lettuce cups. Serve burgers on lettuce wraps, topped with remaining ¼ cup yogurt and peach chutney.

top | *Quinoa Burgers with Spinach, Sun-Dried Tomatoes, and Marinated Feta*

bottom | *Curried Millet Burgers with Peach-Ginger Chutney*

Smoky Carrot Dogs

Smoky Carrot Dogs

VEGAN Makes 16 carrot dogs Total Time 50 minutes, plus 8 hours cooling and chilling

Why This Recipe Works These umami-packed carrot dogs are every bit as versatile as traditional hot dogs, so you'll have some fun serving them. Carrots are simmered until tender and then cooled in a supersavory cooking liquid that includes soy sauce, cider vinegar, vegetable bouillon paste, and liquid smoke. Then the carrots and cooking liquid marinate in the fridge for 6 hours. Once patted dry, the carrots are cooked on the stovetop or grilled until well browned. We had the best success using carrots that are ¾ inch in diameter at their thickest point. Avoid carrots that are larger than 1 inch thick. For toppings, go classic with chopped onion, sauerkraut, ketchup, mustard, or pickle relish.

- 16 carrots, peeled
- 4 cups water
- ½ cup soy sauce
- ¼ cup cider vinegar
- 1 tablespoon liquid smoke
- 1 tablespoon roasted vegetable bouillon paste
- 1 teaspoon red pepper flakes
- 1 teaspoon garlic powder
- 1 teaspoon onion powder
- ½ teaspoon pepper
- ¼ teaspoon nutmeg
- ¼ cup vegetable oil (if using skillet), divided
- Hot dog buns

1. Cut each carrot into 6½-inch length, starting from thickest part of carrot; discard carrot tips or save for another use. Whisk water, soy sauce, vinegar, liquid smoke, bouillon paste, pepper flakes, garlic powder, onion powder, pepper, and nutmeg together in Dutch oven. Add carrots and bring to boil over high heat. Reduce heat to medium-low and simmer until tender and tip of paring knife inserted into thickest carrot meets little resistance, about 15 minutes. Let carrots cool in their cooking liquid until both are at room temperature, about 2 hours.

2. Transfer carrots and cooking liquid to 1-gallon zipper-lock bag and refrigerate for at least 6 or up to 24 hours. Remove carrots from cooking liquid and pat dry with paper towels; discard cooking liquid.

3A. For a stovetop Heat 2 tablespoons oil in 12-inch nonstick skillet over medium heat until shimmering. Place 8 carrots in skillet and cook until brown on all sides, about 5 minutes. Transfer to platter and tent with aluminum foil. Wipe skillet clean with paper towels and repeat with remaining 2 tablespoons oil and remaining 8 carrots; transfer to platter. Serve.

3B. For a grill Prepare hot, single-level fire in gas or charcoal grill. Set cooking grate in place and heat grill until hot, about 5 minutes. Grill carrots until well browned on all sides, about 5 minutes. Serve carrot dogs in buns.

Baja-Style Cauliflower Tacos

VEGAN Serves 4 to 6 Total Time 1 hour

Why This Recipe Works Battered cauliflower bites, drizzled with a creamy sauce, can serve as an incredible stand-in for the fried fish traditionally served in Baja-style tacos. To achieve a crisp exterior without deep frying, we cut the cauliflower into large florets and roast it. To boost the cauliflower's flavor, we dunk the pieces in canned coconut milk seasoned with garlic and spices and then roll them in a mixture of panko and shredded coconut. Not only does this add richness and tropical flavor, but it also mimics the crisp exterior of batter-fried fish. A crunchy slaw with juicy mango and spicy jalapeño provides the perfect balance of sweetness and heat. We whipped up a crema to top it all off by mixing equal parts mayonnaise and sour cream plus cilantro. For a spicier slaw, mince and add the jalapeño ribs and seeds. Serve with lime wedges.

- 3 cups (7½ ounces) coleslaw mix
- ½ mango, peeled and cut into ¼-inch pieces (¾ cup)
- 2 tablespoons lime juice
- 1 tablespoon chopped fresh cilantro
- 1 tablespoon minced jalapeño chile
- 1¼ teaspoons table salt, divided
- 1 cup unsweetened shredded coconut
- 1 cup panko bread crumbs
- 1 cup canned coconut milk
- 1 teaspoon garlic powder
- 1 teaspoon ground cumin
- ¼ teaspoon cayenne
- ½ head cauliflower (1 pound), trimmed and cut into 1-inch pieces
- 12 (6-inch) corn tortillas, warmed
- 1 recipe Cilantro Crema (recipe follows)

1. Adjust oven rack to middle position and heat oven to 450 degrees. Combine coleslaw mix, mango, lime juice, cilantro, jalapeño, and ¼ teaspoon salt in bowl, cover, and refrigerate until ready to serve.

2. Spray rimmed baking sheet with vegetable oil spray. Combine coconut and panko in shallow dish. Whisk coconut milk, garlic powder, cumin, cayenne, and remaining 1 teaspoon salt together in bowl. Add cauliflower to coconut milk mixture; toss to coat well. Working with 1 piece cauliflower at a time, remove from coconut milk, letting excess drip back into bowl, then coat well with coconut-panko mixture, pressing gently to adhere; transfer to prepared sheet.

3. Bake until cauliflower is tender, golden, and crisp, 20 to 25 minutes, flipping cauliflower and rotating sheet halfway through baking.

4. Divide slaw evenly among warm tortillas and top with cauliflower. Drizzle with cilantro crema and serve.

Cilantro Crema

FAST VEGAN Makes ¾ cup Total Time 5 minutes

To make this recipe vegan, substitute plant-based mayo and sour cream for the mayonnaise and dairy sour cream.

- ¼ cup mayonnaise
- ¼ cup sour cream
- 3 tablespoons water
- 3 tablespoons minced fresh cilantro
- ¼ teaspoon table salt

Whisk all ingredients together in bowl. (Crema can be refrigerated for up to 3 days.)

Black Bean, Sweet Potato, and Poblano Tacos

Black Bean and Sweet Potato Tacos

VEGAN Serves 4 Total Time 1 hour

Why This Recipe Works Tacos are often focused on rich meats, but these days you can find all kinds of plant-based fillings, from cauliflower to mushrooms and more. It inspired us to create this delicious pantry-friendly combination of black beans, sweet potatoes, and onion, which we season with fragrant garlic, cumin, coriander, and oregano. Roasting the vegetables produces caramelized exteriors and tender interiors. Adding black beans ramps up the protein for a wonderfully hearty meal. Instead of topping the tacos with queso fresco or sour cream (which you can do, if you prefer), we made an avocado crema. Diced avocado is also nice. For a tangy, spicy finish, serve the tacos with Quick Sweet-and-Spicy Pickled Red Onion (page 213).

- 3 tablespoons extra-virgin olive oil
- 3 garlic cloves, minced
- 1½ teaspoons ground cumin
- 1½ teaspoons ground coriander
- 1 teaspoon minced fresh oregano or ¼ teaspoon dried
- 1 teaspoon table salt
- ½ teaspoon pepper
- 12 ounces sweet potatoes, peeled and cut into ½-inch pieces
- 1 onion, halved and sliced ½ inch thick
- 1 (15-ounce) can black beans, rinsed
- ¼ cup chopped fresh cilantro
- 12 (6-inch) corn or flour tortillas, warmed
- 1 recipe Avocado Crema (recipe follows; optional)

1. Adjust oven racks to upper-middle and lower-middle positions and heat oven to 450 degrees. Whisk oil, garlic, cumin, coriander, oregano, salt, and pepper together in large bowl. Add potatoes and onion and toss to coat.

2. Spread vegetable mixture in even layer over 2 aluminum foil–lined rimmed baking sheets. Roast vegetables until tender and golden brown, about 30 minutes, stirring vegetables and switching and rotating sheets halfway through roasting.

3. Return vegetables to now-empty bowl, add beans and cilantro, and gently toss to combine. Serve with tortillas and crema, if using.

Variation

VEGAN **Black Bean, Sweet Potato, and Poblano Tacos**

Roast 4 poblano chiles, stemmed, seeded, and cut into ½-inch-wide strips, with potatoes and onions.

Avocado Crema

FAST VEGAN Makes ⅔ cup Total Time 10 minutes

To make this recipe vegan, substitute plant-based sour cream for the dairy sour cream.

- ½ avocado, chopped
- ¼ cup chopped fresh cilantro
- ¼ cup sour cream
- ¼ cup water
- ½ serrano chile, seeded and minced
- 1 teaspoon lime juice
- ¼ teaspoon table salt

Process all ingredients in food processor until smooth, about 1 minute, scraping down sides of bowl as needed. Season with salt and pepper to taste. (Crema can be refrigerated for up to 3 days.)

Red Lentil Tacos

VEGAN Serves 4 to 6 Total Time 50 minutes, plus 30 minutes to make pickles

Why This Recipe Works Convenient, vibrant, and nutritious, red lentils are perfect for working into a weeknight dinner. Here we use them for the body of a substantial, savory filling. They cook and break down quickly; combined with warm spices and peppers, the result is a great vegetarian taco filling. We love the refreshing crunch of pickled radishes on these tacos, but you can use your favorite taco toppings.

Spicy Pickled Radishes

- 10 radishes, trimmed and sliced thin
- ½ cup lime juice (4 limes)
- 1 jalapeño chile, stemmed and sliced thin
- 1 teaspoon sugar
- ¼ teaspoon table salt

Taco Filling

- 2 tablespoons vegetable oil
- 1 small onion, chopped fine
- 1 green bell pepper, stemmed, seeded, and chopped fine
- 3 garlic cloves, minced
- 2 tablespoons chili powder
- 2 teaspoons ground cumin
- 2 teaspoons ground coriander
- 1 teaspoon dried oregano
- ½ teaspoon table salt
- ¼ teaspoon cayenne pepper
- 1 cup red lentils, picked over and rinsed
- 3 cups vegetable broth
- 12 (6-inch) corn tortillas, warmed

1. **For the spicy pickled radishes** Combine all ingredients in bowl. Cover and let sit at room temperature for 30 minutes. Drain vegetables in colander. (Drained pickles can be refrigerated for up to 24 hours.)

2. **For the taco filling** Heat oil in 12-inch nonstick skillet over medium heat until shimmering. Add onion and bell pepper and cook until softened, about 5 minutes. Stir in garlic, chili powder, cumin, coriander, oregano, salt, and cayenne and cook until fragrant, about 30 seconds.

3. Stir in lentils and broth and bring to boil. Reduce heat to medium-low, partially cover, and simmer vigorously until lentils have broken down and all liquid has evaporated, 15 to 20 minutes. Serve with tortillas and reserved pickled radishes.

Sheet Pan Cheese Quesadillas

FAST Serves 4 Total Time 40 minutes

Why This Recipe Works Quesadillas are a real crowd-pleaser. To make four in a single go, we bake them on a sheet pan. To prevent the cheese from liquefying and running onto the sheet, we add it only after the first side of each tortilla has been adequately browned. We position the rounded edge of the tortillas toward the center of the baking sheet to best fit four large quesadillas at once. A variation with black beans makes the quesadillas more filling for a quick handheld dinner. Letting the quesadillas cool briefly before cutting them prevents the molten cheese from oozing out. If you're serving quesadillas for a party, you can double the recipe and spread the quesadillas across two sheet pans. Bake the quesadillas on the upper-middle and lower-middle racks and switch and rotate the pans halfway through cooking in step 3. Serve with your favorite accompaniments.

- 4 (10-inch) flour tortillas
- 12 ounces Monterey Jack cheese, shredded (3 cups)

1. Adjust oven rack to middle position and heat oven to 450 degrees. Spray rimmed baking sheet with vegetable oil spray. Fold tortillas in half. Arrange folded tortillas in single layer on prepared sheet with rounded edges facing center of sheet.

2. Bake until tortilla tops and edges begin to turn spotty brown, 4 to 6 minutes. Remove sheet from oven. Flip tortillas over. Using tongs, open each tortilla and fill each with equal amount of Monterey Jack, leaving 1-inch border. Close tortillas and press firmly with spatula to compact.

3. Return quesadillas to oven and continue to bake until crisp around edges and golden brown on second side, 4 to 6 minutes longer. Remove from oven and press quesadillas gently with spatula to deflate any air bubbles. Transfer to wire rack and let cool for 5 minutes. Slice each quesadilla into 4 wedges, and serve.

Variation

FAST **Sheet Pan Black Bean and Jalapeño Quesadillas**

Reduce Monterey Jack to 2 cups. Rinse 1 (15-ounce) can black beans. Using potato masher, mash half of beans in large bowl. Toss mashed beans, remaining black beans, and ¼ cup minced jarred jalapeños with Monterey Jack before filling tortillas in step 2.

Using a Sheet Pan

Arrange folded tortillas on sheet with rounded edge facing center. Flip tortillas once spotty brown. Open tortillas with tongs and fill with cheese.

Spinach and Goat Cheese Quesadillas

FAST Serves 4 Total Time 45 minutes

Why This Recipe Works Making a quesadilla with a complex filling, rather than just cheese, poses a few challenges that could lead to undercooked, bland, or limp and soggy results. We address these issues by using canned red beans along with baby spinach, which is quickly sautéed in a skillet and drained so that it doesn't sog out the quesadilla. Jarred jalapeños deliver superconvenient yet bold flavor, and Monterey Jack and goat cheeses are used not just for their distinctive flavors but also for their ability to easily melt without breaking. Finally, we shallow-fry the quesadillas rather than cooking them in a dry skillet, promoting enhanced browning for flavor and a crispness that can stand up to the heavier filling. If desired, pinto beans or black beans can be used instead of red beans. Two fish spatulas work well for flipping the quesadillas in step 5. For an even quicker meal, prep the filling a day in advance. The quesadillas can be served plain, with your favorite hot sauce, or with Quick Tomato Salsa (page 198).

- 1 tablespoon vegetable oil
- 1 onion, chopped fine
- ½ teaspoon table salt, divided
- 10 ounces (10 cups) baby spinach
- 1 (15-ounce) can small red beans, rinsed
- 4 ounces Monterey Jack cheese, shredded (1 cup)
- 4 ounces goat cheese, crumbled (1 cup)
- ⅓ cup finely chopped jarred jalapeño chiles
- 1½ teaspoons cumin seeds
- 4 (10-inch) flour tortillas
- ¼ cup plus 2 tablespoons vegetable oil for frying, divided

1. Heat 1 tablespoon oil in 12-inch nonstick skillet over medium heat until shimmering. Add onion and ¼ teaspoon salt, and cook, stirring occasionally, until onion is starting to brown, 6 to 7 minutes.

2. Add half of spinach and adjust heat to medium-low. Cover and cook for 1 minute. Add remaining spinach and stir to combine. Cover and cook for 1 minute. Uncover and continue to cook, stirring constantly, until spinach is fully wilted, about 1 minute longer. Transfer spinach mixture to fine-mesh strainer set over medium bowl. Press on spinach with silicone spatula to remove excess water. Wipe out skillet.

top | *Sheet Pan Cheese Quesadillas*
bottom | *Spinach and Goat Cheese Quesadillas*

Chickpea and Poblano Quesadillas

3. Using potato masher, mash beans and remaining ¼ teaspoon salt in large bowl to coarse paste. Add drained spinach mixture, cheeses, jalapeños, and cumin seeds and stir well to combine.

4. Spread one-quarter of filling over half of each tortilla, leaving ½-inch border at edge. Fold tortillas over filling and press firmly to seal. Set wire rack in rimmed baking sheet and line with single layer of paper towels.

5. Heat ¼ cup oil in now-empty skillet over medium heat until shimmering. Place 2 quesadillas in skillet, pressing into pan with thin spatula, and cook until browned on both sides and cheese has melted, 1½ to 2 minutes per side. Transfer to prepared rack. Repeat with remaining 2 tablespoons oil and remaining 2 quesadillas. Cool for at least 3 minutes. Cut into wedges and serve.

Chickpea and Poblano Quesadillas

FAST Serves 4 Total Time 30 minutes

Why This Recipe Works Canned chickpeas add heft, protein, and earthy flavor to these quick weeknight quesadillas. The one-bowl, no-cook filling is a snap to put together. Mashing some of the chickpeas and keeping the rest whole makes for an ideal texture. We add scallions and a poblano to liven up the cheese. Using a heavy saucepan to weigh down the quesadillas while they cook keeps the filling in place and promotes an evenly browned, crisp exterior. An easy avocado sauce makes the perfect accompaniment. If your avocados are not yet ripe, you may need to add an extra 1 to 2 tablespoons of water to the blender when processing the sauce.

- 2 ripe avocados, halved and pitted
- 3 tablespoons water
- 1 tablespoon lime juice
- ¾ teaspoon table salt, divided
- 1 tablespoon chopped fresh cilantro
- 1 (15-ounce) can chickpeas, rinsed
- 8 ounces Monterey Jack cheese, shredded (2 cups)
- 1 poblano chile, stemmed, seeded, and chopped fine
- 3 scallions, sliced thin
- ¼ teaspoon pepper
- 4 (10-inch) flour tortillas
- 2 tablespoons vegetable oil, divided

1. Process avocados, water, lime juice, and ¼ teaspoon salt in blender until smooth, about 30 seconds. Transfer to bowl and stir in cilantro; set aside.

2. Using potato masher, mash half of chickpeas in second bowl. Stir in Monterey Jack, poblano, scallions, pepper, remaining ½ teaspoon salt, and remaining chickpeas until combined. Spread 1 cup chickpea mixture over half of each tortilla, leaving ½-inch border at edge. Fold tortillas over filling and press firmly to seal.

3. Heat 1 tablespoon oil in 12-inch nonstick skillet over medium heat until shimmering. Place 2 quesadillas in skillet. Set large saucepan on top of quesadillas and cook until browned on both sides and cheese is melted, about 2 minutes per side. Transfer to cutting board. Repeat with remaining 1 tablespoon oil and remaining 2 quesadillas. Cut into wedges and serve with avocado sauce.

Cheese Pupusas

Makes 8 pupusas Total Time 1 hour, plus 1 hour 20 minutes chilling and resting

Why This Recipe Works Pupusas are savory stuffed corn cakes that have a long history in Honduras and El Salvador, where they're made by stuffing cheese, beans, braised meat, or a combination thereof into a ball of corn flour dough called masa. The ball is flattened into a disk and cooked on a cast-iron griddle (called a comal) until the tender cake forms a crisp, spotty-brown shell. Served with curtido (a pickled cabbage slaw) and tomato salsa, the result is irresistible. Hydrating the masa harina with boiling (rather than room-temperature) water lets the starches in the flour absorb it quickly and completely, resulting in an easy-to-handle dough. Properly hydrated masa dough should be tacky, requiring damp hands to keep it from sticking. If the dough feels the slightest bit dry at any time, knead in a little warm tap water until the dough is tacky. Pressing the stuffed pupusas between sheets of marked plastic ensures uniform size. An occasional leak while frying the pupusas is to be expected—and the browned cheese is delicious. For an accurate measurement of boiling water, bring a kettle of water to a boil and then measure out the desired amount. For a spicier curtido, add the jalapeño seeds.

Curtido

- 1 cup cider vinegar
- ½ cup water
- 1 tablespoon sugar
- 1½ teaspoons table salt
- ½ head green cabbage, cored and sliced thin (6 cups)
- 1 onion, sliced thin
- 1 carrot, peeled and shredded
- 1 jalapeño chile, stemmed, seeded, and minced
- 1 teaspoon dried oregano
- 1 cup chopped fresh cilantro

Pupusas

- 2 cups (8 ounces) masa harina
- ½ teaspoon table salt
- 2 cups boiling water, plus warm tap water as needed
- 2 teaspoons vegetable oil, divided
- 2 ounces cotija cheese, cut into 2 pieces
- 8 ounces Monterey Jack cheese, cut into 8 pieces
- 1 recipe Quick Tomato Salsa (recipe follows)

1. **For the curtido** Whisk vinegar, water, sugar, and salt in large bowl until sugar has dissolved. Add cabbage, onion, carrot, jalapeño, and oregano and toss to combine. Cover and refrigerate for at least 1 hour or up to 24 hours.

2. **For the pupusas** Mix masa harina and salt together in medium bowl. Add boiling water and 1 teaspoon oil and mix with silicone spatula until soft dough forms. Cover dough and let rest for 20 minutes.

3. While dough rests, draw 4-inch circle in center of 1 side of 1-quart or 1-gallon zipper-lock bag with marker. Cut open seams along both sides of bag, but leave bottom seam intact so that bag opens completely. Line rimmed baking sheet with parchment paper. Process cotija and Monterey Jack in food processor until mixture resembles wet oatmeal, about 30 seconds (it will not form cohesive mass). Remove processor blade. Form cheese into 8 balls, weighing about 1¼ ounces each, and place balls on 1 half of prepared sheet.

4. Knead dough in bowl for 15 to 20 seconds. Test dough's hydration by flattening golf ball–size piece. If cracks larger than ¼ inch form around edges, add warm tap water, 2 teaspoons at a time, until dough is soft and slightly tacky. Transfer dough to counter, shape into large ball, and divide into 8 equal pieces. Using your damp hands, roll 1 dough piece into ball and place on empty half of prepared sheet. Cover with damp dish towel. Repeat with remaining dough pieces.

5. Place open cut bag marked side down on counter. Place 1 dough ball in center of circle. Fold other side of bag over ball. Using glass pie plate or 8-inch square baking dish, gently press dough to 4-inch diameter, using circle drawn on bag as guide. Turn out disk into your palm and place 1 ball cheese filling in center. Bring sides of dough up around filling and pinch top to seal. Remoisten your hands and roll ball until smooth, smoothing any cracks with your damp fingertip. Return ball to bag and slowly press to 4-inch diameter. Pinch closed any small cracks that form at edges. Return pupusa to sheet and cover with damp dish towel. Repeat with remaining dough and filling.

6. Heat remaining 1 teaspoon oil in 12-inch nonstick skillet over medium-high heat until shimmering. Wipe skillet clean with paper towels. Carefully lay 4 pupusas in skillet and cook until spotty brown on both sides, 2 to 4 minutes per side. Transfer to platter and repeat with remaining 4 pupusas. Toss curtido, then drain. Return curtido to bowl and stir in cilantro. Serve pupusas warm with curtido and salsa.

Quick Tomato Salsa

FAST **VEGAN** Makes 2 cups Total Time 10 minutes

For a spicier salsa, add the jalapeño seeds.

- ¼ small red onion
- 2 tablespoons minced fresh cilantro
- ½ small jalapeño chile, seeded and minced
- 1 (14.5-ounce) can diced tomatoes, drained
- 2 teaspoons lime juice, plus extra for seasoning
- 1 small garlic clove, minced
- ¼ teaspoon table salt
- Pinch pepper

Pulse onion, cilantro, and jalapeño in food processor until finely chopped, 5 pulses, scraping down sides of bowl as needed. Add tomatoes, lime juice, garlic, salt, and pepper and process until smooth, 20 to 30 seconds. Season with salt and extra lime juice to taste.

Shaping Pupusas

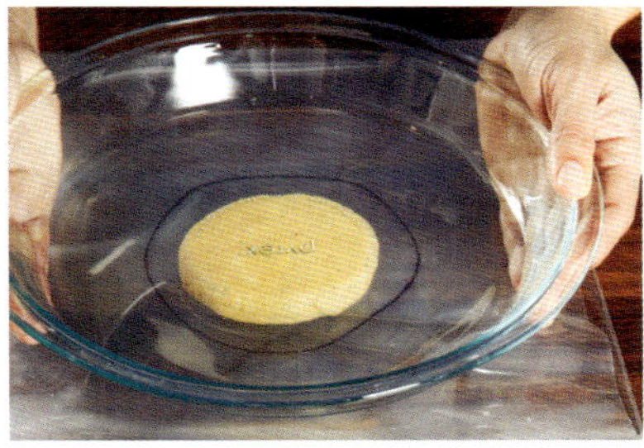

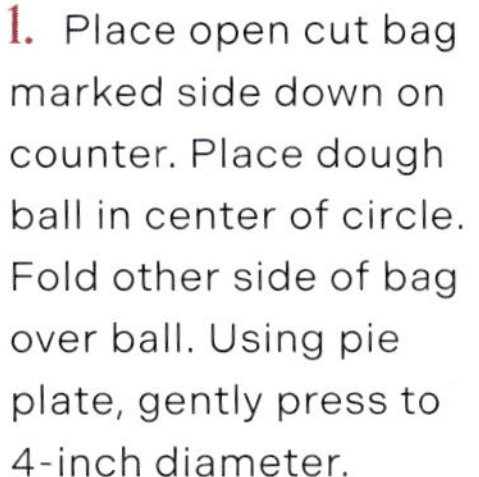

1. Place open cut bag marked side down on counter. Place dough ball in center of circle. Fold other side of bag over ball. Using pie plate, gently press to 4-inch diameter.

2. Turn out disk into your palm and place cheese ball in center. Bring dough up around filling; pinch to seal. Remoisten hands and roll ball, smoothing any cracks with your damp fingertip.

3. Return ball to bag and use pie plate to slowly press to 4-inch diameter. Pinch closed any small cracks that form at edges. Repeat with remaining dough and filling.

Black Bean and Cheese Arepas

FAST Serves 4 Total Time 45 minutes

Why This Recipe Works In Venezuela, arepas—the corn cakes popular in many Latin countries—are served split open and stuffed with different fillings, including cheese, beans, and corn. The arepas come together from a dough made with masarepa blanca (an instant flour made from cooked corn), water, and salt, but getting the consistency right can be tricky. We found that using just a half cup more water than masarepa produced a dough that was easy to shape, and a small amount of baking powder lightened the texture. We shaped the dough into rounds, browned them in a skillet, and finished them in the oven. For a hearty filling, we combined canned black beans with Monterey Jack cheese; cilantro added freshness, lime juice offered an acidic boost, and chili powder brought a hint of heat. Masarepa is also

Cheese Pupusas

known as harina precocida and masa al instante. We had best results using P.A.N. precooked white cornmeal. Do not use Goya brand masarepa blanca.

Arepas

- 2 cups (10 ounces) masarepa blanca
- 1 teaspoon table salt
- 1 teaspoon baking powder
- 2½ cups warm water
- ¼ cup vegetable oil, divided

Black Bean Filling

- 1 (15-ounce) can black beans, rinsed
- 4 ounces Monterey Jack cheese, shredded (1 cup)
- 2 tablespoons minced fresh cilantro
- 2 scallions, sliced thin
- 1 tablespoon lime juice
- ¼ teaspoon chili powder

1. **For the arepas** Adjust oven rack to middle position and heat oven to 400 degrees. Whisk masarepa, salt, and baking powder together in large bowl. Gradually add warm water, stirring until combined. Using generous ⅓ cup dough for each round, form into eight 3-inch rounds, each about ½ inch thick.

2. Heat 2 tablespoons oil in 12-inch nonstick skillet over medium-high heat until shimmering. Add 4 arepas and cook until golden on both sides, about 4 minutes per side. Transfer arepas to wire rack set in rimmed baking sheet. Wipe out skillet with paper towels and repeat with remaining 2 tablespoons oil and remaining 4 arepas. (Fried arepas can be refrigerated for up to 3 days or frozen for up to 1 month. Increase baking time as needed; if frozen, do not thaw before baking.) Bake arepas on wire rack until they sound hollow when tapped on bottom, about 10 minutes.

3. **For the filling** Meanwhile, using potato masher or fork, mash beans in bowl until most are broken. Stir in Monterey Jack, cilantro, scallions, lime juice, and chili powder and season with salt and pepper to taste.

4. Using fork, gently split hot, baked arepas open. Stuff each with 3 heaping tablespoons filling. Serve.

Variation

FAST VEGAN Avocado, Tomato, and Bell Pepper Arepas

Omit black beans and cheese. Increase cilantro to ¼ cup, scallions to 4, lime juice to 3 tablespoons, and chili powder to ½ teaspoon. Add to filling 2 halved and pitted avocados, 1 chopped and 1 mashed; 2 tomatoes, cored and chopped into ½-inch pieces; and 1 yellow bell pepper, stemmed, cored, and cut into ¼-inch pieces.

Cheddar-Crusted Grilled Cheese

FAST Serves 2 Total Time 30 minutes

Why This Recipe Works Here's how to transform a grilled cheese sandwich from good to spectacular. For richness, we spread a little mayonnaise on one side of the bread. Sliced American cheese clings to the bread and melts like a dream, and shredded sharp cheddar adds its distinctive flavor. We melt butter in a nonstick skillet, add the sandwiches, and cover the skillet; this traps the heat and steam, which helps the cheese melt as the bread slowly browns. We then push the limits by sprinkling more shredded cheddar directly into the empty skillet in the shape of the bread and put the sandwiches directly on the cheese. The cheese melts and fuses to the sandwiches, making for a delectable cheesy crust. A 5-minute rest on a wire rack allows the crust to continue to crisp. Use a 12-inch nonstick skillet with a tight-fitting lid here. While crisping the cheese crust in step 5, avoid flipping the sandwiches too early. At first, the cheese will be soft and melty, but it will crisp as it continues to cook. When sprinkling the cheese in the skillet for the crust, be sure to leave enough room between the portions so that the cheese doesn't run together. For the best flavor, buy the American cheese at the deli counter, not the presliced cheese that comes wrapped in cellophane. To serve four, double the ingredients; once the first two grilled cheeses are cooked, transfer them to a wire rack set in a rimmed baking sheet and keep warm in a 200-degree oven.

- 2 teaspoons mayonnaise
- 4 slices hearty white sandwich bread
- 2 slices deli American cheese (1½ ounces)
- 4 ounces sharp white cheddar cheese, shredded (1 cup), divided
- 2 tablespoons unsalted butter, divided

1. Spread mayonnaise evenly on 1 side of each slice of bread. Layer 1 slice American cheese and ¼ cup cheddar on mayonnaise side of each of 2 slices bread. Top with remaining 2 slices bread, mayonnaise side down.

2. Melt 1 tablespoon butter in 12-inch nonstick skillet over medium heat. Place sandwiches in skillet. Cover and cook until deep golden brown on bottom, 4 to 7 minutes.

3. Using spatula, carefully flip sandwiches. Add remaining 1 tablespoon butter to center of skillet between sandwiches and tilt to distribute butter as it melts. Cover and continue to cook until second side is deep golden brown and cheese is visibly melted around edges of sandwiches, 2 to 5 minutes. Transfer sandwiches to wire rack.

4. Remove skillet from heat and wipe clean with paper towels. Sprinkle two ¼-cup portions of remaining cheddar into rectangles just larger than slices of bread, about 6 by 4 inches, on opposite sides of now-empty skillet. Place sandwiches directly on top of cheddar.

5. Return skillet to medium heat and cook until edges of cheddar beneath sandwiches are well browned and crisp, 2 to 4 minutes. (Do not slide spatula under sandwiches before cheddar is crisp; it will pull cheddar and ruin crust.) When cheddar is browned along edges, slide spatula underneath sandwiches and transfer, cheddar crust side up, to rack. (For decorative purposes, you can upturn edges of cheddar crust, if desired.) Let sandwiches sit for 5 minutes to allow cheese to set. Transfer sandwiches to cutting board and cut diagonally. Serve.

Variation

FAST Cheddar-Crusted Grilled Cheese with Tomato

Shingle 2 thin tomato slices on top of American cheese in each sandwich. Sprinkle tomato slices with 1 tablespoon grated Parmesan and pinch each of table salt, pepper, red pepper flakes, dried oregano, and garlic powder. Sprinkle cheddar over tomato layer.

top | *Black Bean and Cheese Arepas*

bottom | *Cheddar-Crusted Grilled Cheese with Tomato*

Mushroom, Lettuce, and Tomato Sandwiches

Marinated Tomato Sandwiches

FAST VEGAN Serves 2 Total Time 30 minutes

Why This Recipe Works This recipe will broaden your tomato sandwich horizons. Slices of vine-ripened tomatoes get an infusion of juicy tang by being submerged in a warm vinegar-sriracha marinade to tenderize them, add moisture, and punch up their flavor. Instead of bread, a toasted English muffin provides a craggy, grippy sandwich base that can absorb the tomato juices. Adding mashed avocado before layering on the tomatoes provides richness. A layer of alfalfa sprouts prevents the tomato slices from slipping against each other, and their earthiness highlights the tomatoes' sweet, fruity flavor. Choose tomatoes that are 2 to 2½ inches in diameter to make the neatest sandwich. If you do not own a microwave, heat the marinade in a small saucepan over medium-high heat. When it registers 160 to 170 degrees, pour it over the tomatoes. You can substitute baby arugula for the watercress. For a spicier sandwich, use the full amount of sriracha.

- ⅓ cup cider vinegar
- ¼ cup water
- 2½ teaspoons sugar
- ½–1 teaspoon sriracha
- ⅛ teaspoon table salt
- 2 vine-ripened tomatoes (4 ounces each), cored and sliced ¼ inch thick
- ½ avocado, sliced thin
- 2 English muffins, split and lightly toasted
- ½ ounce (¼ cup) alfalfa sprouts
- ½ cup watercress

1. Stir together vinegar, water, sugar, sriracha, and salt in 8-inch square microwave-safe baking dish. Add tomatoes in even layer. Microwave until marinade begins to steam, 1½ to 2 minutes. Let tomatoes marinate at room temperature for 10 minutes.

2. Line large plate with single layer of paper towels. Transfer tomatoes to prepared plate. Divide avocado between English muffin bottoms. Using fork, lightly mash avocado.

3. To build each sandwich, top avocado with one-quarter of tomato slices followed by half of alfalfa sprouts, another quarter of tomato slices, half of watercress, and English muffin top. Serve.

Mushroom, Lettuce, and Tomato Sandwiches

VEGAN Serves 4 Total Time 50 minutes

Why This Recipe Works A classic BLT nicely balances a few simple ingredients: salty-crisp bacon, sweet and juicy tomatoes, and refreshing lettuce, all tied together with a slick of mayonnaise. Meet that famous sandwich's equally splendid cousin: the MLT. To create a flavor-packed vegetarian version, we use strips of portobello mushrooms. When sautéed and seasoned with smoked paprika and a little salt, they develop meaty texture, umami character, and even some smokiness. Using a full 1½ pounds of mushrooms provides plenty of substance. We kept the juicy tomatoes but swapped lettuce for arugula, as its peppery bite perks up the other flavors. Finally, for a creamy, tangy spread to slather on, we mix avocado and yogurt to complete the sandwich. To make this recipe vegan, substitute plant-based yogurt for the dairy yogurt.

- 1 tablespoon extra-virgin olive oil
- 1 shallot, minced
- 1½ pounds portobello mushroom caps, gills removed, sliced ½ inch thick
- ½ teaspoon plus ⅛ teaspoon table salt, divided
- 1 garlic clove, minced
- ½ teaspoon smoked paprika
- 1 ripe avocado, halved and pitted
- 2 tablespoons plain yogurt
- 8 slices rustic bread, toasted
- 2 tomatoes, cored and sliced thin
- 2 ounces (2 cups) baby arugula

1. Heat oil in 12-inch nonstick skillet over medium heat until shimmering. Add shallot and cook until softened, about 2 minutes. Add mushrooms and ½ teaspoon salt. Cover and cook, stirring occasionally, until mushrooms have released their liquid, 10 to 12 minutes.

2. Uncover; increase heat to medium-high; and cook, stirring occasionally, until mushrooms are browned, about 10 minutes. Stir in garlic and smoked paprika and cook until fragrant, about 30 seconds. Off heat, let mushrooms cool for 10 minutes.

3. Just before serving, combine avocado, yogurt, and remaining ⅛ teaspoon salt in small bowl and mash until smooth. Spread avocado mixture evenly over 4 toast slices. Layer mushrooms, tomatoes, and then arugula over avocado mixture. Top with remaining 4 toast slices. Serve.

The Power of Pickled Cabbage

Pickles are an expected sandwich garnish. Here we make crunchy and tangy pickled red cabbage a star ingredient, piling it high on a delicious all-veg sandwich.

Tastes Good and Looks Good

Red cabbage is the sweetest of the cabbages. It adds texture to our sandwich and beautiful color, turning a stunning pink when pickled.

Partially Cooked

Pickled cabbage is halfway between raw and cooked. Fermentation has long been a common way to prepare cabbage, turning it into popular foods such as sauerkraut and kimchi. We wanted to be able to make our sandwich on short notice, so we turned to quick pickling. A hot vinegary brine poured over shredded cabbage takes just 30 minutes to turn it pleasingly crisp and suffuse it with great flavor.

It's Healthy

Still something of an underdog in the vegetable world, cabbage is a cruciferous vegetable, which means that it is super-healthy. Cabbage has antioxidant compounds as well as a high concentration of vitamins A and C.

Creamy Mushroom and Pink Pickled Cabbage Sandwiches

Creamy Mushroom and Pink Pickled Cabbage Sandwiches

Serves 4 Total Time 30 minutes, plus 30 minutes pickling

Why This Recipe Works This texturally varied sandwich is a loving vegetarian tribute to a favorite lunch offering at acclaimed Bagelsaurus in Cambridge, Massachusetts. Their hot smoked salmon bagel is served with pickled red cabbage, red onion, and fresh dill. The pickled cabbage is arguably our favorite component, so we decided to make the bright-fuchsia ingredient the star of our sandwich. We soak fiber-packed red cabbage in rice vinegar with a little sugar, which gives us sturdy, chewy pickles with a balanced taste that isn't overly acidic; caraway seeds further deepen the flavor profile. Atop this satisfyingly crisp mound of vegetables, we add a lot of dill, treating the fragrant herb as more of a salad green than a garnish. Searing some maitake or oyster mushrooms—particularly fleshy, meaty varieties—intensifies their umami. We mix the mushrooms with sour cream (letting the mushrooms cool first so the cream doesn't break) and scallions to create a creamy filling with pops of zesty freshness. We like using up to ½ cup of torn fresh dill, but you can use less if you prefer.

- ½ cup unseasoned rice vinegar
- 2 teaspoons sugar
- 1 teaspoon caraway seeds
- ¼ teaspoon table salt for pickling
- 2 cups shredded red cabbage
- 1 tablespoon vegetable oil
- 1 pound maitake or oyster mushrooms, trimmed and torn into 1- to 1½-inch pieces
- ½ teaspoon table salt, divided
- ⅓ cup sour cream
- 3 scallions, sliced thin
- 4 hamburger buns, toasted
- Torn fresh dill

1. Microwave vinegar, sugar, caraway seeds, and ¼ teaspoon salt in medium bowl until simmering, 1 to 2 minutes; whisk to dissolve sugar. Add cabbage; press to submerge; and let sit, stirring occasionally, for 30 minutes. Drain cabbage and set aside.

2. Heat oil in 12-inch nonstick skillet over medium-high heat until shimmering. Add mushrooms and ¼ teaspoon salt. Cover and cook, stirring occasionally, until mushrooms have released their liquid, 3 to 5 minutes. Uncover and cook, stirring occasionally, until mushrooms are well browned, 5 to 10 minutes.

3. Transfer mushrooms to bowl and let cool for 5 minutes. Add sour cream, scallions, and remaining ¼ teaspoon salt and toss to combine. Divide mushroom mixture among bun bottoms and top with pickled cabbage, dill, and bun tops. Serve.

Cutty's-Inspired Eggplant Spuckie

FAST Serves 4 Total Time 40 minutes

Why This Recipe Works This hearty sandwich will make you fall in love with eggplant. A spuckie is what some old-school Bostonians call a sub sandwich. This particular spuckie, inspired by one at the Boston-area sandwich shop Cutty's, is a test kitchen favorite. The star of the show is the eggplant, which we broil until it turns silky-soft and browned. We pair it with thick slices of mozzarella for a satisfying sandwich filling. The briny carrot-olive spread comes together quickly in the food processor and adds flavor and crunch while gluing the sandwich together. Piling it all on chewy, airy ciabatta rolls rounds out every bite. It's OK to use the tender, thin stems at the base of the parsley leaves.

- 1½ pounds eggplant, sliced into ½-inch-thick rounds
- ½ cup extra-virgin olive oil, divided
- 1 teaspoon table salt, divided
- ¾ cup pitted kalamata olives
- ½ cup fresh parsley leaves
- ½ cup jarred roasted red peppers, coarsely chopped
- 1 teaspoon red wine vinegar
- 1 small garlic clove, minced
- ¼ teaspoon red pepper flakes
- 1 cup shredded carrots
- 4 ciabatta sandwich rolls, halved lengthwise
- 8 ounces fresh mozzarella cheese, sliced into ¼-inch-thick rounds

1. Adjust oven rack 6 inches from broiler element and heat broiler. Line rimmed baking sheet with aluminum foil and spray with vegetable oil spray. Brush eggplant slices with 2 tablespoons oil, sprinkle with ¾ teaspoon salt, and arrange on prepared sheet. Broil eggplant until softened and beginning to brown, 10 to 14 minutes, flipping halfway through cooking. Transfer eggplant to plate and set aside.

2. Pulse olives, parsley, red peppers, vinegar, garlic, pepper flakes, and remaining ¼ teaspoon salt in food processor until chopped, 8 to 10 pulses. Transfer to bowl and stir in carrots and 2 tablespoons oil.

3. Arrange rolls on now-empty sheet and brush cut sides with remaining ¼ cup oil. Broil rolls, cut sides up, until golden brown, 2 to 5 minutes. Spread carrot-olive mixture evenly on cut sides of each roll. Distribute mozzarella and eggplant evenly among roll bottoms, then cap with roll tops. Serve.

Beet, Orange, and Chèvre Tartines

FAST Serves 4 Total Time 30 minutes

Why This Recipe Works A thoughtfully designed French open-faced sandwich, called a tartine, displays a range of flavors and textures and caters to the eyes as well as the palate. It is a triple-decker affair: The base is a generous slice of bread that's often toasted. The middle is often a luscious, savory spread. Finally, the crowning layer is a colorful and tasty topping. Here earthy beets are paired with vibrant orange and tangy chèvre to make attractive, flavor-packed tartines. We reduced the usual lengthy cooking time for the beets by slicing them thin, seasoning them well, and steaming them in the microwave. Dressing the beets with white wine vinegar while they are still hot mellows the vinegar's tang. Thinning the snow-white chèvre with water creates a spreadable consistency so that it can be smeared across a baguette before the oranges, beets, and a peppery arugula–olive oil dressing are arranged on top. Finally, a sprinkle of chopped hazelnuts provides nutty sweetness and crunch. Look for beets that are about 4 inches in diameter. Rustic country bread or a fine-crumbed bread such as pain de mie or brioche can be substituted; cut slices that are 6 inches wide and ¾ inch thick and toast. These tartines are substantial enough to be a light lunch or brunch.

- 1 pound medium beets, trimmed, peeled, halved, and sliced ¼ inch thick
- ¾ teaspoon table salt, divided
- 5 tablespoons water, divided
- 2 tablespoons white wine vinegar, divided
- ½ teaspoon pepper, divided
- 2 oranges
- 2 ounces (2 cups) arugula
- 3 tablespoons extra-virgin olive oil
- 1 tablespoon whole-grain mustard
- 10 ounces chèvre, crumbled (2½ cups)
- 2 (6-inch) pieces baguette, halved lengthwise
- 2 tablespoons chopped toasted hazelnuts

1. Toss beets and ½ teaspoon salt in large bowl. Add 1 tablespoon water and cover with plate. Microwave until beets can be easily pierced with paring knife, about 10 minutes, stirring halfway through microwaving. Add 1 tablespoon vinegar and ¼ teaspoon pepper and toss to combine; set aside.

2. Cut away peel and pith from oranges. Cut oranges into ½-inch pieces (you should have about 2 cups) and transfer to second bowl. Process arugula, oil, mustard, remaining ¼ teaspoon salt, remaining 1 tablespoon vinegar, and remaining ¼ teaspoon pepper in food processor until finely chopped, about 10 seconds, scraping down sides of bowl as needed. Transfer to bowl with orange pieces and toss to combine.

3. In separate bowl, whisk chèvre and remaining ¼ cup water until smooth. Divide chèvre mixture evenly among bread pieces and spread into even layer. Distribute half of orange mixture over chèvre spread. Top with beets and remaining orange mixture. Sprinkle with hazelnuts. Serve.

Raw Vegetable Wraps

FAST Serves 4 Total Time 25 minutes

Why This Recipe Works There's nothing more appealing than the cool, crunchy bite of raw vegetables, and this wrap turns them into a quick no-cook meal, perfect on a hot summer night. The recipe calls for chopping up some great-tasting vegetables, mixing together a four-ingredient spread, and wrapping it all up in a large flour tortilla. We've selected the perfect texture combination of crunchy, creamy, and juicy vegetables to create the ultimate raw vegetable wrap. The flavor explosion from the feta spread transforms the big pile of raw vegetables into a deliciously satisfying wrap. If you don't have or like one of the vegetables, double up on another vegetable of the same consistency: carrots, cabbage, cucumber for crunchy; tomatoes and roasted red pepper for soft/juicy. If you don't have avocado, double the feta spread. Look for extra-large 12-inch tortillas for these wraps; if you can only find 10-inch tortillas, divide the ingredients among 6 tortillas. Quickly warming the tortillas in a skillet makes them more pliable and easier to roll into wraps. If you can't find marinated feta, substitute 8 ounces traditional feta, crumbled, plus ¼ cup extra-virgin olive oil. You can substitute ½ English cucumber, halved lengthwise, for the Persian cucumbers; baby arugula for the alfalfa sprouts; and coleslaw mix for the cabbage. A vegetable peeler makes quick work of shaving the carrots into ribbons.

- 2 tomatoes, cored and sliced thin
- ½ teaspoon plus pinch kosher salt, divided
- ¾ teaspoon pepper, divided
- 8 ounces marinated feta cheese (2 cups), plus ¼ cup marinated feta oil
- ¼ cup chopped fresh dill
- 2 tablespoons oil-packed sun-dried tomatoes, chopped
- 4 (12-inch) flour tortillas, warmed
- 6 ounces (3 cups) alfalfa sprouts
- 2 carrots, peeled and shaved into ribbons
- 2 Persian cucumbers, sliced thin on bias
- 1 cup jarred roasted red pepper strips, rinsed, patted dry, and sliced thin
- 2 cups thinly sliced red cabbage
- 2 avocados, halved, pitted, and sliced thin

1. Arrange tomato slices on paper towel–lined plate and sprinkle with ½ teaspoon salt and ½ teaspoon pepper. Using fork, mash feta and feta oil, dill, sun-dried tomatoes, and remaining ¼ teaspoon pepper in bowl until well combined. (Feta spread can be refrigerated for up to 1 week. Bring to room temperature before using.)

2. Divide feta mixture evenly among tortillas and spread into even layer, leaving 3-inch border around edge. Working with one wrap at a time, sprinkle one-quarter sprouts in 3-inch-wide strip just below center of wrap, then top with tomatoes, carrot ribbons, cucumbers, red peppers, cabbage, and avocado; sprinkle with remaining pinch salt. Fold bottom of tortilla over vegetables, then fold in sides over top. Roll bundle tightly away from you, tucking in sides as you roll. Cut wraps in half and serve.

Building the Wrap

Spread circle of feta mixture in center of wrap. Sprinkle sprouts just below center of wrap. Top with layer of tomatoes, carrots, cucumbers, red peppers, and red cabbage, and finish with avocado.

top | *Beet, Orange, and Chèvre Tartines*
bottom | *Raw Vegetable Wraps*

Roasted Vegetable Sandwiches

Roasted Vegetable Sandwiches

VEGAN Serves 4 Total Time 55 minutes

Why This Recipe Works For the filling in these hefty meatless sandwiches, carrots, fennel, and red onion are roasted until creamy-tender with savory browning. Jarred Calabrian chiles add a piquant heat to creamy ricotta, which we spread thickly on both sides of toasted ciabatta rolls to hold these satisfying sandwiches together. Peppery arugula and bright lemon help cut through the richness of the cheese. We developed this recipe using BelGioioso Ricotta con Latte Whole Milk Ricotta Cheese. To make this recipe vegan, substitute plant-based ricotta for the dairy ricotta cheese.

- 10 ounces carrots, peeled and cut into 3-inch sticks
- 1 fennel bulb, stalks discarded, bulb halved, cored, and cut into ½-inch-thick wedges
- 1 small red onion, cut through root end into ½-inch-thick wedges
- 5 tablespoons extra-virgin olive oil, divided
- ¾ teaspoon plus pinch table salt, divided
- ¾ teaspoon plus pinch pepper, divided
- 8 ounces (1 cup) whole-milk ricotta cheese
- 1 tablespoon jarred crushed Calabrian chiles
- 1 teaspoon grated lemon zest, plus 2 teaspoons juice
- 2 cups (2 ounces) baby arugula
- 4 ciabatta sandwich rolls, split

1. Adjust oven rack to upper-middle position and heat oven to 450 degrees. Toss carrots, fennel, onion, 2 tablespoons oil, ½ teaspoon salt, and ½ teaspoon pepper together on rimmed baking sheet. Roast vegetables until well browned and tender, 25 to 30 minutes; transfer to plate and set aside.

2. Stir ricotta, Calabrian chiles, lemon zest, ¼ teaspoon salt, and ¼ teaspoon pepper together in bowl. Toss arugula, lemon juice, and remaining pinch salt and pinch pepper together in second bowl.

3. Arrange rolls cut side up on now-empty sheet and brush cut sides with remaining 3 tablespoons oil. Bake rolls until golden brown, 2 to 5 minutes. Spread ricotta mixture on cut sides of rolls. Distribute vegetable mixture and arugula evenly among roll bottoms, then cap with roll tops. Serve.

Ultimate Grilled Vegetable Sandwiches

Serves 4 to 6 Total Time 1½ hours

Why This Recipe Works Smoky grilled vegetables, melted mozzarella, and basil mayo take this bright sandwich over the top. It starts with a medley of summer vegetables: eggplant, zucchini, red bell pepper, and red onion cut to maximize their surface area for the most flavorful grill marks. We brush the vegetables with a garlicky olive oil and then grill them until charred and tender but not mushy. Tossing the grilled eggplant and zucchini in a balsamic dressing imbues them with tangy flavor throughout and softens them to the perfect silky consistency. Thinly slicing the grilled bell pepper and onion prevents large, slippery pieces from falling out of the sandwich. We start with a punchy basil mayonnaise in a hollowed-out ciabatta loaf, then layer the vegetables with fresh mozzarella on the bottom (to prevent the bread from getting soggy) and grill the whole thing again to toast it. Be sure to use fresh bread here; once ciabatta becomes stale, the crust becomes tough and the sandwiches will be difficult to eat.

- 1 (1-pound) loaf ciabatta, halved horizontally
- ½ cup chopped fresh basil
- ⅓ cup mayonnaise
- ⅔ ounce Parmesan cheese, grated (⅓ cup)
- 2 tablespoons capers, rinsed and chopped
- 1 teaspoon pepper, divided
- 6 tablespoons extra-virgin olive oil
- 5 garlic cloves, minced
- ¼ teaspoon red pepper flakes
- 1 pound eggplant, sliced into ¼-inch-thick rounds
- 1 (8-ounce) zucchini, halved crosswise and sliced lengthwise ¼ inch thick
- 1 red bell pepper, stemmed, seeded, and quartered
- ½ small red onion, cut into 2 wedges through root end
- 1 teaspoon plus ⅛ teaspoon table salt, divided
- 1 tablespoon balsamic vinegar
- 8 ounces fresh mozzarella cheese, sliced into ¼-inch-thick rounds

1. Using your hands, hollow out ciabatta by removing inner crumb, leaving ¼-inch border on sides and bottom; set aside. Combine basil, mayonnaise, Parmesan, capers, and ½ teaspoon pepper in bowl; set aside.

2. Combine oil, garlic, and pepper flakes in 1-cup liquid measuring cup. Microwave, uncovered, until bubbling and fragrant, about 90 seconds. Place eggplant, zucchini, bell pepper, and onion on rimmed baking sheet (vegetables will overlap) and brush all over with ¼ cup garlic oil (brush eggplant last, as it will absorb more oil than other vegetables). Sprinkle vegetables with 1 teaspoon salt and remaining ½ teaspoon pepper.

3A. For a charcoal grill Open bottom vent completely. Light large chimney starter filled with charcoal briquettes (6 quarts). When top coals are partially covered with ash, pour evenly over grill. Set cooking grate in place, cover, and open lid vent completely. Heat grill until hot, about 5 minutes.

3B. For a gas grill Turn all burners to high; cover; and heat grill until hot, about 15 minutes. Turn all burners to medium-high.

4. Clean and oil cooking grate. Arrange eggplant and zucchini on grill and cook (covered if using gas) until well-browned and tender, 6 to 9 minutes, flipping as needed for even browning. Transfer eggplant and zucchini to large bowl as each piece finishes cooking. Add 1 tablespoon garlic oil and vinegar and toss to combine; set aside.

5. Arrange bell pepper and onion on now-empty grill and cook (covered if using gas) until well browned and tender, 12 to 16 minutes, flipping as needed for even browning. Transfer bell pepper and onion to cutting board; slice thin, then sprinkle with remaining ⅛ teaspoon salt. (Grill will be used again in step 7.)

6. Brush ciabatta crust with remaining 1 tablespoon garlic oil. Spread mayonnaise mixture inside ciabatta. Build sandwich by layering mozzarella on bottom, followed by eggplant and zucchini, and finally bell pepper and onion. Cap with ciabatta top. Wrap tightly in aluminum foil.

7. Transfer foil-wrapped sandwich to grill and cook, pressing occasionally with spatula, until bread is dark golden brown and charred in spots, 1 to 3 minutes per side (peel back small piece of foil to check bread color). Transfer to cutting board and let foil-wrapped sandwich rest for 5 minutes. Unwrap sandwich, slice, and serve.

Using Bread Scraps

This recipe calls for hollowing out a loaf of ciabatta. Give the removed bread a blitz in a food processor to make fresh bread crumbs. If you like, season the crumbs and dry them in a low oven.

Chickpea Salad Sandwiches with Quick Pickles

FAST Serves 4 Total Time 20 minutes

Why This Recipe Works This easy bean-based sandwich offers all the satisfaction of a traditional deli-style salad. Protein-packed chickpeas retain a creamy, practically saucy texture. Mayonnaise lends a smooth richness, but using too much of it masks the legumes' earthiness. To ensure more pronounced chickpea flavor in every bite, we blitz a portion of the chickpeas in a food processor with mayo, lemon juice, and salt to make a binder reminiscent of hummus. We then add the remaining chickpeas and, to maintain some textural contrast, pulse the mixture just briefly. This makes for a chunky, extra-satisfying sandwich filling. Dill brings a refreshing grassiness that complements the cool, creamy chickpeas. For a tart dimension, we quickly pickle some cucumber slices by simply tossing them with onion and vinegar. We also add a layer of thinly sliced boiled eggs to up the protein and heartiness of the meal. Loaded onto chewy pumpernickel bread, this chickpea salad makes a luscious sandwich sure to upgrade any lunchtime.

- ½ English cucumber, sliced thin
- ½ small red onion, sliced thin
- ¼ cup cider vinegar
- ½ teaspoon table salt for brining
- 2 (15-ounce) cans chickpeas, rinsed, divided
- ½ cup mayonnaise
- 1 tablespoon lemon juice
- ½ teaspoon table salt
- 2 tablespoons chopped fresh dill
- 8 slices pumpernickel sandwich bread
- 2 Easy-Peel Hard-Cooked Eggs (page 450), sliced thin
- 4 leaves Bibb lettuce

1. Combine cucumber, onion, vinegar, and ½ teaspoon salt in bowl; set aside, tossing occasionally.

2. Process ¾ cup chickpeas, mayonnaise, lemon juice, and salt in food processor until smooth, about 30 seconds, scraping down sides of bowl as needed. Add dill and remaining chickpeas to food processor and pulse until coarsely chopped with some larger pieces remaining, about 4 pulses. Season with salt to taste.

3. Drain cucumber mixture. Spread chickpea salad evenly over 4 bread slices. Layer eggs, cucumber mixture, and then lettuce over salad. Top with remaining 4 bread slices. Serve.

Spiced Smashed Chickpea Wraps

FAST **VEGAN** Serves 4 Total Time 20 minutes

Why This Recipe Works This fresh take on a rolled-up pita sandwich makes canned chickpeas the star of the filling. Mashing the chickpeas lightly breaks their skins and allows them to soak up the warming flavor of the cumin and the zing of the chili-garlic sauce. Taking a cue from Greek gyros, we spread toasted pitas with a generous smear of yogurt sauce before adding the seasoned beans. Bracing red onion, zippy pepperoncini, and cooling cucumber add three different kinds of crunch. For more heat, serve with extra chili-garlic sauce. We like to spread the pitas with our Tahini-Yogurt Sauce, but you can substitute simply seasoned Greek yogurt, if you prefer.

- 2 (15-ounce) cans chickpeas, rinsed
- 2 tablespoons chili-garlic sauce
- 2 teaspoons ground cumin
- ½ teaspoon table salt
- 1 recipe Tahini-Yogurt Sauce (recipe follows)
- 4 (8-inch) pitas, lightly toasted
- ½ English cucumber, halved lengthwise and sliced thin on bias
- ½ cup pepperoncini, stemmed and sliced into thin rings
- ¼ cup thinly sliced red onion

1. Using potato masher, mash chickpeas very coarse in bowl. Stir in chili-garlic sauce, cumin, and salt.

2. Spread ¼ cup tahini-yogurt sauce evenly over 1 side of each pita. Divide chickpea mixture, cucumber, pepperoncini, and onion evenly among pitas. Fold pitas in half, wrap tightly in parchment paper, and serve.

Tahini-Yogurt Sauce

FAST **VEGAN** Makes 1 cup Total Time 5 minutes, plus 30 minutes resting

To make this recipe vegan, substitute plant-based Greek yogurt for the dairy Greek yogurt.

- ⅓ cup tahini
- ⅓ cup plain Greek yogurt
- ¼ cup water
- 3 tablespoons lemon juice
- 1 garlic clove, minced
- ¾ teaspoon table salt

Whisk all ingredients together in bowl. Let sit until flavors meld, about 30 minutes. Season with salt and pepper to taste. (Sauce can be refrigerated for up to 4 days.)

Spiced Smashed Chickpea Wraps

Mumbai Frankie Wraps

VEGAN Serves 4 Total Time 1¼ hours

Why This Recipe Works In Mumbai, India, handheld street foods like frankie wraps are hugely popular. Frankies take many forms but tend to consist of a warm, tender chapati or roti (whole-wheat flatbreads) filled with delectably spiced potatoes along with proteins or vegetables and topped with chutneys, sauces, and pickles. We kept our take on the frankie vegetable-forward: roasted hearty cauliflower and chickpeas seasoned with earthy garam masala. Next, we mash Yukon Gold potatoes with shallot, ginger, garlic, turmeric, and coriander and enrich this mixture with coconut milk. We spread the potato mash over the wrap, layer on the cauliflower-chickpea mixture, and then top it all with sweet-spicy pickled onion and a bright herbal chutney before rolling it into a cone shape. We like to make our own chapati, but you can use store-bought. We do not recommend naan or other thicker flatbreads. For easiest assembly, we suggest making the chapati, pickled onion, and chutney ahead.

- 12 ounces cauliflower florets, cut into 1-inch pieces
- 1 (15-ounce) can chickpeas, rinsed
- 2 tablespoons vegetable oil, divided
- ¾ teaspoon garam masala
- ¾ teaspoon table salt, divided
- 1 pound Yukon Gold potatoes, peeled and cut into 1-inch pieces
- 1 shallot, minced
- 3 garlic cloves, minced
- 1 tablespoon grated fresh ginger
- 1 teaspoon ground turmeric
- ⅛ teaspoon ground coriander
- Pinch cayenne pepper
- ½ cup canned coconut milk
- 1 recipe Chapati (page 213), warmed
- ½ cup Cilantro-Mint Chutney (page 213)
- ½ cup Quick Sweet-and-Spicy Pickled Red Onion (page 213)

1. Adjust oven rack to lowest position and heat oven to 500 degrees. Line rimmed baking sheet with aluminum foil. Toss cauliflower, chickpeas, 1 tablespoon oil, garam masala, and ¼ teaspoon salt together in bowl. Spread cauliflower mixture in even layer on prepared sheet and roast, stirring halfway through roasting, until cauliflower is spotty brown and tender, about 10 minutes; set aside. (Cauliflower mixture can be refrigerated for up to 24 hours; let come to room temperature before serving.)

2. Place potatoes and remaining ½ teaspoon salt in large saucepan, add cold water to cover by 1 inch, and bring to boil over high heat. Reduce heat to medium and simmer until potatoes are tender, about 12 minutes; drain well.

3. Heat remaining 1 tablespoon oil in now-empty saucepan over medium heat until shimmering. Add shallot and cook until softened and lightly browned, 3 to 5 minutes. Stir in garlic, ginger, turmeric, coriander, and cayenne and cook until fragrant, about 30 seconds. Stir in coconut milk, scraping up any browned bits, and bring to simmer. Stir in potatoes, then remove from heat and mash with potato masher until mostly smooth, about 2 minutes. Season with salt to taste; set aside. (Potato mixture can be refrigerated for up to 24 hours; reheat in microwave, covered, before serving.)

4. Divide potato mixture evenly among chapati, then spread in even layer over half of each chapati. Divide cauliflower mixture evenly over potato mixture, then top each with 2 tablespoons chutney and 2 tablespoons pickled onion. Roll into cone shape and serve.

Mumbai Frankie Wraps

Chapati (Whole-Wheat Wraps)

VEGAN Makes 4 wraps Total Time 40 minutes, plus 30 minutes resting

This recipe can easily be doubled. You can use a 12-inch nonstick skillet in place of cast iron. In step 5, heat ½ teaspoon oil over medium heat in the skillet until shimmering, then wipe out the skillet before adding the first dough round.

- ¾ cup (4⅛ ounces) whole-wheat flour
- ¾ cup (3¾ ounces) all-purpose flour
- 1 teaspoon table salt
- ½ cup warm water
- 3 tablespoons plus 2 teaspoons vegetable oil, divided

1. Whisk flours and salt together in bowl. Stir in warm water and 3 tablespoons oil until cohesive dough forms. Transfer dough to lightly floured counter and knead by hand to form smooth ball, 1 minute.

2. Divide dough into 4 pieces and cover with plastic wrap. Form 1 piece of dough into rough ball by stretching dough around your thumb and pinching edges together so that top is smooth (keep remaining pieces covered). Place ball seam side down on clean counter and, using your cupped hand, drag in small circles until dough feels taut and round. Repeat with remaining dough pieces. Place on plate seam side down.

3. Cover dough with plastic wrap and let sit for 30 minutes. (Dough can be refrigerated for up to 3 days.)

4. Line rimmed baking sheet with parchment paper. Roll 1 dough ball into 9-inch circle on lightly floured counter (keep remaining dough balls covered). Transfer to prepared sheet and top with additional sheet of parchment. Repeat with remaining dough balls.

5. Heat 12-inch cast-iron skillet over medium heat for 3 minutes. Add ½ teaspoon oil to skillet, then use paper towels to carefully wipe out skillet, leaving thin film of oil on bottom; skillet should be just smoking. Place 1 dough round in hot skillet and cook until dough is bubbly and bottom is browned in spots, about 2 minutes. Flip dough and press firmly with spatula all over to encourage puffing, cooking until puffed and second side is spotty brown, 1 to 2 minutes. Transfer to clean plate and cover with dish towel to keep warm. Repeat with remaining oil and dough rounds. Serve. (Cooked chapati can be refrigerated for up to 3 days or frozen for up to 3 months. To freeze, layer wraps between parchment and store in zipper-lock bag. To serve, stack wraps on plate, cover with damp dish towel, and microwave until warm, 60 to 90 seconds.)

Quick Sweet-and-Spicy Pickled Red Onion

VEGAN Makes 1 cup Total Time 10 minutes, plus 45 minutes pickling

- 1 cup red wine vinegar
- ⅓ cup sugar
- ¼ teaspoon table salt
- 1 red onion, halved and sliced thin
- 2 jalapeño chiles, stemmed, seeded, and cut into thin rings

Microwave vinegar, sugar, and salt in bowl until steaming, 1 to 2 minutes. Stir in onion and jalapeño and let sit, stirring occasionally, for 45 minutes. Drain vegetables in colander. Serve. (Drained pickled onion can be refrigerated for up to 1 week.)

Cilantro-Mint Chutney

FAST VEGAN Makes 1 cup Total Time 10 minutes

To make this recipe vegan, substitute plant-based yogurt for the dairy yogurt.

- 2 cups fresh cilantro leaves
- 1 cup fresh mint leaves
- ⅓ cup plain yogurt
- ¼ cup finely chopped onion
- 1 tablespoon lime juice
- 1½ teaspoons sugar
- ½ teaspoon ground cumin
- ¼ teaspoon table salt

Process all ingredients in food processor until smooth, about 20 seconds, scraping down sides of bowl as needed. (Chutney can be refrigerated for up to 2 days.)

Grilled Halloumi Wraps

Grilled Halloumi Wraps

Serves 4   Total Time 1¼ hours

Why This Recipe Works Firm, easy to brown, and nuttily delicious, halloumi cheese is a natural on the grill. To offset the cheese's salty richness, we combine it with crisp sumac-spiked onion, smoky-sweet grilled bell pepper, and peppery arugula. While the cheese and peppers cook, we steam some moistened pitas in a foil packet on the cooler side of the grill so that they'll be soft and flexible when it comes time to wrap. For a yogurt spread that's garlicky without being harsh, we combine the garlic with some lemon juice to temper its pungent flavor before combining it with the yogurt. The saltiness of halloumi varies; for the best results, select a product that has less than 260 milligrams of sodium per serving. Because the cooking time is so brief, using a charcoal grill is impractical here; if you don't have a gas grill, cook the halloumi and bell pepper in a grill pan on the stovetop over medium-high heat, and wrap the moistened pitas in paper towels and warm them in the microwave.

- 1 red onion, halved and sliced thin
- 3 tablespoons red wine vinegar
- 1 tablespoon ground sumac
- ¾ teaspoon table salt, divided
- 2 tablespoons lemon juice
- 1 garlic clove, minced
- ½ cup plain Greek yogurt
- 1 large red bell pepper
- 4 (8-inch) pitas
- 12 ounces halloumi cheese, sliced crosswise ½ inch thick
- 1 tablespoon extra-virgin olive oil
- ¼ teaspoon red pepper flakes
- 2 ounces (2 cups) baby arugula

1. Stir onion, vinegar, sumac, and ¼ teaspoon salt in medium bowl until well combined and set aside. Whisk lemon juice, garlic, and ¼ teaspoon salt together in small bowl. Whisk in yogurt until smooth.

2. Slice ½ inch from top and bottom of bell pepper. Gently remove stem from top. Twist and pull out core, using knife to loosen at edges if necessary. Cut slit down 1 side of bell pepper. Turn bell pepper skin side down and gently press so it opens to create long strip. Slide knife along insides to remove remaining ribs and seeds.

3. Lightly moisten 2 pitas with water. Sandwich remaining pitas between moistened pitas and wrap tightly in lightly greased heavy-duty aluminum foil.

4. Turn all burners on gas grill to high; cover; and heat grill until hot, about 15 minutes. Leave primary burner on high and turn off other burner(s). Clean and oil cooking grate. Arrange halloumi slices and bell pepper, skin side up, on hotter side of grill. Cook, covered, until first side of cheese and bell pepper are lightly browned, 3 to 5 minutes. Using tongs, flip halloumi and bell pepper and continue to cook until second side of cheese and bell pepper are lightly browned, 3 to 5 minutes.

5. Meanwhile, place packet of pitas on cooler side of grill. Flip occasionally to heat, about 5 minutes. Transfer halloumi and bell pepper to cutting board. Cut bell pepper into ½-inch pieces and transfer to second small bowl. Add oil, pepper flakes, and remaining ¼ teaspoon salt and toss to combine.

6. Lay each warm pita on 12-inch square of foil or parchment paper. Spread each pita with one-quarter of yogurt mixture. Place one-quarter of halloumi in middle of each pita. Top with bell pepper, onion, and arugula. Drizzle with any remaining onion liquid. Roll pita into cylinder. Wrap in foil and cut in half. Serve.

Falafel

VEGAN Makes 24 falafel Total Time 1 hour, plus 8 hours soaking

Why This Recipe Works To produce really good falafel that are tender, packed with vibrant herbs, and sturdy enough to fry, we start by soaking dried chickpeas overnight to soften them slightly, then grind them into coarse bits along with onion, herbs, garlic, and spices. Though many recipes call for mixing starch into the dough, we found success using a technique from Asian bread baking called tangzhong, a cooked flour paste. This paste adds moisture without making the batter too fragile. Adding a bit of baking powder to the dough helps lighten the fritters as they fry. Frying the fritters at 325 degrees allows the moist interiors to fully cook through just as the exteriors turn brown and crisp. This recipe requires that the chickpeas be soaked for at least 8 hours. Use a Dutch oven that holds 6 quarts or more. An equal amount of chickpea flour can be substituted for the all-purpose flour; if using, increase the amount of water to ½ cup in step 4. Do not substitute canned beans or quick-soaked chickpeas; they will make stodgy falafel. Along with the tahini sauce, you could serve these with lettuce, chopped tomatoes and cucumbers, fresh cilantro, and Tomato-Chile Sauce (page 216). Serve the first batch of falafel immediately or hold them in a 200-degree oven while the second batch cooks. To make this recipe vegan, substitute plant-based Greek yogurt for the dairy Greek yogurt.

Falafel

- 8 ounces dried chickpeas, picked over and rinsed
- ¾ cup fresh cilantro leaves and stems
- ¾ cup fresh parsley leaves
- ½ onion, chopped fine (½ cup)
- 2 garlic cloves, minced
- 1½ teaspoons ground coriander
- 1 teaspoon ground cumin
- 1 teaspoon table salt
- ¼ teaspoon cayenne pepper
- ¼ cup all-purpose flour
- 2 teaspoons baking powder
- 2 quarts vegetable oil for frying

Tahini Sauce

- ⅓ cup tahini
- ⅓ cup plain Greek yogurt
- ¼ cup lemon juice (2 lemons)
- ¼ cup water

1. **For the falafel** Place chickpeas in large container and cover with 2 to 3 inches cold water. Let soak at room temperature for at least 8 hours or up to 24 hours. Drain well.

2. **For the tahini sauce** Whisk tahini, yogurt, and lemon juice together in medium bowl until smooth. Whisk in water to thin sauce as desired. Season with salt to taste; set aside. (Sauce can be refrigerated for up to 4 days. Let come to room temperature and stir to combine before serving.)

3. Process cilantro, parsley, onion, garlic, coriander, cumin, salt, and cayenne in food processor for 5 seconds. Scrape down sides of bowl. Continue to process until mixture resembles pesto, about 5 seconds longer. Add chickpeas and pulse 6 times. Scrape down sides of bowl. Continue to pulse until chickpeas are coarsely chopped and resemble sesame seeds, about 6 pulses more. Transfer mixture to large bowl and set aside.

Tomato-Chile Sauce

FAST VEGAN Makes 1½ cups
Total Time 15 minutes

- 1 (15-ounce) can diced tomatoes, drained
- ½ cup fresh cilantro leaves and stems
- 3 garlic cloves, minced
- 1 tablespoon red pepper flakes
- 1 tablespoon red wine vinegar, plus extra for seasoning
- 3 teaspoons ground cumin
- 1 teaspoon ground coriander
- ¾ teaspoon table salt
- ½ teaspoon smoked paprika
- ⅛ teaspoon sugar
- 2 tablespoons extra-virgin olive oil

Process tomatoes, cilantro, garlic, pepper flakes, vinegar, cumin, coriander, salt, paprika, and sugar in food processor until smooth paste is formed, 20 to 30 seconds. With food processor running, slowly add oil until fully incorporated, about 5 seconds. Transfer to bowl and season with salt and vinegar to taste.

4. Whisk flour and ⅓ cup water in bowl until no lumps remain. Microwave, whisking every 10 seconds, until mixture thickens to stiff, smooth, pudding-like consistency that forms mound when dropped from end of whisk into bowl, 40 to 80 seconds. Stir baking powder into flour paste.

5. Add flour paste to ground chickpea mixture and, using silicone spatula, mix until fully incorporated. Divide mixture into 24 pieces and gently roll into golf ball–size spheres, transferring spheres to parchment paper–lined rimmed baking sheet once they are formed. (Formed falafel can be refrigerated for up to 2 hours.)

6. Heat oil in large Dutch oven over medium-high heat to 325 degrees. Add half of falafel and fry, stirring occasionally, until deep brown, about 5 minutes. Adjust burner, if necessary, to maintain oil temperature of 325 degrees. Using slotted spoon or wire skimmer, transfer to paper towel–lined baking sheet. Return oil to 325 degrees and repeat with remaining falafel. Serve immediately with tahini sauce.

Vospov Kofte (Red Lentil Kofte)

Serves 4 to 6 Total Time 1¼ hours, plus 1 hour cooling and chilling

Why This Recipe Works Vospov (red lentil) kofte is the vegetarian analog to chi kofte, an Armenian dish of minced raw beef or lamb that's bound with bulgur, seasoned with tomato paste and spices, served with chopped herbs, and eaten inside pita or lavash. The meatless version is popular during Lent and is typically served at room temperature with herbs and bread. We opt for a 3:1:1 ratio of water to lentils to bulgur, which yields a mixture that is tender, moist, and easy to shape. Olive oil and butter add complexity, especially since the butter develops nutty flavor as it softens the onion and blooms the spices. For the herb component, we mix some chopped parsley into the kofte and then turn much more of it into a vibrant herb salad. Fine-grind bulgur (labeled "#1") is ideal here but can be hard to find; if you can't find it, process ¾ cup plus 2 tablespoons of any size bulgur in a blender until at least half is finely ground, about 2 minutes. If sumac is unavailable, increase the lemon juice to 1 tablespoon and the salt to ½ teaspoon in the salad. We like the gentle heat and raisiny sweetness of Aleppo pepper here, but if it's unavailable, substitute ¾ teaspoon of paprika and ¼ teaspoon of cayenne pepper in the kofte and ⅜ teaspoon of paprika and ⅛ teaspoon of cayenne pepper in the salad. Serve the kofte on their own or with pita or lavash.

Kofte

- 3 cups water
- 1 cup dried red lentils, picked over and rinsed
- ¼ cup extra-virgin olive oil
- 1¼ teaspoons table salt, divided
- 1 cup fine-grind bulgur
- 4 tablespoons unsalted butter
- 1 onion, chopped fine
- 1 teaspoon ground dried Aleppo pepper
- 1 teaspoon ground cumin
- ¼ teaspoon pepper
- ¼ teaspoon ground allspice
- 2 tablespoons chopped fresh parsley

Salad

- ¾ cup chopped fresh parsley
- 4 scallions, sliced thin
- ¼ cup chopped fresh mint
- 1 tablespoon extra-virgin olive oil
- 2 teaspoons lemon juice
- 1 teaspoon ground sumac
- ½ teaspoon ground dried Aleppo pepper
- ¼ teaspoon table salt

1. For the kofte Bring water, lentils, oil, and 1 teaspoon salt to boil in large saucepan over high heat. Adjust heat to maintain gentle simmer. Cover and cook, stirring occasionally, until lentils are fully broken down, 20 to 25 minutes.

2. Place bulgur in large bowl. Pour lentil mixture over bulgur, stir until uniform, and set aside. Wipe out saucepan with paper towel. Melt butter in now-empty saucepan over medium-high heat. Add onion, Aleppo pepper, cumin, pepper, allspice, and remaining ¼ teaspoon salt. Cook, stirring frequently, until onion is softened and just beginning to brown, 8 to 10 minutes. Add parsley and onion mixture to lentil mixture and stir until uniform. Transfer to bowl and let cool completely, 30 to 45 minutes. Refrigerate until stiffened enough to mold, about 30 minutes.

3. Using ¼-cup dry measuring cup sprayed with vegetable oil spray, divide mixture into 16 portions (respray cup if mixture starts to stick). Using your slightly moistened hands, press and roll each portion into 3-inch log. Arrange around perimeter of platter.

4. For the salad Toss all ingredients together in bowl.

5. Top kofte with salad; serve at room temperature.

top | *Falafel*
bottom | *Vospov Kofte (Red Lentil Kofte)*

Sandwich Spreads

Easily enhance a sandwich, wrap, or burger with one of these quick spreads. Store-bought doesn't compare with a simple homemade version. Be sure to also treat your sandwich to these other sauces: Cilantro Crema (page 191), Avocado Crema (page 193), and Tomato-Chile Sauce (page 216).

Easy Homemade Mayonnaise

FAST Makes 1½ cups Total Time 10 minutes

Do not substitute olive oil for the vegetable oil; the mayonnaise will turn out bitter. Add the oil in a slow, even stream or the mayo won't come together.

- 1 large egg
- 4 teaspoons white wine vinegar
- ¾ teaspoon table salt
- ½ teaspoon Dijon mustard
- ¼ teaspoon sugar
- 1½ cups vegetable oil

Process egg, vinegar, salt, mustard, and sugar in food processor until combined, about 5 seconds. With processor running, slowly drizzle in oil until emulsified and mixture is thick, about 2 minutes. Scrape down sides of bowl with silicone spatula and continue to process for 5 seconds longer. Transfer to airtight container and refrigerate until ready to use. (Mayonnaise can be refrigerated for up to 1 week.)

Variations

FAST Basil-Caper Mayonnaise

Combine ½ cup chopped fresh basil, ½ cup mayonnaise, ⅓ cup grated Parmesan cheese, 2 tablespoons rinsed and drained capers, and 1 teaspoon pepper.

FAST Lemon-Dill Mayonnaise

Combine ½ cup mayonnaise, ¼ cup chopped fresh dill, 2 tablespoons extra-virgin olive oil, 1 tablespoon grated lemon zest, 1 tablespoon lemon juice, 1 minced garlic clove, ¼ teaspoon kosher salt, and ¼ teaspoon pepper.

FAST Spicy Sriracha-Lime Mayonnaise

Whisk ½ cup mayonnaise, 1 tablespoon sriracha, 1 teaspoon grated lime zest, 1 tablespoon lime juice, and ¼ teaspoon smoked paprika.

Herbed Yogurt Sauce

FAST **VEGAN** Makes 1 cup Total Time 35 minutes

To make this recipe vegan, substitute plant-based yogurt for the dairy yogurt.

- 1 cup plain yogurt
- 2 tablespoons minced fresh cilantro
- 2 tablespoons minced fresh mint
- 1 garlic clove, minced

Whisk all ingredients in bowl until combined. Season with salt and pepper to taste. Let sit until flavors meld, about 30 minutes. (Sauce can be refrigerated for up to 2 days.)

Creamy Chipotle Sauce

FAST **VEGAN** Makes ½ cup Total Time 5 minutes

To make this recipe vegan, substitute plant-based mayo and sour cream for the mayonnaise and dairy sour cream.

- ¼ cup mayonnaise
- ¼ cup sour cream
- 1 tablespoon lime juice
- 1 tablespoon minced canned chipotle chile in adobo sauce
- 1 garlic clove, minced

Combine all ingredients in small bowl. (Sauce can be refrigerated for up to 4 days.)

Homemade Nut Butter

Makes 4 cups   Total Time 50 minutes to 1 hour

Making nut butters at home couldn't be simpler—just grind the nuts to a paste in a food processor. Be aware that hard, dense nuts such as almonds can take as long as 20 minutes to process to a smooth paste. We found that toasting the nuts before grinding them not only boosts their flavor but also warms their oils, allowing for faster breakdown during processing. We do not recommend using walnuts in this recipe, as their skins impart a bitter flavor to the butter. You can use blanched, skin-on, raw, or preroasted nuts here, but do not use salted nuts. The weight of 4 cups of nuts may vary depending on the type of nuts you use. Certain nuts may require thinning with vegetable oil or thickening with water. You can customize your nut butter in one of two ways: by using a blend of nuts or by adding ¼ to ½ teaspoon ground cinnamon, nutmeg, or ginger or ⅛ teaspoon cayenne pepper to the nuts before processing in step 2.

- 4 cups (1¼ pounds) whole unsalted nuts
- 1 teaspoon honey, plus extra for seasoning
- ¾ teaspoon kosher salt

1. Adjust oven rack to middle position and heat oven to 375 degrees. Spread nuts in single layer on rimmed baking sheet and roast until fragrant and slightly darkened, 10 to 12 minutes, rotating sheet halfway through roasting. (If using preroasted nuts, place in oven for 5 minutes to warm.) Transfer sheet to wire rack and let nuts cool slightly, about 10 minutes.

2. Process nuts in food processor until oil is released and paste begins to form, scraping down sides of bowl often. Add honey and salt and continue to process to desired smoothness, 2 to 20 minutes longer, depending on nut variety. Season with extra honey and salt to taste. If butter is thicker than desired, thin by adding vegetable oil, 1 teaspoon at a time, pulsing 3 times after each addition, until desired consistency is reached. If butter is thinner than desired, thicken by adding water, 1 teaspoon at a time, pulsing 3 times after each addition, until desired consistency is reached. Transfer to jar with tight-fitting lid. (Butter can be stored at room temperature or refrigerated for up to 2 months.)

Nut Processing Time

NUT	PROCESSING TIME
Almonds	18–20 minutes
Cashews	10–12 minutes
Hazelnuts	3–4 minutes
Peanuts	3–4 minutes
Pecans	2–3 minutes
Pistachios	8–10 minutes

Pizzas, Flatbreads & Savory Tarts

Making Pizza at Home

222 Test Kitchen Tips

223 Topping Know-How

223 No-Cook Pizza Sauce ■ ●

224 One-Hour Pizza

225 Cast Iron Pan Pizza

226 Caprese Sheet-Pan Pizza

228 Philadelphia Tomato Pie ●

229 Corn, Tomato, and Arugula Pizza ■

229 Neapolitan-Style Pizza Margherita
Neapolitan-Style Pizza with Artichoke Hearts and Fontina
Neapolitan-Style Pizza with Mushrooms, Garlic, and Taleggio

232 Pizza al Taglio with Arugula and Fresh Mozzarella

233 Thin-Crust Grilled Pizza with Fontina, Parmesan, and Scallions

235 Fugazzeta (Argentine Cheese-Stuffed Pizza)

236 Focaccia di Recco

238 Avocado Toast ■ ●

238 Lemon-Pickled Radish Toast with Basil and Parmesan

239 Ricotta Toast with Pesto di Prezzemolo and Grapes ■

239 Mana'eesh Za'atar (Za'atar Flatbreads) ●

240 Za'atar ■ ●

240 Alu Parathas (Punjabi Potato-Stuffed Griddle Breads)

242 Tamatya-Kandyachi Koshimbir (Tomato-Onion Salad) ■ ●

242 Socca with Sautéed Onions and Rosemary ●

245 Whole-Wheat Crepes with Creamy Sautéed Mushrooms and Asparagus ■

245 Whole-Wheat Crepes ■

246 Flatbreads with Fontina, Mushrooms, and Chives

246 Cauliflower Chickpea Flatbread with Romesco

247 Upside-Down Caramelized Shallot and Onion Tart

247 Whipped Boursin ■

251 Vidalia Onion Pie

251 Tourte aux Pommes de Terre (French Potato Pie)

252 Eggplant and Tomato Phyllo Pie

254 Mushroom and Leek Galette with Gorgonzola
Butternut Squash Galette with Gruyère

256 Celery Root Galette with Blue Cheese and Walnuts

258 Summer Squash Tart ■

258 Caramelized Onion, Tomato, and Goat Cheese Tart

259 Caramelized Onions ■ ●

258 Upside-Down Tomato Tart

261 Fennel-Apple Tarte Tatin

262 Kol Böreği (Spiraled Spinach and Cheese Pastry)

■ Fast (45 minutes or less) ● Vegan

Making Pizza at Home

Pulling a pizza out of the oven with a burnished crust, bubbling sauce, melted cheese, and great toppings will make anyone feel triumphant. If you've never tried to make pizza at home, start with our Corn, Tomato, and Arugula Pizza (page 229) which uses store-bought dough; or try Cast Iron Pan Pizza (page 225), where you just press the dough into the pan. If you are a more seasoned pizza maker, try one of the Neapolitan pizzas (page 229–231) or Thin-Crust Grilled Pizza (page 233). Any way, our recipes will work for you.

Test Kitchen Tips

Use the Right Flour It's important to use the flour(s) specified in our recipes, as different flours have different protein levels and this has an impact on the crust. For instance, bread flour has a high protein level (12 to 14 percent), which creates a strong gluten web leading to a more resilient, stretchable dough and a chewy crust. All-purpose flour has a lower protein level (10 to 12 percent), which results in a crispier crust. Sometimes we call for more than one flour to get the best results.

Weigh Your Flour A variance in the amount of flour you use will affect the texture of your pizza. Too much flour can result in too much gluten development, which makes shaping the dough extremely difficult. Too little flour, and the dough won't contain enough protein to build structure and chew. In tests, we've found that there can be up to a 20 percent difference in the weight of a cup of flour—a difference that can easily ruin a recipe. So weighing your flour ensures accuracy and consistent results.

Use the Autolyse Technique Salt slows flour's absorption of water so delaying its addition in some pizzas allows the flour to be more thoroughly hydrated, which helps to ensure a chewy crust. Autolysing simply entails mixing the flour, yeast, and liquid and withholding the addition of salt for a few minutes when mixing the dough.

Don't Dismiss Store-Bought Dough Purchased dough works well for simple, straightforward pizza recipes. Be sure to bring the dough to room temperature before using, and scatter some flour over your workstation to keep the dough from sticking.

Preheat the Oven Skip this step and you are apt to end up with an anemic-looking pizza with a soggy crust rather than one with a crisp and perfectly browned crust.

Use a Baking Stone or Steel While a professional brick oven can reach temperatures upwards of 800 degrees, home ovens typically top out at 500 to 550 degrees. That said, heating a good baking stone or steel in a 500- to 550-degree oven for an hour turns out pizzas that come closest to those produced in restaurant ovens. Both ceramic and steel stones work well, though we have a preference for steel as the heat transfer is faster. If you don't have a baking stone, you can use a preheated overturned rimmed baking sheet instead.

Use Pizza Peels Getting your pizza into a really hot oven and onto a baking stone and then removing it from the stone can be tricky and nerve-racking. This is where a pizza peel comes in. We use them to move pizza into, out of, and within hot ovens. If you don't have a pizza peel, use an overturned rimless baking sheet to slide the pizza onto the baking stone.

Topping Know-How

Don't Overload Your Pizza Going light on the sauce, cheese, and veggies allows the crust to shine. Plus an overloaded pizza will just end up soggy. Pay attention to the exact amount of sauce called for on a pizza and stick to that. Use the back of a ladle to swirl it evenly on the dough.

Make a Fresh Sauce It's easy to make a bright, fresh sauce for pizza, so don't be tempted to reach for a jarred sauce. We make our No-Cook Pizza Sauce in the food processor using canned whole tomatoes which are less processed than other commercial choices.

Cook Raw Ingredients (Most of the Time) Many ingredients like bell peppers, broccoli, and onions should be cooked first, otherwise their moisture will transfer to the dough as it bakes and eating them raw will just be unpleasant.

Use the Right Mozzarella For most recipes we use block mozzarella and shred it ourselves (sometimes adding a bit of Parmesan) to create an even, creamy layer of cheese on our pizzas. We stay away from preshredded cheese, which contains added starch and gives the melted cheese a drier, chewier texture. Fresh mozzarella is higher in moisture and has a higher pH, so it softens but doesn't melt as completely, so the pizza is dotted with gooey cheese like our Neapolitan-Style Pizza Margherita (page 229).

Add a Finishing Touch Some toppings are delicate and fare better if added after baking: A final drizzle of olive oil, a sprinkling of fresh herbs or scallions, a bit of chili crisp, some dollops of pesto or ricotta, a scattering of dressed arugula, very thinly sliced red onion, and more.

No-Cook Pizza Sauce

FAST **VEGAN** Makes 2 cups Total Time 10 minutes

In this recipe, the richness of extra-virgin olive oil and acidity of red wine vinegar enhance canned tomatoes to make a simple pizza sauce.

- 1 (28-ounce) can whole peeled tomatoes, drained with juice reserved
- 1 tablespoon extra-virgin olive oil
- 1 teaspoon red wine vinegar
- 2 garlic cloves, minced
- 1 teaspoon dried oregano

Process drained tomatoes with oil, vinegar, garlic, and oregano in food processor until smooth, about 30 seconds. Transfer mixture to 2-cup liquid measuring cup and add tomato juice until sauce measures 2 cups. Season with salt and pepper to taste. (Sauce can be refrigerated for up to 1 week or frozen for up to 1 month.)

top | *One-Hour Pizza*
bottom | *Cast Iron Pan Pizza*

One-Hour Pizza

Serves 4 to 6   Total Time 1 hour

Why This Recipe Works A from-scratch pizza with a crisp and tender crust in just one hour—from start to finish—really is possible with a few ingenious tricks (and smart usage of time). First, we use a high percentage of yeast and warm water in the dough to make sure proofing takes only 30 minutes. To take full advantage of the minimal proofing time, we had to rethink the way we prepare the dough. Instead of the usual process of proofing the dough and then rolling it out, we reverse the order of operations so the dough proofs in its ready round shape. Since the yeast in the dough doesn't have enough time to create rich flavors, we add beer, which contains flavor compounds created by yeast fermentation. We also add vinegar to provide the acetic acid that yeast would produce during a slow rise. A combination of semolina and all-purpose flours makes the dough more extensible than all-purpose alone. Extra sauce can be refrigerated for up to a week or frozen for up to a month.

Dough

- 1⅓ cups (7⅓ ounces) bread flour
- ½ cup (3 ounces) semolina flour
- 2 teaspoons instant or rapid-rise yeast
- 2 teaspoons sugar
- ½ cup plus 2 tablespoons (5 ounces) warm water
- ¼ cup (2 ounces) mild lager
- 2 teaspoons distilled white vinegar
- 1½ teaspoons extra-virgin olive oil
- 1 teaspoon table salt
- Vegetable oil spray

Sauce

- 1 (28-ounce) can whole peeled tomatoes, drained
- 1 tablespoon extra-virgin olive oil
- 1 teaspoon table salt
- 1 teaspoon dried oregano
- ½ teaspoon sugar
- ¼ teaspoon pepper
- ⅛ teaspoon red pepper flakes

Pizza

- 1 ounce Parmesan cheese, grated fine (½ cup), divided
- 6 ounces whole-milk block mozzarella cheese, shredded (1½ cups), divided

1. For the dough Adjust oven rack 4 to 5 inches from broiler element, set baking steel or stone on rack, and heat oven to 500 degrees.

2. While oven heats, process bread flour, semolina flour, yeast, and sugar in food processor until combined, about 2 seconds. With processor running, slowly add warm water, lager, vinegar, and oil and process until dough is just combined and no dry flour remains, about 10 seconds. Let dough rest for 10 minutes. Add salt to dough and process until dough forms satiny, sticky ball that clears sides of bowl, 30 to 60 seconds. Transfer dough to lightly floured counter and knead by hand to form smooth, round ball, about 30 seconds. Divide dough into 2 equal pieces and shape each into smooth ball.

3. Spray 11-inch round in center of large sheet of parchment paper with oil spray. Place 1 ball of dough in center of parchment. Spray top of dough with oil spray. Using rolling pin, roll dough into 10-inch round. Cover with second sheet of parchment. Using rolling pin and your hands, continue to roll and press dough into 11½-inch round. Set aside and repeat rolling with second ball of dough. Let dough sit at room temperature until slightly puffy, about 30 minutes.

4. For the sauce Process all ingredients in food processor until smooth, about 30 seconds. Transfer to medium bowl.

5. For the pizza When dough has rested for 20 minutes, heat broiler for 10 minutes. Remove top piece of parchment from 1 disk of dough and dust top of dough lightly with all-purpose flour. Using your hands or pastry brush, spread flour evenly over dough, brushing off any excess. Liberally dust baking peel with all-purpose flour. Flip dough onto peel, parchment side up. Carefully remove parchment and discard.

6 Using back of spoon or ladle, spread ½ cup sauce in thin layer over surface of dough, leaving ¾-inch border around edge. Sprinkle ¼ cup Parmesan evenly over sauce, followed by ¾ cup mozzarella.

7. Slide pizza carefully onto steel or stone and set oven to 500 degrees. Bake until crust is well browned and cheese is bubbly and beginning to brown, 8 to 12 minutes, rotating pizza halfway through baking. Transfer pizza to wire rack and let cool for 5 minutes before slicing and serving. Repeat steps 5 through 7 to top and bake second pizza.

Cast Iron Pan Pizza

Serves 4 Total Time 1¼ hours, plus 14 hours resting

Why This Recipe Works For an easy, cheesy, ultracrisp pizza, bake it in a cast-iron skillet. We start with a simple stir-together dough of bread flour, salt, yeast, and warm water; the warm water jump-starts yeast activity so that the crumb is open and light. Instead of kneading the dough, we let it rest overnight in the refrigerator. During this rest, the dough's gluten strengthens enough for the crust to support the toppings but still have a tender crumb. Baking the pie in a generously oiled cast-iron skillet "fries" the outside of the crust. We move the skillet to the stove for the last few minutes of cooking to crisp up the underside of the crust. For the crispy cheese edge known as frico, we press shredded Monterey Jack cheese around the edge of the dough and up the sides of the skillet. For the sauce, we crush canned whole tomatoes (which are less processed and therefore fresher-tasting than commercial crushed tomatoes) by hand, which allows some of their juice to drain so the sauce is thick enough to stay put on the pie, and then puree them in the food processor with classic seasonings—no cooking required.

Dough

2 cups (11 ounces) bread flour
1 teaspoon table salt
1 teaspoon instant or rapid-rise yeast
1 cup (8 ounces) warm water (105 to 110 degrees)
Vegetable oil spray

Sauce

1 (14.5-ounce) can whole peeled tomatoes
1 teaspoon extra-virgin olive oil
1 garlic clove, minced
¼ teaspoon sugar
¼ teaspoon table salt
¼ teaspoon dried oregano
Pinch red pepper flakes

Pizza

3 tablespoons extra-virgin olive oil
4 ounces Monterey Jack cheese, shredded (1 cup)
7 ounces whole-milk block mozzarella cheese, shredded (1¾ cups)

1. For the dough Using wooden spoon or spatula, stir flour, salt, and yeast together in bowl. Add warm water and mix until most of flour is moistened. Using your hands, knead dough in bowl until dough forms sticky ball, about 1 minute. Spray 9-inch pie plate or cake pan with oil spray. Transfer dough to prepared plate and press into 7- to 8-inch disk. Spray top of dough with oil spray. Cover tightly with plastic wrap and refrigerate for 12 to 24 hours.

2. For the sauce Place tomatoes in fine-mesh strainer and crush with your hands. Drain well, then transfer to food processor. Add oil, garlic, sugar, salt, oregano, and pepper flakes and process until smooth, about 30 seconds. (Sauce can be refrigerated for up to 3 days.)

3. For the pizza Two hours before baking, remove dough from refrigerator and let sit at room temperature for 30 minutes.

4. Coat bottom of 12-inch cast-iron skillet with oil. Transfer dough to prepared skillet and use your fingertips to flatten dough until it is ⅛ inch from edge of skillet. Cover tightly with plastic and let rest until slightly puffy, about 1½ hours.

5. Thirty minutes before baking, adjust oven rack to lowest position and heat oven to 400 degrees. Spread ½ cup sauce evenly over top of dough, leaving ½-inch border (save remaining sauce for another use). Sprinkle Monterey Jack evenly over border. Press Monterey Jack into side of skillet, forming ½- to ¾-inch-tall wall. (Not all cheese will stick to side of skillet.) Evenly sprinkle mozzarella over sauce. Bake until cheese at edge of skillet is well browned, 25 to 30 minutes.

6. Transfer skillet to stovetop and let sit until sizzling stops, about 3 minutes. Run butter knife around rim of skillet to loosen pizza. Using thin metal spatula, gently lift edge of pizza and peek at underside to assess browning. Cook pizza over medium heat until bottom crust is well browned, 2 to 5 minutes (skillet handle will be hot). Using 2 spatulas, transfer pizza to wire rack and let cool for 10 minutes. Slice and serve.

Caprese Sheet-Pan Pizza

Serves 4 to 6 Total Time 1¼ hours, plus 1 hour 20 minutes resting

Why This Recipe Works For a stunning, easy-to-make sheet-pan pizza with a crisp, airy, focaccia-like crust, we start with a highly hydrated dough, which yields a light, tender crumb. Briefly resting the dough before adding salt (salt inhibits flour hydration) allows the flour to fully hydrate, strengthening the gluten and making it better able to trap carbon dioxide during rising. Then we simply transfer the sticky dough straight to a well-oiled rimmed baking sheet, eliminating the need for extended handling or rolling of the dough. Generously greasing the pan ensures that the dough doesn't stick. After topping the pie with plenty of fresh mozzarella and macerated tomatoes (to eliminate excess moisture), we bake it at 500 degrees on a baking steel which results in a strong oven spring and exceptional browning. A final drizzle of sweet balsamic glaze and a sprinkling of shaved Parmesan and fresh basil add the crowning glory. If you don't own a baking steel, you can use a baking stone or an overturned heavy-duty rimmed baking sheet. We recommend making our Pesto alla Genovese (page 268), but you can also use store-bought pesto here.

Dough

- 3 cups (15 ounces) all-purpose flour
- 2 teaspoons instant or rapid-rise yeast
- 2 teaspoons sugar
- 1⅓ cups (10⅔ ounces) water, room temperature
- 1 teaspoon table salt
- ¼ cup extra-virgin olive oil

Tomatoes

- 10 ounces assorted colored cherry tomatoes, sliced ¼ inch thick
- ½ teaspoon table salt
- ½ teaspoon sugar
- 1 garlic clove, minced

Pizza

- 1¼ cups pesto
- 10 ounces fresh mozzarella cheese, sliced into ¼-inch thick rounds
- ½ teaspoon pepper
- ¼ teaspoon table salt
- ½ cup shaved Parmesan cheese
- ⅓ cup torn fresh basil leaves
- 2 tablespoons balsamic glaze (optional)

1. **For the dough** Whisk flour, yeast, and sugar together in bowl of stand mixer. Fit mixer with dough hook. Mix flour mixture on low speed while slowly adding water until dough forms and no dry flour remains, 2 to 4 minutes, scraping down bowl as needed. Cover bowl with plastic wrap and let dough rest for 10 minutes.

2. Add salt and mix on medium speed until dough forms satiny, sticky ball that clears sides of bowl, 6 to 8 minutes. Lightly spray rimmed baking sheet with vegetable oil spray. Rub bottom and sides of sheet with olive oil. Using dough scraper or your greased hands, transfer dough to oiled sheet and turn to coat. With your greased hands, stretch dough into rough 12 by 8-inch rectangle of even thickness. Cover with plastic and let rise in warm place until puffed and nearly doubled in size, about 1 hour.

3. Meanwhile, adjust oven rack to lowest position, place baking steel on rack, and heat oven to 500 degrees.

4. **For the tomatoes** Toss all ingredients together in bowl. Transfer to colander set over bowl; set aside.

5. Using your greased hands, gently stretch dough to corners of sheet, pressing lightly with your fingertips to deflate dough and carefully lifting corners and edges of dough to pull toward edges of sheet. (It's OK if dough shrinks back slightly from corners of sheet at this point.) Cover loosely with plastic and let rise in warm place until slightly puffed, about 20 minutes.

6. Using your greased hands, press dough all the way to edges and corners of sheet. Using your fingertips, pinch edges of dough against sides of sheet to form small lip.

7. **For the pizza** Using bottom of ½-cup dry measuring cup or large spoon, spread pesto into thin layer over surface of dough, leaving ½-inch border. Evenly distribute mozzarella over entire surface of dough, making sure some cheese sits on edges of dough against pan. Sprinkle with drained tomatoes, pepper, and salt.

8. Bake until cheese is bubbly and well browned, about 15 minutes, rotating sheet halfway through baking. Run knife around edge of sheet to loosen pizza and transfer pizza to wire rack. Let cool for 5 minutes. Top pizza with Parmesan and basil leaves. Drizzle with balsamic glaze, if using. Slice and serve.

Caprese Sheet-Pan Pizza

top | *Corn, Tomato, and Arugula Pizza*
bottom | *Neapolitan-Style Pizza Margherita*

Philadelphia Tomato Pie

VEGAN Serves 4 Total Time 1¼ hours, plus 3 hours resting

Why This Recipe Works This South Philadelphia specialty boasts a tender yet chewy crust topped with a bright, savory tomato sauce. To achieve the signature crust with fine holes and a pleasantly spongy chew, we use less water by weight in proportion to the flour. A technique called autolyse further ensures a chewy crust; this simply entails mixing the flour, yeast, and liquid but withholding the salt for a short period. Salt slows flour's absorption of water, so delaying its addition allows the flour to become more thoroughly hydrated. The result is more gluten formation and a chewier finished crust. For the invigorating, sweet-tart, herby sauce, we start with a savory base of onion and garlic and then add dried oregano along with red pepper flakes for kick. One can of tomato sauce provides just the right tomato flavor and texture, and a tablespoon of sugar contributes the sauce's signature sweetness. When kneading the dough on medium speed, the mixer may wobble and shimmy. To keep it in place, position a dish towel or shelf liner beneath the mixer and keep a close watch on it. You will need a nonstick metal baking pan for this recipe.

Dough

- 2½ cups (12½ ounces) all-purpose flour
- ¾ teaspoon instant or rapid-rise yeast
- 1 cup (8 ounces) water, room temperature
- 1½ tablespoons extra-virgin olive oil
- 1½ teaspoons table salt

Sauce

- 2 tablespoons extra-virgin olive oil
- ¼ cup finely chopped onion
- 2 garlic cloves, minced
- 2 teaspoons dried oregano
- ¼ teaspoon red pepper flakes
- 1 (15-ounce) can tomato sauce
- 1 tablespoon sugar

1. For the dough Spray 13 by 9-inch nonstick baking pan with vegetable oil spray. Using stand mixer fitted with dough hook, mix flour and yeast on medium speed until combined, about 10 seconds. With mixer running, slowly add room-temperature water and oil and mix until dough forms and no dry flour remains, about 30 seconds, scraping down bowl as needed. Cover bowl with plastic wrap and let dough rest for 10 minutes.

2. Add salt to dough and knead on medium speed until dough is satiny and sticky and clears sides of bowl but still sticks to bottom, 6 to 8 minutes. Transfer dough to prepared pan, cover pan tightly with plastic, and let dough rise at room temperature until doubled in size, about 1½ hours.

3. For the sauce While dough rises, heat oil in small saucepan over medium heat until shimmering. Add onion and cook, stirring occasionally, until softened and lightly browned, 3 to 5 minutes. Add garlic, oregano, and pepper flakes and cook until fragrant, about 30 seconds. Add tomato sauce and sugar and bring to boil. Reduce heat to medium-low and simmer until sauce is slightly thickened and measures about 1¼ cups, about 10 minutes. Let sauce cool completely.

4. Using your well-oiled hands, press dough into corners of pan. (If dough resists stretching, let it rest for 10 minutes before trying to stretch again.) Cover pan tightly with plastic and let dough rise at room temperature until doubled in size, about 1½ hours. Adjust oven rack to upper-middle position and heat oven to 450 degrees.

5. Spread sauce evenly over dough, leaving ½- to ¼-inch border. Bake until edges are light golden brown and sauce has reduced in spots, about 20 minutes. Let tomato pie cool in pan on wire rack for 5 minutes. Run knife around edge of pan to loosen pie. Using spatula, slide pie onto cutting board. Cut into 8 pieces and serve.

Corn, Tomato, and Arugula Pizza

FAST Serves 4 Total Time 45 minutes

Why This Recipe Works Store-bought dough keeps prep time to a minimum for this quick, summery pizza that you can easily assemble on a weeknight. Replacing the tomato sauce with a layer of crème fraîche (a rich and tangy cultured cream) flecked with fresh basil and red pepper flakes creates a unique base on which to assemble the rest of the ingredients. For toppings we take full advantage of summer's bounty: plump cherry tomatoes, sweet corn, and peppery arugula create inviting layers of flavor, texture, and color. Adding the arugula once the pizza is out of the oven ensures it retains its fresh, delicately crisp texture. If you can't find crème fraîche, you can substitute ½ cup of sour cream mixed with 1 tablespoon of heavy cream.

- 2 tablespoons extra-virgin olive oil, divided
- ½ cup crème fraîche
- ¼ cup chopped fresh basil
- ¼ teaspoon red pepper flakes
- 1 pound store-bought pizza dough
- 8 ounces fontina cheese, shredded (2 cups)
- 6 ounces cherry tomatoes, quartered
- 1 ear corn, kernels cut from cob, or ¾ cup thawed frozen
- 1 shallot, sliced thin
- ¼ teaspoon table salt
- 2 ounces (2 cups) baby arugula

1. Adjust oven rack to middle position and heat oven to 500 degrees. Brush rimmed baking sheet with 1 tablespoon oil. Combine crème fraîche, basil, and pepper flakes in bowl.

2. Roll dough into 16 by 10-inch rectangle, about ¼ inch thick, on lightly floured counter. Transfer dough to prepared sheet and brush edges with 2 teaspoons oil. Spread crème fraîche mixture over dough, leaving ½-inch border, then sprinkle evenly with fontina, tomatoes, corn, shallot, and salt. Bake until cheese is spotty brown and crust is golden, 15 to 20 minutes, rotating sheet halfway through baking.

3. Let pizza cool for 5 minutes. Toss arugula with remaining 1 teaspoon oil. Top pizza with arugula. Slice and serve.

Neapolitan-Style Pizza Margherita

Serves 4 (makes four 11-inch pizzas) Total Time 2½ hours plus 20 hours 50 minutes resting, chilling, and standing

Why This Recipe Works The tender, lightly crisp, char-speckled crust (a prized feature called leoparding) that defines Neapolitan pizza is typically the result of the blazing heat of a pizza oven. To mimic those results in a tamer home oven, we start by adding lots of water to the dough so that the crust can bake longer without turning dry and tough. Incorporating a cooked paste of flour and water called a tangzhong maximizes the amount of moisture the dough can hold without becoming too wet and loose to handle. By implementing a "press-and-flip" method when stretching the dough into rounds, we're able to form—and then not disturb—the rim that bakes up into the puffy edge called the cornicione. Using a light hand with the sauce, cheese, and vegetables allows the crust to take center stage. Note that the dough ferments in the refrigerator for 18 to 36 hours. We developed this recipe using Caputo 00 Pizzeria Flour, but other brands of 00 pizza flour can be used. Semolina flour is ideal for dusting the dough and peel, but all-purpose flour works. If you have the option, use a baking steel, which produces a crisper, browner crust than a baking stone does. If your oven does not reach 550 degrees, set it to the highest possible temperature and extend the baking time by about 1 minute. You can garnish any baked pizza with dried oregano, red pepper flakes, extra-virgin olive oil, and/or additional grated Parmesan.

Flour Paste

- ⅓ cup water
- 2 tablespoons 00 pizza flour

Dough

- 1½ cups plus 2 tablespoons water, divided
- 2½ teaspoons table salt
- 1¼ teaspoons sugar
- ½ teaspoon instant or rapid-rise yeast
- 4 cups plus 2 tablespoons 00 pizza flour

Sauce

- 1 (28-ounce) can whole peeled tomatoes
- ½ teaspoon table salt

Pizza

- ¼ cup grated Parmesan cheese, divided
- 8 ounces fresh mozzarella cheese, torn into ½-inch pieces, patted dry with paper towels, divided
- Semolina flour for dusting
- Fresh basil

1. **For the flour paste** Whisk water and flour in medium bowl until no lumps remain. Microwave until mixture thickens to stiff, smooth, pudding-like consistency that forms mound when dropped from end of whisk into bowl, about 60 seconds, whisking halfway through microwaving.

2. **For the dough** Add ½ cup water to flour paste and whisk until smooth. Transfer to large bowl. Add salt, sugar, and remaining 1 cup plus 2 tablespoons water and whisk until salt and sugar have dissolved. Whisk in yeast and let sit until yeast has dissolved, about 30 seconds. Add flour. Holding edge of bowl with your hand, use your other hand to mix and squeeze flour into liquid until sticky, shaggy dough forms (dough will be very sticky). Scrape any dough from your hand back into bowl. Cover bowl with plastic wrap and let dough rest for 20 minutes.

3. Grasping edge of dough with your fingertips, gently lift and fold edge toward middle. Rotate bowl 45 degrees; fold again. Rotate bowl and fold 6 more times (total of 8 folds). Cover and let dough rest at room temperature for 1½ hours.

4. Lightly grease rimmed baking sheet. Transfer dough (it will still be very sticky) to well-floured counter and divide into 4 equal pieces. Working with 1 piece at a time, fold edges of dough toward center to form ball. Pinch seams closed and flip over. Cup both hands beneath dough and lift dough from counter; slide your hands forward and back against dough to create smooth, taut ball. Transfer to prepared sheet. Cover tightly with plastic and refrigerate for at least 18 hours or up to 36 hours.

5. **For the sauce** Process tomatoes and salt with immersion blender or food processor until just smooth, 20 to 60 seconds. (This will yield more sauce than needed in recipe. Sauce can be refrigerated for 2 days or frozen for up to 2 months.)

6. **For the pizza** One hour before baking pizza, remove dough, Parmesan, and mozzarella from refrigerator. (Leave dough covered until using to prevent tops from drying out.) Adjust oven rack 9 inches from broiler element, place baking steel or stone on rack, and heat oven to 550 degrees. Set wire rack in rimmed baking sheet.

7. When 1 hour has elapsed, uncover 1 dough ball on sheet and sprinkle heaping tablespoon of semolina over top. Smooth semolina over surface of ball, allowing excess to fall around ball. Slide bench scraper under about one-quarter of dough, pushing excess semolina beneath dough. Remove scraper and repeat, working around ball to release it from sheet. Invert ball onto lightly floured counter. Re-cover sheet and set aside.

8. Lightly flour any sticky areas of dough. Gently press into 7-inch round, popping any bubbles that are larger than ½ inch. Beginning at center of dough and working upward and outward, use your fingertips to firmly flatten and stretch upper half of round, stopping 1 inch from edge of dough to form rim. Slide fingertips of both your hands beneath top of dough and, grasping to avoid rim, flip dough over so rimmed, flattened half is at bottom. Repeat flattening and stretching motion until you have 8- to 9-inch round with 1-inch-wide rim.

9. Make fist with your hand and hold it over center of dough. Using your other hand, pick up top of dough round and drape it over your fist, being careful not to compress rim. Make fist with hand that lifted dough and place it next to fist under dough, then use both fists to lift dough off counter. Letting dough hang down, gently draw your fists away from each other to stretch dough. Rotate dough over your fists while continuing to stretch until dough reaches 11-inch round. Lay dough onto floured peel.

10. Spread 2 tablespoons tomato sauce over surface of dough. Sprinkle one-quarter of Parmesan evenly over sauce, followed by one-quarter of mozzarella.

11. Slide pizza onto steel and turn on broiler. Broil until rim is well browned with charred spots and underside of pizza is spotty brown, 4 to 5 minutes. (If top of pizza is well-browned but underside is pale, turn off broiler for final 1 to 2 minutes of cooking and return oven to 550 degrees.) Transfer pizza to prepared rack. Turn off broiler and return oven to 550 degrees.

12. Top pizza with basil. Let cool until cheese and sauce set up slightly, about 1 minute. Serve immediately. Repeat steps 7 through 12 with remaining dough balls and toppings to make 3 more pizzas.

Variations

Neapolitan-Style Pizza with Artichoke Hearts and Fontina

Combine 6 tablespoons tomato sauce with 2 tablespoons heavy cream. Omit Parmesan and basil. Reduce mozzarella to 4 ounces. For each pizza, spread 2 tablespoons tomato-cream mixture over surface of dough. Sprinkle one-quarter of mozzarella evenly over sauce followed by 1 ounce Swedish-style fontina or fontal cut into ½-inch pieces and 1 marinated artichoke heart cut into 8 wedges.

Neapolitan-Style Pizza with Mushrooms, Garlic, and Taleggio

Omit tomato sauce, Parmesan, and basil. Reduce mozzarella to 4 ounces and add 4 ounces Taleggio, rind removed and cut into ½-inch pieces. Toss 10 ounces white or cremini mushrooms sliced ½ inch thick, 2 thinly sliced garlic cloves, 1 teaspoon extra-virgin olive oil, and pinch of table salt until well combined. For each pizza, drizzle 2 teaspoons extra-virgin olive oil over surface of dough. Sprinkle with one-quarter of mozzarella followed by one-quarter of Taleggio and one-quarter of mushroom mixture. When pizza comes out of oven, sprinkle with lemon zest and lemon juice to taste.

Shaping the Dough

1. Press dough ball into 7-inch round and firmly flatten and stretch upper half of round stopping 1 inch from edge of dough to form rim.

2. Grasping so as to avoid rim, flip dough over so rimmed, flattened half is at bottom.

3. Repeat flattening and stretching motion until you have 8- to 9-inch round with 1-inch rim.

4. Place fist over center of dough. With other hand, drape dough over fist being careful not to compress rim.

5. With both fists now under dough, use them to lift dough off counter. Pulling fists apart, stretch and rotate dough into 11-inch round.

Pizza al Taglio with Arugula and Fresh Mozzarella

Pizza al Taglio with Arugula and Fresh Mozzarella

Serves 4 to 6   Total Time 1¼ hours, plus 18 hours chilling and resting

Why This Recipe Works Roman pizzerias display pizza al taglio behind glass in deli-style cases, where it is sold by the length and cut with scissors (al taglio means "by the cut"). This rectangular pizza has a unique crust: Full of irregular holes, it's both tender and chewy with a crisp, delicate bottom and a complex, yeasty flavor. Sometimes the pizza is topped before going into the oven; other times items such as salad greens or soft cheeses are piled on after baking, as we do here. Because this dough is so wet, you'll fold it by hand to develop gluten and give it a long rest in the refrigerator, where the yeast slowly consumes the sugars in the flour, producing more of the desirable acids that create flavor complexity. We prefer King Arthur bread flour in this recipe.

Dough

- 2⅔ cups (14⅔ ounces) bread flour
- 1 teaspoon instant or rapid-rise yeast
- 1½ cups (12 ounces) water, room temperature
- 2 tablespoons extra-virgin olive oil
- 1¼ teaspoons table salt
- Vegetable oil spray

Sauce

- 1 (14.5-ounce) can whole peeled tomatoes, drained
- 1 tablespoon extra-virgin olive oil
- 1 teaspoon dried oregano
- ½ teaspoon table salt
- ¼ teaspoon red pepper flakes

Pizza

- ¼ cup extra-virgin olive oil, divided
- 4 ounces (4 cups) baby arugula
- 8 ounces fresh mozzarella cheese, torn into bite-size pieces (2 cups)
- 1½ ounces Parmesan cheese, shredded (½ cup)

1. For the dough Whisk flour and yeast together in medium bowl. Add room-temperature water and oil and stir with wooden spoon until shaggy mass forms and no dry flour remains. Cover bowl with plastic wrap and let dough rest for 10 minutes. Sprinkle salt over dough and mix until fully incorporated. Cover bowl with plastic and let dough rest for 20 minutes.

2. Using your wet hands, fold dough over itself by gently lifting and folding edge of dough toward middle. Turn bowl 90 degrees; fold again. Turn bowl and fold dough 4 more times (total of 6 turns). Cover bowl with plastic and let dough rest for 20 minutes. Repeat folding technique, turning bowl each time, until dough tightens slightly, 3 to 6 turns total. Cover bowl with plastic and let dough rest for 10 minutes.

3. Spray bottom of 13 by 9-inch baking pan liberally with oil spray. Transfer dough to prepared pan and spray top of dough lightly with oil spray. Gently press dough into 10 by 7-inch oval of even thickness. Cover pan tightly with plastic and refrigerate for at least 16 hours or up to 24 hours.

4. For the sauce While dough rests, process all ingredients in blender until smooth, 20 to 30 seconds. Transfer sauce to bowl, cover, and refrigerate until needed. (Sauce can be refrigerated for up to 2 days.)

5. For the pizza Brush top of dough with 2 tablespoons oil. Spray rimmed baking sheet (including rim) with oil spray. Invert prepared sheet on top of pan with dough and flip, allowing dough to fall onto sheet (you may need to lift pan and nudge dough at 1 end to release). Using your fingertips, gently dimple dough into even thickness and stretch toward edges of sheet to form 15 by 11-inch oval. Spray top of dough lightly with oil spray, cover loosely with plastic, and let rest until slightly puffy, 1 to 1¼ hours.

6. Thirty minutes before baking, adjust oven rack to lowest position and heat oven to 450 degrees. Just before baking, use your fingertips to gently dimple dough into even thickness, pressing into corners of sheet. Using back of spoon or ladle, spread ½ cup sauce in even layer over surface of dough. (Remaining sauce can be frozen for up to 2 months.)

7. Drizzle 1 tablespoon oil over top of sauce and use back of spoon to spread evenly over surface. Transfer sheet to oven and bake until bottom of crust is evenly browned and top is lightly browned in spots, 20 to 25 minutes, rotating sheet halfway through baking. Transfer sheet to wire rack and let cool for 5 minutes. Run knife around rim of sheet to loosen pizza. Transfer pizza to cutting board and cut into 8 rectangles. Toss arugula with remaining 1 tablespoon oil in bowl. Top pizza with arugula, followed by mozzarella and Parmesan, and serve.

Thin-Crust Grilled Pizza with Fontina, Parmesan, and Scallions

Serves 4 to 6   Total Time 2½ hours, plus 1½ hours resting

Why This Recipe Works Grilled pizza features a thin, light, crisp crust, and the live fire gives it intensely flavorful smokiness and char. Shaping the dough on parchment paper allows you to stack the pieces neatly for easy transport outside. The parchment also provides a no-stress vehicle for transferring the dough to the grill. A two-zone charcoal setup facilitates even cooking by enabling us to slide all or part of the pizzas over to the cooler side to account for hot spots. Topping the grilled pizzas first with garlic oil and a balanced combo of relatively mild, creamy fontina and sharp, salty Parmesan creates a delicious barrier that keeps pizza sauce from making the dough soggy. A final sprinkling of parsley, basil, and scallions adds color and freshness. You can substitute 2 pounds of store-bought pizza dough for the dough in this recipe (and skip steps 1 and 2); the dough balls in step 3 will weigh about 8 ounces each, and the finished pizzas may be slightly thicker than those made with homemade dough. Grilled pizza cooks quickly, so it's important to have all your ingredients and tools ready ahead of time. Two pairs of grill-safe tongs make moving the dough on and off the grill easier.

Dough

- 3 cups (16½ ounces) bread flour
- 1 tablespoon sugar
- ¼ teaspoon instant or rapid-rise yeast
- 1¼ cups plus 2 tablespoons (11 ounces) ice water
- 3 tablespoons extra-virgin olive oil, divided
- 1½ teaspoons table salt

Pizza

- 3 tablespoons extra-virgin olive oil
- 1 garlic clove, minced
- 3 tablespoons chopped fresh basil
- 3 tablespoons chopped fresh parsley
- 2 scallions, sliced thin on bias
- 6 ounces fontina cheese, shredded (1½ cups)
- 6 ounces Parmesan cheese, shredded (2 cups)
- 1⅓ cups jarred marinara sauce

1. For the dough Process flour, sugar, and yeast in food processor until combined, about 2 seconds. With processor running, slowly add ice water; process until dough is just combined and no dry flour remains, about 10 seconds. Let dough rest for 10 minutes.

Thin-Crust Grilled Pizza with Fontina, Parmesan, and Scallions

2. Add 1 tablespoon oil and salt to dough and process until dough forms satiny, sticky ball that clears sides of bowl, 30 to 60 seconds. Transfer dough to lightly oiled counter and knead until smooth, about 1 minute.

3. Divide dough into 4 equal pieces (about 7 ounces each). Shape each piece into tight ball and transfer to lightly oiled rimmed baking sheet. Lightly brush or spray tops of dough balls with oil. Cover sheet tightly with plastic wrap. Let sit at room temperature until dough balls have relaxed and spread to 4 inches in diameter, about 1½ hours. (Alternatively, unrested dough balls can be refrigerated—on sheet wrapped with plastic—for up to 3 days; let sit at room temperature until relaxed and spread to 4 inches in diameter, about 2 hours, before using.)

4. Pour remaining 2 tablespoons oil over dough balls. Coat both sides of 1 ball in oil and transfer to 12 by 16-inch sheet of parchment paper on counter. Using your fingertips and palms, gently press and stretch dough to form rough 13 by 9-inch oval of even thickness; transfer parchment with dough round onto second baking sheet. Repeat stretching dough on parchment with remaining 3 dough balls; stack stretched rounds between parchment on sheet. Press large sheet of plastic directly onto surface of top dough round and let sit at room temperature for up to 1 hour while heating grill.

5. **For the pizza** Combine oil and garlic in bowl. Combine basil, parsley, and scallions in second bowl. Combine fontina and Parmesan in third bowl. Set bowls aside.

6A. **For a charcoal grill** Open bottom vent completely. Light large chimney starter three-quarters filled with charcoal briquettes (4½ quarts). When top coals are partially covered with ash, pour evenly over half of grill. Set cooking grate in place, cover, and open lid vent completely. Heat grill until hot, about 5 minutes.

6B. **For a gas grill** Turn all burners to high, cover, and heat grill until hot, about 15 minutes. Turn all burners to medium-high.

7. Clean and oil cooking grate. Grasp 1 long side of 1 dough round and parchment with both hands (gently holding dough and parchment together between your thumbs and fingers) and carefully flip onto grill, dough side down (over hotter side if using charcoal). Gently peel parchment away from dough with tongs, using second pair of tongs or spatula to secure dough in place on grill. Cook (covered if using gas)

until bottom is well browned and spottily charred, 1 to 2 minutes, rotating dough once during cooking. Invert dough onto cutting board, grilled side up.

8. Brush top of pizza with one-quarter of garlic oil (2 heaping teaspoons). Sprinkle one-quarter of cheese mixture (about ¾ cup) evenly over pizza. Drizzle one-quarter of sauce (⅓ cup) evenly over pizza. Using your hands or 2 sets of tongs, transfer pizza back to grill (over hotter side if using charcoal) and cook (covered if using gas), rotating pizza often, until bottom is well browned and spottily charred and cheese is melted, 1 to 3 minutes. (If cooking over charcoal, middle of pizza will brown faster; to ensure even cooking, check bottom frequently and rotate and reposition pizza as needed to ensure even browning from middle to edges.)

9. Using 2 sets of tongs, transfer pizza to cutting board (if using gas, keep grill covered to conserve heat); sprinkle with one-quarter of herb mixture (about 2 tablespoons).

10. Repeat with remaining dough and toppings, adjusting heat on gas grill as needed to ensure crust reaches visual cues in given time ranges for each pizza. Slice and serve pizzas immediately after removing from grill.

Fugazzeta (Argentine Cheese-Stuffed Pizza)

Serves 4 to 6 Total Time 1¾ hours, plus 1 to 1½ hours resting

Why This Recipe Works Fugazzeta is an Argentine stuffed pizza known for its fluffy, crisp crust; its generous topping of onions seasoned with oregano and red pepper flakes; and its over-the-top cheesy center. To create a stable base for the ample amount of cheese, we use two-thirds of our traditional moist fugazzeta dough as the bottom crust of the pie, reserving only a third for the top crust. A block of whole-milk mozzarella cheese provides milky, melted ooze, while slices of provolone contribute salty sharpness. We concentrate the onions before cooking—salting, resting, and squeezing them—to eliminate moisture that would impede browning and saturate the top crust. Cooking the fugazzeta on the upper-middle rack after firing the broiler ensures that ample heat is concentrated at the top of the oven to brown the onions and bake the top crust through. You can use preshredded cheese, if desired. For a spicier dish, use the larger amount of pepper flakes. Because the slices are large, fugazzeta is typically eaten with a fork and knife.

- 2½ cups (13¾ ounces) bread flour
- 1½ teaspoons sugar
- 1½ teaspoons instant or rapid-rise yeast
- 1 cup plus 2 tablespoons (9 ounces) water, room temperature
- 2½ teaspoons table salt, divided
- 1½ pounds onions, halved and sliced through root end ¼ inch thick
- ¼ cup extra-virgin olive oil, divided
- 4 teaspoons dried oregano, divided
- ¼–½ teaspoon red pepper flakes
- 12 ounces whole-milk block mozzarella cheese, shredded (3 cups)
- 4 ounces sliced provolone cheese
- 7 pitted green olives

1. Using stand mixer fitted with dough hook, mix flour, sugar, and yeast on low speed until combined, about 10 seconds. With mixer running, slowly add water and mix until dough forms and no dry flour remains, about 2 minutes, scraping down bowl as needed. Cover with plastic wrap and let dough rest for 10 minutes.

2. Add 1 teaspoon salt and mix on medium speed until dough forms satiny, sticky ball that clears sides of bowl, 6 to 8 minutes. Turn dough onto lightly floured counter and knead until smooth, about 1 minute. Remove one-third of dough (about 8 ounces) and shape into smooth, tight ball. Shape remaining two-thirds of dough (about 15 ounces) into smooth, tight ball and transfer both to lightly greased large bowl, rolling in oil to coat. Cover tightly with plastic and let rise until dough balls have doubled in size, 1 to 1½ hours.

3. While doughs rests, toss onions and remaining 1½ teaspoons salt together in strainer set over bowl. Let stand for 45 minutes. Using your hands, squeeze out excess moisture from onions; discard liquid and wipe out bowl. Combine onions, 1 tablespoon oil, 2 teaspoons oregano, and pepper flakes in bowl. Set aside.

4. Adjust oven rack to upper-middle position and heat oven to 450 degrees. Coat bottom of 12-inch cast-iron skillet with remaining 3 tablespoons oil. Transfer larger dough ball to lightly floured counter and, using your hands, gently stretch into 12-inch round. Transfer to prepared skillet. Sprinkle mozzarella evenly over top of dough, leaving ½-inch border around edge. Layer provolone evenly on top of mozzarella, tearing slices to fit as needed while maintaining border.

5. Transfer smaller dough ball to lightly floured counter and gently stretch into 12-inch round. Gently place dough directly on top of cheese and, using your fingers, gently press top and bottom dough layers together to seal (it's OK if seal is not tight). Poke dough in several places with fork. Spread onion mixture evenly over entire surface of dough.

6. Turn oven to broil and heat for 5 minutes. Return oven to 450 degrees and bake pizza until bottom is well browned and some onions have begun to brown while others are spottily charred, 35 to 40 minutes, rotating skillet halfway through baking.

7. Remove skillet from oven and top pizza with remaining 2 teaspoons oregano. Let cool for 15 minutes, then remove pizza from skillet and garnish with olives, placing one in center and others around perimeter of pan. Slice (each piece should get an olive on top) and serve.

Focaccia di Recco

Serves 6   Total Time 1¼ hours, plus 45 minutes resting

Why This Recipe Works Focaccia di Recco—the cheese-stuffed flatbread that's focaccia by name and pizza by feel and deeply cherished in its eponymous hometown—consists of two sheets of paper-thin, crisp-chewy dough sandwiching molten cheese. Using high-protein bread flour, moderately high hydration, and a few tablespoons of olive oil makes for an elastic but sturdy dough that can stretch paper-thin without tearing. Briefly baking the focaccia on a stone preheated in a 525-degree oven yields a flatbread with a deeply tanned yet still chewy bottom and a crisp, lightly charred top. Stracchino (also known as Crescenza) is a young, spreadable cow's milk cheese with a delicately tangy, salty flavor; look for it in specialty cheese shops and Italian markets or online. If it's unavailable, substitute Robiola—a young Italian cheese made with a blend of cow's, goat's, and sheep's milk—or a mixture of 8 ounces cream cheese and 4 ounces (1 cup) shredded fontina (use a young Italian cheese) processed in a food processor until combined. Using high-protein King Arthur Bread Flour makes the dough easier to stretch, but other bread flours will work. If your oven does not go to 525 degrees, set it to the highest possible temperature and extend the baking time slightly. Minimize the time between assembling and baking the focaccia to prevent it from sticking to the pan. Serve as a snack with cocktails or as an appetizer.

- 1⅔ cups (9 ounces) bread flour
- ¾ teaspoon table salt
- ½ cup plus 2 tablespoons (5 ounces) water
- ¼ cup plus 2 teaspoons extra-virgin olive oil, divided
- 12 ounces (1¼ cups) stracchino cheese
- ⅛ teaspoon flake sea salt, crumbled

1. Process flour and salt in food processor until combined, about 2 seconds. Combine water and 2 tablespoons oil in liquid measuring cup. With processor running, slowly add water mixture; process until dough forms satiny, sticky ball that clears sides of bowl, 30 to 60 seconds. Transfer dough to lightly floured counter and knead briefly until smooth, about 2 minutes.

2. Divide dough in half. Working with 1 half at a time, cup dough between palms of your hands and work in circular motions on counter to form smooth, taut ball. Wrap each piece with plastic wrap and let rest for 45 minutes to 1 hour.

3. When dough has been resting for 20 minutes, adjust oven rack to lower-middle position, set baking stone on rack, and heat oven to 525 degrees. Invert rimmed baking sheet on counter. Place second rimmed baking sheet, right side up, on top and arrange so that short sides sit parallel to edge of counter (bottom baking sheet will act as platform). Coat bottom and sides of top baking sheet with 1 tablespoon oil.

4. On lightly floured counter, roll 1 dough ball into 12 by 8-inch rectangle. Brush with pastry brush to remove excess flour. Lift dough, drape over your knuckles, and gently stretch into 16 by 12-inch rectangle. Center dough over prepared pan and lower onto pan. Gently stretch dough, rotating pan as needed, until it hangs 2 inches over all sides. Working with 1 side at a time, gently lift dough, let it contract slightly and then relax into pan so just 1 inch remains draped over rim and dough lines bottom of pan.

5. Dollop generous tablespoons of stracchino evenly over surface of dough, leaving 1-inch border from edge of pan. Repeat rolling and stretching second dough ball into 16 by 12-inch rectangle. Place dough directly on top of dollops of cheese. Gently stretch dough (making sure not to disturb cheese) until it hangs 1 inch over all sides of pan. Press firmly around rim of pan to seal edges.

6. Run rolling pin along outside edge of sheet rim to cut away overhanging dough. Using kitchen shears, cut 2-inch hole just to side of each dollop of cheese. Using your fingertips, roll dough edges down into pan to create border. Press to seal. Drizzle with 1 tablespoon oil and sprinkle with flake sea salt.

7. Bake on baking stone until focaccia is crisp and well browned, 8 to 9 minutes, rotating sheet halfway through baking. Slide thin spatula under focaccia to loosen on all sides and transfer to wire rack. Let cool for 1 minute, then transfer bread to cutting board. Drizzle with remaining 2 teaspoons oil, slice into 12 squares, and serve immediately.

Assembling Focaccia di Recco

1. Roll out 1 dough ball and gently stretch into 16 by 12-inch rectangle. Center and lower dough onto pan. Lift and relax dough into pan until just 1 inch drapes over rim.

2. Dollop generous tablespoons of cheese evenly over surface of dough, leaving 1-inch border from edge of pan.

3. Roll and stretch second dough ball into 16 by 12-inch rectangle; place directly on top of cheese. Press around rim to seal edges. Using kitchen shears, cut hole to side of each dollop.

4. Roll dough edges down into pan to create border and press to seal. Drizzle with oil and sea salt.

top | *Fugazzeta (Argentine Cheese-Stuffed Pizza)*
bottom | *Focaccia di Recco*

top | *Lemon-Pickled Radish Toast with Basil and Parmesan*
bottom | *Ricotta Toast with Pesto di Prezzemolo and Grapes*

Avocado Toast

FAST VEGAN Serves 2 Total Time 15 minutes

Why This Recipe Works Eating an avocado when its flesh is smooth and densely creamy might be one of the greatest culinary pleasures. Place it atop a piece of toasted crusty bread and you've got a healthy, delicious, and quick breakfast or lunch. We take ours up a notch by whisking together a lemony vinaigrette and mixing it in as we mash half of the avocado, giving our dish a distinct citrusy punch. You can season the toast minimally with coarse salt and cracked pepper, or try topping it with pickled red onions, crumbled cooked bacon, quartered cherry tomatoes, mashed beans, fresh herbs, chili crisp, fried egg, or a favorite spice blend.

- 1 ripe avocado
- 2 teaspoons extra-virgin olive oil
- 2 teaspoons lemon juice
- ⅛ teaspoon table salt
- Pinch pepper
- 2 (½-inch-thick) slices crusty bread, toasted

1. Halve and pit avocado. Use spoon to scoop flesh from skin onto cutting board. Cut 1 half of avocado into ½-inch pieces. Cut second half into thin slices.

2. In small bowl, whisk together oil, lemon juice, salt, and pepper. Add chopped avocado to bowl and use whisk to mash until mostly smooth and well combined with dressing.

3. Spread mashed avocado evenly over each piece of toast and arrange avocado slices over top. Season with salt and pepper and serve.

Lemon-Pickled Radish Toast with Basil and Parmesan

Serves 4 to 6 Total Time 30 minutes, plus 30 minutes pickling

Why This Recipe Works With their bright pink hue, crisp snap, and peppery bite, radishes make a unique and flavorful topping for toast. Pickling the radishes tames their bite; we use lemon juice in place of the usual vinegar in the pickling liquid for a bit more character. We combine tangy cream cheese and nutty Parmesan to create a rich, creamy spread that's the perfect foil to the pickled radishes. Some basil mixed into the spread and sprinkled on top adds freshness and color. We prefer to slice the radishes using a mandoline, but you could also use a knife. The pickling liquid might not fully cover the radishes at first; they will shrink significantly as they pickle. Be sure to drain the radishes after 30 minutes or they will become too soft. We developed this recipe using a round boule but any rustic, crusty bread will work. Cut into four pieces each, these toasts make excellent party snacks.

- 1 pound radishes, trimmed and sliced ⅛ inch thick (3½ cups)
- ½ teaspoon grated lemon zest plus 6 tablespoons juice (2 lemons), plus lemon wedges for serving
- ¼ cup sugar
- 1 teaspoon table salt
- 8 ounces cream cheese, softened
- 1 ounce Parmesan cheese, grated (½ cup), divided
- 6 tablespoons chopped fresh basil, divided
- 1 garlic clove, minced
- 6 (½-inch-thick) slices rustic boule, toasted
- Extra-virgin olive oil for drizzling
- Flake sea salt

1. Place radishes in medium bowl. Bring lemon juice, ¼ cup water, sugar, and table salt to simmer in small saucepan over medium-high heat, stirring to dissolve sugar. Pour lemon juice mixture over radishes. Let radishes sit in pickling liquid for 30 minutes, stirring occasionally. Drain radishes and refrigerate until ready to serve. (Pickled radishes can be refrigerated for up to 24 hours.)

2. Meanwhile, process cream cheese, ¼ cup Parmesan, ¼ cup basil, garlic, and lemon zest in food processor until smooth, about 1 minute, scraping down sides of bowl as needed. Transfer to bowl. (Cream cheese mixture can be refrigerated for up to 2 days. Let come to room temperature before using.)

3. Spread cream cheese mixture evenly over toast. Shingle radishes evenly over cream cheese mixture. Drizzle radishes with oil and sprinkle with remaining ¼ cup Parmesan and remaining 2 tablespoons basil. Sprinkle with flake sea salt and season with pepper to taste. Serve with lemon wedges.

Ricotta Toast with Pesto di Prezzemolo and Grapes

FAST Serves 6 Total Time 30 minutes

Why This Recipe Works Our Pesto di Prezzemolo (Parsley Pesto) makes an excellent topping for toasted crusty bread. The addition of creamy whole-milk ricotta helps balance the pesto's bold flavors. We drizzle the toasts with extra-virgin olive oil and finish them with a little flake salt and coarsely ground black pepper. We developed this recipe with BelGioioso Ricotta con Latte Whole Milk Ricotta Cheese. Look for that or another good-quality ricotta without stabilizers, or make your own.

- 12 ounces (1½ cups) whole-milk ricotta cheese
- 1 teaspoon grated lemon zest plus 2 teaspoons juice
- ¼ teaspoon table salt
- 6 (½-inch-thick) slices crusty bread, toasted
- ½ cup Pesto di Prezzemolo (Parsley Pesto) (page 268)
- 4½ ounces (1 cup) seedless green grapes, sliced thin
- Extra-virgin olive oil for drizzling

Combine ricotta, lemon zest and juice, and salt in small bowl. Spread ricotta mixture evenly over toast. Spread pesto over ricotta mixture. Arrange grape slices evenly on top of pesto and drizzle with oil. Season with flake sea salt and coarsely ground pepper to taste and serve.

Mana'eesh Za'atar (Za'atar Flatbreads)

VEGAN Serves 4 to 6 (Makes three 9-inch flatbreads)
Total Time 1 hour 10 minutes, plus 2 hours rising

Why This Recipe Works In Lebanon, these flatbreads are a beloved street food and common addition to the daily at-home table. Mana'eesh are typically topped with olive oil and za'atar—the Middle Eastern spice blend featuring thyme, sumac, and sesame seeds—which adds tart, citrusy flavor and delicate crunch. Baking each flatbread on a preheated baking stone in a 500-degree oven gives it a crispy bottom, and tapping the dough all over before baking helps prevent uneven puffing in the oven. (In Lebanese, the word man'oushe—the singular form of mana'eesh—means "engraved" and refers to these indentations.) You can purchase za'atar in the spice section of many grocery stores or online, or you can make your own with our recipe on page 240.

Dough

2½ cups (12½ ounces) all-purpose flour
1½ teaspoons instant or rapid-rise yeast
1 teaspoon table salt
¾ cup plus 2 tablespoons cold water
2 tablespoons extra-virgin olive oil

Topping

3 tablespoons Za'atar (recipe follows)
3 tablespoons extra-virgin olive oil
½ teaspoon table salt

1. **For the dough** Process flour, yeast, and salt in food processor until combined, about 3 seconds. Combine cold water and oil in liquid measuring cup. With processor running, slowly add water mixture and process until dough forms sticky ball that clears sides of bowl, 30 to 60 seconds.

2. Transfer dough to clean counter and knead into cohesive ball, about 1 minute. Place dough in greased bowl. Cover bowl with plastic wrap and let dough rise at room temperature until almost doubled in size, 2 to 2½ hours. One hour before baking, adjust oven rack to middle position, set baking stone on rack, and heat oven to 500 degrees.

3. **For the topping** Meanwhile, combine za'atar, oil, and salt in bowl.

4. On clean counter, divide dough into 3 equal pieces, about 7 ounces each. Shape each piece of dough into ball. Cover loosely with plastic and let rest for 15 minutes.

5. Working with 1 dough ball at a time on lightly floured counter, coat lightly with flour and flatten into 6- to 7-inch disk using your fingertips.

6. Using rolling pin, roll dough into 9- to 10-inch round. Slide dough round onto floured baking peel. Spread one-third of za'atar mixture (about 1½ tablespoons) over surface of dough with back of dinner spoon, stopping ½ inch from edge.

7. Firmly tap dough all over with your fingertips about 6 times. Slide dough onto baking stone and bake until lightly bubbled and brown on top, about 5 minutes. Using baking peel, transfer flatbread to wire rack. Repeat with remaining dough and za'atar mixture. Slice or tear and serve.

Za'atar

FAST VEGAN Makes about ⅓ cup Total Time 15 minutes

The combination of dried herbs, toasted sesame seeds, and tart, citrusy sumac makes for an earthy yet brightly flavored seasoning.

2 tablespoons dried thyme
1 tablespoon dried oregano
1½ tablespoons sumac
1 tablespoon sesame seeds, toasted
¼ teaspoon table salt

Grind thyme and oregano using spice grinder or mortar and pestle until finely ground and powdery. Transfer to bowl and stir in sumac, sesame seeds, and salt. (Za'atar can be stored in airtight container at room temperature for up to 1 year.)

Alu Parathas (Punjabi Potato-Stuffed Griddle Breads)

Serves 4 (Makes 8 parathas) Total Time 1½ hours, plus 1 hour 5 minutes cooling and resting

Why This Recipe Works These potato-stuffed flatbreads from Punjab are a staple across the northern part of the Indian subcontinent and in big cities such as Mumbai and Delhi. Alu parathas are made by wrapping rounds of dough around a boldly spiced potato stuffing, rolling the stuffed balls into slim disks, and browning the disks (brushed with ghee) until crisp brown patches develop. The steamy, pliable breads are typically enjoyed as the center of a meal. We start by making a compact, flavorful potato stuffing of mashed russets, aromatics, and a bold mix of spices and seeds: amchoor, cumin, kalonji, and ajwain. We wrap the potato balls in rounds of dough, roll the packages thin, and griddle them in a cast-iron skillet using plenty of nutty ghee. Flipping the breads only four times ensures that they stay pliable while still developing lots of crisp brown spots. Ghee, kalonji, ajwain, and amchoor can all be purchased at South Asian markets and online. Ajwain has an oregano-like flavor and is often added to fried Indian food to aid digestion; if you can't find it, it's OK to leave it out. If preferred, you can substitute ¼ teaspoon cayenne pepper for the Thai chile in the stuffing. Serve the parathas as an entrée with raita, prepared mango pickle, or Tamatya-Kandyachi Koshimbir (Tomato-Onion Salad, page 242) for breakfast, lunch, or dinner.

Potato Stuffing

- 1 pound russet potatoes, peeled and cut into 1-inch pieces
- 2 tablespoons minced fresh cilantro
- 1 tablespoon grated fresh ginger
- 1½ teaspoons amchoor
- 1 teaspoon ground cumin
- ¾ teaspoon table salt
- 1 Thai chile, stemmed and minced
- ¼ teaspoon kalonji
- ¼ teaspoon ajwain

Dough

- 1⅔ cups (8⅓ ounces) all-purpose flour
- ½ teaspoon table salt
- ½ teaspoon sugar
- 2 tablespoons vegetable oil
- ½ cup plus 1 tablespoon (4½ ounces) cold water
- ¼ cup ghee, melted

1. For the potato stuffing Place potatoes in large saucepan, add cold water to cover by 1 inch, and bring to boil over high heat. Reduce heat to maintain simmer and cook until potatoes are very tender, about 16 minutes. Drain well and process through ricer or mash with potato masher until completely smooth. Set aside and let partially cool, about 20 minutes.

2. Stir cilantro, ginger, amchoor, cumin, salt, Thai chile, kalonji, and ajwain, if using, into potatoes. Season with salt to taste. Cover and set aside. (Potato stuffing can be refrigerated for up to 24 hours; let come to room temperature before using.)

3. For the dough Pulse flour, salt, and sugar in food processor until combined, about 5 pulses. Add oil and pulse until incorporated, about 5 pulses. With processor running, slowly add cold water and process until dough is combined and no dry flour remains, about 30 seconds. Transfer dough to clean counter and knead by hand to form smooth, round ball, about 30 seconds; transfer to bowl, cover with plastic wrap, and let rest for 30 minutes.

Mana'eesh Za'atar (Za'atar Flatbreads)

4. Divide potato stuffing into 8 equal portions and roll into balls (they will be about 1½ inches wide); cover with plastic. Divide dough into 8 equal pieces, about 1¾ ounces each, and cover loosely with plastic. Working with 1 piece of dough at a time, form dough pieces into smooth, taut balls. (To round, set piece of dough on unfloured counter. Loosely cup your hand around dough and, without applying pressure to dough, move your hand in small circular motions. Tackiness of dough against counter and circular motion should work dough into smooth ball.) Let dough balls rest, covered, for 15 minutes. While dough balls rest, line rimmed baking sheet with parchment paper.

5. Roll 1 dough ball into 4-inch disk on lightly floured counter. Place 1 stuffing ball in center of dough disk. Gather edges of dough around stuffing to enclose completely; pinch to seal. Place seam side down on lightly floured counter, gently flatten, and lightly and gently roll to even ⅛-inch-thick round (about 8 inches wide). Transfer to prepared sheet and cover loosely with plastic. Repeat with remaining dough balls and stuffing, stacking parathas between layers of parchment.

6. Heat 10-inch cast-iron skillet over medium heat for 5 minutes, then reduce heat to low. Brush any remaining flour from both sides of 1 paratha, then gently place in hot skillet, being careful not to stretch paratha. Cook until large bubbles begin to form on surface, underside of paratha is light blond, and paratha moves freely in skillet, 30 to 60 seconds. (Paratha may puff.) Using metal spatula, flip paratha, then brush with ghee. Cook until underside is spotty brown and moves freely in skillet, 20 to 60 seconds, pressing any puffed edges firmly onto skillet with spatula to ensure even contact.

7. Flip paratha back onto first side. Repeat brushing with ghee, pressing, cooking, and flipping once more until paratha is even more spotty brown on both sides and no longer looks raw, about 30 seconds per side. Transfer cooked paratha to second rimmed baking sheet, let cool slightly, then cover loosely with dish towel.

8. Repeat with remaining parathas, wiping out skillet with paper towels between each paratha and briefly removing skillet from heat if it begins to smoke or if paratha browns too quickly. Serve hot. (Parathas can be stacked between layers of parchment paper, placed in zipper-lock bag, and refrigerated for up to 2 days. To refresh, heat 10-inch cast-iron skillet over medium heat for 5 minutes, then reduce heat to low. Cook paratha until warmed through, flipping 3 times, 10 to 15 seconds per side.)

Tamatya-Kandyachi Koshimbir (Tomato-Onion Salad)

FAST **VEGAN** Serves 4 Total Time 15 minutes

Alu paratha differs from many other Indian breads in that it is typically served as an entrée rather than as an accompaniment. This refreshing, lightly spiced salad is an ideal way to complete the meal. If you are not fond of raw onion, substitute ¼ cup crushed peanuts.

- 4 large, firm tomatoes, cored and cut into ¼-inch dice
- 1 Thai green chile, sliced
- ½ teaspoon table salt
- Pinch sugar
- 1 large onion, chopped fine
- ¼ teaspoon ground cumin
- 2 tablespoons grated fresh coconut (optional)
- 2 tablespoons finely chopped fresh cilantro (optional)

Stir tomatoes, Thai chile, salt, and sugar together in bowl. Let sit for 5 minutes to allow flavors to meld. Stir in onion and cumin. Garnish with coconut and cilantro, if using, and serve.

Socca with Sautéed Onions and Rosemary

VEGAN Serves 4 (Makes four 10-inch pancakes)
Total Time 1¼ hours

Why This Recipe Works Socca are a kind of pancake or flatbread made from a simple batter of chickpea flour, water, olive oil, and seasonings. They are a beloved street food in Nice, France, and throughout the French Riviera. It's excellent with just a drizzle of extra-virgin olive oil and a sprinkling of flaky salt, but we also love it with a simple topping of onions sautéed with rosemary. Traditionally, the batter is poured in a thin layer into a hot oiled pan and baked in a wood-fired oven until browned and crisp. To make socca at home, we cook the batter like a crepe in a nonstick skillet on the stovetop. After a few minutes over medium-high heat, the underside turns delightfully crispy and beautifully golden brown. Chickpea flour is also sold as garbanzo flour; we do not recommend using besan or gram flour here.

Socca

- 1½ cups (12 ounces) water
- 1⅓ cups (6 ounces) chickpea flour
- ¼ cup extra-virgin olive oil, divided, plus extra for drizzling
- 1 teaspoon table salt
- ¼ teaspoon ground cumin
- Flake sea salt

Sautéed Onions

- 2 tablespoons extra-virgin olive oil
- 2 onions, halved and sliced thin
- ½ teaspoon table salt
- 1 teaspoon chopped fresh rosemary or ¼ teaspoon dried

1. **For the socca** Adjust oven rack to middle position and heat oven to 200 degrees. Set wire rack in rimmed baking sheet and place in oven. Whisk water, flour, 4 teaspoons oil, table salt, and cumin in bowl until no lumps remain. Let batter rest while preparing onions, at least 10 minutes. (Batter will thicken as it sits.)

2. **For the sautéed onions** Heat oil in 10-inch nonstick skillet over medium-high heat until just smoking. Add onions and salt and cook until onions start to brown around edges but still have some texture, 7 to 10 minutes. Add rosemary and cook until fragrant, about 1 minute. Transfer onion mixture to bowl; set aside. Wipe skillet clean with paper towels.

3. Heat 2 teaspoons oil in now-empty skillet over medium-high heat until just smoking. Lift skillet off heat and pour ½ cup batter into far side of skillet; swirl gently in clockwise direction until batter evenly covers bottom of skillet.

4. Return skillet to heat and cook socca, without moving it, until well browned and crisp around bottom edge, 3 to 4 minutes (you can peek at underside of socca by loosening it from side of skillet with rubber spatula).

5. Flip socca with rubber spatula and cook until second side is just cooked, about 1 minute. Transfer socca, browned side up, to prepared wire rack in oven. Repeat 3 times, using 2 teaspoons oil and ½ cup batter per batch.

6. Transfer socca to cutting board and cut each into 8 wedges. Serve, topped with sautéed onions, drizzled with extra oil, and sprinkled with flake sea salt.

top | *Alu Parathas (Punjabi Potato-Stuffed Griddle Breads)*

bottom | *Socca with Sautéed Onions and Rosemary*

Whole-Wheat Crepes with Creamy Sautéed Mushrooms and Asparagus

Whole-Wheat Crepes with Creamy Sautéed Mushrooms and Asparagus

FAST Serves 4 Total Time 45 minutes

Why This Recipe Works The sweet, nutty flavor of whole-wheat crepes pairs well with a filling of meaty cremini mushrooms and tender asparagus in this simple yet elegant dish. We sauté savory cremini mushrooms until they are well browned and then add thinly sliced asparagus and cook just until tender. A bit of cream and grated Parmesan cheese makes the filling rich and creamy.

- 1½ pounds cremini mushrooms, trimmed and sliced ¼ inch thick
- ¼ cup water
- ½ teaspoon vegetable oil
- 1 tablespoon unsalted butter
- 1 shallot, minced
- ½ teaspoon table salt
- ¼ teaspoon pepper
- 8 ounces asparagus, trimmed and cut on bias ¼ inch thick
- ⅔ cup heavy cream
- 6 tablespoons grated Parmesan cheese
- ½ teaspoon grated lemon zest
- 1 recipe Whole-Wheat Crepes (recipe follows)

1. Combine mushrooms and water in 12-inch nonstick skillet and cook over high heat, stirring occasionally, until skillet is almost dry and mushrooms begin to sizzle, 4 to 8 minutes. Reduce heat to medium-high. Add oil and toss until mushrooms are evenly coated. Continue to cook, stirring occasionally, until mushrooms are well browned, 4 to 8 minutes longer. Reduce heat to medium.

2. Push mushrooms to sides of skillet. Add butter to center. Once butter has melted, add shallot, salt, and pepper to center and cook, stirring constantly, until fragrant, about 30 seconds. Add asparagus and cook, stirring occasionally, until just tender, about 1 minute. Reduce heat to medium-low, add cream, and cook, stirring occasionally, until reduced by half, about 1 minute. Off heat, add Parmesan and lemon zest, stirring until cheese is melted and mushroom mixture is creamy.

3. Place crepes on large plate and invert second plate over crepes. Microwave until crepes are warm, 30 to 45 seconds (45 to 60 seconds if crepes have cooled completely). Working with 1 crepe at a time, spread ⅓ cup mushroom mixture across bottom half of crepe. Fold crepe in half and then into quarters. Transfer to plate and serve.

Whole-Wheat Crepes

FAST Makes 10 crepes Total Time 45 minutes

Stacking the crepes on a wire rack allows excess steam to escape so that they don't stick together.

- ½ teaspoon vegetable oil
- 1 cup (5½ ounces) whole-wheat flour
- ½ teaspoon table salt
- 2 cups milk
- 3 large eggs
- 4 tablespoons unsalted butter, melted and cooled

1. Heat oil in 12-inch nonstick skillet over low heat for at least 5 minutes.

2. While skillet heats, whisk flour and salt together in medium bowl. In second bowl, whisk together milk and eggs. Add half of milk mixture to flour mixture and whisk until smooth. Add melted butter and whisk until incorporated. Whisk in remaining milk mixture until smooth.

3. Using paper towel, wipe out skillet, leaving thin film of oil on bottom and sides. Increase heat to medium and let skillet heat for 1 minute. Test heat of skillet by placing 1 teaspoon batter in center and cooking for 20 seconds. If mini crepe is golden brown on bottom, skillet is properly heated; if it is too light or too dark, adjust heat accordingly and retest.

4. Lift skillet off heat and pour ⅓ cup batter into far side of skillet; swirl gently in clockwise direction until batter evenly covers bottom of skillet. Return skillet to heat and cook crepe, without moving it, until surface is dry and crepe starts to brown at edges, loosening crepe from sides of skillet with rubber spatula, about 35 seconds. Gently slide spatula underneath edge of crepe, grasp edge with your fingertips, and flip crepe. Cook until second side is lightly spotted, about 20 seconds. Transfer crepe to wire rack. Return skillet to heat for 10 seconds before repeating with remaining batter. As crepes are done, stack on rack. Serve. (Crepes can be refrigerated for up to 3 days or stacked between sheets of parchment paper and frozen for up to 1 month. Thaw in refrigerator before using.)

Flatbreads with Fontina, Mushrooms, and Chives

Makes two 12-inch flatbreads   Total Time 1¾ hours

Why This Recipe Works These easy flatbreads pair earthy wild mushrooms with buttery, nutty fontina for an elegant main course. We streamline the recipe by starting with store-bought pizza dough which we shape into long ovals, making them easier to cut for a crowd. Cooking the assembled flatbreads on a baking stone in a 500-degree oven ensures they emerge with crisp, well-browned crusts and perfectly roasted mushrooms. You can use your favorite homemade pizza dough, if you prefer. For the wild mushrooms, try shiitake, oyster, chanterelle, and/or maitake. Other great topping combos: pesto, peas, and baby arugula (add the arugula after baking); and peaches and mozzarella with balsamic vinegar drizzled on after baking.

- 2 pounds store-bought pizza dough
- 4 ounces fontina cheese, shredded (1½ cups)
- 8 ounces wild mushrooms, stemmed and roughly torn, if necessary
- 2 tablespoons minced fresh chives

1. One hour before baking flatbreads, adjust oven rack to second highest position (rack should be 4 to 5 inches below broiler), set baking stone on rack, and heat oven to 500 degrees. Divide dough in half and shape each half into smooth, tight ball. Place balls on lightly oiled rimmed baking sheet at least 3 inches apart. Cover loosely with greased plastic wrap and let sit at room temperature for 1 hour.

2. Generously coat 1 dough ball with flour and place on well-floured counter. Using fingertips, gently flatten into 8-inch disk, leaving 1 inch of outer edge slightly thicker than center. Using your hands, continue stretching dough into 16 by 6-inch oval, working along edges and giving dough half turns as you stretch. Transfer dough oval to well-floured baking peel and reshape as needed. Repeat shaping with remaining dough ball. Sprinkle each flatbread with 2 ounces fontina and 4 ounces mushrooms, leaving ½-inch border. as

3. Slide 1 flatbread carefully onto baking stone and bake until crust is well browned and fontina is bubbly and beginning to brown, 5 to 7 minutes, rotating flatbread halfway through baking. Transfer flatbread to wire rack, let cool for 5 minutes, then sprinkle with 1 tablespoon chives. Repeat baking and cooling remaining flatbread, then sprinkle with remaining chives. Slice flatbreads into wedges and serve.

Cauliflower Chickpea Flatbread with Romesco

Makes two 12-inch flatbreads   Total Time 2 hours

Why This Recipe Works The appeal of a cauliflower-based crust is undeniable, but it can be tricky to create one that doesn't crumble or stick to the pan. The addition of chickpea flour helps create a strong, durable structure. We also stir in plenty of grated Parmesan, which essentially fries to create a gloriously crisp crust. Tangy romesco sauce, a sprinkling of golden cauliflower florets, and dollops of rich, creamy ricotta turn these flatbreads into a meal. If you don't have a baking peel, use a rimless or overturned baking sheet to slide the flatbreads onto the stone. If you don't have a baking stone, you can use a preheated rimless or overturned baking sheet, but the breads will be less crisp. Don't top the second flatbread until right before you bake it.

- 1 head cauliflower (2 pounds), cored and cut into ¾-inch florets (about 7 cups), divided
- 1 cup (4½ ounces) chickpea flour
- 2 large eggs
- ½ cup extra-virgin olive oil, divided, plus extra for drizzling
- 3 garlic cloves, minced, divided
- 2 teaspoons chopped fresh oregano or ¾ teaspoon dried
- 1 teaspoon table salt, divided
- 6 ounces Parmesan cheese, grated (3 cups)
- 1¼ cups fresh parsley leaves, divided
- ⅔ cup jarred roasted red peppers, rinsed, patted dry, and chopped
- ¼ cup walnuts, toasted
- 1 tablespoon sherry vinegar
- ¼ cup ricotta cheese

1. One hour before baking, adjust oven rack to upper-middle position, set baking stone on rack, and heat oven to 475 degrees. Process 4 cups cauliflower florets, chickpea flour, eggs, ¼ cup oil, two-thirds garlic, oregano, and ¼ teaspoon salt in food processor until thick, smooth batter forms, about 3 minutes, scraping down sides of bowl as needed. Transfer batter to large bowl and stir in Parmesan.

2. Line baking peel with 16 by 12-inch piece of parchment paper with long edge perpendicular to handle and spray parchment well with vegetable oil spray. Transfer half of batter (about 2 cups) to center of prepared parchment and top with second greased sheet of parchment. Gently press batter into 12-inch round (about ¼ inch thick), then discard top piece of parchment. Carefully slide round, still on parchment,

onto stone and bake until edges are browned and crisp and top is golden, about 12 minutes, rotating flatbread halfway through baking (parchment will darken). Transfer crust to wire rack set in rimmed baking sheet and discard bottom parchment. Repeat with remaining batter to make second crust.

3. In clean, dry processor workbowl, process ¼ cup parsley, red peppers, walnuts, vinegar, remaining garlic, and ¼ teaspoon salt until smooth, about 30 seconds, scraping down sides of bowl as needed. With processor running, slowly add 3 tablespoons oil until incorporated. (Romesco sauce can be refrigerated for up to 3 days.)

4. Heat remaining 1 tablespoon oil in 12-inch nonstick skillet over medium-high heat until shimmering. Add remaining 3 cups cauliflower florets and remaining ½ teaspoon salt and cook, stirring frequently, until florets are spotty brown and crisp-tender, 12 to 15 minutes.

5. Working with 1 crust at a time, spread half of sauce (about ⅓ cup) in thin layer over crust, leaving ¼-inch border. Scatter half of cauliflower evenly over top. Place flatbread (still on wire rack in sheet) on stone and bake until warmed through, about 5 minutes.

6. Transfer flatbread to cutting board. Sprinkle evenly with ½ cup parsley, dollop half of ricotta in small spoonfuls evenly over flatbread, and drizzle with oil to taste. Slice into 8 slices and serve immediately. Repeat topping and baking for second flatbread.

Upside-Down Caramelized Shallot and Onion Tart

Serves 4   Total Time 2¼ hours

Why This Recipe Works Roasted shallots, caramelized onions, and crisp buttery pastry add up to an elegant savory upside-down tart. Roasting halved shallots with their skins on lets them caramelize on the cut sides while staying moist. We arrange the precooked shallots in an attractive circular pattern before topping them with the caramelized onions and puff pastry, then baking until the crust is puffed and golden. A creamy dollop of Boursin whipped with sour cream adds tangy richness. Thaw frozen puff pastry in the refrigerator for 24 hours or on the counter for 30 to 60 minutes. If your puff pastry is longer than what we call for, you may need to trim (rather than roll) the sheet to achieve the dimensions

top | *Flatbreads with Fontina, Mushrooms, and Chives*
bottom | *Cauliflower Chickpea Flatbread with Romesco*

in step 1. Look for shallots that measure 3½ to 4 inches long and 1½ to 2 inches wide. If you get a double shallot, separate the lobes and halve each lengthwise to create a cut surface.

- 1 (9½ by 9-inch) sheet puff pastry, thawed
- 9 large shallots (1¼ pounds)
- 1 tablespoon extra-virgin olive oil
- ¾ teaspoon plus ⅛ teaspoon table salt, divided
- ½ teaspoon plus ⅛ teaspoon pepper, divided
- 1 pound onions, halved and sliced through root end ¼ inch thick
- ½ cup water, plus more as needed
- 2 tablespoons unsalted butter, divided
- Pinch baking soda
- 2 teaspoons minced fresh thyme
- ½ cup cider vinegar
- 2 tablespoons sugar
- 1 recipe Whipped Boursin (recipe follows)

1. Adjust oven rack to middle position and heat oven to 400 degrees. Roll pastry into 10-inch square on lightly floured counter. Using plate, bowl, or skillet lid as template, cut out 10-inch round. Discard trim. Poke pastry round all over with paring knife, then transfer round to large plate. Refrigerate until needed.

2. Trim stem ends of shallots and halve from root end to stem end, leaving skin intact. Trim root ends but leave shallot intact. Brush cut sides with oil and sprinkle with ⅛ teaspoon salt and ⅛ teaspoon pepper. Arrange cut side down on rimmed baking sheet and roast until tender and paring knife meets no resistance when slipped into center, 30 to 33 minutes.

3. While shallots roast, bring onions, water, 1 tablespoon butter, baking soda, ¼ teaspoon salt, and ¼ teaspoon pepper to simmer in 10-inch ovensafe skillet over medium-high heat. Cover and cook until water has evaporated and onions start to sizzle, 10 to 12 minutes.

4. Uncover and, using wooden spoon, spread onions into even layer, pressing into sides and bottom of skillet. Cook, without stirring, for 30 seconds. Stir onions, then spread into even layer, pressing into sides and bottom of skillet. Repeat until dark fond develops in pan. When fond develops, add 1 to 2 tablespoons water, scrape up browned bits, and stir into onions. Repeat process of letting fond develop and deglazing until onions are very soft, well browned, and slightly sticky, 10 to 12 minutes. Stir in thyme and transfer onions to bowl. (Onions can be refrigerated for up to 3 days or frozen for up to 1 month.)

5. In now-empty skillet, bring vinegar, sugar, remaining ½ teaspoon salt, and remaining ¼ teaspoon pepper to simmer over medium-high heat, swirling skillet to dissolve sugar. Simmer vigorously, swirling skillet occasionally, until consistency resembles that of maple syrup, 3 to 4 minutes. Stir in remaining 1 tablespoon butter. Remove skillet from heat.

6. Gently remove outer shallot skin. Arrange shallots, cut side down, in circular pattern around edge of skillet, nestling shallots snugly. Tuck remaining shallots into center (it is not necessary to maintain circular pattern in center; it's OK if 1 or 2 pieces don't fit). Spread caramelized onions evenly over top of shallots, leaving outer inch of shallots exposed. Place pastry round on top. Bake until pastry is puffed, crisp, and deep golden brown, 35 to 38 minutes, rotating skillet halfway through baking.

7. Let tart cool for 8 minutes. Run paring knife around edge of crust to loosen, then invert plate over skillet. Using pot holders, swiftly and carefully invert tart onto plate (if shallots shift or stick to skillet, rearrange with spoon). Let cool for at least 15 minutes. Serve warm or at room temperature. Cut into wedges, passing Whipped Boursin separately.

Whipped Boursin

FAST Makes about 1 cup Total Time 20 minutes

The allium savor and rich creaminess of Boursin pairs naturally with our Upside-Down Caramelized Shallot and Onion Tart. We beat the Boursin with sour cream, which loosens the cheese's dense creaminess so that we can dollop it over each slice. It also makes a great dip or spread for vegetables, crackers, or crostini.

- 1 (5.2-ounce) package Boursin Shallot & Chive cheese, room temperature
- ½ cup sour cream

Using hand mixer set at low speed, beat Boursin and sour cream until smooth and creamy, about 30 seconds.

Showstopping Shallots

Savory upside-down tarts impress with their dramatic unveiling, high-gloss finish, and contrast of softened, brightly glazed vegetables atop a flaky crust. Alliums such as shallots work particularly well in our Upside-Down Caramelized Shallot and Onion Tart thanks to their complex flavor and visually striking cut surfaces.

A Softer, Sweeter Allium

Shallots contain roughly twice as much sugar as onions and about 10 percent less water, and they're milder because they're lower in the precursor sulfur compound isoalliin that leads to pungency when the vegetables' cells are cut open. Also, because shallots are smaller, with thinner layers, they bake up softer.

Shape Matters

Halving the shallots lengthwise before roasting creates an elegant teardrop shape that makes for a beautiful presentation atop the finished tart. This approach also maximizes surface area and allows for plenty of nooks and crannies to be draped with the glossy syrup.

Roast the Shallots Skin-On

Don't peel the shallots before roasting them. The papery "jackets" insulate the flesh during roasting so it stays moist and tender. It's also much faster and easier to pluck the skins off the roasted shallots than it is to peel them when raw.

Upside-Down Caramelized Shallot and Onion Tart

Vidalia Onion Pie

Vidalia Onion Pie

Serves 4 Total Time 1 hour

Why This Recipe Works Vidalia onion pie is a beloved Southern classic: It features slices of the sweet, seasonal onion in a rich custard filling that is tempered with a generous dose of sharp cheddar cheese, all surrounded by a salty, buttery Ritz Cracker crust. In our streamlined version of this summertime favorite, we jump-start the baking by tempering the custard filling with hot sautéed onions. A sprinkling of chives mixed into the filling adds a bit of color and freshness. We like to serve this pie with a mixed green salad dressed in a tangy vinaigrette. You will need about one sleeve of Ritz Crackers.

- 2 large eggs
- ½ cup half-and-half
- ½ teaspoon hot sauce
- ½ teaspoon pepper
- 35 Ritz Crackers
- ½ cup (2½ ounces) all-purpose flour
- ½ teaspoon table salt, divided
- 8 tablespoons unsalted butter, melted, divided
- 4 cups thinly sliced Vidalia onions (about 2 onions)
- 6 ounces sharp cheddar cheese, shredded (1½ cups)
- ¼ cup minced fresh chives

1. Adjust oven rack to middle position and heat oven to 425 degrees. Whisk eggs, half-and-half, hot sauce, and pepper together in large bowl; set aside. Pulse crackers, flour, and ¼ teaspoon salt in food processor until coarsely ground, 8 to 10 pulses. Add 6 tablespoons melted butter and pulse until crumbs are evenly moistened, about 5 pulses. Transfer cracker mixture to 9-inch pie plate. Press crumbs into even layer on bottom and about 1¼ inches up sides of plate. Bake until crust is fragrant and beginning to brown, about 8 minutes.

2. Meanwhile, combine onions, remaining ¼ teaspoon salt, and remaining 2 tablespoons melted butter in 12-inch nonstick skillet. Cover and cook over medium-high heat, stirring occasionally, until onions are softened, about 8 minutes.

3. Stir hot onions into egg mixture. Stir in cheddar and chives. Transfer onion mixture to crust. Bake until set and center of pie registers 165 degrees, 14 to 17 minutes. Let cool for 5 minutes. Serve.

Tourte aux Pommes de Terre (French Potato Pie)

Serves 6 to 8 Total Time 1½ hours, plus 3 hours chilling and cooling

Why This Recipe Works Versions of this decadent and delicious potato and cream pie recipe—also known as pâté aux pommes de terre—exist throughout central France. Though many are made using puff pastry, here we opt for a somewhat less common pâte brisée (aka pie dough), which offers a crisp, sturdy texture. While many traditional recipes call for adding the cream through a vent hole in the top crust, we find it more practical to parboil the potatoes in water, drain, and then return to the pot to simmer for a few minutes with the cream. This eliminates the guesswork of determining exactly how much cream the potato slices can absorb without the pie ending up runny or loose. To ensure that the cream fully coats the potatoes, we add a pinch of baking soda to the cooking water to help break down the potatoes' exteriors and release starch that thickens the cream. We strongly recommend measuring the flour for the pie crust by weight. The potatoes can be sliced on a mandoline. Serve as a main course with a salad or in small slices as a side dish.

Crust

- 20 tablespoons (2½ sticks) unsalted butter, chilled, divided
- 2½ cups (12½ ounces) all-purpose flour, divided
- 1 teaspoon table salt
- ½ cup (4 ounces) ice water, divided

Filling

- 1 onion, halved and sliced thin
- 1½ teaspoons table salt
- 2 pounds Yukon Gold potatoes, peeled and sliced crosswise ⅛ inch thick
- ½ teaspoon baking soda
- 1¼ cups heavy cream
- 3 garlic cloves, minced
- ½ teaspoon pepper
- ¼ teaspoon ground nutmeg
- 2 tablespoons minced fresh parsley
- 1 large egg, lightly beaten

1. For the crust Shred 4 tablespoons butter on large holes of box grater and place in freezer. Cut remaining 16 tablespoons butter into ½-inch cubes.

2. Pulse 1½ cups flour and salt in food processor until combined, 2 pulses. Add cubed butter and process until homogeneous paste forms, 40 to 50 seconds. Using your hands, carefully break paste into 2-inch chunks and redistribute evenly around processor blade. Add remaining 1 cup flour and pulse until mixture is broken into pieces no larger than 1 inch (most pieces will be much smaller), 4 or 5 pulses. Transfer mixture to medium bowl. Add shredded butter and toss until butter pieces are separated and coated with flour.

3. Sprinkle ¼ cup ice water over mixture. Toss with rubber spatula until mixture is evenly moistened. Sprinkle remaining ¼ cup ice water over mixture and toss to combine. Press dough with spatula until dough sticks together. Use spatula to divide dough into 2 portions. Transfer each portion to sheet of plastic wrap. Working with 1 portion at a time, draw edges of plastic over dough and press firmly on sides and top to form compact, fissure-free mass; wrap in plastic and form into 5-inch disk. Refrigerate dough for at least 2 hours or up to 2 days. (Wrapped dough can be frozen for up to 1 month.) Let chilled dough sit on counter until softened slightly, about 10 minutes, before rolling. (If frozen, let dough thaw completely on counter before rolling.)

4. For the filling One hour before baking pie, toss onion and salt in bowl and set aside. Bring 4 quarts water to boil in Dutch oven over high heat. Add potatoes and baking soda, return to boil, and cook for 1 minute. Drain potatoes and return to pot. Add cream, garlic, pepper, nutmeg, and onion and any accumulated liquid and bring to simmer over high heat. Adjust heat to maintain simmer and cook, stirring gently and frequently (it's OK if some slices break), until cream thickens and begins to coat potatoes, about 5 minutes. Let cool off heat for at least 30 minutes or up to 2 hours.

5. Roll 1 disk of dough into 12-inch round on well-floured counter. Loosely roll dough around rolling pin and gently unroll onto 9-inch pie plate, letting excess dough hang over edge. Ease dough into plate by gently lifting edge of dough with your hand while pressing dough into plate bottom with your other hand. Refrigerate until dough is firm, about 30 minutes. Roll second disk of dough into 12-inch round on well-floured counter, then transfer to parchment paper–lined baking sheet; refrigerate for 30 minutes. Adjust oven rack to lower-middle position and heat oven to 450 degrees.

6. Stir parsley into potato mixture (it's OK if potato mixture is still slightly warm). Transfer mixture to dough-lined pie plate and spread into even layer. Using paring knife or round cutter, cut ½-inch hole in center of second dough round. Loosely roll dough round around rolling pin and gently unroll it over filling, aligning hole with center of pie and leaving at least ½-inch overhang all around. Fold dough under itself so edge of fold is flush with outer rim of pie plate. Flute edges using your thumb and forefinger or press with tines of fork to seal. Place pie on parchment-lined rimmed baking sheet and brush with egg. Bake until top is light golden brown, 18 to 20 minutes.

7. Reduce oven temperature to 325 degrees and continue to bake until crust is deep golden brown and potatoes at vent hole are tender when pricked with paring knife, 30 to 40 minutes longer. If pie begins to get too brown before potatoes are softened, cover loosely with aluminum foil. Let pie cool on wire rack for at least 30 minutes. Serve warm or at room temperature.

Eggplant and Tomato Phyllo Pie

Serves 4 to 6 (Makes one 9-inch pie) Total Time 1¾ hours, plus 15 minutes cooling

Why This Recipe Works Phyllo dough is another route to an easy-to-assemble yet visually stunning vegetable tart, with the paper-thin dough layers baking to a beautiful golden-brown color and shatteringly crisp texture. Here phyllo is paired with a mix of eggplant and tomatoes that is layered between mild mozzarella and nutty Parmesan. Broiling the eggplant slices before assembling the tart deepens their flavor and creates a delightful char. To capture the tomatoes' appealing juiciness while avoiding a soggy tart, salt the tomato slices and let them sit in a colander to draw out excess moisture. Layering 12 sheets of phyllo dough creates a crust sturdy enough to stand up to the abundance of vegetables, and doing so in an offset pattern contributes to the beautiful presentation. The insulating layer of shredded mozzarella melts into the phyllo crust for a satisfyingly cheesy layer that also helps keep the crust from getting soggy. Fresh oregano and basil bring bold herbal flavor. Phyllo dough is also available in larger 18 by 14-inch sheets; if using, cut them in half to make 14 by 9-inch sheets. Don't thaw the phyllo in the microwave; let it sit in the refrigerator overnight or on the counter for 4 to 5 hours.

Go for Gold

The rich, buttery flavor and silky texture of Yukon Gold potatoes make them an ideal choice for this elegant, decadent tart.

A Happy Medium

Yukon Golds are considered all-purpose potatoes; they contain less starch than dry, floury baking potatoes but more than firm, waxy boiling varieties.

Shop Carefully

At the grocery, look for Yukon Golds that show no signs of sprouting and avoid any with a greenish tint. Once home, store them in a cool, dry place and away from onions, which give off gases that hasten sprouting.

Give Them a Head Start

Boiling the potatoes for just a few minutes ensures they become sufficiently tender when baked in the assembled pie.

Tourte aux Pommes de Terre (French Potato Pie)

1 pound tomatoes, cored and sliced ¼ inch thick
1¼ teaspoons table salt, divided
1 pound eggplant, sliced into ¼-inch-thick rounds
½ cup extra-virgin olive oil, divided
12 (14 by 9-inch) phyllo sheets, thawed
3 garlic cloves, minced
2 teaspoons minced fresh oregano
¼ teaspoon pepper
6 ounces block mozzarella cheese, shredded (1½ cups)
2 tablespoons grated Parmesan cheese
1 tablespoon chopped fresh basil

1. Adjust oven rack 6 inches from broiler element and heat broiler. Line rimmed baking sheet with aluminum foil. Toss tomatoes and ¾ teaspoon salt together in colander and set aside to drain for 30 minutes.

2. Meanwhile, arrange eggplant in single layer on prepared sheet and brush both sides with 2 tablespoons oil. Broil eggplant until softened and beginning to brown, 10 to 12 minutes, flipping eggplant halfway through broiling. Set aside to cool slightly, about 10 minutes.

3. Heat oven to 375 degrees. Line second rimmed baking sheet with parchment paper. Place ¼ cup oil in small bowl. Place 1 phyllo sheet on prepared sheet, then lightly brush phyllo with prepared oil. Turn baking sheet 30 degrees and place second phyllo sheet on first phyllo sheet, leaving any overhanging phyllo in place. Brush second phyllo sheet with oil. Repeat turning baking sheet and layering remaining 10 phyllo sheets in pinwheel pattern, brushing each with oil (you should have 12 total layers of phyllo).

4. Shake colander to rid tomatoes of excess juice. Combine tomatoes, garlic, oregano, pepper, 1 tablespoon oil, and remaining ½ teaspoon salt in bowl. Sprinkle mozzarella evenly in center of phyllo in 9-inch round. Shingle tomatoes and eggplant on top of mozzarella in concentric circles, alternating tomatoes and eggplant as you go. Sprinkle Parmesan over top.

5. Gently fold edges of phyllo over vegetable mixture, pleating every 2 to 3 inches as needed. Lightly brush edges with remaining 1 tablespoon oil. Bake until phyllo is crisp and golden brown, 30 to 35 minutes. Let galette cool for 15 minutes then sprinkle with basil. Slide onto cutting board or serving platter, cut into pieces, and serve.

Mushroom and Leek Galette with Gorgonzola

Serves 6 Total Time 2 hours, plus 1½ hours chilling

Why This Recipe Works Galettes have a rustic elegance that makes them ideal for a casual dinner party. This one features meaty shiitake mushrooms and tender leeks encased in a delicate yet substantial crust. Most vegetable tarts rely on the same pastry dough used for fruit tarts, but vegetable tarts are more prone to leaking liquid into the crust or falling apart when the tart is sliced. We needed a crust that was extra-sturdy and boasted a complex flavor of its own. To increase the flavor of the crust and keep it tender, we swap out part of the white flour for nutty whole wheat and use butter rather than shortening. To punch up its flaky texture and introduce more structure, we give the dough a series of folds to create numerous interlocking layers. A boldly flavored sauce of Gorgonzola and crème fraîche binds the vegetables together for a rich, cohesive filling. Cutting a few small holes in the dough prevents it from lifting off the pan as it bakes. A baking stone helps to crisp the crust but is not essential; an overturned baking sheet can be used in its place.

Dough

1¼ cups (6¼ ounces) all-purpose flour
½ cup (2¾ ounces) whole-wheat flour
1 tablespoon sugar
¾ teaspoon table salt
10 tablespoons unsalted butter, cut into ½-inch pieces and chilled
7 tablespoons (3½ ounces) ice water
1 teaspoon distilled white vinegar

Filling

1¼ pounds shiitake mushrooms, stemmed and sliced thin
5 teaspoons extra-virgin olive oil, divided
1 pound leeks, white and light green parts only, sliced ½ inch thick and washed thoroughly (3 cups)
1 teaspoon minced fresh thyme
2 tablespoons crème fraîche
1 tablespoon Dijon mustard
3 ounces Gorgonzola cheese, crumbled (¾ cup)
1 large egg, lightly beaten
Kosher salt
2 tablespoons minced fresh parsley

1. **For the dough** Pulse all-purpose flour, whole-wheat flour, sugar, and salt in food processor until combined, 2 to 3 pulses. Add butter and pulse until it forms pea-size pieces, about 10 pulses. Transfer mixture to medium bowl.

2. Sprinkle water and vinegar over mixture. With rubber spatula, use folding motion to mix until loose, shaggy mass forms with some dry flour remaining (do not overwork). Transfer mixture to center of large sheet of plastic wrap, press gently into rough 4-inch square, and wrap tightly. Refrigerate for at least 45 minutes.

3. Transfer dough to lightly floured counter. Roll into 11 by 8-inch rectangle with short side of rectangle parallel to edge of counter. Using bench scraper, bring bottom third of dough up, then fold upper third over it, folding like business letter into 8 by 4-inch rectangle. Turn dough 90 degrees counterclockwise. Roll out dough again into 11 by 8-inch rectangle and fold into thirds again. Turn dough 90 degrees counterclockwise and repeat rolling and folding into thirds. After last fold, fold dough in half to create 4-inch square. Press top of dough gently to seal. Wrap in plastic and refrigerate for at least 45 minutes or up to 2 days.

4. **For the filling** Microwave mushrooms in covered bowl until just tender, 3 to 5 minutes. Transfer to colander to drain; return to bowl. Meanwhile, heat 1 tablespoon oil in 12-inch skillet over medium heat until shimmering. Add leeks and thyme, cover, and cook, stirring occasionally, until leeks are tender and beginning to brown, 5 to 7 minutes. Transfer to bowl with mushrooms. Stir in crème fraîche and mustard. Season with salt and pepper to taste and set aside.

5. Adjust oven rack to lower-middle position, place baking stone on rack, and heat oven to 400 degrees. Line rimmed baking sheet with parchment paper. Remove dough from refrigerator and let stand at room temperature for 15 to 20 minutes. Roll out on generously floured counter (use up to ¼ cup flour) to 14-inch round about ⅛ inch thick. (Trim edges as needed to form rough round.) Transfer dough to prepared baking sheet (dough will hang over edges of sheet). With tip of paring knife, cut five ¼-inch holes in dough (one at center and four evenly spaced halfway from center to edge of dough). Brush top of dough with 1 teaspoon oil.

6. Spread half of filling evenly over dough, leaving 2-inch border around edge. Sprinkle with half of Gorgonzola, cover with remaining filling, and top with remaining Gorgonzola. Drizzle remaining 1 teaspoon oil over filling. Gently grasp 1 edge of dough and fold up outer 2 inches over filling. Repeat around circumference of tart, overlapping dough every 2 to 3 inches; gently pinch pleated dough to secure but do not press dough into filling. Brush dough with egg and sprinkle evenly with kosher salt.

7. Reduce oven temperature to 375 degrees. Place sheet on baking stone and bake until crust is deep golden brown and filling is beginning to brown, 35 to 45 minutes. Transfer galette, still on sheet, to wire rack and let cool for 10 minutes. Using offset or wide metal spatula, loosen galette from parchment and carefully slide it off parchment onto cutting board. Sprinkle with parsley, cut into wedges, and serve.

Variation

Butternut Squash Galette with Gruyère

If desired, you can substitute rye flour for the whole-wheat flour in this variation.

1. Microwave 6 ounces baby spinach and ¼ cup water in covered bowl until spinach is wilted and decreased in volume by half, 3 to 4 minutes. Using pot holders, remove bowl from microwave and keep covered for 1 minute. Carefully remove plate and transfer spinach to colander. Gently press spinach with rubber spatula to release excess liquid. Transfer spinach to cutting board and chop coarse. Return spinach to colander and press again with rubber spatula; set aside.

2. Substitute 1¼ pounds butternut squash, peeled and cut into ½-inch cubes, for mushrooms and increase microwave cooking time to about 8 minutes. Substitute 1 thinly sliced red onion for leeks and ½ teaspoon minced fresh oregano for thyme. Substitute 1 teaspoon sherry vinegar for Dijon mustard and stir reserved spinach and 3 ounces shredded Gruyère cheese into filling along with crème fraîche and vinegar in step 4. Omit Gorgonzola.

Pleating a Free-Form Tart

Gently grasp 1 edge of dough and make 2-inch-wide fold over filling. Lift and fold another segment of dough over first fold to form pleat. Repeat every 2 to 3 inches.

Celery Root Galette with Blue Cheese and Walnuts

Celery Root Galette with Blue Cheese and Walnuts

Serves 4 to 6 Total Time 2 hours, plus 1½ hours chilling

Why This Recipe Works Celery root (also known as celeriac) boasts a crisp, firm, parsnip-like texture under its tough peel and a mild, celery-like flavor that sweetens with cooking. Here we include it in a free-form tart filled with texture and flavor. The roasted celery root is coated with an orange-honey glaze and layered with a filling of leeks and tender baby spinach bound with crème fraîche and Dijon. Walnuts add a rich nuttiness to our tart dough. The addition of a little vinegar and a gentle hand when mixing the dough ensure it remains sturdy yet tender. A process of folding and rolling the dough contributes appealingly flaky layers. A final sprinkle of an orange-parsley gremolata offers a bright, fresh finish.

Dough

- 1 cup (5 ounces) all-purpose flour
- ½ cup (2¾ ounces) whole-wheat or rye flour
- ½ cup chopped walnuts
- 1 tablespoon sugar
- ¾ teaspoon table salt
- 10 tablespoons unsalted butter, cut into ½-inch pieces and chilled
- 7 tablespoons (3½ ounces) ice water
- 1 teaspoon distilled white vinegar

Filling

- 2 tablespoons plus 4 teaspoons extra-virgin olive oil, divided
- 1½ pounds celery root, peeled and cut into ¾-inch pieces
- 1 teaspoon kosher salt, divided
- ⅛ teaspoon pepper
- 6 ounces (6 cups) baby spinach
- 1½ pounds leeks, white and light green parts only, sliced ½ inch thick and washed thoroughly (4½ cups)
- 3 sprigs fresh thyme, plus ½ teaspoon minced
- 2 tablespoons crème fraîche
- 1 tablespoon Dijon mustard
- 3 tablespoons orange juice
- 2 tablespoons honey
- 2 teaspoons distilled white vinegar
- 3 ounces blue cheese, crumbled (¾ cup), divided
- 1 large egg, lightly beaten

Gremolata

- 2 tablespoons minced fresh parsley
- 1 teaspoon grated orange zest
- 1 garlic clove, minced

1. For the dough Pulse all-purpose flour, whole-wheat flour, walnuts, sugar, and salt in food processor until walnuts are finely ground, 8 to 10 pulses. Add butter and pulse until it forms pea-size pieces, about 10 pulses. Transfer mixture to medium bowl and sprinkle with ice water and vinegar. With silicone spatula, use folding motion to mix until loose, shaggy mass forms with some dry flour remaining (do not overwork). Transfer mixture to center of large sheet of plastic wrap, press gently into rough 4-inch square, and wrap tightly. Refrigerate for 45 minutes.

2. Transfer dough to lightly floured counter. Roll into 11 by 8-inch rectangle with short side of rectangle parallel to edge of counter. Using bench scraper, bring bottom third of dough up, then fold upper third over it, folding like business letter into 8 by 4-inch rectangle. Turn dough 90 degrees counterclockwise. Roll out dough again into 11 by 8-inch rectangle and fold into thirds again. Turn dough 90 degrees counterclockwise and repeat rolling and folding into thirds. After last fold, fold dough in half to create 4-inch square. Press top of dough gently to seal. Wrap tightly in plastic wrap and refrigerate for at least 45 minutes or up to 2 days (or freeze for up to 1 month).

3. For the filling Adjust oven rack to lower-middle position, place baking stone on rack, and heat oven to 425 degrees. Heat 1 tablespoon oil in 12-inch skillet over medium heat until shimmering. Add celery root, ½ teaspoon salt, and pepper and cook, stirring occasionally, until softened and lightly browned, 5 to 7 minutes. Place skillet on baking stone in oven and roast celery root until deep golden brown and tender, 8 to 16 minutes, stirring halfway through roasting. Being careful of hot skillet handle, transfer celery root to plate; set aside. (Celery root can be refrigerated for up to 2 days.) Wipe skillet clean with paper towels.

4. Meanwhile, place spinach and ¼ cup water in large microwave-safe bowl. Cover bowl with large dinner plate (plate should completely cover bowl and not rest on spinach). Microwave on high until spinach is wilted and decreased in volume by half, 3 to 4 minutes. Using pot holders, remove bowl from microwave and keep covered for 1 minute. Carefully remove plate and transfer spinach to colander set in sink. Using back of silicone spatula, gently press spinach against colander to release excess liquid. Transfer spinach to cutting board and chop. Return spinach to colander and press again with silicone spatula.

5. Heat 1 tablespoon oil in now-empty skillet over medium heat until shimmering. Add leeks and minced thyme. Cover and cook, stirring occasionally, until leeks are tender and beginning to brown, 5 to 7 minutes. Transfer leek mixture to medium bowl, add spinach, crème fraîche, and mustard, and gently stir to combine. Season with salt and pepper to taste; set aside. Wipe skillet clean with paper towels.

6. Bring 3 tablespoons water, orange juice, honey, vinegar, and thyme sprigs to simmer in again-empty skillet over medium-high heat. Cook, stirring constantly, until reduced to syrupy consistency, about 2 minutes. Off heat, discard thyme sprigs. Add celery root to skillet and gently toss to coat with glaze.

7. Remove dough from refrigerator and let stand at room temperature for 15 to 20 minutes. Roll on generously floured counter (use up to ¼ cup flour) to 14-inch round about ⅛ inch thick. (Trim edges as needed to form rough round.) Transfer dough to parchment paper–lined rimmed baking sheet (dough will hang over edges of sheet). With tip of paring knife, cut five ¼-inch holes in dough (1 at center and 4 evenly spaced midway from center to edge of dough). Brush top of dough with 2 teaspoons oil.

8. Spread half of leek and spinach filling evenly over dough, leaving 2-inch border around edge. Sprinkle with half of blue cheese and top with remaining leek and spinach filling. Evenly distribute celery root over filling. Sprinkle with remaining blue cheese and drizzle with remaining 2 teaspoons oil. Gently grasp 1 edge of dough and fold up outer 2 inches over filling. Repeat around circumference of tart, overlapping dough every 2 to 3 inches; gently pinch pleated dough to secure, but do not press dough into filling. Brush dough with egg and sprinkle with remaining ½ teaspoon salt.

9. Reduce oven temperature to 375 degrees. Place sheet on baking stone and bake until crust is deep golden brown and filling is beginning to brown, 35 to 45 minutes. Transfer galette, still on sheet, to wire rack and let cool for 10 minutes.

10. For the gremolata Combine all ingredients in bowl. Using offset or wide metal spatula, loosen galette from parchment and carefully slide it off parchment onto cutting board. Sprinkle with gremolata, cut into wedges, and serve.

Summer Squash Tart

FAST Serves 4 Total Time 45 minutes

Why This Recipe Works Yellow squash is bountiful in the summer months and makes an ideal filling for a vegetable tart. Starting with store-bought pie dough keeps this dish streamlined enough to assemble on a busy weeknight. Tossing the squash slices with salt and allowing them to drain for a brief period prevents a watery filling—and a soggy crust. Creamy Boursin cheese helps anchor the squash to the crust and provides an easy flavor boost with its garlic and herbs. To make our tart a complete meal, we add a simple arugula salad tossed with a boldly flavored vinaigrette of lemon, honey, and Dijon mustard. Our favorite store-bought crust is Pillsbury Refrigerated Pie Crusts.

- 1 pound yellow summer squash and/or zucchini, ends trimmed and sliced thin crosswise
- 1 teaspoon table salt, divided
- 1 (9-inch) store-bought pie dough round
- 1 (5.2-ounce) package Boursin Garlic & Fine Herbs cheese, room temperature
- ½ teaspoon grated lemon zest plus 1 tablespoon juice
- ¼ cup extra-virgin olive oil, divided
- 1 teaspoon pepper, divided
- 2 teaspoons honey
- ½ teaspoon Dijon mustard
- 5 ounces (5 cups) baby arugula

1. Adjust oven rack to middle position and heat oven to 475 degrees. Toss squash with ½ teaspoon salt in large bowl; transfer to colander and let drain in sink for 10 minutes. Line rimmed baking sheet with parchment paper. Place pie dough round in center of prepared sheet. Spread Boursin evenly over dough, leaving 1-inch border at edge. Sprinkle cheese with lemon zest.

2. Spread squash over clean dish towel; cover with second towel and press firmly to remove as much liquid as possible. Transfer squash to now-empty bowl and toss with 1 tablespoon oil and ½ teaspoon pepper. Arrange squash in even overlapping layer over Boursin. Fold 1-inch edge of dough over filling, pleating every 2 to 3 inches and pinching to secure. Bake tart until crust is golden and squash is tender, about 15 minutes.

3. Whisk lemon juice, honey, mustard, and remaining ½ teaspoon salt, remaining 3 tablespoons oil, and remaining ½ teaspoon pepper together in now-empty bowl. Add arugula and toss. Cut tart into 4 equal pieces and serve with salad.

Caramelized Onion, Tomato, and Goat Cheese Tart

Serves 4 Total Time 1 hour

Why This Recipe Works Here we use just a handful of ingredients to create a light but flavor-packed tart. Sweet caramelized onions provide a savory base that we accent with tangy, creamy goat cheese and bright, fruity tomatoes. Frozen puff pastry is convenient and provides a light, crisp crust. To thaw frozen puff pastry, let it sit either in the refrigerator for 24 hours or on the counter for 30 minutes to 1 hour before using. If your puff pastry is longer than what we call for, you may need to trim (rather than roll) the sheet to achieve the dimensions in step 2.

- 1 (9½ x 9-inch) sheet puff pastry, thawed
- ½ cup Caramelized Onions (page 259)
- ¼ teaspoon minced fresh thyme
- 6 ounces cherry tomatoes, halved
- 2 ounces goat cheese, crumbled (½ cup)

1. Adjust oven rack to upper-middle position and heat oven to 425 degrees. Line baking sheet with parchment paper.

2. Unfold pastry onto lightly floured counter and roll into 10-inch square. Transfer to prepared sheet and lightly brush ½-inch border along edges of pastry with water. Fold edges of pastry over by ½ inch.

3. Stir together caramelized onions and thyme. Spread onion mixture in even layer over pastry, avoiding raised border. Arrange tomatoes and goat cheese evenly over onions. Season with salt and pepper to taste. Bake until pastry is puffed and golden brown, 20 to 24 minutes, rotating sheet halfway through baking. Transfer tart to wire rack and let cool for 15 minutes. Transfer to cutting board, slice, and serve.

Upside-Down Tomato Tart

Serves 4 to 6 Total Time 2¼ hours

Why This Recipe Works For a savory spin on tarte Tatin, we replace the apples with tomatoes; the savory-sweet fruit pairs beautifully with buttery pastry and a tangy-sweet sherry vinegar syrup. To ensure a crisp crust, we remove the jelly and seeds from plum tomatoes and then roast them in the syrup for a full hour, which not only evaporates excess

Caramelized Onions

FAST VEGAN Makes about 2 cups Total Time 45 minutes

We prefer yellow or Spanish onions in this recipe for their complex flavor. Slicing the onions through their root end prevents them from breaking down too much during cooking. In addition to the tart, caramelized onions make a great addition to most any dish. Try them in an omelet or frittata, or with scrambled eggs. They taste fantastic on grilled cheese sandwiches or tossed into pasta dishes and green salads. Try sprinkling them over bruschetta, focaccia, or pizza. They also can be used to spiff up baked and mashed potatoes, rice, risotto, and polenta.

- 3 pounds onions, halved and sliced through root end ¼ inch thick
- ¾ cup plus 1 tablespoon water, divided
- 2 tablespoons vegetable oil
- ¾ teaspoon salt
- ⅛ teaspoon baking soda

1. Bring onions, ¾ cup water, oil, and salt to boil in 12-inch nonstick skillet over high heat. Cover and cook until water has evaporated and onions start to sizzle, about 10 minutes.

2. Uncover, reduce heat to medium-high, and use rubber spatula to gently press onions into sides and bottom of skillet. Cook, without stirring onions, for 30 seconds. Stir onions, scraping up any browned bits, then gently press onions into sides and bottom of skillet again. Repeat pressing, cooking, and stirring until onions are softened, well browned, and slightly sticky, 15 to 20 minutes.

3. Combine baking soda and remaining 1 tablespoon water in bowl. Stir baking soda solution into onions and cook, stirring constantly, until solution has evaporated, about 1 minute. Transfer onions to bowl. (Onions can be refrigerated for up to 3 days or frozen for up to 1 month.)

top | *Summer Squash Tart*

bottom | *Caramelized Onion, Tomato, and Goat Cheese Tart*

Upside-Down Tomato Tart

moisture but concentrates their fruity taste, gives their edges some flavorful browning, and enhances their meaty texture. We top the roasted tomatoes with puff pastry and bake the tart until puffed, crisp, and golden brown. If you don't have sherry vinegar, you can use cider vinegar. Use your fingers or a teaspoon to remove as much of the tomatoes' gel and seeds as you can. To thaw frozen puff pastry, let it sit either in the refrigerator for 24 hours or on the counter for 30 minutes to 1 hour. If your puff pastry is longer than what we call for, you may need to trim (rather than roll) the sheet to achieve the dimensions in step 2. This tart is at its best within a couple of hours of baking. Cut the tart into four wedges and serve with salad as a main course or six wedges for an appetizer.

- ⅓ cup sherry vinegar
- 2½ tablespoons sugar
- ¾ teaspoon table salt, divided
- ½ teaspoon pepper, divided
- 1 shallot, chopped fine
- 1 tablespoon unsalted butter
- 2½ teaspoons minced fresh thyme, divided
- 2 pounds plum tomatoes (about 10), cored, halved lengthwise, seeds and gel removed
- 1 sheet puff pastry, thawed but still cool

1. Adjust oven rack to middle position and heat oven to 400 degrees. Bring vinegar, sugar, ½ teaspoon salt, and ¼ teaspoon pepper to simmer in 10-inch ovensafe skillet over medium-high heat, swirling skillet to dissolve sugar. Simmer vigorously, swirling skillet occasionally, until consistency resembles that of maple syrup, about 2 minutes. Add shallot, butter, and 2 teaspoons thyme and whisk until butter is fully incorporated, about 1 minute. Off heat, add tomatoes and toss to coat lightly with syrup. Arrange tomatoes cut sides up in as close to single layer as possible (some overlap is OK; tomatoes will shrink as they cook) and sprinkle with remaining ¼ teaspoon salt and remaining ¼ teaspoon pepper. Transfer to oven and cook until liquid has evaporated and tomatoes are very lightly browned around edges and softened but not fully collapsed, about 1 hour.

2. Meanwhile, roll pastry to 10-inch square on lightly floured counter. Using plate, bowl, or pot lid as template, cut out 10-inch round. Discard trim. Transfer round to large plate and refrigerate until needed. Remove skillet from oven and place pastry round over tomatoes. Bake until pastry is puffed, crisp, and deep golden brown, about 30 minutes, rotating skillet halfway through baking.

3. Let tart cool for 8 minutes. Run paring knife around edge of crust to loosen and invert plate over skillet. Using pot holders, swiftly and carefully invert tart onto plate (if tomatoes or shallots shift or stick to skillet, arrange with spoon). Let cool for 10 minutes. Sprinkle with remaining ½ teaspoon thyme and serve warm or at room temperature.

Fennel-Apple Tarte Tatin

Serves 4 (Makes one 10-inch tart)   Total Time 1¾ hours

Why This Recipe Works Yes, tarte Tatin is traditionally a dessert, but the technique also translates well to savory applications. This one features wedges of fennel, which caramelize on the outside while the centers turn meltingly dense and silky. We arrange the wedges in an attractive pinwheel in the skillet, fill in the gaps with sliced fennel, and set the pan over high heat to jump-start browning. A layer of Granny Smith apples provides tart contrast and a sprinkle of sage adds an herbaceous note. All that's left to do is to blanket it with puff pastry and finish it in the oven. A salad of watercress and chopped hazelnuts make this tart a meal. Look for fennel bulbs that are about 4 inches tall after trimming. Do not core the fennel bulb that is cut into wedges. To thaw frozen puff pastry, let it sit either in the refrigerator for 24 hours or on the counter for 30 minutes to 1 hour. If your puff pastry is longer than what we call for, you may need to trim (rather than roll) the sheet to achieve the dimensions in step 1.

- 1 sheet puff pastry, thawed
- 3 tablespoons extra-virgin olive oil, divided
- 1 tablespoon sugar
- ½ teaspoon plus pinch table salt, divided
- 2 fennel bulbs, stalks discarded (1 bulb cut into 6 wedges, 1 bulb halved, cored, and sliced lengthwise ½ inch thick)
- 2 Granny Smith apples, peeled, cored, halved, and sliced ½ inch thick
- 4 teaspoons chopped fresh sage
- 2 teaspoons sherry vinegar
- ¼ teaspoon Dijon mustard
- 6 ounces (6 cups) watercress, torn into bite-size pieces
- 2 tablespoons chopped, toasted, and skinned hazelnuts
- 2 ounces goat cheese, crumbled (½ cup) (optional)

1. Adjust oven rack to middle position and heat oven to 375 degrees. Roll pastry into 11-inch square on lightly floured counter. Using plate, bowl, or pot lid as template, cut out 11-inch round. Discard trim. Transfer round to parchment paper–lined rimmed baking sheet, cover loosely with plastic wrap, and refrigerate until needed.

2. Swirl 2 tablespoons oil in bottom of 10-inch ovensafe nonstick skillet, then sprinkle with sugar and ¼ teaspoon salt. Arrange fennel wedges in pinwheel shape, fanning out from center of circle. Fill in gaps with sliced fennel. Cook over high heat, without stirring, until fennel turns deep golden brown, 7 to 9 minutes.

3. Off heat, sprinkle fennel with apple, sage, and ¼ teaspoon salt. Place pastry round over filling. Being careful of hot skillet, gently fold excess dough up against skillet wall (dough should be flush with skillet edge). Using paring knife, pierce dough evenly over surface 10 times. Transfer skillet to oven and bake until crust is deep golden brown, about 45 minutes. Transfer skillet to wire rack and let cool for 10 minutes.

4. Meanwhile, whisk vinegar, mustard, remaining 1 tablespoon oil, and remaining pinch salt together in large bowl. Add watercress and hazelnuts and toss to coat. Season with salt and pepper to taste.

5. Run paring knife around edge of crust to loosen. Using dish towels or pot holders, carefully place serving platter on top of skillet, and, holding platter and skillet firmly together, invert tart onto serving platter. Transfer any fennel slices that stick to skillet to tart. Sprinkle with goat cheese, if using, and serve immediately with salad.

Kol Böreği (Spiraled Spinach and Cheese Pastry)

Serves 4 to 6   Total Time 1½ hours

Why This Recipe Works Börek, an icon of Turkish cuisine, is a category of pastries that are shaped from thin dough, filled, and then baked, fried, boiled, or steamed. This version, known as kol, or "arm," böreği, is a snail shell–style spiral of spinach and cheese encased in flaky pastry. In Turkey, börek is typically made with thin pastry sheets called yufka; we substitute phyllo dough, layering multiple sheets to mimic the thickness of the traditional pastry. We fill the pastry with sautéed spinach and onion as well as feta cheese. Brushing the kol böreği with a mixture (called sos) of oil, egg, and milk ensures that it holds its stunning shape and becomes crisp and golden in the oven. Phyllo dough is also available in larger 18 by 14-inch sheets; if using, cut them in half to make 14 by 9-inch sheets. Don't thaw the phyllo in the microwave; let it sit in the refrigerator overnight or on the counter for 4 to 5 hours. If desired, 8 ounces (8 cups) of fresh spinach can be used in place of frozen; chop the spinach and cook until just wilted, 5 to 6 minutes. Pair with a salad for a light lunch.

- 5 tablespoons vegetable oil, divided
- 1 large egg
- 2 tablespoons milk
- 1 cup finely chopped onion
- 10 ounces frozen chopped spinach, thawed and squeezed dry
- 5 ounces feta cheese, crumbled (1¼ cups)
- 24 (14 by 9-inch) phyllo sheets, thawed
- 1½ teaspoons sesame seeds
- ¾ teaspoon nigella seeds

1. Adjust oven rack to middle position and heat oven to 400 degrees. Line rimmed baking sheet with parchment paper. Whisk ¼ cup oil, egg, and milk together in small bowl and set aside.

2. Heat remaining 1 tablespoon oil in 12-inch nonstick skillet over medium heat until shimmering. Add onion and cook, stirring occasionally, until softened and starting to brown, about 5 minutes. Stir in spinach and cook until any excess liquid has evaporated, 2 to 3 minutes. Remove from heat and let cool slightly, about 10 minutes. Stir in feta until just combined (there should be distinct pieces throughout).

3. Place 1 phyllo sheet on counter (keep remaining sheets covered) with long side parallel to counter edge. Brush oil mixture along 1 short edge of sheet. Overlap with second phyllo sheet by 1 inch and press to seal pieces together. Drizzle 1½ teaspoons oil mixture over entire surface and gently brush to distribute (there will still be dry spots.) Repeat process 2 more times with 4 more phyllo sheets and 1 tablespoon oil mixture (for total of 3 layers).

4. Spread one-quarter of spinach-feta mixture (about heaping ⅓ cup) along bottom of phyllo, leaving ¾-inch border from bottom edge. Fold bottom edge of phyllo over filling. Continue rolling phyllo away from you into firm cylinder, taking care not to roll too tightly. Starting at 1 end, coil cylinder into spiral shape. Transfer to center of prepared sheet.

5. Repeat steps 3 and 4 with remaining phyllo sheets, oil mixture, and filling to create 3 more cylinders. After each cylinder is formed, transfer to prepared sheet and continue to create 1 large spiral by meeting end of previous cylinder and then wrapping it around existing spiral.

6. Lightly brush pastry with oil mixture (you might not use all of it), taking care to coat seams where cylinders connect (gently blot any excess that pools between spiral's creases). Sprinkle with sesame seeds and nigella seeds. Bake until deeply browned, 25 to 30 minutes. Let cool on baking sheet for 10 minutes. Transfer to cutting board, cut into wedges, and serve warm or at room temperature.

Filling and Shaping the Kol Böreği

1. Place 1 phyllo sheet on counter with long side parallel to counter edge. Overlap phyllo sheets by 1 inch and press to seal pieces together.

2. Spread spinach-feta mixture along bottom of phyllo leaving ¾- inch border from bottom edge. Fold bottom edge over filling and continue rolling phyllo into firm cylinder.

3. After additional 3 cylinders are formed, create large spiral by meeting end of previous cylinder and wrapping it around existing spiral.

4. Lightly brush with oil mixture where cylinders connect. Sprinkle with seeds and bake.

Kol Böreği (Spiraled Spinach and Cheese Pastry)

Pasta, Noodles & Dumplings

270 Fresh Pasta Without a Machine

271 Mezzi Rigatoni with Spicy Gojuchang Tomato Sauce ■

272 Rigatoni with Marinated Tomatoes and Burrata ■

272 Garlicky Spaghetti with Lemon and Pine Nuts ■
Garlicky Spaghetti with Artichokes and Hazelnuts ■
Garlicky Spaghetti with Green Olives and Almonds ■

273 Angel Hair Pasta with Sun-Dried Tomato and Mint Sauce ■

274 Linguine with Sun-Dried Tomato and Eggplant Sauce ■ ●

275 Simple Stovetop Macaroni and Cheese ■
Grown-Up Stovetop Macaroni and Cheese ■

277 Spinach-Artichoke Macaroni and Cheese ■

277 Pasta with Creamy Lemon–Sichuan Peppercorn Sauce

278 Pasta Cacio e Uova (Pasta with Cheese and Eggs) ■

278 Creamy Broccoli Pasta with Crispy Panko

279 Tallarines Verdes (Peruvian Green Noodles)

280 Fettuccine with Walnut Sauce ■

280 Cashew e Pepe e Funghi ■ ●

283 Triple Mushroom Pasta

283 Rigatoni with Quick Mushroom Bolognese ■

284 Summer Squash Pasta with Ricotta and Lemon-Parmesan Bread Crumbs

285 Ultracreamy Spaghetti with Zucchini ■

286 Spaghetti all'Assassina ●

289 Farfalle with Beets, Arugula, and Blue Cheese ■

289 Orecchiette and Navy Beans with Brussels Sprouts and Spicy Mustard Crumbs ■ ●

290 Creamy, Spicy Rotini and Red Lentils with Tomatoes and Goat Cheese ■

290 Pasta e Ceci (Pasta with Chickpeas)

291 Fregula with Chickpeas, Tomatoes, and Fennel

292 Meatless "Meat" Sauce with Chickpeas and Mushrooms ●

294 Fideos with Chickpeas, Fennel, and Kale ●

294 Pesto Lasagna

297 Cheesy Stuffed Shells

297 Unstuffed Shells with Butternut Squash and Leeks

298 Cheese Ravioli with Pumpkin Cream Sauce ■

299 Three-Cheese Ravioli with Browned Butter–Pine Nut Sauce

302 Tortellini Salad with Broccoli, Cannellini Beans, and Olive–Banana Pepper Dressing ■

303 Crispy Gnocchi with Shredded Brussels Sprouts and Gorgonzola ■

303 Samosa Gnocchi Chaat ■

304 Potato Gnocchi with Browned Butter and Sage Sauce

306 Gnocchi à la Parisienne with Arugula, Tomatoes, and Olives
Gnocchi à la Parisienne with Browned Butter

308 Spinach and Ricotta Gnudi with Tomato-Butter Sauce

309 Ramen with Shiitakes and Soft Eggs ■

310 Shiitake and Bok Choy Lo Mein ■

310 Shanghai Scallion Oil Noodles ●

313 San Francisco–Style Garlic Noodles ■

313 Gochujang-Tahini Noodles ■ ●

314 Spicy Basil Noodles with Crispy Tofu, Snap Peas, and Bell Pepper ●

314 Japchae (Sweet Potato Noodles with Shiitakes and Spinach) ●
Sweet Potato Noodles with Shiitakes, Spinach, and Eggs

316 Udon with Stir-Fried Portobellos and Soy-Maple Sauce ●

317 Liang Mian (Chilled Sesame Noodles) ●

318 Chilled Soba Noodles with Cucumber, Snow Peas, and Radishes ■ ●

319 Pittsburgh-Style Haluski

321 Savory Noodle Kugel

321 Green Peas and Dumplings

322 Potato-Cheddar Pierogi
Potato-Sauerkraut Pierogi

323 Su Shui Jiao (Northern Chinese–Style Cabbage and Mushroom Dumplings)

325 Chili Crisp Dumpling Sauce ■ ●

325 Sichuan Peppercorn Oil ■ ●

Fast Tomato Sauces

266 Fresh Tomato Sauce ■ ●
Fresh Tomato Puttanesca Sauce ■ ●

266 No-Cook Fresh Tomato Sauce ■ ●

267 Vodka Sauce ■

267 Tomato-Browned Butter Sauce ■

Pesto: Basil and Beyond

268 Pesto alla Genovese (Basil Pesto) ■

268 Pesto di Prezzemolo (Parsley Pesto) ■

269 Pesto Pantesco ■ ●

269 Pesto alla Calabrese ■

■ Fast (45 minutes or less) ● Vegan

Fast Tomato Sauces

Having some speedy sauces in your back pocket means that dinner is never far away. To serve any of these sauces with pasta, reserve 1 cup of the pasta cooking water when draining the pasta. Return the pasta to the pot and toss with the sauce, adding cooking water as needed to reach the desired consistency.

Fresh Tomato Sauce

FAST **VEGAN** Makes 4 cups (enough for 1 pound pasta) Total Time 20 minutes

Here is the essence of a quickly cooked sauce made with fresh tomatoes—just a short simmer produces bright and lively results. Plum tomatoes are the best choice here, as they have meaty flesh and less juice than other varieties, which translates to a thicker, clingier sauce. Plus, their skins simmer up tender and soft, so there's no need to peel them. The success of this sauce depends on using ripe, in-season tomatoes. If using very sweet tomatoes, omit the sugar.

- 3 tablespoons extra-virgin olive oil
- 2 garlic cloves, minced
- 2 pounds ripe plum tomatoes, cored and cut into ½-inch pieces
- ¾ teaspoon table salt
- ½ teaspoon pepper
- ½ teaspoon sugar (optional)
- 2 tablespoons chopped fresh basil

Cook oil and garlic in large saucepan over medium heat until garlic is fragrant but not browned, 1 to 2 minutes. Stir in tomatoes, salt, pepper, and sugar, if using. Increase heat to medium-high and cook until tomatoes are broken down and sauce is slightly thickened, about 10 minutes. Stir in basil and season with salt and pepper to taste.

Variation

FAST **VEGAN** Fresh Tomato Puttanesca Sauce

Add ¼ cup coarsely chopped pitted kalamata olives and ¼ cup rinsed capers to saucepan with tomatoes.

No-Cook Fresh Tomato Sauce

FAST **VEGAN** Makes 4 cups (enough for 1 pound pasta) Total Time 15 minutes, plus 30 minutes marinating

Sometimes luscious, garden-ripe tomatoes need little else besides high-quality extra-virgin olive oil and a smattering of fresh herbs to become a bright, summery dressing for pasta. Instead of the basil, you can use fresh parsley, cilantro, mint, oregano, or tarragon. The success of this sauce depends on using ripe, flavorful, in-season tomatoes.

- ¼ cup extra-virgin olive oil
- 1 shallot, minced
- 2 teaspoons lemon juice, plus extra as needed
- 1 garlic clove, minced
- 1 teaspoon table salt
- ¼ teaspoon pepper
- Pinch sugar, plus extra as needed
- 2 pounds very ripe tomatoes, cored and cut into ½-inch pieces
- 3 tablespoons chopped fresh basil

Stir oil, shallot, lemon juice, garlic, salt, pepper, and sugar together in large bowl. Stir in tomatoes and let marinate at room temperature until very soft and flavorful, about 30 minutes. Before serving, stir in basil and season with salt, pepper, sugar, and extra lemon juice to taste.

Vodka Sauce

FAST Makes 4 cups (enough for 1 pound pasta)
Total Time 30 minutes

The ratio of ingredients in this classic restaurant sauce is important to strike the correct balance of sweet, tangy, spicy, and creamy. To achieve a just-right consistency, we puree half the tomatoes and cut the rest into chunks. For sweetness, we add sautéed onion; for umami, a bit of tomato paste. You do need a liberal pour of vodka to cut through the richness and add "zinginess," but it's important to add it to the tomatoes early on to allow the alcohol to mostly cook off and prevent a boozy flavor.

- 1 (28-ounce) can whole peeled tomatoes, drained with juice reserved
- 2 tablespoons extra-virgin olive oil
- ½ small onion, minced
- 1 tablespoon tomato paste
- 2 garlic cloves, minced
- ¼ teaspoon red pepper flakes
- ½ teaspoon table salt
- ⅓ cup vodka
- ½ cup heavy cream
- 2 tablespoons chopped fresh basil

1. Puree half of tomatoes in food processor until smooth. Dice remaining tomatoes into ½-inch pieces, discarding cores. Combine pureed and diced tomatoes in liquid measuring cup (you should have about 1⅔ cups). Add reserved juice to equal 2 cups; discard remaining juice.

2. Heat oil in large saucepan over medium heat until shimmering. Add onion and tomato paste and cook, stirring occasionally, until onion is light golden around edges, about 3 minutes. Add garlic and pepper flakes; cook, stirring constantly, until fragrant, about 30 seconds.

3. Stir in tomatoes and salt. Off heat, add vodka. Return pan to medium-high heat and simmer briskly until alcohol flavor is mostly cooked off, 8 to 10 minutes; stir frequently and lower heat to medium if simmering becomes too vigorous. Stir in cream and cook until hot, about 1 minute. Stir in basil. Serve immediately.

Tomato–Browned Butter Sauce

FAST Makes 3 cups (enough for 1 pound pasta)
Total Time 15 minutes

Butter mellows the acidity of tomatoes and adds a velvety quality to this rich sauce. Browning the butter creates flavor complexity; we then add garlic for more depth. Processing whole canned tomatoes before incorporating them delivers excellent texture.

- 1 (28-ounce) can whole peeled tomatoes
- 4 tablespoons unsalted butter, divided
- 2 garlic cloves, minced
- ½ teaspoon sugar
- ½ teaspoon table salt
- 2 teaspoons sherry vinegar
- 3 tablespoons chopped fresh basil

1. Process tomatoes and their juice in food processor until smooth, about 30 seconds. Melt 3 tablespoons butter in 12-inch skillet over medium-high heat, swirling occasionally, until butter is dark brown and releases nutty aroma, about 1½ minutes. Stir in garlic and cook for 10 seconds. Stir in tomatoes, sugar, and salt and simmer until sauce is slightly reduced, about 8 minutes.

2. Off heat, whisk in remaining 1 tablespoon butter and vinegar. Stir in basil and season with salt and pepper to taste. Serve immediately.

Pesto: Basil and Beyond

Besides pasta, these pestos are also good on crostini, in sandwiches, stirred into soup, or as a dip with crudités. To serve any of these pestos with pasta, reserve 1 cup of the pasta cooking water when draining the pasta. Return the pasta to the pot and toss with the pesto, adding cooking water as needed to reach the desired consistency.

Pesto alla Genovese (Basil Pesto)

FAST Makes ¾ cup (enough for 1 pound pasta)
Total Time 25 minutes

Hailing from Genoa, Italy, basil pesto is redolent with the fragrance and flavor of fresh basil and enriched with pine nuts and Parmesan. Toasting the garlic mellows its fiery flavor, while toasting the pine nuts boosts their delicate flavor. Use the highest-quality olive oil you can. Pounding the herbs brings out their flavorful oils.

- 3 garlic cloves, unpeeled
- ¼ cup pine nuts
- 2 cups fresh basil leaves
- 2 tablespoons fresh parsley leaves
- ¼ cup plus 3 tablespoons extra-virgin olive oil
- ½ ounce Parmesan cheese, grated (¼ cup)

1. Toast garlic in 8-inch skillet over medium heat, shaking skillet occasionally, until softened and spotty brown, about 8 minutes; transfer to cutting board. When garlic is cool enough to handle, remove and discard skins and chop coarsely. Meanwhile, toast pine nuts in now-empty skillet over medium heat, stirring often, until golden and fragrant, 4 to 5 minutes; transfer to cutting board.

2. Place basil and parsley in 1-gallon zipper-lock bag. Pound bag with flat side of meat pounder or with rolling pin until all leaves are bruised.

3. Process garlic, pine nuts, and herbs in food processor until finely chopped, about 1 minute, scraping down sides of bowl as needed. With processor running, slowly add oil until incorporated. Transfer pesto to bowl, stir in Parmesan, and season with salt and pepper to taste. (To store, press plastic wrap flush to surface or top with thin layer of olive oil to prevent browning. Cover and refrigerate for up to 3 days or freeze for up to 3 months. Bring to room temperature before using.)

Pesto di Prezzemolo (Parsley Pesto)

FAST Makes 1¾ cups (enough for 1 pound pasta)
Total Time 15 minutes

In Liguria, where basil pesto was born, many cooks switch to fresh parsley for pesto when the basil growing season is waning. This vibrant green pesto features handfuls of the grassy, peppery herb, paired with creamy untoasted walnuts (a common substitute for pine nuts in parsley pesto). Use a good-quality, relatively mild extra-virgin olive oil for the best results. You will need about two bunches of parsley to yield 3 ounces of parsley leaves. It's OK to include the tender, thin stems at the base of the parsley sprigs.

- 2 ounces Parmesan cheese
- 3 ounces fresh parsley leaves (about 5 cups)
- 1 cup extra-virgin olive oil
- 1 cup walnuts
- 2 tablespoons capers, rinsed
- 2 tablespoons lemon juice
- 2 garlic cloves, peeled
- ½ teaspoon red pepper flakes
- ½ teaspoon table salt
- ¼ teaspoon pepper

Process Parmesan in food processor until finely ground, about 30 seconds; transfer to medium bowl. Process parsley, oil, walnuts, capers, lemon juice, garlic, pepper flakes, salt, and pepper until smooth, about 1 minute, scraping down sides of bowl as needed. Transfer pesto to bowl, stir in Parmesan, and season with salt and pepper to taste. (To store, press plastic wrap flush to surface or top with thin layer of olive oil to prevent browning. Cover and refrigerate for up to 2 days or freeze for up to 1 month. Bring to room temperature before using.)

Pesto Pantesco

FAST **VEGAN** Makes 3½ cups (enough for 1 pound pasta) Total Time 15 minutes

Salted capers, with their unique funky depth and nuanced pepperiness, are the hallmark of pesto pantesco, which hails from the island of Pantelleria, off the coast of Sicily. It's made by pulverizing locally grown staples such as tomatoes; garlic; basil and/or parsley; almonds; and, most notably, capers with olive oil until the mixture is coarsely pureed. Capers packed in salt are sold at specialty or Italian markets or online. If possible, use ripe local tomatoes. Avoid plum tomatoes; they're not juicy enough.

- ⅔ cup slivered almonds, toasted
- 1¼ pounds tomatoes, cored and quartered
- ¾ cup fresh basil leaves
- ½ cup fresh parsley leaves
- 3 tablespoons salted capers, rinsed well
- 1 garlic clove, peeled
- ½ teaspoon table salt
- ¼ teaspoon red pepper flakes
- ½ cup extra-virgin olive oil

Pulse almonds in food processor until most pieces are no bigger than ¼ inch, 8 to 10 pulses. Add tomatoes, basil, parsley, capers, garlic, salt, and pepper flakes and pulse until cohesive mixture forms, 8 to 10 pulses. Scrape down sides of bowl. With processor running, slowly add oil in steady steam until emulsified, 15 to 20 seconds.

Pesto alla Calabrese

FAST Makes 2 cups (enough for 1 pound pasta) Total Time 45 minutes

Calabria's namesake coral-colored pesto is sweetly spicy and creamy, with a base of red bell peppers, ricotta and Parmesan cheeses, and chiles. Some versions also include tomato, onion or shallot, garlic, or basil. In a departure from most forms of pesto, some of the components are cooked before the mixture is pureed. Calabrian chiles are the traditional heat source, but they aren't readily available in U.S. supermarkets, so red pepper flakes make a reasonable substitute. For a spicier dish, use the larger amount of pepper flakes. A rasp-style grater makes quick work of turning the garlic into a paste.

- 3 red bell peppers, stemmed, seeded, and cut into ¼-inch-wide strips (5 cups), divided
- 3 tablespoons extra-virgin olive oil, divided
- 1 teaspoon table salt, divided
- 1 small onion, chopped
- 1 plum tomato, cored, seeded, and chopped
- ⅓ cup chopped fresh basil
- 1 garlic clove, minced to paste (1 teaspoon), divided
- ½–¾ teaspoon red pepper flakes
- ½ cup whole-milk ricotta cheese
- ¼ cup grated Parmesan cheese, plus extra for serving
- ¼ teaspoon pepper
- 1 teaspoon white wine vinegar

1. Toss two-thirds of bell peppers with 1 tablespoon oil and ¼ teaspoon salt in 12-inch nonstick skillet. Cover and cook over medium-low heat, stirring occasionally, until bell peppers are softened and just starting to brown, about 15 minutes.

2. Add onion, tomato, basil, ½ teaspoon garlic, and pepper flakes and continue to cook, uncovered, until onion is softened and bell peppers are browned in spots, 6 to 7 minutes longer, stirring occasionally. Off heat, let cool for 5 minutes.

3. Place ricotta, Parmesan, remaining one-third of bell peppers, remaining ½ teaspoon garlic, remaining ¾ teaspoon salt, and pepper in bowl of food processor. Add cooked bell pepper mixture and process for 20 seconds. Scrape down sides of bowl. With processor running, add vinegar and remaining 2 tablespoons oil; process for about 20 seconds. Scrape down sides of bowl, then continue to process until smooth, about 20 seconds longer.

top | *Fresh Pasta Without a Machine with Pesto di Prezzemolo*
bottom | *Mezzi Rigatoni with Spicy Gochujang Tomato Sauce*

Fresh Pasta Without a Machine

Serves 4 to 6 (makes 1 pound) Total Time 1½ hours, plus 1 hour resting

Why This Recipe Works To make delicate, golden fresh pasta ribbons with a springy bite, all you really need is a good dough, a sturdy rolling pin, and some elbow grease. This dough rolls out with ease on the first try and cooks up to a silky, tender yet slightly firm texture, ready to add your sauce of choice. Adding six egg yolks in addition to two whole eggs creates a soft dough that's easily rolled out by hand. If using a high-protein flour like King Arthur, use seven egg yolks. The longer the dough rests in step 2, the easier it will be to roll out. Avoid adding too much flour when rolling out the pasta, which may result in excessive snapback.

- 2 cups (10 ounces) all-purpose flour, plus extra as needed
- 2 large eggs plus 6 large yolks
- 2 tablespoons extra-virgin olive oil
- Table salt for cooking pasta

1. Process flour, eggs and yolks, and oil in food processor until mixture forms cohesive dough that feels soft and is barely tacky to touch, about 45 seconds. (Pinch dough between your fingers; if any dough sticks to your fingers, add up to ¼ cup flour, 1 tablespoon at a time, until barely tacky. Process until flour is fully incorporated before retesting. If dough doesn't become cohesive, add up to 1 tablespoon water, 1 teaspoon at a time, until it just comes together; process 30 seconds longer.)

2. Turn out dough onto dry counter and knead until smooth, 1 to 2 minutes. Shape dough into 6-inch-long cylinder. Wrap in plastic wrap and let rest at room temperature for at least 1 hour or up to 4 hours.

3. Cut cylinder crosswise into 6 equal pieces. Working with 1 piece of dough at a time (rewrap remaining dough), dust both sides with flour, place cut side down on clean counter, and press into 3-inch square. Using heavy rolling pin, roll into 6-inch square. Dust both sides of dough lightly with flour.

4. Starting at center of square, roll dough away from you in single motion. Return rolling pin to center of dough and roll toward you in single motion. Repeat rolling steps until dough

sticks to counter and measures roughly 12 inches long. Lightly dust both sides of dough with flour and continue to roll until dough measures roughly 20 inches long and 6 inches wide, frequently lifting dough to release it from counter. (You should be able to easily see outline of your fingers through dough.) If dough firmly sticks to counter and wrinkles when rolled out, carefully lift dough and dust counter lightly with flour.

5. Transfer pasta sheet to clean dish towel and let stand, uncovered, until firm around edges, about 15 minutes; meanwhile, roll out remaining dough.

6. Starting with 1 short end, gently fold pasta sheet at 2-inch intervals until sheet has been folded into flat, rectangular roll. Using sharp chef's knife, slice crosswise into 3/16-inch-thick noodles. Use your fingers to unfurl noodles and transfer to rimmed baking sheet. Repeat folding and cutting remaining sheets of dough. Cook noodles within 1 hour or freeze. (After cutting strands, toss strands with a bit more flour to keep pieces separate. Coil strands into 2- to 4-ounce nests on baking sheet and freeze. Once frozen, transfer pasta nests to zipper-lock bags and freeze for up to 1 month.)

7. **To cook pasta** Bring 4 quarts water to boil in large pot. Add pasta and 1 tablespoon salt and cook until tender but still al dente, about 3 minutes. Drain pasta and toss with sauce; serve.

Mezzi Rigatoni with Spicy Gochujang Tomato Sauce

FAST Serves 4 to 6 Total Time 45 minutes

Why This Recipe Works In this quick weeknight meal, Italian passata and Korean gochujang combine to create a smooth, bold sauce reminiscent of silky Italian vodka sauce, but with a deeper layer of umami and a pleasant hint of heat. Passata, a strained puree of uncooked ripe tomatoes with the skins and seeds removed, is smooth and bright. Gochujang, a deeply savory, fermented chili paste made from glutinous rice, soybeans, and gochugaru (Korean chili powder), brings gentle heat and a touch of sweetness. Together, they form a rich, harmonious sauce that clings beautifully to pasta and delivers depth well beyond the effort it takes to make. A sprinkle of garlicky bread crumbs before serving adds pleasant crunch and another layer of flavor. We like mezzi rigatoni here, but you can use whichever pasta shape you prefer. We like the Pomì brand of passata. If you cannot find it, tomato puree can be used. This recipe uses the paste form of gochujang. Do not substitute gochujang sauce, which contains additional ingredients.

- 1 pound mezzi rigatoni or rigatoni
- ½ teaspoon table salt, plus salt for cooking pasta
- 5 tablespoons unsalted butter, divided
- 2 shallots, minced
- 3 garlic cloves, minced, divided
- 3 tablespoons gochujang
- 1 tablespoon tomato paste
- 1 cup passata
- ½ cup heavy cream
- ⅓ cup panko bread crumbs
- 1 tablespoon chopped fresh chives
- Grated or shaved Parmesan cheese

1. Bring 4 quarts water to boil in large pot. Add pasta and 1 tablespoon salt and cook, stirring often, until al dente. Reserve 1 cup cooking water, then drain pasta and return it to pot.

2. Meanwhile, melt 4 tablespoons butter in 12-inch skillet over medium heat. Add shallots and cook until beginning to brown, 3 to 5 minutes. Stir in half of garlic and cook until fragrant, about 30 seconds. Stir in gochujang and tomato paste and cook until fragrant, about 1 minute. Stir in passata, heavy cream, and salt. Season with salt and pepper to taste.

3. Melt remaining 1 tablespoon butter in 8-inch nonstick skillet over medium heat. Add panko and cook, stirring frequently, until evenly browned and fragrant, 2 to 4 minutes. Transfer panko to small bowl, stir in remaining garlic, and set aside until ready to serve.

4. Add sauce and ½ cup reserved cooking water to pasta in pot and toss to combine. Before serving, adjust consistency with additional reserved cooking water as needed. Sprinkle with panko, chives, and Parmesan. Serve.

Rigatoni with Marinated Tomatoes and Burrata

FAST Serves 4 Total Time 45 minutes

Why This Recipe Works Burrata takes a simple summer pasta dish over the top. Ripe tomatoes briefly marinated in olive oil and garlic (plus the juice they exude) are tossed with rigatoni. Each serving is then dotted with small chunks of burrata and drizzled with the cheese's creamy interior liquid. A sprinkle of torn fresh basil and some extra-virgin olive oil unite the elements. This sauce is liquidy but superflavorful; sop up any extra with crusty bread.

- 1½ pounds ripe tomatoes, cored and cut into ½-inch pieces
- 1½ teaspoons table salt, plus salt for cooking pasta
- ¼ teaspoon pepper
- ¼ teaspoon sugar
- 5 tablespoons extra-virgin olive oil, divided
- 3 garlic cloves, minced
- 1 pound rigatoni
- 8 ounces burrata cheese, room temperature
- ½ cup fresh basil leaves, torn

1. Combine tomatoes, salt, pepper, and sugar in bowl. Heat 1 tablespoon oil and garlic in 8-inch nonstick skillet over medium heat until garlic just begins to turn golden, 3 to 5 minutes. Pour hot oil mixture over tomatoes and toss to combine. Let sit for at least 20 minutes.

2. Meanwhile, bring 4 quarts water to boil in large pot. Add pasta and 1 tablespoon salt and cook, stirring often, until al dente. Drain pasta and return it to pot.

3. Drain tomatoes in colander set over bowl. Add tomatoes and ½ cup drained tomato juice to pasta and toss vigorously until liquid is mostly absorbed. Adjust consistency with extra tomato juice as needed. Transfer pasta to individual serving bowls. Cut burrata into 1-inch pieces, collecting creamy liquid. Sprinkle burrata over pasta and drizzle with creamy liquid. Drizzle with remaining ¼ cup oil. Season with pepper to taste and sprinkle with basil. Serve.

Garlicky Spaghetti with Lemon and Pine Nuts

FAST Serves 4 Total Time 45 minutes

Why This Recipe Works This is a gussied-up version of the simple Southern Italian pasta known as aglio e olio. To that basic formula of garlic and olive oil, this version adds lemon, pine nuts, fresh basil, and Parmesan. In this recipe you use half the usual amount of water to cook the pasta, resulting in a more concentrated starchy cooking water, which lends extra body to the sauce when you incorporate it. Cooking minced garlic over low heat in plenty of olive oil works best for infusing the oil with garlic flavor without over-cooking the garlic. (With sliced garlic, thinner slices often end up turning dark brown and acrid by the time thicker slices become golden.) Stirring in ½ teaspoon of raw minced garlic to the al dente pasta at the last minute adds extra zing. A garlic press makes quick work of uniformly mincing the garlic.

- ¼ cup extra-virgin olive oil
- 2 tablespoons plus ½ teaspoon minced garlic, divided
- ¼ teaspoon red pepper flakes
- 1 pound spaghetti
- Table salt for cooking pasta
- 2 teaspoons grated lemon zest plus 2 tablespoons juice
- 1 cup chopped fresh basil
- 1 ounce Parmesan cheese, grated (½ cup), plus extra for serving
- ½ cup pine nuts, toasted

1. Combine oil and 2 tablespoons garlic in 8-inch nonstick skillet. Cook over low heat, stirring occasionally, until garlic is pale golden brown, 9 to 12 minutes. Off heat, stir in pepper flakes; set aside.

2. Meanwhile, bring 2 quarts water to boil in large pot. Add pasta and 2 teaspoons salt and cook, stirring frequently, until al dente. Reserve 1½ cups cooking water, then drain pasta and return it to pot. Add lemon zest and juice, garlic-oil mixture, 1 cup reserved cooking water, and remaining ½ teaspoon garlic. Stir until pasta is well coated with oil and no water remains in bottom of pot. Add basil, Parmesan, and pine nuts and toss to combine. Adjust consistency with remaining reserved cooking water as needed. Season with salt and pepper to taste. Serve, passing extra Parmesan separately.

Variations

FAST Garlicky Spaghetti with Artichokes and Hazelnuts

Omit basil and lemon zest and reduce lemon juice to 1 tablespoon. Add 1½ teaspoons fennel seeds, coarsely ground, to skillet along with red pepper flakes. Stir 1 cup jarred whole baby artichokes packed in water, rinsed, patted dry, and chopped, into pasta with lemon juice. Substitute ½ cup hazelnuts, toasted, skinned, and chopped, for pine nuts.

FAST Garlicky Spaghetti with Green Olives and Almonds

Omit lemon zest and reduce lemon juice to 1 tablespoon. Stir 1 cup pitted green olives, chopped fine, into pasta with lemon juice. Substitute ½ cup toasted sliced almonds for pine nuts.

Angel Hair Pasta with Sun-Dried Tomato and Mint Sauce

FAST Serves 4 Total Time 30 minutes

Why This Recipe Works Angel hair pasta has particular cooking considerations—or overcooking considerations—as it cooks so quickly that there is barely time to taste-test it for doneness. Because package directions often result in overcooked pasta, we came up with our own cooking times specific to common brands. Instead of tossing the pasta into bubbling sauce before serving and risk overcooking, we toss it with a no-cook pesto-like sauce. Since angel hair pasta absorbs a lot of the cooking water, we make our sauce extra-potent: Sun-dried tomatoes, white wine vinegar, and tomato paste make it umami-rich, while refreshing mint and garlic give it a complex aroma. Boil De Cecco angel hair for 1½ minutes and Barilla or Prince for 3 minutes. Use straight pasta; nests of angel hair tend to tangle in the pot.

- ½ cup oil-packed sun-dried tomatoes
- ½ cup fresh mint leaves
- ⅓ cup extra-virgin olive oil
- 4 teaspoons white wine vinegar
- 1 tablespoon tomato paste
- 2 garlic cloves, minced
- ¾ teaspoon table salt, plus salt for cooking pasta
- ½ teaspoon red pepper flakes
- ⅛ teaspoon sugar
- 12 ounces angel hair pasta
- ¼ cup pine nuts, toasted
- Grated Parmesan cheese

top | *Rigatoni with Marinated Tomatoes and Burrata*

bottom | *Garlicky Spaghetti with Lemon and Pine Nuts*

top | *Linguine with Sun-Dried Tomato and Eggplant Sauce*
bottom | *Simple Stovetop Macaroni and Cheese*

1. Process sun-dried tomatoes, mint, oil, vinegar, tomato paste, garlic, salt, pepper flakes, and sugar in food processor until smooth, about 1 minute, scraping down sides of bowl as needed. Transfer to large heatproof bowl.

2. Bring 4 quarts water to boil in large pot. Add pasta and 1 tablespoon salt and cook, stirring occasionally, until al dente. Reserve 1½ cups pasta cooking water, then drain pasta. While pasta drains, whisk 1 cup reserved pasta cooking water into sauce. Add pasta to sauce and toss gently with tongs, adjusting consistency with remaining reserved pasta cooking water as needed. Sprinkle with pine nuts. Serve with Parmesan.

Linguine with Sun-Dried Tomato and Eggplant Sauce

FAST **VEGAN** Serves 4 Total Time 40 minutes

Why This Recipe Works This pasta is inspired by food journalist, host, and editor Francis Lam's recipe for Pasta with Let-My-Eggplant-Go-Free! Puree. We followed Lam's guidance and embraced eggplant's natural sponginess, letting it cook down to a plush texture and absorb lots of flavor from spicy, herbal, garlicky olive oil. The eggplant's earthy, nutty flavor is further complemented by bursts of intensity from sun-dried tomatoes. One 8-ounce jar of oil-packed sun-dried tomatoes will yield the ¾ cup called for here. We recommend using the shredding disk of a food processor to shred the eggplant.

- 1 pound linguine
- 1¼ teaspoons table salt, plus salt for cooking pasta
- ⅓ cup extra-virgin olive oil, plus extra for serving
- 1½ pounds eggplant, peeled and shredded
- 6 garlic cloves, sliced thin
- 2 sprigs fresh thyme
- ½ teaspoon pepper
- ¼ teaspoon red pepper flakes
- ¾ cup oil-packed sun-dried tomatoes, drained and chopped
- ¾ cup chopped fresh basil

1. Bring 4 quarts water to boil in large pot. Add pasta and 1 tablespoon salt and cook, stirring often, until al dente. Reserve ½ cup cooking water, then drain pasta and return it to pot.

2. Meanwhile, heat oil in 12-inch nonstick skillet over medium-high heat until shimmering. Add eggplant, garlic, thyme sprigs, pepper, pepper flakes, and salt and cook, stirring occasionally, until eggplant is uniformly wilted, about 8 minutes. Add tomatoes and 1½ cups water and bring to simmer. Reduce heat to medium-low, cover, and cook until eggplant begins to break down, about 12 minutes, stirring occasionally.

3. Discard thyme sprigs. Add eggplant mixture, basil, and reserved cooking water to pasta and toss to combine. Serve, passing extra oil separately.

Simple Stovetop Macaroni and Cheese

FAST Serves 4 Total Time 30 minutes

Why This Recipe Works The sauce for this easy, fast mac and cheese is based on American cheese, which contains plenty of emulsifying salts, making it easy to achieve a smooth sauce without needing to make a béchamel. Because American cheese doesn't have a lot of flavor, we combine it with more-flavorful extra-sharp cheddar. A bit of mustard and cayenne pepper add piquancy. Cooking the macaroni in a smaller-than-usual amount of water (along with some milk) means that it doesn't need to be drained; the liquid that is left after the elbows are hydrated is just enough to form the base of the sauce. Rather than bake the mac and cheese to achieve a crunchy topping, we sprinkle cheesy toasted panko bread crumbs on top. Barilla makes our favorite elbow macaroni. Because the macaroni is cooked in a measured amount of liquid, we don't recommend using different shapes or sizes of pasta. Use a 4-ounce block of American cheese from the deli counter rather than presliced cheese, which is formulated differently and will make the sauce too thick.

- 1½ cups water
- 1 cup milk
- 8 ounces elbow macaroni
- 4 ounces American cheese, shredded (1 cup)
- ½ teaspoon Dijon mustard
- Small pinch cayenne pepper
- 4 ounces extra-sharp cheddar cheese, shredded (1 cup)
- ⅓ cup panko bread crumbs
- 1 tablespoon extra-virgin olive oil
- ⅛ teaspoon table salt
- ⅛ teaspoon pepper
- 2 tablespoons grated Parmesan cheese

1. Bring water and milk to boil in medium saucepan over high heat. Stir in macaroni and reduce heat to medium-low. Cook, stirring frequently, until macaroni is slightly past al dente, 6 to 8 minutes. Add American cheese, mustard, and cayenne and cook, stirring constantly, until cheese is completely melted, about 1 minute. Off heat, stir in cheddar until evenly distributed but not melted. Cover saucepan and let stand for 5 minutes.

2. Meanwhile, combine panko, oil, salt, and pepper in 8-inch nonstick skillet until panko is evenly moistened. Cook over medium heat, stirring frequently, until evenly browned, 3 to 4 minutes. Off heat, sprinkle Parmesan over panko mixture and stir to combine. Transfer panko mixture to small bowl.

3. Stir macaroni until sauce is smooth (sauce may look loose but will thicken as it cools). Season with salt and pepper to taste. Transfer to warm serving dish and sprinkle panko mixture over top. Serve immediately.

Variation

FAST Grown-Up Stovetop Macaroni and Cheese

Increase water to 1¾ cups. Substitute ¾ cup shredded Gruyère cheese and 2 tablespoons crumbled blue cheese for cheddar.

Pasta with Creamy Lemon–Sichuan Peppercorn Sauce

Spinach-Artichoke Macaroni and Cheese

FAST Serves 4 Total Time 45 minutes

Why This Recipe Works If you're in the mood for a cheesy comfort pasta but want to green it up, try this version, in which sautéed baby spinach and marinated artichoke hearts add the iconic flavor of spinach-artichoke dip to classic macaroni and cheese. As with our Simple Stovetop Macaroni and Cheese (page 275), American cheese makes the cheese sauce creamy and velvety with very little effort and no fussy béchamel. Use a 4-ounce block of American cheese from the deli counter rather than presliced cheese, which is formulated differently and will make the sauce too thick. Shredding rather than grating the Parmesan adds to the texture of the finished dish. Use the large holes of a box grater to shred the Parmesan.

- 1 tablespoon extra-virgin olive oil
- 3 garlic cloves, minced
- 5 ounces (5 cups) baby spinach, chopped coarse
- 1½ cups water
- 1 cup whole milk
- 8 ounces elbow macaroni
- ¼ teaspoon table salt
- 1 cup marinated artichoke hearts, chopped
- 4 ounces American cheese, shredded (1 cup)
- ½ teaspoon pepper
- 4 ounces extra-sharp cheddar cheese, shredded (1 cup)
- 1½ ounces Parmesan cheese, shredded (½ cup)

1. Heat oil in large saucepan over medium-high heat until shimmering. Add garlic and cook until fragrant, about 30 seconds. Add spinach and cook until wilted, 2 to 3 minutes. Transfer spinach to bowl and set aside.

2. Bring water and milk to boil in now-empty saucepan over high heat. Stir in macaroni and salt and reduce heat to medium-low. Cook, stirring frequently, until macaroni is slightly past al dente, 6 to 8 minutes. Add artichokes, American cheese, and pepper and cook, stirring constantly, until cheese is completely melted, about 1 minute. Off heat, stir in cheddar and Parmesan until evenly distributed but not melted. Cover saucepan and let stand for 5 minutes.

3. Add spinach to macaroni and stir until sauce is smooth (sauce may look loose but will thicken as it cools). Season with salt and pepper to taste. Serve.

Pasta with Creamy Lemon–Sichuan Peppercorn Sauce

Serves 4 to 6 Total Time 50 minutes

Why This Recipe Works This vibrant pasta dish features bright lemon, fragrant miso, and creamy crème fraîche. But the surprising star is Sichuan peppercorns, which create a unique numbing and tingling sensation due to a compound called hydroxy-alpha-sanshool. This compound interacts with our nerve endings, triggering a phenomenon known as chemesthesis. To get even flavor distribution and a pronounced level of that buzzing sensation, we toast and grind Sichuan peppercorns and incorporate them in two ways: Some are gently heated in oil to release their flavorful compounds and form the sauce base, and the rest are stirred into the pasta right before serving. Use high-quality Sichuan peppercorns, and pick through them to remove any debris. You can use a spice grinder instead of a mortar and pestle. Serve with extra lemon juice if you like a very punchy sauce.

- 4 teaspoons red Sichuan peppercorns
- 1 pound spaghetti
- Table salt for cooking pasta
- 3 tablespoons extra-virgin olive oil
- 2 garlic cloves, minced
- 1 cup vegetable broth
- 1 cup crème fraîche
- 3 tablespoons white miso
- 2 teaspoons grated lemon zest plus 2 tablespoons juice
- 1 teaspoon pepper
- 2 tablespoons chopped fresh parsley
- Grated Parmesan cheese (optional)

1. Heat medium saucepan over medium heat for 1 minute. Add Sichuan peppercorns and toast until fragrant, about 1 minute, stirring frequently. Transfer to mortar and pestle and let cool to room temperature, then grind until coarsely ground; set aside.

2. Bring 4 quarts water to boil in large pot. Add pasta and 1 tablespoon salt and cook, stirring often, until al dente. Reserve 1 cup cooking water, then drain pasta and return it to pot.

3. Cook olive oil, garlic, and half of reserved ground Sichuan peppercorns over medium heat in now-empty saucepan until fragrant, about 1 minute. Stir in broth and bring to boil. Reduce heat to medium-low and simmer until reduced by half, 4 to 5 minutes.

4. Whisk in crème fraîche, miso, lemon zest and juice, and pepper. Increase heat to medium-high and return to brief simmer. Season with salt and pepper to taste.

5. Add sauce and ½ cup reserved cooking water to pasta and toss to combine. Adjust consistency with remaining reserved cooking water as needed. Stir in remaining ground Sichuan peppercorns, then season with salt and pepper to taste. Sprinkle with fresh parsley and serve immediately with Parmesan, if using.

Pasta Cacio e Uova (Pasta with Cheese and Eggs)

FAST Serves 4 to 6 Total Time 35 minutes

Why This Recipe Works Don't call this a vegetarian carbonara or you'll risk the wrath of the residents of Naples, where this dish originates. Similar to carbonara, though, this dish features an egg and cheese-based sauce that relies on the heat of the cooked pasta to come together. The pasta (cooked in half the usual amount of water to create extra-starchy cooking water) is returned to the pot and tossed with garlic-infused fat. The magic happens when beaten eggs and Parmesan cheese are poured into the pot—as everything is stirred together, a smooth and glossy sauce forms. Tubetti is traditionally used for this dish, but you can substitute 8 ounces (2 cups) elbow macaroni.

- 6 tablespoons extra-virgin olive oil
- 4 garlic cloves, lightly crushed and peeled
- 4 large eggs
- 4 ounces Parmesan cheese, grated (2 cups)
- ¼ cup minced fresh parsley
- ½ teaspoon table salt, plus salt for cooking pasta
- ½ teaspoon pepper
- 1 pound tubetti

1. Heat oil in 8-inch skillet over medium-low heat. Add garlic and cook, swirling skillet and flipping garlic occasionally, until garlic is pale golden brown, 7 to 10 minutes. (Tiny bubbles will surround garlic, but garlic should not actively fry. Reduce heat if necessary.) Turn off heat, but leave skillet on burner. Discard garlic.

2. Meanwhile, bring 2 quarts water to boil in large pot. Beat eggs in medium bowl until very few streaks of white remain. Stir in Parmesan, parsley, salt, and pepper and set aside.

3. Stir pasta and 1½ teaspoons salt into boiling water and cook, stirring often, until pasta is al dente. Reserve ¼ cup cooking water, then drain pasta and return it to pot. Immediately add garlic oil, egg mixture, and 1 tablespoon reserved cooking water to pasta and toss until cheese is fully melted. Adjust consistency with remaining reserved cooking water, 1 tablespoon at a time, as needed. Serve immediately.

Creamy Broccoli Pasta with Crispy Panko

Serves 6 Total Time 55 minutes

Why This Recipe Works This pasta is luxuriously creamy while at the same time containing an ample amount of broccoli. Blanching the broccoli stems and florets to tenderize them is a convenient technique here, since cooking pasta also requires a pot of boiling water. Blending the cooked stems and some of the florets with a pesto-inspired roster of ingredients makes a light, fresh, vegetal sauce. Adding Greek yogurt gives the sauce creamy body without muting the delicate pesto and broccoli flavors. Combining the sauce, reserved florets, and pasta off the heat ensures that the sauce warms through gently without curdling. A sprinkle of Parmesan and a smattering of toasted panko bread crumbs make a dynamic finishing touch. Using a conventional blender will produce the smoothest sauce, but an immersion blender can be used instead. We prefer the richness of whole-milk yogurt, but low-fat yogurt can also be used. There is no need to peel the broccoli stalks.

- ½ cup plus 1 tablespoon extra-virgin olive oil, divided
- ½ cup panko bread crumbs
- ⅛ teaspoon plus 2 teaspoons table salt, divided, plus salt for cooking broccoli and pasta
- ⅛ teaspoon plus 1 teaspoon pepper, divided
- 1½ pounds broccoli, florets cut into 1-inch pieces, stalks cut into ½-inch pieces
- 2 garlic cloves, smashed and peeled
- 1 pound penne, rigatoni, or other short tubular pasta
- 2 cups fresh basil leaves
- 1 cup plain Greek yogurt
- 1 ounce Parmesan cheese, grated (½ cup), plus extra for serving
- ¼ cup pine nuts, toasted
- 1 teaspoon grated lemon zest plus 2 tablespoons juice

1. Bring 4 quarts water to boil in large pot. While water is coming to boil, heat 1 tablespoon oil in 10-inch skillet over medium heat until shimmering. Add panko and cook, stirring frequently, until golden brown, about 4 minutes. Off heat, stir in ⅛ teaspoon salt and ⅛ teaspoon pepper. Transfer panko to plate to cool.

2. Add broccoli stalks, garlic, and 1 tablespoon salt to boiling water and cook, stirring occasionally, until stalks are tender, about 6 minutes. Using spider skimmer or slotted spoon, transfer stalks and garlic to blender; set aside.

3. Return water to boil. Add florets and cook until bright green and tender, about 3 minutes. Using spider skimmer, transfer two-thirds of florets to bowl. Transfer remaining florets to blender with stalks and garlic. Return water to boil, add pasta, and cook, stirring often, until al dente.

4. While pasta cooks, add basil, yogurt, Parmesan, pine nuts, lemon zest and juice, remaining ½ cup oil, remaining 2 teaspoons salt, and remaining 1 teaspoon pepper to blender and process until mixture resembles pesto, about 20 seconds, scraping down sides of blender jar. With blender running, slowly add ½ cup water and process until sauce is smooth and thick but fluid, about 20 seconds, adding additional water as needed.

5. Reserve 1 cup cooking water, then drain pasta and return it to pot. Add sauce and reserved florets and stir gently to combine. Adjust consistency with reserved cooking water as needed. Season with salt to taste and serve immediately, passing panko and extra Parmesan separately.

Tallarines Verdes (Peruvian Green Noodles)

Serves 4 to 6   Total Time 55 minutes

Why This Recipe Works When Italian immigrants arrived in Lima, Peru, in the 19th century, they re-created their beloved pesto alla Genovese by swapping in a few local ingredients. The result was a creamy emerald-green spinach sauce that generously coated strands of fettuccine. The dish, called tallarines verdes (green noodles), became a staple of the Peruvian kitchen. For our version, we start by blanching spinach and a small amount of basil to tenderize them so that they can blend up silky smooth, since a luxuriously creamy texture is a hallmark of the dish. Next, we sauté

Creamy Broccoli Pasta with Crispy Panko

red onion and garlic to mellow their sulfuric edge. Blending the vegetables with pecans, queso fresco, and evaporated milk—a favorite staple in the Peruvian kitchen—creates a velvety, full-bodied sauce. We prefer queso fresco here, but an equal amount of feta cheese can be substituted. Walnuts can be used in place of the pecans. This rich pasta is typically served alongside fried eggs.

- 1 tablespoon vegetable oil
- ½ cup chopped red onion
- 2 garlic cloves, peeled and halved
- ¾ teaspoon table salt, plus salt for cooking greens and pasta
- 6 ounces (6 cups) baby spinach
- 1 cup (1 ounce) fresh basil leaves
- 2 ounces queso fresco, crumbled (½ cup)
- ½ cup evaporated milk
- ⅓ cup pecans
- ½ teaspoon pepper
- 12 ounces fettuccine

1. Bring 4 quarts water to boil in large pot. While water is coming to boil, heat oil in 10-inch skillet over medium heat until shimmering. Add onion and cook until just starting to soften, 1 to 2 minutes. Add garlic and cook until fragrant, 30 to 60 seconds. Transfer onion and garlic to blender. Set aside.

2. When water comes to boil, add 1 tablespoon salt, spinach, and basil and cook until just wilted, 20 to 30 seconds. Using spider skimmer or slotted spoon, transfer spinach and basil to small bowl. Squeeze out any excess liquid from spinach and basil.

3. Transfer spinach and basil to blender with onion mixture. Add queso fresco, evaporated milk, pecans, pepper, and salt and process until smooth, about 2 minutes, scraping down sides of blender jar as needed. Set aside.

4. Return water to boil; add pasta and cook, stirring often, until al dente. Reserve 1 cup cooking water, then drain pasta and set aside.

5. Add sauce to now-empty pot and cook over medium heat, stirring occasionally, until warmed through, 2 to 3 minutes. Off heat, stir in pasta and ⅓ cup reserved cooking water and stir until sauce just clings to pasta, about 1 minute. Adjust consistency with remaining reserved cooking water as needed and season with salt to taste. Serve immediately.

Fettuccine with Walnut Sauce

FAST Serves 4 Total Time 30 minutes

Why This Recipe Works The creamy walnut sauce that cloaks the fettuccine in this dish comes together quickly in the food processor while the pasta cooks, but it is a powerhouse of rich, nutty flavor. Equal parts cream and Parmesan add thickness and saltiness to the sauce, while lemon juice brightens and lightens the mixture. A touch of nutmeg adds a warm spice element that heightens the nutty flavor of the toasted walnuts. We hold back ¼ cup of walnuts from the sauce, chopping them and sprinkling on top of the finished pasta (along with some parsley) for crunchy contrast.

- 1 pound fettuccine
- 1 teaspoon table salt, plus salt for cooking pasta
- 2¼ cups (9 ounces) walnuts, toasted, divided
- ¼ cup heavy cream
- ¼ cup grated Parmesan cheese, plus extra for serving
- 1 tablespoon lemon juice
- 1 garlic clove, minced
- ⅛ teaspoon nutmeg
- ½ teaspoon pepper
- 2 tablespoons chopped fresh parsley

1. Bring 4 quarts water to boil in large pot. Add pasta and 1 tablespoon salt and cook, stirring often, until al dente. Reserve 1 cup cooking water, then drain pasta and return it to pot.

2. Chop ¼ cup walnuts; set aside. Process remaining 2 cups walnuts, cream, Parmesan, lemon juice, garlic, nutmeg, salt, and pepper in food processor to coarse paste, about 30 seconds.

3. Add walnut sauce and reserved cooking water to pasta and toss to combine. Season with salt and pepper to taste. Sprinkle with parsley and reserved chopped walnuts. Serve, passing extra Parmesan separately.

Cashew e Pepe e Funghi

FAST **VEGAN** Serves 4 to 6 Total Time 45 minutes

Why This Recipe Works This oh-so-creamy and comforting dish is a marriage of the best hallmarks of pasta carbonara and pasta cacio e pepe. Soaked cashews get blitzed in the food processor into a rich sauce base thanks to their uniquely low fiber and high starch content. Breaking up the cashews to increase their surface area shortens the necessary soaking time to just 15 minutes. We process the soaked nuts with nutritional yeast and miso, two powerful umami boosters. Because oyster mushrooms contain very little moisture relative to other mushrooms, they quickly cook into chewy, golden nuggets that infuse every bite of pasta with irresistibly savory character. You can substitute portobello mushrooms for the oyster mushrooms, but the mushrooms won't be nearly as crisp.

- ½ cup roasted cashews
- ¼ cup nutritional yeast
- 2 tablespoons white miso
- ½ teaspoon table salt, plus salt for cooking pasta
- ¼ cup extra-virgin olive oil
- 6 ounces oyster mushrooms, trimmed and chopped
- 5 garlic cloves, sliced thin
- 1 teaspoon coarsely ground pepper
- 1 pound spaghetti
- 2 tablespoons chopped fresh parsley
- 1 teaspoon lemon juice

1. Process cashews in blender on low speed to consistency of fine gravel mixed with sand, 10 to 15 seconds. Add 1½ cups water, nutritional yeast, miso, and salt and process on low speed until combined, about 5 seconds. Scrape down sides of blender jar and let mixture sit for 15 minutes.

2. Process on low speed until all ingredients are well blended, about 1 minute. Scrape down sides of blender jar, then process on high speed until sauce is completely smooth, 3 to 4 minutes.

3. Heat oil in 12-inch skillet over medium-high heat until shimmering. Add mushrooms and cook until deep golden brown and crisp, 7 to 10 minutes. Off heat, stir in garlic and pepper and cook using residual heat of skillet until fragrant, about 1 minute.

4. Meanwhile, bring 4 quarts water to boil in large pot. Add pasta and 1 tablespoon salt and cook, stirring often, until al dente. Reserve ½ cup cooking water, then drain pasta and return it to pot.

5. Add sauce, mushroom mixture, parsley, and lemon juice to pasta and toss until sauce is thickened slightly and pasta is well coated, about 1 minute. Before serving, adjust consistency with reserved cooking water as needed and season with salt and pepper to taste.

top | *Fettuccine with Walnut Sauce*
bottom | *Cashew e Pepe e Funghi*

Mad About Mushrooms

With their hearty texture and deep flavor, mushrooms are an excellent way to add complex meatiness to all kinds of dishes. In our Triple Mushroom Pasta we use three varieties of mushroom in different ways to create a pasta dish with multilayered mushroom flavor.

White Mushrooms

Humble, inexpensive, mild white mushrooms are a workhorse of the vegetarian kitchen. In this recipe, they are chopped so fine that they nearly become a paste, forming the base of the sauce.

Dried Porcini

Shelf-stable dried porcini add potent savoriness. Because the mushrooms are dried, their flavor is more concentrated. Although they are typically reconstituted in water before using, here we process unsoaked dried porcini along with the fresh white mushrooms, which distributes intense flavor throughout the duxelles.

Maitake Mushrooms

Frilly-capped maitakes have a nutty, slightly smoky taste with peppery undertones. Tearing them into pieces and sizzling them in olive oil turns them deep brown with elegantly light and crisp feathery edges—taking this pasta over the top.

| *Triple Mushroom Pasta*

Triple Mushroom Pasta

Serves 4 to 6 Total Time 1 hour

Why This Recipe Works A trio of mushrooms makes for a pasta that's packed with earthy flavor. We make a double-mushroom duxelles by grinding white mushrooms and dried porcini with aromatics and cooking it all together, then finishing it with a touch of cream. To cook the pound of pasta, we use just 5 cups of water to create a superstarchy liquid. Instead of draining the pasta, when it's just shy of al dente we stir in the duxelles to build an ultrarich, clingy sauce. Torn maitakes seared in extra-virgin olive oil create a beautifully crisp topping. If you can't find maitake (hen-of-the-woods) mushrooms, substitute oyster or cremini mushrooms. We prefer campanelle, but rigatoni or medium shells can be used; the pasta cooking time may differ. Cook the pasta after you've made the crispy mushrooms and duxelles.

Crispy Mushrooms

- 2 tablespoons extra-virgin olive oil
- 8 ounces maitake mushrooms, trimmed and torn into ½-inch pieces

Duxelles

- ¼ ounce dried porcini mushrooms, rinsed
- 1 shallot, peeled
- 3 garlic cloves, peeled
- 1 pound white mushrooms, quartered
- 2 tablespoons unsalted butter
- ½ teaspoon table salt
- ½ cup heavy cream
- ⅛ teaspoon pepper
- 1 tablespoon lemon juice

Pasta

- 5 cups water
- 1 pound campanelle
- 1 teaspoon table salt
- 1 ounce Parmesan cheese, grated (½ cup)
- 2 tablespoons chopped fresh parsley

1. **For the crispy mushrooms** Heat oil in 12-inch skillet over medium heat until shimmering. Add maitakes and cook, without stirring, until mushrooms begin to wilt at edges, 2 to 3 minutes. Gently stir and continue to cook, stirring occasionally, until mushrooms are well browned and crisp, 7 to 9 minutes longer. Off heat, season mushrooms with salt and pepper to taste, transfer to bowl, and set aside until serving (do not wash skillet).

2. **For the duxelles** Add porcini mushrooms, shallot, and garlic to food processor and process until finely chopped, 10 to 15 seconds, scraping down sides of bowl halfway through processing. Add white mushrooms and process until very finely chopped, 40 to 55 seconds, scraping down sides of bowl halfway through processing.

3. Add butter to now-empty skillet and heat over medium heat until butter is foaming, 1 to 2 minutes. Add mushroom mixture and salt and cook, stirring occasionally, until mushroom liquid has evaporated and mushrooms have darkened, 10 to 12 minutes. Remove from heat. Stir in cream, pepper, and lemon juice. Set aside.

4. **For the pasta** Bring water to boil in large Dutch oven. Stir in pasta and salt. Adjust heat to medium so water is at gentle boil and cook, partially covered and stirring occasionally, until pasta is just shy of al dente, 6 to 8 minutes (there will be about ½ inch cooking water in bottom of pot). Do not drain pasta.

5. Off heat, add duxelles and Parmesan and stir vigorously until pasta is coated in lightly thickened sauce, 1 to 2 minutes (sauce will thicken as it cools). Transfer pasta to serving bowl. Top with crispy mushrooms and parsley. Serve immediately.

Rigatoni with Quick Mushroom Bolognese

FAST Serves 4 to 6 Total Time 40 minutes

Why This Recipe Works This lush Bolognese-inspired sauce uses mushrooms to their full meat-replacing advantage. Cremini mushrooms, pulsed to small bits, do an excellent job of mimicking ground beef. We cook the mushrooms in a skillet with onion, carrot, tomato paste, and garlic so the cremini can soak up those flavors; to make use of the flavor-packed fond that develops, we deglaze the skillet with white wine. We then add pasta cooking water, which contributes enough starchiness to turn the mushroom mixture into a decadently velvety sauce. Rigatoni is an easy choice: The tubes perfectly capture and hold on to chunky sauces like this mushroom Bolognese. We toss the pasta with the meaty, umami-rich sauce and then stir in Parmesan for additional savory oomph and nuttiness. Garnish with chopped chives and red pepper flakes if desired.

1 pound rigatoni
¾ teaspoon table salt, plus salt for cooking pasta
1 pound cremini mushrooms, trimmed and quartered
3 tablespoons extra-virgin olive oil
1 small onion, chopped fine
1 carrot, peeled and chopped fine
¼ cup tomato paste
3 garlic cloves, minced
¼ cup dry white wine
¼ cup grated Parmesan cheese, plus extra for serving

1. Bring 4 quarts water to boil in Dutch oven. Add pasta and 1 tablespoon salt and cook, stirring occasionally, until al dente. Reserve 1 cup cooking water, then drain pasta and return it to pot.

2. Meanwhile, pulse mushrooms in food processor until finely chopped, about 10 pulses. Heat oil in 12-inch skillet over medium-high heat until just smoking. Add mushrooms, onion, carrot, and salt and cook until mushrooms appear dry and begin to stick to bottom of skillet, about 14 minutes.

3. Stir in tomato paste and garlic and cook until fond forms on bottom of skillet, about 1 minute. Stir in wine, scraping up any browned bits, and cook until evaporated, about 2 minutes. Stir in reserved cooking water and bring to boil. Add sauce and Parmesan to pasta in pot and stir to combine. Serve with extra Parmesan.

Summer Squash Pasta with Ricotta and Lemon-Parmesan Bread Crumbs

Serves 4 Total Time 1 hour

Why This Recipe Works Sweet, lightly grassy summer squash deserves to be celebrated as an emblem of summer produce, and this recipe has plenty of squash-forward flavor. Cutting the squashes into thin half-moons allows for the excess moisture to be cooked out. Adding minced garlic, red pepper flakes, and black pepper makes for a spicy kick that plays well against the vegetable's sweetness. After the squash mixture is added to the pasta, reserved starchy pasta water and Parmesan make it a cohesive dish. Each portion gets a dollop of creamy ricotta cheese (still cool from the refrigerator for a contrast to the warm pasta). A finishing crunch comes from toasted and seasoned panko bread crumbs. Choose squashes no heavier than 8 ounces each; larger squashes have more seeds and can taste watery.

Bread Crumbs

¼ cup panko bread crumbs
1 tablespoon extra-virgin olive oil
¼ teaspoon table salt
1 ounce Parmesan cheese, grated (½ cup)
1 teaspoon grated lemon zest

Pasta

1½ pounds summer squash, halved lengthwise and sliced thin crosswise
6 tablespoons extra-virgin olive oil, divided
1 teaspoon table salt, plus salt for cooking pasta
4 garlic cloves, minced
¾ teaspoon red pepper flakes
½ teaspoon pepper
1 pound fettuccine
1½ ounces Parmesan cheese, grated (¾ cup)
½ cup torn fresh basil, plus extra for sprinkling
2½ tablespoons lemon juice
8 ounces (1 cup) whole-milk ricotta cheese

1. **For the bread crumbs** Combine panko, oil, and salt in 12-inch nonstick skillet and cook over medium heat, stirring frequently, until golden brown, 3 to 6 minutes. Transfer to bowl and stir in Parmesan and lemon zest; set aside.

2. **For the pasta** Combine squash, 3 tablespoons oil, and salt in now-empty skillet. Cook over medium-high heat, stirring occasionally, until squash is fully softened and spotty brown, 15 to 20 minutes. Add garlic, pepper flakes, and pepper and cook until fragrant, about 1 minute. Let sit off heat, covered.

3. Meanwhile, bring 4 quarts water to boil in large pot. Add pasta and 1 tablespoon salt and cook, stirring often, until al dente. Reserve 2 cups cooking water, then drain pasta and return it to pot.

4. Add squash mixture, 1¼ cups reserved cooking water, Parmesan, basil, lemon juice, and remaining 3 tablespoons oil to pasta and toss to combine. Adjust consistency with remaining reserved cooking water as needed. Season with salt and pepper to taste.

5. Transfer pasta to individual serving bowls. Dollop with ricotta and sprinkle with bread crumbs and extra basil. Serve immediately.

Ultracreamy Spaghetti with Zucchini

FAST Serves 4 Total Time 45 minutes

Why This Recipe Works From its verdant hue to its basil-tinged aroma, spaghetti alla Nerano is a celebration of summertime, a dinner for eating al fresco. The dish's summertime appeal is also practical: When gardens and farmers' markets are teeming with zucchini, Nerano is a way to put pounds of the squash to work. Deep frying, the traditional Italian way of cooking the zucchini coins in this dish, can be cumbersome, so in our version, we achieve comparable robust sweet-nuttiness and spotty browning in our zucchini by microwaving and then sautéing the coins. Tossing al dente spaghetti with the zucchini, black pepper, basil, starchy pasta water, and butter creates an emulsion that serves as the base of a sauce, and adding a combination of mild provolone and Parmesan (to replicate the special blend of local cheeses traditionally used) makes the sauce luxuriously silky. Be sure to use zucchini that are smaller than 8 ounces because they contain fewer seeds. Using a mandoline will make quick work of slicing the zucchini. Use a 2½-ounce block of mild provolone from the deli counter rather than presliced cheese.

- 2 pounds small zucchini, sliced ⅛ inch thick
- 1 teaspoon table salt, plus salt for cooking pasta
- 2 tablespoons extra-virgin olive oil
- 12 ounces spaghetti
- 2 tablespoons unsalted butter
- 2 tablespoons chopped fresh basil
- ½ teaspoon pepper
- 2½ ounces mild provolone cheese, shredded (⅔ cup)
- ⅓ cup grated Parmesan cheese

1. In large bowl, stir together zucchini, ¼ cup water, and salt. Cover and microwave until zucchini is softened (some slices will curl at edges) and liquid is released, 10 to 12 minutes, stirring halfway through microwaving. Drain zucchini in colander and let cool slightly, about 5 minutes.

2. Heat oil in 12-inch nonstick skillet over medium-high heat until shimmering. Add zucchini (do not wash colander) and spread into even layer. Cook, stirring every 4 minutes and then reflattening into even layer, until zucchini is very tender and about half of slices have browned, 10 to 12 minutes (it is OK if some pieces fall apart). (Zucchini can be refrigerated for up to 2 days.)

top | *Summer Squash Pasta with Ricotta and Lemon-Parmesan Bread Crumbs*

bottom | *Ultracreamy Spaghetti with Zucchini*

3. Meanwhile, bring 4 quarts water to boil in large pot. Add pasta and 1 tablespoon salt and cook, stirring often, until al dente. Reserve 1½ cups cooking water, then drain pasta and return it to pot.

4. Add 1 cup reserved cooking water, zucchini, butter, basil, and pepper to pasta. Set pot over low heat and cook, stirring and tossing pasta constantly, until ingredients are evenly distributed and butter is melted, about 1 minute. Off heat, add provolone and Parmesan. Stir vigorously until cheeses are melted and pasta is coated in creamy, lightly thickened sauce, about 1 minute, adjusting consistency with remaining reserved cooking water as needed. Serve immediately.

Spaghetti all'Assassina

VEGAN Serves 4 Total Time 1¼ hours

Why This Recipe Works The defining aspects of this deeply satisfying dish from Bari, Italy, are spaghetti strands with textures that run from soft to al dente to crisp (even within a single strand) and a spicy, concentrated tomato sauce that clings tightly to the pasta. The cooking process involves gradually adding a simple tomato broth to raw spaghetti and a seasoned tomato puree. Eventually, the heat is turned up to crisp and char the bottom of the pasta. To achieve these hallmarks, we make a sauce with garlic, red pepper flakes, and passata di pomodoro (uncooked tomato puree) in a skillet. We then add raw spaghetti to the sauce, followed periodically by cupfuls of the tomato broth, adding more as it dries out and not stirring too much, allowing the pasta to start to crisp and char in spots. To finish, we turn the heat to full blast so that some of the strands develop a smoky char. This recipe was developed with De Cecco Spaghetti No. 12. Other brands of spaghetti may vary in thickness, which will affect the cooking time and the amount of broth required. Fish spatulas work well for flipping the pasta in step 4. We like the Pomì brand of passata. If you cannot find it, tomato puree can be used. The sauce will splatter as it cooks, which is why we call for using a long-handled spatula in step 2.

- 6 cups water
- ¼ cup tomato paste
- 1 teaspoon sugar
- ⅓ cup plus 2 tablespoons extra-virgin olive oil, divided
- 2 garlic cloves, minced
- ½–¾ teaspoon red pepper flakes
- 1 cup tomato passata
- 1¾ teaspoons table salt
- 12 ounces spaghetti

1. Whisk water, tomato paste, and sugar together in medium saucepan. Bring to simmer over medium-high heat, then reduce heat to low to keep tomato broth warm.

2. Heat ⅓ cup oil, garlic, and pepper flakes in 12-inch nonstick skillet over medium heat. Cook, stirring frequently with long-handled silicone spatula, until garlic is golden brown, about 2 minutes. Stir in passata and salt. Cook, stirring frequently, until sauce thickens and oil around edges of skillet begins to sizzle, about 4 minutes.

3. Add pasta in even layer and increase heat to medium-high. Add 1 cup tomato broth and cook, pushing between pasta strands frequently with edge of spatula to prevent clumping, until broth has been mostly absorbed by pasta and sauce around edges of skillet begins to sizzle, 4 to 5 minutes. Add 1 cup broth and cook, shaking skillet occasionally and continuing to prod pasta strands with spatula, until broth has been mostly absorbed and sauce begins to sizzle, 5 to 7 minutes.

4. Using 2 thin spatulas, gently flip half of pasta so bottom is on top and spread into even layer. Repeat with remaining half of pasta. Add 1 cup broth and cook, continuing to shake skillet and prod pasta, until broth has been mostly absorbed and sauce begins to sizzle, 5 to 7 minutes. Add 1 cup broth and repeat cooking until sauce begins to sizzle, 5 to 7 minutes. Repeat dividing and flipping pasta.

5. Add 1 cup broth and repeat cooking until sauce begins to sizzle, 5 to 7 minutes. Pasta should be firm but cooked through. If not, add remaining 1 cup broth, ½ cup at a time, and continue to cook, checking frequently, until pasta is cooked through.

6. Increase heat to high and cook pasta, without moving it, until underside is deeply browned and crisp and some strands are beginning to char, 3 to 5 minutes. Remove skillet from heat, drizzle with remaining 2 tablespoons oil, and serve immediately.

Making Spaghetti all'Assassina

1 After adding pasta in even layer, add 1 cup tomato broth and cook, pushing between pasta strands to prevent clumping until broth is mostly absorbed and sauce at edges begins to sizzle.

2 Add 1 cup broth and cook, shaking skillet and prodding pasta strands until broth is mostly absorbed and sauce begins to sizzle.

3 After 2 cups liquid have been absorbed, use 2 thin spatulas to flip half of pasta so bottom is on top and spread into even layer. Repeat with remaining half of pasta.

4 Add 1 cup broth and repeat cooking until sauce begins to sizzle.

5 Repeat dividing and flipping pasta until cooked through. Increase heat to high and cook pasta, without moving it, until underside is deeply browned and crisp and some strands are beginning to char.

Spaghetti all'Assassina

Farfalle with Beets, Arugula, and Blue Cheese

Farfalle with Beets, Arugula, and Blue Cheese

FAST Serves 6 Total Time 45 minutes

Why This Recipe Works Butterfly-shaped pasta takes on a vibrant and fun pink color thanks to combining it with matchstick-size beets. We precook the beets, along with a little onion, in a skillet while the pasta boils so that the meal comes together quickly. Arugula, folded in along with Gorgonzola cheese at the end, adds a peppery bite and a contrasting texture and color, while the Gorgonzola contributes a slightly pungent flavor and creamy body. Just before serving, we garnish the pasta with chopped toasted walnuts for crunch and a final sprinkling of more Gorgonzola to pull it together.

- 1 pound beets, peeled and cut into matchsticks
- 1 red onion, halved and sliced thin
- 3 tablespoons extra-virgin olive oil
- ¼ teaspoon table salt, plus salt for cooking pasta
- ¼ teaspoon pepper
- 2 tablespoons lemon juice, divided
- 1 pound farfalle
- 5 ounces (5 cups) baby arugula
- 6 ounces Gorgonzola cheese, crumbled (1½ cups), divided
- 1 cup walnuts, toasted and chopped

1. Combine beets, onion, oil, salt, and pepper in 12-inch nonstick skillet. Add ⅓ cup water and bring to boil, then cover and reduce heat to medium-high. Cook for 10 minutes, then remove lid and continue to cook, stirring occasionally, until beets are tender, about 15 minutes. Stir in 1 tablespoon lemon juice and season with salt and pepper to taste.

2. Meanwhile, bring 4 quarts water to boil in large pot. Add farfalle and 1 tablespoon salt and cook, stirring often, until al dente. Reserve ½ cup cooking water, then drain pasta and return it to pot.

3. Stir beets and remaining 1 tablespoon lemon juice into pasta in pot, adjusting consistency with reserved cooking water as needed. Stir in arugula and ¾ cup Gorgonzola and season with salt and pepper to taste. Sprinkle with walnuts and remaining ¾ cup Gorgonzola and serve.

Orecchiette and Navy Beans with Brussels Sprouts and Spicy Mustard Crumbs

FAST **VEGAN** Serves 4 Total Time 40 minutes

Why This Recipe Works Pasta and beans are easy, economical, and nutritious comfort. For this hearty dish, we boil the pasta in a smaller volume of water, which leaves the water extra-starchy and thus ideal for building a creamy, full-bodied sauce. The starchy, protein-rich canned bean liquid helps in the same way. A mustardy bread crumb topping adds crunch and a pop of flavor. To maximize efficiency when trimming, halving, and slicing the sprouts, complete one task at a time on all the sprouts. To make this recipe vegan, substitute plant-based sour cream for the dairy sour cream.

- 2 teaspoons vegetable oil
- ¼ cup panko bread crumbs
- 2 teaspoons Dijon mustard
- ⅛ teaspoon plus ½ teaspoon table salt, divided, plus salt for cooking pasta
- Pinch cayenne pepper
- 8 ounces orecchiette
- 4 teaspoons extra-virgin olive oil
- 10 ounces brussels sprouts, trimmed, halved, and sliced thin
- 1 (15-ounce) can navy beans, undrained
- 1 tablespoon cider vinegar
- ½ teaspoon pepper
- ⅓ cup sour cream

1. Bring 2 quarts water to boil in large saucepan. While water is coming to boil, combine vegetable oil, panko, mustard, ⅛ teaspoon salt, and cayenne in 12-inch nonstick skillet. Cook over medium-high heat, stirring frequently, until panko is golden brown, about 5 minutes. Transfer to small bowl and let cool completely (do not wash skillet).

2. Add pasta and 1½ teaspoons salt to boiling water and cook, stirring often, until al dente. Reserve 1 cup cooking water and drain pasta. Return pasta to pot and cover to keep warm.

3. Heat olive oil in now-empty skillet over medium-high heat until shimmering. Add brussels sprouts, 1 tablespoon water, and remaining ½ teaspoon salt and stir to coat. Cover and cook, stirring occasionally, until sprouts are crisp-tender and bright green, about 4 minutes. Stir in beans and their liquid, ¼ cup reserved cooking water, vinegar, and pepper and cook until bubbling.

4. Add brussels sprout mixture and sour cream to pasta and stir until all ingredients are combined. Adjust consistency with remaining reserved cooking water as needed. Season with salt and pepper to taste. Divide among 4 shallow bowls. Sprinkle with bread crumbs and serve.

Creamy, Spicy Rotini and Red Lentils with Tomatoes and Goat Cheese

FAST Serves 4 Total Time 40 minutes

Why This Recipe Works This easy pasta-and-beans combo will make you look at lentils in a whole new way. Mildly sweet and nutty red lentils are cooked in water seasoned with scallion whites, garlic, red pepper flakes, and tomato paste for just 15 minutes, turning soft enough to be whisked by hand into a sauce-like consistency. Stirring in some pasta cooking water and tangy goat cheese completes the sauce. Adding cherry tomatoes and scallion greens before serving brightens the flavor of this weeknight winner. We like tubed tomato pastes, such as those from Cento, Mutti, and Amore.

- 8 ounces cherry tomatoes, halved
- ½ teaspoon sugar
- ⅛ teaspoon plus ¾ teaspoon table salt, plus salt for cooking pasta
- 1 tablespoon extra-virgin olive oil
- 6 scallions, white parts sliced thin, green parts sliced thin on bias
- 2 teaspoons minced garlic
- ¼–½ teaspoon red pepper flakes
- 1 tablespoon tomato paste
- ½ cup red lentils, picked over and rinsed
- ¼ teaspoon pepper
- 8 ounces rotini
- 4 ounces (1 cup) goat cheese, crumbled

1. Stir tomatoes, sugar, and ⅛ teaspoon salt together in small bowl and set aside. Bring 2 quarts water to boil in large saucepan.

2. Meanwhile, heat oil in medium saucepan over medium-high heat until shimmering. Add scallion whites, garlic, and pepper flakes and cook, stirring frequently, until fragrant and scallions are slightly softened, about 1 minute. Stir in tomato paste and cook, stirring constantly, until paste begins to brown, about 2 minutes. Stir in 2 cups water, lentils, pepper, and remaining ¾ teaspoon salt and bring to simmer. Cover and simmer, stirring occasionally, until lentils are soft and about half are broken down, about 15 minutes.

3. While lentils are simmering, add pasta and 1½ teaspoons salt to boiling water and cook, stirring often, until al dente. Reserve 1 cup cooking water, drain pasta, and return it to pot. Cover to keep warm.

4. Whisk lentils vigorously until coarsely pureed, about 30 seconds. Add lentil puree, ¼ cup reserved cooking water, and goat cheese to pasta and stir until combined. Adjust consistency with remaining reserved cooking water as needed. Season with salt and pepper to taste. Gently stir in tomatoes and half of scallion greens. Divide among 4 shallow bowls, sprinkle with remaining scallion greens, and serve.

Pasta e Ceci (Pasta with Chickpeas)

Serves 4 to 6 Total Time 1 hour

Why This Recipe Works Pasta e ceci, a sibling of pasta e fagioli, is a hearty one-pot meal that's simple to prepare yet packed full of satisfying flavor. To keep the cooking time manageable, we use canned chickpeas—along with their starchy liquid—to add body and flavor. Cooking the chickpeas and ditalini in the same pot blends the dish, and the additional starch released by the pasta creates a silky texture. To achieve the perfect creamy softness, we simmer the chickpeas before adding the pasta. Using a food processor produces a finely minced soffritto of onion, garlic, carrot, and celery, giving the dish an earthy backbone. Tomatoes and Parmesan add depth, while parsley and lemon juice provide a bright contrast just before serving. Another short pasta, such as orzo, can be substituted for the ditalini, but make sure to substitute by weight and not by volume.

- 1 small carrot, peeled and cut into ½-inch pieces
- 1 small celery rib, cut into ½-inch pieces
- 4 garlic cloves, peeled
- 1 onion, halved and cut into 1-inch pieces
- 1 (14-ounce) can whole peeled tomatoes, drained
- ¼ cup extra-virgin olive oil, plus extra for serving
- 2 teaspoons minced fresh rosemary
- ¼ teaspoon red pepper flakes
- 2 (15-ounce) cans chickpeas, undrained
- 2 cups water
- 1 teaspoon table salt

8 ounces (1½ cups) ditalini
1 tablespoon lemon juice
1 tablespoon minced fresh parsley
1 ounce Parmesan cheese, grated (½ cup)

1. Pulse carrot, celery, and garlic in food processor until finely chopped, 8 to 10 pulses. Add onion and pulse until onion is cut into ⅛- to ¼-inch pieces, 8 to 10 pulses. Transfer carrot mixture to large Dutch oven. Pulse tomatoes in now-empty food processor until coarsely chopped, 8 to 10 pulses. Set aside.

2. Add oil to carrot mixture in Dutch oven and cook over medium heat, stirring frequently, until fond begins to form on bottom of pot, about 5 minutes. Add rosemary and pepper flakes and cook until fragrant, about 1 minute. Stir in tomatoes, chickpeas and their liquid, water, and salt and bring to boil, scraping up any browned bits. Reduce heat to medium-low and simmer for 10 minutes. Add pasta and cook, stirring frequently, until tender, 10 to 12 minutes. Stir in lemon juice and parsley and season with salt and pepper to taste. Serve, passing Parmesan and extra oil separately.

top | *Pasta e Ceci (Pasta with Chickpeas)*
bottom | *Fregula with Chickpeas, Tomatoes, and Fennel*

Fregula with Chickpeas, Tomatoes, and Fennel

Serves 4 to 6   Total Time 55 minutes

Why This Recipe Works Fregola sarda, or fregula, is a sun-dried and toasted spherical pasta hand-rolled from semolina, with a dense, tender chew. Here, we pair fregula with canned chickpeas to echo the toothsomeness of the pasta. We cook them together with the chickpea liquid, as well as grape tomatoes. The tomatoes contribute bursts of sweet acidity, while their juices, coupled with the chickpea liquid, thicken to a risotto-like texture. Licorice-scented fennel (a fresh bulb for sweetness, and seeds for more intense flavor) and piney rosemary—typical Sardinian aromatics—give the dish earthy underpinnings. A final sprinkling of Pecorino Sardo, made from Sardinian sheep's milk, is traditional, but since it's difficult to find vegetarian pecorino, we substitute Parmesan. The cheese adds just the right amount of richness. A final dash of lemon juice gives this pasta a tart dimension that complements the dish's nutty flavor profile beautifully.

- 3 tablespoons extra-virgin olive oil, plus extra for drizzling
- 1 fennel bulb, ¼ cup fronds minced, stalks discarded, bulb halved, cored, and sliced thin
- 1 onion, chopped fine
- 3 garlic cloves, minced
- 2 teaspoons minced fresh rosemary or ¾ teaspoon dried
- 1 teaspoon fennel seeds
- ½ teaspoon table salt
- ½ teaspoon pepper
- ¼ teaspoon red pepper flakes
- 4 cups water
- 2 (15-ounce) cans chickpeas, undrained
- 10 ounces grape tomatoes
- 8 ounces fregula
- 1 tablespoon lemon juice
- Grated Parmesan cheese

1. Heat oil in Dutch oven over medium heat until shimmering. Add sliced fennel and onion and cook until vegetables are softened, 5 to 7 minutes. Stir in garlic, rosemary, fennel seeds, salt, pepper, and pepper flakes and cook until fragrant, about 30 seconds.

2. Stir in water, chickpeas and their liquid, tomatoes, and fregula and bring to boil. Reduce heat to medium-low and simmer until fregula is tender, about 25 minutes, stirring occasionally. Stir in lemon juice and fennel fronds and season with salt and pepper to taste. Serve, drizzling individual portions with extra oil and passing Parmesan separately.

Meatless "Meat" Sauce with Chickpeas and Mushrooms

VEGAN Makes 6 cups, enough for 2 pounds pasta
Total Time 1 hour

Why This Recipe Works This vegetarian sauce is just as hearty and lush as one made with meat. Starting with cremini mushrooms and tomato paste is a big factor—both are rich sources of savory flavor. A generous amount of our favorite ingredient, extra-virgin olive oil, does double duty, enriching the sauce and helping toast the classic aromatics that we incorporate here: garlic, dried oregano, and red pepper flakes. We bulk up the sauce with chopped chickpeas that are rinsed of their excess starch to maintain their shape and meatiness when mixed in. Vegetable broth thins the sauce without watering down its flavor. Make sure to rinse the chickpeas after pulsing them in the food processor or else their starchy liquid will make the sauce too thick.

- 10 ounces cremini mushrooms, trimmed
- 6 tablespoons extra-virgin olive oil, divided
- 1 teaspoon table salt
- 1 onion, chopped
- 5 garlic cloves, minced
- 1¼ teaspoons dried oregano
- ¼ teaspoon red pepper flakes
- ¼ cup tomato paste
- 1 (28-ounce) can crushed tomatoes
- 2 cups vegetable broth
- 1 (15-ounce) can chickpeas, rinsed
- 2 tablespoons chopped fresh basil

1. Pulse mushrooms in 2 batches in food processor until chopped into ⅛- to ¼-inch pieces, 7 to 10 pulses, scraping down sides of bowl as needed. (Do not clean workbowl.) Heat 5 tablespoons oil in Dutch oven over medium-high heat until shimmering. Add mushrooms and salt and cook, stirring occasionally, until mushrooms are browned and fond has formed on bottom of pot, about 8 minutes.

2. While mushrooms cook, pulse onion in food processor until finely chopped, 7 to 10 pulses, scraping down sides of bowl as needed. (Do not clean workbowl.) Transfer onion to pot with mushrooms and cook, stirring occasionally, until onion is softened, about 5 minutes. Combine garlic, oregano, pepper flakes, and remaining 1 tablespoon oil in bowl.

3. Add tomato paste to pot and cook, stirring constantly, until mixture is rust-colored, 1 to 2 minutes. Reduce heat to medium and push vegetables to sides of pot. Add garlic mixture to center and cook, stirring constantly, until fragrant, about 30 seconds. Stir in tomatoes and broth and bring to simmer over high heat. Reduce heat to low and simmer sauce for 5 minutes, stirring occasionally.

4. While sauce simmers, pulse chickpeas in food processor until chopped into ¼-inch pieces, 7 to 10 pulses. Transfer chickpeas to fine-mesh strainer and rinse under cold running water until water runs clear; drain well. Add chickpeas to pot and simmer until sauce is slightly thickened, about 15 minutes. Stir in basil and season with salt and pepper to taste. (Sauce can be refrigerated for up to 2 days or frozen for up to 1 month.)

Meatless "Meat" Sauce with Chickpeas and Mushrooms

Fideos with Chickpeas, Fennel, and Kale

VEGAN Serves 4 Total Time 55 minutes

Why This Recipe Works A cousin of paella, fideos ("noodles" in Spanish) is a one-pan dish of short, thin, toasted noodles (which are also called fideos) simmered in a smoky sauce with additions such as meat or seafood. Fideos are so flavorful that they also work great in our pantry-friendly vegetarian meal. We first toast the noodles, which contributes nuttiness and color. Onion and fresh fennel provide an aromatic base. We then cook diced tomatoes with garlic and smoked paprika, add wine for complexity, and simmer the pasta with chickpeas until tender. A run under the broiler creates a nice crunchy surface. You will need a 12-inch broiler-safe skillet for this recipe. The skillet will be quite full once you add the pasta; we recommend using a straight-sided skillet or sauté pan for easier stirring.

- 8 ounces fideo noodles
- 3 tablespoons extra-virgin olive oil, divided
- 1 onion, chopped fine
- 1 fennel bulb, 1½ teaspoons fronds minced, stalks discarded, bulb halved, cored, and sliced thin
- ½ teaspoon table salt, divided
- 1 (14.5-ounce) can diced tomatoes, drained with juice reserved, chopped fine
- 3 garlic cloves, minced
- 1½ teaspoons smoked paprika
- 2¾ cups vegetable broth
- 1 (15-ounce) can chickpeas, rinsed
- 8 ounces frozen kale or spinach, thawed and squeezed dry
- ½ cup dry white wine or dry vermouth
- ½ teaspoon pepper
- ¼ cup sliced almonds, toasted
- Lemon wedges

1. Toss noodles and 1 tablespoon oil in broiler-safe 12-inch skillet until pasta is evenly coated. Toast pasta over medium- high heat, stirring frequently, until pasta darkens to color of peanut butter and releases nutty aroma, 6 to 10 minutes; transfer to bowl. Wipe out skillet.

2. Add remaining 2 tablespoons oil to skillet and heat over medium-high heat until shimmering. Add onion, sliced fennel, and ¼ teaspoon salt and cook until onion is softened, about 5 minutes. Stir in tomatoes and cook until mixture is thick, dry, and slightly darkened, 4 to 6 minutes.

3. Reduce heat to medium, stir in garlic and paprika, and cook until fragrant, about 30 seconds. Stir in toasted pasta until thoroughly combined. Stir in broth, chickpeas, kale, wine, pepper, reserved tomato juice, and remaining ¼ teaspoon salt. Increase heat to medium-high and bring to simmer. Cook, stirring occasionally, until liquid is slightly thickened and pasta is just tender, 8 to 10 minutes. Meanwhile, adjust oven rack 5 to 6 inches from broiler element and heat broiler.

4. Transfer skillet to oven and broil until surface of pasta is dry with crisped, browned spots, 5 to 7 minutes. Let cool for 5 minutes, then sprinkle with almonds and fennel fronds and serve with lemon wedges.

Pesto Lasagna

Serves 8 to 10 Total Time 1¾ hours, plus 45 minutes cooling

Why This Recipe Works This dinner party–worthy dish combines what we love about fresh basil pesto and rich, comforting lasagna. For a creamy base, we make a béchamel sauce, and then we make a fresh, fragrant pesto with lots of blanched basil. (Blanching helps the basil retain its vibrant color, while using a blender instead of a food processor results in a finer pesto.) We stir the basil mixture into the béchamel and add Parmesan and lemon zest, and then we simply layer this pesto-béchamel sauce between the noodles. A final sprinkle of Parmesan and toasted pine nuts reinforces the flavors within. Use a good-quality, relatively mild extra-virgin olive oil for the best results. Toast the pine nuts in a dry skillet over medium heat, stirring often, until they are lightly browned and fragrant. A 1-pound box of lasagna noodles should yield enough for this recipe, but sometimes it's best to buy two boxes in case some noodles are broken. Depending on the exact sizes of your noodles and baking dish, you may not need to use the half noodles called for in steps 4 and 5. You can also make this recipe in a 13 by 9-inch metal baking pan.

Béchamel

- 7 tablespoons unsalted butter
- 7 tablespoons all-purpose flour
- 5½ cups whole milk
- 1 teaspoon pepper
- ⅛ teaspoon grated nutmeg

Pesto

- 4 ounces fresh basil leaves
- 1 tablespoon table salt, plus salt for blanching basil
- ½ cup extra-virgin olive oil
- ¼ cup pine nuts, toasted
- 2 garlic cloves, peeled
- 2 ounces grated Parmesan cheese (1 cup)
- 2 teaspoons grated lemon zest

Lasagna

- 17 curly-edged lasagna noodles
- Vegetable oil spray
- 1 ounce grated Parmesan cheese (½ cup), plus extra for serving
- ¼ cup pine nuts, toasted

1. **For the béchamel** Melt butter in medium saucepan over medium heat. Whisk in flour and cook, whisking constantly, until mixture is evenly combined but still very pale in color, about 1 minute. Slowly whisk in milk, increase heat to medium-high, and bring to boil. Add pepper and nutmeg and continue to cook, whisking constantly, until mixture is thickened and smooth, about 1 minute longer. Transfer béchamel to large bowl and let cool while making pesto, about 20 minutes.

2. **For the pesto** Bring 4 quarts water to boil in large pot. Add basil leaves and 1 tablespoon salt and cook until basil is just wilted but still bright green, 5 to 10 seconds. Using spider skimmer or slotted spoon, transfer basil directly to salad spinner and spin to remove excess water; do not discard water in pot. (If you don't have a salad spinner, pat basil dry with clean dish towel and squeeze thoroughly to remove excess water.)

3. Transfer basil to blender. Add oil, pine nuts, garlic, and salt and process until smooth, about 1 minute, scraping down sides of blender jar as needed. Transfer pesto to bowl with béchamel. Stir in Parmesan and lemon zest until combined; set aside.

4. **For the lasagna** Adjust oven rack to middle position and heat oven to 375 degrees. Return water in pot to boil. Add noodles and cook, stirring occasionally, until fully tender. Drain noodles and transfer to rimmed baking sheet. Spray noodles lightly with oil spray and gently toss to coat. Cut 2 noodles in half crosswise.

5. Spread 1 heaping cup béchamel mixture evenly over bottom of 13 by 9-inch baking dish. Arrange 3 noodles in even layer over sauce, with short ends of noodles flush with 1 short side of dish, leaving gap at 1 end. Arrange 1 half noodle crosswise to fill gap. Spread 1 cup béchamel mixture evenly over noodles. Repeat layering of noodles and béchamel mixture 3 more times, switching position of half noodle in each layer.

6. Arrange remaining 3 noodles over top (there is no half noodle for top layer). Spread remaining 1 cup béchamel mixture over noodles, then sprinkle evenly with Parmesan and pine nuts. Bake until top of lasagna is spotty brown and edges are bubbling, 40 to 50 minutes. Let lasagna cool for 45 minutes. Slice and serve with extra Parmesan.

To make ahead After sprinkling top of lasagna with Parmesan and pine nuts in step 6, cover dish with greased aluminum foil and refrigerate for up to 24 hours. Bake lasagna, covered, on middle rack of 375-degree oven for 20 minutes. Remove foil and continue to bake, uncovered, until top is spotty brown and edges are bubbling, 40 to 50 minutes longer.

Pesto Lasagna

| *Cheesy Stuffed Shells*

Cheesy Stuffed Shells

Serves 6 to 8 Total Time 2 hours

Why This Recipe Works Making stuffed shells is admittedly a once-in-a-while occurrence, as they can be labor-intensive. This easier version takes time, but you don't have to boil the shells separately—and it's a one-pan meal. For a supercheesy filling, we mix creamy ricotta, shredded fontina, and grated Parmesan cheeses with minced garlic, chopped fresh basil, and dried oregano. A little cornstarch keeps the ricotta from becoming grainy once it is baked. We also stir in two eggs to make the filling pipeable and to keep it from oozing out of the shells during baking. Covering the filled shells with a thin tomato sauce allows the dried pasta to cook through properly during baking, absorbing liquid while still leaving behind a full-bodied sauce. Shred the fontina on the large holes of a box grater. We developed this recipe using Barilla Jumbo Shells and were able to easily find at least 24 open shells in each 1-pound box we used. You will need a 12-inch ovensafe skillet with a tight-fitting lid for this recipe.

- 2 tablespoons extra-virgin olive oil
- 1 onion, chopped
- ¾ teaspoon table salt, divided
- 6 garlic cloves, minced, divided
- ¼ teaspoon red pepper flakes
- 1 (28-ounce) can tomato puree
- 2 cups water
- 1 teaspoon sugar
- ½ teaspoon pepper
- 10 ounces (1¼ cups) whole-milk ricotta cheese
- 8 ounces fontina cheese, shredded (2 cups), divided
- 2 ounces Parmesan cheese, grated (1 cup)
- 2 large eggs
- ¼ cup chopped fresh basil, divided
- 4 teaspoons cornstarch
- 1 teaspoon dried oregano
- 24 jumbo pasta shells

1. Adjust oven rack to middle position and heat oven to 400 degrees. Heat oil in 12-inch ovensafe skillet over medium heat until shimmering. Add onion and ½ teaspoon salt and cook until onion is softened and lightly browned, 5 to 7 minutes. Stir in two-thirds of garlic and pepper flakes and cook until fragrant, about 30 seconds. Stir in tomato puree, water, sugar, and pepper and bring to simmer. Reduce heat to medium-low and cook until flavors have melded, about 5 minutes. Off heat, measure out and reserve 2 cups sauce; leave remaining sauce in skillet.

2. Stir ricotta, 1 cup fontina, Parmesan, eggs, 3 tablespoons basil, cornstarch, oregano, remaining ¼ teaspoon salt, and remaining garlic in bowl until thoroughly combined. Transfer filling to pastry bag or large zipper-lock bag (if using zipper-lock bag, cut 1 inch off 1 corner of bag). Place shells open side up on counter. Pipe filling into shells until each is about three-quarters full. Divide remaining filling evenly among shells.

3. Arrange shells open side up in skillet and spoon reserved sauce evenly over tops. Cover and bake until shells are tender, about 45 minutes.

4. Using pot holders, remove skillet from oven. Being careful of hot skillet handle, sprinkle shells with remaining 1 cup fontina. Return skillet to oven and bake, uncovered, until fontina is spotty brown, about 15 minutes. Let shells cool for 10 minutes. Sprinkle with remaining 1 tablespoon basil before serving.

Unstuffed Shells with Butternut Squash and Leeks

Serves 4 Total Time 1¼ hours

Why This Recipe Works For times when the appeal of cheesy jumbo stuffed shells is calling to you but the thought of making them seems like too much of an ordeal, turn to this easier unstuffed version, in which the shells cook directly in the sauce and the "filling" gets dolloped on top. Cooking the squash and leeks briefly before adding the pasta and liquid deepens the vegetables' flavors and ensures that the pasta and squash finish cooking at the same time. Instead of stuffing the shells with cheese, we sprinkle Parmesan on top and dollop a lemony ricotta mixture over everything. We then slide the skillet into the oven to brown and melt the cheesy toppings. You can substitute large or medium shells, ziti, farfalle, campanelle, or orecchiette for the jumbo shells. The skillet will be very full when you add the shells in step 3 (stir gently to start) but will become more manageable as the liquid evaporates and the shells become more malleable. You will need a 12-inch ovensafe nonstick skillet for this recipe.

- 8 ounces (1 cup) whole-milk ricotta cheese
- 2 ounces Parmesan cheese, grated (1 cup), divided
- 1 teaspoon grated lemon zest
- ¾ teaspoon table salt, divided
- ¼ teaspoon pepper
- 1 tablespoon extra-virgin olive oil
- 1½ pounds butternut squash, peeled, seeded, and cut into ½-inch pieces (5 cups)
- 1 pound leeks, white and light green parts only, halved lengthwise, sliced thin, and washed thoroughly
- 2 garlic cloves, minced
- Pinch cayenne pepper
- ¼ cup dry white wine
- 4 cups water
- 1 cup heavy cream
- 12 ounces jumbo pasta shells
- 2 tablespoons chopped fresh basil

1. Adjust oven rack to middle position and heat oven to 375 degrees. Combine ricotta, ½ cup Parmesan, lemon zest, ¼ teaspoon salt, and pepper in bowl; cover and refrigerate until needed.

2. Heat oil in 12-inch ovensafe nonstick skillet over medium heat until shimmering. Add squash, leeks, and remaining ½ teaspoon salt and cook until leeks are softened, about 5 minutes. Stir in garlic and cayenne and cook until fragrant, about 30 seconds. Stir in wine and cook until almost completely evaporated, about 1 minute.

3. Stir in water and cream, then add pasta and bring to vigorous simmer. Reduce heat to medium, cover, and cook, stirring gently and often, until pasta is tender and liquid has thickened, about 15 minutes.

4. Season with salt and pepper to taste. Sprinkle remaining ½ cup Parmesan over top, then dollop evenly with ricotta mixture. Transfer skillet to oven and bake until Parmesan is melted and spotty brown, about 5 minutes. Let cool for 10 minutes, then sprinkle with basil and serve.

Cheese Ravioli with Pumpkin Cream Sauce

FAST Serves 4 Total Time 45 minutes

Why This Recipe Works Packaged ravioli never had it so good. This showstopper of a dish looks like something you'd order in a restaurant, but it's easily made at home with store-bought cheese ravioli. The ravioli is cloaked with a creamy pumpkin sauce and then topped with browned butter infused with hazelnuts and crispy sage leaves for a dish that captures the essence of autumn. The hazelnuts toast right in the butter as the butter browns, making for a deeply flavored finishing drizzle. And the crispy sage leaves are an elegant garnish. Make sure to purchase unsweetened pumpkin puree, which contains no sweeteners or added spices.

- 1½ pounds fresh cheese ravioli
- ⅛ teaspoon plus ½ teaspoon table salt, divided, plus salt for cooking pasta
- 5 tablespoons unsalted butter, divided
- ¼ cup blanched hazelnuts, chopped
- 12 fresh sage leaves
- 1 teaspoon sherry vinegar
- ¼ cup finely chopped shallot
- ¼ teaspoon ground nutmeg
- 1 cup heavy cream
- ½ cup canned unsweetened pumpkin puree
- 1 ounce Parmesan cheese, grated (½ cup)

1. Bring 4 quarts water to boil in large pot. Add pasta and 1 tablespoon salt and cook, stirring often, until al dente. Reserve ½ cup cooking water, then drain pasta.

2. Meanwhile, melt 4 tablespoons butter in 12-inch nonstick skillet over medium heat. Add hazelnuts and sage and cook, swirling skillet constantly, until sage is crispy, about 3 minutes. Using tongs, transfer sage to paper towel–lined plate; continue to cook butter and hazelnuts until both are browned and fragrant, about 1 minute longer. Transfer to heatproof bowl and stir in vinegar and ⅛ teaspoon salt.

3. Melt remaining 1 tablespoon butter in now-empty skillet over medium heat. Add shallot, nutmeg, and remaining ½ teaspoon salt and cook, stirring occasionally, until shallot is softened, about 3 minutes. Stir in cream and pumpkin and bring to simmer. Cook until thickened, about 5 minutes. Off heat, stir in Parmesan. Add pasta and toss to combine. Adjust consistency with reserved cooking water as needed. Serve, topped with sage and hazelnut butter.

Three-Cheese Ravioli with Browned Butter–Pine Nut Sauce

Serves 4 to 6 (makes 36 ravioli)   Total Time 2¼ hours, plus 1 hour resting

Why This Recipe Works To make homemade ravioli approachable, we developed a three-ingredient pasta dough that is quick to make in a food processor and easy to roll thin by hand. Our method for portioning the filling, cutting the dough into rectangles, and folding the dough over the filling makes it easy to ensure that all air bubbles are removed from the ravioli so they won't burst open during cooking. If using King Arthur All-Purpose Flour, which is higher in protein, increase the number of egg yolks to seven. To ensure proper dough texture, use large eggs and weigh the flour. The longer the dough rests in step 2, the easier it will be to roll out. When rolling, don't add too much flour; it can cause excessive snapback. You may use a pasta machine if you like. If you don't have a pot that holds 6 quarts or more, cook the ravioli in two batches; toss the first batch with some sauce in a serving bowl, cover it with aluminum foil, and keep it warm in a 200-degree oven while the second batch cooks.

Pasta Dough

- 2 cups (10 ounces) all-purpose flour, plus extra as needed
- 2 large eggs plus 6 large yolks
- 2 tablespoons extra-virgin olive oil

Filling

- 8 ounces (1 cup) whole-milk ricotta
- 4 ounces Italian fontina cheese, cut into ¼-inch pieces (1 cup)
- 2 ounces Parmesan cheese, grated (1 cup), plus extra for serving
- 1 large egg
- ½ teaspoon pepper
- ¼ teaspoon table salt
- ⅛ teaspoon ground nutmeg

Ravioli

- 1 large egg white, lightly beaten
- Table salt for cooking

Sauce

- 8 tablespoons unsalted butter
- ½ cup pine nuts, toasted
- 2 tablespoons chopped fresh parsley
- ½ teaspoon table salt

top | *Unstuffed Shells with Butternut Squash and Leeks*
bottom | *Cheese Ravioli with Pumpkin Cream Sauce*

1. For the pasta dough Process flour, eggs and yolks, and oil in food processor until mixture forms cohesive dough that feels soft and is barely tacky to touch, about 45 seconds. (Pinch dough between your fingers; if any dough sticks to your fingers, add up to ¼ cup extra flour, 1 tablespoon at a time, until barely tacky. Process until flour is fully incorporated after each addition, 10 to 15 seconds, before retesting. If dough doesn't become cohesive, add up to 1 tablespoon water, 1 teaspoon at a time, until it just comes together; process 30 seconds longer.)

2. Turn out dough onto dry counter and knead until smooth, 1 to 2 minutes. Shape dough into 6-inch-long cylinder. Wrap in plastic wrap and let rest at room temperature for at least 1 hour or up to 4 hours. Wipe processor bowl clean.

3. For the filling Process ricotta, fontina, Parmesan, egg, pepper, salt, and nutmeg in processor until smooth paste forms, 25 to 30 seconds, scraping down sides of bowl as needed. Transfer filling to medium bowl, cover with plastic, and refrigerate until needed.

4. For the ravioli Line rimmed baking sheet with parchment paper. Cut dough cylinder crosswise into 6 equal pieces. Working with 1 piece of dough at a time (rewrap remaining dough), dust both sides with flour, place cut side down on counter, and press into 3-inch square. Using heavy rolling pin, roll into 6-inch square. Dust both sides of dough lightly with flour.

5. Starting at center of square, roll dough away from you in single motion. Return rolling pin to center of dough and roll toward you in single motion. Repeat rolling steps until dough sticks to counter and measures roughly 12 inches long. Lightly dust both sides of dough with flour and continue to roll until dough measures roughly 20 inches long and 6 inches wide, frequently lifting dough to release it from counter. (You should be able to easily see outline of your fingers through dough.) If dough firmly sticks to counter and wrinkles when rolled out, carefully lift dough and dust counter lightly with flour. Transfer dough sheet to prepared baking sheet and cover with plastic. Repeat rolling process with remaining 5 dough pieces and transfer to prepared sheet (2 dough sheets per layer; place parchment between layers). Keep dough covered with plastic.

6. Line second baking sheet with parchment. Lay 1 dough sheet on clean counter with long side parallel to counter edge (keep others covered). Trim ends of dough with sharp knife so that corners are square and dough is 18 inches long. Brush bottom half of dough with egg white. Starting 1½ inches from left edge of dough and 1 inch from bottom, deposit 1 tablespoon filling. Repeat placing 1-tablespoon mounds of filling, spaced 1½ inches apart, 1 inch from bottom edge of dough. You should be able to fit 6 mounds of filling on 1 dough sheet.

7. Cut dough sheet at center points between mounds of filling, separating it into 6 equal pieces. Working with 1 piece at a time, lift top edge of dough over filling and extend it so that it lines up with bottom edge. Keeping top edge of dough suspended over filling with your thumbs, use your fingers to press dough layers together, working around each mound of filling from back to front and pressing out as much air as possible before sealing completely.

8. Once all edges are sealed, use sharp knife or fluted pastry wheel to cut excess dough from around filling, leaving ¼- to ½-inch border around each mound (it's not necessary to cut folded edge of ravioli, but you may do so, if desired). (Dough scraps can be frozen and added to soup.) Transfer ravioli to prepared baking sheet. Refrigerate until ready to cook. Repeat shaping process with remaining dough and remaining filling. (Uncooked ravioli can be frozen in single layer on parchment paper–lined rimmed baking sheet. Transfer ravioli to zipper-lock bag and freeze for up to 1 month. Cook from frozen with no change to cooking time.)

9. Bring 6 quarts water to boil in large pot. Add ravioli and 1 tablespoon salt. Cook, maintaining gentle boil, until ravioli are just tender, about 13 minutes. (To test, pull 1 ravioli from pot, trim off corner without cutting into filling, and taste. Return ravioli to pot if not yet tender.) Drain well.

10. For the sauce While ravioli cook, melt butter in 10-inch skillet over medium-high heat. Continue to cook, swirling skillet constantly, until butter is dark golden brown and has nutty aroma, 1 to 3 minutes longer. Off heat, add pine nuts, parsley, and salt. Using spider skimmer or slotted spoon, transfer ravioli to warmed bowls or plates; top with sauce. Serve immediately, passing extra Parmesan separately.

Filling Ravioli

1. Starting 1½ inches from left edge of dough and 1 inch from bottom, evenly space six 1-tablespoon mounds of filling. Cut sheet at center points between mounds.

2. Lift top edge of dough over filling to line up with bottom edge. Holding top edge suspended with your thumbs, press layers together with your fingers.

3. Working around filling from back to front, press out air before sealing closed.

4. Using sharp knife or pastry wheel, cut away excess dough, leaving ¼- to ½-inch border.

Three-Cheese Ravioli with Browned Butter–Pine Nut Sauce

top | *Tortellini Salad with Broccoli, Cannellini Beans, and Olive–Banana Pepper Dressing*

bottom | *Samosa Gnocchi Chaat*

Tortellini Salad with Broccoli, Cannellini Beans, and Olive–Banana Pepper Dressing

FAST Serves 4 to 6 Total Time 45 minutes

Why This Recipe Works For a pasta salad that's hearty enough for a main course, we swap some of the pasta for creamy white beans and crunchy blanched broccoli. The ring shape of the tortellini nicely captures the olive oil–based vinaigrette, which we thicken with pureed olives, banana peppers, and garlic. Cooking the pasta until it is slightly past al dente means that as it cools and firms up, it will develop just the right tender texture. Juicy cherry tomatoes supply pops of cheery color. A quick, thin Parmesan and black pepper crisp made in the microwave and crumbled over the top completes this pasta salad in style. Sliced pickled cherry peppers or pepperoncini can be substituted for the banana peppers. We like mild, meaty Castelvetrano olives for this recipe, but any pitted green olives will work. If making this salad ahead, dress the salad and garnish it with the cheese crisps right before serving.

- 12 ounces frozen cheese tortellini
- ¾ teaspoon table salt, plus salt for cooking pasta
- 1 pound broccoli crowns, stems sliced ¼ inch thick, florets cut into bite-size pieces
- 1 (15-ounce) can cannellini beans, drained
- 1 ounce Parmesan cheese, grated (½ cup)
- 2 tablespoons panko bread crumbs
- ¼ teaspoon pepper
- ½ cup jarred sliced banana peppers, divided, plus ¼ cup brine
- ½ cup pitted Castelvetrano olives, halved, divided
- 2 garlic cloves, chopped
- ½ cup extra-virgin olive oil
- 10 ounces multicolor cherry tomatoes, halved

1. Line rimmed baking sheet with dish towel. Bring 2 quarts water to boil in large saucepan. Add pasta and 1½ teaspoons salt and cook until tender, about 5 minutes. Add broccoli and beans to saucepan with pasta and cook until broccoli is crisp-tender, 1 to 2 minutes. Drain well and transfer to prepared sheet.

2. Combine Parmesan, panko, and pepper in small bowl and toss until well mixed. Spray large plate lightly with vegetable oil spray. Transfer Parmesan mixture to plate and spread into 8-inch round. Microwave for 2 minutes. Continue to microwave in 30-second increments until mixture is golden brown. Run thin metal spatula under cheese crisp and turn over (it's OK if cheese breaks). Microwave for 30 seconds. Set aside.

3. Combine ¼ cup banana peppers, brine, ¼ cup olives, garlic, and salt in blender and process until coarse paste forms, about 30 seconds. With blender running, drizzle in oil and continue to process until dressing is emulsified and smooth, about 1 minute.

4. Combine pasta, broccoli, beans, tomatoes, remaining ¼ cup banana peppers, and remaining ¼ cup olives in large bowl. Add dressing and toss to coat. Transfer to serving bowl. Crumble cheese crisp over salad and serve.

Crispy Gnocchi with Shredded Brussels Sprouts and Gorgonzola

FAST Serves 4 Total Time 40 minutes

Why This Recipe Works This recipe makes grocery store gnocchi feel like something you might be served in a restaurant. In a hot skillet with a glug of oil, they transform into crispy nuggets with lacy edges and chewy interiors. We build a dry "sauce" in the pan by softening sweet red onions and sautéing brussels sprouts. Off heat, we add an abundant amount of creamy Gorgonzola and then white wine vinegar to temper its richness. A little sage pairs beautifully with the shaved brussels sprouts and cheese. For a crowning touch, we drizzle the final dish with honey and sprinkle on toasted walnuts and more cheese. The partially cooked, vacuum-packed gnocchi found in the pasta aisle work best here. A food processor's slicing blade can be used to slice the brussels sprouts; do not halve them before processing.

- 3 tablespoons extra-virgin olive oil, divided
- 1 pound shelf-stable gnocchi
- 1 red onion, halved and sliced thin
- 1 pound brussels sprouts, trimmed, halved, and sliced thin
- ½ teaspoon table salt
- 3 ounces Gorgonzola cheese, crumbled (¾ cup), divided
- 1 tablespoon white wine vinegar
- 2 teaspoons minced fresh sage
- 1 tablespoon honey, plus extra for serving
- 3 tablespoons chopped toasted walnuts

1. Heat 2 tablespoons oil in 12-inch nonstick skillet over medium-high heat until shimmering. Add gnocchi, separating pieces with wooden spoon. Cook, without moving gnocchi, until well browned on first side, 5 to 7 minutes. Stir gnocchi and continue to cook until heated through, about 2 minutes; transfer to bowl.

2. Heat remaining 1 tablespoon oil in now-empty skillet over medium-high heat until shimmering. Add onion and cook until starting to soften, about 3 minutes. Stir in brussels sprouts and salt and spread into even layer. Cook, stirring occasionally, until sprouts are spotty brown and just tender, 5 to 7 minutes.

3. Off heat, stir in gnocchi, ½ cup Gorgonzola, vinegar, and sage until Gorgonzola is melted and coats gnocchi. Season with salt and pepper to taste. Drizzle with honey and sprinkle with walnuts and remaining ¼ cup Gorgonzola. Serve, passing extra honey for drizzling.

Samosa Gnocchi Chaat

FAST Serves 4 Total Time 45 minutes

Why This Recipe Works Pantry-friendly gnocchi are a blank slate for whatever flavors are thrown at them; crisped in a skillet, they're a world apart from boiled versions. For this colorful and flavorful dinner, we take inspiration from Indian samosas: The crispy gnocchi capture the texture of the fried dough wrapper, while a blend of spices, garlic, and ginger paired with peas and cilantro evoke the flavors of the traditional pea and potato filling. To make the dish heartier, we add canned chickpeas and baby spinach. For a simple yet stunning presentation, we take further inspiration from Indian chaat, a family of street-food snacks characterized by a glorious tumble of diverse yet balanced flavors, textures, and colors, and serve the gnocchi with toppings. Be sure to use shelf-stable gnocchi in this recipe. A rasp grater makes quick work of turning the garlic into a paste. In a pinch, you can use yellow mustard seeds in place of the brown mustard seeds or simply omit them. Store-bought tamarind, coriander, and/or mango chutneys add bright finishing flavor; they're a great addition and we recommend using one or a combination of the three in this dish.

- 1 cup plain yogurt
- ⅛ teaspoon plus ½ teaspoon table salt, divided
- 1 pound shelf-stable gnocchi
- 6 tablespoons vegetable oil
- 2 teaspoons cumin seeds
- 1 teaspoon coriander seeds
- 1 teaspoon brown mustard seeds
- ½ teaspoon garam masala
- ¼ teaspoon ground turmeric
- ⅛ teaspoon cayenne pepper
- 1 red onion, chopped fine, divided
- 2 garlic cloves, minced to paste
- 2 teaspoons grated fresh ginger
- 1 (15-ounce) can chickpeas, rinsed
- 3 ounces (3 cups) baby spinach
- 1 cup frozen peas
- ½ cup chopped fresh cilantro, divided
- 2 teaspoons lemon juice
- Tamarind, coriander, and/or mango chutney

1. Whisk yogurt and ⅛ teaspoon salt together in bowl; set aside until ready to serve. Separate gnocchi and arrange in single layer in 12-inch nonstick skillet. Drizzle oil evenly over gnocchi. Place skillet over medium-high heat and cook, without moving gnocchi, until well browned on 1 side, 5 to 8 minutes.

2. Stir gnocchi and continue to cook until second side of most pieces is lightly crisp, 1 to 2 minutes longer. Using slotted spoon, transfer gnocchi to large plate, leaving oil in skillet.

3. Reduce heat to medium. Add cumin seeds, coriander seeds, mustard seeds, garam masala, turmeric, and cayenne to skillet and cook until fragrant, about 30 seconds. Add three-quarters of red onion and remaining ½ teaspoon salt and cook until onion softens, 3 to 5 minutes. Stir in garlic and ginger and cook until fragrant, about 30 seconds.

4. Stir in chickpeas, spinach, and peas and cook until chickpeas and peas are warmed through, about 3 minutes. Stir in reserved gnocchi, ¼ cup cilantro, and lemon juice.

5. Spread half of reserved yogurt on serving platter, then mound gnocchi mixture on top. Sprinkle with remaining onion and remaining ¼ cup cilantro. Serve immediately, passing remaining yogurt separately.

Potato Gnocchi with Browned Butter and Sage Sauce

Serves 4 Total Time 1¼ hours

Why This Recipe Works Impossibly light and ethereal from-scratch gnocchi with unmistakable potato flavor need only the simplest of sauces to make them shine. Baking russet potatoes (streamlined by parcooking them in the microwave) produces intensely flavored spuds—an excellent start to our gnocchi base. To avoid lumps, which can cause gnocchi to break apart during cooking, we use a ricer for a smooth, supple mash. While many recipes offer a range of flour amounts, this ups the chances of overworking the dough and producing leaden gnocchi, so instead we call for an exact amount based on the ratio of potato to flour so that the gnocchi dough is mixed as little as possible. An egg, while not traditional, tenderizes the gnocchi further, delivering delicate, pillowlike dumplings. For the most accurate measurements, weigh the potatoes and flour. After processing, you may have more than the 3 cups (1 pound) of potatoes required. Reserve any extra for another use.

Gnocchi

- 2 pounds russet potatoes
- 1 large egg, lightly beaten
- ¾ cup plus 1 tablespoon (4 ounces) all-purpose flour
- 1 teaspoon table salt, plus salt for cooking gnocchi

Sauce

- 4 tablespoons unsalted butter, cut into 4 pieces
- 1 small shallot, minced
- 1 teaspoon minced fresh sage
- 1½ teaspoons lemon juice
- ¼ teaspoon table salt

1. **For the gnocchi** Adjust oven rack to middle position and heat oven to 450 degrees. Poke each potato 8 times with paring knife. Microwave potatoes until slightly softened at ends, about 10 minutes, flipping potatoes halfway through cooking. Transfer potatoes directly to oven rack and bake until skewer glides easily through flesh and potatoes yield to gentle pressure, 18 to 20 minutes.

2. Holding potatoes with dish towel, peel with paring knife. Process potatoes through ricer or food mill onto rimmed baking sheet. Gently spread potatoes into even layer and let cool for 5 minutes.

3. Transfer 3 cups (1 pound) warm potatoes to bowl. Using fork, gently stir in egg until just combined. Sprinkle flour and salt over top and gently combine using fork until no pockets of dry flour remain. Press mixture into rough ball, transfer to lightly floured counter, and gently knead until smooth but slightly sticky, about 1 minute, lightly dusting counter with flour as needed to prevent sticking.

4. Line 2 rimmed baking sheets with parchment paper and dust liberally with flour. Cut dough into 8 pieces. Lightly dust counter with flour. Gently roll 1 piece of dough into ½-inch-thick rope, dusting with flour to prevent sticking. Cut rope into ¾-inch lengths.

5. Holding fork with tines upside down in 1 hand, press each dough piece cut side down against tines with thumb of other hand to create indentation. Roll dough down tines to form ridges on sides. If dough sticks, dust thumb or fork with flour. Transfer formed gnocchi to prepared sheets and repeat with remaining dough.

6. For the sauce Melt butter in 12-inch skillet over medium-high heat, swirling pan occasionally, until butter is browned and releases nutty aroma, about 1½ minutes. Off heat, add shallot and sage, stirring until shallot is fragrant, about 1 minute. Stir in lemon juice and salt and cover to keep warm.

7. Bring 4 quarts water to boil in large pot. Add 1 tablespoon salt. Using parchment paper as sling, add half of gnocchi and cook until firm and just cooked through, about 1½ minutes (gnocchi should float to surface after about 1 minute). Remove gnocchi with slotted spoon, transfer to skillet with sauce, and cover to keep warm. Repeat with remaining gnocchi and transfer to skillet. Gently toss gnocchi with sauce to combine and serve.

Creating Gnocchi Ridges

To help gnocchi hold on to sauce, hold fork tines upside down and press each dough piece (cut side down) against tines to make indentation. Roll gnocchi down tines to create ridges on sides.

Potato Gnocchi with Browned Butter and Sage Sauce

Gnocchi à la Parisienne with Arugula, Tomatoes, and Olives

Serves 4 Total Time 1¼ hours, plus 30 minutes resting

Why This Recipe Works These French gnocchi are made with pate a choux, the eggy pastry dough also used to make profiteroles and beignets. The dough comes together on the stovetop and is then transferred to a food processor to incorporate eggs. We pipe and cut the dough directly into simmering water to puff up and then sear the gnocchi in a hot skillet to brown and puff them further to melt-in-your-mouth perfection. Tossing the gnocchi with sweet tomatoes, briny olives, and peppery arugula dressed with lemon results in a dish as colorful as it is flavorful. Emmentaler can be used in place of the Gruyère. You'll need a pastry bag and a ½-inch round tip. Or substitute a large zipper-lock bag with one corner snipped off to create a ½-inch opening.

- 3 large eggs
- 9 tablespoons unsalted butter, divided
- 1 teaspoon table salt, divided
- ¾ cup (3¾ ounces) all-purpose flour
- 2 ounces Gruyère cheese, shredded (½ cup)
- ⅛ teaspoon pepper
- 20 cherry tomatoes, quartered
- 20 pitted kalamata olives, quartered
- 2 teaspoons minced fresh thyme
- 2 teaspoons lemon juice
- 1½ ounces (1½ cups) baby arugula
- 1 tablespoon minced fresh chives
- Grated Parmesan cheese

1. Fit pastry bag with ½-inch round tip. Beat eggs in 2-cup liquid measuring cup.

2. Bring ¾ cup water, 4 tablespoons butter, and ¾ teaspoon salt to boil in small saucepan over medium heat, stirring occasionally. As soon as mixture boils, remove saucepan from heat and stir in flour until incorporated. Return saucepan to low heat and cook, stirring constantly, using smearing motion, until mixture looks like shiny, wet sand, about 2 minutes.

3. Immediately transfer mixture to food processor. Add Gruyère and pepper and process, with feed tube open, for 10 seconds. With processor running, gradually add eggs in steady stream. When all eggs have been added, scrape down sides of bowl with silicone spatula. Continue to process until smooth, thick, sticky paste forms, about 30 seconds longer.

4. Fill prepared pastry bag with warm mixture. Twist top of bag to close and let rest at room temperature for at least 30 minutes or up to 1 hour.

5. Lightly grease rimmed baking sheet. Bring 4 quarts water to boil in large Dutch oven. Reduce heat to maintain gentle simmer. Using 1 hand, hold pastry bag at 45-degree angle so tip is about 3 inches away from surface of water and squeeze bag to force dough out of tip. Using paring knife, cut off ¾-inch lengths and let them fall into water. Continue to pipe until 20 to 30 gnocchi are in pot. Simmer until gnocchi float and are slightly firm, about 2 minutes. Using spider skimmer or slotted spoon, transfer gnocchi to prepared sheet. Repeat until all dough is cooked (4 to 6 batches). (If not proceeding immediately, allow gnocchi to cool completely. Transfer to airtight container and refrigerate for up to 3 days. Alternatively, freeze on sheet until solid, then transfer to zipper-lock bag and freeze for up to 2 months; sauté from frozen, adding 1 to 2 minutes to sautéing time.)

6. Melt 3 tablespoons butter in 12-inch nonstick skillet over medium heat. Add all gnocchi and shake skillet gently until gnocchi fall into single layer. Cook, tossing every 2 minutes, until gnocchi are golden brown and slightly puffed, about 6 minutes. Return cooked gnocchi to sheet.

7. Melt remaining 2 tablespoons butter in now-empty skillet over medium heat. Add tomatoes, olives, thyme, and remaining ¼ teaspoon salt and cook, tossing occasionally, until tomatoes start to soften, about 2 minutes. Add lemon juice and gnocchi and gently stir until gnocchi are evenly glazed. Off heat, add arugula and stir until it just starts to wilt, about 15 seconds. Top with chives and serve immediately, passing Parmesan separately.

Variation

Gnocchi à la Parisienne with Browned Butter

Follow recipe through step 6. Instead of making sauce in step 7, melt 4 tablespoons butter in now-empty skillet over medium-high heat. Continue to cook, swirling skillet constantly, until butter is dark golden brown and has nutty aroma, 1 to 3 minutes longer. Stir in 2 teaspoons minced fresh sage and pinch salt. Add gnocchi and gently stir until gnocchi are evenly coated.

Gnocchi à la Parisienne with Arugula, Tomatoes, and Olives

top | *Spinach and Ricotta Gnudi with Tomato-Butter Sauce*
bottom | *Ramen with Shiitakes and Soft Eggs*

Spinach and Ricotta Gnudi with Tomato-Butter Sauce

Serves 4 Total Time 1¼ hours

Why This Recipe Works Pillowy, verdant, milky-rich gnudi are Italian dumplings cobbled together from ricotta and greens (often spinach or chard), delicately seasoned, and bound with egg and flour and/or bread crumbs. The trick to making this comforting dish well is water management: Both the cheese and the greens are loaded with moisture, much of which needs to be either removed or bound up—otherwise, the dough can be too difficult to handle or require so much binder that the dumplings are leaden instead of light. Drying the ricotta on a paper towel–lined rimmed baking sheet increases its surface area, causing it to drain quickly and effectively. Frozen spinach readily gives up its water when it thaws and is easily squeezed dry. Protein-rich egg whites, flour, and panko bread crumbs bind the mixture into a tender dough that's just cohesive enough to scoop and roll into rounds and gently poach. Taking inspiration from two traditional sauces (bright tomato sugo and rich browned butter), we toast garlic in browning butter and add halved fresh cherry tomatoes, which collapse and spill their bright juices into the rich backdrop. Squeezing the spinach should remove ½ to ⅔ cup of liquid; you should have ⅔ cup of finely chopped spinach.

Gnudi

- 12 ounces (1½ cups) whole-milk ricotta cheese
- ½ cup all-purpose flour
- 1 ounce Parmesan cheese, grated (½ cup), plus extra for garnishing
- 1 tablespoon panko bread crumbs
- ¾ teaspoon table salt, plus salt for cooking gnudi
- ½ teaspoon pepper
- ¼ teaspoon grated lemon zest
- 10 ounces frozen whole-leaf spinach, thawed and squeezed dry
- 2 large egg whites, lightly beaten

Sauce

- 4 tablespoons unsalted butter
- 3 garlic cloves, sliced thin
- 12 ounces cherry or grape tomatoes, halved
- 2 teaspoons cider vinegar
- ¼ teaspoon table salt
- ¼ teaspoon pepper
- 2 tablespoons shredded fresh basil

1. For the gnudi Line rimmed baking sheet with double layer of paper towels. Spread ricotta in even layer over towels; set aside and let sit for 10 minutes. Place flour, Parmesan, panko, salt, pepper, and lemon zest in large bowl and stir to combine. Process spinach in food processor until finely chopped, about 30 seconds, scraping down sides of bowl as needed. Transfer spinach to bowl with flour mixture. Grasp paper towels and fold ricotta in half; peel back towels. Rotate sheet 90 degrees and repeat folding and peeling 2 more times to consolidate ricotta into smaller mass. Using paper towels as sling, transfer ricotta to bowl with spinach mixture. Discard paper towels but do not wash sheet. Add egg whites to bowl and mix gently until well combined.

2. Transfer heaping teaspoons of dough to now-empty sheet (you should have 45 to 50 portions). Using your dry hands, gently roll each portion into 1-inch ball.

3. For the sauce Melt butter in small saucepan over medium heat. Add garlic and cook, swirling saucepan occasionally, until butter is very foamy and garlic is pale golden brown, 2 to 3 minutes. Off heat, add tomatoes and vinegar; cover and set aside.

4. Bring 1 quart water to boil in Dutch oven. Add 1½ teaspoons salt. Using spider skimmer or slotted spoon, transfer all gnudi to water. Return water to gentle simmer. Cook, adjusting heat to maintain gentle simmer, for 5 minutes, starting timer once water has returned to simmer (to confirm doneness, cut 1 dumpling in half; center should be firm).

5. While gnudi simmer, add salt and pepper to sauce and cook over medium-high heat, stirring occasionally, until tomatoes are warmed through and slightly softened, about 2 minutes. Divide sauce evenly into 4 individual serving bowls. Using spider skimmer or slotted spoon, remove gnudi from pot, drain well, and transfer to bowls with sauce. Garnish with basil and extra Parmesan. Serve immediately.

Ramen with Shiitakes and Soft Eggs

FAST Serves 4 Total Time 45 minutes

Why This Recipe Works This deeply flavored soup, while it can't approach the long-simmered complexity of restaurant ramen, is miles above any supermarket variety. Start with good-quality store-bought broth, adding miso and shiitake mushrooms for umami and ginger and scallions for zesty freshness. Letting the yolks from soft-cooked eggs seep into the broth adds rich body. Crispy shallots will up the flavor ante even more. If you can't find fresh ramen noodles, you can substitute 9 ounces of dried ramen noodles. The finished broth in step 3 will taste overseasoned; adding the noodles will temper its flavor.

Soft Eggs

4 large eggs

Ramen

3 tablespoons toasted sesame oil
8 ounces shiitake mushrooms, stemmed and sliced thin
6 scallions, white parts minced, green parts sliced thin on bias
1 (2-inch) piece ginger, peeled and cut into matchsticks
2 tablespoons white miso
8 cups vegetable broth
1 pound fresh ramen noodles
2 ounces (2 cups) baby spinach
1 recipe Microwave-Fried Shallots (page 89) (optional)
Chili-garlic sauce

1. For the eggs Bring 1 inch water to rolling boil in medium or large saucepan over high heat. Place eggs in steamer basket and transfer basket to saucepan. Cover, reduce heat to medium-high, and cook eggs for 6½ minutes.

2. When eggs are almost finished cooking, combine 2 cups ice cubes and 2 cups cold water in bowl. Using tongs or slotted spoon, transfer eggs to ice bath and let sit until just cool enough to handle, about 30 seconds. (Soft-cooked eggs can be refrigerated in their shells for up to 3 days.) Peel eggs and cut in half before adding to soup.

3. For the ramen Heat oil in Dutch oven over medium-high heat until just smoking. Add mushrooms and cook until softened and lightly browned, about 5 minutes. Stir in scallion whites, ginger, and miso and cook until fragrant, about 30 seconds. Whisk in broth, bring to simmer, and cook until flavors meld, about 15 minutes.

4. Meanwhile, bring 4 quarts water to boil in large pot. Add noodles and cook until noodles are tender but still chewy. Drain noodles and distribute evenly into individual serving bowls.

5. Off heat, stir spinach into broth and let sit until wilted, about 2 minutes. Season with salt to taste. Ladle hot broth into each bowl and top with fried shallots, if using, and halved soft-cooked eggs. Serve immediately, topped with scallion greens, passing chili-garlic sauce separately.

Shiitake and Bok Choy Lo Mein

FAST Serves 4 Total Time 30 minutes

Why This Recipe Works The lightly grassy flavor and delicate crunch of bok choy complements the earthiness of shiitake mushrooms, which is enhanced by cooking the mushrooms until they're browned. Ginger, garlic, and hoisin and soy sauces add loads of flavor. Fresh Chinese egg noodles have an irresistible bouncy chewiness, and cooking the parboiled noodles in the skillet without moving them lets them develop a light, flavorful char. Look for the noodles in Asian grocery stores or in the produce section of large supermarkets. For a spicy kick, serve with additional chili-garlic sauce.

- 12 ounces fresh Chinese egg noodles
- 2 tablespoons vegetable oil, divided
- 8 ounces shiitake mushrooms, stemmed, halved if small or quartered if large
- 4 heads baby bok choy (4 ounces each), halved and cut into 1-inch pieces
- 1 tablespoon grated fresh ginger
- 3 garlic cloves, minced
- 3 tablespoons hoisin sauce
- 2 tablespoons soy sauce
- 1 tablespoon toasted sesame oil
- 1 teaspoon chili-garlic sauce, plus extra for serving (optional)

1. Bring 4 quarts water to boil in large pot. Add noodles and cook until tender, about 3 minutes. Drain noodles, rinse under cold running water, and drain again; set aside.

2. Heat 1 tablespoon vegetable oil in 12-inch nonstick skillet over medium-high heat until just smoking. Add mushrooms and cook until browned, about 5 minutes. Add bok choy, ginger, garlic, and remaining 1 tablespoon vegetable oil and cook until bok choy begins to soften, about 2 minutes.

3. Add hoisin, soy sauce, and noodles. Stir to combine, then cook for 2 minutes without stirring to develop light char on noodles. Stir noodles again, then cook for 2 more minutes without stirring. Stir in sesame oil and chili-garlic sauce. Serve, passing extra chili-garlic sauce separately.

Shanghai Scallion Oil Noodles

VEGAN Serves 4 to 6 Total Time 1 hour

Why This Recipe Works For our take on this popular Shanghainese dish, we cook scallion whites, shallot, and ginger to draw out their aromas, then add dark and light soy sauces and sugar to form a glossy, savory-sweet noodle sauce. The dish may be served plain or enhanced with toppings such as blanched baby bok choy, crispy fried eggs, or crispy scallion greens. Look for fresh, egg-free wheat noodles, preferably a Chinese brand, that are about the thickness of cooked spaghetti; thinner noodles will not work.

- ¼ cup light soy sauce
- 2 tablespoons dark soy sauce
- 5 teaspoons sugar
- 15–18 scallions (6 ounces), white and green parts separated
- 1 (1-inch) piece ginger, peeled
- 1 pound fresh Chinese wheat noodles
- ⅔ cup peanut or vegetable oil
- ⅛ teaspoon table salt
- 1 shallot, halved and sliced thin

1. Combine light soy sauce, dark soy sauce, and sugar in small bowl; set aside. Halve scallion whites lengthwise, then slice into 1½-inch segments. Slice green parts into 1½-inch segments; reserve white and green parts separately. Slice ginger crosswise into thin rounds. Stack rounds and slice into thin matchsticks.

2. Bring 4 quarts water to boil in large pot. Add noodles and cook, stirring often, until just tender. Drain noodles, rinse well, and drain again; set aside.

3. Meanwhile, heat oil and scallion greens in 14-inch flat-bottomed wok or 12-inch nonstick skillet over medium-high heat and cook, stirring constantly, until most scallions are browned and crispy, 8 to 10 minutes. Off heat, use slotted spoon to transfer scallion greens to small bowl; sprinkle with salt and set aside.

4. Add shallot, scallion whites, and ginger to oil remaining in wok and cook over medium-low heat, stirring often, until shallot and scallion whites are golden and wilted, 11 to 13 minutes.

5. Stir soy sauce mixture to recombine and add to scallion mixture in wok. Cook, stirring often, until sugar is dissolved and sauce is rapidly bubbling, 1 to 2 minutes. Add noodles and toss until evenly coated in sauce and heated through, 2 to 3 minutes. Transfer noodles to individual serving bowls and top with scallion greens. Serve.

Shanghai Scallion Oil Noodles

A Garlic Trifecta

Depending on how it's prepared, garlic can blitz your palate or pervade a dish with mellow, sweet savor. In our San Francisco–Style Garlic Noodles, we build deeply complex flavor by infusing a butter sauce with three forms of garlic.

Slow Cooked: Nutty-Sweet Depth

Gently sautéing most of the minced garlic mellows the sharp taste of its polysulfide compounds. Cooked low and slow, the garlic's sugars and amino acids also undergo the Maillard reaction, turning complex and sweet.

Raw: Pungent Bite

Raw minced garlic's fiery burn can easily overwhelm a dish. But in concert with slow-cooked garlic, its bite adds balance. To soften rather than erase its sharp edge, we stir a small amount into the cooked garlic as it's coming off the heat.

Garlic Powder: Toasty Savor

Drying garlic to make powder develops its toasty, round taste and also destroys much of the enzyme (alliinase) responsible for the formation of its sharp bite. Mixing the powder with a little water rehydrates it and reactivates the remaining enzyme, yielding fuller and richer garlic flavor.

San Francisco–Style Garlic Noodles

San Francisco–Style Garlic Noodles

FAST Serves 6 as a side dish Total Time 45 minutes

Why This Recipe Works As a Vietnamese refugee in 1970s San Francisco, Helene An created the original version of this Asian-European fusion dish for her family's restaurant, Thanh Long. For our take on what has become a beloved and legendary dish, we treat the garlic in multiple ways to capture its range of flavor. Gently sautéing most of the minced garlic mellows its sharp-tasting compounds while its sugars and amino acids also undergo the Maillard reaction, turning it complex and sweet. A small amount of raw minced garlic added at the end of cooking contributes a hint of bite. Garlic powder, rehydrated with water to create a paste, adds roasty, round depth. Clarifying the butter (using our easy microwave method) and then using only the butterfat to sauté the garlic prevents the butter's milk solids from browning and altering the flavor of the dish. A combination of ultrasavory Maggi Seasoning, a touch of sugar, crumbly bits of Parmesan cheese, and scallions complement the garlic and butter. Fresh lo mein noodles have springy, satisfying chew, and simmering them gently prevents the strands from absorbing too much water and bloating. Use the large holes of a box grater to shred the Parmesan. You can substitute fresh Chinese egg noodles (about ⅛ inch thick) or 8 ounces of dried spaghetti for the lo mein, and liquid soy aminos for the Maggi Seasoning. Do not replace the Maggi Seasoning with soy sauce or coconut aminos, or the garlic powder with granulated garlic.

- 8 tablespoons unsalted butter, cut into 4 pieces
- 2 teaspoons garlic powder
- 1½ ounces Parmesan cheese, shredded (½ cup)
- 5 teaspoons minced garlic, divided
- ½ teaspoon kosher salt
- 1 pound fresh lo mein noodles
- 1 tablespoon Maggi Seasoning
- 3 scallions, sliced thin
- ¼ teaspoon sugar

1. Microwave butter, covered, in 1-cup liquid measuring cup at 50 percent power until melted, 1 to 2 minutes. Let sit until whey and yellow butterfat separate, 3 to 5 minutes. Combine garlic powder and 1½ teaspoons water in small bowl and stir until smooth paste forms. Stir in additional 1½ teaspoons water and set aside. Crumble Parmesan into approximately ¼-inch pieces; set aside.

2. Bring 4 quarts water to boil in large pot. While water comes to boil, transfer 3 tablespoons butterfat to 12-inch skillet (it's OK if small amount of whey ends up in skillet). Add 4 teaspoons garlic and salt and cook over medium-low heat, stirring occasionally, until garlic is pale golden brown, 7 to 10 minutes. Add remaining 1 teaspoon garlic, stir well, and remove skillet from heat.

3. When water comes to boil, add noodles. Reduce heat to maintain very gentle simmer; cook, stirring occasionally, until almost tender (center of noodles should be firm with slightly opaque dot), 5 to 7 minutes. Drain well.

4. Add noodles and Maggi to skillet. Cook over medium-high heat, tossing with tongs, until Maggi is absorbed and any large garlic clumps are broken up, about 30 seconds. Add scallions, sugar, remaining 5 tablespoons butter (whey and butterfat), and garlic powder mixture and toss until well combined, about 30 seconds. Off heat, season with pepper to taste. Add 2 tablespoons Parmesan and toss to combine. Serve immediately, passing remaining Parmesan separately.

Gochujang-Tahini Noodles

FAST **VEGAN** Serves 4 Total Time 35 minutes

Why This Recipe Works This craveable noodle bowl uses gochujang, rice vinegar, and hoisin for a pantry-friendly sauce that's a little zingy and a little sweet. The addition of tahini and sesame oil provides richness. We always have some packets of ramen hanging around, so we often reach for those to pair with this sauce, but other wheat noodles work equally well. No matter what you choose, cook them until tender but still resilient and rinse them to remove excess starch so they don't stick together. This recipe uses the paste form of gochujang. Don't substitute gochujang sauce, which contains additional ingredients. Enjoy these noodles served simply or with as many toppings as you like.

- 5 tablespoons gochujang
- 3 tablespoons unseasoned rice vinegar
- 2 tablespoons tahini
- 2 tablespoons hoisin sauce
- 2 tablespoons soy sauce
- 1 tablespoon toasted sesame oil
- 2 garlic cloves, minced
- 4 (3-ounce) packages ramen noodles, seasoning packets discarded
- 4 scallions, sliced thin (optional)
- 1 tablespoon toasted sesame seeds

1. Whisk gochujang, vinegar, tahini, hoisin, soy sauce, oil, and garlic together in large bowl.

2. Meanwhile, bring 4 quarts water to boil in large pot. Add noodles and cook, stirring occasionally, until noodles are cooked through but still retain some chew. Drain noodles, rinse under warm water, and drain again. Toss noodles in bowl with sauce to thoroughly combine. Portion noodles into individual bowls and top with scallions, if using, and sesame seeds. Serve.

Spicy Basil Noodles with Crispy Tofu, Snap Peas, and Bell Pepper

VEGAN Serves 4 Total Time 50 minutes

Why This Recipe Works Spicy basil noodles are like a wake-up call for the sleepy palate. This brightly flavored Thai-inspired dish combines tender rice noodles with fragrant fresh basil and a spicy, aromatic sauce. Pan-fried tofu offers both creamy and crispy textures that pair well with the tender rice noodles, and stir-fried snap peas and red bell pepper strips add some crunch. We infuse the dish with subtle heat by creating a paste of hot chiles, garlic, and shallots in the food processor. Cooking the mixture briefly deepens its flavor and mellows the harshness of the raw aromatics. Vegetarian fish sauce, brown sugar, lime juice, and vegetable broth add sweet and savory flavors and give the sauce a bit of body. We stir in a generous 2 cups of basil at the very end, which keep its trademark fresh flavor and color intact.

- 12 ounces (⅜-inch-wide) rice noodles
- 14 ounces extra-firm tofu, cut into 1-inch pieces
- 8 Thai, serrano, or jalapeño chiles, stemmed and seeded
- 6 garlic cloves, peeled
- 4 shallots, peeled
- 2 cups vegetable broth
- ¼ cup vegetarian fish sauce
- ¼ cup packed brown sugar
- 3 tablespoons lime juice (2 limes)
- ¼ teaspoon table salt
- ⅛ teaspoon pepper
- ½ cup cornstarch
- 7 tablespoons vegetable oil, divided
- 6 ounces snap peas, strings removed
- 1 red bell pepper, stemmed, seeded, sliced into ¼-inch- wide strips, and halved crosswise
- 2 cups fresh Thai basil leaves or sweet basil leaves

1. Cover noodles with very hot tap water in large bowl and stir to separate. Let noodles soak until softened, pliable, and limp but not fully tender, 35 to 40 minutes; drain. Spread tofu out over paper towel–lined baking sheet and let drain for 20 minutes.

2. Meanwhile, pulse chiles, garlic, and shallots in food processor into smooth paste, about 30 pulses, scraping down bowl as needed; set aside. Whisk broth, fish sauce, sugar, and lime juice together in bowl.

3. Adjust oven rack to upper-middle position and heat oven to 200 degrees. Gently pat tofu dry with paper towels, sprinkle with salt and pepper, and toss with cornstarch in bowl. Transfer coated tofu to strainer and shake gently over bowl to remove excess cornstarch. Heat 3 tablespoons oil in 12-inch nonstick skillet over medium-high heat until just smoking. Add tofu and cook, turning as needed, until all sides are crisp and browned, about 8 minutes; transfer to paper towel–lined plate and keep warm in oven.

4. Wipe out skillet with paper towels, add 1 tablespoon oil, and heat over high heat until just smoking. Add snap peas and bell pepper and cook, stirring often, until vegetables are crisp-tender and beginning to brown, 3 to 5 minutes; transfer to separate bowl.

5. Add remaining 3 tablespoons oil to now-empty skillet and heat over medium-high heat until shimmering. Add processed chile mixture and cook until moisture evaporates and color deepens, 3 to 5 minutes. Add drained noodles and broth mixture and cook, tossing gently, until sauce has thickened and noodles are well coated and tender, 5 to 10 minutes.

6. Stir in cooked vegetables and basil and cook until basil wilts slightly, about 1 minute. Top individual portions with crispy tofu and serve.

Japchae (Sweet Potato Noodles with Shiitakes and Spinach)

VEGAN Serves 4 to 6 Total Time 50 minutes

Why This Recipe Works One of Korea's most beloved celebratory dishes is made using sweet potato starch noodles and vegetables for a result that is both stunning and delicious. The flavorful, balanced sauce made from sesame oil, soy sauce, sugar, sesame seeds, and garlic makes it clear why throughout much of history, Korean royalty kept japchae to themselves. Staggering the cooking times of the multiple vegetables ensures that they are properly cooked. After cooking the noodles, we stir-fry earthy shiitake mushrooms, sweet carrots, and an onion. We then add scallions and spinach, which need less time to cook. This dish often includes a thin egg omelet, and we have included a variation if you would like to try it. If you can't find sweet potato noodles (sometimes sold as sweet potato starch noodles or sweet potato glass noodles), substitute another type of glass or cellophane noodles. Toast the sesame seeds in a dry skillet over medium heat until fragrant (about 1 minute), then quickly remove the seeds from the pan to prevent them from scorching.

- 8 ounces (⅛-inch-wide) dried sweet potato noodles, broken into 12-inch lengths
- 2 teaspoons plus 2 tablespoons toasted sesame oil, divided
- 3 garlic cloves, minced, divided
- 2 teaspoons plus 1 tablespoon vegetable oil, divided
- ¼ cup soy sauce
- 3 tablespoons sugar
- 1 tablespoon sesame seeds, toasted
- 8 ounces shiitake mushrooms, stemmed and sliced thin
- 2 carrots, peeled and cut into 2-inch-long matchsticks
- 1 small onion, halved and sliced ½ inch thick
- 2 scallions, sliced thin
- 8 ounces (8 cups) baby spinach

1. Bring 4 quarts water to boil in large pot. Remove from heat, add noodles, and let sit, stirring occasionally, until noodles are soft and pliable but not fully tender. Drain noodles and rinse under cold running water until chilled. Drain noodles again and toss with 2 teaspoons sesame oil; set aside.

2. Combine two-thirds of garlic and 2 teaspoons vegetable oil in small bowl; set aside. Whisk soy sauce, sugar, sesame seeds, remaining 2 tablespoons sesame oil, and remaining garlic in second small bowl until sugar has dissolved; set aside.

3. Heat remaining 1 tablespoon vegetable oil in 12-inch nonstick skillet over high heat until just smoking. Add mushrooms, carrots, and onion and cook, stirring constantly, until carrots and onion are crisp-tender, 4 to 6 minutes. Add scallions and spinach and cook until wilted, about 2 minutes.

top | *Spicy Basil Noodles with Crispy Tofu, Snap Peas, and Bell Pepper*

bottom | *Japchae (Sweet Potato Noodles with Shiitakes and Spinach)*

4. Push vegetables to 1 side of skillet. Add garlic mixture to clearing and cook, mashing mixture into skillet, until fragrant, about 30 seconds. Stir garlic mixture into vegetables. Add noodles and sauce and cook, stirring constantly, until mixture is thoroughly combined and noodles are well coated and tender, 2 to 4 minutes. Serve.

Variation

Sweet Potato Noodles with Shiitakes, Spinach, and Eggs

Lightly beat 2 large eggs in bowl. After step 2, heat 1 teaspoon vegetable oil in 12-inch nonstick skillet over medium heat until shimmering. Using paper towel, wipe out skillet, leaving thin film of oil on bottom and sides. Add beaten eggs and gently tilt and shake skillet until mixture forms even 10-inch round omelet. Cover and cook until bottom of omelet is spotty brown and top is just set, about 30 seconds. Loosen edges of omelet with silicone spatula and slide onto cutting board. Cut omelet into 2-inch-wide strips. Slice each strip crosswise ¼ inch thick. Sprinkle omelet strips over finished dish before serving.

Udon with Stir-Fried Portobellos and Soy-Maple Sauce

VEGAN Serves 4 to 6 Total Time 1 hour

Why This Recipe Works Hefty, meaty portobello mushrooms in conjunction with snow peas and carrots are tossed with udon noodles to make for a super-satisfying meal. Cooking the mushrooms in two batches keeps them from steaming in their own juices, guaranteeing even cooking and good browning, and adding a boldly flavored glaze gives the mushrooms a sweet-salty flavor boost. We stir-fry the snow peas and carrots until crisp-tender, add garlic and ginger and cook them until just fragrant, and then stir in the glazed mushrooms and a simple stir-fry sauce to coat everything with its glossy goodness. Some udon noodles may not be vegetarian or vegan, so be sure to check the ingredient list.

Glaze

- 3 tablespoons maple syrup
- 2 tablespoons mirin
- 1 tablespoon soy sauce

Sauce

- ½ cup vegetable broth
- 2 tablespoons soy sauce
- 1½ tablespoons mirin
- 2 teaspoons rice vinegar
- 2 teaspoons cornstarch
- 2 teaspoons toasted sesame oil

Noodles and Vegetables

- 1 pound fresh or frozen udon noodles
- 3 tablespoons vegetable oil, divided
- 2 garlic cloves, minced
- 2 teaspoons grated fresh ginger
- ¼ teaspoon red pepper flakes
- 2 pounds portobello mushroom caps, gills removed, cut into 2-inch wedges, divided
- 8 ounces snow peas, strings removed and sliced ¼ inch thick on bias
- 2 carrots, peeled and cut into 2-inch-long matchsticks

1. **For the glaze** Whisk all ingredients together in bowl.

2. **For the sauce** Whisk all ingredients together in bowl.

3. **For the noodles and vegetables** Bring 2 quarts water to boil in large saucepan. Add noodles and cook, stirring often, until tender. Drain noodles and rinse under hot running water, tossing gently, for 1 minute. Drain noodles again and set aside in large bowl.

4. Combine 1 teaspoon vegetable oil, garlic, ginger, and pepper flakes in small bowl. Heat 1 tablespoon vegetable oil in 12-inch nonstick skillet over high heat until shimmering. Add half of mushrooms and cook, without stirring, until browned on one side, 2 to 3 minutes. Flip mushrooms, reduce heat to medium, and cook until second side is browned and mushrooms are tender, about 5 minutes. Transfer to separate bowl. Repeat with 1 tablespoon vegetable oil and remaining mushrooms.

5. Return all mushrooms to pan, add glaze, and cook over medium-high heat, stirring frequently, until glaze is thickened and mushrooms are coated, 1 to 2 minutes. Transfer mushrooms back to same bowl. Wipe skillet clean with paper towels.

6. Heat remaining 2 teaspoons vegetable oil in now-empty skillet over high heat until shimmering. Add snow peas and carrots and cook, stirring occasionally, until vegetables are crisp-tender, about 5 minutes. Clear center of skillet, add garlic mixture, and cook, mashing mixture into skillet, until fragrant, about 30 seconds. Stir garlic mixture into vegetables.

7. Return mushrooms to skillet. Whisk sauce to recombine, then add to skillet. Cook, stirring constantly, until sauce is thickened, 1 to 2 minutes. Add vegetables and sauce to noodles in bowl and gently toss to combine. Serve.

Liang Mian (Chilled Sesame Noodles)

VEGAN Serves 4 Total Time 30 minutes, plus 20 minutes chilling

Why This Recipe Works For our riff on this Chinese classic, we cook wheat noodles at a bare simmer until they are just tender at the center and then refrigerate them to evaporate their moisture and keep them springy. We coat these resilient noodles with a savory dressing based on Chinese sesame paste, which is made from heavily toasted sesame seeds. We temper the sesame paste's earthy flavors with ginger and garlic, season the dressing with soy sauce, and give it a kick with chili oil, including just enough mayonnaise to create creamy emulsification. Customize these noodles by adjusting the amount of garlic and chili oil and by varying the toppings: Try sliced red bell pepper or avocado, blanched edamame or bean sprouts, or thin strips of omelet. The noodles, sesame paste, Chinkiang (or Zhenjiang) black vinegar, and chili oil can be found at most Asian markets. We prefer the chewy texture of fresh noodles that are about ⅛ inch thick, but if they are unavailable, substitute 8 ounces of dried Chinese wheat noodles or spaghetti and increase the cooking time to 6 to 10 minutes. Look for sesame paste that is dark and smooth; stir before using. If Chinese sesame paste is unavailable, use unsalted, unsweetened natural peanut butter. To make this recipe vegan, substitute plant-based mayo for the mayonnaise.

Liang Mian (Chilled Sesame Noodles)

top | *Chilled Soba Noodles with Cucumber, Snow Peas, and Radishes*

bottom | *Pittsburgh-Style Haluski*

- 1 pound fresh Chinese wheat noodles
- 2 teaspoons toasted sesame oil, divided
- ¼ cup Chinese sesame paste
- 1 tablespoon mayonnaise
- 1 tablespoon chili oil, divided
- 3 tablespoons soy sauce
- 5 teaspoons Chinese black vinegar
- 4 teaspoons water
- 4 teaspoons sugar
- 1½ teaspoons minced garlic, divided
- 1 teaspoon grated fresh ginger
- 1 Persian cucumber, cut into 3-inch-long matchsticks
- 1 scallion, sliced thin
- Toasted sesame seeds (optional)

1. Bring 4 quarts water to boil in large pot. Add noodles; reduce heat to maintain very gentle simmer; and cook, stirring occasionally, until almost tender (center of noodles should be firm with slightly opaque dot), 3 to 5 minutes. Meanwhile, place 1 teaspoon sesame oil in large bowl.

2. Drain noodles very well in colander. Transfer noodles to bowl with oil and toss with tongs until lightly coated. Transfer noodles to rimmed baking sheet and spread into even layer. Refrigerate until cold, about 20 minutes.

3. Whisk sesame paste, mayonnaise, 2 teaspoons chili oil, and remaining 1 teaspoon sesame oil together in now-empty bowl. Add soy sauce, vinegar, water, sugar, 1 teaspoon garlic, and ginger and whisk until smooth. Season dressing to taste with remaining 1 teaspoon chili oil and ½ teaspoon garlic. Add noodles and toss until well combined. Divide noodles evenly into individual serving bowls; garnish with cucumber, scallion, and sesame seeds, if using. Serve immediately.

Chilled Soba Noodles with Cucumber, Snow Peas, and Radishes

FAST **VEGAN** Serves 4 to 6 Total Time 45 minutes

Why This Recipe Works Soba noodles, made from buckwheat flour or a buckwheat-wheat flour blend, have a chewy texture and nutty flavor and are often enjoyed chilled. We cook soba noodles in unsalted boiling water until tender but still resilient and rinse them under cold running water to remove excess starch and prevent sticking. We then toss the soba with a miso-based dressing, which clings to and flavors the noodles without overpowering their distinct taste. We also cut a mix of vegetables into varying sizes so they incorporate nicely into the noodles while adding crunch and color. Sprinkling strips of toasted nori over the top adds umami, a touch of brininess, and crisp textural interest. Plain pre-toasted seaweed snacks can be substituted for the toasted nori, and yellow, red, or brown miso can be substituted for the white miso, if desired. This dish isn't meant to be overtly spicy, but if you prefer more heat, use the full ½ teaspoon of red pepper flakes. These chilled noodles pair nicely with tofu.

- 8 ounces dried soba noodles
- 1 (8-inch square) sheet nori (optional)
- 3 tablespoons white miso
- 3 tablespoons mirin
- 2 tablespoons toasted sesame oil
- 1 tablespoon sesame seeds
- 1 teaspoon grated fresh ginger
- ¼–½ teaspoon red pepper flakes
- ⅓ English cucumber, quartered lengthwise, seeded, and sliced thin on bias
- 4 ounces snow peas, strings removed, cut lengthwise into matchsticks
- 4 radishes, trimmed, halved, and sliced thin
- 3 scallions, sliced thin on bias

1. Bring 4 quarts water to boil in large pot. Add noodles and cook, stirring often, until tender. Drain noodles and rinse under cold running water until chilled. Drain noodles again.

2. Grip nori sheet, if using, with tongs and hold about 2 inches above low flame on gas burner. Toast nori, flipping every 3 to 5 seconds, until nori is aromatic and shrinks slightly, about 20 seconds. If you do not have a gas stove, toast nori on rimmed baking sheet in 275-degree oven until it is aromatic and shrinks slightly, 20 to 25 minutes, flipping nori halfway through toasting. Using scissors, cut nori into four 2-inch strips. Stack strips and cut crosswise into thin strips.

3. Whisk miso, mirin, oil, 1 tablespoon water, sesame seeds, ginger, and pepper flakes together in large bowl. Add noodles and toss to combine. Add cucumber; snow peas; radishes; scallions; and nori, if using, and toss well to evenly distribute. Season with salt to taste and serve.

Pittsburgh-Style Haluski

Serves 4 to 6   Total Time 55 minutes

Why This Recipe Works This buttery blend of tender cabbage, onions, and egg noodles draws inspiration from the Hungarian haluski served at the now-closed Józsa Corner in Pittsburgh. We slowly cook the cabbage and onions in butter until deeply golden and imbued with richness. Frequent stirring incorporates the browning vegetables back into the mix and keeps the sugars from burning. After tossing the cabbage mixture with egg noodles, as well as more butter for extra richness, we shower it all with fresh dill and serve it with cooling sour cream. Use a sharp knife or a food processor fitted with a slicing blade to slice the cabbage.

- 8 tablespoons unsalted butter, cut into 1-tablespoon pieces, divided
- 1 head green cabbage (2 pounds), cored and sliced thin
- 2 onions, halved and sliced thin
- 1 cup water
- 2 garlic cloves, minced
- 1¼ teaspoons table salt, plus more for cooking noodles
- 12 ounces (6 cups) wide egg noodles
- 2 tablespoons minced fresh dill, divided
- Sour cream

1. Melt 4 tablespoons butter in 12-inch nonstick skillet over medium-high heat. Add cabbage, onions, water, garlic, and salt. Cover and cook, stirring occasionally, until cabbage is softened, about 15 minutes. (Pan will be very full and lid may not fit at first; vegetables will decrease in volume as they cook.)

2. Remove lid and continue to cook, stirring often, until vegetables are deep golden brown and sticky, about 25 minutes longer.

3. Meanwhile, bring 4 quarts water to boil in large pot. Add noodles and 1 tablespoon salt and cook, stirring often, until tender. Drain noodles and return to pot.

4. Add 1 tablespoon dill, cooked cabbage mixture, and remaining 4 tablespoons butter to noodles and toss until butter is melted and vegetables and noodles are evenly combined. Season with salt and pepper to taste. Transfer to platter and sprinkle with remaining 1 tablespoon dill. Serve, dolloping individual portions with sour cream.

Savory Noodle Kugel

Savory Noodle Kugel

Serves 8 to 10   Total Time 1¾ hours

Why This Recipe Works Kugel can be savory or sweet; savory versions are often made with potatoes, while sweet versions feature noodles. Although rendered chicken fat (schmaltz) is sometimes included in savory kugels, butter or olive oil can also be used, as we do here. Onions caramelized in the oil build a rich and rounded base of flavor into which we mix eggs and some parsley. Tossing the egg mixture with just-cooked, still-warm noodles helps thicken the eggs slightly so they cling to the noodles; transferring the eggy, oniony noodles to a baking dish and popping the casserole into the oven helps it set up. A pass under the broiler gives the kugel its characteristic crunchy top. You will need a broiler-safe 13 by 9-inch baking dish for this recipe.

- 3 tablespoons extra-virgin olive oil
- 3 onions, chopped fine
- 1½ teaspoons table salt, divided, plus salt for cooking noodles
- 6 large eggs
- 2 tablespoons minced fresh parsley
- ¾ teaspoon pepper
- 1 pound wide egg noodles

1. Adjust 1 oven rack to middle position and second rack 6 inches from broiler element. Heat oven to 350 degrees. Grease broiler-safe 13 by 9-inch baking dish. Heat olive oil in 12-inch skillet over medium-low heat. Add onions and ½ teaspoon salt and cook, stirring occasionally, until caramelized, 30 to 40 minutes. Transfer onions to large bowl and let cool for 10 minutes. (Cooled caramelized onions can be refrigerated for up to 3 days.) Whisk eggs, parsley, pepper, and remaining 1 teaspoon salt into onions; set aside.

2. Bring 4 quarts water to boil in large pot. Add noodles and 1 tablespoon salt and cook, stirring often, until al dente. Reserve 3 tablespoons cooking water, then drain noodles and let cool for 5 minutes. Whisk reserved cooking water into onion mixture. Stir still-warm noodles into onion mixture until well combined.

3. Transfer noodle mixture to prepared dish. (Kugel can be refrigerated for up to 24 hours. Increase baking time to 25 minutes.) Bake on middle oven rack until set, about 20 minutes. Remove kugel from oven and heat broiler. Once broiler is hot, broil kugel on upper rack until top noodles are browned and crispy, 1 to 3 minutes, rotating dish as needed for even browning. Serve.

Green Peas and Dumplings

Serves 6 to 8   Total Time 1 hour

Why This Recipe Works This Southern classic was inspired by Mildred Cotton Council, beloved North Carolina country cook and founder (in 1976) of the celebrated Mama Dip's Kitchen restaurant in Chapel Hill, North Carolina. In her book *Mama Dip's Kitchen* (1999), Council encouraged readers to "Treat the recipes like sewing patterns—stretch or alter them to fit." We took that to heart with her recipe for Country Bonnet Green Peas with Dumplings, which calls for just five ingredients to create a flavorful and comforting pot of brothy peas and tender, pasta-like dumplings. For our hearty version, we ultimately settled on just a few small adjustments—using frozen peas and adding sautéed onion and garlic, plus nutmeg and black pepper in the dumplings. We prefer the sweet flavor and creamy texture of frozen petite peas, but you can substitute regular frozen peas. We recommend weighing the flour for the best results.

- 8 tablespoons unsalted butter
- 1 onion, chopped fine
- 3 garlic cloves, minced
- 6 cups water
- 2 pounds frozen petite peas
- 2 teaspoons table salt
- 1⅔ cups (8⅓ ounces) all-purpose flour
- ⅛ teaspoon ground nutmeg
- ⅛ teaspoon pepper

1. Melt butter in Dutch oven over medium heat. Add onion and cook until softened, 4 to 6 minutes. Stir in garlic and cook until fragrant, about 30 seconds. Add water, peas, and salt and bring to boil over high heat. Reduce heat to medium-low and simmer until peas are tender and plump, about 15 minutes. Off heat, scoop out and reserve ½ cup cooking liquid; cover pot to keep warm.

2. Whisk flour, nutmeg, and pepper together in large bowl. Drizzle reserved cooking liquid over flour mixture and, using silicone spatula or wooden spoon, stir mixture until dough comes together in shaggy clumps and some dry flour remains. Continue to stir, pressing and smearing clumps of dough with back of spatula and scraping dry flour from bottom of bowl, until dough comes together to form shaggy mass and no dry flour remains, about 2 minutes longer. Using your hands, squeeze dough together in bowl, then transfer to clean counter. Knead dough until smooth, about 2 minutes.

3. Roll dough into rough 16-inch square; dough should be thinner than ⅛ inch, and you should just see counter through dough. (If dough feels slightly stiff while rolling, let it relax for about 1 minute before continuing to roll.) Using chef's knife or pizza cutter, slice dough horizontally into 8 equal strips. Cut strips vertically at 1-inch intervals to create 2 by 1-inch pieces (it's OK to have some smaller dough scraps or to cut dough slightly unevenly; you should have about 120 dumplings).

4. Return pea mixture to vigorous simmer over medium-high heat. Drop dumplings into pot and gently stir to submerge and distribute dumplings. (Use dough scraper or knife to release dumplings from counter as needed.) Return pea mixture to vigorous simmer. Reduce heat to medium-low, cover, and simmer gently, stirring occasionally, until dumplings are very tender, about 10 minutes. Off heat, season with salt and pepper to taste. Serve peas and dumplings in bowls with broth.

Potato-Cheddar Pierogi

Makes 30 pierogi   Total Time 1½ hours, plus 1 hour chilling

Why This Recipe Works These Polish dumplings, which combine potatoes and cheese tucked into a tender dough, make a hearty bite. We combine boiled russet potatoes, shredded cheddar cheese, and butter in a stand mixer. The heat from the potatoes melts the butter and cheese for an even consistency. We create a pliable, rollable dough using higher-protein bread flour, sour cream, and egg and stamp out rounds with a biscuit cutter. The filling is sealed in by pinching the edges together before boiling the pierogi. A caramelized onion topping mixed with the dumplings gives a traditional sweet-savory finish. When rolling the dough in step 4, be sure not to dust the top surface with too much flour, as that will prevent the edges from forming a tight seal when pinched.

Filling

- 1 pound russet potatoes, peeled and sliced ½ inch thick
- ½ teaspoon table salt, plus salt for cooking potatoes
- 4 ounces sharp cheddar cheese, shredded (1 cup)
- 2 tablespoons unsalted butter
- ½ teaspoon pepper

Dough

- 2½ cups (13¾ ounces) bread flour
- 1 teaspoon baking powder
- ½ teaspoon table salt, plus salt for cooking pierogi
- 1 cup sour cream
- 1 large egg plus 1 large yolk

Topping

- 4 tablespoons unsalted butter
- 1 large onion, chopped fine
- ½ teaspoon table salt

1. **For the filling** Combine potatoes and 1 tablespoon salt in large saucepan and cover with water by 1 inch. Bring to boil over medium-high heat; reduce heat to medium and cook at vigorous simmer until potatoes are very tender, about 15 minutes.

2. Drain potatoes in colander. While still hot, combine potatoes, cheddar, butter, pepper, and salt in bowl of stand mixer. Fit mixer with paddle and mix on medium speed until potatoes are smooth and all ingredients are fully combined, about 1 minute. Transfer filling to 8-inch square baking dish and refrigerate until fully chilled, about 30 minutes.

3. **For the dough** Whisk flour, baking powder, and salt together in clean bowl of stand mixer. Add sour cream, egg, and egg yolk. Fit mixer with dough hook and knead on medium-high speed for 8 minutes (dough will be smooth and elastic). Transfer dough to floured bowl, cover with plastic, and refrigerate for at least 30 minutes until ready to assemble.

4. Line rimmed baking sheet with parchment paper and dust with flour. Roll dough on lightly floured counter into 18-inch circle, about ⅛ inch thick. Using 3-inch biscuit cutter, cut 20 to 24 circles from dough. Place 1 tablespoon chilled filling in center of each dough round. Fold dough over filling to create half-moon shape and pinch edges firmly to seal. Transfer to prepared sheet. (Uncooked pierogi can be frozen for several weeks. Freeze them on baking sheet, about 3 hours. Transfer frozen pierogi to zipper-lock freezer bag. When ready to cook, extend boiling time in step 7 to about 7 minutes.)

5. Gather dough scraps and reroll to ⅛-inch thickness. Cut 6 to 10 more circles from dough and repeat with remaining filling. (It may be necessary to reroll dough once more to yield 30 pierogi.)

6. For the topping Melt butter in 12-inch skillet over medium-low heat. Add onion and salt and cook until onion is caramelized, 15 to 20 minutes. Remove skillet from heat and set aside.

7. Bring 4 quarts water to boil in Dutch oven. Add 1 tablespoon salt and half of pierogi and cook until tender, about 5 minutes. Using spider skimmer or slotted spoon, remove pierogi from water and transfer to skillet with caramelized onion. Return water to boil, cook remaining pierogi, and transfer to skillet with first batch.

8. Add 2 tablespoons cooking water to pierogi in skillet. Cook over medium-low heat, stirring gently, until onion mixture is warmed through and adhered to pierogi. Serve.

Variation

Potato-Sauerkraut Pierogi

Omit cheddar and pepper. In step 2, combine 1¼ cups sauerkraut, drained and chopped fine, and ¼ teaspoon white pepper with potatoes.

Su Shui Jiao (Northern Chinese–Style Cabbage and Mushroom Dumplings)

Makes 48 dumplings Total Time 1¾ hours, plus 1 hour resting

Why This Recipe Works In Northern China, dumplings are traditionally eaten on the first day of the year. With their shape resembling the gold ingots used as currency in ancient China, dumplings symbolize wealth and unity. Northern-style dumplings are made with a thicker dough than potstickers, and they taste best when boiled rather than fried. We recommend weighing the flour for the dough to ensure the best texture. You can substitute 48 store-bought dumpling wrappers for the homemade wrappers: Look for round, white (not egg-based or wonton) Chinese wheat wrappers. Dried mung bean glass noodles are also known as bean thread noodles or cellophane noodles. If you can't find seitan puffs, you can substitute tofu puffs. Do not substitute store-bought peppercorn oil for the Sichuan Peppercorn Oil (page 325). Periodically adding cold water to the pot in step 9 slows the boiling and promotes more even cooking. We like to serve these dumplings with Chinese black vinegar or our Chili Crisp Dumpling Sauce (page 325).

top | *Potato-Cheddar Pierogi*

bottom | *Su Shui Jiao (Northern Chinese–Style Cabbage and Mushroom Dumplings)*

Dough

- 3 cups (15 ounces) all-purpose flour
- 1 cup water, room temperature

Filling

- 3 large eggs
- ¾ teaspoon table salt, divided
- 2 tablespoons vegetable oil
- 1 ounce dried mung bean glass noodles
- 4 ounces shiitake mushrooms, stemmed and chopped coarse
- 4 ounces spiced pressed tofu, chopped coarse
- 1½ ounces seitan puffs, chopped fine
- ⅓ cup minced fresh cilantro
- ⅓ cup minced scallions
- 3 tablespoons Sichuan Peppercorn Oil (page 325) or vegetable oil
- 2 tablespoons toasted sesame oil
- 2 tablespoons light soy sauce
- 2 teaspoons grated fresh ginger
- ½ teaspoon white pepper
- 5 cups chopped napa cabbage leaves and stems

1. **For the dough** Place flour in food processor. With processor running, add room-temperature water and process until dough forms ball and clears sides of bowl, 30 to 45 seconds. Transfer dough to counter and knead until smooth, 2 to 3 minutes. Wrap dough tightly in plastic wrap and let rest at room temperature for at least 1 hour or up to 3 hours. (Tightly wrapped dough can be refrigerated for up to 24 hours; return dough to room temperature before shaping.)

2. **For the filling** Beat eggs and ¼ teaspoon salt in small bowl until no streaks of white remain. Heat vegetable oil in 12-inch nonstick skillet over medium-high heat until just smoking. Add egg mixture and, using silicone spatula, scrape constantly and firmly along bottom of skillet until eggs are fully set and dry, 2 to 3 minutes. Transfer eggs to clean bowl and break into ¼-inch pieces; let cool for at least 5 minutes.

3. Place noodles in large bowl, cover with boiling water, and let sit until tender and translucent, 6 to 8 minutes. Drain noodles and rinse under cold running water. Drain noodles again, spread onto cutting board, and pat dry with paper towels. Chop noodles into ¼-inch pieces and transfer to large bowl.

4. Pulse mushrooms and tofu in food processor until finely chopped, 8 to 10 pulses; transfer to bowl with noodles. Fold in seitan puffs, cilantro, scallions, Sichuan peppercorn oil, sesame oil, soy sauce, ginger, white pepper, remaining ½ teaspoon salt, and cooked eggs until evenly incorporated. (Mushroom mixture can be refrigerated for up to 24 hours.)

5. Pulse cabbage in food processor until finely chopped, 8 to 10 pulses. Transfer cabbage to center of clean dish towel. Gather ends of towel and twist tightly to wring out excess moisture. Fold cabbage into mushroom mixture until evenly combined. Use filling to stuff dumplings within 2 hours.

6. To roll wrappers: Unwrap dough and transfer to counter. Cut dough into 4 quarters. Working with 1 dough quarter at a time (keeping remaining quarters loosely covered with plastic), roll into 12-inch cylinder, lightly flouring counter as needed. Slice cylinder crosswise into twelve 1-inch pieces (about ½ ounce each). Using palms of your hands, roll each piece into rough ball, then press each ball into 2-inch disk; cover with plastic.

7. Using small rolling pin, gently roll and press each disk into 3¼-inch round wrapper (they needn't be perfectly round). Roll from outside of dough disk inward to center, rotating dough about a quarter turn between each stroke. This results in finished wrappers that are a little thicker in very center, creating sturdy and stable dumpling bottoms. Collect wrappers in single layer (without overlapping) on lightly floured counter; cover with plastic. (If counter space is limited, transfer wrappers to lightly floured parchment paper–lined baking sheets.)

8. To fill dumplings: Line 2 rimmed baking sheets with parchment paper and dust lightly with flour; set aside. Working with 1 wrapper at a time (keeping remaining wrappers covered), place wrapper in palm of your nondominant hand. Spoon scant 1 tablespoon filling onto center of wrapper, then lift opposite sides of wrapper and pinch together to form small seam in center. Using your index finger and thumb, gently form 2 pleats along first open side, pressing gently to seal; repeat pleating and sealing on second open side. Arrange dumplings in single layer on prepared sheets. (Uncooked dumplings can be frozen on baking sheets until solid. Transfer to zipper-lock bag and freeze for up to 1 month. Cook dumplings from frozen, increasing cooking time as needed until dough is fully tender and filling is cooked through.)

9. Bring 4 quarts water to boil in large pot over high heat. Add 24 dumplings, a few at a time, stirring gently to prevent sticking. Return water to boil; boil dumplings for 15 seconds. Add 1 cup cold water, return water to boil, and boil dumplings for 15 seconds longer. Repeat adding cold water and boiling for 15 seconds once or twice more, until dumpling dough is fully tender and filling is cooked through (entire process should take 5 to 8 minutes). Using slotted spoon or spider skimmer, transfer dumplings to serving platter. Repeat to cook remaining 24 dumplings.

10. Return water to boil and repeat boiling process with remaining dumplings. Serve dumplings hot.

Chili Crisp Dumpling Sauce

FAST **VEGAN** Serves 6 to 8 (makes 1½ cups)
Total Time 10 minutes

- ½ cup unseasoned rice vinegar
- ½ cup light soy sauce
- ⅓ cup water
- 2 tablespoons Chinese chili crisp
- 2 tablespoons sugar
- 2 tablespoons toasted sesame seeds
- 6 garlic cloves, minced

Combine all ingredients in bowl, stirring to dissolve sugar. (Sauce can be refrigerated for up to 3 days.)

Sichuan Peppercorn Oil

FAST **VEGAN** Serves 4 to 6 (makes ½ cup)
Total Time 35 minutes

Either red or green Sichuan peppercorns work well.

- ⅓ cup Sichuan peppercorns
- ⅔ cup peanut or vegetable oil

Heat peppercorns and oil in small saucepan over medium-low heat, swirling occasionally, until peppercorns are fully blackened and oil is fragrant and smoking, about 20 minutes. Remove from heat and let sit for 10 minutes. Strain oil through fine-mesh strainer into bowl; discard peppercorns. Let cool and transfer to airtight container. (Oil can be refrigerated for up to 3 months.)

Pleating Dumplings

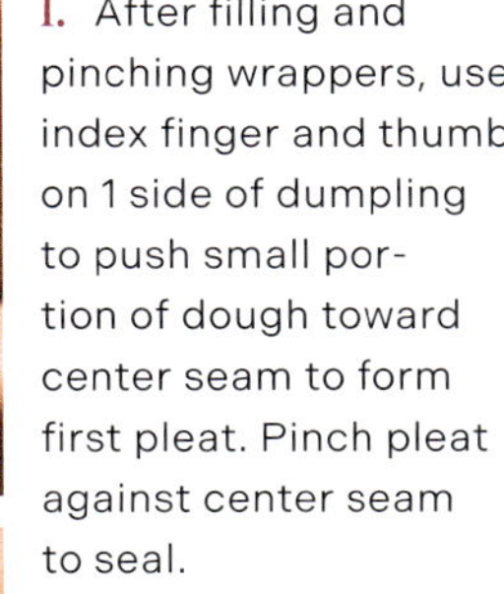

1. After filling and pinching wrappers, use index finger and thumb on 1 side of dumpling to push small portion of dough toward center seam to form first pleat. Pinch pleat against center seam to seal.

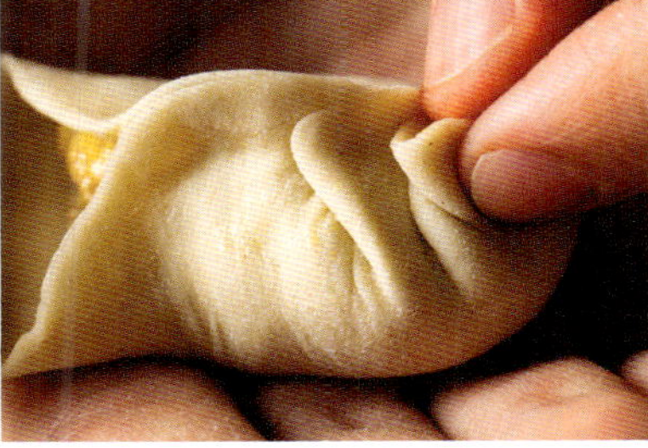

2. On same side of dumpling, repeat pushing small portion of dough toward first pleat to create second pleat.

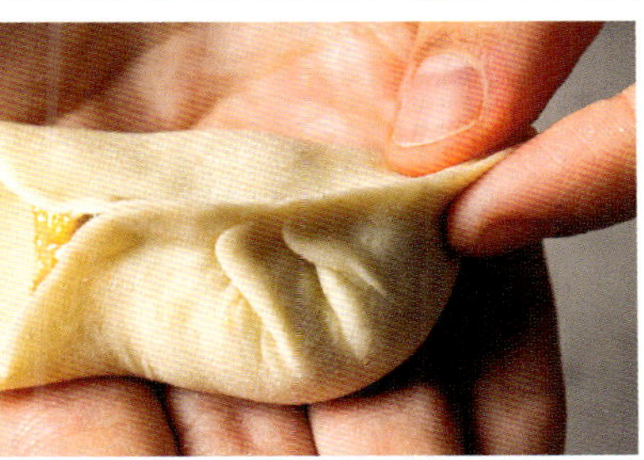

3. Pinch second pleat to seal, then pinch together remaining opening to fully seal first side.

4. Repeat pleating and sealing on opposite side of dumpling.

5. Lightly compress dumpling in your palm to reinforce crescent shape and pinch along seams to reinforce seals.

Rice & Grains

328 Simple Rice Pilaf ■ ●
Basmati Rice Pilaf with Whole Spices
Basmati Rice Pilaf with Peas, Scallions, and Lemon ●

329 Easy Mexican Rice ●

329 Spinach Rice

330 Javaher Polo (Jeweled Rice) ●

333 Cauliflower Biryani ●

334 Paella de Verduras (Cauliflower and Bean Paella) ●

334 Vegetable Bibimbap with Tempeh ●

337 Garlicky Fried Rice with Bok Choy

337 Stir-Fried Rice Cakes with Bok Choy and Snow Peas ■ ●

338 Risotto alla Milanese

338 Miso Mushroom Risotto ●

341 Corn Risotto

341 Cơm Đỏ (Vietnamese Red Rice) ■

342 Hung Kao Mun Gati (Thai Coconut Rice) ■ ●

342 Arroz con Titoté (Colombian Coconut Rice) ●

343 Congee ●

344 Wild Rice Pilaf with Pecans and Cranberries ●
Wild Rice with Scallions, Cilantro, and Almonds ●

346 California Barley Bowls with Lemon-Yogurt Sauce ●

347 Barley with Lemon and Herbs ●
Barley with Celery and Miso Dressing ●
Barley with Fennel, Dried Apricots, and Orange ●

348 Beet and Barley Risotto

348 Barley and Lentils with Mushrooms and Tahini-Yogurt Sauce ●

349 Farro with Wild Mushroom Ragout ■ ●

350 Jollof-Inspired Fonio ■

352 Curried Fonio with Roasted Vegetables

353 Hibiscus Vinaigrette ■ ●

353 Spring Freekeh and Halloumi Bowls

354 Tahini-Garlic Sauce ■ ●

354 Maftoul with Carrots and Chickpeas ■ ●

356 Oat Berry Pilaf with Walnuts and Gorgonzola

357 Quinoa Bowls with Snap Peas, Strawberries, and Basil Vinaigrette ■

357 Quinoa, Black Bean, and Mango Salad with Lime Dressing ●

358 Quinoa Lettuce Wraps with Feta and Olives

359 Herbed Quinoa Cakes with Whipped Feta

360 Creamy Polenta with Fennel and Chickpeas

363 Creamy Polenta with Radicchio Agrodolce

363 Spicy Polenta with White Beans and Kale ■

364 Grits with Fresh Corn

365 Savory Oatmeal with Peas, Parmesan, and Pepper

Cooking Rice

366 Easy Baked White Rice ■ ●

366 Easy Baked Brown Rice ●

367 Rice Cooking Chart

Cooking Grains

369 Grain Cooking Chart

■ Fast (45 minutes or less) ● Vegan

top | *Simple Rice Pilaf*
bottom | *Easy Mexican Rice*

Simple Rice Pilaf

FAST **VEGAN** Serves 4 to 6 Total Time 45 minutes

Why This Recipe Works Basmati rice is an aromatic variety of long-grain rice. It cooks up light and fluffy with firm, distinct grains, making it good for pilafs. Our pilaf method calls for cooking the rice over an even, gentle heat. It is important to first rinse the rice, which removes excess starch and ensures separate grains. For an easy flavor boost, we sauté an onion in the saucepan before adding the rice. Toasting the rice for a few minutes in the pan deepens its flavor. A little less liquid than the traditional ratio of 1 cup of rice to 2 cups of water delivers better results. We place a dish towel under the lid while the rice finishes steaming off the heat; it absorbs excess moisture in the pan and guarantees fluffy, light, and tender rice. You can substitute conventional long-grain white, jasmine, or Texmati rice for the basmati.

- 1 tablespoon extra-virgin olive oil
- 1 small onion, chopped
- ¼ teaspoon table salt
- 1½ cups basmati rice, rinsed
- 2¼ cups water

1. Heat oil in large saucepan over medium heat until shimmering. Add onion and salt and cook until softened, about 5 minutes. Add rice and cook, stirring constantly, until grains become chalky and opaque, 1 to 3 minutes.

2. Stir in water and bring to boil. Reduce heat to low, cover, and simmer gently until rice is tender and water has been fully absorbed, 16 to 18 minutes.

3. Off heat, lay clean dish towel underneath lid and let sit, covered, for 10 minutes. Fluff rice with fork and serve.

Variations

Basmati Rice Pilaf with Whole Spices

Omit oil and onion and increase salt to 1 teaspoon. Melt 3 tablespoons unsalted butter in medium saucepan over medium heat. Add 1 teaspoon cumin seeds; 3 green cardamom pods, lightly crushed; and 3 whole cloves and cook, stirring constantly, until fragrant, about 1 minute. Add rice and cook, stirring constantly, until fragrant, about 1 minute. Add 1 cinnamon stick, 1 bay leaf, and salt when stirring in water. Before fluffing cooked rice, discard cardamom, cloves, cinnamon stick, and bay leaf.

VEGAN Basmati Rice Pilaf with Peas, Scallions, and Lemon

Add 2 minced garlic cloves, 1 teaspoon grated lemon zest, and ⅛ teaspoon red pepper flakes to saucepan with rice. Before covering rice with dish towel, sprinkle ½ cup thawed frozen peas over top. When fluffing cooked rice, stir in 2 thinly sliced scallions and 1 tablespoon lemon juice.

Easy Mexican Rice

VEGAN Serves 4 to 6 Total Time 55 minutes

Why This Recipe Works This easy version of Mexican rice yields tender, fluffy rice with a deep savoriness and refreshing brightness. It's beauty lies in its simplicity and a careful balance of fresh flavors. Achieving fluffy rice with separate, intact grains boils down to applying a few easy techniques: rinsing the rice, toasting it in oil to coat the grains, and cooking it in just enough liquid. For a cooking liquid that is infused with flavor, we use a food processor to combine a quartered fresh tomato, jalapeño chile, and chopped garlic until smooth; this mixture becomes the base of the liquid in which the rice is cooked, along with the addition of vegetable broth, which adds more savory flavor than just water. After toasting the rice in oil, we add tomato paste, which both colors the rice and adds a deep umami flavor. Finishing with a fistful of fresh cilantro and a bit of lime juice provides bursts of brightness. To make this dish spicier, include the jalapeño seeds.

- 1½ cups long-grain white rice
- 1 tomato, cored and quartered
- 1 jalapeño chile, stemmed, halved, and seeded
- 1 garlic clove, chopped
- 1½ teaspoons table salt
- ¼ teaspoon pepper
- 1–1¾ cups vegetable broth
- 3 tablespoons extra-virgin olive oil
- 1 tablespoon tomato paste
- ¼ cup chopped fresh cilantro
- Lime wedges

1. Place rice in fine-mesh strainer and rinse under cold running water until water runs clear. Drain well and set aside.

2. Process tomato, jalapeño, garlic, salt, and pepper in food processor until smooth, about 30 seconds, scraping down sides of bowl as needed. Transfer mixture to 4-cup liquid measuring cup. Stir to deflate foam, if necessary, then add enough broth to equal 2½ cups.

3. Heat oil in large saucepan over medium-high heat until shimmering. Add rice and cook, stirring frequently, until edges begin to turn translucent, about 2 minutes. Add tomato paste and cook, stirring constantly, until mixture is uniformly colored, about 1 minute. Add tomato mixture and bring to boil. Stir rice, cover, and reduce heat to low. Cook for 20 minutes.

4. Let stand off heat, covered, for 10 minutes. Stir in cilantro and season with salt and pepper to taste. Serve with lime wedges.

Spinach Rice

Serves 4 to 6 Total Time 1¼ hours

Why This Recipe Works This Greek-inspired rice is bursting with flavor thanks to not only frozen spinach but also aromatics, mint, and tangy feta cheese. The key to achieving a foolproof pilaf chock-full of greens while also ensuring evenly cooked rice is to add the thawed chopped spinach at the very end. When cooking it with the rice, the spinach floats in the cooking liquid, carrying a layer of rice up with it. So we add the spinach to the pilaf as it rests after cooking, which ensures that the greens get hot without turning mushy or slimy. Stirring in mint, scallions, and lemon juice brightens the flavor of the cooked greens.

- 3 tablespoons extra-virgin olive oil, plus extra for serving
- 1 onion, chopped fine
- ½ teaspoon table salt
- ¼ teaspoon pepper
- 1½ cups long-grain white rice
- 2 garlic cloves, minced
- 1 teaspoon dried oregano
- 2½ cups vegetable broth
- 10 ounces frozen spinach, thawed, squeezed dry, and chopped
- 2 scallions, sliced thin
- 2 tablespoons chopped fresh mint
- 1 tablespoon lemon juice, plus wedges for serving
- 2 ounces feta cheese, crumbled (½ cup)

1. Heat oil in large saucepan over medium-high heat until shimmering. Add onion, salt, and pepper and cook until softened, 3 to 5 minutes. Add rice and cook, stirring frequently, until edges begin to turn translucent, about 2 minutes. Add garlic and oregano and cook until fragrant, about 30 seconds.

2. Stir in broth and bring to boil. Cover, reduce heat to low, and cook until liquid is absorbed and rice is tender, about 20 minutes.

3. Off heat, sprinkle spinach on top of rice, cover, and let stand for 10 minutes. Uncover and fluff rice with fork. Stir in scallions, mint, and lemon juice, tossing until any clumps of spinach are broken up and thoroughly mixed into rice. Season with salt and pepper to taste. Transfer to platter and sprinkle with feta. Serve, drizzled with extra oil and lemon wedges.

Javaher Polo (Jeweled Rice)

VEGAN Serves 6 Total Time 2 hours, plus 20 minutes soaking and resting

Why This Recipe Works Fluffy rice bedazzled with nuts and dried fruits, Persian Javaher Polo is simply astonishing. This classic and festive dish is composed of light and fluffy steamed rice that's studded with nuts and dried fruit and served with a golden-brown, crispy crust known as tahdig. Rinsing the rice, soaking it for 15 minutes in hot salted water, parboiling it, and then steaming it to finish cooking creates the fluffiest texture. Combining a portion of the rice with yogurt and oil ensures a nicely browned, flavorful crust, and chunks of butter added during steaming enriches the rice. The yogurt also makes the tahdig easier to remove from the pot, as does brushing the bottom of the pot with a little extra oil and letting the pot rest on a damp dish towel after cooking. Lightly toasted nuts, soaked barberries, and candied carrots and orange peel serve as the "jewels" and add crunch, sweetness, and tartness. Coloring a portion of the rice yellow with saffron makes for a stunning finishing touch on the artfully decorated and arranged dish. Stunningly tart barberries (zereshk) can be found in Middle Eastern markets and online. If you cannot find them, substitute ⅓ cup chopped pistachios. Greek yogurt can be substituted for the plain yogurt if desired. For the best results, use a Dutch oven with a bottom diameter of 8½ to 10 inches. If you own a nonstick pot, you can use that instead; skip brushing the bottom and sides of the pot with 1 tablespoon of oil in step 4. To make this recipe vegan, substitute plant-based yogurt for the dairy yogurt.

- ¼ cup dried barberries
- Pinch saffron threads, crumbled
- 1 orange, scrubbed and dried
- 2 cups basmati rice
- 2 tablespoons plus 1 teaspoon table salt, plus salt for soaking rice
- 5 tablespoons vegetable oil, divided
- ¼ cup plain yogurt
- 4 tablespoons plus 1 teaspoon unsalted butter, divided
- 2 carrots, peeled and cut into 2-inch-long matchsticks (1 cup)
- ½ cup sugar
- ¼ cup slivered almonds, lightly toasted
- ¼ cup slivered pistachios, lightly toasted

1. Remove any stems from barberries and place in bowl. Cover with cold water. In small bowl, stir together saffron and 1 tablespoon water. Use vegetable peeler to remove strips of zest from orange (reserve flesh for another use). Cut zest into 2-inch-long matchsticks. Place orange strips in medium saucepan and cover with cold water. Bring to boil over high heat. Drain strips in fine-mesh strainer. Repeat boiling and draining 2 more times. Transfer strips to bowl. (Blanched orange strips can be refrigerated for up to 1 week.)

2. Place rice in fine-mesh strainer and rinse under cold running water until water runs clear. Drain well. Place rice and 1 tablespoon salt in medium bowl and cover with 4 cups hot water. Stir gently to dissolve salt; let stand for 15 minutes. Drain rice in fine-mesh strainer.

3. Bring 8 cups water to boil in large Dutch oven over high heat. Add rice and 2 tablespoons plus 1 teaspoon salt. Boil briskly until rice is mostly tender with slight bite in center and grains are floating toward top of pot, 3 to 5 minutes.

4. Drain rice in fine-mesh strainer and rinse with cold running water to stop cooking, about 30 seconds. Rinse and dry pot well to remove any residual starch. Brush bottom and 1 inch up sides of pot with 1 tablespoon oil.

5. Combine yogurt, 2 cups rice, and remaining ¼ cup oil in medium bowl. Stir until rice is evenly coated. Spread yogurt-rice mixture evenly over bottom of prepared pot, packing it down well.

6. Mound remaining rice in center of pot on top of yogurt-rice base (it should look like a cone or a small hill). Poke 8 equally spaced holes through rice mound but not into yogurt-rice base. Cut 2 tablespoons butter into 8 cubes. Place 1 butter cube in each hole. Drizzle ⅓ cup water over rice mound.

7. Wrap pot lid with clean dish towel and cover pot tightly, making sure towel is secure on top of lid and away from heat. Cook over medium-high heat until rice on bottom is crackling and steam is coming out from beneath lid, 8 to 10 minutes, rotating pot halfway through for even cooking.

8. Reduce heat to medium-low and continue to cook until rice is tender and fluffy, 30 to 35 minutes longer. While rice cooks, scoop barberries from bowl, leaving any grit behind in water. Pat dry. Melt 1 teaspoon butter in 10-inch skillet over medium heat. Add barberries and cook, stirring frequently, until color darkens slightly, 2 to 3 minutes (watch carefully, as barberries burn easily). Transfer to small bowl.

9. Wipe out now-empty skillet with paper towel and melt remaining 2 tablespoons butter over medium heat. Add carrots and cook, stirring occasionally, until they begin to soften, 2 to 3 minutes. Add orange peel, sugar, and 6 tablespoons water, stirring to dissolve sugar. Simmer, stirring occasionally, until carrots are tender and orange peel is translucent, 5 to 7 minutes. Drain carrots and orange in fine-mesh strainer and transfer to bowl. Discard syrup.

10. Remove pot from heat and place on damp dish towel set in rimmed baking sheet; let stand, covered, for 5 minutes. Transfer ½ cup rice to bowl. Add saffron water and toss until rice is evenly colored.

11. On large round serving platter, gently spoon remaining rice in large circle (leave crust on bottom of pot intact). Spoon yellow rice in center of platter, shaping it into small circle. Arrange alternating additions of carrot-orange mixture, almonds, pistachios, and barberries so each radiates from "crown" of yellow rice. Using thin metal spatula, loosen edges of crust from pot, then break crust into large pieces. Transfer pieces to separate serving platter. To serve, scoop some of each topping with rice and mix on individual plates, passing crust separately.

Javaher Polo (Jeweled Rice)

Cauliflower Biryani

Cauliflower Biryani

VEGAN Serves 4 to 6 Total Time 1½ hours

Why This Recipe Works Roasted cauliflower, warm spices, and saffron give this aromatic rice dish complex flavor. Traditional biryani recipes often take a long time to develop such flavor, steeping whole spices and cooking each component separately before marrying them. However this recipe is easier and faster, while staying true to the original's hearty warmth and home-style appeal. We cut the cauliflower into small florets to speed up roasting and toss them with warm spices for vibrant flavor. While the cauliflower roasts, we sauté onion, jalapeño, garlic, and more spices; we then add rice to this spicy, flavor-packed mixture and simmer it until tender. Once the rice finishes cooking, we let the residual heat plump a handful of currants and bloom the saffron. Finally, we stir in lots of bright mint and cilantro and fold in our roasted cauliflower. Biryani is traditionally served with a cooling yogurt sauce, which we make before starting the biryani to allow the flavors in the sauce time to meld. You can substitute long-grain white, jasmine, or Texmati rice for the basmati, if you prefer. To make this recipe vegan, substitute plant-based yogurt for the dairy yogurt.

- 1 cup plain whole-milk yogurt
- 1 teaspoon grated lemon zest plus 2 tablespoons juice
- ¼ cup minced fresh cilantro, divided
- ¼ cup minced fresh mint, divided
- 5 garlic cloves, minced, divided
- 1 head cauliflower (2 pounds), cored and cut into ½-inch florets
- ¼ cup extra-virgin olive oil, divided
- 1 teaspoon table salt, divided
- ¼ teaspoon pepper
- ¼ teaspoon ground cardamom, divided
- ¼ teaspoon ground cumin, divided
- 1 onion, sliced thin
- 1 jalapeño chile, stemmed, seeded, and minced
- ⅛ teaspoon ground cinnamon
- ⅛ teaspoon ground ginger
- 1½ cups basmati rice, rinsed
- 2¼ cups water
- ½ teaspoon saffron threads, lightly crumbled
- ¼ cup dried currants or raisins

1. Adjust oven rack to middle position and heat oven to 425 degrees. Whisk yogurt, lemon zest and juice, 2 tablespoons cilantro, 2 tablespoons mint, and 1 teaspoon garlic together in bowl. Cover and refrigerate while cooking biryani, or at least 30 minutes.

2. Toss cauliflower florets, 2 tablespoons oil, ½ teaspoon salt, pepper, ⅛ teaspoon cardamom, and ⅛ teaspoon cumin together in bowl. Spread florets onto rimmed baking sheet and roast until tender 15 to 20 minutes.

3. Meanwhile, heat remaining 2 tablespoons oil in large saucepan over medium-high heat until shimmering. Add onion and cook, stirring often, until soft and dark brown around edges, 10 to 12 minutes.

4. Stir in jalapeño, cinnamon, ginger, remaining garlic, remaining ⅛ teaspoon cardamom, and remaining ⅛ teaspoon cumin and cook until fragrant, about 1 minute. Stir in rice and cook until well coated, about 1 minute. Add water, saffron, and remaining ½ teaspoon salt and bring to simmer. Reduce heat to low, cover, and simmer until all liquid is absorbed, 16 to 18 minutes.

5. Off heat, sprinkle currants over rice. Cover, laying clean dish towel underneath lid, and let sit for 10 minutes. Fold in remaining 2 tablespoons cilantro, remaining 2 tablespoons mint, and roasted cauliflower. Season with salt and pepper to taste and serve with yogurt sauce.

Rinsing Rice

It is important to rinse rice before cooking to remove excess surface starch, which leads to clumpy rice. Place rice in a fine-mesh strainer and run cold water over it until the water runs clear. Drain well.

Paella de Verduras (Cauliflower and Bean Paella)

VEGAN Serves 4 Total Time 1¼ hours

Why This Recipe Works Paella de verduras—a beloved rice dish that's prepared throughout Spain—showcases vegetables rather than merely using them to flavor the rice. Here we feature green beans and butter beans, plus cauliflower florets. We add a complex savory backbone with a retooled Spanish sofrito, using browned bell pepper, umami-rich tomato paste, and lots of garlic. Smoked paprika, saffron, and nutty-tasting dry sherry add brightness and depth. We parcook the beans and cauliflower on their own and then place the vegetables on top of the rice so they can finish cooking with the rest of the dish. Continuing to cook the rice after the liquid in the pan has evaporated creates a caramelized, crisp-chewy layer called socarrat that adds even more complexity. Letting the paella rest for a few minutes before serving helps the socarrat layer firm up so it is even crispier and releases easily from the pan. You can use Bomba or arborio rice in place of the Calasparra.

- 3 tablespoons extra-virgin olive oil, divided
- 2½ cups 2- to 2½-inch cauliflower florets
- ¾ teaspoon table salt, divided
- 6 ounces green beans, trimmed and cut into 2- to 2½-inch pieces
- 1 red bell pepper, stemmed, seeded, and chopped fine
- 1 tablespoon tomato paste
- 3 garlic cloves, minced
- 1 teaspoon smoked paprika
- ¼ teaspoon saffron threads, crumbled
- ¼ cup dry sherry
- 1 cup Calasparra rice
- 1 (15-ounce) can butter beans, rinsed
- 3½ cups vegetable broth
- Lemon wedges

1. Heat 1½ tablespoons oil in 12-inch skillet over medium heat until shimmering. Add cauliflower and ¼ teaspoon salt and cook, stirring frequently, until cauliflower is spotty brown, 3 to 5 minutes. Add green beans and ¼ teaspoon salt. Continue to cook, stirring frequently, until green beans are dark green, 2 to 4 minutes. Transfer vegetables to bowl.

2. Heat remaining 1½ tablespoons oil in now-empty skillet over medium heat until shimmering. Add bell pepper and remaining ¼ teaspoon salt and cook, stirring occasionally, until bell pepper starts to brown, 7 to 10 minutes. Add tomato paste and cook, stirring constantly, until bell pepper pieces are coated in tomato paste, about 1 minute. Add garlic, paprika, and saffron and cook, stirring constantly, until fragrant, about 30 seconds. Stir in sherry and cook, stirring frequently, until excess moisture has evaporated and bell pepper mixture forms large clumps, 1 to 2 minutes.

3. Add rice and stir until very well combined. Off heat, smooth into even layer. Scatter butter beans evenly over rice. Scatter cauliflower and green beans evenly over butter beans. Gently pour broth over all, making sure rice is fully submerged (it's OK if parts of vegetables aren't submerged).

4. Bring to boil over high heat. Adjust heat to maintain gentle simmer and cook until broth is just below top of rice, 12 to 17 minutes. Cover and cook until rice is cooked through, about 5 minutes. Uncover and cook until rice pops and sizzles and all excess moisture has evaporated (to test, use butter knife to gently push aside some rice and vegetables), 3 to 7 minutes. (If socarrat is desired, continue to cook, rotating skillet quarter turn every 20 seconds, until rice on bottom of skillet is well browned and slightly crusty [use butter knife to test], 2 to 5 minutes.) Let rest off heat for 5 minutes. Serve, passing lemon wedges separately.

Vegetable Bibimbap with Tempeh

VEGAN Serves 6 Total Time 1½ hours

Why This Recipe Works Korean bibimbap might just be the ultimate rice bowl. It features a crispy rice crust and a variety of lively toppings—some savory, some acidic, some spicy. ("Bibim" means "mixed" and "bap" means "rice.") We learned that a Dutch oven holds heat well enough to create the desired crust. Some recipes include eggs and meat, but we didn't miss them one bit in our vegetable version. We did want to add some heft, so we incorporate tempeh; its nutty and pleasantly bitter notes play nicely with the dish's parade of sweet and sour flavors. The ingredient list is long, but don't be intimidated. Prepare the pickles, chile sauce, and vegetables a day ahead and warm the vegetables to room temperature in the microwave before adding them to the rice. You can also substitute store-bought kimchi for the pickles. For a true bibimbap experience, bring the pot to the table before stirring the vegetables and tempeh into the rice in step 8.

Pickles

- 1 cup cider vinegar
- 2 tablespoons sugar
- 1½ teaspoons table salt
- 1 cucumber, peeled, quartered lengthwise, seeded, and sliced thin on bias
- 4 ounces (2 cups) bean sprouts

Rice

- 2½ cups short-grain white rice
- 2½ cups water
- ¾ teaspoon table salt

Vegetables and Tempeh

- 2 tablespoons vegetable oil, divided
- 8 ounces tempeh, cut into ½-inch pieces
- ¼ cup soy sauce, divided
- ¼ teaspoon table salt
- ¼ teaspoon pepper
- ½ cup water
- 3 scallions, minced
- 3 garlic cloves, minced
- 1 tablespoon sugar
- 3 carrots, peeled and shredded (2 cups)
- 8 ounces shiitake mushrooms, stemmed and sliced thin
- 10 ounces curly-leaf spinach, stemmed and chopped coarse

Bibimbap

- 2 tablespoons vegetable oil
- 1 tablespoon toasted sesame oil
- 1 recipe Gochujang Sauce (page 527)

1. **For the pickles** Whisk vinegar, sugar, and salt together in bowl. Add cucumber and bean sprouts and toss to combine. Press vegetables to submerge, cover, and refrigerate for at least 30 minutes or up to 24 hours.

2. **For the rice** Bring rice, water, and salt to boil in medium saucepan over high heat. Cover, reduce heat to low, and cook for 7 minutes. Let sit, covered, off heat until rice is tender, about 15 minutes.

3. **For the vegetables and tempeh** While rice cooks and rests, heat 1 tablespoon oil in 12-inch nonstick skillet over medium-high heat until just smoking. Add tempeh, 1 tablespoon soy sauce, salt, and pepper and cook until well browned, 4 to 6 minutes. Off heat, cover to keep warm.

4. Combine water, scallions, garlic, sugar, and remaining 3 tablespoons soy sauce in bowl. Heat 1 teaspoon oil in Dutch oven over high heat until shimmering. Add carrots, stirring to coat. Stir in ⅓ cup scallion mixture and cook until carrots are slightly softened and liquid has evaporated, about 1 minute; transfer to bowl.

5. Heat 1 teaspoon oil in now-empty pot until shimmering. Add mushrooms, stirring to coat. Stir in ⅓ cup scallion mixture and cook until mushrooms are tender and liquid has evaporated, about 3 minutes; transfer to second bowl.

6. Heat remaining 1 teaspoon oil in now-empty Dutch oven until shimmering. Stir in spinach and remaining scallion mixture and cook until spinach is just wilted, about 1 minute. Transfer spinach to third bowl, discard any remaining liquid, and wipe out pot with paper towel.

7. **For the bibimbap** Heat vegetable oil and sesame oil in now-empty pot over high heat until shimmering. Carefully add cooked rice and press into even layer. Cook, without stirring, until rice begins to form crust on bottom of pot, about 2 minutes. Transfer tempeh, carrots, mushrooms, and spinach to pot and arrange in piles to cover surface of rice. Reduce heat to low and cook until golden brown crust forms on bottom of rice, about 5 minutes.

8. Drizzle 2 tablespoons gochujang sauce over top. Without disturbing crust, stir rice, vegetables, and tempeh until combined. Scrape large pieces of crust from bottom of pot and stir into rice. Serve in individual bowls, passing pickles and remaining gochujang sauce separately.

Vegetable Bibimbap with Tempeh

A Diminutive Star

Baby bok choy, with its bright green leaves and overlapping white stems, is an alluring vegetable. It can be used with many cooking techniques, stir-frying foremost among them. Stir-fries are meant to be fast-paced affairs, and baby bok choy obliges because it can be prepped easily and cooked quickly, but also because of the crisp-tender texture between the stems and leaves.

The Flavor Equation

The leaves of baby bok choy have a mild mustardy, grassy flavor that is subtle but noticeable. After all, it's part of the cabbage family. It won't overpower other ingredients, but it stands up to and balances out the intense flavors in our Garlicky Fried Rice (10 cloves of garlic and 2 tablespoons fish sauce). We intentionally use a generous amount of baby bok choy here so that you taste it in every bite.

Baby Versus Large Bok Choy

So why use baby bok choy instead of its much larger cousin? Its flavor is less assertive and its leaves are more tender since it is harvested earlier in the season. In our fried rice recipe, we preferred it for its flavor profile, easy prep, and shorter cooking time.

Garlicky Fried Rice with Bok Choy

Garlicky Fried Rice with Bok Choy

Serves 4 to 6 Total Time 40 minues, plus 45 minutes resting, cooling, and chilling

Why This Recipe Works Garlic does the heavy lifting flavor-wise in this savory, vegetable-packed rice dish, with help from fish sauce and baby bok choy. We love the bright green the bok choy adds to the rice plus its hint of mustardy flavor. But the best part of this dish is the crunchy hits of rice peppered throughout, where lime juice and fish sauce concentrate into tiny pops of umami. Cooking the rice undisturbed at the end is key to getting those magical crispy bits, so don't go stir-crazy. You will need a 14-inch flat-bottomed wok or a 12-inch nonstick skillet for this recipe. If using a wok, make sure that it is well seasoned so that the rice doesn't stick. You can use 4 cups day-old cooked rice in place of making the rice in this recipe; skip step 1 and bring the leftover rice to room temperature before using.

- 1½ cups short-grain white rice, rinsed
- 1½ cups water
- 1 teaspoon table salt, divided
- 3 tablespoons vegetable oil, divided
- 6 heads (1½ pounds) baby bok choy, halved lengthwise and sliced crosswise ½ inch thick
- 10 garlic cloves, minced
- 2 tablespoons vegetarian fish sauce
- 1 teaspoon grated lime zest plus 1½ tablespoons juice
- ¼ teaspoon pepper

1. Combine rice, water, and ½ teaspoon salt in medium saucepan and bring to boil over high heat. Reduce heat to low, cover, and simmer for 7 minutes. Let sit off heat, covered, for 15 minutes. Spread rice onto rimmed baking sheet and let cool on wire rack for 10 minutes. Transfer sheet to refrigerator and let rice chill for 20 minutes.

2. Heat 1 tablespoon oil in 14-inch flat-bottomed wok or 12-inch nonstick skillet over medium-high heat until just smoking. Add bok choy and remaining ½ teaspoon salt and cook until beginning to soften and char in spots, 2 to 4 minutes. Stir in garlic and cook until fragrant, about 30 seconds. Stir in rice, remaining 2 tablespoons oil, fish sauce, lime zest and juice, and pepper.

3. Firmly press rice mixture into compact, even layer. Cover and cook, without stirring, until rice begins to crisp, about 2 minutes. Uncover, reduce heat to medium, and continue to cook until bottom of rice is golden brown, 4 to 6 minutes. Season with salt and pepper to taste and serve.

Stir-Fried Rice Cakes with Bok Choy and Snow Peas

FAST VEGAN Serves 4 Total Time 30 minutes

Why This Recipe Works If you are not familiar with Korean rice cakes, this simple stir-fry is a great way to get to know them. In addition to the rice cakes, it features lots of baby bok choy, snow peas, scallions, and a flavor bomb of a sauce thanks to a bit of gochujang. Rice cakes are made from a mixture of rice flour and water that's pounded and kneaded into a pliable dough and rolled into a long, thick cylinder. Then, it's sliced into thin, oblong disks or cut into smaller cylinders. What's delightful to the uninitiated is rice cakes' gummy texture—like a chewier gnocchi, with enough surface area to cling to whatever sauce you toss its way. If using frozen Korean rice cakes, be sure to thaw them before cooking. You can find rice cakes in many supermarkets or in Korean markets. This recipe uses the paste form of gochujang. Don't substitute gochujang sauce, which contains additional ingredients. If you like things spicy, use the full amount of gochujang.

- 3 tablespoons soy sauce
- 1 tablespoon sugar
- 1 tablespoon toasted sesame oil
- 1 tablespoon hoisin sauce
- ½–1 teaspoon gochujang
- 1 tablespoon vegetable oil
- 3 scallions, cut into 1-inch pieces
- 3 garlic cloves, minced
- 1 pound Korean rice cakes (sliced or tube-shaped)
- 4 heads (1 pound) baby bok choy, chopped
- ⅓ cup water
- 4 ounces snow peas, strings removed and cut in half crosswise

1. In small bowl, whisk soy sauce, sugar, sesame oil, hoisin, and gochujang until combined.

2. Heat vegetable oil in 12-inch nonstick skillet over medium-high heat until shimmering. Add scallions and cook, stirring occasionally, until just beginning to brown, about 2 minutes. Add garlic and cook for 30 seconds. Stir in rice cakes, separating any that are stuck together, and bok choy. Add water, cover, and cook until bok choy is bright green and liquid has begun to evaporate, about 3 minutes.

3. Add soy sauce mixture and snow peas and stir until well combined. Cook, stirring occasionally, until sauce is thickened, 1 to 2 minutes. Serve.

Risotto alla Milanese

Serves 6 Total Time 1 hour

Why This Recipe Works Risotto alla Milanese is an Italian staple with a dazzling yellow color. Rather than babysitting the risotto for half an hour on the stove, we adopt our "almost hands-free" method, allowing the rice to simmer with only minimal stirring in a heavy-bottomed Dutch oven. This method cooks the risotto slowly, keeping the rice creamy yet al dente, without the arm work of constant stirring. For easy pairing, we use a hefty amount of dry white wine and vegetable broth to keep our risotto bright, tangy, and well balanced. The result is a creamy risotto that is excellent with any staple protein or vegetable or devoured simply on its own. Gently crumbling the saffron makes it easier to achieve an accurate measurement. For a softer, creamier risotto, you can substitute carnaroli rice for the arborio. You can substitute 1 tablespoon of kosher salt for the table salt, if desired. Note that this method of making risotto is more hands-off than traditional versions and requires precise timing, so we highly recommend using a timer.

- 5 cups vegetable broth, plus extra warm broth as needed
- 1½ teaspoons saffron threads, crumbled
- 8 tablespoons unsalted butter, cut into 1-tablespoon pieces, divided
- 1 onion, chopped fine
- 1½ teaspoons table salt
- 2 cups arborio rice
- 1¼ cups dry white wine
- 2 ounces Parmesan cheese, grated (1 cup)

1. Bring broth to boil in large saucepan over high heat, then reduce heat to low. Add saffron and cover to keep warm.

2. Meanwhile, melt 3 tablespoons butter in large Dutch oven over medium heat. Add onion and salt and cook, stirring occasionally, until onion is softened but not browned, 3 to 4 minutes. Add rice and cook, stirring frequently, until edges of grains are translucent, about 2 minutes.

3. Add wine and cook, stirring frequently, until wine is nearly absorbed, about 1 minute. Stir in 4 cups warm broth. Reduce heat to low, cover, and simmer, stirring every 5 minutes, until nearly all liquid has been absorbed and rice is just al dente, 15 to 19 minutes.

4. Add remaining 1 cup warm broth and cook, stirring constantly, until grains of rice are cooked through but still slightly firm in center and cooking liquid is thick and creamy, 3 to 5 minutes. Stir in Parmesan. Let risotto stand off heat, covered, for 5 minutes.

5. Stir in remaining 5 tablespoons butter and season with salt and pepper to taste. Adjust consistency with up to ½ cup warm broth as needed. (Texture of risotto should be somewhat loose; it will thicken slightly as it sits.) Serve.

Miso Mushroom Risotto

VEGAN Serves 4 Total Time 1¼ hours

Why This Recipe Works The ideal risotto is beloved for its plush creaminess, usually a result of copious amounts of butter and Parmesan. We wanted a version that was completely plant based, but we found all the options, many using cashew cheese, extra olive oil, or even chia seeds (for body), to be heavy and gluey. This creamy mushroom risotto relies on miso, made from fermented soybeans, instead of butter and Parm. A powerhouse ingredient, miso gives the risotto its savor and umami, acts as a thickener, and coats it in a satiny gloss. To ensure that the mushroom flavor really shines we use two kinds: a full pound of cremini mushrooms as well as dried porcini. We brown the cremini mushrooms, which adds lots of flavor, then set them aside to add at the end. Dried porcini mushrooms are known for their intense earthiness, which ups the umami quotient; we add them along with the garlic just before incorporating the rice and liquid. They add beautiful background flavor notes as they meld with the rice mixture. Note that this method of making risotto is more hands-off than traditional versions and requires precise timing, so we highly recommend using a timer.

- 4 cups vegetable broth
- 3 cups water
- ⅓ cup white miso
- ¼ cup extra-virgin olive oil, divided
- 1 pound cremini mushrooms, trimmed and sliced ¼ inch thick
- 1 onion, chopped fine
- 4 garlic cloves, minced
- 1 ounce dried porcini mushrooms, rinsed and minced
- 2 cups arborio rice
- ½ cup dry white wine
- ¼ cup chopped fresh parsley

1. Bring broth, water, and miso to boil in large saucepan over high heat; reduce heat to medium-low and simmer, whisking occasionally, until miso is dissolved, about 5 minutes. Reduce heat to lowest setting and cover to keep warm.

2. Meanwhile, heat 1 tablespoon oil in Dutch oven over medium heat until shimmering. Add cremini mushrooms, cover, and cook until mushrooms have released their liquid, about 5 minutes. Uncover and continue to cook until well browned, 10 to 12 minutes longer; transfer to bowl.

3. Heat 2 tablespoons oil in now-empty pot over medium heat until shimmering. Stir in onion and cook until softened, about 5 minutes. Add garlic and porcini mushrooms and cook until fragrant, about 30 seconds. Add rice and cook, stirring frequently, until edges of grains are translucent, about 3 minutes.

4. Add wine and cook, stirring constantly, until fully absorbed, 2 to 3 minutes. Stir in 5 cups hot broth mixture, then reduce heat to medium-low, cover, and simmer until almost all liquid has been absorbed and rice is just al dente, 16 to 18 minutes, stirring twice during simmering. Add ¾ cup hot broth mixture and browned cremini mushrooms and stir gently and constantly until risotto becomes creamy, about 3 minutes. Cover pot and let sit off heat for 5 minutes.

5. Stir in parsley and remaining 1 tablespoon oil and season with salt and pepper to taste. Before serving, adjust consistency with additional hot broth mixture as needed.

top | *Risotto alla Milanese*

bottom | *Miso Mushroom Risotto*

Corn Puree Transforms Risotto

Our Corn Risotto uses corn kernels in two ingenious ways: pureed and raw. It is the formula for the freshest corn flavor and creates the most luxurious pot of risotto we've ever had.

Liquid Gold

We make corn an integral part of the dish by stirring in a puree made from the kernels and the "milk" we scrape from the cobs. This liquid not only saturates every bite with corn flavor but also adds naturally occurring starch from the corn, which, when heated, thickens to a sauce-like consistency. This gives the risotto exceptionally silky body. We add the puree toward the end of cooking to preserve the corn's fresh flavor.

Cutting the Richness

White wine is usually used in risotto to brighten up the starchy rice, but in this instance it simply overwhelmed the corn flavor. Instead, we add lemon juice for brightness and finish the dish with crème fraîche. The cultured dairy contributes some acidity, but far less than wine, and its dairy flavor complements the corn.

Adding Corn Kernels

After the puree simmers briefly with the rice mixture, we add a cup of raw corn kernels, which contribute just enough snap, sweetness, and color.

Corn Risotto

Serves 6 to 8 Total Time 1 hour

Why This Recipe Works When fresh corn is available, try something a bit different and make it the centerpiece of a risotto. To make risotto that features truly vibrant corn flavor, we start by blending 3 cups of fresh corn kernels with a little water and the pulpy "milk" we scrape from the cobs to yield a supersweet, bright-tasting puree. If crème fraîche is unavailable, you can substitute sour cream. A large ear of corn should yield 1 cup of kernels, but if the ears you find are smaller, buy at least six.

- 4–6 ears corn, kernels cut from cobs (4 cups), divided, cobs reserved
- 5½ cups hot water, divided
- 2 tablespoons unsalted butter
- 1 shallot, minced
- 1 garlic clove, minced
- 2 teaspoons table salt
- ½ teaspoon pepper
- 1½ cups arborio rice
- 3 sprigs fresh thyme
- 1 ounce Parmesan cheese, grated (½ cup)
- ¼ cup crème fraîche
- 2 tablespoons chopped fresh chives
- ½ teaspoon lemon juice

1. Stand 1 reserved corn cob on end on cutting board and firmly scrape downward with back of butter knife to remove any pulp remaining on cob. Repeat with remaining cobs. Transfer pulp to blender. Add 3 cups corn kernels.

2. Process corn and pulp on low speed until thick puree forms, about 30 seconds. With blender running, add ½ cup hot water. Increase speed to high and continue to process until smooth, about 3 minutes longer. Pour puree into fine-mesh strainer set over large liquid measuring cup or bowl. Using back of ladle or silicone spatula, push puree through strainer, extracting as much liquid as possible (you should have about 2 cups corn liquid). Discard solids.

3. Melt butter in large Dutch oven over medium heat. Add shallot, garlic, salt, and pepper and cook, stirring frequently, until softened but not browned, about 1 minute. Add rice and thyme sprigs and cook, stirring frequently, until edges of grains are translucent, 2 to 3 minutes.

4. Stir in 4½ cups hot water. Reduce heat to medium-low, cover, and simmer until liquid is slightly thickened and rice is just al dente, 16 to 19 minutes, stirring twice during cooking.

5. Add corn liquid and continue to cook, stirring gently and constantly, until risotto is creamy and thickened but not sticky, about 3 minutes longer (risotto will continue to thicken as it sits). Stir in Parmesan and remaining 1 cup corn kernels. Cover pot and let stand off heat for 5 minutes. Stir in crème fraîche, chives, and lemon juice. Discard thyme sprigs and season with salt and pepper to taste. Adjust consistency with remaining ½ cup hot water as needed. Serve.

Cơm Đỏ (Vietnamese Red Rice)

FAST Serves 4 to 6 Total Time 45 minutes

Why This Recipe Works Red rice is an ultrasavory Vietnamese side dish. It's normally made as a fried rice by stir-frying precooked rice, but we make ours from scratch in one pot. To re-create the slightly drier texture of a fried rice, we hold back slightly on the water. And to ensure the dish has the depth of flavor that it should, we use lots of tomato paste and soy sauce for umami and butter for richness and complexity. This recipe is based on a version made by Vietnamese cooking authority Andrea Nguyen. If jasmine rice is unavailable, substitute another long-grain white rice. Maggi Seasoning can be used in place of the soy sauce, if desired.

- 1½ cups jasmine rice
- 2 tablespoons unsalted butter
- 4 garlic cloves, minced
- 3 tablespoons tomato paste
- 1¾ cups water
- 2 teaspoons soy sauce
- ½ teaspoon table salt

1. Place rice in fine-mesh strainer and rinse under cold running water until water runs clear. Drain well. Melt butter in medium saucepan over medium-high heat. Add rice and cook, stirring constantly, until grains become chalky and opaque, 1 to 3 minutes. Add garlic and cook, stirring constantly, until fragrant, about 30 seconds. Add tomato paste and cook, stirring constantly, until tomato paste is evenly distributed, about 1 minute.

2. Add water, soy sauce, and salt and bring to boil. Cover, reduce heat to low, and cook until liquid is absorbed and rice is tender, about 20 minutes. Let stand off heat, covered, for 10 minutes. Fluff rice with fork and stir to combine. Serve.

Hung Kao Mun Gati (Thai Coconut Rice)

FAST **VEGAN** Serves 4 to 6 Total Time 40 minutes

Why This Recipe Works Every region that grows coconuts and rice marries them to make the grains rich and fragrant. This coconut rice is an elegant dish, one that will take your meal up a notch, and making it is as simple as making plain white rice. Though many recipes use a full can of coconut milk, we found that doing so makes the rice too greasy; the sweet spot is 1½ cups rice cooked in 1 cup coconut milk and 1½ cups water; this leads to a luxuriously rich and perfumed rice that is not too heavy. Letting the rice sit for 10 minutes after cooking allows the delicate grains to firm up a bit so they don't break when served. Gently stirring the rested rice redistributes any coconut oil that has risen to the top of the saucepan during cooking. Do not use low-fat coconut milk in this recipe. Many brands of coconut milk separate during storage; be sure to stir yours until smooth before measuring it. We like the delicately clingy texture of jasmine rice here, but regular long-grain white rice can be substituted. Avoid basmati; the grains will remain too separate. Chopped toasted peanuts, toasted sesame seeds, fried shallots, and pickled chiles are great toppings for this rice. Serve with stir-fries.

- 1½ cups jasmine rice
- 1 cup canned coconut milk
- 1 tablespoon sugar
- ¾ teaspoon table salt

1. Place rice in fine-mesh strainer and rinse under cold running water until water runs clear. Drain well. Stir rice, 1½ cups water, coconut milk, sugar, and salt together in large saucepan. Bring to boil over high heat. Reduce heat to maintain bare simmer. Cover and cook until all liquid is absorbed, 18 to 20 minutes.

2. Let sit off heat, covered, for 10 minutes. Mix rice gently but thoroughly with silicone spatula and serve.

Arroz con Titoté (Colombian Coconut Rice)

VEGAN Serves 4 Total Time 1 hour

Why This Recipe Works This coconut rice is popular in restaurants along the Caribbean coast of Colombia; it's a knockout dish with stunning flavor. We start by boiling pure coconut milk in a partially covered saucepan until the water evaporates, leaving the fat behind. After browning the particles of coconut that are suspended in the fat, we add the rice, which we rinse to remove excess surface starch that would otherwise make the finished product sticky. Adding just enough water to hydrate and gel the starches in the rice ensures that the cooked grains are light and fluffy. A small amount of brown sugar and raisins, which are traditional ingredients, enhance the natural sweetness of the coconut. Finishing with a spritz of lime juice brings all the sweet, salty, nutty flavors into focus. Do not use a coconut milk with additives, which can interfere with the reducing process. Do not use low-fat coconut milk. The coconut solids may bond to the surface of your saucepan in step 2, but they will release as the rice cooks. Browning the coconut milk adds nutty depth, so the small amount of sugar and raisins do not make the dish taste particularly sweet. Do not omit the lime wedges; they bring all the flavors into focus.

- 1 (14-ounce) can coconut milk
- 1½ cups long-grain white rice
- 2¼ cups water, divided
- ⅓ cup raisins
- 2 tablespoons packed dark brown sugar
- 1 teaspoon table salt
- Lime wedges, for serving

1. Pour coconut milk into large saucepan. Cover, leaving lid slightly ajar so steam can escape. Cook over medium-high heat, stirring occasionally, until coconut milk is reduced by about three-quarters and begins to sputter, 10 to 12 minutes. While coconut milk cooks, place rice in fine-mesh strainer and rinse under cold running water until water runs clear. Drain well.

2. Reduce heat to medium. Uncover saucepan and cook, stirring frequently, until fat separates from coconut solids, about 2 minutes. Continue to cook, stirring frequently, until coconut solids turn deep brown (solids will stick to

saucepan), about 3 minutes longer. Add rice and cook, stirring constantly, until grains are well coated with fat. Stir in ½ cup water (mixture may sputter) and scrape bottom and sides of saucepan with wooden spoon to loosen coconut solids. Stir in raisins, sugar, salt, and remaining 1¾ cups water. Bring mixture to boil. Adjust heat to maintain low simmer. Cover and cook until all liquid is absorbed, 18 to 20 minutes.

3. Let sit off heat, covered, for 10 minutes. Mix rice gently but thoroughly. Serve with lime wedges.

Congee

VEGAN Serves 4 to 6 Total Time 1 hour

Why This Recipe Works Congee, and every other version of rice porridge that's made across East and Southeast Asia, is one of the most enduring forms of culinary thrift. Endlessly variable, this savory rice porridge is great for both breakfast and dinner. It features soft, barely intact grains gently bound by their silky, viscous cooking liquid; the result should be fluid but thick and creamy enough to suspend any toppings. Our formula starts with a 13:1 ratio of liquid to long-grain white rice, which produces an appropriately loose porridge. We simmer the rice vigorously to encourage the grains to break down in about 45 minutes (instead of a more typical 90-minute gentle simmer), partially covering the pot to help the contents cook quickly while minimizing evaporation. To prevent the congee from boiling over, we rinse excess starch from the raw rice and wedge a wooden spoon between the lid and the rim of the pot, giving the water bubbles a chance to escape. Jasmine rice can be substituted for regular long-grain white rice; do not use basmati. We prefer the distinctive flavor of Chinese black vinegar here; look for it in Asian supermarkets. Serve with Microwave-Fried Shallots (page 89) and Soft-Cooked Eggs (page 450), if desired.

- ¾ cup long-grain white rice
- 1 cup vegetable broth
- ¾ teaspoon table salt
- Scallions, sliced thin on bias
- Fresh cilantro leaves
- Dry-roasted peanuts, chopped coarse
- Chili oil
- Soy sauce
- Chinese black vinegar

top | *Hung Kao Mun Gati (Thai Coconut Rice)*
bottom | *Arroz con Titoté (Colombian Coconut Rice)*

1. Place rice in fine-mesh strainer and rinse under cold running water until water runs clear. Drain well and transfer to Dutch oven. Add broth, salt, and 9 cups water and bring to boil over high heat. Reduce heat to maintain vigorous simmer. Cover pot, tucking wooden spoon horizontally between pot and lid to hold lid ajar. Cook, stirring occasionally, until mixture is thickened, glossy, and reduced by half, 45 to 50 minutes.

2. Portion congee into individual serving bowls and serve, passing scallions, cilantro, peanuts, oil, soy sauce, and vinegar separately.

Wild Rice Pilaf with Pecans and Cranberries

VEGAN Serves 6 to 8 Total Time 1 hour

Why This Recipe Works Wild rice is tricky. Its sleek, ebony coating masks a chewy interior tasting of little but the marsh where it is grown. So how could we make it taste as good as it looks? First, we needed a technique for ensuring that the rice turns out tender and fluffy, never crunchy or gluey. Simmering it in a flavorful liquid and then draining off the excess is the surest way to that end. Cooking it in a combination of vegetable broth and water along with a bundle of fresh thyme and aromatic bay leaves (for finesse and complexity) is a start, but even with this method the rice alone was too overwhelming. To tame it but still keep the essence of its flavor, we pair it with long-grain white rice. For the most flavorful white rice possible, we enlist the pilaf method: sautéing minced carrot and onion in oil, then adding the rice and water plus a second bundle of fresh thyme. To finish this combo of perfectly cooked wild and white rice, we add a hefty amount of toasted pecans and tart-sweet dried cranberries. Now the marriage of flavors and textures hits all the high notes. Do not use quick-cooking or presteamed wild rice in this recipe (check the ingredient list on the package to determine this).

- 2½ cups water, divided
- 1¾ cups vegetable broth
- 2 bay leaves
- 8 sprigs fresh thyme, divided into 2 bundles, each tied together with kitchen twine
- 1 cup wild rice, rinsed
- 2 tablespoons extra-virgin olive oil
- 1 onion, chopped fine
- 1 large carrot, peeled and chopped fine
- 1 teaspoon table salt
- 1½ cups long-grain white rice, rinsed
- ¾ cup dried cranberries
- ¾ cup pecans, toasted and chopped coarse
- 2 tablespoons minced fresh parsley

1. Bring ¼ cup water, broth, bay leaves, and 1 bundle thyme to boil in medium saucepan over medium-high heat. Add wild rice and reduce heat to low. Cover and simmer gently until rice is plump and tender and most of liquid has been absorbed, 35 to 45 minutes. Drain rice and discard bay leaves and thyme. Transfer rice to large bowl, cover, and set aside.

2. Meanwhile, heat oil in large saucepan over medium-high heat until shimmering. Add onion, carrot, and salt and cook until vegetables are softened, about 5 minutes. Add white rice and cook, stirring constantly, until grains become chalky and opaque, 1 to 3 minutes.

3. Stir in remaining 2¼ cups water and second thyme bundle and bring to boil. Reduce heat to low, cover, and simmer gently until rice is tender and water has been fully absorbed, 16 to 18 minutes. Off heat, lay clean dish towel underneath lid and let sit, covered, for 10 minutes. Discard thyme and fluff rice with fork.

4. Add white rice, cranberries, pecans, and parsley to bowl with wild rice and toss to combine. Season with salt and pepper to taste. Serve.

Variation

VEGAN Wild Rice Pilaf with Scallions, Cilantro, and Almonds

Omit dried cranberries. Substitute toasted sliced almonds for pecans and cilantro for parsley. Add 2 thinly sliced scallions and 1 teaspoon lime juice to pilaf before serving.

Wild Rice Pilaf with Pecans and Cranberries

California Barley Bowls with Lemon-Yogurt Sauce

California Barley Bowls with Lemon-Yogurt Sauce

VEGAN   Serves 4   Total Time 50 minutes

Why This Recipe Works Sweet snow peas are the vegetable of choice for this bowl; their flavor contrasts perfectly with nutty barley, a great alternative to the usual rice. We also add chunks of ripe avocado and toasted, spiced sunflower seeds. For the barley we use easy-to-find pearl barley, which is processed to remove its hull and bran. To keep the cooking method easy, we simply boil the barley until tender and then toss it with a simple dressing. While the barley cooks, we sauté the snow peas with coriander and toast the sunflower seeds with lots of warm spices. To pull it all together, a yogurt sauce infused with bright lemon and refreshing mint adds zestiness and color. Do not substitute hulled or hull-less barley in this recipe. If using quick-cooking or presteamed barley (check the ingredient list on the package to determine this), you will need to alter the barley cooking time in step 1. The cooking time for barley will vary from product to product, so start checking for doneness after 25 minutes. Be sure to cover the pot when bringing the water to a boil in step 1; any water loss due to evaporation will affect how the barley cooks. To make this recipe vegan, substitute plant-based yogurt for the dairy yogurt.

- 1 cup pearl barley, rinsed
- 1 teaspoon table salt, divided, plus salt for cooking barley
- ¼ cup extra-virgin olive oil, divided
- 8 ounces snow peas, strings removed, halved lengthwise
- 1 teaspoon ground coriander, divided
- ¾ cup sunflower seeds
- ½ teaspoon ground cumin
- ⅛ teaspoon ground cardamom
- 1 cup plain yogurt
- 2 teaspoons grated lemon zest plus 3 tablespoons juice, divided
- 2 tablespoons minced fresh mint, divided
- ¼ teaspoon pepper
- 2 avocados, halved, pitted, and cut into ½-inch pieces

1. Bring 4 quarts water to boil in large pot. Add barley and 1 tablespoon salt and cook until tender, 20 to 25 minutes; drain and transfer to large bowl.

2. Meanwhile, heat 1½ teaspoons oil in 12-inch skillet over medium-high heat until just smoking. Add snow peas and ½ teaspoon coriander and cook until peas are spotty brown, about 3 minutes; transfer to plate.

3. Add 1½ teaspoons oil to now-empty skillet and heat over medium heat until shimmering. Stir in sunflower seeds, cumin, cardamom, remaining ½ teaspoon coriander, and ½ teaspoon salt. Cook, stirring constantly, until seeds are toasted, about 2 minutes; let cool off heat.

4. Whisk yogurt, 1 teaspoon lemon zest and 2 tablespoons juice, 1 tablespoon mint, remaining ½ teaspoon salt, and pepper together in small bowl; cover and refrigerate until needed.

5. Whisk remaining 3 tablespoons oil, remaining 1 teaspoon lemon zest and 1 tablespoon juice, and remaining 1 tablespoon mint together in separate bowl and season with salt and pepper to taste. Pour dressing over barley, add snow peas, and toss well to coat. Portion barley into individual serving bowls, top with avocados and spiced sunflower seeds, and drizzle with yogurt sauce. Serve.

Barley with Lemon and Herbs

VEGAN Serves 6 to 8 Total Time 50 minutes

Why This Recipe Works Warm barley tossed with a pleasantly mouth-puckering, citrusy dressing is sure to perk up your senses with a taste of sunshine. We love barley for its nuttiness and light chew. Using the pasta method—boiling the barley in plenty of salted water and then draining it—rids it of the excess starch that causes clumping. An acid-heavy dressing using a 1:1 ratio of lemon juice to oil, plus fragrant lemon zest and sharp Dijon mustard, gives this winter salad its punch. A few fresh elements—shallot, scallions, and herbs—give our satisfying salad a truly light and lively flavor profile. The cooking time for barley will vary from product to product, so start checking for doneness after 25 minutes. Be sure to cover the pot when bringing the water to a boil in step 1; any water loss due to evaporation will affect how the barley cooks.

- 1½ cups pearl barley, rinsed
- ½ teaspoon table salt, plus salt for cooking barley
- 3 tablespoons extra-virgin olive oil
- 2 tablespoons minced shallot
- 1 teaspoon grated lemon zest plus 3 tablespoons juice
- 1 teaspoon Dijon mustard
- ¼ teaspoon pepper
- 6 scallions, sliced thin on bias
- ¼ cup minced fresh mint
- ¼ cup minced fresh cilantro

1. Line rimmed baking sheet with parchment paper and set aside. Bring 4 quarts water to boil in Dutch oven. Add barley and 1 tablespoon salt. Stir and cook, adjusting heat to maintain gentle boil, until barley is tender with slight chew, 25 to 45 minutes.

2. While barley cooks, whisk oil, shallot, lemon zest and juice, mustard, salt, and pepper together in large bowl.

3. Drain barley. Transfer to prepared sheet and spread into even layer. Let stand until no longer steaming, 5 to 7 minutes. Add barley to bowl with dressing and toss to coat. Add scallions, mint, and cilantro and stir to combine. Season with salt and pepper to taste. Serve. (Barley can be refrigerated for up to 3 days. Allow to come to room temperature before serving.)

Variations

VEGAN Barley with Celery and Miso Dressing

Substitute 3 tablespoons seasoned rice vinegar, 1 tablespoon white miso paste, 1 tablespoon soy sauce, 1 tablespoon toasted sesame oil, 1 tablespoon vegetable oil, 2 teaspoons grated fresh ginger, 1 minced garlic clove, 1 teaspoon packed brown sugar, and ¼ to ½ teaspoon red pepper flakes for olive oil, shallot, lemon zest and juice, mustard, salt, and pepper in step 2. Substitute 2 celery ribs, sliced thin on bias, and 2 peeled and grated carrots for scallions. Omit mint and increase cilantro to ½ cup.

VEGAN Barley with Fennel, Dried Apricots, and Orange

Substitute 3 tablespoons red wine vinegar and ½ teaspoon grated orange zest plus 2 tablespoons juice for lemon zest and juice. Omit mustard. Reduce olive oil to 2 tablespoons and add 1 minced garlic clove to dressing in step 2. Substitute 20 chopped dried California apricots and 1 small fennel bulb, 2 tablespoons fronds minced, stalks discarded, bulb halved, cored, and chopped fine, for scallions. Omit mint and substitute parsley for cilantro.

Beet and Barley Risotto

Serves 4 Total Time 1¼ hours

Why This Recipe Works One wonderful thing about beets (apart from their flavor and beautiful color) is that you can use the leaves as well. Here shredded beets and their tender leaves are incorporated into a vibrant barley risotto. Pearl barley has had its outer hull and bran removed, exposing the starchy interior. The starch helps the barley cooking liquid thicken into a velvety sauce as it simmers. Simmering the barley just until the grains are still somewhat firm in the center helps them retain some of their satisfying bite. Cooking the grains with white wine and vegetable broth delivers complex flavor and savoriness. We stir grated raw beets into the barley in two stages—half at the beginning for a base of flavor and half at the end for freshness, color, and pleasant chew. Do not substitute hulled, hull-less, quick-cooking, or presteamed barley for the pearl barley (check the ingredient list on the package to determine this). You can use the large holes of a box grater or a food processor fitted with a shredding disk to shred the beets. You can replace the beet greens with 2 cups stemmed and chopped Swiss chard if necessary.

- 3 cups vegetable broth
- 3 cups water
- 2 tablespoons extra-virgin olive oil
- 1 pound beets with greens attached, beets trimmed, peeled, and shredded, divided, greens stemmed and cut into 1-inch pieces (2 cups)
- 1 onion, chopped
- ½ teaspoon table salt
- 1½ cups pearl barley, rinsed
- 4 garlic cloves, minced
- 1 teaspoon minced fresh thyme or ¼ teaspoon dried
- 1 cup dry white wine
- 1 ounce Parmesan cheese, grated (½ cup)
- 2 tablespoons chopped fresh parsley

1. Bring broth and water to simmer in medium saucepan. Reduce heat to lowest setting and cover to keep warm.

2. Heat oil in large saucepan over medium heat until shimmering. Add half of shredded beets, onion, and salt and cook until vegetables are softened, 5 to 7 minutes. Stir in barley and cook, stirring often, until fragrant, about 4 minutes. Stir in garlic and thyme and cook until fragrant, about 30 seconds. Stir in wine and cook until fully absorbed, about 2 minutes.

3. Stir in 3 cups warm broth mixture. Simmer, stirring occasionally, until liquid is absorbed and bottom of pan is dry, 22 to 25 minutes. Stir in 2 cups warm broth mixture and simmer, stirring occasionally, until liquid is absorbed and bottom of pan is dry, 15 to 18 minutes.

4. Add beet greens and continue to cook, stirring often and adding remaining warm broth mixture as needed to prevent bottom of pan from becoming dry, until greens are softened and barley is cooked through but still somewhat firm in center, 5 to 10 minutes. Off heat, stir in remaining shredded beets and Parmesan. Season with salt and pepper to taste and sprinkle with parsley. Serve.

Barley and Lentils with Mushrooms and Tahini-Yogurt Sauce

VEGAN Serves 4 Total Time 50 minutes

Why This Recipe Works This superhearty dish is a great way to pair black lentils with dried and fresh mushrooms, both of which have deep, robust flavors. The lentils and barley go especially well with porcini and portobello mushrooms, onion, and a creamy tahini-yogurt sauce that we enliven with lemon and garlic. Slightly smaller than brown lentils, black lentils have a great ability to hold their shape even when tender (which means we can cook them in the same pot as the barley). While the lentils simmer and stay warm in the pot, we sauté the onion and brown the portobellos in a skillet. Then the umami-rich porcini and their flavorful soaking liquid go in, pairing beautifully with the meaty portobellos. Fresh dill and strips of lemon peel brighten and balance the earthiness, and drizzling the garlicky tahini-yogurt sauce over the barley and lentils before serving works perfectly to balance all the hearty flavors and textures. While we prefer black lentils here, lentilles du Puy, brown lentils, and green lentils can be substituted.

- ½ ounce dried porcini mushrooms, rinsed
- 1 cup pearl barley, rinsed
- ½ cup black lentils, picked over and rinsed
- ½ teaspoon table salt, plus salt for cooking barley and lentils
- 2 tablespoons extra-virgin olive oil
- 1 onion, chopped fine
- 2 large portobello mushroom caps, cut into 1-inch pieces

3 (2-inch) strips lemon zest, sliced thin lengthwise
¾ teaspoon ground coriander
¼ teaspoon pepper
2 tablespoons chopped fresh dill
Tahini-Yogurt Sauce (page 211)

1. Microwave 1½ cups water and porcini mushrooms in covered bowl until steaming, about 1 minute. Let sit until softened, 5 minutes. Drain in fine-mesh strainer lined with coffee filter, reserving liquid, and chop porcini.

2. Bring 4 quarts water to boil in Dutch oven. Add barley, lentils, and 1 tablespoon salt, return to boil, and cook until tender, 20 to 40 minutes. Drain barley and lentils, return to now-empty pot, and cover to keep warm.

3. Meanwhile, heat oil in 12-inch nonstick skillet over medium heat until shimmering. Add onion and cook until softened, about 5 minutes. Stir in portobello mushrooms, cover, and cook until portobellos have released their liquid and begin to brown, about 4 minutes.

4. Uncover, stir in lemon zest, coriander, salt, and pepper, and cook until fragrant, about 30 seconds. Stir in porcini and porcini soaking liquid, bring to boil, and cook, stirring occasionally, until liquid is thickened slightly and reduced to ½ cup, about 5 minutes. Stir mushroom mixture and dill into barley-lentil mixture and season with salt and pepper to taste. Serve, drizzling individual portions with sauce.

Farro with Wild Mushroom Ragout

FAST **VEGAN** Serves 4 Total Time 45 minutes

Why This Recipe Works Whole-grain farro is popular in Italy, and we love it for its slightly sweet, nutty flavor and chewy texture. We give this dish a simple Italian profile by pairing it with a mushroom ragout. Chunks of portobellos and other mushrooms add texture, while dried porcini add flavor and depth. For the best flavor, we prefer to use a combination of white, shiitake, and oyster mushrooms; however, you can choose just one or two varieties if you like. The woody stems of shiitakes are unpleasant to eat, so be sure to remove them. Drizzle individual portions with good balsamic vinegar before serving, if desired. We prefer the flavor and texture of whole farro in this recipe. Do not substitute pearl, quick-cooking, or presteamed farro (check the ingredient list on the package to determine this) for the whole farro.

top | *Beet and Barley Risotto*

bottom | *Barley and Lentils with Mushrooms and Tahini-Yogurt Sauce*

- 3½ cups vegetable broth
- 1½ cups whole farro, rinsed
- 1 pound portobello mushroom caps, halved and sliced ½ inch thick
- 1½ pounds assorted mushrooms, trimmed and halved if small or quartered if large
- 2 tablespoons extra-virgin olive oil
- 1 onion, chopped fine
- ½ ounce dried porcini mushrooms, rinsed and minced
- 3 garlic cloves, minced
- 1 teaspoon minced fresh thyme or ¼ teaspoon dried
- ¼ cup dry Madeira
- 1 (14.5-ounce) can diced tomatoes, drained and chopped
- 2 tablespoons minced fresh parsley

1. Combine broth and farro in large saucepan and bring to simmer over medium heat. Cook until farro is tender and creamy, 20 to 25 minutes. Season with salt and pepper to taste; cover and keep warm.

2. Meanwhile, microwave portobellos and assorted mushrooms in covered bowl until tender, 6 to 8 minutes. Drain, reserving mushroom juices.

3. Heat oil in Dutch oven over medium-high heat until shimmering. Add onion and porcini and cook until softened and lightly browned, 5 to 7 minutes. Stir in drained mushrooms and cook, stirring often, until mushrooms are dry and lightly browned, about 5 minutes.

4. Stir in garlic and thyme and cook until fragrant, about 30 seconds. Stir in Madeira and reserved mushroom juices, scraping up any browned bits. Stir in tomatoes and simmer gently until sauce is slightly thickened, about 8 minutes. Off heat, stir in parsley and season with salt and pepper to taste. Portion farro into individual serving bowls and top with mushroom mixture. Serve.

Jollof-Inspired Fonio

FAST Serves 4 to 6 Total Time 40 minutes

Why This Recipe Works Jollof rice is a beloved West African specialty, the foundational ingredients of which are rice, tomatoes, onions, and spices, though many variations exist throughout the region. We set out to apply jollof's signature bright, savory flavors to fonio, an ancient variety of millet that also hails from West Africa. We begin by blitzing canned tomatoes and an assortment of aromatics in a blender to create a smooth, flavorful cooking liquid for the fonio. As the grains simmer, the fonio takes on a rouge color, characteristic of jollof rice as it drinks up the tomatoes' savory brightness. We enrich this concoction with butter and top it with sweet, soft caramelized onions and fresh parsley. Hearty, comforting, and deeply flavorful, this dish works equally well as a hearty side or a meal on its own. Fonio is widely available online.

- 3 cups vegetable broth, divided
- 1 (14.5-ounce) can whole peeled tomatoes
- 1 red onion (½ onion quartered, ½ onion sliced thin)
- 4 garlic cloves, peeled
- 1 teaspoon table salt
- 1 teaspoon packed brown sugar
- ½ teaspoon red pepper flakes
- ¼ cup vegetable oil, divided
- 1 cup fonio
- 2 bay leaves
- 2 tablespoons unsalted butter
- 2 tablespoons chopped fresh parsley

1. Process 1 cup broth, tomatoes and their juice, quartered onion, garlic, salt, sugar, and pepper flakes in blender on high speed until smooth, 1 to 2 minutes.

2. Heat 2 tablespoons oil in 12-inch nonstick skillet over medium heat until shimmering. Add tomato mixture and cook, stirring occasionally, until slightly thickened, 5 to 7 minutes.

3. Add fonio, bay leaves, and remaining 2 cups broth and stir well. Cook, stirring occasionally, until most liquid has been absorbed, 3 to 4 minutes. Stir in butter, remove from heat, and cover. Let stand until all liquid has been absorbed, 10 to 15 minutes.

4. While fonio stands, heat remaining 2 tablespoons oil in 10-inch nonstick skillet over medium heat until shimmering. Add sliced onion and cook, stirring occasionally, until it begins to brown at edges, 2 to 3 minutes. Reduce heat to low and continue to cook, stirring occasionally, until onion is soft and deeply brown, 15 to 20 minutes.

5. Fluff fonio with fork and top with caramelized onion and parsley. Serve.

Jollof-Inspired Fonio

top | *Curried Fonio with Roasted Vegetables and Hibiscus Vinaigrette*

bottom | *Spring Freekeh and Halloumi Bowls*

Curried Fonio with Roasted Vegetables and Hibiscus Vinaigrette

VEGAN Serves 4 Total Time 1 hour

Why This Recipe Works This curried fonio is topped with a bonanza of roasted vegetables: sweet butternut squash, grassy okra, and wedges of red onion. We roast them at the same time but on separate baking sheets so that we can steam the okra first by covering the baking sheet with foil before it gets crispy and brown. Fonio cooks up quickly but is also light and fluffy and absorbs flavors well. To create a punchy and flavorful foundation for this fonio pilaf, we use curry powder along with fresh garlic and ginger. We add extra crunch and richness by stirring in chopped roasted cashews to finish, then we drizzle everything with a sweet-tart vinaigrette made with dried hibiscus flowers. The bright fuchsia flowers—from a plant related to okra and native to Africa—add a unique cranberry-like flavor and color that pulls this striking plate together. Fonio is widely available online.

- 1 pound butternut squash, peeled, seeded, and cut into ¾-inch pieces (2½ cups)
- 1 red onion, cut through root end into 1-inch wedges
- 2 tablespoons plus 2 teaspoons extra-virgin olive oil, divided
- 1¼ teaspoons table salt, divided
- ¼ teaspoon pepper, divided
- 12 ounces okra, trimmed and halved lengthwise
- 2 garlic cloves, minced
- 1½ teaspoons curry powder
- 1 teaspoon grated fresh ginger
- 2 cups water
- 1 cup fonio
- ⅓ cup roasted cashews, chopped
- ½ cup Hibiscus Vinaigrette (page 353)
- ¼ cup chopped fresh parsley

1. Adjust oven racks to upper-middle and lower-middle positions and heat oven to 425 degrees. Line 2 rimmed baking sheets with aluminum foil.

2. Toss squash and onion with 1 tablespoon oil, ½ teaspoon salt, and ⅛ teaspoon pepper in bowl, then arrange in even layer on 1 prepared sheet. Toss okra with 2 teaspoons oil, ¼ teaspoon salt, and remaining ⅛ teaspoon pepper in now-empty bowl, then arrange cut side down on second prepared sheet. Cover sheet with okra tightly with aluminum foil.

3. Place sheet with squash and onion on lower rack and sheet with okra on upper rack. Roast for 15 minutes, then remove foil from sheet with okra. Continue to roast vegetables until squash and onion are tender and browned and cut sides of okra are well browned, 7 to 12 minutes.

4. Meanwhile, heat remaining 1 tablespoon oil in medium saucepan over medium heat until shimmering. Add garlic, curry powder, and ginger and cook until fragrant, about 30 seconds. Stir in water, fonio, and remaining ½ teaspoon salt and bring to simmer. Cover, reduce heat to low, and simmer until liquid is absorbed, about 3 minutes. Off heat, let fonio sit, covered, for 10 minutes, then gently fluff with fork, breaking up any large clumps. Stir in cashews.

5. Portion fonio into individual serving bowls. Top with roasted vegetables and drizzle with vinaigrette. Sprinkle with parsley and serve.

Hibiscus Vinaigrette

FAST **VEGAN** Makes 1 cup
Total Time 20 minutes

For an accurate measurement of boiling water, bring a kettle of water to a boil and then measure out the desired amount. Dried hibiscus flowers are widely available online.

- ½ ounce (½ cup) whole dried hibiscus flowers
- ½ cup boiling water
- ½ cup extra-virgin olive oil
- 2 tablespoons red wine vinegar
- 2 tablespoons sugar
- 1 teaspoon table salt
- 1 teaspoon Dijon mustard
- ½ teaspoon pepper
- 1 tablespoon minced shallot

Combine hibiscus flowers and boiling water in blender jar; let sit for 10 minutes. Add oil, vinegar, sugar, salt, mustard, and pepper and process until only small pieces of flowers remain, about 1 minute. Transfer to small bowl and stir in shallot. (Vinaigrette can be refrigerated for up to 5 days.)

Spring Freekeh and Halloumi Bowls

Serves 4 Total Time 1¼ hours

Why This Recipe Works Carrots, asparagus, peas, and fresh herbs are a sweet foil for chewy, slightly smoky freekeh, a nutty nutritious grain used in eastern Mediterranean and North African kitchens. Balancing them is the appealing richness of halloumi cheese, with its briny, savory flavor and a springy, meaty mouthfeel that makes it very satisfying to eat. We sear cubes of halloumi to crisp the exteriors and amplify the ingredient's richly milky flavor. We use cracked freekeh because it cooks faster than whole freekeh, and also has a sturdy yet tender bite that further enhances the heartiness of this bowl. The grain is also a flavor sponge, readily absorbing the warmth of allspice and cinnamon. We drizzle the bowls with a creamy, tangy tahini-garlic sauce and then, for a fresh crunch, we toss pea tendrils across the top. A final drizzle of pomegranate molasses adds a zesty element that pulls all the flavors together. Do not substitute whole freekeh for the cracked freekeh in this recipe.

- 2 tablespoons plus 1 teaspoon extra-virgin olive oil, divided
- 3 onions, cut into ¾-inch-thick pieces
- 2 teaspoons ground allspice
- 2 teaspoons ground cinnamon
- ¾ teaspoon pepper
- 2 cups cracked freekeh, rinsed
- 2¼ cups vegetable broth
- 3 carrots, peeled and cut ½ inch thick on bias
- 1 pound asparagus, trimmed and sliced ½ inch thick
- ½ cup frozen peas
- 2 tablespoons lemon juice
- 8 ounces halloumi, cut into ¾-inch pieces
- 1 recipe Tahini-Garlic Sauce (page 354)
- 3 tablespoons torn fresh dill, chervil, and/or mint
- Pea tendrils (optional)
- Pomegranate molasses

1. Heat 2 tablespoons oil in large saucepan over medium heat until shimmering. Add onions and cook until golden brown, about 10 minutes, stirring occasionally. Stir in allspice, cinnamon, and pepper and cook until fragrant, about 30 seconds. Add freekeh and toast until fragrant and nutty, about 3 minutes, stirring often. Stir in broth and bring to simmer. Reduce heat to medium-low, cover, and cook, stirring occasionally and scraping bottom of saucepan with wooden spoon, for 15 minutes (freekeh will not be fully cooked).

2. Stir in carrots, cover, and cook until freekeh is almost tender, about 10 minutes. Stir in asparagus, cover, and cook until asparagus is vibrant green and crisp-tender, about 5 minutes. Stir in peas and lemon juice and season with salt to taste. Cover and let sit off heat while cooking halloumi.

3. Pat halloumi dry with paper towels. Heat remaining 1 teaspoon oil in 10-inch skillet over medium-high heat until shimmering. Add halloumi and cook, turning as needed, until halloumi is deep golden brown on multiple sides, about 4 minutes.

4. Portion freekeh into individual serving bowls. Top with seared halloumi, drizzle with tahini sauce, and sprinkle with herbs and pea tendrils, if using. Drizzle with pomegranate molasses to taste and serve.

Tahini-Garlic Sauce

FAST VEGAN Makes ¼ cup Total Time 10 minutes

To make this recipe vegan, substitute plant-based yogurt for the dairy yogurt.

- ⅓ cup tahini
- 3 tablespoons plain yogurt
- 2 tablespoons lemon juice
- 2 tablespoons water
- 2 teaspoons pomegranate molasses
- 1 garlic clove, minced
- ½ teaspoon table salt

Whisk all ingredients in bowl until well combined. Season with salt and pepper to taste. (Sauce can be refrigerated for up to 3 days. Thin with extra water as needed before serving.)

Maftoul with Carrots and Chickpeas

FAST VEGAN Serves 4 Total Time 40 minutes

Why This Recipe Works Maftoul, also known as Palestinian couscous, is traditionally made by hand-rolling bulgur in moistened wheat flour (generally a mix of whole-wheat and white flours) to create small balls of pasta. Its beige color and extra-nutty flavor make maftoul a unique addition to the hand-rolled pastas of the Mediterranean, like North African couscous (from which maftoul was likely derived) and Sardinian fregula, both made from semolina. While maftoul is traditionally served with a brothy stew of chicken, onions, and chickpeas ("maftoul" refers to both the pasta and the finished dish), we leaned on the heartiness of this nutty, wholesome ingredient to create a legume- and vegetable-forward dish, fragrant with warm spices. We prefer our homemade baharat, but you may use store-bought. Because the size of maftoul can vary considerably, we provide a wide range of cook times. You can use an equal amount (by weight) of fregula or moghrabieh in place of the maftoul.

- 8 ounces (1⅓ cups) maftoul
- ½ teaspoon table salt, plus salt for cooking maftoul
- 2 tablespoons extra-virgin olive oil
- 1 red onion, sliced ½ inch thick
- 2 garlic cloves, minced
- 1 tablespoon Baharat (page 57)
- 1 pound carrots, peeled, cut crosswise into 1½- to 2-inch lengths, and halved lengthwise or quartered if thick
- 2 cups vegetable broth
- 1 (15-ounce) can chickpeas, rinsed
- ½ cup minced fresh parsley
- 1 tablespoon lemon juice

1. Bring 2 quarts water to boil in medium saucepan. Add maftoul and 1½ teaspoons salt and cook, stirring occasionally, until just tender, 10 to 25 minutes. Drain and set aside.

2. While maftoul cooks, heat oil in large saucepan over medium-high heat until shimmering. Add onion and cook until softened and beginning to brown, 5 to 7 minutes. Reduce heat to medium, stir in garlic and baharat, and cook until fragrant, about 30 seconds. Add carrots, broth, chickpeas, and salt and bring to boil. Reduce heat to maintain simmer and cook, stirring occasionally, until carrots are tender, 8 to 10 minutes.

3. Off heat, stir in reserved maftoul and let sit, covered, until most of broth has been absorbed but dish is still saucy, 3 to 5 minutes. Stir in parsley and lemon juice and season with salt and pepper to taste. Serve.

Maftoul with Carrots and Chickpeas

Quinoa Bowls with Snap Peas, Strawberries, and Basil Vinaigrette

Oat Berry Pilaf with Walnuts and Gorgonzola

Serves 4 to 6 Total Time 1¼ hours

Why This Recipe Works While we think of oats mostly in cut or rolled form as part of a wholesome breakfast, oat berries (sometimes called oat groats) have a pleasantly chewy texture and a hearty, mildly nutty flavor that bring a new dimension to pilafs. Oat berries are whole oats that have been hulled and cleaned but not processed. (Other forms of oat are processed further, such as being ground, cut, or rolled flat.) Because they haven't been processed, oat berries retain a high nutritional value and take longer to cook than other types of oats. Thanks to their naturally nutty flavor, there's no need to toast them before using them in a pilaf, as you would with rice or other grains. Here, we add water and oat berries to a saucepan after sautéing minced shallot. Creamy, pungent Gorgonzola nicely balances the earthy taste of the oat berries, and sprinkling the cheese over the oat berries just before serving prevents the pilaf from becoming too thick. Tart dried cherries and tangy balsamic vinegar cut through the richness, while parsley gives the pilaf freshness.

- 1 tablespoon extra-virgin olive oil
- 1 shallot, minced
- 2 cups water
- 1½ cups oat berries (groats), rinsed and drained
- ¼ teaspoon table salt
- ¾ cup walnuts, toasted and chopped
- ½ cup dried cherries
- 2 tablespoons minced fresh parsley
- 1 tablespoon balsamic vinegar
- 2 ounces Gorgonzola cheese, crumbled (½ cup)

1. Heat oil in large saucepan over medium heat until shimmering. Add shallot and cook, stirring occasionally, until softened, about 2 minutes. Stir in water, oat berries, and salt and bring to simmer. Reduce heat to low, cover, and continue to simmer until oat berries are tender but still slightly chewy, 30 to 40 minutes.

2. Off heat, lay clean dish towel underneath lid and let sit for 10 minutes. Fluff oat berries with fork and fold in walnuts, cherries, and parsley. Drizzle with vinegar. Transfer pilaf to serving bowl. Sprinkle Gorgonzola over top and season with salt and pepper to taste. Serve.

Quinoa Bowls with Snap Peas, Strawberries, and Basil Vinaigrette

FAST Serves 4 Total Time 45 minutes

Why This Recipe Works This colorful, fresh grain bowl radiates summer vibes. Nutty and nutritious quinoa is the perfect base for strawberries and snap peas dressed with a basil vinaigrette. We make the vinaigrette in the blender to integrate the fresh herbs and aromatics perfectly. To deepen the flavor of the bowl and introduce aromatic warmth, we toast slivered almonds with coriander and fennel seeds until golden and fragrant. Salty ricotta salata provides creamy richness and a firm bite that holds up well against the softer ingredients. If you buy unwashed quinoa, rinse it and then spread it out on a clean dish towel to dry for 15 minutes.

- 8 ounces sugar snap peas, strings removed and halved crosswise
- 1¼ teaspoons table salt, divided, plus salt for cooking peas and quinoa
- 1½ cups prewashed white quinoa
- 1 cup packed fresh basil leaves
- 3 tablespoons chopped fresh chives
- 2 tablespoons white wine vinegar
- 2 garlic cloves, minced
- 2 teaspoons sugar
- ⅔ cup plus 1 tablespoon vegetable oil, divided
- ½ cup slivered almonds
- ½ teaspoon coriander seeds
- ½ teaspoon fennel seeds
- 10 ounces strawberries, hulled and quartered
- 3 ounces ricotta salata, crumbled (¾ cup)

1. Bring 2 quarts water to boil in large saucepan. Fill bowl halfway with ice and water. Add peas and 2 teaspoons salt to boiling water and cook until crisp-tender, about 1 minute. Using slotted spoon, transfer peas to ice bath. Once peas are chilled, transfer to paper towel–lined plate.

2. Return water to boil. Add quinoa and cook until tender with slight chew, 10 to 15 minutes. Drain quinoa and return to pot; cover and set aside.

3. Pulse basil, chives, vinegar, garlic, sugar, and 1 teaspoon salt in blender until roughly chopped, 5 to 7 pulses. With blender running, slowly drizzle in ⅔ cup oil until emulsified, about 1 minute. Season with salt and pepper to taste. (Vinaigrette can be refrigerated for up to 3 days.)

4. Cook almonds, coriander seeds, fennel seeds, remaining ¼ teaspoon salt, and remaining 1 tablespoon oil in 10-inch skillet over medium heat, stirring constantly, until lightly toasted and fragrant, about 3 minutes; transfer to bowl.

5. Portion quinoa into individual serving bowls. Top with snap peas, strawberries, and ricotta salata. Drizzle with vinaigrette and sprinkle with nut mixture. Serve.

Quinoa, Black Bean, and Mango Salad with Lime Dressing

VEGAN Serves 4 to 6 Total Time 40 minutes, plus 25 minutes resting and cooling

Why This Recipe Works Mango and black beans are a brilliant savory-sweet combo. Add red bell pepper, creamy avocado, and an easy-to-whip-up lime-based dressing and you have a protein-packed salad that tastes as good as it looks. To highlight its delicate texture and nuttiness, we toast the quinoa to bring out its flavor before adding liquid to the pan and simmering the grains until they are nearly tender. Then we spread the quinoa on a rimmed baking sheet to cool without clumping, giving us fluffy grains. Black beans, mango, and bell pepper add heartiness, flavor, and color to the salad, and the blended dressing is a refreshing mix of jalapeño, cilantro, and lime juice. Scallions bring bite, and avocado provides creaminess. If you buy unwashed quinoa, rinse it and then spread it out on a clean dish towel to dry for 15 minutes.

- 1½ cups prewashed white quinoa
- 2¼ cups water
- 1½ teaspoons table salt, divided
- 5 tablespoons lime juice (3 limes)
- ½ jalapeño chile, seeded and chopped
- ¾ teaspoon ground cumin
- ½ cup extra-virgin olive oil
- ⅓ cup fresh cilantro leaves
- 1 red bell pepper, stemmed, seeded, and chopped
- 1 mango, peeled, pitted, and cut into ¼-inch pieces
- 1 (15-ounce) can black beans, rinsed
- 2 scallions, sliced thin
- 1 avocado, halved, pitted, and sliced thin

1. Toast quinoa in large saucepan over medium-high heat, stirring often, until very fragrant and quinoa makes continuous popping sound, 5 to 7 minutes. Stir in water and ½ teaspoon salt and bring to simmer. Cover, reduce heat to low, and simmer gently until most of water has been absorbed and quinoa is nearly tender, about 15 minutes. Let sit off heat, covered, for 10 minutes. Spread quinoa onto rimmed baking sheet and let cool for 15 minutes.

2. Meanwhile, process lime juice, jalapeño, cumin, and remaining 1 teaspoon salt in blender until jalapeño is finely chopped, about 15 seconds. With blender running, add oil and cilantro and process until smooth and emulsified, about 20 seconds.

3. Combine cooled quinoa, bell pepper, mango, beans, scallions, and dressing in large bowl and toss to combine. Season with salt and pepper to taste. Serve, topping individual portions with avocado.

Preparing a Mango

1. Cut thin slice from one end of mango. Rest mango on trimmed bottom, then cut off skin in thin strips, top to bottom.

2. Cut down along each side of flat pit to remove flesh.

3. Trim around pit to remove any remaining flesh. Cut flesh into pieces according to recipe.

Quinoa Lettuce Wraps with Feta and Olives

Serves 4 Total Time 45 minutes, plus 20 minutes cooling

Why This Recipe Works Lettuce wraps are incredibly appealing. Quinoa makes a perfect base for the filling, with its nutty flavor and a texture that easily absorbs dressings of all kinds. That said, it demands bold partners to bring it to life; here, tomatoes and cucumber (cut into very small pieces so there is some in every bite) add bulk, while shallot and briny olives give it pungency. But we did not stop there. The crowning touch is a creamy vinaigrette made with tangy feta, yogurt, herbs, red wine vinegar, and olive oil. One taste and you'll be coming back for more. After combining a portion of it with the salad, we drizzle it over each stuffed lettuce leaf. The large, crisp leaves of Boston or Bibb lettuce make perfectly sized cups. If you buy unwashed quinoa, rinse it and then spread it out on a clean dish towel to dry for 15 minutes.

Vinaigrette

- 4 ounces feta cheese, crumbled (1 cup)
- ½ cup plain yogurt
- ¼ cup minced fresh mint
- 3 tablespoons red wine vinegar
- 2 tablespoons minced fresh oregano or 1½ teaspoons dried
- ½ teaspoon table salt
- ¼ teaspoon pepper
- ½ cup extra-virgin olive oil

Salad

- 1½ cups prewashed white quinoa
- 2¼ cups water
- ½ teaspoon table salt
- 2 tomatoes, cored, seeded, and cut into ¼-inch pieces
- 1 cucumber, halved lengthwise, seeded, and cut into ¼-inch pieces
- 1 shallot, minced
- ¼ cup pitted kalamata olives, chopped
- 2 heads Boston or Bibb lettuce (1 pound), leaves separated

1. **For the vinaigrette** Process feta, yogurt, mint, vinegar, oregano, salt, and pepper in blender until smooth, about 15 seconds. With blender running, slowly add oil until emulsified, about 30 seconds. (Vinaigrette can be refrigerated for up to 24 hours.)

2. For the salad Toast quinoa in large saucepan over medium-high heat, stirring often, until very fragrant and quinoa makes continuous popping sound, 5 to 7 minutes. Stir in water and salt and bring to simmer. Cover, reduce heat to low, and simmer gently until most of water has been absorbed and quinoa is nearly tender, about 15 minutes. Spread quinoa onto rimmed baking sheet and let cool for 20 minutes; transfer to large bowl.

3. Add tomatoes, cucumber, shallot, olives, and ⅔ cup vinaigrette to quinoa and toss to combine. Season with salt and pepper to taste. Serve with lettuce leaves, spooning ⅓ cup quinoa mixture into each leaf and drizzling with remaining vinaigrette.

Herbed Quinoa Cakes with Whipped Feta

Serves 4 Total Time 1¾ hours, plus 1 hour cooling and chilling

Why This Recipe Works Quinoa's unique texture makes for hearty vegetarian cakes, and its neutral flavor benefits from pairing with bold and exciting ingredients. A tangy perk comes from the addition of apple cider vinegar and lemon juice, while a hint of sweetness comes from soaked raisins. We also add a generous amount of herbs to give the mixture a fresh note. The quinoa cakes are bound together with eggs and panko bread crumbs. When pan-seared, these satisfying cakes develop a tasty browned crust on each side. We accompany them with a tangy whipped feta and recommend serving with a green salad for either lunch or a light dinner. If you buy unwashed quinoa, rinse it and then spread it out on a clean dish towel to dry for 15 minutes. The patties hold together but tend to be delicate, so flip them carefully in step 6.

Whipped Feta

- ¾ teaspoon lemon juice
- 1 small garlic clove, minced
- 4 ounces feta cheese, crumbled (1 cup)
- 1½ tablespoons milk
- 1 tablespoon extra-virgin olive oil
- 1½ teaspoons minced fresh oregano
- 1½ teaspoons minced fresh parsley

top | *Quinoa Lettuce Wraps with Feta and Olives*
bottom | *Herbed Quinoa Cakes with Whipped Feta*

Quinoa Cakes

- ¼ cup golden raisins, chopped
- 3 tablespoons cider vinegar
- ⅛ teaspoon saffron threads, crumbled (optional)
- 3 tablespoons plus 2 cups water, divided
- 3 tablespoons extra-virgin olive oil, divided
- 1 small red onion, chopped fine
- 4 garlic cloves, minced
- 1 cup prewashed white quinoa
- 1 teaspoon table salt
- ½ cup panko bread crumbs
- 2 large eggs, lightly beaten
- ½ teaspoon grated lemon zest plus 2 teaspoons juice
- 2 ounces Parmesan cheese, grated (1 cup)
- ⅓ cup chopped fresh parsley and/or dill
- 2 tablespoon chopped fresh oregano
- ¼ teaspoon pepper
- ¼ teaspoon ground allspice

1. **For the whipped feta** Combine lemon juice and garlic in bowl and let sit for 10 minutes. Process feta, milk, and lemon juice mixture in food processor until feta mixture resembles ricotta cheese, about 15 seconds. Scrape down sides of bowl. With processor running, slowly drizzle in oil. Continue to process until mixture has Greek yogurt–like consistency (some small lumps will remain), 1½ to 2 minutes longer, stopping once to scrape down bottom and sides of bowl. Add oregano and parsley and pulse to combine. Set aside until ready to serve. If whipped feta is very loose, you may need to refrigerate it for up to 1½ hours. (Whipped feta can be refrigerated for up to 3 days. If refrigerated for longer than 1½ hours, let sit at room temperature for 30 minutes before serving.)

2. **For the quinoa cakes** Microwave raisins; vinegar; saffron, if using; and 3 tablespoons water in small bowl until steaming, about 2 minutes. Let sit until raisins are soft and plump, about 30 minutes. Drain raisins and set aside.

3. Meanwhile, heat 1 tablespoon oil in large saucepan over medium heat until shimmering. Add onion and cook until softened, 3 to 5 minutes. Stir in garlic and cook until fragrant, about 30 seconds. Stir in remaining 2 cups water, quinoa, and salt and bring to simmer. Cover, reduce heat to medium-low, and cook until quinoa is tender, 10 to 15 minutes. Off heat, let quinoa sit, covered, until liquid is fully absorbed, about 10 minutes. Uncover and let cool for 30 minutes.

4. Line rimmed baking sheet with parchment paper. Process panko in clean, dry food processor until finely ground, about 30 seconds. Add eggs and lemon zest and pulse until mixture forms paste, about 5 pulses. Transfer panko mixture to large bowl and stir in cooled quinoa, reserved raisins, lemon juice, Parmesan, parsley, dill, oregano, pepper, and allspice.

5. Divide quinoa mixture into 8 equal portions. Using your lightly moistened hands, firmly pack each portion into tight ball, then flatten into 3-inch-wide patty; transfer to prepared sheet. Cover with plastic wrap and refrigerate until chilled and firm, at least 30 minutes or up to 24 hours.

6. Heat 1½ teaspoons oil in 12-inch nonstick skillet over medium-low heat until shimmering. Carefully place 4 chilled quinoa patties in skillet and cook until crisp and golden brown on first side, 5 to 7 minutes. Gently flip patties using 2 spatulas, add 1½ teaspoons oil to skillet, and cook until crisp and browned on second side, 4 to 6 minutes. Transfer to platter and tent with aluminum foil. Repeat with remaining 1 tablespoon oil and remaining chilled quinoa patties. Serve with whipped feta.

Creamy Polenta with Fennel and Chickpeas

Serves 4 Total Time 1¼ hours

Why This Recipe Works Polenta is something to cozy up to: It's creamy, cheesy, and undeniably rich, all the attributes of comfort food. And when it comes to vegetarian cooking, polenta is a blank canvas for all manner of vegetable-centric toppings to suit any mood. As an added bonus, our baking soda trick cuts the cooking time in half. This is because baking soda causes the pectin in polenta to break down rapidly so it is creamy and lush in just 30 minutes. Our full-flavored vegetarian topping starts with browning fennel to mellow its anise aroma. We build a fond from garlic and tomato paste to add depth to crushed tomatoes. To round out the flavors, we deglaze the pan with sweet and slightly fruity dry Marsala. After adding the crushed tomatoes to the skillet, we simmer chickpeas and the browned fennel in the rich sauce until tender. Before serving, we scatter shavings of umami-rich Parmesan over the top. We developed this recipe with Bob's Red Mill yellow corn polenta. Coarse-ground grits also work well. Avoid quick-cooking or instant polenta or cornmeal. Look for a fennel bulb that measures 3½ to 4 inches in diameter and weighs around 1 pound with the stalks (12 to 14 ounces without); trim the base very slightly so that the bulb remains intact. Cannellini beans may be used in place of the chickpeas.

Creamy Polenta

- 4½ cups water
- 1 cup coarse-ground polenta
- 1 teaspoon table salt
- Pinch baking soda
- 1 tablespoon unsalted butter
- 1 ounce Parmesan cheese, grated (½ cup)

Fennel and Chickpeas

- 1 fennel bulb, base slightly trimmed, 1 tablespoon fronds chopped coarse, stalks discarded
- 2 tablespoons extra-virgin olive oil, plus extra for serving
- ¼ teaspoon table salt
- 4 garlic cloves, minced
- 1 tablespoon tomato paste
- ¼ teaspoon red pepper flakes
- ⅓ cup dry Marsala
- 1 (15-ounce) can chickpeas, undrained
- 1 (14.5-ounce) can crushed tomatoes
- Shaved Parmesan cheese

1. For the polenta Bring water to boil in medium saucepan over high heat. Whisk in polenta, salt, and baking soda. Bring mixture to boil, stirring frequently. Reduce heat to lowest possible setting, cover, and cook for 5 minutes. Whisk until smooth, cover, and continue to cook until grains are tender but slightly al dente, about 25 minutes longer. (Polenta should be loose and barely hold its shape when drizzled from whisk; it will continue to thicken as it cools.)

2. Off heat, whisk in butter and Parmesan and season with salt and pepper to taste. Keep covered until ready to serve.

3. For the fennel and chickpeas While polenta cooks, cut fennel bulb lengthwise through core into 8 wedges (do not remove core). Heat oil in 12-inch skillet over medium heat until shimmering. Arrange fennel wedges cut-side down in skillet and season with salt. Brown both cut sides, 3 to 4 minutes per side. Transfer to plate.

Cooking Polenta

A whisk swiped through freshly cooked polenta will leave a faint trail. After a short rest, it will be just thick enough to be scooped with a spoon.

Creamy Polenta with Fennel and Chickpeas

Creamy Polenta with Radicchio Agrodolce

4. Reduce heat to medium-low. Add garlic, tomato paste, and pepper flakes to now-empty skillet and cook, stirring constantly, until dark fond forms on bottom of skillet, about 2 minutes. Stir in Marsala, scraping up any browned bits.

5. Stir in chickpeas and tomatoes. Return fennel to skillet, nestling wedges into sauce. Bring to boil over high heat. Adjust heat to maintain simmer, cover, and cook until fennel is just tender, 15 to 20 minutes. Transfer polenta to platter and top with fennel-chickpea mixture. Serve, passing oil, Parmesan, and fennel fronds separately.

Creamy Polenta with Radicchio Agrodolce

Serves 4 Total Time 1 hour

Why This Recipe Works Cheesy polenta is often topped with a meat or mushroom ragu, but here we counter the creamy grain with pleasingly bitter radicchio and celery in an agrodolce sauce, a sweet-and-sour reduction of vinegar and sugar with an eye-catching luster. We add a pinch of baking soda to the polenta, which cuts the cooking time in half and eliminates the need for constant stirring. While the polenta cooks, we sauté celery and shallots until they're softened, add fresh thyme for slightly peppery notes, and reduce red wine vinegar and sugar in the same pan. The vinegar and sugar thicken into the signature agrodolce glaze. Grapes provide pops of appropriately winey sweetness. Charring the radicchio slightly counterbalances the sweetness from the grapes with smoky bitterness. You can use fresh parsley if your celery doesn't come with leaves.

- 5 cups water
- ½ teaspoon table salt, divided
- Pinch baking soda
- 1 cup coarse-ground cornmeal
- ¼ cup extra-virgin olive oil, divided, plus extra for drizzling
- 1 ounce Parmesan cheese, grated (1 cup), plus extra for serving
- 3 celery ribs, cut into ½-inch pieces, plus ½ cup celery leaves
- 2 shallots, sliced thin
- 1 teaspoon minced fresh thyme or ¼ teaspoon dried
- 1 cup red wine vinegar
- 3 tablespoons sugar
- 3 ounces seedless red grapes, halved (½ cup)
- 1 head radicchio (10 ounces), halved, cored, and cut into ½-inch pieces
- ¼ cup whole almonds, toasted and chopped coarse

1. Bring water to boil in large saucepan over medium-high heat. Stir in ¼ teaspoon salt and baking soda. Slowly add cornmeal in steady stream, stirring constantly. Bring mixture to boil, stirring constantly. Reduce heat to lowest possible setting, cover, and cook for 5 minutes.

2. Whisk cornmeal to smooth out any lumps, making sure to scrape down sides and bottom of saucepan. Cover and continue to cook, without stirring, until cornmeal is tender but slightly al dente, about 25 minutes. (Polenta should be loose and barely hold its shape but will continue to thicken as it cools.) Off heat, stir in 2 tablespoons oil and Parmesan and season with salt and pepper to taste. Cover and keep warm.

3. Meanwhile, heat 1 tablespoon oil in 12-inch nonstick skillet over medium heat until shimmering. Add celery ribs, shallots, and remaining ¼ teaspoon salt and cook, stirring occasionally, until softened and lightly browned, 7 to 9 minutes. Stir in thyme and cook until fragrant, about 30 seconds. Stir in vinegar and sugar, bring to simmer, and cook until liquid is thickened to syrupy glaze, about 10 minutes. Transfer to large bowl and stir in grapes. Cover with aluminum foil to keep warm.

4. Heat remaining 1 tablespoon oil in now-empty skillet over medium-high heat until shimmering. Add radicchio and cook until browned, about 5 minutes. Transfer to bowl with celery mixture and toss to combine. Transfer polenta to platter and top with radicchio mixture. Sprinkle with almonds, extra Parmesan, and celery leaves and drizzle with extra oil. Serve.

Spicy Polenta with White Beans and Kale

FAST Serves 4 Total Time 35 minutes

Why This Recipe Works When you want polenta in a hurry, this is the recipe to turn to as it uses instant polenta, which needs only about 3 minutes to cook once the broth comes to a boil. For a bit of heat, we use fire-roasted tomatoes in the topping and infuse olive oil with red pepper flakes and garlic. The topping is a snap to make in a large skillet; first we sauté onion in shimmering olive oil and then add the earthy chopped kale, white beans, and tomatoes. It takes just 10 minutes for this beautiful topping to thicken to just the right consistency. Making this dish even more appealing and rich is the fresh mozzarella, which we tear and scatter over each serving.

6 tablespoons extra-virgin olive oil, divided, plus extra for drizzling
1 onion, chopped
12 ounces lacinato kale, stemmed and chopped
1 (15-ounce) can white beans, rinsed
1 (14.5-ounce) can fire-roasted diced tomatoes
1 teaspoon table salt, divided
3 garlic cloves, minced
½ teaspoon red pepper flakes, plus extra for serving
4 cups vegetable broth
1 cup instant polenta
8 ounces fresh mozzarella cheese, torn into 1-inch pieces

1. Heat 3 tablespoons oil in 12-inch nonstick skillet over medium-high heat until shimmering. Add onion and cook until softened and lightly browned, 5 to 7 minutes. Stir in kale, beans, tomatoes and their juice, and ¾ teaspoon salt. Cover and cook, stirring occasionally, until kale is very tender and sauce is thickened, 8 to 10 minutes.

2. Meanwhile, cook garlic, pepper flakes, and remaining 3 tablespoons oil in large saucepan over medium heat, stirring frequently, until garlic begins to turn straw-colored, about 4 minutes. Add broth and bring to boil over high heat. Whisk in polenta and remaining ¼ teaspoon salt, reduce heat to medium-low, and cook until thickened, about 3 minutes. Season with salt and pepper to taste.

3. Portion polenta into individual serving bowls and top with bean mixture and mozzarella. Drizzle with extra oil and sprinkle with extra pepper flakes. Serve.

Grits with Fresh Corn

Serves 4 to 6 Total Time 1 hour

Why This Recipe Works Corn on corn is a recipe for success. Grits are mild on their own since they are made from dried corn, so we dress them up and double down on the corn flavor with fresh corn and aromatics. The corn cobs come in especially handy: We scrape off the pulp left behind with a butter knife for a sweet, flavor-packed addition to the grits. We add milk, water, some corn kernels, and the corn pulp to a saucepan and bring the mixture to a boil. Next we stir in the grits, minced garlic, salt, and pepper and bring the mixture to a boil again. Then we lower the heat and cook the grits covered—whisking often to avoid scorching—until they thicken. We add a knob of butter off the heat and season the grits to taste before moving on to the savory topping. Sautéing some reserved corn kernels in more butter with garlic and scallion whites for just a few minutes allows them to lose their raw crunch. Then we stir scallion greens into the sautéed corn and top portions of the grits with this delightful sweet-savory mixture. If you use fresh-milled grits such as Anson Mills Colonial Coarse Pencil Cob Grits, you will need to increase the simmering time by 25 minutes and may need to add more water during simmering in step 2.

3 ears corn, husks and silk removed
2¼ cups whole milk
2 cups water
1 cup old-fashioned grits
2 garlic cloves, minced, divided
1¾ teaspoons table salt, divided
¼ teaspoon plus ⅛ teaspoon pepper, divided
4 tablespoons unsalted butter, divided
2 scallions, white parts sliced thin, green parts sliced thin on bias

1. Cut kernels from cobs (you should have about 2¼ cups). Scrape pulp from cobs, keeping separate from kernels.

2. Combine milk, water, two-thirds of kernels (about 1½ cups), and pulp in large saucepan. Bring to boil over medium-high heat. Whisk in grits, half of garlic, 1½ teaspoons salt, and ¼ teaspoon pepper and return to boil. Reduce heat to low, cover, and simmer, whisking often, until thick and creamy, about 25 minutes. Off heat, stir in 2 tablespoons butter and season with salt and pepper to taste. Cover to keep warm.

3. Meanwhile, melt remaining 2 tablespoons butter in 10-inch nonstick skillet over medium heat. Add scallion whites, remaining garlic, remaining ¼ teaspoon salt, and remaining ⅛ teaspoon pepper and cook until fragrant, about 30 seconds. Add remaining one-third of kernels (about ¾ cup) and cook until tender, 2 to 3 minutes, stirring occasionally.

4. Off heat, stir scallion greens into skillet. If grits are too thick, adjust consistency by gradually whisking in additional hot water as needed until creamy. Serve grits, topping individual portions with corn-scallion mixture.

Savory Oatmeal with Peas, Parmesan, and Pepper

Serves 4   Total Time 30 minutes, plus 2 hours soaking

Why This Recipe Works Savory oatmeal is another way to enjoy steel-cut oats. It can work as a powerhouse breakfast or even lunch or dinner. Most oatmeal fans agree that the steel-cut version of the grain offers the best flavor and texture, but many balk at the 40-minute cooking time. In this recipe, we decrease the cooking time to only 10 minutes by stirring steel-cut oats into boiling water the night before. This enables the grains to hydrate and soften. In the morning, we add more water and a bit of lemon juice and simmer the mixture for 4 to 6 minutes, until thick and creamy. Stirring in generous amounts of Parmesan and pepper gives these oats a savory flavor, and a topping of peas provides visual appeal and pops of grassy sweetness. A final sprinkle of Parmesan and pepper and a drizzle of olive oil seals the deal. The oatmeal thickens as it cools; thin with boiling water for a looser consistency. For a heartier meal, top each serving with a Perfect Fried Egg (page 451) or Soft-Cooked Egg (page 450).

- 4 cups water, divided
- 1 cup steel-cut oats
- ¼ teaspoon table salt
- 2 teaspoons lemon juice
- 4 ounces Parmesan cheese, grated (2 cups), plus extra for serving
- 1½ teaspoons pepper
- 1 cup frozen peas
- 4 teaspoons extra-virgin olive oil

1. Bring 3 cups water to boil in large saucepan over high heat. Off heat, stir in oats and salt. Cover saucepan and let stand for at least 2 hours or up to 10 hours.

2. Stir remaining 1 cup water and lemon juice into oats and bring to boil over medium-high heat. Reduce heat to medium and cook, stirring occasionally, until oats are softened but still retain some chew and mixture thickens and resembles warm pudding, 4 to 6 minutes. Off heat, whisk in Parmesan and pepper until fully incorporated. Let sit for 5 minutes.

3. While oatmeal rests, microwave peas until warm, 1 to 2 minutes. Stir oatmeal and season with salt and pepper to taste. Divide evenly into 4 individual serving bowls. Top each portion with ¼ cup peas and drizzle with 1 teaspoon oil. Sprinkle with additional Parmesan and pepper, if desired, and serve.

Savory Oatmeal with Peas, Parmesan, and Pepper

Cooking Rice

Rice can be surprisingly difficult to cook perfectly. Here are three simple methods for basic rice cooking: boiling, pilaf-style, and microwaving. Pilaf-style cooking is our favorite (though boiling rice in ample amounts of water is a great easy method when you want rice to round out a meal or fill a burrito). To make rice for a crowd, use the boiling method and double the amount of rice (do not add more water or salt).

Boiling Directions Bring water to a boil in large saucepan. Stir in rice and 2½ teaspoons salt. Return to a boil, reduce to a simmer, and cook until rice is tender, following cooking times in chart. Drain.

Pilaf-Style Directions Rinse rice and drain well. Heat 1 tablespoon oil in medium saucepan (preferably nonstick) over medium-high heat until shimmering. Stir in rice and cook until edges of grains begin to turn translucent, about 3 minutes. Stir in water and ¼ teaspoon salt. Bring mixture to a simmer, reduce heat to low, cover, and continue to simmer until rice is tender and all water is absorbed, following cooking times in chart. Off heat, place clean dish towel under lid and let rice sit for 10 minutes. Fluff rice with fork.

Microwave Directions Rinse rice and drain well. Combine water, rice, 1 tablespoon oil, and ¼ teaspoon salt in bowl. Cover and microwave on high (full power) until water begins to boil, 5 to 10 minutes. Reduce microwave heat to medium (50 percent power) and continue to cook until rice is just tender, following cooking times in chart. Remove from microwave and fluff with fork. Cover bowl with plastic wrap, poke several vent holes in plastic with tip of knife, and let sit until completely tender, about 5 minutes.

Easy Baked White Rice

FAST VEGAN Serves 6 to 8 Total Time 45 minutes

This hands-off recipe uses the gentle heat of the oven to cook foolproof rice.

4½ cups boiling water
2⅔ cups long-grain white rice, rinsed
1 tablespoon extra-virgin olive oil
¾ teaspoon table salt

Adjust oven rack to middle position and heat oven to 450 degrees. Combine boiling water, rice, oil, and salt in 13 by 9-inch baking dish. Cover dish tightly with double layer of aluminum foil. Bake until liquid is absorbed and rice is tender, 20 to 25 minutes. Remove dish from oven, uncover, and fluff rice with fork, scraping up any rice that has stuck to bottom. Re-cover dish with foil and let rice sit for 10 minutes. Season with salt and pepper to taste. Serve.

Easy Baked Brown Rice

VEGAN Serves 4 Total Time 1¾ hours

Medium-grain or short-grain brown rice can be substituted for the long-grain rice. To double the recipe, use a 13 by 9-inch baking dish; the baking time need not be increased.

2⅓ cups boiling water
1½ cups long-grain brown rice, rinsed
2 teaspoons extra-virgin olive oil
½ teaspoon table salt

Adjust oven rack to middle position and heat oven to 375 degrees. Combine boiling water, rice, oil, and salt in 8-inch square baking dish. Cover dish tightly with double layer of aluminum foil. Bake until rice is tender and water is absorbed, about 1 hour. Remove dish from oven, uncover, and gently fluff rice with fork, scraping up any rice that has stuck to bottom. Cover dish with clean dish towel and let rice sit for 5 minutes. Uncover and let rice sit for 5 minutes longer. Season with salt and pepper to taste. Serve.

Rice Cooking Chart

Yield 1 cup raw rice yields 2 cups cooked

TYPE OF RICE	COOKING METHOD	AMOUNT OF RICE	AMOUNT OF WATER	COOKING TIME
Short- and Medium-Grain White Rice	Boiled	1 cup	4 quarts	10 to 15 minutes
	Pilaf-Style	1 cup	1¾ cups	10 to 15 minutes
	Microwave	X	X	X
Long-Grain White Rice	Boiled	1 cup	4 quarts	12 to 17 minutes
	Pilaf-Style	1 cup	1¾ cups	16 to 18 minutes
	Microwave	1 cup	2 cups	10 to 15 minutes
Short- and Medium-Grain Brown Rice	Boiled	1 cup	4 quarts	22 to 27 minutes
	Pilaf-Style	1 cup	1¾ cups	40 to 50 minutes
	Microwave	1 cup	2 cups	25 to 30 minutes
Long-Grain Brown Rice	Boiled	1 cup	4 quarts	25 to 30 minutes
	Pilaf-Style	1 cup	1¾ cups	40 to 50 minutes
	Microwave	1 cup	2 cups	25 to 30 minutes
Black Rice	Boiled	1½ cups	4 quarts	20 to 25 minutes
	Pilaf-Style	X	X	X
	Microwave	X	X	X
Red Rice	Boiled	1½ cups	4 quarts	27 to 31 minutes
	Pilaf-Style	X	X	X
	Microwave	X	X	X
Wild Rice	Boiled	1 cup	4 quarts	45 to 40 minutes
	Pilaf-Style	X	X	X
	Microwave	X	X	X
Basmati or Jasmine Rice	Boiled	1 cup	4 quarts	12 to 17 minutes
	Pilaf-Style	1 cup	1¾ cups	16 to 18 minutes
	Microwave	1 cup	2 cups	10 to 15 minutes

X = Not recommended

Cooking Grains

Some grains, such as bulgur, cook in minutes, while others, such as barley, take much longer. We have perfected three basic methods for cooking grains. When given a choice, pilaf-style is our favorite option because it produces grains with a light, fluffy texture and a slightly toasted flavor. That said, some grains requiring prolonged cooking are best boiled.

Boiling Directions Bring water to boil in large saucepan. Stir in grain and ½ teaspoon salt. Return to a boil, then reduce to a simmer and cook until grain is tender, following cooking times in chart. Drain.

Pilaf-Style Directions Rinse and then dry the grains on a towel. Heat 1 tablespoon oil in a medium saucepan (preferably nonstick) over medium-high heat until shimmering. Stir in the grain and toast until lightly golden and fragrant, 2 to 3 minutes. Stir in the water and ¼ teaspoon salt. Bring the mixture to a simmer, then reduce the heat to low, cover, and continue to simmer until grain is tender and has absorbed all of the water, following cooking times in the chart. Off heat, let grain stand for 10 minutes, then fluff with fork.

Microwave Directions Rinse grain and drain well. Combine the water, grain, 1 tablespoon oil, and ¼ teaspoon salt in bowl. Cover and cook following times and temperatures in chart. Remove from microwave and fluff with fork. Cover bowl with plastic wrap, poke several vent holes in plastic with tip of knife, and let sit until completely tender, about 5 minutes.

Cooling Grains To cool cooked grains, spread on rimmed baking sheet and let cool for at least 15 minutes before using.

Reheating Grains To reheat cooked grains, microwave in covered microwave-safe bowl until hot throughout, fluffing with fork halfway through cooking. (Timing will vary depending on quantity and type of grains used.)

Storing Grains and Rice

The pantry To prevent open boxes and bags of grains and rice from spoiling, store in airtight container.

The refrigerator Cooked grains can be refrigerated for up to three days.

The freezer Store uncooked grains and rice in the freezer in an airtight container. Store cooked grains and rice in the freezer for up to three months. When completely cooled, transfer cooked grains to a zipper-lock bag and lay bag flat to freeze.

Grain Cooking Chart

The chart below contains all you need to know to cook our favorite grains. The recipes can be scaled up by increasing the amounts proportionally. The cooking times will remain the same.

Yield 1 cup dry grains yields 2½ cups cooked
1½ cups dry grains yields 4 cups cooked

TYPE OF GRAIN	COOKING METHOD	AMOUNT OF GRAIN	AMOUNT OF WATER	COOKING TIME
Pearl Barley	Boiled	1½ cups	4 quarts	20 to 40 minutes
	Pilaf-Style	X	X	X
	Microwave	X	X	X
Bulgur (medium- to coarse-grind)	Boiled	1 cup	4 quarts	15 to 20 minutes
	Pilaf-Style*	1 cup	1 cup	16 to 18 minutes
	Microwave	1 cup	1 cup	5 to 10 minutes
Bulgur (fine-grind)	Boiled	X	X	X
	Pilaf-Style	X	X	X
	Microwave	1 cup	2 cups	4 minutes
Farro	Boiled	1 cup	4 quarts	15 to 20 minutes
	Pilaf-Style	X	X	X
	Microwave	X	X	X
Fonio	Boiled	X	X	X
	Pilaf-Style	X	X	X
	Microwave	1 cup	2 cups	5 minutes
Freekeh	Boiled	1½ cups	4 quarts	30 to 45 minutes
	Pilaf-Style	X	X	X
	Microwave	X	X	X
Kamut	Boiled	1 cup	2 quarts	55 minutes to 1¼ hours
	Pilaf-Style	X	X	X
	Microwave	X	X	X
Millet	Boiled	X	X	X
	Pilaf-Style**	1 cup	2 cups	15 to 20 minutes
	Microwave	X	X	X
Oat Berries	Boiled	1 cup	4 quarts	30 to 40 minutes
	Pilaf-Style	1 cup	1½ cups	30 to 40 minutes
	Microwave	X	X	X
Quinoa (any color)	Boiled	X	X	X
	Pilaf-Style	1 cup	1 cup + 3 tablespoons	18 to 20 minutes
	Microwave	1 cup	2 cups	5 minutes on medium, then 5 minutes on high
Wheat Berries	Boiled	1 cup	4 quarts	1 hour
	Pilaf-Style	X	X	X
	Microwave	X	X	X

* For pilaf, do not rinse, and skip the toasting step, adding the grain to the pot with the liquid.
** For pilaf, increase the toasting time until the grains begin to pop, about 12 minutes.
X = Not recommended

Beans & Legumes

372 Cacio e Pepe Beans with Squash, Sage, and Walnuts ■

373 Bean Bourguignon ●

374 Gigantes Plaki

374 Calabrian Chile White Beans with Almond Romesco ■

375 Sicilian White Beans and Escarole ■ ●

377 Stewed Cranberry Beans with Tomatoes and Sage

378 Jackfruit and Chickpea Makhani

378 Chickpea Bouillabaisse

380 Chana Masala ●

382 Chickpea Curry ■ ●

382 Espinacas con Garbanzos (Andalusian Spinach and Chickpeas) ■ ●

383 Crispy Chickpea Cakes with Zucchini Ribbon Salad

384 Sautéed Fava Beans, Asparagus, and Leek ■ ●

386 Edamame Salad with Mint and Parmesan ■

387 Cuban-Style Black Beans and Rice ●

387 Skillet Rice and Beans with Corn and Fresh Tomatoes ●

Skillet Rice and Chickpeas with Coconut Milk ●

Spanish-Style Skillet Rice and Chickpeas ●

388 Tacu Tacu with Salsa Criolla ●

391 Gallo Pinto (Costa Rican Beans and Rice) ●

391 Jamaican Rice and Peas

393 Crispy Coconut Rice and Pigeon Peas with Tropical Fruit ■ ●

394 Mujaddara ●

394 Crispy Onions ■ ●

395 Koshari ●

396 Lentils with Roasted Broccoli and Lemony Bread Crumbs ●

397 Lentilles du Puy with Spinach and Crème Fraîche

399 Palak Dal (Spinach-Lentil Dal with Cumin and Mustard Seeds)

399 Red Lentil Kibbeh

400 Harissa ■ ●

400 Misir Wot ■ ●

402 Cooking Dried Beans

■ Fast (45 minutes or less) ● Vegan

Cacio e Pepe Beans with Squash, Sage, and Walnuts

Cacio e Pepe Beans with Squash, Sage, and Walnuts

FAST Serves 4 Total Time 45 minutes

Why This Recipe Works Inspired by cacio e pepe, the classic Roman pasta dish featuring generous amounts of Pecorino Romano cheese and black pepper, we swapped the pasta for beans and the Pecorino Romano for Parmesan (since traditional Pecorino Romano isn't vegetarian) for a dish so flavorful we didn't even miss the pasta. Navy beans are a good choice here as they hold their petite shape beautifully, even with additional cooking. We leave one can of beans undrained to take advantage of the starchy canning liquid to help give the dish a bit of thickening and creaminess once we add the cheese. A generous dose of black pepper accentuates the beans' mild flavor. To add heft to our meal, we roast chunks of sweet butternut squash, a great counterpoint to the peppery beans. And to make it feel as luxe as the real deal, we drizzle each portion with a mixture of browned butter, sage, and walnuts. You can use 1½ pounds precut butternut squash if desired, or you can substitute delicata squash, quartered lengthwise and sliced 1 inch thick. We prefer navy beans here, but any mild, creamy bean like cannellini, great northern, or pinto can be used. You can substitute almonds, hazelnuts, or pine nuts for the walnuts.

- 2 pounds butternut squash, peeled, seeded, and cut into 1-inch pieces (6 cups)
- 2 tablespoons extra-virgin olive oil, divided
- ½ teaspoon table salt, divided
- 1½ teaspoons pepper, divided
- 4 tablespoons unsalted butter
- ⅓ cup chopped walnuts
- ¼ cup fresh sage leaves
- ½ teaspoon lemon juice
- 2 (15-ounce) cans navy beans (1 can rinsed, 1 can undrained)
- ¼ cup water
- 2 ounces Parmesan cheese, grated (1 cup), plus extra for serving
- 2 garlic cloves, minced to paste (1 teaspoon)

1. Adjust oven rack to middle position and heat oven to 450 degrees. Toss squash with 1 tablespoon oil, ¼ teaspoon salt, and ⅛ teaspoon pepper and spread in even layer on rimmed baking sheet. Roast until tender and side touching sheet is well browned, about 25 minutes.

2. Meanwhile, melt butter in large saucepan over medium heat. Add walnuts, sage leaves, ⅛ teaspoon pepper, and remaining ¼ teaspoon salt and cook, stirring frequently, until nuts are lightly toasted and butter is browned, about 3 minutes. Stir in lemon juice, then transfer to bowl and cover to keep warm.

3. Heat remaining 1 tablespoon oil in now-empty saucepan over medium heat until shimmering. Add remaining 1¼ teaspoons pepper and cook until fragrant, about 30 seconds. Add beans and bean liquid and water and bring to simmer. Reduce heat to low, cover, and gently simmer for 5 minutes.

4. Off heat, stir in Parmesan and garlic, stirring in 1 to 2 tablespoons hot water if sauce begins to thicken. Transfer beans and squash to platter or divide among individual serving bowls, then drizzle with walnut mixture. Sprinkle with additional pepper and Parmesan and serve.

Bean Bourguignon

VEGAN Serves 4 to 6 Total Time 1 hour, plus 8 hours brining

Why This Recipe Works Creamy, chestnut-like Christmas lima beans meet tender, earthy portobello mushrooms in a rich, velvety sauce, as luxurious and satisfying as the French classic. The ability of mushrooms to create fond, plus umami-boosting miso, soy sauce, and tomato paste, create a supremely savory sauce. Simmering beans in this acidic sauce would slow down their cook time and lead to uneven results, so we cook them separately and add them to the sauce for the last 15 minutes to infuse them with the stew's flavors. You can substitute dried shiitake mushrooms for the porcini and yellow or red miso for white. Leave the portobello mushroom gills intact; they enhance the stew's color and flavor. You can use dried large lima beans in place of the Christmas lima beans. Serve over polenta.

- 1½ tablespoons table salt for brining
- 8 ounces (1⅓ cups) dried Christmas lima beans, picked over and rinsed
- ½ teaspoon table salt, plus salt for cooking beans
- ¼ cup extra-virgin olive oil, divided
- 1½ pounds portobello mushroom caps, cut into 1-inch pieces
- ¼ teaspoon pepper
- 2 carrots, peeled and chopped fine
- 1 large shallot, minced
- ½ ounce dried porcini mushrooms, rinsed and minced
- 4 garlic cloves, minced
- 2 teaspoons minced fresh thyme or ¾ teaspoon dried
- 3 tablespoons all-purpose flour
- 1 cup plus 2 tablespoons dry red wine, divided
- 2 tablespoons white miso
- 2 tablespoons soy sauce
- 1 tablespoon tomato paste
- 2 bay leaves
- 1 cup frozen pearl onions, thawed
- ¼ cup minced fresh parsley

1. Dissolve 1½ tablespoons salt in 2 quarts cold water in large container. Add beans and soak at room temperature for at least 8 hours or up to 24 hours. Drain and rinse well. (If you're pressed for time, see page 403 for information on quick brining your beans.)

2. Bring beans and 7 cups water to simmer in large saucepan. Simmer, partially covered, over medium-low heat until beans are tender, 20 to 30 minutes. Off heat, stir in 1½ teaspoons salt, cover, and let sit for 15 minutes. Drain beans and set aside.

3. While beans cook, add ¼ cup water and 2 tablespoons oil to Dutch oven and bring to simmer over medium-high heat. Add portobello mushrooms, salt, and pepper. Cover and cook for 5 minutes, stirring occasionally (mushrooms will release liquid).

4. Uncover and continue to cook, stirring occasionally, until pot is dry and dark fond forms, 6 to 8 minutes longer. Add carrots, shallot, and remaining 2 tablespoons oil and cook, stirring frequently, until vegetables start to brown, 3 to 4 minutes. Add porcini mushrooms, garlic, and thyme and cook until fragrant, about 30 seconds. Stir in flour and cook for 30 seconds. Whisk in 1 cup wine, scraping up any browned bits.

5. Whisk in miso, soy sauce, and tomato paste, then stir in 5 cups water and bay leaves. Bring to boil over high heat. Reduce heat to maintain vigorous simmer and cook, stirring occasionally and scraping bottom of pot to loosen any browned bits, until sauce is reduced and has consistency of heavy cream, 20 to 25 minutes.

6. Stir in beans, pearl onions, and remaining 2 tablespoons wine. Cover and cook over low heat, stirring occasionally, until pearl onions are tender, about 15 minutes. Discard bay leaves and stir in parsley. Serve.

Gigantes Plaki

Serves 4 to 6 Total Time 2½ hours, plus 8¼ hours brining and cooling

Why This Recipe Works Gigantes plaki is a popular dish found both as a meze at tavernas throughout Greece and on family dining tables, most often during Lent. The name simply refers to the type of bean (gigantes) and the style of cooking them in a baking dish in the oven (plaki). The beans absorb the juices and flavors of generous amounts of olive oil, tomatoes, and aromatics, becoming creamy and luxurious within a scrumptious casserole with caramelized edges and an intoxicating aroma. Onion, celery, carrots, and garlic form the base of the aromatics, along with beloved Greek oregano; hints of warmth from cinnamon and sweetness from a touch of honey balance the acidity of the tomato-heavy sauce. Gigantes plaki is a hearty, delicious meal that can be eaten warm or at room temperature. If you can't find gigante beans, you can substitute dried large lima beans.

- 3 tablespoons table salt for brining
- 1 pound (2½ cups) dried gigante beans, picked over and rinsed
- ¼ cup extra-virgin olive oil, plus extra for drizzling
- 1 onion, chopped
- 2 carrots, peeled and chopped
- 2 celery ribs, chopped
- 1 teaspoon table salt
- 2 tablespoons tomato paste
- 4 garlic cloves, minced
- 1 tablespoon chopped fresh oregano or 1 teaspoon dried
- ¼ teaspoon ground cinnamon
- 1 (14.5-ounce) can whole peeled tomatoes, drained with juice reserved, chopped
- 1 tablespoon honey
- 2 bay leaves
- 2 tablespoons chopped fresh dill

1. Dissolve 3 tablespoons salt in 4 quarts cold water in large container. Add beans and soak at room temperature for at least 8 hours or up to 24 hours. Drain and rinse well. (If you're pressed for time, see page 403 for information on quick brining your beans.)

2. Bring beans and 3 quarts water to boil in Dutch oven. Reduce heat and simmer, stirring occasionally, until beans are tender, 1 to 1½ hours. (Skim any loose bean skins or foam from surface of liquid as beans cook.) Drain beans and set aside. Wipe out pot with paper towels.

3. Adjust oven rack to middle position and heat oven to 400 degrees. Heat oil in now-empty pot over medium heat until shimmering. Add onion, carrots, celery, and salt and cook until softened and beginning to brown, 7 to 10 minutes. Stir in tomato paste, garlic, oregano, and cinnamon and cook until fragrant, about 30 seconds. Add tomatoes and their juice and 1¼ cups water, scraping up any browned bits. Stir in beans, honey, and bay leaves and bring to simmer. Season with salt and pepper to taste.

4. Transfer bean mixture to 13 by 9-inch baking dish, smoothing top with silicone spatula. Transfer dish to oven and bake until beans are cooked through and edges are golden brown and bubbling, 30 to 45 minutes. Let cool for 15 minutes. Discard bay leaves, then sprinkle with dill and drizzle with extra oil. Serve.

Calabrian Chile White Beans with Almond Romesco

FAST Serves 4 to 6 Total Time 45 minutes

Why This Recipe Works Two regions of Spain and Italy inspire this smoky, spicy, and incredibly delicious combo of creamy white beans and romesco sauce, which Calabrian chiles tilt into new territory. To make the romesco, first we broil a red bell pepper and a few handfuls of cherry tomatoes until both develop a smoky char. We puree the vegetables with an array of ingredients: a hefty dose of Parmesan, for richness and body; almonds, for the hallmark texture; the chiles, for a kick of heat and a touch of fruitiness; tomato paste, for umami and color; vinegar, for base notes of tanginess; and of course, garlic. This bold, rich red paste captures the essence of the traditional Catalonian version. Paired with cannellini beans, it is a new and brilliant way to create a vegetarian meal. Often romesco is just drizzled over beans or layered under them. Instead we simmer it all in a Dutch oven, giving the dish a slick of romesco everywhere with creamy beans throughout. Jarred, crushed Calabrian chiles are available in the condiment section of some specialty markets or online. You can use other canned beans, such as great northern or chickpeas, in place of the cannellini beans.

- 1 red bell pepper, stemmed, seeded, and halved lengthwise
- 8 ounces cherry or grape tomatoes, halved
- ¼ cup extra-virgin olive oil, divided
- 1 cup fresh basil leaves, plus 2 tablespoons chopped

- 1½ ounces Parmesan cheese, grated (¾ cup), plus extra for serving
- ⅔ cup sliced blanched almonds
- 2 tablespoons jarred crushed Calabrian chiles, plus extra for serving
- 2 tablespoons tomato paste
- 2 tablespoons cider vinegar
- 2 garlic cloves, chopped
- ¾ teaspoon table salt, divided
- 1 onion, chopped fine
- 2 (15-ounce) cans cannellini beans, rinsed
- 2 cups vegetable broth

1. Adjust oven rack 6 inches from broiler element and heat broiler. Toss bell pepper and cherry tomatoes with 2 tablespoons oil in bowl, then spread in even layer, skin side up, on rimmed baking sheet. Broil until well charred, 8 to 12 minutes. Transfer vegetables and any juices to food processor.

2. Add whole basil leaves, Parmesan, almonds, Calabrian chiles, tomato paste, vinegar, garlic, and ½ teaspoon salt and process to coarse paste, 15 to 20 seconds, scraping down sides of bowl halfway through processing. Season with salt to taste. (Romesco can be refrigerated for up to 24 hours.)

3. Heat remaining 2 tablespoons oil in Dutch oven over medium heat until shimmering. Add onion and remaining ¼ teaspoon salt and cook until softened, about 5 minutes. Stir in beans, romesco, and broth, increase heat to medium-high, and bring to boil. Reduce heat to medium-low and simmer until thickened slightly, about 10 minutes. Season with salt to taste, then sprinkle with chopped basil. Serve with extra Parmesan and extra Calabrian chiles.

Sicilian White Beans and Escarole

FAST **VEGAN** Serves 4 Total Time 40 minutes

Why This Recipe Works White beans and escarole are a classic pairing in Italian cooking, and no wonder. Combining buttery, mild cannellini beans with tender, slightly bitter escarole results in a simple but well-balanced dish. Canned beans make this dish speedy and convenient, and their creamy texture is a perfect counterpoint to the greens. Sautéed onions give the dish a rich, deep flavor base, and red pepper flakes provide a bit of heat. We like the combo of broth and water here as it adds a flavorful backbone. We add the escarole and beans along with the liquid and then cook

top | *Gigantes Plaki*
bottom | *Calabrian Chile White Beans with Almond Romesco*

| *Sicilian White Beans and Escarole*

the greens just until the leaves are wilted before cranking up the heat so the liquid quickly evaporates. This short stint on the heat prevents the beans from breaking down and becoming mushy. Once we take the pot off the heat, we stir in lemon juice for a bright finish and drizzle each portion with olive oil for richness. Chicory can be substituted for the escarole; however, its flavor is stronger.

- 1 tablespoon extra-virgin olive oil, plus extra for serving
- 2 onions, chopped fine
- ½ teaspoon table salt
- 4 garlic cloves, minced
- ⅛ teaspoon red pepper flakes
- 1 head escarole (1 pound), trimmed and sliced 1 inch thick
- 1 (15-ounce) can cannellini beans, rinsed
- 1 cup vegetable broth
- 1 cup water
- 2 teaspoons lemon juice

1. Heat oil in Dutch oven over medium heat until shimmering. Add onions and salt and cook until softened and lightly browned, 5 to 7 minutes. Stir in garlic and pepper flakes and cook until fragrant, about 30 seconds.

2. Stir in escarole, beans, broth, and water and bring to simmer. Cook, stirring occasionally, until escarole is wilted, about 5 minutes. Increase heat to high and cook until liquid is nearly evaporated, 10 to 15 minutes. Stir in lemon juice and season with salt and pepper to taste. Drizzle with extra oil and serve.

Stewed Cranberry Beans with Tomatoes and Sage

Serves 4 to 6 Total Time 2 hours, plus 8 hours 20 minutes brining and resting

Why This Recipe Works Our version of this classic one-pot bean dish showcases the delicate flavor and creamy texture of cranberry beans. While pancetta is traditionally used to add savory flavor to this dish, we lean heavily on tomato paste (which adds umami), whole canned tomatoes, and vegetable broth instead. We cook the beans halfway through before adding the tomatoes to the pot since the calcium chloride in canned tomatoes can toughen their skins. Soaking the beans in brine for at least 8 hours results in creamier beans that cook more evenly than if soaked in just water. Cranberry beans are also sold as borlotti or Roman beans.

- 1½ tablespoons table salt for brining
- 1 pound (2 cups) dried cranberry beans, picked over and rinsed
- 6 tablespoons extra-virgin olive oil, divided, plus extra for drizzling
- 1 onion, chopped fine
- 2 tablespoons tomato paste
- 6 garlic cloves, chopped
- 4 cups vegetable broth
- ⅓ cup fresh sage leaves
- 2 teaspoons table salt
- ½ teaspoon pepper
- 1 (14.5-ounce) can whole peeled tomatoes, crushed by hand into small pieces, juice reserved
- 1 ounce Parmesan cheese, shaved with vegetable peeler

1. Dissolve 1½ tablespoons salt in 2 quarts cold water in large container. Add beans and soak at room temperature for at least 8 hours or up to 24 hours. Drain and rinse well. (If you're pressed for time, see page 403 for information on quick brining your beans.)

2. Adjust oven rack to middle position and heat oven to 325 degrees. Heat ¼ cup oil in Dutch oven over medium-high heat until shimmering. Add onion and cook, stirring occasionally, until lightly browned, about 6 minutes. Stir in tomato paste and garlic and cook, stirring often, until tomato paste begins to darken, about 2 minutes.

3. Stir in broth, scraping up any browned bits. Add sage, salt, pepper, and beans and bring to boil. Cover pot, transfer to oven, and cook for 40 minutes. Remove pot from oven and stir in tomatoes and their juice. Cover pot, return to oven, and continue to cook until beans are fully tender, about 30 minutes longer.

4. Remove pot from oven. Stir beans, then let sit, covered, until liquid thickens slightly, about 20 minutes. (Cooking liquid may seem brothy at first; it will thicken as it rests.) Stir in remaining 2 tablespoons oil until liquid is creamy and glossy, about 1 minute. Season with salt and pepper to taste. Sprinkle individual portions with Parmesan and drizzle with extra oil and serve.

Jackfruit and Chickpea Makhani

Serves 4 Total Time 1 hour

Why This Recipe Works Makhani, meaning butter, refers to a North Indian preparation that involves blanketing a protein—often paneer or legumes—in a velvety spiced sauce. For a hearty riff that channels this preparation's luscious richness and tomatoey tang, we turn to jackfruit and chickpeas. Young jackfruit, when cooked and shredded, has a tender, stringy texture, which plays well with dense, creamy chickpeas. To create a flavorful base, we cook the aromatics and spices until fragrant and then deglaze the pan with the canned chickpea liquid to scrape up the flavor-packed browned bits. We then blitz this mixture with yogurt, butter, and sugar to produce a luscious, subtly sweet sauce. Coating the jackfruit in yogurt before charring it in the oven makes the fruit crisp while locking in the interior tenderness. Be sure to use young (unripe) jackfruit packed in brine or water; do not use mature jackfruit packed in syrup. Jackfruit seeds are edible. For a spicier dish, do not remove the chile seeds. Serve with rice and/or warm naan.

- 2 tablespoons vegetable oil
- 1 onion, chopped fine
- 5 garlic cloves, minced
- 4 teaspoons grated fresh ginger
- 1 serrano chile, stemmed, seeded, and minced
- ⅓ cup tomato paste
- 1 tablespoon garam masala
- 1 teaspoon ground coriander
- ½ teaspoon ground cumin
- ½ teaspoon pepper
- 2 (15-ounce) cans chickpeas, drained with liquid reserved
- 1 cup plain Greek yogurt, divided
- 2 tablespoons unsalted butter
- 1 tablespoon sugar
- 1 (20-ounce) can young green jackfruit packed in brine or water, drained and cut into ¾-inch pieces (2 cups)
- ½ teaspoon table salt, divided
- 3 tablespoons chopped fresh cilantro, divided

1. Heat oil in large saucepan over medium heat until shimmering. Add onion, garlic, ginger, and serrano and cook, stirring frequently, until onion is softened and lightly browned, 6 to 8 minutes. Add tomato paste, garam masala, coriander, cumin, and pepper and cook, stirring frequently, until fragrant and tomato paste begins to brown, about 2 minutes. Stir in chickpea canning liquid, scraping up any browned bits.

2. Transfer mixture to blender. Add ½ cup yogurt, butter, and sugar and process until smooth, about 30 seconds, scraping down sides of blender jar as needed. Return sauce to now-empty saucepan and bring to brief simmer over medium heat. Off heat, season with salt and pepper to taste and cover to keep warm.

3. Adjust oven rack 6 inches from broiler element and heat broiler. Line rimmed baking sheet with aluminum foil and spray with vegetable oil spray. Pat jackfruit dry with paper towels, then toss with remaining ½ cup yogurt and salt until well coated. Spread jackfruit evenly over prepared sheet and broil until lightly charred, 10 to 12 minutes, flipping jackfruit halfway through broiling.

4. Stir jackfruit and chickpeas into saucepan and bring to simmer over medium heat. Cover; reduce heat to low; and cook, stirring and scraping bottom of saucepan occasionally, until chickpeas are softened, about 15 minutes. Stir in 2 tablespoons cilantro and season with salt to taste. Transfer to platter and sprinkle with remaining 1 tablespoon cilantro. Serve.

Chickpea Bouillabaisse

Serves 4 to 6 Total Time 1½ hours

Why This Recipe Works The flavors of Provence come to life in this meatless version of bouillabaisse. To re-create the classic flavors, we start with a base of fennel, garlic, tomato paste, and saffron for the broth. In lieu of fish stock, we use vegetable broth and canned chickpea liquid to create the dish's traditional body. Chickpeas add heft and an ultrasavory presence, while potatoes, white wine, pastis, and orange zest stay true to the Provençal flavors. A bit of tarragon, a favorite herb in French cuisine, infuses the dish with its sweet anise flavor. And we did not skip the rouille, the saffron-scented sauce that is the crowning glory of bouillabaisse. Using a baguette, we bind the lush rouille and also make large croutons. The vibrant rouille-topped croutons add acidity and brightness. We prefer the robust flavor of extra-virgin olive oil in the rouille; you can use a combination of vegetable oil and extra-virgin olive oil if you prefer a more neutral flavor.

Bouillabaisse

- 2 tablespoons extra-virgin olive oil
- 1 large leek, white and light green parts only, halved lengthwise, sliced thin, and washed thoroughly
- 1 fennel bulb, stalks discarded, bulb halved, cored, and sliced thin
- ¼ teaspoon table salt
- 4 garlic cloves, minced
- 1 tablespoon tomato paste
- 1 tablespoon unbleached all-purpose flour
- ¼ teaspoon saffron threads, crumbled
- ¼ teaspoon ground cayenne pepper
- 2 (15-ounce) cans chickpeas, undrained
- 3 cups vegetable broth
- 1 (14.5-ounce) can diced tomatoes, drained
- 12 ounces Yukon Gold potatoes, cut into ¾-inch pieces
- ½ cup dry white wine
- ¼ cup pastis or Pernod
- 1 (3-inch) strip orange zest
- 1 tablespoon chopped fresh tarragon or parsley

Rouille and Croutons

- 3 tablespoons water
- ¼ teaspoon saffron threads, crumbled
- 1 (12-inch) baguette
- 4 teaspoons lemon juice
- 2 teaspoons Dijon mustard
- 1 large egg yolk
- 2 small garlic cloves, minced
- ¼ teaspoon cayenne pepper
- Pinch table salt
- ½ cup plus 2 tablespoons extra-virgin olive oil, divided

1. For the bouillabaisse Adjust oven rack to lower-middle position and heat oven to 375 degrees. Heat oil in Dutch oven over medium-high heat until shimmering. Add leek, fennel, and salt and cook, stirring often, until vegetables begin to soften, about 5 minutes. Stir in garlic, tomato paste, flour, saffron, and cayenne and cook until fragrant, about 30 seconds. Stir in chickpeas and their liquid, broth, tomatoes, potatoes, wine, pastis, and orange zest. Bring to simmer and cook over medium-low heat, partially covered, until potatoes are tender, about 20 minutes.

2. For the rouille and croutons While bouillabaisse cooks, microwave water and saffron in medium bowl until water is steaming, 15 to 30 seconds; set aside for 5 minutes. Cut 4-inch piece of baguette; remove and discard crust. Tear crustless bread into 1-inch pieces (you should have about 1 cup). Stir bread pieces and lemon juice into saffron-infused

Jackfruit and Chickpea Makhani

water and let sit for 5 minutes. Using whisk, mash soaked bread mixture until uniform paste forms, 1 to 2 minutes. Whisk in mustard, egg yolk, garlic, cayenne, and salt. Whisking constantly, slowly drizzle in ¼ cup oil in steady stream until smooth, mayonnaise-like consistency is reached, about 4 minutes, scraping down bowl as necessary. Slowly whisk in ¼ cup oil until smooth; set aside until ready to serve.

3. Cut remaining baguette into ¾-inch-thick slices. Toss slices with remaining 2 tablespoons oil until coated, then arrange in single layer on rimmed baking sheet. Bake until light golden brown, 10 to 15 minutes.

4. Discard orange zest from bouillabaisse. Stir in tarragon and season with salt and pepper to taste. Serve, dolloping individual serving bowls with rouille and spreading rouille over croutons.

Chana Masala

VEGAN Serves 4 to 6 Total Time 50 minutes

Why This Recipe Works Chana masala is arguably one of North India's most popular vegetarian dishes, and it can be quick and easy to prepare. We start by using a food processor to grind the aromatic paste that forms the base of our dish. We opt for canned chickpeas because their flavor and texture are nearly indistinguishable from those of chickpeas that are cooked from dried, and we don't drain them because the canning liquid adds body and savory depth to the dish. The canned chickpeas still retain a bit of snap, so we simmer them in the sauce until they turn soft. Adding stronger foundational spices such as cumin, turmeric, and fennel seeds at the beginning of cooking ensures that they permeate the dish, and reserving the sweet, delicate garam masala until near the end preserves its aroma. A generous garnish of chopped onion, sliced chile, and fresh cilantro adds so much vibrancy, texture, and freshness that you'd never guess that most of the ingredients in the recipe are from the pantry. Because the sodium contents of canned chickpeas and tomatoes vary, we include only a small amount of salt in this recipe; season with additional salt at the end of cooking if needed. If you prefer a spicier dish, leave the seeds in the serrano chiles. If you can't find Kashmiri chile powder, substitute 1 teaspoon paprika. This dish is often paired with bhature, deep-fried breads that puff up as they cook; alternatively, serve it with rice or naan.

- 1 small red onion (¾ onion chopped coarse, ¼ onion chopped fine)
- 10 sprigs fresh cilantro, stems cut into 1-inch lengths and leaves reserved
- 1 (1½-inch) piece ginger, peeled and chopped coarse
- 2 garlic cloves, chopped coarse
- 2 serrano chiles, stemmed, halved, seeded, and sliced thin crosswise, divided
- 3 tablespoons vegetable oil
- 1 (14.5-ounce) can whole peeled tomatoes
- 1 teaspoon Kashmiri chile powder
- 1 teaspoon ground cumin
- ½ teaspoon ground turmeric
- ½ teaspoon fennel seeds
- 2 (15-ounce) cans chickpeas, undrained
- 1½ teaspoons garam masala
- ½ teaspoon table salt
- Lime wedges

1. Process coarsely chopped onion, cilantro stems, ginger, garlic, and half of serranos in food processor until finely chopped, scraping down sides of bowl as necessary, about 20 seconds. Combine onion mixture and oil in large saucepan. Cook over medium-high heat, stirring frequently, until onion is fully softened and beginning to stick to saucepan, 5 to 7 minutes.

2. While onion mixture cooks, process tomatoes and their juice in now-empty food processor until smooth, about 30 seconds. Add chile powder, cumin, turmeric, and fennel seeds to onion mixture and cook, stirring constantly, until fragrant, about 1 minute. Stir in chickpeas and their liquid and processed tomatoes and bring to boil. Adjust heat to maintain simmer, then cover and simmer for 15 minutes.

3. Stir in garam masala and salt and continue to cook, uncovered and stirring occasionally, until chickpeas are softened and sauce is thickened, 8 to 12 minutes longer. Season with salt to taste. Transfer to wide, shallow serving bowl. Sprinkle with finely chopped onion, remaining serranos, and cilantro leaves and serve, passing lime wedges separately.

Chana Masala

Chickpea Curry

FAST **VEGAN** Serves 4 Total Time 40 minutes

Why This Recipe Works This simple, speedy weeknight curry uses pantry ingredients plus a few fresh ones to punch far above its weight in terms of flavor payoff. You can make it with any number of different vegetables, but to keep it easy, we cut up a generous amount of green bell peppers and add a minced jalapeño to bring a little spiciness to the green pepper vibe. We sauté the bell peppers first until they are starting to brown and then add the jalapeño, garlic, ginger, and curry powder to bloom briefly in the hot oil. Next we add canned chickpeas, tomatoes, and coconut milk, and after a quick simmer, dinner is served. To make this curry spicier, add the seeds from the chile. Serve with rice.

- 2 tablespoons vegetable oil
- 2 green bell peppers, stemmed, seeded, and cut into 1-inch pieces
- 1½ teaspoons table salt
- ½ teaspoon pepper
- 1 jalapeño chile, stemmed, seeded, and minced
- 4 garlic cloves, minced
- 1 tablespoon grated fresh ginger
- 1 tablespoon curry powder
- 2 (15-ounce) cans chickpeas, rinsed
- 1 (14.5-ounce) can diced tomatoes
- 1 (14-ounce) can coconut milk

1. Heat oil in Dutch oven over medium-high heat until shimmering. Add bell peppers, salt, and pepper and cook until bell peppers are beginning to brown, 5 to 7 minutes. Add jalapeño, garlic, ginger, and curry powder and cook until fragrant, about 30 seconds.

2. Add chickpeas, tomatoes and their juice, and coconut milk and bring to boil. Cover, reduce heat to medium-low, and simmer until bell peppers are tender and flavors meld, about 20 minutes, stirring occasionally. Serve.

Espinacas con Garbanzos (Andalusian Spinach and Chickpeas)

FAST **VEGAN** Serves 4 Total Time 40 minutes

Why This Recipe Works Espinacas con garbanzos is Southern Spain's best-kept secret—a merger of meltingly soft chickpeas, fruity oil, and garlic with tender spinach and spices. It may be visually unassuming, but its enticing aroma will stop you in your tracks. To make it, we briefly simmer canned chickpeas in a combination of vegetable broth and chickpea canning liquid, which tenderizes them and ensures extra-savory flavor. We use a picada (a paste of garlic and bread cooked in plenty of olive oil), which thickens and seasons the sauce like magic. Smoked paprika, cumin, cinnamon, cayenne, and saffron imbue this special picada with heady aromas, and tomatoes and vinegar boost its tang. Since spinach and chickpeas are a beloved combo in Spain, we follow that tradition. Thawed frozen chopped spinach is perfect here; already fine and tender, it disperses beautifully throughout the dish and provides plenty of surface area to hold the flavorful juices in place so the dish isn't soupy. Red wine vinegar can be substituted for the sherry vinegar.

- 1 loaf crusty bread, divided
- 2 (15-ounce) cans chickpeas (1 can drained and rinsed, 1 can undrained)
- 1½ cups vegetable broth
- 6 tablespoons extra-virgin olive oil, divided
- 6 garlic cloves, minced
- 1 tablespoon smoked paprika
- 1 teaspoon ground cumin
- ¼ teaspoon table salt
- ⅛ teaspoon ground cinnamon
- ⅛ teaspoon cayenne pepper
- Small pinch saffron threads, crumbled
- 2 small plum tomatoes, halved lengthwise, flesh shredded on large holes of box grater and skins discarded
- 4 teaspoons sherry vinegar, plus extra for seasoning
- 10 ounces frozen chopped spinach, thawed and squeezed dry

1. Cut 1½-ounce piece from loaf of bread (thickness will vary depending on size of loaf) and tear into 1-inch pieces. Process in food processor until finely ground (you should have ¾ cup crumbs). Combine chickpeas and broth in large saucepan and bring to boil over high heat. Adjust heat to maintain simmer and cook until level of liquid is just below top layer of chickpeas, about 10 minutes.

2. While chickpeas cook, heat ¼ cup oil in 10-inch nonstick skillet over medium heat until just shimmering. Add bread crumbs and cook, stirring frequently, until deep golden brown, 3 to 4 minutes. Add garlic, paprika, cumin, salt, cinnamon, cayenne, and saffron and cook until fragrant, 30 seconds. Stir in tomatoes and vinegar and remove from heat.

3. Stir bread mixture and spinach into chickpeas in saucepan. Continue to simmer, stirring occasionally, until mixture is thick and stew-like, 5 to 10 minutes longer. Off heat, stir in remaining 2 tablespoons oil. Cover and let sit for 5 minutes. Season with salt and extra vinegar to taste. Serve with remaining bread.

Crispy Chickpea Cakes with Zucchini Ribbon Salad

Crispy Chickpea Cakes with Zucchini Ribbon Salad

Serves 4 to 6   Total Time 50 minutes

Why This Recipe Works For something a bit different to do with the canned chickpeas in your pantry, try making these delightful patties, which are a fresh take on falafel. They come together easily after pulsing chickpeas and binders in a food processor with loads of fresh cilantro, onion, coriander, cumin, and cayenne. We then shape this cohesive mixture into disks and pan-fry them. Taking this meal up a notch is a quick sauce of yogurt, tahini, lemon, and mint. To make the patties a complete meal, we add an elegant ribboned-zucchini salad with briny kalamata olives, lemony yogurt, and mint. Niçoise olives can be used in place of kalamata. Use a vegetable peeler or a mandoline to shave the zucchini.

Zucchini Salad

- ¼ cup minced fresh mint
- 3 tablespoons extra-virgin olive oil
- 2 tablespoons lemon juice
- 1 tablespoon plain Greek yogurt
- ½ teaspoon honey
- 3 small zucchini (6 ounces each), shaved lengthwise into ribbons
- 2 tablespoons finely chopped pitted kalamata olives

Chickpea Cakes

- 1½ cups fresh cilantro leaves and stems
- ½ onion, chopped
- 1½ teaspoons ground coriander
- 1 teaspoon ground cumin
- 1 teaspoon table salt
- ½ teaspoon baking powder
- ¼ teaspoon cayenne pepper
- 1 large egg
- 2 (15-ounce) cans chickpeas, rinsed and patted dry
- ¼ cup all-purpose flour
- 3 tablespoons extra-virgin olive oil
- 1 recipe Tahini-Yogurt Sauce (page 211)

1. **For the zucchini salad** Whisk mint, oil, lemon juice, yogurt, and honey together in medium bowl. Add zucchini ribbons and toss gently to coat. Sprinkle with olives and refrigerate until needed.

2. **For the chickpea cakes** Process cilantro, onion, coriander, cumin, salt, baking powder, and cayenne in food processor for 5 seconds. Scrape down sides of bowl. Continue to process until mixture resembles pesto, about 5 seconds longer. Add egg and process for 5 seconds. Add chickpeas and flour and pulse 4 times. Scrape down sides of bowl. Continue to pulse until chickpeas are coarsely chopped and flour is fully incorporated, about 4 more pulses.

3. Spray rimmed baking sheet with vegetable oil spray. Remove food processor blade and, using ½ cup measure, drop 6 even portions (about scant ½ cup each) onto prepared sheet. Gently shape into patties about 3 inches in diameter.

4. Line cutting board with single layer of paper towels. Heat oil in 12-inch nonstick skillet over medium-high heat until shimmering. Using thin spatula, transfer patties to skillet. Cook for 4 minutes, then reduce heat to medium-low, cover, and continue to cook until tops are firm to touch and patties register 185 degrees, 7 to 9 minutes. Transfer patties to prepared board, browned side down. Invert cakes to browned side up and serve with sauce and salad.

Sautéed Fava Beans, Asparagus, and Leek

FAST **VEGAN** Serves 6 Total Time 45 minutes

Why This Recipe Works For the ultimate spring sauté, we pair fava beans with crisp-tender asparagus, softened leek, lemon, and herbs. It takes some work to get to the good part of favas, but these luxuriously creamy, protein-rich nuggets are worth it. We blanch and shell the favas and then add them to the skillet after the leek and asparagus have been sautéed to preserve their vibrant color and creamy bite. This recipe works best with fresh fava beans; look for them at farmers' markets or supermarkets and choose bright green, unblemished pods. You can use 12 ounces (2½ cups) frozen shelled fava beans, thawed, in place of the fresh favas. Be sure to remove the sheaths. Skip step 1 if using frozen favas. We like fresh parsley here, but mint, tarragon, or cilantro will also work.

- 2½ pounds fava beans, shelled (2½ cups)
- 2 tablespoons extra-virgin olive oil
- 1 leek, white and light green parts only, sliced thin, and washed thoroughly (1½ cups)
- 1 pound asparagus, trimmed and cut on bias into 1-inch lengths
- ½ teaspoon table salt
- ⅛ teaspoon pepper
- 1 teaspoon grated lemon zest, plus lemon wedges for serving
- 1 tablespoon chopped fresh parsley

1. Bring 1 quart water to boil in medium saucepan. Fill large bowl halfway with ice and water. Nestle fine-mesh strainer into ice bath. Add beans to boiling water and cook for 4 minutes. Using spider skimmer or slotted spoon, transfer beans to strainer set in ice water and let cool, about 2 minutes. Transfer fava beans to double layer of paper towels and dry well. Using paring knife, make small cut along edge of each bean through waxy sheath, then gently squeeze sheath to release bean; discard sheath.

2. Heat oil in 12-inch nonstick skillet over medium heat until shimmering. Add leek and cook, stirring frequently until softened, about 4 minutes. Add asparagus, salt, and pepper and stir well. Continue to cook, stirring occasionally, until asparagus is crisp-tender, 3 to 6 minutes. Stir in beans and cook just until beans are warmed through, about 2 minutes. Off heat, stir in lemon zest. Season with salt to taste and top with parsley. Serve with lemon wedges.

Preparing Fresh Fava Beans

1. To shell favas, use paring knife and your thumb to snip off tip of pod and pull apart sides to release beans. Blanch beans and dry well.

2. Use paring knife to make small cut along edge of bean through waxy sheath, then gently squeeze sheath to release bean. Discard sheath.

A Spring Sensation

Fava beans are a rite of spring, available in markets only from March through May. We are always eager to get our hands on them for their freshness, flavor, and vibrant color. Remarkably versatile and delicious, we guarantee they are worth seeking out. Our Sautéed Fava Beans, Asparagus, and Leek recipe is a mélange of very green vegetables, with the beans taking center stage. They need very little to make them shine.

Naturally Creamy

The glistening favas are hidden in long leathery pods, but do not be intimidated—you can shell them quite easily, after which you will see a neatly arranged and beautiful row of beans. Their delicate and almost nutty, buttery flavor as well as a natural creaminess make any fava bean dish a luxurious treat. What makes them so creamy? Water-soluble proteins within the beans. As an added bonus, you only need to cook them for mere minutes.

Blanch and Shock

Once these culinary gems are removed from their pods, we blanch them in boiling water and then shock them in an ice bath so they retain their bright green color; this also makes it easier to remove their waxy sheath. The cooking process softens the pectin in the coating, making it flexible enough to be squeezed or peeled away.

Sautéed Fava Beans, Asparagus, and Leek

top | *Edamame Salad with Mint and Parmesan*
bottom | *Cuban-Style Black Beans and Rice*

Edamame Salad with Mint and Parmesan

FAST Serves 4 Total Time 40 minutes

Why This Recipe Works Edamame are young soybeans, and they shine brightly in this salad. The recipe springs from our love of Italian fava bean salads. Here we pair the verdant beans with a garlicky lemon dressing, Parmesan, and refreshing fresh mint and parsley. We blanch the edamame in heavily salted water to season them all the way through and soften them just a bit, allowing the dressing to cling to their exteriors. Frozen shelled edamame come in a wide range of package sizes. If you can find only a 10-ounce package, there's no need to buy a second package to make up the extra 2 ounces; just make the recipe with 10 ounces of edamame. You do not need to thaw the edamame before boiling. Use the large holes of a box grater to shred the Parmesan.

- 3 tablespoons extra-virgin olive oil
- 1 small shallot, minced
- 1 tablespoon lemon juice
- 1 garlic clove, minced
- ½ teaspoon table salt, plus salt for blanching edamame
- ½ teaspoon pepper
- 12 ounces (2 cups) frozen shelled edamame
- 1½ ounces Parmesan cheese, shredded (½ cup)
- ⅓ cup coarsely chopped fresh mint
- ¼ cup coarsely chopped fresh parsley

1. Combine oil, shallot, lemon juice, garlic, salt, and pepper in bowl; set aside.

2. Bring 2 quarts water to boil in large saucepan over high heat. Fill large bowl halfway with ice and water. Line large plate with double layer of paper towels.

3. Add edamame and 1 tablespoon salt to boiling water and cook for 5 minutes (water may not return to boil; this is OK). Drain edamame in colander. Nestle colander into ice bath, submerging edamame. Let sit until edamame are chilled, 3 to 5 minutes.

4. Lift colander from ice bath, allowing excess water to drain, and transfer edamame to prepared plate. Pat dry with additional paper towels.

5. Transfer edamame to bowl with dressing and toss to coat. Add Parmesan, mint, and parsley and toss to combine. Season with salt and pepper to taste. Serve.

Cuban-Style Black Beans and Rice

VEGAN Serves 6 to 8 Total Time 2¼ hours, plus 8 hours brining

Why This Recipe Works Beans and rice is a familiar combination the world over, but the Cuban dish is unique in that the rice is cooked in the inky concentrated liquid left over from cooking the beans, thus rendering the grains flavorful too. We simmer a portion of the sofrito (the traditional combination of garlic, bell pepper, and onion) with our beans to infuse them with flavor and then use the liquid to cook our rice and beans together. Lightly browning the remaining sofrito and spices with tomato paste deepens the flavor, and finishing the dish in the oven eliminates the crusty bottom that can form when the dish is cooked on the stove. You will need a Dutch oven with a tight-fitting lid for this recipe.

- 1½ tablespoons table salt for brining
- 1 cup dried black beans, picked over and rinsed
- 2 cups water
- 2 large green bell peppers, halved and seeded, divided
- 1 large onion, halved crosswise and peeled, root end left intact, divided
- 1 head garlic, 5 cloves removed and minced, remaining head halved crosswise with skin left intact
- 2 bay leaves
- 2½ teaspoons table salt, divided
- 2 tablespoons extra-virgin olive oil
- 4 teaspoons ground cumin
- 1 tablespoon minced fresh oregano
- 1 tablespoon tomato paste
- 1½ cups long-grain white rice, rinsed
- 2 tablespoons red wine vinegar
- 2 scallions, sliced thin
- Lime wedges

1. Dissolve 1½ tablespoons salt in 2 quarts cold water in large container. Add beans and soak at room temperature for at least 8 hours or up to 24 hours. Drain and rinse well. (If you're pressed for time, see page 403 for information on quick brining your beans.)

2. Combine beans, water, 1 bell pepper half, 1 onion half (with root end), halved garlic head, bay leaves, and 1 teaspoon salt in Dutch oven. Bring to simmer over medium-high heat, cover, and reduce heat to low. Cook until beans are just soft, 30 to 40 minutes. Discard bell pepper, onion, garlic, and bay leaves, then drain beans in colander set over large bowl, reserving 2½ cups bean cooking liquid. (If you don't have enough bean cooking liquid, add water to equal 2½ cups.) Do not wash out Dutch oven.

3. Adjust oven rack to middle position and heat oven to 350 degrees. Cut remaining bell peppers and onion into 2-inch pieces and process in food processor until broken into rough ¼-inch pieces, about 8 pulses, scraping down sides of bowl as necessary; set vegetables aside.

4. In now-empty Dutch oven, heat oil over medium-low heat until shimmering. Add reserved processed vegetables, cumin, oregano, and tomato paste. Increase heat to medium and cook, stirring frequently, until vegetables are softened and beginning to brown, 10 to 15 minutes. Add minced garlic and cook, stirring constantly, until fragrant, about 1 minute. Add rice and stir to coat, about 30 seconds.

5. Stir in beans, reserved bean cooking liquid, vinegar, and remaining 1½ teaspoons salt. Increase heat to medium-high and bring to simmer. Cover and transfer to oven. Bake until liquid is absorbed and rice is tender, about 30 minutes. Fluff with fork and let rest, uncovered, for 5 minutes. Serve, passing scallions and lime wedges separately.

Skillet Rice and Beans with Corn and Fresh Tomatoes

VEGAN Serves 6 Total Time 1 hour

Why This Recipe Works We love skillet meals where you need only one pan. This recipe lets the beans steal the limelight but pairs them with rice (of course), fresh summer corn, and grape tomatoes, and gives them a bit of a Tex-Mex slant by including cilantro, lime, garlic, cumin, and a little cayenne. The result is a summery recipe with plump beans, soft rice, and fresh-tasting vegetables. We begin by sautéing onion and corn. Toasting the rice briefly before stirring in broth and black beans ensures that the grains soak up all the flavors and become fat and tender. We finish by sprinkling tomatoes, scallions, cilantro, and lime juice over the dish before serving. We prefer the flavor of fresh corn; however, 1½ cups frozen corn, thawed and patted dry, can be substituted.

- 2 tablespoons extra-virgin olive oil, divided
- 12 ounces grape tomatoes, quartered
- 5 scallions, sliced thin
- ¼ cup minced fresh cilantro
- 1 tablespoon lime juice
- 1 onion, chopped fine
- 2 ears corn, kernels cut from cobs
- 4 garlic cloves, minced
- 1 teaspoon ground cumin
- Pinch cayenne pepper
- 1 cup long-grain white rice, rinsed
- 3 cups vegetable broth
- 2 (15-ounce) cans black beans, rinsed

1. Combine 1 tablespoon oil, tomatoes, scallions, cilantro, and lime juice in bowl and season with salt and pepper to taste; set aside for serving.

2. Heat remaining 1 tablespoon oil in 12-inch nonstick skillet over medium-high heat until shimmering. Add onion and cook until softened and lightly browned, 5 to 7 minutes. Stir in corn and cook until lightly browned, about 4 minutes.

3. Stir in garlic, cumin, and cayenne and cook until fragrant, about 30 seconds. Stir in rice and coat with spices, about 1 minute. Stir in broth and beans and bring to simmer. Cover and simmer gently, stirring occasionally, until rice is tender and liquid is absorbed, about 20 minutes.

4. Season with salt and pepper to taste, sprinkle tomato mixture over top, and serve.

Variations

VEGAN Skillet Rice and Chickpeas with Coconut Milk

Substitute 2 finely chopped yellow bell peppers for corn, 1½ teaspoons garam masala for cumin, and canned chickpeas for black beans. Substitute 1 cup coconut milk for 1 cup broth.

VEGAN Spanish-Style Skillet Rice and Chickpeas

Substitute 2 finely chopped red bell peppers for corn, pinch crumbled saffron threads for cumin, and canned chickpeas for black beans.

Tacu Tacu with Salsa Criolla

VEGAN Serves 4 Total Time 2¾ hours, plus 8½ hours brining and resting

Why This Recipe Works Tacu tacu is a Peruvian rice and bean cake commonly served at breakfast or lunch, often topped with eggs. Regardless of time of day, tacu tacu is normally accompanied by salsa criolla, a Peruvian onion salsa. The bean of choice is the canary bean, a creamy mild-flavored variety. Following traditional preparation, we blend a portion of the beans to help bind the mixture together. Tacu tacu has a mild kick thanks to the addition of aji amarillo paste, a yellow chili pepper paste that is a staple in Peruvian cuisine (and widely available online or in specialty markets). This is a great way to use up leftover rice; substitute 2 cups day-old cooked rice for the cup of uncooked rice. You can use dried cannellini beans or two (15-ounce) cans rinsed cannellini beans in place of the dried canary beans; skip steps 1 and 3 if using canned beans.

Tacu Tacu

- 1½ tablespoons table salt for brining
- 8 ounces (1 cup) dried canary beans, picked over and rinsed
- ¾ teaspoon plus ⅛ teaspoon table salt, divided, plus salt for cooking beans
- 1 cup long-grain white rice, rinsed
- 6 tablespoons extra-virgin olive oil, divided
- ½ red onion, chopped fine
- 2 tablespoons aji amarillo paste
- 3 garlic cloves, minced to paste
- 1 teaspoon ground cumin
- ¾ teaspoon dried oregano
- ¼ teaspoon pepper, divided
- 1 cup vegetable broth
- 3 tablespoons chopped fresh cilantro
- 4 large eggs (optional)
- Lime wedges

Salsa Criolla

- ½ red onion, sliced thin
- 1 tablespoon lime juice
- ¼ teaspoon table salt
- Pinch pepper
- 2 tablespoons chopped fresh cilantro

1. **For the tacu tacu** Dissolve 1½ tablespoons salt in 2 quarts cold water in large container. Add beans and soak at room temperature for at least 8 hours or up to 24 hours. Drain and rinse well. (If you're pressed for time, see page 403 for information on quick brining your beans.)

2. **For the salsa criolla** Soak onion in ice water for 10 minutes. Drain well and pat dry with paper towels. Combine onion, lime juice, salt, and pepper in bowl. Cover with plastic wrap and refrigerate for at least 30 minutes or up to 2 days. Stir in cilantro just before serving.

3. Bring beans and 7 cups water to simmer in large saucepan. Simmer, partially covered, over medium-low heat until beans are tender, 30 to 40 minutes. Remove from heat, stir in 1½ teaspoons salt, cover, and let sit until completely tender, about 15 minutes.

4. Drain beans and transfer to large bowl. Process 1 cup beans in food processor until smooth, about 30 seconds, scraping sides of processor bowl as needed. Transfer to large bowl with remaining beans, stirring and mashing as needed to combine; set aside.

5. While beans are cooking, bring rice, 1½ cups water, and ¼ teaspoon salt to simmer in medium saucepan over medium-high heat. Reduce heat to medium-low, cover, and simmer gently until rice is tender and all liquid has been absorbed, 11 to 13 minutes. Let sit off heat, covered, for 10 minutes. Fluff rice with fork and set aside.

6. Adjust oven racks to upper-middle and lower-middle positions and heat oven to 200 degrees. Heat 1 tablespoon oil in 12-inch nonstick skillet over medium heat until shimmering. Add onion and cook, stirring occasionally, until softened and just beginning to brown, 5 to 7 minutes. Stir in aji amarillo paste, garlic, cumin, oregano, ⅛ teaspoon pepper, and ½ teaspoon salt and cook until fragrant, about 1 minute. Off heat, add reserved bean mixture and reserved rice and stir to combine. Return skillet to medium heat, stir in broth, and bring to simmer. Cook until liquid is absorbed and rice mixture thickens, 3 to 5 minutes, stirring frequently; mixture should be sticky. Transfer to bowl, stir in cilantro, and let sit for 10 minutes.

7. In clean, dry skillet, heat 1½ teaspoons oil over medium heat until shimmering. Add one-quarter rice and bean mixture and, using silicone spatula, press mixture against 1 side of skillet while tilting skillet toward tacu tacu (tilting makes it easier to pack rice and bean mixture firmly). Firmly press mixture until it is a rough oval and measures about 8 inches in length. Cook until golden brown along edges, 2 to 4 minutes.

8. Place skillet flat on stovetop and, using 2 spatulas, carefully flip tacu tacu. (If it breaks, firmly press into side of skillet matching shape of tacu tacu to bring back together.) Add 1½ teaspoons oil to skillet and nestle tacu tacu into side of skillet that matches its shape. Repeat firmly pressing tacu tacu into side of skillet while tilting skillet slightly. Cook until golden brown along edges, 2 to 4 minutes. Carefully slide tacu tacu onto serving plate and transfer to oven to keep warm. Repeat with remaining rice and bean mixture and 3 tablespoons oil.

9. Heat remaining 1 tablespoon oil in clean, dry skillet over medium heat until shimmering. Add eggs, if using, and sprinkle with remaining ⅛ teaspoon salt and remaining ⅛ teaspoon pepper. Cover and cook for 1 minute. Let sit off heat, covered, for 15 to 45 seconds for runny yolks, 45 to 60 seconds for soft but set yolks, or about 2 minutes for medium-set yolks. Top each tacu tacu with 1 egg and serve with salsa criolla and lime wedges.

Tacu Tacu with Salsa Criolla

Gallo Pinto (Costa Rican Beans and Rice)

An Herb with Attitude

Some people cannot imagine a world without cilantro, while others have an aversion to it. In the test kitchen, we love cilantro, as no other herb possesses the same bright citrusy flavor and distinctive aroma. It plays a starring role in many Mexican and Latin American dishes, such as Gallo Pinto, in which leftover rice and beans are transformed into a lively, hearty meal infused with cilantro.

Fresh and Dried Coriander

The entire plant is known as coriander, but the stems and leaves are commonly referred to as cilantro. The seeds from the plant are called coriander and are dried and sold whole or ground.

Using It All

Gallo Pinto calls for 30 sprigs of fresh cilantro (one large bunch) and ½ teaspoon dried coriander. Cilantro has both tender thin stems and thicker ones. We chop the thin stems along with the leaves as they are edible too. Instead of discarding the thicker stems, we use them to flavor the black beans by adding an herb bundle of these stems along with thyme sprigs and bay leaves. To make the potent base for this dish, we cook onion and garlic along with the aromatics. When we fold together the beans, rice, and some of the bean cooking liquid, we also fold in the hefty amount of reserved and finely chopped thin cilantro stems and leaves for a final fresh finish.

Gallo Pinto (Costa Rican Beans and Rice)

VEGAN Serves 4 to 6 Total Time 1½ hours, plus 8 hours brining

Why This Recipe Works Considered the national dish of Costa Rica, a bowl of gallo pinto is unpretentious and soul satisfying. Gallo pinto is traditionally the foundation of a hearty breakfast, often accompanied by eggs, cheese, avocado, and tortillas. To make it, we cook leftover rice with spices, onions, garlic, peppers, and cilantro. To infuse the dish with maximum bean flavor, we use dried black beans, soaking them overnight to soften them. The next day, we cook the beans in a scant amount of flavored liquid to make a concentrated bean broth. We finish the dish with finely chopped bell peppers for subtle vegetal sweetness, a shower of fresh cilantro for freshness, and a few dashes of the bottled Costa Rican condiment Salsa Lizano for a final touch of bracing acidity. Day-old rice works best, as it absorbs the bean broth and other flavors so readily; in a pinch, cook the rice 2 hours ahead, spread it on a rimmed baking sheet, and let it cool before chilling it for 30 minutes. Vegetarian Worcestershire sauce can replace the Salsa Lizano.

- ½ teaspoon table salt for brining
- ¾ cup dried black beans, picked over and rinsed
- 30 sprigs fresh cilantro (1 bunch)
- 8 sprigs fresh thyme
- 2 bay leaves
- 3 tablespoons vegetable oil, divided
- 1 large white onion, chopped fine (1½ cups), divided
- 6 garlic cloves, minced, divided
- 1¼ teaspoons table salt, divided
- 1 teaspoon chili powder
- ½ teaspoon pepper
- ½ teaspoon ground coriander
- ½ teaspoon ground cumin
- 1 large red bell pepper, stemmed, seeded, and cut into ¼-inch pieces (about 1⅓ cups), divided
- 1 large yellow bell pepper, stemmed, seeded, and cut into ¼-inch pieces (about 1¼ cups), divided
- 3 tablespoons Salsa Lizano, plus extra for serving
- 3 cups cooked long-grain white rice, cold
- Hot sauce

1. Dissolve ½ teaspoon salt in 1 quart cold water in large container. Add beans and soak at room temperature for at least 8 hours or up to 24 hours. Drain and rinse well. (If you're pressed for time, see page 403 for information on quick brining your beans.)

2. Remove thick stems from cilantro sprigs and reserve. Chop leaves and thin stems fine (you should have about ¾ cup) and refrigerate until needed. Using kitchen twine, tie reserved stems, thyme sprigs, and bay leaves into bundle.

3. Heat 1 tablespoon oil in medium saucepan over medium heat until shimmering. Add half of onion, half of garlic, 1 teaspoon salt, chili powder, pepper, coriander, and cumin and cook, stirring frequently, until softened, 5 to 7 minutes. Increase heat to high; add beans, cilantro bundle, and 1¾ cups water; and bring to boil. Cover, reduce heat, and simmer, stirring occasionally, until beans are just soft and liquid begins to thicken, 1 to 1¼ hours. (Beans can be refrigerated in their cooking liquid for up to 3 days.) Strain beans through fine-mesh strainer, reserving ½ cup cooking liquid.

4. Heat remaining 2 tablespoons oil in 12-inch nonstick skillet over medium heat until shimmering. Add 1 cup red bell pepper, 1 cup yellow bell pepper, remaining ¼ teaspoon salt, remaining onion, and remaining garlic and cook, stirring occasionally, until softened and lightly browned, 10 minutes. Stir in Salsa Lizano. Add rice and cook, stirring constantly and breaking up rice clumps, until mixture is heated through, 1 to 2 minutes.

5. Add beans and reserved cooking liquid. Gently fold beans into rice until combined and warmed through, 1 to 2 minutes. Off heat, add reserved chopped cilantro and remaining bell peppers. Season with salt and pepper to taste. Serve, passing hot sauce and Salsa Lizano separately.

Jamaican Rice and Peas

Serves 6 Total Time 2¼ hours, plus 8 hours soaking

Why This Recipe Works This dish features fluffy white rice and creamy red kidney beans (Jamaicans call them peas) enriched with coconut milk and seasoned with scallions, garlic, a Scotch bonnet chile, thyme, and pimento (allspice). We remain faithful to traditional recipes, soaking dried red kidney beans before simmering them until tender in just enough broth and coconut milk to leave the right amount of liquid to cook the rice. If you can't find a Scotch bonnet chile, you can substitute a habanero.

Crispy Coconut Rice and Pigeon Peas with Tropical Fruit

- 1 cup dried red kidney beans, picked over and rinsed
- 3 cups vegetable broth
- 1 (14-ounce) can coconut milk
- 10 sprigs fresh thyme
- 2 scallions, sliced thin
- 4 garlic cloves, chopped coarse
- 1 Scotch bonnet chile
- 2 teaspoons table salt
- ½ teaspoon pepper
- ¼ teaspoon whole allspice berries
- 2 cups long-grain white rice, rinsed
- 2 tablespoons unsalted butter

1. Combine 1 quart cold water and beans in bowl and soak at room temperature for at least 8 hours or up to 24 hours.

2. Drain beans and transfer to large saucepan. Add broth, coconut milk, thyme sprigs, scallions, garlic, Scotch bonnet, salt, pepper, and allspice berries. Bring to boil over high heat. Cover, reduce heat to medium-low, and simmer until beans are tender, 45 minutes to 1 hour.

3. Drain bean mixture in fine-mesh strainer set over 8-cup liquid measuring cup or large bowl. Discard thyme sprigs and Scotch bonnet. Return bean mixture to saucepan along with 3½ cups bean cooking liquid (add water to compensate if necessary; reserve any excess for another use or discard).

4. Stir rice and butter into bean mixture. Bring to boil over high heat. Once boiling, stir, then place large sheet of aluminum foil over saucepan and cover tightly with lid. Reduce heat to low and cook for 20 minutes. Let rest off heat, covered, for 10 minutes. Fluff rice with fork and serve.

Crispy Coconut Rice and Pigeon Peas with Tropical Fruit

FAST **VEGAN** Serves 4 Total Time 45 minutes

Why This Recipe Works In the Dominican Republic, as in many cultures, the most cherished part of a pot of rice is the crispy layer that sticks to the bottom. To maximize surface area for crisping, we cook long-grain white rice in a nonstick skillet rather than a saucepan. Once all the water and coconut milk are absorbed, we drizzle oil around the edge so it seeps below the rice and promotes a crispy brown crust. Then we flip the rice in sections and compress it with the back of a spatula to brown the other side. Pigeon peas, a common bean in the Caribbean, hold their shape well and add heft to the dish. Chunks of juicy mango, sweet papaya, and colorful red cabbage create a textural symphony of tropical flavors. A tart and savory dressing of lime juice, brown sugar, and soy sauce ties the dish together, while allspice gives a subtle nod to Caribbean jerk flavors. You can use preshredded coleslaw mix in place of the sliced red cabbage. If you can't find a papaya, try substituting pineapple chunks, cut cantaloupe, or even halved cherry tomatoes. Give the can of coconut milk a good shake before opening; this will make it easier to measure.

- 1 cup long-grain white rice, rinsed
- 1 cup water
- ⅔ cup canned coconut milk
- 1 teaspoon table salt, divided
- 3 tablespoons vegetable oil
- 3 tablespoons lime juice
- 1 tablespoon packed brown sugar
- 1 tablespoon soy sauce
- 1 teaspoon ground allspice
- 2 cups thinly sliced red cabbage
- 2 cups ½-inch ripe papaya pieces
- 2 cups ½-inch mango pieces
- 1 (15-ounce) can pigeon peas, rinsed
- 1 cup fresh cilantro leaves
- ½ red onion, chopped fine
- 1 serrano chile, stemmed and sliced thin
- ½ cup unsweetened flaked coconut, toasted (optional)

1. Bring rice, water, coconut milk, and ½ teaspoon salt to boil in 12-inch nonstick skillet over high heat. Reduce heat to low, cover, and simmer until all liquid has been absorbed, 18 to 20 minutes, adjusting heat as needed to maintain bare simmer.

2. Uncover and drizzle oil around edge of skillet. Increase heat to medium-high and cook, undisturbed, until rice is lightly browned and crisp on bottom and makes continuous popping sounds, about 4 minutes. With large spatula, flip rice in sections and compress in skillet, trying to keep clumps intact. Cook until lightly browned and crisp on second side, about 4 minutes. Transfer rice to large plate and cool for 10 minutes.

3. Whisk lime juice, sugar, soy sauce, allspice, and remaining ½ teaspoon salt together in large bowl. Add cabbage, papaya, mango, pigeon peas, cilantro, onion, serrano, and rice and gently toss to combine. Sprinkle with toasted coconut, if using, and serve.

Mujaddara

VEGAN Serves 4 to 6 Total Time 1½ hours

Why This Recipe Works Essentially the "rice and beans" of the Middle East, mujaddara might be the most spectacular example of how a few humble ingredients can add up to a dish that's satisfying, complex, and deeply savory. This warm-spiced rice and lentil pilaf contains large brown or green lentils and crispy fried onion strings. So that all the elements are perfectly cooked, we precook the lentils and soak the rice in hot water before combining them. For the crispiest possible onions, we remove some moisture by salting and microwaving them before frying. When preparing the onions, be sure to reserve 3 tablespoons oil after cooking and draining. Using some of the oil from the onions to dress our pilaf gives it ultrasavory depth. A bracing garlicky yogurt sauce is the final touch. Large green or brown lentils will work interchangeably in this recipe; do not substitute smaller French lentils. To make this recipe vegan, substitute plant-based yogurt for the dairy yogurt.

Yogurt Sauce

- 1 cup plain whole-milk yogurt
- 2 tablespoons lemon juice
- ½ teaspoon minced garlic
- ½ teaspoon table salt

Rice and Lentils

- 8½ ounces (1¼ cups) green or brown lentils, picked over and rinsed
- 1 teaspoon table salt, plus salt for cooking lentils
- 1¼ cups basmati rice
- 1 recipe Crispy Onions, plus 3 tablespoons reserved oil (recipe follows)
- 3 garlic cloves, minced
- 1 teaspoon ground coriander
- 1 teaspoon ground cumin
- ½ teaspoon ground cinnamon
- ½ teaspoon ground allspice
- ¼ teaspoon pepper
- ⅛ teaspoon cayenne pepper
- 1 teaspoon sugar
- 3 tablespoons minced fresh cilantro

1. **For the yogurt sauce** Whisk all ingredients together in bowl. Refrigerate while preparing rice and lentils.

2. **For the rice and lentils** Bring lentils, 4 cups water, and 1 teaspoon salt to boil in medium saucepan over high heat. Reduce heat to low and cook until lentils are tender, 15 to 17 minutes. Drain and set aside. While lentils cook, place rice in medium bowl and cover by 2 inches with hot tap water; let stand for 15 minutes.

3. Using your hands, gently swish rice grains to release excess starch. Carefully pour off water, leaving rice in bowl. Add cold tap water to rice and pour off water. Repeat adding and pouring off cold tap water 4 or 5 times, until water runs almost clear. Drain rice in fine-mesh strainer.

4. Heat reserved onion oil, garlic, coriander, cumin, cinnamon, allspice, pepper, and cayenne in Dutch oven over medium heat until fragrant, about 2 minutes. Add rice and cook, stirring occasionally, until edges of rice begin to turn translucent, about 3 minutes. Add 2¼ cups water, sugar, and salt and bring to boil. Stir in lentils, reduce heat to low, cover, and cook until all liquid is absorbed, about 12 minutes.

5. Off heat, remove lid, fold clean dish towel in half, and place over pot; replace lid. Let stand for 10 minutes. Fluff rice and lentils with fork and stir in cilantro and half of crispy onions. Transfer to serving platter, top with remaining crispy onions, and serve, passing yogurt sauce separately.

Crispy Onions

FAST **VEGAN** Makes 1½ cups
Total Time 45 minutes

Thoroughly dry the microwaved onions after rinsing.

- 2 pounds onions, halved and sliced crosswise into ¼-inch-thick pieces
- 2 teaspoons table salt, for salting onions
- 1½ cups vegetable oil

1. Toss onions and salt together in large bowl. Microwave for 5 minutes. Rinse thoroughly, transfer to paper towel–lined baking sheet, and dry well.

2. Cook onions and oil in Dutch oven over high heat, stirring frequently, until onions are golden brown, 25 to 30 minutes. Drain onions in colander set in large bowl and reserve oil as needed for recipe. Transfer onions to paper towel–lined baking sheet to drain. (Remaining oil may be refrigerated for up to 4 weeks.)

Koshari

VEGAN Serves 4 to 6 Total Time 1¾ hours

Why This Recipe Works Considered the national dish of Egypt, koshari evolved as a way to use up leftovers and became a popular street food. This hearty dish usually features lentils, rice, pasta, and chickpeas smothered in a spiced tomato sauce and topped with crispy fried onions. Although it takes some time to put together, each element is fairly simple. We cook the lentils and pasta in boiling water and drain them, then set them aside while we prepare the rice and sauce. Soaking the rice in hot water before cooking eliminates excess starch so it doesn't clump. Using the same spices—coriander, cumin, cinnamon, nutmeg, and cayenne—in the sauce and the rice creates a layered flavor profile. Adding the chickpeas directly to the sauce to simmer infuses them with flavor. The finishing touch: a generous amount of ultrasavory, crunchy fried onions. You can use store-bought crispy onions and extra-virgin olive oil in place of the Crispy Onions if you prefer.

- 1 cup elbow macaroni
- 1 teaspoon table salt, divided, plus salt for cooking pasta and lentils
- 1 cup dried green or brown lentils, picked over and rinsed
- 1 recipe Crispy Onions (page 394), plus ¼ cup reserved oil, divided
- 4 garlic cloves, minced, divided
- 1½ teaspoons ground coriander, divided
- 1½ teaspoons ground cumin, divided
- ¾ teaspoon ground cinnamon, divided
- ¼ teaspoon ground nutmeg, divided
- ¼ teaspoon cayenne pepper, divided
- 1 (28-ounce) can tomato sauce
- 1 (15-ounce) can chickpeas, rinsed
- 1 cup basmati rice
- 1 tablespoon red wine vinegar
- 3 tablespoons minced fresh parsley

1. Bring 2 quarts water to boil in Dutch oven. Add pasta and 1½ teaspoons salt and cook, stirring often, until al dente. Drain pasta, rinse with water, then drain again. Transfer to bowl and set aside.

2. Meanwhile, bring lentils, 4 cups water, and 1 teaspoon salt to boil in medium saucepan over high heat. Reduce heat to low and cook until lentils are just tender, 15 to 17 minutes. Drain and set aside.

top | *Mujaddara*
bottom | *Koshari*

3. Cook 1 tablespoon reserved onion oil, 1 teaspoon garlic, ½ teaspoon coriander, ½ teaspoon cumin, ¼ teaspoon cinnamon, ⅛ teaspoon nutmeg, ⅛ teaspoon cayenne, and ½ teaspoon salt in now-empty saucepan over medium heat until fragrant, about 1 minute. Stir in tomato sauce and chickpeas, bring to simmer, and cook until slightly thickened, about 10 minutes. Cover and keep warm.

4. While sauce cooks, place rice in medium bowl, cover with hot tap water by 2 inches, and let sit for 15 minutes. Using your hands, gently swish grains to release excess starch. Carefully pour off water, leaving rice in bowl. Add cold tap water to rice and pour off water. Repeat adding and pouring off cold water 4 or 5 times, until water runs almost clear. Drain rice in fine-mesh strainer.

5. Cook remaining 3 tablespoons reserved onion oil, remaining garlic, remaining 1 teaspoon coriander, remaining 1 teaspoon cumin, remaining ½ teaspoon cinnamon, remaining ⅛ teaspoon nutmeg, and remaining ⅛ teaspoon cayenne in now-empty pot over medium heat until fragrant, about 2 minutes. Add rice and cook, stirring occasionally, until grain edges begin to turn translucent, about 3 minutes. Stir in 2 cups water and remaining ½ teaspoon salt and bring to boil. Stir in reserved lentils, reduce heat to low, cover, and simmer gently until all liquid is absorbed, about 12 minutes.

6. Off heat, sprinkle pasta over rice mixture. Cover, laying clean dish towel underneath lid, and let sit for 10 minutes.

7. Return sauce to simmer over medium heat. Stir in vinegar and season with salt and pepper to taste. Fluff rice and lentils with fork and stir in parsley and half of onions. Transfer to serving platter and top with half of sauce and remaining onions. Serve, passing remaining sauce separately.

Sorting Lentils

Using a baking sheet or plate, spread lentils out into single layer. Check over to remove any small stones or other foreign matter.

Lentils with Roasted Broccoli and Lemony Bread Crumbs

VEGAN Serves 4 to 6 Total Time 1 hour

Why This Recipe Works This supersavory dish elevates earthy French green lentils and humble broccoli to a whole new level—an abundant dish that's a company-worthy main. By preheating the sheet pan in a 500-degree oven and laying the broccoli on it in a single layer, we impart deep, flavorful browning to the stalks and florets in a short amount of time so you'll jump to eat your broccoli. While the lentils cook, we quickly make a bright, crispy, lemony bread-crumb topping in a skillet, then we reduce some balsamic vinegar in the same skillet to transform its flavor from sharp and assertive to luxurious, sweet, and drizzleable for a stunning, shining finishing touch. Lentilles du Puy (or French green lentils) hold their shape quite well during cooking; we do not recommend substituting other types of lentils in this dish.

- 6 tablespoons extra-virgin olive oil, divided, plus extra for drizzling
- 1 onion, chopped fine
- ¾ teaspoon table salt, divided
- 2 garlic cloves, minced
- 1 teaspoon minced fresh thyme or ½ teaspoon dried
- 12 ounces (1¾ cups) dried lentilles du Puy (French green lentils), picked over and rinsed
- 3¾ cups water
- ½ cup panko bread crumbs
- 2 teaspoons grated lemon zest
- ½ cup balsamic vinegar
- 2 pounds broccoli, florets cut into 1-inch pieces, stalks peeled and sliced lengthwise into ½-inch-thick planks

1. Adjust oven rack to lowest position, place aluminum foil-lined rimmed baking sheet on rack, and heat oven to 500 degrees. Heat 1 tablespoon oil in large saucepan over medium heat until shimmering. Add onion and ¼ teaspoon salt and cook until softened, about 5 minutes. Stir in garlic and thyme and cook until fragrant, about 30 seconds.

2. Stir in lentils and water and bring to simmer over high heat. Reduce heat to low, cover, and simmer, stirring occasionally, until lentils are just tender, about 25 minutes. Uncover, increase heat to medium, and continue to cook until lentils are completely tender and most of liquid has evaporated, 10 to 15 minutes. Season with salt and pepper to taste, cover to keep warm, and set aside.

3. While lentils cook, combine panko and 2 tablespoons oil in 8-inch skillet, stirring to coat. Cook over medium-low heat, stirring frequently, until light golden brown, 5 to 7 minutes; transfer to bowl and stir in lemon zest. Wipe skillet clean with paper towels. Cook vinegar in now-empty skillet, scraping bottom of skillet with silicone spatula, until thickened and reduced to 2 tablespoons, about 5 minutes.

4. Toss broccoli with remaining 3 tablespoons oil and remaining ½ teaspoon salt in bowl. Working quickly, lay broccoli in single layer, flat sides down, on preheated sheet. Roast until florets are browned, 9 to 11 minutes. Divide lentils among individual serving bowls and top with broccoli mixture. Sprinkle with panko mixture, drizzle with balsamic reduction, and serve, drizzling with extra oil.

Lentils with Roasted Broccoli and Lemony Bread Crumbs

Lentilles du Puy with Spinach and Crème Fraîche

Serves 4 to 6 Total Time 1 hour

Why This Recipe Works This satisfying lentil dish is both humble and extravagant. The carefully crafted ingredient list captures the vibe of French cooking beautifully, including lentilles du Puy, mirepoix, Dijon, and crème fraîche. To start, we build flavor the classical way by sautéing our mirepoix—a mix of finely diced onion, carrot, and celery—in fruity olive oil. Once the vegetables turn soft, we add the broth and lentils and let them simmer unattended for 30 minutes, during which time they absorb the flavors of the mirepoix and become beautifully creamy. Taking things up a notch, we fold in baby spinach and a couple tablespoons of Dijon, which lends its bold mustardy kick to the mix and helps make the dish creamy. A dollop of crème fraîche is a luxurious and unexpected final touch. You can substitute other French green lentils for the lentilles du Puy, but do not substitute other types of green lentils or black, brown, or red lentils—the cooking times of the other lentil varieties can vary greatly. By the end of step 2, the lentils should have absorbed most, but not all, of the vegetable broth. If the bottom of the saucepan looks dry and the lentils are still somewhat firm, add hot water, ¼ cup at a time, and continue to cook until the lentils are tender. You can substitute sour cream for the crème fraîche.

top | *Lentilles du Puy with Spinach and Crème Fraîche*

bottom | *Palak Dal (Spinach-Lentil Dal with Cumin and Mustard Seeds)*

- 1 tablespoon extra-virgin olive oil
- ½ cup finely chopped onion
- ¼ cup finely chopped carrot
- ¼ cup finely chopped celery
- ½ teaspoon table salt
- 2 cups vegetable broth
- 1 cup dried lentilles du Puy, picked over and rinsed
- Hot water
- 2 ounces (2 cups) baby spinach
- 2 tablespoons Dijon mustard
- ¼ cup crème fraîche

1. Heat oil in large saucepan over medium heat until shimmering. Add onion, carrot, celery, and salt and cook until vegetables are tender, about 5 minutes.

2. Add broth and lentils and bring to simmer. Reduce heat to medium-low; cover; and cook, stirring occasionally, until lentils are tender but still hold their shape, about 30 minutes. (Add hot water, ¼ cup at a time, if saucepan becomes dry before lentils are cooked through.)

3. Gently fold in spinach and mustard. Let sit off heat for 5 minutes. Transfer to serving bowl and dollop with crème fraîche. Serve.

Palak Dal (Spinach-Lentil Dal with Cumin and Mustard Seeds)

Serves 4 to 6   Total Time 1 hour

Why This Recipe Works Dal is an Indian staple that is quick, easy, nourishing, inexpensive, and—most important—incredibly flavorful. Quick-cooking red lentils are the centerpiece of our palak dal ("palak" means "spinach" in Hindi). Once they soften, we give them a vigorous whisk, which transforms them into a rustic, porridge-like stew without requiring us to break out the blender or food processor. Seasoning the lentils with a tadka (whole spices sizzled in ghee with aromatics) right before serving gives the dish loads of complexity, a gorgeous appearance, and an enticing aroma. For less heat, remove the ribs and seeds of the serrano. Fresh curry leaves add a wonderful aroma to this dal, but if they're unavailable, you can omit them. Yellow mustard seeds can be substituted for brown. Monitor the spices and aromatics carefully during frying, reducing the heat if necessary to prevent scorching. Serve the dal with naan and basmati or another long-grain white rice.

4½ cups water
1½ cups (10½ ounces) dried red lentils, picked over and rinsed
1 tablespoon grated fresh ginger
¾ teaspoon ground turmeric
6 ounces (6 cups) baby spinach
1½ teaspoons table salt
3 tablespoons ghee
1½ teaspoons brown mustard seeds
1½ teaspoons cumin seeds
1 large onion, chopped
15 curry leaves, roughly torn (optional)
6 garlic cloves, sliced
4 whole dried arbol chiles
1 serrano chile, halved lengthwise
1½ teaspoons lemon juice, plus extra for seasoning
⅓ cup chopped fresh cilantro

1. Bring water, lentils, ginger, and turmeric to boil in large saucepan over medium-high heat. Reduce heat to maintain vigorous simmer. Cook, stirring occasionally, until lentils are soft and starting to break down, 18 to 20 minutes.

2. Whisk lentils vigorously until coarsely pureed, about 30 seconds. Continue to cook until lentils have consistency of loose polenta or oatmeal, up to 5 minutes longer. Stir in spinach and salt and continue to cook until spinach is fully wilted, 30 to 60 seconds longer. Cover and set aside off heat.

3. Melt ghee in 10-inch skillet over medium-high heat. Add mustard seeds and cumin seeds and cook, stirring constantly, until seeds sizzle and pop, about 30 seconds. Add onion and cook, stirring frequently, until onion is just starting to brown, about 5 minutes. Add curry leaves, if using; garlic; arbols; and serrano and cook, stirring frequently, until onion and garlic are golden brown, 3 to 4 minutes.

4. Add lemon juice to lentils and stir to incorporate. (Dal should have consistency of loose polenta. If too thick, loosen with hot water, adding 1 tablespoon at a time.) Season with salt and extra lemon juice to taste. Transfer dal to serving bowl and spoon onion mixture on top. Sprinkle with cilantro and serve.

Red Lentil Kibbeh

Serves 4 Total Time 1 hour

Why This Recipe Works Kibbeh is a popular Middle Eastern dish made from bulgur, minced onion, varying spices, and (traditionally) ground meat. Here, we enhance both the color and flavor of the red lentils with two red pastes: tomato paste and harissa. We give the bulgur a head start before adding the lentils so both finish cooking at the same time. You can serve the spoonable mixture on its own with some Bibb lettuce and yogurt, or it makes a showstopping addition to a larger spread, alongside dips or with nuts, pickled radishes, and pita. We prefer our homemade harissa, but you may use store-bought.

3 tablespoons extra-virgin olive oil, divided
1 onion, chopped fine
1 red bell pepper, stemmed, seeded, and chopped fine
1 teaspoon table salt
2 tablespoons Harissa (page 400)
2 tablespoons tomato paste
½ teaspoon cayenne pepper (optional)
4 cups water
1 cup medium-grind bulgur, rinsed
¾ cup dried red lentils, picked over and rinsed
½ cup chopped fresh parsley
2 tablespoons lemon juice, plus lemon wedges for serving
1 head Bibb lettuce (8 ounces), leaves separated
½ cup plain yogurt

1. Heat 1 tablespoon oil in large saucepan over medium heat until shimmering. Add onion, bell pepper, and salt and cook until softened, about 5 minutes. Stir in harissa; tomato paste; and cayenne, if using, and cook, stirring frequently, until fragrant, about 1 minute.

2. Stir in water and bulgur and bring to simmer. Reduce heat to low, cover, and simmer gently until bulgur is barely tender, about 8 minutes. Stir in lentils; cover; and continue to cook, stirring occasionally, until lentils and bulgur are tender, 8 to 10 minutes.

3. Off heat, lay clean dish towel underneath lid and let mixture sit for 10 minutes. Stir in 1 tablespoon oil, parsley, and lemon juice and stir vigorously until mixture is cohesive. Season with salt and pepper to taste. Transfer to platter and drizzle with remaining 1 tablespoon oil. Spoon kibbeh into lettuce leaves and drizzle with yogurt. Serve with lemon wedges.

Harissa

FAST **VEGAN** Makes ½ cup
Total Time 10 minutes

This traditional North African condiment is great for flavoring soups, sauces, and dressings or dolloping on hummus, sandwiches, and eggs. If you can't find Aleppo pepper, you can substitute ¾ teaspoon paprika and ¾ teaspoon finely chopped red pepper flakes.

- 6 tablespoons extra-virgin olive oil
- 6 garlic cloves, minced
- 2 tablespoons paprika
- 1 tablespoon ground coriander
- 1 tablespoon ground dried Aleppo pepper
- 1 teaspoon ground cumin
- ¾ teaspoon caraway seeds
- ½ teaspoon table salt

Combine all ingredients in bowl and microwave until bubbling and very fragrant, about 1 minute, stirring halfway through microwaving; let cool to room temperature. (Harissa can be refrigerated for up to 4 days.)

Misir Wot

FAST **VEGAN** Serves 4 Total Time 45 minutes

Why This Recipe Works One of Ethiopia's most famous vegetarian dishes, misir wot is a deeply flavored lentil dish traditionally seasoned with the spice blend berbere, which delivers intense warmth alongside sweet and citrusy notes. Since it's not always easy to find, we make it ourselves. Premade berbere often contains powdered ginger, which has a strong peppery aroma; we vastly prefer the floral sweetness of fresh ginger. To start, we cook our aromatics—red onion, umami-rich tomato paste, and fresh ginger and garlic—before adding our berbere blend to bloom. Next we add the red lentils, as well as some plum tomatoes, which bring a necessary freshness. We finish with a drizzle of red wine vinegar, the acidity of which helps cut through the many layers of delicious heat. Do not substitute other types of lentils for the red lentils here; they have a very different texture. Adjust the amount of cayenne according to your preference. Serve with injera, an Ethiopian flatbread made with teff flour.

- 3 tablespoons extra-virgin olive oil
- 1 red onion, chopped fine
- 2 tablespoons tomato paste
- 4 teaspoons grated fresh ginger
- 3 garlic cloves, minced
- 2½ teaspoons paprika
- 1¼ teaspoons ground coriander
- ¾ teaspoon ground cardamom
- ¾ teaspoon ground cumin
- ½–1 teaspoon cayenne pepper
- 2 cups water
- 1 cup dried red lentils, picked over and rinsed
- 4 plum tomatoes, cored and chopped fine
- 1 teaspoon table salt
- Red wine vinegar

1. Heat oil in large saucepan over medium-high heat until shimmering. Add onion and cook, stirring occasionally, until softened and lightly browned, 5 to 7 minutes. Add tomato paste, ginger, garlic, paprika, coriander, cardamom, cumin, and cayenne and cook until fragrant, about 1 minute.

2. Stir in water, lentils, tomatoes, and salt and bring to simmer. Reduce heat to low and simmer, stirring occasionally, until lentils are tender and beginning to break down, 15 to 25 minutes. Season with salt, pepper, and vinegar to taste. Serve.

Misir Wot

Cooking Dried Beans

Cooking dried beans does take more time than opening a can, but it isn't difficult to do and the results are unbeatable in terms of the heightened flavor and creamy texture of from-scratch beans. The cooking method is the same for all beans, and the test kitchen's tried-and-true method could not be easier, as outlined in the five steps below. We prefer to cook beans on the stovetop because you can adjust the heat, and you can easily monitor the beans' cooking and test them for doneness. Since it's impossible to know the age of your beans (which can have a large impact on how long it takes for the beans to cook), it's important to taste the beans for doneness rather than relying solely on recipe cook times.

1. Pick Over and Rinse

Before cooking, pick over 1 pound of dried beans to remove any small stones or debris and then rinse them.

How to The easiest way to check the beans is to spread them on a large plate or rimmed baking sheet.

2. Brine and Then Rinse

To brine or not to brine? We definitely recommend brining dried beans prior to cooking. Overnight brining will give you the most tender beans, with skins that stay in place. Brining (and soaking generally) speeds up cooking. Brining also helps beans maintain their shape throughout cooking, seasons them, and results in tender skins. Getting the skins to soften reduces the number of beans that explode during cooking, which is key for beans that cook up creamy rather than starchy. Note that some recipes may call for simply soaking beans in water without any salt.

How to Dissolve 1½ tablespoons salt in 2 quarts cold water in a large container. Use a deep container (a bowl rather than a wide Dutch oven) to ensure that the beans remain submerged as they hydrate and swell. Add rinsed beans and soak at room temperature for at least 8 hours or up to 24 hours. Drain and rinse them well before using.

3. Simmer Gently

Maintaining a gentle simmer prevents the beans from rupturing and helps avoid too much water evaporating during cooking, ensuring that the beans stay submerged. Cooking them uncovered on the stovetop allows you to watch and taste them as they cook.

How to Bring soaked beans and 7 cups water to simmer in large saucepan or Dutch oven. Simmer, uncovered, over medium-low heat until the beans are tender, about 40 minutes.

4. Test for Doneness

Taste the texture of the beans. After approximately 40 minutes of simmering, the beans should be just tender.

How to To check for doneness, simply bite into a few beans. Be sure to taste more than one bean in the pot. It's a good idea to start checking your beans after 30 minutes.

5. Finish off the Heat

Turning off the heat, covering the pot, and letting the beans steep after simmering allows them to gently finish cooking through without rupturing their skins.

How to Remove the pan from the heat, stir in 1½ teaspoons salt, cover, and let sit for 15 minutes. Drain the beans.

Quick Brining

When pressed for time, a quick brine (water plus salt) for an hour works, but we strongly recommend overnight brining. Quick-brined beans will be less creamy and may take longer to cook.

To quick brine beans Combine 1 pound dried beans with 1½ tablespoons salt and 2 quarts cold water in a large Dutch oven and bring to a boil. Remove from the heat, cover, and let sit for 1 hour. Drain, rinse, and continue with the recipe.

Baking Soda and Acid

Baking soda raises the pH of cooking liquid, making an alkaline environment. This weakens the beans' cell walls and helps them absorb water faster; as a result, the beans cook faster.

The acid in some ingredients like tomatoes and wine also affects how beans cook. Acids can prevent beans from becoming tender, so we don't add them too early in the cooking process.

Tofu & Tempeh

406 Homestyle Tofu ■

407 Spicy Cold Tofu ■ ●

407 Crispy Tofu ●

410 Tofu Sushi Bowls ■ ●

410 Tofu Katsu ■

413 Seared Tofu with Panch Phoron, Green Beans, and Pickled Shallot ●

413 Panch Phoron ■ ●

414 Tofu Rancheros ●

414 Saag Tofu

417 Crispy Tofu Salad with Cherry Tomatoes

417 Crispy Tofu and Kale Salad with Miso-Ginger Dressing ■ ●

418 Pita Salad with Za'atar Tofu and Chickpeas ■ ●

418 Charred Cabbage Salad with Torn Tofu and Plantain Chips

419 Garlicky Tofu Tabbouleh ●

420 Chile-Spiced Crumbled Tofu with Pineapple Salsa ■ ●

421 Crispy Teriyaki Tofu ■ ●

422 Stir-Fried Tofu and Bok Choy ■ ●

424 Panko-Crusted Tofu with Cabbage Salad ■

425 Sweet and Spicy Glazed Tofu with Coconut-Braised Mustard Greens and Winter Squash ■ ●

425 Caribbean Tofu with Rice and Pigeon Peas ●

426 East African Tofu and Coconut Curry ■ ●

427 Thai Red Curry with Tofu and Lentils

428 Bulgur with Vegetables and Marinated Tofu

431 Shawarma-Spiced Tofu Wraps with Sumac Onions

431 Sumac Onions ●

431 Tofu Summer Rolls with Spicy Almond Butter Sauce ●

432 Mapo Tofu ●

433 Overstuffed Sweet Potatoes with Tofu and Red Curry Vinaigrette ●

434 Tofu and Chickpea Flour Frittata with Mushrooms ●

435 Grilled Tofu with Vegetable Skewers ●

436 Crispy Tempeh ■ ●

436 Crispy Tempeh with Sambal Sauce ■ ●

437 Seared Tempeh with Tomato Jam

439 Ras el Hanout ■ ●

439 Pan-Seared Tempeh Steaks with Chimichurri Sauce ●

440 Stir-Fried Tempeh, Napa Cabbage, and Carrots ■ ●

441 Stir-Fried Tempeh with Orange Sauce ■ ●

441 Sweet Potato Red Flannel Hash with Tempeh

442 Loaded Sweet Potato Wedges with Tempeh ●

443 Tempeh Tacos ■ ●

445 Tempeh Reubens ●

446 Sauerkraut ●

447 Korean Barbecue Tempeh Wraps ●

All About Tofu

408 Choosing the Right Tofu

409 Homemade Tofu ●

■ Fast (45 minutes or less) ● Vegan

top | *Homestyle Tofu*
bottom | *Spicy Cold Tofu*

Homestyle Tofu

FAST Serves 4 Total Time 45 minutes

Why This Recipe Works The "homestyle" in homestyle tofu holds real meaning beyond "comforting" or "homemade," definitions that are often associated with the word in Western culture. Here homestyle refers to a specific flavor combination popular in Sichuan cooking—a little spicy, a little savory, a little sweet. Though tofu is the star of the show, we're just as fond of the crunchy vegetal supporting cast: bell peppers, bamboo shoots, and carrots, lightly dressed by the piquant sauce. This recipe can also be made using a 12-inch nonstick skillet; increase the oil to 2 cups in step 2.

- 14 ounces firm tofu
- 2 teaspoons soy sauce
- 2 teaspoons cornstarch
- 1 teaspoon sugar
- 1 teaspoon vegetarian oyster sauce
- 1 cup vegetable oil
- 1 green bell pepper, stemmed, seeded, and cut into 1-inch pieces
- 1 carrot, peeled and sliced ¼ inch thick on bias
- ½ cup canned sliced bamboo shoots, drained, rinsed, and patted dry
- 3 garlic cloves, sliced
- 2 scallions, white and green parts separated and sliced thin
- 1 (1-inch) piece ginger, peeled and sliced into thin matchsticks
- 1 tablespoon doubanjiang (broad bean chile paste)
- ¾ cup water

1. Halve tofu lengthwise, then cut crosswise into ¾-inch-thick slabs. Spread tofu over paper towel–lined plate and let drain for 20 minutes. Gently pat dry with paper towels. In small bowl combine soy sauce, cornstarch, sugar, and oyster sauce; set aside.

2. Line large plate with triple layer of paper towels. Heat oil in 14-inch flat-bottomed wok over medium-high heat to 375 degrees. Using spider skimmer or slotted spoon, carefully add tofu in even layer and cook until crisp and well browned on both sides, about 10 minutes, flipping tofu halfway through cooking. Transfer tofu to prepared plate to drain.

3. Pour off all but 3 tablespoons oil from wok. Heat oil left in wok over medium-high heat until just smoking. Add bell pepper, carrot, and bamboo shoots and cook, tossing slowly but constantly, until crisp-tender, about 3 minutes. Push vegetables to 1 side of wok and add garlic, scallion whites, ginger, and doubanjiang to clearing. Cook, mashing garlic mixture into wok, until fragrant, about 30 seconds. Stir garlic mixture into vegetables. Add water and tofu and cook, tossing slowly but constantly, until tofu has warmed through and absorbed some liquid, 3 to 5 minutes.

4. Whisk soy sauce mixture to recombine, then add to wok and cook, tossing gently, until sauce has thickened, about 30 seconds. Sprinkle with scallion greens and serve.

Spicy Cold Tofu

FAST **VEGAN** Serves 4 Total Time 20 minutes

Why This Recipe Works Chilled silken tofu is an experience: Its texture is luxurious and its presentation is refined. It's also one of the most effortless preparations of tofu. Because it's so simple, we can focus our energy on the presentation of this satisfying dish. We shingle slabs of the silken tofu uniformly, carefully spoon the dressing over the tofu dominos and around the plate, and garnish the tofu and the dressing artfully with whole fresh cilantro leaves. The spicy part comes from a Thai chile. For a milder dish, remove the chile seeds before slicing.

- 2 tablespoons soy sauce
- 1 tablespoon toasted sesame oil
- 1½ teaspoons Chinese white rice vinegar
- 1 teaspoon sugar
- 1 teaspoon minced fresh ginger
- 1 garlic clove, minced
- 1 Thai chile, stemmed and sliced thin
- 1 scallion, white and green parts separated and sliced thin
- 14 ounces silken tofu, chilled
- ¼ cup fresh cilantro leaves and tender stems
- ½ teaspoon sesame seeds, toasted

1. Whisk soy sauce, oil, vinegar, sugar, ginger, and garlic in medium bowl until sugar has dissolved. Stir in Thai chile and scallion whites.

2. Slice tofu crosswise into ¾-inch-thick slabs or cut into 1-inch pieces. Arrange tofu attractively on serving platter. Spoon dressing over tofu and sprinkle with scallion greens, cilantro, and sesame seeds. Serve.

Crispy Tofu

VEGAN Serves 6 Total Time 40 minutes, plus 20 minutes draining

Why This Recipe Works A wonderful way to use soft tofu is to give it a coating of cornstarch with a bit of cornmeal, which after pan-frying becomes a superlatively crispy-crunchy foil to the interior texture of the tofu. Here we cut the tofu into ½- nch batons, draining them on paper towels and then patting them dry before tossing them gently in the coating mixture using our hands. We cook them in two batches, which ensures that there is room in the skillet for them to get crispy. Crispy tofu can be used in many ways and is especially nice as a topping for warm grains or salad or simply enjoyed alone with a dipping sauce. You can also use firm tofu in this recipe.

- 28 ounces soft tofu, cut into 3-inch-long by ½-inch-thick fingers
- ¾ cup cornstarch
- ¼ cup cornmeal
- 2 tablespoons extra-virgin olive oil

1. Spread tofu over paper towel–lined baking sheet and let drain for 20 minutes. Gently pat dry with paper towels. Adjust oven rack to middle position, place paper towel–lined platter on rack, and heat oven to 200 degrees.

2. Set wire rack in rimmed baking sheet. Whisk cornstarch and cornmeal together in shallow dish. Season tofu with salt and pepper. Working with several pieces of tofu at a time, coat tofu thoroughly with cornstarch mixture, pressing gently to adhere, then transfer to wire rack.

3. Heat 1 tablespoon oil in 12-inch nonstick skillet over medium-high heat until shimmering. Gently add half of tofu to skillet and cook, using spatula to carefully turn pieces, until crisp and lightly golden on all sides, 10 to 12 minutes. Transfer tofu to plate in oven. Repeat with remaining 1 tablespoon oil and remaining tofu. Serve.

All About Tofu

Tofu is an important food choice because it is high in protein as well as calcium and iron. Available in many varieties, tofu is made from soy milk that has been coagulated to form curds and then pressed to extract liquid. Its neutral flavor makes it a clean and versatile canvas for added flavors.

Choosing the Right Tofu

Tofu is available in a variety of textures: extra-firm, firm, medium, soft, and silken. Reaching for the right variety will be key to the success of any given recipe. In general, firmer varieties hold their shape when cooking, while softer varieties do not, so it follows that each type of tofu is best when used in specific ways. Regardless of type, tofu is highly perishable and is best when it is fresh. To store an opened package, cover the tofu with water and refrigerate in a covered container, changing the water daily. Any hint of sourness means the tofu is past its prime.

Extra-Firm and Firm Tofu We prefer extra-firm or firm tofu for stir-fries and noodle dishes, as they hold their shape in high-heat cooking applications and when tossed with pasta. These two varieties of tofu are also great marinated (they absorb marinade better compared with softer varieties) or tossed raw into salads.

Medium and Soft Tofu Medium and soft tofu boast a creamy, custardy texture; we love to pan-fry these kinds of tofu, often coated with cornstarch, to achieve a crisp exterior, which makes a nice textural contrast to the silky interior. Soft tofu is also great scrambled like eggs.

Silken Tofu Silken tofu has a very soft, ultracreamy texture and is often used as a base for smoothies and dips, in desserts such as puddings, or as an egg replacement in vegan baked goods.

Cutting Tofu

To cut into slabs, slice block crosswise into planks of desired width. To cut tofu into fingers, cut each plank into fingers of size desired.

Drying Tofu

Spread tofu pieces evenly over rimmed baking sheet lined with paper towels and let drain for 20 minutes. Gently pat tofu dry with paper towels.

Homemade Tofu

VEGAN Makes 14 ounces Total Time 1¼ hours, plus 13 hours soaking and resting

Tofu is an important food in the diets of one-third of the world's population. Made from cooking ground soybeans in liquid and pressing the curds into custardy blocks, tofu is supremely versatile (as you'll see in the recipes). By itself it doesn't taste like much, but it's a true chameleon ingredient in that it takes on the flavor of its surroundings. It can be served hot, cold, or at room temperature, and it's so adaptable that it can be made into a crispy fried appetizer, stew, or the centerpiece entrée at a dinner party. While truly fresh tofu is hard to come by, tofu is no more difficult to make than yogurt. We do it in a few relatively easy steps: making soy milk from soy beans, curdling the hot soy milk with the mineral salt nigari, and then pressing the resulting curds. Liquid nigari can be found online and at Asian supermarkets. It's important to bring the strained soy milk in step 4 to at least 165 degrees before adding the nigari, because otherwise the tofu might not coagulate properly. We developed this recipe using a 5½ by 4-inch tofu mold and press kit; other mold sizes and styles may affect the pressing time in step 7.

- 8 ounces (1¼ cups) dried soybeans, picked over and rinsed
- 2 teaspoons liquid nigari

1. Place soybeans in large bowl or container and add enough water to cover by 2 inches. Soak soybeans at room temperature for at least 12 hours or up to 18 hours. Drain and rinse well.

2. Working in batches, process one-third of soaked soybeans and 3 cups water in blender until mostly smooth, about 3 minutes; transfer mixture to large Dutch oven. Repeat processing twice more with remaining soybeans and 3 cups water for each batch.

3. Set colander over large bowl and line with triple layer of cheesecloth. Bring soybean mixture to simmer over medium-high heat, stirring frequently with rubber spatula to prevent scorching and boiling over, and cook until slightly thickened, about 10 minutes.

4. Slowly pour soybean mixture into prepared colander and let drain. Being careful of hot liquid, pull edges of cheesecloth together and twist to form pouch. Using tongs, firmly squeeze soybean pulp to extract as much liquid as possible. (You should have about 8 cups of soy milk; discard soybean pulp or reserve for another use.) Return soy milk to clean Dutch oven and heat to gentle simmer (165 to 175 degrees) over medium-high heat, stirring frequently to prevent scorching. Remove pot from heat.

5. Combine ½ cup water and nigari in 1-cup liquid measuring cup. While slowly stirring milk in figure-eight motion, add ¼ cup nigari mixture. Immediately stop stirring, cover, and let milk mixture sit undisturbed for 2 minutes. Drizzle remaining ¼ cup nigari mixture on surface of milk mixture and gently stir using figure-eight motion until combined, about 6 stirs. Cover and let sit undisturbed until curds form and whey is pooling on top and around sides of pot, about 20 minutes.

6. Line tofu mold with triple layer of cheesecloth and place in colander set over large bowl. Using slotted spoon, gently transfer milk curds to prepared mold, retaining as much of curds' natural structure as possible. Cover top of curds with excess cheesecloth and arrange mold press plate on top.

7. Weight plate with heavy brick or large can and press tofu until desired firmness is reached, about 30 minutes for medium-firm and 40 minutes for firm. Gently transfer tofu to storage container and cover with water. Let sit until tofu is fully set, at least 10 minutes. (Tofu can be refrigerated for up to 1 week; change water daily.)

Pressing Homemade Tofu

1. Gently transfer milk curds to mold. Use slotted spoon with small holes or fine-mesh strainer to avoid disturbing structure of curds.

2. Arrange mold press plate on top of curds and weight with heavy brick or large can until desired firmness is reached.

Tofu Sushi Bowls

FAST **VEGAN** Serves 2 Total Time 45 minutes

Why This Recipe Works Here we've deconstructed the classic sushi roll, making it essentially a tofu-rice bowl with all the flavors that make sushi so popular. We coat long fingers of tofu with cornstarch to help them brown to crispy perfection. Brown rice isn't typical for sushi rolls, but we like its nutty chew and how filling it is for the base of our bowls. We super-season the rice with a sesame-scallion vinaigrette instead of the classic sushi rice seasoning. Sliced radishes and cucumber finish the bowls with freshness and satisfying crunch, and avocado contributes creamy richness. Some crumbled nori, scattered across the top, makes our bowl mimic the roll. We like this bowl with either warm or room-temperature rice. You can add pickled ginger for an extra kick.

- 7 ounces firm tofu, cut into 3-inch-long by ½-inch-thick fingers
- ⅛ teaspoon table salt
- ⅛ teaspoon pepper
- 3 tablespoons cornstarch
- 1 tablespoon vegetable oil
- 2 cups cooked brown rice
- ¼ cup Sesame-Scallion Vinaigrette (page 139)
- 3 radishes, sliced thin
- ½ cucumber, halved lengthwise, seeded, and sliced thin
- ½ ripe avocado, cubed
- 1 (8 by 7½-inch) sheet nori, crumbled

1. Spread tofu over paper towel–lined plate and let drain for 20 minutes. Gently pat dry with paper towels. Sprinkle with salt and pepper.

2. Gently toss drained tofu with cornstarch in bowl. Heat oil in 12-inch nonstick skillet over medium-high heat until shimmering. Add tofu and brown lightly on all sides, 12 to 15 minutes; transfer to clean paper towel–lined plate to drain.

3. Toss rice with half of vinaigrette to coat then season with salt and pepper to taste. Divide among individual serving bowls then top with tofu, radishes, cucumber, and avocado. Drizzle with remaining vinaigrette and sprinkle with nori. Serve.

Tofu Katsu

FAST Serves 4 Total Time 45 minutes

Why This Recipe Works Here we make tofu the centerpiece of katsu, a deep-fried Japanese specialty. To get an ultracrispy panko coating, we skip the usual three-step bound breading process, given tofu's slick surface; instead, we dredge slabs of tofu in an egg-flour mixture, which helps lock in the panko. This achieves the wonderful contrast between the interior of the tofu and the ultracrispy exterior. We pair the tofu with thinly sliced raw cabbage, as is traditional, tenderizing the shreds with a little lemon juice and salt. Serve with rice, if desired.

- ½ head green cabbage, halved, cored, and sliced thin (6 cups)
- 3 scallions, sliced thin on bias
- 1 tablespoon lemon juice
- 1¼ teaspoons table salt, divided
- 2 large eggs
- 2 tablespoons soy sauce
- 1 tablespoon all-purpose flour
- 1½ cups panko bread crumbs
- 14 ounces extra-firm tofu, cut crosswise into 8 slabs
- ½ cup vegetable oil for frying
- ¼ cup bottled tonkatsu sauce, plus extra for serving

1. Combine cabbage, scallions, lemon juice, and ¼ teaspoon salt in bowl. Squeeze and massage with your hands until cabbage is slightly wilted, about 1 minute. Set wire rack in rimmed baking sheet and line half of rack with triple layer of paper towels.

2. Whisk eggs, soy sauce, flour, and remaining 1 teaspoon salt together in shallow dish. Place panko in large zipper-lock bag and lightly crush with rolling pin; transfer to second shallow dish. Pat tofu dry with paper towels. Working with 1 tofu slab at a time, dredge in egg mixture, allowing excess to drip off, then coat all sides with panko, pressing gently to adhere. Transfer to unlined side of wire rack.

3. Heat oil in 12-inch nonstick skillet over medium-high heat until shimmering. Add tofu and cook until deep golden brown, about 3 minutes per side. Transfer to lined side of wire rack. Season cabbage salad with salt to taste and serve with tofu drizzled with tonkatsu sauce, passing extra sauce separately.

Tofu Katsu

A World Traveler

A supermarket staple year-round, green beans are inexpensive and easy to cook. They are trending upward in popularity, with all sorts of adventurous recipes and cooking methods available. And while they are still a Thanksgiving legacy for American families, how they appear now on the table can be very exciting. That said, green beans have traveled the world, finding a unique place in the cuisines of many cultures. Our recipe for Seared Tofu with Panch Phoron, Green Beans, and Pickled Shallot is one with roots in eastern India, Bangladesh, and Nepal, where an aromatic five-spice blend (panch phoron) is often used; here the hearty bean is paired with torn tofu and both are tossed with the spice blend, infusing the dish with unmistakable flavor.

Steam Then Brown

When you are incorporating green beans into a recipe that moves quickly in and out of the skillet, like this one (and of course many stir-fries), they need a little help to cook through quickly but still retain their snap. The trick is to add a bit of water to the skillet along with the beans and cover it, giving the skillet an occasional shake until the water evaporates and the beans have time to take on a little flavorful browning.

Versatility in Spades

We especially like to cook green beans in one of two ways: either slow or fast. They're terrific after a quick roast in the oven or a speedy blanch-and-shock treatment on the stovetop. They also hold up wonderfully to long braises without turning to mush like other green vegetables. And we include lots of ideas about how to use them in many varied dishes, including cold salads.

Seared Tofu with Panch Phoron, Green Beans, and Pickled Shallot

Seared Tofu with Panch Phoron, Green Beans, and Pickled Shallot

VEGAN Serves 4 Total Time 1¼ hours

Why This Recipe Works In this fragrant tofu dish, we hand-tear it to create craggy edges—all the more surface area for each chunk to absorb flavor. The edges turn pleasingly crisp as we sear the tofu in the skillet. For a hearty vegetable to pair with the tofu, we use green beans, cooking them with a little water to help them steam-cook; when the water evaporates, we sear them to encourage flavorful browning. We toss everything with panch phoron, an aromatic five-spice blend of whole fenugreek, mustard, cumin, fennel, and nigella seeds often used in regions of eastern India, Bangladesh, and Nepal. To release maximum flavor from the spices, we use the Indian method of tadka—meaning tempering or blooming. To serve, we spread a serving plate with cilantro- and lime-spiked yogurt and top it with the tofu and beans as well as quick-pickled shallot slices. You will need a 12-inch nonstick skillet with a tight-fitting lid for this recipe. To make this recipe vegan, substitute plant-based yogurt for the dairy yogurt.

- 28 ounces extra-firm or firm tofu torn into rough 1½-inch pieces
- ⅓ cup red wine vinegar
- 2 tablespoons sugar
- 1⅛ teaspoons table salt, divided
- 1 large shallot, sliced thin
- 1 cup plain whole-milk yogurt
- ¾ cup minced fresh cilantro
- 1 teaspoon grated lime zest plus 1 tablespoon juice
- 2 garlic cloves, minced
- 1 pound green beans, trimmed and halved
- 2 tablespoons water
- ¼ cup vegetable oil, divided
- ¾ teaspoon ground turmeric
- 4 teaspoons Panch Phoron (recipe follows)

1. Spread tofu over paper towel–lined baking sheet and let drain for 20 minutes. Gently pat dry with paper towels.

2. Microwave vinegar, sugar, and ⅛ teaspoon salt in medium bowl until steaming, about 2 minutes. Add shallot and stir until submerged. Let sit for 10 minutes, stirring occasionally. Drain shallot and set aside for serving.

3. Meanwhile, combine yogurt, cilantro, lime zest and juice, and garlic in separate bowl and season with salt to taste; set sauce aside for serving.

4. Combine green beans, water, 1 tablespoon oil, and ¼ teaspoon salt in 12-inch nonstick skillet. Cover and cook over medium-high heat, tossing occasionally, until beans are nearly tender, 6 to 8 minutes. Uncover and continue to cook until water has evaporated and beans are just beginning to brown in spots, 2 to 4 minutes; transfer to large bowl.

5. Sprinkle tofu with turmeric and remaining ¾ teaspoon salt. Heat 1 tablespoon oil in now-empty skillet over medium-high heat until shimmering. Add tofu and cook until golden brown, 8 to 10 minutes, turning as needed and adding 1 tablespoon oil halfway through cooking. Transfer tofu to bowl with green beans.

6. Add panch phoron and remaining 1 tablespoon oil to again-empty skillet and cook over medium-high heat until fragrant and seeds start to pop, about 1 minute. Off heat, immediately add green beans and tofu and toss gently to combine.

7. Spread reserved yogurt sauce over surface of serving platter. Arrange tofu and green bean mixture attractively on top, sprinkle with pickled shallot, and serve.

Panch Phoron

FAST **VEGAN** Makes ¼ cup Total Time 5 minutes

- 1 tablespoon cumin seeds
- 1 tablespoon fennel seeds
- 1 tablespoon mustard seeds
- 1 tablespoon nigella seeds
- 1½ teaspoons fenugreek seeds

Combine all ingredients in bowl. (Panch phoron can be stored for up to 1 month.)

Tofu Rancheros

VEGAN Serves 4 Total Time 1¼ hours

Why This Recipe Works Tofu rancheros, a riff on huevos rancheros, with warm corn tortillas nestled alongside makes for a hearty, zesty way to start (or end) the day. The backbone of any rancheros dish is really the sauce, so for maximum flavor with little effort, we roast canned diced tomatoes with brown sugar, lime juice, onion, green chiles, garlic, and chili powder; roasting on a sheet pan allows moisture to quickly evaporate and a nice char to form on the vegetables. We sear the tofu while the sauce cooks for a beautiful golden color. To supercharge the toppings we add a vibrant salad of avocado, cilantro, and scallions.

- 2 (28-ounce) cans diced tomatoes
- 4 teaspoons lime juice, divided, plus lime wedges for serving
- 1 tablespoon packed brown sugar
- 1 onion, chopped
- ½ cup chopped canned green chiles
- ¼ cup extra-virgin olive oil, divided
- 2 tablespoons plus ½ teaspoon chili powder, divided
- 4 garlic cloves, sliced thin
- 14 ounces firm tofu, halved lengthwise, then cut crosswise into twelve ½-inch-thick slabs
- ¼ teaspoon table salt
- ⅛ teaspoon pepper
- 1 cup fresh cilantro leaves
- 4 scallions, white parts sliced thin, green parts cut into 1-inch pieces
- 1 avocado, halved, pitted, and diced
- 8 (6-inch) corn tortillas, warmed

1. Adjust oven rack to middle position and heat oven to 500 degrees. Line rimmed baking sheet with parchment paper. Drain tomatoes in fine-mesh strainer set over bowl, pressing to extract as much juice as possible. Reserve 1¼ cups tomato juice and discard remainder. Whisk 1 tablespoon lime juice and sugar into tomato juice.

2. Combine onion, chiles, 2 tablespoons oil, 2 tablespoons chili powder, garlic, and drained tomatoes in second bowl. Transfer tomato mixture to prepared baking sheet and spread in even layer to edges of sheet. Roast until charred in spots, 35 to 40 minutes, stirring and redistributing into even layer halfway through baking.

3. Meanwhile, spread tofu over paper towel–lined plate and let drain for 20 minutes. Gently pat dry with paper towels. Sprinkle with salt and pepper, and sprinkle both sides with remaining ½ teaspoon chili powder.

4. Heat 1 tablespoon oil in 12-inch nonstick skillet over medium-high heat until just smoking. Add tofu and cook until golden and crisp on both sides, 5 to 7 minutes; transfer to paper towel–lined plate.

5. Transfer roasted tomato mixture to now-empty skillet and stir in reserved tomato juice mixture. Season with salt and pepper to taste, then nestle tofu into sauce. Bring to simmer over medium heat, cover, and cook until tofu is warmed through and sauce thickens slightly, about 2 minutes.

6. Whisk remaining 1 tablespoon oil and remaining 1 teaspoon lime juice together in large bowl. Add cilantro, scallions, and avocado and toss to coat. Season with salt and pepper to taste. Serve rancheros with warm tortillas and lime wedges, topped with herb and avocado salad.

Saag Tofu

Serves 4 to 6 Total Time 45 minutes, plus 20 minutes draining

Why This Recipe Works A spicy sauce of pureed stewed spinach studded with pieces of fresh cheese and often finished with cream or butter, saag paneer is a revered—and comforting—Indian dish. The dense, mild paneer is texturally reminiscent of firm tofu, so we thought using tofu would make a delicious rendition. We build layers of flavor by frying an assortment of spices and caramelizing onion, jalapeño, garlic, ginger, and tomatoes. We blitz half of this mixture in a food processor—along with milk and cashews, for buttery richness—until smooth, which gives our dish an appealing chunky consistency. Mustard greens, which are often used in this dish, add mildly spicy pungency; we puree half and chop half for a balance of smoothness and bite. All we need to do with the tofu cubes is heat them in the sauce. We prefer firm tofu here, but you can substitute extra-firm tofu; do not use soft tofu, as it will disintegrate. For a spicier dish, include the ribs and seeds from the jalapeño. Serve over rice.

- 14 ounces firm tofu, cut into ½-inch pieces
- ⅛ teaspoon plus ¾ teaspoon table salt, divided
- Pinch pepper

- 12 ounces curly-leaf spinach, stemmed
- 12 ounces mustard greens, stemmed
- 3 tablespoons vegetable oil
- 1 teaspoon cumin seeds
- 1 teaspoon ground coriander
- 1 teaspoon paprika
- ½ teaspoon ground cardamom
- ¼ teaspoon ground cinnamon
- 1 onion, chopped fine
- 1 jalapeño chile, stemmed, seeded, and minced
- 3 garlic cloves, minced
- 1 tablespoon grated fresh ginger
- 1 (14.5-ounce) can diced tomatoes, drained and chopped
- 1½ cups milk, divided
- ½ cup roasted cashews, chopped, divided
- 1 teaspoon sugar
- 1½ tablespoons lemon juice
- 3 tablespoons minced fresh cilantro

1. Spread tofu over paper towel–lined plate and let drain for 20 minutes. Gently pat dry with paper towels. Sprinkle with ⅛ teaspoon salt and pepper.

2. Meanwhile, microwave spinach in covered bowl until wilted, about 3 minutes; transfer ½ cup spinach to blender. Chop remaining spinach; set aside. Microwave mustard greens in now-empty covered bowl until wilted, about 4 minutes; transfer ½ cup to blender with spinach. Chop remaining mustard greens; set aside.

3. Heat oil in 12-inch skillet over medium-high heat until shimmering. Add cumin seeds, coriander, paprika, cardamom, and cinnamon and cook until fragrant, about 30 seconds. Add onion and remaining ¾ teaspoon salt and cook, stirring frequently, until softened, about 3 minutes. Stir in jalapeño, garlic, and ginger and cook until lightly browned and just beginning to stick to pan, about 3 minutes. Stir in tomatoes, scraping up any browned bits, and cook until pan is dry and tomatoes are beginning to brown, about 4 minutes.

4. Transfer half of onion-tomato mixture, ¾ cup milk, ¼ cup cashews, and sugar to blender with greens and process until smooth, about 1 minute. Add pureed greens mixture, chopped greens, lemon juice, and remaining ¾ cup milk to skillet with remaining onion-tomato mixture and bring to simmer over medium-high heat. Reduce heat to low and season with salt and pepper to taste. Stir in tofu and cook until warmed through, about 2 minutes. Sprinkle with cilantro and remaining ¼ cup cashews and serve.

top | *Tofu Rancheros*
bottom | *Saag Tofu*

Crispy Tofu and Kale Salad and Miso-Ginger Dressing

Crispy Tofu Salad with Cherry Tomatoes

Serves 4   Total Time 1 hour

Why This Recipe Works In this salad, the "crispy" doesn't come just from the fried tofu but also from the crispy shallots, a flavor star of the show. Ingredients common to Thai salads—the shallots, cherry tomatoes, basil and mint, and a pungent fish sauce–based dressing—make this an incredibly vibrant tofu dish with dimension in every bite. We fry the shallots and then use the same allium-infused oil to cook the tofu, which we tear roughly to create craggy surfaces for crisping. The shallots and the dressing create deep savor in this otherwise light and refreshing salad. We prefer to use a mandoline to slice the shallots evenly so that they'll brown at the same rate. Serve this salad with steamed rice and/or Bibb lettuce leaves.

- 14 ounces extra-firm tofu, torn into rough 1-inch pieces
- 2 tablespoons vegetarian fish sauce
- 2 tablespoons lime juice
- 2 tablespoons water
- 2 teaspoons sugar
- 1 Thai chile, stemmed and sliced thin
- 10 ounces cherry tomatoes, halved
- ½ cup vegetable oil
- ½ cup very thinly sliced shallots (2 to 3 shallots)
- ¼ cup fresh mint leaves, torn, divided
- ¼ cup fresh Thai basil leaves, torn, divided

1. Spread tofu over paper towel–lined plate and let drain for 20 minutes. Gently pat dry with paper towels. Whisk fish sauce, lime juice, water, sugar, and Thai chile together in large bowl, then stir in tomatoes.

2. Meanwhile, cook oil and shallots in 12-inch nonstick skillet over medium heat, stirring often, until shallots turn light golden brown and bubbling subsides, 5 to 10 minutes (watch shallots carefully to avoid burning). Off heat, use slotted spoon to quickly transfer shallots to paper towel–lined plate, then season with salt to taste.

3. Heat oil left in skillet over medium-high heat. Add tofu and cook until light golden brown and crispy all over, 8 to 10 minutes. Transfer tofu to paper towel–lined plate and season with salt to taste. Gently stir tofu and half of mint, basil, and crispy shallots into tomato mixture. Top with remaining mint, basil, and shallots. Serve.

Crispy Tofu and Kale Salad with Miso-Ginger Dressing

FAST   VEGAN   Serves 4   Total Time 35 minutes

Why This Recipe Works This hearty kale salad is bright and pungent with the flavors of miso, ginger, and toasted sesame oil and features crispy tofu, shredded carrots, and an abundance of avocado chunks. It is so easy to make: simply assemble the dressing and add the kale; while it is soaking and softening in the dressing we fry the cornstarch-coated tofu until really crisp. Sprinkle the salad with fresh cilantro leaves before serving.

- ¼ cup seasoned rice vinegar
- 3 tablespoons toasted sesame oil
- 3 tablespoons white miso
- 1 tablespoon grated fresh ginger
- 1 pound curly kale, stemmed and chopped coarse
- 2 carrots, peeled and shredded
- 14 ounces firm tofu, cut into ½-inch pieces
- ½ teaspoon table salt
- ⅓ cup cornstarch
- ¼ cup vegetable oil for frying
- 2 avocados, halved, pitted, and cut into ½-inch pieces
- ½ cup roasted cashews, chopped coarse

1. Whisk vinegar, sesame oil, miso, and ginger together in large bowl. Add kale and carrots and toss to combine.

2. Spread tofu over paper towel–lined plate and let drain for 20 minutes. Gently pat dry with paper towels. Sprinkle with salt. Toss tofu with cornstarch in bowl.

3. Heat vegetable oil in 12-inch nonstick skillet over medium-high heat until shimmering. Add tofu and cook, turning as needed, until crispy and browned on all sides, 10 to 15 minutes, breaking up any pieces that stick together. Transfer to paper towel–lined plate. Divide kale salad among 4 serving bowls; top with avocados, cashews, and tofu. Serve.

Pita Salad with Za'atar Tofu and Chickpeas

FAST **VEGAN** Serves 4 Total Time 40 minutes

Why This Recipe Works With a mix of crunchy and chewy textures, the Levantine bread salad fattoush is a refreshing summer meal, and we love the idea of adding protein to make it a complete dinner. For this spin on fattoush, which like other bread dishes gets its name from the Arabic word "fatteh" (crumbs), we cook pieces of tofu with a coating of za'atar, the spice blend beloved in the region, and also toss in some chickpeas. A tahini dressing clings beautifully to all of the mix-ins, and pepperoncini provide piquant bite to the salad. For an extra-briny kick, top this salad with kalamata olives.

- 14 ounces extra-firm tofu, cut into ¾-inch pieces
- 5 tablespoons extra-virgin olive oil, divided
- 2 tablespoons tahini
- 2 teaspoons grated lemon zest plus 3 tablespoons juice
- 1¼ teaspoons table salt, divided
- 1 (15-ounce) can chickpeas, rinsed
- 10 ounces cherry tomatoes, halved
- 3 tablespoons za'atar
- 2 romaine lettuce hearts (12 ounces), cut into 1-inch pieces
- 2 cups pita chips, broken into ½-inch pieces
- ½ cup pepperoncini, stemmed and sliced into rings, divided

1. Spread tofu over paper towel–lined plate and let drain for 20 minutes. Gently pat dry with paper towels. Whisk 3 tablespoons oil, tahini, lemon zest and juice, and ¼ teaspoon salt together in large bowl. Add chickpeas and tomatoes and toss to coat; set aside.

2. Sprinkle tofu pieces with za'atar and remaining 1 teaspoon salt. Heat remaining 2 tablespoons oil in 12-inch nonstick skillet over medium-high heat until shimmering. Add tofu and cook until first side is lightly browned, 3 to 4 minutes. Flip tofu and cook until second side is lightly browned, 3 to 4 minutes.

3. Add lettuce, pita chips, and half of pepperoncini to bowl with chickpea mixture and toss to combine. Transfer salad to serving plates and top with tofu and remaining pepperoncini. Serve.

Charred Cabbage Salad with Torn Tofu and Plantain Chips

Serves 4 Total Time 45 minutes, plus 35 minutes marinating and cooling

Why This Recipe Works This showstopping salad seasons cabbage and tofu with beloved Southeast Asian flavors for a flavor-packed meal. We first cut a whole head of red cabbage into eight substantial wedges, then coat them in oil, Thai red curry paste, and turmeric before roasting. The oven time tenderizes the cabbage while charring the edges, giving us textural variation and imbuing the leaves with potent flavor. Like cabbage, tofu is also adept at absorbing seasonings; tearing it gives us lots of craggy surfaces for a marinade—a sweet-savory concoction of vinegar, lime juice, ginger, honey, and fish sauce—to sink into. For a warm dressing, we bloom more curry paste, turmeric, and ginger in the microwave, then add rice vinegar. Crushed plantain chips make a perfect sweet-salty garnish. The tofu can be marinated for up to 24 hours. Note that this recipe uses seasoned rice vinegar; we don't recommend using unseasoned rice vinegar in its place. If you don't have plantain chips or banana chips, you can substitute chopped macadamia nuts or cashews.

- 14 ounces firm tofu, torn into bite-size pieces
- 3 tablespoons seasoned rice vinegar, divided
- 2 tablespoons lime juice
- 4 teaspoons grated fresh ginger, divided
- 1 tablespoon honey
- 1 tablespoon vegetarian fish sauce
- 1 head red cabbage (2 pounds)
- 7 tablespoons vegetable oil, divided
- 4 teaspoons Thai red curry paste, divided
- 1 tablespoon ground turmeric, divided
- ½ teaspoon table salt
- 1 tablespoon water
- 1 cup bean sprouts
- ¼ cup chopped fresh basil
- 2 scallions, sliced thin on bias
- ¼ cup plantain or banana chips, crushed

1. Adjust oven rack to lowest position and heat oven to 500 degrees. Spread tofu over paper towel–lined plate and let drain for 20 minutes. Gently pat dry with paper towels. Whisk 1 tablespoon vinegar, lime juice, 2 teaspoons ginger, honey, and fish sauce together in medium bowl. Add tofu and toss gently to coat; set aside for 20 minutes.

2. Halve cabbage through core and cut each half into 4 approximately 2-inch-wide wedges, leaving core intact (you will have 8 wedges). Whisk ¼ cup oil, 1 teaspoon curry paste, 2 teaspoons turmeric, and salt together in bowl. Arrange cabbage wedges in single layer on aluminum foil–lined rimmed baking sheet, then brush cabbage all over with oil mixture. Cover tightly with foil and roast for 10 minutes. Remove foil and drizzle 2 tablespoons oil evenly over wedges. Return sheet to oven and roast, uncovered, until cabbage is tender and sides touching sheet are well browned, 10 to 15 minutes. Let cool slightly, about 15 minutes.

3. Whisk remaining 2 teaspoons ginger, remaining 1 tablespoon oil, remaining 1 tablespoon curry paste, and remaining 1 teaspoon turmeric together in bowl. Microwave until fragrant, about 30 seconds. Whisk water and remaining 2 tablespoons vinegar into ginger mixture.

4. Chop cabbage coarse and spread over serving platter, then top with bean sprouts, basil, scallions, and reserved tofu. Drizzle with vinaigrette and sprinkle with plantain chips. Serve.

Garlicky Tofu Tabbouleh

VEGAN Serves 4 to 6 Total Time 35 minutes, plus 2 hours resting

Why This Recipe Works Tabbouleh made from bulgur, tomatoes, lemon, and heaps of fresh herbs is often served as a meze. But with just a little help, tabbouleh becomes more substantial. Enter tofu: Garlicky, savory sautéed tofu transforms this classic into a light summer meal or hearty addition to a picnic spread. Rather than using pieces of tofu, we pulse it in the food processor to mimic the texture of bulgur. Salting our tomatoes rids them of excess liquid, and we use their juice (rather than water) to soak the bulgur. Meanwhile, we sauté the tofu with a hefty dose of toasted garlic. As the tofu cools, we make a lemony dressing and then toss everything with liberal amounts of parsley, mint, and scallions and let the whole thing sit for about an hour to let the flavors mingle. When shopping, don't confuse bulgur with cracked wheat, which has a much longer cooking time and will not work in this recipe.

Pita Salad with Za'atar Tofu and Chickpeas

- 3 tomatoes, cored and cut into ½-inch pieces
- ¾ teaspoon table salt, divided
- ½ cup medium-grind bulgur, rinsed
- ¼ cup lemon juice (2 lemons), divided
- 14 ounces extra-firm or firm tofu, cut into 2-inch pieces
- ¼ cup extra-virgin olive oil, divided
- 3 garlic cloves, minced
- ⅛ teaspoon cayenne pepper
- 1½ cups minced fresh parsley
- ½ cup minced fresh mint
- 2 scallions, sliced thin

1. Toss tomatoes with ¼ teaspoon salt in fine-mesh strainer set over bowl and let drain, tossing occasionally, for 30 minutes; reserve 2 tablespoons drained tomato juice. Toss bulgur with 2 tablespoons lemon juice and reserved tomato juice in bowl and let sit until grains begin to soften, 30 to 40 minutes.

2. Meanwhile, spread tofu over paper towel–lined plate and let drain for 20 minutes. Gently pat dry with paper towels and season with salt and pepper. Pulse tofu in food processor until coarsely chopped, 3 or 4 pulses. Line baking sheet with clean paper towels. Spread processed tofu over prepared sheet and press gently with paper towels to dry.

3. Heat 2 teaspoons oil in 12-inch nonstick skillet over medium-high heat until shimmering. Add tofu and cook, stirring occasionally, until tofu is lightly browned, 10 to 12 minutes. (Tofu should start to sizzle after about 1½ minutes; adjust heat as needed.) Push tofu to sides of skillet. Add 1 teaspoon oil and garlic to center and cook, mashing garlic into skillet, until fragrant, about 1 minute. Stir mixture into tofu. Transfer to bowl and let cool for 10 minutes.

4. Whisk remaining ½ teaspoon salt, remaining 2 tablespoons lemon juice, remaining 3 tablespoons oil, and cayenne together in large bowl. Add drained tomatoes, soaked bulgur, cooled tofu, parsley, mint, and scallions and toss to combine. Cover and let sit until bulgur is tender, about 1 hour. Toss to recombine and season with salt and pepper to taste before serving.

Chile-Spiced Crumbled Tofu with Pineapple Salsa

FAST **VEGAN** Serves 4 Total Time 30 minutes

Why This Recipe Works Spiced tofu crumbles give you lots of options for a fast dinner. But first, to make these crumbles, we build a flavor base in a skillet by sautèing a finely chopped sweet red bell pepper and then blooming a host of spices: chile powder, paprika, cumin, oregano, and cinnamon. A bright hit of sharp apple cider vinegar, a touch of balancing sugar, and minced garlic round out the base to which we add the tofu. Mashing the tofu into the skillet allows it to absorb these incredible flavors, while at the same time it breaks the tofu into perfectly sized crumbles. You can use these crumbles as a taco filling topped with our sweet-spicy pineapple salsa, in a burrito, or simply spooned over rice. If you don't have a large silicone spatula, use a wooden spoon for mashing.

Salsa

- 1 cup ½-inch pineapple pieces
- ½ cup finely chopped white onion
- 2 tablespoons chopped fresh cilantro
- 1 jalapeño chile, stemmed, seeded, and minced
- 2 tablespoons lime juice
- ¼ teaspoon table salt

Tofu Crumbles

- ¼ cup extra-virgin olive oil
- 1 red bell pepper, stemmed, seeded, and chopped fine
- 2 teaspoons ancho chile powder
- 1 tablespoon paprika
- 1¼ teaspoons table salt
- 1 teaspoon ground cumin
- 1 teaspoon dried oregano
- ¼ teaspoon ground cinnamon
- Pinch ground allspice
- 2 tablespoons cider vinegar
- 2 teaspoons sugar
- 2 garlic cloves, minced
- 14 ounces extra-firm or firm tofu, cut crosswise into 8 equal pieces

1. **For the salsa** Combine all ingredients in bowl. Season with salt and pepper to taste; set aside for serving.

2. **For the tofu crumbles** Heat oil in 12-inch skillet over medium heat until shimmering. Add bell pepper and cook until tender, about 3 minutes. Add chile powder, paprika, salt, cumin, oregano, cinnamon, and allspice and cook, stirring constantly, until mixture is bubbling and fragrant, about 1 minute. Stir in vinegar, sugar, and garlic.

3. Add tofu and mash with silicone spatula until it has broken into fine crumbles. Continue to cook until juices are bubbling, about 3 minutes. Season with salt and pepper to taste. Serve with salsa.

Crispy Teriyaki Tofu

FAST **VEGAN** Serves 4 Total Time 40 minutes

Why This Recipe Works The bold flavors and textures of this 10-ingredient meal will have you second-guessing everything you thought you knew about tofu. We start with firm tofu, which has a meaty yet tender bite. Next, we tear it. This carefree preparation serves a double purpose; not only is it quick and easy, but it also dramatically increases the tofu's surface area. This creates endless nooks and crannies that pan-fry beautifully over high heat, resulting in maximally crispy tofu morsels with soft, chewy centers. The textured edges beg for a sauce to cling to, and we opt for a bold yet comforting Japanese teriyaki sauce. Teriyaki sauce is traditionally made with just three ingredients—soy sauce, sugar, and sake or mirin. We include mirin in this recipe for its sweetness and slight umami flavor that lends a subtle complexity to this relatively simple sauce. Fresh ginger adds a zingy boost, and cornstarch helps the sauce thicken and perfectly glaze the awaiting crispy caves on the tofu's surface. This attention-grabbing tofu is complemented by nutty sesame seeds and fresh scallions, and we like to pair it with rice to soak up the punchy sauce.

- 6 tablespoons soy sauce
- 3 tablespoons water
- 6 tablespoons mirin
- 3 tablespoons sugar
- 3 tablespoons grated fresh ginger
- 28 ounces firm or extra-firm tofu, torn into rough ¾-inch pieces
- 6 tablespoons vegetable oil, divided
- ¾ teaspoon cornstarch
- 2 scallions, sliced thin
- 1 tablespoon toasted sesame seeds

top *Chile-Spiced Crumbled Tofu with Pineapple Salsa*

bottom *Crispy Teriyaki Tofu*

1. Combine soy sauce, water, mirin, sugar, and ginger in small bowl. Microwave until sugar is dissolved, about 1 minute, stirring halfway through; set aside. Spread tofu over paper towel–lined baking sheet and let drain for 20 minutes. Gently pat dry with paper towels.

2. Heat 3 tablespoons oil in 12-inch nonstick skillet over high heat until just smoking. Add half of tofu and cook, stirring and turning occasionally, until well browned and crispy on all sides, 8 to 10 minutes; transfer to large bowl.

3. Reduce heat to medium-high, add remaining 3 tablespoons oil and remaining tofu to skillet, and cook, stirring and turning occasionally, until well browned and crispy on all sides, 8 to 10 minutes; add to bowl with first batch of browned tofu. Meanwhile, whisk cornstarch into reserved soy sauce mixture.

4. Wipe out skillet with paper towels. Add soy sauce mixture to now-empty skillet and cook over low heat until sauce has thickened slightly, 1 to 2 minutes. Off heat, return tofu to skillet and toss to coat. Transfer to serving platter and sprinkle with scallions and toasted sesame seeds. Serve immediately with rice.

Stir-Fried Tofu and Bok Choy

FAST **VEGAN** Serves 4 Total Time 45 minutes

Why This Recipe Works This simple stir-fry features crispy browned tofu, mustardy bok choy (stems and leaves), carrots, and an easy whisk-together sauce thickened with cornstarch. Several key techniques help produce creamy tofu with a browned crust and crisp-tender vegetables, all lightly coated in a flavorful sauce. Coating the pieces in cornstarch further promotes a crispy crust while keeping the interior creamy and also makes a craggy surface that holds the sauce nicely. We stir-fry the tofu in a wok first, over high heat, before removing it and adding the slower-cooking vegetables, which ensures that the bok choy and carrots don't get soggy. Clearing the vegetables to the side of the pan, we then mash into the wok a classic trio of stir-fry aromatics with a bit of oil: scallions, garlic, and ginger, essentially the Chinese equivalent of a mirepoix. Once they become fragrant, we combine them with the vegetables, add back the tofu, and then pour in the sauce until it thickens and clings beautifully to the tofu and vegetables.

Sauce

- ½ cup vegetable broth
- ¼ cup soy sauce
- 2 tablespoons Shaoxing wine
- 1 tablespoon sugar
- 2 teaspoons cornstarch
- 1 teaspoon toasted sesame oil

Stir-Fry

- 14 ounces extra-firm tofu, cut into 1-inch pieces
- ⅓ cup cornstarch
- 3 scallions, minced
- 3 garlic cloves, minced
- 1 tablespoon grated fresh ginger
- 3 tablespoons vegetable oil, divided
- 1 small head bok choy (1 pound), stalks and greens separated, stalks sliced thin, and greens cut into 1-inch pieces
- 2 carrots, peeled and cut into matchsticks

1. **For the sauce** Whisk all ingredients together in bowl.

2. **For the stir-fry** Spread tofu over paper towel–lined plate and let drain for 20 minutes. Gently pat dry with paper towels, then toss with cornstarch in bowl. Transfer coated tofu to strainer and shake gently over bowl to remove excess cornstarch.

3. Combine scallions, garlic, ginger, and 1 teaspoon oil in bowl; set aside. Heat 2 tablespoons oil in 14-inch flat-bottomed wok or 12-inch nonstick skillet over high heat until just smoking. Add tofu and cook until crisp and well browned on all sides, 10 to 15 minutes; transfer to bowl.

4. Add remaining 2 teaspoons oil to wok and return to high heat until shimmering. Add bok choy stalks and carrots and cook until vegetables are crisp-tender, about 4 minutes. Clear center of wok; add garlic mixture; and cook, mashing mixture into wok, until fragrant, about 30 seconds. Stir garlic mixture into vegetables.

5. Return tofu to wok. Stir in bok choy greens. Whisk sauce to recombine, then add to wok. Cook, stirring constantly, until sauce is thickened, 1 to 2 minutes. Serve.

Stir-Fried Tofu and Bok Choy

top | *Panko-Crusted Tofu with Cabbage Salad*

bottom | *Sweet and Spicy Glazed Tofu with Coconut-Braised Mustard Greens and Winter Squash*

Panko-Crusted Tofu with Cabbage Salad

FAST Serves 4 Total Time 35 minutes

Why This Recipe Works Inspired by Japanese katsu, we give tofu planks a panko breading and make a quick katsu sauce to go with them. To help the panko crust adhere, we dredge the tofu slices in a mixture of flour and egg, creating a glue-like paste that locks the panko in place. Ketchup, Worcestershire, soy sauce, garlic powder, and a bit of sugar make up our homemade tonkatsu sauce. Last but not least is a crunchy cabbage salad, which needs nothing more than a quick toss with some rice vinegar, toasty sesame oil, and a touch more sugar for seasoning.

- 14 ounces extra-firm tofu, cut lengthwise into four ½-inch-thick slabs
- ¼ cup ketchup
- 4 teaspoons vegetarian Worcestershire sauce
- 2 teaspoons soy sauce
- 1 teaspoon garlic powder
- 1 teaspoon sugar, divided
- 2 large eggs
- 2 tablespoons all-purpose flour
- 1⅓ cups panko bread crumbs
- ½ teaspoon table salt
- 1 cup vegetable oil, for frying
- 2½ teaspoons unseasoned rice vinegar
- 1½ teaspoons toasted sesame oil
- 3 cups shredded red or green cabbage

1. Spread tofu over paper towel–lined plate and let drain for 20 minutes. Whisk ketchup, Worcestershire, soy sauce, garlic powder, and ½ teaspoon sugar together in small bowl; set aside.

2. Whisk eggs and flour together in shallow dish. Place panko in large zipper-lock bag and lightly crush with rolling pin; transfer crumbs to second shallow dish. Gently pat tofu dry with paper towels and sprinkle with salt. Working with 1 slab at a time, dip tofu in egg mixture, allowing excess to drip off, then coat all sides with panko, pressing gently to adhere; transfer to large plate.

3. Place wire rack in rimmed baking sheet and line rack with triple layer of paper towels. Heat vegetable oil in 12-inch nonstick skillet over medium-high heat until shimmering. Add tofu and cook until deep golden brown, 2 to 3 minutes per side. Transfer tofu to prepared rack and let drain.

4. Combine vinegar, sesame oil, and remaining ½ teaspoon sugar in small bowl. Add cabbage, toss to coat, and season with salt and pepper to taste. Drizzle tofu with reserved sauce. Serve.

Sweet and Spicy Glazed Tofu with Coconut-Braised Mustard Greens and Winter Squash

FAST **VEGAN** Serves 4 Total Time 45 minutes

Why This Recipe Works Glazing tofu either separately or as part of a stir-fry offers many flavoring options and is easy to do. In this hearty dish, perfect for the winter months, we cook the tofu separately and combine it later with braised squash and pungent mustard greens simmered with creamy coconut milk. We tear the tofu into chunks to create craggy edges—and textural variation when crisped up in a skillet. It is also a great way to give the tofu more places for the glaze to stick. A sweet-tangy mixture of brown sugar and vinegar as well as soy sauce is responsible for its umami. And as this mixture reduces in the skillet, it clings appetizingly to the uneven surfaces of the tofu.

- 14 ounces firm or extra-firm tofu, torn into rough ¾-inch pieces
- 2 tablespoons plus 1 teaspoon vegetable oil, divided
- 4 scallions, white and green parts separated and sliced thin
- 1 Scotch bonnet or habanero chile, stemmed, seeded, and minced, divided
- 5 garlic cloves, minced
- 2 teaspoons minced fresh thyme, divided
- 2 cups water
- 2 pounds butternut squash, peeled, seeded, and cut into ½-inch pieces (5 cups)
- ¾ teaspoon table salt, divided
- 1 pound mustard greens, stemmed and cut into 1-inch pieces
- 2 tablespoons soy sauce
- 1 tablespoon packed brown sugar
- 1 tablespoon cider vinegar
- ½ teaspoon ground allspice
- ¼ teaspoon ground ginger
- ¾ cup coconut milk
- Lime wedges

1. Spread tofu over paper towel–lined plate and let drain for 20 minutes. Gently pat dry with paper towels.

2. Heat 1 tablespoon oil in Dutch oven over medium heat until shimmering. Add scallion whites, half of chile, garlic, and 1 teaspoon thyme and cook until fragrant, about 1 minute. Add water, squash, and ½ teaspoon salt and bring to boil. Stir in mustard greens (mustard greens will not be fully submerged); reduce heat to medium-low; and simmer, covered, stirring occasionally until vegetables are just tender, 12 to 15 minutes.

3. Meanwhile, combine soy sauce, sugar, and vinegar in bowl. Combine 1 teaspoon oil, allspice, ginger, remaining half of chile, and remaining 1 teaspoon thyme in second bowl. Press tofu dry with paper towels.

4. Heat remaining 1 tablespoon oil in 12-inch nonstick skillet over medium-high heat until shimmering. Add tofu and cook until golden brown, 8 to 10 minutes, turning as needed. Clear space in skillet and add allspice mixture. Cook, stirring frequently, until fragrant, about 30 seconds. Stir in soy sauce mixture and cook, stirring frequently, until sauce is reduced and tofu is coated, 2 to 4 minutes. Set aside off heat until ready to serve.

5. Stir coconut milk and remaining ¼ teaspoon salt into squash mixture and bring to brief boil. Simmer, uncovered, until thickened slightly, 3 to 5 minutes. Season with salt and pepper to taste. Serve with tofu and lime wedges, sprinkling individual portions with scallion greens.

Caribbean Tofu with Rice and Pigeon Peas

VEGAN Serves 4 Total Time 1 hour, plus 20 minutes resting

Why This Recipe Works This comforting dish is a study in flavor and texture contrasts: crisp, spicy-sweet tofu accompanied by creamy, savory rice and hearty pigeon peas. Incorporating the earthy, nutty flavor of pigeon peas is as easy as opening a can. We start our rice and peas side dish while the tofu drains, boosting savoriness with jalapeños and onion and adding coconut milk to the cooking liquid for creaminess. We cook the tofu until golden and crisp and then coat it with a glaze of pineapple preserves, lime juice, and pepper flakes. Served alongside our rich rice, the tofu is anything but mild-mannered.

28 ounces firm tofu, cut in half lengthwise then crosswise into 6 slices
1 tablespoon curry powder
1½ teaspoons table salt, divided
¼ teaspoon pepper
1 onion, chopped fine
2 jalapeño chiles, stemmed, seeded, and minced
¼ cup vegetable oil, divided
1½ cups long-grain white rice
1 (15-ounce) can pigeon peas, rinsed
1 (14-ounce) can coconut milk
1 cup plus 3 tablespoons water, divided
½ cup pineapple preserves
2 tablespoons lime juice
¼ teaspoon red pepper flakes
2 scallions, sliced thin

1. Spread tofu over paper towel–lined baking sheet and let drain for 20 minutes. Gently pat dry with paper towels and sprinkle with curry powder, ½ teaspoon salt, and pepper.

2. Meanwhile, cook onion, jalapeño, and 2 tablespoons oil in large saucepan over medium-high heat until softened, about 3 minutes. Stir in rice and cook until opaque, about 1 minute. Stir in peas, coconut milk, 1 cup water, and remaining 1 teaspoon salt. Bring to boil, then reduce heat to low, cover, and cook until rice is tender, about 20 minutes. Season with salt and pepper to taste.

3. Microwave pineapple preserves until bubbling, about 1 minute, then whisk in lime juice, pepper flakes, and remaining 3 tablespoons water.

4. Heat remaining 2 tablespoons oil in 12-inch nonstick skillet over medium-high heat until just smoking. Add half of tofu and cook until golden and crisp on all sides, about 5 minutes; transfer to paper towel–lined plate. Repeat with remaining tofu, then return first batch of tofu to skillet. Add pineapple mixture and simmer, turning tofu to coat, until glaze thickens, about 1 minute. Sprinkle with scallions and serve with rice.

East African Tofu and Coconut Curry

FAST **VEGAN** Serves 4 Total Time 45 minutes

Why This Recipe Works The food from across East Africa reflects the region's early role in the spice trade and its many colonizations. This delightfully mild curry with a touch of sweetness is infused with cinnamon, a common ingredient in Indian cooking, and gets its lushness from coconut milk. Butternut squash, which we brown and then braise with the tofu, pairs perfectly with the aromatic ginger and garlic. As the tofu braises it picks up great flavor and becomes tender while the sauce turns creamy. We finish by topping the curry with chopped tomatoes and a handful of mint leaves.

3 tablespoons extra-virgin olive oil, divided
1 pound butternut squash, peeled, seeded, and cut into ½-inch pieces
1½ teaspoons table salt, divided
1 onion, chopped fine
2 tablespoons curry powder
2 cinnamon sticks
¼ cup tomato paste
2 tablespoons grated fresh ginger
2 garlic cloves, minced
1½ teaspoons sugar
1 (15-ounce) can coconut milk
1 cup water
14 ounces firm tofu, cut into 1-inch pieces
¼ cup chopped roasted cashews
1 tablespoon lime juice
2 tomatoes, cored and cut into ½-inch pieces
¼ cup torn mint leaves

1. Heat 1 tablespoon oil in 12-inch nonstick skillet over medium-high heat until shimmering. Add squash and ¼ teaspoon salt and cook until spotty brown and beginning to soften, 7 to 10 minutes; transfer to bowl.

2. Add 1 tablespoon oil, onion, and ¼ teaspoon salt to now-empty skillet and cook over medium heat until onion is softened, about 5 minutes. Add curry powder and cinnamon sticks and cook until fragrant, about 30 seconds. Stir in tomato paste, remaining 1 tablespoon oil, ginger, garlic, sugar, and remaining 1 teaspoon salt and cook until fragrant, about 1 minute. Stir in coconut milk and water and bring to boil. Gently stir in tofu and squash, reduce heat to medium-low, cover, and cook until butternut squash is tender, about 10 minutes, stirring occasionally.

3. Off heat, discard cinnamon sticks, stir in cashews and lime juice, and season with salt and pepper to taste. Top with chopped tomatoes and mint and serve.

Thai Red Curry with Tofu and Lentils

Serves 4 Total Time 1 hour, plus 20 minutes resting

Why This Recipe Works Thai curries embrace a delicate balance of flavors, textures, temperatures, and colors to produce lively, satisfying meals. This fresh-tasting curry features hearty lentils and tofu and uses just enough coconut milk to create a rich, fragrant sauce. We start by cooking the lentils in an aromatic red curry broth until they're tender but still slightly al dente and have absorbed most of the liquid. Then we stir in the coconut milk and add vibrant red bell pepper slices, snow peas, and cubes of tofu at the very end, simply warming them through to maintain the vegetables' color and crisp-fresh texture. A generous handful of fresh basil and a sprinkle of scallions gives the dish a brisk, heady finish. Do not use light coconut milk. You will need a 12-inch skillet with a tight-fitting lid. You can use brown, black, or regular green lentils in place of the lentilles de Puy, but cooking times will vary. Do not use red or yellow lentils in this recipe.

- 14 ounces extra-firm tofu, cut into ½-inch pieces
- ¼ teaspoon table salt
- ⅛ teaspoon pepper
- 1 tablespoon vegetable oil
- 1 tablespoon Thai red curry paste
- 2½ cups water
- 2 tablespoons vegetarian fish sauce
- 1 cup dried lentilles du Puy, picked over and rinsed
- ½ cup canned coconut milk
- 1 red bell pepper, stemmed, seeded, and cut into ¼-inch-wide strips
- 4 ounces snow peas, strings removed, halved crosswise
- ½ cup coarsely chopped fresh basil
- 1 tablespoon lime juice
- 2 scallions, sliced thin

1. Spread tofu over paper towel–lined plate and let drain for 20 minutes. Gently pat dry with paper towels and sprinkle with salt and pepper.

East African Tofu and Coconut Curry

2. Heat oil in 12-inch skillet over medium heat until shimmering. Add curry paste and cook, stirring constantly, until fragrant, about 1 minute. Stir in water, fish sauce, and lentils and bring to simmer. Cover, reduce heat to low, and simmer gently, stirring occasionally, until lentils are tender and about two-thirds of liquid has been absorbed, 30 to 35 minutes.

3. Stir in coconut milk until well combined. Add tofu, bell pepper, and snow peas, and increase heat to medium-high. Cover and cook, stirring occasionally, until tofu is warmed through and vegetables are crisp-tender, about 2 minutes.

4. Off heat, stir in basil and lime juice. Season with salt to taste, and sprinkle with scallions. Serve.

Bulgur with Vegetables and Marinated Tofu

Serves 4 Total Time 1¼ hours

Why This Recipe Works A riot of colors and flavors, this multidimensional bulgur dish features sweet-and-spicy marinated tofu, roasted carrots and broccolini, pickled cabbage, and an irresistible garnish of crispy shallots. Taking things up a notch, we combine a portion of the cabbage pickling liquid with the shallot-infused oil and sriracha to make a zippy dressing for the warm bulgur. Stop cooking the shallots once they turn light golden brown; they will continue to darken and crisp as they cool. Placing the broccolini in a pile on the baking sheet creates textural contrast and prevents the broccolini from drying out.

- 5 tablespoons extra-virgin olive oil, divided
- 3 shallots, sliced into thin rounds
- 1¾ teaspoons plus pinch table salt, divided, plus salt for cooking bulgur
- 3 tablespoons sriracha, divided
- 2 tablespoons honey, divided
- 14 ounces firm tofu, cut into ¾-inch pieces
- ½ cup rice vinegar
- 1½ cups thinly sliced red cabbage
- 1 pound carrots, peeled and sliced on bias ½ inch thick
- 1 pound broccolini, trimmed and cut into 1-inch pieces
- 1¼ cups medium-grind bulgur
- 2 tablespoons mayonnaise

1. Adjust oven rack to middle position and heat oven to 425 degrees. Heat ¼ cup oil and shallots in large saucepan over medium heat, stirring constantly once shallots start to sizzle. Cook until shallots are deep golden, 6 to 10 minutes. Drain shallots in fine-mesh strainer set over bowl; reserve oil. Transfer shallots to paper towel–lined plate and sprinkle with pinch salt; set aside until ready to serve. (Do not wash saucepan or strainer.)

2. Whisk 2 tablespoons sriracha, 1 tablespoon honey, and ½ teaspoon salt together in second bowl. Add tofu and gently toss to coat. Cover and refrigerate until ready to serve. Combine vinegar, ½ teaspoon salt, and remaining 1 tablespoon honey in third bowl. Microwave until simmering, 1 to 2 minutes. Stir in cabbage; set aside until ready to serve, stirring occasionally.

3. Toss carrots with 1½ teaspoons oil and ¼ teaspoon salt and spread on half of rimmed baking sheet. Toss broccolini with remaining 1½ teaspoons oil and remaining ½ teaspoon salt and pile on other half of sheet. Roast until carrots are tender and broccolini is crisp in spots, 15 to 20 minutes, stirring vegetables halfway through roasting.

4. While vegetables roast, add 6 cups water to now-empty saucepan and bring to boil over high heat. Add bulgur and 1 teaspoon salt and return to simmer. Reduce heat to maintain gentle simmer and cook until tender, about 5 minutes. Drain bulgur, then return to saucepan; cover and set aside.

5. Measure out 2 tablespoons cabbage liquid and add to reserved shallot oil. Whisk in mayonnaise and remaining 1 tablespoon sriracha. Mix 3 tablespoons dressing into bulgur. Divide bulgur among individual bowls. Top with tofu, carrots, broccolini, and cabbage (leaving behind pickling liquid), then drizzle with remaining dressing. Sprinkle with shallots and serve.

Broccoli's Slimmer Cousin

A hybrid of broccoli and Chinese broccoli (gai lan), broccolini was developed by a Japanese seed company in the 1900s. It has long, svelte stalks and smaller loose florets. Unlike broccoli, there is no need to peel the thin stems—simply trim the woody ends and you're ready to cook. In our recipe for Bulgur with Vegetables and Marinated Tofu we roast broccolini as a topping for nutty bulgur and chilled marinated tofu.

We Love Roasting It

For this recipe we cut the broccolini into 1-inch pieces and toss them with olive oil and salt. We spread carrot pieces on one side of the baking sheet and then pile the broccolini on the other half. Placing it in a pile prevents it from drying out and at the same time creates a textural contrast that is most appealing. What we love about roasting broccolini is that its delicate flowering ends turn wonderfully crispy, rendering them even more flavorful. After just about 15 minutes, it is perfectly cooked.

A Unique Flavor

Broccolini is frequently served as a side dish in Italian restaurants. It has a slightly peppery edge, a bit of grassiness (some call it a cross between spinach and asparagus), and a touch of bitterness. Its boldness means it needs little embellishment and so can be cooked simply, such as roasting it as we do here or pan-steaming it.

Bulgur with Vegetables and Marinated Tofu

top | *Shawarma-Spiced Tofu Wraps with Sumac Onions*
bottom | *Tofu Summer Rolls with Spicy Almond Butter Sauce*

Shawarma–Spiced Tofu Wraps with Sumac Onions

Serves 4 to 6 Total Time 1 hour, plus 1 hour marinating

Why This Recipe Works Crispy charred tofu fingers burst with bold spices and garlic in this satisfying and texturally varied vegetarian sandwich. The flavors of street cart Middle Eastern shawarma are the inspiration, and the dish includes a marinade to deeply season the tofu that relies on classic shawarma spices of sumac, fenugreek, paprika, cumin, and garlic. Lemon juice and honey provide well-rounded, complex flavor, the latter also delivering that impeccable caramelization. The intense heat of the broiler ably blooms the flavors, burnishing them on the crispy tofu. Tossing the finished tofu in some reserved marinade amplifies the smoky flavor. We wrap the tofu in warm, fluffy pita and then pile on some shawarma topping treats: tomatoes, sumac onions, pickles, and fresh herbs, plus a finishing drizzle of cooling, creamy tahini-yogurt sauce. The tofu fingers are delicate and may break while turning; this will not affect the final wraps. We really enjoy the sumac onions here; however, an equal amount of thinly sliced red onion can be substituted. Try using items in these wraps in other contexts; they're great on top of a salad or as a plated meal.

- 28 ounces firm or extra-firm tofu, cut crosswise into ½-inch-thick slabs then lengthwise into ½-inch-thick fingers
- ½ cup extra-virgin olive oil
- 6 garlic cloves, minced
- 1½ tablespoons ground sumac
- 1 tablespoon ground fenugreek
- 2 teaspoons smoked paprika
- 1½ teaspoons ground cumin
- 1 teaspoon table salt
- ¼ cup lemon juice (2 lemons)
- 3 tablespoons honey
- 4–6 (8-inch) pita, warmed
- 1 tomato, cored and chopped
- ½ cup chopped fresh parsley and/or mint
- ½ cup dill pickle slices
- ½ cup Sumac Onions (page 431)
- ½ cup Tahini-Yogurt Sauce (page 211)

1. Spread tofu over paper towel–lined baking sheet and let drain for 20 minutes. Gently pat dry with paper towels.

2. Microwave oil, garlic, sumac, fenugreek, paprika, cumin, and salt in medium bowl, stirring occasionally, until fragrant, 30 to 60 seconds. Whisk in lemon juice and honey until honey has dissolved. Measure out and reserve ¼ cup marinade. (Reserved marinade can be refrigerated for up to 24 hours; bring to room temperature and whisk to recombine before using.)

3. Arrange tofu in single layer on second rimmed baking sheet and spoon marinade evenly over top. Using your hands, gently turn tofu to coat with marinade. Cover and refrigerate for at least 1 hour or up to 24 hours.

4. Adjust oven rack 6 inches from broiler element and heat broiler. Line rimmed baking sheet with aluminum foil. Transfer tofu to prepared sheet and arrange in single layer, spaced evenly apart. Broil tofu until well browned on first side, 10 to 15 minutes, rotating sheet halfway through broiling. Gently flip tofu and continue to broil until well browned on second side, 10 to 15 minutes, rotating sheet halfway through broiling. Transfer tofu and reserved marinade to large bowl and gently toss to coat. Divide tofu evenly among pitas and top with tomato, parsley, pickles, sumac onions, and tahini sauce. Serve.

Sumac Onions

VEGAN Makes 2 cups Total Time 15 minutes, plus 1 hour marinating

These generously sized marinated onion slices are a robust sandwich or salad accompaniment. In addition to being dressed with lemon juice and red wine vinegar, the Middle Eastern condiment also gets a generous seasoning of puckery sumac. Olive oil and a little sugar and salt balance the flavors.

- 1 red onion, halved and sliced through root end into ¼-inch pieces
- 2 tablespoons lemon juice
- 2 tablespoons red wine vinegar
- 1 tablespoon extra-virgin olive oil
- 1 tablespoon ground sumac
- ½ teaspoon sugar
- ¼ teaspoon table salt

Combine all ingredients in bowl. Let sit, stirring occasionally, for 1 hour. (Onions can be refrigerated for up to 1 week).

Tofu Summer Rolls with Spicy Almond Butter Sauce

VEGAN Serves 4 Total Time 50 minutes, plus 1 hour marinating

Why This Recipe Works We love how the pleasantly chewy rice paper wrappers in Vietnamese gỏi cuốn, also known as summer rolls, give way to an ensemble of flavors: soft rice noodles, crisp vegetables, and here, tofu. We marinate strips of the tofu in rice vinegar, soy sauce, and sriracha. We also skip the noodles in favor of a rainbow of veggies: red cabbage, red bell pepper, cucumber, carrots, and basil. For dipping, we whisk up a sriracha-spiked almond butter sauce, a rich, thick condiment that clings to our rolls. Be sure to make one roll at a time to keep the wrappers moist and pliable. Different brands of rice paper wrappers may vary in the time it takes to soak and become pliable. For the nut butter, you can use a smooth or chunky variety.

Sauce

- 3 tablespoons almond or peanut butter
- 3 tablespoons water
- 1 tablespoon rice vinegar
- 1 tablespoon soy sauce
- 2 teaspoons grated fresh ginger
- 1 teaspoon sriracha
- 1 garlic clove, minced

Rolls

- 6 tablespoons unseasoned rice vinegar, divided
- 1 tablespoon soy sauce
- 2 teaspoons sriracha
- 2 scallions, sliced thin on bias
- 7 ounces extra-firm tofu, cut into 3-inch-long by ½-inch-thick strips
- ½ small head red cabbage, halved, cored, and sliced thin (3½ cups)
- 12 (8-inch) round rice paper wrappers
- 1 cup fresh basil leaves
- 1 red bell pepper, stemmed, seeded, and cut into 2-inch-long matchsticks
- ½ seedless English cucumber, cut into 3-inch matchsticks
- 2 carrots, peeled and shredded

1. **For the sauce** Whisk all ingredients in bowl until well combined; set aside until ready to serve.

2. For the rolls Whisk 2 tablespoons vinegar, soy sauce, sriracha, and scallions in shallow dish until well combined. Add tofu and let sit for 1 hour. Toss cabbage with remaining ¼ cup vinegar and let sit for 1 hour.

3. Drain cabbage in fine-mesh strainer, pressing gently with back of spatula to remove as much liquid as possible. Transfer to large plate and pat dry with paper towels.

4. Spread clean, damp dish towel on work surface. Fill 9-inch pie plate with 1 inch room-temperature water. Submerge 1 wrapper in water until just pliable, 10 seconds to 2 minutes; lay softened wrapper on towel. Scatter 3 basil leaves over wrapper. Arrange 5 matchsticks each of bell pepper and cucumber horizontally on wrapper, leaving 2-inch border at bottom. Top with 1 tablespoon carrots, then arrange 2 tablespoons cabbage on top of carrots. Place 1 strip tofu horizontally on top of vegetables, being sure to shake off excess marinade.

5. Fold bottom of wrapper over filling, pulling back on it firmly to tighten it around filling, then fold sides of wrapper in and continue to roll tightly into spring roll. Transfer to platter and cover with second damp dish towel.

6. Repeat with remaining wrappers and filling. Serve with reserved almond butter sauce. (Rolls are best eaten immediately but can be covered with a clean, damp dish towel and refrigerated for up to 4 hours.)

Mapo Tofu

VEGAN Serves 4 to 6 Total Time 1¼ hours

Why This Recipe Works Mapo tofu is a spicy Sichuan classic, traditionally containing minced or ground pork or beef. Our vegetarian rendition is equally bold in flavor, with a balanced spiciness and a complex sauce. We start with cubed soft tofu, poached gently in salted water to firm up the cubes and help them stay intact in the braise. For the sauce base, we use plenty of ginger and garlic along with four Sichuan pantry powerhouses: broad bean chili paste, fermented black beans, Sichuan chili powder, and Sichuan peppercorns. A small amount of finely chopped mushrooms brings umami depth. In place of the chili oil often called for, we use a generous amount of vegetable oil, extra Sichuan chili powder, and toasted sesame oil. We finish the dish with just the right amount of cornstarch to create a velvety texture. If you can't find Sichuan chili powder, an equal amount of gochugaru (Korean red pepper flakes) is a good substitute. In a pinch, use 2½ teaspoons ancho chile powder and ½ teaspoon cayenne pepper. If you can't find fermented black beans, you can use an equal amount of fermented black bean paste or sauce or 2 additional teaspoons of broad bean chili paste. Serve with white rice.

- 2 cups water
- ½ teaspoon table salt
- ½ ounce dried shiitake mushrooms
- 1 tablespoon Sichuan peppercorns
- 12 scallions
- 28 ounces soft tofu, cut into ½-inch pieces
- 9 garlic cloves, peeled
- 1 (3-inch) piece ginger, peeled and cut into ¼-inch rounds
- ⅓ cup broad bean chili paste
- 1 tablespoon fermented black beans
- ½ cup vegetable oil, divided
- 1 tablespoon Sichuan chili powder
- 4 ounces fresh shiitake mushrooms, stemmed, or oyster mushrooms, trimmed
- 2 tablespoons hoisin sauce
- 2 teaspoons toasted sesame oil
- 2 tablespoons soy sauce
- 1 tablespoon cornstarch

1. Microwave water, salt, and dried mushrooms in covered large bowl until steaming, about 1 minute. Let sit until softened, about 5 minutes. Drain mushrooms in fine-mesh strainer, reserving liquid; set aside soaked mushrooms and return liquid to large bowl.

2. Place peppercorns in small bowl and microwave until fragrant, 15 to 30 seconds. Let cool completely. Once cool, grind in spice grinder or mortar and pestle (you should have 1½ teaspoons).

3. Using side of chef's knife, lightly crush white parts of scallions, then cut scallions into 1-inch pieces. Place tofu and scallions in bowl with reserved mushroom liquid and microwave until steaming, 5 to 7 minutes. Let sit while preparing remaining ingredients.

4. Process garlic, ginger, chili paste, and black beans in food processor until coarse paste forms, 1 to 2 minutes, scraping down sides of bowl as needed. Add ¼ cup vegetable oil, chili powder, and 1 teaspoon peppercorns and continue to process until smooth paste forms, 1 to 2 minutes. Transfer spice paste to second bowl.

5. Place reserved soaked mushrooms and fresh shiitake mushrooms in now-empty processor and pulse until finely chopped, 15 to 20 pulses (do not overprocess). Heat 2 tablespoons vegetable oil and mushroom mixture in large saucepan over medium heat, breaking up mushrooms with wooden spoon, until mushrooms begin to brown and stick to bottom of saucepan, 5 to 7 minutes. Transfer mushroom mixture to third bowl.

6. Add remaining 2 tablespoons vegetable oil and spice paste to now-empty saucepan and cook, stirring frequently, until paste darkens and oil begins to separate from paste, 2 to 3 minutes. Gently pour tofu with mushroom liquid into saucepan, followed by hoisin, sesame oil, and mushroom mixture. Cook, gently stirring frequently, until dish comes to simmer, 2 to 3 minutes. Whisk soy sauce and cornstarch together in small bowl. Add cornstarch mixture to saucepan and continue to cook, stirring frequently, until thickened, 2 to 3 minutes. Transfer to serving dish, sprinkle with remaining peppercorns, and serve. (Mapo tofu can be refrigerated for up to 24 hours.)

Overstuffed Sweet Potatoes with Tofu and Red Curry Vinaigrette

VEGAN Serves 4 Total Time 1¼ hours

Why This Recipe Works This fresh take on stuffed potatoes takes its cue from the tangy and sweet flavors of Thai-style curries. All of the elements—rich, earthy sweet potato halves along with morsels of tofu, broccoli, mushrooms, and bell peppers—are roasted to perfection on a single baking sheet. To create extra-crispy tofu, we toss pieces of tofu with cornstarch, and then we arrange them on one side of an oiled baking sheet and place the sweet potato halves on the other side. (Halving the sweet potatoes reduces the roasting time from an hour for whole potatoes to a mere 20 minutes.) Once the potatoes are done, we add the other vegetables to the space left on the baking sheet and roast them until tender in the time it takes to finish the crispy tofu. After stuffing the potatoes with the tofu and vegetables, we drizzle them with a curry vinaigrette packed with the bold flavors of lime and curry paste. Do not substitute soft tofu here. If you can't find Thai basil, you can substitute Italian basil. Green and red curry paste work equally well here.

top *Mapo Tofu*

bottom *Overstuffed Sweet Potatoes with Tofu and Red Curry Vinaigrette*

- 14 ounces firm tofu, cut into ¾-inch pieces
- ½ cup plus 1 teaspoon vegetable oil, divided
- 1 teaspoon table salt, divided
- ½ teaspoon pepper, divided
- 6 tablespoons cornstarch
- 2 sweet potatoes (12 ounces each), unpeeled, halved lengthwise
- 8 ounces broccoli florets, cut into ½-inch pieces
- 8 ounces white or cremini mushrooms, trimmed and quartered
- 1 red bell pepper, stemmed, seeded, and cut into ¼-inch-wide strips
- 1 teaspoon grated lime zest plus 2 tablespoons juice
- 2 teaspoons Thai green or red curry paste
- ¼ cup shredded fresh Thai basil

1. Spread tofu over paper towel–lined plate and let drain for 20 minutes. Adjust oven rack to lower-middle position and heat oven to 450 degrees. Brush rimmed baking sheet with 3 tablespoons oil.

2. Gently pat tofu dry with paper towels, sprinkle with ½ teaspoon salt and ¼ teaspoon pepper, then toss with cornstarch in bowl. Arrange tofu in even layer on half of sheet. Arrange potato halves cut side down on other half of sheet and brush skins with 1 teaspoon oil. Roast until potato halves yield to gentle pressure and centers register 200 degrees, 20 to 25 minutes, flipping tofu with spatula halfway through roasting.

3. Toss broccoli, mushrooms, and bell pepper with 1 tablespoon oil, ¼ teaspoon salt, and ⅛ teaspoon pepper in bowl. Remove sheet from oven, transfer potato halves to plate, and cover with aluminum foil to keep warm. Arrange broccoli mixture in even layer on now-empty side of sheet and roast until vegetables are tender and beginning to brown and tofu is crisp and lightly browned, 10 to 15 minutes, tossing vegetables and flipping tofu halfway through roasting.

4. Whisk lime zest and juice, curry paste, remaining ¼ cup oil, remaining ¼ teaspoon salt, and remaining ⅛ teaspoon pepper together in bowl. Arrange potato halves cut side up on individual serving plates, top with tofu and vegetable mixture, drizzle with vinaigrette, and sprinkle with basil. Serve.

Tofu and Chickpea Flour Frittata with Mushrooms

VEGAN Serves 6 to 8 Total Time 1¼ hours

Why This Recipe Works Simpler and more substantial than omelets and less fussy than quiche, frittatas—in this case minus the eggs and filled with vegetables and tofu—are a favorite. Silken tofu is too wet to use here, but firm tofu becomes perfectly smooth and "eggy" after a few seconds in a food processor. For additional structure to balance the frittata's softness, we add some chickpea flour, which also heightens the savory flavor profile. Turmeric gives the frittata a pleasing color, and garlic powder provides umami flavor depth. After sautéing mushrooms and aromatics until deeply caramelized, we stir the tofu puree into the vegetables and bake the frittata until it's golden and set throughout. Given a 5-minute rest in the pan, the frittata slides right out and slices into neat wedges. Do not use silken, soft, or extra-firm tofu in this recipe. You will need a 12-inch ovensafe nonstick skillet for this recipe.

- 28 ounces firm tofu
- 3 tablespoons extra-virgin olive oil, divided
- 1¼ teaspoons table salt, divided
- ½ teaspoon ground turmeric
- ½ teaspoon garlic powder
- ⅛ teaspoon pepper
- ¼ cup chickpea flour
- 8 ounces cremini mushrooms, trimmed and sliced thin
- 2 shallots, minced
- 1 garlic clove, minced
- 1 teaspoon minced fresh thyme
- 1 tablespoon minced fresh parsley

1. Spread tofu over paper towel–lined baking sheet and let drain for 20 minutes. Adjust oven rack to middle position and heat oven to 350 degrees. Process tofu, 1 tablespoon oil, 1 teaspoon salt, turmeric, garlic powder, and pepper in food processor until smooth, about 30 seconds, scraping down sides of bowl as needed. Add chickpea flour and process until well combined, about 15 seconds.

2. Heat remaining 2 tablespoons oil in 12-inch ovensafe nonstick skillet over medium-high heat until shimmering. Add mushrooms and remaining ¼ teaspoon salt and cook until mushrooms have released their liquid and are beginning to brown, 5 to 7 minutes. Stir in shallots and cook until mushrooms are well browned, 5 to 7 minutes. Stir in garlic and thyme and cook until fragrant, about 30 seconds.

3. Off heat, stir in tofu mixture and spread into even layer. Transfer skillet to oven and bake until center is set and surface is slightly puffed, dry, and lightly golden, 30 to 35 minutes, rotating skillet halfway through baking.

4. Using pot holder, remove skillet from oven and let frittata sit for 5 minutes. Being careful of hot skillet handle, use spatula to loosen frittata from skillet and slide onto cutting board. Sprinkle with parsley, cut into wedges, and serve.

Grilled Tofu with Vegetable Skewers

VEGAN Serves 4 Total Time 50 minutes

Why This Recipe Works For a supersavory grilled vegetable and tofu entrée, we cut the tofu into planks so that they would hold their shape when grilled. A potent sauce of umami-rich soy sauce, Worcestershire sauce, Dijon mustard, garlic, and balsamic vinegar does double duty here, with part of it dressing the vegetables (bell peppers, onion, and mushrooms), which we parcook in the microwave; drizzling the tofu with the remaining sauce after grilling (instead of marinating it beforehand) prevents it from sticking to the grill. Be sure to thoroughly oil the grill grate so that the tofu doesn't stick. You will need four 12-inch skewers for this recipe. Serve with rice or quinoa, if desired.

- 28 ounces firm or extra-firm tofu, sliced lengthwise into 1-inch-thick planks
- 2 red bell peppers, seeded and cut into 1½-inch pieces
- 1 red onion, cut into 1½-inch pieces
- 10 ounces cremini mushrooms, stemmed
- 5 tablespoons extra-virgin olive oil, divided
- ¼ cup soy sauce
- 2 tablespoons vegetarian Worcestershire sauce
- 1 tablespoon Dijon mustard
- 3 garlic cloves, minced
- 2 teaspoons balsamic vinegar
- ½ teaspoon table salt

1. Spread tofu over paper towel–lined baking sheet and let drain for 20 minutes. Gently pat dry with paper towels. Place bell peppers, onion, and mushrooms in large microwave-safe bowl. Whisk 3 tablespoons oil, soy sauce, Worcestershire, mustard, garlic, and vinegar together in second bowl; transfer ⅓ cup marinade to bowl with vegetables. Cover and microwave until onion is translucent at edges, 3 to 6 minutes, shaking bowl to redistribute vegetables halfway through microwaving. Let cool slightly.

top | *Tofu and Chickpea Flour Frittata with Mushrooms*
bottom | *Grilled Tofu with Vegetable Skewers*

2. Thread vegetables evenly onto four 12-inch skewers. Brush with remaining 2 tablespoons oil and sprinkle with salt.

3A. **For a charcoal grill** Open bottom vent completely. Light large chimney starter filled with charcoal briquettes (6 quarts). When top coals are partially covered with ash, pour evenly over grill. Set cooking grate in place, cover, and open lid vent completely. Heat grill until hot, about 5 minutes.

3B. **For a gas grill** Turn all burners to high; cover; and heat grill until hot, about 15 minutes. Leave all burners on high.

4. Clean cooking grate, then repeatedly brush grate with well-oiled paper towels until grate is black and glossy, 5 to 10 times. Place kebabs and tofu on grill. Cook (covered if using gas), flipping as needed, until tofu is well browned and vegetables are tender, 10 to 14 minutes. Transfer to platter and drizzle tofu with remaining marinade, turning tofu to coat. Serve.

Crispy Tempeh

FAST **VEGAN** Makes 1 cup Total Time 45 minutes

A two-step method—boiling in soy sauce–seasoned water followed by frying—turns typically bland and slightly bitter tempeh into a crunchy umami bomb that is great sprinkled on grain bowls or salads.

- 3 tablespoons soy sauce
- 8 ounces tempeh, crumbled into ¼-inch pieces
- 1 cup peanut or vegetable oil for frying

1. Bring 4 cups water and soy sauce to boil in large saucepan. Add tempeh, return to boil, and cook for 10 minutes. Drain tempeh well and wipe saucepan dry with paper towels.

2. Set wire rack in rimmed baking sheet and line with triple layer paper towels. Heat oil in now-empty dry saucepan over medium-high heat until shimmering. Add tempeh and cook until golden brown and crisp, about 12 minutes, adjusting heat as needed if tempeh begins to scorch. Using spider skimmer or slotted spoon, transfer tempeh to prepared sheet to drain, then season with salt and pepper to taste. Serve immediately.

Crispy Tempeh with Sambal Sauce

FAST **VEGAN** Serves 4 Total Time 40 minutes

Why This Recipe Works Sambals are hugely popular throughout Indonesia. These condiment sauces, which can be served cooked or raw, are typically made from chiles and aromatics such as onion, fresh herbs, and spices. Here, a mouth-warming but not exceedingly hot sambal makes an intensely flavorful sauce for coating cubes of tempeh. We quickly combine all the sambal ingredients in a food processor, stopping when the mixture reaches a pleasingly coarse texture. We then fry the tempeh until it is golden brown and slightly crispy on the outside but still rather firm on the inside. We use a small portion of the remaining oil from frying the tempeh to cook the sambal, which partially tames the heat of the Fresno chiles and renders the onion and garlic tender and sweet. Then, it is just a matter of tossing the crispy tempeh in the sambal sauce and stirring in plenty of fresh basil. Lemon basil is traditional in Indonesia, but Thai and Italian basil are both excellent substitutes. If you can't find kecap manis, a thick, sweet soy sauce used in Indonesia, you can substitute a combination of 1½ tablespoons dark brown sugar and 1 teaspoon soy sauce. Serve with rice.

- 12 ounces Fresno chiles, stemmed, seeded, and chopped coarse
- 1 small onion, chopped coarse
- 5 garlic cloves, peeled
- ¼ teaspoon table salt
- 1 cup vegetable oil for frying
- 1 pound tempeh, cut into ½-inch pieces
- ½ cup water
- 2 tablespoons kecap manis
- 1½ cups fresh Thai basil leaves

1. Process chiles, onion, garlic, and salt in food processor until finely chopped, about 30 seconds, scraping down sides of bowl as needed; transfer to bowl.

2. Adjust oven rack to middle position and heat oven to 200 degrees. Set wire rack in rimmed baking sheet and line rack with triple layer of paper towels. Heat oil in 14-inch flat-bottomed wok or 12-inch nonstick skillet over medium-high heat to 375 degrees. Carefully add half of tempeh to hot oil and increase heat to high. Cook, turning as needed, until golden brown, 3 to 5 minutes. Adjust burner, if necessary, to maintain oil temperature between 350 and 375 degrees. Off heat, using slotted spoon, transfer tempeh to prepared rack

and keep warm in oven. Return oil to 375 degrees over medium-high heat and repeat with remaining tempeh; transfer to rack.

3. Carefully pour off all but 2 tablespoons oil from wok. Add chile mixture to oil left in wok and cook over medium-high heat, tossing slowly but constantly, until darkened in color and completely dry, 7 to 10 minutes. Off heat, stir in water and kecap manis until combined. Add tempeh and basil and toss until well coated. Serve.

Seared Tempeh with Tomato Jam

Serves 4 Total Time 1 hour plus 2 hours marinating and cooling

Why This Recipe Works Tempeh, like tofu, is excellent at absorbing flavors, so in this recipe we cut it into slabs, marinate them, and then sear them in a skillet. Marinating the tempeh in a seasoned vinegar-and-water base infuses it with flavor. And patting the marinated tempeh dry and pan-searing it creates a delectably crisp edge and a cohesive interior texture. The bright tomato jam made with warm spice notes from the fresh ginger and ras el hanout balances the tempeh's earthy flavor. Serve alongside something verdant, such as green beans or sautéed spinach.

- 1 pound tomatoes, cored and cut into ½-inch pieces
- 2 tablespoons honey
- ½ cup plus 2 tablespoons red wine vinegar, divided
- 7 garlic cloves, minced, divided
- 1 tablespoon grated fresh ginger
- 1 teaspoon Ras el Hanout (page 439)
- ½ teaspoon ground dried Aleppo pepper, divided
- ¼ cup water
- 1 teaspoon dried oregano
- ½ teaspoon table salt
- 1 pound tempeh, cut crosswise into 4 even pieces, each piece halved horizontally into ¼-inch slabs and slabs cut into triangles
- 3 tablespoons extra-virgin olive oil
- 2 tablespoons chopped fresh cilantro

1. Combine tomatoes, honey, 6 tablespoons vinegar, half of garlic, ginger, ras el hanout, and ¼ teaspoon Aleppo pepper in 12-inch nonstick skillet. Bring to boil over medium-high heat, then reduce to simmer and cook, stirring often, until tomatoes have broken down and begun to thicken, 15 to 20 minutes.

Seared Tempeh with Tomato Jam

Pan-Seared Tempeh Steaks with Chimichurri Sauce

2. Mash jam with potato masher to even consistency. Continue to cook until mixture has thickened and darkened in color, 5 to 10 minutes. Let jam cool completely, about 1 hour. Season with salt and pepper to taste; set aside. (Jam can be refrigerated for up to 4 days; bring to room temperature before serving.) Meanwhile, whisk water, oregano, salt, remaining ¼ cup vinegar, remaining garlic, and remaining ¼ teaspoon Aleppo pepper together in bowl. Transfer marinade to 1-gallon zipper-lock bag. Add tempeh, press out air, seal, and toss gently to coat. Refrigerate tempeh for at least 1 hour or up to 24 hours, flipping bag occasionally.

3. Remove tempeh from marinade and pat dry with paper towels. Heat oil in 12-inch nonstick skillet over medium heat until shimmering. Add 8 pieces tempeh and cook until golden brown on first side, 2 to 4 minutes. Flip tempeh, reduce heat to medium-low, and continue to cook until golden brown on second side, 2 to 4 minutes. Transfer to serving platter and tent with aluminum foil to keep warm. Repeat with remaining tempeh. Serve tempeh steaks with tomato jam, sprinkling individual portions with cilantro.

Ras el Hanout

FAST **VEGAN** Makes ½ cup Total Time 15 minutes

If you can't find Aleppo pepper, you can substitute ½ teaspoon paprika and ½ teaspoon red pepper flakes.

- 16 cardamom pods
- 4 teaspoons coriander seeds
- 4 teaspoons cumin seeds
- 2 teaspoons anise seeds
- ½ teaspoon allspice berries
- ¼ teaspoon black peppercorns
- 4 teaspoons ground ginger
- 2 teaspoons ground nutmeg
- 2 teaspoons ground dried Aleppo pepper
- 2 teaspoons ground cinnamon

1. Toast cardamom, coriander, cumin, anise, allspice, and peppercorns in small skillet over medium heat until fragrant, shaking skillet occasionally to prevent scorching, about 2 minutes. Let cool completely.

2. Transfer toasted spices, ginger, nutmeg, Aleppo pepper, and cinnamon to spice grinder and process to fine powder. (Ras el hanout can be stored at room temperature for up to 1 year.)

Pan-Seared Tempeh Steaks with Chimichurri Sauce

VEGAN Serves 4 Total Time 35 minutes plus 1 hour marinating

Why This Recipe Works The earthy flavor of tempeh really shines when it is paired with a bright sauce. Here we use a classic chimichurri sauce combining parsley, wine vinegar, oil, lots of garlic, oregano, and a good dose of red pepper flakes. Marinating the tempeh in a seasoned vinegar-and-water base infuses it with flavor. Patting the marinated tempeh dry and pan-searing it creates a delectably crisp edge and helps the interior hold together.

- 5 tablespoons red wine vinegar, divided
- ¼ cup water
- 4 garlic cloves, minced, divided
- 1½ teaspoons dried oregano, divided
- ½ teaspoon red pepper flakes, divided
- 1 pound tempeh, cut into 3½-inch-long by ⅜-inch-thick slabs
- 1 cup fresh parsley leaves
- ½ cup extra-virgin olive oil, divided
- ½ teaspoon table salt

1. Combine ¼ cup vinegar, water, half of garlic, 1 teaspoon oregano, and ¼ teaspoon pepper flakes in 1-gallon zipper-lock bag. Add tempeh, press out air, seal, and toss to coat. Refrigerate tempeh for at least 1 hour or up to 24 hours, flipping bag occasionally.

2. Pulse parsley, ¼ cup oil, salt, remaining 1 tablespoon vinegar, remaining garlic, remaining ½ teaspoon oregano, and remaining ¼ teaspoon pepper flakes in food processor until coarsely chopped, about 10 pulses, scraping down sides of bowl as needed. Transfer to bowl and season with salt and pepper to taste.

3. Remove tempeh from marinade and pat dry with paper towels. Heat 2 tablespoons oil in 12-inch nonstick skillet over medium heat until shimmering. Add 4 pieces tempeh and cook until golden brown on first side, 2 to 4 minutes.

4. Flip tempeh, reduce heat to medium-low, and continue to cook until golden brown on second side, 2 to 4 minutes; transfer to platter. Wipe out skillet with paper towels and repeat with remaining 2 tablespoons oil and remaining tempeh. Serve with parsley sauce.

top | *Stir-Fried Tempeh, Napa Cabbage, and Carrots*
bottom | *Stir-Fried Tempeh with Orange Sauce*

Stir-Fried Tempeh, Napa Cabbage, and Carrots

FAST **VEGAN** Serves 4 Total Time 45 minutes

Why This Recipe Works This stir-fry delivers golden-brown tempeh; caramelized carrots; and crisp, fresh cabbage in a lustrous, tangy-sweet sauce. First, we sear the tempeh it in a hot skillet with soy sauce to give it a flavor boost and a crisp brown crust. Carrots add a sweet element and crunch, and we crank the heat to high for good caramelization. Since napa cabbage can go from tender-crisp to limp and watery in a matter of seconds, we cook it just until it achieves a little browning and heats throughout. We pair these ingredients with a full-bodied sweet-sour orange sauce made with equal amounts of vinegar, sugar, and orange juice with ketchup for additional zinginess. Serve over rice.

Sauce

- 6 tablespoons red wine vinegar
- 6 tablespoons orange juice
- 6 tablespoons sugar
- 3 tablespoons ketchup
- 1 teaspoon cornstarch
- ½ teaspoon salt

Stir-Fry

- 3 tablespoons vegetable oil, divided
- 4 scallions, white and green parts separated and sliced thin on bias
- 3 garlic cloves, minced
- 1 tablespoon grated fresh ginger
- ½ teaspoon red pepper flakes
- 12 ounces tempeh, cut into ½-inch pieces
- 2 tablespoons soy sauce
- 3 carrots, peeled and sliced on bias ¼ inch thick
- ½ head napa cabbage (about 1 pound), cored and cut into 1½-inch pieces

1. **For the sauce** Whisk all ingredients together in bowl.

2. **For the stir-fry** Combine 1 teaspoon oil, scallion whites, garlic, ginger, and pepper flakes in bowl. Heat 2 tablespoons oil in 14-inch flat-bottomed wok or 12-inch nonstick skillet over high heat until just smoking. Add tempeh and soy sauce, and cook, stirring occasionally, until well browned, 4 to 6 minutes; transfer to plate.

3. Heat remaining 2 teaspoons oil in now-empty wok over high heat until shimmering. Add carrots and cook, stirring occasionally, until spotty brown, about 4 minutes. Stir in cabbage and cook until vegetables are crisp-tender, about 4 minutes.

4. Push vegetables to sides of pan. Add garlic mixture to center and cook, mashing mixture into pan, until fragrant, about 30 seconds. Stir garlic mixture into vegetables. Add browned tempeh and stir to combine. Whisk sauce to recombine, then add to wok and cook, stirring constantly, until sauce is thickened, about 2 minutes. Transfer to platter, sprinkle with scallion greens, and serve.

Stir-Fried Tempeh with Orange Sauce

FAST **VEGAN** Serves 4 Total Time 35 minutes

Why This Recipe Works The sauce for this stir-fried tempeh is bursting with flavor thanks to a great lineup of ingredients that includes orange juice and zest, which tames the slightly bitter flavor of the tempeh. First, we sear the tempeh with soy sauce to give it an umami flavor boost and a crisp brown crust. Red bell pepper adds sweetness and crunch. Broccoli florets also stand up well to the quick, high heat, adding their vegetal essence and bright color. Serve with rice and garnish with toasted sesame seeds.

Sauce

- ¼ cup Shaoxing wine or dry sherry
- ¼ cup water
- 2 tablespoons soy sauce
- 1 tablespoon cornstarch
- 1 tablespoon grated fresh ginger
- 3 garlic cloves, minced
- 1½ teaspoons toasted sesame oil
- ¼ teaspoon grated orange zest, plus ¾ cup juice (2 oranges)

Stir-Fry

- 2 tablespoons vegetable oil, divided
- 12 ounces tempeh, cut into ½-inch pieces
- 2 tablespoons soy sauce
- 1 pound broccoli, florets cut into ½-inch pieces, stalks peeled, halved, and sliced thin
- 1 red bell pepper, stemmed, seeded, and cut into ¼-inch-wide strips
- 6 scallions, sliced thin on bias

1. **For the sauce** Whisk all ingredients together in bowl.

2. **For the stir-fry** Heat 1 tablespoon oil in 14-inch flat-bottomed wok or 12-inch nonstick skillet over high heat until just smoking. Add tempeh and soy sauce, and cook, stirring occasionally, until well browned, 4 to 6 minutes; transfer to plate.

3. Return now-empty pan to high heat, add remaining 1 tablespoon oil, and heat until just smoking. Add broccoli and bell pepper, and cook, stirring occasionally, until vegetables are spotty brown and crisp-tender, about 4 minutes.

4. Stir in browned tempeh. Whisk sauce to recombine, then add to wok and cook, stirring constantly, until sauce is thickened, about 30 seconds. Off heat, sprinkle with scallions and serve.

Sweet Potato Red Flannel Hash with Tempeh

Serves 4 Total Time 50 minutes

Why This Recipe Works Red flannel hash gets its name from the deep red beets scattered throughout, reminiscent of the check on a flannel plaid. This version features tempeh instead of eggs and sweet potato in addition to the classic combination of beets and russet potatoes for a dish that is true weekend comfort food. We season and brown tempeh cubes to provide a satisfyingly hearty bite and a savory flavor. To make the process speedy, we parcook the vegetables in the microwave until tender and then move them to the skillet to brown and crisp, rounding out the flavors with onion, garlic, and thyme and stirring in some cream for richness and binding. As for the tempeh, cooking it along with the vegetables keeps the hash from cohering. Instead, we sear the tempeh separately, build the hash, and then scatter the cubes over the top along with a handful of scallions. The hash stays together, and the salty richness of the tempeh perfectly balances the sweet vegetables underneath for a hearty, colorful meal.

- 1 russet potato (8 ounces), peeled and cut into ½-inch pieces
- 1 small sweet potato (8 ounces), peeled and cut into ½-inch pieces
- 8 ounces beets, peeled and cut into ½-inch pieces
- ¼ cup vegetable oil, divided
- ¾ teaspoon table salt, divided
- ¾ teaspoon pepper, divided
- 8 ounces tempeh, cut into ½-inch pieces
- 1 tablespoon soy sauce
- 1 onion, chopped fine
- 2 garlic cloves, minced
- ½ teaspoon minced fresh thyme or ¼ teaspoon dried
- ⅓ cup heavy cream
- 2 scallions, sliced thin

1. Combine russet potato, sweet potato, beets, 1 tablespoon oil, ½ teaspoon salt, and ½ teaspoon pepper in bowl. Microwave, covered, stirring occasionally, until russet potato is translucent around edges and sweet potato and beets are fork-tender, 8 to 10 minutes.

2. Meanwhile, heat 1 tablespoon oil in 12-inch nonstick skillet over medium-high heat until just smoking. Add tempeh, soy sauce, remaining ¼ teaspoon salt, and remaining ¼ teaspoon pepper and cook, stirring occasionally, until well browned, 4 to 6 minutes. Transfer to bowl and cover with foil.

3. Heat remaining 2 tablespoons oil in now-empty skillet over medium-high heat until shimmering. Add onion and cook until softened, about 5 minutes. Stir in garlic and thyme and cook until fragrant, about 30 seconds.

4. Stir in microwaved vegetables and any accumulated juices and cream. Using back of spatula, firmly pack vegetables into skillet and cook undisturbed for 2 minutes. Flip hash, 1 portion at a time, and repack into pan. Repeat flipping process every few minutes until vegetables are nicely browned, 6 to 8 minutes. Top with reserved tempeh, sprinkle with scallions, and serve.

Loaded Sweet Potato Wedges with Tempeh

VEGAN Serves 4 Total Time 55 minutes

Why This Recipe Works Sturdy, caramelized wedges of sweet potatoes make a satisfyingly starchy base for a filling meal. To further amp up the satiation factor, we pair the hearty root vegetable with crisp crumbles of equally hearty tempeh. While the sweet potatoes roast in the oven, we brown ground tempeh on the stovetop, seasoning it with a quartet of spices: cumin, coriander, paprika, and cinnamon. After topping the potato wedges with the tempeh mixture, we load them with vegetables—sweet cherry tomatoes, crisp radishes, spicy jalapeño, and fresh cilantro. A quick avocado-yogurt sauce brightens up the dish. You can also serve it with Quick Sweet-and-Spicy Pickled Red Onion (page 213). To make this recipe vegan, substitute plant-based yogurt for the dairy yogurt.

- 1 ripe avocado, halved, pitted, and cut into ½-inch pieces
- ¼ cup plain yogurt, plus extra for serving
- 1 teaspoon lime juice, plus wedges for serving
- 1½ teaspoons ground cumin, divided
- ⅛ teaspoon plus ¾ teaspoon table salt, divided
- ⅛ teaspoon pepper
- 2 pounds sweet potatoes, unpeeled, cut lengthwise into 2-inch-wide wedges
- 5 tablespoons extra-virgin olive oil, divided
- 8 ounces tempeh, crumbled into pea-size pieces
- 1 teaspoon ground coriander
- 1 teaspoon smoked paprika
- ⅛ teaspoon ground cinnamon
- 4 ounces cherry tomatoes, halved
- 4 radishes, trimmed, halved, and sliced thin
- 1 jalapeño, stemmed and sliced into thin rings
- ¾ cup chopped fresh cilantro
- 3 scallions, sliced thin

1. Using sturdy whisk, mash and stir avocado, yogurt, lime juice, ½ teaspoon cumin, ⅛ teaspoon salt, and pepper together in bowl until as smooth as possible. Season with salt and pepper to taste and set aside until ready to serve.

2. Adjust oven rack to middle position and heat oven to 450 degrees. Line rimmed baking sheet with aluminum foil and spray with vegetable oil spray. Toss potatoes with 1 tablespoon oil and ½ teaspoon salt in bowl, then arrange potato wedges, cut sides down, in single layer on prepared sheet. Roast until tender and sides in contact with sheet are well browned, about 30 minutes.

3. Meanwhile, heat remaining ¼ cup oil in 12-inch skillet over medium heat until shimmering. Add tempeh, coriander, paprika, cinnamon, remaining 1 teaspoon cumin, and remaining ¼ teaspoon salt and cook until well browned, 8 to 12 minutes, stirring often; set aside until ready to serve.

4. Transfer sweet potatoes to platter or individual serving plates and top with crispy tempeh, cherry tomatoes, radishes, jalapeño, cilantro, and scallions. Serve with reserved avocado sauce, extra yogurt, and lime wedges.

Tempeh Tacos

FAST **VEGAN** Serves 4 to 6 Total Time 30 minutes

Why This Recipe Works Much more than just a stand-in for more traditional beef or chicken versions, these tempeh tacos have their own nutty flavor and tender but firm texture. Chili powder and dried oregano add the right depth without overpowering the tempeh. To make their flavor fuller and rounder, we bloom the spices briefly in hot oil. For a light sauce to carry the flavors of the spices and keep the filling cohesive, we use a combination of tomato sauce and vegetable broth. To give the sauce sweet-and-sour balance, we add brown sugar and lime juice.

- 1 tablespoon vegetable oil
- 1 onion, chopped fine
- 3 tablespoons chili powder
- 4 garlic cloves, minced
- 1 teaspoon dried oregano
- 1 pound tempeh, crumbled into ¼-inch pieces
- 1 (8-ounce) can tomato sauce
- 1 cup vegetable broth
- 1 teaspoon packed brown sugar
- 2 tablespoons minced fresh cilantro
- 1 tablespoon lime juice
- 12 taco shells, warmed

1. Heat oil in 12-inch skillet over medium heat until shimmering. Add onion and cook until softened, about 5 minutes. Stir in chili powder, garlic, and oregano and cook until fragrant, about 30 seconds. Stir in tempeh and cook until lightly browned, about 5 minutes.

2. Stir in tomato sauce, broth, and sugar and simmer until thickened, about 2 minutes. Off heat, stir in cilantro and lime juice and season with salt and pepper to taste. Serve with taco shells.

Making Taco Shells

In 8-inch skillet, heat ¾ cup vegetable oil to 350 degrees. Using tongs, slip half of corn tortilla into hot oil and submerge it with metal spatula. Fry until just set but not brown, about 30 seconds. Flip tortilla. Hold tortilla open about 2 inches while keeping bottom submerged in oil. Fry until golden brown, about 1½ minutes. Flip again and fry other side until golden brown. Transfer shell, upside down, to paper towel–lined baking sheet to drain. Repeat with remaining tortillas, keeping oil temperature between 350 and 375 degrees. For best results, use homemade taco shells immediately.

Tempeh Tacos

Tempeh Reubens

Tempeh Reubens

VEGAN Serves 4 Total Time 1 hour

Why This Recipe Works This clever recipe uses hearty tempeh instead of corned beef for a vegetarian reuben with all the fixings. We "corn" the tempeh in just a 10-minute simmer in a traditional corning brine, which imparts the distinctive flavor without making the tempeh too salty. Then, we brown the tempeh in a skillet to give it a nice crust. To make a quick Russian dressing, we mix prepared cocktail sauce with creamy mayonnaise, crunchy pickles, and some tart pickle juice. The result is a dressing with great flavor and a satisfying crunch. We top the sandwiches with sauerkraut and Swiss cheese and toast them in a skillet until the cheese is melted and the bread is crisp and golden brown. You can make homemade Sauerkraut (page 446) or use store-bought. To make this recipe vegan, substitute plant-based mayo for the dairy mayonnaise.

- 10 tablespoons cider vinegar, divided
- ½ cup water
- 2 teaspoons ground allspice
- 1½ teaspoons table salt
- 1 teaspoon black peppercorns, cracked
- 1 teaspoon dried thyme
- 1 teaspoon paprika
- 1 pound tempeh, cut into 3½-inch-long by ⅜-inch-thick slabs
- 1 cup sauerkraut, drained and rinsed
- 1 teaspoon packed brown sugar
- ¼ cup vegetable oil, divided
- ¼ cup mayonnaise
- ¼ cup finely chopped sweet pickles plus 1 teaspoon pickle brine
- 2 tablespoons cocktail sauce
- 4 tablespoons unsalted butter, melted
- 8 slices hearty rye bread
- 4 ounces Swiss cheese, shredded (1 cup)

1. Combine ½ cup vinegar, water, allspice, salt, peppercorns, thyme, and paprika in large saucepan and bring to simmer over medium heat. Add tempeh, cover, reduce heat to medium-low, and simmer until liquid is mostly absorbed, 10 to 15 minutes, turning tempeh halfway through cooking. Transfer tempeh to plate and let cool for 10 minutes.

2. Meanwhile, cook sauerkraut, remaining 2 tablespoons vinegar, and sugar in 12-inch nonstick skillet over medium-high heat, stirring occasionally, until liquid evaporates, about 3 minutes; transfer to bowl. Wipe out skillet with paper towels.

3. Heat 2 tablespoons oil in now-empty skillet over medium heat until shimmering. Add 4 pieces tempeh and cook until golden brown on first side, 2 to 4 minutes. Flip tempeh, reduce heat to medium-low, and continue to cook until golden brown on second side, 2 to 4 minutes; transfer to clean plate. Wipe out skillet with paper towels and repeat with remaining 2 tablespoons oil and remaining tempeh. Wipe out skillet with paper towels.

4. Whisk mayonnaise, pickles and brine, and cocktail sauce together in bowl. Brush melted butter evenly over 1 side of each slice of bread. Flip bread over and spread mayonnaise mixture evenly over second side. Assemble 4 sandwiches by layering ingredients as follows between prepared bread (with mayonnaise mixture inside sandwich): half of Swiss, tempeh, sauerkraut, remaining Swiss. Press gently on sandwiches to set.

5. Heat now-empty skillet over medium-low heat for 2 minutes. Place 2 sandwiches in pan and cook until golden brown on first side, about 2 minutes. Flip sandwiches, cover skillet and cook until second side is golden brown and cheese is melted, about 2 minutes. Transfer sandwiches to serving platter. Wipe out skillet with paper towels and cook remaining 2 sandwiches. Serve.

Making Tempeh Reubens

1. After simmering tempeh in flavorful liquid, brown it in now-empty skillet. Flip it when first side is golden brown, lower the heat, and cook until second side browns.

2. To assemble reubens, layer Swiss, tempeh, sauerkraut, and remaining Swiss between prepared bread. Cook first side until golden brown. Flip, cover skillet, and brown second side.

Sauerkraut

VEGAN Makes 6 cups Total Time 30 minutes, plus 6 days fermenting

To help the cabbage stay submerged, we place a bag of brine on top to weigh it down. We use brine (rather than water) because if the bag breaks it won't ruin the careful balance of salinity inside the jar. For a balanced flavor, we prefer fermenting at a cool room temperature of 65 degrees (consider locations such as a basement, den, or cabinet in an air-conditioned room). We don't recommend fermenting above 70 degrees as the flavor suffers, and above 75 degrees food safety becomes a concern. You will need cheesecloth for this recipe.

- 1 head green cabbage (2½ pounds), quartered, cored, and shredded
- 2 tablespoons pickling and canning salt
- 1½ teaspoons juniper berries
- 2 cups water

1. Cut out parchment paper round to match diameter of ½-gallon glass or ceramic container. Toss cabbage with 4 teaspoons salt in large bowl. Using your hands, forcefully knead salt into cabbage until it has softened and begins to release moisture, about 3 minutes. Stir in juniper berries.

2. Tightly pack cabbage mixture and any accumulated liquid in jar, pressing down firmly with your fist to eliminate air pockets as you pack. Press parchment round flush against surface of cabbage.

3. Dissolve remaining 2 teaspoons salt in water and transfer to 1-quart zipper-lock bag; squeeze out air and seal bag well. Place bag of brine on top of parchment and gently press down. Cover jar with triple layer of cheesecloth and secure with rubber band.

4. Place jar in cool location (50 to 70 degrees; do not expose cabbage to temperatures above 70 degrees) away from direct sunlight and let ferment for 6 days; check jar daily, skimming residue and mold from surface and pressing to keep cabbage submerged. After 6 days, taste sauerkraut daily until it has reached desired flavor (this may take up to 7 days longer; sauerkraut should be pale and translucent with a tart and floral flavor).

5. When sauerkraut has reached desired flavor, remove cheesecloth, bag of brine, and parchment and skim off any residue or mold. Serve. (Sauerkraut and accumulated juices can be transferred to clean jar, covered, and refrigerated for up to 2 months; once refrigerated, flavor of sauerkraut will continue to mature.)

Korean Barbecue Tempeh Wraps

VEGAN Serves 4 Total Time 50 minutes

Why This Recipe Work These tempeh wraps deliver all the bold flavors and sweet, sticky sauce that make Korean barbecue so sought after. To give the tempeh a flavorful browned crust, we sear it in a skillet before tossing it with the barbecue sauce. To make the Korean-style sauce, we use a combination of soy sauce, sugar, and spicy sriracha. Adding some cornstarch and simmering the sauce for 5 minutes gives it a thick, luscious consistency that clings nicely to the tempeh. Thinly sliced baby bok choy, whole cilantro leaves, sliced radishes, and scallions lend the wraps bright flavor and freshness.

- ¾ cup sugar
- 6 tablespoons soy sauce
- 6 tablespoons water
- 5 garlic cloves, minced
- 1½ tablespoons rice vinegar
- 1½ teaspoons sriracha
- 1½ teaspoons cornstarch
- ¼ cup vegetable oil, divided
- 1 pound tempeh, cut crosswise into ½-inch-thick strips
- 4 (10-inch) flour tortillas
- 2 heads baby bok choy (4 ounces each), sliced thin crosswise
- 1 cup fresh cilantro leaves
- 3 radishes, trimmed, halved, and sliced thin
- 2 scallions, sliced thin

1. Whisk sugar, soy sauce, water, garlic, rice vinegar, sriracha, and cornstarch together in bowl; set aside. Heat 2 tablespoons oil in 12-inch nonstick skillet over medium heat until shimmering. Add half of tempeh and cook until golden brown on both sides, 2 to 4 minutes per side. Transfer to paper towel–lined plate. Repeat with remaining 2 tablespoons oil and remaining tempeh.

2. Add sugar-soy mixture to now-empty skillet and bring to simmer over medium-low heat. Cook until thickened and reduced to about 1 cup, about 5 minutes. Transfer tempeh to bowl, add half of sauce, and toss to coat. Lay tortillas on counter, then divide tempeh evenly among tortillas. Top evenly with bok choy, cilantro, radishes, and scallions, then drizzle each wrap with 1 tablespoon sauce. Fold sides of tortilla over filling, fold bottom of tortilla over sides and filling, and roll tightly. Slice in half and serve, passing remaining sauce separately.

Korean Barbecue Tempeh Wraps

Eggs All Day

452 Creamy French-Style Scrambled Eggs ■
453 Xīhóngshì Chao Jīdàn (Chinese Stir-Fried Tomatoes and Eggs) ■
453 Scrambled Eggs with Shiitake Mushrooms and Feta Cheese ■
454 Menemen (Turkish Scrambled Eggs with Vegetables) ■
454 Australian Folded Eggs ■
457 Coddled Eggs ■
457 Çılbır (Turkish Poached Eggs with Yogurt and Spiced Butter) ■
458 Make-Ahead Cheese Soufflés
459 Pickled Mustard Seeds ●
460 Biscuits with Creamy Tomato Gravy and Fried Eggs
461 Shakshuka (Eggs in Spicy Tomato and Roasted Red Pepper Sauce)
462 Green Shakshuka
462 Microwave-Fried Garlic ■ ●
464 Chickpea Shakshuka ■
464 Tomato and Corn Tostadas with Baked Eggs
465 Vegetarian Refried Beans ■ ●
466 Easy Cheddar Omelet ■
Easy Feta and Dill Omelet ■
Easy Tex-Mex Omelet ■
466 Family-Size Spinach and Herb Cream Cheese Omelet with Home Fries
467 Spanish Tortilla with Roasted Red Peppers and Peas
468 Garlic Mayonnaise ■
468 Potato and Zucchini Spanish Tortilla
471 Broccoli and Feta Frittata ■
471 Pesto Potato Frittata with Peas and Goat Cheese ■
472 Kuku Sabzi
474 Frittata Bites with Broccoli and Sun-Dried Tomatoes
Frittata Bites with Peas, Goat Cheese, and Basil
475 Asparagus, Leek, and Goat Cheese Quiche
476 Fried Egg Sandwiches with Hummus and Sprouts ■
477 Egg, Kimchi, and Avocado Sandwiches
478 Breakfast Tacos with Pinto Beans and Cotija Cheese ■
479 Kale and Black Bean Breakfast Burritos ■
479 Breakfast Burritos with Poblano, Beans, Corn, and Crispy Potatoes
480 Brussels Sprout Hash with Poached Eggs ■

Put an Egg on It

450 Easy-Peel Hard-Cooked Eggs ■
Soft-Cooked Eggs ■
450 Jammy Eggs ■
451 Perfect Fried Eggs ■
451 Perfect Poached Eggs ■

■ Fast (45 minutes or less) ● Vegan

Put an Egg on It

Protein-rich eggs are an easy and delicious addition to many vegetarian meals. Along with protein they provide healthy fats and plenty of vitamins that are necessary for a balanced diet. Try chopped hard-cooked eggs on salad, add a jammy egg to your ramen, slide a fried egg on top of rice, or perch a poached egg on toast.

Easy-Peel Hard-Cooked Eggs

FAST Makes 2 to 6 eggs Total Time 35 minutes

Use large eggs that have no cracks and are cold from the refrigerator.

2–6 large eggs

1. Bring 1 inch water to rolling boil in medium saucepan over high heat. Place eggs in steamer basket. Transfer basket to saucepan. Cover, reduce heat to medium-low, and cook eggs for 13 minutes.

2. When eggs are almost finished cooking, combine 2 cups ice cubes and 2 cups cold water in medium bowl. Using tongs or spoon, transfer eggs to ice bath; let sit for 15 minutes. Peel before serving. (Eggs can be refrigerated in their shells in airtight container for up to 5 days.)

Variation

FAST Soft-Cooked Eggs

Precise timing is critical, so use a digital timer. You can use this method for one to six large, extra-large, or jumbo eggs without altering the timing. After adding steamer basket with eggs to saucepan of boiling water, cover, reduce heat to medium-high, and cook for 6½ minutes. Remove lid, transfer saucepan to sink, and place under cold running water for 30 seconds. Peel before serving.

Jammy Eggs

FAST Makes 2 to 6 eggs Total Time 15 minutes

Just as we do for soft- and hard-boiled eggs, we steam our jammy eggs over boiling water. Steam reaches the same 212 degrees as boiling water, cooking the eggs exactly the same way as when they're submerged. But because steaming involves so little liquid, the water returns to a boil within seconds, no matter how many eggs you add to the pot.

2–6 large eggs

1. Bring ½ inch water to boil in medium saucepan over medium-high heat. Using tongs, gently place eggs in boiling water (eggs will not be submerged). Cover and cook for 8 minutes.

2. Remove lid, transfer saucepan to sink, and place under cold running water for 30 seconds. Peel before serving. (Jammy eggs can be refrigerated in their shells in their original egg carton for up to 3 days.)

Perfect Fried Eggs

FAST Serves 2 Total Time 15 minutes

When checking the eggs for doneness, lift the lid just a crack to prevent loss of steam should they need further cooking. When cooked, the thin layer of white surrounding the yolk will turn opaque, but the yolk should remain runny. To cook two eggs, use an 8- or 9-inch nonstick skillet and halve the amounts of oil and butter. You can use this method with extra-large or jumbo eggs without altering the timing.

- 2 teaspoons vegetable oil
- 4 large eggs, divided
- 2 teaspoons unsalted butter, cut into 4 pieces and chilled

1. Heat oil in 12-inch nonstick skillet over low heat for 5 minutes. Meanwhile, crack 2 eggs into small bowl. Repeat with remaining 2 eggs and second small bowl.

2. Increase heat to medium-high and heat until oil is shimmering. Add butter to skillet and quickly swirl to coat pan. Working quickly, pour 1 bowl of eggs into 1 side of pan and second bowl of eggs into other side. Cover and cook for 1 minute. Let stand off heat, covered, for 15 to 45 seconds for runny yolks (white around edge of yolk will be barely opaque), 45 to 60 seconds for soft but set yolks, and about 2 minutes for medium-set yolks. Season with salt and pepper to taste. Using fish spatula, transfer eggs to plates and serve.

Perfect Poached Eggs

FAST Makes 1 to 4 eggs Total Time 15 minutes

Once the cover is removed, you can check the eggs individually, removing them once the white nearest the yolk is just set. For the best results, be sure to use the freshest eggs possible. This recipe can be used to cook from one to four eggs. To make two batches of eggs to serve all at once, transfer four cooked eggs directly to a large pot of 150-degree water and cover them. This will keep them warm for 15 minutes or so while you return the poaching water to a boil and cook the next batch.

- 1–4 large eggs
- 1 tablespoon distilled white vinegar
- Table salt for poaching eggs

1. Bring 6 cups water to boil in Dutch oven over high heat. Meanwhile, crack eggs, one at a time, into colander. Let stand until loose, watery whites drain away from eggs, 20 to 30 seconds. Gently transfer eggs to 2-cup liquid measuring cup.

2. Add vinegar and 1 teaspoon salt to boiling water. With lip of measuring cup just above surface of water, gently tip eggs into water, one at a time, leaving space between them. Cover pot and let stand off heat until whites closest to yolks are just set and opaque, about 3 minutes. If after 3 minutes whites are not set, let stand in water, checking every 30 seconds, until eggs reach desired doneness. (For medium-cooked yolks, let eggs sit in pot, covered, for 4 minutes, then begin checking for doneness.)

3. Using slotted spoon, carefully lift and drain each egg over pot. Season with salt and pepper to taste and serve.

top | *Creamy French-Style Scrambled Eggs*
bottom | *Xīhóngshì Chǎo Jīdàn (Chinese Stir-Fried Tomatoes and Eggs)*

Creamy French-Style Scrambled Eggs

FAST Serves 4 Total Time 20 minutes

Why This Recipe Works French-style scrambled eggs have a rich, velvety texture that makes them a luxurious choice for breakfast—or any meal. To cut down a bit on all the fat used in a traditional recipe, we use steaming water rather than melted butter to indicate when our nonstick skillet is hot enough to begin cooking the eggs very slowly over low heat. Stirring constantly controls the coagulation of the proteins so that some form delicate curds while the rest thicken into a saucy consistency. Adding a tablespoon of water at the end of cooking dilutes the proteins, giving our eggs the perfect texture. For the creamiest, richest-tasting result, be sure to cook these eggs slowly, following the visual cues provided. It should take 12 to 14 minutes total. Though the eggs will be rather loose, their extended cooking time ensures that they reach a safe temperature. You can prepare two servings by halving the amounts of all the ingredients and using an 8-inch skillet. Fresh chives or tarragon can be substituted for the parsley, if desired. Serve with buttered toast.

- 8 large eggs
- ½ teaspoon table salt
- 3 tablespoons water
- 1 teaspoon minced fresh parsley

1. Using fork, beat eggs and salt in bowl until blended. Heat 2 tablespoons water in 10-inch nonstick skillet over low heat until steaming. Add egg mixture and immediately stir with silicone spatula. Cook, stirring slowly and constantly, scraping edges and bottom of skillet, for 4 minutes. (If egg mixture is not steaming after 4 minutes, increase heat slightly.)

2. Continue to stir slowly until eggs begin to thicken and small curds begin to form, about 4 minutes longer. (If curds have not begun to form, increase heat slightly.) If any large curds form, mash with spatula. As curds start to form, stir vigorously, scraping edges and bottom of skillet, until eggs are thick enough to hold their shape when pushed to side of skillet, 4 to 6 minutes. Off heat, add remaining 1 tablespoon water and parsley and stir vigorously until incorporated, about 30 seconds. Serve.

Xīhóngshì Chao Jīdàn (Chinese Stir-Fried Tomatoes and Eggs)

FAST Serves 4 Total Time 25 minutes

Why This Recipe Works Stir-fried tomatoes and eggs is such a simple dish that it is often the first thing that children in China learn how to cook for themselves. But just because it's easy and fast doesn't mean it isn't also delicious—in fact, it makes a great low-effort vegetarian meal for cooks of all ages. Sesame oil and Shaoxing wine add nutty flavor and help the eggs stay tender by diluting the egg proteins to keep them from bonding too closely. For the sauce, garlic, ginger, and scallions provide savoriness to canned tomatoes, and simmering the tomatoes with some sugar makes the base concentrated and rich. Serve with steamed white rice.

- 4 scallions, white parts sliced thin, green parts cut into 1-inch lengths
- 3 tablespoons vegetable oil, divided
- 3 garlic cloves, sliced thin
- 2 teaspoons grated fresh ginger
- 8 large eggs
- 2 tablespoons Shaoxing wine or dry sherry
- 1 teaspoon toasted sesame oil
- 1 teaspoon table salt, divided
- 1 (28-ounce) can whole peeled tomatoes, drained with juice reserved, cut into 1-inch pieces
- 2 teaspoons sugar

1. Combine scallion whites, 1 tablespoon vegetable oil, garlic, and ginger in small bowl; set aside. Whisk eggs, Shaoxing wine, sesame oil, and ½ teaspoon salt together in separate bowl.

2. Heat remaining 2 tablespoons vegetable oil in 14-inch flat-bottomed wok or 12-inch nonstick skillet over medium-high heat until shimmering. Add egg mixture. Using silicone spatula, slowly but constantly scrape along bottom and sides of pan until eggs just form cohesive mass, 1 to 2 minutes (eggs will not be completely dry); transfer to clean bowl.

3. Add garlic mixture to now-empty pan and cook over medium heat, mashing mixture into pan, until fragrant, about 30 seconds. Add tomatoes and their juice, sugar, and remaining ½ teaspoon salt and simmer until almost completely dry, 5 to 7 minutes. Stir in egg mixture and scallion greens and cook, breaking up any large curds, until heated through, about 1 minute. Serve.

Scrambled Eggs with Shiitake Mushrooms and Feta Cheese

FAST Serves 4 Total Time 30 minutes

Why This Recipe Works The addition of earthy shiitake mushrooms and briny feta takes these scrambled eggs from basic to deluxe. To tenderize and lend richness to the eggs without adding moisture, we skip dairy in favor of olive oil. Stirring the eggs quickly over medium-high heat creates large curds, which we then fold the mushrooms into so that it can all set into a cohesive mix. Oyster or cremini mushrooms can be substituted for the shiitake mushrooms, if desired; to prepare the oyster or cremini mushrooms, trim the stems but do not remove them. Precrumbled feta is often coated with cellulose to keep it from caking; for the best results, buy a block of feta and crumble it yourself. This recipe can be easily halved, if desired; use a 10-inch skillet.

- 8 large eggs
- 3 tablespoons extra-virgin olive oil, divided
- ¼ teaspoon table salt, divided
- ¼ teaspoon pepper
- 1 shallot, minced
- 1 teaspoon minced fresh thyme
- 8 ounces shiitake mushrooms, stemmed and sliced thin
- ¼ cup water
- 1 ounce feta cheese, crumbled (¼ cup)

1. In medium bowl, beat eggs, 2 tablespoons oil, ⅛ teaspoon salt, and pepper with fork until no streaks of white remain. Heat 1 teaspoon oil, shallot, thyme, and remaining ⅛ teaspoon salt in 12-inch nonstick skillet over medium heat, stirring occasionally, until shallot is softened and beginning to brown, 2 to 3 minutes. Add mushrooms and water, cover, and cook, stirring frequently, until mushrooms are softened, 5 to 8 minutes. Uncover and continue to cook until moisture has evaporated, 2 to 3 minutes longer. Transfer mushroom mixture to bowl and set aside. Wipe skillet clean with paper towels.

2. Heat remaining 2 teaspoons oil in skillet over medium-high heat until shimmering. Add egg mixture and, using silicone spatula, constantly and firmly scrape along bottom and sides of skillet until eggs begin to clump and spatula just leaves trail on bottom of skillet, 30 to 60 seconds. Reduce heat to low and gently but constantly fold eggs until clumped and just slightly wet, 30 to 60 seconds. Fold in mushroom mixture. Transfer to serving dish, sprinkle with feta, and serve.

Menemen (Turkish Scrambled Eggs with Vegetables)

FAST Serves 4 Total Time 45 minutes

Why This Recipe Works Menemen is a hearty Turkish breakfast of eggs combined with peppers, tomatoes, and often onion. The most popular style of menemen features eggs that are tender and softly set. The vegetables in the dish need to be cooked long enough to soften and evaporate excess moisture. Removing the skillet from the heat after sautéing the vegetables allows the skillet to cool slightly before the eggs are added, preventing the eggs from setting too quickly. Cooking the eggs very slowly over low heat while constantly stirring heats the eggs gently and evenly, turning them deliciously creamy and cooking them to a safe temperature. To finish the dish, we sprinkle it with fresh parsley, tulum (a crumbly Turkish sheep or goat's milk cheese), and pul biber chile flakes for mild heat and a smoky essence. Cubanelle peppers can be used in place of the Anaheim chiles. Tulum can be found online or at specialty cheese shops; feta can be substituted. If not using cheese, season with salt to taste before serving. We strongly recommend seeking out the mild Turkish red pepper flakes pul biber or Aleppo pepper; however, ½ teaspoon paprika may be substituted. Menemen is a traditional breakfast dish but can be enjoyed for lunch or dinner as well.

- 5 tablespoons extra-virgin olive oil, divided
- 1 small onion, chopped fine
- 2 Anaheim chiles, stemmed, seeded, and cut into ½-inch pieces
- 1 teaspoon pul biber, divided
- ¾ teaspoon dried oregano
- ¾ teaspoon table salt, divided
- ¼ teaspoon pepper, divided
- 2 large tomatoes, cored and cut into ½-inch pieces (2½ cups)
- 6 large eggs
- 2 ounces tulum cheese, crumbled (½ cup) (optional)
- 1 tablespoon minced fresh parsley
- Crusty bread, flatbread, or pita

1. Heat 3 tablespoons oil in 10-inch nonstick skillet over medium-low heat until shimmering. Add onion, Anaheims, ½ teaspoon pul biber, oregano, ¼ teaspoon salt, and ⅛ teaspoon pepper and stir to combine. Cover and cook until vegetables are soft, about 10 minutes, stirring once halfway through cooking. Add tomatoes. Increase heat to medium and cook uncovered, stirring occasionally, until tomatoes are soft and excess moisture has evaporated, 5 to 8 minutes.

2. Move skillet off heat for 2 minutes to cool slightly. While skillet is cooling, whisk eggs in medium bowl with remaining ½ teaspoon salt and remaining ⅛ teaspoon pepper.

3. Return skillet to heat and adjust heat to low. Add eggs. Cook, stirring slowly and constantly, scraping edges and bottom of skillet with silicone spatula, for 4 minutes. (If egg mixture is not steaming after 4 minutes, increase heat slightly.)

4. Continue to stir slowly until eggs thicken and are just set (spatula drawn across bottom of skillet should leave clean trail), 5 to 6 minutes longer. Remove skillet from heat. Drizzle remaining 2 tablespoons oil over top and sprinkle with cheese, if using; parsley; and remaining ½ teaspoon pul biber. Serve immediately, passing bread separately.

Australian Folded Eggs

FAST Serves 1 Total Time 10 minutes

Why This Recipe Works Popularized in Australian cafés, this butter-yellow egg rosette offers the luxury of a creamy French omelet with the speed of a scramble. A simple series of folds reshapes the eating experience into something unique and decadent. We use a small skillet so that the eggs settle into a thick layer that doesn't cook through too quickly and prevent us from shaping them, and we use a spatula to wind the eggs into a rosette. The glistening golden swirl is particularly nice to eat draped over toast, vegetables, or rice. This recipe moves very quickly, so read carefully and have your ingredients and equipment ready before you begin. For the best results, cook the eggs in a nonstick skillet that's in good condition and has a matching lid. Alternatively, you may use a small, well-seasoned carbon-steel skillet or a flat-bottomed wok (these will also require lids). These eggs are meant to be very soft and moist. If you prefer more fully cooked eggs, add the optional teaspoon of water as the recipe directs; the captured steam will set the top of the eggs. Whether or not you add water, steam will cause the eggs to puff and lose some of their shape; if necessary, tidy the edges of the eggs before serving. Top with crumbled cheese, sautéed or roasted vegetables, sriracha, freshly ground pepper, fresh herbs, and/or chili flakes.

- 2 large eggs
- ⅛ teaspoon table salt
- 1 teaspoon water (optional)
- 1½ teaspoons unsalted butter

1. Beat eggs and salt in bowl until few streaks of white remain. Rap bowl on counter to pop large bubbles on surface. Place water, if using, in small bowl near stovetop.

2. Melt butter in 8-inch nonstick skillet over high heat, swirling skillet to distribute butter across bottom. When butter sizzles evenly, add eggs and let sit until set around edges and partially set on bottom, about 10 seconds. With silicone spatula, draw eggs from 1 side of skillet to opposite side, tilting skillet slightly so uncooked egg fills in empty space. Let sit until set around new edge, about 8 seconds.

3. Use spatula to push newly set edge toward edge of skillet (this will be center of rosette). Roll center of rosette around perimeter of skillet, collecting more egg as you go and tilting skillet so uncooked egg flows away from rosette. Continue rolling until all egg has been worked into rosette (top of eggs will still be loose). Add water, if using. Immediately cover skillet and slide pan off heat; let sit until top of eggs is set but still translucent, about 1 minute. Tidy edges of rosette if necessary, transfer to plate, and serve.

Shaping Folded Eggs

1. Pour egg into sizzling butter; let set briefly. Draw some of egg from 1 side to other, tilting pan so eggs fill space. Let sit briefly.

2. Push some of set egg toward pan edge. This will form center of rosette. Start rolling rosette around pan's perimeter, collecting more egg as you roll. Tilt pan so raw egg flows away from rosette.

3. Midway through rolling, rosette fully forms. Roll until all egg is worked into rosette. Top of eggs will look loose. Cover skillet.

Australian Folded Eggs

Coddled Eggs

Coddled Eggs

FAST Serves 4 Total Time 25 minutes

Why This Recipe Works Coddling is an old-school egg tradition that's loaded with modern appeal: tender whites and runny yolks, a hands-off method, and endless flavor potential. We crack one or two eggs into a greased ramekin or cup and then nestle the ramekin into a simmering water bath on the stove and cover the pot. The ramekin's walls insulate the egg, and the hot water from below and steam from above efficiently but softly set the white and thicken the yolk so that it's just a notch tighter than runny. To ensure uniform cooking from top to bottom—and keep our hands out of harm's way—we add the filled ramekins to the pot and pour boiling water around them; that way, the water instantly cools when it hits the pan, giving the eggs a gentler start to cooking. Salting the bottom of the ramekin as well as the eggs before cooking seasons every bite. Use a large saucepan with high sides and a tight-fitting lid. The diameter of the ramekin impacts the cooking time; use ramekins that are 3 to 3¼ inches wide at their base. The eggs will continue to cook off the heat, so serve them promptly. Instead of herbs, you can top the eggs with your favorite compound butter, Sichuan chili crisp, or grated cheese.

8 large eggs, cold from refrigerator
8 pinches table salt, divided
4 teaspoons unsalted butter
Minced fresh tarragon or dill (optional)

1. Spray four 4-ounce ramekins with vegetable oil spray. Sprinkle bottom of each ramekin with pinch of salt. Crack 2 eggs into each ramekin and sprinkle eggs with pinch of salt. Line bottom of large saucepan with thin dish towel or double layer of paper towels, folding to fit in bottom of pan. Place filled ramekins on top of towel. Bring kettle of water to boil. Pour boiling water into pot, avoiding ramekins, until it comes halfway up sides of ramekins (about 1 inch deep).

2. Cover pot and cook over medium heat until egg whites are just set and opaque and yolks are pale yellow and covered by thin film, 9 to 10 minutes. (If after 2 minutes, no steam is escaping from beneath lid, increase heat until steam is visible.) Using tongs, grasp ramekin and shake gently; center should jiggle slightly. If eggs slosh rather than jiggle, continue to cook, covered, checking every 30 seconds.

3. Off heat, using tongs and sturdy, thin spatula, transfer ramekins to cutting board. Gently blot top of eggs with paper towel to remove any condensation. Top each portion with 1 teaspoon butter and herbs, if using. Season with salt and pepper to taste and serve immediately.

Çılbır (Turkish Poached Eggs with Yogurt and Spiced Butter)

FAST Serves 4 Total Time 30 minutes

Why This Recipe Works Çılbır, a favorite of Turkish home cooks in need of a quick and ultrasatisfying meal, consists of a just-set egg, garlicky yogurt, and swirls of spiced butter—a preparation both simple and special that was once served to Ottoman royalty. To make it, we start with a base of strained yogurt, which provides a plush, creamy bed for the poached egg. Minced garlic mixes seamlessly with the yogurt. For perfect poached eggs, we drain the loose whites before dropping the eggs into water seasoned with salt and vinegar. This helps the whites set up quickly, ensuring that the yolks remain liquid, as does gently cooking the eggs off the heat. For the finishing touch, we melt butter until it starts to sizzle and turn nutty before adding fruity red pepper flakes, which turns the butter bright red. This spiced butter is used throughout Turkish cuisine; try it drizzled over roasted vegetables, spooned over grilled corn, or stirred into yogurt dip or hummus. Strained yogurt has had some of the whey removed so that it's thicker than regular yogurt. Turkish strained yogurt is ideal for çılbır, but if you can't find it, Greek yogurt works well, too; do not use labneh, which is too thick for this recipe. A rasp-style grater makes quick work of turning the garlic into a paste. We strongly recommend seeking out the mild Turkish red pepper flakes pul biber or Aleppo pepper; however, ½ teaspoon of paprika can be substituted. For the tidiest presentation, use the freshest eggs possible. Çılbır can be eaten at any time of day; we like to pair it with a salad when serving it for lunch or dinner.

1 cup plain whole-milk strained yogurt
½ teaspoon garlic, minced to paste
⅛ teaspoon table salt, plus salt for cooking eggs
4 large eggs
1 tablespoon distilled white vinegar
2 tablespoons unsalted butter
1 teaspoon pul biber or ground dried Aleppo pepper
¼ teaspoon dried mint (optional)
Pita, flatbread, or crusty bread

1. Stir yogurt, garlic, and salt in medium bowl until just combined. Divide yogurt mixture evenly among 4 serving plates or shallow bowls, spreading each portion with small spatula or back of spoon to make flat bed large enough to hold 1 poached egg. Set aside plates and allow yogurt to warm up while you prepare eggs.

2. Bring 6 cups water to boil in Dutch oven over high heat. Meanwhile, crack eggs, one at a time, into colander. Let stand until loose, watery whites drain away from eggs, 20 to 30 seconds. Gently transfer eggs to 2-cup liquid measuring cup.

3. Add vinegar and 1 teaspoon salt to boiling water. With lip of measuring cup just above surface of water, gently tip eggs into water, one at a time, leaving space between them. Cover pot and let stand off heat until whites closest to yolks are just set and opaque, about 3 minutes. If after 3 minutes whites are not set, let stand in water, checking every 30 seconds, until eggs reach desired doneness. (For medium-cooked yolks, let eggs sit in pot, covered, for 4 minutes, then begin checking for doneness.)

4. While eggs cook, heat butter in small saucepan over medium heat until it sputters, 2 to 3 minutes. Stir in pepper flakes (butter will foam) and remove from heat.

5. Using slotted spoon, carefully lift and drain 1 egg over pot. Pat bottom of spoon dry with paper towel and gently place egg on yogurt bed. Repeat with remaining eggs. Drizzle butter evenly over eggs. Sprinkle each serving with pinch dried mint, if using, and season with salt and pepper to taste. Serve immediately, passing pita separately.

Make-Ahead Cheese Soufflés

Serves 6   Total Time 1¾ hours, plus 1 hour chilling

Why This Recipe Works Rich, airy, and delightfully cheesy, these soufflés can be made ahead as a vegetarian meal to suit any schedule. We begin with a standard béchamel sauce and then add plenty of nutty Comté, which we supplement with Parmesan to add extra-cheesy oomph without a lot of moisture that might otherwise cause the soufflé to collapse. After folding in egg whites whipped to stiff peaks, we portion the mixture into individual ramekins, which we bake in a water bath until the structure is softly set. The water bath ensures that the soufflés cook evenly from edge to edge instead of becoming dry and stiff on the sides. When they're cool, we remove them from their ramekins and refrigerate them on a baking sheet. Just before serving, we transfer the baking sheet to a hot oven, where the soufflés puff and crisp. You'll need six 4-ounce ramekins for this recipe. Greasing the ramekins generously ensures that the soufflés emerge cleanly. Sharp cheddar, Gruyère, or gouda can be substituted for the Comté. Serve the soufflés with Pickled Mustard Seeds (recipe follows) and lightly dressed salad greens, if desired.

- 2 tablespoons unsalted butter
- 3 tablespoons all-purpose flour
- ¼ teaspoon table salt
- Pinch ground nutmeg
- 1 cup milk, divided
- 3 ounces Comté cheese, shredded (¾ cup)
- 1 ounce Parmesan cheese, grated (½ cup)
- 3 large eggs, separated
- 2 teaspoons minced fresh parsley
- ¼ teaspoon cream of tartar

1. Adjust oven rack to middle position and heat oven to 350 degrees. Generously spray six 4-ounce ramekins with vegetable oil spray.

2. Melt butter in medium saucepan over medium heat. Stir in flour, salt, and nutmeg and cook for 1 minute. Add half of milk and whisk until smooth. Whisk in remaining milk and cook, whisking constantly, until mixture is thickened and bubbling, about 2 minutes. Off heat, whisk in Comté and Parmesan until melted and smooth (mixture will be thick). Transfer to large bowl and whisk in egg yolks and parsley.

3. Using stand mixer fitted with whisk attachment, whip egg whites and cream of tartar on medium-low speed until foamy, about 1 minute. Increase speed to medium-high and whip until stiff peaks form, about 2 minutes. Gently whisk one-third of whites into cheese mixture. Using silicone spatula, gently fold in remaining whites.

4. Distribute mixture evenly among prepared ramekins and smooth tops. Transfer ramekins to 13 by 9-inch baking pan and add boiling water until it comes halfway up sides of ramekins. Bake until soufflés are puffed and register 170 to 175 degrees, 14 to 17 minutes. Using tongs, transfer ramekins to wire rack and let cool completely, 30 to 40 minutes (soufflés will shrink). While soufflés cool, line rimmed baking sheet with parchment paper and grease parchment lightly.

5. Invert 1 ramekin onto your hand and shake sharply until soufflé releases. Reinvert soufflé onto prepared sheet. Repeat with remaining soufflés. Cover tightly with plastic wrap and refrigerate for at least 1 hour or up to 3 days. (The cooled soufflés can be frozen for up to 2 weeks before the second bake; thaw them at room temperature before baking.)

6. Adjust oven rack to middle position and heat oven to 400 degrees. Bake soufflés until puffed and deeply browned, 15 to 18 minutes. Using thin spatula, transfer soufflés to individual serving plates. Serve immediately.

Pickled Mustard Seeds

VEGAN Makes ½ cup Total Time 50 minutes, plus 20 minutes cooling

You can substitute cider vinegar for the white wine vinegar, if desired.

- ½ cup white wine vinegar
- ½ cup water
- ⅓ cup yellow mustard seeds
- 2 tablespoons maple syrup
- ½ teaspoon table salt

1. Whisk all ingredients together in small saucepan and bring to boil over medium-high heat. Lower heat to maintain simmer and cook, stirring frequently, until mustard seeds are swollen and softened and mixture is nearly dry, about 40 minutes. (If mixture starts to dry out before mustard seeds have softened, add extra water, 1 tablespoon at a time.)

2. Transfer to container and let cool completely. Cover and refrigerate for up to 1 month. Let come to room temperature before serving.

top | *Çılbır (Turkish Poached Eggs with Yogurt and Spiced Butter)*
bottom | *Make-Ahead Cheese Soufflés*

Biscuits with Creamy Tomato Gravy and Fried Eggs

Biscuits with Creamy Tomato Gravy and Fried Eggs

Serves 4 Total Time 1 hour

Why This Recipe Works A vegetarian alternative to the ubiquitous sausage gravy, tomato gravy is a Southern sauce typically eaten for breakfast over biscuits (though it's also delicious over grits). Made mostly of pantry staples, including convenient canned diced tomatoes, it's a prime example of how simple cooking can turn out something greater than the sum of its parts. We start by making a small batch of easy cream biscuits. We then build our tomato gravy in a skillet, starting with a base of butter, onion, and the canned tomatoes—including the liquid. Flour thickens the mixture, then vegetable broth and heavy cream give it creamy gravy texture. Pepper, salt, and sugar round out the flavor. We then cook a few eggs sunny-side up and plate it all together for a decadent comfort meal. Sprinkle with chives, if desired.

- 1½ cups (7½ ounces) plus 2 tablespoons all-purpose flour, divided
- 2½ teaspoons sugar, divided
- 1½ teaspoons table salt, divided
- 1½ teaspoons baking powder
- 1 cup plus 6 tablespoons heavy cream, divided
- 5 tablespoons unsalted butter, divided
- ½ onion, chopped fine
- 1 (14.5-ounce) can diced tomatoes
- 1 cup vegetable broth
- ½ teaspoon pepper
- 4 large eggs

1. Adjust oven rack to upper-middle position and heat oven to 450 degrees. Whisk 1½ cups flour, 2 teaspoons sugar, ¾ teaspoon salt, and baking powder together in bowl. Stir in 1 cup plus 2 tablespoons cream. Transfer dough to lightly floured counter and knead until smooth, about 30 seconds. Pat dough into 6-inch square, then cut into 4 squares. Arrange squares on parchment-lined baking sheet. Bake biscuits until golden, 15 to 20 minutes; let cool.

2. While biscuits cool, melt 4 tablespoons butter in large saucepan over medium-high heat. Add onion and cook until softened, about 5 minutes. Stir in tomatoes and their juice and cook until thickened, about 5 minutes. Whisk in remaining 2 tablespoons flour and cook for 1 minute. Whisk in broth, pepper, ½ teaspoon salt, remaining ½ teaspoon sugar, and remaining ¼ cup cream. Simmer until slightly thickened, 3 to 7 minutes then set aside off heat, covered, until ready to serve.

3. Melt remaining 1 tablespoon butter in 12-inch nonstick skillet over medium-high heat. Crack eggs into skillet and sprinkle with remaining ¼ teaspoon salt. Cover and cook until whites are just set, 2 to 3 minutes. To serve, top each biscuit with some of the tomato gravy and a fried egg.

Shakshuka (Eggs in Spicy Tomato and Roasted Red Pepper Sauce)

Serves 4   Total Time 1 hour

Why This Recipe Works The North African dish shakshuka (eggs poached in tomato sauce flavored with peppers, spices, and garlic) makes a great meatless meal any time, from brunch to dinner. For the sauce, we blend whole peeled tomatoes and jarred roasted red peppers for a mix of sweetness, smokiness, and acidity. Adding pita bread keeps the silky-smooth sauce from weeping. A combination of garlic, tomato paste, and ground spices creates shakshuka's distinct flavor profile. To cook the eggs perfectly, we add them to the skillet off the heat and cook them in a smooth rather than chunky sauce. A chunky sauce impedes the convection currents that transfer heat, so an egg surrounded by large pieces will cook more slowly than an egg sitting in a smooth sauce. We also cover the whites with sauce just after adding them to the pan to help speed their cooking from both directions. Chopped fresh cilantro, crumbled feta, and sliced kalamata olives on top provide brightness, texture, and contrasting flavor. Use a glass lid if you have it. If not, peek at the eggs frequently as they cook. Top with Zhoug (Spicy Middle Eastern Herb Sauce) (page 524), if desired.

- 4 (8-inch) pita breads, divided
- 1 (28-ounce) can whole peeled tomatoes, drained
- 3 cups jarred roasted red peppers, divided
- ¼ cup extra-virgin olive oil
- 4 garlic cloves, sliced thin
- 1 tablespoon tomato paste
- 2 teaspoons ground coriander
- 2 teaspoons smoked paprika
- 1 teaspoon ground cumin
- ½ teaspoon table salt
- ¼ teaspoon pepper
- ¼ teaspoon cayenne pepper
- 8 large eggs
- ½ cup coarsely chopped fresh cilantro leaves and stems
- 1 ounce feta cheese, crumbled (¼ cup)
- ¼ cup pitted kalamata olives, sliced

1. Cut enough pita bread into ½-inch pieces to equal ½ cup (about one-third of 1 pita bread). Cut remaining pita breads into wedges for serving. Process pita pieces, tomatoes, and half of red peppers in blender until smooth, 1 to 2 minutes. Cut remaining red peppers into ¼-inch pieces and set aside.

2. Heat oil in 12-inch skillet over medium heat until shimmering. Add garlic and cook, stirring occasionally, until golden, 1 to 2 minutes. Add tomato paste, coriander, paprika, cumin, salt, pepper, and cayenne and cook, stirring constantly, until rust-colored and fragrant, 1 to 2 minutes. Stir in tomato–red pepper puree and reserved red peppers (mixture may sputter) and bring to simmer. Reduce heat to maintain simmer; cook, stirring occasionally, until slightly thickened (spatula will leave trail that slowly fills in behind it, but sauce will still slosh when skillet is shaken), 10 to 12 minutes.

3. Off heat, using back of spoon, make 8 shallow indentations (about 1 inch wide) in sauce (7 around perimeter and 1 in center). Crack 1 egg into small bowl and pour into 1 indentation (it will hold yolk in place but not fully contain egg). Repeat with remaining 7 eggs. Spoon sauce over edges of egg whites so that whites are partially covered and yolks are exposed.

4. Bring to simmer over medium heat (there should be small bubbles across entire surface). Cover and cook until yolks film over, 4 to 5 minutes, adjusting heat to maintain gentle simmer. Continue to cook, covered, until whites are softly but uniformly set (if skillet is shaken lightly, each egg should jiggle as a single unit), 1 to 2 minutes longer. Off heat, sprinkle with cilantro, feta, and olives. Serve immediately, passing pita wedges separately.

Poaching Eggs in Thick Sauce

Moving the pan off the heat allows the sauce to cool slightly so the eggs cook at an even rate. The indents hold the yolks in place and keep them evenly spaced. Spooning sauce over the whites just after adding the eggs provides immediate direct heat to help the whites set faster.

Green Shakshuka

Serves 4 Total Time 1 hour

Why This Recipe Works The classic shakshuka has a greener cousin packed with nutritious vegetables. For a vibrant, earthy green shakshuka, we replace the robust tomato and pepper sauce from red shakshuka with a mix of leafy greens and herbs: savory, mineral-y Swiss chard; baby spinach; and fresh parsley. We start by softening the thinly sliced stems of the chard with onion and garlic in olive oil and then add cumin and coriander before wilting the chard leaves, parsley, and spinach. Next, we puree a portion of the cooked greens with water and bread. The smooth puree evenly transfers heat to the eggs, while the portion of unblended greens provides a sturdy bed for them. Cooking the eggs covered lets them be heated from above and below. If sumac is unavailable, omit it in the steps and serve with lemon wedges (lemon juice may dull the color of the greens). Use a glass lid if you have one. If not, peek at the eggs frequently as they cook. Serve with hot sauce and garnish with Microwave-Fried Garlic (recipe follows).

- 6 tablespoons extra-virgin olive oil
- 1 pound Swiss chard, stems sliced ¼ inch thick (2 cups), leaves cut into 1½- to 2-inch pieces (8 cups)
- 1 onion, chopped fine
- 8 garlic cloves, sliced thin
- 1 teaspoon table salt, divided
- 2 teaspoons ground coriander
- 2 teaspoons ground cumin
- 2 cups plus 2 tablespoons chopped fresh parsley leaves and stems, divided
- 1 pound (16 cups) baby spinach
- 1 ounce country-style bread, cut into ½-inch pieces (½ cup), plus bread for serving
- 1¼ cups water
- 1½ teaspoons ground sumac, divided
- 8 large eggs
- 1 ounce goat cheese or feta cheese, crumbled (¼ cup)

1. Heat oil in 12-inch nonstick skillet over medium heat until shimmering. Add chard stems, onion, garlic, and ½ teaspoon salt. Cook, stirring occasionally, until vegetables are soft and lightly browned, 8 to 10 minutes.

2. Add coriander and cumin and cook until fragrant, about 1 minute. Add chard leaves and 2 cups parsley. Adjust heat to medium-low, cover, and cook, stirring occasionally, until greens are just wilted but still bright green, 2 to 3 minutes.

3. Add half of spinach, cover, and cook until just wilted. Add remaining spinach and cook, covered, stirring occasionally, until all spinach is wilted but still bright green, 3 to 5 minutes. Off heat, transfer 1½ cups greens mixture to blender. Add bread, water, 1 teaspoon sumac, and remaining ½ teaspoon salt. Process until smooth puree forms, about 1 minute, scraping sides of blender jar as needed. Stir puree into skillet and smooth into even layer.

4. Using back of spoon, make 8 shallow indentations (about 1 inch wide) in surface of greens (7 around perimeter and 1 in center). Crack 1 egg into each indentation (it will hold yolk in place but not fully contain egg). Spoon greens over edges of egg whites so whites are partially covered and yolks are exposed.

5. Bring to simmer over medium heat. Cover and cook until yolks film over, 3 to 5 minutes, adjusting heat to maintain gentle simmer. Continue to cook, covered, until whites are softly but uniformly set (if skillet is shaken lightly, each egg should jiggle as single unit), 1 to 2 minutes longer. Off heat, sprinkle with goat cheese, remaining 2 tablespoons parsley, and remaining ½ teaspoon sumac. Season with salt to taste and serve, passing bread separately.

Microwave-Fried Garlic

FAST VEGAN Makes ½ cup
Total Time 20 minutes

- ½ cup thinly sliced garlic
- ½ cup vegetable oil
- 1 teaspoon confectioners' sugar

1. Stir garlic into oil in medium bowl.

2. Microwave for 3 minutes. If garlic hasn't begun to brown, stir and microwave for 1½ minutes longer.

3. Repeat stirring and microwaving in 30-second increments until slices are golden brown, keeping in mind that garlic will continue to darken and crisp as it cools.

4. Using slotted spoon, transfer garlic to paper towel–lined plate. Dust garlic with sugar (to offset any bitterness) and season with salt to taste. (Fried garlic can be stored at room temperature for up to 2 days.)

Swiss Superstar

Savory, earthy Swiss chard is a robust, glossy leafy green that adds mineral freshness to many dishes. In the same family as spinach and beets, chard is high in antioxidants and fiber. The tough stems of chard are often discarded, but in our Green Shakshuka we use both the stalks and leaves to contribute flavor and body.

Time It Right

Swiss chard stems and leaves cook at very different rates, which makes incorporating the entire vegetable into a dish challenging. But by separating the stems from the leaves and then roughly chopping them, smaller pieces are created that can easily be thrown into a simple one-pot recipe without fiddling with the temperature. In our Green Shakshuka, we cook the chopped stems first, then add the leaves in a later step.

Taste the Rainbow

Swiss chard is available year-round and comes in several varieties: The classic white-stemmed, white-veined kind with dark green leaves is the most popular, though "ruby" or "rhubarb" Swiss chard, with its vivid, deep-red stalks, can also be found. The variety gaining the most popularity in recent times is rainbow chard. If you need any other reason to incorporate this vegetable into your next meal, its bouquet of hues, from yellow to pink, white, and crimson, gives any dish a pop of mesmerizing color.

Green Shakshuka

Chickpea Shakshuka

FAST Serves 4 Total Time 45 minutes

Why This Recipe Works The untraditional but appealing addition of chickpeas gives this shakshuka nutty depth and substance, making it an even heartier choice for a weeknight family meal. We keep the ingredient list short and incorporate canned chickpeas into the sauce to maintain the ease that convenience products such as canned tomatoes and jarred peppers lend to many versions of shakshuka. Eggs poached in the sauce and a sprinkle of goat cheese on top add richness. Spooning sauce over the egg whites as they cook ensures they cook evenly. We like to sprinkle the shakshuka with parsley leaves and serve it with crusty bread.

- 2 tablespoons extra-virgin olive oil, plus extra for drizzling
- 1 onion, chopped fine
- 1 cup jarred roasted red peppers, rinsed, patted dry, and chopped coarse
- 1 teaspoon table salt
- ½ teaspoon pepper
- 1 (15-ounce) can chickpeas, rinsed
- 1½ teaspoons smoked paprika
- 1 teaspoon ground cumin
- 1 (28-ounce) can crushed tomatoes
- 8 large eggs
- 2 ounces goat cheese, crumbled (½ cup)

1. Heat oil in 12-inch nonstick skillet over medium-high heat until shimmering. Add onion, red peppers, salt, and pepper and cook until onion is softened, stirring occasionally, about 4 minutes. Add chickpeas, paprika, and cumin and cook until fragrant, about 1 minute. Stir in tomatoes and bring to simmer. Cover, reduce heat to medium-low, and cook until flavors meld, about 5 minutes.

2. Off heat, using back of spoon, make 8 shallow indentations (about 1 inch wide) in sauce (7 around perimeter and 1 in center). Crack 1 egg into small bowl and pour into 1 indentation (it will hold yolk in place but not fully contain egg). Repeat with remaining 7 eggs. Spoon sauce over edges of egg whites so that whites are partially covered and yolks are exposed.

3. Bring to simmer over medium-high heat. Cover, reduce heat to medium-low, and cook until egg whites are fully set, about 8 minutes, rotating skillet occasionally for even cooking. Sprinkle shakshuka evenly with goat cheese. Serve, drizzled with extra oil.

Tomato and Corn Tostadas with Baked Eggs

Serves 4 Total Time 55 minutes

Why This Recipe Works For a vegetarian dinner full of Mexican-inspired flavors, we liked the idea of pairing crunchy, crisp corn tostadas with creamy beans; soft, rich eggs; and flavorful roasted vegetables. We start by roasting cherry tomatoes, corn, and onion with smoky chipotle and aromatic spices: cumin, coriander, and oregano (plus salt and pepper). To keep things easy, we bake the eggs directly in divots made in the vegetable mixture. A slather of warm refried beans (made meat-free and supersavory by the addition of extra spices and tomato paste rather than pork) and a sprinkle of queso fresco and cilantro finish off our tostadas perfectly. We prefer our homemade Vegetarian Refried Beans (recipe follows), but you may use store-bought.

- 1½ pounds cherry tomatoes, halved
- 1½ cups fresh or thawed frozen corn
- 1 onion, halved and sliced thin
- 2 tablespoons vegetable oil
- 3 garlic cloves, minced
- 2 teaspoons minced canned chipotle chile in adobo sauce
- 2 teaspoons minced fresh oregano or ½ teaspoon dried
- 1 teaspoon ground cumin
- ½ teaspoon ground coriander
- ½ teaspoon table salt
- ¼ teaspoon pepper
- 8 (6-inch) corn tortillas
- ¾ cup vegetable oil for frying
- 8 large eggs
- 1 cup vegetarian refried beans, warmed
- 2 ounces queso fresco, crumbled (½ cup)
- 3 tablespoons chopped fresh cilantro

1. Adjust oven rack to middle position and heat oven to 500 degrees. Line rimmed baking sheet with aluminum foil. Toss tomatoes, corn, onion, 2 tablespoons oil, garlic, chipotle, oregano, cumin, coriander, salt, and pepper together, then spread onto prepared sheet. Roast tomato mixture, stirring occasionally, until tomatoes are softened and skins begin to shrivel, 10 to 15 minutes. Remove from oven.

2. Meanwhile, using fork, poke center of each tortilla 3 or 4 times (to prevent puffing and allow for even cooking). Heat ¾ cup oil in 8-inch skillet over medium heat to 350 degrees. Line second rimmed baking sheet with several layers of paper towels.

3. Working with 1 tortilla at a time, add to hot oil and place metal potato masher on top to keep tortilla flat and submerged in oil. Fry until crisp and lightly browned, 45 to 60 seconds (no flipping is necessary). Transfer fried tortilla to paper towel–lined sheet. Repeat with remaining tortillas.

4. Using spoon, make 8 indentations, 2 to 3 inches wide, in tomato mixture in sheet. Crack 1 egg into each indentation. Bake until egg whites are just set and yolks are still runny, 5 to 7 minutes, rotating sheet halfway through baking.

5. Spread 2 tablespoons warm refried beans over each tostada, then top with tomato mixture and eggs. Sprinkle with queso fresco and cilantro and serve immediately.

Tomato and Corn Tostadas with Baked Eggs

Vegetarian Refried Beans

FAST **VEGAN** Makes 1¾ cup Total Time 30 minutes

For more spice, add the ribs and seeds from the jalapeño and/or poblano chile.

- 1 cup water
- 2 (15-ounce) cans pinto beans, rinsed, divided
- 1 tablespoon vegetable oil
- 1 small onion, chopped fine
- 1 jalapeño chile, stemmed, seeded, and minced
- 1 poblano chile, stemmed, seeded, and minced
- ¼ teaspoon table salt
- 3 small garlic cloves, minced
- 2 tablespoons tomato paste
- ½ teaspoon ground cumin
- ½ teaspoon dried oregano
- ½ teaspoon chipotle chile powder
- 1 tablespoon minced fresh cilantro
- 2 teaspoons lime juice (optional)

1. Process water and all but 1 cup beans in food processor until smooth, about 15 seconds, scraping down sides of bowl as needed. Add remaining beans and pulse until slightly chunky, about 10 pulses.

2. Heat oil in 12-inch nonstick skillet over medium heat until shimmering. Add onion, jalapeño, poblano, and salt. Adjust heat to medium-high and cook, stirring occasionally, until softened and beginning to brown, about 5 minutes.

3. Stir in garlic, tomato paste, cumin, oregano, and chipotle powder and cook until fragrant, about 30 seconds. Stir in processed beans, reduce heat to medium, and cook, stirring often, until beans are thick and creamy, about 5 minutes. Stir in cilantro and lime juice, if using, and adjust consistency with extra hot water as needed. Season with salt and pepper to taste. Serve. (Beans can be refrigerated for up to 2 days.)

Easy Cheddar Omelet

FAST Makes 1 omelet Total Time 15 minutes

Why This Recipe Works Omelets are well-known diner staples that can be endlessly customized for a filling meal. But they can be a challenge to make well at home. Our simple method takes the guesswork out of omelet making. We use a 10-inch nonstick skillet to ensure that our omelet will come out easily. After stirring the eggs until large curds form, we briefly tilt the skillet to allow any uncooked egg to run around the pan and finish by letting the omelet cook undisturbed until just set. We add shredded cheddar cheese and let the omelet sit in the pan, covered, until the cheese is melted for a tender, cheesy omelet worthy of any diner. For a few adventurous variations of this omelet, we swap in mix-ins such as briny feta, pickled jalapeños, and fresh herbs.

- 3 large eggs
- ⅛ teaspoon salt
- ⅛ teaspoon pepper
- 1 tablespoon unsalted butter
- 1 ounce cheddar cheese, shredded (¼ cup)

1. Whisk eggs, salt, and pepper in bowl until eggs are thoroughly combined and mixture is pure yellow.

2. Melt butter in 10-inch nonstick skillet over medium-high heat, swirling to coat skillet bottom. Add eggs and cook, gently stirring and scraping bottom of skillet with silicone spatula in circular motion until large curds begin to form and bare spots are visible on bottom of skillet, about 20 seconds.

3. Tilt skillet so uncooked eggs fill bare spots. Run spatula around edge of skillet and push cooked eggs down off sides. Let cook, undisturbed, until bottom of omelet is just set but top is still slightly wet, about 30 seconds.

4. Remove skillet from heat. Sprinkle cheddar over half of omelet. Cover and let sit until cheese has melted, about 1 minute. Fold unfilled half of omelet over filled half to create half-moon shape. Holding plate in 1 hand, tilt skillet to slide omelet onto plate. Serve.

Variations

FAST Easy Feta and Dill Omelet

Decrease salt to pinch. Substitute ¼ cup crumbled feta cheese for cheddar and add 1 tablespoon chopped fresh dill before covering skillet in step 4.

FAST Easy Tex-Mex Omelet

Substitute shredded Monterey Jack cheese for cheddar and add 1 tablespoon minced pickled jalapeños and 1 tablespoon minced fresh cilantro before covering skillet in step 4.

Family-Size Spinach and Herb Cream Cheese Omelet with Home Fries

Serves 4 Total Time 55 minutes

Why This Recipe Works When the desire for breakfast for dinner strikes, making a single omelet that is big enough for four people rather than dishing out omelets one by one will keep you from feeling like a line cook on the clock. Our sheet pan method for cooking a side of home fries reduces the hands-on time even further—and is much easier than keeping a careful eye on two stovetop pans at once. We toss cubed Yukon Gold potatoes with butter and seasoning before popping them in the oven to roast. While those cook, we make a crave-worthy filling of spinach, cream cheese, and alliums. Then we pour seasoned whisked eggs into a 12-inch skillet and, once the eggs are just about set, spread the filling over the top and fold the supersized omelet in half just as the home fries turn tender and browned. It's a filling meal that leaves just a handful of dishes to do.

- 2 pounds Yukon Gold potatoes, unpeeled, cut into ½-inch pieces
- 3 tablespoons unsalted butter, melted, plus 3 tablespoons unsalted butter, divided
- 1¼ teaspoons plus ⅛ teaspoon table salt, divided
- 1 teaspoon pepper, divided
- ½ teaspoon smoked paprika
- 6 ounces (6 cups) baby spinach, chopped coarse
- 2 garlic cloves, minced
- 3 ounces cream cheese, softened
- 2 tablespoons chopped fresh dill
- 2 tablespoons chopped fresh chives
- 8 large eggs

1. Adjust oven rack to middle position and heat oven to 475 degrees. Toss potatoes with melted butter, 1 teaspoon salt, ½ teaspoon pepper, and paprika on rimmed baking sheet. Roast until potatoes are tender and browned, 25 to 28 minutes.

2. Meanwhile, melt 1 tablespoon butter in 12-inch nonstick skillet over medium-high heat. Add spinach and garlic and cook until wilted and skillet is dry, stirring occasionally, about 4 minutes. Stir in cream cheese, dill, chives, ⅛ teaspoon salt, and ¼ teaspoon pepper. Transfer spinach mixture to bowl and cover to keep warm.

3. Whisk eggs, remaining ¼ teaspoon salt, and remaining ¼ teaspoon pepper together in separate bowl. Melt remaining 2 tablespoons butter in now-empty skillet over medium heat. Add eggs and cook, stirring, until mixture is thickened, about 2 minutes. Spread eggs into even layer and cook until bottom of omelet is just set but top is still runny, about 1 minute. Cover skillet, reduce heat to low, and cook until top of omelet begins to set but is still moist, 4 to 5 minutes. Spread spinach mixture evenly over eggs and fold omelet in half. Cut into wedges and serve with potatoes.

Spanish Tortilla with Roasted Red Peppers and Peas

Serves 4 to 6 Total Time 1 hour

Why This Recipe Works The classic Spanish omelet is immensely appealing, but typical recipes call for up to 4 cups of extra-virgin olive oil to cook the potatoes, which can lead to an overly oily—and expensive—tortilla. We wanted an intensely rich, velvety, melt-in-your-mouth egg-and-potato omelet that doesn't require using a quart of oil. We use Yukon Gold potatoes, which are starchy enough to become meltingly tender as they cook, but sturdy enough to stir and flip halfway through cooking with few breaks. We pair them with standard yellow onions, which have a sweet, mellow flavor, and enough eggs for the tortilla to set firm and tender, with the eggs and potatoes melding into one another. To flip the tortilla, we simply slide it out of the pan and onto one plate. Then, placing another plate upside down over the tortilla, we easily flip the whole thing and slide the tortilla back into the pan, making a once-messy task easy and foolproof. Spanish tortillas are often served warm or at room temperature with olives, pickles, and Garlic Mayonnaise (page 468). This tortilla can be served as a light entrée or as an appetizer. For the most traditional tortilla, omit the roasted red peppers and peas.

top | *Family-Size Spinach and Herb Cream Cheese Omelet with Home Fries*

bottom | *Spanish Tortilla with Roasted Red Peppers and Peas*

6 tablespoons plus 1 teaspoon extra-virgin olive oil, divided
1½ pounds Yukon Gold potatoes, peeled, quartered, and cut into ⅛-inch-thick slices
1 small onion, halved and sliced thin
1 teaspoon table salt, divided
¼ teaspoon pepper
8 large eggs
½ cup jarred roasted red peppers, rinsed, dried, and cut into ½-inch pieces
½ cup frozen peas, thawed
Garlic Mayonnaise (optional; recipe follows)

1. Toss ¼ cup oil, potatoes, onion, ½ teaspoon salt, and pepper in large bowl until potato slices are thoroughly separated and coated in oil. Heat 2 tablespoons oil in 10-inch nonstick skillet over medium-high heat until shimmering. Reduce heat to medium-low, add potato mixture to skillet, and set bowl aside (do not rinse). Cover and cook, stirring occasionally with silicone spatula, until potatoes offer no resistance when poked with paring knife, 22 to 28 minutes (some potato slices may break into smaller pieces).

2. Meanwhile, whisk eggs and remaining ½ teaspoon salt in reserved bowl until just combined. Using silicone spatula, fold hot potato mixture, red peppers, and peas into eggs until combined, making sure to scrape all of potato mixture out of skillet. Return skillet to medium-high heat, add remaining 1 teaspoon oil, and heat until just beginning to smoke. Add egg-potato mixture and cook, shaking pan and folding mixture constantly for 15 seconds; smooth top of mixture with silicone spatula. Reduce heat to medium, cover, and cook, gently shaking pan every 30 seconds, until bottom is golden brown and top is lightly set, about 2 minutes.

3. Using silicone spatula, loosen tortilla from pan, shaking it back and forth until tortilla slides around. Slide tortilla onto large plate. Invert tortilla onto second large plate and slide it, browned side up, back into skillet. Tuck edges of tortilla into skillet. Return pan to medium heat and continue to cook, gently shaking pan every 30 seconds, until second side is golden brown, about 2 minutes longer. Slide tortilla onto cutting board; let cool for at least 15 minutes. Cut tortilla into cubes or wedges and serve with garlic mayonnaise, if using.

Garlic Mayonnaise

FAST Makes 1¼ cups Total Time 15 minutes

2 large egg yolks
2 teaspoons Dijon mustard
2 teaspoons lemon juice
1 garlic clove, minced
¾ cup vegetable oil
1 tablespoon water
¼ cup extra-virgin olive oil
½ teaspoon table salt
¼ teaspoon pepper

Process yolks, mustard, lemon juice, and garlic in food processor until combined, about 10 seconds. With machine running, slowly drizzle in vegetable oil, about 1 minute. Transfer mixture to medium bowl and whisk in water. Whisking constantly, slowly drizzle in olive oil, about 30 seconds. Whisk in salt and pepper. (Mayonnaise can be refrigerated in airtight container for up to 4 days.)

Potato and Zucchini Spanish Tortilla

Serves 4 Total Time 1 hour

Why This Recipe Works A traditional Spanish tortilla contains only four ingredients: olive oil, potatoes, eggs, and salt. In this version, we add onion for its sweetness and zucchini for its meltingly tender texture. We use a large amount of oil to poach the potatoes and zucchini and turn them soft and creamy rather than crispy and fried. The vegetables absorb some of the oil, but most of it gets strained out. Cooking the vegetables until tender before combining them with the eggs means we only need to cook the tortilla long enough to set the eggs and achieve a light-colored exterior. It is important to use a nonstick pan so that the tortilla doesn't stick. Strain the leftover oil through a fine-mesh strainer and drizzle it over individual portions or reserve it for another use. (It's great for drizzling over toast, making croutons, or whisking into a vinaigrette.) Avoid large zucchini in this recipe as they tend to be more watery and full of seeds. Serve the tortilla warm or at room temperature.

- 1 cup extra-virgin olive oil
- 1 small onion, chopped fine
- 1 pound Yukon Gold potatoes, peeled, halved lengthwise and sliced crosswise ⅛-inch thick
- 8 ounces zucchini, cut into ½-inch pieces
- 1¼ teaspoons table salt, divided
- 5 large eggs

1. Heat oil in 10-inch nonstick skillet over medium heat until shimmering. Add onion and cook until just softened but not browned, stirring occasionally, 3 to 5 minutes. Stir in potatoes, zucchini, and ¾ teaspoon table salt. Compress vegetables to submerge in oil as much as possible (it's OK if vegetables aren't fully submerged; as they cook they will shrink and become submerged). Cook until potatoes and zucchini are very tender and lightly caramelized, 25 to 30 minutes, stirring occasionally (zucchini should be falling apart). Remove from heat.

2. Whisk eggs and remaining ½ teaspoon table salt together in large bowl. Strain vegetable-oil mixture through fine-mesh strainer set over clean bowl. Transfer vegetables to bowl with eggs, stirring to combine, and set strained oil aside.

3. Heat 1 tablespoon strained oil in now-empty skillet over medium heat until shimmering. Add egg-vegetable mixture and cook, stirring center to scramble eggs lightly, until edges are set, about 1 minute. Run silicone spatula along edges of pan, then shake skillet gently to loosen tortilla from skillet. Cook for additional 1 to 2 minutes, until set but not browned.

4. Remove skillet from heat. Run silicone spatula along edges of pan, then shake skillet gently to loosen tortilla from skillet. Slide tortilla onto large plate. Invert tortilla onto second large plate and slide it, browned side up, back into skillet, tucking edges of tortilla as needed around perimeter of skillet. Cook over medium-high heat until second side is just set, 1 to 2 minutes. Gently slide tortilla onto serving plate and let rest for 10 minutes. Serve warm or at room temperature, drizzling with extra strained oil if desired.

Potato and Zucchini Spanish Tortilla

Pesto Potato Frittata with Peas and Goat Chaese

Broccoli and Feta Frittata

FAST Serves 4 to 6 Total Time 40 minutes

Why This Recipe Works For a tender, evenly cooked, cohesive frittata that is big and hearty enough to serve at least four for dinner, we start with a well-seasoned filling made with bold ingredients and combine it with a dozen eggs. To ensure that the frittata is cohesive, we chop the filling ingredients small so that they can be surrounded and held in place by the eggs. To help the eggs stay tender even when cooked to a relatively high temperature, we add milk and salt. The liquid and salt weaken the interactions between the proteins, making it harder for them to coagulate and turn the eggs rubbery and tough. For eggs that are cooked fully and evenly, we start the frittata on the stovetop and then transfer the skillet to the oven to gently finish.

- 12 large eggs
- ⅓ cup whole milk
- ¾ teaspoon table salt, divided
- 1 tablespoon extra-virgin olive oil
- 12 ounces broccoli florets, cut into ½-inch pieces (4 cups)
- Pinch red pepper flakes
- 3 tablespoons water
- ½ teaspoon grated lemon zest plus ½ teaspoon juice
- 4 ounces feta cheese, crumbled into ½-inch pieces (1 cup)

1. Adjust oven rack to middle position and heat oven to 350 degrees. Whisk eggs, milk, and ½ teaspoon salt in bowl until well combined.

2. Heat oil in 12-inch ovensafe nonstick skillet over medium-high heat until shimmering. Add broccoli, pepper flakes, and remaining ¼ teaspoon salt; cook, stirring frequently, until broccoli is crisp-tender and spotty brown, 7 to 9 minutes. Add water and lemon zest and juice; continue to cook, stirring constantly, until broccoli is just tender and no water remains in skillet, about 1 minute longer.

3. Add feta and egg mixture and cook, using silicone spatula to stir and scrape bottom of skillet until large curds form and spatula leaves trail through eggs but eggs are still very wet, about 30 seconds. Smooth curds into even layer and cook, without stirring, for 30 seconds. Transfer skillet to oven and bake until frittata is slightly puffy and surface bounces back when lightly pressed, 6 to 9 minutes. Using silicone spatula, loosen frittata from skillet and transfer to cutting board. Let stand for 5 minutes before slicing and serving.

Pesto Potato Frittata with Peas and Goat Cheese

FAST Serves 4 Total Time 45 minutes

Why This Recipe Works It's easy to pack a frittata full of vegetables; just start the veg on the stove, pour a whisked egg mixture over top, and let the oven do the rest of the work. This frittata (which serves four—a perfect low-effort dinner) combines the light tenderness of cooked eggs with the firm, starchy bite of Yukon Gold potatoes for a meal that won't leave you hungry again a few hours later. Cooking the potatoes in pesto imbues them with a garlicky, herbal flavor. Adding a cup of frozen peas is a convenient way to fit in an extra serving of vegetables, plus the peas provide pops of color and sweet earthiness. A generous amount of goat cheese rounds out the flavor and adds creaminess to the finished frittata. You can use our homemade Basil Pesto (page 268) or store-bought here.

- 10 large eggs
- ½ cup half-and-half
- ¾ teaspoon table salt, divided
- ¼ teaspoon pepper
- 2 tablespoons unsalted butter
- 1 pound Yukon Gold potatoes, peeled and cut into ½-inch pieces
- ½ cup basil pesto
- 1 cup frozen peas
- 4 ounces goat cheese, crumbled (1 cup)

1. Adjust oven rack to upper-middle position and heat over to 375 degrees. Whisk eggs, half-and-half, ¼ teaspoon salt, and pepper together in bowl.

2. Melt butter in 12-inch ovensafe nonstick skillet over medium-high heat. Add potatoes, pesto, and remaining ½ teaspoon salt and cook, stirring frequently, until potatoes are tender and lightly browned, 12 to 15 minutes. Stir in peas and cook until warmed through, about 1 minute. Stir in egg mixture and sprinkle evenly with goat cheese. Transfer skillet to oven and bake until frittata is just set in center, 10 to 12 minutes. Let rest for 5 minutes. Serve.

Kuku Sabzi

Serves 8 Total Time 1½ hours

Why This Recipe Works Kuku sabzi is a savory Persian herb cake that's enjoyed at Nowruz celebrations (and year-round). It requires a precise ratio of finely chopped greens to egg to be uniformly verdant and cohesive, and we finely chop the greens by hand so that the texture of the cake is light and moist, not damp or dense. Cooking the batter in an oiled skillet over gentle heat encourages even browning without burning. Use only the tender stems and leaves of the herbs; buy 8 ounces each of parsley and cilantro and 4 ounces of dill so that you have enough once the tough stems are removed. It's best to measure the prepped herbs by weight to ensure the proper ratio of greens to eggs, wash and dry the herbs a day before using, and chop them by hand with a sharp knife to produce a lighter, drier texture. If using a food processor, pulse the herbs in batches to avoid overprocessing. If using an electric stovetop, preheat a second burner to medium heat and use that to cook the kuku in step 3. Kuku is typically served as part of a larger meal with a main protein and rice. You can also serve it as a light meal with flatbread and a mix of pickles, or with thick yogurt. It's also great between halves of a split roll with tomatoes, pickles, and onions.

- 1 large leek, chopped fine and washed thoroughly (3 cups)
- 4 ounces finely chopped fresh parsley (2 cups)
- 4 ounces finely chopped fresh cilantro (2 cups)
- 4 ounces (1½ cups) finely chopped romaine lettuce
- 2 ounces finely chopped fresh dill (1 cup)
- 6 garlic cloves, minced
- 6 large eggs
- 1¼ teaspoons table salt
- 1 teaspoon pepper
- ¼ cup vegetable oil, divided

1. Combine leek, parsley, cilantro, romaine, dill, and garlic in large bowl. Whisk eggs, salt, and pepper in medium bowl until well combined and no streaks of white remain. Add eggs to leek mixture and stir until evenly moistened and mixture is cohesive (it will be very thick).

2. Heat 3 tablespoons oil in 10-inch nonstick skillet over medium-high heat until shimmering. Add small amount of leek mixture to skillet. When it sizzles, quickly add remaining mixture (if there's any liquid at bottom of bowl, stir it back into leek mixture before adding to skillet) and spread into even layer, smoothing top with spatula.

3. Reduce heat to medium. Cover and cook until top is set (it should give a little and leave a slight indent when gently pressed) and bottom and sides are deeply browned, 18 to 22 minutes, rotating skillet every 4 to 5 minutes for even browning and adjusting heat as necessary to ensure kuku isn't getting too dark (oil around edges of skillet should be gently but actively sizzling).

4. Uncover. Using silicone spatula, loosen kuku from skillet, gently shaking back and forth until kuku moves around freely from sides. Off heat, invert plate over skillet. Using pot holders, swiftly and carefully invert kuku onto plate.

5. Add remaining 1 tablespoon oil to skillet and slide kuku, browned side up, back into skillet. Tuck edges of kuku into skillet with silicone spatula. Return skillet to medium heat and continue to cook, uncovered, until bottom is browned, about 10 minutes longer.

6. Invert plate over skillet and, using pot holders, invert kuku onto plate. Slide kuku onto cutting board or serving plate and let stand for at least 5 minutes before slicing and serving. Kuku can be served hot, warm, at room temperature, or cold.

Chopping a Big Batch of Herbs

1. Gather washed, dried herbs (as much as you can comfortably hold) into a tight pile with your nondominant hand. Using sharp chef's knife in a rocking motion, slice herbs thin, working your way through pile. Turn sliced herbs 90 degrees and repeat.

2. Place fingers of nondominant hand flat on top of knife's tip and, moving blade up and down with other hand while using knife's tip as a pivot, chop through pile until herbs are as fine as desired.

The Romaine Event

Romaine lettuce is more versatile than you might think. Thanks to the thick rib in the center of each leaf, romaine is sturdy and crisp, with a slight bitterness when raw. Though it's great in salads, where it can handle assertive dressings and mix-ins, it has surprising uses in cooked dishes as well—it can even be grilled.

It Can Take the Heat

Unlike more delicate leafy greens, romaine can stand up to heat without completely wilting—and is subtly transformed by cooking. Heat concentrates romaine's natural sugars, bringing out a slight sweetness. In our Kuku Sabzi, we utilize romaine by chopping it finely and mixing it with herbs and leeks, then cooking it all together with egg to form a cohesive cake. The romaine adds airy structure and a clean, neutral flavor that plays well with the aromatic herbs and leek.

King of Lettuce

Romaine lettuce is the most popular lettuce in the American market, with yearly sales totaling more than $1.5 billion. And for good reason—romaine combines the refreshing crunch of iceberg lettuce with the nutrient-density of spinach and kale. It's especially rich in Vitamin A and potassium.

Kuku Sabzi

top | *Frittata Bites with Broccoli and Sun-Dried Tomatoes*
bottom | *Asparagus, Leek, and Goat Cheese Quiche*

Frittata Bites with Broccoli and Sun-Dried Tomatoes

Makes 12 frittatas Total Time 1 hour

Why This Recipe Works These grab-and-go frittatas blow coffeehouse egg bites out of the water. Not to mention, they're full of protein and vegetables that will give you a great start to the day or supply you with a much-needed afternoon energy boost. By making a muffin tin's worth, you can prepare multiple meals (or snacks) at once. We supplement the protein-packed eggs and hearty potatoes with convenient frozen broccoli, which has the bonus of being frozen at the peak of its freshness. Sun-dried tomatoes bring concentrated umami flavor to each frittata bite, while mozzarella adds cheesy goodness. Paired with whole-grain toast, they make a nutritious on-the-go breakfast.

- 8 ounces Yukon Gold potatoes, peeled and cut into ½-inch pieces
- 1 onion, chopped fine
- 1 tablespoon extra-virgin olive oil
- ¼ teaspoon table salt, divided
- ⅛ teaspoon pepper
- 8 ounces frozen broccoli florets, thawed, patted dry, and cut into ½-inch pieces
- 1½ ounces shredded part-skim mozzarella cheese (⅓ cup)
- ¼ cup oil-packed sun-dried tomatoes, patted dry and chopped fine
- 8 large eggs
- ¼ cup 1 percent low-fat milk
- 8 (2-ounce) slices rustic whole-grain bread, about ½ inch thick, toasted

1. Adjust oven rack to lower-middle position and heat oven to 425 degrees. Toss potatoes and onion with oil, ⅛ teaspoon salt, and pepper and microwave in covered bowl until potatoes are tender and translucent around edges, 5 to 8 minutes, stirring halfway through microwaving. Remove from microwave and let cool slightly, about 2 minutes. Stir in broccoli, cheese, and tomatoes.

2. Generously spray 12-cup nonstick muffin tin with vegetable oil spray, then divide potato mixture evenly among cups. Whisk eggs, milk, and remaining ⅛ teaspoon salt together in large bowl until well combined and uniform yellow color; do not overbeat. Using ladle, evenly distribute egg mixture over filling in muffin cups.

3. Bake until frittatas are lightly puffed and just set in center, 15 to 20 minutes. Transfer muffin tin to wire rack and let cool slightly, about 10 minutes. Run butter knife around edges of frittatas to loosen, then gently remove from muffin tin. Serve with toasted bread. (Frittatas can be refrigerated for up to 2 days.)

Variation

Frittata Bites with Peas, Goat Cheese, and Basil

Substitute 8 ounces thawed frozen peas for broccoli, ⅓ cup crumbled goat cheese for mozzarella, and 2 tablespoons chopped fresh basil for sun-dried tomatoes.

Asparagus, Leek, and Goat Cheese Quiche

Serves 6 to 8 Total Time 2½ hours, plus 3¼ hours chilling and cooling

Why This Recipe Works For a light, bright, springtime quiche, we fill a luscious egg custard with crisp-tender asparagus, buttery sautéed leek, a bit of fresh lemon zest, and vibrant, creamy goat cheese. We parbake the crust to ensure that it remains structurally sound. We then layer the raw asparagus tips on top of the quiche just before baking to keep them from overcooking and to make for an elegant presentation. To prevent the crust from sagging, in step 4 make sure the crimped edge overhangs the edge of the pie plate slightly, and in step 5 use plenty of pie weights (3 to 4 cups). Do not use asparagus that is thinner than ½ inch in diameter. Shred the Parmesan on the large holes of a box grater. To keep from overfilling the quiche, be sure to use the volume measurements given for the leek and asparagus spears.

Crust

- 3 tablespoons ice water
- 2 tablespoons sour cream
- 1¼ cups (6¼ ounces) all-purpose flour
- 1½ teaspoons sugar
- ½ teaspoon table salt
- 8 tablespoons unsalted butter, cut into ½-inch pieces and chilled

Filling

- 1 pound asparagus, trimmed
- 2 tablespoons unsalted butter
- 1 leek, white and light-green parts only, halved lengthwise, sliced thin, and washed thoroughly (about 1½ cups)
- ¾ teaspoon table salt, divided
- ¾ teaspoon pepper, divided
- ¾ cup heavy cream, divided
- 2 teaspoons cornstarch
- 4 large eggs
- 2 teaspoons grated lemon zest
- 2 garlic cloves, minced
- 4 ounces goat cheese, crumbled (1 cup), divided
- 1 ounce Parmesan cheese, shredded (⅓ cup)

1. For the crust Combine ice water and sour cream in bowl. Process flour, sugar, and salt in food processor until combined, about 5 seconds. Scatter butter over top and pulse until butter pieces are no larger than peas, about 10 pulses. Add ice water mixture and pulse until dough forms clumps and no dry flour remains, about 12 pulses, scraping down sides of bowl as needed.

2. Transfer dough to counter and knead briefly until it comes together. Form into 5-inch disk, pressing any cracked edges back together. Wrap in plastic wrap and refrigerate for 1 hour. (Wrapped dough can be refrigerated for up to 2 days or frozen for up to 1 month. If frozen, let dough thaw completely on counter before rolling.)

3. Adjust oven rack to middle position and heat oven to 350 degrees. Let chilled dough sit on counter to soften slightly, about 10 minutes, before rolling. Roll dough into 12-inch circle on lightly floured counter. Loosely roll dough around rolling pin and gently unroll it onto 9-inch pie plate, letting excess dough hang over edge. Ease dough into plate by gently lifting edge of dough with one hand while pressing into plate bottom with your other hand.

4. Trim overhang to ½ inch beyond lip of plate. Tuck overhang under itself; folded edge should be flush with edge of plate. Crimp dough evenly around edge of plate using your fingers. Push protruding crimped edge so it slightly overhangs edge of plate. Wrap dough-lined plate loosely in plastic and freeze until dough is firm, about 15 minutes.

5. Place chilled pie shell on rimmed baking sheet. Line shell with double layer of parchment paper, covering edges to prevent burning, and fill with pie weights. Bake until edges are light golden brown, about 20 minutes. Remove parchment and weights; rotate plate; and bake until crust bottom dries out and turns light golden brown, about 20 minutes. If crust begins to puff, pierce gently with tip of paring knife. Set aside. (Crust needn't cool completely before adding filling.)

6. For the filling Meanwhile, cut tips from asparagus; set aside. Slice asparagus spears ½ inch thick. (You should have 1¾ cups ½-inch asparagus spear slices; reserve any extra for another use.) Melt butter in 12-inch nonstick skillet over medium heat. Add leek, ¼ teaspoon salt, and ¼ teaspoon pepper and cook until leek is softened, 3 to 5 minutes. Stir in sliced asparagus spears and cook until asparagus is bright green and crisp-tender, about 3 minutes. Set aside to cool slightly.

7. Whisk ¼ cup cream and cornstarch in large bowl until cornstarch dissolves. Whisk in eggs, lemon zest, garlic, remaining ½ teaspoon salt, remaining ½ teaspoon pepper, and remaining ½ cup cream until mixture is smooth.

8. Sprinkle ½ cup goat cheese evenly over crust, followed by asparagus-leek mixture, spreading into even layer. Slowly pour custard evenly over top. Sprinkle remaining ½ cup goat cheese evenly over top. Arrange asparagus tips in single layer on top of custard. Press tips gently to submerge partially in custard. Sprinkle evenly with Parmesan.

9. Bake on baking sheet until top of quiche is lightly browned and center registers 170 degrees, 40 to 50 minutes, rotating sheet halfway through baking. Transfer to wire rack and let rest until cool to touch, about 2 hours. Slice and serve. (Quiche can be refrigerated for up to 3 days.)

Fried Egg Sandwiches with Hummus and Sprouts

FAST Serves 4 Total Time 25 minutes

Why This Recipe Works This satisfying, texturally dynamic egg sandwich tastes fresh and light while still containing several different vegetables: cucumber, tomato, red onion, and alfalfa sprouts. We start by smearing sandwich bread (multigrain, if you want extra fiber) with creamy, garlicky hummus and tart, spicy sambal oelek. The nuttiness of the hummus and heat of the sambal harmonizes nicely with the richness of the eggs. We layer the sandwiches with the crunchy vegetables and briny feta. If you can't find sambal oelek, you can substitute chili-garlic sauce or sriracha.

- 2 teaspoons extra-virgin olive oil
- ½ cup garlic hummus
- 8 slices hearty sandwich bread, lightly toasted
- 2 Persian cucumbers, sliced thin on bias
- 4 teaspoons sambal oelek
- 4 large eggs
- ¼ teaspoon table salt, divided
- ¼ teaspoon pepper, divided
- 2 ounces feta cheese, crumbled (½ cup)
- Thinly sliced tomato
- Thinly sliced red onion
- 2 ounces (2 cups) alfalfa sprouts

1. Heat oil in 12-inch nonstick skillet over low heat for 5 minutes. While pan heats, spread hummus on 1 side of 4 slices bread, then arrange cucumber slices on top of hummus. Spread sambal on one side of remaining 4 slices bread.

2. Crack 2 eggs into small bowl and season with ⅛ teaspoon salt and ⅛ teaspoon pepper. Repeat with remaining 2 eggs, remaining ⅛ teaspoon salt, and remaining ⅛ teaspoon pepper in second small bowl.

3. Increase heat to medium-high and heat until oil is shimmering. Working quickly, pour 1 bowl of eggs into 1 side of pan and second bowl of eggs into other side. Cover and cook for 1 minute. Let stand off heat, covered, for 15 to 45 seconds for runny yolks (white around edge of yolk will be barely opaque), 45 to 60 seconds for soft but set yolks, and about 2 minutes for medium-set yolks.

4. Using spatula, place eggs on top of cucumbers. Top each egg with feta, tomato slices, onion slices, and sprouts. Top with remaining bread slices and serve.

Egg, Kimchi, and Avocado Sandwiches

Serves 4 Total Time 1¼ hours

Why This Recipe Works For a hearty egg sandwich, we tuck squares of baked eggs, zippy kimchi, creamy avocado, and tangy mayonnaise into lightly toasted rolls and add a generous sprinkle of cilantro to freshen the flavors. This recipe requires an 8-inch square metal baking pan. Avoid using a ceramic or glass baking dish, which will increase the cooking time and could cause the eggs to overcook during cooling. We like the flavor and texture of kaiser rolls for these sandwiches, but you can substitute 4-inch bulkie rolls, English muffins, or burger buns, if desired. For maximum efficiency, gather and prepare the sandwich fillings while the eggs cook, and toast the rolls while the eggs cool.

- 8 large eggs
- ¼ teaspoon table salt
- ¾ cup cabbage kimchi, drained and chopped coarse
- ¼ cup mayonnaise
- 4 kaiser rolls, halved and lightly toasted
- ¼ cup chopped fresh cilantro
- 1 ripe avocado, halved, pitted, and sliced thin

1. Adjust oven rack to middle position and heat oven to 300 degrees. Whisk eggs and salt in large bowl until well combined. Whisk in ⅔ cup water. Spray 8-inch square metal baking pan with vegetable oil spray. Pour egg mixture into prepared pan and set pan on rimmed baking sheet. Add 1½ cups water to sheet. Transfer sheet to oven and bake until eggs are fully set, 35 to 40 minutes, rotating pan halfway through baking. While eggs bake, blot kimchi with paper towels. Remove pan from sheet, transfer to wire rack, and let cool for 10 minutes.

2. Run knife around edges of pan and, using dish towel or pot holders, invert eggs onto cutting board (if eggs stick to pan, tap bottom of pan firmly to dislodge). Cut into 4 equal squares. (Egg squares can be stacked in an airtight container and refrigerated for up to 3 days. To reheat, arrange the egg square[s] on a plate and microwave at 50 percent power until they're warm, about 45 seconds for a single square or 2 to 3 minutes for four squares.) Spread mayonnaise on roll bottoms. Sprinkle cilantro over mayonnaise. Using spatula, transfer 1 egg square to each sandwich. Top each egg square with avocado and then kimchi. Set roll tops over kimchi and serve.

Fried Egg Sandwiches with Hummus and Sprouts

top | *Breakfast Tacos with Pinto Beans and Cotija Cheese*

bottom | *Breakfast Burritos with Poblano, Beans, Corn, and Crispy Potatoes*

Breakfast Tacos with Pinto Beans and Cotija Cheese

FAST Serves 4 Total Time 20 minutes

Why This Recipe Works We wanted a vegetarian option for boldly flavored breakfast tacos that would come together quickly and keep us satisfied until lunchtime. Beans are often served alongside Mexican egg dishes such as huevos rancheros or migas, so we thought, why not put them directly into the eggs? We add olive oil to the mixture to keep the eggs tender and add richness, cooking them quickly over medium-high heat for large, airy curds. We then fold in the beans and cilantro once the curds are well established but still a little wet so that the eggs can set up around the beans and pull the dish together. A bit of crumbly, salty cotija cheese is a worthy addition. Served with a stack of warm tortillas and a bottle of hot sauce, these eggs make a quick, fresh meal. This recipe can be easily halved, if desired; use a 10-inch skillet.

- 3 tablespoons extra-virgin olive oil, divided
- ¼ cup jarred sliced jalapeños, chopped coarse
- 2 garlic cloves, minced
- 1 (15-ounce) can pinto beans, rinsed
- ¼ cup chopped fresh cilantro, divided
- 8 large eggs
- ¼ teaspoon table salt
- ¼ teaspoon pepper
- 1 ounce cotija or feta cheese, crumbled (¼ cup)
- 12 (6-inch) corn or flour tortillas, warmed

1. Cook 1 teaspoon oil, jalapeños, and garlic in 12-inch nonstick skillet over medium heat until fragrant, about 1 minute. Stir in beans and 3 tablespoons cilantro and cook until moisture has evaporated, about 1 minute. Transfer bean mixture to bowl and set aside. Wipe skillet clean with paper towels.

2. Beat eggs, 2 tablespoons oil, salt, and pepper with fork in bowl until eggs are thoroughly combined and color is pure yellow. Heat remaining 2 teaspoons oil in now-empty skillet over medium-high heat until shimmering. Add egg mixture and, using silicone spatula, constantly and firmly scrape along bottom and sides of skillet until eggs begin to clump and spatula just leaves trail on bottom of skillet, 1 to 2 minutes. Reduce heat to low and gently but constantly fold eggs until clumped and just slightly wet, 30 to 60 seconds. Fold in reserved bean mixture. Transfer to serving dish and sprinkle with cotija and remaining 1 tablespoon cilantro. Serve with tortillas.

Kale and Black Bean Breakfast Burritos

FAST Serves 6 Total Time 45 minutes

Why This Recipe Works Black beans, kale, and fluffy scrambled eggs fill these burritos with flavorful protein and superfood greens for a nutritious and filling meal. To build a flavorful base, we sauté aromatic onion, garlic, a poblano chile, and cumin and then add our beans, mashing half of them to create a cohesive mixture. Next, we quickly braise kale until tender, then use the same skillet to scramble the eggs before folding in the kale. We spread the bean mixture onto tortillas, add the kale-egg scramble, and finish with chopped tomato and a drizzle of olive oil. Softening the tortillas in the microwave makes them easy to roll. Serve with hot sauce, if desired.

- 2 tablespoons extra-virgin olive oil, divided, plus extra for drizzling
- 1 small onion, chopped fine
- 1 poblano chile, stemmed, seeded, and chopped fine
- ¾ teaspoon table salt, divided
- 2 garlic cloves, minced
- ½ teaspoon ground cumin
- 1 (15-ounce) can black beans, rinsed
- ¾ cup water, divided
- 12 ounces kale, stemmed and chopped
- 8 large eggs
- 2 tablespoons milk
- ¼ teaspoon pepper
- 6 (10-inch) flour tortillas
- 1 tomato, cored and chopped fine

1. Heat 1 tablespoon oil in 12-inch nonstick skillet over medium-high heat until shimmering. Add onion, poblano, and ¼ teaspoon salt and cook until softened, about 5 minutes. Stir in garlic and cumin and cook until fragrant, about 30 seconds. Stir in beans and ½ cup water and cook until beans are warmed through, about 4 minutes. Off heat, mash half of beans to chunky paste; transfer to bowl and cover to keep warm; set aside. Wipe out skillet with paper towels.

2. In now-empty skillet, heat 2 teaspoons oil over medium-high heat until shimmering. Add kale and ¼ teaspoon salt, cover, and cook until kale begins to wilt, about 2 minutes. Stir in remaining ¼ cup water, cover, and cook until kale is tender, 2 to 4 minutes; transfer to second bowl. Wipe out skillet with paper towels.

3. Beat eggs, milk, pepper, and remaining ¼ teaspoon salt with fork in bowl until eggs are thoroughly combined and color is pure yellow. Heat remaining 1 teaspoon oil in now-empty skillet over medium-high heat until shimmering. Add egg mixture and, using silicone spatula, constantly and firmly scrape along bottom and sides of skillet until eggs begin to clump and spatula leaves trail on bottom of skillet, 1 to 2 minutes. Off heat, gently stir in kale and constantly fold eggs and kale until clumped and just slightly wet, 30 to 60 seconds. Cover to keep warm.

4. Wrap tortillas in damp dish towel and microwave until warm and pliable, about 1 minute. Arrange tortillas on counter. Spread reserved bean mixture evenly across center of each tortilla. Top with kale-egg mixture, then sprinkle with tomato and drizzle with extra oil to taste. Working with 1 burrito at a time, fold sides of tortilla over filling, then fold up bottom of tortilla and roll tightly around filling. Serve immediately.

Breakfast Burritos with Poblano, Beans, Corn, and Crispy Potatoes

Serves 4 Total Time 50 minutes

Why This Recipe Works For a potato-y breakfast burrito, we ensure extra-crispy potatoes by using frozen Tater Tots, thawed and then smashed flat in the skillet. Along with the taters, we add fluffy scrambled eggs, pinto beans, sharp cheddar cheese, and sautéed vegetables for a hearty vegetarian filling. A potent chipotle sour cream sauce provides tang and heat without adding excess moisture, keeping the burritos neat and portable. Browning the rolled burritos in a hot skillet right before serving produces a crispy golden exterior and helps them stay sealed. If you are spice averse, omit the cayenne pepper and reduce the chipotle chile to 1 tablespoon. To thaw frozen Tater Tots, either let them sit in the refrigerator for 24 hours or arrange them on a paper towel–lined plate and microwave them for 1½ minutes.

Chipotle Sour Cream

- ¼ cup sour cream
- 2 tablespoons minced canned chipotle chile in adobo sauce
- 2 teaspoons lime juice
- 1 garlic clove, minced
- ¼ teaspoon cayenne pepper
- ¼ teaspoon table salt

Burritos

- 6 tablespoons vegetable oil, divided
- 2 cups frozen Tater Tots, thawed and patted dry
- 1 poblano chile, stemmed, seeded, and chopped
- ½ cup canned pinto beans, rinsed
- ½ cup frozen corn
- ¼ cup chopped onion
- 1 teaspoon chili powder
- ½ teaspoon table salt
- 8 large eggs, lightly beaten
- 3 ounces sharp cheddar cheese, shredded (¾ cup)
- 4 (10-inch) flour tortillas

1. **For the chipotle sour cream** Combine all ingredients in bowl; set aside.

2. **For the burritos** Heat 3 tablespoons oil in 12-inch nonstick skillet over medium-high heat until shimmering. Add Tater Tots to skillet and press with spatula or underside of dry measuring cup to flatten slightly. Cook until crispy and deep golden brown, about 4 minutes per side. Transfer Tater Tots to paper towel–lined plate and set aside. Wipe skillet clean with paper towels.

3. Heat 2 tablespoons oil in now-empty skillet over medium heat until shimmering. Add poblano, beans, corn, onion, chili powder, and salt and cook until softened, 6 to 8 minutes. Add eggs and, using silicone spatula, constantly and firmly scrape along bottom and sides of skillet until eggs begin to clump and spatula leaves trail on bottom of skillet, 1 to 2 minutes. Off heat, gently stir in cheddar and constantly fold eggs and cheddar until clumped and just slightly wet, 30 to 60 seconds. Cover to keep warm.

4. Wrap tortillas in damp dish towel and microwave until warm and pliable, about 1 minute. Arrange tortillas on counter. Spread about 1½ tablespoons reserved chipotle sour cream across bottom third of each tortilla, leaving 1-inch border. Top chipotle sour cream with Tater Tots and eggs. Working with 1 burrito at a time, fold sides of tortilla over filling, then fold up bottom of tortilla and roll tightly around filling.

5. Wipe skillet clean with paper towels. Heat remaining 1 tablespoon oil in skillet over medium heat until shimmering. Arrange burritos in skillet seam side down and cook until crisp and golden, about 1 minute per side. Serve.

Filling, Rolling, and Crisping a Burrito

1. Divide filling among tortillas, then fold sides of tortillas over filling.

2. Fold up bottom and roll tightly.

3. Arrange burritos seam side down in skillet and cook until crisp and golden.

Brussels Sprout Hash with Poached Eggs

FAST Serves 4 Total Time 35 minutes

Why This Recipe Works Earthy brussels sprouts and sweet carrots combine with potatoes in this fast and hearty hash. But hashing together different vegetables presents a challenge: The potatoes and carrots take longer than the brussels sprouts to soften. Starting the potatoes and carrots in the microwave with a little oil solves the problem, turning them tender in only 5 minutes. Meanwhile, we cook the brussels sprouts in a skillet to get good browning. Sliced or shredded sprouts tend to steam rather than brown, so we cut the sprouts into wedges, providing nice flat surfaces that pick up flavorful browning. Next, we add the microwaved carrots and potatoes along with onion, garlic, thyme, and a little water to help the brussels sprouts finish cooking through. Look for small brussels sprouts no bigger than a golf ball, as they're likely to be sweeter and more tender than large sprouts. If you can find only large sprouts, halve them and cut each half into thirds.

- 1 pound red potatoes, unpeeled, cut into ½-inch pieces
- 2 carrots, peeled and cut into ½-inch pieces
- 3 tablespoons extra-virgin olive oil, divided
- 1½ teaspoons table salt, divided
- ½ teaspoon plus ⅛ teaspoon pepper, divided
- 1 pound brussels sprouts, trimmed and quartered lengthwise
- 1 onion, chopped fine
- 2 tablespoons water
- 1 tablespoon minced fresh thyme
- 1 garlic clove, minced
- 1 tablespoon refined coconut oil or unsalted butter
- 4 eggs
- 2 scallions, sliced thin

1. Combine potatoes, carrots, 1 tablespoon olive oil, ½ teaspoon salt, and ¼ teaspoon pepper in large bowl. Microwave, covered, until vegetables are tender, 5 to 7 minutes, stirring occasionally.

2. Meanwhile, heat 1 tablespoon olive oil in 12-inch nonstick skillet over medium-high heat until shimmering. Add brussels sprouts and cook until browned, 6 to 8 minutes, stirring occasionally. Add microwaved vegetables and any accumulated juices, onion, water, thyme, garlic, remaining 1 tablespoon olive oil, ¾ teaspoon salt, and ¼ teaspoon pepper. Reduce heat to medium, cover, and cook until brussels sprouts are just tender, 5 to 7 minutes longer, stirring halfway through cooking.

3. Off heat, stir in coconut oil and season with salt and pepper to taste. Make 4 shallow indentations (about 2 inches wide) in surface of hash using back of spoon. Crack 1 egg into each indentation and sprinkle eggs with remaining ¼ teaspoon salt and remaining ⅛ teaspoon pepper. Cover and cook over medium-low heat until egg whites are just set and yolks are still runny, 5 to 10 minutes. Sprinkle with scallions and serve.

Brussels Sprout Hash with Poached Eggs

Small Plates & Snacks

484 Garam Masala Peanuts
Chaat Masala Peanuts

485 Garam Masala ■ ●

485 Warm Marinated Olives ■ ●

485 Marinated Manchego

486 Homemade Yogurt
Labneh
Lemon-Dill Labneh

489 Whipped Feta Dip ■
Whipped Feta and Roasted Red Pepper Dip ■
Whipped Feta Dip with Dill and Parsley ■

489 Frico ■

490 Pan-Seared Halloumi with Cherry Pepper Glaze ■

490 Bouyourdi (Spicy Greek Baked Feta)

491 Baked Pimento Cheese Dip

493 Classic Guacamole ■ ●

493 Hummus with Crispy Mushrooms and Sumac ■ ●

494 Ultracreamy Hummus ●

494 Fattet Hummus (Crispy Pita with Garlicky Yogurt and Chickpeas) ■

497 Biscuit Crackers with Red Lentil Dip

498 Beet Dip with Yogurt and Tahini

498 Corn Cheese ■

499 Slow-Roasted Eggplant Dip with Pomegranate Molasses and Aleppo Pepper ●

501 Fresh Leek and Spinach Dip

501 Southern Cheese Straws
Parmesan–Black Pepper Cheese Straws

502 Pa amb Tomàquet (Catalan Tomato Bread) ■ ●

503 Fava Bean Crostini with Manchego and Pine Nuts

504 Cranberry and Goat Cheese Crostini ■

504 Buffalo Cauliflower Bites ■ ●

506 Vegan Ranch Dressing ■ ●

506 Vegan Mayonnaise ■ ●

507 Portobello Mushroom Fries with Cherry Pepper Sauce

509 Patatas Bravas ●

510 Zucchini Chips with Tzatziki

511 Chickpea Fries ●

512 Lemon and Herb Dipping Sauce ■ ●
Calabrian Chile Dipping Sauce ■ ●
Honey and Spice Dipping Sauce ■

512 Scallion Pancakes

514 Spring Rolls (Cantonese Egg Rolls) ●

515 Plum Sauce ■ ●

516 Pakoras (South Asian Spiced Vegetable Fritters) ●

516 Carrot-Tamarind Chutney ■ ●

517 Sweet Potato Fritters with Feta, Dill, and Cilantro
Sweet Potato Fritters with Cheddar and Chipotle

519 Sesame Balls ●

No-Fuss Appetizers

520 Blistered Shishito Peppers ■ ●

520 Buttered Popcorn ■
Parmesan-Pepper Popcorn ■
Garlic and Herb Popcorn ■
Hot and Sweet Popcorn ■
Cajun-Spiced Popcorn ■

521 Sun-Dried Tomato Tapenade with Farmer's Cheese ■

521 Melted Brie with Honey and Herbs ■

■ Fast (45 minutes or less) ● Vegan

top | *Garam Masala Peanuts*
bottom | *Warm Marinated Olives*

Garam Masala Peanuts

Serves 8 to 10 Total Time 50 minutes, plus 30 minutes cooling

Why This Recipe Works A powerfully flavorful spice blend anchors these crunchy spiced peanuts. Garam masala ("warm spice blend")—an incredibly aromatic, sweet, and lightly spicy blend of ingredients such as cinnamon, cardamom, black pepper, coriander, and cumin—perfectly complements sweet-salty, earthy roasted peanuts. Tossing the peanuts (we call for dry-roasted peanuts since raw are difficult to source) in a mixture of sugar, egg white, and water before roasting them low and slow yields peanuts that are uniformly coated with a delicious, crunchy shell. Seasoning the nuts before and after baking ensures that they have the full spectrum of flavors, since some spices can be muted with long cooking. We developed this recipe using Planters Unsalted Dry Roasted Peanuts. You can substitute lightly salted dry-roasted peanuts; if you do, reduce the salt to 1 teaspoon. Do not substitute salted dry-roasted peanuts. You can make our homemade Garam Masala (recipe follows) or use store-bought. This recipe can be doubled: Adjust the oven racks to the upper-middle and lower-middle positions and bake the nuts on two baking sheets, switching and rotating the sheets halfway through baking.

- ½ cup sugar
- 1 large egg white
- 4 teaspoons garam masala, divided
- 1 tablespoon water
- 1¾ teaspoons table salt
- 3¼ cups (1 pound) unsalted dry-roasted peanuts

1. Adjust oven rack to middle position and heat oven to 300 degrees. Line rimmed baking sheet with parchment paper and spray with vegetable oil spray. Whisk sugar, egg white, 2 teaspoons garam masala, water, and salt together in large bowl. Add peanuts and toss until evenly coated with sugar mixture.

2. Spread peanut mixture evenly over prepared sheet and bake until peanuts are deep golden brown, dry, and crisp, about 40 minutes, rotating sheet halfway through baking.

3. Immediately sprinkle remaining 2 teaspoons garam masala evenly over hot peanuts. Transfer peanuts to bowl and stir to incorporate spices and break up any large clumps. Let cool completely, about 30 minutes. Serve. (Nuts can be stored in airtight container for up to 3 weeks.)

Variation

Chaat Masala Peanuts

You can find chaat masala in Indian supermarkets or online.

Reduce salt to 1½ teaspoons. Sprinkle 2 teaspoons chaat masala on peanuts with garam masala in step 3.

Garam Masala

FAST VEGAN Makes ⅓ cup Total Time 10 minutes

Use a rasp-style grater to grate a whole nutmeg or substitute an equal amount of ground nutmeg.

- 2 tablespoons coriander seeds
- 4 teaspoons black peppercorns
- 1 tablespoon cumin seeds
- 2 cinnamon sticks
- 1½ teaspoons green cardamom pods (about 14 total)
- 4 whole cloves
- ½ teaspoon ground nutmeg

Toast coriander seeds, peppercorns, cumin seeds, cinnamon sticks, cardamom pods, and cloves in dry 8-inch skillet over medium heat until just fragrant, about 3 minutes. Transfer seed mixture to spice grinder, add nutmeg, and process until ground to fine powder, 1 to 2 minutes. (Garam masala can be stored in an airtight container for up to 1 month.)

Warm Marinated Olives

FAST VEGAN Serves 6 to 8 Total Time 25 minutes

Why This Recipe Works We make these boldly flavored olives in a skillet; first we infuse olive oil with thinly sliced strips of orange zest, then add the olives, herbes de Provence, coriander seeds, and red pepper flakes. We allow the olives and spices to cook for 5 minutes, while toasting the spices. A combination of black and green olives creates diverse flavors and textures. (Black olives offer a softer texture with slightly floral or smoky flavors, some with hints of red wine or whiskey. Green olives have a meatier texture and a flavor varying from buttery to ultrabriny, some with hints of vermouth.) Using pitted olives allows the spices to get trapped in the holes left by the removed pits, flavoring the olives inside and out. These olives create a bonus spiced dipping oil for crusty bread. To crush the coriander seeds, place them in a zipper-lock bag and press or gently pound with a skillet, rolling pin, or meat mallet.

- 1 orange
- ½ cup extra-virgin olive oil
- 2 cups pitted brine-cured green olives
- 2 cups pitted brine-cured black olives
- 1 tablespoon herbes de Provence
- 2 teaspoons coriander seeds, crushed
- ¼–½ teaspoon red pepper flakes
- 6 garlic cloves, minced
- 1 tablespoon red wine vinegar
- Crusty bread

1. Using vegetable peeler, remove four 2-inch strips of zest from orange. Slice each strip thin lengthwise. Heat oil and zest in 12-inch skillet over medium heat until zest is fragrant and begins to curl, about 3 minutes. Add olives, herbes de Provence, coriander seeds, and pepper flakes and cook until spices are toasted and olives are sizzling, about 5 minutes.

2. Stir in garlic and cook until fragrant, about 30 seconds. Off heat, stir in vinegar. Let olive mixture sit in skillet until cooled slightly, about 5 minutes. Serve (directly from skillet or in large shallow serving bowl) with crusty bread. (Marinated olives can be refrigerated for up to 4 days. Let sit at room temperature for about 10 minutes before serving.)

Marinated Manchego

Serves 6 to 8 Total Time 35 minutes, plus 24 hours marinating

Why This Recipe Works Marinating Manchego cheese is an easy way to add more depth to an already flavorful cheese. It's great to serve as an appetizer, and you get the added bonus of making an infused oil that can be used in a salad dressing or for sautéing vegetables. To make it, we gently heat garlic, orange zest, thyme, bay leaves, and red pepper flakes in oil. The garlic softens slightly and infuses the oil with nutty-sweet flavor. Once the mixture cools, we pour it over the Manchego and allow the cheese to marinate in the deeply flavored oil. Use a good-quality extra-virgin olive oil here. Remove the strips of orange zest with a vegetable peeler. Serve the cheese with crusty bread for dipping or use it in a salad.

- ¾ cup extra-virgin olive oil, plus extra as needed
- 8 garlic cloves, smashed and peeled
- 6 (3-inch) strips orange zest
- 8 sprigs fresh thyme
- 3 bay leaves
- ½ teaspoon table salt
- ¼ teaspoon red pepper flakes
- 8 ounces Manchego cheese, cut into rough ¾-inch cubes

1. Combine oil, garlic, orange zest, thyme sprigs, bay leaves, salt, and pepper flakes in small saucepan and cook over medium-low heat until garlic begins to turn golden, about 10 minutes. Set aside and let cool completely.

2. Place Manchego in 16-ounce jar with tight-fitting lid. Using tongs or fork, transfer garlic, orange zest, thyme sprigs, and bay leaves to jar with Manchego. Pour oil mixture over Manchego to cover, pressing down cheese as needed to submerge it. If needed, add extra oil to cover cheese. Affix jar lid and refrigerate for at least 24 hours or up to 1 week. Let come to room temperature before serving.

Homemade Yogurt

Makes 2 quarts Total Time 40 minutes, plus 13 hours fermenting and chilling

Why This Recipe Works For tangy, creamy yogurt, we skip the usual preliminary scalding and cooling steps by starting with ultra-pasteurized milk, which has already been rapidly heated and chilled. This lets bacterial cultures turn it into an especially thick and silky yogurt. We bring the milk to 115 degrees and stir in store-bought yogurt with live cultures, strains of bacteria that digest the lactose in milk, producing lactic acid. This acid is what gives yogurt its flavor and causes the proteins in milk to gradually form a gel, turning liquid milk into creamy yogurt. To provide those bacteria with a cozy environment to do their work, we place a covered pot of boiling water in the oven beside the pot of warm water holding the jars of milk. This setup helps the oven maintain a temperature of 100 to 115 degrees for hours. After that, it is just a matter of tasting for tartness and thickness to decide when to pop the jars into the fridge to let the yogurt set. This recipe will work only with ultra-pasteurized milk. Most organic milk is ultra-pasteurized; this will be noted on the label. Be sure to use freshly opened containers of milk. Any type of plain yogurt (whole-milk, low-fat, Greek, etc.) that contains live cultures can be used. You can halve this recipe, if preferred. Be sure to save ½ cup of yogurt to use as the starter for a subsequent batch.

- 7½ cups ultra-pasteurized whole, 2 percent low-fat, 1 percent low-fat, or skim milk
- ½ cup plain yogurt

1. Bring milk to 115 degrees in saucepan over medium heat, 2 to 5 minutes. (If milk gets hotter than 115 degrees, let it cool to 115 degrees before proceeding. Higher temperatures can kill some cultures.) Off heat, whisk yogurt into milk until very well combined. Divide mixture evenly between two 1-quart Mason jars (they will be very full; a funnel can be helpful for this step). Add lids, then screw on rings until just finger-tight.

2. Adjust oven rack to lowest position and turn on oven light. Bring 5 quarts water to boil in large covered pot. Place jars in second large pot. Add room-temperature water until jars are submerged to their necks. (If jars are taller than pot, add water to 1¼ inches from rim of pot.) Remove jars and bring water to 120 degrees over medium heat. Return jars to pot of 120-degree water. Transfer both pots to oven. Incubate yogurt, without opening oven door, for 5 hours.

3. Remove 1 jar from water bath. Using clean spoon, taste yogurt for tartness and consistency. If tarter, thicker yogurt is desired, return jar to water bath and shut oven door. (Bear in mind that yogurt will thicken significantly as it cools but can be loosened up by stirring prior to serving.) Set oven to 350 degrees and heat for 3 minutes (start your timer as soon as you set the dial; oven will not reach 350 degrees). Turn off oven and let incubate for up to 10 more hours, repeating heating step each time oven door is opened. Remove jars from water bath and refrigerate until fully cooled and set, about 8 hours. (Yogurt can be refrigerated for up to 2 weeks.)

Variations

Labneh

Makes ½ cup   Total Time 15 minutes, plus overnight straining

Labneh is yogurt that's been drained of most of its whey so that it takes on a thick, lush consistency akin to that of whipped cream cheese. Drizzled with olive oil and sprinkled with za'atar, labneh can be part of a meze offering. You can substitute drained Greek yogurt for homemade.

Strain ¾ cup homemade yogurt through cheesecloth overnight. Line plate with triple layer of paper towels and spread yogurt over top. Fold paper towels over yogurt. Peel off paper towels and rotate plate 90 degrees. Repeat folding and peeling twice to remove excess moisture from yogurt. (Labneh can be refrigerated for up to 2 weeks.)

Lemon-Dill Labneh

Makes 1 cup   Total Time 15 minutes, plus 1 hour chilling

You will need 1 cup labneh for this recipe. Serve with crudités or pita chips.

Stir 1 tablespoon minced fresh dill, 2 teaspoons grated lemon zest, ⅛ teaspoon salt, and pinch pepper into labneh. Cover and refrigerate until flavors have blended, about 1 hour. Season with salt and pepper to taste before serving.

Making Labneh

1. Line large plate with triple layer of paper towels. Spread ⅔ cup homemade or commercial strained yogurt evenly over top; set aside and let sit for 10 minutes.

2. Use paper towels to fold yogurt in half; peel back towels. Rotate plate 90 degrees and repeat folding and peeling 2 more times to make a smaller, drier mass.

| *Homemade Yogurt*

Whipped Feta Dip with Dill and Parsley

Whipped Feta Dip

FAST Serves 8 Total Time 15 minutes

Why This Recipe Works We defy tradition with this lush, salty Greek-style dip by using cow's-milk feta instead of a true Greek feta made with sheep's- or goat's-milk or a combination thereof. The reason: Cow's-milk feta produces a firmer dip that holds up well at room temperature. But we also wanted a dip that was loose enough to easily scoop up with soft pita, so we process the cheese with a few tablespoons of milk in addition to the traditional extra-virgin olive oil. We also rinse the feta in water to avoid an overly salty dip. A little garlic and lemon juice, along with fresh oregano, round out the flavors. Do not substitute sheep's-milk feta, which is softer. Because feta is quite salty, avoid serving this dip with salted chips; serve with crudités and pita bread.

- 1½ teaspoons lemon juice
- ¼ teaspoon minced garlic
- 8 ounces cow's-milk feta cheese
- 3 tablespoons milk
- 2 tablespoons plus 2 teaspoons extra-virgin olive oil, divided
- 2 teaspoons minced fresh oregano

1. Combine lemon juice and garlic in small bowl and set aside. Break feta into rough ½-inch pieces and place in medium bowl. Add water to cover, then swish briefly to rinse. Transfer to fine-mesh strainer and drain well.

2. Transfer feta to food processor. Add milk and reserved lemon juice mixture and process until feta mixture resembles ricotta cheese, about 15 seconds. With processor running, slowly drizzle in 2 tablespoons oil. Continue to process until mixture has Greek yogurt–like consistency (some small lumps will remain), 1½ to 2 minutes longer, stopping once to scrape down bottom and sides of bowl. Add oregano and pulse to combine. Transfer dip to bowl. If serving immediately, drizzle with remaining 2 teaspoons oil. (Dip can be refrigerated for up to 3 days. If refrigerated, let sit at room temperature for 30 minutes and drizzle with oil before serving.)

Variations

FAST Whipped Feta and Roasted Red Pepper Dip

Substitute red wine vinegar for lemon juice. Reduce milk to 2 tablespoons. Add ¼ cup jarred roasted red peppers, chopped; ½ teaspoon smoked paprika; and pinch cayenne pepper with milk. Omit oregano.

FAST Whipped Feta Dip with Dill and Parsley

Substitute 1 tablespoon minced fresh dill (or mint, if desired) and 1 tablespoon minced fresh parsley for oregano.

Frico

FAST Makes 8 large wafers Total Time 45 minutes

Why This Recipe Works As an accompaniment to cocktails or eaten just as a snack, frico is a simple, crisp wafer of flavorful cheese, usually Montasio, that has been melted and browned. We set out to find the secret behind great frico, and then to determine the best substitute for Montasio cheese, which isn't available in many supermarkets. Many recipes suggest Parmesan as a substitute for Montasio, but we found Asiago cheese to be a better stand-in—though the real thing is even better. Cheese simply grated into a hot pan could turn into a sticky mess, but we found that using a nonstick skillet allows us to cook the frico without adding butter or oil. We discovered that it was easy to turn the frico to the other side once the first side browned if we first took the skillet off the heat, the slightly cooled cheese didn't stretch or tear when we flipped it. Turning the heat down to cook the second side gave the best results; a pan that is too hot turned the cheese bitter. Serve frico with a bowl of marinated olives or marinated sun-dried tomatoes. Frico is also good crumbled into a salad, crouton-style.

- 1 pound Montasio or aged Asiago cheese, grated fine (about 8 cups)

1. Sprinkle 2 ounces (about 1 cup) of grated cheese over bottom of 10-inch nonstick skillet set over medium-high heat. Use heat-resistant silicone spatula or wooden spoon to tidy lacy outer edges of cheese. Cook, shaking pan occasionally to ensure even distribution of cheese over pan bottom, until edges are lacy and toasted, about 4 minutes. Remove pan from heat and allow cheese to set for about 30 seconds.

2. Using fork on top and heat-resistant spatula underneath, carefully flip cheese wafer and return pan to medium heat. Cook until second side is golden brown, about 2 minutes. Slide cheese wafer out of pan and transfer to plate. Repeat with remaining cheese. Serve within 1 hour.

Pan-Seared Halloumi with Cherry Pepper Glaze

FAST Serves 6 Total Time 25 minutes

Why This Recipe Works Pan-seared halloumi makes an excellent (and easy) appetizer to whip up—as long as you know how to make the best of the cheese's browning properties and how to accommodate its saltiness. We start by cutting our cheese into ½-inch-thick slices to increase the surface area to be browned. A slick of oil in a nonstick skillet facilitates the rapid transfer of heat to the cheese, so it browns thoroughly before drying out, and ensures that the browning remains on the cheese, not on the skillet. The cheese exudes some water as it cooks, which interferes with browning; we turn the slices frequently so that every bit of the cheese makes contact with the oiled skillet for the best browning. Because halloumi has plenty of salt, we took care not to add any in our glaze: Minced cherry peppers add sweet heat, lemon juice contributes a refreshing brightness, and honey provides not just sweetness but also viscosity. A fragrant shower of mint brings welcome freshness. The saltiness of halloumi varies; for the best results, select a product that has less than 260 milligrams of sodium per serving. Red cherry peppers look nice here, but pepperoncini also work.

- 1 tablespoon extra-virgin olive oil
- 8 ounces halloumi cheese, sliced crosswise ½ inch thick
- 3 tablespoons honey
- 3 tablespoons minced jarred hot cherry peppers
- 2 tablespoons lemon juice
- 1 tablespoon chopped fresh mint

1. Heat oil in 10-inch nonstick skillet over medium-high heat until shimmering. Arrange halloumi in even layer in skillet and cook, flipping frequently, until deeply browned and crisp on both sides, about 6 minutes. Transfer cheese to cutting board. Wipe out skillet with paper towel.

2. Add honey, cherry peppers, and lemon juice to now-empty skillet. Cook over low heat, stirring occasionally, until syrupy, about 1 minute. While glaze cooks, cut cheese into bite-size pieces. Return cheese to skillet and increase heat to medium. Continue to cook, stirring gently, until glaze coats cheese, 4 to 6 minutes longer. Transfer to platter, sprinkle with mint, and serve.

Bouyourdi (Spicy Greek Baked Feta)

Serves 4 to 6 Total Time 55 minutes

Why This Recipe Works To make this beloved Greek meze, we use sheep's-milk feta, ripe tomato, and green bell pepper. The heat from fresh chiles and dried chile flakes balances the creamy dairy. Extra-virgin olive oil enhances the dish's richness and unifies its components. Use sheep's-milk feta in brine if possible, which will be moister. Do not use precrumbled feta; it is too dry. If your block of feta is thicker than 1 inch, slice it into 1-inch slabs before using. This dish is meant to be spicy. Bukovo pepper flakes are traditional, but any red pepper flakes can be used. Use an 8-inch square broiler-safe baking dish or shallow earthenware dish or cazuela to mimic the traditional clay vessel. Serve with crusty bread as an appetizer or with other meze as a meal.

- 1 large tomato, cored
- 1 longhorn chile or ½ jalapeño, stemmed
- ¼ green bell pepper, cut into ¼-inch pieces
- 3 tablespoons extra-virgin olive oil, divided
- 1½ teaspoons dried oregano, divided
- 1 (7-ounce) block feta cheese
- ½ teaspoon bukovo or red pepper flakes

1. Adjust oven rack to upper-middle position and heat oven to 350 degrees.

2. Slice two ¼-inch-thick rounds from tomato and set aside. Chop remaining tomato into ½-inch pieces and place in small bowl. Cut longhorn chile in half crosswise (reserve 1 half for other use). Slice two ¼-inch-thick rings from longhorn chile half and set aside. Mince remaining longhorn chile and add to chopped tomato, along with bell pepper, 2 tablespoons oil, and 1 teaspoon oregano. Stir to combine, pour into baking dish, and smooth into even layer.

3. Center feta block on top of vegetables. Arrange tomato slices and longhorn chile rings in single layer on top of feta. Drizzle with remaining 1 tablespoon oil and sprinkle with remaining ½ teaspoon oregano. Cover dish tightly with aluminum foil and bake until diced vegetables have softened and tomato slices are beginning to soften at edges, about 25 minutes.

4. Remove foil and return dish to oven. Turn on broiler. Broil until edges of tomato and longhorn chile slices are browned, 4 to 7 minutes. Remove dish from oven, sprinkle with pepper flakes, and serve.

Baked Pimento Cheese Dip

Serves 6 to 8 Total Time 1 hour

Why This Recipe Works Pimento cheese, often called the caviar of the South, is the ultimate refrigerator condiment for snacking or slathering on bread or crackers. It's been adapted into many variations, including a hot, melty dip. Because such a cheesy mixture has the potential to curdle or exude excess oil when heated, we make a few adjustments to ensure a cohesive, smooth result. For one, we microwave the cream cheese to jump-start the warming process, which helps maintain a creamy, cohesive consistency. We opt for extra-sharp cheddar for a strong, cheesy flavor, along with a generous amount of pimento peppers to permeate the dip. Mayonnaise keeps the mixture creamy, and Worcestershire sauce and cayenne pepper add subtle heat and savoriness. We bake the dip just briefly at a high temperature, which gently warms it without overcooking it and browns the edges. After the dip has rested, serve it with tortilla chips, crackers, and/or pickle spears for a craveable, shareable snack. We prefer the flavor of extra-sharp cheddar in this recipe, but sharp cheddar also works.

- 8 ounces cream cheese
- ⅔ cup mayonnaise
- 2 teaspoons Worcestershire sauce
- ¼ teaspoon cayenne pepper
- 8 ounces yellow extra-sharp cheddar cheese, shredded (2 cups)
- 2 (4-ounce) jars pimentos, drained, patted dry, and minced

1. Adjust oven rack to middle position and heat oven to 400 degrees. Microwave cream cheese in large bowl until warmed and very soft, about 1 minute, stirring with silicone spatula halfway through microwaving.

2. Using silicone spatula, fold mayonnaise, Worcestershire, and cayenne into softened cream cheese until evenly combined and no lumps remain. Fold in cheddar and pimentos. Transfer mixture to 1-quart baking dish and smooth top with silicone spatula. (Dish can be covered with plastic wrap and refrigerated for up to 24 hours. Let sit at room temperature for about 30 minutes before baking. Increase baking time to 30 to 35 minutes.)

3. Bake until mixture is browned at edges, 20 to 25 minutes. Let cool for 10 minutes. Serve.

top | *Bouyourdi (Spicy Greek Baked Feta)*
bottom | *Baked Pimento Cheese Dip*

The Best Guac

Choose the Right Avocado

At the grocery you might see Fuerte avocados, which are also known as Florida or skinny avocados. These avocados are large, with a smooth, bright green exterior; their high water content and relatively low fat content give them a mild, sweet flavor. But the most common variety is Hass; these avocados are small, rough-skinned, and dark green in color. They have a rich flavor and buttery texture that make them a superior choice for guacamole.

Ripeness Is Key

Although color alone isn't an indication of ripeness, Hass avocados do start out green and become progressively purple-black as they ripen. Avocados ripen unevenly, starting at the stem end, so gently squeezing the bottom of the fruit is the best indication of ripeness; it should yield slightly to the pressure.

Creamy but Chunky

Achieving the best texture is essential for really great guacamole, and we like a dip that's both creamy and chunky. To get the best of both worlds, we use a whisk to mash our avocados: The rounded top where the wires meet mashes the avocado efficiently, while the spaces between the wires allow many of the chunks to remain intact.

Classic Guacamole

Classic Guacamole

FAST **VEGAN** Makes 2 cups Total Time 15 minutes

Why This Recipe Works To make a smooth guacamole without relying on the coarse surface of a molcajete, a three-legged Mexican mortar made of volcanic rock, we mince the onion and chile by hand with kosher salt; the coarse crystals break down the aromatics, releasing their juices and flavors and transforming them into a paste that is easy to combine with the avocado and other ingredients. (The salt also helps the aromatics break down in a regular mortar and pestle.) A bit of lime zest adds further brightness without acidity. We use a whisk to mix and mash the avocado into the paste, creating a creamy but still chunky dip. Chopped tomato and cilantro add fruity flavor and freshness. For a spicier version, mince and add the serrano ribs and seeds to the onion mixture. A mortar and pestle can be used to process the onion mixture. Be sure to use Hass avocados here; Florida, or "skinny," avocados are too watery for dips. We used Diamond Crystal kosher salt when developing this recipe. If using Morton kosher salt, reduce salt to ¾ teaspoon.

- 2 tablespoons finely chopped onion
- 1 serrano chile, stemmed, seeded, and minced
- 1 teaspoon kosher salt
- ¼ teaspoon grated lime zest plus 1½–3 tablespoons juice
- 3 ripe avocados, halved, pitted, and cut into ½-inch pieces
- 1 plum tomato, cored, seeded, and cut into ⅛-inch dice
- 2 tablespoons chopped fresh cilantro

Place onion, serrano, salt, and lime zest on cutting board and chop until very finely minced. Transfer onion mixture to medium bowl and stir in 1½ tablespoons lime juice. Add avocados and, using sturdy whisk, mash and stir mixture until well combined with some ¼- to ½-inch chunks of avocado remaining. Stir in tomato and cilantro. Season with salt and up to 1½ teaspoons additional lime juice to taste. Serve.

Hummus with Crispy Mushrooms and Sumac

FAST **VEGAN** Serves 4 Total Time 35 minutes

Why This Recipe Works This hummus meal is super-satisfying, and is all about plants. Here, we opt for sautéed mushrooms, made irresistible by selecting oyster mushrooms; when roughly shredded, these mushrooms take on lacy, crispy edges, and you'll want to eat them straight from the pan. Chickpeas tossed in sumac with a squeeze of caramelized lemon offer a bright flavor counterpoint to the rich hummus and well-textured mushrooms. More texture and a slight sweetness come from a final sprinkling of chopped pistachios. You can substitute halved portobello mushrooms, sliced thin, for the oyster mushrooms.

- 12 ounces oyster mushrooms, trimmed and torn into 1½-inch pieces
- ¼ cup water
- 2 tablespoons extra-virgin olive oil, divided, plus extra for drizzling
- ⅛ teaspoon table salt
- 1 lemon, quartered
- 1 (15-ounce) can chickpeas, rinsed
- 2 teaspoons sumac, plus extra for serving
- 3 cups Ultracreamy Hummus (page 494)
- ¼ cup fresh parsley leaves
- 2 tablespoons chopped toasted pistachios

1. Cook mushrooms and water in 12-inch nonstick skillet over high heat, stirring occasionally, until mushrooms begin to stick to bottom of skillet, 6 to 8 minutes. Reduce heat to medium-high and stir in 1 tablespoon oil and salt. Cook, stirring occasionally, until mushrooms are crisp and well browned, 8 to 12 minutes. Transfer to plate.

2. Add remaining 1 tablespoon oil and lemon quarters, cut sides down, to now-empty skillet and cook over medium-high heat until well browned on cut sides, 2 to 3 minutes; transfer to plate with mushrooms. Add chickpeas to oil left in again-empty skillet and cook until lightly browned, about 2 minutes. Off heat, add sumac and toss to coat. Season with salt and pepper to taste.

3. Divide hummus among individual bowls. Top with mushrooms, chickpeas, parsley, and pistachios. Sprinkle with extra sumac and drizzle with extra oil. Serve with seared lemon quarters.

Ultracreamy Hummus

VEGAN Makes 3 cups Total Time 1 hour

Why This Recipe Works To achieve a perfectly velvety-smooth, buttercream-like texture, we simmer canned (yes, canned) chickpeas with water and baking soda for 20 minutes, which allows us to quickly remove their grainy skins by gently swishing them under water. Tahini made with heavily roasted seeds can contribute bitterness, so choose a light- colored tahini (avoid versions that look like peanut butter). The hummus will thicken slightly over time; add warm water, 1 tablespoon at a time, as needed to restore its creamy consistency.

- 2 (15-ounce) cans chickpeas, rinsed
- ½ teaspoon baking soda
- ⅓ cup lemon juice (2 lemons), plus extra for seasoning
- 1 teaspoon table salt
- 1 tablespoon minced garlic
- ¼ teaspoon ground cumin, plus extra for garnish
- ½ cup tahini, stirred well
- 2 tablespoons extra-virgin olive oil, plus extra for drizzling
- 1 tablespoon minced fresh parsley

1. Combine chickpeas, baking soda, and 6 cups water in medium saucepan and bring to boil over high heat. Reduce heat to maintain simmer and cook, stirring occasionally, until chickpea skins begin to float to surface and chickpeas are creamy and very soft, 20 to 25 minutes.

2. While chickpeas cook, whisk lemon juice, salt, and garlic together in small bowl and let sit for 10 minutes. Strain garlic-lemon mixture through fine-mesh strainer set over separate bowl, pressing on solids to extract as much liquid as possible; discard solids.

3. Drain chickpeas in colander and return to saucepan. Fill saucepan with cold water and gently swish chickpeas with your fingers to release skins. Pour off most of water into colander to collect skins, leaving chickpeas behind in saucepan. Repeat filling, swishing, and draining 3 or 4 times until most skins have been removed (this should yield about ¾ cup skins); discard skins. Transfer chickpeas to colander to drain.

4. Set aside 2 tablespoons whole chickpeas for garnish. Process garlic-lemon mixture, ¼ cup water, cumin, and remaining chickpeas in food processor until smooth, about 1 minute, scraping down sides of bowl as needed. Add tahini and oil and process until hummus is smooth, creamy, and light, about 1 minute, scraping down sides of bowl as needed. (Hummus should have pourable consistency similar to yogurt. If too thick, loosen with water, adding 1 teaspoon at a time.) Season with salt and extra lemon juice to taste. (Hummus can be refrigerated for up to 5 days; bring to room temperature before serving and stir in 1 tablespoon warm water to loosen hummus texture if necessary.) Transfer hummus to serving bowl and sprinkle with parsley, reserved chickpeas, and extra cumin. Drizzle with extra oil and serve.

Fattet Hummus (Crispy Pita with Garlicky Yogurt and Chickpeas)

FAST Serves 4 to 6 Total Time 45 minutes

Why This Recipe Works Fatteh is a popular Middle Eastern dish that ensures that leftover pita bread will be put to good use. Chickpea fatteh is commonly eaten for breakfast or brunch, but we like it as a light dinner or appetizer. We created our fatteh from the bottom up, starting with crispy pita chips that we make by tearing the bread into bite-size pieces, tossing them with oil and salt, and baking them until crisp. Next, we briefly simmer canned chickpeas to soften them a bit and then season the legumes with cumin and garlic tempered with lemon juice. The last component is a yogurt sauce flavored with tahini. Along with the tahini, we mix pomegranate molasses, lemon juice, and garlic into whole-milk yogurt to create a bright, creamy, pourable sauce. To serve, we arrange the pita chips on a platter with the seasoned chickpeas on top. We pour the yogurt sauce over the chickpeas before finishing the dish with toasted pine nuts, fresh parsley, and drizzles of extra-virgin olive oil. Use thinner pitas that have an inside pocket as opposed to ones that are thicker and not hollow. We don't recommend using store-bought pita chips. We like the viscosity of regular whole-milk yogurt in this recipe, but you can substitute ½ cup of whole-milk Greek yogurt mixed with 3 tablespoons of water. Though not traditional, pomegranate seeds add color and fruitiness. Fattet hummus is eaten with a spoon.

- 3 (8-inch) pitas, torn into 1-inch pieces (5 cups)
- ¼ cup extra-virgin olive oil, plus extra for drizzling
- 1¼ teaspoons table salt, divided
- 6 tablespoons lemon juice (2 lemons), divided
- 4 teaspoons minced garlic, divided
- ⅔ cup plain whole-milk yogurt
- ⅓ cup tahini
- 2 tablespoons minced fresh mint
- 1 tablespoon pomegranate molasses
- 2 (15-ounce) cans chickpeas, undrained
- 1½ teaspoons ground cumin
- ¼ cup pomegranate seeds (optional)
- ¼ cup pine nuts, toasted
- 2 tablespoons minced fresh parsley

1. Adjust oven rack to middle position and heat oven to 375 degrees. Toss pita pieces with oil and ½ teaspoon salt. Spread pita on wire rack set in rimmed baking sheet. Bake until crisp and golden brown, 15 to 18 minutes, rotating sheet halfway through baking. Set aside to cool. (Pita can be stored at room temperature for 24 hours.)

2. Meanwhile, combine ¼ cup lemon juice and 2 teaspoons minced garlic in small bowl. Combine remaining 2 tablespoons lemon juice and remaining 2 teaspoons minced garlic in medium bowl. Let both stand for 10 minutes.

3. Add yogurt, tahini, mint, pomegranate molasses, and ½ teaspoon salt to small bowl of lemon juice mixture and whisk to form thick, pourable sauce. Set aside.

4. Bring chickpeas and their liquid to boil in medium saucepan over medium-high heat. Adjust heat to medium-low and simmer until chickpeas are tender and heated through, about 5 minutes. Drain chickpeas well and add to medium bowl of lemon juice mixture along with cumin and remaining ¼ teaspoon salt. Stir well to combine.

5. In wide, shallow serving bowl, arrange pita chips in even layer. Spoon chickpea mixture over chips. Spoon yogurt sauce evenly over chickpeas. (If sauce has thickened so it doesn't easily pour from spoon, stir in water, 1 teaspoon at a time, until just pourable.) Sprinkle with pomegranate seeds, if using; pine nuts; and parsley. Drizzle with extra oil to finish. Serve.

top | *Hummus with Crispy Mushrooms and Sumac*

bottom | *Fattet Hummus (Crispy Pita with Garlicky Yogurt and Chickpeas)*

Biscuit Crackers with Red Lentil Dip

Biscuit Crackers with Red Lentil Dip

Serves 6 to 8 Total Time 1 hour 50 minutes, plus 40 minutes chilling and sitting

Why This Recipe Works The rich flavor and tender texture of biscuits both shine through when compacted into a crisp cracker form. The browning highlights their buttery qualities in a very satisfying way. Usually biscuit dough should be kneaded as little as possible to keep the dough crumbly and flaky, but for these crackers more kneading is better to make it cohesive and easier to roll out thin. The crackers nicely tame the spicy flavor of the hearty red lentil dip, which is great served either warm or at room temperature. (Its spiciness comes through more strongly when it's warm.) If you prefer a smoother dip, process the mixture using a food processor or immersion blender in step 6 before stirring in the parsley. Harissa spiciness varies by brand. If your harissa is spicy, omit the cayenne. You can sub any kind of seeds, such as sesame seeds, or a seed blend for the coarse salt topping on the crackers.

Biscuit Crackers

- ¾ cup (3¾ ounces) all-purpose flour
- 1½ teaspoons sugar
- 1 teaspoon baking powder
- ⅛ teaspoon baking soda
- ¼ teaspoon table salt
- 4 tablespoons unsalted butter, chilled, plus 1 tablespoon, melted
- 5 tablespoons buttermilk
- 2 teaspoons coarse sea salt

Red Lentil Dip

- 2 tablespoons extra-virgin olive oil, divided
- 1 red bell pepper, stemmed, seeded, and chopped fine
- ½ onion, chopped fine
- 1 teaspoon table salt
- 2 tablespoons harissa
- 2 tablespoons tomato paste
- ¼ teaspoon cayenne pepper (optional)
- 2 cups water
- ⅔ cup dried red lentils, picked over and rinsed
- 2 tablespoons lemon juice
- 2 tablespoons plain yogurt
- ½ cup chopped fresh parsley

1. **For the crackers** Whisk flour, sugar, baking powder, baking soda, and table salt together in large bowl. Grate 3½ tablespoons chilled butter on large holes of box grater; reserve excess chilled butter for another use. Add grated butter to flour mixture and toss gently to combine.

2. Add buttermilk to flour mixture and fold with spatula until just combined (dough will look dry). Transfer dough to liberally floured counter. Dust surface of dough with flour. Using your floured hands, knead dough until cohesive mass forms. Transfer dough to sheet of plastic wrap. Wrap in plastic and flatten to form 5-inch disk. Refrigerate dough for at least 30 minutes or up to 2 days. (Wrapped dough can be frozen for up to 1 month. Let dough thaw completely in refrigerator.) Let chilled dough sit on counter to soften slightly, about 10 minutes, before rolling.

3. Adjust oven rack to upper-middle position and heat oven to 375 degrees. Roll dough into 11-inch square on lightly floured counter. Using pizza cutter or chef's knife, cut dough into rough 2 by 1-inch pieces (you should have about 40 pieces). Arrange pieces at least ¼ inch apart on parchment paper–lined rimmed baking sheet. Prick dough pieces 1 or 2 times with fork. Brush tops with melted butter and sprinkle with sea salt. Cover crackers with second sheet of parchment, then second rimmed baking sheet.

4. Bake crackers until golden brown, about 30 minutes, rotating sheet halfway through cooking. Let crackers cool completely on wire rack between sheets. (Crackers can be stored in an airtight container for up to 24 hours.)

5. **For the dip** Heat 1 tablespoon oil in medium saucepan over medium heat until shimmering. Add bell pepper, onion, and salt and cook until softened, 5 to 7 minutes. Stir in harissa; tomato paste; and cayenne, if using; cook, stirring frequently, until fragrant, about 1 minute. Stir in water, scraping up any browned bits. Stir in lentils and bring to simmer. Reduce heat to low, cover, and simmer, stirring occasionally, until lentils begin to break down, about 15 minutes.

6. Off heat, lay clean dish towel underneath lid and let lentil mixture sit for 10 minutes. Add lemon juice, yogurt, and remaining 1 tablespoon oil and stir vigorously until mixture is cohesive. Stir in parsley and season with salt and pepper to taste. Serve warm or at room temperature. (Dip can be refrigerated for up to 3 days; bring to room temperature and stir to recombine before serving.)

Beet Dip with Yogurt and Tahini

Serves 6 to 8 Total Time 2 hours, plus 55 minutes cooling and chilling

Why This Recipe Works This bright dip is inspired by beet dips found in Middle Eastern cuisine. We roast and shred beets and then mix them with creamy Greek yogurt, nutty tahini, oil, garlic, lemon juice, and seasonings. The tahini adds a little bitterness and the lemon juice adds tang to balance the sweetness of the beets. Letting the dip sit for 30 minutes allows the flavors to meld and the beets' color to fully come through. A sprinkle of fresh dill adds contrasting color and freshness. To ensure even cooking, look for beets of similar size—roughly 2 to 3 inches in diameter. If you can't find Aleppo pepper, you can substitute ½ teaspoon of paprika plus ⅛ teaspoon of red pepper flakes. Serve this dip with cucumber slices, pita chips, or crackers.

- 1¼ pounds red or golden beets, trimmed
- 1 cup plain whole-milk Greek yogurt
- 5 tablespoons extra-virgin olive oil, divided
- ¼ cup tahini
- ¼ cup lemon juice (2 lemons)
- 3 garlic cloves, minced
- 2 teaspoons dried mint
- 1½ teaspoons table salt
- 1 teaspoon ground dried Aleppo pepper, plus extra for seasoning
- ¼ teaspoon ground cumin
- 1 tablespoon chopped fresh dill

1. Adjust oven rack to middle position and heat oven to 350 degrees. Wrap beets in aluminum foil packet and place on rimmed baking sheet. Roast until beets offer no resistance when pierced through foil with paring knife, 1¼ to 1½ hours. Carefully open packet and set beets aside to cool completely, about 25 minutes. Rub off skins with paper towels.

2. Meanwhile, whisk yogurt, ¼ cup oil, tahini, lemon juice, garlic, mint, salt, Aleppo pepper, and cumin together in large bowl.

3. Shred cooled beets on large holes of box grater or using shredding disk of food processor. Stir beets into yogurt mixture and refrigerate for 30 minutes to allow flavors to meld. (Dip can be refrigerated for up to 3 days.)

4. Stir dip to recombine and season with salt and Aleppo pepper to taste. Transfer to serving bowl, drizzle with remaining 1 tablespoon oil, and sprinkle with dill. Serve chilled or at room temperature.

Corn Cheese

FAST Serves 6 Total Time 25 minutes

Why This Recipe Works Gooey, stretchy corn cheese, a popular anju (Korean drinking snack) and barbecue side dish, is a dream for cheese-pull enthusiasts and anyone looking for a crowd-pleasing snack. The richness and relatively low pH of low-moisture whole-milk mozzarella makes it a great melter, and commercial preshredded mozzarella is coated with a starch that helps it melt more smoothly than freshly shredded cheese. Stirring some of the cheese into the mayonnaise-dressed corn and sprinkling more on the surface makes the dish cohesive and ensures gooeyness in every bite. Cooking and serving in a cast-iron skillet is key: Its superior heat retention keeps the cheese hotter and gooier longer than pans made from other materials. If you do not have a cast-iron skillet, use a stainless-steel skillet. Three cups of fresh or thawed frozen corn can be substituted for the canned. This recipe was developed with Cabot Low-Moisture Whole Milk Shredded Mozzarella Cheese; the starch added to prevent the shreds from clumping also helps the cheese stay soft and fluid out of the oven. If grating a block of whole-milk mozzarella, toss the cheese with ¼ teaspoon of cornstarch before using. Do not use fresh mozzarella. For a spicy dish, add 1 tablespoon of gochujang with the mayonnaise. Serve this as a dip with corn chips or as a side with grilled vegetables.

- 2 tablespoons unsalted butter
- 2 (15-ounce) cans corn, drained
- 1½ teaspoons sugar
- ¼ teaspoon table salt
- 6 ounces preshredded whole-milk mozzarella cheese (1½ cups), divided
- ⅓ cup mayonnaise
- 1 scallion, sliced thin

1. Adjust oven rack 8 inches from broiler element and heat broiler.

2. Melt butter in 10-inch cast-iron skillet over medium-high heat. Add corn, sugar, and salt and cook, stirring frequently, until pan is almost dry and fond begins to form at edges of pan, 5 to 6 minutes.

3. Off heat, stir in ⅔ cup of cheese and mayonnaise. Spread into even layer and top with remaining ⅓ cup cheese. Broil until surface is bubbling and cheese is browned in spots, about 3 minutes. Garnish with scallion and serve immediately.

Slow-Roasted Eggplant Dip with Pomegranate Molasses and Aleppo Pepper

VEGAN Serves 6 to 8 (makes 3 cups) Total Time 1½ hours

Why This Recipe Works Reminiscent of a Sicilian caponata, this slow-roasted eggplant is garlicky, smoky, a little spicy, a little sweet, and a little sour. It also couldn't be simpler to make. We toss all the ingredients in a Dutch oven and roast them until tender. Scraping down the sides of the pot once during cooking minimizes the amount of eggplant that gets stuck to the sides. This dip is delicious eaten with flatbread or pita, but its adaptability is the recipe's real win: It's great as a sandwich spread, served with labneh and a runny egg for a light dinner, or as a poaching sauce for eggs, shakshuka-style. You can mash the dip to your desired consistency before serving.

- 2 pounds eggplant, cut into ½-inch pieces
- 1 onion, chopped
- 1 garlic head, outer papery skins removed and top third of head cut off and discarded
- ½ cup extra-virgin olive oil
- 3 tablespoons pomegranate molasses
- 2 tablespoons tomato paste
- 1½ teaspoons table salt
- 1½ teaspoons ground dried Aleppo pepper
- 1 teaspoon smoked paprika
- 1 teaspoon paprika
- ½ teaspoon saffron threads, crumbled (optional)
- ½ teaspoon ground coriander
- ½ teaspoon ground cumin
- 1 bay leaf

top | *Beet Dip with Yogurt and Tahini*
bottom | *Corn Cheese*

Love for Leeks

Leeks may be a less commonly used member of the allium family—which includes onions, shallots, scallions, chives, garlic, and ramps—but they have a lot to offer. They're sweeter and milder than onions, making them ideal for a starring role.

A Trio of Colors

The color of leeks ranges from white to dark green. For most recipes (our Fresh Leek and Spinach Dip included) we use only the white and light green portions; they are more tender than the dark greens, which are best reserved for soups and stocks.

Leeks Cooked and Raw

For our dip, we gently cook most of the leeks in a little olive oil, which results in a silky texture and sweet, mellow flavor. But we reserve a portion of the leeks to add to our dip raw, giving it a fresh oniony edge that's pleasant but not overpowering.

Fresh Leek and Spinach Dip

1. Adjust oven rack to lower-middle position and heat oven to 400 degrees. Combine all ingredients (including saffron, if using) in Dutch oven, tossing until vegetables are evenly coated. Cover pot, transfer to oven, and roast for 30 minutes.

2. Remove pot from oven and stir eggplant mixture well, being sure to scrape corners and sides of pot. Return covered pot to oven and roast until eggplant is very tender, about 45 minutes.

3. Remove pot from oven and discard bay leaf. Transfer garlic to cutting board and, using fork, mash root end of head to extrude garlic cloves; discard skins and return garlic to pot. Using potato masher, mash and stir vegetable mixture in pot until coarsely mashed, being sure to scrape corners and sides of pot. Season with salt and pepper to taste. Serve warm or at room temperature. (Dip can be refrigerated for up to 3 days; bring to room temperature before serving.)

Fresh Leek and Spinach Dip

Serves 10 to 12 Total Time 25 minutes, plus 30 minutes chilling

Why This Recipe Works For a fresh take on classic spinach dip, which is typically made with dehydrated soup mix, we skip the mix and re-create the dip using fresh spinach and leeks. We found that sweating a portion of the leeks and reserving some raw leeks added savory onion flavor. We add the hot leek mixture straight to the food processor with the cream cheese (so there is no need to soften it) and pulse with other ingredients until the leeks are finely chopped. To avoid fibrous texture in our dip, we opt out of the traditional frozen spinach and use 3 ounces of fresh baby spinach instead. The baby spinach adds fresh notes and vibrant green color. After pulsing the spinach with the leeks and cream cheese, along with soy sauce and white wine vinegar for umami and acidity, we add sour cream for a cooling and tangy addition and Parmesan cheese for more savory flavor. After chilling, this delicious dip is ready to be served. Look for smaller leeks that are about 1 inch in diameter; they're usually more tender. If you can find only larger leeks, discard any fibrous outer layers. Serve the dip with crudités, crackers, or pita chips, or as a spread on sandwiches.

- 1 pound leeks, white and light green parts only, sliced thin crosswise and washed thoroughly (3 cups), divided
- 2 tablespoons extra-virgin olive oil
- ¾ teaspoon table salt, divided
- 3 garlic cloves, minced
- 4 ounces cream cheese, cut into 4 pieces
- 3 ounces (3 cups) baby spinach
- 1½ tablespoons soy sauce
- 2 teaspoons white wine vinegar
- ½ teaspoon pepper
- 1½ cups sour cream
- ¼ cup grated Parmesan cheese

1. Add 2½ cups leeks, oil, and ¼ teaspoon salt to 12-inch nonstick skillet. Cover and cook over medium heat, stirring occasionally, until leeks are softened, 6 to 8 minutes. Stir in garlic and cook until fragrant, about 30 seconds.

2. Pulse hot leek mixture, cream cheese, spinach, soy sauce, vinegar, pepper, remaining ½ cup leeks, and remaining ½ teaspoon salt in food processor until well combined and spinach is finely chopped, about 10 pulses, scraping down sides of bowl as needed. Add sour cream and Parmesan and pulse until just combined, about 5 pulses.

3. Transfer dip to serving bowl. Cover and refrigerate until chilled, about 30 minutes. Serve. (Dip can be refrigerated for up to 2 days; stir to recombine before serving.)

Southern Cheese Straws

Makes 48 cheese straws Total Time 1 hour, plus 20 minutes cooling

Why This Recipe Works These delicate, crumbly, cheesy, buttery crackers have a cult following in the South. To make a version that mimics their signature straw shape without using a cookie press, we roll out the dough into a square and then cut it into strips before baking. Using a food processor to buzz the grated cheese, chilled butter, flour, and baking powder together results in crackers with a short, extra-tender texture. A generous helping of extra-sharp cheddar provides bold flavor, while a little cayenne adds just enough pleasant heat. Flour the counter and the top of the dough as needed to prevent sticking. Be sure to use unsalted butter here.

8 ounces extra-sharp cheddar cheese, shredded (2 cups)
1½ cups (7½ ounces) all-purpose flour
8 tablespoons unsalted butter, cut into 8 pieces and chilled
¾ teaspoon table salt
¾ teaspoon paprika
½ teaspoon baking powder
¼ teaspoon cayenne pepper
3 tablespoons ice water

1. Adjust oven rack to middle position and heat oven to 350 degrees. Line rimmed baking sheet with parchment paper. Process cheddar, flour, butter, salt, paprika, baking powder, and cayenne in food processor until mixture resembles wet sand, about 20 seconds. Add ice water and process until dough ball starts to form, about 25 seconds.

2. Turn out dough onto lightly floured counter. Knead briefly until dough fully comes together, 2 to 3 turns. Using your hands, pat dough into rough 4-inch square. Roll dough into 10-inch square, about ¼ inch thick, flouring counter as needed to prevent sticking.

3. Position dough so 1 edge is parallel to edge of counter. Using rounded side of fork, drag tines across entire surface of dough to make decorative lines.

4. Using pizza cutter or chef's knife, trim away and discard outer ½ inch of dough to make neat square. Cut dough into 3 equal pieces perpendicular to decorative lines. Working with 1 section of dough at a time, cut into ½-inch-wide strips in direction of lines.

5. Evenly space cheese straws on prepared sheet, about ½ inch apart. Bake until edges of straws are light golden brown, 30 to 35 minutes, rotating sheet halfway through baking. Let straws cool completely on sheet. Serve. (Straws can be stored in airtight container at room temperature for up to 1 week.)

Variation

Parmesan–Black Pepper Cheese Straws

Reduce extra-sharp cheddar to 1½ cups. Add 1 cup grated Parmesan to food processor with flour in step 1. Substitute 1 teaspoon black pepper for cayenne pepper.

Shaping Cheese Straws

1. Roll out dough into 10-inch square, then drag tines of fork across dough to make decorative lines.

2. Cut square into thirds, then cut each rectangle into ½-inch-wide strips with pizza cutter.

Pa amb Tomàquet (Catalan Tomato Bread)

FAST **VEGAN** Serves 4 to 6 Total Time 30 minutes

Why This Recipe Works Pa amb tomàquet—Catalan bread with tomato—is as simple as cooking gets. Ciabatta mimics the airy, open structure of traditional pan de cristal. Halving the loaf laterally, opening it like a book, and cutting the halves into slices maximizes its surface area. Toasted dry under the broiler, the bread chars lightly and quickly so that its interior crumb remains tender—a textural contrast that is just right for both supporting and absorbing the tomatoes' liquid. Rubbing a garlic clove over the toasts infuses them with subtle savoriness. Halving and grating ripe round tomatoes on a box grater yields loads of sweet, skin-free pulp that can be uniformly seasoned and spooned onto the toasts. Great olive oil, drizzled over the tomato bread for serving, complements the bright tomato and lean bread. Avoid plum tomatoes here; they're not juicy enough. If ciabatta is unavailable, substitute a crusty baguette, cut into 4-inch pieces. Use a fresh, robust, high-quality olive oil here. Serve as an appetizer or snack or as an accompaniment to any meal.

- 2 large ripe tomatoes, halved through equator
- ½ teaspoon table salt
- 1 loaf ciabatta, halved horizontally and sliced crosswise 2 inches thick
- 1 large garlic clove, peeled and halved crosswise
- 3 tablespoons extra-virgin olive oil, plus extra for serving
- Flake sea salt

1. Place box grater in medium bowl. Rub cut side of tomatoes against large holes of grater until tomato flesh is reduced to pulp (skins should remain intact). Discard skins. (You should have about 1½ cups pulp.) Stir in table salt.

2. Adjust oven rack 6 inches from broiler element and heat broiler. Set wire rack in rimmed baking sheet and arrange bread slices cut side up on rack. Broil until browned, crisp, and starting to char at edges, 2 to 4 minutes. Rub toasts with cut side of garlic (apply more pressure for more-potent flavor; rub lightly for delicate flavor).

3. Arrange toasts on serving plate. Distribute tomato pulp evenly among toasts and spread to edges. Drizzle with oil and season lightly with flake sea salt. Serve immediately, passing extra oil and sea salt separately.

Fava Bean Crostini with Manchego and Pine Nuts

Serves 8 to 10 Total Time 1¾ hours, plus 20 minutes cooling

Why This Recipe Works Fava beans, also known as broad beans, do require some prep work, but the fresh beans popular in the Mediterranean (and beyond) are so special they're well worth it. These artful crostini showcase the rich, creamy-tangy flavor and buttery texture of fava beans. First the beans must be removed from their tough outer pod, then the translucent waxy sheath covering each bean should also be removed. To preserve the beans' flavor, we simmer them with aromatic shallot, garlic, and cumin. Then we use a potato masher to turn them into a smooth, creamy topping. Stirring in lemon juice and parsley adds more freshness. We spread the puree onto thin crispy-toasted baguette slices and garnish them with Manchego cheese and toasted pine

Pa amb Tomàquet (Catalan Tomato Bread)

nuts. These are lovely as a meal starter, but you can certainly serve more per person for a fun, delicious lunch. This recipe works best with fresh fava beans, but if you can't find them, you can substitute 1 pound (3 cups) frozen shucked fava beans, thawed. Skip step 2 if using frozen favas.

- 24 (¼-inch-thick) slices baguette (1 baguette)
- 5 tablespoons extra-virgin olive oil, divided, plus extra for drizzling
- 3 pounds fava beans, shelled (3 cups)
- 1 shallot, minced
- 1 garlic clove, minced
- ½ teaspoon ground cumin
- ½ teaspoon table salt
- 3 tablespoons minced fresh parsley
- 1 tablespoon lemon juice
- 1 ounce Manchego cheese, shaved
- 2 tablespoons pine nuts, toasted

1. Adjust oven rack to middle position and heat oven to 400 degrees. Place baguette slices in single layer on rimmed baking sheet. Bake until golden and crisp, 8 to 10 minutes, flipping slices halfway through baking. Brush bread with 1 tablespoon oil and season with salt to taste. Let cool completely on sheet, about 30 minutes.

2. Meanwhile, bring 4 quarts water to boil in large pot. Fill large bowl halfway with ice and water. Add fava beans to boiling water and cook for 1 minute. Using slotted spoon, transfer fava beans to ice water and let cool, about 2 minutes. Transfer fava beans to triple layer of paper towels and dry well. Using paring knife, make small cut along edge of each bean through waxy sheath, then gently squeeze sheath to release bean; discard sheath.

3. Heat remaining ¼ cup oil in medium saucepan over medium heat until shimmering. Add shallot and cook until softened, about 3 minutes. Stir in garlic and cumin and cook until fragrant, about 30 seconds. Stir in fava beans, 1 cup water, and salt and bring to simmer. Cook until fava beans are softened and most of liquid has evaporated, 12 to 15 minutes. Off heat, using potato masher, mash bean mixture until mostly smooth. Stir in parsley and lemon juice and let cool completely, about 20 minutes.

4. Spread fava bean mixture evenly over toasted baguette slices and top with Manchego and pine nuts. Drizzle with extra oil. Serve.

Cranberry and Goat Cheese Crostini

FAST Serves 6 to 8 Total Time 20 minutes

Why This Recipe Works For a superfast Thanksgiving-flavored appetizer, we start by doctoring whole-berry canned cranberry sauce: Grated orange zest and minced fresh rosemary add wintry flavor to complement the tart berries. We make quick crostini by toasting baguette slices under the broiler, then top them with creamy goat cheese and a dollop of the cranberry mixture.

- 20 (¼-inch-thick) slices baguette (1 baguette)
- 2 tablespoons extra-virgin olive oil, plus extra for drizzling
- ½ cup canned whole-berry cranberry sauce
- 1 teaspoon minced fresh rosemary
- ¼ teaspoon grated orange zest
- ⅛ teaspoon table salt
- ⅛ teaspoon pepper
- 4 ounces goat cheese, softened

1. Adjust oven rack 4 inches from broiler element and heat broiler. Arrange baguette slices in single layer on rimmed baking sheet. Brush tops of slices with oil. Broil until golden, 1 to 2 minutes. Transfer sheet to wire rack. (Cooled baguette slices can be transferred to zipper-lock bag and stored for up to 24 hours.)

2. Combine cranberry sauce, rosemary, orange zest, salt, and pepper in bowl. (Cranberry mixture can be refrigerated for up to 24 hours.)

3. Spread goat cheese evenly on toasted baguette slices and top with cranberry mixture. Arrange on serving platter, drizzle with extra oil, and season with pepper to taste. Serve.

Buffalo Cauliflower Bites

FAST **VEGAN** Serves 4 to 6 Total Time 40 minutes

Why This Recipe Works Deemed "better than wings" by anyone who tries them, these crunchy, tangy, spicy cauliflower bites will be the new star of your game day table. The key was to come up with a crunchy coating that would hold up under the buffalo sauce. A mixture of cornstarch and cornmeal gives us an ultracrisp exterior. Because cauliflower

Cranberry and Goat Cheese Crostini

is not naturally moist, the mixture didn't adhere; so we dunked the florets in canned coconut milk, which has the right viscosity. Frying helps achieve an unbelievably crackly crust and tender interior. Since these cauliflower bites are vegan, we developed a ranch dressing that uses homemade vegan mayonnaise (recipes follow). We used Frank's RedHot Original Cayenne Pepper Sauce, but other hot sauces can be used. Use a Dutch oven that holds 6 quarts or more for this recipe.

Buffalo Sauce

- ¼ cup coconut oil
- ½ cup hot sauce
- 1 tablespoon packed dark brown sugar
- 2 teaspoons cider vinegar

Cauliflower

- 1–2 quarts peanut or vegetable oil for frying
- ¾ cup cornstarch
- ¼ cup cornmeal
- ½ teaspoon table salt
- ¼ teaspoon pepper
- ⅔ cup canned coconut milk
- 1 tablespoon hot sauce
- 1 pound cauliflower florets, cut into 1½-inch pieces
- 1 recipe Vegan Ranch Dressing (recipe follows)

1. **For the buffalo sauce** Melt coconut oil in small saucepan over low heat. Whisk in hot sauce, brown sugar, and vinegar until combined. Remove from heat and cover to keep warm; set aside.

2. **For the cauliflower** Line platter with triple layer of paper towels. Add oil to large Dutch oven until it measures about 1½ inches deep and heat over medium-high heat to 400 degrees. While oil heats, combine cornstarch, cornmeal, salt, and pepper in small bowl. Whisk coconut milk and hot sauce together in large bowl. Add cauliflower and toss to coat well. Sprinkle cornstarch mixture over cauliflower; fold with silicone spatula until thoroughly coated.

3. Fry half of cauliflower, adding 1 or 2 pieces to oil at a time, until golden and crisp, gently stirring as needed to prevent pieces from sticking together, about 3 minutes. Using slotted spoon, transfer fried cauliflower to prepared platter.

4. Return oil to 400 degrees and repeat with remaining cauliflower. Transfer ½ cup sauce to clean large bowl, add fried cauliflower, and toss gently to coat. Serve immediately with dressing and remaining sauce.

Vegan Ranch Dressing

FAST VEGAN Makes ½ cup Total Time 10 minutes

We prefer our homemade vegan mayonnaise (recipe follows), but you can use store-bought; our favorite brand is Just Mayo.

- ½ cup vegan mayonnaise
- 2 tablespoons unsweetened plain coconut milk yogurt
- 1 teaspoon white wine vinegar
- 1½ teaspoons minced fresh chives
- 1½ teaspoons minced fresh dill
- ¼ teaspoon garlic powder
- ⅛ teaspoon table salt
- ⅛ teaspoon pepper

Whisk all ingredients in bowl until smooth. (Dressing can be refrigerated for up to 4 days.)

Vegan Mayonnaise

FAST VEGAN Makes 1 cup Total Time 15 minutes

Aquafaba is the liquid found in a can of chickpeas.

- ⅓ cup aquafaba
- 1½ teaspoons lemon juice
- ½ teaspoon table salt
- ½ teaspoon sugar
- ½ teaspoon Dijon mustard
- 1¼ cups vegetable oil
- 3 tablespoons extra-virgin olive oil

1. Process aquafaba, lemon juice, salt, sugar, and mustard in food processor for 10 seconds. With processor running, gradually add vegetable oil in slow, steady stream until mixture is thick and creamy, scraping down sides of bowl as needed, about 3 minutes.

2. Transfer mixture to bowl. Whisking constantly, slowly add olive oil until emulsified. If pools of oil form on surface, stop adding oil and whisk mixture until well combined, then resume adding oil. Mayonnaise should be thick and glossy with no oil pools on surface. (Mayonnaise can be refrigerated for up to 1 week.)

Portobello Mushroom Fries with Cherry Pepper Sauce

Serves 4 Total Time 1 hour

Why This Recipe Works These mushroom fries deliver perfectly seasoned, crispy exteriors and tender (not soggy or wet) interiors. Because smaller varieties of mushrooms can overcook and sog out, we chose to use portobello mushrooms cut into ½-inch-thick slices. These meaty slices can withstand enough time in the hot oil for the crispy coating to become golden brown without overcooking. For a breading that adheres to the mushrooms and stays crispy, we coat the mushrooms with a light batter of flour, water, egg, and salt, followed by a crispy, cheesy mixture of panko and Parmesan cheese seasoned with oregano and red pepper flakes. We found that shallow frying the mushrooms in just 2 cups of oil in a skillet resulted in even browning, while deep frying made the mushrooms float, and when we tried to flip them, they just flipped right back, so we couldn't get browning on both sides. These fries are delicious with jarred marinara sauce, but we also developed a creamy dip to pair with them. The mixture of sour cream, jarred hot cherry peppers, parsley, garlic, honey, and salt makes the perfect companion to our mushroom fries. If you can find only portobello mushrooms with stems, buy 1 pound to ensure that you'll end up with 12 ounces of caps after trimming.

Sauce

- ¾ cup sour cream
- ⅓ cup minced seeded jarred hot cherry peppers, plus 1 tablespoon brine
- 1 tablespoon minced fresh parsley
- 2 garlic cloves, minced
- 2 teaspoons honey
- ¼ teaspoon table salt

Mushrooms

- 12 ounces portobello mushroom caps
- 2 cups panko bread crumbs
- 1 ounce Parmesan cheese, grated (½ cup)
- 2 teaspoons dried oregano
- 1¾ teaspoons table salt, divided
- ¾ teaspoon red pepper flakes
- ½ cup all-purpose flour
- ½ cup water
- 2 large eggs
- 2 cups vegetable oil for frying

Portobello Mushroom Fries with Cherry Pepper Sauce

Patatas Bravas

1. **For the sauce** Whisk all ingredients together in bowl. Season with salt and pepper to taste. Refrigerate until ready to serve. (Sauce can be refrigerated for up to 2 days.)

2. **For the mushrooms** Using a spoon, gently scrape gills from underside of mushroom caps. Slice mushrooms ½ inch thick.

3. Combine panko, Parmesan, oregano, 1 teaspoon salt, and pepper flakes in medium bowl. Transfer half of panko mixture to shallow dish; reserve remaining panko mixture in bowl.

4. Whisk flour, water, eggs, and remaining ¾ teaspoon salt in large bowl until smooth. Add half of mushrooms to batter and gently turn to coat. Working with 1 mushroom piece at a time, remove from batter, letting excess drip back into bowl, and transfer to dish with panko mixture, turning to coat and pressing gently to adhere. Arrange breaded mushrooms on rimmed baking sheet. Discard used panko mixture, then add reserved panko mixture to now-empty shallow dish and repeat breading with remaining mushrooms. (Breaded mushrooms can be refrigerated, uncovered, for up to 2 hours.)

5. Set wire rack in second rimmed baking sheet and line with triple layer of paper towels. Add oil to 12-inch nonstick skillet and heat over medium-high heat to 350 degrees. Add half of mushrooms, one at a time, to hot oil. Fry until mushrooms are golden brown, 2 to 3 minutes per side.

6. Transfer mushrooms to prepared rack and let drain briefly, about 30 seconds per side. Transfer drained mushrooms to serving platter. Return oil to 350 degrees and repeat with remaining mushrooms. Serve with sauce.

Scraping Out Gills

Gently scrape underside of mushroom cap with dinner spoon to remove feathery gills, which can impart a muddy taste and soggy texture to fries.

Patatas Bravas

VEGAN   Serves 4 to 6   Total Time 1 hour

Why This Recipe Works Patatas bravas, crispy potatoes served with a smoky, spicy tomatoey sauce, are hugely popular in tapas bars. To create well-browned potatoes with an ultracrispy crust without double frying, we first parboil russet potatoes with baking soda, which triggers a chain reaction that causes the pectin on the potatoes' surface to release a layer of starch that develops into a thick crust when fried. We also toss the parcooked potatoes with kosher salt, which roughs up the surfaces of the potatoes, creating many nooks and crannies through which steam can escape. As the steam escapes, the nooks and crannies trap oil, helping to make an even more substantial crunchy crust. For the sauce, we cook tomato paste, cayenne, sweet smoked paprika, garlic, and water to make a smooth, smoky, and spicy mixture, finishing with sherry vinegar for tang. Finally, adding mayonnaise allows us to combine the bravas sauce and another common accompaniment, aioli, into a single sauce. While this dish is traditionally served as part of a tapas spread, it can also be served as a side dish. Bittersweet or hot smoked paprika can be used in place of sweet, if desired. If you make this substitution, be sure to taste the sauce before deciding how much cayenne to add, if any. A rasp-style grater makes quick work of turning the garlic into a paste. For efficiency, get the water boiling while you make the sauce, and get the oil heating while you parcook the potatoes. Use a Dutch oven that holds 6 quarts or more. To make this recipe vegan, substitute plant-based mayo for the mayonnaise.

Sauce

- 1 tablespoon vegetable oil
- 2 teaspoons garlic, minced to paste
- 1 teaspoon sweet smoked paprika
- ½ teaspoon kosher salt
- ½–¾ teaspoon cayenne pepper
- ¼ cup tomato paste
- ½ cup water
- 2 teaspoons sherry vinegar
- ¼ cup mayonnaise

Potatoes

- 2¼ pounds russet potatoes, peeled and cut into 1-inch pieces
- ½ teaspoon baking soda
- 1½ teaspoons kosher salt
- 3 cups peanut or vegetable oil for frying

1. For the sauce Heat oil in small saucepan over medium-low heat until shimmering. Add garlic, paprika, salt, and cayenne and cook until fragrant, about 30 seconds. Add tomato paste and cook for 30 seconds. Whisk in water and bring to boil over high heat. Reduce heat to medium-low and simmer until slightly thickened, 4 to 5 minutes. Transfer sauce to bowl, stir in vinegar, and let cool completely. Once cool, whisk in mayonnaise. (Sauce can be refrigerated for up to 24 hours. Bring to room temperature before serving.)

2. For the potatoes Bring 8 cups water to boil in large saucepan over high heat. Add potatoes and baking soda. Return to boil and cook for 1 minute. Drain potatoes.

3. Return potatoes to saucepan and place over low heat. Cook, shaking saucepan occasionally, until any surface moisture has evaporated, 30 to 60 seconds. Off heat, add 1½ teaspoons salt and stir with silicone spatula until potatoes are coated with thick, starchy paste, about 30 seconds. Transfer potatoes to rimmed baking sheet in single layer to cool. (Potatoes can stand at room temperature for up to 2 hours.)

4. Heat oil in large Dutch oven over high heat to 375 degrees. Add all potatoes (they should just be submerged in oil) and cook, stirring occasionally with wire skimmer or slotted spoon, until deep golden brown and crispy, 20 to 25 minutes.

5. Transfer potatoes to paper towel–lined wire rack set in rimmed baking sheet. Season with salt to taste. Spoon ½ cup sauce onto bottom of large platter or 1½ tablespoons sauce onto individual plates. Arrange potatoes over sauce and serve immediately, passing remaining sauce separately.

Zucchini Chips with Tzatziki

Serves 4 to 6 Total Time 50 minutes, plus 30 minutes salting

Why This Recipe Works Many Greek American restaurants serve up delicate, ethereally light rounds of fried zucchini. Salting the zucchini ahead of time pulls out water and seasons it, which ensures crisp, well-seasoned slices. Thoroughly drying the slices before battering and frying results in the crispiest chips. Use a box grater to shred the cucumber for the tzatziki. We prefer to cut the zucchini with a mandoline for even slices, but you can use a chef's knife. Use a Dutch oven that holds 6 quarts or more for this recipe.

Tzatziki

- ¾ cup plain Greek yogurt
- ⅓ cup shredded English cucumber
- 1 tablespoon extra-virgin olive oil
- 1 tablespoon chopped fresh dill
- 2 garlic cloves, minced
- 1½ teaspoons lemon juice
- ½ teaspoon pepper
- ¼ teaspoon table salt

Zucchini Chips

- 2 (8-ounce) zucchini, sliced ⅛ inch thick
- 2 teaspoons table salt
- ½ teaspoon pepper
- 2 quarts vegetable oil for frying
- 1¼ cups water
- 1 cup all-purpose flour
- ½ cup cornstarch
- 1 teaspoon baking powder

1. For the tzatziki Stir all ingredients together in bowl. Cover and refrigerate until ready to serve. (Tzatziki can be refrigerated for up to 4 days; stir to recombine and season with salt and pepper to taste before serving.)

2. For the zucchini chips Toss zucchini with salt in large bowl to combine. Transfer to colander and set colander over now-empty bowl. Let sit for 30 minutes.

3. Spread zucchini over clean dish towel. Cover with second clean dish towel and press to remove as much moisture as possible. Sprinkle with pepper.

4. Add oil to Dutch oven and heat over medium-high heat to 375 degrees. Line large platter with triple layer of paper towels. Set wire rack in rimmed baking sheet. Whisk water, flour, cornstarch, and baking powder in large bowl until smooth.

5. Add one-third of zucchini to batter. Using silicone spatula, stir to evenly coat. Using both your hands and working quickly, transfer batch of coated zucchini to hot oil 2 pieces at a time. Fry until deep golden brown, stirring occasionally with spider skimmer or slotted spoon, 6 to 8 minutes. Adjust burner, if necessary, to maintain oil temperature between 350 and 375 degrees. Transfer zucchini to prepared platter and let drain for about 1 minute. Transfer drained zucchini to wire rack. Return oil to 375 degrees and repeat with remaining zucchini in 2 batches. Serve warm or at room temperature, with tzatziki.

Chickpea Fries

VEGAN Serves 6 to 8 Total Time 1½ hours, plus 1 hour chilling

Why This Recipe Works Creamy, crispy chickpea fries—known as panisse in France and panissa or panelle in Italy—are a popular European street snack perfect for batch-making at home and sharing with friends. These black pepper–forward fries are nicely browned on the outside, with soft, custardy centers. To maintain the light flavors of our chickpea fries, we stick to the most foundational ingredients, staying away from distracting add-ins. We combine the ingredients and simmer them on the stovetop to remove the moisture, essential for hydrating the chickpea flour and keeping the fries intact. We let the batter solidify in the refrigerator before slicing it into batons and then frying the batons until they are crisp and golden.

- 1 cup (4½ ounces) chickpea flour
- ¾ teaspoon table salt
- ¼ teaspoon pepper
- 2¼ cups water
- 2 tablespoons extra-virgin olive oil
- 2 quarts vegetable oil for frying
- Lemon wedges
- 1 recipe dipping sauce (page 512)

1. Spray 8-inch square baking pan with vegetable oil spray. Combine chickpea flour, salt, and pepper in medium saucepan. Slowly whisk in water and olive oil until smooth. Bring to simmer over medium heat and cook, whisking constantly, until mixture is bubbling and slightly thickened, 3 to 4 minutes.

2. Stirring constantly with wooden spoon or silicone spatula, continue to cook over medium-low heat until batter is thickened to consistency of thick mashed potatoes and is no longer glossy, 6 to 8 minutes longer (spatula dragged through mixture should leave distinct trail).

3. Transfer batter to prepared pan and spread into even layer using greased silicone spatula. Let batter cool slightly, about 10 minutes. Cover with plastic wrap and refrigerate until batter is firm and fully set, at least 1 hour or up to 24 hours.

4. Turn mixture out onto cutting board. Cut into thirds to form 3 strips. Then cut each strip crosswise into 12 fries (you should have 36 fries).

top | *Zucchini Chips with Tzatziki*
bottom | *Chickpea Fries*

5. Adjust oven rack to middle position and heat oven to 200 degrees. Set wire rack in rimmed baking sheet. Heat vegetable oil in large Dutch oven over medium-high heat to 375 degrees. Using spider skimmer or slotted spoon, carefully add half of fries to hot oil. Cook, without moving them, until fries begin to develop color, 30 seconds to 1 minute.

6. Continue to fry, stirring gently to prevent fries from sticking together or to bottom of pot, until fries are golden brown and crispy, 7 to 10 minutes longer. Adjust heat as needed to maintain oil temperature between 350 and 375 degrees.

7. Using spider skimmer or slotted spoon, transfer fries to prepared rack and season with salt and pepper to taste. Transfer to oven to keep warm. Return oil to 375 degrees and repeat frying with remaining fries. Serve with lemon wedges and dipping sauce.

Lemon and Herb Dipping Sauce

FAST **VEGAN** Makes 1 cup Total Time 10 minutes

To make this recipe vegan, substitute plant-based mayo for the mayonnaise.

- 1 cup mayonnaise
- 2 tablespoons capers, minced
- 1 tablespoon grated lemon zest plus 2 teaspoons juice
- 1 tablespoon minced fresh tarragon

Whisk all ingredients together in small bowl. Season with salt and pepper to taste. (Sauce can be refrigerated for up to 2 days.)

Variations

FAST VEGAN Calabrian Chile Dipping Sauce

Substitute 3 tablespoons minced fresh chives and 2 tablespoons jarred crushed Calabrian chiles for capers, lemon zest, and tarragon. Reduce lemon juice to 1 teaspoon.

FAST Honey and Spice Dipping Sauce

Substitute 1 tablespoon honey, 2 teaspoons cider vinegar, and 2 teaspoons ras el hanout for capers, lemon zest and juice, and tarragon.

Scallion Pancakes

Serves 4 to 6 Total Time 1¼ hours, plus 30 minutes resting

Why This Recipe Works The best scallion pancakes (cōngyóubǐng) are crispy and browned on the outside and multilayered and delicately chewy inside. The dough must be rolled very thin, so we opt for a boiling-water dough that stretches easily but does not spring back. To form alternating layers of dough and fat, we roll the dough into a large, thin round, brush it with a mixture of oil and flour, and sprinkle it with salt and scallions before rolling it into a cylinder. We coil the cylinder into a spiral and then roll it out into a round again. Making a small slit in the center of the pancake before frying it in a skillet prevents steam from building up underneath the pancake, so it lies flat and cooks evenly. A stir-together sauce complements the richness of the pancakes. The pancakes may be served as an appetizer or a side dish. For this recipe, we prefer the steady, even heat of a cast-iron skillet. A heavy stainless-steel skillet may be used, but you may have to increase the heat slightly. For an accurate measurement of boiling water, bring a kettle of water to a boil and then measure out the desired amount. We used Diamond Crystal kosher salt when developing this recipe. If using Morton kosher salt, reduce salt to ¾ teaspoon.

Dipping Sauce

- 2 tablespoons soy sauce
- 1 scallion, sliced thin
- 1 tablespoon water
- 2 teaspoons rice vinegar
- 1 teaspoon honey
- 1 teaspoon toasted sesame oil
- Pinch red pepper flakes

Pancakes

- 1½ cups (7½ ounces) plus 1 tablespoon all-purpose flour
- ¾ cup boiling water
- 7 tablespoons vegetable oil
- 1 tablespoon toasted sesame oil
- 1 teaspoon kosher salt
- 4 scallions, sliced thin

1. For the dipping sauce Whisk all ingredients together in small bowl; set aside.

2. For the pancakes Using wooden spoon, mix 1½ cups flour and boiling water in bowl to form rough dough. When cool enough to handle, transfer dough to lightly floured counter and knead until tacky (but not sticky) ball forms, about 4 minutes (dough will not be perfectly smooth). Cover loosely with plastic wrap and let rest for 30 minutes.

3. While dough is resting, stir together 1 tablespoon vegetable oil, sesame oil, and remaining 1 tablespoon flour. Set aside.

4. Place 10-inch cast-iron skillet over low heat to preheat. Divide dough in half. Cover 1 half of dough with plastic wrap and set aside. Roll remaining dough into 12-inch round on lightly floured counter. Drizzle with 1 tablespoon oil-flour mixture and use pastry brush to spread evenly over entire surface. Sprinkle with ½ teaspoon salt and half of scallions. Roll dough into cylinder. Coil cylinder into spiral, tuck end underneath, and flatten spiral with your palm. Cover with plastic and repeat with remaining dough, oil-flour mixture, salt, and scallions.

5. Roll first spiral into 9-inch round. Cut ½-inch slit in center of pancake. Cover with plastic. Roll and cut slit in second pancake. Place 2 tablespoons vegetable oil in skillet and increase heat to medium-low. Place 1 pancake in skillet (oil should sizzle). Cover and cook, shaking skillet occasionally, until pancake is slightly puffy and golden brown on underside, 1 to 1½ minutes. (If underside is not browned after 1 minute, turn heat up slightly. If it is browning too quickly, turn heat down slightly.) Drizzle 1 tablespoon vegetable oil over pancake. Use pastry brush to distribute over entire surface. Carefully flip pancake. Cover and cook, shaking skillet occasionally, until second side is golden brown, 1 to 1½ minutes. Uncover skillet and continue to cook until bottom is deep golden brown and crispy, 30 to 60 seconds longer. Flip and cook until deep golden brown and crispy, 30 to 60 seconds. Transfer to wire rack. Repeat with remaining 3 tablespoons vegetable oil and remaining pancake. Cut each pancake into 8 wedges and serve, passing dipping sauce separately. (Uncooked pancakes can be stacked between layers of parchment paper, wrapped tightly in plastic wrap, and refrigerated for up to 24 hours or frozen for up to 1 month. If frozen, thaw pancakes in single layer for 15 minutes before cooking.)

Shaping Scallion Pancakes

1. Brush 12-inch dough round with oil-flour mixture and sprinkle with salt and scallions. Roll up round into cylinder.

2. Coil cylinder tucking end underneath, then flatten. Roll out flattened spiral into 9-inch round and cut ½-inch slit in center.

| *Scallion Pancakes*

| *Spring Rolls (Cantonese Egg Rolls)*

Spring Rolls (Cantonese Egg Rolls)

VEGAN Makes 16 spring rolls Total Time 1¼ hours

Why This Recipe Works Spring rolls are a dim sum staple from Singapore to San Francisco. This vegetarian Cantonese version is similar to what the Western world calls egg rolls only they are thinner, with a smooth and crisp exterior. Make sure you get the correct spring roll wrappers (and here's where it gets confusing): The ones you want are square, flour-based wrappers, not translucent circular wrappers, though both might be labeled "spring roll wrappers." The easiest way to confirm is to look at the photo on the packaging—if the rolls look crispy and fried, those wrappers are the ones you want. This recipe can easily be doubled; fry the spring rolls in six batches, keeping fried spring rolls warm in a 200-degree oven. Serve with Plum Sauce for dipping (page 515).

- 1½ ounces dried shiitake mushrooms, rinsed
- 2 ounces dried mung bean glass noodles
- 2 tablespoons vegetable oil
- 6 scallions, white and green parts separated and sliced thin
- 4 garlic cloves, minced
- 4 teaspoons grated fresh ginger
- 2 tablespoons soy sauce
- 1 tablespoon Shaoxing wine
- 1 teaspoon toasted sesame oil
- ½ teaspoon table salt
- ¼ teaspoon white pepper
- 4 cups shredded napa cabbage
- 3 carrots, peeled and cut into 2-inch-long matchsticks
- 2 tablespoons cornstarch
- 16 (8-inch) square spring roll wrappers
- 2 quarts peanut or vegetable oil for frying

1. Microwave 1 cup water and mushrooms in covered bowl until steaming, about 1 minute. Let sit until softened, about 5 minutes. Lift mushrooms from bowl with fork and discard liquid. Squeeze mushrooms dry, remove stems, and chop. Soak noodles in 4 cups hot water in bowl for 15 minutes. Drain and rinse under cold water until chilled. Drain noodles again and chop into 1-inch lengths; set aside.

2. Heat empty 14-inch flat-bottomed wok over high heat until just beginning to smoke, about 3 minutes. Reduce heat to medium-high, drizzle vegetable oil around perimeter of wok, and heat until just smoking. Add mushrooms and cook, stirring constantly, until heated through, about 2 minutes. Add scallion whites, garlic, and ginger and cook, stirring constantly, until fragrant, about 1 minute. Stir in soy sauce, Shaoxing wine, sesame oil, salt, and pepper and cook until thickened to glaze, about 30 seconds.

3. Add cabbage and carrots and cook, tossing slowly but constantly, until cabbage is just softened, about 2 minutes. Off heat, add scallion greens and noodles and toss to combine. Transfer vegetable mixture to large plate, spread into even layer, and refrigerate until cool enough to handle, about 5 minutes.

4. Whisk cornstarch and 2 tablespoons water in bowl until combined. Arrange 1 wrapper on counter so 1 corner points toward edge of counter. Place 2 heaping tablespoons filling on lower half of wrapper and mold it with your fingers into neat 4-inch-long cylinder parallel to edge of counter. Using pastry brush, apply light layer of cornstarch slurry onto top corner of wrapper, being sure to coat edges.

5. Fold bottom corner of wrapper over filling and press gently along length of filling to remove air pockets. Fold side corners over to enclose filling snugly; gently roll to form cylinder. Transfer spring roll seam side down to parchment paper–lined platter. Press gently on spring roll to flatten slightly, then cover with damp paper towel while shaping remaining spring rolls; do not stack. Wipe any excess moisture from counter and repeat with remaining wrappers and filling. (Spring rolls can be frozen until solid, then transferred to zipper-lock bag and stored in freezer for up to 1 month. Do not thaw before frying; increase frying time by 2 minutes.)

6. Set wire rack in rimmed baking sheet and line half of rack with triple layer of paper towels. Add peanut oil to clean, dry, 14-inch flat-bottomed wok or large Dutch oven until it measures about 1½ inches deep and heat over medium-high heat to 375 degrees. Using tongs, carefully add 5 spring rolls to hot oil and cook until light golden brown, 5 to 7 minutes, turning as needed for even browning. Adjust burner, if necessary, to maintain oil temperature between 350 and 375 degrees.

7. Using spider skimmer or slotted spoon, transfer spring rolls to paper towel–lined side of prepared rack and let drain for 1 minute, then move to unlined side of rack. Return oil to 375 degrees and repeat with remaining spring rolls in 2 batches. (Before cooking each batch of spring rolls, line rack with fresh layer of paper towels.) Let cool for 5 minutes. Serve.

Plum Sauce

FAST **VEGAN** Makes 1 cup Total Time 45 minutes

Sour pickled plums offset the sweetness and mellow the acidity of this sauce. If pickled plums are not available, they can be omitted; add an extra 1 tablespoon vinegar to the sauce mixture before simmering.

- 1 cup apricot preserves or jam
- ½ cup Chinese white rice vinegar
- ½ cup water
- 2 salted pickled plums, pitted and mashed (2 tablespoons)
- 1 (1-inch) piece ginger, sliced thin
- ⅛ teaspoon Sichuan chili flakes

Whisk apricot preserves, vinegar, and water together in small saucepan until combined. Stir in plums, ginger, and chili flakes. Bring to simmer over medium heat and cook, stirring occasionally, until slightly thickened and sauce coats back of spoon, about 15 minutes. Discard ginger. Let sauce cool to room temperature before serving, about 15 minutes. (Sauce can be refrigerated for up to 1 week; let come to room temperature before serving.)

Pakoras (South Asian Spiced Vegetable Fritters)

VEGAN Makes 15 pakoras Total Time 1 hour

Why This Recipe Works Pakoras, from the Indian subcontinent, are crispy spiced vegetable fritters that make a satisfying snack. For ours we use a 4:1 ratio of chopped and shredded vegetables—a colorful trio of spinach, potato, and red onion. The thick batter is made of besan (flour milled from skinned and split brown chickpeas) and water. These pakoras are generously spiced with earthy cumin, citrusy coriander, ocher turmeric, mildly spicy Kashmiri chile powder, fenugreek, and ajwain, which is frequently added to fried foods to support digestion. Serrano chile adds bright heat. Baking powder keeps the pakoras light and fluffy. Use the large holes of a box grater to shred the potato. For the best texture, measure the prepped onion and potato by weight. Besan is also known as gram flour. To substitute standard chickpea flour (made from white chickpeas), add an additional 2 tablespoons of water to the batter. Besan, ajwain, and Kashmiri chile powder can be found in South Asian markets. If ajwain is unavailable, substitute dried thyme. If fenugreek is unavailable, it can be omitted. Use a Dutch oven that holds 6 quarts or more. Serve with Carrot-Tamarind Chutney (recipe follows) and/or Cilantro-Mint Chutney (page 213).

- 1 large red onion, halved and sliced thin (1½ cups/5 ounces)
- 1 large russet potato, peeled and shredded (1½ cups/6½ ounces)
- 1 cup baby spinach, chopped
- 1 serrano chile, stemmed and minced
- 1 teaspoon ground cumin
- 1 teaspoon ground coriander
- 1 teaspoon ajwain
- ½ teaspoon table salt
- ½ teaspoon Kashmiri chile powder
- ¼ teaspoon ground fenugreek
- ¾ cup besan
- 1 teaspoon baking powder
- ½ teaspoon ground turmeric
- ¼ cup water
- 2 quarts vegetable oil for frying

1. In large bowl, combine onion, potato, spinach, serrano, cumin, coriander, ajwain, salt, chile powder, and fenugreek. Toss vegetables until coated with spices. Using your hands, squeeze mixture until vegetables are softened and release some liquid, about 45 seconds (do not drain).

2. In small bowl, mix together besan, baking powder, and turmeric. Sprinkle over vegetable mixture and stir until besan is no longer visible and mixture forms sticky mass. Add water and stir vigorously until well incorporated.

3. Adjust oven rack to middle position and heat oven to 200 degrees. Set wire rack in rimmed baking sheet. Add oil to large Dutch oven until it measures about 1½ inches deep and heat over medium-low heat to 375 degrees.

4. Transfer heaping tablespoonful of batter to oil, using second spoon to ease batter out of spoon. Stir batter briefly and repeat portioning until there are 5 pakoras in oil. Fry, adjusting burner, if necessary, to maintain oil temperature of 370 to 380 degrees, until pakoras are deep golden brown, 1½ to 2 minutes per side. Using spider skimmer or slotted spoon, transfer pakoras to prepared rack and place in oven. Return oil to 375 degrees and repeat with remaining batter in 2 batches. Serve immediately.

Carrot-Tamarind Chutney

FAST VEGAN Makes 1 cup Total Time 15 minutes

This sweet-tart chutney comes together easily in the food processor. Cumin and coriander echo the earthy, citrusy notes of the pakoras. Tamarind juice concentrate can be found in South Asian markets.

- ½ cup chopped peeled carrot
- ¼ cup chopped red onion
- 3 tablespoons tamarind juice concentrate
- 2 tablespoons water
- 1 tablespoon lemon juice
- 2 teaspoons sugar
- ½ teaspoon ground cumin
- ½ teaspoon ground coriander
- ½ teaspoon table salt

Process carrot and onion in food processor until finely chopped, about 20 seconds, scraping down sides of bowl halfway through processing. Add tamarind concentrate, water, lemon juice, sugar, cumin, coriander, and salt and process until combined, about 20 seconds, scraping down sides of bowl halfway through processing (mixture will not be completely smooth). Transfer to bowl and serve. (Chutney can be refrigerated for up to 3 days.)

Sweet Potato Fritters with Feta, Dill, and Cilantro

Serves 4 to 6 Total Time 1¼ hours, plus 30 minutes cooling

Why This Recipe Works These lightly crisp sweet potato fritters are a delicious combo of mashed sweet potatoes and sweet potato fries. They have savory exteriors and creamy, sweet insides. To create them, we start by following a tried-and-true method for making mashed sweet potatoes that calls for steaming the spuds in a small amount of water (rather than boiling them in an abundance of water, which dilutes their flavor). After cooking the potatoes, we mash them, purposefully leaving a few small chunks for contrasting texture. Adding eggs and flour to the mash makes the fritters fluffier, with extra-crunchy edges. Shallow frying is easier to manage—and clean up—than deep frying. Sliced scallions, chopped fresh cilantro and dill, and some briny feta cheese make each bite of these fritters exciting. Using two spatulas to flip the fritters helps prevent splattering.

- 1½ pounds sweet potatoes, peeled and sliced ¼ inch thick
- ¼ cup water
- 1½ teaspoons table salt
- 3 ounces feta cheese, crumbled (¾ cup)
- ½ cup all-purpose flour
- 2 large eggs
- 4 scallions, sliced thin
- ¼ cup chopped fresh cilantro
- ¼ cup chopped fresh dill
- 1 teaspoon ground cumin
- ½ teaspoon pepper
- ½ cup peanut or vegetable oil for frying
- Sour cream
- Lemon or lime wedges

1. Combine potatoes, water, and salt in large saucepan. Cover and cook over medium-low heat, stirring occasionally, until paring knife inserted into potatoes meets no resistance, about 20 minutes.

2. Remove from heat. Using potato masher, mash potatoes until mostly smooth with some small chunks remaining. Let cool until no longer hot to touch, about 30 minutes. (Mashed sweet potatoes can refrigerated for up to 2 days.)

3. Set wire rack in rimmed baking sheet and line half of rack with triple layer of paper towels. Stir feta, flour, eggs, scallions, cilantro, dill, cumin, and pepper into potato mixture until fully combined.

4. Heat oil in 12-inch nonstick skillet over medium heat to 350 degrees (to take temperature, tilt skillet so oil pools on 1 side). Using greased ¼-cup dry measuring cup, place 6 portions of potato mixture in skillet. Press portions into approximate 3-inch disks with back of spoon.

5. Cook fritters until deep brown, 2 to 3 minutes per side, using 2 spatulas to carefully flip. Transfer fritters to paper towel–lined side of prepared rack to drain for 15 seconds on each side, then move to unlined side of rack. Return oil to 350 degrees and repeat with remaining potato mixture. Serve with sour cream and lemon wedges.

Variation

Sweet Potato Fritters with Cheddar and Chipotle

Substitute shredded sharp cheddar for feta and 2 tablespoons minced canned chipotle chile in adobo sauce for dill.

Sweet Potato Fritters with Feta, Dill, and Cilantro

Sesame Balls

Sesame Balls

VEGAN Makes 8 balls Total Time: 1½ hours, plus 30 minutes resting

Why This Recipe Works Sesame balls are irresistibly crisp and chewy fried balls with a sweet red bean paste center. Cantonese home cooks always make fried sesame balls around Chinese New Year. They are a superstitious food that will hopefully bring gold and silver rolling into the household. Glutinous rice flour is also sold as sweet rice flour. We developed this recipe using Mochiko brand rice flour. Lotus seed paste, black sesame seed paste, or mung bean paste can be used in place of the red bean paste. This recipe can be easily doubled; fry the sesame balls in two batches.

- 1½ cups (8¼ ounces) glutinous rice flour
- ½ teaspoon baking powder
- ⅛ teaspoon table salt
- ⅓ cup (2⅓ ounces) sugar
- 8 teaspoons smooth sweetened red bean paste
- ½ cup sesame seeds
- 2 quarts peanut or vegetable oil for frying

1. Whisk flour, baking powder, and salt together in large bowl. Bring ¾ cup water and sugar to boil in small saucepan over high heat until sugar has dissolved. Using silicone spatula, stir hot syrup into flour mixture until combined and no dry flour remains. Transfer dough to clean counter and knead with hands until smooth, about 3 minutes. Return dough to bowl, cover tightly with plastic wrap, and let rest for 30 minutes.

2. Meanwhile, divide bean paste into 1 teaspoon portions. Using lightly moistened hands, roll each portion into ball and transfer to plate. Cover loosely with plastic and refrigerate until ready to use.

3. Divide dough into 8 equal pieces (about 2 ounces each). Cover with damp towel. Working with 1 piece of dough at a time, use hands to roll into ball. Place ball on counter and flatten with palm of hand into 2-inch-wide circle. Place 1 portion of bean paste in center of circle. Gather sides of dough around paste, pushing out air pockets, and pinch top to seal, enclosing paste in center. Remoisten hands and roll ball, smoothing any cracks with your fingertips. Cover with damp towel.

4. Place ½ cup water in small bowl. Place sesame seeds in shallow dish. Working with 1 ball at a time, roll in water, letting excess drip off, then coat with sesame seeds, pressing gently to adhere. Transfer to plate.

5. Line rimmed baking sheet with triple layer of paper towels. Add oil to 14-inch flat-bottomed wok or large Dutch oven until it measures about 1½ inches deep and heat over medium-high heat to 325 degrees. Using spider skimmer or slotted spoon, carefully add balls, 1 at a time, to hot oil. Cook, stirring constantly, until balls begin to float, about 4 minutes. Adjust burner, if necessary, to maintain oil temperature between 300 and 325 degrees.

6. Using spider skimmer, fully submerge each ball, gently pressing it against side or bottom of wok to deflate by about ½ inch, then release. Continuously submerge, press, and release balls until puffy and light golden brown, about 4 minutes. Using spider skimmer, transfer sesame balls to prepared sheet. Let cool for 5 minutes. Serve.

Shaping Sesame Balls

1. Place 1 portion of bean paste on dough circle, then gather sides of dough around paste, pushing out air pockets.

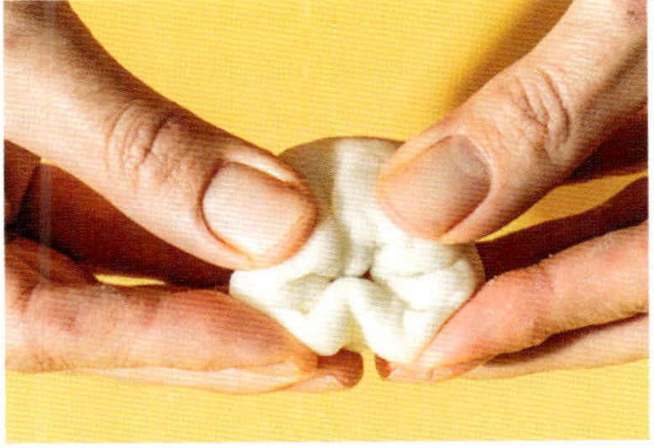

2. Pinch top of dough to seal, enclosing paste in center.

3. Working with 1 ball at a time, roll in water, letting excess drip off, then coat with sesame seeds, pressing gently to adhere.

No-Fuss Appetizers

Appetizers help set the mood for the main meal, or they can serve as the centerpiece of a gathering. Here are a few of our favorite fast and easy appetizers to welcome your guests and keep them happily occupied.

Blistered Shishito Peppers

FAST VEGAN Serves 6 Total Time 15 minutes

Japanese shishito peppers are a popular vegetable appetizer that you pick up by the stem and eat whole. Slender, 3- to 4-inch-long shishitos boast thin skins; delicate flesh; and a fruity, grassy flavor reminiscent of jalapeño or serrano chiles, minus the heat. We cook them in a small amount of oil until they blister.

- 2 tablespoons vegetable oil
- 8 ounces shishito peppers

Heat oil in 12-inch skillet over medium-high heat until just smoking. Add peppers and cook, without stirring, until skins are blistered, 3 to 5 minutes. Using tongs, flip peppers; continue to cook until blistered on second side, 3 to 5 minutes longer. Transfer to serving bowl, season with kosher salt to taste, and serve immediately.

Buttered Popcorn

FAST Makes 14 cups Total Time 15 minutes

Popcorn is a great whole-grain snack. The key to perfectly popped buttery stovetop popcorn is to heat three test kernels with vegetable oil in a saucepan until the kernels pop—that means the oil is hot enough. Adding the rest of the kernels off the burner and letting them sit for 30 seconds ensures all of the kernels heat up evenly. After that, it just takes a few minutes over medium-high heat with the lid slightly ajar for all the corn to pop—no shaking required. If you're looking to mix things up, we've got you covered with several irresistible flavor combinations.

- 3 tablespoons vegetable oil
- ½ cup popcorn kernels
- 2 tablespoons unsalted butter, melted
- ¼ teaspoon table salt

1. Heat oil and 3 popcorn kernels in large saucepan over medium-high heat until kernels pop. Remove pan from heat, add remaining kernels, cover, and let sit for 30 seconds.

2. Return pan to medium-high heat. Continue to cook with lid slightly ajar until popping slows to about 2 seconds between pops. Transfer popcorn to large bowl. Add melted butter and toss to coat popcorn. Add salt and toss to combine. Serve.

Variations

FAST Parmesan-Pepper Popcorn
Add ½ teaspoon pepper to butter before melting. Add ½ cup grated Parmesan to popcorn when tossing with butter.

FAST Garlic and Herb Popcorn
Add 2 minced garlic cloves and 1 tablespoon minced fresh or 1 teaspoon dried rosemary, thyme, or dill to butter before melting.

FAST Hot and Sweet Popcorn
Add 2 tablespoons sugar, 1 teaspoon ground cinnamon, and ½ teaspoon chili powder to butter before melting.

FAST Cajun-Spiced Popcorn
Add 1 teaspoon red pepper flakes, 1 teaspoon minced fresh thyme, ¾ teaspoon hot sauce, ½ teaspoon garlic powder, ½ teaspoon paprika, and ¼ teaspoon onion powder to butter before melting.

Sun-Dried Tomato Tapenade with Farmer's Cheese

FAST Serves 8 Total Time 10 minutes

For a twist on this popular Mediterranean spread, we swap in tart-sweet sun-dried tomatoes for a portion of the olives. The addition of some capers underscores the brininess of the kalamata olives, and a small handful of parsley contributes freshness. You can substitute goat cheese for the farmer's cheese if you prefer. Serve with crackers or thinly sliced baguette.

- 1 cup oil-packed sun-dried tomatoes, rinsed and patted dry
- ¼ cup extra-virgin olive oil
- 1 cup pitted kalamata olives
- ¼ cup coarsely chopped parsley
- 1 tablespoon capers, rinsed
- 8 ounces farmer's cheese

1. Pulse sun-dried tomatoes and oil in food processor until finely chopped, about 25 pulses; transfer to small serving bowl.

2. Add olives, parsley, and capers to now-empty food processor and pulse until finely chopped, about 10 pulses; stir into chopped tomatoes. Season with salt and pepper to taste and serve with farmer's cheese.

Melted Brie with Honey and Herbs

FAST Serves 8 Total Time 10 minutes

For a streamlined take on this cocktail party classic, we ditch both the puff pastry and the oven. Microwaving the Brie ensures that it delivers all the warm, gooey appeal of the original with minimal fuss. We cut off the top rind (starting with chilled Brie makes it easy to do this) but leave the sides intact so the cheese can soften without oozing all over the place. A drizzle of honey and a sprinkle of fresh thyme balance the richness of the cheese. Serve this Brie with crackers or a thinly sliced baguette and you won't miss the puff pastry.

- 1 (8-ounce) wheel firm Brie cheese
- 2 tablespoons honey
- ½ teaspoon chopped fresh thyme or rosemary

1. Using serrated knife, carefully slice rind off top of Brie; leave rind on sides and bottom. Place Brie, cut side up, on microwave-safe platter.

2. Drizzle honey over Brie, then sprinkle thyme over honey. Microwave until Brie is warm and just begins to bubble, 1 to 2 minutes. Serve immediately.

Simple Vegetables A to Z

Simple Sauces

524 All-Purpose Herb Sauce ●
Smoked Paprika Sauce ●
Chile-Coriander Sauce ●

524 Zhoug (Spicy Middle Eastern Herb Sauce) ■ ●

525 Chermoula ●

525 Peanut-Sesame Sauce ■ ●

526 Pumpkin Seed Sauce ■ ●

526 Miso-Ginger Sauce ■ ●

526 Infinite Sauce ■

527 Gochujang Sauce ■ ●

527 Romesco ■ ●

527 Spicy Avocado–Sour Cream Sauce ■ ●

527 Beurre Blanc ■

528 Stir-Fried Amaranth with Garlic ■ ●

528 Roasted Artichokes ●
Roasted Artichokes with Lemon Vinaigrette ●

529 Braised Asparagus with Lemon and Chives ■ ●
Braised Asparagus with Orange and Tarragon ■ ●
Braised Asparagus with Sherry Vinegar and Marjoram ■ ●

530 Pan-Seared Beets with Horseradish Cream ■

530 Baby Bok Choy with Ginger and Garlic ■

531 Roasted Broccoli ■ ●
Roasted Broccoli with Garlic ■ ●
Roasted Broccoli with Olives, Garlic, Oregano, and Lemon ■ ●

532 Broiled Broccoli Rabe ■ ●

532 Skillet-Roasted Brussels Sprouts with Cider Vinegar and Honey ■
Skillet-Roasted Brussels Sprouts with Maple Syrup and Smoked Almonds ■ ●
Skillet-Roasted Brussels Sprouts with Pomegranate and Pistachios ■ ●

534 Fried Brussels Sprouts with Sriracha Dipping Sauce ■ ●
Fried Brussels Sprouts with Lemon-Chive Dipping Sauce ■ ●

535 Roasted Cabbage ●
Roasted Cabbage with Bread Crumbs, Sage, and Parmesan
Roasted Cabbage with Gochujang, Sesame, and Scallions ●

536 Suan La Bai Cai (Sour and Hot Napa Cabbage) ■

536 Boiled Carrots with Lemon and Chives ■
Boiled Carrots with Cumin, Lime, and Cilantro ■ ●
Boiled Carrots with Fennel Seeds and Citrus ■ ●
Boiled Carrots with Mint and Paprika ■

537 Butter-Roasted Carrots with Hazelnut Crumble and Goat Cheese

538 Cauliflower Rice ■ ●

540 Skillet-Roasted Cauliflower with Garlic and Lemon ■ ●
Skillet-Roasted Cauliflower with Capers and Pine Nuts ■ ●
Skillet-Roasted Cauliflower with Cumin and Pistachios ■ ●

541 Modern Cauliflower Gratin

542 Roasted Celery Root with Chimichurri

543 Quick Collard Greens ■ ●

544 Foolproof Boiled Corn ■

544 Chili-Lime Salt ■ ●

545 Flavored Butters ■
Cilantro-Chipotle Butter
Spicy Old Bay Butter
Hot Honey Butter
Basil-Lemon Butter

545 Sautéed Corn with Cherry Tomatoes, Ricotta Salata, and Basil ■

546 Coconut Creamed Corn ■ ●
Coconut Creamed Corn with Ginger and Crispy Shallots ■ ●

546 Grilled Corn with Basil-Lemon Butter ■

549 Pai Huang Gua (Smashed Cucumbers) ■ ●

549 Marinated Eggplant with Capers and Mint ●

550 Braised Eggplant with Paprika, Coriander, and Yogurt ●

Braised Eggplant with Soy, Garlic, and Ginger ●

551 Roasted Fennel

551 Orange-Honey Dressing ■

552 Crunchy Oil-Cured Olives ■ ●

552 Gai Lan with Oyster Sauce ■

552 Skillet-Charred Green Beans ■ ●
Skillet-Charred Green Beans with Crispy Bread-Crumb Topping ■ ●

554 Quick Cast-Iron Skillet Green Bean Casserole ■

555 Simple Sautéed Kale ●

555 Roasted Kale with Garlic, Red Pepper Flakes, and Lemon ■ ●
Roasted Kale with Coriander, Ginger, and Coconut ■ ●
Roasted Kale with Parmesan, Shallot, and Nutmeg ■

556 Leeks Vinaigrette

557 Sautéed Mushrooms with Red Wine and Rosemary ■
Sautéed Mushrooms with Mustard and Parsley ■
Sautéed Mushrooms with Soy, Scallion, and Ginger ■

559 Roasted Okra ■ ●

559 Spicy Red Pepper Mayonnaise ■ ●

561 Braised Vidalia Onions with Chile, Lime, and Cilantro ■
Braised Vidalia Onions with Honey, Lemon, and Oregano ■

561 Rajas Poblanas con Crema (Charred Poblano Strips with Cream)

Rajas Poblanas con Crema y Elote (Charred Poblano Strips with Cream and Corn)

562 Three-Cheese Potato Frico

563 Best Baked Potatoes ●

563 Herbed Goat Cheese Topping ■

563 Creamy Egg Topping ■

565 Fastest, Easiest Mashed Potatoes ■

565 Braised Red Potatoes with Lemon and Chives
Braised Red Potatoes with Dijon and Tarragon
Braised Red Potatoes with Miso and Scallions

566 Creamy Potatoes and Leeks

566 Sichuan Hot and Sour Potatoes ■ ●

567 Cheddar Scalloped Potatoes

568 Thick-Cut Oven Fries ●

569 Better Hash Browns ●

570 Lemony Roasted Radicchio, Fennel, and Root Vegetables ●

571 Roasted Radishes with Yogurt-Tahini Sauce ■

571 Sugar Snap Peas with Pine Nuts, Fennel, and Lemon Zest ■ ●
Sugar Snap Peas with Almonds, Coriander, and Orange Zest ■ ●
Sugar Snap Peas with Sesame, Ginger, and Lemon Zest ■ ●

572 Roasted Delicata Squash

572 Tximitxurri (Basque-Style Herb Sauce) ■ ●

573 Spicy Honey ■

573 Best Baked Sweet Potatoes ●

574 Garam Masala Yogurt ■ ●

574 Garlic and Chive Sour Cream ■ ●

575 Mashed Sweet Potatoes ■
Mashed Sweet Potatoes with Chipotle and Lime ■
Mashed Sweet Potatoes with Curry and Golden Raisins ■
Mashed Sweet Potatoes with Jalapeño, Garlic, and Scallions ■
Mashed Sweet Potatoes with Maple and Orange ■

575 Honey-Garlic Melting Sweet Potatoes
Miso-Maple Melting Sweet Potatoes

576 Swiss Chard and Kale Gratin

577 Fried Red Tomatoes

579 Pan-Seared Zucchini with Spicy Honey and Scallion ■
Pan-Seared Zucchini with Raisin, Caper, and Parsley Sauce and Pine Nuts ■ ●
Pan-Seared Zucchini with Yogurt, Red Pepper Paste, and Preserved Lemon ■ ●

580 Broiled Smashed Zucchini with Garlicky Yogurt ●
Broiled Smashed Zucchini with Herbed Sour Cream ●
Broiled Smashed Zucchini with Ricotta and Parmesan

■ Fast (45 minutes or less) ● Vegan

Simple Sauces

Nearly any vegetable dish can be enhanced with a drizzle of flavorful sauce, making even the simplest of vegetables feel luxurious. From spicy and savory to bright and fresh, these sauces are easy to whip up and sure to please.

All-Purpose Herb Sauce

VEGAN Makes ¾ cup Total Time 10 minutes, plus 1 hour resting

This easily customizable sauce is the perfect way to use up fresh herbs and take any veggie dish to the next level of flavor.

- 2 cups fresh parsley, basil, cilantro, tarragon, chives, and/or dill leaves
- 1 slice bread, lightly toasted and cut into ½-inch pieces (about ¾ cup)
- 1 small garlic clove, minced
- ⅛ teaspoon table salt
- 2 tablespoons lemon juice
- ½ cup extra-virgin olive oil

1. Pulse parsley, bread, garlic, and salt in food processor until finely chopped, about 5 pulses. Add lemon juice and pulse briefly to combine.

2. Transfer mixture to medium bowl and slowly whisk in oil until incorporated. Cover and let sit at room temperature for at least 1 hour to allow flavors to meld. Season with salt and pepper to taste. (Sauce can be refrigerated for up to 2 days. Bring to room temperature and whisk to recombine before serving.)

Variations

VEGAN **Smoked Paprika Sauce**

Choose combination of parsley and basil. Add ½ teaspoon smoked paprika to processor with remaining ingredients.

VEGAN **Chile-Coriander Sauce**

Choose combination of parsley and cilantro. Add 2 stemmed and seeded jalapeños (or 4 stemmed and seeded Thai chiles), ½ teaspoon coriander, and ½ teaspoon cumin to processor with remaining ingredients.

Zhoug (Spicy Middle Eastern Herb Sauce)

FAST VEGAN Makes 1 cup Total Time 15 minutes

While this herby, spicy, green sauce (which some sources say originated in Yemen) is often served as an accompaniment to Shakshuka (page 461), it's hard to imagine what it wouldn't taste good on.

- 2 cups fresh cilantro leaves and stems
- 4 Thai chiles, stemmed
- 3 garlic cloves, peeled
- ½ teaspoon ground coriander
- ½ teaspoon ground cumin
- ½ teaspoon table salt
- ½ cup extra-virgin olive oil

Pulse cilantro, Thai chiles, garlic, coriander, cumin, and salt in food processor until coarsely chopped, 8 to 10 pulses. Transfer to small bowl. Add oil and stir until sauce has consistency of loose paste. Season with salt to taste. (Sauce can be refrigerated for up to 2 weeks. Let come to room temperature before serving.)

Chermoula

VEGAN Makes 1½ cups Total Time 15 minutes, plus 1 hour resting

Traditionally used as a marinade, chermoula is also excellent as a bright, herby sauce or dressing for grilled vegetables or protein.

- 2¼ cups fresh cilantro leaves
- 8 garlic cloves, minced
- 1½ teaspoons ground cumin
- 1½ teaspoons paprika
- ½ teaspoon cayenne pepper
- ½ teaspoon table salt
- 6 tablespoons lemon juice (2 lemons)
- ¾ cup extra-virgin olive oil

1. Pulse cilantro, garlic, cumin, paprika, cayenne, and salt in food processor until coarsely chopped, about 10 pulses. Add lemon juice and pulse briefly to combine.

2. Transfer mixture to medium bowl and slowly whisk in oil until incorporated. Cover and let sit at room temperature for at least 1 hour to allow flavors to meld. Season with salt and pepper to taste. (Sauce can be refrigerated for up to 2 days. Bring to room temperature and whisk to recombine before serving.)

Peanut-Sesame Sauce

FAST VEGAN Makes ⅔ cup Total Time 10 minutes

This versatile sauce brings nutty depth, slight sweetness, and a touch of heat that is great on tofu, grains, or greens.

- 3 tablespoons chunky peanut butter
- 3 tablespoons toasted sesame seeds
- 2 tablespoons soy sauce
- 1½ tablespoons rice vinegar
- 1½ tablespoons packed light brown sugar
- 1½ teaspoons grated fresh ginger
- 1 garlic clove, minced
- ¾ teaspoon hot sauce

Process all ingredients in blender until smooth and mixture has consistency of heavy cream, about 1 minute (adjust consistency with warm water, 1 tablespoon at a time, as needed). Season with salt and pepper to taste. (Sauce can be refrigerated for up to 3 days; add warm water as needed to loosen before serving.)

Pumpkin Seed Sauce

FAST **VEGAN** Makes 2 cups Total Time 45 minutes

Pumpkin seed sauce, or pipián verde, is a traditional Pueblan green mole sauce that's made with tangy fresh tomatillos and nutty toasted pumpkin seeds. Try it stirred into white beans.

- ⅓ cup raw pepitas
- ¼ cup sesame seeds
- 2 tablespoons vegetable oil
- 1 onion, chopped fine
- ½ teaspoon table salt
- 1 jalapeño chile, stemmed, seeded, and chopped
- 3 garlic cloves, minced
- 1 teaspoon minced fresh thyme or ¼ teaspoon dried
- 6 ounces tomatillos, husks and stems removed, rinsed well, dried, and chopped
- 1½ cups vegetable broth
- 1 cup fresh cilantro leaves
- 1 tablespoon lime juice
- Pinch sugar

1. Toast pepitas and sesame seeds in dry 12-inch nonstick skillet over medium heat until seeds are golden and fragrant, about 5 minutes; transfer to bowl.

2. Add oil, onion, and salt to now-empty skillet and cook over medium heat until onion is softened, about 5 minutes. Stir in jalapeño, garlic, and thyme and cook until fragrant, about 30 seconds. Stir in tomatillos, broth, and toasted seeds and bring to simmer. Reduce heat to medium-low, cover, and cook until tomatillos begin to soften, about 10 minutes.

3. Transfer mixture to food processor. Add cilantro, lime juice, and sugar and process until mostly smooth, about 2 minutes. Season with salt and pepper to taste. (Sauce can be refrigerated for up to 2 days; bring to room temperature before serving.)

Miso-Ginger Sauce

FAST **VEGAN** Makes ¾ cup Total Time 5 minutes

For a thick, saucy dressing packed with flavor, we turn to miso and potent fresh ginger. To make this recipe vegan, substitute plant-based mayo for the mayonnaise.

- ¼ cup mayonnaise
- 3 tablespoons red miso
- 2 tablespoons water
- 1 tablespoon maple syrup
- 1 tablespoon sesame oil
- 1½ teaspoons sherry vinegar
- 1½ teaspoons grated fresh ginger

Whisk all ingredients together in bowl. (Sauce can be refrigerated for up to 3 days.)

Infinite Sauce

FAST Makes ½ cup Total Time 15 minutes

Browned butter and soy sauce, balanced by a splash of lemon juice, combine into a rich, salty, and savory sauce that is delicious drizzled over an infinite number of dishes.

- 8 tablespoons unsalted butter
- 1 tablespoon soy sauce
- 1 teaspoon lemon juice

Melt butter in 10-inch skillet over medium-high heat. Reduce heat to low and continue to cook, swirling skillet constantly, until butter is dark golden brown and has nutty aroma, 6 to 8 minutes longer. Off heat, stir in soy sauce. Transfer sauce to heatproof bowl, making sure to scrape out butter solids with rubber spatula. Stir in lemon juice. (Sauce can be stored at room temperature for up to 5 days or refrigerated for up to 2 weeks.)

Gochujang Sauce

FAST **VEGAN** Makes ½ cup Total Time 5 minutes

Gochujang, a thick, spicy chile paste, forms the base of this Korean-inspired sauce. We thin it with water and season with toasted sesame oil and a bit of sugar to make a spicy-salty-sweet condiment that can be drizzled over a number of dishes.

- ¼ cup gochujang
- 3 tablespoons water
- 2 tablespoons toasted sesame oil
- 1 teaspoon sugar

Whisk all ingredients together in bowl. (Sauce can be refrigerated for up to 3 days.)

Romesco

FAST **VEGAN** Makes 2 cups Total Time 15 minutes

This sauce is traditionally served with fish but also goes well with chicken, meat, or vegetables, and makes a great dip for rustic bread.

- 1 slice hearty white sandwich bread, crusts removed, bread lightly toasted and cut into ½-inch pieces (½ cup)
- 3 tablespoons slivered almonds, toasted
- 1¾ cups jarred roasted red peppers, rinsed, patted dry, and chopped coarse
- 1 small tomato, cored, seeded, and chopped
- 2 tablespoons extra-virgin olive oil
- 1½ tablespoons sherry vinegar
- 1 large garlic clove, minced
- ½ teaspoon table salt
- ¼ teaspoon cayenne pepper

Process bread and almonds in food processor until finely ground, about 30 seconds. Add red peppers, tomato, oil, vinegar, garlic, salt, and cayenne. Process until smooth and mixture has texture similar to mayonnaise, 20 to 30 seconds, scraping down sides of bowl as needed. Season with salt and pepper to taste. (Sauce can be refrigerated for up to 2 days; bring to room temperature before serving.)

Spicy Avocado–Sour Cream Sauce

FAST **VEGAN** Makes 1 cup Total Time 5 minutes

For a spicy, rich sauce that can stand up to hefty toppings, we combine avocado and sour cream with jalapeño and a touch of citrus. To make this recipe vegan, substitute plant-based sour cream for the dairy sour cream.

- 1 cup sour cream
- ½ ripe avocado, cut into 1-inch pieces
- 1 jalapeño chile, stemmed, seeded, and chopped
- 1 teaspoon lime juice

Process all ingredients in food processor until smooth, scraping down sides of bowl as needed. Season with salt and pepper to taste. (Sauce can be refrigerated for up to 2 days.)

Beurre Blanc

FAST Makes ½ cup Total Time 20 minutes

This delicately flavored butter sauce is a good way to add richness to vegetables. You'll need about 2 tablespoons sauce per 4-ounce serving of vegetables.

- 3 tablespoons dry white wine
- 2 tablespoons white wine vinegar
- 1 small shallot, minced
- Pinch table salt
- 1 tablespoon heavy cream
- 8 tablespoons unsalted butter, cut into 8 pieces and chilled
- ⅛ teaspoon sugar

1. Bring wine, vinegar, shallot, and salt to simmer in small saucepan and cook until about 2 scant tablespoons of liquid remain, 3 to 5 minutes.

2. Reduce heat to medium-low and whisk in cream. Add butter, 1 piece at a time, whisking vigorously after each addition, until butter is incorporated and forms thick pale-yellow sauce, 30 to 60 seconds. Off heat, whisk in sugar. Strain sauce through fine-mesh strainer into bowl. Season with salt to taste and serve immediately.

top | *Stir-Fried Amaranth with Garlic*
bottom | *Braised Asparagus with Lemon and Chives*

Stir-Fried Amaranth with Garlic

FAST VEGAN Serves 4 Total Time 20 minutes

Why This Recipe Works In this simple stir-fry, amaranth is the undisputed star. This dish is an example of ching chau, which in Cantonese means "clear stir-fry." It is considered the purest form of stir-fry, in which usually only a single ingredient is cooked with light seasoning to allow the flavors, freshness, and colors of that ingredient to shine. There is no sauce in the dish, but we infuse the stir-fry oil with a little garlic. Once our amaranth starts to wilt we sprinkle in some salt to allow the seasoning to better adhere to the tender leaves. The greens then need just a little extra time before they are fully cooked. Any tender green can be cooked by this simple method, but none will look more dazzling than amaranth, or xiancai, sometimes called yin choy or Chinese spinach. Cooking in very high heat gives the earthy, slightly bitter greens a vivid, bright color that otherwise can be achieved only through blanching.

- 4 teaspoons vegetable oil, divided
- 2 garlic cloves, chopped, divided
- 1 pound red or green amaranth, watercress, or stemmed flat-leaf spinach, divided
- ¼ teaspoon table salt, divided

1. Heat 2 teaspoons oil in 12-inch nonstick skillet or 14-inch flat-bottomed wok over high heat until just smoking. Add half of garlic, then immediately add half of greens. Cook, tossing greens slowly but constantly, until just beginning to wilt, about 30 seconds. Sprinkle with ⅛ teaspoon salt and continue to cook until greens are vibrant and just tender, 30 seconds to 2 minutes; transfer to bowl.

2. Repeat with remaining 2 teaspoons oil, remaining garlic, remaining greens, and remaining ⅛ teaspoon salt. Off heat, return first batch of greens to skillet and toss to combine. Serve.

Roasted Artichokes

VEGAN Serves 4 Total Time 55 minutes

Why This Recipe Works While artichokes are great boiled, roasting helps to accentuate their nutty flavor. This hybrid steam-and-roast method yields artichokes that are tender, deeply flavorful, and nicely browned. To prevent the artichokes from discoloring and drying out in the heat of the oven, we give them a quick dip in lemon water, toss with olive oil and salt, and cover the roasting dish with foil. If your artichokes are larger than 8 to 10 ounces, strip away another layer or two of the toughest outer leaves. Serve the artichokes plain with a squeeze of lemon or pair them with Lemon-Dill Mayonnaise (page 218). To eat, use your teeth to scrape the flesh from the cooked tough outer leaves. The inner tender leaves, heart, and stem are entirely edible.

- 1 lemon, plus lemon wedges for serving
- 4 artichokes (8 to 10 ounces each)
- 3 tablespoons extra-virgin olive oil, divided
- ¾ teaspoon table salt

1. Adjust oven rack to lower-middle position and heat oven to 475 degrees. Cut lemon in half, squeeze halves into 2 quarts water, and drop in spent halves.

2. Cut off most of stem of 1 artichoke, leaving about ¾ inch attached. Cut off top quarter. Pull tough outer leaves downward toward stem and break off at base; continue until first three or four rows of leaves have been removed. Using paring knife, trim outer layer of stem and rough areas around base, removing any dark green parts. Cut artichoke in half lengthwise. Using spoon, remove fuzzy choke. Pull out inner, tiny purple-tinged leaves, leaving small cavity in center. Drop prepped halves into lemon water. Repeat with remaining artichokes.

3. Brush 13 by 9-inch baking dish with 1 tablespoon oil. Remove artichokes from lemon water, shaking off some excess lemon water (some should be left clinging to leaves). Toss artichokes with remaining 2 tablespoons oil and salt and season with pepper to taste, gently working some oil and seasonings between leaves. Arrange artichoke halves cut side down in baking dish and cover tightly with aluminum foil.

4. Roast until cut sides of artichokes start to brown and both bases and leaves are tender when poked with tip of paring knife, 25 to 30 minutes. Transfer artichokes to serving dish. Serve artichokes warm or at room temperature, passing lemon wedges separately.

Variation

VEGAN Roasted Artichokes with Lemon Vinaigrette

Cut very thin slices off both ends of 2 additional lemons and cut lemons in half crosswise. Place lemon halves, flesh side up, in baking dish with artichokes before covering with foil in step 3. Roast artichokes as directed. Once roasted lemon halves are cool enough to handle, squeeze into fine-mesh strainer set over bowl. Press on solids to extract all liquid; discard solids. Measure 1½ tablespoons strained lemon juice into small bowl. Whisk in ½ teaspoon finely grated garlic, ½ teaspoon Dijon mustard, and ½ teaspoon salt and season with pepper to taste. Whisking constantly, gradually drizzle 6 tablespoons extra-virgin olive oil into lemon mixture. Whisk in 2 tablespoons minced fresh parsley. Serve vinaigrette with artichokes.

Braised Asparagus with Lemon and Chives

FAST **VEGAN** Serves 4 Total Time 30 minutes

Why This Recipe Works Braising produces asparagus with a tender, silky texture and sweet, nutty flavor. To achieve consistently cooked spears, we eschew the tradition of slow cooking in a minimal amount of liquid. Instead we vigorously simmer the vegetable in a larger amount of liquid. To maximize infusion of the braising liquid, we peel off the asparagus's tough outer skin—this skin is covered with an impermeable waxy cuticle that protects the spears from water loss. When the skin is removed, the braising liquid is better able to penetrate the asparagus, seasoning it throughout. We also allow the braising liquid to evaporate, leaving behind a light glaze that coats the asparagus. Finishing the dish with a small amount of acidity and fresh herbs accentuates the vegetable's sweet flavor. This recipe is best with asparagus spears that are at least ¾ inch thick.

- 1 pound thick asparagus
- 1 cup water
- ¼ cup vegetable broth
- 2 tablespoons extra-virgin olive oil
- ¼ teaspoon table salt
- ¼ teaspoon grated lemon zest plus 1 teaspoon juice
- 2 teaspoons minced fresh chives, divided

1. Trim bottom inch of asparagus spears; discard trimmings. Peel bottom two-thirds of spears until white flesh is exposed. Bring water, broth, oil, and salt to simmer in 12-inch skillet over high heat. Add asparagus in even layer. Reduce heat to maintain vigorous simmer and cover. Cook, gently shaking skillet occasionally, until asparagus is tender and can be easily pierced with tip of paring knife, 8 to 10 minutes.

2. Remove lid and continue to cook, shaking and swirling skillet, until skillet is almost dry and asparagus is glazed, 1 to 3 minutes longer. Off heat, add lemon zest and juice and half of chives and toss to coat. Transfer asparagus to platter, sprinkle with remaining chives, season with salt to taste, and serve.

Variations

FAST VEGAN Braised Asparagus with Orange and Tarragon

Substitute orange zest and juice for lemon, increasing amount of orange juice to 1 tablespoon. Substitute minced fresh tarragon for chives.

FAST VEGAN Braised Asparagus with Sherry Vinegar and Marjoram

Substitute 1 teaspoon sherry vinegar for lemon zest and juice and 1 teaspoon minced fresh marjoram for chives.

Pan-Seared Beets with Horseradish Cream

FAST Serves 4 Total Time 30 minutes

Why This Recipe Works Using vacuum-packed beets makes beets a possibility for a busy weeknight. Pan-searing and then glazing them with a mix of balsamic, garlic, and thyme absolutely transforms them, while a stir-together sauce of sour cream and horseradish makes a tangy, creamy counterpart. A garnish of everything bagel seasoning finishes our weeknight beets with flair. You will need three 8-ounce packages of vacuum-packed cooked beets.

- 1½ pounds cooked and peeled beets, sliced ½ inch thick and patted dry
- ¾ teaspoon pepper, divided
- ½ teaspoon table salt, divided
- ½ cup sour cream
- 1½ tablespoons prepared horseradish
- ¼ cup extra-virgin olive oil, divided
- 1½ tablespoons balsamic vinegar
- 4 teaspoons fresh thyme leaves, divided
- 1 garlic clove, minced
- 2 teaspoons everything bagel seasoning

1. Toss beets, ½ teaspoon pepper, and ¼ teaspoon salt together in bowl. Whisk sour cream, horseradish, remaining ¼ teaspoon pepper, and remaining ¼ teaspoon salt together in second bowl; set aside. Combine 2 tablespoons oil, vinegar, 1 tablespoon thyme, and garlic in small bowl; set aside.

2. Heat remaining 2 tablespoons oil in 12-inch nonstick skillet over medium-high heat until just smoking. Transfer beets to skillet and spread into even layer (some beets will overlap). Cook beets, without stirring, until deeply browned and charred in spots on first side, 5 to 7 minutes. Flip beets and spread into even layer. Continue to cook, flipping and stirring beets occasionally, until beets are deeply browned all over and charred in spots, 5 to 7 minutes longer. Stir in vinegar mixture and cook until fragrant, about 30 seconds.

3. Transfer beets to serving platter and sprinkle with everything bagel seasoning and remaining 1 teaspoon thyme. Dollop with horseradish cream and serve.

Baby Bok Choy with Ginger and Garlic

FAST Serves 4 Total Time 45 minutes

Why This Recipe Works The key to cooking bok choy is in striking a textural balance by softening the stalks to a tender crispness before the green leaves get too limp. Cooking baby bok choy—as opposed to its larger counterpart—solves some of the dilemma. We cut the baby bok choy in half lengthwise, which has the added benefit of providing more direct access to where most of the dirt and grit hide, making the vegetable easier to clean. We briefly steam the bok choy, then quickly stir-fry it with the flavor powerhouse combination of ginger, garlic, sesame oil, and vegetarian oyster sauce. If using heads larger than 2 ounces each, quarter them instead of halving. Spin the bok choy dry after washing to avoid adding too much water to the pan.

- 4 teaspoons vegetable oil, divided
- 1 tablespoon grated fresh ginger
- 1 garlic clove, minced
- 2 tablespoons vegetarian oyster sauce
- 2 teaspoons toasted sesame oil
- ½ teaspoon cornstarch
- 8 small heads baby bok choy (1½ to 2 ounces each), halved lengthwise, washed thoroughly, and spun dry
- 2 tablespoons water

1. Combine 1 teaspoon vegetable oil, ginger, and garlic in small bowl; set aside. Whisk oyster sauce, sesame oil, and cornstarch together in second small bowl; set aside.

2. Heat remaining 1 tablespoon vegetable oil in 12-inch nonstick skillet or 14-inch flat-bottomed wok over high heat until just smoking. Reduce heat to medium. Add bok choy and water (water will sputter), cover, and cook, shaking skillet occasionally, for 2 minutes.

3. Uncover, toss bok choy, then push to 1 side of skillet. Add ginger-garlic mixture to clearing and cook, mashing mixture into skillet, until fragrant, about 20 seconds. Stir ginger-garlic mixture into bok choy and continue to cook, tossing slowly but constantly, until all water has evaporated, stems are crisp-tender, and leaves are wilted, 1 to 2 minutes. Add oyster sauce mixture and cook, stirring constantly, until sauce is thickened and coats bok choy, about 15 seconds. Serve.

Roasted Broccoli

FAST VEGAN Serves 4 Total Time 30 minutes

Why This Recipe Works Roasting can concentrate flavor to turn dull vegetables into something great. Our method for roasted broccoli turns out perfectly browned and deeply flavorful florets every time. To ensure even browning, we cut the crown into uniform wedges that lay flat, increasing contact with the pan. To promote even cooking of the stem, we slice away the exterior and cut the stalk into rectangular pieces slightly smaller than the more delicate wedges. Preheating the baking sheet helps the broccoli cook faster, while a very hot oven delivers the best browning. Sprinkling a little sugar over the broccoli helps it brown even more deeply. It is important to trim away the outer peel from the broccoli stalks; otherwise, they will turn tough when cooked.

- 1¾ pounds broccoli (1 large bunch)
- 3 tablespoons extra-virgin olive oil
- ½ teaspoon table salt
- ½ teaspoon sugar
- Lemon wedges

1. Adjust oven rack to lowest position, place rimmed baking sheet on rack, and heat oven to 500 degrees. Cut broccoli at juncture of florets and stems; remove outer peel from stalk. Cut stalk into 2- to 3-inch lengths and each length into ½-inch-thick pieces. Cut crowns into 4 wedges (if 3 to 4 inches in diameter) or 6 wedges (if 4 to 5 inches in diameter). Place broccoli in large bowl; drizzle with oil and toss well until evenly coated. Sprinkle with salt and sugar and season with pepper to taste; toss to combine.

top | *Pan-Seared Beets with Horseradish Cream*
bottom | *Baby Bok Choy with Ginger and Garlic*

2. Carefully remove baking sheet from oven. Working quickly, transfer broccoli to sheet and spread into even layer, placing flat sides down. Return sheet to oven and roast until stalks are well browned and tender and florets are lightly browned, 9 to 11 minutes. Transfer to serving dish and serve with lemon wedges.

Variations

FAST **VEGAN** Roasted Broccoli with Garlic

Add 1 minced garlic clove to oil before drizzling it over broccoli in step 1.

FAST **VEGAN** Roasted Broccoli with Olives, Garlic, Oregano, and Lemon

While broccoli roasts, cook 2 tablespoons extra-virgin olive oil, 5 thinly sliced garlic cloves, and ½ teaspoon red pepper flakes in 8-inch skillet over medium-low heat, stirring often, until garlic softens and is beginning to brown, 5 to 7 minutes. Off heat, stir in 2 tablespoons finely chopped pitted black olives, 1 teaspoon minced fresh oregano, and 2 teaspoons lemon juice. Toss cooked broccoli with olive mixture before serving.

Broiled Broccoli Rabe

FAST **VEGAN** Serves 4 Total Time 20 minutes

Why This Recipe Works Most recipes for broccoli rabe call for blanching and shocking the green before cooking it in order to tame its bitterness—a fussy method that washes out all of its distinctive flavor. We skip stovetop methods and broil the rabe, which creates deep caramelization without overcooking the pieces. Plus, broiling the rabe takes just minutes and requires no more equipment than a rimmed baking sheet. Most of the vegetable's bitterness comes from an enzymatic reaction triggered when the florets are cut or chewed, so we keep the leafy parts of the vegetable whole. The heat from cooking then deactivates the enzyme, reducing much of the bitterness. Because the amount of heat generated by a broiler varies from oven to oven, we recommend keeping an eye on the broccoli rabe as it cooks. If the leaves are getting too dark or not browning in the time specified in the recipe, adjust the distance of the oven rack from the broiler element.

- 3 tablespoons extra-virgin olive oil, divided
- 1 pound broccoli rabe
- 1 garlic clove, minced
- ¼ teaspoon table salt
- ¼ teaspoon red pepper flakes
- Lemon wedges

1. Adjust oven rack 4 inches from broiler element and heat broiler. Brush rimmed baking sheet with 1 tablespoon oil.

2. Trim and discard bottom 1 inch of broccoli rabe stems. Wash broccoli rabe with cold water, then dry with clean dish towel. Cut tops (leaves and florets) from stems, then cut stems into 1-inch pieces (keep tops whole). Transfer broccoli rabe to prepared sheet.

3. Combine remaining 2 tablespoons oil, garlic, salt, and pepper flakes in small bowl. Pour oil mixture over broccoli rabe and toss to combine.

4. Broil until half of leaves are well browned, 2 to 2½ minutes. Using tongs, toss to expose unbrowned leaves. Return sheet to oven and continue to broil until most leaves are lightly charred and stems are crisp-tender, 2 to 2½ minutes longer. Transfer to serving platter and serve immediately, passing lemon wedges.

Skillet-Roasted Brussels Sprouts with Cider Vinegar and Honey

FAST Serves 4 Total Time 20 minutes

Why This Recipe Works To create stovetop brussels sprouts that are deeply browned on the cut sides while still bright green on the uncut sides and crisp-tender within, we start the sprouts in a cold skillet with plenty of oil and cook them covered. This gently heats the sprouts and creates a steamy environment that cooks them through without adding any extra moisture. We then remove the lid and continued to cook the sprouts cut sides down so they have time to develop a substantial, caramelized crust. Using enough oil to completely coat the skillet ensures that all the sprouts make full contact with the fat to brown evenly from edge to edge. Look for brussels sprouts that are similar in size, with small, tight heads that are no more than 1½ inches in diameter, as they're likely to be sweeter and more tender than larger sprouts.

- 1 pound small (1 to 1½ inches in diameter) brussels sprouts, trimmed and halved
- 5 tablespoons extra-virgin olive oil
- 2 teaspoons cider vinegar
- 2 teaspoons honey
- ¼ teaspoon red pepper flakes
- ¼ teaspoon table salt

1. Arrange brussels sprouts in single layer, cut sides down, in 12-inch nonstick skillet. Drizzle oil evenly over sprouts. Cover skillet, place over medium-high heat, and cook until sprouts are bright green and cut sides have started to brown, about 5 minutes.

2. Uncover and continue to cook until cut sides of sprouts are deeply and evenly browned and paring knife slides in with little to no resistance, 2 to 3 minutes longer, adjusting heat and moving sprouts as necessary to prevent them from overbrowning. While sprouts cook, combine vinegar, honey, pepper flakes, and salt in small bowl.

3. Off heat, add vinegar mixture to skillet and stir to evenly coat sprouts. Season with salt to taste. Transfer sprouts to large plate and serve.

Variations

FAST VEGAN Skillet-Roasted Brussels Sprouts with Maple Syrup and Smoked Almonds

Substitute 1 tablespoon maple syrup and 1 tablespoon sherry vinegar for cider vinegar, honey, and red pepper flakes. Before serving, sprinkle sprouts with ¼ cup smoked almonds, chopped fine.

FAST VEGAN Skillet-Roasted Brussels Sprouts with Pomegranate and Pistachios

Substitute 1 tablespoon pomegranate molasses and ½ teaspoon ground cumin for cider vinegar, honey, and red pepper flakes. Before serving, sprinkle sprouts with ¼ cup shelled pistachios, toasted and chopped fine, and 2 tablespoons pomegranate seeds.

Skillet-Roasted Brussels Sprouts with Cider Vinegar and Honey

top | *Fried Brussels Sprouts with Sriracha Dipping Sauce*
bottom | *Roasted Cabbage*

Fried Brussels Sprouts with Sriracha Dipping Sauce

FAST **VEGAN** Serves 4 to 6 Total Time 40 minutes

Why This Recipe Works Fried brussels sprouts can be delightfully crispy, nutty, and salty. Yet when we first attempted to make them at home, the sprouts splattered every time they hit the hot oil. We then tried submerging the sprouts in cold oil and heating the oil and sprouts together over high heat. We found that as long as we cook the brussels sprouts until they are deep brown, this method produces beautifully crisped sprouts. An easy stir-together sriracha sauce offers a spicy, creamy counterpoint. Be sure to choose sprouts that are similar in size to ensure even cooking. For this recipe, we prefer larger brussels sprouts, about the size of golf balls, because they're easier to dip in the sauce. To keep the sprouts' leaves intact and attached to their cores, trim just a small amount from the stems before cutting the sprouts in half. If you choose to wash your sprouts before cooking, do so before trimming and halving them. Stir gently and not too often in step 2; excessive stirring will cause the leaves to separate from the sprouts. To make the dipping sauce and the recipe variation vegan, substitute plant-based mayo for the mayonnaise.

Sriracha Dipping Sauce

- ½ cup mayonnaise
- 1½ tablespoons sriracha
- 2 teaspoons lime juice
- ¼ teaspoon garlic powder

Brussels Sprouts

- 2 pounds brussels sprouts, trimmed and halved through stem
- 1 quart vegetable oil
- Kosher salt

1. **For the sriracha dipping sauce** Whisk all ingredients together in bowl. Cover and refrigerate until ready to serve.

2. **For the brussels sprouts** Line rimmed baking sheet with triple layer of paper towels. Combine brussels sprouts and oil in large Dutch oven. Cook over high heat, gently stirring occasionally, until dark brown throughout and crispy, 20 to 25 minutes.

3. Using spider or slotted spoon, lift brussels sprouts from oil and transfer to prepared sheet. Roll gently so paper towels absorb excess oil. Season with salt to taste. Serve immediately with sauce.

Variation

FAST VEGAN **Fried Brussels Sprouts with Lemon-Chive Dipping Sauce**

Whisk together ½ cup mayonnaise, 2 tablespoons minced fresh chives, 1 teaspoon grated lemon zest plus 1 tablespoon juice, 1 teaspoon vegetarian Worcestershire sauce, 1 teaspoon Dijon mustard, and ¼ teaspoon garlic powder in bowl. Cover and refrigerate until needed. Serve as directed in step 3 in place of Sriracha Dipping Sauce.

Roasted Cabbage

VEGAN Serves 4 to 6 Total Time 50 minutes

Why This Recipe Works For roasted cabbage that is well seasoned, attractively caramelized outside, and meltingly tender inside, we start by cutting the head straight through the core to create eight structurally sound wedges. Brushing oil over the cut surfaces and laying those surfaces flush against the sheet pan gives the edge of each leaf its best chance at deep caramelization. We cover the pan tightly with foil for the first 20 minutes of roasting to foster a steamy environment, which cooks the wedges through. We then remove the foil and allow the exterior to dry out and caramelize. A quick flip halfway through the uncovered roasting period ensures that each cut side is equally browned. A dense cabbage, one that's heavier than it looks, will hold together best when cut into eight wedges. We developed this recipe with Diamond Crystal kosher salt. If using Morton kosher salt, which is denser, use only ¾ teaspoon.

- 1 head green cabbage (2 to 2½ pounds)
- 3 tablespoons vegetable oil, divided
- 1 teaspoon kosher salt, divided
- ¼ teaspoon pepper

1. Adjust oven rack to upper-middle position and heat oven to 500 degrees. Quarter cabbage through core and cut each quarter into 2 wedges, leaving core intact. Arrange wedges, 1 flat side down, on rimmed baking sheet. Brush 1½ tablespoons oil on exposed cut sides of wedges and sprinkle with ½ teaspoon salt. Flip wedges so oiled sides are flush with sheet. Brush second cut sides with remaining 1½ tablespoons oil and sprinkle with pepper and remaining ½ teaspoon salt. Cover sheet tightly with aluminum foil and roast for 20 minutes.

2. Remove foil (be careful of escaping steam) and continue to cook until cabbage wedges begin to brown on underside, 5 to 10 minutes. Using tongs and thin metal spatula, flip each wedge. Roast until edges are very well browned and some leaves have crisped, 5 to 10 minutes. Transfer to serving platter, season with salt and pepper to taste, and serve.

Variations

Roasted Cabbage with Bread Crumbs, Sage, and Parmesan

While cabbage roasts, melt 1 tablespoon unsalted butter in 10-inch skillet over medium heat. Add 2 tablespoons chopped fresh sage and cook, stirring constantly, until fragrant, about 1 minute. Add ¼ cup panko bread crumbs and cook, stirring frequently, until crumbs are golden brown, about 2 minutes. Transfer to small bowl to cool. Stir in ½ cup grated Parmesan cheese. Sprinkle half of topping over platter. Transfer cabbage to platter, sprinkle with remaining topping, and serve.

VEGAN **Roasted Cabbage with Gochujang, Sesame, and Scallions**

While cabbage roasts, stir 2 tablespoons gochujang paste, 1 tablespoon unseasoned rice vinegar, 2 teaspoons water, 1 teaspoon toasted sesame oil, and ½ teaspoon sugar together in small bowl. Drizzle half of gochujang mixture over serving platter. Transfer cabbage to platter and drizzle with remaining gochujang mixture. Sprinkle with 1 tablespoon toasted sesame seeds and 2 thinly sliced scallions (green parts only) and serve.

Flipping the Cabbage

To keep the wedges intact as you flip them, grip each one with tongs and then slide thin metal spatula underneath to help gently turn it over.

Suan La Bai Cai (Sour and Hot Napa Cabbage)

FAST Serves 4 to 6 Total Time 45 minutes

Why This Recipe Works This napa cabbage stir-fry prepared in the sour-hot style (suan means sour and la means spicy) is iconic in Sichuan and northern Chinese cuisines. It is fast, economical, and glossed with an aromatic, vinegary, gently spicy, savory-sweet sauce. Separating the cabbage's white ribs from the more tender greens and staggering their additions to the skillet ensures that both components cook quickly and evenly and prevents the cabbage from shedding too much water and diluting the sauce. Sichuan Facing Heaven chiles (dried round chiles) are traditional, but you can use any small, dried hot chile such as arbol. For a spicier dish, use the larger amount of chiles. Serve with white rice.

- 1 head napa cabbage (2 pounds)
- 2 tablespoons soy sauce
- 2 tablespoons Chinese black vinegar
- 1 tablespoon vegetarian oyster sauce
- 1 tablespoon cornstarch
- 2½ teaspoons sugar
- 2 tablespoons peanut or vegetable oil
- 3–5 small dried chiles, stemmed, halved, and seeded
- 1 scallion, white and green parts separated and sliced thin
- 1 tablespoon grated fresh ginger
- 1 tablespoon minced garlic

1. Discard any outer leaves from cabbage that are bruised or torn. Peel away enough leaves to yield 1½ pounds (16 to 20 leaves). Reserve smaller leaves near core for other use. Stack three similar-size leaves and, using sharp knife, remove white portion from center. Keeping pieces stacked, cut cabbage whites crosswise at 45-degree angle into 1-inch-thick slices and place in medium bowl. Cut cabbage greens into 2-inch pieces and place in second medium bowl. Repeat with remaining leaves.

2. Whisk soy sauce, vinegar, oyster sauce, cornstarch, and sugar together in small bowl; set aside.

3. Heat oil in 12-inch nonstick skillet or 14-inch flat-bottomed wok over medium heat until just smoking. Add chiles and cook, stirring constantly with wooden spoon or wok spatula, until they begin to brown, about 30 seconds. Add scallion whites, ginger, and garlic and cook, stirring constantly, until fragrant, about 1 minute.

4. Increase heat to high and add sliced cabbage whites. Cook, stirring constantly, until cabbage begins to turn translucent at edges, about 2 minutes. Add chopped cabbage greens and cook, tossing with tongs constantly, until greens begin to collapse and wilt, about 2½ minutes longer.

5. Whisk soy sauce mixture to recombine and pour over cabbage. Cook, stirring constantly, until cabbage is evenly coated and sauce has thickened, about 30 seconds. Immediately transfer cabbage to large serving bowl. Garnish with scallion greens and serve.

Angle-Cutting Napa Cabbage

Holding thick white ribs in stack, cut crosswise at a 45-degree angle into 1-inch-thick slices. This exposes more surface area for sauce to cling to.

Boiled Carrots with Lemon and Chives

FAST Serves 4 Total Time 30 minutes

Why This Recipe Works Carrots are inexpensive, available year-round, and easy to prepare, making them a great go-to vegetable on a weeknight. Boiling them simply in very salty water is super-easy and beneficial: It seasons the carrots as they cook so they become more flavorful, and also helps them cook faster. Plus, seasoning the cooking water helps the salt penetrate deeper through the skin of the vegetables and makes them tastier than carrots that merely receive a sprinkle of salt after cooking. Finishing touches of butter for richness, lemon juice for brightness, and a sprinkle of freshly chopped chives and black pepper for flavor make this simple side dish a great complement to any meal.

- 1 pound carrots, peeled
- 2 teaspoons table salt
- 1 tablespoon unsalted butter, cut into 4 pieces
- 1 teaspoon lemon juice, plus extra for serving
- ⅛ teaspoon pepper
- 1 tablespoon chopped fresh chives

1. Cut carrots into 1½- to 2-inch lengths. Leave thin pieces whole, halve medium pieces lengthwise, and quarter thick pieces lengthwise.

2. Bring 2 cups water to boil in medium saucepan over high heat. Add carrots and salt, cover, and cook until tender throughout, about 6 minutes (start timer as soon as carrots go into water).

3. Drain carrots and return to saucepan. Add butter, lemon juice, and pepper and stir until butter is melted. Stir in chives, season with extra lemon juice to taste, and serve.

Variations

FAST **VEGAN** Boiled Carrots with Cumin, Lime, and Cilantro

Substitute extra-virgin olive oil for butter; ½ teaspoon grated lime zest plus 1 teaspoon lime juice for lemon juice; ½ teaspoon cumin seeds, crushed (use mortar and pestle or spice grinder to crush) for pepper; and cilantro for chives.

FAST **VEGAN** Boiled Carrots with Fennel Seeds and Citrus

Substitute extra-virgin olive oil for butter; ½ teaspoon fennel seeds, crushed (use mortar and pestle or spice grinder to crush) for pepper; and parsley for chives. Add ½ teaspoon grated orange zest to carrots with lemon juice.

FAST Boiled Carrots with Mint and Paprika

Substitute sherry vinegar for lemon juice, ½ teaspoon paprika for pepper, and mint for chives.

Butter-Roasted Carrots with Hazelnut Crumble and Goat Cheese

Serves 6 to 8   Total Time 1½ hours

Why This Recipe Works Roasting carrots brings out their natural sweetness and gives them both great flavor and texture. To dress them up, we make a crumble with toasted hazelnuts, sesame seeds, and coriander seeds along with fresh thyme and lemon zest. A final topping of pepperoncini and goat cheese adds some tang and a creamy element. Look for carrots that are 1 to 1½ inches in diameter at the larger end; larger or smaller carrots may need to be cooked for a slightly longer or slightly shorter time, respectively. The carrots may appear crowded on the baking sheet in step 4; this is OK.

top | *Suan La Bai Cai (Sour and Hot Napa Cabbage)*

bottom | *Butter-Roasted Carrots with Hazelnut Crumble and Goat Cheese*

Hazelnut Crumble

- ¼ cup skinned hazelnuts
- 1 tablespoon sesame seeds
- 2 teaspoons coriander seeds
- 1 teaspoon minced fresh thyme
- 1 teaspoon grated lemon zest
- ¼ teaspoon table salt

Carrots

- 5 tablespoons unsalted butter, melted, divided
- 3 pounds carrots, peeled
- 2 teaspoons table salt
- 2 teaspoons pepper
- 4 ounces goat cheese, crumbled (1 cup)
- 3 tablespoons pepperoncini, stemmed and sliced into thin rings
- 2 tablespoons extra-virgin olive oil
- 2 tablespoons chopped fresh parsley

1. For the hazelnut crumble Adjust oven rack to lowest position and heat oven to 350 degrees. Spread hazelnuts, sesame seeds, and coriander seeds in even layer on rimmed baking sheet and bake until hazelnuts are deep golden brown and seeds are fragrant, 7 to 9 minutes. Let mixture cool on sheet for 10 minutes.

2. Transfer hazelnut mixture to food processor. Add thyme, lemon zest, and salt and pulse until finely chopped, 8 to 10 pulses. Transfer hazelnut crumble to small bowl; set aside. (Crumble can be stored at room temperature for up to 1 month.)

3. For the carrots Increase oven temperature to 450 degrees. Pour 4 tablespoons melted butter onto rimmed baking sheet; tilt and swirl sheet until surface is evenly coated with butter.

4. Cut carrots in half crosswise, then cut each piece in half lengthwise. Toss carrots, salt, pepper, and remaining 1 tablespoon melted butter together in large bowl, then arrange in even layer on prepared sheet. Roast carrots on lowest rack until well browned on bottoms and paring knife inserted into thickest carrots meets with little resistance, 40 to 50 minutes.

5. Using spatula, transfer carrots to serving platter. Sprinkle with hazelnut crumble, goat cheese, and pepperoncini. Drizzle with oil and sprinkle with parsley. Serve warm or at room temperature.

Cauliflower Rice

FAST VEGAN Serves 4 to 6 Total Time 35 minutes

Why This Recipe Works Cauliflower is a true shape-shifter of a vegetable. This method of preparing it results in a light, neutral-flavored but nutrient-dense side dish that works in nearly any meal where you would use white rice. The key is to blitz the florets in a food processor until transformed into perfect rice-size granules. To make our cauliflower rice foolproof, we process the cauliflower in batches, making sure all the florets break down evenly. Cooking the rice in oil seasoned with shallot and a small amount of vegetable broth boosts the flavor. To ensure that the cauliflower is tender but still maintains a rice-like chew, we first steam it in a covered pot, then finish cooking it uncovered to evaporate any remaining moisture, for beautifully fluffy cauliflower rice.

- 1 head cauliflower (2 pounds), cut into 1-inch florets (6 cups)
- 1 tablespoon extra-virgin olive oil
- 1 shallot, minced
- ½ cup vegetable broth
- ¾ teaspoon table salt
- 2 tablespoons minced fresh parsley

1. Working in 2 batches, pulse cauliflower florets in food processor until finely ground into ¼- to ⅛-inch pieces, 6 to 8 pulses, scraping down sides of bowl as needed; transfer to bowl.

2. Heat oil in large saucepan over medium-low heat until shimmering. Add shallot and cook until softened, about 3 minutes. Stir in cauliflower, broth, and salt. Cover and cook, stirring occasionally, until cauliflower is tender, 12 to 15 minutes.

3. Uncover and continue to cook, stirring occasionally, until cauliflower rice is almost completely dry, about 3 minutes. Off heat, stir in parsley and season with salt and pepper to taste. Serve.

Cauliflower Rice

top | *Skillet-Roasted Cauliflower with Garlic and Lemon*
bottom | *Modern Cauliflower Gratin*

Skillet-Roasted Cauliflower with Garlic and Lemon

FAST **VEGAN** Serves 4 to 6 Total Time 45 minutes

Why This Recipe Works For a simple and fresh way to prepare cauliflower without turning on the oven, we turn to skillet roasting. Cutting the cauliflower into planks and then into flat-sided florets maximizes surface area for plenty of flavorful browning. We start the cauliflower in a cold pan and allow it to steam in its own moisture before removing the lid and letting it brown. Because the cauliflower is steaming for the first 5 minutes of cooking, it is important not to lift the lid during this time.

- 1 head cauliflower (2 pounds)
- 1 slice hearty white sandwich bread, torn into 1-inch pieces
- 5 tablespoons extra-virgin olive oil, divided
- 1 teaspoon plus pinch table salt, divided
- ½ teaspoon plus pinch pepper, divided
- 1 garlic clove, minced
- 1 teaspoon grated lemon zest, plus lemon wedges for serving
- ¼ cup chopped fresh parsley

1. Trim outer leaves of cauliflower and cut stem flush with bottom of head. Turn head so stem is facing down and cut head into ¾-inch-thick slices. Cut around core to remove florets; discard core. Cut large florets into 1½-inch pieces. Transfer florets to bowl, including any small pieces that may have been created during trimming, and set aside.

2. Pulse bread in food processor to coarse crumbs, about 10 pulses. Heat bread crumbs, 1 tablespoon oil, pinch salt, and pinch pepper in 12-inch nonstick skillet over medium heat, stirring frequently, until bread crumbs are golden brown, 3 to 5 minutes. Transfer crumbs to bowl and wipe out skillet.

3. Combine 2 tablespoons oil and cauliflower florets in now-empty skillet and sprinkle with remaining 1 teaspoon salt and remaining ½ teaspoon pepper. Cover skillet and cook over medium-high heat until florets start to brown and edges just start to become translucent (do not lift lid), about 5 minutes.

4. Remove lid and continue to cook, stirring every 2 minutes, until florets turn golden brown in many spots, about 12 minutes.

5. Push cauliflower to edges of skillet. Add remaining 2 tablespoons oil, garlic, and lemon zest to center and cook, stirring with rubber spatula, until fragrant, about 30 seconds. Stir garlic mixture into cauliflower and continue to cook, stirring occasionally, until cauliflower is tender but still firm, about 3 minutes longer.

6. Remove skillet from heat and stir in parsley. Transfer cauliflower to serving platter and sprinkle with bread crumb topping. Serve, passing lemon wedges separately.

Variations

FAST VEGAN Skillet-Roasted Cauliflower with Capers and Pine Nuts

Omit bread crumb topping and reduce oil to ¼ cup. Reduce salt in step 3 to ¾ teaspoon. Substitute 2 tablespoons capers (rinsed and minced) for garlic and 2 tablespoons minced fresh chives for parsley. Stir in ¼ cup toasted pine nuts with chives in step 6.

FAST VEGAN Skillet-Roasted Cauliflower with Cumin and Pistachios

Omit bread crumb topping and reduce oil to ¼ cup. Heat 1 teaspoon cumin seeds and 1 teaspoon coriander seeds in 12-inch nonstick skillet over medium heat, stirring frequently, until lightly toasted and fragrant, 2 to 3 minutes. Transfer to spice grinder or mortar and pestle and coarsely grind. Wipe out skillet. Substitute ground cumin-coriander mixture, ½ teaspoon paprika, and pinch cayenne pepper for garlic; lime zest for lemon zest; and 3 tablespoons chopped fresh mint for parsley. Sprinkle with ¼ cup pistachios, toasted and chopped, before serving with lime wedges.

Modern Cauliflower Gratin

Serves 8 to 10 Total Time 1¼ hours, plus 20 minutes resting

Why This Recipe Works For a rich and flavorful cauliflower gratin without the heft, we rely on cauliflower's natural ability to become an ultracreamy puree, turning some of it into a sauce to bind the remaining florets together. To ensure that we have enough cauliflower to use in two ways, we use two heads. We cook the core, stems, and some florets until supersoft, then blend it into a velvety puree. Butter and Parmesan (plus a little cornstarch) give the sauce a rich flavor and texture without making it too heavy, and a few pantry spices lend some complexity. We save most of the florets to steam in a basket over the simmering cauliflower until tender, then toss the florets in the sauce to coat. We top the gratin with more Parmesan and some panko for savory crunch and minced chives for color. When buying cauliflower, look for heads without many leaves. Alternatively, if your cauliflower does have a lot of leaves, buy slightly larger heads—about 2¼ pounds each. This recipe can be halved to serve 4 to 6; cook the cauliflower in a large saucepan and bake the gratin in an 8-inch square baking dish.

- 2 heads cauliflower (2 pounds each)
- 3 cups water
- 8 tablespoons unsalted butter, divided
- ½ cup panko bread crumbs
- 2 ounces Parmesan cheese, grated (1 cup), divided
- 2 teaspoons table salt
- ½ teaspoon pepper
- ½ teaspoon dry mustard
- ⅛ teaspoon ground nutmeg
- Pinch cayenne pepper
- 1 teaspoon cornstarch dissolved in 1 teaspoon water
- 1 tablespoon minced fresh chives

1. Adjust oven rack to middle position and heat oven to 400 degrees.

2. Pull off outer leaves of 1 head of cauliflower and trim stem. Using paring knife, cut around core to remove; halve core lengthwise and slice thin crosswise. Slice head into ½-inch-thick slabs. Cut stems from slabs to create florets that are about 1½ inches tall; slice stems thin and reserve along with sliced core. Transfer florets to bowl, including any small pieces that may have been created during trimming, and set aside. Repeat with remaining head of cauliflower. (After trimming you should have about 3 cups of sliced stems and cores and 12 cups of florets.)

3. Combine sliced stems and cores, 2 cups florets, water, and 6 tablespoons butter in Dutch oven and bring to boil over high heat. Place remaining florets in steamer basket (do not rinse bowl). Once mixture is boiling, place steamer basket in pot, cover, and reduce heat to medium. Steam florets in basket until translucent and stem ends can be easily pierced with paring knife, 10 to 12 minutes. Remove steamer basket and drain florets. Transfer drained florets to now-empty bowl. Re-cover pot, reduce heat to low, and continue to cook stem mixture until very soft, about 10 minutes longer.

4. While cauliflower is cooking, melt remaining 2 tablespoons butter in 10-inch skillet over medium heat. Add panko and cook, stirring frequently, until golden brown, 3 to 5 minutes. Transfer to bowl and let cool. Once cool, add ½ cup Parmesan and toss to combine.

5. Transfer stem mixture and cooking liquid to blender and add salt, pepper, mustard, nutmeg, cayenne, and remaining ½ cup Parmesan. Process until smooth and velvety, about 1 minute (puree should be pourable; adjust consistency with additional water as needed). With blender running, add cornstarch slurry. Season with salt and pepper to taste. Pour puree over cauliflower florets and toss gently to evenly coat. Transfer mixture to 13 by 9-inch baking dish (it will be quite loose) and smooth top with spatula. (Gratin and bread crumb mixture can be refrigerated separately for up to 24 hours. To serve, assemble and bake gratin as directed in step 6, increasing baking time by 13 to 15 minutes.)

6. Scatter bread crumb mixture evenly over top. Transfer dish to oven and bake until sauce bubbles around edges, 13 to 15 minutes. Let stand for 20 to 25 minutes. Sprinkle with chives and serve.

Prepping Cauliflower for Gratin

1. Cut out each core, halve lengthwise, and slice thin crosswise. Reserve for sauce. Slice each head into ½-inch-thick slabs.

2. Cut stems from slabs to create flat, 1½-inch-tall florets. Slice stems thin and reserve with sliced cores for sauce.

Roasted Celery Root with Chimichurri

Serves 6 to 8   Total Time 1¾ hours

Why This Recipe Works An innovative but easy two-step oven- and pan-roasting method creates a rustic, satisfying dish that highlights the flavor and texture of celery root. We start by halving the root—no peeling required. We wrap both halves in tightly sealed foil packets with butter, water, salt, and pepper. After a little more than an hour in a 400-degree oven, the rough and tough exterior of the vegetable breaks down and the entire root is rendered creamy, tender, and aromatic. After removing the cooled halves from the foil packets, we break them apart by hand into jagged chunks, which provide greater surface area for crisping up during the final stovetop step. We pair the celery root with a chimichurri that anchors bright red wine vinegar and fresh herbs in rich and fruity extra-virgin olive oil, spooning a generous amount over the tops of the roasted pieces.

- 1 large celery root (2 pounds), trimmed and halved, divided
- 2 teaspoons table salt, divided
- ¼ teaspoon pepper, divided
- 6 tablespoons hot water, divided
- 2 tablespoons unsalted butter, melted, divided
- 2 teaspoons dried oregano
- 1⅓ cups fresh parsley leaves
- ⅔ cup fresh cilantro leaves
- 6 garlic cloves, minced
- ½ teaspoon red pepper flakes
- ¼ cup red wine vinegar
- ½ cup plus 3 tablespoons extra-virgin olive oil, divided

1. Adjust oven rack to middle position and heat oven to 400 degrees. Stack two 16 by 12-inch sheets of aluminum foil. Sprinkle 1 celery root half with ¼ teaspoon salt and ⅛ teaspoon pepper, place cut side down in center of foil, and drizzle with 1 tablespoon hot water and 1 tablespoon melted butter. Crimp foil tightly around celery root to seal; transfer to rimmed baking sheet. Repeat with 2 sheets of foil, remaining celery root half, ¼ teaspoon salt, remaining ⅛ teaspoon pepper, 1 tablespoon hot water, and remaining 1 tablespoon melted butter.

2. Roast celery root until tender and skewer inserted in center meets little resistance (you will need to unwrap foil to test), 1 hour to 1 hour 20 minutes, rotating sheet halfway through roasting.

3. Meanwhile, combine oregano, 1 teaspoon salt, and remaining ¼ cup hot water in small bowl; let sit for 5 minutes to soften oregano. Pulse parsley, cilantro, garlic, and pepper flakes in food processor until coarsely chopped, about 10 pulses. Add oregano mixture and vinegar and pulse until combined. Transfer to bowl and slowly whisk in ½ cup oil until incorporated. Set aside chimichurri.

4. Carefully open foil packets to allow steam to escape and let sit until cool enough to handle, about 15 minutes. Using your hands, break celery root into rough 1-inch chunks. Heat 1½ tablespoons oil in 12-inch nonstick skillet over high heat until shimmering. Add half of celery root chunks and sprinkle with ¼ teaspoon salt. Cook, turning occasionally, until well browned on all sides, 6 to 8 minutes. Transfer celery root to serving platter and tent with foil to keep warm. Repeat with remaining 1½ tablespoons oil, remaining celery root, and remaining ¼ teaspoon salt. Drizzle roasted celery root with chimichurri and serve.

Roasted Celery Root with Chimichurri

Quick Collard Greens

FAST **VEGAN** Serves 4 to 6 Total Time 40 minutes

Why This Recipe Works Collard greens are typically braised for at least an hour to soften their tough leaves, but we devised a quick recipe that gives us the same results. Stemming the greens is a necessary first step, and blanching the leaves in salt water tenderizes them and removes their bitterness in minutes. However, blanching leaves us with waterlogged greens, so we use a spatula to press out excess water, and then we roll the greens up in a dish towel to dry them further. We chop the compressed collards into thin slices perfect for sautéing. And since we aren't infusing the greens with flavor during a long braise, we add some aromatic garlic and spicy red pepper flakes to the hot oil for a quick, well-seasoned dish. You can substitute mustard or turnip greens for the collards; reduce their boiling time to 2 minutes.

- Table salt for cooking collard greens
- 2½ pounds collard greens, stemmed, leaves halved lengthwise
- 3 tablespoons extra-virgin olive oil
- 2 garlic cloves, minced
- ¼ teaspoon red pepper flakes

1. Bring 4 quarts water to boil in large pot over medium-high heat. Stir in 1 tablespoon salt, then add collard greens, 1 handful at a time. Cook until tender, 4 to 5 minutes. Drain and rinse with cold water until greens are cool, about 1 minute. Press greens with rubber spatula to release excess liquid. Place greens on dish towel and compress into 10-inch log. Roll up towel tightly, then remove greens from towel. Cut greens crosswise into ¼-inch slices. (Greens can be refrigerated for up to 2 days before continuing.)

2. Heat oil in 12-inch nonstick skillet over medium-high heat until just smoking. Scatter greens in skillet and cook, stirring frequently, until just beginning to brown, 3 to 4 minutes. Stir in garlic and pepper flakes and cook until greens are spotty brown, 1 to 2 minutes. Season with salt and pepper to taste, transfer to bowl, and serve.

top *Foolproof Boiled Corn*

bottom *Sautéed Corn with Cherry Tomatoes, Ricotta Salata, and Basil*

Foolproof Boiled Corn

FAST Serves 4 to 6 Total Time 30 minutes

Why This Recipe Works To produce perfectly crisp, juicy corn every time, we figured out that the ideal doneness range is 150 to 170 degrees—when the starches have gelatinized but a minimum amount of the pectin (the glue that holds the cell walls together) has dissolved. Consistently cooking the corn to that temperature is easy with a hack sous vide method: Bring a measured amount of water (4 quarts) to a boil, shut off the heat, drop in six ears of corn, and let the corn stand for at least 10 minutes. The temperature of the water decreases quickly enough that there is never any chance of the corn overcooking, while the temperature of the corn increases to the ideal zone. Even better, the method is flexible: It can accommodate between six and eight ears of different sizes, and the corn can sit in the water for as long as 30 minutes without overcooking. The result: perfectly sweet, snappy kernels every time. Serve with one of the flavored butters (page 545), if desired.

- 6 ears corn, husks and silk removed
- Unsalted butter, softened
- 1 recipe Chili-Lime Salt (optional) (recipe follows)

1. Bring 4 quarts water to boil in large Dutch oven. Turn off heat, add corn to water, cover, and let stand for at least 10 minutes or up to 30 minutes.

2. Transfer corn to large platter and serve immediately, passing butter, salt (or Chili-Lime Salt, if using), and pepper separately.

Chili-Lime Salt

FAST **VEGAN** Makes 3 tablespoons
Total Time 5 minutes

This salt mixture can be refrigerated for up to 1 week.

- 1 tablespoon table salt
- 4 teaspoons chili powder
- ¾ teaspoon grated lime zest

Combine all ingredients in small bowl.

Flavored Butters

FAST Makes about ½ cup Total Time 10 minutes

Flavored butters are great for spreading on boiled corn or tossing with sautéed corn or other vegetables. To make the following butters, combine 6 tablespoons softened unsalted butter and seasonings in a small bowl. (Butters can be refrigerated for up to 4 days or frozen for up to 2 months.)

Cilantro-Chipotle Butter

- 2 tablespoons minced fresh cilantro
- 1 tablespoon minced fresh parsley
- 1 teaspoon minced canned chipotle chile in adobo sauce
- ½ teaspoon finely grated orange zest
- ½ teaspoon table salt

Spicy Old Bay Butter

- 1 tablespoon hot sauce
- 1 tablespoon minced fresh parsley
- 1½ teaspoons Old Bay seasoning
- 1 teaspoon finely grated lemon zest

Hot Honey Butter

- 2 tablespoons honey
- ½ teaspoon table salt
- ¼ teaspoon red pepper flakes

Basil-Lemon Butter

- 2 tablespoons chopped fresh basil
- 1 tablespoon minced fresh parsley
- 1 teaspoon finely grated lemon zest
- ½ teaspoon table salt
- ¼ teaspoon pepper

Sautéed Corn with Cherry Tomatoes, Ricotta Salata, and Basil

FAST Serves 4 to 6 Total Time 30 minutes

Why This Recipe Works To take advantage of the summer corn season, we wanted a quick recipe for sautéed corn bursting with fresh flavor. First we cut the kernels from the raw ears. To replicate the lightly charred, smoky flavor and satisfying texture of grilled corn, we sear the corn, without stirring it, in a little oil in a skillet. This caramelizes the corn, contributing a rich sweetness and a deep toasted quality while ensuring the kernels retain some crunch. Then, to balance the sweetness, we add toasted garlic chips, ricotta salata, and lemon juice. Cherry tomatoes and basil freshen the dish. We call for a range of lemon juice because fresh corn can vary in sweetness. If ricotta salata is unavailable, substitute a mild feta cheese.

- 2 tablespoons vegetable oil
- 3 garlic cloves, sliced thin
- 4 ears corn, kernels cut from cobs (3 cups)
- ½ teaspoon table salt
- 6 ounces cherry tomatoes, halved
- 1½ ounces ricotta salata cheese, crumbled (⅓ cup), divided
- ¼ cup shredded fresh basil
- 1–2 tablespoons lemon juice
- ¼ teaspoon pepper

1. Cook oil and garlic in 12-inch nonstick skillet over medium heat, stirring frequently, until garlic is light golden brown and fragrant, 2 to 3 minutes. Using slotted spoon, transfer garlic to large bowl, leaving oil in skillet.

2. Return skillet to medium-high heat and heat until shimmering. Add corn and sprinkle with salt. Cook, without stirring, until corn is browned on bottom and beginning to pop, about 3 minutes. Stir and continue to cook, stirring once or twice, until corn is spotty brown all over, 2 to 3 minutes. Transfer corn to bowl with garlic.

3. Stir tomatoes, half of ricotta salata, basil, 1 tablespoon lemon juice, and pepper into corn. Season with salt, pepper, and remaining lemon juice to taste. Sprinkle with remaining ricotta salata and serve.

Coconut Creamed Corn

FAST **VEGAN** Serves 4 to 6 Total Time 35 minutes

Why This Recipe Works Silky coconut milk is a fitting substitute for the traditional heavy cream in creamed corn, taking the standard American side into new territory. We simmer corn directly in coconut milk and salt to create a deeply seasoned, flavorful mixture. We then blend part of the cooked mixture to help thicken the overall dish and boost fresh corn flavor. A hint of pepper and cayenne stirred in at the end adds complexity to the buttery sweetness of the dish. We prefer to use fresh corn here; frozen kernels turn mushy when blended. Be sure to use unsweetened coconut milk, not sweetened coconut milk or coconut cream.

- 9 ears corn, kernels cut from cobs (6¾ cups)
- 1 (14-ounce) can coconut milk
- 1¼ teaspoons table salt
- ¼ teaspoon pepper
- ⅛ teaspoon cayenne pepper

1. Combine corn, coconut milk, and salt in large saucepan and bring to vigorous simmer over high heat (bubbles should be visible around edges of saucepan). Reduce heat to medium-low and cook, stirring occasionally, until corn is crisp-tender, about 20 minutes, adjusting heat as needed to maintain gentle simmer.

2. Off heat, carefully transfer 1½ cups corn mixture to blender. Process until smooth, about 30 seconds. Return pureed corn mixture to saucepan with remaining corn mixture and bring to simmer over medium heat. Off heat, stir in pepper and cayenne and season with salt to taste. Serve.

Variation

FAST **VEGAN** **Coconut Creamed Corn with Ginger and Crispy Shallots**

While corn simmers in step 1, combine ¼ cup vegetable oil, 3 thinly sliced shallots, 3 thinly sliced garlic cloves, 1 tablespoon grated fresh ginger, 1 thinly sliced jalapeño, ½ teaspoon paprika, and ¼ teaspoon table salt in 8-inch nonstick skillet. Cook over medium-high heat, stirring constantly, until shallots are softened and garlic begins to turn golden, 5 to 7 minutes. Reserve 2 tablespoons shallot mixture in small bowl; stir remaining oil mixture into corn mixture along with pepper and cayenne in step 2. Sprinkle with 2 tablespoons chopped fresh cilantro, drizzle with reserved oil mixture, and serve.

Grilled Corn with Basil-Lemon Butter

FAST Serves 4 to 6 Total Time 25 minutes

Why This Recipe Works To infuse grilled corn with the flavor of herbed butter, we first char ears of corn over a hot fire, then transfer them to a roasting pan with flavored butter. We cover the pan with aluminum foil and continue to cook the sweet, toasted ears on the grill until they pick up flavor. Charring the ears before cooking in the butter flavors the corn without causing flare-ups. We recommend using a disposable aluminum pan that measures at least 2¾ inches deep.

Butter

- 6 tablespoons unsalted butter, softened
- 2 tablespoons chopped fresh basil
- 1 tablespoon minced fresh parsley
- 1 teaspoon finely grated lemon zest, plus lemon wedges for serving
- ½ teaspoon table salt
- ¼ teaspoon pepper

Corn

- 8 ears corn, husks and silk removed
- 2 tablespoons vegetable oil

1. **For the butter** Combine all ingredients in small bowl and transfer to 13 by 9-inch disposable aluminum pan.

2. **For the corn** Brush corn evenly with oil and season with salt and pepper to taste.

3A. **For a charcoal grill** Open bottom vent completely. Light large chimney starter three-quarters filled with charcoal briquettes (4½ quarts). When top coals are partially covered with ash, pour evenly over grill. Set cooking grate in place, cover, and open lid vent completely. Heat grill until hot, about 5 minutes.

3B. **For a gas grill** Turn all burners to high, cover, and heat grill until hot, about 15 minutes. Turn all burners to medium-high.

4. Clean and oil cooking grate. Place corn on grill and cook, turning occasionally, until lightly charred on all sides, 5 to 9 minutes. Transfer corn to disposable pan and cover tightly with aluminum foil.

Coconut Creamed Corn with Ginger and Crispy Shallots

The Cooling Cucumber

Crunchy, refreshing, and more than 90 percent water, cucumbers are a vegetable best served raw. Their mild flavor makes them a wonderful canvas for a boldly seasoned dressing, such as in our Pai Huang Gua (Smashed Cucumbers).

Smashing Success

Smashing exposes more surface area than chopping or slicing, and the irregular shapes hold on to the dressing better than smooth surfaces. Smashing also creates varied textures with desirable nooks and crannies. Larger pieces are crunchy, while mushed bits of the gel-like cucumber insides meld with the dressing (in pai huang gua, that's a mix of soy sauce, vinegar, sesame oil, and garlic) and thicken for better coating and more pickle-like flavor.

A Tale of Two Cucumbers

The two most popular types of cucumber you'll find in grocery stores are American cucumbers, which have thick, waxy skin; and English cucumbers, which have thin, crisp skin and are usually wrapped in plastic. American cucumbers are quite seedy and usually have to be peeled, while English cucumbers are practically seedless and can be eaten skin-and-all. We like the texture and ease of English cucumbers better for this recipe.

Pai Huang Gua (Smashed Cucumbers)

5. Place disposable pan on grill and cook corn, shaking pan frequently, until butter is sizzling, about 3 minutes. Remove pan from grill and remove foil, allowing steam to escape away from you. Serve with lemon wedges, spooning butter in pan over individual ears.

Pai Huang Gua (Smashed Cucumbers)

FAST VEGAN Serves 4 Total Time 35 minutes

Why This Recipe Works Smashed cucumbers, or pai huang gua, is a Sichuan dish that is typically served with rich, spicy food. We start with English cucumbers, which are nearly seedless and have thin, crisp skins. Placing them in a zipper-lock bag and smashing them into large, irregular pieces speeds up the salting step that helps expel excess water. The craggy pieces also do a better job of holding on to the dressing. Using black vinegar (an aged rice-based vinegar) adds a mellow complexity to the soy and sesame dressing. We recommend using Chinese Chinkiang (or Zhenjiang) black vinegar in this dish for its complex flavor. If you can't find it, you can substitute 2 teaspoons rice vinegar plus 1 teaspoon balsamic vinegar. A rasp-style grater makes quick work of turning the garlic into a paste.

- 2 (14-ounce) English cucumbers, ends trimmed
- ¾ teaspoon table salt
- 4 teaspoons Chinese black vinegar
- 1 teaspoon garlic minced to paste
- 1 tablespoon soy sauce
- 2 teaspoons toasted sesame oil
- 1 teaspoon sugar
- 1 teaspoon sesame seeds, toasted
- Chili oil (optional)

1. Cut cucumbers crosswise into 3- to 4-inch lengths and place in 1-gallon zipper-lock bag. Using small skillet or rolling pin, firmly but gently smash cucumbers until flattened and split lengthwise into 3 or 4 spears each. Tear spears into rough 1-inch pieces and transfer to colander set in large bowl. Toss cucumbers with salt and let stand for at least 15 minutes or up to 30 minutes.

2. Meanwhile, whisk vinegar and garlic together in medium bowl and let sit for at least 5 minutes or up to 15 minutes.

3. Whisk soy sauce, oil, and sugar into vinegar mixture until sugar has dissolved. Add cucumbers, discarding any extracted liquid, and sesame seeds to bowl with dressing and toss to combine. Drizzle with chili oil, if using, and serve immediately.

Marinated Eggplant with Capers and Mint

VEGAN Serves 4 to 6 Total Time 1 hour, plus 1 hour marinating

Why This Recipe Works Marinated eggplant is a classic meze dish popular for sharing and right at home as a side to any number of main dishes. It has a creamy texture and a deep yet tangy flavor. We use Italian eggplant here, which is smaller than the standard supermarket size and more readily available year-round. Broiling the eggplant before marinating helps us achieve flavorful browning while cooking it through perfectly. To encourage even more browning, we first salt the eggplant, which draws out excess moisture. As for the marinade, a Greek-inspired combination of extra-virgin olive oil, red wine vinegar, capers, lemon zest, oregano, garlic, and mint works perfectly.

- 1½ pounds Italian eggplant, sliced into 1-inch-thick rounds
- ¼ teaspoon table salt
- ¼ cup extra-virgin olive oil, divided
- 4 teaspoons red wine vinegar
- 1 tablespoon capers, rinsed and minced
- 1 garlic clove, minced
- ½ teaspoon grated lemon zest
- ½ teaspoon minced fresh oregano
- ¼ teaspoon pepper
- 3 tablespoons minced fresh mint

1. Spread eggplant on paper towel–lined baking sheet, sprinkle both sides with salt, and let sit for 30 minutes.

2. Adjust oven rack 4 inches from broiler element and heat broiler. Line rimmed baking sheet with aluminum foil. Thoroughly pat eggplant dry with paper towels, arrange on prepared sheet in single layer, and lightly brush both sides with 1 tablespoon oil. Broil eggplant until mahogany brown and lightly charred, 6 to 8 minutes per side.

3. Whisk remaining 3 tablespoons oil, vinegar, capers, garlic, lemon zest, oregano, and pepper together in large bowl. Add eggplant and mint and gently toss to combine. Marinate eggplant until cooled to room temperature, about 1 hour. Season with pepper to taste and serve. (Marinated eggplant can be refrigerated for up to 3 days. Bring to room temperature before serving.)

Braised Eggplant with Paprika, Coriander, and Yogurt

VEGAN Serves 4 to 6 Total Time 50 minutes

Why This Recipe Works Eggplant is easy to prep and mild in flavor, with extremely porous flesh that soaks up seasonings. When braised, it develops a meltingly tender, creamy texture, yet the pieces remain meaty and intact. Here, we cut the eggplant into slim wedges, making sure that each piece has some skin attached to it, which gives it structural integrity even after the flesh becomes tender. We then braise the eggplant in a single batch in a skillet. As it cooks, the unique air-filled flesh collapses and becomes denser and firmer. We cook the eggplant until it softens and the savory braising liquid—made with tomato paste, garlic, and a mix of warm spices—reduces to a thick sauce. We serve our eggplant and sauce with a drizzle of cool yogurt and a refreshing sprinkle of cilantro. Large globe and Italian eggplants disintegrate when braised, so do not substitute a single larger (1 to 1¼ pounds) eggplant here. You can substitute 1 to 1¼ pounds of long, slim Chinese or Japanese eggplants if they are available; cut them as directed. To make this recipe vegan, substitute plant-based yogurt for the dairy yogurt.

- 2 (8- to 10-ounce) globe or Italian eggplants
- 3 tablespoons vegetable oil
- 2 garlic cloves, minced
- 1 tablespoon tomato paste
- 2 teaspoons paprika
- 1 teaspoon table salt
- 1 teaspoon ground coriander
- ½ teaspoon sugar
- ½ teaspoon ground cumin
- ½ teaspoon ground cinnamon
- ½ teaspoon ground nutmeg
- ½ teaspoon ground ginger
- 2¾ cups water
- ⅓ cup plain whole-milk yogurt
- 2 tablespoons minced fresh cilantro

top | *Braised Eggplant with Paprika, Coriander, and Yogurt*
bottom | *Roasted Fennel*

1. Trim ½ inch from top and bottom of 1 eggplant. Halve eggplant crosswise. Cut each half lengthwise into 2 pieces. Cut each piece into ¾-inch-thick wedges. Repeat with remaining eggplant.

2. Heat oil in 12-inch nonstick skillet over medium heat until shimmering. Add garlic and cook, stirring constantly, until fragrant, about 30 seconds. Add tomato paste, paprika, salt, coriander, sugar, cumin, cinnamon, nutmeg, and ginger and cook, stirring constantly, until mixture starts to darken, 1 to 2 minutes. Spread eggplant evenly in skillet (pieces will not form single layer). Pour water over eggplant, increase heat to high, and bring to boil. Reduce heat to maintain gentle boil and cover. Cook until eggplant is soft and has decreased in volume enough to form single layer on bottom of skillet, about 15 minutes, gently shaking skillet to settle eggplant halfway through cooking (some pieces will remain opaque).

3. Uncover and continue to cook, swirling skillet occasionally, until liquid is thickened and reduced to just a few tablespoons, 12 to 14 minutes longer. Off heat, season with salt and pepper to taste. Transfer to platter, drizzle with yogurt, sprinkle with cilantro, and serve.

Variation

VEGAN **Braised Eggplant with Soy, Garlic, and Ginger**

Omit tomato paste, paprika, salt, ground spices, sugar, yogurt, and cilantro. Before step 1, whisk 1½ cups water, ¼ cup Shaoxing wine, 2 tablespoons soy sauce, 4 teaspoons sugar, 2 teaspoons doubanjiang (broad bean chile paste), and 1 teaspoon cornstarch in medium bowl until sugar is dissolved. Use this mixture in place of water to braise the eggplant in step 2. Before serving, drizzle eggplant with ½ teaspoon toasted sesame oil and sprinkle with 2 sliced scallions.

Roasted Fennel

Serves 4 to 6 Total Time 50 minutes

Why This Recipe Works When roasted, fennel's crunchy texture and anise-y flavor transform into a sweet, nutty dish that is tender and silky. We cut the bulbs into wedges to provide good surface area for browning while the attached core keeps the pieces intact. Tossing the wedges with salted water provides moisture for steaming and seasons between the layers. We cover the fennel with foil first so it steams and turns creamy, then remove the foil so the fennel caramelizes. Look for fennel bulbs that measure 3½ to 4 inches in diameter and weigh around 1 pound with stalks (12 to 14 ounces without); trim the bases slightly in order to keep the bulbs intact. A tart dressing made with orange juice and honey is a perfect complement to the fennel.

- 2 fennel bulbs, bases slightly trimmed, 2 tablespoons fronds chopped coarse, stalks discarded
- 2 tablespoons water
- ½ teaspoon table salt
- 3 tablespoons vegetable oil
- ¼ teaspoon pepper
- Orange-Honey Dressing (recipe follows)
- 1 recipe Crunchy Oil-Cured Olives (optional) (page 552)

1. Adjust oven rack to lower-middle position and heat oven to 450 degrees. Spray rimmed baking sheet with vegetable oil spray.

2. Cut each fennel bulb lengthwise through core into 8 wedges (do not remove core). Whisk water and salt in large bowl until salt is dissolved. Add fennel wedges to bowl and toss gently to coat. Drizzle with oil, sprinkle with pepper, and toss again. Arrange fennel wedges cut side down along 2 longer sides of prepared sheet. Drizzle any water in bowl evenly over fennel wedges. Cover sheet tightly with aluminum foil and roast for 20 minutes.

3. Remove foil from sheet and continue to roast until sides of fennel touching sheet are browned, 5 to 8 minutes longer, rotating sheet halfway through roasting. Flip each fennel wedge to second cut side. Continue to roast until second sides are browned, 3 to 5 minutes longer. Transfer to plate; sprinkle with topping, if using, and fennel fronds; and serve.

Orange-Honey Dressing

FAST Makes ¼ cup Total Time 5 minutes

This dressing complements sweet roasted fennel as well as other vegetables.

- 1 tablespoon extra-virgin olive oil
- 2 teaspoons honey
- 1½ teaspoons white wine vinegar
- ⅛ teaspoon grated orange zest plus 1 tablespoon juice
- Pinch kosher salt

Whisk all ingredients together in bowl.

Crunchy Oil-Cured Olives

FAST **VEGAN** Makes 2 tablespoons
Total Time 20 minutes

The olives will crisp as they cool.

- 2 tablespoons coarsely chopped oil-cured black olives
- ¼ teaspoon grated lemon zest

Line plate with double layer of paper towels. Spread olives on towels. Microwave, stirring every 30 seconds, until olives start to dry and no longer clump together, 2½ to 3 minutes. Let cool for 10 minutes. Transfer olives to cutting board, sprinkle with lemon zest, and chop until olives are finely chopped and mixture is homogeneous.

Gai Lan with Oyster Sauce

FAST Serves 4 Total Time 30 minutes

Why This Recipe Works Gai lan, also called Chinese broccoli or Chinese kale, is a common element of many stir-fries—but we think it deserves a starring role. We love the crunchiness of the stalks and the vibrant taste of the leaves, and it's one of the more nutrition-dense vegetables you can cook. This dish is a simple and classic Cantonese treatment for gai lan, using vegetarian oyster sauce, broth, and a touch of cornstarch (to help the sauce lightly cling to the greens). If you can't find gai lan, broccolini is a good substitute; trim the broccolini stems and cut the tops (leaves and florets) from the stems, keeping them separate, and halve any stems thicker than ½ inch.

- 5 teaspoons vegetable oil, divided
- 1 garlic clove, minced
- ¼ teaspoon Sichuan chili flakes
- 3 tablespoons vegetable broth
- 3 tablespoons vegetarian oyster sauce
- 1 tablespoon Shaoxing wine
- 1 teaspoon dark soy sauce
- 1 teaspoon toasted sesame oil
- 1 teaspoon cornstarch
- 1½ pounds gai lan, trimmed
- ¼ cup water

1. Combine 1 teaspoon vegetable oil, garlic, and chili flakes in small bowl; set aside. Whisk broth, oyster sauce, Shaoxing wine, soy sauce, sesame oil, and cornstarch in second small bowl; set aside.

2. Trim leaves from bottom 3 inches of gai lan stalks and reserve. Cut tops (leaves and florets) from stalks. Quarter stalks lengthwise if more than 1 inch in diameter, and halve stalks if less than 1 inch in diameter. Keep leaves and tops separate from stalks.

3. Heat 2 teaspoons oil in 12-inch nonstick skillet or 14-inch flat-bottomed wok over high heat until just smoking. Reduce heat to medium and add gai lan stalks and water (water will sputter). Cover and cook until gai lan is bright green, about 5 minutes. Uncover, increase heat to high, and continue to cook, tossing slowly but constantly, until all water has evaporated and stalks are crisp-tender, 1 to 3 minutes; transfer to separate bowl.

4. Add remaining 2 teaspoons vegetable oil to now-empty skillet and heat until just smoking. Add half of gai lan tops and reserved leaves and cook, tossing slowly but constantly, until beginning to wilt, 1 to 3 minutes. Add remaining gai lan tops and reserved leaves and continue to cook, tossing slowly but constantly, until completely wilted, about 3 minutes.

5. Push gai lan to 1 side of skillet. Add garlic mixture to clearing and cook, mashing mixture into wok, until fragrant, about 30 seconds. Stir garlic mixture into gai lan. Whisk broth mixture to recombine, then add to skillet with stalks and any accumulated juices and cook, tossing constantly, until sauce has thickened and coats gai lan, about 30 seconds. Serve.

Skillet-Charred Green Beans

FAST **VEGAN** Serves 4 Total Time 35 minutes

Why This Recipe Works Deep-frying green beans evenly softens and blisters them, leaving them with a soft, appealingly dense, satisfying chew and concentrated flavor. To achieve those results without the hassle of frying, we first soften the beans by steaming them in the microwave. Then we char them in a skillet with just a couple tablespoons of hot oil. We don't stir the beans for the first few minutes so that they develop deep color and flavor on one side; then we toss them in the pan so that they soften and blister all over.

Once they are charred, we season them with a lemony salt-and-pepper mixture. Microwave thinner, more tender beans for 6 to 8 minutes and thicker, tougher beans for 10 to 12 minutes. To make the beans without a microwave, bring ¼ cup water to a boil in a skillet over high heat. Add the beans, cover, and cook for 5 minutes. Transfer the beans to a paper towel–lined plate to drain and wash the skillet before proceeding with the recipe.

- ½ teaspoon grated lemon zest plus 1 teaspoon juice
- ¼ teaspoon table salt
- ¼ teaspoon pepper
- 1 pound green beans, trimmed
- 2 tablespoons vegetable oil

1. Combine lemon zest, salt, and pepper in small bowl. Set aside.

2. Rinse green beans but do not dry. Place in medium bowl, cover, and microwave until fully tender, 6 to 12 minutes, stirring every 3 minutes. Using tongs, transfer green beans to paper towel–lined plate and let drain.

3. Heat oil in 12-inch nonstick skillet over high heat until just smoking. Add green beans in single layer. Cook, without stirring, until green beans begin to blister and char, 4 to 5 minutes. Toss green beans and continue to cook, stirring occasionally, until green beans are softened and charred, 4 to 5 minutes longer. Using tongs, transfer green beans to serving bowl, leaving any excess oil in skillet. Sprinkle with lemon-salt mixture and lemon juice and toss to coat. Serve.

Variation

FAST VEGAN Skillet-Charred Green Beans with Crispy Bread-Crumb Topping

Process 2 tablespoons panko bread crumbs in spice grinder or mortar and pestle until uniformly ground to a medium-fine consistency that resembles couscous. Cook panko and 1 tablespoon vegetable oil in 12-inch nonstick skillet over medium-low heat, stirring frequently, until light golden brown, 5 to 7 minutes. Remove skillet from heat. Add ¾ teaspoon kosher salt, ¼ teaspoon pepper, and ¼ teaspoon red pepper flakes and stir to combine. Transfer panko mixture to bowl and set aside. Wash out skillet thoroughly and dry with paper towels. Proceed with recipe as directed, substituting panko mixture for lemon-salt mixture.

Skillet-Charred Green Beans

top | *Quick Cast-Iron Skillet Green Bean Casserole*
bottom | *Roasted Kale with Garlic, Red Pepper Flakes, and Lemon*

Quick Cast-Iron Skillet Green Bean Casserole

FAST Serves 6 to 8 Total Time 35 minutes

Why This Recipe Works Green bean casserole is a beloved Thanksgiving side of tender green beans coated in a creamy mushroom sauce with a crispy topping of fried onions. Here, we reengineer the casserole to be made sequentially in a cast-iron skillet, without the need to take things in and out of the skillet. First we cook the mushrooms, followed by the aromatics (onion, garlic, and fresh thyme). Then we add the green beans, cover the skillet, and steam until the beans are tender. A mixture of flour, heavy cream, vegetable broth, and soy sauce is added to thicken into a luscious sauce that binds our skillet casserole together. To keep things simple we sprinkle canned fried onions on top and serve the casserole directly from the skillet. We recommend using a 12-inch cast-iron skillet because of its large cooking surface, tall sides, and ability to retain heat. If you don't have a cast-iron skillet, you can use a 12-inch nonstick skillet. In either case, you will need a tight-fitting lid. Note that the skillet will be very full when adding the green beans in step 2.

- 8 tablespoons unsalted butter
- 12 ounces white or cremini mushrooms, trimmed, halved, and sliced thin
- 1 onion, chopped fine
- 3 garlic cloves, minced
- 5 sprigs fresh thyme
- 2 pounds green beans, trimmed
- 1½ teaspoons table salt
- 1 cup heavy cream
- ¾ cup vegetable broth
- 2 tablespoons all-purpose flour
- 1 tablespoon soy sauce
- 1 teaspoon pepper
- 2 cups canned fried onions

1. Melt butter in 12-inch cast-iron skillet over medium-high heat. Add mushrooms and cook, stirring occasionally, until beginning to brown, 8 to 10 minutes. Stir in onion, garlic, and thyme sprigs and cook until onion is just softened, 1 to 2 minutes.

2. Stir green beans and salt into mushroom mixture until evenly combined. Cover skillet and cook, tossing with tongs occasionally to redistribute, until green beans are fully tender but still bright green, 10 to 12 minutes.

3. Whisk cream, broth, flour, soy sauce, and pepper together in 4-cup liquid measuring cup until flour is dissolved. Stir cream mixture into green bean mixture until evenly combined. Bring green bean mixture to simmer; cook, uncovered, tossing with tongs occasionally, until sauce is thick and glossy and just coats green beans, 1 to 2 minutes. (Sauce will thicken slightly as it cools.) Off heat, discard thyme sprigs. Sprinkle green bean mixture evenly with fried onions and serve.

Simple Sautéed Kale

VEGAN Serves 6 to 8 Total Time 50 minutes

Why This Recipe Works Notoriously fibrous and tough, kale is often long-cooked. For a faster way to sauté the hearty greens, we first cut the leaves into rough 2-inch pieces and the woody stems into smaller ½-inch pieces so they cook in the same amount of time. To jump-start the sautéing, we soften all the kale at once by blanching it in salted water. Once it is drained and pressed of excess water, we heat sliced garlic and a dash of red pepper flakes in extra-virgin olive oil in the now-empty Dutch oven and add the kale. After 5 minutes of stirring, the kale is completely tender and infused with garlicky flavor. A final drizzle of olive oil gives it a glossy sheen and extra richness. You can substitute lacinato kale (also known as dinosaur or Tuscan kale) for the curly kale in this recipe. It's important to boil the kale in the full 4 quarts of water; with less water it can become too salty.

- 1½ pounds curly kale
- Table salt for cooking kale
- 6 tablespoons extra-virgin olive oil, divided
- 4 garlic cloves, sliced thin
- ¼ teaspoon red pepper flakes

1. Bring 4 quarts water to boil in Dutch oven over medium-high heat.

2. Meanwhile, stem kale by grasping leaves between your thumb and index finger at base of stem and pulling from bottom to top of stem to strip off leaves. Cut leaves into 2-inch pieces. Trim and discard bases of stems thicker than ½ inch. Cut remaining stems into ½-inch pieces. Transfer kale to large bowl and wash thoroughly.

3. Add 2 tablespoons salt to boiling water. Add kale to pot, 1 handful at a time, submerging with tongs as needed. Cook, stirring occasionally, until leaves are tender and stems are just al dente, about 5 minutes. Drain in colander and let sit for 5 minutes, occasionally pressing on kale with rubber spatula to release excess moisture. (Drained kale can be refrigerated for up to 3 days.)

4. Heat ¼ cup oil in now-empty pot over medium heat until shimmering. Add garlic and pepper flakes and cook until garlic is lightly browned, 30 to 60 seconds. Add kale and cook, stirring frequently, until stems are tender, about 5 minutes. Season with salt and pepper to taste. Transfer to serving platter, drizzle with remaining 2 tablespoons oil, and serve.

Roasted Kale with Garlic, Red Pepper Flakes, and Lemon

FAST **VEGAN** Serves 4 Total Time 30 minutes

Why This Recipe Works We use curly kale for roasting because it retains some volume and featheriness, even when cooked. Massaging oil and seasonings into the kale directly on the baking sheet evenly seasons all the leaves and kick-starts the wilting process before cooking. Roasting the kale in a hot oven cooks it relatively quickly and encourages browning. By skipping any stirring while roasting, we end up with kale that has a delightful mix of textures: tender, crisp, and crunchy. The classic combination of garlic, red pepper flakes, and lemon brightens up the earthy green. Washing the kale and drying it in a salad spinner leaves it with just the right amount of surface moisture to facilitate cooking. Kneading and squeezing helps soften the kale's texture—do not skip these steps. Kale bunches can vary in the amount of usable leaves; buy 1 pound to ensure that you end up with 12 cups (10 ounces) of kale pieces. To minimize waste, look for bunches where leaves run the length of the stem. Serve the kale as a side dish or mix it into pastas, scrambles, or grain bowls.

- 1 pound curly kale, stemmed and torn into 1½- to 2-inch pieces (12 cups)
- 2 tablespoons vegetable oil
- 2 garlic cloves, minced
- 1 teaspoon grated lemon zest
- ½ teaspoon table salt
- ¼ teaspoon red pepper flakes

1. Adjust oven rack to upper-middle position and heat oven to 400 degrees. Working in 3 batches, wash kale and spin in salad spinner until leaves are mostly dry. Transfer to rimmed baking sheet.

2. Combine oil, garlic, lemon zest, salt, and pepper flakes in small bowl and drizzle over kale. Gently knead and squeeze kale until leaves are evenly coated in oil mixture, have started to soften, and are slightly wilted, about 1 minute.

3. Roast kale until leaves are tender and some edges of leaves are crisp and brown, about 10 minutes. Serve immediately (leaves will soften as they stand).

Variations

FAST VEGAN Roasted Kale with Coriander, Ginger, and Coconut

Omit lemon zest. Substitute 2 teaspoons grated fresh ginger for garlic and ½ teaspoon ground coriander for pepper flakes. Sprinkle ½ cup unsweetened coconut chips over kale after roasting.

FAST Roasted Kale with Parmesan, Shallot, and Nutmeg

Substitute ½ cup grated Parmesan for garlic, 2 tablespoons minced shallot for lemon zest, and ground nutmeg for pepper flakes.

Leeks Vinaigrette

Serves 4 Total Time 1¼ hours

Why This Recipe Works In this simple, classic French preparation, silky sweet, tender leeks are overlaid with a veil of mustardy dressing, which permeates the alliums' layers, especially if you let the dish sit for a few hours before serving. We trim away the dark-green tops and then halve each leek lengthwise, leaving the base intact to preserve the shape, and rinse each thoroughly to remove any grit concealed between the layers. Though some recipes call for steaming, we prefer simmering leeks in heavily salted water, which seasons them all the way to their base. Tying up each leek with a piece of kitchen twine keeps the layers together during cooking and a brief squeeze after cooling removes any excess water. Crispy bread crumbs spiked with Parmesan add savor, richness, and a pleasing textural contrast. You can use almost any unseeded bread for the bread crumbs; remove crusts before making crumbs.

- 3 leeks (1 to 1½ inches in diameter, with 8 to 9 inches of white and light-green parts)
- Table salt for simmering leeks
- 2 teaspoons plus 3 tablespoons extra-virgin olive oil, divided
- ¾ cup fresh bread crumbs
- 2 tablespoons finely grated Parmesan cheese
- 2 tablespoons finely chopped fresh parsley, divided
- ¼ teaspoon pepper
- 1½ tablespoons red wine vinegar
- 1 tablespoon Dijon mustard
- 1 garlic clove, minced to paste

1. Bring 3 quarts water to boil in Dutch oven. Trim large green tops from leeks. Trim roots from leeks, leaving base intact so layers stay together. Starting 1 inch above base, halve leeks lengthwise (they should still be joined at base). Rinse thoroughly between layers to remove any dirt. Tie halves of each leek together with kitchen twine about 2 inches from top.

2. Add leeks and 3 tablespoons salt to boiling water and return to boil. Adjust heat to maintain simmer. Cover and cook until area just above base can be pierced easily with paring knife, 15 to 20 minutes. Using tongs, grasp 1 leek close to base and hold vertically over pot to drain briefly. Transfer to paper towel–lined plate and repeat with remaining leeks. Let sit until cool enough to handle, about 10 minutes. While leeks cool, make crumbs and vinaigrette.

3. Heat 2 teaspoons oil in 8-inch nonstick skillet over medium heat until shimmering. Add bread crumbs and cook, stirring frequently, until deep golden brown, 4 to 5 minutes. Off heat, sprinkle with Parmesan and let sit until crumbs are just warm, about 5 minutes. Add 1 tablespoon parsley and pepper and stir, breaking up any clumps.

4. Whisk vinegar, mustard, garlic, and 1 tablespoon water in small bowl until combined. Whisking constantly, drizzle in remaining 3 tablespoons oil. Whisk in remaining 1 tablespoon parsley. Squeeze leeks over sink to remove excess water. Remove twine and finish cutting leeks in half lengthwise. Cut each half crosswise into thirds (do not remove bases of leeks; they're delicious). Spread half of vinaigrette over bottom of serving platter. Arrange leeks on platter, cut side up, opening layers slightly. Drizzle evenly with remaining vinaigrette. (Dressed leeks can be covered loosely and stored at room temperature for up to 3 hours.) Sprinkle with bread crumb mixture and serve.

Preparing Leeks for Leeks Vinaigrette

1. Trim dark green tops from leeks. Trim roots, leaving base intact. Starting 1 inch above base, halve leeks lengthwise (they should still be joined at base).

2. Tie halves of each leek with kitchen twine 2 inches from top to keep leeks intact during cooking.

Sautéed Mushrooms with Red Wine and Rosemary

FAST Serves 4 Total Time 35 minutes

Why This Recipe Works Sautéing mushrooms the usual way means waiting patiently for them to release their moisture, which then must evaporate before the mushrooms can brown. We accelerate the process by steaming the mushrooms in a small amount of water in the pan, which allows them to release their moisture more quickly. It also keeps the mushrooms from absorbing much oil; in fact, ½ teaspoon of oil is enough to prevent sticking and encourage browning. And because we use so little fat to sauté the mushrooms, we are able to sauce them with a butter-based reduction without making them overly rich. Adding broth to the sauce and simmering the mixture ensures that the butter emulsifies, creating a flavorful glaze that clings well to the mushrooms. Use one variety of mushroom or a combination. Stem and halve portobello mushrooms and cut each half crosswise into ½-inch pieces. Trim white or cremini mushrooms; quarter them if large or medium or halve them if small. Tear trimmed oyster mushrooms into 1- to 1½-inch pieces. Stem shiitake mushrooms; quarter large caps and halve small caps. Cut trimmed maitake (hen-of-the-woods) mushrooms into 1- to 1½-inch pieces.

Leeks Vinaigrette

- 1¼ pounds mushrooms
- ¼ cup water
- ½ teaspoon vegetable oil
- 1 tablespoon unsalted butter
- 1 shallot, minced
- 1 teaspoon minced fresh rosemary
- ¼ teaspoon table salt
- ¼ teaspoon pepper
- ¼ cup red wine
- 1 tablespoon cider vinegar
- ½ cup vegetable broth

1. Cook mushrooms and water in 12-inch nonstick skillet over high heat, stirring occasionally, until skillet is almost dry and mushrooms begin to sizzle, 4 to 8 minutes. Reduce heat to medium-high, add oil, and toss until mushrooms are evenly coated. Continue to cook, stirring occasionally, until mushrooms are well browned, 4 to 8 minutes longer.

2. Reduce heat to medium and push mushrooms to sides of skillet. Add butter to center. When butter has melted, add shallot, rosemary, salt, and pepper to center and cook, stirring constantly, until aromatic, about 30 seconds. Add wine and vinegar and stir mushrooms into mixture. Cook, stirring occasionally, until liquid has evaporated, 2 to 3 minutes. Add broth and cook, stirring occasionally, until glaze is reduced by half, about 3 minutes. Season with salt and pepper to taste, and serve.

Variations

FAST Sautéed Mushrooms with Mustard and Parsley

Omit rosemary. Substitute 1 tablespoon Dijon mustard for wine and increase vinegar to 1½ tablespoons (liquid will take only 1 to 2 minutes to evaporate). Stir in 2 tablespoons chopped fresh parsley before serving.

FAST Sautéed Mushrooms with Soy, Scallion, and Ginger

Substitute 1 thinly sliced scallion for shallot and grated fresh ginger for rosemary. Omit salt. Substitute 2 tablespoons soy sauce for wine and sherry vinegar for cider vinegar.

top | *Sautéed Mushrooms with Red Wine and Rosemary*
bottom | *Roasted Okra*

Roasted Okra

FAST **VEGAN** Serves 4 Total Time 45 minutes

Why This Recipe Works Roasted okra is a revelation: The pods emerge from the oven tender, brown, and lightly crisp at the edges, with a nutty-sweet, green bean–esque flavor. We split similar-size pods lengthwise, toss them with oil and salt, and arrange the halved pods cut sides down on a rimmed baking sheet. We cover them with foil so that the thicker parts can steam and turn tender before the thin tips wither and scorch. Finally, we uncover the okra to allow their cut sides, which rest flush against the baking sheet, to brown and crisp lightly. Don't use frozen okra in this recipe. For even cooking and browning, select okra pods that have approximately the same diameter. If you use a dark baking sheet, the browning time after removing the foil will be on the shorter end of the range. If desired, serve with Spicy Red Pepper Mayonnaise (recipe follows) by spreading the mayonnaise on a serving platter and arranging the okra on top. Alternatively, simply squeeze lemon or lime juice onto the roasted okra and/or sprinkle with your favorite spice blend.

- 1 pound fresh okra, caps trimmed and halved lengthwise
- 2 teaspoons vegetable oil
- ½ teaspoon table salt

1. Adjust oven rack to middle position and heat oven to 425 degrees.

2. Toss okra with oil and salt in bowl until well combined. Arrange okra, cut sides down, in single layer on rimmed baking sheet. Cover sheet tightly with aluminum foil and roast until okra is bright green, 12 to 15 minutes (cut sides of a few pieces may be beginning to brown). Remove foil and roast until cut sides are well browned, 7 to 12 minutes.

3. Let okra rest on sheet for 5 minutes. Serve.

Spicy Red Pepper Mayonnaise

FAST **VEGAN** Serves 4 Total Time 25 minutes

Why This Recipe Works For a creamy, flavorful accompaniment to roasted okra, combine minced jarred roasted red peppers with sautéed garlic and vibrant spices, then stir in mayonnaise and tangy lime juice and zest. For less spice, use just a pinch of cayenne pepper. To make this recipe vegan, substitute plant-based mayo for the dairy mayonnaise.

- 2 teaspoons vegetable oil
- 5 garlic cloves, minced
- ¾ teaspoon smoked paprika
- ¾ teaspoon ground coriander
- ¾ teaspoon ground cumin
- Pinch to ⅛ teaspoon cayenne pepper
- ⅓ cup jarred roasted red peppers, patted dry and minced
- ½ teaspoon table salt
- ¼ teaspoon sugar
- 3 tablespoons mayonnaise
- ¼ teaspoon grated lime zest plus ½ teaspoon juice

1. Heat oil in 8-inch skillet over medium heat until shimmering. Add garlic and cook, stirring frequently, until garlic just starts to brown, about 2 minutes. Add paprika, coriander, cumin, and cayenne and cook, stirring constantly, until fragrant, about 30 seconds. Immediately transfer to bowl. Stir in red peppers, salt, and sugar and refrigerate for at least 5 minutes.

2. Stir mayonnaise and lime zest and juice into red pepper mixture and serve.

Braised Vidalia Onions with Chile, Lime, and Cilantro

Braised Vidalia Onions with Chile, Lime, and Cilantro

FAST Serves 4 to 6 Total Time 40 minutes

Why This Recipe Works Vidalia onions, which are sweet onions regionally grown in Georgia, have a uniquely mild, floral flavor. As a result, they require little treatment to be delicious. Here, we cut the onions into petite wedges, then sear them over medium-high heat to create a golden-brown crust. To further soften and flavor the onions, we flip them, add a mixture of water, vegetarian fish sauce, sugar, and lime zest, and cook everything with the lid on, letting the sauce soften and thoroughly flavor the onions. We lift the lid to let the sauce thicken slightly and then remove and plate the wedges. The remaining sauce is mixed with butter and lime juice and emulsified into a creamy, bright mixture to coat the onions. For pops of flavor complexity, we sprinkle the onions with fresh cilantro, minced Thai chiles, and flake sea salt. To help keep the onion wedges intact, take care to avoid over-trimming the root end when peeling. You can substitute other sweet onion varieties, such as Maui or Walla Walla, for the Vidalias. Do not substitute yellow or red onions.

- ½ cup water
- 1½ tablespoons vegetarian fish sauce
- 1 tablespoon packed brown sugar
- 1 teaspoon grated lime zest plus 1 teaspoon juice
- 1½ pounds Vidalia onions, peeled and cut into 1¼-inch wedges
- 5 teaspoons vegetable oil, divided
- 1 teaspoon table salt
- 2 tablespoons unsalted butter, cut into 4 pieces
- ¼ cup fresh cilantro leaves
- 2 Thai chiles, stemmed, seeded, and minced
- ½ teaspoon flake sea salt

1. Whisk water, fish sauce, sugar, and lime zest together in small bowl; set aside. In large bowl, gently toss onion wedges with 2 teaspoons oil and table salt.

2. Heat remaining 1 tablespoon oil in 12-inch nonstick skillet over medium-high heat until shimmering. Arrange onion wedges in single layer in skillet, flat side down. Cook onions, without moving, until well browned on first side, 5 to 7 minutes, adjusting position of skillet as needed to encourage even browning.

3. Off heat, using tongs and spatula, carefully flip onion wedges to second flat side. Pour fish sauce mixture over onions, then bring to simmer over medium-low heat. Cover skillet and cook until onions begin to soften and turn translucent, 5 to 7 minutes. Remove lid and increase heat to medium-high. Continue to cook until sauce is reduced by about half and slightly thickened, 2 to 3 minutes longer.

4. Off heat, carefully transfer onions to serving platter. Add lime juice to sauce left in skillet and bring to simmer over medium-low heat. Add butter and cook, stirring constantly, until butter is melted and sauce has consistency of thin gravy, about 1 minute. Spoon sauce over onions; sprinkle with cilantro, chiles, and flake sea salt; and serve.

Variation

FAST Braised Vidalia Onions with Honey, Lemon, and Oregano

Omit Thai chiles. Substitute ⅔ cup vegetable broth for water, 1 tablespoon sherry vinegar for fish sauce, 1 tablespoon honey for brown sugar, an equal volume of lemon zest and juice for lime zest and juice, and 1 tablespoon oregano for cilantro. Add ¼ teaspoon table salt to broth mixture in step 1.

Rajas Poblanas con Crema (Charred Poblano Strips with Cream)

Serves 4 Total Time 50 minutes

Why This Recipe Works A Mexican favorite, these tender strips of roasted chiles and sliced onion cooked with crema can be enjoyed alongside rice or beans, or used as a filling for tacos or quesadillas. We start by broiling poblanos until they are completely charred and then wrapping them in foil to steam. This imbues the chiles with smoky flavor and makes them easy to peel. White onion gently cooked in butter adds a bit of sweetness, and garlic contributes savoriness. Just under a cup of Mexican crema makes the dish creamy, lightly salty, and tangy and balances the mild heat of the poblanos without overpowering them. Cooking times will vary depending on the broiler, so watch the chiles carefully. Mexican crema (or crema mexicana) can be found in the dairy section of the grocery store. If you don't have crema, substitute heavy cream.

1 pound (3 to 4) poblano chiles, stemmed, halved, and seeded
2 tablespoons unsalted butter
½ white onion, sliced ¼ inch thick through root end
2 garlic cloves, minced
½ teaspoon table salt
¼ teaspoon pepper
¾ cup Mexican crema

1. Line rimmed baking sheet with aluminum foil. Adjust oven rack 3 to 4 inches from broiler element and heat broiler. Arrange poblanos skin side up on prepared sheet and press to flatten. Broil until skin is puffed and most of surface is well charred, 5 to 10 minutes, rotating sheet halfway through broiling.

2. Using tongs, pile poblanos in center of foil. Gather foil over poblanos and crimp to form pouch. Let steam for 10 minutes. Open foil packet carefully and spread out poblanos. When cool enough to handle, peel poblanos (it's OK if some bits of skin remain intact) and discard skins. Slice lengthwise into ½-inch-thick strips. (Rajas can be refrigerated for up to 3 days.)

3. Melt butter in 12-inch nonstick skillet over medium heat. Add onion and cook, stirring occasionally, until softened and edges are just starting to brown, 6 to 8 minutes. Add garlic and cook until fragrant, about 30 seconds. Add rajas, salt, and pepper and cook until warmed through, about 1 minute. Add crema and cook, stirring gently but frequently, until crema has thickened and clings to vegetables, 2 to 3 minutes. Serve immediately.

Variation

Rajas Poblanas con Crema y Elote (Charred Poblano Strips with Cream and Corn)

Add ¾ cup fresh or frozen corn to onion mixture with rajas in step 3.

Three-Cheese Potato Frico

Serves 4 to 6   Total Time 1¼ hours

Why This Recipe Works Potato frico hails from the Friuli region in northeastern Italy, where the thick, crispy pancake was created to use up scraps left over from making Montasio, an Alpine sheep's cheese. To make our version of this crowd-pleasing dish, we soften onion and then add russet potatoes (sliced thin to cook quickly) and a measured amount of water. Then we stir in the cheeses: melty fontina, mellow cheddar, and sharp Parmesan. When we toss the cheeses with the cooked potatoes, some of their starch releases and mixes with the cheeses, forming a gooey amalgamation of melted cheese and potato. We cook this mixture until browned and crispy on both sides (using a plate to help flip it). You will need a 10-inch nonstick skillet with a tight-fitting lid for this recipe. If you can find Montasio cheese, use 4 ounces of it instead of the fontina and cheddar.

2 tablespoons extra-virgin olive oil
1 onion, halved and sliced thin
¾ teaspoon table salt, divided
1 pound russet potatoes, peeled, quartered lengthwise, and sliced crosswise ¼ inch thick
⅓ cup water
½ teaspoon pepper
1½ ounces Parmesan cheese, grated (¾ cup)
2½ ounces fontina cheese, shredded (⅔ cup)
1½ ounces sharp white cheddar cheese, shredded (⅓ cup)

1. Heat oil in 10-inch nonstick skillet over medium heat until shimmering. Add onion and ¼ teaspoon salt and cook, stirring often, until softened, 8 to 10 minutes. Stir in potatoes, water, pepper, and remaining ½ teaspoon salt. Spread potatoes into even layer, cover skillet, and bring mixture to vigorous simmer. Reduce heat to medium-low and simmer, stirring occasionally, until potatoes are tender and beginning to fall apart and pan is completely dry, 18 to 22 minutes.

2. Stir in cheeses with silicone spatula and cook, folding and stirring mixture constantly, until cheese is melted and potatoes are mostly broken down, about 2 minutes. Smooth top of mixture. Increase heat to medium and cook until edges and bottom are deep golden brown, 8 to 10 minutes, gently lifting edges with spatula to check color of bottom.

3. Loosen edges of frico from pan with spatula, then vigorously shake pan in circular motion until frico slides around freely in pan. Remove pan from heat. Slide frico, browned side down, onto large plate (make sure plate is larger than skillet). Invert second large plate over frico, then flip frico onto second plate. Slide frico, browned side up, back into skillet, using spatula to loosen frico from plate as needed. Neaten edges of frico with spatula.

4. Return pan to medium heat and cook until second side is deep golden brown, 4 to 6 minutes. Slide frico onto cutting board and let cool for 5 minutes (crust will continue to crisp as it cools). Cut frico into wedges and serve immediately.

Best Baked Potatoes

VEGAN Serves 4 Total Time 1½ hours

Why This Recipe Works To produce perfect baked potatoes with an evenly fluffy interior, we figured out their ideal doneness temperature: 205 degrees. To season the skin, we coat the potatoes in salty water before baking; we then crisp the skins by painting on oil before a brief second bake. Be sure to open up the potatoes immediately after removing them from the oven in step 3 so that steam can escape. Top the baked potatoes as desired, or with our Herbed Goat Cheese Topping or Creamy Egg Topping (recipes follow).

Table salt for seasoning potatoes
4 (7- to 9-ounce) russet potatoes, unpeeled, each lightly pricked with fork in 6 places
1 tablespoon vegetable oil

1. Adjust oven rack to middle position and heat oven to 450 degrees. Dissolve 2 tablespoons salt in ½ cup water in large bowl. Place potatoes in bowl and toss so exteriors of potatoes are evenly moistened. Transfer potatoes to wire rack set in rimmed baking sheet. Bake until center of largest potato registers 205 degrees, 45 minutes to 1 hour.

2. Remove potatoes from oven and brush tops and sides with oil. Return potatoes to oven and continue to bake 10 minutes longer.

3. Remove potatoes from oven and, using paring knife, make 2 slits, forming X, in each potato. Using clean dish towel, hold ends and squeeze slightly to push flesh up and out. Season with salt and pepper to taste and serve immediately.

Herbed Goat Cheese Topping

FAST Makes ¾ cup Total Time 10 minutes

4 ounces goat cheese, softened
2 tablespoons extra-virgin olive oil
2 tablespoons minced fresh parsley
1 tablespoon minced shallot
½ teaspoon grated lemon zest

Mash goat cheese with fork. Stir in oil, parsley, shallot, and lemon zest. Season with salt and pepper to taste.

Creamy Egg Topping

FAST Makes 1 cup Total Time 10 minutes

3 hard-cooked large eggs, chopped
¼ cup sour cream
1½ tablespoons minced cornichons
1 tablespoon minced fresh parsley
1 tablespoon Dijon mustard
1 tablespoon capers, rinsed and minced
1 tablespoon minced shallot

Stir together eggs, sour cream, cornichons, parsley, mustard, capers, and shallot. Season with salt and pepper to taste.

Best Baked Potatoes

Braised Red Potatoes with Lemon and Chives

Fastest, Easiest Mashed Potatoes

FAST Serves 4 Total Time 25 minutes

Why This Recipe Works You can make great mashed potatoes any way you like—smooth or chunky, fluffy or creamy, earthy or buttery—as long as you start with properly cooked spuds. It's crucial to avoid overcooking, which results in too much free starch that gelatinizes and renders the mash gluey. To avoid overcooking and speed up the process, we start by slicing the potatoes thin to ensure that they cook through quickly and evenly. We also pack them tightly into a moderately sized pot, which reduces the amount of water needed to cover them and thus the time it takes for the water to come to a boil. Choosing the potato variety, processing tool, and ratio of dairy to potato allows you to adjust the flavor and consistency to your liking. Yukon Gold potatoes will deliver buttery flavor and color; for earthier flavor, use russets. For a smooth mash, use a ricer or food mill; for a chunkier texture, use a potato masher. For lean mashed potatoes, use milk; for a richer result, use half-and-half.

- 2 pounds Yukon Gold or russet potatoes, peeled and sliced ¼ inch thick
- 8–10 tablespoons half-and-half or milk
- 4 tablespoons unsalted butter, cut into ¼-inch slices
- 1 teaspoon table salt

1. Bring 1 quart water to boil in medium saucepan over high heat. Add potatoes, making sure they are fully submerged in water. (If not, add just enough water to cover). Return water to boil, then adjust heat to maintain very gentle simmer. Cover and cook until paring knife meets no resistance when slipped into center of potatoes, about 12 minutes.

2. Drain potatoes and return to saucepan. Use potato masher, ricer, or food mill to process potatoes to desired consistency. Stir in ½ cup half-and-half, butter, and salt until combined. Adjust consistency with remaining half-and-half as desired. Season with salt and pepper to taste, and serve.

Braised Red Potatoes with Lemon and Chives

Serves 4 to 6 Total Time 50 minutes

Why This Recipe Works Braising is a fantastic way to deliver red potatoes with creamy interiors and crispy exteriors. We combine halved small red potatoes, butter, and salted water (plus thyme and garlic cloves for flavoring) in a 12-inch skillet and simmer until the potatoes are perfectly creamy and the water is fully evaporated. Then we let the potatoes continue to cook in the now-dry skillet until their cut sides brown in the butter, developing rich flavor and crispy edges. These potatoes are so good that they need only minimal seasoning: We simply mince the softened garlic to toss with the crisped potatoes, along with lemon juice, chives, and pepper. Use small red potatoes measuring 1 to 2 inches in diameter. You will need a 12-inch nonstick skillet with a tight-fitting lid for this recipe.

- 1½ pounds small red potatoes, unpeeled, halved
- 2 cups water
- 3 tablespoons unsalted butter
- 3 garlic cloves, peeled
- 3 sprigs fresh thyme
- ¾ teaspoon table salt
- 1 teaspoon lemon juice
- ¼ teaspoon pepper
- 2 tablespoons minced fresh chives

1. Arrange potatoes in single layer cut side down in 12-inch nonstick skillet. Add water, butter, garlic, thyme sprigs, and salt and bring to simmer over medium-high heat. Reduce heat to medium, cover, and simmer until potatoes are just tender, about 15 minutes.

2. Remove lid and use slotted spoon to transfer garlic to cutting board; discard thyme sprigs. Increase heat to medium-high and simmer vigorously, swirling skillet occasionally, until water evaporates and butter starts to sizzle, 15 to 20 minutes. When cool enough to handle, mince garlic to paste. Transfer paste to bowl and stir in lemon juice and pepper.

3. Continue to cook potatoes, swirling skillet frequently, until butter browns and cut sides of potatoes turn spotty brown, 4 to 6 minutes. Off heat, add chives and garlic mixture, toss to coat thoroughly, and serve.

Variations

Braised Red Potatoes with Dijon and Tarragon

Substitute 2 teaspoons Dijon mustard for lemon juice and 1 tablespoon minced fresh tarragon for chives.

Braised Red Potatoes with Miso and Scallions

Reduce salt to ½ teaspoon. Substitute 1 tablespoon red miso paste for lemon juice and 3 thinly sliced scallions for chives.

Creamy Potatoes and Leeks

Serves 6 Total Time 1 hour

Why This Recipe Works Potatoes and leeks are a classic pairing. This rustic yet elegant dish uses one skillet to make rich, creamy potatoes and meltingly tender leeks with a crispy panko topping. We start by toasting panko bread crumbs in butter. Then we soften leeks in more butter before adding chunks of potatoes to cook in vegetable broth and wine (instead of water), which gives the dish depth and brightness. To enrich the final dish, we add some heavy cream and allow the potatoes to cook past al dente, creating an even creamier consistency. Just as the cream reduces, we stir in a handful of nutty Gruyère cheese, then top it all with the buttery toasted bread crumbs and earthy fresh thyme leaves. We prefer to use leeks measuring about 1 inch in diameter for this recipe because they're more tender than larger leeks. Larger leeks will work, but discard their more fibrous outer layers.

- 4 tablespoons unsalted butter, cut into 4 pieces, divided
- ½ cup panko bread crumbs
- 1¼ teaspoons table salt, divided
- 2 pounds leeks, white and light-green parts only, halved lengthwise, sliced ½ inch thick, and washed thoroughly
- 1½ pounds Yukon Gold potatoes, unpeeled, cut into ¾-inch pieces
- 1½ cups vegetable broth
- ¼ cup dry white wine
- ¾ cup heavy cream
- ½ teaspoon pepper
- 2 ounces Gruyère cheese, shredded (⅔ cup)
- 2 teaspoons chopped fresh thyme or oregano

1. Melt 2 tablespoons butter in 12-inch nonstick skillet over medium heat. Add panko and ½ teaspoon salt and cook, stirring often, until golden brown, 3 to 6 minutes. Transfer to bowl; set aside. Wipe skillet clean with paper towels.

2. Melt remaining 2 tablespoons butter in now-empty skillet over medium heat. Add leeks and ¼ teaspoon salt and cook, covered, until softened, about 6 minutes, stirring halfway through cooking.

3. Stir in potatoes, broth, wine, and remaining ½ teaspoon salt and spread into even layer. Cover and bring to vigorous simmer over medium-high heat. Reduce heat to medium-low and simmer, covered, until potatoes are fork-tender, 20 to 25 minutes.

4. Stir in cream and pepper and return to simmer. Continue to cook, uncovered, until spatula leaves trail when dragged through mixture, 4 to 6 minutes longer. Off heat, stir in Gruyère. Sprinkle evenly with panko mixture and thyme and serve.

Sichuan Hot and Sour Potatoes

FAST VEGAN Serves 4 Total Time 30 minutes

Why This Recipe Works In Sichuanese cuisine, potatoes are often enjoyed for their semiraw bite and crunchiness—much like fresh jicama in a salad. In this version, we slice potatoes into matchsticks and briefly soak them, which draws out excess starch and prevents them from becoming gummy, clumping, or sticking to the pan. The cold water also stiffens the potatoes, ensuring their signature crisp-tender texture. We then give them a quick stir-fry—just enough for the spuds to start crisping and pick up the tingly aromatics of Sichuan peppercorns and Thai chile. Look for potatoes that are about 4 inches in length. Slicing the potatoes into thin matchsticks is crucial for the success of this dish. You can do this with a sharp knife; however, a mandoline ensures even slices; we use it to slice ⅛-inch planks and then cut those into matchsticks by hand. We prefer yellow waxy potatoes such as Yukon Golds for this recipe, but any potato will work.

- 1 pound large yellow waxy potatoes, peeled
- 1½ tablespoons vegetable oil
- ¾ teaspoon Sichuan peppercorns
- 1 Thai chile, stemmed and sliced thin
- 2 scallions, sliced into 3-inch-long thin matchsticks
- 1 teaspoon table salt
- ½ teaspoon sugar
- 4 teaspoons Chinese white rice vinegar

1. Slice potatoes into ⅛-inch-thick planks, then cut planks into ⅛-inch matchsticks. Transfer potatoes to bowl, submerge in cold water, and soak for 10 minutes. Drain in colander, transfer to paper towel–lined plate, and set aside.

2. Heat oil and peppercorns in 12-inch nonstick skillet or 14-inch flat-bottomed wok over medium heat, stirring constantly, until peppercorns are sizzling and fragrant but not darkened, about 2 minutes. Using slotted spoon, remove peppercorns and discard, reserving oil. Add Thai chile to oil in skillet and cook, stirring constantly, until fragrant, about 15 seconds. Increase heat to high, add potatoes, and cook, tossing slowly but constantly, until potatoes are crisp-tender, about 2 minutes. Add scallions, salt, and sugar and toss to combine. Off heat, add vinegar and toss to combine. Serve warm or at room temperature.

Cheddar Scalloped Potatoes

Serves 6 Total Time 1 hour

Why This Recipe Works We love scalloped potatoes, but most recipes call for more than an hour of oven time to soften the potatoes. We developed a streamlined recipe that can be made any night of the week. We start by parboiling sliced russet potatoes in a combination of heavy cream and vegetable broth on the stovetop. Then we stir in some sharp cheddar cheese and transfer the gooey, cheesy potato mixture to a baking dish to finish cooking in the oven. Do not prepare the potatoes ahead of time or store them in water; the potato starch is essential for thickening the sauce. A mandoline makes quick work of slicing the potatoes. We prefer sharp cheddar for this recipe, but mild or extra-sharp cheddar can also be used. This recipe can easily be doubled. To do so, use a large Dutch oven instead of a large saucepan in step 1 and let the casserole cool for 30 minutes before serving in step 3.

- 2 pounds russet potatoes, peeled and sliced ¼ inch thick
- 1¼ cups heavy cream
- 1 cup vegetable broth
- 1 teaspoon table salt
- ½ teaspoon pepper
- 8 ounces sharp cheddar cheese, shredded (2 cups), divided

1. Adjust oven rack to upper-middle position and heat oven to 425 degrees. Bring potatoes, cream, broth, salt, and pepper to simmer in large saucepan over medium-high heat.

Creamy Potatoes and Leeks

top | *Thick-Cut Oven Fries*
bottom | *Better Hash Browns*

2. Reduce heat to medium, cover, and cook, stirring occasionally, until paring knife can be slipped in and out of potatoes with no resistance, about 8 minutes, adjusting heat as necessary to maintain gentle simmer. Off heat, gently stir in 1 cup cheddar. (Potato mixture can be transferred to 13 by 9-inch baking dish, cooled completely, covered with aluminum foil, and refrigerated for up to 24 hours. To serve, keep covered with foil and bake until heated through, about 20 minutes. Uncover, sprinkle with remaining 1 cup cheddar, and continue to bake, uncovered, until bubbling around edges and top is spotty brown, about 20 minutes longer.)

3. Transfer potato mixture to 13 by 9-inch baking dish, spread into even layer, and sprinkle with remaining 1 cup cheddar. Bake until bubbling around edges and top is golden brown, about 20 minutes. Let cool for 15 minutes and serve.

Thick-Cut Oven Fries

VEGAN Serves 4 Total Time 55 minutes

Why This Recipe Works When traditional french fries are fried, water is rapidly driven out of the starch cells at the surface of the potato, leaving behind tiny cavities. It's these cavities that create a delicate, crispy crust. Since oven fries don't heat fast enough for air pockets to form, we instead coat the potatoes in a cornstarch slurry that crisps up like a deep-fried fry would. We arrange the coated planks on a rimmed baked sheet coated with both vegetable oil spray and vegetable oil; the former contains a surfactant called lecithin, which prevents the oil from pooling and, in turn, prevents the potatoes from sticking. Using the oil spray also allows us to use only 3 tablespoons oil, just enough to evenly coat the fries. Covering the baking sheet with aluminum foil for the first half of cooking ensures that the potatoes are fully tender by the time they are browned. Choose potatoes that are 4 to 6 inches in length to ensure well-proportioned fries. Trimming thin slices from the sides of the potatoes in step 2 ensures that each fry has two flat surfaces for even browning. This recipe's success is dependent on a heavy-duty rimmed baking sheet that will not warp in the heat of the oven. The rate at which the potatoes brown is dependent on your baking sheet and oven. After removing the foil from the baking sheet in step 5, monitor the color of the potatoes carefully to prevent scorching.

3 tablespoons vegetable oil
2 pounds Yukon gold potatoes, unpeeled
3 tablespoons cornstarch
½ teaspoon table salt

1. Adjust oven rack to lowest position and heat oven to 425 degrees. Generously spray rimmed baking sheet with vegetable oil spray. Pour oil into prepared sheet and tilt sheet until surface is evenly coated with oil.

2. Halve potatoes lengthwise and turn halves cut sides down on cutting board. Trim thin slice from both long sides of each potato half; discard trimmings. Slice potatoes lengthwise into ⅓- to ½-inch-thick planks.

3. Combine ¾ cup water and cornstarch in large bowl, making sure no lumps of cornstarch remain on bottom of bowl. Microwave, stirring every 20 seconds, until mixture begins to thicken, 1 to 3 minutes. Remove from microwave and continue to stir until mixture thickens to pudding-like consistency. (If necessary, add up to 2 tablespoons water to achieve correct consistency.)

4. Transfer potatoes to bowl with cornstarch mixture and toss until each plank is evenly coated. Arrange planks on prepared sheet, leaving small gaps between planks. (Some cornstarch mixture will remain in bowl.) Cover sheet tightly with lightly greased aluminum foil and bake for 12 minutes.

5. Remove foil from sheet and bake until bottom of each fry is golden brown, 10 to 18 minutes. Remove sheet from oven and, using thin metal spatula, carefully flip each fry. Return sheet to oven and continue to bake until second sides are golden brown, 10 to 18 minutes longer. Sprinkle fries with salt. Using spatula, carefully toss fries to distribute salt. Transfer fries to paper towel–lined plate, season with salt to taste, and serve.

Better Hash Browns

VEGAN Serves 4 to 6 Total Time 1¼ hours

Why This Recipe Works Making good hash browns can be tricky: The shredded potatoes discolor quickly, the potato cake falls apart when you try to flip it, and the exterior often burns before the interior is cooked. We prevent discoloration by rinsing the grated potatoes in salted water. This also seasons the potatoes and lowers the gelatinization temperature of the potato starch, which helps the shreds stick together. We parcook the potatoes in the microwave, which removes more moisture and jump-starts the gelatinization process so that the potatoes are cohesive even before they go into the skillet. Molding the hash browns in a cake pan makes things easy and delivers a smoother potato cake that is less likely to stick to the pan We prefer using the shredding disk of a food processor to shred the potatoes, but you can use the large holes of a box grater if you prefer.

Table salt for seasoning potatoes
2½ pounds Yukon Gold potatoes, peeled and shredded
¼ teaspoon pepper
¼ cup vegetable oil, divided

1. Spray 8-inch round cake pan with vegetable oil spray. Whisk 2 cups water and 4 teaspoons salt in large bowl until salt dissolves. Transfer potatoes to salt water and toss briefly to coat. Immediately drain in colander. Place 2½ cups potatoes in center of clean dish towel. Gather ends together and twist tightly to wring out excess moisture. Transfer dried potatoes to large bowl, add pepper, and toss to combine. Microwave until very hot and slightly softened, about 5 minutes. Place remaining potatoes in towel and wring out excess moisture. Add to microwaved potatoes and toss with two forks until mostly combined (potatoes will not combine completely). Continue to microwave until potatoes are hot and form cohesive mass when pressed with spatula, about 6 minutes, stirring halfway through microwaving.

2. Transfer potatoes to prepared pan and let cool until no longer steaming, about 5 minutes. Using your lightly greased hands, press potatoes firmly into pan to form smooth disk. Refrigerate until cool, at least 20 minutes or up to 24 hours (if refrigerating longer than 30 minutes, wrap pan with plastic wrap once potatoes are cool).

3. Heat 2 tablespoons oil in 10-inch skillet over medium heat until shimmering. Invert potato cake onto plate and carefully slide cake into pan. Cook, swirling pan occasionally to distribute oil evenly and prevent cake from sticking, until bottom of cake is brown and crispy, 6 to 8 minutes. (If not browning after 3 minutes, turn heat up slightly. If browning too quickly, reduce heat.) Slide cake onto large plate. Invert onto second large plate. Heat remaining 2 tablespoons oil in skillet until shimmering. Carefully slide cake, browned side up, back into skillet. Cook, swirling pan occasionally, until bottom of cake is brown and crispy, 5 to 6 minutes. Carefully slide cake onto large plate and invert onto serving plate. Cut into wedges and serve.

Roasted Radishes with Yogurt-Tahini Sauce

Lemony Roasted Radicchio, Fennel, and Root Vegetables

VEGAN Serves 4 to 6 Total Time 55 minutes

Why This Recipe Works A medley of radicchio, fennel, potatoes, parsnips, and shallots creates an intriguing balance of flavors and textures in this hearty winter sheet-pan vegetable dish. Arranging the radicchio in the center of the baking sheet, with the other vegetables around the perimeter, keeps the more delicate radicchio from charring in the hot oven. Before roasting, we toss the vegetables with olive oil, garlic, thyme, rosemary, and a little sugar (to promote browning). Once all the vegetables are perfectly tender and caramelized, we toss the whole shebang with a bright-tasting lemony dressing. When coring the radicchio, leave just enough core to hold each wedge together.

- 2 fennel bulbs, stalks discarded, bulbs halved, cored, and sliced into ½-inch-thick wedges
- 1 pound red potatoes, unpeeled, cut into 1-inch pieces
- 1 head radicchio (10 ounces), halved, cored, and cut into 2-inch-thick wedges
- 8 ounces parsnips, peeled and cut into 2-inch pieces
- 8 shallots, halved
- 3 tablespoons extra-virgin olive oil, divided
- 6 garlic cloves, peeled
- 2 teaspoons minced fresh thyme
- 1 teaspoon minced fresh rosemary
- 1 teaspoon sugar
- ¾ teaspoon table salt
- ¼ teaspoon pepper
- 2 tablespoons chopped fresh basil
- 2 tablespoons minced fresh chives
- 1 tablespoon lemon juice, plus extra for seasoning

1. Adjust oven rack to middle position and heat oven to 450 degrees. Toss fennel, potatoes, radicchio, parsnips, shallots, 1 tablespoon oil, garlic, thyme, rosemary, sugar, salt, and pepper together in bowl.

2. Spread vegetables into single layer on rimmed baking sheet, arranging radicchio in center and other vegetables around perimeter. Roast until the vegetables are tender and golden brown, 30 to 35 minutes, rotating sheet halfway through roasting.

3. Whisk basil, chives, lemon juice, and remaining 2 tablespoons oil together in large serving bowl. Add vegetables and toss to combine. Season with salt, pepper, and extra lemon juice to taste, and serve.

Roasted Radishes with Yogurt-Tahini Sauce

FAST Serves 4 to 6 Total Time 30 minutes

Why This Recipe Works The crisp texture of radishes holds up well to high-heat roasting, yielding a tender but meaty interior. Roasting also mellows the spiciness of the roots, concentrating their natural sugars for nutty sweetness. To facilitate browning and complement the nuttiness of the radishes, we toss them in a mixture of melted butter and white miso and then roast them on the bottom rack of the oven. The butter produces superior browning on the cut sides while the miso adds a pleasing savory quality. To make the most of our radishes, we used the mild, peppery green tops in a simple salad, pairing them with a tangy yogurt-tahini sauce and a sprinkling of pistachios and sesame seeds. If you can only find radishes without greens, you can use baby arugula or watercress instead.

- ½ cup plain whole-milk yogurt
- 2 tablespoons tahini
- 1 teaspoon grated lemon zest plus 4 teaspoons juice, divided
- 1 garlic clove, minced
- ¾ teaspoon plus ⅛ teaspoon table salt, divided
- ¼ teaspoon pepper, divided
- 2 tablespoons chopped toasted pistachios or almonds
- 1½ teaspoons sesame seeds, toasted
- ⅛ teaspoon ground cumin
- 3 tablespoons unsalted butter, melted
- 5½ teaspoons white miso, divided
- 1½ teaspoons honey, divided
- 2 pounds radishes with their greens, radishes trimmed and halved lengthwise, 8 cups greens reserved
- 1 teaspoon extra-virgin olive oil

1. Adjust oven rack to lowest position and heat oven to 500 degrees. Whisk yogurt, tahini, lemon zest and 1 tablespoon juice, garlic, ¼ teaspoon salt, and ⅛ teaspoon pepper together in bowl; set sauce aside for serving. Combine pistachios, sesame seeds, cumin, and ⅛ teaspoon salt in small bowl; set aside for serving.

2. Line rimmed baking sheet with aluminum foil. Whisk melted butter, 5 teaspoons miso, 1 teaspoon honey, and ¼ teaspoon salt in large bowl until smooth. Add radishes and toss to coat. Arrange radishes cut side down on prepared sheet and roast until tender and well browned on cut side, 10 to 15 minutes.

3. Whisk oil, remaining 1 teaspoon lemon juice, remaining ¼ teaspoon salt, remaining ⅛ teaspoon pepper, remaining ½ teaspoon miso, and remaining ½ teaspoon honey in clean large bowl until smooth. Add radish greens and toss to coat. Season with salt and pepper to taste.

4. To serve, spread portions of yogurt-tahini sauce over bottom of individual serving plates. Top with roasted radishes and radish greens, then sprinkle with pistachio mixture.

Sugar Snap Peas with Pine Nuts, Fennel, and Lemon Zest

FAST **VEGAN** Serves 4 Total Time 25 minutes

Why This Recipe Works A quick sauté is an excellent way to cook sweet, crisp sugar snap peas. To ensure that the pods and peas cook through at the same rate, we steam the sugar snap peas briefly before sautéing them; the trapped steam transfers heat more efficiently than air does so that the peas cook through more quickly. Cutting the peas in half further reduces the cooking time, so the pods retain more of their snap, and the pockets capture the seasonings rather than letting them slide to the bottom of the platter. Sprinkling the pods with dukkah—an Egyptian condiment made of finely chopped nuts, seeds, and seasonings—dresses up the simple preparation with distinct (but not overwhelming) flavor and crunch. Do not substitute ground fennel for the fennel seeds in this recipe.

- 3 tablespoons pine nuts
- 1 teaspoon fennel seeds
- ½ teaspoon grated lemon zest
- ¼ teaspoon table salt
- ⅛ teaspoon red pepper flakes
- 2 teaspoons vegetable oil
- 12 ounces sugar snap peas, strings removed, halved crosswise on bias
- 2 tablespoons water
- 1 garlic clove, minced
- 3 tablespoons chopped fresh basil

1. Toast pine nuts in dry 12-inch skillet over medium heat, stirring frequently, until just starting to brown, about 3 minutes. Add fennel seeds and continue to toast, stirring constantly, until pine nuts are lightly browned and fennel is fragrant, about 1 minute longer. Transfer pine nut mixture to cutting board. Sprinkle lemon zest, salt, and pepper flakes over pine nut mixture and chop until finely minced and well combined. Transfer to bowl and set aside.

2. Heat oil in now-empty skillet over medium heat until shimmering. Add snap peas and water, immediately cover, and cook for 2 minutes. Uncover, add garlic, and continue to cook, stirring frequently, until moisture has evaporated and snap peas are crisp-tender, about 2 minutes longer. Remove skillet from heat; stir in three-quarters of pine nut mixture and basil. Transfer snap peas to serving platter, sprinkle with remaining pine nut mixture, and serve.

Variations

FAST VEGAN Sugar Snap Peas with Almonds, Coriander, and Orange Zest

Substitute sliced almonds for pine nuts, coriander seeds for fennel seeds, ¼ teaspoon orange zest for lemon zest, and cilantro for basil. Omit red pepper flakes.

FAST VEGAN Sugar Snap Peas with Sesame, Ginger, and Lemon Zest

Substitute 2 tablespoons black or white sesame seeds for pine nuts, ½ teaspoon grated fresh ginger for garlic, and 1 thinly sliced scallion for basil. Omit fennel seeds and red pepper flakes.

Roasted Delicata Squash

Serves 4 to 6 Total Time 1 hour

Why This Recipe Works Roasting brings out the naturally sweet and toasty flavor in delicata squash. For this recipe, we spread the squash slices on a rimmed baking sheet and cover the sheet tightly with aluminum foil to trap steam and ensure that each bite of squash cooks up creamy and moist. Placing the sheet on the oven's lowest rack puts the slices close to the heating element and thus speeds up cooking and browning. During the final minutes of cooking, we dot the slices with butter and let them brown to reinforce the squash's subtle flavor. To ensure that the flesh cooks evenly, choose squashes that are similar in size and shape. Delicata have thin, edible skin that needn't be removed; simply use a vegetable peeler to pare away any tough brown blemishes. You can substitute chives for parsley, if desired. Serve the squash as is, or drizzled with Tximitxurri (Basque-Style Herb Sauce; recipe follows) or Spicy Honey (page 573).

- 3 delicata squashes (12 to 16 ounces each), ends trimmed, halved lengthwise, seeded, and sliced crosswise ½ inch thick
- 4 teaspoons vegetable oil
- ½ teaspoon table salt
- 2 tablespoons unsalted butter, cut into 8 pieces
- 1 tablespoon minced fresh parsley

1. Adjust oven rack to lowest position and heat oven to 425 degrees. Toss squash with oil and salt until evenly coated. Arrange squash on rimmed baking sheet in single layer and cover sheet tightly with aluminum foil. Roast until squash is tender when pierced with tip of paring knife, 18 to 20 minutes.

2. Remove foil and continue to roast until sides touching sheet are golden brown, 8 to 11 minutes longer. Remove sheet from oven and, using thin metal spatula, flip squash. Scatter butter over squash. Return to oven and continue to roast until sides touching sheet are golden brown, 8 to 11 minutes longer. Transfer squash to serving platter, sprinkle with parsley, and serve.

Tximitxurri (Basque-Style Herb Sauce)

FAST VEGAN Makes ½ cup
Total Time 25 minutes

For a sauce with some heat, substitute hot smoked paprika for the regular smoked paprika.

- ¼ cup minced fresh parsley
- ¼ cup extra-virgin olive oil
- 2 tablespoons sherry vinegar
- 2 garlic cloves, minced
- 1 teaspoon smoked paprika
- ¼ teaspoon table salt

Stir all ingredients together in bowl and let stand for at least 15 minutes before serving.

Spicy Honey

FAST Makes ½ cup Total Time 20 minutes

We prefer vinegary Frank's RedHot Original Cayenne Pepper Sauce here. Do not substitute a thick hot sauce, such as sriracha; it will make the honey too thick to drizzle. Microwaving in 20-second intervals will prevent the mixture from boiling over.

- ¼ cup honey
- 2 tablespoons hot sauce

Stir honey and hot sauce together in 1-cup liquid measuring cup. Microwave until sauce comes to boil, about 1 minute. Continue to microwave in 20-second intervals until sauce is reduced to ¼ cup. Let cool for at least 10 minutes before serving.

Best Baked Sweet Potatoes

VEGAN Serves 4 Total Time 1½ hours

Why This Recipe Works Producing baked sweet potatoes with creamy, deeply flavorful interiors isn't just about cooking the spuds to a particular temperature (200 degrees or so). We discovered that we need to hold them at that temperature for about an hour, which allows time for the cell walls to break down, starches to gelatinize, and moisture to evaporate so that flavor concentrates. That process could take about 3 hours of baking time. Instead, we jump-start the potatoes by zapping them in the microwave until they hit 200 degrees, then transfer them to a 425-degree oven for just an hour to finish cooking. Any variety of orange- or red-skinned, orange-fleshed sweet potato can be used in this recipe, but we highly recommend using Garnet (also sold as Diane). Avoid varieties with tan or purple skin, which are starchier and less sweet than those with orange and red skins. When shopping, look for sweet potatoes that are uniform in size and weigh between 8 and 12 ounces (we prefer smaller potatoes). Top potatoes as desired, or with one of our two sauces, Garam Masala Yogurt or Garlic and Chive Sour Cream (page 574).

- 4 small sweet potatoes (8 ounces each), unpeeled, each pricked lightly with fork in 3 places

top | *Roasted Delicata Squash*
bottom | *Best Baked Sweet Potatoes*

top | *Mashed Sweet Potatoes*
bottom | *Honey-Garlic Melting Sweet Potatoes*

1. Adjust oven rack to middle position and heat oven to 425 degrees. Set wire rack in aluminum foil–lined rimmed baking sheet and spray rack with vegetable oil spray. Place potatoes on large plate and microwave until potatoes yield to gentle pressure and centers register 200 degrees, 6 to 9 minutes, flipping potatoes every 3 minutes.

2. Using tongs, transfer potatoes to prepared rack and bake for 1 hour (exteriors of potatoes will be lightly browned and potatoes will feel very soft when squeezed).

3. Slit each potato lengthwise; using clean dish towel, hold ends and squeeze slightly to push flesh up and out. Transfer potatoes to serving platter, season with salt and pepper to taste, and serve.

Garam Masala Yogurt

FAST **VEGAN** Makes ½ cup Total Time 5 minutes

To make this recipe vegan, substitute plant-based yogurt for the dairy yogurt.

- ½ cup plain yogurt
- 2 teaspoons lemon juice
- ½ teaspoon garam masala
- ⅛ teaspoon table salt

Combine all ingredients in bowl.

Garlic and Chive Sour Cream

FAST **VEGAN** Makes ½ cup Total Time 5 minutes

To make this recipe vegan, substitute plant-based sour cream for the dairy sour cream.

- ½ cup sour cream
- 1 tablespoon minced fresh chives
- 1 garlic clove, minced
- ⅛ teaspoon table salt

Combine all ingredients in bowl.

Mashed Sweet Potatoes

FAST Serves 4 Total Time 40 minutes

Why This Recipe Works We wanted mashed sweet potatoes that actually tasted like sweet potatoes, which meant that we needed to maximize their flavor. Because their structure is looser than other potatoes and they absorb more moisture during boiling (which dilutes their flavor), we steam the potatoes in just 6 tablespoons of water over medium-low heat. This allows the potatoes to release their liquid, which produces more steam to cook them. We add some butter, sugar, salt, and pepper to the potatoes before cooking. Once they are cooked, we simply mash all the ingredients together in the same saucepan. This recipe can be easily doubled and prepared in a Dutch oven; increase the cooking time to 40 to 50 minutes.

- 2 pounds sweet potatoes, peeled and sliced ¼ inch thick
- 6 tablespoons water
- 4 tablespoons unsalted butter, cut into 4 pieces
- 1 teaspoon sugar
- 1 teaspoon table salt
- ½ teaspoon pepper

1. Combine potatoes, water, butter, sugar, salt, and pepper in large saucepan. Cover and cook over medium-low heat, stirring occasionally, until potatoes crumble easily when poked with paring knife, 25 to 30 minutes.

2. Remove from heat. Using potato masher, mash potatoes thoroughly until smooth and no lumps remain. Season with salt and pepper to taste, and serve.

Variations

FAST Mashed Sweet Potatoes with Chipotle and Lime

Add 2 teaspoons minced canned chipotle chile in adobo sauce to saucepan with potatoes in step 1. Stir 2 tablespoons minced fresh chives and 1 teaspoon grated lime zest into potato mixture after mashing in step 2.

FAST Mashed Sweet Potatoes with Curry and Golden Raisins

Add 2 teaspoons curry powder to saucepan with potatoes in step 1. Stir ½ cup golden raisins and 2 tablespoons minced fresh cilantro into potato mixture after mashing in step 2.

FAST Mashed Sweet Potatoes with Jalapeño, Garlic, and Scallions

Add 1 stemmed, seeded, and minced jalapeño chile and 2 minced garlic cloves to saucepan with potatoes in step 1. Stir 2 thinly sliced scallions into potato mixture after mashing in step 2.

FAST Mashed Sweet Potatoes with Maple and Orange

Omit sugar. Stir 2 tablespoons maple syrup, 1 teaspoon minced fresh thyme, and ½ teaspoon grated orange zest into potato mixture after mashing in step 2.

Honey-Garlic Melting Sweet Potatoes

Serves 6 to 8 Total Time 1½ hours

Why This Recipe Works Melting potatoes (also known as fondant potatoes or pommes de terre fondantes) come from a French technique for searing coins of potatoes and finishing them in broth, yielding ultracreamy interiors. We apply the same philosophy to sweet potatoes, balancing their natural sweetness with a savory pan sauce. Instead of using a skillet, we opt for a baking pan to fit enough sweet potatoes for a crowd and roast them at 450 degrees for maximum browning. We then flip the potatoes and add an aromatic broth mixture to finish tenderizing and seasoning them while also creating a velvety pan sauce. Since sweet potatoes are less starchy than regular potatoes, we add cornstarch to help the sauce thicken in the oven. Look for sweet potatoes that are 2 to 3 inches in diameter. We do not recommend using a glass or ceramic baking dish in place of the metal baking pan called for here; hot baking dishes are prone to cracking when cooler liquid is added (as in step 2). Sprinkle flake sea salt over the potatoes just before serving, if desired.

- 1¼ cups vegetable broth
- 2 tablespoons honey
- 2 teaspoons cornstarch
- 1¼ teaspoons table salt, divided
- ⅛ teaspoon cayenne pepper
- 3 pounds sweet potatoes, peeled and ends trimmed
- 6 tablespoons unsalted butter, melted
- ½ teaspoon pepper
- 3 garlic cloves, smashed and peeled
- 1 teaspoon fresh thyme leaves

1. Adjust oven rack to upper-middle position and heat oven to 450 degrees. Whisk broth, honey, cornstarch, ¼ teaspoon salt, and cayenne together in small bowl; set aside. Cut potatoes crosswise into 1-inch-thick rounds. Toss potatoes with melted butter, pepper, and remaining 1 teaspoon salt in large bowl.

2. Arrange potatoes in single layer in 13 by 9-inch metal baking pan. Roast until potatoes are tender when pierced with paring knife and bottoms are lightly browned, 30 to 35 minutes. Remove pan from oven. Using flat metal spatula and tongs, loosen potatoes from bottom of pan and flip. Add garlic to pan. Whisk broth mixture to recombine, then pour around potatoes, avoiding tops of potatoes. Continue to roast until liquid has reduced slightly, about 15 minutes longer.

3. Carefully transfer potatoes to serving platter, browned side up; discard garlic. Stir sauce in pan to recombine, then spoon over potatoes. Sprinkle potatoes with thyme; serve.

Variation

Miso-Maple Melting Sweet Potatoes

Omit ¼ teaspoon salt and cayenne pepper from sauce. Substitute 1 cup water for vegetable broth, 3 tablespoons maple syrup for honey, and 3 tablespoons white or red miso for cornstarch. Stir 2 teaspoons lemon juice into sauce before spooning over potatoes in step 3. Substitute 2 thinly sliced scallions for thyme.

Swiss Chard and Kale Gratin

Serves 8 to 10 Total Time 1½ hours

Why This Recipe Works For a creamy, rich green gratin with a crisp, flavorful bread crumb topping, we start with a mixture of kale and Swiss chard. Sturdy kale keeps the gratin fluffy and tall; Swiss chard leaves collapse when cooked, but the plentiful tender stems add bulk. Steaming the greens in a Dutch oven cooks them quickly and eliminates the need for blanching or sautéing in multiple batches. To keep the gratin from being too liquid-y or sogging out the crumb topping, we keep the amount of cream to 1 cup, just enough to give the dish a silky richness. For a craggy, crisp, and flavorful topping, we use rustic bread, pulsed to a coarse texture in a food processor, along with Parmesan and garlic. Do not use rainbow chard for this recipe; it will have a muddy-brown color when cooked. The greens should not be completely dry after pressing in step 4.

- 2 pounds Swiss chard
- 1 pound curly kale, stemmed and cut into 1-inch-wide strips
- 2 garlic cloves, peeled
- 4 ounces rustic white bread, cut into ¾-inch cubes (3 cups)
- 5 tablespoons extra-virgin olive oil, divided
- 2 ounces Parmesan cheese, grated (1 cup)
- ¾ teaspoon table salt, divided
- ½ teaspoon pepper, divided
- 1 onion, chopped coarse
- 1½ teaspoons minced fresh thyme
- 1 cup heavy cream
- ⅛ teaspoon ground nutmeg

1. Adjust oven rack to upper-middle position and heat oven to 375 degrees. Stem chard, then cut stems into 2-inch lengths and set aside. Slice leaves into 1-inch-wide strips. Bring 2 cups water to boil in Dutch oven over high heat. Add kale, cover, and reduce heat to medium-high. Cook until kale is wilted, about 5 minutes, stirring halfway through cooking. Add chard leaves, cover, and continue to cook until chard is wilted, about 4 minutes longer, stirring halfway through cooking. Transfer to colander set in sink and let drain. (Do not wash pot.)

2. Pulse garlic in food processor until coarsely chopped, 5 to 7 pulses. Add bread and 3 tablespoons oil and pulse until largest crumbs are smaller than ¼ inch (most will be much smaller), 8 to 10 pulses. Add Parmesan, ¼ teaspoon salt, and ¼ teaspoon pepper and pulse to combine. Transfer to bowl.

3. Add onion and chard stems to now-empty processor and process until finely chopped, scraping down sides of bowl as needed, 20 to 30 seconds. Transfer to now-empty pot. Add thyme, remaining 2 tablespoons oil, remaining ½ teaspoon salt, and remaining ¼ teaspoon pepper. Cook over medium-high heat, stirring occasionally, until moisture has evaporated and mixture is just beginning to brown, 8 to 10 minutes.

4. Using spatula, press gently on greens in colander to remove excess moisture. Transfer greens to pot with onion mixture. Add cream and nutmeg and stir to combine. (Filling and bread crumb topping can be refrigerated separately for up to 24 hours. Increase baking time by 5 to 10 minutes.) Transfer greens mixture to 13 by 9-inch baking dish. Sprinkle bread crumb mixture evenly over surface. Bake until topping is golden brown and filling bubbles around edges, 20 to 25 minutes. Let cool for 10 minutes before serving.

Fried Red Tomatoes

Serves 4 Total Time 35 minutes, plus 40 minutes draining

Why This Recipe Works Fried green tomatoes may be more well known, but we think red tomatoes also deserve some time in the skillet. Moisture is the enemy of a crispy crust on a fried ripe tomato. To eliminate excess moisture, we slice plum tomatoes thin and let them drain on layers of paper towels. To help a light coating adhere to the tomatoes, we mix buttermilk and egg together and dip the tomatoes into the mixture before dredging them in the breading of cornmeal, flour, and Parmesan. We quickly shallow-fry the tomato slices in hot oil to sear the crust but not overcook the interior. Use two forks to turn the tomatoes quickly. This recipe can easily be doubled and cooked in two batches; change the oil and wipe out the skillet between batches.

- 8 ounces plum tomatoes, ends trimmed, sliced ¼ inch thick
- ½ teaspoon granulated garlic
- ⅓ cup buttermilk
- 1 large egg
- ⅔ cup cornmeal
- ⅓ cup all-purpose flour
- 1 ounce Parmesan cheese, grated (½ cup)
- ¾ teaspoon table salt
- ¼ teaspoon pepper
- ⅛ teaspoon cayenne pepper
- ½ cup vegetable oil for frying
- 2 tablespoons chopped fresh basil
- Lemon wedges

1. Line wire rack with triple layer of paper towels. Evenly space tomato slices on rack, sprinkle with granulated garlic, and let drain for 40 minutes, flipping halfway through draining.

2. Line rimmed baking sheet with parchment paper. Whisk buttermilk and egg together in shallow dish. Combine cornmeal, flour, Parmesan, salt, pepper, and cayenne in second shallow dish. Lightly pat tops of tomatoes with paper towels to remove any accumulated liquid. Working with one at a time, dip tomato slices in buttermilk mixture, then dredge in cornmeal mixture, pressing firmly to adhere; transfer to prepared sheet.

3. Heat oil in 12-inch nonstick skillet over medium-high heat until just smoking. Add all tomato slices to skillet and fry until golden brown, 2 to 4 minutes per side. Transfer to platter and sprinkle with basil. Serve with lemon wedges.

Fried Red Tomatoes

Pan-Seared Zucchini with Spicy Honey and Scallion

Zucchini Has the Range

In the height of summer, you can't escape zucchini. These squashes are very easy to grow, thriving in many different climates and soil conditions. They're so easy to grow, in fact, that come midsummer, home gardeners usually have more zucchini than they know what to do with. Luckily for the home cook, zucchini is remarkably versatile—you can use it for everything from zucchini bread to zoodles.

Steam and Sear

In our Pan-Seared Zucchini with Spicy Honey and Scallion, we give zucchini the showstopper treatment by steaming and searing it at the same time. In a moist-heat environment, the pectin and hemicellulose in the vegetable's cell walls dissolve and its flesh collapses, allowing air to escape and creating a dense structure. (In an uncovered pan, the zucchini would dry out without compressing, resulting in a more porous and desiccated texture.) The result is lush, fork-tender zucchini.

A Cut Above

Cross-hatching the zucchini is for more than just appearances. It's a technique that helps draw more moisture out of the zucchini before searing it. We rub salt into the slits and briefly microwave the zucchini to remove excess water and prime the surface for beautiful, flavorful browning.

Pan-Seared Zucchini with Spicy Honey and Scallion

FAST Serves 4 Total Time 45 minutes

Why This Recipe Works For dense, meltingly soft, and dramatically browned zucchini, we start by halving the squashes and scoring the cut surfaces, rubbing them with salt, and then briefly microwaving. The salt and heat draw moisture from the flesh, and the slits provide escape routes for the water so that the surfaces are primed for browning. Cooking in a well-oiled cast-iron skillet encourages rich browning; the metal holds the heat really well, and the fat facilitates heat transfer between the pan and the food. Covering the skillet for most of the cooking time traps moist heat that forces air out of the flesh and also dissolves its pectin, rendering the flesh fork-tender. A mixture of honey and hot sauce, microwaved to a glaze consistency, adds sweetness with a bit of heat; sliced scallion brings fresh crunch and color. We use Diamond Crystal kosher salt. If using Morton kosher salt, which is denser, use only 1½ teaspoons. If desired, omit the honey, hot sauce, and scallion and serve with lemon wedges. Be sure to use a cast-iron skillet, which encourages rich browning.

- 2 tablespoons honey
- 1 tablespoon hot sauce
- 3 zucchini (8 ounces each), halved lengthwise
- 2 teaspoons kosher salt
- 3 tablespoons vegetable oil
- 1 scallion, sliced thin on bias

1. Whisk honey and hot sauce together in 1-cup liquid measuring cup. Microwave until mixture comes to boil, 30 to 45 seconds. Continue to microwave, stirring every 30 seconds, until sauce is slightly thickened, about 1 minute (sauce will continue to thicken as it cools).

2. Using sharp paring knife, score cut sides of zucchini diagonally, about ¼ inch deep, at ½-inch intervals. Turn zucchini 90 degrees and score again in opposite direction. Place scored zucchini halves close to each other cut sides up on cutting board. Sprinkle salt evenly over halves. Rub salt into cut sides until mostly dissolved.

3. Line large plate with double layer of paper towels. Place zucchini cut side down on paper towels and press gently. Microwave until zucchini has exuded water and is hot to touch, about 3 minutes. Cut each piece in half crosswise.

4. Spread oil over surface of cold 12-inch cast-iron skillet. Arrange zucchini cut side down in skillet and press to ensure that cut sides are flush with skillet surface (reserve paper towel–lined plate). Cover skillet. Cook over medium-high heat, rotating skillet one-quarter turn every 2 minutes for even cooking, until cut sides are deeply browned, 8 to 10 minutes.

5. Slide skillet off heat. Uncover and turn zucchini cut side up. Return to medium-high heat and continue to cook, uncovered, until paring knife meets little to no resistance when slipped into center of squash, 2 to 3 minutes longer. Transfer zucchini cut side up to reserved paper towel–lined plate to drain for 5 minutes.

6. Transfer zucchini cut side up to platter. Drizzle with spicy honey, sprinkle with scallion, and serve.

Variations

FAST VEGAN Pan-Seared Zucchini with Raisin, Caper, and Parsley Sauce and Pine Nuts

Omit honey, hot sauce, and scallion. Before scoring zucchini, combine ⅓ cup golden raisins, 2 tablespoons water, and 1½ tablespoons white wine vinegar in 2-cup liquid measuring cup. Microwave until simmering, about 1 minute. Stir well, then set aside to cool while zucchini cooks. While zucchini is draining in step 5, add ½ cup chopped fresh parsley, 2 tablespoons capers, and 1 tablespoon pine nuts to raisin mixture. Using immersion blender in mashing, up-and-down motion, blend to coarse puree. Spread half of parsley sauce over platter. Transfer zucchini cut side up to platter. Drizzle with remaining parsley sauce. Sprinkle with 2 teaspoons chopped parsley and 2 teaspoons pine nuts.

FAST VEGAN Pan-Seared Zucchini with Yogurt, Red Pepper Paste, and Preserved Lemon

Omit honey, hot sauce, and scallion. While zucchini is draining in step 5, spread ½ cup plain dairy or plant-based Greek yogurt on platter. Dollop 3 tablespoons ajvar (red pepper paste, available in Eastern European markets) on yogurt and swirl with back of spoon. Sprinkle with 1 tablespoon chopped preserved lemon and 2 teaspoons chopped fresh mint. Transfer zucchini cut side up to platter. Sprinkle with 1 tablespoon chopped preserved lemon and 2 teaspoons chopped mint.

Broiled Smashed Zucchini with Garlicky Yogurt

VEGAN   Serves 4   Total Time 50 minutes

Why This Recipe Works This dish showcases the full spectrum of zucchini flavor and texture; we use a meat pounder to smash the squash and then break it into a couple of large pieces by hand. After seasoning the craggy pieces, we broil them until they are charred in spots and then let the pieces cool before cutting into chunks. We serve them atop a schmear of creamy garlic dressing and garnish with crunchy nuts, spicy pepper, fresh herbs, and a drizzle of extra-virgin olive oil. For this recipe, we prefer zucchini that are 7 to 12 ounces each. We developed this recipe using an electric broiler. If using a gas broiler, adjust the oven rack 4 inches from the broiler element and use tongs to rearrange the zucchini pieces halfway through cooking instead of rotating the pan in step 2. We developed this recipe with Diamond Crystal kosher salt. If using Morton kosher salt, which is denser, use only 1¾ teaspoons. To make this recipe, and the first variation, vegan, substitute plant-based yogurt for the dairy yogurt and plant-based sour cream for the dairy sour cream.

- 2 pounds zucchini
- 2 tablespoons extra-virgin olive oil, plus extra for drizzling
- 4 teaspoons lemon juice
- 2¼ teaspoons kosher salt, divided
- ½ cup plain Greek yogurt
- 2 tablespoons water
- ½ teaspoon minced garlic
- ¼ cup hazelnuts, toasted, skinned, and chopped
- Chopped fresh dill, basil, parsley, or chives
- Aleppo pepper

1. Adjust oven rack 5 inches from broiler element and heat broiler. Line rimmed baking sheet with aluminum foil. Using meat pounder or rolling pin, firmly but gently smash zucchini until flattened and cracked lengthwise. Trim and discard ends. Break each zucchini into 2 to 4 large pieces. Transfer zucchini pieces to large bowl, including any smaller pieces that have been created during smashing and breaking. Add oil and lemon juice and toss until zucchini is evenly coated.

2. Arrange zucchini skin side down on prepared sheet. Sprinkle with 2 teaspoons salt, making sure to season thicker pieces more heavily than thinner pieces. Broil until zucchini are lightly charred in spots, 9 to 12 minutes, rotating sheet halfway through broiling. Let cool until zucchini are warm to touch, 15 to 20 minutes.

3. Meanwhile, stir yogurt, water, garlic, and remaining ¼ teaspoon salt together in small bowl. Let sit at room temperature so flavors meld, about 10 minutes. Spread yogurt mixture on serving platter. Cut zucchini into bite-size pieces and arrange on top of yogurt mixture. Sprinkle with hazelnuts, dill, and Aleppo pepper. Drizzle with extra oil and serve.

Variations

VEGAN Broiled Smashed Zucchini with Herbed Sour Cream

Omit yogurt, water, and garlic. Combine ½ cup sour cream, 2 teaspoons water, 1 tablespoon minced fresh chives, 1 tablespoon minced fresh dill, and ¼ teaspoon grated lemon zest with remaining ¼ teaspoon salt in small bowl. Substitute ¼ cup toasted, chopped pine nuts for hazelnuts. Top with more fresh dill. Substitute coarsely ground pepper for Aleppo pepper.

Broiled Smashed Zucchini with Ricotta and Parmesan

Omit yogurt, water, and garlic. Combine ½ cup whole-milk ricotta cheese, 2 tablespoons grated Parmesan, and 2 teaspoons water with remaining ¼ teaspoon salt in small bowl. Substitute ¼ cup toasted sliced almonds for hazelnuts. Substitute parsley for dill and coarsely ground pepper for Aleppo pepper.

Smashing Zucchini

1. Using meat pounder or rolling pin, firmly but gently smash zucchini until it flattens and cracks develop along its length. Trim and discard ends.

2. Break each zucchini into 2 to 4 large pieces.

Broiled Smashed Zucchini with Garlicky Yogurt

Nutritional Information for Our Recipes

We calculate the nutritional values of our recipes per serving; if there is a range in the serving size, we used the highest number of servings to calculate the nutritional values. We entered all the ingredients, using weights for important ingredients such as meat, cheese, and most vegetables. We also used our preferred brands in these analyses. We did not include additional salt or pepper for food that's "seasoned to taste."

	Cal	Total Fat (g)	Sat Fat (g)	Chol (mg)	Sodium (mg)	Carbs (g)	Fiber (g)	Total Sugar (g)	Protein (g)	Gluten Free
01 VEGETABLES FRONT AND CENTER										
Curry Roasted Cabbage Wedges with Tomatoes and Chickpeas	490	29	2.5	0	1230	45	16	10	14	✓
Butternut Squash Steaks with Honey-Nut Topping	400	20	5	5	610	55	8	19	7	✓
Garlic Yogurt Sauce	25	1.5	1.5	5	5	1	0	1	1	✓
Cauliflower Steaks with Salsa Verde	300	29	4	0	470	10	4	3	4	✓
King Trumpet Mushrooms with Smoked Paprika Vinaigrette	284	28	4	0	436	7	2	3	5	✓
Spicy Chile-Honey Glazed Eggplant with Burrata and Greens	488	34	13	56	747	34	7	25	17	✓
Hasselback Eggplant with Muhammara	440	25	3.5	5	800	51	12	26	10	
Whole Pot-Roasted Cauliflower with Tomatoes and Olives	208	10	3	12	885	24	9	14	11	✓
Whole Romanesco with Berbere and Yogurt-Tahini Sauce	339	28	12	50	688	12	6	9	13	✓
Stir-Fried Asparagus with Shiitake Mushrooms	93	5	0	0	227	10	3	5	4	
Eggplant with Black Bean Sauce	460	32	2.5	0	550	31	5	16	8	
Stir-Fried Portobellos with Ginger-Oyster Sauce	568	49	3	0	1253	31	6	9	5	
Stir-Fried Portobellos with Sweet Chili-Garlic Sauce	316	17	1	0	1182	37	5	22	9	
Aloo Gobi	329	22	2	0	784	32	6	5	5	✓
Sautéed Eggplant with Polenta	501	29	4	0	1610	57	8	17	7	✓
Green Curry with Kale and Butternut Squash	820	67	41	0	1160	53	12	12	18	✓
Madras Okra Curry	258	22	8	0	128	15	5	4	3	✓
Mushroom Bourguignon	172	8	1	0	568	17	3	5	7	
Potato Vindaloo	222	6	1	0	1035	40	8	10	5	✓
Silky Roasted Eggplant with Tomato and Feta	423	30	9	45	1021	27	9	14	12	
Baharat Cauliflower and Eggplant with Chickpeas	570	28	3.5	0	1220	70	13	10	20	
Baharat	20	1	0	0	0	5	2	0	1	✓
Walkaway Ratatouille	178	11	2	0	752	19	6	9	3	✓
Vegetable Lasagna	606	36	17	77	958	44	6	9	29	
Eggplant Parmesan	479	27	8	122	918	41	9	10	21	
Baked Pumpkin Kibbeh	480	20	6	25	860	64	11	6	14	
Skillet Tomato Cobbler	239	15	7	56	431	22	2	7	4	
Savory Dutch Baby with Portobellos, Roasted Red Peppers, Walnuts, and Feta	694	38	13	324	1028	64	4	12	27	
Cheesy Tomato and Bean Bake	358	13	4	18	899	45	10	7	18	
Mushroom and White Bean Gratin	428	20	3	0	757	49	9	6	15	

	Cal	Total Fat (g)	Sat Fat (g)	Chol (mg)	Sodium (mg)	Carbs (g)	Fiber (g)	Total Sugar (g)	Protein (g)	Gluten Free
01 VEGETABLES FRONT AND CENTER										
Swiss Chard, Pinto Bean, and Monterey Jack Enchiladas	490	28	5	15	1270	57	10	12	12	✓
Herb Vegetable and Lentil Bake	460	28	7	25	850	41	11	13	14	✓
Broccoli Rabe and Farro Gratin	400	12	2	4	760	59	12	5	18	
Teff-Stuffed Acorn Squash with Lime Crema and Roasted Pepitas	436	13	2	0	1210	73	12	10	13	✓
Stuffed Delicata Squash	479	27	11	45	1028	54	10	3	13	
Eggplant Involtini	330	23	6	36	1020	22	9	10	12	
Stuffed Peppers with Chickpeas, Goat Cheese, and Herbs	530	31	10	21	961	48	10	12	20	
Chiles Rellenos	350	19	8	35	890	32	3	6	12	
Stuffed Portobello Mushrooms with Spinach and Gorgonzola	420	28	7	20	700	29	6	7	15	
Chipotle Lentil-Stuffed Sweet Potatoes	345	7	4	19	901	56	14	10	15	✓
Stuffed Tomatoes with Couscous and Zucchini	420	19	6	15	560	48	9	16	18	✓
Beet Poke Bowls	673	29	4	0	1317	97	12	18	19	
Cauliflower Rice Bowls with Sweet Potatoes, Avocados, and Spicy Chickpeas	500	30	4.5	0	880	54	18	11	12	✓
Spiced Roasted Chickpeas	150	9	1	0	310	14	5	0	5	✓
Roasted Vegetable Bowls with Bulgur, White Beans, and Arugula	595	31	6	7	913	65	13	7	19	
Hearty Vegetable and Farro Bowls with Goat Cheese	630	27	5	5	620	85	11	10	18	
Roasted Sweet Potato and Tofu Bowls with Snap Pea Salad	560	25	3	0	2160	58	9	20	28	
Rainbow Bowls with Crispy Tempeh	560	29	3.5	0	460	58	10	25	21	✓
Orange-Ginger Vinaigrette	70	3.5	0.5	0	210	9	0	7	1	✓
Tarragon-Lemon Gremolata	30	1.5	0	0	75	4	4	2	3	✓
Shichimi Togarashi	15	1	0	0	0	2	1	0	1	✓
Savory Seed Brittle	80	5	1	0	135	6	1	2	3	✓
Dukkah	60	4	0	0	240	5	2	0	3	✓
Microwave-Fried Shallots	30	2	0	0	2	2	0	1	0	✓
02 SALADS BIG AND SMALL										
Easiest Salad, Ever	30	2.5	0	0	20	0	0	0	0	✓
Kale Caesar Salad	592	52	11	33	878	18	4	3	16	
Crispy and Creamy Kale Salad	404	37	4	9	403	12	7	3	11	✓
Horiatiki Salata (Hearty Greek Salad)	398	33	11	50	1008	16	4	8	11	✓
Cobb Salad	593	36	7	377	920	44	12	9	26	
Hearty Green Salad with Chickpeas, Pickled Cauliflower, and Seared Halloumi	590	38	12	54	1127	47	9	24	20	✓
Bitter Greens, Carrot, and Chickpea Salad with Warm Lemon Dressing	490	23	4	11	803	62	16	26	16	✓
Marinated Bean and Asparagus Salad with Preserved Lemon Dressing	296	17	2	0	337	30	7	6	8	✓
White Bean and Arugula Salad with Frico Crumble	240	13	4	15	600	19	5	2	11	✓
Beet Salad with Spiced Yogurt and Watercress	212	13	3	8	580	19	5	13	9	✓
Beet Salad with Blue Cheese and Endive	265	18	8	34	591	19	6	12	9	✓
Quick-Cooking Beets	65	0	0	0	312	14	4	10	2	✓

02 SALADS BIG AND SMALL

	Cal	Total Fat (g)	Sat Fat (g)	Chol (mg)	Sodium (mg)	Carbs (g)	Fiber (g)	Total Sugar (g)	Protein (g)	Gluten Free
Broccoli Salad with Avocado Dressing	225	14	2	0	423	25	7	13	6	✓
Roasted Butternut Squash Salad with Creamy Tahini Dressing	309	24	3	2	615	24	6	5	5	✓
Roasted Cauliflower Salad with Arugula and Pear	169	10	2	1	641	18	5	9	4	✓
Charred Shaved Brussels Sprout Salad with Sweet Chili–Lime Dressing	250	18	2	0	448	18	7	5	8	✓
Charred Shaved Brussels Sprout Salad with Apricot Dressing	284	21	2	0	438	22	7	8	7	✓
Charred Shaved Brussels Sprout Salad with Sherry-Honey Dressing	290	20	2	0	456	27	7	15	7	✓
Chopped Carrot Salad with Mint, Pistachios, and Pomegranate Seeds	238	17	2	0	345	21	6	12	5	✓
Lao Hu Cai (Tiger Salad)	60	4	1	0	181	5	2	2	2	✓
Shaved Celery Salad with Pomegranate-Honey Vinaigrette	226	14	3	11	362	20	4	11	7	✓
Apple–Celery Root Salad	86	6	1	3	131	8	2	5	1	✓
Esquites (Mexican Corn Salad)	183	12	4	18	265	16	2	5	6	✓
Buffalo Cucumber Salad	201	14	6	19	692	13	1	8	7	✓
Avocado and Cucumber Salad with Sriracha Mayo	210	18	3	2	355	11	5	2	8	
Shaved Vegetable Salad with Creamy Miso Dressing	191	13	1	0	638	16	4	8	4	✓
Green Bean Salad with Creamy Lemon Sauce and Crispy Capers	278	27	4	8	363	9	3	4	2	✓
Three-Bean Salad	206	8	1	0	402	27	8	7	9	✓
Napa Cabbage Slaw with Carrots and Sesame	92	6	1	0	260	7	2	4	2	
Napa Cabbage Slaw with Apple and Walnuts	131	10	1	0	303	9	2	6	3	✓
Napa Cabbage Slaw with Jicama and Pepitas	120	9	1	0	272	8	3	4	4	✓
Coleslaw Potato Salad	261	17	3	9	464	25	4	4	3	✓
Spicy Green Pea Salad	41	1	0	2	258	7	2	4	2	✓
Radicchio Chopped Salad with White Beans, Oranges, and Olives	395	27	5	17	638	30	8	7	13	✓
Romaine and Radicchio Salad with Roasted Squash and Pickled Pears	220	15	2.5	0	720	20	4	9	3	✓
Cast Iron–Seared Romaine with Oyster Sauce, Ginger, and Sesame	115	10	1	0	352	7	3	2	2	✓
Torn Potato Salad with Toasted Garlic and Herb Dressing	233	13	2	2	395	27	3	1	3	✓
Fingerling Potato Salad with Sun-Dried Tomato Dressing	223	11	2	0	424	30	4	2	4	✓
Herbes de Provence	5	0	0	0	0	1	0	0	0	✓
Cherry Tomato Salad with Pita Chips and Spicy Citrus Dressing	148	11	1	0	132	13	3	4	2	
Tomatillo and Bibb Lettuce Salad with Tomatillo Ranch	213	18	3	8	485	11	4	7	3	✓
Wheat Berry Salad with Radicchio, Dried Cherries, and Pecans	263	15	3	4	195	30	5	6	6	
Chopped Vegetable and Stone Fruit Salad	110	5	0.5	0	250	15	3	11	2	✓
Bulgur Salad with Curry Roasted Sweet Potatoes and Chickpeas	560	32	7	15	920	59	12	11	15	
Farro Salad with Asparagus, Radishes, and Parmesan	266	15	3	5	281	27	5	4	9	
Basic Farro	189	6	1	0	118	31	5	3	6	
Kale and Farro Salad with Fennel, Olives, and Parmesan	270	11	2	5	380	36	5	2	10	
Sweet Potato, Lentil, and Kale Salad with Fried Shallots	541	27	6	14	623	57	11	7	21	✓

	Cal	Total Fat (g)	Sat Fat (g)	Chol (mg)	Sodium (mg)	Carbs (g)	Fiber (g)	Total Sugar (g)	Protein (g)	Gluten Free
02 SALADS BIG AND SMALL										
Butternut Squash and Apple Fattoush	310	19	2.5	0	460	33	4	7	4	
Red Cabbage and Grapefruit Salad	182	12	2	0	404	17	3	10	4	✓
Cantaloupe Salad with Olives and Red Onion	58	1	0	0	268	13	2	10	1	✓
Honeydew Salad with Peanuts and Lime	149	4	1	0	473	28	3	22	4	✓
Caramelized Plums with Spicy Herb Salad	172	12	1	0	208	15	4	11	3	✓
Grilled Peach and Tomato Salad with Burrata and Basil	341	28	11	48	530	14	2	11	10	✓
Grilled Stone Fruit	68	4	2	10	4	9	1	0	0	✓
Grilled Watermelon, Halloumi, and Olive Salad	378	19	7	34	713	49	3	39	9	✓
Make-Ahead Vinaigrette	100	11	1.5	0	100	1	0	1	0	✓
Make-Ahead Sherry-Shallot Vinaigrette	110	11	1.5	0	100	1	0	1	0	✓
Make-Ahead Balsamic-Fennel Vinaigrette	110	11	1.5	0	100	2	0	2	0	✓
Raspberry Vinaigrette	80	7	1	0	70	4	0	4	0	✓
Sesame-Scallion Vinaigrette	20	0	0	0	610	2	0	2	1	
Creamless Creamy Herb Dressing	50	4	0.5	0	180	3	0	1	2	✓
Creamless Creamy Roasted Red Pepper and Tahini Dressing	50	4	0.5	0	280	4	0	1	1	✓
Creamy Avocado Dressing	35	3.5	0.5	0	110	1	1	0	0	✓
03 SOUPS AND STEWS										
Pappa al Pomodoro	240	15	2	0	537	23	4	8	5	
Caramelized Carrot Soup with Coriander-Lemon Browned Butter	274	18	10	46	967	25	5	14	6	✓
Cauliflower Soup	188	16	10	41	886	11	4	4	4	✓
Hawaij Cauliflower Soup with Zhoug	270	24	3.5	0	740	12	4	4	4	✓
Sweet Potato Soup with Maple Sour Cream	260	10	6	28	97	38	5	11	3	✓
Roasted Garlic Soup with Parmesan Croutons	526	30	8	29	965	42	3	8	24	
Carabaccia (Tuscan Onion Soup)	358	18	4	153	798	38	7	12	14	
Zucchini Soup with Dill and Sour Cream	271	17	5	17	721	28	5	13	6	✓
Super Greens Soup with Lemon-Tarragon Cream	172	11	4	15	936	17	4	3	5	✓
Hearty Cabbage Soup	100	4	2.5	10	660	14	2	3	2	✓
Spiced Eggplant and Kale Soup	310	27	6	5	730	14	6	6	5	✓
Kimchi and Tofu Soup	130	6	0	0	1260	10	1	2	8	
Shiitake, Tofu, and Mustard Greens Soup	174	9	1	0	1190	14	5	3	15	
Lemongrass-Coconut Soup with Oyster Mushrooms	523	47	38	0	1499	20	3	3	17	✓
Quick Food Processor Gazpacho	100	2	0	0	988	20	4	12	4	
Chilled Peach and Cucumber Soup	206	10	2	8	911	27	4	21	5	✓
Wild Rice and Mushroom Soup	248	12	7	32	883	27	2	3	8	
Creamy White Bean Soup with Herb Oil and Crispy Capers	393	23	6	15	817	35	8	4	14	✓
Red Lentil Soup with Warm Spices	320	10	5	25	777	42	6	5	17	✓
Lentil and Escarole Soup	330	13	3	9	1114	38	8	7	17	✓
Classic Minestrone	205	2	1	2	1142	37	10	6	13	
Ribollita	467	20	3	0	1662	60	12	11	15	

	Cal	Total Fat (g)	Sat Fat (g)	Chol (mg)	Sodium (mg)	Carbs (g)	Fiber (g)	Total Sugar (g)	Protein (g)	Gluten Free
03 SOUPS AND STEWS										
Butternut Squash and White Bean Soup with Sage Pesto	659	38	9	25	1294	63	15	7	22	✓
Acquacotta (Tuscan White Bean and Escarole Soup)	451	21	4	42	1237	51	11	9	17	✓
Tanabour (Armenian Yogurt and Barley Soup)	289	15	8	65	686	27	5	6	13	
Turkish Bulgur and Lentil Soup	330	9	1.5	0	740	49	9	3	16	
Tomato, Bulgur, and Red Pepper Soup	129	4	1	0	856	20	5	5	3	
Harira (Moroccan Lentil and Chickpea Soup)	363	13	2	4	1136	49	10	10	16	
Chickpea Noodle Soup	326	9	1	0	1067	48	13	9		✓
Creamy Chickpea and Sweet Potato Stew	544	34	15	0	735	49	13	11	19	✓
Thai-Spiced Red Lentil Stew with Spinach and Corn	336	20	13	0	791	34	6	7	10	✓
Green Gumbo	243	15	1	0	909	23	6	3	7	✓
Best Vegetarian Chili	439	14	1	0	1252	66	16	10	20	
Black Bean Chili	326	8	1	0	975	53	14	10	17	✓
Roasted Poblano and White Bean Chili	411	10	1	0	1278	68	15	10	19	✓
Classic Vegetable Broth	70	1	0	0	360	15	4	6	4	✓
Vegetable Broth Base	10	0	0	0	350	2	0	1	0	
Vegetable Scrap Broth	15	0	0	0	470	4	1	2	0	✓
Umami Broth	35	0.5	0	0	240	4	1	0	3	
Classic Croutons	60	4	0.5	0	60	5	0	1	1	
Herbed Croutons	70	2	1	5	75	11	0	2	2	
Umami Croutons	50	3	0	0	80	5	0	0	1	
Tofu Croutons	20	1.5	0	0	20	0	0	0	1	✓
Spiced Seeds	60	5	1	0	75	1	1	0	2	✓
Pickled Celery	5	0	0	0	80	1	0	1	0	✓
Quick Chili Oil	130	14	2.5	0	260	3	1	1	1	
Lemon-Herb Sauce	70	8	1	5	70	0	0	0	0	✓
04 BURGERS, TACOS, AND MORE										
Ultimate Veggie Burgers	383	15	2	3	411	52	5	6	13	
Black Bean Burgers	372	11	2	62	531	52	11	4	16	
Classic Burger Sauce	38	4	1	2	57	1	0	1	0	✓
Sheet Pan White Bean and Sun-Dried Tomato Patties with Lemony Spinach Salad	450	28	9	70	1020	34	8	5	18	
Pinto Bean–Beet Burgers	448	21	2	0	448	55	8	6	13	
Quinoa Burgers with Spinach, Sun-Dried Tomatoes, and Marinated Feta	580	41	10	111	538	37	4	2	19	
Curried Millet Burgers with Peach-Ginger Chutney	452	19	2	50	1005	61	9	18	11	✓
Smoky Carrot Dogs	170	8	1	0	1080	22	6	11	4	
Baja-Style Cauliflower Tacos	438	28	17	7	643	45	8	12	8	
Cilantro Crema	51	5	1	6	81	1	0	1	1	✓
Black Bean and Sweet Potato Tacos	600	18	2	0	1660	83	9	14	17	✓
Black Bean, Sweet Potato, and Poblano Tacos	580	21	5	0	1660	83	9	14	17	✓

	Cal	Total Fat (g)	Sat Fat (g)	Chol (mg)	Sodium (mg)	Carbs (g)	Fiber (g)	Total Sugar (g)	Protein (g)	Gluten Free
04 BURGERS, TACOS, AND MORE										
Avocado Crema	20	2	0	0	0	1	1	0	0	✓
Red Lentil Tacos	292	7	1	0	414	49	9	3	12	✓
Sheet Pan Cheese Quesadillas	530	31	18	75	1140	37	0	2	27	
Sheet Pan Black Bean and Jalapeño Quesadillas	540	25	14	110	1100	37	0	2	42	
Spinach and Goat Cheese Quesadillas	770	49	15	50	1072	54	9	7	31	
Chickpea and Poblano Quesadillas	770	48	16	59	1031	59	15	7	30	
Cheese Pupusas	490	26	14	65	577	44	4	0	22	✓
Quick Tomato Salsa	20	0	0	0	156	5	2	3	1	✓
Black Bean and Cheese Arepas	530	23	7	25	1110	66	3	0	15	✓
Avocado, Tomato, and Bell Pepper Arepas	560	29	4	0	720	71	8	4	8	✓
Cheddar-Crusted Grilled Cheese	592	42	22	102	878	31	2	4	23	
Cheddar-Crusted Grilled Cheese with Tomato	616	43	23	105	934	33	3	4	25	
Marinated Tomato Sandwiches	217	5	1	0	408	38	6	9	7	
Mushroom, Lettuce, and Tomato Sandwiches	450	13	2	0	1190	56	9	9	16	
Creamy Mushroom and Pink Pickled Cabbage Sandwiches	240	9	2.5	10	600	35	5	8	8	
Cutty's-Inspired Eggplant Spuckie	679	47	14	50	928	48	8	10	20	
Beet, Orange, and Chèvre Tartines	510	37	18	52	824	23	6	15	25	
Raw Vegetable Wraps	790	48	15	50	1730	74	11	13	23	
Roasted Vegetable Sandwiches	461	26	6	28	689	48	6	8	12	
Ultimate Grilled Vegetable Sandwiches	592	37	11	46	989	46	5	9	19	
Chickpea Salad Sandwiches with Quick Pickles	679	32	5	49	978	77	16	13	23	
Spiced Smashed Chickpea Wraps	380	16	3.5	5	1470	46	9	3	15	
Tahini-Yogurt Sauce	40	3	1	0	115	2	0	0	1	✓
Mumbai Frankie Wraps	630	29	7	0	1150	82	11	5	16	
Chapati (Whole-Wheat Wraps)	310	14	1	0	580	41	4	0	7	
Quick Sweet-and-Spicy Pickled Red Onion	10	0	0	0	10	2	0	2	0	✓
Cilantro-Mint Chutney	156	12	1	0	242	9	3	2	3	✓
Grilled Halloumi Wraps	437	25	13	80	1188	36	5	6	20	
Falafel	500	30	4	0	1020	57	1	2	16	
Tomato-Chile Sauce	117	10	1	0	381	8	4	4	2	✓
Vospov Kofte (Red Lentil Kofte)	379	20	7	20	548	42	8	2	12	
Easy Homemade Mayonnaise	127	14	1	8	40	0	0	0	0	✓
Basil-Caper Mayonnaise	160	16	3	15	250	0	0	0	3	✓
Lemon-Dill Mayonnaise	160	18	2.5	10	150	0	0	0	0	✓
Spicy Sriracha-Lime Mayonnaise	130	14	2	10	115	1	0	0	0	✓
Herbed Yogurt Sauce	40	2	1.5	10	30	3	0	1	2	✓
Creamy Chipotle Sauce	317	30	8	34	582	7	1	3	5	✓
Homemade Nut Butter	201	17	2	0	83	6	3	2	9	✓

	Cal	Total Fat (g)	Sat Fat (g)	Chol (mg)	Sodium (mg)	Carbs (g)	Fiber (g)	Total Sugar (g)	Protein (g)	Gluten Free
05 PIZZA, FLATBREADS, AND SAVORY TARTS										
No-Cook Pizza Sauce	40	2	0	0	210	4	1	2	1	✓
One-Hour Pizza	634	28	10	48	1016	70	6	8	28	
Cast Iron Pan Pizza	713	38	15	68	784	62	4	3	30	
Caprese Sheet-Pan Pizza	742	41	12	50	951	65	4	4	26	
Philadelphia Tomato Pie	477	13	2	0	675	79	5	8	11	
Corn, Tomato, and Arugula Pizza	658	33	15	79	1152	65	4	11	27	
Neapolitan-Style Pizza Margherita	640	16	9	45	1970	95	1	4	27	
Neapolitan-Style Pizza Margherita with Artichoke Hearts and Fontina	690	21	12	60	2140	96	2	4	26	
Neapolitan-Style Pizza with Mushrooms, Garlic, and Taleggio	740	27	11	50	1720	94	0	3	28	
Pizza al Taglio with Arugula and Fresh Mozzarella	613	34	10	43	664	55	4	3	23	
Thin-Crust Grilled Pizza with Fontina, Pecorino, and Scallions	708	33	12	64	1330	73	5	11	28	
Fugazzeta (Argentine Cheese-Stuffed Pizza)	853	48	25	129	1119	63	4	8	42	
Focaccia di Recco	416	24	9	45	312	32	1	0	18	
Avocado Toast	279	20	3	0	300	23	8	3	5	
Lemon-Pickled Radish Toast with Basil and Parmesan	330	20	10	47	453	29	3	12	10	
Ricotta Toast with Pesto di Prezzemolo and Grapes	719	62	12	35	551	29	5	6	16	
Mana'eesh Za'atar (Za'atar Flatbreads)	323	12	2	0	264	46	2	0	7	
Za'atar	5	0	0	40	1	0	0	0	0	✓
Alu Parathas (Punjabi Potato-Stuffed Griddle Breads)	490	21	9	33	561	68	3	2	9	
Tamatya-Kandyachi Koshimbir (Tomato-Onion Salad)	51	1	1	0	300	10	3	6	2	✓
Socca with Sautéed Onions and Rosemary	245	15	2	0	324	20	4	5	7	✓
Whole-Wheat Crepes with Creamy Sautéed Mushrooms and Asparagus	641	42	24	248	892	48	7	13	25	
Whole-Wheat Crepes	147	8	4	73	160	14	2	3	6	
Flatbreads with Fontina, Mushrooms, and Chives	340	8	3.5	15	780	56	0	8	13	
Cauliflower Chickpea Flatbread with Romesco	170	13	3	30	400	7	2	2	9	✓
Upside-Down Caramelized Shallot and Onion Tart	487	30	15	69	817	44	6	22	14	
Whipped Boursin	205	18	10	53	250	3	0	1	9	✓
Vidalia Onion Pie	704	50	27	207	791	46	3	12	19	
Tourte aux Pommes de Terre (French Potato Pie)	643	43	27	138	607	56	4	3	9	
Eggplant and Tomato Phyllo Pie	528	37	14	60	687	30	4	5	19	
Mushroom and Leek Galette with Gorgonzola	507	31	16	97	613	48	6	7	13	
Butternut Squash Galette with Gruyère	496	30	16	99	588	48	5	5	12	
Celery Root Galette with Blue Cheese and Walnuts	630	41	18	100	870	55	6	12	13	
Summer Squash Tart	336	28	9	36	493	12	2	7	11	
Caramelized Onion, Tomato, and Goat Cheese Tart	93	6	4	10	206	5	1	2	5	
Caramelized Onions	132	5	0	0	328	21	4	10	2	✓
Upside-Down Tomato Tart	97	4	2	5	311	15	2	10	2	
Fennel-Apple Tarte Tatin	319	20	6	10	530	29	8	16	8	
Kol Böreği (Spiraled Spinach and Cheese Pastry)	456	25	7	59	776	46	3	2	13	

	Cal	Total Fat (g)	Sat Fat (g)	Chol (mg)	Sodium (mg)	Carbs (g)	Fiber (g)	Total Sugar (g)	Protein (g)	Gluten Free
06 PASTA, NOODLES, AND DUMPLINGS										
Fresh Tomato Sauce	91	7	1	0	299	7	2	4	1	✓
Fresh Tomato Puttanesca Sauce	98	8	1	0	399	7	2	4	2	✓
No-Cook Fresh Tomato Sauce	170	14	2	0	590	11	3	7	2	✓
Vodka Sauce	204	16	6	27	378	8	2	5	4	✓
Tomato-Browned Butter Sauce	100	7	4.5	20	380	6	1	4	1	✓
Pesto alla Genovese (Basil Pesto)	205	21	3	3	86	2	0	0	3	✓
Pesto di Prezzemolo (Parsley Pesto)	340	35	5	5	195	5	2	1	5	✓
Pesto Pantesco	270	26	3	0	300	7	3	3	4	✓
Pesto alla Calabrese	150	11	3.5	15	490	6	2	3	5	✓
Fresh Pasta Without a Machine	280	11	3	245	130	35	0	0	10	
Mezzi Rigatoni with Spicy Gojuchang Tomato Sauce	482	19	11	48	431	69	6	6	13	
Rigatoni with Marinated Tomatoes and Burrata	835	38	13	56	844	94	6	8	29	
Garlicky Spaghetti with Lemon and Pine Nuts	738	31	6	13	413	90	5	4	24	
Garlicky Spaghetti with Artichokes and Hazelnuts	778	30	6	13	632	101	11	5	28	
Garlicky Spaghetti with Green Olives and Almonds	723	30	6	17	712	91	6	4	23	
Angel Hair Pasta with Sun-Dried Tomato and Mint Sauce	637	32	6	17	381	71	5	3	19	
Linguine with Sun-Dried Tomato and Eggplant Sauce	673	23	3	0	769	101	10	9	18	
Simple Stovetop Macaroni and Cheese	563	28	14	70	656	52	2	5	26	
Grown-Up Stovetop Macaroni and Cheese	559	27	14	70	690	51	2	5	27	
Spinach-Artichoke Macaroni and Cheese	678	38	16	79	938	55	5	6	33	
Pasta with Creamy Lemon-Sichuan Peppercorn Sauce	455	16	5	23	408	64	4	5	13	
Pasta Cacio e Uova (Pasta with Cheese and Eggs)	177	15	5	82	353	1	0	0	10	
Creamy Broccoli Pasta with Crispy Panko	621	30	6	12	665	71	6	6	20	
Tallarines Verdes (Peruvian Green Noodles)	343	11	3	13	333	48	3	5	12	
Fettuccine with Walnut Sauce	929	51	9	23	485	95	8	5	28	
Cashew e Pepe e Funghi	480	16	3	0	336	68	7	4	19	
Triple Mushroom Pasta	507	20	10	44	764	66	5	6	18	
Rigatoni with Quick Mushroom Bolognese	609	14	3	9	724	97	6	9	21	
Summer Squash Pasta with Ricotta and Lemon-Parmesan Bread Crumbs	946	43	14	59	1001	101	6	7	38	
Ultracreamy Spaghetti with Zucchini	592	23	11	39	841	72	5	8	24	
Spaghetti all'Assassina	578	26	4	0	1187	74	5	8	13	
Farfalle with Beets, Arugula, and Blue Cheese	550	26	3	0	510	68	4	2	13	
Orecchiette and Navy Beans with Brussels Sprouts and Spicy Mustard Crumbs	493	13	4	21	652	74	10	4	21	
Creamy, Spicy Rotini and Red Lentils with Tomatoes and Goat Cheese	420	11	5	13	420	62	5	5	19	
Pasta e Ceci (Pasta with Chickpeas)	534	20	5	15	923	676	13	10	22	
Fregula with Chickpeas, Tomatoes, and Fennel	436	11	1	0	1063	70	14	9	16	
Meatless "Meat" Sauce with Chickpeas and Mushrooms	176	10	1	0	523	20	5	7	6	✓
Fideos with Chickpeas, Fennel, and Kale	490	18	2.5	0	860	64	16	9	15	

	Cal	Total Fat (g)	Sat Fat (g)	Chol (mg)	Sodium (mg)	Carbs (g)	Fiber (g)	Total Sugar (g)	Protein (g)	Gluten Free
06 PASTA, NOODLES, AND DUMPLINGS										
Pesto Lasagna	540	37	13	50	544	34	2	8	18	
Cheesy Stuffed Shells	568	26	14	128	808	55	4	8	29	
Unstuffed Shells with Butternut Squash and Leeks	630	28	16	80	1213	73	6	8	23	
Cheese Ravioli with Pumpkin Cream Sauce	1006	58	32	189	931	90	6	6	34	
Three-Cheese Ravioli with Browned Butter–Pine Nut Sauce	691	46	21	191	534	42	2	1	27	
Tortellini Salad with Broccoli, Cannellini Beans, and Olive-Banana Pepper Dressing	403	25	6	12	721	32	8	5	15	
Crispy Gnocchi with Shredded Brussels Sprouts and Gorgonzola	458	22	7	41	683	53	8	8	16	
Samosa Gnocchi Chaat	490	32	7	25	940	41	6	7	11	
Potato Gnocchi with Browned Butter and Sage	663	18	10	103	986	111	7	3	16	
Gnocchi à la Parisienne with Arugula, Tomatoes, and Olives	480	38	20	225	1040	21	1	3	12	
Gnocchi à la Parisienne with Browned Butter	460	38	23	240	770	16	0	0	11	
Spinach and Ricotta Gnudi with Tomato-Butter Sauce	407	26	15	85	727	26	3	3	20	
Ramen with Shiitakes and Soft Eggs	513	27	8	186	1670	52	5	5	17	
Shiitake and Bok Choy Lo Mein	491	15	2	72	667	75	6	8	16	
Shanghai Scallion Oil Noodles	553	28	3	64	697	63	4	6	13	
San Francisco–Style Garlic Noodles	486	22	12	113	267	57	3	2	16	
Gochujang-Tahini Noodles	470	11	2.5	0	1030	77	1	7	16	
Spicy Basil Noodles with Crispy Tofu, Snap Peas, and Bell Pepper	533	18	2	0	1084	77	6	15	18	✓
Japchae (Sweet Potato Noodles with Shiitakes and Spinach)	315	21	6	41	1147	20	5	11	16	
Sweet Potato Noodles with Shiitakes, Spinach, and Eggs	250	14	2	60	690	27	3	12	6	
Udon with Stir-Fried Portobellos and Soy-Maple Sauce	460	9	1	0	500	77	3	16	14	
Liang Mian (Chilled Sesame Noodles)	592	18	3	97	706	89	5	7	19	
Chilled Soba Noodles with Cucumber, Snow Peas, and Radishes	215	6	1	0	620	34	1	2	8	
Pittsburgh-Style Haluski	421	20	11	94	694	52	6	7	11	
Savory Noodle Kugel	269	9	2	150	274	36	2	3	11	
Green Peas and Dumplings	309	12	7	31	598	41	8	7	10	
Potato-Cheddar Pierogi	440	22	12	105	750	49	2	2	12	
Potato-Sauerkraut Pierogi	390	17	9	90	810	50	3	3	9	
Su Shui Jiao (Northern Chinese–Style Cabbage and Mushroom Dumplings)	84	5	0	12	71	8	1	0	2	
Chili Crisp Dumpling Sauce	43	1	0	0	579	6	1	3	2	
Sichuan Peppercorn Oil	157	17	1	0	1	2	1	0	1	✓
07 RICE AND GRAINS										
Simple Rice Pilaf	337	9	6	23	532	57	1	1	5	✓
Basmati Rice Pilaf with Whole Spices	223	6	4	15	333	38	1	0	3	✓
Basmati Rice Pilaf with Peas, Scallions, and Lemon	190	3	0	0	100	37	1	1	4	✓
Easy Mexican Rice	264	8	1	2	323	43	1	2	5	✓
Spinach Rice	329	11	3	14	568	48	2	3	9	✓
Javaher Polo (Jeweled Rice)	559	25	7	23	390	77	3	24	7	✓

	Cal	Total Fat (g)	Sat Fat (g)	Chol (mg)	Sodium (mg)	Carbs (g)	Fiber (g)	Total Sugar (g)	Protein (g)	Gluten Free
07 RICE AND GRAINS										
Cauliflower Biryani	339	11	2	5	831	54	5	9	8	✓
Paella de Verduras (Cauliflower and Bean Paella)	517	14	3	6	804	78	9	9	19	✓
Vegetable Bibimbap with Tempeh	590	21	2	0	2050	87	8	15	20	
Garlicky Fried Rice with Bok Choy	190	3	0	0	500	35	2	2	5	✓
Stir-Fried Rice Cakes with Bok Choy and Snow Peas	556	11	1	0	966	105	7	8	13	
Risotto Milanese	522	22	13	58	859	57	2	1	14	✓
Miso Mushroom Risotto	600	17	2	0	1090	90	4	9	20	✓
Corn Risotto	273	8	4	18	683	44	3	5	8	✓
Cơm Đỏ (Vietnamese Red Rice)	213	4	2	10	307	39	1	1	4	
Hung Kao Mun Gati (Thai Coconut Rice)	251	8	7	0	301	40	1	2	4	✓
Arroz con Titoté (Colombian Coconut Rice)	522	22	19	0	606	77	1	15	7	✓
Congee	134	4	0	1	205	21	0	1	3	
Wild Rice Pilaf with Pecans and Cranberries	249	12	3	11	350	34	4	14	6	✓
Wild Rice Pilaf with Scallions, Cilantro, and Almonds	300	9	3	10	430	46	3	2	7	✓
California Barley Bowls with Lemon-Yogurt Sauce	550	34	5	5	750	55	14	6	13	
Barley with Lemon and Herbs	185	6	1	0	145	31	7	1	4	
Barley with Celery and Miso Dressing	181	4	0	0	212	33	7	2	4	
Barley with Fennel, Dried Apricots, and Orange	218	4	1	0	378	42	9	9	5	
Beet Barley Risotto	332	9	3	8	1012	46	11	7	12	
Barley and Lentils with Mushrooms and Tahini-Yogurt Sauce	340	5	1	0	330	61	14	3	15	
Farro with Wild Mushroom Ragout	394	10	1	0	1539	66	13	14	19	
Jollof-Inspired Fonio	186	15	3	14	530	10	2	5	4	✓
Curried Fonio with Roasted Vegetables and Hibiscus Vinaigrette	540	30	5	0	1050	67	7	8	7	✓
Hibiscus Vinaigrette	140	14	2	0	310	3	0	3	0	✓
Spring Freekeh and Halloumi Bowls	760	32	12	45	1120	90	22	11	32	
Tahini-Garlic Sauce	45	3.5	0.5	0	100	3	0	1	1	✓
Maftoul with Carrots and Chickpeas	410	9	1	0	930	70	7	6	13	
Oat Berry Pilaf with Walnuts and Gorgonzola	234	16	3	8	400	21	3	14	5	✓
Quinoa Bowls with Snap Peas, Strawberries, and Basil Vinaigrette	780	56	10	20	1090	57	9	9	17	✓
Quinoa, Black Bean, and Mango Salad with Lime Dressing	454	24	3	0	770	52	11	9	12	✓
Quinoa Lettuce Wraps with Feta and Olives	441	28	7	25	908	38	6	4	13	✓
Herbed Quinoa Cakes with Whipped Feta	560	29	10	130	1260	53	5	14	21	
Creamy Polenta with Fennel and Chickpeas	496	18	6	20	1269	64	11	9	18	✓
Creamy Polenta with Radicchio Agrodolce	370	25	6	20	860	20	2	15	15	✓
Spicy Polenta with White Beans and Kale	690	37	12	50	1550	67	13	6	27	✓
Grits with Fresh Corn	266	12	7	30	603	35	2	8	7	✓
Savory Oatmeal with Peas, Parmesan, and Pepper	398	24	12	69	990	21	4	3	26	✓
Easy Baked White Rice	206	0	0	0	374	45	0	0	4	✓
Easy Baked Brown Rice	200	4	1	0	200	37	2	1	4	✓

	Cal	Total Fat (g)	Sat Fat (g)	Chol (mg)	Sodium (mg)	Carbs (g)	Fiber (g)	Total Sugar (g)	Protein (g)	Gluten Free
08 BEANS AND LEGUMES										
Cacio e Pepe Beans with Squash, Sage, and Walnuts	422	12	6	35	411	58	3	2	19	✓
Bean Bourguignon	246	10	1	0	618	25	5	6	9	
Gigantes Plaki	390	10	1.5	0	620	60	16	14	18	✓
Calabrian Chile White Beans with Almond Romesco	439	23	5	13	833	40	10	5	22	✓
Sicilian White Beans and Escarole	201	4	1	0	669	34	10	3	10	✓
Stewed Cranberry Beans with Tomatoes and Sage	309	18	4	8	835	28	10	6	12	✓
Jackfruit and Chickpea Makhani	410	17	4.5	20	1220	48	11	9	18	✓
Chickpea Bouillabaisse	740	33	5	30	1680	85	11	9	20	
Chana Masala	291	11	1	0	576	39	11	8	11	✓
Chickpea Curry	596	35	20	0	1141	60	18	13	19	✓
Espinacas con Garbanzos (Andalusian Spinach and Chickpeas)	571	28	4	3	908	62	17	12	21	
Crispy Chickpea Cakes with Zucchini Ribbon Salad	478	27	4	34	799	46	12	10	17	
Sautéed Fava Beans, Asparagus, and Leek	103	5	1	0	210	13	5	6	6	✓
Edamame Salad with Mint and Parmesan	271	19	5	17	321	11	6	3	16	✓
Cuban-Style Black Beans and Rice	307	22	7	18	596	22	5	3	8	✓
Skillet Rice and Beans with Corn and Fresh Tomatoes	345	6	1	0	968	62	12	5	13	✓
Skillet Rice and Chickpeas with Coconut Milk	300	10	3	0	500	46	7	4	8	✓
Spanish-Style Skillet Rice and Chickpeas	260	6	1	0	630	46	6	6	8	✓
Tacu Tacu with Salsa Criolla	603	23	4	186	611	77	9	3	23	✓
Gallo Pinto (Costa Rican Beans and Rice)	291	8	1	0	564	47	7	4	9	✓
Jamaican Rice and Peas	557	20	15	14	706	79	6	3	16	✓
Crispy Coconut Rice and Pigeon Peas with Tropical Fruit	530	20	9	0	1020	81	7	25	11	
Mujaddara (Rice and Lentils with Crispy Onions)	460	14	3	5	810	70	9	9	14	✓
Crispy Onions	90	5	1	0	100	13	2	6	1	✓
Koshari	450	8	1	0	1080	81	12	10	17	
Lentils with Roasted Broccoli and Lemony Bread Crumbs	417	15	2	0	364	56	11	8	19	
Lentilles de Puy with Spinach and Crème Fraîche	170	10	2	7	732	14	1	6	7	✓
Palak Dal (Spinach-Lentil Dal with Cumin and Mustard Seeds)	273	8	4	16	348	40	7	4	14	✓
Red Lentil Kibbeh	264	8	2	3	460	40	7	5	11	
Harissa	208	21	3	0	75	5	3	1	1	✓
Misir Wot	303	11	2	0	660	40	8	5	14	✓
09 TOFU AND TEMPEH										
Homestyle Tofu	250	19	1.5	0	390	10	1	3	10	
Spicy Cold Tofu	123	8	1	0	453	5	1	2	10	
Crispy Tofu	220	10	0.5	0	0	20	0	0	11	✓
Homemade Tofu	124	5	0	0	7	9	5	3	13	✓
Tofu Sushi Bowls	530	22	2	0	840	73	9	3	17	
Tofu Katsu	472	35	3	93	618	26	4	4	16	

	Cal	Total Fat (g)	Sat Fat (g)	Chol (mg)	Sodium (mg)	Carbs (g)	Fiber (g)	Total Sugar (g)	Protein (g)	Gluten Free
09 TOFU AND TEMPEH										
Seared Tofu with Panch Phoron, Green Beans, and Pickled Shallots	554	36	5	8	727	28	10	14	40	✓
Panch Phoron	40	2.5	0	0	5	4	2	0	2	✓
Tofu Rancheros	520	29	4	0	1554	52	18	16	25	✓
Saag Tofu	293	20	3	0	826	19	8	5	18	✓
Crispy Tofu Salad with Cherry Tomatoes	370	32	3	0	727	13	3	7	11	
Crispy Tofu and Kale Salad with Miso-Ginger Dressing	738	58	8	0	980	38	16	5	27	✓
Pita Salad with Za'atar Tofu and Chickpeas	534	29	4	0	1042	52	14	9	23	
Charred Cabbage Salad with Torn Tofu and Plantain Chips	514	36	5	0	752	34	9	17	22	✓
Garlicky Tofu Tabbouleh	198	12	2	0	431	16	4	3	9	
Chile-Spiced Crumbled Tofu with Pineapple Salsa	290	20	3	0	920	18	5	10	12	✓
Crispy Teriyaki Tofu	450	30	4	0	1590	26	2	16	21	
Stir-Fried Tofu and Bok Choy	300	14	2	0	610	28	3	8	14	
Panko-Crusted Tofu with Cabbage Salad	410	23	3	95	800	37	1	9	16	
Sweet and Spicy Glazed Tofu with Coconut-Braised Mustard Greens and Winter Squash	380	22	9	0	960	37	9	9	17	
Caribbean Tofu with Rice and Pigeon Peas	750	24	3	0	1250	102	4	33	29	✓
East African Tofu and Coconut Curry	360	28	15	0	690	23	5	6	10	✓
Thai Red Curry with Tofu and Lentils	197	14	6	0	840	10	3	4	12	✓
Bulgur with Vegetables and Marinated Tofu	663	33	4	3	1217	73	16	21	28	
Shawarma-Spiced Tofu Wraps with Sumac Onions	510	24	3	0	800	53	2	10	23	
Sumac Onions	35	3	0	0	100	3	0	1	0	✓
Tofu Summer Rolls with Spicy Almond Butter Sauce	268	9	2	0	441	41	4	7	10	
Mapo Tofu	331	26	2	0	758	16	3	4	13	
Overstuffed Sweet Potatoes with Tofu and Red Curry Vinaigrette	569	39	3	0	696	47	7	9	15	✓
Tofu and Chickpea Flour Frittata with Mushrooms	218	14	2	0	352	9	3	2	19	✓
Grilled Tofu with Vegetable Skewers	371	26	4	0	1061	19	4	8	22	
Crispy Tempeh	60	3	0	0	80	4	0	2	5	
Crispy Tempeh with Sambal Sauce	588	49	5	3	617	20	2	5	26	
Seared Tempeh with Tomato Jam	300	12	2	5	710	31	2	6	17	✓
Ras el Hanout	30	1	0	0	0	5	3	0	1	✓
Pan-Seared Tempeh Steaks with Chimichurri Sauce	595	53	9	0	492	12	1	0	24	✓
Stir-Fried Tempeh, Napa Cabbage, and Carrots	404	20	3	0	672	41	3	27	21	
Stir-Fried Tempeh with Orange Sauce	333	18	3	0	562	22	4	4	23	
Sweet Potato Red Flannel Hash with Tempeh	393	25	6	0	672	32	5	8	15	
Loaded Sweet Potato Wedges with Tempeh	520	27	4.5	0	710	55	10	15	13	✓
Tempeh Tacos	300	12	2	0	650	38	6	5	13	
Tempeh Reubens	770	50	16	6C	1720	54	7	7	27	
Sauerkraut	15	0	0	0	200	3	1	2	1	✓
Korean Barbecue Tempeh Wraps	667	30	4	0	1749	76	2	40	30	

10 EGGS ALL DAY

	Cal	Total Fat (g)	Sat Fat (g)	Chol (mg)	Sodium (mg)	Carbs (g)	Fiber (g)	Total Sugar (g)	Protein (g)	Gluten Free
Easy-Peel Hard-Cooked Eggs	72	5	2	186	71	0	0	0	6	✓
Soft-Cooked Eggs	72	5	2	186	71	0	0	0	6	✓
Jammy Eggs	72	5	2	186	71	0	0	0	6	✓
Perfect Fried Eggs	219	18	6	382	255	1	0	0	13	✓
Perfect Poached Eggs	145	10	3	372	251	1	0	0	13	✓
Creamy French-Style Scrambled Eggs	143	10	3	372	259	1	0	0	13	✓
Xīhóngshì Chao Jīdàn (Chinese Stir-Fried Tomatoes and Eggs)	296	22	4	372	764	11	4	8	14	
Scrambled Eggs with Shiitake Mushrooms and Feta Cheese	288	22	6	380	402	8	2	3	16	✓
Menemen (Turkish Scrambled Eggs with Vegetables)	406	31	8	295	576	15	2	5	16	
Australian Folded Eggs	193	15	7	387	261	1	0	0	13	✓
Coddled Eggs	177	13	6	382	244	1	0	0	13	✓
Çılbır (Turkish Poached Eggs with Yogurt and Spiced Butter)	188	14	8	211	311	3	0	3	12	
Make-Ahead Cheese Soufflés	215	15	8	130	292	6	0	2	13	
Pickled Mustard Seeds	296	12	1	0	723	36	4	27	9	✓
Biscuits with Creamy Tomato Gravy and Fried Eggs	742	50	30	319	907	57	4	10	17	
Shakshuka (Eggs in Spicy Tomato and Roasted Red Pepper Sauce)	492	28	7	380	1061	44	9	12	22	
Green Shakshuka	473	34	8	377	990	22	6	4	22	
Microwave-Fried Garlic	280	28	2	0	0	6	0	1	1	✓
Chickpea Shakshuka	501	25	8	382	1165	45	12	16	28	✓
Tomato and Corn Tostadas with Baked Eggs	370	23	8	365	600	22	1	4	19	✓
Vegetarian Refried Beans	230	5	0.5	0	560	36	10	3	11	✓
Easy Cheddar Omelet	431	35	17	616	448	2	0	1	26	✓
Easy Feta and Dill Omelet	416	34	17	622	642	3	0	1	24	✓
Easy Tex-Mex Omelet	442	36	18	618	475	2	0	1	27	✓
Family-Size Spinach and Herb Cream Cheese Omelet with Home Fries	482	26	13	416	943	44	6	3	20	✓
Spanish Tortilla with Roasted Red Peppers and Peas	486	31	6	372	754	35	5	4	17	✓
Garlic Mayonnaise	104	12	1	18	34	0	0	0	0	✓
Potato and Zucchini Spanish Tortilla	268	24	4	93	283	9	1	1	4	✓
Broccoli and Feta Frittata	237	16	6	390	463	5	1	2	17	✓
Pesto Potato Frittata with Peas and Goat Cheese	615	42	18	514	903	29	5	4	31	✓
Kuku Sabzi	137	11	2	140	222	5	1	1	6	✓
Frittata Bites with Broccoli and Sun-Dried Potatoes	610	21	6	380	840	68	11	11	34	
Frittata Bites with Peas, Goat Cheese, and Basil	590	40	16	505	1120	29	2	4	28	
Asparagus, Leek, and Goat Cheese Quiche	434	32	19	173	454	24	2	3	14	
Fried Egg Sandwiches with Hummus and Sprouts	195	9	3	99	338	20	3	3	9	
Egg, Kimchi, and Avocado Sandwiches	459	27	6	378	616	35	4	2	19	
Breakfast Tacos with Pinto Beans and Cotija Cheese	385	23	6	379	540	23	6	1	22	✓

	Cal	Total Fat (g)	Sat Fat (g)	Chol (mg)	Sodium (mg)	Carbs (g)	Fiber (g)	Total Sugar (g)	Protein (g)	Gluten Free
10 EGGS ALL DAY										
Kale and Black Bean Breakfast Burritos	383	16	4	248	754	43	9	4	19	
Breakfast Burritos with Poblano, Beans, Corn, and Crispy Potatoes	700	45	11	401	723	48	6	4	28	
Brussels Sprout Hash with Poached Eggs	420	24	8	370	1090	35	8	7	19	✓
11 SMALL PLATES AND SNACKS										
Garam Masala Peanuts	300	22	3	0	142	18	4	12	12	✓
Chaat Masala Peanuts	301	22	3	0	143	18	4	12	12	✓
Garam Masala	61	2	0	0	8	14	6	0	2	✓
Warm Marinated Olives	216	22	3	0	716	6	2	2	1	
Marinated Manchego	303	30	8	28	186	3	1	0	7	✓
Homemade Yogurt	36	0	0	3	51	5	0	5	3	✓
Labneh	70	4	2.5	15	55	6	0	6	4	✓
Lemon-Dill Labneh	80	4	2.5	15	130	6	0	6	4	✓
Whipped Feta Dip	119	11	5	26	326	2	0	0	4	✓
Whipped Feta and Roasted Red Pepper Dip	119	11	4	26	325	2	0	0	4	✓
Whipped Feta Dip with Dill and Parsley	119	11	4	26	326	1	0	0	4	✓
Frico	222	14	8	4	669	2	0	0	20	✓
Pan-Seared Halloumi with Cherry Pepper Glaze	155	10	5	34	433	11	0	9	6	✓
Bouyourdi (Spicy Greek Baked Feta)	154	14	5	29	379	3	1	1	5	✓
Baked Pimento Cheese Dip	354	34	13	64	407	4	1	2	9	
Classic Guacamole	124	11	2	0	205	7	5	1	2	✓
Hummus with Crispy Mushrooms and Sumac	550	36	5	0	1270	44	13	2	19	✓
Ultracreamy Hummus	218	12	1	0	287	23	7	4	8	✓
Fattet Hummus (Crispy Pita with Garlicky Yogurt and Chickpeas)	496	26	3	4	587	56	13	12	17	
Biscuit Crackers with Red Lentil Dip	170	9	4	15	670	18	2	3	4	
Beet Dip with Yogurt and Tahini	187	15	3	5	318	11	3	6	5	✓
Corn Cheese	306	22	8	37	501	22	3	7	10	✓
Slow-Roasted Eggplant Dip with Pomegranate Molasses and Aleppo Pepper	194	14	2	0	377	18	4	11	2	✓
Fresh Leek and Spinach Dip	149	12	6	29	214	8	1	3	3	
Southern Cheese Straws	52	4	2	10	35	4	0	0	2	
Parmesan–Black Pepper Cheese Straws	60	4	2	11	64	4	0	0	2	
Pa amb Tomàquet (Catalan Tomato Bread)	208	8	1	0	332	28	2	4	6	
Fava Bean Crostini with Manchego and Pine Nuts	380	11	2	5	400	59	10	14	1	
Cranberry and Goat Cheese Crostini	163	7	3	7	217	20	1	7	5	
Buffalo Cauliflower Bites	555	48	15	1	756	29	3	4	4	✓
Vegan Ranch Dressing	90	10	1	0	120	0	0	0	0	✓
Vegan Mayonnaise	180	20	2	0	75	0	0	0	0	✓
Portobello Mushroom Fries with Cherry Pepper Sauce	720	54	10	131	720	43	3	8	18	

	Cal	Total Fat (g)	Sat Fat (g)	Chol (mg)	Sodium (mg)	Carbs (g)	Fiber (g)	Total Sugar (g)	Protein (g)	Gluten Free
11 SMALL PLATES AND SNACKS										
Patatas Bravas	320	22	2	5	630	29	2	2	4	✓
Zucchini Chips with Tzatziki	389	28	3	5	528	30	2	3	6	
Chickpea Fries	518	57	4	0	58	2	0	0	1	✓
Lemon and Herb Dipping Sauce	202	22	3	11	217	0	0	0	0	✓
Calabrian Chile Dipping Sauce	201	22	3	11	167	0	0	0	0	✓
Honey and Spice Dipping Sauce	210	22	3	11	167	2	0	2	0	✓
Scallion Pancakes	313	20	2	0	296	30	1	1	4	
Spring Rolls (Cantonese Egg Rolls)	120	6	0	0	250	16	1	1	2	
Plum Sauce	50	0	0	0	200	13	0	9	0	✓
Pakoras (South Asian Spiced Vegetable Fritters)	172	12	1	0	213	14	2	2	4	✓
Carrot-Tamarind Chutney	69	0	0	0	211	17	2	11	1	✓
Sweet Potato Fritters with Feta, Dill, and Cilantro	378	25	4	79	454	32	4	5	8	
Sweet Potato Fritters with Cheddar and Chipotle	386	25	4	76	449	32	4	5	8	
Sesame Balls	260	12	2	0	45	37	2	11	4	✓
Blistered Shishito Peppers	49	5	0	0	1	2	1	1	0	✓
Buttered Popcorn	60	5	5	40	5	1	0	0	1	✓
Parmesan Pepper Popcorn	80	2	5	115	5	1	0	0	2	✓
Garlic and Herb Popcorn	70	1	5	40	5	1	0	0	1	✓
Hot and Sweet Popcorn	70	1	5	45	7	1	2	2	1	✓
Cajun-Spiced Popcorn	70	1	5	50	5	1	0	0	1	✓
Sun-Dried Tomato Tapenade with Farmer's Cheese	180	16	5	15	250	4	1	0	6	✓
Melted Brie with Honey and Herbs	160	13	8	45	290	2	0	2	9	✓
12 SIMPLE VEGETABLES A to Z										
All-Purpose Herb Sauce	100	10	1.5	0	60	3	0	0	0	
Smoked Paprika Sauce	100	10	1.5	0	60	3	0	0	0	
Chile-Coriander Sauce	100	10	1.5	0	60	3	0	0	0	
Zhoug (Spicy Middle Eastern Herb Sauce)	88	9	1	0	64	2	0	1	0	✓
Chermoula	167	18	3	0	71	2	0	0	0	✓
Peanut-Sesame Sauce	110	7	1.5	0	400	8	1	5	4	
Pumpkin Seed Sauce	120	9	1.5	0	150	7	2	2	4	✓
Miso-Ginger Sauce	313	24	3	0	1580	19	2	11	7	✓
Infinite Sauce	100	11	7	30	150	0	0	0	0	
Gochujang Sauce	39	3	0	0	257	2	0	1	1	✓
Romesco	43	3	0	0	75	3	1	1	1	
Spicy Avocado-Sour Cream Sauce	70	6	2.5	15	25	2	1	1	1	✓
Beurre Blanc	220	23	15	65	290	1	0	1	0	✓
Stir-Fried Amaranth with Garlic	50	5	0	0	190	2	1	0	2	✓
Roasted Artichokes	146	10	1	0	672	13	6	2	4	✓
Roasted Artichokes with Lemon Vinaigrette	339	31	4	0	820	18	8	3	4	✓

	Cal	Total Fat (g)	Sat Fat (g)	Chol (mg)	Sodium (mg)	Carbs (g)	Fiber (g)	Total Sugar (g)	Protein (g)	Gluten Free
12 SIMPLE VEGETABLES A to Z										
Braised Asparagus with Lemon and Chives	88	7	1	0	172	5	2	2	3	✓
Braised Asparagus with Orange and Tarragon	91	7	1	0	172	6	3	2	3	✓
Braised Asparagus with Sherry Vinegar and Marjoram	88	7	1	0	172	5	2	2	3	✓
Pan-Seared Beets with Horseradish Cream	262	19	5	17	458	20	5	14	4	✓
Baby Bok Choy with Ginger and Garlic	80	7	1	0	320	4	1	1	2	
Roasted Broccoli	161	11	2	0	357	14	5	4	6	✓
Roasted Broccoli with Garlic	140	11	1.5	0	330	9	3	3	3	✓
Roasted Broccoli with Olives, Garlic, Oregano, and Lemon	250	22	3	0	350	12	4	3	4	✓
Broiled Broccoli Rabe	116	11	1	0	293	4	3	1	4	✓
Skillet-Roasted Brussels Sprouts with Cider Vinegar and Honey	210	18	2.5	0	170	12	4	5	3	✓
Skillet-Roasted Brussels Sprouts with Maple Syrup and Smoked Almonds	263	22	3	0	344	15	5	6	6	✓
Skillet-Roasted Brussels Sprouts with Pomegranate and Pistachios	262	21	3	0	346	17	5	8	6	✓
Fried Brussels Sprouts with Sriracha Dipping Sauce	435	42	4	8	471	14	6	3	5	✓
Fried Brussels Sprouts with Lemon-Chive Dipping Sauce	435	42	4	8	468	14	6	4	5	
Roasted Cabbage	105	7	1	0	345	10	4	5	2	✓
Roasted Cabbage with Bread Crumbs, Sage, and Parmesan	187	13	4	14	458	14	5	6	7	
Roasted Cabbage with Gochujang, Sesame, and Scallions	135	9	1	0	452	12	5	6	3	✓
Suan La Bai Cai (Sour and Hot Napa Cabbage)	82	5	0	0	474	8	2	4	3	
Boiled Carrots with Lemon and Chives	73	3	2	8	277	11	3	5	1	✓
Boiled Carrots with Cumin, Lime, and Cilantro	78	4	1	0	274	11	3	5	1	✓
Boiled Carrots with Fennel Seeds and Citrus	78	4	1	0	278	11	3	5	1	✓
Boiled Carrots with Mint and Paprika	74	3	2	8	279	11	3	5	1	✓
Butter-Roasted Carrots with Hazelnut Crumble and Goat Cheese	260	19	9	29	502	18	6	8	7	✓
Cauliflower Rice	94	4	1	1	491	12	4	5	4	✓
Skillet-Roasted Cauliflower with Garlic and Lemon	154	12	2	0	401	11	4	3	4	
Skillet-Roasted Cauliflower with Capers and Pine Nuts	158	13	2	0	399	9	4	3	4	✓
Skillet-Roasted Cauliflower with Cumin and Pistachios	152	12	2	0	398	10	4	3	4	✓
Modern Cauliflower Gratin	199	14	8	35	493	12	4	4	9	
Roasted Celery Root with Chimichurri	240	22	4	8	391	11	2	2	2	✓
Quick Collard Greens	167	8	3	13	686	14	8	4	9	✓
Foolproof Boiled Corn	98	3	1	3	241	19	2	6	3	✓
Chili-Lime Salt	3	0	0	0	173	0	0	0	0	✓
Cilantro-Chipotle Butter	80	8	5	25	150	0	0	0	0	✓
Spicy Old Bay Butter	80	8	5	25	170	0	0	0	0	✓
Hot Honey Butter	90	8	5	25	150	4	0	4	0	✓
Basil-Lemon Butter	80	8	5	25	150	0	0	0	0	✓
Sautéed Corn with Cherry Tomatoes, Ricotta Salata, and Basil	129	7	1	7	281	16	2	5	4	✓

	Cal	Total Fat (g)	Sat Fat (g)	Chol (mg)	Sodium (mg)	Carbs (g)	Fiber (g)	Total Sugar (g)	Protein (g)	Gluten Free
12 SIMPLE VEGETABLES A to Z										
Coconut Creamed Corn	262	16	13	0	510	31	3	10	6	✓
Coconut Creamed Corn with Ginger and Crispy Shallots	358	26	14	0	574	34	4	11	7	✓
Grilled Corn with Basil-Lemon Butter	262	18	8	31	366	26	3	9	5	✓
Pai Huang Gua (Smashed Cucumbers)	61	3	0	0	493	9	1	4	2	
Marinated Eggplant with Capers and Mint	95	8	1	0	120	5	2	3	1	
Braised Eggplant with Paprika, Coriander, and Yogurt	98	8	1	2	423	7	3	4	2	✓
Braised Eggplant with Soy, Garlic, and Ginger	72	3	0	0	298	9	2	5	1	
Roasted Fennel	86	7	1	0	209	6	2	3	1	✓
Orange-Honey Dressing	29	2	0	0	16	2	1	2	0	✓
Crunchy Oil-Cured Olives	4	0	0	0	7	0	1	0	0	✓
Gai Lan with Oyster Sauce	130	8	1	0	650	11	4	4	3	
Skillet-Charred Green Beans	98	7	1	0	242	8	3	4	2	✓
Skillet-Charred Green Beans with Crispy Bread-Crumb Topping	135	11	1	0	293	9	3	4	2	
Quick Cast-Iron Skillet Green Bean Casserole	421	31	17	65	703	33	5	6	7	
Simple Sautéed Kale	121	11	2	0	224	4	4	1	3	✓
Roasted Kale with Garlic, Red Pepper Flakes, and Lemon	104	9	1	0	285	6	5	1	3	✓
Roasted Kale with Coriander, Ginger, and Coconut	173	16	7	0	308	8	6	2	4	✓
Roasted Kale with Parmesan, Shallot, and Nutmeg	179	13	3	13	335	7	5	2	10	✓
Leeks Vinaigrette	191	14	2	3	239	14	2	3	4	
Sautéed Mushrooms with Red Wine and Rosemary	97	4	2	9	199	9	2	5	6	
Sautéed Mushrooms with Mustard and Parsley	88	4	2	9	242	9	2	5	6	✓
Sautéed Mushrooms with Soy, Scallion, and Ginger	96	5	2	9	496	11	4	4	5	
Roasted Okra	58	3	0	0	269	8	4	2	2	✓
Spicy Red Pepper Mayonnaise	109	11	1	4	70	3	1	1	1	✓
Braised Vidalia Onions with Chile, Lime, and Cilantro	121	8	3	10	383	12	1	9	1	
Braised Vidalia Onions with Honey, Lemon, and Oregano	127	8	3	11	362	13	1	9	2	
Rajas Poblanas con Crema (Charred Poblano Strips with Cream)	191	15	8	41	316	14	2	8	4	✓
Rajas Poblanas con Crema y Elote (Charred Poblano Strips with Cream and Corn)	213	15	8	41	317	19	3	9	4	
Three-Cheese Potato Frico	249	15	7	33	361	16	1	1	13	✓
Best Baked Potatoes	167	4	0	0	537	31	2	1	4	✓
Creamy Egg Topping	83	6	2	147	152	2	0	1	5	✓
Herbed Goat Cheese Topping	137	13	5	13	132	1	0	0	5	✓
Fastest, Easiest Mashed Potatoes	321	16	10	42	618	41	5	3	6	✓

	Cal	Total Fat (g)	Sat Fat (g)	Chol (mg)	Sodium (mg)	Carbs (g)	Fiber (g)	Total Sugar (g)	Protein (g)	Gluten Free
12 SIMPLE VEGETABLES A to Z										
Braised Red Potatoes with Lemon and Chives	135	6	4	15	316	19	2	2	2	✓
Braised Red Potatoes with Dijon and Tarragon	137	6	4	15	334	19	2	1	3	✓
Braised Red Potatoes with Miso and Scallions	141	6	4	15	325	20	2	2	3	✓
Creamy Potatoes and Leeks	446	24	14	69	710	48	5	9	11	
Sichuan Hot and Sour Potatoes	140	5	0.5	0	590	22	2	1	3	✓
Cheddar Scalloped Potatoes	455	31	19	95	648	32	2	3	14	✓
Thick-Cut Oven Fries	290	11	1	0	669	45	5	2	5	✓
Better Hash Browns	228	10	1	0	461	33	4	2	4	✓
Lemony Roasted Radicchio, Fennel, and Root Vegetables	242	7	1	0	369	42	9	13	6	✓
Roasted Radishes with Yogurt-Tahini Sauce	160	12	5	18	458	11	4	6	4	✓
Sugar Snap Peas with Pine Nuts, Fennel, and Lemon Zest	102	7	0	0	240	8	3	4	3	✓
Sugar Snap Peas with Almonds, Coriander, and Orange Zest	98	6	0	0	240	8	3	4	4	✓
Sugar Snap Peas with Sesame, Ginger, and Lemon Zest	83	5	0	0	236	8	3	3	3	✓
Roasted Delicata Squash	122	7	3	10	199	16	2	0	1	✓
Tximitxurri (Basque-Style Herb Sauce)	84	9	1	0	42	1	0	0	0	✓
Spicy Honey	43	0	0	0	127	12	0	12	0	✓
Best Baked Sweet Potatoes	142	0	0	0	529	33	5	7	3	✓
Garam Masala Yogurt	20	1	1	4	78	2	0	1	1	✓
Garlic and Chive Sour Cream	58	6	3	17	70	2	0	1	1	✓
Mashed Sweet Potatoes	303	12	7	31	616	47	7	11	4	✓
Mashed Sweet Potatoes with Maple and Orange	325	12	7	31	638	53	7	16	4	✓
Mashed Sweet Potatoes with Chipotle and Lime	304	12	7	31	624	47	7	11	4	✓
Mashed Sweet Potatoes with Curry and Golden Raisins	361	12	7	31	662	62	8	22	5	✓
Mashed Sweet Potatoes with Jalapeño, Garlic, and Scallions	307	12	7	31	636	48	7	11	4	✓
Honey-Garlic Melting Sweet Potatoes	257	9	6	24	513	41	5	12	4	✓
Swiss Chard and Kale Gratin	269	20	9	37	480	13	4	3	10	
Fried Red Tomatoes	446	29	5	60	393	33	2	3	13	
Pan-Seared Zucchini with Spicy Honey and Scallion	154	11	1	0	461	14	2	13	2	✓
Pan-Seared Zucchini with Raisin, Caper, and Parsley Sauce and Pine Nuts	185	14	1	0	515	16	3	12	3	✓
Pan-Seared Zucchini with Yogurt, Red Pepper Paste, and Preserved Lemon	173	15	2	5	548	9	2	5	5	✓
Broiled Smashed Zucchini with Garlicky Yogurt	184	15	3	5	676	10	3	7		✓
Broiled Smashed Zucchini with Herbed Sour Cream	215	19	4	17	644	10	3	7	5	✓
Broiled Smashed Zucchini with Ricotta and Parmesan	194	14	4	18	658	12	3	6	8	✓

Conversions and Equivalents

Some say cooking is a science and an art. We would say that geography has a hand in it too. Flours and sugars manufactured in the United Kingdom and elsewhere will feel and taste different from those manufactured in the United States. So we cannot promise that the loaf of bread you bake in Canada or England will taste the same as a loaf baked in the States, but we can offer guidelines for converting weights and measures. We also recommend that you rely on your instincts when making our recipes. Refer to the visual cues provided.

The recipes in this book were developed using standard U.S. measures following U.S. government guidelines. The charts below offer equivalents for U.S. and metric measures. All conversions are approximate and have been rounded up or down to the nearest whole number.

> 1 teaspoon = 4.9292 milliliters, rounded up to 5 milliliters
> 1 ounce = 28.3495 grams, rounded down to 28 grams

Volume Conversions

U.S.	Metric
1 teaspoon	5 milliliters
2 teaspoons	10 milliliters
1 tablespoon	15 milliliters
2 tablespoons	30 milliliters
¼ cup	59 milliliters
⅓ cup	79 milliliters
½ cup	118 milliliters
¾ cup	177 milliliters
1 cup	237 milliliters
1¼ cups	296 milliliters
1½ cups	355 milliliters
2 cups (1 pint)	473 milliliters
2½ cups	591 milliliters
3 cups	710 milliliters
4 cups (1 quart)	0.946 liter
1.06 quarts	1 liter
4 quarts (1 gallon)	3.8 liters

Weight Conversions

Ounces	Grams
½	14
¾	21
1	28
1½	43
2	57
2½	71
3	85
3½	99
4	113
4½	128
5	142
6	170
7	198
8	227
9	255
10	283
12	340
16 (1 pound)	454

Conversions for Common Baking Ingredients

Because measuring by weight is far more accurate than measuring by volume, and thus more likely to achieve reliable results, in our recipes we provide ounce measures in addition to cup measures for many ingredients. Refer to the chart below to convert these measures into grams.

Ingredient	Ounces	Grams
Flour		
1 cup all-purpose flour*	5	142
1 cup cake flour	4	113
1 cup whole-wheat flour	5½	156
Sugar		
1 cup granulated (white) sugar	7	198
1 cup packed brown sugar (light or dark)	7	198
1 cup confectioners' sugar	4	113
Cocoa Powder		
1 cup cocoa powder	3	85
Butter†		
4 tablespoons (½ stick, or ¼ cup)	2	57
8 tablespoons (1 stick, or ½ cup)	4	113
16 tablespoons (2 sticks, or 1 cup)	8	227

* U.S. all-purpose flour, the most frequently used flour in this book, does not contain leaveners, as some European flours do. These leavened flours are called self-rising or self-raising. If you are using self-rising flour, take this into consideration before adding leavening to a recipe.

† In the United States, butter is sold both salted and unsalted. We generally recommend unsalted butter. If you are using salted butter, take this into consideration before adding salt to a recipe.

Oven Temperature

Fahrenheit	Celsius	Gas Mark
225	105	¼
250	120	½
275	135	1
300	150	2
325	165	3
350	180	4
375	190	5
400	200	6
425	220	7
450	230	8
475	245	9

Converting Temperatures from an Instant-Read Thermometer

We include doneness temperatures in many of the recipes in this book. We recommend an instant-read thermometer for the job. Refer to the table above to convert Fahrenheit degrees to Celsius. Or, for temperatures not represented in the chart, use this simple formula:

Subtract 32 degrees from the Fahrenheit reading, then divide the result by 1.8 to find the Celsius reading.

EXAMPLE
"Roast chicken until thighs register 175 degrees."

TO CONVERT
175°F − 32 = 143°
143° ÷ 1.8 = 79.44°C, rounded down to 79°C

Index

Note: Page references in *italics* indicate photographs.

A

Acidic Flavors, about, 10

Acquacotta (Tuscan White Bean and Escarole Soup), 164, *165*

All-Purpose Herb Sauce, 524

Almond(s)

- Calabrian Chile White Beans with Almond Romesco, 374–75, *375*
- Garlicky Spaghetti with Green Olives and Almonds, 273
- Skillet-Roasted Brussels Sprouts with Maple Syrup and Smoked Almonds, 533
- Sugar Snap Peas with Almonds, Coriander, and Orange Zest, 572
- Tofu Summer Rolls with Spicy Almond Butter Sauce, *430,* 431–32
- Wild Rice Pilaf with Scallions, Cilantro, and Almonds, 344

Aloo Gobi, *48,* 48–49

Alu Parathas (Punjabi Potato-Stuffed Griddle Breads), 240–42, *243*

Amaranth with Garlic, Stir-Fried, 528, *528*

Andalusian Spinach and Chickpeas (Espinacas con Garbanzos), 382–83

Angel Hair Pasta with Sun-Dried Tomato and Mint Sauce, 273–74

Appetizers

- Baked Pimento Cheese Dip, 491, *491*
- Beet Dip with Yogurt and Tahini, 498, *499*
- Biscuit Crackers with Red Lentil Dip, *496,* 497
- Bouyourdi (Spicy Greek Baked Feta), 490, *491*
- Buffalo Cauliflower Bites, 504–5
- Calabrian Chile Dipping Sauce, 512
- Carrot-Tamarind Chutney, 516
- Chaat Masala Peanuts, 485
- Chickpea Fries, *511,* 511–12
- Classic Guacamole, 492, *492,* 493
- Corn Cheese, 498–99, *499*
- Cranberry and Goat Cheese Crostini, 504, *505*
- Fattet Hummus (Crispy Pita with Garlicky Yogurt and Chickpeas), 494–95, *495*
- Fava Bean Crostini with Manchego and Pine Nuts, 503–4
- Fresh Leek and Spinach Dip, *500,* 500–501
- Frico, 489
- Garam Masala, 485
- Garam Masala Peanuts, 484, *484*
- Homemade Yogurt, 486, *487*
- Honey and Spice Dipping Sauce, 512
- Hummus with Crispy Mushrooms and Sumac, 493
- Labneh, 487
- Lemon and Herb Dipping Sauce, 512

Appetizers (cont.)

- Lemon-Dill Labneh, 487
- Marinated Manchego, 485–86
- No-Fuss
  - Blistered Shishito Peppers, 520
  - Buttered Popcorn, about, 520
  - Buttered Popcorn, Cajun-Spiced, 520
  - Buttered Popcorn, Garlic and Herb, 520
  - Buttered Popcorn, Hot and Sweet, 520
  - Buttered Popcorn, Parmesan-Pepper, 520
  - Melted Brie with Honey and Herbs, 521
  - Sun-Dried Tomato Tapenade with Farmer's Cheese, 521
- Pa amb Tomàquet (Catalan Tomato Bread), 502–3, *503*
- Pakoras (South Asian Spiced Vegetable Fritters), 516
- Pan-Seared Halloumi with Cherry Pepper Glaze, 490
- Parmesan–Black Pepper Cheese Straws, 502
- Patatas Bravas, *508,* 509–10
- Plum Sauce, 515, *515*
- Portobello Mushroom Fries with Cherry Pepper Sauce, *507,* 507–9, *509*
- Scallion Pancakes, *7,* 512–13, *513*
- Sesame Balls, *518,* 519, *519*
- Slow-Roasted Eggplant Dip with Pomegranate Molasses and Aleppo Pepper, 499
- Southern Cheese Straws, 501–2, *502*
- Spring Rolls (Cantonese Egg Rolls), *514,* 514–15
- Sweet Potato Fritters with Cheddar and Chipotle, 517
- Sweet Potato Fritters with Feta, Dill, and Cilantro, 517, *517*
- Ultracreamy Hummus, 494, *495*
- Vegan Mayonnaise, 506
- Vegan Ranch Dressing, 506
- Warm Marinated Olives, *484,* 485
- Whipped Feta and Roasted Red Pepper Dip, 489
- Whipped Feta Dip, 489
- Whipped Feta Dip with Dill and Parsley, *488,* 489
- Zucchini Chips with Tzatziki, 510, *511*

Apple(s)

- Butternut Squash and Apple Fattoush, *130,* 131
- –Celery Root Salad, 110
- Chile-Spiced Crumbled Tofu with Pineapple Salsa, *14,* 420–21, *421*
- Fennel-Apple Tarte Tatin, 261–62
- Napa Cabbage Slaw with Apple and Walnuts, 116

Argentine Cheese-Stuffed Pizza (Fugazzeta), 235–36, *237*

Armenian Yogurt and Barley Soup (Tanabour), *166,* 166–67
Arroz Con Titoté (Colombian Coconut Rice), 342–43, *343*
Artichoke(s)
Garlicky Spaghetti with Artichokes and Hazelnuts, 273
Neapolitan-Style Pizza with Artichoke Hearts and Fontina, 231
Roasted Artichokes, 528–29
Roasted Artichokes with Lemon Vinaigrette, 529
Spinach-Artichoke Macaroni and Cheese, 277
Asparagus
about, 26, *26*
Braised Asparagus with Lemon and Chives, *528,* 529–30
Braised Asparagus with Orange and Tarragon, 530
Braised Asparagus with Sherry Vinegar and Marjoram, 530
Farro Salad with Asparagus, Radishes, and Parmesan, 128, *129*
Marinated Bean and Asparagus Salad with Preserved Lemon Dressing, *99,* 99–100
Quiche, Leek, and Goat Cheese, *474,* 475–76
Sautéed Fava Beans, Asparagus, and Leek, 384, *384,* 385, *385*
Stir-Fried Asparagus with Shiitake Mushrooms, 43
Whole-Wheat Crepes with Creamy Sautéed Mushrooms and Asparagus, *244,* 245
Australian Folded Eggs, 454–55, *455*
Avocado(s)
about, 26, *26,* 113, *113,* 492, *492*
Arepas, Tomato, and Bell Pepper, 200
Broccoli Salad with Avocado Dressing, 103–4, *105*
Cauliflower Rice Bowls with Sweet Potatoes, Avocados, and Chickpeas, 81–82, *83*
Classic Guacamole, 492, *492,* 493
Creamy Avocado Dressing, 139
Crema, 193, *193*
and Cucumber Salad with Sriracha Mayo, *112,* 112–13, *113*
Egg, Kimchi, and Avocado Sandwiches, 477, *477*
Spicy Avocado–Sour Cream Sauce, 527
Toast, 238

B

Baharat, 57
Baharat Cauliflower and Eggplant with Chickpeas, 57
Baja-Style Cauliflower Tacos, 191
Baked Pimento Cheese Dip, 491, *491*
Baked Pumpkin Kibbeh, 62
Barley
Beet and Barley Risotto, 348, *349*
California Barley Bowls with Lemon-Yogurt Sauce, *346,* 346–47
with Celery and Miso Dressing, 347
with Fennel, Dried Apricots, and Orange, 347
with Lemon and Herbs, 347
Barley (cont.)
and Lentils with Mushrooms and Tahini-Yogurt Sauce, 348–49, *349*
Tanabour (Armenian Yogurt and Barley Soup), *166,* 166–67
Basic Farro, 128
Basil
-Caper Mayonnaise, 218
Frittata Bites with Peas, Goat Cheese, and Basil, 475
Grilled Corn with Basil-Lemon Butter, 546–49
Grilled Peach and Tomato Salad with Burrata and Basil, *135,* 135–36
-Lemon Flavored Butter, 545
Lemon-Pickled Radish Toast with Basil and Parmesan, *238,* 238–39
Pesto alla Genovese (Basil Pesto), 268
Quinoa Bowls with Snap Peas, Strawberries, and Basil Vinaigrette, *356,* 357
Sautéed Corn with Cherry Tomatoes, Ricotta Salata, and Basil, *544,* 545
Spicy Basil Noodles with Crispy Tofu, Snap Peas, and Bell Pepper, 314, *315*
Basmati Rice
Pilaf with Peas, Scallions, and Lemon, 329
Pilaf with Whole Spices, 328
Basque-Style Herb Sauce (Tximitxurri), 572
Bean(s). *see also* Black Bean(s); Chickpea(s); Lentil(s); Red Lentil(s); White Bean(s)
about dried beans, *402,* 402–3, *403*
Bourguignon, 373
Breakfast Burritos with Poblano, Beans, Corn, and Crispy Potatoes, *478,* 479–80, *480*
Cacio e Pepe Beans with Squash, Sage, and Walnuts, *372,* 372–73
Edamame Salad with Mint and Parmesan, 386, *386*
Fava Bean Crostini with Manchego and Pine Nuts, 503–4
Gallo Pinto (Costa Rican Beans and Rice), 390, *390,* 391
Gigantes Plaki, 374, *375*
Marinated Bean and Asparagus Salad with Preserved Lemon Dressing, *99,* 99–100
Orecchiette and Navy Beans with Brussels Sprouts and Spicy Mustard Crumbs, 289–90
Paella de Verduras (Cauliflower and Bean Paella), 334
Pinto
–Beet Burgers, 186, *186,* 187
Breakfast Tacos with Pinto Beans and Cotija Cheese, 478, *478*
Gallo Pinto (Costa Rican Beans and Rice), 390, *390,* 391
Swiss Chard, Pinto Bean, and Monterey Jack Enchiladas, 67–68
Ribollita, *162,* 162–63
Sautéed Fava Beans, Asparagus, and Leek, 384, *384,* 385, *385*
Skillet Rice and Beans with Corn and Fresh Tomatoes, 387–88
Stewed Cranberry Beans with Tomatoes and Sage, 377
Tacu Tacu with Salsa Criolla, 388–89, *389*
Three-Bean Salad, 114–15, *115*
Tortellini Salad with Broccoli, Cannellini Beans, and Olive–Banana Pepper Dressing, *302,* 302–3
Vegetarian Refried Beans, 465

Beet(s)
and Barley Risotto, 348, *349*
Dip with Yogurt and Tahini, 498, *499*
Farfalle with Beets, Arugula, and Blue Cheese, *288,* 289
Pan-Seared Beets with Horseradish Cream, 530, *531*
Pinto Bean–Beet Burgers, 186, *186,* 187
Poke Bowls, *80,* 81
Quick-Cooking Beets, 103
Salad with Blue Cheese and Endive, 103
Salad with Spiced Yogurt and Watercress, 100–103, *102*
Tartines, Orange, and Chèvre, 206, *207*
Bell Pepper(s) and Red Pepper(s)
about, 27, *27*
Avocado, Tomato, and Bell Pepper Arepas, 200
Hasselback Eggplant with Muhammara, 41
Savory Dutch Baby with Portobellos, Roasted Red Peppers, Walnuts, and Feta, *64,* 65
Spicy Basil Noodles with Crispy Tofu, Snap Peas, and Bell Pepper, 314, *315*
Berbere and Yogurt-Tahini Sauce, Whole Romanesco with, 42, *43*
Berry(ies)
Oat Berry Pilaf with Walnuts and Gorgonzola, 356
Quinoa Bowls with Snap Peas, Strawberries, and Basil Vinaigrette, *356,* 357
Raspberry Vinaigrette, 138
Wild Rice Pilaf with Pecans and Cranberries, 344, *345*
Best Baked Potatoes, 563, *563*
Best Baked Sweet Potatoes, *573,* 573–74
Best Vegetarian Chili, 172–73, *173*
Better Hash Browns, *568,* 569
Biscuit Crackers with Red Lentil Dip, *496,* 497
Biscuits with Creamy Tomato Gravy and Fried Eggs, *460,* 460–61
Bitter Greens, Carrot, and Chickpea Salad with Warm Lemon Dressing, 98, *99*
Black Bean(s)
Burgers, *182,* 183–84
and Cheese Arepas, 199–200, *201*
Chili, 173–74, *174*
Cuban-Style Black Beans and Rice, *386,* 387
Eggplant with Black Bean Sauce, *14, 44,* 45
Kale and Black Bean Breakfast Burritos, 479, *480*
Quinoa, Black Bean, and Mango Salad with Lime Dressing, 357–58, *358*
Sheet Pan Black Bean and Jalapeño Quesadillas, 194
and Sweet Potato Tacos, *192,* 193
Tacos, Sweet Potato, and Poblano, 193
Blistered Shishito Peppers, 520
Blue Cheese
Beet Salad with Blue Cheese and Endive, 103
Celery Root Galette with Blue Cheese and Walnuts, *256,* 256–57
Farfalle with Beets, Arugula, and Blue Cheese, *288,* 289
Boiled Carrots
with Cumin, Lime, and Cilantro, 537
with Fennel Seeds and Citrus, 537
with Lemon and Chives, 536–37
with Mint and Paprika, 537
Bok Choy
about, 27, *27*
Baby Bok Choy with Ginger and Garlic, 530–31, *531*
Garlicky Fried Rice with Bok Choy, 336, *336,* 337
Shiitake and Bok Choy Lo Mein, 310
Stir-Fried Tofu and Bok Choy, 422, *423*
Bourguignon, Bean, 373
Bouyourdi (Spicy Greek Baked Feta), 490, *491*
Bowls
about combinations for, 21, *21*
Beet Poke Bowls, *80,* 81
California Barley Bowls with Lemon-Yogurt Sauce, *346,* 346–47
Cauliflower Rice Bowls with Sweet Potatoes, Avocados, and Chickpeas, 81–82, *83*
Hearty Vegetable and Farro Bowls with Goat Cheese, 85
Quinoa Bowls with Snap Peas, Strawberries, and Basil Vinaigrette, *356,* 357
Rainbow Bowls with Crispy Tempeh, 86, *87*
Roasted Tofu and Sweet Potato Bowls with Snap Pea Salad, *84,* 85–86
Roasted Vegetable Bowls with Bulgur, White Beans, and Arugula, 84, *84*
Spring Freekeh and Halloumi Bowls, *352,* 353–54
Tofu Sushi Bowls, 410
Vegetable Bibimbap with Tempeh, 334–35, *335*
Braised Asparagus
with Lemon and Chives, *528,* 529–30
with Orange and Tarragon, 530
with Sherry Vinegar and Marjoram, 530
Braised Eggplant with Paprika, Coriander, and Yogurt, *550,* 550–51
Braised Eggplant with Soy, Garlic, and Ginger, 551
Braised Red Potatoes
with Dijon and Tarragon, 566
with Lemon and Chives, *564,* 565
with Miso and Scallions, 566
Braised Vidalia Onions with Chile, Lime, and Cilantro, *560,* 561
Braised Vidalia Onions with Honey, Lemon, and Oregano, 561
Breads, Tarts, and Pies (Savory). *see also* Pizza
Alu Parathas (Punjabi Potato-Stuffed Griddle Breads), 240–42, *243*
Avocado Toast, 238
Butternut Squash Galette with Gruyère, 255
Caramelized Onion, Tomato, and Goat Cheese Tart, 258, *259*
Caramelized Onions, 259
Cauliflower Chickpea Flatbread with Romesco, 246–47, *247*
Celery Root Galette with Blue Cheese and Walnuts, *256,* 256–57
Eggplant and Tomato Phyllo Pie, 252–54
Fennel-Apple Tarte Tatin, 261–62
Flatbreads with Fontina, Mushrooms, and Chives, 246, *247*

Breads, Tarts, and Pies (Savory). ***see also*** **Pizza (cont.)**
Focaccia di Recco, 236–37, *237*
Kol Böreği (Spiraled Spinach and Cheese Pastry), 262–63, *263*
Lemon-Pickled Radish Toast with Basil and Parmesan, *238,* 238–39
Mana'eesh Za'atar (Za'atar Flatbreads), 239–40, *241*
Mushroom and Leek Galette with Gorgonzola, 254–55, *255*
Philadelphia Tomato Pie, 228–29
Ricotta Toast with Pesto di Prezzemolo and Grapes, *238,* 239
Socca with Sautéed Onions and Rosemary, 242–43, *243*
Summer Squash Tart, 258, *259*
Tamatya-Kandyachi Koshimbir (Tomato-Onion Salad), 242
Tourte aux Pommes de Terre (French Potato Pie), 251–52, *253*
Upside-Down Caramelized Shallot and Onion Tart, 247–48, *249*
Upside-Down Tomato Tart, 258–61, *260*
Vidalia Onion Pie, *250,* 251
Whole-Wheat Crepes, 245
Whole-Wheat Crepes with Creamy Sautéed Mushrooms and Asparagus, *244,* 245
Breakfast Burritos with Poblano, Beans, Corn, and Crispy Potatoes, *478,* 479–80, *480*
Breakfast Tacos with Pinto Beans and Cotija Cheese, 478, *478*
Broccoli
about, 27, *27*
Creamy Broccoli Pasta with Crispy Panko, 278–79, *279*
and Feta Frittata, 471
Frittata Bites with Broccoli and Sun-Dried Tomatoes, *474,* 474–75
Lentils with Roasted Broccoli and Lemony Bread Crumbs, *396,* 396–97, *397*
Roasted Broccoli, 531–32
Roasted Broccoli with Olives, Garlic, Oregano, and Lemon, 532
Salad with Avocado Dressing, 103–4, *105*
Tortellini Salad with Broccoli, Cannellini Beans, and Olive-Banana Pepper Dressing, *302,* 302–3
Broccolini, about, 429, *429*
Broccoli Rabe and Farro Gratin, *70,* 70–71
Broiled Broccoli Rabe, 532
Broiled Smashed Zucchini with Garlicky Yogurt, 580, *580, 581*
Broiled Smashed Zucchini with Herbed Sour Cream, 580
Brussels Sprout(s)
about, 28, *28*
Brussels Sprout Hash with Poached Eggs, 480–81, *481*
Charred Shaved Brussels Sprout Salad with Apricot Dressing, 107
Charred Shaved Brussels Sprout Salad with Sherry-Honey Dressing, 107
Charred Shaved Brussels Sprout Salad with Sweet Chili-Lime Dressing, 106–7
Fried Brussels Sprouts with Lemon-Chive Dipping Sauce, 535
Fried Brussels Sprouts with Sriracha Dipping Sauce, 534, *534*
Orecchiette and Navy Beans with Brussels Sprouts and Spicy Mustard Crumbs, 289–90
Skillet-Roasted Brussels Sprouts with Cider Vinegar and Honey, 532–33, *533*

Brussels Sprout(s) (cont.)
Skillet-Roasted Brussels Sprouts with Maple Syrup and Smoked Almonds, 533
Skillet-Roasted Brussels Sprouts with Pomegranate and Pistachios, 533
Buffalo Cauliflower Bites, 504–5
Buffalo Cucumber Salad, 111, *111*
Bulgur
Red Lentil Kibbeh, 399
Roasted Vegetable Bowls with Bulgur, White Beans, and Arugula, 84, *84*
Salad with Curry Roasted Sweet Potatoes and Chickpeas, 126
Tomato, Bulgur, and Red Pepper Soup, 167–68
Turkish Bulgur and Lentil Soup, *166,* 167
with Vegetables and Marinated Tofu, 428, *429*
Burgers
Black Bean Burgers, *182,* 183–84
Classic Burger Sauce, 184
Curried Millet Burgers with Peach-Ginger Chutney, 188–89, *189*
Pinto Bean-Beet Burgers, 186, *186,* 187
Quinoa Burgers with Spinach, Sun-Dried Tomatoes, and Marinated Feta, 187–88, *189*
Ultimate Veggie Burgers, *7, 182,* 182–83
Burrata
Grilled Peach and Tomato Salad with Burrata and Basil, *135,* 135–36
Rigatoni with Marinated Tomatoes and Burrata, 272, *273*
Spicy Chile-Honey Glazed Eggplant with Burrata and Greens, 40, *40*
Burritos
about preparation of, 480, *480*
Breakfast Burritos with Poblano, Beans, Corn, and Crispy Potatoes, *478,* 479–80, *480*
Kale and Black Bean Breakfast Burritos, 479, *480*
Buttered Popcorn
about, 520
Cajun-Spiced Popcorn, 520
Garlic and Herb Popcorn, 520
Hot and Sweet Popcorn, 520
Parmesan-Pepper Popcorn, 520
Butternut Squash
about, 28, *28*
and Apple Fattoush, *130,* 131
Galette with Gruyère, 255
Green Curry with Kale and Butternut Squash, 50, *50, 51*
Roasted Butternut Squash Salad with Creamy Tahini Dressing, 104–5
Steaks with Honey-Nut Topping, 37
Unstuffed Shells with Butternut Squash and Leeks, 297–98, *299*
and White Bean Soup with Sage Pesto, 163–64
Butter-Roasted Carrots with Hazelnut Crumble and Goat Cheese, *537,* 537–38
Butters, Flavored. see Flavored Butters

C

Cabbage. *see also* Napa Cabbage
- about preparing, 28, *28*
- about roasting and flipping, 535, *535*
- Charred Cabbage Salad with Torn Tofu and Plantain Chips, 418–19
- Creamy Mushroom and Pink Pickled Cabbage Sandwiches, 204, *204*, 205
- Curry Roasted Cabbage Wedges with Tomatoes and Chickpeas, *36*, 36–37
- Egg, Kimchi, and Avocado Sandwiches, 477, *477*
- Hearty Cabbage Soup, 151, *151*
- Kimchi and Tofu Soup, 153
- Panko-Crusted Tofu with Cabbage Salad, *424*, 424–25
- Pittsburgh-Style Haluski, *318*, 319
- Potato-Sauerkraut Pierogi, 323
- Red Cabbage and Grapefruit Salad, 132, *132*, *133*
- Roasted Cabbage, *534*, 535, *535*
- Roasted Cabbage with Bread Crumbs, Sage, and Parmesan, 535
- Roasted Cabbage with Gochujang, Sesame, and Scallions, 535
- Sauerkraut, 446, *446*
- Su Shui Jiao (Northern Chinese–Style Cabbage and Mushroom Dumplings), *323*, 323–25

Cacio e Pepe Beans with Squash, Sage, and Walnuts, *372*, 372–73

Cajun-Spiced Popcorn, 520

Calabrian Chile Dipping Sauce, 512

Calabrian Chile White Beans with Almond Romesco, 374–75, *375*

California Barley Bowls with Lemon-Yogurt Sauce, *346*, 346–47

Cantaloupe Salad with Olives and Red Onion, 132–33

Cantonese Egg Rolls (Spring Rolls), *514*, 514–15

Caprese Sheet-Pan Pizza, 226–27, *227*

Carabaccia (Tuscan Onion Soup), *148*, 149

Caramelized Carrot Soup with Coriander-Lemon Browned Butter, 143

Caramelized Onion, Tomato, and Goat Cheese Tart, 258, *259*

Caramelized Onions, 259

Caramelized Plums with Spicy Herb Salad, 134–35, *135*

Caribbean Tofu with Rice and Pigeon Peas, 425–26

Carrot(s)
- about, 29, *29*
- Bitter Greens, Carrot, and Chickpea Salad with Warm Lemon Dressing, 98, *99*
- Boiled
  - with Cumin, Lime, and Cilantro, 537
  - with Fennel Seeds and Citrus, 537
  - with Lemon and Chives, 536–37
  - with Mint and Paprika, 537
- Butter-Roasted Carrots with Hazelnut Crumble and Goat Cheese, *537*, 537–38
- Caramelized Carrot Soup with Coriander-Lemon Browned Butter, 143
- Chopped Carrot Salad with Mint, Pistachios, and Pomegranate Seeds, 107, *107*
- Maftoul with Carrots and Chickpeas, 354, *355*

Carrot(s) (cont.)
- Napa Cabbage Slaw with Carrots and Sesame, 115–17, *116*, *117*
- Smoky Carrot Dogs, *190*, 190–91
- Stir-Fried Tempeh, Napa Cabbage, and Carrots, *440*, 440–41
- -Tamarind Chutney, 516

Cashew e Pepe e Funghi, 280–81, *281*

Cast Iron Pan Pizza, *224*, 225–26

Cast Iron–Seared Romaine with Oyster Sauce, Ginger, and Sesame, *120*, 121

Catalan Tomato Bread (Pa amb Tomàquet), 502–3, *503*

Cauliflower
- about, 29, *29*, 38, *38*, 542, *542*
- Baharat Cauliflower and Eggplant with Chickpeas, 57
- Baja-Style Cauliflower Tacos, 191
- Biryani, *332*, 333
- Buffalo Cauliflower Bites, 504–5
- Charred Cauliflower and Crispy Chickpeas with Romesco, *69*, 69–70
- Chickpea Flatbread with Romesco, 246–47, *247*
- Hawaij Cauliflower Soup with Zhoug, 144
- Modern Cauliflower Gratin, *540*, 541–42, *542*
- Paella de Verduras (Cauliflower and Bean Paella), 334
- Rice, 538, *539*
- Rice Bowls with Sweet Potatoes, Avocados, and Chickpeas, 81–82, *83*
- Roasted Cauliflower with Arugula and Pear, *105*, 105–6
- Skillet-Roasted
  - with Capers and Pine Nuts, 541
  - with Cumin and Pistachios, 541
  - with Garlic and Lemon, *540*, 540–41
- Soup, 144–45, *145*
- Steaks with Salsa Verde, 38, *38*
- Whole Pot-Roasted Cauliflower with Tomatoes and Olives, 41–42

Celery
- Barley with Celery and Miso Dressing, 347
- Lao Hu Cai (Tiger Salad), *108*, 109
- Pickled Celery, 179
- Shaved Celery Salad with Pomegranate-Honey Vinaigrette, 109

Celery Root
- about, 29, *29*
- Apple–Celery Root Salad, 110
- Galette with Blue Cheese and Walnuts, *256*, 256–57
- Roasted Celery Root with Chimichurri, 542–43, *543*

Chaat Masala Peanuts, 485

Chana Masala, 380, *381*

Chapati (Whole-Wheat Wraps), 213

Charred Cabbage Salad with Torn Tofu and Plantain Chips, 418–19

Charred Cauliflower and Crispy Chickpeas with Romesco, *69*, 69–70

Charred Poblano Strips with Cream and Corn (Rajas Poblanas con Crema y Elote), 562

Charred Poblano Strips with Cream (Rajas Poblanas con Crema), 561–62

Charred Shaved Brussels Sprout Salad
with Apricot Dressing, 107
with Sherry-Honey Dressing, 107
with Sweet Chili-Lime Dressing, 106–7
Cheddar-Crusted Grilled Cheese, 200–201
Cheddar-Crusted Grilled Cheese with Tomato, 201, *201*
Cheddar Scalloped Potatoes, 567–68
Cheese. *see also* Feta Cheese; Goat Cheese
Baked Pimento Cheese Dip, 491, *491*
Beet, Orange, and Chèvre Tartines, 206, *207*
Black Bean and Cheese Arepas, 199–200, *201*
Blue
Beet Salad with Blue Cheese and Endive, 103
Celery Root Galette with Blue Cheese and Walnuts, *256,* 256–57
Farfalle with Beets, Arugula, and Blue Cheese, *288,* 289
Breakfast Tacos with Pinto Beans and Cotija Cheese, 478, *478*
Burrata
Grilled Peach and Tomato Salad with Burrata and Basil, *135,* 135–36
Rigatoni with Marinated Tomatoes and Burrata, 272, *273*
Spicy Chile-Honey Glazed Eggplant with Burrata and Greens, 40, *40*
Butternut Squash Galette with Gruyère, 255
Cheddar-Crusted Grilled Cheese, 200–201
Cheddar-Crusted Grilled Cheese with Tomato, 201, *201*
Cheesy Stuffed Shells, *296,* 297
Cheesy Tomato and Bean Bake, 65–66, *66*
Corn Cheese, 498–99, *499*
Family-Size Spinach and Herb Cream Cheese Omelet with Home Fries, 466–67, *467*
Fava Bean Crostini with Manchego and Pine Nuts, 503–4
Frico
recipe for, 489
Three-Cheese Potato Frico, 562
White Bean and Arugula Salad with Frico Crumble, 100, *101*
Fugazzeta (Argentine Cheese-Stuffed Pizza), 235–36, *237*
Grown-Up Stovetop Macaroni and Cheese, 275
Kol Böreği (Spiraled Spinach and Cheese Pastry), 262–63, *263*
Make-Ahead Cheese Soufflés, 458–59, *459*
Marinated Manchego, 485–86
Parmesan–Black Pepper Cheese Straws, 502
Pasta Cacio e Uova (Pasta with Cheese and Eggs), 278
Pupusas, 197–99, *199*
Ravioli with Pumpkin Cream Sauce, 298, *299*
Ricotta Toast with Pesto di Prezzemolo and Grapes, *238,* 239
Sautéed Corn with Cherry Tomatoes, Ricotta Salata, and Basil, *544,* 545
Scrambled Eggs with Shiitake Mushrooms and Feta Cheese, 453
Sheet Pan Cheese Quesadillas, 194, *194, 195*
Simple Stovetop Macaroni and Cheese, *274,* 275
Cheese. *see also* Feta Cheese; Goat Cheese (cont.)
Southern Cheese Straws, 501–2, *502*
Spinach and Ricotta Gnudi with Tomato-Butter Sauce, *308,* 308–9
Spinach-Artichoke Macaroni and Cheese, 277
Summer Squash Pasta with Ricotta and Lemon-Parmesan Bread Crumbs, 284, *285*
Sun-Dried Tomato Tapenade with Farmer's Cheese, 521
Three-Cheese Ravioli with Browned Butter–Pine Nut Sauce, 299–301, *301*
Cherries, Dried, Wheat Berry Salad with Radicchio, and Pecans, 125
Cherry Tomato Salad with Pita Crisps and Spicy Citrus Dressing, 123, *123*
Chèvre Tartines, Beet, Orange, and, 206, *207*
Chickpea(s)
Baharat Cauliflower and Eggplant with Chickpeas, 57
Bitter Greens, Carrot, and Chickpea Salad with Warm Lemon Dressing, 98, *99*
Bouillabaisse, 378–80
Bulgur Salad with Curry Roasted Sweet Potatoes and Chickpeas, 126
Cauliflower Chickpea Flatbread with Romesco, 246–47, *247*
Cauliflower Rice Bowls with Sweet Potatoes, Avocados, and Chickpeas, 81–82, *83*
Charred Cauliflower and Crispy Chickpeas with Romesco, *69,* 69–70
Creamy Chickpea and Sweet Potato Stew, 170, *170*
Creamy Polenta with Fennel and Chickpeas, 360–63, *361*
Crispy Chickpea Cakes with Zucchini Ribbon Salad, *383,* 383–84
Curry, 382
Curry Roasted Cabbage Wedges with Tomatoes and Chickpeas, *36,* 36–37
Espinacas con Garbanzos (Andalusian Spinach and Chickpeas), 382–83
Fattet Hummus (Crispy Pita with Garlicky Yogurt and Chickpeas), 494–95, *495*
Fideos with Chickpeas, Fennel, and Kale, 294
Fregula with Chickpeas, Tomatoes, and Fennel, *291,* 291–92
Fries, *511,* 511–12
Harira (Moroccan Lentil and Chickpea Soup), 168
Hearty Green Salad with Chickpeas, Pickled Cauliflower, and Seared Halloumi, 97–98
Jackfruit and Chickpea Makhani, 378, *379*
Maftoul with Carrots and Chickpeas, 354, *355*
Meatless "Meat" Sauce with Chickpeas and Mushrooms, 292, *293*
Noodle Soup, 169, *169*
Pasta e Ceci (Pasta with Chickpeas), 290–91, *291*
Pita Salad with Za'atar Tofu and Chickpeas, 418, *419*
and Poblano Quesadillas, *196,* 197
Shakshuka, 464
Skillet Rice and Chickpeas with Coconut Milk, 388
Spanish-Style Skillet Rice and Chickpeas, 388
Spiced Roasted Chickpeas, 82, *83*

Chickpea(s) (cont.)
Spiced Smashed Chickpea Wraps, 211, *211*
Stuffed Peppers with Chickpeas, Goat Cheese, and Herbs, *74,* 75
Tofu and Chickpea Flour Frittata with Mushrooms, 434–35, *435*
Chile(s)
about, 29, *29*
Braised Vidalia Onions with Chile, Lime, and Cilantro, *560,* 561
Calabrian Chile Dipping Sauce, 512
Calabrian Chile White Beans with Almond Romesco, 374–75, *375*
-Coriander Sauce, 524
Rellenos, 75–77, *76, 77*
-Spiced Crumbled Tofu with Pineapple Salsa, *14,* 420–21, *421*
Spicy Chile-Honey Glazed Eggplant with Burrata and Greens, *12,* 40, *40*
Tomato-Chile Sauce, 216, *216*
Chili
Best Vegetarian Chili, 172–73, *173*
Black Bean Chili, 173–74, *174*
Roasted Poblano and White Bean Chili, *174,* 175
Chili Crisp Dumpling Sauce, 325
Chili-Lime Salt, 544
Chilled Peach and Cucumber Soup, 156, *157*
Chilled Sesame Noodles (Liang Mian), *317,* 317–18
Chilled Soba Noodles with Cucumber, Snow Peas, and Radishes, *318,* 318–19
Chinese Stir-Fried Tomatoes and Eggs (Xīhóngshì Chao Jīdàn), *452,* 453
Chipotle(s)
Cilantro-Chipotle Flavored Butter, 545
Creamy Chipotle Sauce, 218
Lentil-Stuffed Sweet Potatoes, 78, *79*
Mashed Sweet Potatoes with Chipotle and Lime, 575
Sweet Potato Fritters with Cheddar and Chipotle, 517
Chopped Carrot Salad with Mint, Pistachios, and Pomegranate Seeds, 107, *107*
Chopped Vegetable and Stone Fruit Salad, *15,* 126, *127*
Cilantro. *see also* Coriander
Boiled Carrots with Cumin, Lime, and Cilantro, 537
Braised Vidalia Onions with Chile, Lime, and Cilantro, *560,* 561
-Chipotle Flavored Butter, 545
Crema, 191, *191*
-Mint Chutney, 213
Sweet Potato Fritters with Feta, Dill, and Cilantro, 517, *517*
Wild Rice Pilaf with Scallions, Cilantro, and Almonds, 344
Citrus
cutting, 132, *132* (*see also* Lemon(s); Orange(s))
Red Cabbage and Grapefruit Salad, 132, *133*
Çılbır (Eggs with Yogurt and Spiced Butter), 457–58, *459*
Classic Burger Sauce, 184
Classic Croutons, 178
Classic Guacamole, 492, *492,* 493
Classic Minestrone, 161, *161*
Classic Vegetable Broth, 176
Cobb Salad, *96,* 97
Coconut
Arroz con Titoté (Colombian Coconut Rice), 342–43, *343*
Creamed Corn, 546
Creamed Corn with Ginger and Crispy Shallots, 546, *547*
Crispy Coconut Rice and Pigeon Peas with Tropical Fruit, *392,* 393
East African Tofu and Coconut Curry, 426–27, *427*
Hung Kao Mun Gati (Thai Coconut Rice), 342, *343*
Lemongrass-Coconut Soup with Oyster Mushrooms, 154–55, *155*
Roasted Kale with Coriander, Ginger, and Coconut, 556
Skillet Rice and Chickpeas with Coconut Milk, 388
Sweet and Spicy Glazed Tofu with Coconut-Braised Mustard Greens and Winter Squash, *424,* 425
Coddled Eggs, *456,* 457
Coleslaw Potato Salad, 116–17
Collard Greens, about, 31, *31*
Collard Greens, Quick, 543
Colombian Coconut Rice (Arroz con Titoté), 342–43, *343*
Cơm Đỏ (Vietnamese Red Rice), 341–42
Congee, 343–44
Coriander
about, 390, *390*
Braised Eggplant with Paprika, Coriander, and Yogurt, *550,* 550–51
Caramelized Carrot Soup with Coriander-Lemon Browned Butter, 143
Chile-Coriander Sauce, 524
Roasted Kale with Coriander, Ginger, and Coconut, 556
Sugar Snap Peas with Almonds, Coriander, and Orange Zest, 572
Corn. *see also* Buttered Popcorn; Polenta
about, 30, *30*
Breakfast Burritos with Poblano, Beans, Corn, and Crispy Potatoes, *478,* 479–80, *480*
Cheese, 498–99, *499*
Coconut Creamed Corn, 546
Coconut Creamed Corn with Ginger and Crispy Shallots, 546, *547*
Esquites (Mexican Corn Salad), 110
Foolproof Boiled Corn, 544, *544*
Grilled Corn with Basil-Lemon Butter, 546–49
Grits with Fresh Corn, 364
Pasta with Creamy Lemon–Sichuan Peppercorn Sauce, *276,* 277–78
Pizza, Tomato, and Arugula, *228,* 229
Rajas Poblanas con Crema y Elote (Charred Poblano Strips with Cream and Corn), 562
Risotto, 340, *340,* 341
Sautéed Corn with Cherry Tomatoes, Ricotta Salata, and Basil, *544,* 545
Skillet Rice and Beans with Corn and Fresh Tomatoes, 387–88
Teff-Stuffed Acorn Squash with Lime Crema and Roasted Pepitas, 71–72
Thai-Spiced Red Lentil Stew with Spinach and Corn, 171
Tomato and Corn Tostadas with Baked Eggs, 464–65, *465*

Costa Rican Beans and Rice (Gallo Pinto), 390, *390,* 391
Cranberries, Wild Rice Pilaf with Pecans and, 344, *345*
Cranberry and Goat Cheese Crostini, 504, *505*
Creamy, Spicy Rotini and Red Lentils with Tomatoes and Goat Cheese, 290
Creamy Broccoli Pasta with Crispy Panko, 278–79, *279*
Creamy Chickpea and Sweet Potato Stew, 170, *170*
Creamy Chipotle Sauce (sandwich spread), 218
Creamy Egg Topping, 563
Creamy Flavors, about, 10
Creamy French-Style Scrambled Eggs, 452, *452*
Creamy Mushroom and Pink Pickled Cabbage Sandwiches, 204, *204,* 205
Creamy Polenta with Fennel and Chickpeas, 360–63, *361*
Creamy Polenta with Radicchio Agrodolce, *362,* 363
Creamy Potatoes and Leeks, 566, *567*
Creamy White Bean Soup with Herb Oil and Crispy Capers, *158,* 159
Crispy and Creamy Kale Salad, 93–94, 95, *95*
Crispy and Crunchy Foods, about, 10
Crispy Chickpea Cakes with Zucchini Ribbon Salad, *383,* 383–84
Crispy Coconut Rice and Pigeon Peas with Tropical Fruit, *392,* 393
Crispy Gnocchi with Shredded Brussels Sprouts and Gorgonzola, 303
Crispy Onions, 394
Crispy Pita with Garlicky Yogurt and Chickpeas (Fattet Hummus), 494–95, *495*
Crispy Tempeh, 436
Crispy Tempeh with Sambal Sauce, 436–37
Crispy Tofu
- and Kale Salad with Miso-Ginger Dressing, *416,* 417
- recipe for, 407
- Salad with Cherry Tomatoes, 417
- Spicy Basil Noodles with Crispy Tofu, Snap Peas, and Bell Pepper, 314, *315*
- Teriyaki, *421,* 421–22

Crunchy Oil-Cured Olives, 552
Cuban-Style Black Beans and Rice, *386,* 387
Cucumber(s)
- about, 30, *30,* 548, *548*
- Avocado and Cucumber Salad with Sriracha Mayo, *112,* 112–13, *113*
- Buffalo Cucumber Salad, 111, *111*
- Chilled Peach and Cucumber Soup, 156, *157*
- Chilled Soba Noodles with Cucumber, Snow Peas, and Radishes, *318,* 318–19
- Pai Huang Gua (Smashed Cucumbers), 548, *548,* 549

Curried Fonio with Roasted Vegetables and Hibiscus Vinaigrette, *352,* 352–53
Curried Millet Burgers with Peach-Ginger Chutney, 188–89, *189*
Curry Roasted Cabbage Wedges with Tomatoes and Chickpeas, *36,* 36–37
Cutty's-Inspired Eggplant Spuckie, 205–6

D

Delicata Squash, Roasted, 572, *573*
Delicata Squash, Stuffed, 72, *73*
Di San Xian (Stir-Fried Three Treasures), 45–46, *46*
Dressings and Vinaigrettes
- about, 21, 138
- Creamless Creamy Roasted Red Pepper and Tahini Dressing, 139
- Creamy Avocado Dressing, 139
- Creamy Tahini Dressing, Roasted Butternut Squash Salad with, 104–5
- Hibiscus Vinaigrette, 353
- Leeks Vinaigrette, 556, *557*
- Make-Ahead Balsamic-Fennel Vinaigrette, 138
- Make-Ahead Sherry-Shallot Vinaigrette, 138
- Orange-Ginger Vinaigrette, 86, *86*
- Orange-Honey Dressing, 551
- Preserved Lemon Dressing, Marinated Bean and Asparagus Salad with, *99,* 99–100
- Raspberry Vinaigrette, 138
- Sesame-Scallion Vinaigrette, 139
- Sweet Chili-Lime Dressing, Charred Shaved Brussels Sprout Salad with, 106–7
- Vegan Ranch Dressing, 506
- Warm Lemon Dressing, Bitter Greens, Carrot, and Chickpea Salad with, 98, *99*

Dried Beans, *402,* 402–3, *403*. *see also* Bean(s)
Drizzles, about, 17. *see also* Dressings and Vinaigrettes; Sauces; Toppings for Vegetable Dishes
Dukkah, 89

E

Easiest Salad, Ever, 92, *92*
East African Tofu and Coconut Curry, 426–27, *427*
Easy Baked Brown Rice, 366
Easy Baked White Rice, 366
Easy Cheddar Omelet, 466
Easy Feta and Dill Omelet, 466
Easy Homemade Mayonnaise
- about, 218
- Basil-Caper Mayonnaise, 218
- Lemon-Dill Mayonnaise, 218
- Spicy Sriracha-Lime Mayonnaise, 218

Easy Mexican Rice, *328,* 329
Easy-Peel Hard-Cooked Eggs, 450
Easy Tex-Mex Omelet, 466
Edamame Salad with Mint and Parmesan, 386, *386*

Eggplant
about, 44, *44*
Baharat Cauliflower and Eggplant with Chickpeas, 57
with Black Bean Sauce, *14, 44,* 45
Braised Eggplant with Paprika, Coriander, and Yogurt, *550,* 550–51
Braised Eggplant with Soy, Garlic, and Ginger, 551
Cutty's-Inspired Eggplant Spuckie, 205–6
Hasselback Eggplant with Muhammara, 41
Involtini, 72–75, *74*
Linguine with Sun-Dried Tomato and Eggplant Sauce, *274,* 274–75
Marinated Eggplant with Capers and Mint, 549–50
Parmesan, 60–62, *61*
Sautéed Eggplant with Polenta, 49–50
Silky Roasted Eggplant with Tomato and Feta, 55–56, *56*
Slow-Roasted Eggplant Dip with Pomegranate Molasses and Aleppo Pepper, 499
Spiced Eggplant and Kale Soup, *152,* 153
Spicy Chile-Honey Glazed Eggplant with Burrata and Greens, *12,* 40, *40*
and Tomato Phyllo Pie, 252–54
Walkaway Ratatouille, 58, *59*
Egg(s). ***see also*** **Frittata; Omelet(s)**
about poaching, 461, *461*
Asparagus, Leek, and Goat Cheese Quiche, *474,* 475–76
Australian Folded Eggs, 454–55, *455*
Biscuits with Creamy Tomato Gravy and Fried Eggs, *460,* 460–61
Brussels Sprout Hash with Poached Eggs, 480–81, *481*
Chickpea Shakshuka, 464
Çılbır (Eggs with Yogurt and Spiced Butter), 457–58, *459*
Coddled Eggs, *456,* 457
Creamy Egg Topping, 563
Creamy French-Style Scrambled Eggs, 452, *452*
Easy-Peel Hard-Cooked Eggs, 450
Fried Egg Sandwiches with Hummus and Sprouts, 476
Green Shakshuka, 462, 463, *463*
Jammy Eggs, 450
Menemen (Turkish Scrambled Eggs with Vegetables), 454
Neapolitan-Style Pizza with Mushrooms, Garlic, and Taleggio, 231
Pasta Cacio e Uova (Pasta with Cheese and Eggs), 278
Perfect Fried Eggs, 451
Perfect Poached Eggs, 451
Ramen with Shiitakes and Soft Eggs, 309
Sandwiches, Kimchi, and Avocado, 477, *477*
Scrambled Eggs with Shiitake Mushrooms and Feta Cheese, 453
Shakshuka (Eggs in Spicy Tomato and Roasted Red Pepper Sauce), 461, *461*
Soft-Cooked Eggs, 450
Spring Rolls (Cantonese Egg Rolls), *514,* 514–15
Sweet Potato Noodles with Shiitakes, Spinach, and Eggs (Japchae), 316
Tomato and Corn Tostadas with Baked Eggs, 464–65, *465*
Ultimate Veggie Burgers, *7, 182,* 182–83
Xīhóngshì Chao Jīdàn (Chinese Stir-Fried Tomatoes and Eggs), *452,* 453
Entertaining and Menu Ideas, 22, *23–25,* 24
Espinacas con Garbanzos (Andalusian Spinach and Chickpeas), 382–83
Esquites (Mexican Corn Salad), 110

F

Falafel, 215–16, *217*
Family-Size Spinach and Herb Cream Cheese Omelet with Home Fries, 466–67, *467*
Farfalle with Beets, Arugula, and Blue Cheese, *288,* 289
Farro
Basic Farro, 128
Broccoli Rabe and Farro Gratin, *70,* 70–71
Hearty Vegetable and Farro Bowls with Goat Cheese, 85
Kale and Farro Salad with Fennel, Olives, and Parmesan, 129, *129*
Salad with Asparagus, Radishes, and Parmesan, 128, *129*
with Wild Mushroom Ragout, 349–50
Fastest, Easiest Mashed Potatoes, 565
Fast Tomato Sauces
about, 266
Fresh Tomato Puttanesca Sauce, 266
Fresh Tomato Sauce, 266
No-Cook Fresh Tomato Sauce, 266
Tomato-Browned Butter Sauce, 267
Vodka Sauce, 267
Fattet Hummus (Crispy Pita with Garlicky Yogurt and Chickpeas), 494–95, *495*
Fava Bean(s)
about, 384, *384*
Crostini with Manchego and Pine Nuts, 503–4
Sautéed Fava Beans, Asparagus, and Leek, 384, *384,* 385, *385*
Fennel
about, 30, *30*
-Apple Tarte Tatin, 261–62
Barley with Fennel, Dried Apricots, and Orange, 347
Boiled Carrots with Fennel Seeds and Citrus, 537
Creamy Polenta with Fennel and Chickpeas, 360–63, *361*
Fideos with Chickpeas, Fennel, and Kale, 294
Fregula with Chickpeas, Tomatoes, and Fennel, *291,* 291–92
Kale and Farro Salad with Fennel, Olives, and Parmesan, 129, *129*
Lemony Roasted Radicchio, Fennel, and Root Vegetables, *570,* 570–71
Make-Ahead Balsamic-Fennel Vinaigrette, 138
Roasted Fennel, *550,* 551
Sugar Snap Peas with Pine Nuts, Fennel, and Lemon Zest, 571–72
Feta Cheese
Bouyourdi (Spicy Greek Baked Feta), 490, *491*
Broccoli and Feta Frittata, 471
Easy Feta and Dill Omelet, 466
Herbed Quinoa Cakes with Whipped Feta, *359,* 359–60

Feta Cheese (cont.)
Quinoa Burgers with Spinach, Sun-Dried Tomatoes, and Marinated Feta, 187–88, *189*
Quinoa Lettuce Wraps with Feta and Olives, 358–59, *359*
Savory Dutch Baby with Portobellos, Roasted Red Peppers, Walnuts, and Feta, *64*, 65
Scrambled Eggs with Shiitake Mushrooms and Feta Cheese, 453
Silky Roasted Eggplant with Tomato and Feta, 55–56, *56*
Sweet Potato Fritters with Feta, Dill, and Cilantro, 517, *517*
Whipped Feta and Roasted Red Pepper Dip, 489
Whipped Feta Dip, 489
Whipped Feta Dip with Dill and Parsley, *488*, 489
Fettuccine with Walnut Sauce, 280, *281*
Fideos with Chickpeas, Fennel, and Kale, 294
Fingerling Potato Salad with Sun-Dried Tomato Dressing, 122, *124*
Flatbreads
Cauliflower Chickpea Flatbread with Romesco, 246–47, *247*
with Fontina, Mushrooms, and Chives, 246, *247*
Mana'eesh Za'atar (Za'atar Flatbreads), 239–40, *241*
Flavored Butters
about, 545
Basil-Lemon, 545
Cilantro-Chipotle, 545
Hot Honey, 545
Spicy Old Bay, 545
Focaccia di Recco, 236–37, *237*
Food Scraps, Cooking with, 5
Foolproof Boiled Corn, 544, *544*
Freekeh, Spring, and Halloumi Bowls, *352*, 353–54
Freezing, about, 5, *5*, 6
Fregula with Chickpeas, Tomatoes, and Fennel, *291*, 291–92
French Potato Pie (Tourte aux Pommes de Terre), 251–52, *253*
Fresh Leek and Spinach Dip, *500*, 500–501
Fresh Pasta Without a Machine, *270*, 270–71
Fresh Tomato Puttanesca Sauce, 266
Fresh Tomato Sauce, 266
Frico
recipe for, 489
Three-Cheese Potato Frico, 562
White Bean and Arugula Salad with Frico Crumble, 100, *101*
Fried Brussels Sprouts with Lemon-Chive Dipping Sauce, 535
Fried Brussels Sprouts with Sriracha Dipping Sauce, 534, *534*
Fried Egg Sandwiches with Hummus and Sprouts, 476
Fried Red Tomatoes, 577, *577*
Frittata
Bites with Broccoli and Sun-Dried Tomatoes, *474*, 474–75
Bites with Peas, Goat Cheese, and Basil, 475
Broccoli and Feta Frittata, 471
Pesto Potato Frittata with Peas and Goat Cheese, *470*, 471–72
Tofu and Chickpea Flour Frittata with Mushrooms, 434–35, *435*
Fruit. *see also specific names of fruits*
Crispy Coconut Rice and Pigeon Peas with Tropical Fruit, *392*, 393
Jackfruit and Chickpea Makhani, 378, *379*
produce planning and storage, 4–6, *5*
Quinoa, Black Bean, and Mango Salad with Lime Dressing, *357*, 357–58
Wheat Berry Salad with Radicchio, Dried Cherries, and Pecans, 125
Fugazzeta (Argentine Cheese-Stuffed Pizza), 235–36, *237*

G

Gai Lan with Oyster Sauce, 552
Galette, Butternut Squash, with Gruyère, 255
Galette, Mushroom and Leek, with Gorgonzola, 254–55, *255*
Gallo Pinto (Costa Rican Beans and Rice), 390, *390*, 391
Game Day Gathering (menu), 22
Garam Masala
Garam Masala Peanuts, 484, *484*
Garam Masala Yogurt, 574
recipe for, 485
Garlic
about mincing, 30, *30*
about peeling, 147, *147*
Baby Bok Choy with Ginger and Garlic, 530–31, *531*
Braised Eggplant with Soy, Garlic, and Ginger, 551
Broiled Smashed Zucchini with Garlicky Yogurt, 580, *580*, *581*
and Chive Sour Cream, 574
Fattet Hummus (Crispy Pita with Garlicky Yogurt and Chickpeas), 494–95, *495*
Garlicky Fried Rice with Bok Choy, 336, *336*, 337
Garlicky Spaghetti with Artichokes and Hazelnuts, 273
Garlicky Spaghetti with Green Olives and Almonds, 273
Garlicky Spaghetti with Lemon and Pine Nuts, 272, *273*
Garlicky Tofu Tabbouleh, 419–20
and Herb Popcorn, 520
Honey-Garlic Melting Sweet Potatoes, 575–76
Mashed Sweet Potatoes with Jalapeño, Garlic, and Scallions, 575
Mayonnaise, 468
Microwave-Fried Garlic, 462
Neapolitan-Style Pizza with Mushrooms, Garlic, and Taleggio, 231
Roasted Broccoli with Garlic, 532
Roasted Broccoli with Olives, Garlic, Oregano, and Lemon, 532
Roasted Garlic Soup with Parmesan Croutons, *146*, 147, *147*
Roasted Kale with Garlic, Red Pepper Flakes, and Lemon, *554*, 555–56
San Francisco–Style Garlic Noodles, 312, *312*, 313
Skillet-Roasted Cauliflower with Garlic and Lemon, *540*, 540–41
Stir-Fried Amaranth with Garlic, 528, *528*
Stir-Fried Portobellos with Sweet Chili-Garlic Sauce, 48
Tahini-Garlic Sauce, 354
Torn Potato Salad with Toasted Garlic and Herb Dressing, 121–22
Yogurt Sauce, 37

Garnishes and Toppings
about, 11, 17, 21
Creamy Egg Topping, 563
Garlic, Microwave-Fried, 462
Herbed Goat Cheese Topping, 563
Onions, Caramelized, 259
Onions, Crispy, 394
Shallots, Microwave-Fried, 89
Soups and Stews
about, 178
Croutons, Classic, 178
Croutons, Herbed, 178
Croutons, Umami, 178
grab-and-go toppings, 178
Lemon-Herb Sauce, 179
Pickled Celery, 179
Quick Chili Oil, 179
Spiced Seeds, 179
Tofu Croutons, 178
Vegetable Dishes
Dukkah, 89
Savory Seed Brittle, 88
Shichimi Togarashi, 88
store-bought, 89
Tarragon-Lemon Gremolata, 88
Gazpacho, Quick Food Processor, 155–56
Gigantes Plaki, 374, *375*
Ginger
about, 31, *31*
Baby Bok Choy with Ginger and Garlic, 530–31, *531*
Braised Eggplant with Soy, Garlic, and Ginger, 551
Cast Iron–Seared Romaine with Oyster Sauce, Ginger, and Sesame, *120,* 121
Coconut Creamed Corn with Ginger and Crispy Shallots, 546
Crispy Tofu and Kale Salad and Miso-Ginger Dressing, *416,* 417
Curried Millet Burgers with Peach-Ginger Chutney, 188–89, *189*
Miso-Ginger Sauce, 526
Orange-Ginger Vinaigrette, 86, *86*
Roasted Kale with Coriander, Ginger, and Coconut, 556
Sautéed Mushrooms with Soy, Scallion, and Ginger, 558
Stir-Fried Portobellos with Ginger-Oyster Sauce, 46–48, *47*
Sugar Snap Peas with Sesame, Ginger, and Lemon Zest, 572
Gnocchi à la Parisienne with Arugula, Tomatoes, and Olives, 306, *307*
Gnocchi à la Parisienne with Browned Butter, 306
Gnudi with Tomato-Butter Sauce, Spinach and Ricotta, *308,* 308–9
Goat Cheese
Asparagus, Leek, and Goat Cheese Quiche, *474,* 475–76
Butter-Roasted Carrots with Hazelnut Crumble and Goat Cheese, *537,* 537–38
Caramelized Onion, Tomato, and Goat Cheese Tart, 258, *259*
Cranberry and Goat Cheese Crostini, 504, *505*
Goat Cheese (cont.)
Creamy, Spicy Rotini and Red Lentils with Tomatoes and Goat Cheese, 290
Frittata Bites with Peas, Goat Cheese, and Basil, 475
Hearty Vegetable and Farro Bowls with Goat Cheese, 85
Herbed Goat Cheese Topping, 563
Pesto Potato Frittata with Peas and Goat Cheese, *470,* 471–72
Savory Oatmeal with Peas, Parmesan, and Pepper, 365, *365*
Spinach and Goat Cheese Quesadillas, *195,* 195–96
Stuffed Peppers with Chickpeas, Goat Cheese, and Herbs, *74,* 75
Gochujang
Mezzi Rigatoni with Spicy Gochujang Tomato Sauce, *270,* 271
Roasted Cabbage with Gochujang, Sesame, and Scallions, 535
Sauce, 527
-Tahini Noodles, 313–14
Grab-and-Go Toppings, about, 178. *see also* Garnishes and Toppings
Grain Dishes. *see also* Rice
about cooking, 368. 369
Barley and Lentils with Mushrooms and Tahini-Yogurt Sauce, 348–49, *349*
Barley with Celery and Miso Dressing, 347
Barley with Fennel, Dried Apricots, and Orange, 347
Barley with Lemon and Herbs, 347
California Barley Bowls with Lemon-Yogurt Sauce, *346,* 346–47
Cauliflower Biryani, *332,* 333
Congee, 343–44
Creamy Polenta with Fennel and Chickpeas, 360–63, *361*
Creamy Polenta with Radicchio Agrodolce, *362,* 363
Curried Fonio with Roasted Vegetables and Hibiscus Vinaigrette, *352,* 352–53
Farro with Wild Mushroom Ragout, 349–50
Grits with Fresh Corn, 364
Herbed Quinoa Cakes with Whipped Feta, *359,* 359–60
Jollof-Inspired Fonio, 350, *351*
Maftoul with Carrots and Chickpeas, 354, *355*
Oat Berry Pilaf with Walnuts and Gorgonzola, 356
Paella de Verduras (Cauliflower and Bean Paella), 334
Quinoa, Black Bean, and Mango Salad with Lime Dressing, 357–58, *358*
Quinoa Bowls with Snap Peas, Strawberries, and Basil Vinaigrette, *356,* 357
Quinoa Lettuce Wraps with Feta and Olives, 358–59, *359*
Savory Oatmeal with Peas, Parmesan, and Pepper, 365, *365*
Spicy Polenta with White Beans and Kale, 363–64
Spring Freekeh and Halloumi Bowls, *352,* 353–54
Tahini-Garlic Sauce, 354
Vegetable Bibimbap with Tempeh, 334–35, *335*
Green Bean(s)
Salad with Creamy Lemon Sauce and Crispy Capers, 114, *115*
Seared Tofu with Panch Phoron, Green Beans, and Pickled Shallot, *412,* 413
Skillet-Charred Green Beans, 552–53, *553*
Skillet-Charred Green Beans with Crispy Bread-Crumb Topping, 553

Green Curry with Kale and Butternut Squash, 50, *50, 51*
Green Gumbo, *170,* 171–72
Green Peas and Dumplings, 321–22
Greens. *see also* Kale; Salads; Spinach
about, 31, *31*
Bitter Greens, Carrot, and Chickpea Salad with Warm Lemon Dressing, 98, *99*
Gai Lan with Oyster Sauce, 552
Green Gumbo, *170,* 171–72
Green Shakshuka, 462, 463, *463*
Quick Collard Greens, 543
Shiitake, Tofu, and Mustard Greens Soup, 154, *155*
Spicy Chile-Honey Glazed Eggplant with Burrata and Greens, *12,* 40, *40*
Super Greens Soup with Lemon-Tarragon Cream, 150
Sweet and Spicy Glazed Tofu with Coconut-Braised Mustard Greens and Winter Squash, *424,* 425
Swiss Chard
about, 31, *31,* 463, *463*
and Kale Gratin, 576
Pinto Bean, and Monterey Jack Enchiladas, 67–68
Grilled Corn with Basil-Lemon Butter, 546–49
Grilled Halloumi Wraps, *214,* 214–15
Grilled Peach and Tomato Salad with Burrata and Basil, *135,* 135–36
Grilled Stone Fruit, 136
Grilled Tofu with Vegetable Skewers, *435,* 435–36
Grilled Watermelon, Halloumi, and Olive Salad, 136–37, *137*
Grits with Fresh Corn, 364
Grown-Up Stovetop Macaroni and Cheese, 275

H

Haluski, Pittsburgh-Style, *318,* 319
Harira (Moroccan Lentil and Chickpea Soup), 168
Harissa, 400, *400*
Hasselback Eggplant with Muhammara, 41
Hawaij Cauliflower Soup with Zhoug, 144
Hazelnut(s)
Butter-Roasted Carrots with Hazelnut Crumble and Goat Cheese, *537,* 537–38
Garlicky Spaghetti with Artichokes and Hazelnuts, 273
Hearty Cabbage Soup, 151, *151*
Hearty Greek Salad (Horiatiki Salata), 94
Hearty Green Salad with Chickpeas, Pickled Cauliflower, and Seared Halloumi, 97–98
Hearty Vegetable and Farro Bowls with Goat Cheese, 85
Herb(s). *see also* Pesto; *specific names of herbs*
about chopping, 472, *472*
about freezing, 5, *5*
All-Purpose Herb Sauce, 524
Herb(s). *see also* Pesto; *specific names of herbs* (cont.)
Barley with Lemon and Herbs, 347
Broiled Smashed Zucchini with Herbed Sour Cream, 580
Caramelized Plums with Spicy Herb Salad, 134–35, *135*
Creamless Creamy Herb Dressing, 139
Creamy White Bean Soup with Herb Oil and Crispy Capers, *158,* 159
Family-Size Spinach and Herb Cream Cheese Omelet with Home Fries, 466–67, *467*
Garlic and Herb Popcorn, 520
Herbed Croutons, 178
Herbed Goat Cheese Topping, 563
Herbed Quinoa Cakes with Whipped Feta, *359,* 359–60
Herbed Yogurt Sauce, 218
Herbes de Provence, 122
Hibiscus Vinaigrette, 353
Hibiscus Vinaigrette, Curried Fonio with Roasted Vegetables and, *352,* 352–53
Lemon and Herb Dipping Sauce, 512
Lemon-Herb Sauce, 179
Melted Brie with Honey and Herbs, 521
Stuffed Peppers with Chickpeas, Goat Cheese, and Herbs, *74,* 75
Torn Potato Salad with Toasted Garlic and Herb Dressing, 121–22
Tximitxurri (Basque-Style Herb Sauce), 572
Vegetable and Lentil Bake, 68–69, *69*
Zhoug, Hawaij Cauliflower Soup with, 144
Zhoug (Spicy Middle Eastern Herb Sauce), 524
Hibiscus Vinaigrette, 353
Hibiscus Vinaigrette, Curried Fonio with Roasted Vegetables and, *352,* 352–53
Homemade Nut Butter (sandwich spread), 219
Homemade Tofu, 409, *409*
Homemade Yogurt, 486, *487*
Homestyle Tofu, *406,* 406–7
Honey
Braised Vidalia Onions with Honey, Lemon, and Oregano, 561
Butternut Squash Steaks with Honey-Nut Topping, 37
Charred Shaved Brussels Sprout Salad with Sherry-Honey Dressing, 107
-Garlic Melting Sweet Potatoes, 575–76
Hot Honey Flavored Butter, 545
Melted Brie with Honey and Herbs, 521
Orange-Honey Dressing, 551
Pan-Seared Zucchini with Spicy Honey and Scallion, 578, *578,* 579
Shaved Celery Salad with Pomegranate-Honey Vinaigrette, 109
Skillet-Roasted Brussels Sprouts with Cider Vinegar and Honey, 532–33, *533*
and Spice Dipping Sauce, 512
Spicy Chile-Honey Glazed Eggplant with Burrata and Greens, *12,* 40, *40*
Spicy Honey, 573
Honeydew Salad with Peanuts and Lime, *133,* 133–34, *134*
Horiatiki Salata (Hearty Greek Salad), 94

Hot and Sweet Popcorn, 520
Hummus
with Crispy Mushrooms and Sumac, 493
Fattet Hummus (Crispy Pita with Garlicky Yogurt and Chickpeas), 494–95, *495*
Fried Egg Sandwiches with Hummus and Sprouts, 476
Ultracreamy Hummus, 494, *495*
Hung Kao Mun Gati (Thai Coconut Rice), 342, *343*

J

Jackfruit and Chickpea Makhani, 378, *379*
Jalapeño, Garlic, and Scallions, Mashed Sweet Potatoes with, 575
Jalapeño Quesadillas, Sheet Pan Black Bean and, 194
Jamaican Rice and Peas, 391–93
Jammy Eggs, 450
Japchae (Sweet Potato Noodles with Shiitakes, Spinach, and Eggs), 316
Japchae (Sweet Potato Noodles with Shiitakes and Spinach), 314–16, *315*
Javaher Polo (Jeweled Rice), 330–31, *331*
Jollof-Inspired Fonio, 350, *351*
July 4th Barbecue (menu), 22, *23*

K

Kale
about, 31, *31*
and Black Bean Breakfast Burritos, 479, *480*
Caesar Salad, *92,* 92–93
Crispy and Creamy Kale Salad, 93–94, 95, *95*
Crispy Tofu and Kale Salad and Miso-Ginger Dressing, *416,* 417
and Farro Salad with Fennel, Olives, and Parmesan, 129, *129*
Fideos with Chickpeas, Fennel, and Kale, 294
Green Curry with Kale and Butternut Squash, 50, *50, 51*
Roasted Kale with Coriander, Ginger, and Coconut, 556
Roasted Kale with Garlic, Red Pepper Flakes, and Lemon, *554,* 555–56
Roasted Kale with Parmesan, Shallot, and Nutmeg, 556
Simple Sautéed Kale, 555
Spiced Eggplant and Kale Soup, *152,* 153
Spicy Polenta with White Beans and Kale, 363–64
Sweet Potato, Lentil, and Kale Salad with Fried Shallots, 130–31
Swiss Chard and Kale Gratin, 576
Kibbeh, Red Lentil, 399
Kimchi
about, 11
Egg, and Avocado Sandwiches, 477, *477*
and Tofu Soup, 153
King Trumpet Mushrooms with Smoked Paprika Vinaigrette, 38–39, *39*
Kol Böreği (Spiraled Spinach and Cheese Pastry), 262–63, *263*
Korean Barbecue Tempeh Wraps, 447, *447*
Koshari, *395,* 395–96, *396*
Kuku Sabzi, *472,* 472–74, *473*

L

Labels, reading, 11
Labneh, 487
Lao Hu Cai (Tiger Salad), *108,* 109
Leek(s)
about, 31, *31,* 500, 557
Asparagus, Leek, and Goat Cheese Quiche, *474,* 475–76
Creamy Potatoes and Leeks, 566, *567*
Fresh Leek and Spinach Dip, *500,* 500–501
Mushroom and Leek Galette with Gorgonzola, 254–55, *255*
Sautéed Fava Beans, Asparagus, and Leek, 384, *384,* 385, *385*
Unstuffed Shells with Butternut Squash and Leeks, 297–98, *299*
Vinaigrette, 556, *557*
Legume(s). ***see*** **Black Bean(s); Chickpea(s); Lentil(s); Red Lentil(s); White Bean(s);** ***specific pigeon peas recipes***
Lemongrass
about trimming, 50, *50*
Lemongrass-Coconut Soup with Oyster Mushrooms, 154–55, *155*
Lemon(s)
Barley with Lemon and Herbs, 347
Basil-Lemon Flavored Butter, 545
Basmati Rice Pilaf with Peas, Scallions, and Lemon, 329
Bitter Greens, Carrot, and Chickpea Salad with Warm Lemon Dressing, 98, *99*
Boiled Carrots with Lemon and Chives, 536–37
Braised Asparagus with Lemon and Chives, *528,* 529–30
Braised Red Potatoes with Lemon and Chives, *564,* 565
Braised Vidalia Onions with Honey, Lemon, and Oregano, 561
California Barley Bowls with Lemon-Yogurt Sauce, *346,* 346–47
Caramelized Carrot Soup with Coriander-Lemon Browned Butter, 143
-Dill Labneh, 487
-Dill Mayonnaise, 218
Fried Brussels Sprouts with Lemon-Chive Dipping Sauce, 535
Garlicky Spaghetti with Lemon and Pine Nuts, 272, *273*
Green Bean Salad with Creamy Lemon Sauce and Crispy Capers, 114, *115*
Grilled Corn with Basil-Lemon Butter, 546–49
and Herb Dipping Sauce, 512
-Herb Sauce, 179
Lemony Roasted Radicchio, Fennel, and Root Vegetables, 570–71
Lentils with Roasted Broccoli and Lemony Bread Crumbs, *396,* 396–97, *397*

Lemon(s) (cont.)
Marinated Bean and Asparagus Salad with Preserved Lemon Dressing, *99*, 99–100
Pan-Seared Zucchini with Yogurt, Red Pepper Paste, and Preserved Lemon, 579
Pasta with Creamy Lemon–Sichuan Peppercorn Sauce, *276*, 277–78
-Pickled Radish Toast with Basil and Parmesan, *238*, 238–39
Roasted Artichokes with Lemon Vinaigrette, 529
Roasted Broccoli with Olives, Garlic, Oregano, and Lemon, 532
Roasted Kale with Garlic, Red Pepper Flakes, and Lemon, *554*, 555–56
Sheet Pan White Bean and Sun-Dried Tomato Patties with Lemony Spinach Salad, 184, *185*
Skillet-Roasted Cauliflower with Garlic and Lemon, *540*, 540–41
Sugar Snap Peas with Pine Nuts, Fennel, and Lemon Zest, 571–72
Sugar Snap Peas with Sesame, Ginger, and Lemon Zest, 572
Summer Squash Pasta with Ricotta and Lemon-Parmesan Bread Crumbs, 284, *285*
Super Greens Soup with Lemon-Tarragon Cream, 150
Tarragon-Lemon Gremolata, 88
Lentil(s). ***see also*** **Red Lentil(s)**
about sorting, 396, *396*
Barley and Lentils with Mushrooms and Tahini-Yogurt Sauce, 348–49, *349*
Chipotle Lentil–Stuffed Sweet Potatoes, 78, *79*
and Escarole Soup, 160, *161*
Harira (Moroccan Lentil and Chickpea Soup), 168
Herb Vegetable and Lentil Bake, 68–69, *69*
Lentilles du Puy with Spinach and Crème Fraîche, 397–98, *398*
Mujaddara, 394, *395*
Palak Dal (Spinach-Lentil Dal with Cumin and Mustard Seeds), *398*, 398–99
with Roasted Broccoli and Lemony Bread Crumbs, *396*, 396–97, *397*
Sweet Potato, Lentil, and Kale Salad with Fried Shallots, 130–31
Turkish Bulgur and Lentil Soup, *166*, 167
Liang Mian (Chilled Sesame Noodles), *317*, 317–18
Linguine with Sun-Dried Tomato and Eggplant Sauce, *274*, 274–75
Loaded Sweet Potato Wedges with Tempeh, 442–43

M

Madras Okra Curry, *52*, 53
Maftoul with Carrots and Chickpeas, 354, *355*
Maitake Mushrooms, about, 282
Make-Ahead Cheese Soufflés, 458–59, *459*
Make-Ahead Sherry-Shallot Vinaigrette, 138
Mana'eesh Za'atar (Za'atar Flatbreads), 239–40, *241*
Mango
about, 358, *358*
Salad with Lime Dressing, Quinoa, Black Bean, and, *357*, 357–58
Mapo Tofu, 432–33, *433*
Marinated Bean and Asparagus Salad with Preserved Lemon Dressing, *99*, 99–100
Marinated Eggplant with Capers and Mint, 549–50
Marinated Manchego, 485–86
Marinated Tomato Sandwiches, 203
Mashed Sweet Potatoes
with Chipotle and Lime, 575
with Curry and Golden Raisins, 575
with Jalapeño, Garlic, and Scallions, 575
with Maple and Orange, 575
recipe for, *573*, 574
Mayonnaise
Basil-Caper Mayonnaise, 218
Easy Homemade Mayonnaise, 218
Garlic Mayonnaise, 468
Lemon-Dill Mayonnaise, 218
Spicy Red Pepper Mayonnaise, 559, *559*
Spicy Sriracha-Lime Mayonnaise, 218
Vegan Mayonnaise, 506
Meal Planning Ideas. ***see*** **Vegetarianism**
Meatless "Meat" Sauce with Chickpeas and Mushrooms, 292, *293*
Melons
about cutting, 134, *134*
Cantaloupe Salad with Olives and Red Onion, 132–33
Grilled Watermelon, Halloumi, and Olive Salad, 136–37, *137*
Honeydew Salad with Peanuts and Lime, *133*, 133–34, *134*
Melted Brie with Honey and Herbs, 521
Memorial Day Cookout (menu), 22
Menemen (Turkish Scrambled Eggs with Vegetables), 454
Menu Ideas, for Entertaining, 22, *23–25*, 24
Mexican Corn Salad (Esquites), 110
Mezzi Rigatoni with Spicy Gochujang Tomato Sauce, *270*, 271
Microwave-Fried Garlic, 462
Microwave-Fried Shallots, 89
Minestrone, Classic, 161, *161*
Misir Wot, 400, *401*
Miso
Barley with Celery and Miso Dressing, 347
Braised Red Potatoes with Miso and Scallions, 566
Crispy Tofu and Kale Salad and Miso-Ginger Dressing, *416*, 417
-Ginger Sauce, 526
-Maple Melting Sweet Potatoes, 576
Mushroom Risotto, 338–39, *339*
Shaved Vegetable Salad with Creamy Miso Dressing, *112*, 113–14
Modern Cauliflower Gratin, *540*, 541–42, *542*
Moroccan Lentil and Chickpea Soup (Harira), 168
Mujaddara, 394, *395*
Mumbai Frankie Wraps, 212, *212*

Mushroom(s)
about preparing, 32, *32*
about scraping out gills, 509, *509*
about types of, 282
Barley and Lentils with Mushrooms and Tahini-Yogurt Sauce, 348–49, *349*
Bourguignon, 53–54, *54*
Creamy Mushroom and Pink Pickled Cabbage Sandwiches, 204, *204*, 205
Farro with Wild Mushroom Ragout, 349–50
Flatbreads with Fontina, Mushrooms, and Chives, 246, *247*
Hummus with Crispy Mushrooms and Sumac, 493
King Trumpet Mushrooms with Smoked Paprika Vinaigrette, 38–39, *39*
and Leek Galette with Gorgonzola, 254–55, *255*
Lemongrass-Coconut Soup with Oyster Mushrooms, 154–55, *155*
Meatless "Meat" Sauce with Chickpeas and Mushrooms, 292, *293*
Miso Mushroom Risotto, 338–39, *339*
Neapolitan-Style Pizza with Mushrooms, Garlic, and Taleggio, 231
Portobello Mushroom Fries with Cherry Pepper Sauce, *507*, 507–9, *509*
Rigatoni with Quick Mushroom Bolognese, 283–84
Sandwiches, Lettuce, and Tomato, *202*, 203
Sautéed Mushrooms with Mustard and Parsley, 558
Sautéed Mushrooms with Red Wine and Rosemary, 557–58, *558*
Sautéed Mushrooms with Soy, Scallion, and Ginger, 558
Scrambled Eggs with Shiitake Mushrooms and Feta Cheese, 453
Stir-Fried Asparagus with Shiitake Mushrooms, 43
Stuffed Portobello Mushrooms with Spinach and Gorgonzola, 77–78
Su Shui Jiao (Northern Chinese-Style Cabbage and Mushroom Dumplings), *323*, 323–25
Tofu and Chickpea Flour Frittata with Mushrooms, 434–35, *435*
Triple Mushroom Pasta, 282, *282*, 283
and White Bean Gratin, 66–67
Whole-Wheat Crepes with Creamy Sautéed Mushrooms and Asparagus, *244*, 245
Wild Rice and Mushroom Soup, 156–57
Mustard Greens and Winter Squash, Sweet and Spicy Glazed Tofu with Coconut-Braised, *424*, 425
Mustard Greens Soup, Shiitake, Tofu, and, 154, *155*
Mustard Seeds, Pickled, 459

N

Napa Cabbage
about cutting and slicing, 116, *116*, 536, *536*
Slaw with Apple and Walnuts, 116
Slaw with Carrots and Sesame, 115–17, *116*, *117*
Slaw with Jícama and Pepitas, 116
Stir-Fried Tempeh, Napa Cabbage, and Carrots, *440*, 440–41
Suan La Bai Cai (Sour and Hot Napa Cabbage), 536, *536*, *537*
Neapolitan-Style Pizza
with Artichoke Hearts and Fontina, 231
Margherita, *228*, 229–31, *231*
with Mushrooms, Garlic, and Taleggio, 231
New Year's Eve Cocktail Party/New Year's Day Brunch (menus), 22
No-Cook Fresh Tomato Sauce, 266
No-Cook Pizza Sauce, 223
Noodle Dishes
Chickpea Noodle Soup, 169, *169*
Chilled Soba Noodles with Cucumber, Snow Peas, and Radishes, *318*, 318–19
Gochujang-Tahini Noodles, 313–14
Japchae (Sweet Potato Noodles with Shiitakes and Spinach), 314–16, *315*
Liang Mian (Chilled Sesame Noodles), *317*, 317–18
San Francisco–Style Garlic Noodles, 312, *312*, 313
Savory Noodle Kugel, *320*, 321
Shanghai Scallion Oil Noodles, 310, *311*
Spicy Basil Noodles with Crispy Tofu, Snap Peas, and Bell Pepper, 314, *315*
Sweet Potato Noodles with Shiitakes, Spinach, and Eggs (Japchae), 316
Tallarines Verdes (Peruvian Green Noodles), 279–80
Northern Chinese–Style Cabbage and Mushroom Dumplings (Su Shui Jiao), *323*, 323–25
Nut(s). *see also* Peanut(s); Pine Nut(s)
Almonds
Calabrian Chile White Beans with Almond Romesco, 374–75, *375*
Garlicky Spaghetti with Green Olives and Almonds, 273
Skillet-Roasted Brussels Sprouts with Maple Syrup and Smoked Almonds, 533
Sugar Snap Peas with Almonds, Coriander, and Orange Zest, 572
Tofu Summer Rolls with Spicy Almond Butter Sauce, *430*, 431–32
Wild Rice Pilaf with Scallions, Cilantro, and Almonds, 344
Cashew e Pepe e Funghi, 280–81, *281*
Hazelnuts
Butter-Roasted Carrots with Hazelnut Crumble and Goat Cheese, *537*, 537–38
Garlicky Spaghetti with Artichokes and Hazelnuts, 273
Homemade Nut Butter, 219
Pistachios
Chopped Carrot Salad with Mint, Pistachios, and Pomegranate Seeds, 107, *107*
Skillet-Roasted Brussels Sprouts with Pomegranate and Pistachios, 533
Skillet-Roasted Cauliflower with Cumin and Pistachios, 541
Walnuts
Cacio e Pepe Beans with Squash, Sage, and Walnuts, *372*, 372–73
Celery Root Galette with Blue Cheese and Walnuts, *256*, 256–57
Fettuccine with Walnut Sauce, 280, *281*
Napa Cabbage Slaw with Apple and Walnuts, 116

Nut(s). *see also* Peanut(s); Pine Nut(s) (cont.)
Oat Berry Pilaf with Walnuts and Gorgonzola, 356
Savory Dutch Baby with Portobellos, Roasted Red Peppers, Walnuts, and Feta, *64,* 65

Oat Berry Pilaf with Walnuts and Gorgonzola, 356
Oatmeal with Peas, Parmesan, and Pepper, Savory, 365, *365*
Okra
about, 52, *52*
Green Gumbo, *170,* 171–72
Madras Okra Curry, *52,* 53
Roasted Okra, *558,* 559
Olive(s)
Cantaloupe Salad with Olives and Red Onion, 132–33
Crunchy Oil-Cured Olives, 552
Fresh Tomato Puttanesca Sauce, 266
Garlicky Spaghetti with Green Olives and Almonds, 273
Gnocchi à la Parisienne with Arugula, Tomatoes, and Olives, 306, *307*
Grilled Watermelon, Halloumi, and Olive Salad, 136–37, *137*
Kale and Farro Salad with Fennel, Olives, and Parmesan, 129, *129*
Quinoa Lettuce Wraps with Feta and Olives, 358–59, *359*
Radicchio Chopped Salad with White Beans, Oranges, and Olives, 118
Roasted Broccoli with Olives, Garlic, Oregano, and Lemon, 532
Tortellini Salad with Broccoli, Cannellini Beans, and Olive-Banana Pepper Dressing, *302,* 302–3
Warm Marinated Olives, *484,* 485
Whole Pot-Roasted Cauliflower with Tomatoes and Olives, 41–42
Omelet(s)
Easy Cheddar Omelet, 466
Easy Feta and Dill Omelet, 466
Easy Tex-Mex Omelet, 466
Family-Size Spinach and Herb Cream Cheese Omelet with Home Fries, 466–67, *467*
One-Hour Pizza, *224,* 224–25
Onion(s). *see also* Leek(s); Scallion(s); Shallot(s)
about, 32, *32,* 148, *148*
Braised Vidalia Onions with Chile, Lime, and Cilantro, *560,* 561
Braised Vidalia Onions with Honey, Lemon, and Oregano, 561
Cantaloupe Salad with Olives and Red Onion, 132–33
Carabaccia (Tuscan Onion Soup), *148,* 149
Caramelized Onion, Tomato, and Goat Cheese Tart, 258, *259*
Caramelized Onions, 259
Quick Sweet-and-Spicy Pickled Red Onion, 213
Shawarma-Spiced Tofu Wraps with Sumac Onions, *430,* 430–31
Socca with Sautéed Onions and Rosemary, 242–43, *243*
Sumac Onions, 431
Onion(s). *see also* Leek(s); Scallion(s); Shallot(s) (cont.)
Tamatya-Kandyachi Koshimbir (Tomato-Onion Salad), 242
Upside-Down Caramelized Shallot and Onion Tart, 247–48, *249*
Vidalia Onion Pie, *250,* 251
Orange(s)
Barley with Fennel, Dried Apricots, and Orange, 347
Beet, Orange, and Chèvre Tartines, 206, *207*
Braised Asparagus with Orange and Tarragon, 530
-Ginger Vinaigrette, 86, *86*
-Honey Dressing, 551
Mashed Sweet Potatoes with Maple and Orange, 575
Radicchio Chopped Salad with White Beans, Oranges, and Olives, 118
Stir-Fried Tempeh with Orange Sauce, *440,* 441
Sugar Snap Peas with Almonds, Coriander, and Orange Zest, 572
Orecchiette and Navy Beans with Brussels Sprouts and Spicy Mustard Crumbs, 289–90
Overstuffed Sweet Potatoes with Tofu and Red Curry Vinaigrette, 433–34, *434*
Oyster Sauce, Gai Lan with, 552

P

Pa amb Tomàquet (Catalan Tomato Bread), 502–3, *503*
Paella de Verduras (Cauliflower and Bean Paella), 334
Pai Huang Gua (Smashed Cucumbers), 548, *548,* 549
Pakoras (South Asian Spiced Vegetable Fritters), 516
Palak Dal (Spinach-Lentil Dal with Cumin and Mustard Seeds), *398,* 398–99
Panch Phoron, 413, *413*
Panch Phoron, Green Beans, and Pickled Shallot, Seared Tofu with, *412,* 413
Panko-Crusted Tofu with Cabbage Salad, *424,* 424–25
Pan-Seared Beets with Horseradish Cream, 530, *531*
Pan-Seared Halloumi with Cherry Pepper Glaze, 490
Pan-Seared Tempeh Steaks with Chimichurri Sauce, *438,* 439
Pan-Seared Zucchini with Raisin, Caper, and Parsley Sauce and Pine Nuts, 579
Pan-Seared Zucchini with Spicy Honey and Scallion, 578, *578,* 579
Pan-Seared Zucchini with Yogurt, Red Pepper Paste, and Preserved Lemon, 579
Pappa al Pomodoro, *142,* 142–43, *143*
Parmesan-Black Pepper Cheese Straws, 502
Parmesan-Pepper Popcorn, 520
Pasta. *see also* Noodle Dishes
Angel Hair Pasta with Sun-Dried Tomato and Mint Sauce, 273–74
Cacio e Uova (Pasta with Cheese and Eggs), 278
Cashew e Pepe e Funghi, 280–81, *281*
Cheese Ravioli with Pumpkin Cream Sauce, 298, *299*

Pasta. ***see also*** **Noodle Dishes (cont.)**
Cheesy Stuffed Shells, *296,* 297
Creamy, Spicy Rotini and Red Lentils with Tomatoes and Goat Cheese, 290
Creamy Broccoli Pasta with Crispy Panko, 278–79, *279*
with Creamy Lemon–Sichuan Peppercorn Sauce, *276,* 277–78
e Ceci (Pasta with Chickpeas), 290–91, *291*
Farfalle with Beets, Arugula, and Blue Cheese, *288,* 289
Fettuccine with Walnut Sauce, 280, *281*
Fideos with Chickpeas, Fennel, and Kale, 294
Fregula with Chickpeas, Tomatoes, and Fennel, *291,* 291–92
Fresh Pasta Without a Machine, *270,* 270–71
Gnocchi
Crispy Gnocchi with Shredded Brussels Sprouts and Gorgonzola, 303
Gnocchi à la Parisienne with Arugula, Tomatoes, and Olives, 306, *307*
Gnocchi à la Parisienne with Browned Butter, 306
Potato Gnocchi with Browned Butter and Sage Sauce, 304–5, *305*
Samosa Gnocchi Chaat, *302,* 303–4
Green Peas and Dumplings, 321–22
Linguine with Sun-Dried Tomato and Eggplant Sauce, *274,* 274–75
Macaroni
Grown-Up Stovetop Macaroni and Cheese, 275
Simple Stovetop Macaroni and Cheese, *274,* 275
Spinach-Artichoke Macaroni and Cheese, 277
Meatless "Meat" Sauce with Chickpeas and Mushrooms, 292, *293*
Mezzi Rigatoni with Spicy Gochujang Tomato Sauce, *270,* 271
Orecchiette and Navy Beans with Brussels Sprouts and Spicy Mustard Crumbs, 289–90
Pesto Lasagna, 294–95, *295*
Pittsburgh-Style Haluski, *318,* 319
Potato-Cheddar Pierogi, 322–23, *323*
Potato-Sauerkraut Pierogi, 323
Ramen with Shiitakes and Soft Eggs, 309
Rigatoni with Marinated Tomatoes and Burrata, 272, *273*
Rigatoni with Quick Mushroom Bolognese, 283–84
Shiitake and Bok Choy Lo Mein, 310
Spaghetti
Garlicky Spaghetti with Artichokes and Hazelnuts, 273
Garlicky Spaghetti with Green Olives and Almonds, 273
Garlicky Spaghetti with Lemon and Pine Nuts, 272, *273*
Spaghetti all'Assassina, 286–87, *287*
Ultracreamy Spaghetti with Zucchini, *285,* 285–86
Spinach and Ricotta Gnudi with Tomato-Butter Sauce, *308,* 308–9
Summer Squash Pasta with Ricotta and Lemon-Parmesan Bread Crumbs, 284, *285*
Su Shui Jiao (Northern Chinese–Style Cabbage and Mushroom Dumplings), *323,* 323–25
Three-Cheese Ravioli with Browned Butter–Pine Nut Sauce, 299–301, *301*

Pasta. ***see also*** **Noodle Dishes (cont.)**
Tomato Sauces, Fast, 266
Fresh Tomato Puttanesca Sauce, 266
Fresh Tomato Sauce, 266
No-Cook Fresh Tomato Sauce, 266
Tomato-Browned Butter Sauce, 267
Vodka Sauce, 267
Tortellini Salad with Broccoli, Cannellini Beans, and Olive-Banana Pepper Dressing, *302,* 302–3
Triple Mushroom Pasta, 282, *282,* 283
Udon with Stir-Fried Portobellos and Soy-Maple Sauce, 316–17
Unstuffed Shells with Butternut Squash and Leeks, 297–98, *299*
Patatas Bravas, *508,* 509–10
Peanut(s)
Chaat Masala Peanuts, 485
Garam Masala Peanuts, 484, *484*
Honeydew Salad with Peanuts and Lime, *133,* 133–34, *134*
-Sesame Sauce, 525
Pear, Roasted Cauliflower with Arugula and, *105,* 105–6
Pears, Pickled, Romaine and Radicchio Salad with Roasted Squash and, 118–19, *119*
Pea(s)
about snap peas and snow peas, 33, *33*
Basmati Rice Pilaf with Peas, Scallions, and Lemon, 329
Chilled Soba Noodles with Cucumber, Snow Peas, and Radishes, *318,* 318–19
Frittata Bites with Peas, Goat Cheese, and Basil, 475
Green Peas and Dumplings, 321–22
Jamaican Rice and Peas, 391–93
Pesto Potato Frittata with Peas and Goat Cheese, *470,* 471–72
Quinoa Bowls with Snap Peas, Strawberries, and Basil Vinaigrette, *356,* 357
Roasted Tofu and Sweet Potato Bowls with Snap Pea Salad, *84,* 85–86
Savory Oatmeal with Peas, Parmesan, and Pepper, 365, *365*
Spanish Tortilla with Roasted Red Peppers and Peas, 467–68, *468*
Spicy Basil Noodles with Crispy Tofu, Snap Peas, and Bell Pepper, 314, *315*
Stir-Fried Rice Cakes with Bok Choy and Snow Peas, 337
Sugar Snap Peas with Almonds, Coriander, and Orange Zest, 572
Sugar Snap Peas with Pine Nuts, Fennel, and Lemon Zest, 571–72
Sugar Snap Peas with Sesame, Ginger, and Lemon Zest, 572
Peppercorn(s)
Pasta with Creamy Lemon–Sichuan Peppercorn Sauce, *276,* 277–78
Sichuan Peppercorn Oil, 325
Pepper(s). ***see also*** **Bell Pepper(s) and Red Pepper(s); Chipotle(s)**
Blistered Shishito Peppers, 520
Cherry Pepper Glaze, Pan-Seared Halloumi with, 490
Mashed Sweet Potatoes with Jalapeño, Garlic, and Scallions, 575
Sheet Pan Black Bean and Jalapeño Quesadillas, 194
Perfect Fried Eggs, 451
Perfect Poached Eggs, 451

Peruvian Green Noodles (Tallarines Verdes), 279–80
Pesto
about, 268
alla Calabrese, 269
alla Genovese (Basil Pesto), 268
Butternut Squash and White Bean Soup with Sage Pesto, 163–64
di Prezzemolo (Parsley Pesto), 268
Lasagna, 294–95, *295*
Pantesco, 269
Potato Frittata with Peas and Goat Cheese, *470,* 471–72
Ricotta Toast with Pesto di Prezzemolo and Grapes, *238,* 239
Philadelphia Tomato Pie, 228–29
Pickled Celery, 179
Pickled Mustard Seeds, 459
Pierogi, Potato-Sauerkraut, 323
Pies. *see* Breads, Tarts, and Pies (Savory)
Pigeon Peas, Caribbean Tofu with Rice and, 425–26
Pigeon Peas with Tropical Fruit, Crispy Coconut Rice and, *392,* 393
Pimento Cheese Dip, Baked, 491, *491*
Pine Nut(s)
Fava Bean Crostini with Manchego and Pine Nuts, 503–4
Garlicky Spaghetti with Lemon and Pine Nuts, 272, *273*
Pan-Seared Zucchini with Raisin, Caper, and Parsley Sauce and Pine Nuts, 579
Skillet-Roasted Cauliflower with Capers and Pine Nuts, 541
Sugar Snap Peas with Pine Nuts, Fennel, and Lemon Zest, 571–72
Three-Cheese Ravioli with Browned Butter–Pine Nut Sauce, 299–301, *301*
Pinto Bean(s)
–Beet Burgers, 186, *186,* 187
Breakfast Tacos with Pinto Beans and Cotija Cheese, 478, *478*
Gallo Pinto (Costa Rican Beans and Rice), 390, *390,* 391
Swiss Chard, Pinto Bean, and Monterey Jack Enchiladas, 67–68
Pistachios
Chopped Carrot Salad with Mint, Pistachios, and Pomegranate Seeds, 107, *107*
Skillet-Roasted Brussels Sprouts with Pomegranate and Pistachios, 533
Skillet-Roasted Cauliflower with Cumin and Pistachios, 541
Pita Salad with Za'atar Tofu and Chickpeas, 418, *419*
Pittsburgh-Style Haluski, *318,* 319
Pizza
about, 222, 223
al Taglio with Arugula and Fresh Mozzarella, *232,* 232–33
Caprese Sheet-Pan Pizza, 226–27, *227*
Cast Iron Pan Pizza, *224,* 225–26
Corn, Tomato, and Arugula Pizza, *228,* 229
Fugazzeta (Argentine Cheese-Stuffed Pizza), 235–36, *237*
Neapolitan-Style Pizza Margherita, *228,* 229–31, *231*
Neapolitan-Style Pizza with Artichoke Hearts and Fontina, 231
Neapolitan-Style Pizza with Mushrooms, Garlic, and Taleggio, 231
No-Cook Pizza Sauce, 223
Pizza (cont.)
One-Hour Pizza, *224,* 224–25
Thin-Crust Grilled Pizza with Fontina, Parmesan, and Scallions, 233–35, *234*
Plum Sauce, 515, *515*
Poaching of Eggs. *see also* Shakshuka
about, 461, *461*
Perfect Poached Eggs, 451
Poblanas and Poblano(s)
Black Bean, Sweet Potato, and Poblano Tacos, 193
Breakfast Burritos with Poblano, Beans, Corn, and Crispy Potatoes, *478,* 479–80, *480*
Chickpea and Poblano Quesadillas, *196,* 197
Chiles Rellenos, 75–77, *76, 77*
Rajas Poblanas con Crema (Charred Poblano Strips with Cream), 561–62
Rajas Poblanas con Crema y Elote (Charred Poblano Strips with Cream and Corn), 562
Roasted Poblano and White Bean Chili, *174,* 175
Poke Bowls, Beet, *80,* 81
Polenta
about, 361, *361*
Creamy Polenta with Fennel and Chickpeas, 360–63, *361*
Creamy Polenta with Radicchio Agrodolce, *362,* 363
Sautéed Eggplant with Polenta, 49–50
Spicy Polenta with White Beans and Kale, 363–64
Porcini (Dried) Mushrooms, about, 282
Portobello Mushroom Fries with Cherry Pepper Sauce, *507,* 507–9, *509*
Potato(es)
about, 32, *32*
Aloo Gobi, *48,* 48–49
Alu Parathas (Punjabi Potato-Stuffed Griddle Breads), 240–42, *243*
Best Baked Potatoes, 563, *563*
Better Hash Browns, *568,* 569
Braised Red Potatoes with Dijon and Tarragon, 566
Braised Red Potatoes with Lemon and Chives, *564,* 565
Braised Red Potatoes with Miso and Scallions, 566
Breakfast Burritos with Poblano, Beans, Corn, and Crispy Potatoes, *478,* 479–80, *480*
-Cheddar Pierogi, 322–23, *323*
Cheddar Scalloped Potatoes, 567–68
Chipotle Lentil-Stuffed Sweet Potatoes, 78, *79*
Coleslaw Potato Salad, 116–17
Creamy Potatoes and Leeks, 566, *567*
Family-Size Spinach and Herb Cream Cheese Omelet with Home Fries, 466–67, *467*
Fastest, Easiest Mashed Potatoes, 565
Fingerling Potato Salad with Sun-Dried Tomato Dressing, 122, *124*
Gnocchi with Browned Butter and Sage Sauce, 304–5, *305*
Patatas Bravas, *508,* 509–10
Pesto Potato Frittata with Peas and Goat Cheese, *470,* 471–72
-Sauerkraut Pierogi, 323

Potato(es) (cont.)
Sichuan Hot and Sour Potatoes, 566–67
Thick-Cut Oven Fries, *568*, 568–69
Three-Cheese Potato Frico, 562
Torn Potato Salad with Toasted Garlic and Herb Dressing, 121–22
Tourte aux Pommes de Terre (French Potato Pie), 251–52, *253*
Vindaloo, *54*, 55
and Zucchini Spanish Tortilla, 468–69, *469*
Produce, Planning and Storage, 4–6, *5*. *see also* Fruit; Vegetables
Pumpkin
Baked Pumpkin Kibbeh, 62
Cheese Ravioli with Pumpkin Cream Sauce, 298, *299*
Pumpkin Seed Sauce, 526
Punjabi Potato-Stuffed Griddle Breads (Alu Parathas), 240–42, *243*

Q

Quesadillas
Chickpea and Poblano Quesadillas, *196*, 197
Sheet Pan Black Bean and Jalapeño Quesadillas, 194
Sheet Pan Cheese Quesadillas, 194, *194*, *195*
Spinach and Goat Cheese Quesadillas, *195*, 195–96
Quick Cast-Iron Skillet Green Bean Casserole, *554*, 554–55
Quick Chili Oil, 179
Quick Collard Greens, 543
Quick-Cooking Beets, 103
Quick Food Processor Gazpacho, 155–56
Quick Sweet-and-Spicy Pickled Red Onion, 213
Quick Tomato Salsa, 198
Quinoa
Black Bean and Mango Salad with Lime Dressing, 357–58, *358*
Bowls with Snap Peas, Strawberries, and Basil Vinaigrette, *356*, 357
Burgers with Spinach, Sun-Dried Tomatoes, and Marinated Feta, 187–88, *189*
Herbed Quinoa Cakes with Whipped Feta, *359*, 359–60
Lettuce Wraps with Feta and Olives, 358–59, *359*

R

Radicchio
Chopped Salad with White Beans, Oranges, and Olives, 118
Creamy Polenta with Radicchio Agrodolce, *362*, 363
Lemony Roasted Radicchio, Fennel, and Root Vegetables, *570*, 570–71
Romaine and Radicchio Salad with Roasted Squash and Pickled Pears, 118–19, *119*
Wheat Berry Salad with Radicchio, Dried Cherries, and Pecans, 125
Rainbow Bowls with Crispy Tempeh, 86, *87*
Rajas Poblanas con Crema (Charred Poblano Strips with Cream), 561–62
Rajas Poblanas con Crema y Elote (Charred Poblano Strips with Cream and Corn), 562
Ramen with Shiitakes and Soft Eggs, 309
Ranch Dressing
Tomatillo, Tomatillo and Bibb Lettuce Salad with, 124, *124*, 125
Vegan, 506
Ras el Hanout, 439
Raspberry Vinaigrette, 138
Ravioli, Cheese, with Pumpkin Cream Sauce, 298, *299*
Ravioli, Three-Cheese, with Browned Butter–Pine Nut Sauce, 299–301, *301*
Raw Vegetable Wraps, 206–7, *207*
Red Cabbage and Grapefruit Salad, 132, *132*, *133*
Red Lentil(s)
Biscuit Crackers with Red Lentil Dip, *496*, 497
Creamy, Spicy Rotini and Red Lentils with Tomatoes and Goat Cheese, 290
Kibbeh, 399
Misir Wot, 400, *401*
Soup with Warm Spices, 159–60
Tacos, 193–94
Thai Red Curry with Tofu and Lentils, 427–28
Thai-Spiced Red Lentil Stew with Spinach and Corn, 171
Vospov Kofte (Red Lentil Kofte), 216–17, *217*
Ribollita, *162*, 162–63
Rice
about, 333, 366, 367
Arroz con Titoté (Colombian Coconut Rice), 342–43, *343*
Basmati Rice Pilaf with Peas, Scallions, and Lemon, 329
Basmati Rice Pilaf with Whole Spices, 328
Caribbean Tofu with Rice and Pigeon Peas, 425–26
Cauliflower Biryani, *332*, 333
Cơm Đỏ (Vietnamese Red Rice), 341–42
Crispy Coconut Rice and Pigeon Peas with Tropical Fruit, *392*, 393
Cuban-Style Black Beans and Rice, *386*, 387
Easy Baked Brown Rice, 366
Easy Baked White Rice, 366
Easy Mexican Rice, *328*, 329
Gallo Pinto (Costa Rican Beans and Rice), 390, *390*, 391
Garlicky Fried Rice with Bok Choy, 336, *336*, 337
Hung Kao Mun Gati (Thai Coconut Rice), 342, *343*
Jamaican Rice and Peas, 391–93
Javaher Polo (Jeweled Rice), 330–31, *331*
Jollof-Inspired Fonio, 350, *351*
Mujaddara, 394, *395*
Paella de Verduras (Cauliflower and Bean Paella), 334
Risotto
Beet and Barley Risotto, 348, *349*
Corn Risotto, 340, *340*, 341
Milanese, 338, *339*
Miso Mushroom Risotto, 338–39, *339*

Rice (cont.)
Simple Rice Pilaf, 328, *328*
Skillet Rice and Beans with Corn and Fresh Tomatoes, 387–88
Skillet Rice and Chickpeas with Coconut Milk, 388
Spanish-Style Skillet Rice and Chickpeas, 388
Spinach Rice, 329–30
Stir-Fried Rice Cakes with Bok Choy and Snow Peas, 337
Tacu Tacu with Salsa Criolla, 388–89, *389*
Vegetable Bibimbap with Tempeh, 334–35, *335*
Wild Rice and Mushroom Soup, 156–57
Wild Rice Pilaf with Pecans and Cranberries, 344, *345*
Wild Rice Pilaf with Scallions, Cilantro, and Almonds, 344
Rich Flavors, about, 10
Ricotta Toast with Pesto di Prezzemolo and Grapes, *238*, 239
Rigatoni
with Marinated Tomatoes and Burrata, 272, *273*
Mezzi Rigatoni with Spicy Gochujang Tomato Sauce, *270*, 271
with Quick Mushroom Bolognese, 283–84
Risotto
Beet and Barley Risotto, 348, *349*
Corn Risotto, 340, *340*, 341
Milanese, 338, *339*
Miso Mushroom Risotto, 338–39, *339*
Roasted Artichokes, 528–29
Roasted Artichokes with Lemon Vinaigrette, 529
Roasted Broccoli
with Garlic, 532
with Olives, Garlic, Oregano, and Lemon, 532
recipe for, 531–32
Roasted Butternut Squash Salad with Creamy Tahini Dressing, 104–5
Roasted Cabbage
about, 535, *535*
with Bread Crumbs, Sage, and Parmesan, 535
with Gochujang, Sesame, and Scallions, 535
recipe for, *534*, 535
Roasted Cauliflower with Arugula and Pear, *105*, 105–6
Roasted Celery Root with Chimichurri, 542–43, *543*
Roasted Delicata Squash, 572, *573*
Roasted Fennel, *550*, 551
Roasted Garlic Soup with Parmesan Croutons, *146*, 147, *147*
Roasted Kale with Coriander, Ginger, and Coconut, 556
Roasted Kale with Garlic, Red Pepper Flakes, and Lemon, *554*, 555–56
Roasted Kale with Parmesan, Shallot, and Nutmeg, 556
Roasted Okra, *558*, 559
Roasted Poblano and White Bean Chili, *174*, 175
Roasted Radishes with Yogurt-Tahini Sauce, 571, *571*
Roasted Tofu and Sweet Potato Bowls with Snap Pea Salad, *84*, 85–86
Roasted Vegetable Bowls with Bulgur, White Beans, and Arugula, 84, *84*
Roasted Vegetable Sandwiches, *208*, 209
Romaine Lettuce
about, 473, *473*
Romaine Lettuce (cont.)
Cast Iron–Seared Romaine with Oyster Sauce, Ginger, and Sesame, *120*, 121
and Radicchio Salad with Roasted Squash and Pickled Pears, 118–19, *119*
Romanesco, Whole, with Berbere and Yogurt-Tahini Sauce, 42, *43*

S

Saag Tofu, 414–15, *415*
Salads
Apple–Celery Root Salad, 110
Avocado and Cucumber Salad with Sriracha Mayo, *112*, 112–13, *113*
Beet Salad with Blue Cheese and Endive, 103
Beet Salad with Spiced Yogurt and Watercress, 100–103, *102*
Bitter Greens, Carrot, and Chickpea Salad with Warm Lemon Dressing, 98, *99*
Broccoli Salad with Avocado Dressing, 103–4, *105*
Buffalo Cucumber Salad, 111, *111*
Bulgur Salad with Curry Roasted Sweet Potatoes and Chickpeas, 126
Butternut Squash and Apple Fattoush, *130*, 131
Cantaloupe Salad with Olives and Red Onion, 132–33
Caramelized Plums with Spicy Herb Salad, 134–35, *135*
Cast Iron–Seared Romaine with Oyster Sauce, Ginger, and Sesame, *120*, 121
Charred Shaved Brussels Sprout Salad with Apricot Dressing, 107
Charred Shaved Brussels Sprout Salad with Sherry-Honey Dressing, 107
Charred Shaved Brussels Sprout Salad with Sweet Chili-Lime Dressing, 106–7
Cherry Tomato Salad with Pita Crisps and Spicy Citrus Dressing, 123, *123*
Chopped Carrot Salad with Mint, Pistachios, and Pomegranate Seeds, 107, *107*
Chopped Vegetable and Stone Fruit Salad, *15*, 126, *127*
Cobb Salad, *96*, 97
Coleslaw Potato Salad, 116–17
Crispy and Creamy Kale Salad, 93–94, 95, *95*
Easiest Salad, Ever, 92, *92*
Esquites (Mexican Corn Salad), 110
Farro Salad with Asparagus, Radishes, and Parmesan, 128, *129*
Fingerling Potato Salad with Sun-Dried Tomato Dressing, 122, *124*
Green Bean Salad with Creamy Lemon Sauce and Crispy Capers, 114, *115*
Grilled Peach and Tomato Salad with Burrata and Basil, *135*, 135–36
Grilled Watermelon, Halloumi, and Olive Salad, 136–37, *137*
Hearty Green Salad with Chickpeas, Pickled Cauliflower, and Seared Halloumi, 97–98
Honeydew Salad with Peanuts and Lime, *133*, 133–34, *134*
Horiatiki Salata (Hearty Greek Salad), 94
Kale and Farro Salad with Fennel, Olives, and Parmesan, 129, *129*
Kale Caesar Salad, *92*, 92–93
Lao Hu Cai (Tiger Salad), *108*, 109
Marinated Bean and Asparagus Salad with Preserved Lemon Dressing,

Salads (cont.)
99, 99–100
Napa Cabbage Slaw with Apple and Walnuts, 116
Napa Cabbage Slaw with Carrots and Sesame, 115–17, *116, 117*
Napa Cabbage Slaw with Jícama and Pepitas, 116
Radicchio Chopped Salad with White Beans, Oranges, and Olives, 118
Red Cabbage and Grapefruit Salad, 132, *132, 133*
Roasted Butternut Squash Salad with Creamy Tahini Dressing, 104–5
Roasted Cauliflower with Arugula and Pear, *105,* 105–6
Romaine and Radicchio Salad with Roasted Squash and Pickled Pears, 118–19, *119*
Shaved Celery Salad with Pomegranate-Honey Vinaigrette, 109
Shaved Vegetable Salad with Creamy Miso Dressing, *112,* 113–14
Sweet Potato, Lentil, and Kale Salad with Fried Shallots, 130–31
Three-Bean Salad, 114–15, *115*
Tomatillo and Bibb Lettuce Salad with Tomatillo Ranch, 124, *124,* 125
Torn Potato Salad with Toasted Garlic and Herb Dressing, 121–22
Wheat Berry Salad with Radicchio, Dried Cherries, and Pecans, 125
White Bean and Arugula Salad with Frico Crumble, 100, *101*
Samosa Gnocchi Chaat, *302,* 303–4
Sandwiches and Handheld Foods. *see also* Burgers; Quesadillas; Tacos; Wraps
Avocado, Tomato, and Bell Pepper Arepas, 200
Black Bean and Cheese Arepas, 199–200, *201*
Cheese Pupusas, 197–99, *199*
Creamy Mushroom and Pink Pickled Cabbage Sandwiches, 204, *204,* 205
Cutty's-Inspired Eggplant Spuckie, 205–6
Egg, Kimchi, and Avocado Sandwiches, 477, *477*
Falafel, 215–16, *217*
Fried Egg Sandwiches with Hummus and Sprouts, 476
Marinated Tomato Sandwiches, 203
Mushroom, Lettuce, and Tomato Sandwiches, *202,* 203
Roasted Vegetable Sandwiches, *208,* 209
Sandwich Spreads
about, 218
Creamy Chipotle Sauce, 218
Easy Homemade Mayonnaise, 218
Herbed Yogurt Sauce, 218
Homemade Nut Butter, 219
Smoky Carrot Dogs, *190,* 190–91
Ultimate Grilled Vegetable Sandwiches, 209–10, *210*
San Francisco–Style Garlic Noodles, 312, *312,* 313
Sauces
about, 17, 21
Browned Butter and Sage Sauce, Potato Gnocchi with, 304–5, *305*
Browned Butter–Pine Nut Sauce, Three-Cheese Ravioli with, 299–301, *301*
Cherry Pepper Sauce, Portobello Mushroom Fries with, *507,* 507–9, *509*
Chili Crisp Dumpling Sauce, 325
Classic Burger Sauce, 184
Sauces (cont.)
Creamy Chipotle Sauce (sandwich spread), 218
Creamy Lemon Sauce and Crispy Capers, Green Bean Salad with, 114, *115*
Dipping Sauce(s)
Calabrian Chile, 512
Honey and Spice, 512
Lemon and Herb, 512
Sriracha, Fried Brussels Sprouts with, 534, *534*
Garlic Yogurt Sauce, 37
Ginger-Oyster Sauce, Stir-Fried Portobellos with, 46–48, *47*
Herbed Yogurt Sauce (sandwich spread), 218
Lemon-Herb Sauce, 179
Meatless "Meat" Sauce with Chickpeas and Mushrooms, 292, *293*
No-Cook Pizza Sauce, 223
Orange Sauce, Stir-Fried Tempeh with, *440,* 441
Plum Sauce, 515, *515*
Simple Sauces
about, 524
All-Purpose Herb Sauce, 524
Beurre Blanc, 527
Chermoula, 525
Gochujang Sauce, 527
Infinite Sauce, 526
Miso-Ginger Sauce, 526
Peanut-Sesame Sauce, 525
Pumpkin Seed Sauce, 526
Romesco, 527
Spicy Avocado–Sour Cream Sauce, 527
Zhoug (Spicy Middle Eastern Herb Sauce), 524
Soy-Maple Sauce, Udon with Stir-Fried Portobellos and, 316–17
Spicy Almond Butter Sauce, Tofu Summer Rolls with, *430,* 431–32
Tahini-Garlic Sauce, 354
Tahini-Yogurt Sauce, 211
Tomato-Butter Sauce, Spinach and Ricotta Gnudi with, *308,* 308–9
Tomato-Chile Sauce, 216, *216*
Tomato Sauces, Fast
about, 266
Fresh Tomato Puttanesca Sauce, 266
Fresh Tomato Sauce, 266
No-Cook Fresh Tomato Sauce, 266
Tomato–Browned Butter Sauce, 267
Vodka Sauce, 267
Tximitxurri (Basque-Style Herb Sauce), 572
Yogurt-Tahini Sauce, Whole Romanesco with Berbere and, 42, *43*
Sauerkraut
Pierogi, Potato-, 323
recipe for, 446, *446*
Sautéed Corn with Cherry Tomatoes, Ricotta Salata, and Basil, *544,* 545
Sautéed Eggplant with Polenta, 49–50
Sautéed Fava Beans, Asparagus, And Leek, 384, *384,* 385, *385*
Sautéed Mushrooms with Mustard and Parsley, 558

Sautéed Mushrooms with Red Wine and Rosemary, 557–58, *558*
Sautéed Mushrooms with Soy, Scallion, and Ginger, 558
Savory Dutch Baby with Portobellos, Roasted Red Peppers, Walnuts, and Feta, *64,* 65
Savory Noodle Kugel, *320,* 321
Savory Oatmeal with Peas, Parmesan, and Pepper, 365, *365*
Savory Seed Brittle, 88
Scallion(s)
Basmati Rice Pilaf with Peas, Scallions, and Lemon, 329
Braised Red Potatoes with Miso and Scallions, 566
Mashed Sweet Potatoes with Jalapeño, Garlic, and Scallions, 575
Pancakes, *7,* 512–13, *513*
Pan-Seared Zucchini with Spicy Honey and Scallion, 578, *578,* 579
Roasted Cabbage with Gochujang, Sesame, and Scallions, 535
Sautéed Mushrooms with Soy, Scallion, and Ginger, 558
Sesame-Scallion Vinaigrette, 139
Shanghai Scallion Oil Noodles, 310, *311*
Thin-Crust Grilled Pizza with Fontina, Parmesan, and Scallions, 233–35, *234*
Wild Rice Pilaf with Scallions, Cilantro, and Almonds, 344
Scrambled Eggs with Shiitake Mushrooms and Feta Cheese, 453
Seared Tempeh with Tomato Jam, *437,* 437–39
Seared Tofu with Panch Phoron, Green Beans, and Pickled Shallot, *412,* 413
Seed(s). *see also* Pine Nut(s); Sesame
Boiled Carrots with Fennel Seeds and Citrus, 537
Chopped Carrot Salad with Mint, Pistachios, and Pomegranate Seeds, 107, *107*
Palak Dal (Spinach-Lentil Dal with Cumin and Mustard Seeds), *398,* 398–99
Pickled Mustard Seeds, 459
Pumpkin Seed Sauce, 526
Savory Seed Brittle, 88
Spiced Seeds, 179
Sesame. *see also* Tahini
Balls, *518,* 519, *519*
Cast Iron–Seared Romaine with Oyster Sauce, Ginger, and Sesame, *120,* 121
Liang Mian (Chilled Sesame Noodles), *317,* 317–18
Napa Cabbage Slaw with Carrots and Sesame, 115–17, *116, 117*
Peanut-Sesame Sauce, 525
Roasted Cabbage with Gochujang, Sesame, and Scallions, 535
-Scallion Vinaigrette, 139
Sugar Snap Peas with Sesame, Ginger, and Lemon Zest, 572
Shakshuka
Chickpea Shakshuka, 464
Green Shakshuka, 462, *463* 463
Shakshuka (Eggs in Spicy Tomato and Roasted Red Pepper Sauce), 461, *461*
Shallot(s)
about, 33, *33*
Coconut Creamed Corn with Ginger and Crispy Shallots, 546
Make-Ahead Sherry-Shallot Vinaigrette, 138
Microwave-Fried Shallots, 89
Roasted Kale with Parmesan, Shallot, and Nutmeg, 556
Seared Tofu with Panch Phoron, Green Beans, and Pickled Shallot, *412,* 413
Sweet Potato, Lentil, and Kale Salad with Fried Shallots, 130–31
Upside-Down Caramelized Shallot and Onion Tart, 247–48, *249*
Shanghai Scallion Oil Noodles, 310, *311*
Shaved Celery Salad with Pomegranate-Honey Vinaigrette, 109
Shaved Vegetable Salad with Creamy Miso Dressing, *112,* 113–14
Shawarma-Spiced Tofu Wraps with Sumac Onions, *430,* 430–31
Sheet Pan Meals
about, 13, *18–19,* 18–21
Black Bean and Jalapeño Quesadillas, 194
Cheese Quesadillas, 194, *194, 195*
White Bean and Sun-Dried Tomato Patties with Lemony Spinach Salad, 184, *185*
Shichimi Togarashi, 88
Shiitake Mushrooms
and Bok Choy Lo Mein, 310
Japchae (Sweet Potato Noodles with Shiitakes and Spinach), 314–16, *315*
Ramen with Shiitakes and Soft Eggs, 309
Scrambled Eggs with Shiitake Mushrooms and Feta Cheese, 453
Stir-Fried Asparagus with Shiitake Mushrooms, 43
Sweet Potato Noodles with Shiitakes, Spinach, and Eggs (Japchae), 316
Tofu and Mustard Greens Soup, 154, *155*
Shishito Peppers, Blistered, 520
Sichuan Hot and Sour Potatoes, 566–67
Sichuan Peppercorn Oil, 325
Sicilian White Beans and Escarole, 375–77, *376*
Silky Roasted Eggplant with Tomato and Feta, 55–56, *56*
Simple Dinner Party for 6 (menu), 22
Simple Rice Pilaf, 328, *328*
Simple Sauces
about, 524
All-Purpose Herb Sauce, 524
Beurre Blanc, 527
Chermoula, 525
Chile-Coriander Sauce, 524
Gochujang Sauce, 527
Infinite Sauce, 526
Miso-Ginger Sauce, 526
Peanut-Sesame Sauce, 525
Pumpkin Seed Sauce, 526
Romesco, 527
Smoked Paprika Sauce, 524
Spicy Avocado–Sour Cream Sauce, 527
Zhoug (Spicy Middle Eastern Herb Sauce), 524

Simple Sautéed Kale, 555
Simple Stovetop Macaroni and Cheese, *274,* 275
Skillet-Charred Green Beans, 552–53, *553*
Skillet-Charred Green Beans with Crispy Bread-Crumb Topping, 553
Skillet Rice and Beans with Corn and Fresh Tomatoes, 387–88
Skillet Rice and Chickpeas with Coconut Milk, 388
Skillet-Roasted Brussels Sprouts with Cider Vinegar and Honey, 532–33, *533*
Skillet-Roasted Brussels Sprouts with Maple Syrup and Smoked Almonds, 533
Skillet-Roasted Brussels Sprouts with Pomegranate and Pistachios, 533
Skillet-Roasted Cauliflower
with Capers and Pine Nuts, 541
with Cumin and Pistachios, 541
with Garlic and Lemon, *540,* 540–41
Skillet Tomato Cobbler, 63, *63*
Slow-Roasted Eggplant Dip with Pomegranate Molasses and Aleppo Pepper, 499
Small Plates/Snacks. *see* Appetizers
Smashed Cucumbers (Pai Huang Gua), 548, *548,* 549
Smoky Carrot Dogs, *190,* 190–91
Snap Pea(s)
about, 33, *33*
Quinoa Bowls with Snap Peas, Strawberries, and Basil Vinaigrette, *356,* 357
Roasted Tofu and Sweet Potato Bowls with Snap Pea Salad, *84,* 85–86
Spicy Basil Noodles with Crispy Tofu, Snap Peas, and Bell Pepper, 314, *315*
Socca with Sautéed Onions and Rosemary, 242–43, *243*
Soft-Cooked Eggs, 450
Soufflés, Make-Ahead Cheese, 458–59, *459*
Soups and Stews
about vegetable broths, building-block, 176–77
Acquacotta (Tuscan White Bean and Escarole Soup), 164, *165*
Best Vegetarian Chili, 172–73, *173*
Black Bean Chili, 173–74, *174*
Butternut Squash and White Bean Soup with Sage Pesto, 163–64
Carabaccia (Tuscan Onion Soup), *148,* 149
Caramelized Carrot Soup with Coriander-Lemon Browned Butter, 143
Cauliflower Soup, 144–45, *145*
Chickpea Noodle Soup, 169, *169*
Chilled Peach and Cucumber Soup, 156, *157*
Classic Minestrone, 161, *161*
Creamy Chickpea and Sweet Potato Stew, 170, *170*
Creamy White Bean Soup with Herb Oil and Crispy Capers, *158,* 159
Green Gumbo, *170,* 171–72
Harira (Moroccan Lentil and Chickpea Soup), 168
Hawaij Cauliflower Soup with Zhoug, 144
Hearty Cabbage Soup, 151, *151*
Kimchi and Tofu Soup, 153
Lemongrass-Coconut Soup with Oyster Mushrooms, 154–55, *155*
Soups and Stews (cont.)
Lentil and Escarole Soup, 160, *161*
Pappa al Pomodoro, *142,* 142–43, *143*
Quick Food Processor Gazpacho, 155–56
Red Lentil Soup with Warm Spices, 159–60
Ribollita, *162,* 162–63
Roasted Garlic Soup with Parmesan Croutons, *146,* 147, *147*
Roasted Poblano and White Bean Chili, *174,* 175
Shiitake, Tofu, and Mustard Greens Soup, 154, *155*
Spiced Eggplant and Kale Soup, *152,* 153
Super Greens Soup with Lemon-Tarragon Cream, 150
Sweet Potato Soup with Maple Sour Cream, *146,* 146–47
Tanabour (Armenian Yogurt and Barley Soup), *166,* 166–67
Thai-Spiced Red Lentil Stew with Spinach and Corn, 171
Tomato, Bulgur, and Red Pepper Soup, 167–68
Turkish Bulgur and Lentil Soup, *166,* 167
Wild Rice and Mushroom Soup, 156–57
Zucchini Soup with Dill and Sour Cream, 149–50, *151*
Sour and Hot Napa Cabbage (Suan La Bai Cai), 536, *536, 537*
South Asian Spiced Vegetable Fritters (Pakoras), 516
Southern Cheese Straws, 501–2, *502*
Soy. *see also* Miso; Tempeh; Tofu
Braised Eggplant with Soy, Garlic, and Ginger, 551
Sautéed Mushrooms with Soy, Scallion, and Ginger, 558
Udon with Stir-Fried Portobellos and Soy-Maple Sauce, 316–17
Spaghetti all'Assassina, 286–87, *287*
Spanish-Style Skillet Rice and Chickpeas, 388
Spanish Tortilla with Roasted Red Peppers and Peas, 467–68, *468*
Spiced Eggplant and Kale Soup, *152,* 153
Spiced Roasted Chickpeas, 82, *83*
Spiced Seeds, 179
Spiced Smashed Chickpea Wraps, 211, *211*
Spice Mixtures. *see also* Dressings and Vinaigrettes; Garnishes and Toppings; Sauces; *specific names of herbs; specific names of spices*
about spicy and smoky flavors, 9
All-Purpose Herb Sauce, 524
Baharat, 57
Chili-Lime Salt, 544
Dukkah, 89
Garam Masala, 485
Harissa, 400, *400*
Herbes de Provence, 122
Panch Phoron, 413, *413*
Quick Chili Oil, 179
Ras el Hanout, 439
Shichimi Togarashi, 88
Sichuan Peppercorn Oil, 325
Spiced Seeds, 179
Tarragon-Lemon Gremolata, 88
Za'atar, 240
Zhoug (Spicy Middle Eastern Herb Sauce), 524

Spicy Basil Noodles with Crispy Tofu, Snap Peas, and Bell Pepper, 314, *315*
Spicy Chile-Honey Glazed Eggplant with Burrata and Greens, *12*, 40, *40*
Spicy Cold Tofu, *406*, 407
Spicy Greek Baked Feta (Bouyourdi), 490, *491*
Spicy Honey, 573
Spicy Middle Eastern Herb Sauce (Zhoug), 524
Spicy Polenta with White Beans and Kale, 363–64
Spicy Red Pepper Mayonnaise, 559, *559*
Spicy Sriracha-Lime Mayonnaise, 218
Spinach
-Artichoke Macaroni and Cheese, 277
Espinacas con Garbanzos (Andalusian Spinach and Chickpeas), 382–83
Family-Size Spinach and Herb Cream Cheese Omelet with Home Fries, 466–67, *467*
Fresh Leek and Spinach Dip, *500*, 500–501
and Goat Cheese Quesadillas, *195*, 195–96
Japchae (Sweet Potato Noodles with Shiitakes, Spinach, and Eggs), 316
Japchae (Sweet Potato Noodles with Shiitakes and Spinach), 314–16, *315*
Kol Böreği (Spiraled Spinach and Cheese Pastry), 262–63, *263*
Lentilles du Puy with Spinach and Crème Fraîche, 397–98, *398*
Palak Dal (Spinach-Lentil Dal with Cumin and Mustard Seeds), *398*, 398–99
Quinoa Burgers with Spinach, Sun-Dried Tomatoes, and Marinated Feta, 187–88, *189*
Rice, 329–30
and Ricotta Gnudi with Tomato-Butter Sauce, *308*, 308–9
Sheet Pan White Bean and Sun-Dried Tomato Patties with Lemony Spinach Salad, 184, *185*
Stuffed Portobello Mushrooms with Spinach and Gorgonzola, 77–78
Thai-Spiced Red Lentil Stew with Spinach and Corn, 171
Spiraled Spinach and Cheese Pastry (Kol Böreği), 262–63, *263*
Spring Freekeh and Halloumi Bowls, *352*, 353–54
Spring Rolls (Cantonese Egg Rolls), *514*, 514–15
Squash. *see also* Butternut Squash; Pumpkin; Zucchini
Cacio e Pepe Beans with Squash, Sage, and Walnuts, *372*, 372–73
Roasted Delicata Squash, 572, *573*
Romaine and Radicchio Salad with Roasted Squash and Pickled Pears, 118–19, *119*
Stuffed Delicata Squash, 72, *73*
Summer Squash Pasta with Ricotta and Lemon-Parmesan Bread Crumbs, 284, *285*
Summer Squash Tart, 258, *259*
Sweet and Spicy Glazed Tofu with Coconut-Braised Mustard Greens and Winter Squash, *424*, 425
Teff-Stuffed Acorn Squash with Lime Crema and Roasted Pepitas, 71–72
Stewed Cranberry Beans with Tomatoes and Sage, 377
Stir-Fry Dishes
Amaranth with Garlic, 528, *528*
Asparagus with Shiitake Mushrooms, 43
Di San Xian (Stir-Fried Three Treasures), 45–46, *46*
Portobellos with Ginger-Oyster Sauce, 46–48, *47*
Stir-Fry Dishes (cont.)
Portobellos with Sweet Chili-Garlic Sauce, 48
Rice Cakes with Bok Choy and Snow Peas, 337
Tempeh, Napa Cabbage, and Carrots, *440*, 440–41
Tempeh with Orange Sauce, *440*, 441
Tofu and Bok Choy, 422, *423*
Udon with Stir-Fried Portobellos and Soy-Maple Sauce, 316–17
Xīhóngshì Chao Jīdàn (Chinese Stir-Fried Tomatoes and Eggs), *452*, 453
Stone Fruit(s)
Barley with Fennel, Dried Apricots, and Orange, 347
Caramelized Plums with Spicy Herb Salad, 134–35, *135*
Charred Shaved Brussels Sprout Salad with Apricot Dressing, 107
Chilled Peach and Cucumber Soup, 156, *157*
Chopped Vegetable and Stone Fruit Salad, *15*, 126, *127*
Curried Millet Burgers with Peach-Ginger Chutney, 188–89, *189*
Grilled Peach and Tomato Salad with Burrata and Basil, *135*, 135–36
Grilled Stone Fruit, 136
Plum Sauce, 515, *515*
Wheat Berry Salad with Radicchio, Dried Cherries, and Pecans, 125
Strawberries, and Basil Vinaigrette, Quinoa Bowls with Snap Peas, *356*, 357
Stuffed Delicata Squash, 72, *73*
Stuffed Peppers with Chickpeas, Goat Cheese, and Herbs, *74*, 75
Stuffed Portobello Mushrooms with Spinach and Gorgonzola, 77–78
Stuffed Tomatoes with Couscous and Zucchini, 78–80
Suan La Bai Cai (Sour and Hot Napa Cabbage), 536, *536*, *537*
Sugar Snap Peas
about, 33, *33*
with Almonds, Coriander, and Orange Zest, 572
with Pine Nuts, Fennel, and Lemon Zest, 571–72
with Sesame, Ginger, and Lemon Zest, 572
Sumac Onions, 431
Summer Squash Pasta with Ricotta and Lemon-Parmesan Bread Crumbs, 284, *285*
Summer Squash Tart, 258, *259*
Sun-Dried Tomato(es)
Angel Hair Pasta with Sun-Dried Tomato and Mint Sauce, 273–74
Fingerling Potato Salad with Sun-Dried Tomato Dressing, 122, *124*
Frittata Bites with Broccoli and Sun-Dried Tomatoes, *474*, 474–75
Linguine with Sun-Dried Tomato and Eggplant Sauce, *274*, 274–75
Quinoa Burgers with Spinach, Sun-Dried Tomatoes, and Marinated Feta, 187–88, *189*
Sheet Pan White Bean and Sun-Dried Tomato Patties with Lemony Spinach Salad, 184, *185*
Sun-Dried Tomato Tapenade with Farmer's Cheese, 521
Sun-Dried Tomato Tapenade with Farmer's Cheese, 521
Super Greens Soup with Lemon-Tarragon Cream, 150
Su Shui Jiao (Northern Chinese–Style Cabbage and Mushroom Dumplings), *323*, 323–25
Sweet and Spicy Glazed Tofu with Coconut-Braised Mustard Greens and Winter Squash, *424*, 425

Sweet and Sweet-Tart Flavors, about, 9
Sweet Potato(es)
Best Baked Sweet Potatoes, *573*, 573–74
Black Bean, Sweet Potato, and Poblano Tacos, 193
Black Bean and Sweet Potato Tacos, *192*, 193
Bulgur Salad with Curry Roasted Sweet Potatoes and Chickpeas, 126
Cauliflower Rice Bowls with Sweet Potatoes, Avocados, and Chickpeas, 81–82, *83*
Fritters with Cheddar and Chipotle, 517
Fritters with Feta, Dill, and Cilantro, 517, *517*
Honey-Garlic Melting Sweet Potatoes, 575–76
Japchae (Sweet Potato Noodles with Shiitakes, Spinach, and Eggs), 316
Japchae (Sweet Potato Noodles with Shiitakes and Spinach), 314–16, *315*
Lentil and Kale Salad with Fried Shallots, 130–31
Loaded Sweet Potato Wedges with Tempeh, 442–43
Mashed
with Chipotle and Lime, 575
with Curry and Golden Raisins, 575
with Jalapeño, Garlic, and Scallions, 575
with Maple and Orange, 575
recipe for, *573*, 574
Miso-Maple Melting Sweet Potatoes, 576
Overstuffed Sweet Potatoes with Tofu and Red Curry Vinaigrette, 433–34, *434*
Red Flannel Hash with Tempeh, 441–42
Roasted Tofu and Sweet Potato Bowls with Snap Pea Salad, *84*, 85–86
Soup with Maple Sour Cream, *146*, 146–47
Swiss Chard
about, 31, *31*, 463, *463*
and Kale Gratin, 576
Pinto Bean, and Monterey Jack Enchiladas, 67–68

T

Tacos
about taco shells, 443, *443*
Baja-Style Cauliflower Tacos, 191
Black Bean, Sweet Potato, and Poblano Tacos, 193
Black Bean and Sweet Potato Tacos, *192*, 193
Breakfast Tacos with Pinto Beans and Cotija Cheese, 478, *478*
Red Lentil Tacos, 193–94
Tempeh Tacos, 443, *443*
Tacu Tacu with Salsa Criolla, 388–89, *389*
Tahini
Barley and Lentils with Mushrooms and Tahini-Yogurt Sauce, 348–49, *349*
Beet Dip with Yogurt and Tahini, 498, *499*
Creamless Creamy Roasted Red Pepper and Tahini Dressing, 139
-Garlic Sauce, 354
Tahini (cont.)
Gochujang-Tahini Noodles, 313–14
Roasted Butternut Squash Salad with Creamy Tahini Dressing, 104–5
Roasted Radishes with Yogurt-Tahini Sauce, 571
Whole Romanesco with Berbere and Yogurt-Tahini Sauce, 42, *43*
-Yogurt Sauce, 211
Tallarines Verdes (Peruvian Green Noodles), 279–80
Tamatya-Kandyachi Koshimbir (Tomato-Onion Salad), 242
Tanabour (Armenian Yogurt and Barley Soup), *166*, 166–67
Tangy Flavors, about, 10
Tarragon-Lemon Gremolata, 88
Tarts. *see* Breads, Tarts, and Pies (Savory)
Teff-Stuffed Acorn Squash with Lime Crema and Roasted Pepitas, 71–72
Tempeh
Crispy Tempeh, 436
Crispy Tempeh with Sambal Sauce, 436–37
Korean Barbecue Tempeh Wraps, 447, *447*
Loaded Sweet Potato Wedges with Tempeh, 442–43
Pan-Seared Tempeh Steaks with Chimichurri Sauce, *438*, 439
Rainbow Bowls with Crispy Tempeh, 86, *87*
Reubens, *444*, 445, *445*, 446
Seared Tempeh with Tomato Jam, *437*, 437–39
Stir-Fried Tempeh, Napa Cabbage, and Carrots, *440*, 440–41
Stir-Fried Tempeh with Orange Sauce, *440*, 441
Sweet Potato Red Flannel Hash with Tempeh, 441–42
Tacos, 443, *443*
Vegetable Bibimbap with Tempeh, 334–35, *335*
Thai Coconut Rice (Hung Kao Mun Gati), 342, *343*
Thai Red Curry with Tofu and Lentils, 427–28
Thai-Spiced Red Lentil Stew with Spinach and Corn, 171
Thanksgiving (menus), 24, *24*, *25*
Thick-Cut Oven Fries, *568*, 568–69
Thin-Crust Grilled Pizza with Fontina, Parmesan, and Scallions, 233–35, *234*
Three-Bean Salad, 114–15, *115*
Three-Cheese Potato Frico, 562
Three-Cheese Ravioli with Browned Butter–Pine Nut Sauce, 299–301, *301*
Tiger Salad (Lao Hu Cai), *108*, 109
Tofu
about, 408, *408*
Bulgur with Vegetables and Marinated Tofu, 428, *429*
Caribbean Tofu with Rice and Pigeon Peas, 425–26
Charred Cabbage Salad with Torn Tofu and Plantain Chips, 418–19
and Chickpea Flour Frittata with Mushrooms, 434–35, *435*
Chile-Spiced Crumbled Tofu with Pineapple Salsa, *14*, 420–21, *421*
Crispy Teriyaki Tofu, *421*, 421–22
Crispy Tofu, 407
Crispy Tofu and Kale Salad with Miso-Ginger Dressing, *416*, 417
Crispy Tofu Salad with Cherry Tomatoes, 417
Croutons, 178
East African Tofu and Coconut Curry, 426–27, *427*

Tofu (cont.)
Garlicky Tofu Tabbouleh, 419–20
Grilled Tofu with Vegetable Skewers, *435*, 435–36
Homemade Tofu, 409, *409*
Homestyle Tofu, *406*, 406–7
Katsu, 410, *411*
Kimchi and Tofu Soup, 153
Mapo Tofu, 432–33, *433*
Overstuffed Sweet Potatoes with Tofu and Red Curry Vinaigrette, 433–34, *434*
Panko-Crusted Tofu with Cabbage Salad, *424*, 424–25
Pita Salad with Za'atar Tofu and Chickpeas, 418, *419*
Rancheros, 414, *415*
Roasted Tofu and Sweet Potato Bowls with Snap Pea Salad, *84*, 85–86
Saag Tofu, 414–15, *415*
Seared Tofu with Panch Phoron, Green Beans, and Pickled Shallot, *412*, 413
Shawarma-Spiced Tofu Wraps with Sumac Onions, *430*, 430–31
Shiitake, Tofu, and Mustard Greens Soup, 154, *155*
Spicy Basil Noodles with Crispy Tofu, Snap Peas, and Bell Pepper, 314, *315*
Spicy Cold Tofu, *406*, 407
Stir-Fried Tofu and Bok Choy, 422, *423*
Summer Rolls with Spicy Almond Butter Sauce, *430*, 431–32
Sushi Bowls, 410
Sweet and Spicy Glazed Tofu with Coconut-Braised Mustard Greens and Winter Squash, *424*, 425
Thai Red Curry with Tofu and Lentils, 427–28
Tomatillos
about, 124, *124*
Tomatillo and Bibb Lettuce Salad with Tomatillo Ranch, 124, *124*, 125
Tomato(es)
about cutting, 33, *33*
about grating, 143, *143*
Avocado, Tomato, and Bell Pepper Arepas, 200
Biscuits with Creamy Tomato Gravy and Fried Eggs, *460*, 460–61
-Browned Butter Sauce, 267
Bulgur and Red Pepper Soup, 167–68
Caramelized Onion, Tomato, and Goat Cheese Tart, 258, *259*
Cheddar-Crusted Grilled Cheese with Tomato, 201, *201*
Cheesy Tomato and Bean Bake, 65–66, *66*
Cherry Tomato Salad with Pita Crisps and Spicy Citrus Dressing, 123, *123*
-Chile Sauce, 216, *216*
Corn, Tomato, and Arugula Pizza, *228*, 229
and Corn Tostadas with Baked Eggs, 464–65, *465*
Creamy, Spicy Rotini and Red Lentils with Tomatoes and Goat Cheese, 290
Crispy Tofu Salad with Cherry Tomatoes, 417
Curry Roasted Cabbage Wedges with Tomatoes and Chickpeas, *36*, 36–37
Eggplant and Tomato Phyllo Pie, 252–54
Fregula with Chickpeas, Tomatoes, and Fennel, *291*, 291–92

Tomato(es) (cont.)
Fried Red Tomatoes, 577, *577*
Gnocchi à la Parisienne with Arugula, Tomatoes, and Olives, 306, *307*
Grilled Peach and Tomato Salad with Burrata and Basil, *135*, 135–36
Marinated Tomato Sandwiches, 203
Mezzi Rigatoni with Spicy Gochujang Tomato Sauce, *270*, 271
Mushroom, Lettuce, and Tomato Sandwiches, *202*, 203
Pa amb Tomàquet (Catalan Tomato Bread), 502–3, *503*
Philadelphia Tomato Pie, 228–29
Quick Tomato Salsa, 198
Rigatoni with Marinated Tomatoes and Burrata, 272, *273*
Sauces, Fast
about, 266
Fresh Tomato Puttanesca Sauce, 266
Fresh Tomato Sauce, 266
No-Cook Fresh Tomato Sauce, 266
Tomato-Browned Butter Sauce, 267
Vodka Sauce, 267
Sautéed Corn with Cherry Tomatoes, Ricotta Salata, and Basil, *544*, 545
Seared Tempeh with Tomato Jam, *437*, 437–39
Shakshuka (Eggs in Spicy Tomato and Roasted Red Pepper Sauce), 461, *461*
Silky Roasted Eggplant with Tomato and Feta, 55–56, *56*
Skillet Rice and Beans with Corn and Fresh Tomatoes, 387–88
Skillet Tomato Cobbler, 63, *63*
Spinach and Ricotta Gnudi with Tomato-Butter Sauce, *308*, 308–9
Stewed Cranberry Beans with Tomatoes and Sage, 377
Stuffed Tomatoes with Couscous and Zucchini, 78–80
Tamatya-Kandyachi Koshimbir (Tomato-Onion Salad), 242
Upside-Down Tomato Tart, 258–61, *260*
Whole Pot-Roasted Cauliflower with Tomatoes and Olives, 41–42
Xīhóngshì Chao Jīdàn (Chinese Stir-Fried Tomatoes and Eggs), *452*, 453
Toppings, Types of. *see* Dressings and Vinaigrettes; Garnishes and Toppings; Sauces
Toppings for Vegetable Dishes
Dukkah, 89
Savory Seed Brittle, 88
Shichimi Togarashi, 88
store-bought, 89
Tarragon-Lemon Gremolata, 88
Torn Potato Salad with Toasted Garlic and Herb Dressing, 121–22
Tortellini Salad with Broccoli, Cannellini Beans, and Olive-Banana Pepper Dressing, *302*, 302–3
Tourte aux Pommes de Terre (French Potato Pie), 251–52, *253*
Triple Mushroom Pasta, 282, *282*, 283
Turkish Bulgur and Lentil Soup, *166*, 167
Tuscan Onion Soup (Carabaccia), *148*, 149
Tuscan White Bean and Escarole Soup (Acquacotta), 164, *165*
Tximitxurri (Basque-Style Herb Sauce), 572

U

Udon with Stir-Fried Portobellos and Soy-Maple Sauce, 316–17

Ultimate Grilled Vegetable Sandwiches, 209–10, *210*

Ultimate Veggie Burgers, *7, 182,* 182–83

Ultracreamy Hummus, 494, *495*

Ultracreamy Spaghetti with Zucchini, *285,* 285–86

Umami Broth, 177

Umami Croutons, 178

Umami Flavors, about, 8

Unstuffed Shells with Butternut Squash and Leeks, 297–98, *299*

Upside-Down Caramelized Shallot and Onion Tart, 247–48, *249*

Upside-Down Tomato Tart, 258–61, *260*

V

Vegan Mayonnaise, 506

Vegan Ranch Dressing, 506

Vegetable Bibimbap with Tempeh, 334–35, *335*

Vegetable Broths, Building-Block, 176

Classic Vegetable Broth, 176

Umami Broth, 177

Vegetable Broth Base, 176

Vegetable Scrap Broth, 177

Vegetable Lasagna, 58–60

Vegetables. *see also specific names of vegetables*

about buying, storing, using up, 4–6, *5*

about roll cutting, 46, *46*

about turning into main dishes, *16,* 16–17, *17*

about vegetable preparation basics, 26–33, *26–33*

Bulgur with Vegetables and Marinated Tofu, 428, *429*

Chopped Vegetable and Stone Fruit Salad, *15,* 126, *127*

Curried Fonio with Roasted Vegetables and Hibiscus Vinaigrette, *352,* 352–53

Grilled Tofu with Vegetable Skewers, *435,* 435–36

Hearty Vegetable and Farro Bowls with Goat Cheese, 85

Herb Vegetable and Lentil Bake, 68–69, *69*

Lemony Roasted Radicchio, Fennel, and Root Vegetables, *570,* 570–71

Menemen (Turkish Scrambled Eggs with Vegetables), 454

Pakoras (South Asian Spiced Vegetable Fritters), 516

Raw Vegetable Wraps, 206–7, *207*

Roasted Vegetable Bowls with Bulgur, White Beans, and Arugula, 84, *84*

Roasted Vegetable Sandwiches, *208,* 209

Shaved Vegetable Salad with Creamy Miso Dressing, *112,* 113–14

Toppings for Vegetable Dishes

Dukkah, 89

Savory Seed Brittle, 88

Shichimi Togarashi, 88

store-bought, 89

Tarragon-Lemon Gremolata, 88

Vegetables. *see also specific names of vegetables* (cont.)

Ultimate Grilled Vegetable Sandwiches, 209–10, *210*

Vegetable Bibimbap with Tempeh, 334–35, *335*

Vegetable Broths, Building-Block, 176

Classic Vegetable Broth, 176

Umami Broth, 177

Vegetable Broth Base, 176

Vegetable Scrap Broth, 177

Vegetable Lasagna, 58–60

Vegetarianism, 1–33

bowl combinations, 21, *21*

entertaining and menu ideas, 22, *23–25,* 24

flavorful vegetarian meals, 8–11

freezer-friendly meals, 6, *7*

freezing building-block ingredients, *5,* 6

ingredient labels, reading, 11

meal planning for vegetarian dinners, 2

meal planning go-to meals, 13–14

meal planning tips, 3

meal planning with ingredients on hand, 15

popularity of, 1

produce planning and storage, 4–5

sheet pan meals, improvising, *18–19,* 18–21

vegetable preparation basics, 26–33, *26–33*

vegetables as main dishes, *16,* 16–17, *17*

Vegetarian Refried Beans, 465

Vidalia Onion(s)

Braised Vidalia Onions with Chile, Lime, and Cilantro, *560,* 561

Braised Vidalia Onions with Honey, Lemon, and Oregano, 561

Vidalia Onion Pie, *250,* 251

Vietnamese Red Rice (Cơm Đỏ), 341–42

Vinaigrettes. *see* Dressings and Vinaigrettes

Vindaloo, Potato, *54,* 55

Vodka Sauce, 267

Vospov Kofte (Red Lentil Kofte), 216–17, *217*

W

Walkaway Ratatouille, 58, *59*

Walnut(s)

Cacio e Pepe Beans with Squash, Sage, and Walnuts, *372,* 372–73

Celery Root Galette with Blue Cheese and Walnuts, *256,* 256–57

Fettuccine with Walnut Sauce, 280, *281*

Napa Cabbage Slaw with Apple and Walnuts, 116

Oat Berry Pilaf with Walnuts and Gorgonzola, 356

Savory Dutch Baby with Portobellos, Roasted Red Peppers, Walnuts, and Feta, *64,* 65

Warm Marinated Olives, *484,* 485

Wheat. *see also* Bulgur
Chapati (Whole-Wheat Wraps), 213
Wheat Berry Salad with Radicchio, Dried Cherries, and Pecans, 125
Whole-Wheat Crepes, 245
Whole-Wheat Crepes with Creamy Sautéed Mushrooms and Asparagus, *244,* 245
Whipped Boursin, 248
Whipped Feta and Roasted Red Pepper Dip, 489
Whipped Feta Dip, 489
Whipped Feta Dip with Dill and Parsley, *488,* 489
White Bean(s)
Acquacotta (Tuscan White Bean and Escarole Soup), 164, *165*
and Arugula Salad with Frico Crumble, 100, *101*
Butternut Squash and White Bean Soup with Sage Pesto, 163–64
Calabrian Chile White Beans with Almond Romesco, 374–75, *375*
Creamy White Bean Soup with Herb Oil and Crispy Capers, *158,* 159
Mushroom and White Bean Gratin, 66–67
Radicchio Chopped Salad with White Beans, Oranges, and Olives, 118
Roasted Poblano and White Bean Chili, *174,* 175
Roasted Vegetable Bowls with Bulgur, White Beans, and Arugula, 84, *84*
Sheet Pan White Bean and Sun-Dried Tomato Patties with Lemony Spinach Salad, 184, *185*
Sicilian White Beans and Escarole, 375–77, *376*
Spicy Polenta with White Beans and Kale, 363–64
White Mushrooms, about, 282
Whole Pot-Roasted Cauliflower with Tomatoes and Olives, 41–42
Whole Romanesco with Berbere and Yogurt-Tahini Sauce, 42, *43*
Whole-Wheat Crepes, 245
Whole-Wheat Crepes with Creamy Sautéed Mushrooms and Asparagus, *244,* 245
Whole-Wheat Wraps (Chapati), 213
Wild Rice
and Mushroom Soup, 156–57
Pilaf with Pecans and Cranberries, 344, *345*
Pilaf with Scallions, Cilantro, and Almonds, 344
Wraps
Chapati (Whole-Wheat Wraps), 213
Grilled Halloumi Wraps, *214,* 214–15
Korean Barbecue Tempeh Wraps, 447, *447*
Mumbai Frankie Wraps, 212, *212*
Quinoa Lettuce Wraps with Feta and Olives, 358–59, *359*
Raw Vegetable Wraps, 206–7, *207*
Shawarma-Spiced Tofu Wraps with Sumac Onions, *430,* 430–31
Spiced Smashed Chickpea Wraps, 211, *211*

Xīhóngshì Chao Jīdàn (Chinese Stir-Fried Tomatoes and Eggs), *452,* 453

Yogurt
Homemade Yogurt, 486, *487*
Labneh, 487
Lemon-Dill Labneh, 487

Z

Za'atar
Mana'eesh Za'atar (Za'atar Flatbreads), 239–40, *241*
Pita Salad with Za'atar Tofu and Chickpeas, 418, *419*
recipe for, 240
Zhoug, Hawaij Cauliflower Soup with, 144
Zhoug (Spicy Middle Eastern Herb Sauce), 524
Zucchini
about, 30, *30,* 578, *578,* 580, *580*
Broiled Smashed Zucchini with Garlicky Yogurt, 580, *580, 581*
Broiled Smashed Zucchini with Herbed Sour Cream, 580
Chips with Tzatziki, 510, *511*
Crispy Chickpea Cakes with Zucchini Ribbon Salad, *383,* 383–84
Pan-Seared Zucchini with Raisin, Caper, and Parsley Sauce and Pine Nuts, 579
Pan-Seared Zucchini with Spicy Honey and Scallion, 578, *578,* 579
Pan-Seared Zucchini with Yogurt, Red Pepper Paste, and Preserved Lemon, 579
Potato and Zucchini Spanish Tortilla, 468–69, *469*
Soup with Dill and Sour Cream, 149–50, *151*
Stuffed Tomatoes with Couscous and Zucchini, 78–80
Ultracreamy Spaghetti with Zucchini, *285,* 285–86